THE ANCIENT NEAR EAST

'In the original Italian edition of this work, Liverani defined and applied, with the touch of a master, the criteria for proper historical writing as it relates to the ancient Near East. This English version will extend the reach of a classic to the much wider audience it deserves.'

Giorgio Buccellati, *Professor Emeritus, University of California, USA*

'Mario Liverani's classic text is as unusual in its ambitious chronological scope as in its clarity of vision: from the Neolithic to the emergence of the Persian Empire, his analysis of the history of the Middle East is firmly focused on the interplay between society, economy and ideology. And yet, the vast learning is lightly worn and the volume offers a hugely enjoyable and eye-opening read for novice and expert alike. A must have for anyone with an interest in world history.'

Karen Radner, *University College London, UK*

'The English translation of Mario Liverani's *Antico Oriente: Storia, Societa', Economia* is a welcomed addition to the publishing world and Routledge has truly done us a great service in making this project possible. Since its appearance in 1988, *Antico Oriente* has become *the* introduction to the ancient Near East ... The author breezes through an astonishing amount of data and material with ease, and he makes it accessible to the scholarly and general public alike. This is a wonderful book, which will make readers fall in love with the wonders of the ancient Near East, and at the same time provide them with a firm grasp on the methodological problems one faces when dealing with such a complex but fascinating world.'

Alhena Gadotti, *Towson University, USA*

The Ancient Near East reveals three millennia of history (c. 3500–500 BC) in a single work. Liverani draws upon over 45 years' worth of experience and this personal odyssey has enabled him to retrace the history of the peoples of the Ancient Near East. The history of the Sumerians, Hittites, Assyrians, Babylonians and more is meticulously detailed by one of the leading scholars of Assyriology.

Utilizing research derived from the most recent archaeological finds, the text has been fully revised for this English edition and explores Liverani's current thinking on the history of the Ancient Near East. The rich and varied illustrations for each historical period, augmented by new images for this edition, provide insights into the material and textual sources for the Ancient Near East. Many highlight the ingenuity and technological prowess of the peoples in the Ancient Near East. Never before available in English, *The Ancient Near East* represents one of the greatest books ever written on the subject and is a must read for students who will not have had the chance to explore the depth of Liverani's scholarship.

Mario Liverani is Emeritus Professor of Ancient Near East History at Sapienza University of Rome, Italy.

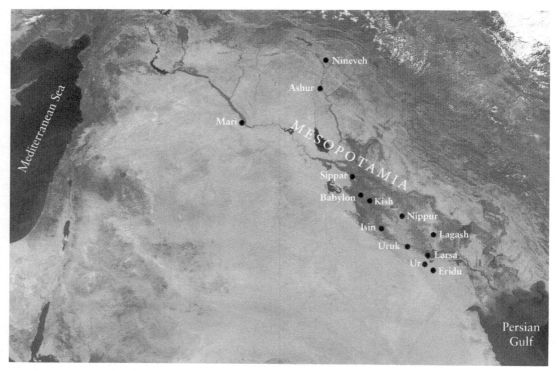

Figure 0.1. Satellite image of Mesopotamia (NASA).

THE ANCIENT NEAR EAST

History, society and economy

Mario Liverani
Translated by Soraia Tabatabai

Routledge
Taylor & Francis Group

LONDON AND NEW YORK

First published in English 2014
by Routledge
2 Park Square, Milton Park, Abingdon, Oxon OX14 4RN

and by Routledge
711 Third Avenue, New York, NY 10017

Routledge is an imprint of the Taylor & Francis Group, an informa business

Originally published in Italian as *Antico Oriente*

© 1988, 2011, Gius. Laterza and Figli, all rights reserved.
English language edition published by agreement of Marco Vigevani Agenzia Letteraria, Milano.

British Library Cataloguing in Publication Data
A catalogue record for this book is available from the British Library

Library of Congress Cataloging in Publication Data
Liverani, Mario.
[Antico Oriente. English]
The Ancient Near East: history, society and ecnomy / Mario Liverani ; translated by Soraia Tabatabai
pages cm
"Originally published in Italian as Antico Oriente © 1988, 2011, Gius. Laterza & Figli."
Includes bibliographical references and index.
1. Middle East–History–To 622. I. Title.
DS62.23.L5813 2013
939.4–dc23
2013018121

ISBN: 978–0–415–67905–3 (hbk)
ISBN: 978–0–415–67906–0 (hbk)
ISBN: 978–1–315–87989–5 (ebk)

Typeset in Bembo & Minion
by Swales & Willis Ltd, Exeter, Devon

CONTENTS

FIGURES

TABLES

TEXTS

My illustrious Friend and Joy of my Liver!

The thing you ask of me is both difficult and useless. Although I have passed all my days in this place, I have neither counted the houses, nor have I inquired into the number of inhabitants; and as to what one person loads on his mules and the other stows away in the bottom of his ship, that is no business of mine. But, above all, as to the previous history of this city, God only knows the amount of dirt and confusion that the infidels may have eaten before the coming of the sword of Islam. It were unprofitable for us to inquire into it.

[Letter of the mayor of Kuyunjik to the first archaeologists working in Nineveh
(from A. H. Layard, Nineveh and Babylon, *London, 1882, p. 401)]*

PREFACE

To the first edition

As absurd as it may seem, to this day [1988] there is no true history of the Ancient Near East that on the one hand is sufficiently detailed, and on the other follows a coherent methodological approach. Admittedly, there are numerous (not always reliable) popular accounts. However, these are more meant to captivate (maybe even amaze) the reader, rather than providing him with a solid historical reconstruction. At the same time, there are more analytical accounts (which have been translated and are well known in Italy), like the *Cambridge Ancient History* and the *Fischer Weltgeschichte*. However, these books are the result of the collaboration of several authors. Therefore, they seem to be born out of the ingenuous illusion that, in order to reconstruct history, it is sufficient to analyse the available documentary 'material' in chronological order.

For this reason, these books show a preference (which is already visible in the decision to involve a variety of authors) for a specialised and philological kind of competence, rather than providing a solid historical background. Moreover, these works were written in the 1960s. However, in the past 20 years, our knowledge of the history of the Ancient Near East has been radically revised and improved. This is due to the discovery of new archaeological and textual evidence and the inclusion of areas considered to be 'marginal' and largely secondary. Finally, further developments have been brought by the introduction in Ancient Near Eastern scholarship of broader research interests and more advanced historiographical methodologies.

Compared to other fields of ancient history, the Ancient Near East has experienced an unparalleled and dramatic increase of evidence. An overview of Greek or Roman history written in the 1960s can to a certain degree be 'valid' today both in its general lines and in its specific details. The history of the Ancient Near East, however, requires radical revisions at least every generation or so. Twenty years ago, entire chapters of the history of the Near East could not have been even imagined. In this regard, the case of Ebla might be the most widely known, but is certainly not the only one.

The same can be said in terms of historical approach. 'Classical' ancient history is based on an influential and complex historiographical tradition. On the contrary, over the past twenty years Ancient Near Eastern history has been influenced by a variety of historical approaches and research interests. On the one hand, this phenomenon still shows a certain degree of enthusiastic improvisation in the field. On the other hand, it has the merit of having transformed Ancient Near Eastern history into a sort of advanced 'workshop'. The sheer nature of Ancient Near Eastern history as a field between archaeology (especially for prehistoric phases) and history, and its use of a wide range of sources has had liberating effects. The latter were more strongly opposed (if not rejected) elsewhere, due to the strong influence of historical traditions in those fields.

Today, writing a history of the Ancient Near East is a necessary task. At the same time, however, it is a dangerous, almost presumptuous, task. In order to fulfil this ambition, yet minimise its risks, I have been able to rely on over 25 years of research and teaching. This experience has allowed me to gather information on a variety of fields, from current archaeological trends to philology and historical methodology. I have also tried to expand the scope of my initial research interests (from prehistory to the late empires). Consequently, I have researched a variety of aspects, from political ideologies to modes of production, social structures, systems of exchange, technology and demography. As a result, I have acquired a set of competences than can certainly be criticised for each specialised sector. However, overall these competences have allowed me to embark on a venture that in its own nature cannot be anything but a work of organisation and general evaluation of the evidence.

I believe that it is not by chance that this attempt was initiated in Italy. Other countries even more involved in this sector have maintained far more philological approaches (especially in Germany), or anthropological ones (especially in the United States). Italy, however, has recently focused on a more historical approach to the cultures of the Ancient Near East. This country is perhaps the only country in the world in which the 'History of the Ancient Near East' is not just formally, but is by all means, a discipline in its own right with respect to philology and archaeology. Having been directly involved (around the 1960s) in archaeological excavations and the publication of texts from the Near East, Italy is now ready for the less immediate and less natural task that is the historical reconstruction of the Near East.

The balance between the various components at the heart of this historical reconstruction is entirely my responsibility. Obviously, it can become the object of criticism and improvements. Even the limits of this work are arguable: not so much in its chronological delimitations – in-between the two great historical divisions of the Urban Revolution and the Axial Age – but for its geographic delimitations. The visible progress of scholarly research into the so-called marginal areas and into local characteristics, and the increasing number of ancient centres discovered has created a polycentric image of the Near East. This view makes the approach used in this book seem reductive and somehow too centred on Mesopotamia. However, a historical work covering the Aegean, Egypt, Central Asia and the Indus Valley constitutes a different type of project. Moreover, it requires a type of competence that is difficult to acquire, and a completely different methodology.

Regarding the internal components of the historical reconstruction, I have used, as my basic structure, the triangle ideology/society/economy. The analysis of the interaction of these three elements is already quite challenging. If I have left out several artistic, religious and literary aspects (among others) from the reconstruction, this is not because they are considered secondary. They are left out because they have to be considered individually before being successfully included in this historical reconstruction.

If these are the main premises of the present work, I have to add that its concrete realisation (the two years of 'mad' work) has been possible largely thanks to a number of people whom I would like to acknowledge here. First, there are my friends from Laterza. They not only accepted my manuscript, but even suggested, as a sort of 'challenge', the publication of a difficult and demanding book. Then, there are a number of colleagues and friends (M. G. Biga, G. del Monte, F. M. Fales, M. Marazzi, L. Milano, A. Palmieri, F. Pomponio, C. Zaccagnini), who have greatly contributed to the materials used in this book through their helpful advice (each in their own specialised area). Finally, I am grateful to my mother for having prepared the entire final typewritten manuscript, to Dr Barbara Cifola for having prepared the chronological tables, and to Giacinto Giuliani and Dario Terzi for the maps. Finally, to the numerous Italian and foreign colleagues, I owe them their consensus to use some original drawings.

Mario Liverani
Rome, February 1988

Preface to the second edition

After more than 20 years from the first edition and several re-editions with only few, relatively marginal, corrections, it is time to provide a systematically revised edition of this book to the reader. The main reason behind these revisions is not only the publication of the new Italian edition, but also of the English and German editions, which make this volume accessible on an international level. I have to say that the lateness of these translations (which follow the Spanish one, published in 1995), testify that through the years this work has gradually acquired and preserved the character of a unique and internationally acknowledged reference point. This is both due to its methodological approach and its size, unparalleled among the works of an individual author in this field.

I have to add that the recent (but now established) changes in university courses (in Italy and elsewhere) make a book of this size a somehow anomalous manual for the purpose of teaching a subject that cannot claim a large number of course credits. As a result, this book has been recently moved from the 'Manuals' series to the 'Historical Library' (*Biblioteca Storica*) series. Nonetheless, in recent years, the distribution of this book has continued. This fact indicates that there is an audience outside universities interested in a more detailed and reliable account of the Near East than that which is provided by more commercial accounts. At the same time, it indicates that within universities themselves there is a concrete need for a reference work of this size.

After all, when one of my students complains that the book is 'too long' for the final exam, I answer that the number of pages is not the only factor to take into account. One also has to take into consideration a book's readability. A smaller volume full of names, dates, and events to memorise becomes far more difficult to remember than a longer volume that simply needs to be read. This book indeed needs to be read. I distinctly remember that, when I wrote it, I forced myself not to include anything that I did not know already without having to consult anything else. Admittedly, the book comes with a whole set of chronological tables, maps, texts and bibliographies. However, this is simply for consultation.

The publication of a revised edition has also become necessary due to the amount of time (20 years) that has passed from the first edition. This period has been filled with discoveries. In the study of the Ancient Near East, these discoveries appear at a much faster pace than in any other field of ancient history. This is true despite the many difficulties the current wars and political events provide to archaeological activities in many countries of the Middle East. Unfortunately, these 'new discoveries' are not evenly distributed, but mainly concern areas in which it has been possible to excavate.

I have to point out that the revisions (which only affect some chapters, while others have remained almost unchanged) mainly consist in the addition of new information. The revisions, then, consist in the inclusion of new discoveries, the reformulation of certain problems, and the inclusion of new considerations and debates. Whenever possible, I have tried to simplify the text as a whole. I have not deemed it necessary to modify the overall structure of the book. Therefore, its methodological premises, the balance of political, economic and cultural aspects, and its main chronological divisions have essentially remained the same. In other words, I have not written a new book, and I did not do it for a series of reasons closely related to each other.

A book like this requires a degree of effort, time and energy that can only be achieved once in a lifetime. Moreover, if the structure of the book seems dated, this task would befall on a scholar from the new generation and with a different background. Personally, I believe that the overall structure of this book is still valid. The period between 1965 and 1985 has been innovative in terms of historical methodology, which was applied to the study of the history of the Near East for the first time. However, the same cannot be said for the years between 1985 and 2005. Apart from new discoveries, I believe that the greatest innovation of the last 20 years has been the implementation of a 'systematic' way of reasoning and analysing problems. We owe these changes to the spread of electronic resources for historical purposes. However, this is an innovation that affected more the way we work than the general evaluation of the Near East. Consequently, I have kept the same structure the book had 20 years ago, and I do not regret this choice.

M. L.

PART I

Introduction

1
THE ANCIENT NEAR EAST AS A HISTORICAL PROBLEM

1 The myth of the Ancient Near East

Over the past century and a half, excavations have provided the archaeological and textual evidence necessary for the study of Ancient Near Eastern cultures. Prior to these excavations, many of these populations had been completely forgotten, not only in terms of their history and cultural traits, but also in terms of their names, languages and written sources. Their rediscovery constitutes one of the greatest achievements and developments in ancient history. This rediscovery, however, has only just begun and continues to provide new information, requiring the revision or the first writing of these long and often complex chapters of history. Admittedly, Western culture always retained a sort of mythicised memory of the Near East, based on preconceptions rather than on actual historical evidence. To a certain extent, these views continue to influence historical research today. Consequently, a brief but critical reference to this phenomenon can be a useful premise for the delineation of current historiographical trends.

One of the main sources that preserved a historical memory of the Near East through time (that is without interruption) is the Old Testament. However, this complex collection of writings, which vary both in terms of dating and type, was compiled according to the ideological intentions of its editors. Moreover, the Bible is closely linked to the development of two religions, namely, Judaism and Christianity. Both these religions initially developed in the Near East, and then managed to spread beyond their spatial and chronological boundaries.

On the one hand, this link has allowed the survival of a distant memory of the Near East, despite the general disappearance of its literature. The latter had to be rediscovered, alas only partially, through archaeological investigations. On the other hand, being a holy book (and thus a divine revelation), the Old Testament has given this memory a sense of authority and an appearance of 'truth'. This overall impression has been accepted by Western culture without substantial revisions. Consequently, the conviction of the uniqueness of the Israelites as the 'chosen' people has negatively influenced the presentation of the surrounding cultures cited in the Old Testament – from the Assyrians to the Chaldeans, Canaanites, and the Philistines. These surrounding cultures were therefore seen as instrumental participants (in the hands of divine will) of the salvation story of the human race in its initial phase.

Originally, the archaeological rediscovery of the Ancient Near East was itself part of an attempt at recovering data and images of the so-called 'historical context' of the Old Testament. Only at a later stage, and undoubtedly as a reaction against a historical and textual analysis of the Old Testament, archaeological activities intensified in order to demonstrate its substantial accuracy. Using a famous expression of obvious ideological brutality, these activities were aimed at documenting that 'the Bible was right'. Indeed, it has been noted that the majority of the earliest archaeological investigations pursued in the region were motivated, financed, and advertised for their (true or supposed) relevance in the exegesis of the Old Testament.

The majority of researchers involved (philologists, historians and archaeologists, to name a few) were initially spurred by common motivations. This was because they were mainly Jewish, Protestant pastors and, to a lesser degree, Catholic priests. Setting aside their intellectual integrity, these scholars were not entirely impartial in their research. Their main interest lay in the results of their investigations being able to confirm or deny the premises of their own worldview. From the nineteenth century onwards, however, a more secular approach has slowly managed to prevail, despite its occasional involvement in historically misleading controversies and debates – from the 'Babel und Bibel' of the nineteenth century, to the recent debates on Ebla.

The classical authors were another source guaranteeing the survival of information and images of the Near East in Western culture. These authors were representatives of a world (Ancient Greek, then Hellenistic and Roman world) that was contemporary, yet in a way in opposition to late Near Eastern cultures. From Herodotus onwards, the East began to be depicted as the polar opposite of 'our' West. As a result, several myths were centred on the despotism of the Near East (in opposition to Western democracy), its technological and cultural immobility (in opposition to the growing progress of the Western world), and the occult and magical nature of its wisdom (in opposition to the secular and rational sciences of the Ancient Greeks and their successors).

The shift from this anthropology by contraposition to a more historical anthropology of diversity – according to which each culture is different, including our own, the latter not being superior to the others – developed, and is still developing, along a difficult path. The latter fits within the general process of historicity and cultural relativism, characteristic of modern culture. Therefore, if this mythology of 'the different' as polar opposite seems to have disappeared today, it is not due to the rejection of the myth per se. It is rather due to its displacement elsewhere, perhaps in the extra-terrestrial and the futuristic, which have substituted the 'Oriental' and 'Ancient'. In fact, the latter are now known well enough to preclude any utopic assumption, or their interpretation as opposites of Western culture.

With the significant increase of information on the Near East, however, new myths have replaced the old ones. I am mainly referring to the modern version of the origin myth that sees the Ancient Near East as the 'cradle' or the 'dawn' of civilisation. This view sees the Near East as the initial place that developed those technological and operational instruments, and forms of organisations typical of a 'high culture' which, through constant modifications and improvements, has survived to this day. It is not by chance that the Ancient Near East has become one of those privileged periods of history that constitutes the backbone of a Eurocentric world history, followed by Ancient Greece, Ancient Rome, Medieval Europe, and Modern Western Europe. On the one hand, this backbone tends to give a sense of unity and progress in history. On the other hand, it inevitably causes the marginalisation of other historical phases that are left out and considered irrelevant.

This view is partly true, yet dangerous in its implications. It is undeniable that the range of phenomena which allowed the development of complex societies (the origin of the state, the city, writing, and so on) first appeared in the Near East, and that the reconstruction of the history of their transmission to our time is complex, yet possible. However, it is dangerous and misleading to imagine a monogenesis of civilisation, which instead had several starting points and different paths. Equally, one cannot underestimate the influence of the continuous and substantial changes that institutions, technologies, and ideologies underwent in their history. Historical phenomena do not have a single 'origin', but are always modelled upon the structure of the society in which they are found. This supposed origin, then, is only one of the rings in a chain (among the many rings in the many chains of history) that has to be reconstructed in its total length, which is neither short nor univocal. This is even more the case today, with the broadening of our knowledge of the world and the drastic changes in the systems of transmission of ideas and concepts. This forces us to put our own ethnocentric point of view aside and to take advantage of the experiences and paths previously ignored by other ethnocentric worldviews.

The Near Eastern contribution to human history is certainly not the earliest one. It is preceded by other equally fundamental prehistoric phases. Therefore, the Near East is only one of many phases, and equal to any other period of history, including those that are not part of that privileged backbone of history established by modern Western historiography. Nevertheless, the history of the Near East attracts particular attention due to its crucial place in history, as a threshold or starting point of fundamental constitutive processes characteristic of complex societies. Moreover, these myths and misconceptions characterising the traditional image of the Near East need to be reconsidered and clarified with a critical eye, rather than ignored or all too easily removed from our memory.

2 Historiographical approaches to the Ancient Near East

Modern historiography has long abandoned those mythical motivations emphasising the uniqueness of the Near East (for theological reasons, as an anthropological categorisation, or as an issue of 'original' primacy). It now aims, at least in its most conscious trends, for a normalisation of this phase of history, to be analysed and evaluated in the same way as other phases and other cultures. This process of normalisation implies the abandonment of simplistic models (often too easy to apply, and thus tempting), in order to gain a variety of perspectives, allowing a more holistic reconstruction of the history of the Near East. Consequently, landscapes and material remains are analysed in conjunction with social, economic, and political aspects, as well as ideologies and symbolic systems, in an attempt to reconstruct the whole network of interconnections and motivations linking these elements to each other.

Unlike other ancient periods of history (Ancient Greece and Rome in particular), for the Near East this task is influenced, both positively and negatively, by two factors: one of absence, and one of presence. On the one hand, we lack an ancient historiography able to provide a sort of guideline for our reconstruction. This substantial, yet not total, lack is, however, a useful aspect. It forces the reconstruction of a guideline from a responsible evaluation of the sources, rather than encouraging a lazy reliance on pre-existing guidelines that are often unrealistic, biased, and reductive. In fact, when such a biased picture exists (such as in the case of Greco-Roman history), it turns a large part of modern historical research into a mere exegesis of ancient historiography. On the contrary, the history of the Near East has to be reconstructed *ex novo* from primary sources, unmediated by later historians. It is here that the availability of primary sources becomes an influential factor. In this regard, administrative texts (as well as commercial, legal, and, in general, archival material) have survived in large amounts. This is due to the trivial, yet essential, fact that the writing material used (i.e. clay tablets) has endured fire and burial much better than other materials in use later or elsewhere (for example papyrus, parchment, and paper). The disadvantage of this fortunate availability of sources is the fact that every year new excavations, both legal and illegal, uncover new material. This forces – even with the inconvenience of a considerable and growing delay in publications – a constant revision of entire chapters of history with new details and more secure data.

Therefore, the absence of ancient historiographical guidelines, the constant publication of new sources, and the progress of philological knowledge and excavation methods make the history of the Near East a young and wide-ranging field of research, relatively free of traditional historiographical problems. The disadvantage of this situation is not really the constant out-datedness of current historical research (which is, on the contrary, a proof of its fast progress). It is the need for a vast array of specialised fields to access the primary sources, and the constant effort in the publication of the first editions of these sources. In fact, the majority of researchers specialised in the study of the Near East are focused on finding and publishing new material: they are therefore predominantly archaeologists and philologists. Fully-fledged historians – separate from the other two categories – are almost non-existent, and Italy is in this case a positive exception. The history produced is therefore anchored in strong philological foundations, and more faithful to the sources (possibly in the hope that they would speak for themselves), rather than guided by problems and issues of interpretation. The general histories of the Near East published today are a clear demonstration of this, since they convert more specialised studies in the field into a general synthesis.

However, this historiographical delay is contrasted by this field's enormous potential, which has now begun to be applied. The lack of historiographical traditions and the constant influx of new material allows for the development of new approaches and methodologies, at times close to the most naïve and reckless of improvisations. However, this field's eclecticism and receptiveness for schemes developed elsewhere (for other phases in history, as well as completely different anthropological situations) are in great danger of causing misunderstandings and superficial approaches in the study of the Near East. Nonetheless, these schemes have to be considered constructive – at least for the phase of history that we can rightly consider as 'pre-paradigmatic' – for the potential reactions and innovative approaches they unleash in the field. It can be said that there has not been a single analytical method or theme in historiography, recent or not so recent, which has not been applied to the Near East: from neo-geographic spatial analysis to the structural analysis of the narratives; from acculturation to frontier studies; from modes of production to systems of exchange; from the structure of myths to political discourse; from settlement patterns to historical semantics; from systems theory to mental maps, and so on. This experimental phase will sooner or later have to be consolidated into coherent lines of research, and become a mature and less adventurous 'paradigmatic' historiography. However, the first essential objective towards an enrichment of the overall picture of this phase has been achieved, having overcome the restrictions that a too-strong tradition is still enforcing on other phases of ancient history.

Therefore, the history of the Near East also constitutes a sort of 'fringe discipline', creating the right environment for the circulation of different experiences and interpretations. In this regard, the complex set of materials available and the complementarity of the archaeological and textual evidence have prompted a more holistic reconstruction of the past (from material culture to ideology). This should long have been part of the work of the historian, but is so hard to find in many historical works. Therefore, the historian of the Ancient Near East is forced to take on the role of field archaeologist as well as philologist, to a degree unknown to other fields of research, whose areas of expertise appear better defined and seem to be working in a sort of consolidated production chain.

The reconstruction of late prehistoric phases in particular – characterised by the difficult task of reconstructing complex social structures on the basis of non-textual evidence – has acted as an incentive for the coordinated and in-depth application of all the clues and evidence available: from data regarding ecology to pedology, paleo-botany, archaeo-zoology, ethno-archaeological comparisons, and experimental archaeology, along with all the refinements in prehistoric excavations (stratigraphic investigations as well as surveys), and all the problematic complexity of social, political, and economic anthropology. On the one hand, the results remain outside the margins of history, since the lack of textual evidence hinders an access to the historical events. On the other hand, these results open up a sort of 'New History', characterised by a desire to establish 'laws' (in a way similar to other, typically American, new sciences such as New Archaeology, New Geography, and New Economic History), aimed more at 'predicting' the past rather than reconstructing it. These trends manifest a tendency to detect laws instead of identifying exceptions. Moreover, the introduction of electronic programs has opened up a range of possibilities (and risks) through 'simulations' applied to the uncertainties of the past, rather than the uncertainties of the future. This has formed a generation of 'demiurge' historians who prefer to creatively construct the past, rather than reconstructing it.

In many respects, then, the history of the Near East is increasingly becoming a workshop for the study of highly interesting phenomena characterising the history of human societies. The concept of 'workshop' has to be understood as a place that allows the breaking down of complex phenomena in their constitutive factors, analysed on their own, in order to detect norms and recreate patterns of behaviour. Moreover, due to its place at the 'dawn' of history, the Near East can be considered a privileged workshop, since it deals with phenomena at the time when they were starting to become more complex. Yet this phase remains distant enough from our times to prevent an emotional or cultural attachment. The latter could in fact hinder a full understanding of the real development of the various factors. Therefore, apart from the immediate results gathered from an understanding of the historical facts examined, the study of the Near East constitutes an opportunity to gain a wider perspective on the results gathered, allowing a reconstruction of influential historical and anthropological patterns.

3 Unity and variety, centre and periphery

The chronological and spatial delimitations of the Near East (in other words, this book's delimitations) constitute a problem both in practical and historical terms. Practical difficulties certainly bear a considerable weight on the matter, such as the specialised expertise (especially philological expertise) of the researchers, or their discipline's traditions. In terms of chronology, the emergence of the history of the Near East out of its prehistoric phase is linked to the appearance of written sources in addition to the archaeological evidence. Conversely, the end of Near Eastern history, separating Pre-Classical from Classical history, is marked by the appearance of Greco-Roman sources, which differed in language, typology, and scholarly traditions from Near Eastern sources. The same is true for the geographical delimitations of the Ancient Near East in relation to the surrounding regions, which remained less structurally complex for a longer period of time.

However, these practical aspects are linked to wider historical phenomena, which need to be emphasised here in order to allow a periodisation into historical phases without excessive conventionalisms and artificial assumptions. The invention of writing is not an isolated phenomenon. It developed within the framework of social differentiation, the division of labour, and the rise of complex administrative and political units, as well as larger settlements. Therefore, the development of writing belongs to the process of city and state formation, as well as socio-economic stratification. Thus, it is the culmination of that process defined by Gordon Childe as the 'Urban Revolution'. Due to its long-term implications, this 'revolution' deserves to be considered as a fundamental moment in history. The Near Eastern cultures considered in this book emerged from this Urban Revolution, which reached completion, after a long formation period, around 3500 BC. Before and at the periphery of these cultures, prehistoric communities had a different (and less complex) level of political structure, technological development and social control, as well as a different mode of production. Even the final phase of the period under study, marked here by the rise of the Persian empire (ca. 500 BC), followed by the Hellenistic period, coincides with an important historical phenomenon. This is the approximation of the Near East in supra-regional historical events and political entities. With the appearance of these phenomena, then, it becomes clear that an isolated study of the history of the Near East becomes inadequate and needs to be abandoned in favour of a wider approach.

This first level of approximation is, however, not enough, since it leaves aside the problem of the plurality and interconnection of the various centres of urbanisation. In fact, the early nucleus of urbanisation in Lower Mesopotamia is contemporary to other centres attested in Egypt, Iran, Central Asia, the Indus Valley, the Aegean, and southern Arabia, not to mention other comparable centres, not linked to the area under study, such as China, Mexico, or Peru. Despite the fact that all these areas are characterised by unique features, they nonetheless remain, to a lesser or larger degree, interlinked depending on their location and sphere of influence. Another factor that cannot be underestimated is the role of regions located in between these urban centres. These areas were less densely populated and less involved in the history of the Near East, but played a crucial role as buffer zones or as resources for workforce and technological developments. Consequently, their study is fundamental for the understanding of the developments taking place in neighbouring urban centres. Therefore, while the selection of a specific area highlights the unique character of the chosen region, a wider perspective allows for an appreciation of the plurality of centres and their mutual relations.

This book's choice to specifically focus on the Lower Mesopotamian area – alongside its links with Upper Mesopotamia, the Syro-Palestinian area, Anatolia, the Transcaucasian area, and western Iran – is mainly due to the author's expertise in the area and the size of this volume. However, this choice is not meant to support the idea of the primacy of Mesopotamia in the Near East. On the contrary, its historical value will be presented only within the wider perspective of the history of the surrounding regions, characterised by other important centres and border regions rich in resources, and the network of relations existing between these areas.

Despite this attempt at delineating the Near East, the area remains difficult to define. Its geographic borders are clear to the west (with the Mediterranean) and north-west (with the Black Sea), but unclear to the north (the Caucasus and the steppes of Central Asia) and the south (the Arabic desert), and more flexible to the east (the Iranian plateau and the Persian Gulf). In terms of chronology, the first process initiating the periodisation of this phase (that is the rise of urban centres) takes place at different times in different areas. These chronological and spatial variations interact with and influence each other. The entire region is held together by strong cultural, political, and commercial interactions. Nonetheless, each area maintains deeply embedded traits that allow a clear distinction between, for instance, the cultural context of Syria and Central Anatolia, or Lower Mesopotamia and Elam, and so on. Therefore, even on a local level (though only to a certain extent), one finds those contrapositions between unity and difference, centre and periphery, singularity and interrelation. These contrapositions have also characterised the wider region, including Egypt and the Aegean, the Indus Valley, Central Asia, and southern Arabia.

A similar situation can be envisioned on a diachronic level: the long span of time (three millennia: from 3500 to 500 BC) considered here has its own fundamental continuity and solidity, mainly arising from the increasing spread and development of the urban model and state formation. However, this apparent unity does not preclude interruptions, at times quite dramatic (often due to the rise or reappearance of non-urban and non-palatial features), or distinctions into phases (and 'centuries'). These can be identified thanks to the long process of enrichment and re-elaboration of the evidence. Phases are often so typified that they promote a solid and chronologically defined image of the Near East, in marked contrast with the history of each individual region, which developed over a long period of time. On the whole, the geographical and chronological delimitations laid out in this book seem to be the ones which best underline the socio-cultural unity of the Near East. However, the internal division into chapters allows an evaluation of the geographic and chronological structure and uniqueness of each area, whose interaction allows a better view of the overall history of the Near East.

Apart from chronological and geographical difficulties, there are internal complexities and variables due to the social context, economic and technological knowledge, and political participation of the areas under study. Some of these variables, such as the opposition between nomadic and sedentary communities, or between urban and rural settlements, create a series of interfaces that are very close to each other, yet distinctly located in space. Despite the low density of occupation, this area therefore experienced the close coexistence of very different lifestyles and technologies. In addition to these variables, there is also a network of 'invisible frontiers'. These cannot be traced on a map, since they separate cultural spaces rather than geographic ones and are the result of the coexistence, interaction, and conflict of different ideologies.

On a practical level, there is a series of 'documentary boundaries', allowing certain characteristics to emerge more (or better) than others. This distorts many aspects of our image of the Near East, and condemns entire sections into oblivion. Through the partial survival of ancient sources, as well as the bias of modern interpretation, a world that was mostly made of villages and agro-pastoral economy runs the risk of being considered by us as a world of cities, palaces, and luxury goods. A world that was 90 per cent (if not 99 per cent) illiterate runs the risk of being remembered for its writings and literature. Finally, a world that had to deal with an endemic scarcity (of food, resources, and workforce) runs the risk of being remembered as the opulent paradise of an abstract 'civilisation'. Thus, the duty of modern historiography is to balance this biased picture of the Near East, providing a historical reconstruction with a certain degree of quantitative evidence, and a more critical evaluation of the sources, making it more understandable and accessible to us.

4 The problem of chronology

From a technical point of view, it is necessary to clarify ancient chronology and the methods used to reconstruct it. Anyone interested in Near Eastern history immediately notices the existence of two types of dating systems: one is an archaeological chronology, characterised by round numbers, which are obvious approximations (such as 'Ghassulian, ca. 3700–3300 BC', or 'Akkadian period, twenty-fourth–twenty-second century BC', or 'Late Bronze Age III A, 1365–1300 BC'); and there is a historical kind of chronology, with precise numbers (such as 'Sennacherib, 704–681 BC', or 'Third Dynasty of Ur, 2112–2004 BC'). The latter differ from book to book (for instance, in the case of Hammurabi, one can find dates such as 1792–1750, or 1848–1806, or 1728–1696 BC), a fact that raises the issue of the effective value of such dates.

These two kinds of dating systems are complementary in principle, but one prevails in prehistoric periods, while the other prevails in historical phases. Archaeological chronology is based on more objective and scientific data. It tends to reconstruct the dating of ancient artefacts (or, better, of their finding spots) in relation to one another, and to the present (dates BP, 'before present'). Historical chronology is more cultural in character. It tends to reconstruct ancient dating systems and chronological sequences and then place them within our own chronological framework and sequence in order to make them useful to us. For both procedures, the first step consists of placing the elements to be dated in a reciprocal relationship of before and after, or even of contemporaneity (relative chronology). The second step consists of linking the sequence obtained through the relative chronology to one or more fixed dates, transforming it into a sequence of dates (absolute chronology). These can be more or less precise, down to the century or the decade, the year or even the day, according to the level of detail provided by the available evidence.

In archaeology, relative chronology relies heavily on stratigraphic evidence gathered from excavated settlements. Stratigraphy allows the reconstruction of the various layers found in the ground (formed either by accumulation or deposition), the recovery of the remains found in each layer, and the establishment of relations between the layers (such as 'covers', 'cuts' and so on), allowing a diachronic reconstruction of the site. This evidence is then summarised on grids showing the sequence of interventions on the ground through time – both voluntary (constructions, the deposit of objects, evidence for destruction, etc.); and involuntary (such as waste deposits, wind deposits, floods and so on). A rigorous method used by virtually all archaeologists excavating in the Near East to analyse this process is the Harris matrix, which compares sequences obtained through the stratigraphic analysis of each excavated area. In this way, it becomes possible to reconstruct the overall stratigraphic history of the site. Therefore, the comparison of various sequences gathered from several sites (and here the typology of the artefacts comes into play) allows the reconstruction of a comparative stratigraphy of an entire area as well as a relative chronology of a certain period (thus becoming a chronology of the material culture, since it is based on the archaeological evidence). This leads to a sequence that encompasses the whole of the Near East (and beyond), including all its historical and prehistoric phases.

There are two ways to turn this archaeological relative chronology into an absolute chronology. First, the discovery of written documents within the excavated layers can become a useful link of the stratigraphic sequence with the historical chronology, which will be considered later. Second, there are scientific methods to date some kinds of materials, mostly organic. Some methods, though useful for the earliest prehistoric phases (such as thermoluminescence dating), are too imprecise for late prehistoric and historical phases. For the latter, carbon-14 (or radiocarbon) analysis is used, along with the increasing use of dendrochronology.

Radiocarbon dating is based on the fact that the radioactive isotope of carbon (^{14}C), which occurs in living organic material in a known quantity, progressively decays through time and, according to Willard

Libby, is halved in 5568 years (*lower half-life*). Measuring the quantity of ^{14}C contained in an organic remain therefore allows us to establish the age of the sample, with an approximation which varies according to the state of the sample and the accuracy of the process. Therefore, dates established through radiocarbon analysis are always written with a '± 50' or '± 70', or simply with a ± sign to show that the date is an approximation (Figure 1.1).

Dates can be more or less reliable, or even completely wrong if gathered from samples contaminated by other organic materials, or a certain type of soil. Moreover, dates gathered from carbonised grains found on the floor of a burnt building are the most precise, and refer to the moment of the fire. Conversely, dates gathered from the timber frames of the same building refer to the moment of construction and will be less precise, since the material could have been recycled or used years after it was cut. Nonetheless, a good number of matching dates recovered through radiocarbon analysis from the same layer allow a relatively precise dating. Currently, the use of the accelerator allows an even more precise dating from a small amount of carbon.

Dendrochronology (or tree-ring dating) is based on the fact that the width of tree-rings (which grow yearly and are visible in a horizontal cross section of a tree's trunk) is proportional to the humidity absorbed by the tree in that same year (i.e. the intensity of rainfall). Therefore, tree-rings belonging to different trees growing in the same area should be equally wide each year, but different year by year. Cross sections thus become *bona fide* graphs documenting rainfall variability, following a fixed pattern in a certain amount of years. This pattern can then be recognised and used on new trees. Starting from sequences obtained from

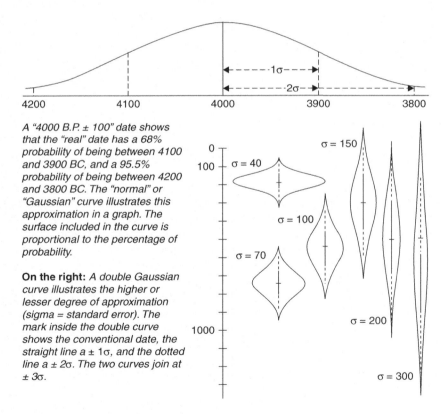

A "4000 B.P. ± 100" date shows that the "real" date has a 68% probability of being between 4100 and 3900 BC, and a 95.5% probability of being between 4200 and 3800 BC. The "normal" or "Gaussian" curve illustrates this approximation in a graph. The surface included in the curve is proportional to the percentage of probability.

On the right: A double Gaussian curve illustrates the higher or lesser degree of approximation (sigma = standard error). The mark inside the double curve shows the conventional date, the straight line a ± 1σ, and the dotted line a ± 2σ. The two curves join at ± 3σ.

Figure 1.1 Radiocarbon dating approximations.

living trees (thus with a known final date) and comparing them with each other and back in time (through a partial and progressive overlapping of the various samples) with ancient tree-ring samples (timber beams used in buildings, churches, mosques, for example), it has been possible to establish a sequence for the Near East reaching as far back as the Classical period.

Despite a considerable chronological gap of several centuries, a long sequence has been established for the Iron Age (and Late Bronze Age) in Anatolia, initially developed from the data found in the funerary tumuli at Gordion (modern Yassihüyük). This and other sequences disconnected from the present are dated through radiocarbon dating (taking a sample from the earliest and latest tree-rings), leading to the development of sequences going as far back as the Bronze Age. Only when these sequences are successfully linked to each other and to the principal sequence (which can be precisely dated), will it be possible to have an exact chronology (by year). However, this chronology is based on a specific type of material (trunks, even burnt ones) and is thus only useful for dating buildings in which these remains were found.

While dendrochronology is still working towards a reconstruction of an entire sequence for the Near East, it has already brought an important, yet indirect, development. In fact, radiocarbon analysis of trunks accurately dated through dendrochronology has revealed that the dates obtained were too early for later periods and too late for ancient periods (especially between 2000 and 7000 BC, that is the pre-historical phases). The reason for this is that the rate of radioactive decay of ^{14}C has not been homogenous through time, but has experienced fluctuations, detected through dendrochronology. Therefore, dates gathered through radiocarbon dating have to be re-calibrated, even when they were obtained from materials other than timber or for other periods that could not be covered by dendrochronology (Figure 1.2).

These are not inconspicuous differences in dating. For instance, the same sample (from the late Ubaid period) has been dated ± 4133 with the *lower half-life*, ± 4322 with the *higher half-life*, and ± 5072 through calibration. Since this calibration develops into a series of complex percentages of probability spread through time, laboratories continue to follow the convention of using B.P. dates according to the *lower half-life*. Nevertheless, thanks to computer programmes specifically developed for this purpose, anyone can calculate the calibrated date.

Regarding historical phases, this archaeological and scientific chronology has to be integrated and improved (to the level of the actual events) through the data derived from written sources (Table 1.1). In fact, every culture has some form of chronological structure, not necessarily for historiographical reasons, but mainly for legal and administrative purposes, in order to be able to refer back to previous legal and administrative documents. Such chronologies are based on 'eras', namely, temporal sequences linked to a known initial date. Our own sequence (which calculates time according to the year Jesus Christ was allegedly born) has been in use for such an extended period of time – to the point that it has become retrospective (with the establishment of dates 'before Christ') – that we have almost forgotten that it is only one possible convention among the infinite ways to establish time, and the many ways which were in use before and at the same time as our system (both in Christian and non-Christian contexts).

In the Near East, the 'eras' used were short, normally based on the enthronement year of a ruling king, thus varying between cities and between reigns. In order to make use of the chronological data reported in ancient sources, it is therefore necessary to reconstruct the complex network of dynastic sequences found in each state. A text mentioning a precise date, such as 'fourth day, third month, sixth year of Nebuchadnezzar', is not datable for us, unless we are able to relate that specific chronological phase (that is Nebuchadnezzar's reign) to our own time. Thankfully, our difficulty is not substantially different (though with a different purpose and scope of research) from the problem encountered by ancient scribes and archivists. The latter had to establish concordances between the various dating systems used in their recent past, and which continued to be used in their own documents. Therefore, they developed specific tools that we can use again today.

11

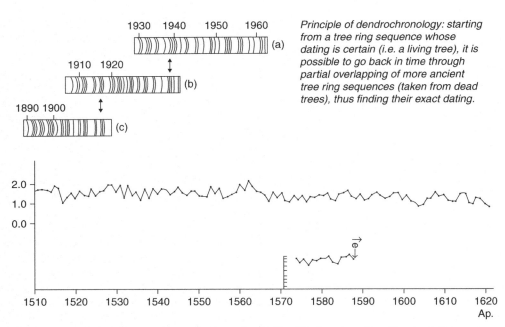

Principle of dendrochronology: starting from a tree ring sequence whose dating is certain (i.e. a living tree), it is possible to go back in time through partial overlapping of more ancient tree ring sequences (taken from dead trees), thus finding their exact dating.

Dendrochronological diagram: the y-axis shows the width of the tree rings (in millimetres), the x-axis the years (here: AD). A short sequence is dated by matching it with the main sequence.

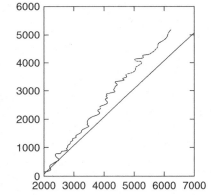

Radiocarbon calibration. The y-axis shows the "calendar" (real) years gathered through dendrochronology (in this case, the dates are all AD), the x-axis shows radiocarbon dates (compared to the half-life of radiocarbon at 5568 years), counted from the present (BP).

Figure 1.2   Dendrochronology and radiocarbon calibration.

In Mesopotamia, there were three main ways to identify a year: 1) through an eponymous official (*līmu*), a system in use in Assyria throughout its history; 2) through a year name (for instance 'year of the construction of the walls of Sippar'), a system in use in Sumer and Babylonia until the mid–second millennium BC; 3) by referring back to the enthronement year of the ruling king, a system in use in Babylonia from the Kassite dynasty onwards. Therefore, in order to make use of their chronology, Assyrian scribes composed and kept up-to-date a list of eponyms. Similarly, Sumerian and Babylonian scribes developed lists of year names and ruling kings, either for a single or several dynasties, reaching the compilation of lists

Table 1.1 Chronology of the Ancient Near East

Dates BC	Archaeological phases	Syria – Palestine	Anatolia	Upper Mesopotamia	Lower Mesopotamia	Iran
3000	"Urban Revolution"	Late Chalcolithic Uruk colonies	Late Chalcolithic Uruk colonies	Late Chalcolithic Uruk colonies	Late Uruk 3300–3100	Uruk colonies
	I	Amuq G			Jemdet Nasr 3100–2900	Proto-Elamite period 3100–2700
					I 2900–2750	
	II	Amuq H		Nineveh 5	II 2750–2600	
2500	III	Ebla 2500–2300 Amuq I			III 2600–2350 (Early Dynastic period)	
		Sakkanakku in Mari Amuq J		Urkish and Nawar	Akkad 2350–2200	Awan 2350–2200
	intermediary period Early/ Middle Bronze Age	Amorites 2000		Amorites 2000	Gutians 2200–2120 Ur III 2120–2000 Amorites 2000	Simash 2050–1950
	Early Bronze Age	Mari 1850–1750	Assyrian colonies 1900–1750	Old Assyrian kingdom 1950–1750	Isin 2017–1794 Larsa 2025–1763	Sukkalmah 1900–1750
2000		Yamhad 1800–1600 Alalah VII		Dark Age 1750–1550	Babylon 1894–1595	
		★Hyksos	Old Hittite kingdom 1650–1550	Hana	Sealand	

Table 1.1 Continued

Dates BC	Archaeological phases	Syria – Palestine	Anatolia	Upper Mesopotamia	Lower Mesopotamia	Iran
1500	Late Bronze Age	Egyptian and Mitannian rule 1550–1370	Middle Hittite period – Kizzuwatna 1550–1370	Mitannian rule 1550–1360	Kassites	
		Egyptian and Hittite rule 1370–1190	Hittite empire 1370–1190	Middle Assyrian kingdom 1360–1050	1600–1150	Middle Elamite kingdom
		"Sea Peoples" 1200				
1000	Iron Age I	Arameans 1100–720		Assyrian crisis 1050–900	Isin II 1150–1025	
	Iron Age II	Neo-Hittites 1100–720	Phrygia 750–650	Assyrian empire 900–615	Various dynasties 1025–725	
	Iron Age III	Assyrian rule	Lydia 650–550		Assyrian rule 725–625	Neo-Elamite kingdom 750–650
		Median and Chaldean rule	Nairi			
			Utartu 800–600		Chaldeans 625–539	Media 650–550
500		Persian empire (from 550 BC onwards)				

including neighbouring dynasties, such as the 'Sumerian King List' and the Assyro-Babylonian 'Synchronistic King List'.

If we had all these chronological texts today, we would be able to reconstruct a complete chronology of the Near East that included all the eras that had been used, and their sequence or overlap. Unfortunately, the lists that have arrived to us are incomplete, fragmentary and with considerable mistakes (especially in terms of numbers). The latter only appear when more lists or copies of the same list are available, but otherwise remain unknown to us. Mesopotamian lists often contain deliberate mistakes: for instance, the omission of certain kings or dynasties for political reasons; the listing as a sequence of dynasties which were instead completely, or in part, contemporary to each other; and the inclusion (at the beginning of the Sumerian King List) of mythical and legendary data. Despite these difficulties, through these sources it has been possible to broadly reconstruct the chronology of Mesopotamia from the mid-third millennium BC (any time before that has to be reconstructed through archaeological evidence) all the way to the Greek and Persian chronology of the first millennium BC.

This chronology is relatively precise and quite established between 1500 and 500 BC, while for the first millennium BC there is additional evidence from chronicles (especially Babylonian) and annals (mostly Assyrian). In the mid-second millennium BC, some gaps in the Assyrian King List (which is the longest unbroken sequence available) and some overlaps between Babylonian dynasties have caused a more or less long hiatus. In fact, there are differences by decennia in the period between 2500 and 1500 BC, gradually increasing in the phases preceding 2500 BC, due to the many uncertainties and gaps in our evidence. While it has been previously believed that it was possible to measure the length of the hiatus through several allusions to astronomical phenomena recorded in Old Babylonian texts (from the reign of Ammi-saduqa), we now know that these allusions are uncertain (since different astronomers have interpreted them in different ways) and not entirely reliable. In fact, these astronomical references pertain to cyclical phenomena with various possible dates, all equally valid from an astronomical point of view.

As mentioned above, the dates of the reign of Hammurabi can be 1848–1806 BC, according to the so-called long chronology, 1792–1750 BC using the middle chronology, and 1728–1696 BC with the short chronology. These dates are the result of a different choice of astronomical cycle, and have to be understood as conventions rather than actual dates. In this volume, the chosen chronology is the middle one, which has long been the most widely accepted and which fits the archaeological and radiocarbon chronology best. The recent tendency of implementing the short chronology clashes, in my opinion, against unacceptable shortenings of the Hittite and Syrian chronologies, and should be considered a (hopefully) passing trend. The most pressing matter in terms of chronology, however, is the establishment of a coherent relation between the scientific absolute chronology and the historical one. This is a difficult problem, due to the degree of conventionality and the variety of options available for both systems.

Nonetheless, the overall chronological reconstruction of the Near East is more or less adequate for the sources it refers to, and from which it has been developed. For periods and regions with more evidence (and thus requiring a more precise chronology) it is possible to establish a relatively detailed chronology, while for periods and areas with fewer sources, the chronology remains approximate. There are also strictly cultural factors hindering a chronological reconstruction. For instance, in Late Bronze Age Syria and Hittite Anatolia legal documents are (so to speak) dated through formulae such as 'from today onwards' and 'forever', thus indicating that the validity of the text is closely linked to the physical survival of the tablet. These kinds of documents did not need to have a chronological reference and are testaments to a culture that composed undated administrative texts. Consequently, it is not surprising that the scribes belonging to these cultures did not provide any form of chronological list (since they did not need it), a fact that has resulted in our own difficulty in reconstructing their dynastic sequence and the length of each reign. Generally speaking, Mesopotamia provides us (due to the abundance of sources and the precision of its scribes) with the most detailed and reliable chronology, while the surrounding areas can be reconstructed through synchronisms. These synchronisms increase in number as new documents are discovered and published.

For the study of particular concentrations of sources (such as archives), there is prosopography (the study of specific individuals and their connections), which can also be of aid for a chronological reconstruction. It is here that more detail is needed, bringing about the study of calendric systems (if the texts provide the month and the day). In archives of cuneiform tablets (just like later archives), texts were either stored because of their importance, or were destroyed. For this reason, legal texts (real-estate transactions, adoptions and loans, for example) had to be stored over a long period of time, at least as long as they were valid. Bookkeeping records were often stored for shorter periods, but their data was kept in summaries (covering a year or even longer periods), meant to be stored for longer.

In this volume, the chronology used for prehistoric periods is the one derived from calibrated radiocarbon dating. The conventional middle chronology is used for the analysis of Mesopotamian history from the beginning of the third millennium all the way to the mid-second millennium BC, and to which all the chronologies from the surrounding regions are connected. After the mid-second millennium, the differences between chronologies are virtually irrelevant. All dates are BC, unless otherwise specified.

2
THE GEOGRAPHY OF THE ANCIENT NEAR EAST

1 Ecological reality and mental maps

The Ancient Near East (to the extent considered in this book) covers a relatively confined area of roughly 2,000,000 km^2. It is therefore slightly smaller than Western Europe. Despite its limited size, this region contains a variety of areas characterised by different types of land, rainfall levels, climates, vegetation, and habitability levels (Figure 2.1). Mountain ranges can reach 3,500 m and 4,000 m in the Taurus, Pontic, and Zagros Mountains, 5,000 m in Armenia (Mount Ararat), while the land depression of the Dead Sea (–395 m below sea level) is the deepest in the world. The landscape of the Near East is thus composed of a mixture of mountain ranges, alluvial plains, and desert plateaus. The Mediterranean climate of the western coasts swiftly changes into the arid climate of the Syro-Arabian desert or, elsewhere, into a cold mountain climate. Rivers, such as the Tigris and Euphrates, cross regions otherwise condemned to total aridity. Similarly, densely populated areas are in close contact with sparsely populated ones.

A common simplification of the geography of the Near East is that of the 'Fertile Crescent', namely, a semicircle of fertile irrigated lands prone to agricultural and urban settlements extending from the Levant to Syria and Mesopotamia. This area borders the Syro-Arabian desert to the south and the Anatolian, Armenian, and Iranian highlands to the north. A closer look at this territory, however, reveals a more complex situation, characterised by an intricate mixture of eco-regions. For instance, highlands contain several basins that recreate, on a smaller scale, the characteristic features of the Fertile Crescent. Similarly, fertile areas are interrupted by hills, mountains, and deserts, while arid plateaus present a constellation of oases and *wadis*. This ecological variety is a structural trait of the Near East and is particularly important from a historical point of view, since it entails a close interaction between areas with different potential. For this reason, the concepts of interfaces, borders, and niches become useful tools for the understanding of this network of relations.

An interface is the conjunction of two different zones. Through an interface, a range of products, people, expertise, technologies, and developments that belong to one area, but are not available in the other, can be exchanged. The exchange process normally causes a visible change in expressions and valuations, from which both parties gain mutual enrichment, comparison, and adjustment. This interaction, then, contributed to the evolution of communities from their earliest stages. At times, phenomena resulting from the intersection of two areas lead to the movement of human groups, such as in the case of seasonal migrations, very common in pastoral groups exploiting interfaces between mountains and plains, or fertile valleys and arid lands. More often than not, sedentary communities take advantage of their convenient position

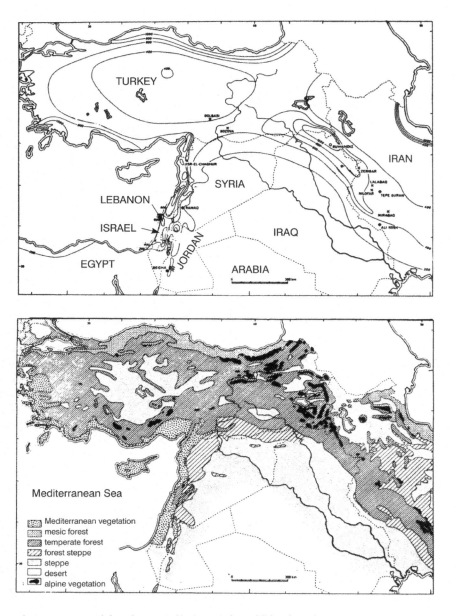

Figure 2.1 The environmental foundations. *Above*: Annual rainfall levels. *Below*: Natural (post-glacial) vegetation.

near an interface, benefiting from its privileged access to different, yet complementary resources. In terms of cultural development, then, the presence of many interfacing areas close to each other made the Near East a highly dynamic environment.

While interfacing areas are an environmental phenomenon, borders are more historical and cultural in nature, being a concept rather than a feature of the environment. A border zone is located along the boundaries of a given community, beyond which – according to the members of that community – there is nothing, or the generally inferior 'other'. This is an appealing area for its raw materials, accessed through unequal exchange, or military conquest and imperialistic expansion. While an interfacing area works both ways, a border is univocal, being a point of view or, better, an idea.

An interface is relatively stable and centred on its natural resources and their exploitation. On the contrary, a border can be moved, becoming the object of outward expansion if its central community is strong. However, a border is also prone to being violated and removed if the 'chaotic' forces from the outside prevail over the stability of the community within that border. In addition to that, there can be internal borders within the community itself that can become, in the course of time, 'invisible frontiers'. These frontiers are untraceable on maps, but can only be detected in the community's degree of cultural diversity. 'Invisible frontiers' can include linguistic and religious frontiers, and differences in modes of production and lifestyle, as well as social and political structures.

The niche (ecological or cultural) constitutes a completely different concept, which stresses the value of well-defined and relatively isolated zones with their own social structures, resources, and modes of production. Niches can be small territorial units (a valley or an oasis) whose impact seems minor when compared to the large-scale economic and historical processes that we know today. However, the processes affecting the history of the Near East were of a much smaller scale than the processes we see today. Therefore, the development and location of human settlements, the accumulation of surplus, craftsmanship, and trade had a strong influence on the history of the area despite their relatively limited scale.

Consequently, a secluded and protected area, well connected to its surroundings, could experience a more effective and productive development than a larger, but fragmented area. The latter could only arise after the development of a more organised and efficient network of communication, a more compact population, and a more pressing need for imported materials and resources. The optimal size of a niche is therefore prone to changes in response to its historical context. For instance, the oasis of Jericho was an optimal niche for the Neolithic period, while Assyria, which included a large number of cities, became an optimal niche in the Iron Age.

Through this articulation in niches, interfaces and borders, the Ancient Near East acquires a considerable degree of complexity. This explains (as will be explored in detail in the analysis of its history) its varying degrees of development, its versatility in terms of political structures, and its constant cultural interactions. However, in the case of a general overview of Near Eastern history, this complexity also runs the risk of becoming an inextricable mess. Simplifications can therefore illuminate this complex picture in a viable and powerful way, providing clarifications and explanations for many aspects of the history of the Near East. The protagonists of the history of the Near East themselves already put forward similar ideological simplifications of this complex reality through their own worldview. Some of these ideologies were to be picked up by modern historiography, at times unaware of their ideological nature.

This is the case of the most powerful of these ideas, namely, the one that sees the Near East as a contraposition of centre and periphery. The centre constitutes the settled and civilised space. Its ideal nucleus is the city (with its main temple or palace), which is at the heart of a network of irrigated fields and villages. The periphery is the area surrounding the centre. This area is characterised by steppes or mountains, and a sparse, nomadic population of shepherds, refugees, and robbers. Being further away from the centre, the periphery is less inhabited and acts as a mere supplier of natural resources such as timber, metals, and semi-precious stones. Similar 'mental maps' can be easily found in ancient sources (Figure 2.2), such as in the case of Gudea (ca. 2100 BC), ruler of the city of Lagash. He saw his own city as the centre of the world, and the temple of the god Ningirsu as the centre of Lagash. The materials needed for the construction of the temple came from the surrounding areas. This periphery was seen as a series of territories each providing a specific type of metal or wood, and each linked to the central plain by a river that conveniently brought the raw materials to the centre. In this way, the surrounding lands were seen as being provided with a purpose they would have lacked otherwise.

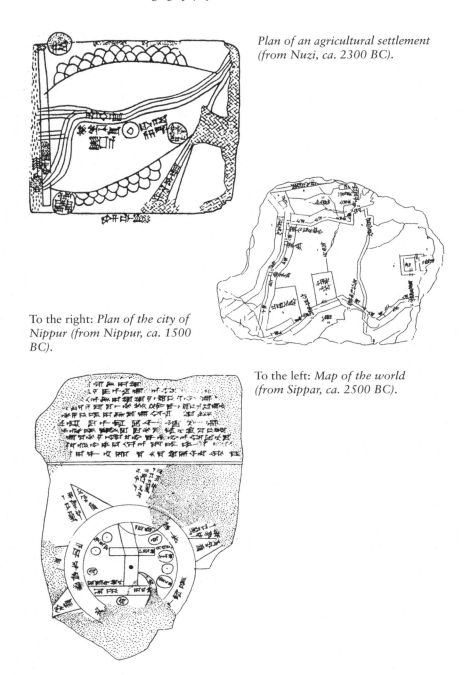

Plan of an agricultural settlement (from Nuzi, ca. 2300 BC).

To the right: *Plan of the city of Nippur (from Nippur, ca. 1500 BC).*

To the left: *Map of the world (from Sippar, ca. 2500 BC).*

Figure 2.2 Maps from the Ancient Near East.

Modern historiography has implemented a similar point of view, envisioning the Ancient Near East as centred in the Lower Mesopotamian plain. This area had the largest fields and urban settlements, and was surrounded by sparsely populated steppes and mountains. The latter provided raw materials and were culturally and politically dependent on the centre. It is clear that this kind of simplification can be fairly acceptable from the viewpoint of the centre, but cannot be accepted for the periphery. In fact, in terms of written sources, this was a typically Mesopotamian worldview.

However, the communities living elsewhere also felt at the centre of their own world, which they organised, with more or less success, in response to their own needs. They therefore protected their identity even at the cost of drastically changing the characteristics and traditions of other communities. Consequently, this opposition of centre and periphery runs the risk of forcing modern historiography to focus too much on Mesopotamia (clearly visible in the modern use of the term 'Greater Mesopotamia', indicating Mesopotamia and the surrounding regions). This approach, however, flattens out the unique traits of the surrounding communities and regions, the diverse and reciprocal nature of cultural interactions, and the complexity of trade, exchange, and politics. Despite still using, at least partly, a similar point of view on the Near East, it is necessary to adjust it in its articulation. Therefore, one must take into consideration the diversity of the territory and its diachronic development, locating the many rising centres that were emerging through time, and bearing in mind the subjectivity and relativity of the concept of periphery.

From a purely descriptive point of view, a strong complementarity between the areas with high concentrations of people and those rich in raw materials remains. This makes the opposition between centre and periphery a useful, yet simplified, model. In fact, population density is directly correlated to agriculture and is therefore found in fertile areas (i.e. plains), especially if irrigated. Alluvial plains consequently attract the majority of cultivations and urban settlements. However, such areas lack a wide range of raw materials, such as forests for wood, pasturelands for wool, metals and stone. These resources are predominantly located on the mountains and semi-arid plateaus, areas that are unsuitable for urban settlements and agricultural activities.

These two complementary areas experience an unequal level of exchange. The periphery, rich in resources, provides goods to the densely populated centre. In turn, the centre provides a return in the form of ideologies and cultural influence. Since history is concerned with human groups, this unbalanced perspective favouring the densely populated areas and marginalising the areas providing material resources is both reasonable and inevitable. However, if taken too far, this dichotomy would result in a loss of the overall balance between the two, and an impoverishment of the wealth of different experiences that shaped the history of the Near East.

So far, we have considered the Near East as a complex environment in geographical terms, but seemingly stable through time. This apparent stability, however, is only a rough approximation. It is true that the climate of the Near East in its 10,000 years of history was similar to today's climate, indicating that the whole history of the area developed within the same interglacial phase. However, within this phase there have been medium-sized fluctuations in rainfall levels and temperature. The latter had a particularly strong impact on areas with critical habitability levels, thus shifting the borders of a number of eco-regions (such as the western edge of the Syro-Arabian Desert, located between Syria and the Transjordan plateau) and causing fluctuations between the presence of sedentary and transhumant communities. Modern historiography is very aware of the historical impact of these fluctuations, and has often considered climate factors as the main reason for regional collapses and migrations of people. However, the effects of these climatic factors were not always as immediate as is often believed.

Be that as it may, the most significant factors influencing the changing landscape of the Near East were human activities. At times, these activities led to a savage exploitation of certain resources, kick-starting often irreversible processes of decline. In this regard, the process of deforestation was particularly damaging. Its impact can be noted when comparing maps reconstructing the original forested areas with their extension today. From the Neolithic period, the creation of farmlands and pasturelands through the removal of forests constituted a factor that has deeply marked the history of the Near East. The first acts of deforestation from that time were mainly aimed at clearing limited portions of land in a virtually intact territory. They were followed by the deforestation of wider areas in the Bronze Age. In fact, the needs of urban centres led to the deforestation of mountain forests for building purposes, as well as the remainders of forests on the plains for agricultural purposes.

In the Iron Age, the agro-pastoral exploitation of the mountains and hills increased. Deforested areas were now used for intensive grazing, causing an irreversible damage to the land both in terms of vegetation and soil depth. On the irrigated plains, interventions were mainly focused on the construction of canals, the regulation of water flow, and the drainage and diffusion of water. These interventions first affected specific areas, then vast portions of the territory. Consequently, the irrigation system of the Near East experienced various stages of growth and decline (especially in Lower Mesopotamia), including the retransformation of vast areas into marshes. Moreover, the intensive cultivation of the land led to a salinisation of the soil. Due to these constant fluctuations, it is necessary to reconstruct the landscape of each historical period analysed, at least as far as possible. While in certain cases the ancient landscape is very similar to the current one, in others it is drastically different, especially if the modern landscape is the outcome of decline and desertification processes, or modern interventions in the land.

In this regard, paleobotanic and palynologic data play an essential role in a historical reconstruction of the Near Eastern landscape. This evidence allows us to identify the most common plant species (both natural and cultivated) in the area, and their fluctuations. In addition to that, archaeological evidence provides useful insights on the chronology of human interventions, such as the construction of canal systems, agricultural terraces, wells, and so on. Written sources and depictions are normally given great importance for a reconstruction of the landscape, despite the fact that this evidence is intrinsically biased. Administrative texts are far more reliable and play a fundamental role in the understanding of agriculture and livestock in the Near East, often providing us with quantitative data. From a linguistic point of view, however, this kind of evidence is difficult to interpret, since an exact and reliable translation of ancient terminology (botanical, zoological and technological) is not always available.

Literary accounts and depictions portray a highly deformed reality, both culturally and ideologically, and require careful interpretation. The landscapes presented are usually misrepresented, both in terms of size and of exotic and unusual features. They often present utopic connotations, depicting or describing landscapes which were an interpretation of real landscapes, with strong political, celebrative, or normative overtones. They consequently do not faithfully describe a landscape, but show how this landscape was seen. These literary and iconographic landscapes therefore belong more to the realm of art and literature than to a solid reconstruction of a specific environment. Nonetheless, if appropriately interpreted, they can provide useful information that can be used for a historical reconstruction.

2 Population

The environmental diversity of the Near East caused its population to be distributed more unevenly than today. Communities mainly settled in the alluvial plains and the intermontane niches. In some phases, they even moved into vast hilly areas and plateaus, and avoided the mountains and steppes, which were accessible on a seasonal basis, and by smaller, nomadic communities. The alluvial plains themselves were not evenly populated and were inhabited insofar as the land was cultivated and free from marshes. Therefore, even within these densely populated areas, the discontinuity of population levels remains, with irrigated patches of land (cultivated by sedentary and even urbanised communities) emerging from a territory potentially exploitable, but largely left uncultivated.

Overall, there are three principles worth bearing in mind. First of all, the amount of land was higher than the number of people living in it. Second, agriculture depended on the availability of water. Third, human intervention was the main factor allowing the development of infrastructures for the exploitation of land and water. Moreover, human intervention was proportional to population density and the level of socio-political organisation. These three core elements – land, water, and labour – strongly influenced each other. Consequently, population density was influenced by the availability of food, but was also the main factor causing food production. Therefore, population growth was a gradual and difficult process, and no single factor could be responsible for it without the intervention of other contributing factors. Similarly, the process could be put to a halt or even reverted in case of a crisis.

The spatial discontinuity of the population was parallel to a diachronic discontinuity in time. The archaeological evidence shows that the history of each settlement was characterised by an alternation between phases of construction and destruction, of occupation and definitive, or prolonged, abandonment; this evidence makes it possible to compile the specific histories of each settlement into a regional and demographic history. This allows for a better understanding of local alternations between phases of development, during which positive factors (such as production and reproduction) significantly prevailed, and phases of decline, or even collapse, during which negative factors prevailed.

Crises were often caused by natural phenomena, such as earthquakes, droughts, epidemics and floods, which could not be averted, at least considering the levels of technological development of the period. However, apart from these natural causes, which were outside human control, there were crucial human factors. These constituted effective development strategies, even though the people implementing them were largely unaware of them. First, there is a strictly quantitative factor. A small community has fewer chances to survive over a prolonged period of time, being more vulnerable to a violent crisis. Moreover, a small community is less able to maintain its cultural and physical bonds over time, such as in the case of marriage incompatibilities, endogamy, the unsuitable marriageable age of its members, and so on. In this regard, a larger community is better equipped to cope with minor crises, being affected by them, but not destroyed. A larger community therefore has the ability to recover from minor crises, while at the same time providing its members with a wider range of choices and more frequent adjustments. However, in order to function properly, a larger community has to be structurally and socially complex. Therefore, a larger community is more exposed to dangerous and unrecoverable crises, affecting those not directly involved in food production in particular.

Second, there is a strictly strategic factor, based on a choice between two possible models. One developmental model is slow – almost imperceptible – but safer, being more inclined towards safeguarding the community, rather than quantitative growth and qualitative improvements. This model is generally found in small agricultural and pastoral communities (such as villages and semi-nomadic groups). The model is centred on subsistence rather than progress, and it aims at maintaining its reserve of resources (land, livestock, and so on) virtually intact. There is, however, an accelerated model, primarily found in urban settlements. This model focuses on the accumulation of surplus and the specialisation of labour, with a marked tendency towards the increase and diversification of resources. In order to achieve this, the model requires the maximisation of profits from the available resources, and thus the over-exploitation of its means of production and labour: decimating herds, over-irrigating lands, cultivating without interruptions (causing soil salinisation and land degradation). These measures lead to the expectation of amounts of labour and food surplus that, if excessive, can become detrimental. This second model allowed the greatest achievements of the history of the Near East (cities with temples and palaces, the development of craftsmanship, archives, city-walls, canals, and so on). However, it was also the ultimate reason for the dramatic collapses and disasters in the Near East, caused by projects that expected too much from the scarce and variable human and material resources available at the time.

An important factor that played a major role in this progressive model was war, understood here as an extreme means to obtain resources and to expand one's sphere of political control. Military campaigns always have a negative effect on the population (bloodshed and lower birth rates) and on production (destruction of settlements and farmlands). However, through the annexation and re-organisation of conquered lands, war can have positive effects, though strictly in the sense of allowing the enlargement of a community and the integration of different territories. These effects respond to the two factors mentioned above, namely, the establishment of boundaries and of a certain pace of development. In terms of demography and production, it is clear that war is convenient to the winner and detrimental to the loser. Therefore, it is necessary to consider the effects of war over people and lands from both sides, and evaluate whether its immediate negative impact is compensated through time and contributes to the overall progress of the defeated community.

In general, the first model can be represented on a chart with a line that slowly but continuously increases through time. On the other hand, the fast-paced model can be represented with a line that rises rapidly, but abruptly drops from time to time. Considering the peaks reached by this second line, it is undeniable that they are far higher than the ones achieved in the first model. At the same time, considering the lowest points of the second line, they roughly coincide with the ones of the first model. This is because phases of accelerated development (generally urban, political, and economically and militarily aggressive) cannot continue indefinitely in time. Their eventual collapse is a structural aspect of their existence and is not accidental, but lays the groundwork for new phases of development.

It remains true, however, that peaks of development in the second model – and it has to be pointed out that we tend to overestimate them, due to their better attestation both in archaeological and written evidence – are rare and isolated in time and space. Overall, then, the average demographic development of the Near East follows the slow pace of the first model. This slower rate of growth is due to two factors: 1) the high infant mortality rate, which virtually cancelled out the high birth rates (also because the high birth rates were aimed at compensating for infant mortality); 2) an average life expectancy so low as to affect fertility rates. In a community in which the average life expectancy is 25 or 30 years, a couple's main problem is whether or not they will be able to give birth to enough children. In this way, they would be able to leave at least two of them alive long enough to be able to generate offspring themselves (since many of them would have died in infancy). Otherwise, a community would eventually die out. The solution found was to lower the marriageable age of women, in order to benefit the most from their fertility, and to balance endogamy with exogamy, monogamy, and polygamy, in order to make full use of the range of marriageable individuals available.

However, these social and cultural measures could not completely remove the physical and biological risks linked to childbirth. The latter was determined by two main factors, namely, health and diet. Infant and maternal mortality, frequent epidemics, and famines were insurmountable plagues for the Near Eastern levels of health and diet. Therefore, the already low and discontinuous population density of the Near East was further reduced by short life expectancy and poor quality of life, which was worsened by malnutrition and endemic diseases (gastro-enteric illnesses in particular, due to the low water quality of rivers and wells).

In the Near East, then, people had a short life span, lived badly, with little food and many illnesses. Consequently, they produced at rates and in quantities that may seem insignificant to us, but were the reflection of bad health and diet. However, given the achievements of these communities despite their low quality of life, the frequent crises affecting them are not as surprising as their ability to even reach such levels of growth. The accomplishments of these people with their cities and temples, as well as their high-quality artefacts and technological developments, are the result of a tenacious fight for survival and a forceful sourcing of food and labour. These efforts should be attributed to the ruling socio-political structures, which managed to control the population both physically and ideologically.

Finally, it is important to note the anthropological and linguistic features of the Near East. In terms of anthropology (as far as the available evidence can provide us with diachronic data), the stability of the population is striking and is an aspect still present today. This characteristic indicates that the Near East began to be populated very early on, and from the Neolithic period onwards experienced considerable internal movements, such as seasonal and permanent migration. The invasions and migrations emphasised by historians of the nineteenth century (AD) must have been quite modest in scale. They therefore influenced genetic diversity only marginally, allowing the leading human species to survive. The impact of migratory movements was more cultural than genetic, especially in the case of movements of elite groups (i.e. specialised military, technological, religious, or administrative groups). The latter were both culturally and politically influential, but too limited in size compared to the rest of the population, made of sedentary agro-pastoral communities.

A similar overview can be gathered from the distribution of languages in the Near East. Languages are crucial cultural phenomena, being both transferable and versatile. From a linguistic point of view, then, the earliest written attestations document the presence of Semitic groups, located on the concave side of the Fertile Crescent, where they live to this day. These groups were to stay within this area throughout their existence, spreading all the way to the Taurus and Zagros Mountains, but not beyond these boundaries. Within this compact Semitic area, however, a variety of Semitic languages developed with considerable differences and in a variety of dialects. This is the case of the ancient Eblaite and Proto-Akkadian languages, which were slowly replaced by waves of Amorite, Aramaic, and Arabic. By the third millennium BC, the borders of this Semitic area were already established. These were not much different from the ones that separate Arabic-speaking people from those speaking Turkish and Iranian languages today.

Populations speaking Indo-European languages can be found outside the Fertile Crescent, especially in Anatolia and the Iranian plateau. These populations, which were slowly but progressively spreading to the south, managed to move into those intermediary zones standing between them and the Semitic area. In these intermediary zones, people initially spoke a variety of different languages (neither Semitic, nor Indo-European), partly related to each other, such as Sumerian, Elamite, Hurrian, and others that are not sufficiently documented in the sources. However, this linguistic buffer zone was destined to disappear, and was slowly assimilated and replaced by the two predominant linguistic groups (although these other languages lasted longer in Armenia and on the Transcaucasian highlands).

As can be seen, these changes in the ethno-linguistic groups of the area were long-term phenomena affecting the Near East as a whole. The individual migrations attested in the sources were cultural phenomena rather than movements of large ethnical groups. Substantial changes in the Near East, from the assimilation of entire groups, to the shift of linguistic boundaries, and the rise of internal subdivisions, took place without the full awareness of the people experiencing them. Consequently, they remain undocumented in the sources. However, scholars have too often drawn simplistic connections between the available documentation and these changes.

3 Technological developments

In the traditional stereotypes regarding the Ancient Near East there seems to be a contradiction between the image of stagnation and inventiveness. On the one hand, there is the old-fashioned view of the East in general as being always the same socio-political context determined to suppress originality and creativity, a situation that only changed through its later contacts with the West. Leaving aside the theoretical foundations of this stereotype and considering any current book on Ancient Near Eastern history, one gets the impression that throughout its long history nothing changed in terms of lifestyle and technology. In other words, one gets the impression that no one would even realise if the book happened to mix up a part regarding Sargon of Akkad with one concerning the Assyrian king Sargon II. The difficulty of understanding in the form of a sequence the rise and fall of dynasties, the construction and destruction of cities, and the appearance and assimilation of entire populations, gives a sense of cyclicality and repetitiveness to Near Eastern history, which seems not to have benefited from the significant cultural changes (from ideology to technology) taking place in the area.

On the other hand, there is still an idea of the Near East as the birthplace of many fundamental techniques and technologies of the Ancient World: from food production to writing, city and state organisation, metallurgy, architecture, and so on. Therefore, by tracing the history of each technique, one can find its Near Eastern 'origin'. This makes this region the 'cradle' of civilisation, the birthplace of all cultural factors constituting, with modifications and improvements, the core of our own culture.

Both points of view are highly idealised. First, the myth of oriental stagnation exists as a counterpart of the myth of that 'Greek miracle' which gave birth to Western culture, and which was later used to justify colonialism. Second, the myth of the Near East as the 'cradle' of civilisation emphasises our position at the end of a long process of change and continuity, and at the forefront of world progress. A partial and approximate contextualisation of these two myths thus results in a view of the Near East as a creative and propulsive force in history, yet confined to material culture and placed in a remote past. Moreover, the Near East appears as constituted by a creative phase followed by a phase of immobilisation, when established practices were maintained, but were made ineffective and unsuitable as a basis for further progress by magic and despotic attitudes.

A more radical and less biased interpretation of the technological and cultural developments of the Near East allows a more balanced overview of its history (Table 2.1). The Near East is characterised by many areas and environments prone to innovation and development, and suitable phases for the development of more durable systems. The technological developments of the Near East are remarkable, but constituted a process that took place over millennia. This is the case not only because technological developments required a long time to be implemented, but also because demographic and economic conditions caused the majority of resources to be directed towards subsistence. Moreover, crises, sudden collapses, and abrupt interruptions (both in time and space) constituted another element slowing down the process. Alongside these, there were reciprocal influences between different cultural entities and political, ideological, religious, and production systems. Religious ideologies (from the magical interpretation of events and healing practices to the belief in salvation in the afterlife) were closely linked to the lack of human control over natural phenomena. However, they slowly began to influence technological developments, the monopolisation of resources, and so on.

There are essentially three innovative phases in the history of the Near East. The first one covers a long

Table 2.1 Technological progress in the Ancient Near East

	Farming	Agriculture	Architecture/craftsmanship	Written records
8000				
	goats, sheep, pigs	grains, legumes	unbaked bricksplaster, drainage	first signs
7000				
	cattle, donkeys		hammered metal, weaving (wool) handmade pottery	
6000				
5000		linen		first stamp seals
		irrigation in the alluvial plains, animal-drawn ploughs	molten metal	
4000				
		vine, olive tree, date palm	arsenical copper	cretula + signs
3500				
		extensive irrigation	wheel-made pottery, bronze	cylinder seals, weights and measurements, logographic writing
3000				
2500				syllabic writing
2000			baked bricks	
1500	horse		glass	
	camel, dromedary	mountain irrigation terraces	iron	alphabet
1000				
		cotton		
500				

period of its early history and took place slightly earlier than the period considered in this book. It is the so-called Neolithic Revolution, when fundamental techniques for food production (agriculture and farming), the necessary instruments (tools and containers), and the earliest forms of housing (houses, villages, and farms) were first developed. The second phase is the Urban Revolution of the Early Bronze Age. This phase saw the development of recording techniques (which culminated with the development of writing), the introduction of specialised labour (such as full-time craftsmanship) and mass production, as well as the development of cities and the rise of the concept of the state. The third phase took place between the Late Bronze Age and the Early Iron Age, when a number of innovations, such as the alphabet and the increasing use of iron were developed. This led to a sort of 'democratisation' of the former palace and temple economies, and a stronger presence of socially and geographically marginal areas compared to the former supremacy of the city. The intermediary phases between these innovative phases, however, were not characterised by stagnation: after all, innovations never appear all of a sudden, but always follow a slow and difficult path of development.

In any case, it is clear that the central and innovative role of the Near East in world history needs to be re-defined and toned down. The Neolithic Revolution affected a vast region over a long period of time (including areas outside the borders of the Near East), and evolved in a variety of ways. The Urban Revolution brought Lower Mesopotamia to be imitated (though in different ways) by other centres elsewhere. Finally, in the Iron Age, at the beginning of the first millennium BC, the Near East began to interact with, re-elaborate, and provide influential innovations to a wider network of cultural contacts. Therefore, if there was an imaginary line of development marking areas particularly prone to technological developments, this line would go from the interfacing areas between complementary eco-regions in the Neolithic period, to the urban centres as hubs for the innovations of the Bronze Age (the rise of temple and palaces in the production and political and administrative control of communities). Finally, the line would reach the trade routes (through land and water), which were the privileged locations for the elaboration and diffusion of the technological innovations of the Iron Age.

This line of development cuts across the opposition and complementarity of different working environments, which were the main areas for the diffusion of technological innovations. In the initial stages of urbanisation, palace workshops constituted privileged areas for these developments. This was due to the availability of specialised workforce able to work full-time, and the influx of raw materials through tributes and long distance trade. Therefore, the presence of institutions such as the palace (or the temple) laid those unprecedented bases for the development of specialised technologies, more refined and suitable for large-scale production.

However, outside these workshops there were other, more marginal (both geographically and socially), environments able to develop their own techniques. They therefore became potential reservoirs for more politically and economically centralised systems. This happened whenever changes in inter-regional relations, social situations, processes of acculturation, or de-culturation, took place. Placing these (and other) factors within the wider network of interactions of the Near East is a difficult task, one that is far from being fully understood and remains largely to the imagination. It is not possible to synthesise here the various theories about this issue, although certain points will be mentioned within the treatment of the history of specific communities. In order to clarify the kind of approach that should be used, it may be worth considering briefly the example of animal husbandry.

The Neolithic period saw the slow development of the domestication of several animal species (including experiments later abandoned because they were too difficult) by village communities. This activity was pursued for a variety of necessities, from food to textile production, and support in cultivation and transport. However, this process took place at a household and village level. In the early stages of urbanisation, production became an activity overseen by larger institutions. This led to a steep rise in the farming of sheep and goats for textile production, the development of mechanisms for the concentration and conservation of products for large urban centres, and the organisation of production units and draught animals for transport and agriculture. In the Late Bronze Age, the larger urban centres assimilated new species of animals, namely, the horse (in the Middle Bronze Age), the camel, and the dromedary. These had been previously domesticated in marginal areas, but gradually became essential for military and commercial needs.

A second example is the development of metalworking. The Chalcolithic period saw the development of basic casting techniques and the first alloys, though on a village level and in modest quantities. With the rise of urbanisation, bronze gradually became the preferred metal, and began to be produced on a larger scale in palace workshops. The higher demand for bronze led to a sharp increase in long-distance trade (supervised by the palace administration) for the metals needed to produce it (primarily copper and tin). The situation also led to a particular focus on metalwork, in order to meet the demands of the palace and the army. Finally, with the collapse of palace workshops and inter-palatial trade of copper and tin at the end of the Bronze Age, iron emerged as a 'democratising' metal. This was due to the fact that its production required less equipment and the raw material was more readily available.

Many other examples can be mentioned. If one could place them in columns next to each other, they would emphasise, despite their unique traits, the basic common characteristics and trends of each historical phase. However, the Near East did not have a homogeneous history of technological development. On the contrary, this process was marked by strong regional diversity, different socio-economic contexts, and a diachronic variability between areas. Despite the crises and collapses that took place throughout the history of the Near East, the main tendency was towards an improvement of the ability to master the surrounding environment, and to benefit from the scarce resources available.

Two strategies thus coexisted: one towards the selection and concentration of techniques, and the other towards a diversification of experimentation. Depending on the socio-political and economic situation of a given community, the two strategies interacted and alternatively prevailed over each other. Overall, the adaptations applied on Near Eastern technologies once they were borrowed elsewhere were not higher than the adaptations they had already experienced throughout the previous three millennia of their existence. The technological variable is therefore neither univocal nor independent, and has to be linked to other variables that might have influenced a given community. However, technology remains of primary importance in the understanding of the factors influencing historical events, from political and military changes, to the development of economic systems, and the establishment of social relations.

4 Modes of production

For a long time, the interpretation of socio-economic issues in the Near East has remained largely pragmatic. For instance, it avoided delving into the whole debate (once central to the study of ancient history) between 'modernists' and 'primitivists' – in other words, between the supporters of a reconstruction through concepts and models taken from modern economics, and the supporters of a reconstruction based on elementary forms of socio-economic developments. In the last fifty years, however, the preference for theoretical models has become more popular. Previously, there was a period characterised by a stronger support for the 'Asiatic mode of production' model developed by Marx, and/or Polányi's 'marketless trading' model. They both were non-modernist models that were historical without being primitivist. Then, classical economics experienced a revival, supporting the idea of the universality of economic concepts. In all these periods, prevailing interpretative trends were highly influenced by current political affairs and ideologies.

Admittedly, the so-called 'laws' of economics were developed from a relatively limited set of historical evidence and for other historical contexts. In fact, they are based on concepts such as markets and currencies that are quite anachronistic when applied to the Near East. Nonetheless, Near Eastern modes of production and exchange were considerably sophisticated and not directly comparable to elementary systems of exchange. It is therefore necessary to reconstruct operational models specifically designed around the societies considered, taking into consideration their uniqueness and complexity.

Regarding modes of production, it has to be borne in mind that the Marxist model concerns a capitalistic type of economy (with its formative and transformative processes). Therefore, when it was applied to ancient economies it was through few, largely unsubstantiated, references. In fact, nineteenth century researchers only had indirect and largely irrelevant evidence on the Ancient Near East. Therefore, theories on the Asiatic mode of production and its relations to other modes (such as the slave and feudal ones) belong to the realm of Marxist studies rather than to the study of the Near East.

What remains a useful concept in the context of the Near East is the 'mode of production' itself. This model, though maybe out-dated for the analysis of complex economies like the current one, can provide useful insights into less complex economies. Certain aspects remain particularly important such as the identification of types of ownership of the means of production (especially in terms of land), the relationship between means of production and workforce, the size of production units, and the accumulation of surplus. It is the highly variable combination of these basic factors that characterises what Marx defined as the foundation of the economic structure of society. Within it, many 'modes of production' (which interact following patterns of hegemony and subordination), systems of exchange, forms of consumption (as well as accumulation, ostentation, and destruction) can be detected. Modes of production and systems of exchange are, however, only ideal constructions, mere interpretative tools. The study of the economic formation of society therefore remains a historical reconstruction, concrete and variable both in time and space.

The most influential modes of production that can be found in the Near East are the palace and the household models. The first came about through the Urban Revolution, and is characterised by the rise of the 'great organisations' (the temple and the palace) as centres of production, and the servile state of the producers of food towards those holding political and administrative control. Moreover, this mode of production led to the strong and dynamic specialisation of labour, a centripetal and redistributive influx of goods, and the resulting hierarchic distribution of sectors related to production. The second mode, the household, is instead residual of the Neolithic period, when the workforce and the owners of the means of production were the same people. Moreover, the household model features the absence of a full-time labour specialisation (or, better, it is still unstructured) and the relatively equal status of its members and sectors. The two models interact with each other in a clear 'hegemony vs. subordination' kind of dynamic, since the palace model could not exist without the household one. The latter was in fact gradually absorbed and restructured (due to its relation to the palace), thus losing its former independence and autonomy.

The establishment of these two models, and of the hegemonic character of the palace model, does not eliminate the problem of the diachronic evolution of economic development and of the existence of other (more marginal) modes of production. This issue will have to be dealt with in the following chapters. For now, it may be sufficient to mention the fact that the two models evolved through mutual influences. Moreover, regional variations and the existence of other modes of production constitute an alternative development strategy, partly influenced by the specific context in which they developed. The main developmental current of the fertile plains was influenced by factors such as urbanisation, irrigation, the cultivation of grains and the farming of sheep and goats, organised trade, palace workshops, and the religious nature of political organisation. However, there were environments and strategies for production that were more centred on the exploitation of local resources (such as metal, wood and semiprecious stones), transhumance, and rain-fed agriculture. These were usually managed by communal groups ruled by an elite.

The idea of 'modes of production' as theoretical concepts that find their concrete application in the way they interact with each other (not just in the realm of production) in a specific historical context is even truer in the case of systems of exchange. In this regard, Karl Polányi's view of ancient economies has strongly influenced the study of the Near East. This is due to his definition of integrative models of reciprocity, redistribution, and markets. It is quite clear that the concept of reciprocity is best suited for a household mode of production, while redistribution is closely linked to palace administration. However, a market-centred analysis continues to be unsuitable for the type of economies found in the Ancient Near East, with the exception of the relatively early emergence of certain elements related to market economies in certain areas.

Just as with modes of production, so with systems of exchange the redistributive system prevailed. This system displays an application of reciprocal relations mainly in marginal areas, with the marked exception of inter-state commercial exchanges. Nonetheless, it is clear that these models are more interpretative than descriptive. Consequently, they belong to the study of ideologies rather than the study of economies. In fact, depending on its value and purpose, the same act of exchange can belong to both the reciprocal and redistributive model. Apart from its political, administrative, ceremonial, and other purposes, which only marked the way in which it was pursued, exchange always constituted a strictly economic reality (also in terms of exchanged commodities and technologies). Unfortunately, this fundamental role can only be understood from quantitative evaluations, with regards to which our sources are far too limited and selective (except for trade in the Old Assyrian period).

In this regard, through the scientific analysis of materials found in ancient sites, the archaeological evidence is increasingly supporting the study of the materials both for issues of production and exchange. This allows for a more precise establishment of their origins, their structure, and diffusion. Moreover, the analysis of paleobotanical and paleozoological evidence (crucial for a reliable reconstruction of agricultural and farming activities), as well as of materials (crucial for the reconstruction of technologies and trading networks), is much more common for the study of prehistoric and proto-historic phases. However, it is underestimated for historical phases, as if the availability of written sources would make scientific data less relevant. Naturally, the contrary is true: only through the comparison of the entire set of available evidence will it become possible to gain a reliable understanding of the communities considered. The analysis of sources and administrative texts remains in fact relatively abstract if we cannot find out to what they were referring. Similarly, scientific evidence becomes difficult to contextualise historically if the ancient systems used at the time cannot be recovered.

5 Ideologies

A historical reconstruction of the ecology, demography, technology, and modes of production of the Ancient Near East follows the slow pace of development of macro-phenomena and the medium pace of social ones. It does not, however, follow the fast pace of the events that characterised its history. The available documentation (environmental, archaeological, and textual) does not allow a thorough understanding of the history of the Near East. This is because its evidence does not document every aspect of ancient life. Nonetheless, the knowledge of influential individuals, dynasties, or battles remains useful for the establishment of a chronological framework. Through the latter, it becomes possible to link equally historically important long-term phenomena shaping the Near East, especially since they can be linked to each other according to their development in time.

The reconstruction of events in the history of the Near East is generally sourced from royal inscriptions, as well as the deriving chronicles and annals recording important events, and ancient pseudo-historical literature. However, this event-based analysis often becomes overbearing, limiting the reconstruction of the history of the Near East and obscuring, if not obliterating, a thorough understanding of cultural processes. Reduced to a sequence of events, the history of the Near East loses its charm and interesting characteristics. Due to considerable gaps in the available evidence, the history of the Near East thus becomes repetitive, overall banal, too limited in its breadth, and schematic.

It is crucial to bear in mind that the use of royal inscriptions to reconstruct the sequence of events marking the political history of the Near East is based on a fundamental misunderstanding: that of considering royal inscriptions, annals, chronicles, and even literary sources as 'historical sources'. This kind of writing is neither objectively nor subjectively 'historical'. Our interest is in reconstructing past events, but ancient sources were not written for the same purpose. From our point of view, then, these sources do not provide us with a straightforward reconstruction. They also fail to provide all the kinds of information needed for our historical reconstruction, unless we give up on our cultural background and historiographical interests to take on the completely different viewpoint of ancient societies.

In fact, there was no proper historiography in the Near East in the way we understand it today. Royal inscriptions and annals were political texts aimed at celebrating specific individuals. Thus, they were part of a propagandistic plan, rather than an accurate account of events. This, however, does not mean that in the Near East there was no sense of history and no interest in the past, seen as the causal relation between events and their meaning. After all, every culture has its own sense of history, and so each text, despite being written for particular purposes, relies and transmits crucial elements of a society's worldview. Interestingly enough, the influence of political propaganda and a specific worldview on ancient texts is often overlooked. As a result, sources are given a historical meaning that they do not always have. For instance, today no one would write sentences such as 'in my reign grain was growing two meters high' or 'cows gave birth to twins' (sentences which also appear on celebratory inscriptions) for a reconstruction of economic history. These are obvious propagandistic statements, useful for an analysis of a society's ideology of kingship, rather than its agricultural and farming techniques. However, similar statements on military victories, political consensus or the administration of justice are taken as genuine and used as the basis for a historical event-based framework.

It is clear, then, that these celebratory inscriptions do not contain historical facts, but are using them for propaganda (i.e. aimed at gaining political consensus). An immediate reaction to this would be to start the historical reconstruction of the Near East anew, avoiding the primary sources due to their tendentious and biased nature, to which one could easily apply the popular disclaimer 'any resemblance to real events is purely coincidental'.

This approach, however, would impoverish our own approach towards a historical reconstruction of the Near East. Despite the fact that these sources cannot be considered providers of historiographical information, they nonetheless provide useful information about the ideologies (not only political) of their authors and their cultural context. In fact, when dealing with these sources, our task is not to understand whether or not they recounted the truth or were based on real events. On the contrary, we have to use this material, and in particular its cultural bias, in order to reconstruct the aims and reasons for its existence, the range of ideas employed and the worldview they derive from and transmit. Therefore, ancient sources primarily document ideologies, and not facts.

From this point of view, then, this kind of documentation is not an obstacle, but an enrichment of our historical investigation. In fact, in the understanding of historical events, if one refuses to take into consideration a recorded event because the account may be unreliable, it is still possible to recognise the underlying reasons and political concerns surrounding its mention. Moreover, such an approach benefits our understanding of the overall context, making the written evidence an essential source for the understanding of social structures and the set of values which a certain community responded to and identified with. Political history should therefore not be relegated to the understanding of its events, but can and has to aim for a systematic reconstruction. This eventually leads to its integration with cultural history, enriching the latter's technological aspect with the knowledge of ancient ideologies.

Royal inscriptions and other texts related to the palace were written with a propagandistic tone for clear political reasons: from legitimacy to celebration, comparison with other rulers and states, and communication. Legitimacy is a constant issue in the exercise of kingship, but is more evident in the initial phases of a king's reign. After all, legitimacy is a problem that affects most rulers, especially usurpers, or, more generally, those transitional stages that cannot rely on a secure dynastic line. Therefore, legitimacy becomes a central topic in the apologetic tone employed by usurpers on their inscriptions. Their statements are frequently more or less extravagant justifications, which by contrast can reveal the traditional ideology of kingship and the common means of accession to power. If the normal procedure consisted in inheriting the office through the male line (and this is frequently the case), the usurper would have attempted to claim his descent from a former, disinherited branch of the royal family. In case the usurper lacked any such proof of legitimacy, he would have stated his divine appointment, being the one chosen among the people for merits that were not evident to humans. The actual legitimacy of a king would arise anyway from his rule. After all, a king that could successfully rule his state proved to his subjects that his rise to power was legitimate. Otherwise, why would the gods have granted him success and prosperity?

Legitimacy is therefore closely linked to the celebration of power, simply because he who is able to rule is the legitimate ruler. However, this aspect is only visible during the reign itself. Consequently, a ruler that already managed to claim his legitimacy (through inheritance or usurpation), had to continuously demonstrate that his reign was prosperous and successful. Any aspect of kingship could therefore become a useful means for the assertion of power. Military campaigns had to be successful, through the ruler's prowess and divine support. Similarly, commercial activities had to emphasise the quantity and rarity of the imported products without mentioning exports.

In this way, the cities at the centre of one's kingdom could be portrayed as the centre of the known world, receiving raw materials and products, and employing all available resources for the king's needs. Consequently, such centralisation of resources constituted proof of the ruler's 'universal' control, real or potential. Even natural phenomena (such as rain and floods, crucial for a successful harvest), despite being outside the king's sphere of influence, were associated with his positive influence. This is because of the common idea that the divine governed natural phenomena. The gods were beneficial towards their communities only if the king, as representative of the human sphere, and the community as a whole were able to please them.

The celebration of a king's deeds was also expressed through the presentation of contrasting situations (both in terms of time and space) to his rule. In other words, all positive qualities were located in the centre of the realm, while all negative aspects were relegated to the periphery. This mirrored the opposition between order and chaos, civilised and barbarian, life and death, and between active players and passive receivers of political, military, and economic achievements. At the heart of the idea of the superiority of the centre, there was its clear link to the divine sphere. A successful king was one who could ensure positive relations with the gods at the expense of the surrounding populations. The latter were considered to be godless, absurdly contrary to being subjugated, and thus condemned to provide materials and workforce to the centre. Whenever the chaotic periphery rose against the centre, the king formed a protective barrier to ensure the safety of his subjects.

The same contrast between the positive centre and the negative periphery can be seen on a chronological level, with a tripartite division of time. First, there was the origin of the world, considered as a positive period when the world was created by the gods and ruled by the first mythical kings and heroes. Then, there was a negative period governed by inefficient (thus, illegitimate) successors, which brought chaos (which should have been relegated to the periphery) to the state. The situation was only solved in the third phase, when the celebrated king, just and successful, driven by his legitimacy of rule and his personal strength, managed to re-establish the right relations between the human and the divine spheres. Only then could order and prosperity return, and the king stood as a living insurance of the end of the negative phase and the return of stability.

The ruler's celebration was always directed towards his subjects, who could not have known what actually happened outside the centre and were not able to make suitable comparisons, since all the information was monopolised by the ones in power. On the contrary, when diplomatic and commercial needs required cooperation with other centres of power, the tone had to change completely. It became much more focused on reciprocity and equality of status. In this case, the language used was one of kinship and brotherhood, aimed at the acknowledgement of mutual interests and spheres of influence.

In these inter-state interactions, then, the preservation of one's power was linked to the acknowledgement of the surrounding powers. The same commercial, military, and political endeavours internally celebrated as proof of hegemonic power and the subordination of the periphery, were then externally presented in terms of equality. There is nothing more indicative of the internal and external political ideology of a state than the possibility to compare opposing versions of the same episode in sources directed to the subjects (royal inscriptions) and to other rulers (letters and treaties). Both versions are intrinsically biased, though in different ways: both employ facts as a way to construct the respective system of diplomatic networks, and use strong metaphors and connotations, depicting a different political situation from the real one.

Political propaganda can therefore provide a historical framework that is coherent, maybe too coherent, despite its strongly biased tone. However, this historical framework cannot possibly be an integral part of our own reconstruction. A political kind of discourse is intrinsically biased, mentioning certain events and forgetting others, while emphasising or minimising important elements. In this way, it influences, positively or negatively, historical information for its own purposes. Moreover, it always provides only the point of view belonging to the one in power, and never that of enemies or subjects. In other words, it is the view of the winner and never of the defeated.

Those in power effectively monopolised the means to record ideologies and historical events, thus shaping a community's memories. The point of view of the defeated, their political strategies, and marginal ideologies run the risk of being completely invisible in the sources, except for very few cases. As a result, the only way to recover this information is a reversed reading of the official propaganda, paying attention to the concerns lurking behind the bold statements and the receivers of its criticism. Assurances also inform us of opposing opinions, political dissent, and potential oppositions to the ruling power. Therefore, through the confutation and demonisation of threats, ruling entities have involuntarily made sure that we know about their enemies.

However, how did political propaganda reach its audience? And who exactly was its audience? It has been often noted that in a world in which literacy (which required the knowledge of an ideographic and syllabic writing, in use before the development of alphabetic systems) was limited to a small, specialised group, the expression of political ideas in writing made the overall message inaccessible to a large portion of the population, and thus somehow pointless. The real problem, however, is that today we only have access to written sources, despite the fact that there were other means of large-scale communication that have not survived as well. In fact, written political propaganda was only accessible to a small group of scribes, administrators, and courtiers constituting the ruling class, in a sort of self-indoctrination process. On this level of society, a political statement can be more complex and sophisticated, since only among the ruling class would such a message be fully understood.

For a wider audience (such as a city's inhabitants), there were other forms of communication, from oral transmission to iconography and festivals. These were designed to be less complex, and easier to spread and understand. In the case of a more marginal portion of society, such as villages outside the centre, this political message would only be delivered indirectly. In fact, it was sufficient for them to know of the presence of a legitimate ruler at the centre of their world, loved by the gods and caring towards his people, victorious in military campaigns, as well as able to obtain from nature and men fertility, prosperity, wealth and peace. Each layer of society, then, was reached through the appropriate channels of communication, and the corresponding message was designed accordingly. Royal inscriptions were accessible to few privileged individuals, but they constituted only the tip of an iceberg made of a wider political propaganda (which was also ideological with strong religious connotations). The latter held the community together on both a social and a political level, providing security and cohesion.

It is our task to understand the place of ideologies in the wider historical framework of the Near East, since, unlike the study of historical events, they allow us to recognise the cultural character of ancient communities and their values and worries. It is first necessary, however, to categorise specific ideologies by period, area, and social context. At the same time, it is crucial to find and bear in mind the underlying reasons, or the function, of the ideologies considered. Then, a community's ideology needs to be convincingly linked to its social structure and material culture. This is not purely because the ideological level is more important than other levels, but because these various levels are interrelated and influence each other in a way which, if discovered, can become the key for the understanding of ancient cultures.

3

THE NEOLITHIC AND CHALCOLITHIC PERIODS

1 The earliest experiments in food production

In order to trace the development of cultural elements and regional differences influencing the history of the Ancient Near East, it is necessary to start from what has been defined as the 'Neolithic Revolution' (Gordon Childe) (Table 3.1). In this case, the term 'revolution' does not indicate a sudden change, but a radical change within the socio-economic structures of the time. However, this change, which took place over a couple of millennia, was relatively fast compared to the previous two and a half million years of hunter-gathering activities.

The main characteristic of the Neolithic Revolution was the progressive development of food production techniques (agriculture and farming), gradually overtaking foraging activities, such as hunting and gathering.

Table 3.1 Chronology of the 'Neolithic Revolution'

	General definition	Palestine	Syria	Taurus	Anatolia	Kurdistan	Luristan	Khuzistan
15.000	Intensive hunter-gathering activities	Kebara				Zarzi		
10.000	Incipient food production	Natufian (10,000–8500 BC) Pre-Pottery Neolithic A (8000–7300 BC)			Pre-ceramic Hacilar (7500–7000 BC)	Zawi Chemi Shanidar (9000–8000 BC) Kamir Shahir (7500–7000 BC)	Ganjdareh Asiab (8000–7500 BC)	Bus Mordeh (7500–6500 BC)
7000	Pre-Pottery Neolithic	Pre-Pottery Neolithic B (Jericho) (7000–6000 BC) Beidha (7000–6000 BC)	Pre-Pottery Neolithic B (Mureibet) (ca. 6500 BC) Buqros, el-Kom (6500–6000 BC)	Çayönü (7500–6500 BC) Cafer Hüyük	Pre-ceramic Çatal Hüyük 6000	Pre-ceramic Jarmo (6500–6000 BC)	Tepe Guran (6500–6000 BC)	Ali Kosh (6500–6000 BC)
6000								

34

Unfortunately, the initial stages of this process are still under speculation and remain largely unknown. The traditional features of Neolithic societies, such as their agro-pastoral activities, the sedentarisation of village communities, and pottery production are considered inseparable and largely contemporaneous. However, these traits need to be re-examined when considering the Near East. This area provides contemporary evidence for both intensive harvesting and the initial phases of production processes, and non-sedentary agriculture and Neolithic communities where pottery was still unknown. Moreover, the so-called 'Broad-spectrum Revolution' (L. Binford) of the Upper Palaeolithic period, when resources were gathered through specialised hunter-gathering techniques, may have preceded the formation of these typically Neolithic features.

Since the earliest evidence for these changes comes from the Near East, the varying degrees of development in the area, through stages of trial and error, can be explained. Looking at the history of the Near East, it becomes possible to catch a glimpse of the variety of strategies put forward by different communities in different environments, even when they were relatively close to each other (both geographically and chronologically). In this period, then, communities with different degrees of technological and economic development coexisted. This is mainly known from radiocarbon evidence. Comparative stratigraphic and typological reconstructions tend to minimise regional developments, interpreting the presence of similar features in different communities as an indication of their contemporaneity in time.

In this regard, interfacing regions, located in-between eco-zones, appear to have been the most successful in testing innovative techniques. The earliest communities developing food production techniques were located right outside the border of the Fertile Crescent, along an arch stretching from Palestine to the foothills of the Taurus and Zagros Mountains, and reaching Khuzistan. Successively, in the seventh millennium BC, the great ceramic cultures of the Neolithic period either spread to the Lower Mesopotamian plain, or established their presence in the Anatolian and Iranian plateaus. Mesopotamia (as well as Egypt) only gained a central role in the process around the fourth millennium BC. This centrality would characterise Mesopotamia throughout the later stages of its history, especially in relation to its own 'periphery'.

The Levant and the Anatolian and Iranian foothills were particularly suitable regions for the Neolithic Revolution. These areas were all characterised by ecologically stable and well-protected niches (valleys and intermontane basins) suitable for the socio-cultural phenomena of the time, which benefited from close contacts between different ecosystems. This interaction facilitated the exploitation of different resources and the seasonal movement of human groups for farming and agricultural needs. Overall, bearing in mind that from 10,000 BC the climate became warmer and more humid than before, these were rainier zones, mainly characterised by herbaceous zones with sparse forests (with oak and pistachio trees). In these areas, the plant and animal species that would be at the centre of the Neolithic Revolution (such as cereals, legumes, goats and sheep) grew naturally.

The previous period (ca. 15,000–10,000 BC), corresponding to the Epipaleolithic Age in the periodisation based on stone production, has been considered a time of intensive hunting and gathering activities (R. Braidwood). Settlements were still made of shelters for small communities of forty to fifty people, whose mobility in the territory followed the animals at the centre of their diet. Survival was a daily issue, since there were no techniques for food production or for its conservation. Hunting was mainly focused on smaller species than those hunted in the Palaeolithic: gazelles in Palestine, sheep in the Zagros and goats throughout the area. People began to practise a more specialised type of hunting, focused on the selection of species to be removed in order not to weaken wild herds. In this way, communities began to control herds without farming them in full.

Gathering activities, especially of cereals and legumes, also intensified and became increasingly specialised, causing, albeit involuntarily, the first effects of human selection and diffusion of certain plants. Therefore, basic concepts of food production were laid down through an increased knowledge of the most effective practices for the exploitation of the land. Nomadism became more confined, since it depended on the availability and location of resources. At times (such as in the case of lake fishing or even in areas with a large concentration of wild cereals) these aspects facilitated the development of a sedentary lifestyle. The large and roughly cut Palaeolithic stone tools were abandoned in favour of geometric microliths used for specific purposes, such as pestles to grind cereals.

The main cultures of this phase were the ones at Kebara in Palestine and Zarzi in Iraqi Kurdistan. It is there that the first innovative processes appeared, opening up a new phase of development in the Near East. While in the Zagros area small, mobile communities mainly focused on the domestication of sheep and goats, in the Levantine and Taurus areas larger and more settled communities brought about the domestication of cereals.

The critical phase of this development, called the era of 'incipient food production' (R. Braidwood), took place between 10,000 and 7500 BC. Some species of small ruminating mammals, already the object of specialised hunting activities (in 10,000 BC the dog was already domesticated for hunting and guarding purposes, and not as food), became an increasingly important part of a sort of human-animal symbiosis. This close interaction, however, only worked with certain species (for example sheep and goats), which would eventually be domesticated, but did not work with other species (for example gazelles), which continued to be hunted. This 'symbiosis' and early phase of domestication brought about the systematic use of milk and fell (and eventually of wool), the selective killing of male animals, and the protection and guiding of herds (which by now had become human property) to seasonal pasturelands.

These animals began to experience morphological changes, allowing us to recognise their domestication from bone remains and from the assessment of their age and gender. Naturally, physical changes in these animals only appeared after long periods of domestication. Therefore, they are very difficult to recognise in the earliest phases of this process. The same is true for the domestication of cereals (mainly spelt wheat, emmer in Syria and Palestine, einkorn in Anatolia and Iran) and legumes (Figure 3.1). The continuous harvesting of wild cereals and the subsequent concentration of the discarded seeds around settlements must have led (following observations on their life cycle) to the first experiments in cultivation. This happened through the delimitation of the 'cultivated' space, protecting it from animals. Even in the case of cereals and legumes, domestication caused considerable morphological changes and genetic mutations, which remained incomplete in the earliest stages. Therefore, this type of early agriculture was a sort of 'cultivation of wild plants'.

Already in its incipient phases (10,000–7500 BC), this new mode of production had a visible impact on the social structure of human groups and the organisation of resources. Communities began to build roundhouses, partly set in the ground and with a tent-shaped roof. Therefore, the earliest permanent base-camps appeared (particularly where the first attempts at cultivation also took place), alongside seasonal camps for hunting purposes (which remained a fundamental activity) and other seasonal activities. The appearance of the first silos for the conservation of food and seeds from one year to the next indicates how these communities had by now overcome the daily dimension of nutrition. Moreover, herds and camps also raised the issue of property and inheritances. This led to the development of tombs, either for individuals or family groups.

This incipient food production era mainly corresponds to the Natufian culture and then the Pre-Pottery Neolithic A in Palestine (and in Syria up to the Middle Euphrates). It also appeared in the Zagros foothills in sites such as Zawi, Chemi and Shanidar, and then in Kamir Shahir (Kurdistan), Ganj Dareh and Asiab (Luristan) and Bus Mordeh (Khuzistan). There are considerable chronological differences between these sites, since the Palestinian sequence seems to pre-date the one in the Zagros. There are also ecological differences, such as the presence of sheep in the Zagros and not in the Syro-Palestinian area.

Stone tools also varied, though they were still geometric microliths designed for specific purposes, such as arrowheads for hunting, flint-bladed sickles for harvesting cereals and burins. Tools were also built from other materials, such as bone, used for fishing hooks and harpoons. While at the beginning of this phase communities still relied on specialised hunting activities and the intensive harvesting of wild plants, by the end of this period (the Pre-Pottery Neolithic A) we have the first concrete evidence for cultivation. The discovery of einkorn and wild spelt wheat in Mureibet, in the Middle Euphrates, indicates the development of agricultural activities because they are found outside their natural habitat. This is also the case for emmer and spelt in Jericho and Netiv Hagdud, in the Jordan Valley. Soon after, the avail-

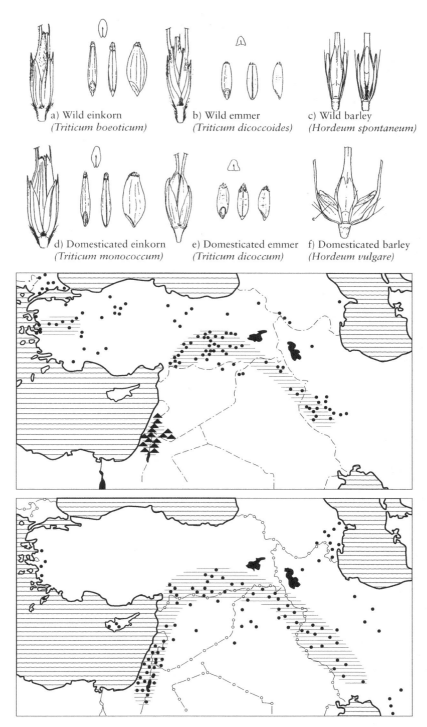

Figure 3.1 The origins of agriculture. *Above*: Morphological changes in cultivated crops; *Centre*: Original habitat of wild einkorn (•) and emmer (▲); *Below*: Original habitat of wild barley.

able evidence clearly shows the first domestication of sheep and goats in many areas of Khuzistan and Kurdistan.

A clear periodisation of this phase is evidently difficult, due to the geographical variations and the different pace of development of these phenomena. Nonetheless, the phase between 8000 and 7000 BC can be considered fully Neolithic. Sedentary village communities began to have between 250 and 500 inhabitants, rectangular mud-brick houses, and an economy based on agriculture and the farming of sheep, goats and pigs (and cattle by the end of the period). These kinds of groups are mostly found in the Pre-Pottery Neolithic B in Syria (Mureibet, Buqras), Palestine (Jericho, 'Ain Ghazal), the Taurus foothills (Çayönü, Cafer Hüyük, Nevali Çori), Kurdistan (Jarmo), Luristan (Tepe Guran) and Khuzistan (Ali Kosh).

From a social point of view, the introduction of a rectangular plan for households is an important change. While the circular plan, which could not be easily enlarged, indicated a family structure that could not be expanded, the rectangular plan allowed the construction of extensions to the main plan. This allowed the development of a series of interlinked buildings surrounding a courtyard, or of more complex plans (see Can Hasan III in Anatolia and Buqras in the Middle Euphrates), or even larger buildings with stone foundations (see Çayönü). There is also evidence for increased cooperation between families in this period, a case in point being the fortification walls and towers at Jericho. The ownership of means of production, such as land and herds, and its hereditary transmission thus began to have a considerable impact: communities become larger, expanding from the 2000 to 3000 m² of the Natufian period to the 2 or 3 ha of the Pre-Pottery Neolithic A and B.

The Pre-Pottery Neolithic B also provides the first clearly ideological (i.e. religious) expressions of a patriarchal structure, from the skulls of dead ancestors whose features had been moulded in clay or chalk (at Jericho and other Palestinian sites), to the statuettes from 'Ain Ghazal. However, the imposing cultic buildings from the Taurus foothills (one at Nevali Çori, and a whole complex at Göbekli, near Urfa) constitute the most impressive evidence. They were characterised by a round or rectangular plan, polished floors, and anthropomorphic steles, which indicate the practice of ancestor cults. From the same period, we have evidence for houses built on robust substructures (possibly to separate the harvested crops from the ground), and specifically designed for family units living in larger villages (for instance, at Çayönü, north of Diyarbakir). Naturally, alongside these more advanced settlements, there were still less economically developed groups living in more difficult areas, such as Beidha in Jordan, a sedentary village that continued to subsist on hunting. Similarly, many sites in the Negev and Judaean Desert continued to be seasonal camps for hunters.

This phase also experienced a significant development in interregional contacts, visible from the spread of obsidian from Anatolia and Armenia, and seashells from the Mediterranean, the Red Sea and the Persian Gulf. In this way, the Neolithic era of the Near East began to take form. Village communities began to produce their own food, though in varying degrees according to the type of resources available or their degree of technological development. These communities also interacted with each other through the exchange (also over long distances) of small, valuable materials.

The issue of the 'causes' leading to the shift from hunter-gathering to food production (the latter requiring a considerable increase in the amount of work needed) cannot be solved with a single answer (and certainly not here). The multiple causes and effects, and independent and inter-dependent factors, undoubtedly contributed to this change. However, all these factors are difficult to estimate in terms of their impact, due to the lack of evidence and the breadth and duration of the phenomenon. Nonetheless, the idea that the main cause of this change was the dramatic rise of the population cannot be accepted: both in the phase of intensive and specialised hunting and gathering, and of incipient food production, communities were small enough to be able to survive with the resources available to them. Regarding the climatic and, consequently, ecological changes mentioned above, they constitute more the framework of this technological and economic change, rather than its cause. In fact, different communities could have reacted to these changes in different ways, and it is this variety of possible choices and strategies that characterises human history.

Be that as it may, there are two main factors worth bearing in mind: a temporal and a spatial one (Figures 3.2 and 3.3). In terms of time, the desire to maintain a durable system for the procurement of food made cultivation,

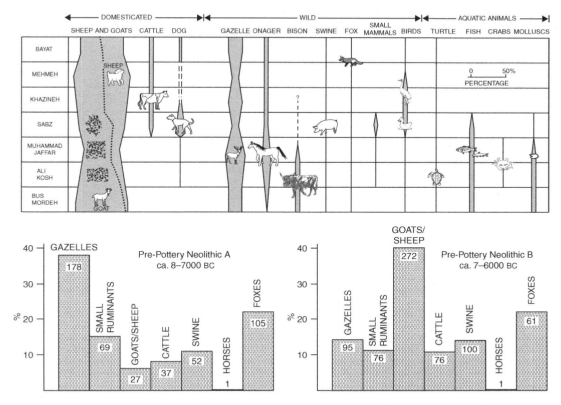

Figure 3.2   The beginnings of farming. *Above*: The distribution of animal remains in prehistoric Khuzistan (from the Bus Mordeh phase, ca. 7500–6500 BC, to the Bayat phase, ca. 4000 BC). *Below*: The transition from Pre-Pottery A to B in Palestine saw a marked decline of wild species and a marked increase of sheep and goats.

the management of herds, food storage, and sedentarisation effective means for the development of a long-term solution for the management of food resources. In terms of space, the movement of human groups across different ecosystems led many resources and means of production, which grew naturally in one area, to be transferred to another area, allowing the development of new techniques. These factors heavily influenced the availability of resources, leading to the rise of more stable and interacting communities. These communities thus began to actively change cycles for reproduction and consumption rather than being influenced by them.

2 The Neolithic period

By the end of the eighth millennium BC, the Near East (from the Fertile Crescent to Anatolia) had already developed the basic technological advances characterising the Neolithic period: households, base-camps, village communities, the cultivation of cereals and legumes, and the farming of goats, sheep, pigs and cattle. Other typically Neolithic techniques also rose to prominence in the area. For instance, there was the rise of textile production (mainly wool and linen) for clothes, worn instead of fell, and pottery (which first developed in the Zagros area, at Ganj Dareh and Tepe Guran), crucial for the conservation of food. In addition to that, some areas began to create tools out of hammering copper, especially at Çayönü, located close to the large copper ores at Ergani Maden.

By the first half of the seventh millennium BC, however, at the peak of this important cultural development, archaeological evidence becomes more difficult to find. This gap in the evidence might not have

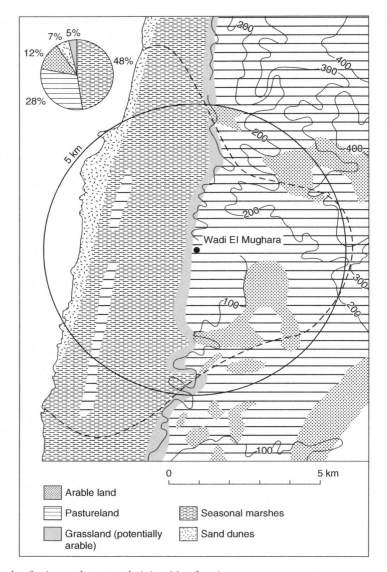

Figure 3.3 Example of a site-catchment analysis in a Natufian site.
The dotted line delimitates the area that could be reached in an hour on foot.

been accidental, and could correspond to a real population crisis throughout the Fertile Crescent. The interpretation of this crisis as a result of climatic changes (such as severe drought) is purely hypothetical. However, it is clear that a demographic and cultural development of this scale could not have been an easy and unstoppable process, but a difficult one, liable to backlashes and in need of constant re-adaptations.

The revival after this critical phase laid down the foundations for a visible demographic and techno-logical development. From 7000 to 5200 BC, fully Neolithic cultures rose to prominence, with periods of great prosperity. This was due to the spread of those techniques, initially developed in the Anatolian highlands, in the Iranian plateau and Mesopotamia. These areas began to implement the new agro-pastoral techniques, with the deforestation, drainage and irrigation of the land. Therefore, they were suddenly able to provide a significantly larger space for farming and agriculture compared to the original mountain niches. For this reason, a uniform view of the Near Eastern Neolithic period presents considerable difficulties, overshadowing the progressive pace of technological development, regional variations, differences in production strategies, the degree of experimentation and the slower pace of marginalised areas. Nonetheless, as an introduction to the history of the Near East, this period has to be considered here as a large-scale phenomenon, defining the Neolithic period in its most characteristic features.

Agriculture and farming were the main sources of economic growth, based on a drastic selection of domesticated plants and animals. Among cereal crops, spelt, emmer and einkorn (plants belonging to the wheat family) became the most commonly grown. In this regard, there were already regional variations and preferences in cultivation that would become more marked in the following periods. These grains were now fully domesticated and their appearance in the alluvial plains owes much to the earliest irrigation techniques. Artificial irrigation, in oases (Jericho), or through drainage and the construction of canals in the alluvial plains (Eridu), or in the plateaus (Çatal Hüyük), was first implemented in this phase. This intervention ensured the availability of water and distributed it throughout the year. Irrigation, hybridisation and selection (at times involuntary) produced visible morphological changes. Diets were integrated through the consumption of legumes, while, among the 'industrial' plants, linen became increasingly widespread. Alongside agriculture, a substantial part of the diet was still provided by the harvesting of those wild plants that were not yet domesticated, but were still regularly consumed.

A similar point can be made with regards to the domestication of animals. Only a few species were domesticated. The dog began to be used for the defence of villages and herds, as well as hunting. There were also sheep and goats (now present throughout the area and farmed in mixed herds), pigs, cattle and donkeys (used as pack animals). Farming was either sedentary (in the case of cattle and pigs), or transhumant (goats and sheep), both horizontally (with riverside pasturelands in the summer and the nearby plains in winter), and vertically (summer pasturelands in the highlands, and in the valleys during winter). Farmed animals were not just important for meat (mainly pigs, male goats and rams), but also for milk (in the case of cows, sheep and goats), textile fibres and their role as pack animals. This was a clear outcome of the so-called 'secondary products revolution' (A. Sherrat). Alongside farming, those species that had not been domesticated (such as onagers in Upper Mesopotamia, gazelles in Palestine, wild goats on the Zagros), or were a threat to the fields and herds, continued to be hunted. In some areas, river and lake fishing, as well as the collection of shellfish, constituted a further contribution to the provision of food.

Vegetable or animal fibres (linen and wool), which were treated to form threads, led to the development of weaving. This technique is attested through imprints of fabrics on clay or remains of the equipment used (weights used on looms). Therefore, weaving began to fulfil most needs in terms of clothing, largely replacing the use of animal hide. Other secondary production techniques regarded alimentation. The grinding of grains through stone pestles, already used for wild grains, became an essential part of a household's equipment. Pottery became crucial in the cooking and consumption of food and to contain liquids. Small plastered pits still played an important role in the conservation of food (in large jars) over long periods of time. They had to be frequently abandoned or renovated, however, due to their quick decay and infestations.

Stone containers were rare, while wooden or woven containers are badly preserved, but were potentially more widespread (just like woven mats). Stone tools quickly adapted to the production needs of the time. Therefore, the macrolithic tools of the Palaeolithic (percussors, scrapers, and others) and the microlithic tools of the Mesolithic ceased to be used. Tools became more specialised, for instance, in the case of arrowheads for hunting, and burins and bodkins for leatherwork. Similarly, the first types of sickles for the harvesting of cereals, and long blades for butchery and other similar tasks also became a fundamental part of the Neolithic equipment. Unfortunately, wooden tools have not survived, but must have been essential in agricultural activities such as ploughing and sowing.

These processes of production and transformation of resources normally took place in rectangular houses. These houses had wells dug in the ground and plastered pits, hearths, ovens and areas for milling, weaving and any other activity. The main building material was clay mixed with hay, first stacked in shapeless blocks, then in bricks formed by hand or through moulds. Stones (for the foundations) and wood were used depending on local availability. Regional variations, which will be explored later on, led to the development of different households, centred on a courtyard or spread out in a network of individual units. Thus, settlement plans varied from a largely open layout to a protected terraced plan. The latter form the earliest examples of fortified villages, protected either through fortification walls or a clever layout of buildings, so as to delimitate the edge of the village.

Villages were normally relatively small, an aspect that, combined with the matrimonial strategies of the time, indicates that settlements only had a few large families or even just one. The social structure of these communities was thus characterised by few heads of households (elders), marked gender, age and provenance barriers, but few socio-political differences. Consequently, burials do not display any significant differences in status.

Communities were united and motivated by common religious beliefs, visible from the various cultic artefacts and objects found (Figure 3.4). This religiosity had two main complementary aspects: a funerary aspect, linked, through ancestral cults, to the patriarchal structure of these communities (an aspect that was already visible in the Pre-Pottery Neolithic B); and a fertility aspect (human, animal and agrarian), brought to the fore by the development of food production techniques. These two aspects are closely linked to each

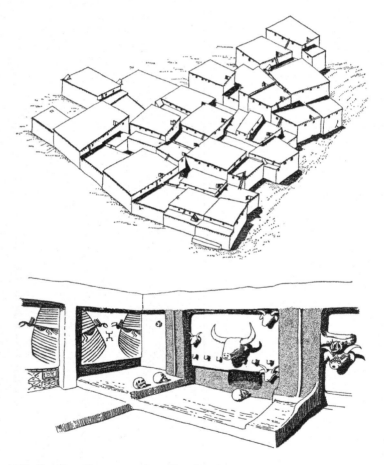

Figure 3.4 Çatal Hüyük. *Above*: Reconstruction of level VI B, ca. 5900 BC. *Below*: One of the buildings with cultic decorations.

other, since Neolithic ideology saw a parallelism between the reproduction of animals (based on sexual penetration) and plants (based on the sowing of seeds) and the burying of the dead. The latter was seen as an act somehow similar to the burial and rebirth of seeds. The term 'religiosity' has been preferred to religion here, since its symbolism (largely animal and sexual) and female representations (the Venus figurines) address more natural problems of fertility and mortality, rather than specific divine figures.

The social structure of these communities was therefore based on kinship, with family units (each with its own household), linked to each other through more or less strong ties, acting as an enlarged family. In terms of status, there was little stratification among families, thus constituting a collective community. The same families producing food also pursued secondary activities such as weaving and pottery, without full-time labour specialisation. While there were shared warehouses, certain fundamental expressions of communal life were still lacking, such as temples or other cultic buildings. The earliest communal sanctuaries, though still relatively small compared to the following developments (up until the early stages of urbanisation), only appeared towards the end of this period in Lower Mesopotamia (Eridu).

Regarding the use of the term and concept of 'city' for Neolithic settlements, it is important to point out that this is only an anachronistic attempt at finding the 'earliest city'. Cases such as Jericho, with its walls and tower, or Çatal Hüyük with its 'sanctuaries' have been often misrepresented in this way. Defence systems were certainly the result of a highly coordinated and organised community. However, that is not enough evidence to postulate the existence of a centralised political power, or an indication of typically urban characteristics. Ethnographic studies have demonstrated that egalitarian communities, with few signs of an established social hierarchy, can attain similar results (Figure 3.5).

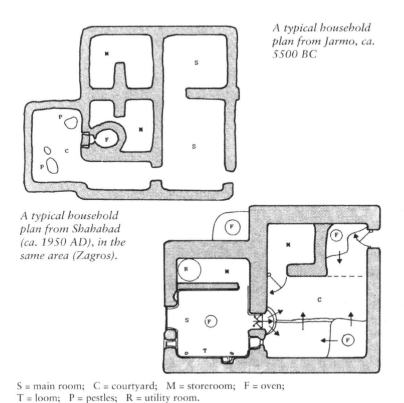

A typical household plan from Jarmo, ca. 5500 BC

A typical household plan from Shahabad (ca. 1950 AD), in the same area (Zagros).

S = main room; C = courtyard; M = storeroom; F = oven;
T = loom; P = pestles; R = utility room.

Figure 3.5 A Neolithic household and a comparative ethnographic example.

Regarding the so-called 'sanctuaries' of Çatal Hüyük (see the following paragraph), their conspicuous number demonstrates the exact opposite of a specialisation and centralisation of cultic activities. It is certainly not possible to deduce the existence of a (very large!) priestly caste. On the contrary, cultic activities were pursued on a family level, by each family in their own household or in the house of its 'patriarch'. Thus, these 'sanctuaries' are not the result of a centralised or specialised (and hierarchically organised) cultic system. They were the result of a disaggregation of cultic activities, indicating their close connection to the families that performed them.

In terms of territory, another characteristic element is the existence of numerous non-colonised marginal areas used for hunting and gathering activities. Their existence kept each Neolithic village largely isolated. For this reason, the degree of conflict between communities, despite being difficult to trace in terms of evidence, must have been quite low. Moreover, weapons (arrowheads, knives and daggers) were still not specialised enough. Therefore, it remains difficult to establish whether certain weapons were for hunting or for war. The same is true with regards to defence systems, both in terms of the concentration of households and the presence of protective walls. The latter were mainly implemented to guard the community from wild animals, rather than from potential enemy attacks. There were certainly elements of conflict between human groups, but it seems like war was still not essential for modes of production or the interactions among different groups.

Therefore, Neolithic communities were characterised by the limited hierarchy of the socio-economic structure of Neolithic communities, the modest influence of political and cultic leadership, the low density of the population, the availability of resources and the local dimension of production and of family relations. All these aspects pose the problem of whether or not a regional form of aggregation that was above the village level existed. Looking at the material evidence, which is the only well attested type of evidence for this phase, it is quite clear that there were some forms of regional influences. Some features clearly originated from environmental factors and thus have little relevance to the investigation of human interactions on a regional level. Other characteristics, unrelated to the environmental factors, were transmitted both in time (from generation to generation) and space (through imitation, technical and cultural hegemony and so on) from the centres in which these characteristics initially developed.

These aspects are visible from the typological and decorative classification of pottery remains, which allow the individuation of Neolithic cultural units on a regional scale. An even more indicative feature would have been language, which is however unrecorded. It is nonetheless worth deducing that already in this period there were linguistic distributions similar to the ones that would develop later on in the area (except for migrations, subdivisions and syncretisms that took place in the course of time). These cultural elements allow us to locate, at least partially, those ideological boundaries between 'us' and 'them', which were at the heart of Neolithic social identity: 'we' decorate pottery in this way, 'they' do it differently; 'we' speak the same language, 'they' do not (but speak incomprehensible languages).

The correspondence between material, linguistic and ethnic (namely, as the awareness or assumption of a common origin) boundaries varied in time and even in later phases it is still relatively low. Ethnographic examples, however, show that even in less complex environments there can be a close correspondence between culture, language and ethnicity. It is impossible to say whether this was the case for the Neolithic period. Previous historians (or archaeologists) took these correspondences between cultural, linguistic and ethnic boundaries for granted. They therefore believed that communities with the same material culture belonged to the same ethno-linguistic group. Only later on, more critical approaches removed these identifications, thus eliminating the problem.

Admittedly, this radical elimination may have been excessive, but can be explained by the danger of implementing a methodology that equates culture, language and people. In fact, it is not impossible to think that this was a phase of colonisation with signs of a sort of Darwinian selection process between more or less technologically strong groups. The subsequent settlement of groups closer to each other and the appearance of some elements of unity through language or provenance must have influenced the acceptance or rejection of cultural elements. These aspects certainly formed a certain awareness of a group's identity. Not much else can be inferred and it would be wrong to interpret the material evidence as an indicator of a political system on a regional level. At this stage, communities still acted on a local level.

The economy of these communities was still as local as their political organisation, while cultural as well as environmental features existed on a regional level. However, there were also what could be defined, albeit anachronistically, as commercial interactions. There is no contradiction between the local aspect of production and the existence of long-distance exchange. Basic materials and resources needed for survival were still gathered within a radius of few kilometres from the settlement itself. Moreover, the transport of food and heavy materials over long distances was not yet possible. However, there were precious materials (precious for that period), generally small and light to carry, which were transported over very long distances considering their place of origin.

The extent of the movement of precious materials across the Near East can be studied from non-perishable materials that can be traced back to their place of origin. The typical example of this is obsidian, a volcanic glass whose colour (from black to dark green or brown) and composition varies according to the area it comes from (in the case of the Near East, that would be Anatolia or Armenia). A laboratory analysis can therefore determine the presence of certain elements, which varied from area to area, to establish the origin of a given artefact. This allows us to delineate the network of exchange of obsidian, a highly valued material for the production of blades. Semiprecious stones, seashells and metals also provide valuable information on their place of origin. In any case, these were all materials that were traded in small quantities and mainly used for the construction of decorative objects or tools (semiprecious stone and seashells) of a higher quality (blades were also made of flint, which was readily available throughout the Near East).

Regarding the issue of how exchange took place, it is too simplistic to imply that it was barter. At least two other possibilities can be put forward. First, exchange could have happened from village to village, thus allowing materials to move across the territory. Second, travellers could have brought the materials from their place of origin to the destination site. In this latter case, there could have been two further alternatives. The traveller could have come from the place of origin of the material, or the other way round. The first possibility is a more 'primitive' one, requiring a long time and a high degree of chance. Moreover, this would also mean that materials could not travel very far from the centre. However, the evidence does not support this possibility for two main reasons. First, the rise of competing centres for certain desirable materials (such as obsidian) did not decrease with distance, but shows the existence of privileged routes of exchange. Second, the concentration of these materials did not decrease as the distance from the place of origin increased.

If the available evidence provides a reliable picture of the distribution of materials, it is possible to infer that the second scenario, that of trade with specific villages, is the more likely one. However, on the basis of simple distribution (whose evidence still remains in need of an appropriate methodology for this phase), it remains difficult to decide between the 'export' model (from the places of origin) and the 'import' model (from the destination of the materials). Scholars researching prehistoric trade prefer the idea of a system mainly based on export, due to the semi-manufactured or manufactured condition of the semiprecious stones from Iran. Nevertheless, in the case of trade in historical phases, the import system is well documented. However, this system requires a certain degree of political and economic organisation from the centre pursuing importation, a fact that was closely linked to urbanisation processes.

Therefore, despite its structure as a local network of independent and self-subsistent entities, the Neolithic Near East certainly began to develop an organised regional system. This system featured different complementary areas in terms of resources and potential, characterised by specific cultural traits and with more or less technologically developed and populated environments.

3 Regional variations

In the course of the Neolithic period (Table 3.2), those areas close to the highlands that had initially kick-started the Neolithic Revolution gradually lost their innovating role. Production techniques and domesticated plants and animals were transferred to regions where they were not naturally available. Moreover, interfaces began to be less close to each other and the niches larger. Consequently, the colonisation of plateaus and of the Mesopotamian alluvial plains allowed a wider distribution of cultural traits and knowledge throughout the Near East.

Nonetheless, this large-scale diffusion was not unitary, and cultivated areas remained surrounded by vast portions of forested areas or marshes. Anatolia, for instance, presents a mixed picture. The region had already experienced the innovations developed during the Mesolithic, especially as the main provider of obsidian. However, during the era of incipient food production only the areas south of the Taurus Mountains were at the forefront of this progress. In the following phase, occupation visibly expanded, spreading all the way north of the Taurus. However, the areas in the far north remained wild, largely deserted, and cut off from the wave of innovation taking place in the region. The Neolithic cultures of Anatolia are some of the better attested ones in the Near East, thanks to the large-scale excavations of sites such as Çatal Hüyük, Hacilar, Can Hasan and Mersin. However, the archaeological exploration of these phases throughout the Near East is not systematic enough to allow a complete reconstruction of the Neolithic populations inhabiting the area.

Çatal Hüyük is the most impressive site of this period (600 m long and 350 m wide), with a sequence of fourteen levels from 7300 to 6200 BC. The site was located on the southern edge of the Konya plain. In this position, it benefited from a fertile niche and the interface between the semi-arid plain and the forested mountains. The economy of Çatal Hüyük was based on agriculture and farming. It was also characterised by a better range of resources (wheat instead of spelt, cattle instead of sheep or goats), beautiful stone craftsmanship (predominantly in obsidian), and a large amount of pottery (first polished and light or dark in colour, then red and engobed, but never painted like the pottery from the following period).

The settlement's plan was compact, with houses attached to each other, creating a protective wall to the outside. The lack of streets shows that circulation took place through terraced roofs. The latter provided

Table 3.2 Chronology of the Neolithic period in the Ancient Near East

	Khabur	Jebel Sinjar Assyria	Middle Tigris	Lower Mesopotamia	Khuzistan	Anatolia	Syria
7000							
		Umm Dabaghiya			Muhammad Jaffar	Çatal Hüyük (6300–5500 BC)	Amuq A
6300							
	Early Halaf	Hassuna	Early Samarra (5600–5400 BC) Middle Samarra		Susiana A	Hacilar Mersin 24–22	Amuq B
5800			(5400–5000 BC)				
	Middle Halaf	Late Hassuna Gawta 20	Late Samarra (5400–4800 BC)	Eridu (= Ubaid I) Eridu 19–15	Tepe Sabz	Hacilar Mersin 22–20	Amuq C
5400							
	Late Halaf	Gawra 19–18		Hajji Muhammad (= Ubaid II) Eridu 14–12	Khazineh Susiana B	Can Hasan Mersin 19–17	Amuq D
5000							

the main access to households and were the place where some domestic activities took place. Households had a uniform plan, with beds placed against walls (and under which the dead were buried), hearths, ovens, niches and a ladder to access the building. Despite the fact that houses were all similar to each other, about a third of them indicate the presence of decorations and furniture.

A prominent feature is the bull skull wall decoration, accompanied by symbols of fertility and prosperity and clay female figurines. These buildings were not sanctuaries looked after by priests, but households in which domestic cults were observed. Çatal Hüyük is one of the few sites in the area providing rich evidence on the life of a Neolithic village and clearly displays the symbolic and ritual obsession of its inhabitants. The latter lived in close contact with their dead and with the divine in order to ensure a successful reproductive cycle, considered to be closely linked to the act of sowing and animal penetration.

Other important sites in Anatolia display different features. Hacilar is smaller in size, with a diameter of 100 m, and had a shorter history, made of six levels spanning from 6200 to 5700 BC. Chronologically, Hacilar eventually reached the pace of development of Çatal Hüyük, although the two settlements are very different. Households at Hacilar were grouped units surrounding a courtyard. Circulation through the settlement was on ground level. The domestic equipment was characteristic of the period, but without benches attached to the walls or cultic decorations. It was a poor village with rough stone craftsmanship and painted pottery (red on cream clay). The excavated levels show drastic changes in the settlement: starting from an open village inhabited by many families (Level VI), the village became a settlement inhabited by a single family and surrounded by a rectangular enclosure (Level II), and then a compact set of houses with access from the terrace (Level I).

Level I in Hacilar is contemporary to the site of Can Hasan (5800–5400 BC), characterised by a compact settlement layout with one-room houses. The walls of these houses were internally supported by pillars, reducing the space for domestic activities. Cream-coloured pottery with red decorations continued to be in use here until the appearance of polychrome ware, possibly an influence from further east (Tell Halaf). The site of Mersin provides a different example of a Neolithic settlement. The village had some connections to Upper Mesopotamia (Tell Halaf, then Tell Ubaid) and had a fortress (Level XVI from ca. 5000–4800 BC, with polychrome as well as polished pottery). The latter was actually a juxtaposition of houses to form a barrier to the outside – another example of social organisation, but not necessarily with a political purpose.

Mersin, located in the Cilician plain, had links with the Levant (Syria and Palestine). In the latter area, a number of ceramic cultures developed between 6500 and 5400 BC, but remained quite marginal compared to their Anatolian and Upper Mesopotamian contemporaries. There were three densely populated (or better documented) areas. There was northern Syria, both around the Middle Euphrates and along the coast (Ras Shamra). Syria had links with Anatolia, and its pottery was influenced by the Amuq phases (A, B and C) and, later on, the middle and late Halaf culture, whose final collapse affected the whole area. Then, there were Central Syria (Bequa and Damascus), Lebanon (whose key-site was Byblos) and northern Palestine (most importantly Munhata in the Jordan Valley). The arid areas of southern Palestine (Negev and the Judaean Desert) and the Transjordan plateau remained sparsely populated.

Overall, the Syro-Levantine Neolithic ceramic cultures spread from north to south and display a marked revival from the crisis of the seventh millennium BC. However, despite implementing all characteristic techniques of the Neolithic (such as the farming of sheep, which was not a local animal), settlements remained small in size, with archaic features (such as round tents), and relatively poor. This might indicate a difficult situation in the area, which would culminate in another crisis at the end of the sixth millennium BC.

Alongside Pre-Pottery Natufian Palestine, the Zagros foothills (from the eastern side of the Taurus to Khuzistan) were another area formerly at the forefront of the incipient food production phase that experienced a critical period in the ceramic Neolithic phase, though this was manifested in a different way. Palestine, located on the edge of the Fertile Crescent, experienced a crisis caused by resource depletion. On the contrary, the Zagros, surrounded by areas more suitable for agriculture and farming, experienced a crisis caused by migration. Its inhabitants moved down to the Mesopotamian plains (the semi-arid ones in the north and the wetter ones in the south), where they found a suitable environment for further developments.

Umm Dabaghiyah (6900–6300 BC), located south of Jebel Sinjar, between the Tigris and the nearby steppes, is the earliest Upper Mesopotamian ceramic culture attested. The settlement was made of a few rectangular houses with more than one room and large storehouses made of several square rooms built close to each other. Due to the arid climate, agriculture and farming was not prosperous. This situation made the hunting of wild onagers (constituting 70% of the bone remains found, alongside 20% belonging to gazelles and only 10% belonging to domesticated goats and sheep) the main resource for survival. Pottery is both painted and polished, with incised or applied decorations.

Between 6300 and 5200 BC, three more complex cultures emerged, whose relations were formerly envisioned diachronically, despite their contemporaneity: Halaf in the north, Samarra in the south, and Hassuna between the two. The culture of Hassuna emerged after the one of Umm Dabaghiyah. It was located in the same area, between Jebel Sinjar, the Tigris and the Wadi Tharthar. The main sites of the area were Hassuna itself and Yarim Tepe, close to the Sinjar. Hassuna culture (6300–5800 BC) was contemporary to the first phases of the Samarran and Halaf ones, and was then absorbed by the latter in its middle and late phases. Buildings were of a similar type to the ones found at Umm Dabaghiyah. They were therefore characterised by large rectangular houses and large communal storehouses. The main means for subsistence were non-irrigated cultivations, farming, and hunting. Pottery production was more advanced than in Umm Dabaghiyah, but was not particularly developed, due to the limited range of stone equipment available.

The contemporary Samarran culture is divided into an early phase (6300–6000 BC, attested at Samarra, on the Tigris, and Tell es-Sawwan, located a bit more to the south), a middle one (6000–5600 BC, stretching to the north at Tell Shemshara along the Lower Zab river, to the south-east at Choga Mami on the other side of the Diyala river, and to the west at Baghuz, along the Euphrates), and a late phase (5600–5200 BC, only attested at Choga Mami). Samarran culture was considerably more sophisticated, in terms of settlements (such as the large houses of Tell es-Sawwan and their enclosure walls), pottery, decorated with complex and at times artistic motifs (such as the rotating patterns drawn on the ware, often with naturalistic subjects), and of subsistence methods. In fact, this culture depended less on hunting and more on irrigated agriculture (which is first attested for certain at Choga Mami).

After an early phase (6100–5800 BC) in the heart of the Jezira region, from Arpachiya (in Assyria) to Sabi Abyad (in the Balikh Valley), Halaf culture spread in Upper Mesopotamia (Figure 3.6). In the Upper and Middle Euphrates region, the Mediterranean coast, and Central Anatolia, Halaf culture also developed into different, yet related, cultures. To the south-east, it co-existed with the late Hassuna settlements (corresponding to the Middle Halaf phase, ca. 5800–5400 BC) and the latter was eventually absorbed into the final phase of Halaf culture (Late Halaf, ca. 5400–5100 BC).

Therefore, the impact of this culture was much more far-reaching than any other culture of the period. It affected the foothills extending from the Euphrates to the Zab and beyond, and had links with the nearby mountainous areas. It is widely believed that Halaf culture owes greatly to those highland groups who descended to the surrounding plains to find vaster spaces for agriculture and farming. However, this descent could have been a seasonal form of transhumance from the mountains to the plains, rather than a fully-fledged migration of people. Halaf culture was mainly sustained through agricultural and farming activities, centred on the cultivation of spelt (without irrigation) and the farming of goats and sheep. This kind of subsistence constituted the final stage of the previous experiments in the area and would remain fundamental to the non-irrigated foothills.

Halaf settlements kept several archaic traits, such as the small circular houses with domed roofs (*tholoi*) preceded by a long rectangular antechamber. In contrast to rectangular buildings, which had already been around for centuries, this kind of architecture certainly indicates a regression in the Neolithic way of using

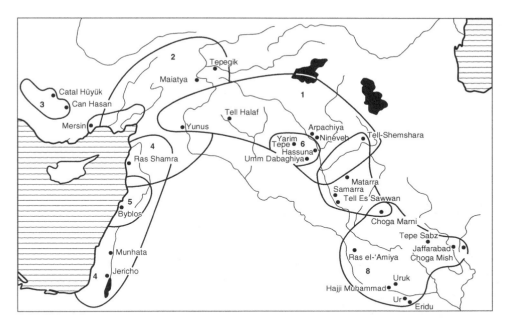

Figure 3.6 The diffusion of ceramic cultures in the Late and Middle Halaf period (ca. 5800–5100 BC): 1: Halaf; 2: Halaf-type; 3: contemporary Anatolian pottery; 4: Amuq D and Palestinian Ceramic Neolithic B; 5: Middle Neolithic of Byblos; 6: Hassuna; 7: Samarra; 8: Hajji Muhammad.

up space. Round buildings prevented the development of building complexes through extensions. Despite this and other archaic features, Halaf culture undoubtedly managed to have a considerable impact on the area, as shown by the diffusion of its characteristic pottery (Figure 3.7). The latter was at the forefront of this kind of production in the Near Eastern Neolithic in terms of workmanship, types, and polychrome decoration.

Lower Mesopotamia was yet another case in terms of ecologic and cultural development. Prior to the centuries-long works of drainage and irrigation, it was largely covered by marshes (Figure 3.8). While in nearby Khuzistan the fully Neolithic cultures of Muhammad Jaffar and Tepe Sabz continued the local sequence (following the culture of Ali Kosh, mentioned above), Eridu culture almost suddenly emerged in the Lower Euphrates area. The quality of its ware, which was of the same quality as the best pottery from Samarra or Halaf, indicates that Eridu must have had a formative stage that remains unknown to us. This is either because it is still buried *in situ*, or because it developed elsewhere (Khuzistan?), and was subsequently brought to Eridu by groups already in possession of core production techniques. The latter, such as irrigated agriculture, are fully Neolithic in character, and were practised alongside fishing, which was prominent due to the settlement's location.

A further development from Eridu culture is that of Hajji Muhammad (near Uruk), which developed in the south (Eridu), reached the area of Kish (Ras el-'Amiya). From there, it spread beyond the Tigris to Choga Mami (where it influenced late Halaf culture) and to the Khuzistan settlements of the Khazineh phase. This area of cultural unity (an area which would later on comprise Sumer, Akkad and Elam) was thriving. It was different from contemporary Halaf culture, mainly because it had to adapt to a different ecosystem. The latter facilitated the irrigated cultivation of grains and cattle farming (which at Ras el-'Amiya constituted 45% of bone remains). This was the initial phase of Ubaid culture, through which Lower Mesopotamia would eventually take the lead in terms of technological and organisational

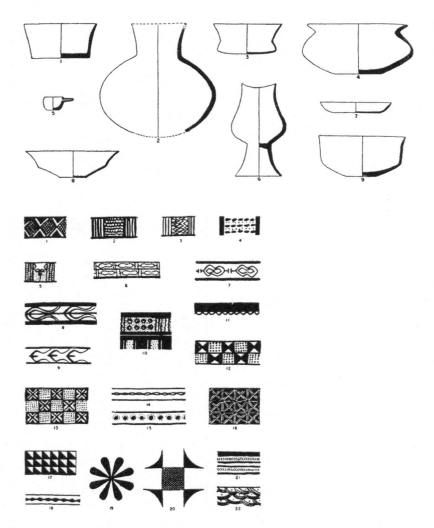

Figure 3.7 Halaf pottery: types and decorative motifs.

development in the Near East. On the contrary, Halaf culture would experience a progressive crisis. In terms of periodisation, the rise of Ubaid culture marks the end of the Neolithic and the beginning of the Chalcolithic period (Table 3.3).

Although the leading cultures of the Neolithic period in the Near East extended from Anatolia to Khuzistan, it is necessary to bear in mind the existence of less rich and advanced cultures on the edge of this area: from the above-mentioned ones in Palestine to the ones in Cyprus (Khirokitia culture, with circular houses and no pottery despite its production economy), in the Zagros (Tepe Giyan and Dalma Tepe), and south of the Caucasus. Through these marginal cultures, located in more difficult areas in terms of agriculture, the Fertile Crescent came into contact with other Neolithic communities outside the geographical limits of this book. Beyond Palestine there were the Egyptian cultures of the Fayyum. Beyond Cyprus and Anatolia there were the cultures of the Aegean and Macedonia. Finally, beyond the Zagros there were the Neolithic cultures of Central Iran (Tepe Siyalk) and Central Asia.

Figure 3.8 The marshes of Lower Mesopotamia, with the typical reed buildings.

Table 3.3 Chronology of the Chalcolithic period in the Ancient Near East

	Mesopotamia		Khuzistan	Syria	Anatolia
	South	North			
4500					
	Early Ubaid (=Ubaid 3)	Nineveh 3 Gawra 17–14	Susiana C Mehmeh	Amuq D	Mersin 16
4000	Eridu 11–9				
	Late Ubaid (=Ubaid 4)	Nineveh 3 Gawra 13–12	Bayat Susa A	Amuq E	Mersin 15
3500	Eridu 8–6 Uruk 18–15				

4 The first steps towards urbanisation

In Levels 17 to 15 excavated at Eridu (ca. 5800 BC), a number of small buildings have been found. Due to their type and location (underneath later temples of the Ubaid and Uruk phases), these buildings have been interpreted as the earliest Mesopotamian buildings exclusively dedicated to cultic activities. These small chapels constitute a modest beginning that would eventually lead to a remarkable development. At this stage, however, the dedication of specific spaces to cultic activities is significant, since in other areas such activities were still pursued on a family level (see Çatal Hüyük). This development would become a characteristic feature of the following phase of the Ubaid period, when it grew considerably and reached Upper Mesopotamia, but not the surrounding areas (Figure 3.9).

Ubaid culture lasted a long period of time, from 5100 to 4500 BC in its early phase, and 4500 to 4000 BC in its late phase. Initially, it remained confined to the same area as Eridu and Hajji Muhammad, displaying a marked continuity in terms of settlement and pottery types. This led to the alternative periodisation of the Eridu, Hajji Muhammad, Early Ubaid, and Late Ubaid phases as Ubaid 1, 2, 3, and 4. The main sites of this phase are Eridu itself, Ur, Tell Weyli, and the eponymous site of Tell Ubaid (near Ur) in the far south. Later on, Tell Uqair (near Kutha), Ras el-'Amiya (near Kish), Tell Abada and Tell Madhur (in the

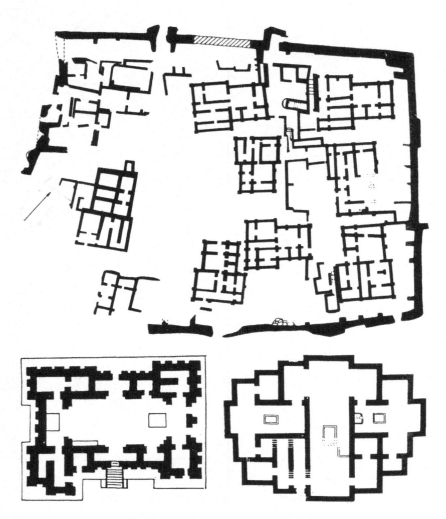

Figure 3.9 *Above*: The enclosure wall of Tell es-Sawwan, Samarra period. *Below, left*: Temple 7, Eridu, Late Ubaid period. *Below, right*: A typical private household plan of the Ubaid period.

Hamrin area) rose to prominence in the north. Pottery finds from field surveys indicate a marked proliferation of settlements. Unfortunately, archaeologists are rarely able to reveal Neolithic levels. This is because more often than not their main purpose is to excavate later historical settlements. To make matters worse, these ancient levels are difficult to find in settlements that did not survive beyond the Neolithic, since they were completely concealed by later alluvial deposits.

The inhabitants of the Mesopotamian lowlands were the first to master, yet still on a local level, the construction of canals for the irrigation of areas which were not arable otherwise, and the drainage of excess water from marshes to drainage basins. As a result, the first fully-fledged agricultural settlements began to appear along irrigation canals. Apart from pottery, the best indicators of agricultural activities found in these centres were clay sickles, more suitable than flint sickles for the harvesting of grain on a larger scale. Alongside agriculture, there was farming (sheep, goats and cattle) and the initial stages of arboriculture (mainly the date palm) and horticulture (onions and various legumes). This development was certainly the result of the increased availability of water. In some centres close to ponds or lagoons (such as in the case of Eridu), fishing also provided a considerable contribution to the diet, and offerings of fish and fishing tools (fish hooks and curved nails to fix fishing nets) were made to the nearby temples.

In certain areas, household architecture remained quite simple, with huts made of twigs and clay. In other areas, it became much more solid and complex (Tell Weyli, Tell Abada and Tell Madhur). At the heart of these more sophisticated settlements there was the temple. As recorded in the archaeological sequences found at Eridu, sanctuaries were reconstructed and expanded after each collapse, and their remains formed a raised platform on which new temples were constructed. Unlike the small chapels of the Eridu phase, the temples of the Ubaid period (Levels 11–8) were larger, with a central room flanked by smaller chambers. In the late Ubaid period (Levels 7–6), temples displayed a tripartite structure (a central hall with two rows of rooms on each side) with buttressed facades (a feature that would become characteristic of Mesopotamian temples for three millennia) and access through a long staircase along the raised platform.

These imposing buildings (20 × 12 m), which by far superseded anything ever built until then, indicate how the unification of cultic activities outside the household immediately led to a significant change. This change affected both the political and economic organisation of these settlements, and the centralisation of resources and activities (offerings, cults as communal activities, use of workforce for building activities and the possible existence of specialised priests).

There were other clues indicating this tendency towards unification and social stratification. Admittedly, these are not yet fully visible, but are still discernible in the wider context of later developments. One clue is the increased number of precious artefacts, clearly the product of specialised labour both in terms of craftsmanship and procurement of resources, even if not necessarily on a full-time basis. The presence of these artefacts, such as metal objects and semi-precious stones (used for necklaces and stamp seals), potentially indicates the existence of trade and specialised craftsmanship. A second clue is the investment of an increasing amount of resources gathered from household activities for communal and symbolic purposes. This shift indicates a conscious strategy of investment of surplus not towards family consumption, but the development of the community as a whole. As a result of this change, households and burials maintained a visible degree of homogeneity and austerity.

A third clue can be found in the early traces of mass production. On the one hand, this required full-time workers. On the other, it required the existence of some form of political leadership to organise the economic activities of a community, and commission certain products. While the presence of clay sickles does not necessarily imply a certain degree of centralisation, pottery evidence constitutes a better case in point. The ceramic remains of the Ubaid period is hand-made, very refined in terms of technique (from the type of clay to the firing temperature and thinness of the ware) and decoration (which developed from the previous phases, adding new subjects such as animals). By the late Ubaid period, however, pottery became less refined, due to its production in large quantities. This led to the introduction of the potter's wheel, irregular firing, and less care in the decoration of vases. The process would culminate in the following period (Early Uruk), with a more consistent implementation of the potter's wheel for serial pottery production.

With Ubaid culture, then, it becomes possible to detect the first steps towards the creation of socio-economic and political structures more complex than the ones characterising villages. The starting point of this process has to be the progress in agriculture, which in the Mesopotamian alluvial plain had become possible through extensive irrigation and the introduction of the cattle-drawn plough. These changes led to the beginnings of labour specialisation, the subsequent emergence of agents responsible for the coordination of social organisation and decision-making processes (mainly centred on the leading role of temples), and the progressive social stratification of communities.

From Lower Mesopotamia, Ubaid culture spread to the north, where it took over the now declining Late Halaf culture. The area that is best attested for this phase is the region that would eventually become Assyria. The main sites for this period are Tepe Gawra, in the foothills, and Tell Arpachiya and Nineveh, on the Tigris. Other centres were located in the area of Nuzi, Shemshara, Jebel Sinjar (Telul el-Thalalat) and Khabur (Tell Brak). Tepe Gawra had a sequence of temples similar to the one found at Eridu, although slightly later in date. The sequence reached its peak in the temple complex of Level 13, characterised by a large courtyard flanked by three sanctuaries and combining southern elements with local ones. The temples of Level 13 feature thin and highly decorated buttressed walls, coloured plaster, a tripartite plan and a lateral entrance. They therefore are equal in quality to the most impressive buildings found at Eridu, showing that in the Ubaid period the two areas were equally advanced both economically and technologically.

However, the two areas were not equal in terms of their landscape and cultural traditions. The buildings of Tepe Gawra continued to be circular in plan from the Late Halaf period (Level 20) to the Early Uruk phase (Level 11). This was possibly due to the settlement's proximity to those mountain settlements where this kind of architecture was characteristic. Moreover, Tepe Gawra reveals an alternation between levels with *tholoi* constructions, and ones with temples in the Lower Mesopotamian style (Figure 3.10). There-fore, in the levels where the former can be found, the latter are absent, and vice versa. This could possibly indicate some sort of competition and incompatibility between the traditions coming from the mountains (continuing the Halaf tradition) and from the southern alluvial plains (with the new Ubaid culture). The settlements of the north relied much more on commercial contacts than on agriculture, which was pros-perous, obviating the need to implement irrigation canals. There was an abundance of Afghan lapis lazuli, Iranian carnelian, turquoise, hematite, diorite and Anatolian obsidian and copper.

Just like in the south, socio-political changes followed a similar path in the north. An example of this is the development of the stone industry, with seals decorated with the characteristic geometric designs of the Ubaid culture (in the following period these designs would be substituted by human and animal figures). The developments in the stone industry indicate a type of economic interaction requiring the identification of individuals and a confirmation of their role. However, the discovery of a *tholos* (Level 11) in the middle of a residential area indicates the presence of a leader from one of the mountain communities. His authority was probably the result of military interventions and his control over inter-regional relations.

Although Ubaid culture did not spread beyond the Khabur region, some communities with Ubaid-like pottery have been found outside its boundaries. For instance, there were the communities in northern Syria (Amuq E, Ras Shamra), south-eastern Anatolia (Mersin XV–XII, whose levels with Ubaid-like pottery alternate levels with Central Anatolian type of pottery; Domuztepe), in the Euphrates Valley (Hammam et-Turkman, Kurban Hüyük, Degirmen Tepe) and Iran (Siyalk II–III, with beautiful pottery decorated with animal designs, as well as evidence for wheel-made pottery and copper smelting; and Tepe Hissar I, a commercial centre with links to Turkmenistan). Ubaid-like pottery was also produced in Oman, a promising mining area (mainly for copper).

Despite being at times used for tools and weapons (and not just for small decorative objects) requiring a higher level of technical knowledge, metalworking (smelting of pure copper or arsenical copper) is poorly attested in Ubaid settlements, both in the south and the north. However, this may be due to the continuous

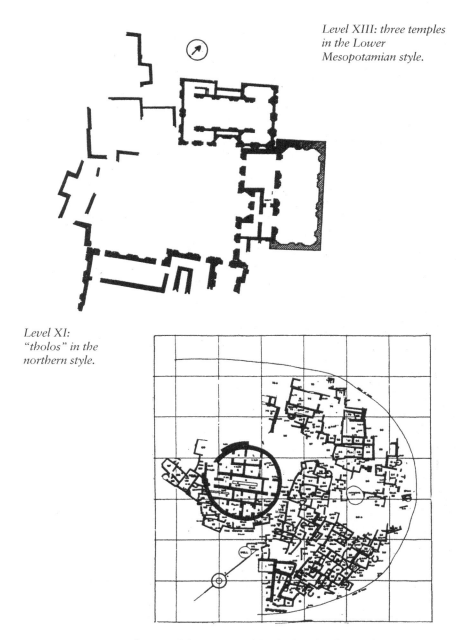

Level XIII: *three temples in the Lower Mesopotamian style.*

Level XI: *"tholos" in the northern style.*

Figure 3.10 Tepe Gawra: interstratification of alternative models of political and social development.

re-use of these metals. The newly developed techniques for copper are far better attested in areas close to metal deposits, such as eastern Anatolia, near the mines at Ergani Maden, and southern Palestine, near the mines at Arabah.

These two areas had different characteristics that deserve to be mentioned. In the case of Late Chalcolithic eastern Anatolia, settlements were predominantly agricultural. However, they were the main providers of copper for the northern section of the Ubaid area. Local metalworking activities thus allowed the development of a culture displaying the first signs of a transition into a more complex organisational structure and characterised by mass-produced pottery (lower quality bowls with potter's stamps). The most important site of the Anatolian Chalcolithic was Arslantepe, which will be considered later on.

In Palestine, Ghassulian culture (named after the site of Tulaylat al-Ghassul) was predominantly pastoral and generally located in the semi-arid areas surrounding the Sinai, Negev and the Judaean Desert. In the summer, however, these communities moved to the rainier areas of the central West Bank and the Jordan Valley. Evidence from burials, caves, and settlements attest to a rich production in arsenical copper weapons (also for ceremonial purposes). This indicates the emergence of leaders whose authority was probably ensured militarily, as well as through their control over herds and copper mines. Therefore, it is possible to see the emergence of an interregional system, which juxtaposes the more densely populated, agriculturally and socially developed Mesopotamian area, with marginal areas responsible for the provision of metal and stone. The latter were strongly influenced by Mesopotamian developments on an organisational level, although power was not yet delegated to a temple, but to the authority of charismatic leaders.

With Late Chalcolithic Anatolia and Ghassulian Palestine (4100–3500 BC) we have reached the end of the Late Ubaid period and the beginning of a phase defined as Early Uruk in the Mesopotamian alluvial plain. There is no clear break between the Ubaid and Uruk period and developments continued in a similar way. However, the different periodisation is needed in view of changes in pottery style. Following the painted ware of the Late Ubaid (Figure 3.11), new polished types appeared, in grey and red, as well as unpolished light coloured pottery, typical of the Uruk phase. Moreover, there are several important indications of progress towards a more centralised economic and political organisation. Unfortunately, we do not possess enough data to determine the pace of development of each settlement, not even on a regional level. It is only possible to establish the various stages of technological development and the degree of growth of temple complexes.

The most important sites for the Early Uruk phase can be found south of Uruk itself (which substitutes Eridu as main site of the period, both archaeologically and historically). In the north, Tepe Gawra remains an important settlement, leading to the definition of the Early Uruk phase in the north as the Gawra phase. At Uruk, the division into stages of development follows the levels of the Eanna, an area that in the Late Uruk phase would become a large temple complex. While Levels 18 to 15 still belong to the Ubaid phase, Levels 14 to 6 are datable to the Early Uruk period. Level 12 indicates the development of a typical kind of ware for this period, defined as the 'bevelled-rim bowl'. This type of bowl was moulded in large quantities and clearly destined for distribution and usage outside the family context, mainly large temple complexes. This aspect will be taken into consideration later on, with the late Uruk phase, when the system reached its zenith.

For now, it is important to note that this type of pottery and its requirement for a certain type of social organisation and production was already in existence around 3800 BC. A large concentration of ovens for ceramic production, as well as the first potter's wheel (which first appeared in the Late Ubaid period), was found at Ur. This evidence indicates the mass production of wares outside the context of households. The use of the potter's wheel spread to all forms of pottery (not just mass-produced types) in Level 8 of the Eanna. With Level 6, at the peak of the Early Uruk phase, there are two architectural innovations: the use of the prismatic *Riemchen* bricks (named by the German excavators at Uruk) instead of the larger and squared bricks used before; and the decoration of temple facades with coloured clay cones.

Levels earlier than Level 4 at the Eanna at Uruk have not yet been investigated in depth, making the understanding of the architectural development of this temple complex difficult to follow in full. However, at Tell Uqair, in Mesopotamia, a temple complex from this period (the so-called 'Painted Temple') has been excavated. The imposing complex was surrounded by an enclosure and placed on a raised platform. This complex gives us an idea of the remarkable growth temple complexes and economic and political structures must have experienced in the second half of the fourth millennium BC. The contemporary temple complex of Eridu presents a similar development. These temples constitute the centre of a unified social organisation that experienced a considerable evolution in this period.

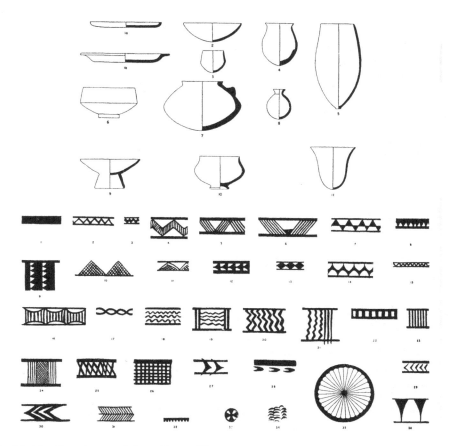

Figure 3.11 Ubaid pottery: types and decorative motifs.

These new settlements began to develop in marked contrast to villages – an opposition that had already begun at this stage, but that will be taken into consideration later on, when it would reach its peak. In the north, a few centres also experienced this development. In particular, Tell Brak and Nineveh seem to have been already on the path to become large cities. However, Tepe Gawra remains our best source for the development of temple areas in this period. The area includes various tripartite sanctuaries. The recession of the main room compared to the side parts of these sanctuaries, and the change of orientation of the entrance (which was from the shorter side), gave them an 'in antis' plan, thus distinguishing them from southern temples.

Differences between north and south are not just limited to temple plans. The potential in productivity, and demographic growth of the newly drained and cultivated lands of Lower Mesopotamia, allowed the development of a large environmental niche. In this way, the area managed to become the centre of a remarkable expansion and to dominate the marginal areas. The north, which on a cultural and technological level was not inferior to the south, had however less potential in terms of agricultural and demographic growth. Just like Late Ubaid culture, Early Uruk culture eventually managed to influence more distant regions (such as Upper Mesopotamia and Khuzistan). For now, however, this growth happened locally, within each Late Chalcolithic culture. In fact, a more visible and innovative transmission of typical elements of Uruk culture to the surrounding areas would only take place later on, in the Late Uruk phase.

In eastern Anatolia, north of the Taurus Mountains, where the Euphrates forms vast basins, the Late Chalcolithic culture contemporary to the Early Uruk phase in Mesopotamia can be best explored through the recent excavations at Arslantepe (near Malatya). Arslantepe is a privileged site, at the centre of a well-watered and protected ecologic niche, close to the forests and pasturelands in the mountains (Figure 3.12). The site already had a long history by the mid-fourth millennium BC, but peaked in the Late Chalcolithic phase. At that time, the site had a temple complex of considerable size and quality, as well as a centre for the production of large quantities of bowls and stamped cretulae (small clay nodules). This development, contemporary to the Early Uruk phase of Lower Mesopotamia, precedes the rise of southern settlements and indicates that some marginal centres had already grown on a local level. This evolution was probably caused by the first commercial interactions with the Early Uruk centres. This was definitely a proto-urban development, but entirely local in this case.

In the mid-fourth millennium BC, certain important political and cultural elements began to appear in the Near East. The Lower Mesopotamian alluvial plain took on a leading role in the technological and organisational development of the area, polarising the surrounding areas. The increasing complexity of interregional relations was mirrored in the increasing complexity of local settlements. Consequently, temple complexes became the socio-economic, political and ideological centres of their communities. The emerging new role of temples has to be linked to the appearance of new forms of religiosity. Offerings, the communal character of cultic buildings, and the presence of more than one temple in a settlement indicate that by this stage there were established divine 'personalities' (who would only be named in texts from the following periods) that the community could address for its expectations and fears. Therefore, communities effectively traded earlier generic worldviews about uncontrollable forces guiding nature and fertility, in favour of established divine characters. Already from these early stages, the emerging class of priests and religious officials mediated the interaction between local communities and deities. Therefore, this class took on the privilege and duty of overseeing not only this human–divine intermediation, but also the political and economic decisions of the community.

Figure 3.12   Aerial view of Arslantepe, ancient Melid (Courtesy: the Italian Archaeological Mission in Eastern Anatolia).

PART II

The Early Bronze Age

4
THE URBAN REVOLUTION

1 Labour specialisation and the 'great organisations'

The slow process leading to the development of agriculture, craftsmanship, long-distance trade, and cultic centres peaked in the mid-fourth millennium BC. Gordon Childe defined this period as the 'Urban Revolution'. The centre of this revolution was Lower Mesopotamia, and specifically Uruk (Middle Uruk period, ca. 3800–3400 BC, and Late Uruk period, ca. 3400–3000 BC). The definition of this phase as the 'Urban Revolution' has been widely criticised, but remains a meaningful notion. The 'Urban Revolution' was part of a long process that partly relied on very ancient premises. Nonetheless, it was a revolutionary event both in terms of time and impact. Time-wise, it constitutes a quick acceleration, if not a proper 'jump', preceded and followed by slower stages of development with long-lasting implications. In terms of the impact of these changes, they pervaded every aspect of society – from demography to technology, socio-economic structures and ideologies. These changes affected society so radically that they changed its core structure. They developed a kind of organisation that would survive throughout the Bronze Age and beyond, and would provide the Ancient Near East with its characteristic traits.

This 'revolution' was a complex phenomenon. The main problem for scholars has been that of deciding which of the various factors contributing to the process were the fundamental and primary ones and which were the secondary ones affecting this change. The earliest scholarly explanations for this phenomenon favoured one of three decisive factors: technology, demography or social organisation. It is now clear, however, that we are dealing with a systemic phenomenon, in which various factors interacted with each other, thus stimulating further growth. For instance, innovations in the exploitation of resources certainly constituted a powerful drive for development. However, these could not have taken place without labour specialisation and urbanisation. Equally, demographic growth was undoubtedly an important factor. Nonetheless, it would have been a slow-acting factor on its own, requiring new conditions in order to develop prominently over a short period of time. Similarly, while technological innovations were probably stimulated by increased production needs, at the same time they facilitated the latter.

It is therefore necessary to simplify this systemic process and establish some sort of logical, rather than chronological, order of priority for these factors. It is clear that the increase in agricultural productivity was the most influential prerequisite guaranteeing food surplus. Only the latter allowed the establishment of redistributive centres and the maintenance of full-time specialised workers. The most noticeable change was undoubtedly the demographic and urban one. However, the organisational change remains the most substantial one. The origin of the city marked the origin of the State and of socio-economic stratification.

It therefore marks the beginning of history. This is not just because the development of writing provides us with clearer and more detailed sources of information. For the first time, more complex types of human interaction began to develop within the community (such as social stratification, the development of political leadership and the socio-political role of ideologies) and between communities. The latter were now structured on a larger scale (city-states and regional States) and equipped with specific strategies and rivalries to access resources and secure territorial control.

Throughout the Neolithic and Chalcolithic periods, communities only developed at a village level (or as nomadic communities). Each community was generally quite homogeneous, both externally and internally. This was mainly because it was a self-sufficient entity. There were differences in terms of rank, with wealthier or larger families compared to others, as well as larger or more prosperous villages. There were also some forms of labour specialisations (of individuals or entire communities). The latter, however, remained rather limited. The organisational 'jump' consisted of the systematic separation between primary production and secondary specialisation. This distinction polarised human groups, leading to the concentration of labour specialists in larger proto-urban centres. Consequently, food production was left in the hands of the villages in the countryside.

This complementary relation immediately became hierarchical, inextricably linking villages to the larger cities. Thus, the flow of food surplus moved from the food producers to the specialised craftsmen. This allowed the latter to survive without having to produce food themselves. In return, a flow of products and services moved from the specialised craftsmen to the food producers. The relation therefore worked both ways, benefiting communities both in the cities and the villages. However, internal relations eventually became uneven enough to greatly benefit the specialised groups, who monopolised rare and more advanced technologies. They therefore had considerable contractual abilities. This was a social and cultural privilege distinguishing them from food producers, who carried out rather basic and common tasks in terms of technological advancement (food producers constituted 80% or more of the population). Moreover, specialised groups acted further down in the production process, and were thus in a more favourable position to gain better percentages of income, and to influence strategic decisions.

Those who carried out administrative (scribes, administrators, keepers) and ceremonial duties (priests) stood at the top of the hierarchy of these specialised urban centres. Their duties were meant to ensure the community's cohesion and the organisation of labour and retribution. The traditional activities that once belonged to the heads of households on a family and village level now became a specialised duty (possibly the most specialised task of all). This duty became accountable for choices that were neither obvious nor insignificant, since they were based on inequality and were aimed at accentuating it. In village communities, each self-sufficient household was able to disagree or disappear without any particular effect on the other households. On the contrary, solidarity in urban centres was not cumulative or optional any more. In the urban and specialised system, solidarity became organic and necessary: complementarity and sequentiality made the labour of each household necessary for other households. No one would have been able to leave without compromising the entire system. Strategic choices affected everyone and had to be accepted by everyone, either through persuasion or coercion.

The organisation of specialised labour, its spatial concentration in specific areas and the formation of communal decisional centres created those institutions defined by Leo Oppenheim as the 'great organisations', namely, the temple and the palace. These large architectural and organisational complexes physically separated villages from cities. The latter were settlements housing large organisations, while the former were deprived of such institutions. There was a marked difference between the temple and the palace. The temple was primarily a centre for cultic activities. It was the house of a deity, where the community performed daily and seasonal (festivals) cults to its symbolic leader. On the other hand, the palace housed a community's human leader, namely, the king, along with his closest social circle (the royal family and the court).

However, the similarities between the two institutions are equally important. Both the palace and the temple were centres for administrative and decision-making activities, as well as for the accumulation of surplus, the core of the whole redistributive system. Apart from being the human or divine household of the community's representatives, and the centre of the public manifestations of political and religious ideologies, the palace and the temple were also surrounded by workshops, warehouses, scribal schools and archives. They were the hearts of the cities both logistically, with areas specifically dedicated to economic activities, and structurally, since they were surrounded by other buildings for storage, administrative and crafting purposes. Therefore, the complex constituted by the palace or temple and the presence of specialised buildings and residences for the personnel (such as religious officials, merchants, craftsmen, guards) represent that 'public' sector that prevailed in urban societies. However, this sector was entirely absent on a village level.

As a response to the rise of these great organisations, the population began to be differentiated into two separate groups. Specialised groups lacked the means to support themselves. They therefore worked on commission for the palace, which supported them through a system of rations and land allocations. These specialised workmen thus constituted the socio-economic and political elite of the State. However, as direct beneficiaries of this redistributive system, they remained both legally and economically subservient to the king (or the deity), since they were supported by the State. The rest of the population, made of food producing families, was to a certain degree 'freer'. These groups owned their lands and animals, and were largely self-subsistent.

However, this part of society was still obliged to provide its surplus to the State, thus becoming a fundamental part of the redistributive system. Despite being involved in this system, the larger part of the population never received a concrete return for their contributions. This return would often be purely ideological (religious or for political propaganda), with a modest influence on specialised production and the all-essential military service. The most effective State intervention in the surrounding countryside was the construction of canals. These infrastructures were specifically designed for the improvement of agricultural activities. Canals required a certain degree of coordination both in terms of labour and resources. They therefore necessitated the support of a great organisation.

Within the palace, labour specialisation was prominent. This is attested on the many detailed lists of professions from the Late Uruk period. The marked increase in labour specialisation led to important implications. Full-time workers managed to improve their technical knowledge and become more efficient in their chosen field of expertise, providing significant improvements. This centralisation of labour therefore generated a more favourable environment for technological innovations. Similarly, the needs of the commissioning groups provided new opportunities for high-quality craftsmanship. Conversely, craftsmanship directed towards a larger and less specialised group became more repetitive and homogeneous, compromising quality for quantity.

Mass production led to the development of more efficient processes. For instance, pottery, shaped on the potter's wheel or even in moulds, was simpler and less personalised, but faster and less expensive to make (Figure 4.1). Similarly, casting moulds began to be used in metallurgy. Textile production moved from households into larger workshops, engaging a large share of female workers and children. In other words, technological developments were mainly driven by economic and quantitative needs, although they were still at times devoted to quality and luxury goods.

The second impact of the Urban Revolution was predominantly social. Each specialised sector developed a hierarchy of masters, trainees, overseers and workmen. Similarly, relations of dependence and the earliest ambitions in terms of career advancement effectively became substitutes for traditional family relations. Remuneration was closely linked to the kind of workplace an individual worked in, as well as to his ability to provide the service required. On a family or village level, an individual was provided from birth with a profession on the basis of his position in the family. Therefore, each individual already knew which social and professional role he would inherit at his father's death. On the contrary, remuneration now became a personal endeavour, with the development of ideas such as individual merit and accountability, as well as personal possession of goods (not family possessions anymore).

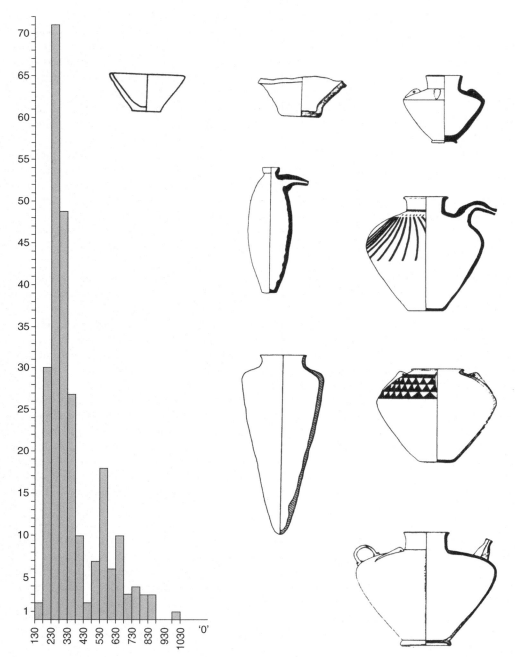

Figure 4.1 Characteristic pottery of the Late Uruk period; the graph shows the degree of standardisation of the capacity of ration bowls (Malatya).

However, the most striking development towards hierarchy took place between categories of professions. This hierarchy was based on the degree of remuneration received and the prestige of the work provided, being either more or less specialised, or requiring more or less training, or closer or further away from the ruling centre. Class differences were not occasional anymore, but became a fundamental aspect of society. Consequently, this new society of specialists automatically became stratified, with considerable class differences.

2 The city and its villages

If the Urban Revolution peaked in Lower Mesopotamia between 3500 and 3200 BC, one may wonder why it took place there and then. Evidently, the necessary premises for this profound social change found this particular historical context appropriate for further developments. First of all, as already mentioned, there must have been an availability of surplus able to support the great organisations and their specialised staff. In other words, agriculture had to be particularly developed. Agriculture in small ecological niches had been perfectly adequate for the initial stimulation of technical and economic progress, mostly favoured by the proximity of different eco-regions.

Lower Mesopotamia was a far larger 'niche'. However, it was a niche that, if not properly equipped, could not allow the rise of human settlements. This was due to the presence of two large rivers (the Tigris and the Euphrates), whose meanders and seasonal floods created marshes and inaccessible lands. Its distance from the raw materials needed for the construction of tools (such as metal, semiprecious stones and timber) was a hindrance in the initial stages of development. After all, long-distance journeys were expensive and largely unreliable. However, once properly organised, Lower Mesopotamia had its advantages in terms of size and quality. Once drained, its lands provided high yields and a network of economic relations via rivers and large spaces, which facilitated the evolution of villages into larger settlements.

Admittedly, Lower Mesopotamia experienced a unique progress. The area had initially remained on the margins of the general developmental trends of the Neolithic period. It only rose in the Ubaid period and in the transitional phase between the Chalcolithic and the Bronze Age. It is possible that the lower sea levels of the Persian Gulf at the time, either because of earthquakes or the increasing amount of sediments accumulated in the rivers, had been an important factor in this sudden rise. This led to the construction of canals, both to drain excess water from the marshes and to distribute it more evenly across the territory (Figure 4.2). Therefore, water began to be managed more effectively, minimising the differences both in its seasonal and annual availability.

Water management developed through various technical and organisational stages. Large canals carrying water on a regional level were for now still impossible to construct and would only appear several centuries later, as a result of political unification and increased mobility. The initial hydric interventions were strictly local in nature and required little technical expertise. However, these interventions already led to the creation and constant upkeep of drained stretches of land. Consequently, hydric factors began to heavily influence the development of relations between these drained stretches of land. For instance, land located higher up influenced the location of drained areas in the foothills, the creation of a canal, the deviation of a river and the use of a depression in the land as a basin. If these factors benefited certain areas, they hindered others. This situation led to an increased need for coordination between local initiatives, in order to avoid potential conflicts. Be that as it may, the first hydric interventions already took place in the Ubaid period. They moved at the same pace as the agricultural activities of the alluvial plain. Only by the mid-fourth millennium BC did these interventions increase in scale, and were then used to create a network of inter-regional connections, since river transport was less expensive than land transport.

Aside from the construction of canals, agricultural activities also benefited from the technological progress of the period. Due to the increased availability of water, irrigated agriculture provided higher and more regular yields than those in the surrounding foothills, which still relied on rainfed agriculture. For the cultivation of the alluvial plains, a tool was developed which would continue to be used in Meso-potamia for three millennia. This tool was the scratch plough (*apin* in Sumerian and *epinnu* in Akkadian), which allowed a significantly faster cultivation than hoe farming. The Mesopotamian scratch plough was

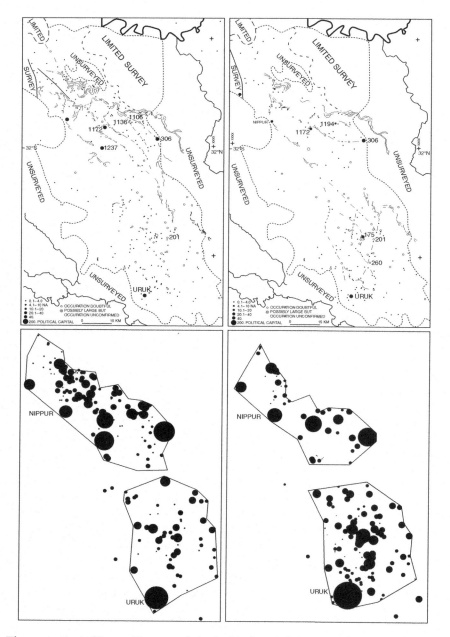

Figure 4.2 The occupation of Lower Mesopotamia in the Uruk period. Settlements and canals in the Early Uruk period (*above, left*) and Late Uruk period (*above, right*); simulation of cultivated areas in the Early Uruk period (*below, left*) and Late Uruk period (*below, right*).

a complex piece of equipment. It allowed a more precise type of sowing, placing the seeds deep in the ground, away from animals feeding on them. Naturally, the scratch plough required the availability of draught animals (four or six) able to pull the plough and specialised workmen. This kind of activity was best suited for agriculture on the plains, with long fields of similar size spread along irrigation canals (Figure 4.3). This division of the land indicates a planned and organised kind of agricultural production. Irrigation, the scratch plough, high yields in cereal cultivation (with a 1:30 – and higher – ratio between seeds sown and harvested) and long fields provided Lower Mesopotamia with a large and stable availability of surplus. The latter could then sustain a wide and diversified range of specialised workmen and administrators living in the cities.

Settlements were not uniformly distributed across an undifferentiated territory that pursued the same kinds of activities anymore. First of all, settlements developed close to water resources, both for irrigation purposes and for transport. The latter became an essential aspect for the centralisation of surplus, which was delivered from the fields to the warehouses in the cities. Moreover, settlements began to be divided into a hierarchy of two and, soon after, three groups. The division into two groups included the villages, characterised by their small size and agro-pastoral activities, and the cities. The latter were responsible for the transformation of raw materials, trade and services. The size of cities did not depend on the degree of exploitation of the surrounding lands anymore. This is because they could benefit from their newly developed ability to gather resources on a regional level. The third group was made of intermediary centres, which performed urban kind of activities, both in terms of craftsmanship and administration, away from the centre.

The development of a hierarchy of settlements with different specialisations is only a marginal aspect of this new political organisation, which moved from a local scale to a regional one. This is visible from the rise of capitals as well as a number of centres in the periphery and a vast amount of tributary villages. Capitals were centres of political control (centred on the palace, the temple or temples, and the ruling class) and of the majority of specialised activities. This intricate structure was separated from other similar structures

Figure 4.3   Landscape of the southern Iraq region, with long fields on both sides of the river (NASA).

67

by stretches of land left untouched, covered with marshes, or arid steppes unreached by irrigation canals. These territories had a political function, keeping regional complexes separate, as well as an economic role, providing marginal, yet important resources through seasonal pastoralism, fishing and gathering activities.

Urbanisation developed alongside a rapid demographic growth. The latter was not due to immigration flows, as previously hypothesised, but to an internal demographic growth caused by the improvements in food production processes. However, within this overarching growth, which demonstrates the positive effects of the Urban Revolution (able to sustain a larger number of inhabitants living in the same territory), there were considerable differentiations and fluctuations. The rise of an urban centre led to the abandonment of the surrounding countryside. A case in point is Uruk, whose growth (of ca. 70 hectares) in the Early Uruk phase (levels XIV–VI of the Eanna, ca. 3500–3200 BC) led to the concentration of the population within its walls and to the disappearance of the nearby villages. Further north, in the area of Nippur and Adab, where urban concentration is less visible, demographic growth was spread across numerous villages. Later on, however, in the Late Uruk phase (levels V–III of the Eanna, ca. 3400–3000 BC) the opposite happened: the large centre of Uruk (ca. 100 hectares) also attracted people from the north, leading to a crisis of the villages in the Nippur-Adab area. It is hard to tell to what extent these demographic fluctuations were the result of actual movements of people or of different rates of growth in different areas. However, these rates, originally applied to populations with similar starting points, modify quantitative relations when applied over long periods of time.

Finally, it is worth bearing in mind that, in order to be effective and productive, the exploitation of the land through canals and allotments relied on demographic growth. The construction of a canal itself required the accumulation of food to cover the costs (in the form of food rations to be given to the workers). Moreover, it required the availability of a workforce able to take time off farming, as long as it was not damaging the cultivations already in process. Moreover, once the canal was completed, it was crucial to find families ready to settle and cultivate the new lands. This repopulation ensured the availability of resources (in terms of further surplus), a fact that would justify the creation of the canal in the first place. Therefore, the intervention becomes cyclical, requiring a surplus of people and food and increasing productivity and surplus. Internal political structures were equally cyclical, requiring a wide consensus and technical and economic expertise to plan the infrastructures needed, but at the same time building consensus and making the surrounding settlements more dependent on the centre. Therefore, demography, technology and politics did not develop independently from each other. This interconnection, then, prevents us from considering one aspect as more influential than the others.

The hierarchical and interdependent relations developing in the area also changed the urban and agricultural landscape on closer inspection. In the countryside, land began to be diversified on a legal level. In the pre-urban phase, all the lands had the same legal status, since they belonged to the families cultivating them. In those communities, there were mechanisms to guarantee that the land would continue to be owned by the family living in it (since land ownership was mainly passed on through inheritance). Moreover, there were plots of land managed by the village, namely, pasturelands and lands belonging to extinct family lines. Now, however, urbanisation brought a significant change to the legal status of land: some fields continued to be owned by 'free' families; others belonged to the temple or the palace. With time, the latter acquired an increasing amount of land, either through economic processes or by colonising new territories. After all, the long fields lined along irrigation canals would have been unthinkable without the intervention of these central structures.

The management of land belonging to the temple and the palace was organised in two ways. One part of the land was directly exploited by these organisations through servile labour, thus becoming part of a larger agricultural centre. The other part was divided into lots and allotted to individuals in exchange for their services to the organisation. Therefore, the lands owned by the temple and the palace created a new agricultural landscape. The latter began to characterise the immediate surroundings of the cities and the newly colonised land, thus causing a dispersion of the population and the marginalisation of villages mentioned above. The various types of land management of temple or palace land caused the tribute system to develop in different ways: villages had to pay a tithe (or anyway a low percentage); the lands directly linked to the organisations had to give up their whole produce (minus whatever was needed for the following cultivation and for the rations to be given to the workmen and livestock); and specialised services had to be provided in exchange of plots of land. In addition to that, individual plots of land began to develop economic types of interactions. In the temple and the palace lands, seasonal tasks requiring a large workforce were performed by the inhabitants from the villages as an obligation (*corvée*). This system allowed the great organisation to cut costs.

A parallel diversification, though in a different form, also affected urban settlements. In villages, the equal status of family units was architecturally visible through the uniformity of household plans, which maintained a similar size and function. In the cities, however, social stratification and specialisation led to the development of a complex urban plan. The palace and the temple (characterised by a particular care for the exterior facades, meant to arouse the admiration of the population) constituted the centre of the settlement, along with other, often public, buildings such as warehouses, workshops and so on. The varying degrees of prestige and the economic means of family units led households to reflect the social status of the families living in them, both in terms of size and wealth. In this increasingly complex urban plan, the temple and its surrounding area (with many smaller temples, reflecting the polytheistic nature of each city's pantheon) undoubtedly remained the core of the settlement. For instance, the Eanna at Uruk was characterised by many sacred buildings linked to each other by colonnades and courtyards, as well as the nearby artificial mound with the temple of Anu (Figure 4.4). It therefore constitutes a case of its own in terms of complexity and elaborateness, but not an unusual one.

Urbanisation also brought about a vast concentration of wealth, enough to require the construction of defensive walls. The costs of an endeavour of such magnitude were clearly meant to protect the wealth accumulated in the city. Defensive walls required many working days for the production of bricks and the erection of walls, as well as for the construction of the foundations and the accumulation of the soil needed. This wealth was not only made of food supplies gathered through taxation and of luxury goods that had reached the city through long distance trade. There were also the knowledge and technical expertise of the urban workshops, as well as the ideologies expressed through the temples and their furnishings. All these resources had to be protected from potential attacks from nearby cities or foreign invaders.

By contrast, villages were too numerous and small, and their wealth too modest to justify the construction of defensive walls. The real wealth of villages was their inhabitants, either as workforce for the palaces they depended upon, or for eventual invaders. In case of invasions, the population would have fled, rather than invest in fortification walls. The cities, then, were in marked contrast to the villages, which were located in the open countryside, sparsely inhabited with simple, non-durable houses. The cities' fortification walls visibly separated urban settlements from their surroundings, creating a compact city plan. Moreover, their large and architecturally complex buildings were meant to last through time. They also had to be frequently restored and rebuilt, due to their functional and symbolic value for the entire community. Therefore, urbanisation also meant monumental architecture (from temples to city walls), aimed at protecting the community's prosperity both physically and ideologically.

3 From quality to quantity

The great organisations were large redistributive centres: surplus, wages, services and commodities were accumulated and redistributed to a degree that easily superseded interactions on a village and family level. The enlarged scale of these interactions made the older means of interaction through habit and personal acquaintances inadequate. In other words, a more objective and impersonal system was needed in order to ensure and guarantee that exchange would remain constant in every direction. This brought to the development of counting and measuring systems, and systems meant to give a concrete value to commodities, labour, time and land.

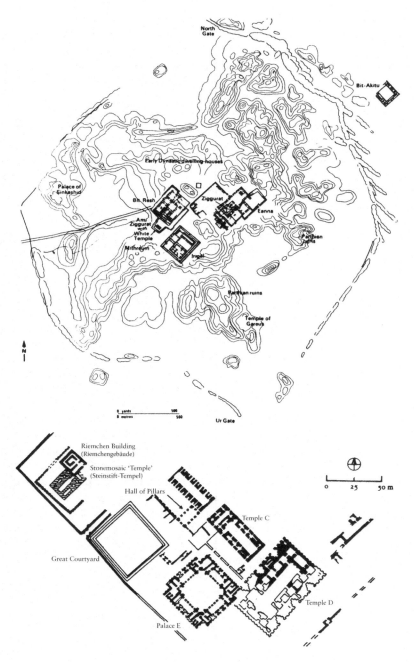

Figure 4.4 Plan of Uruk (*above*); the district of Eanna in Uruk, level 4 (*below*).

Systems of measurement (weight, mass, length and area) already existed. They were predominantly based on body parts: the thumb (inch), cubit or foot for linear measurements, or the talent (the weight of a person), or the weight of a donkey and so on. These conventional and concrete systems were difficult to implement in a complex counting system. This was due to their unreliability and their different standardisation from place to place. The decisive step towards a more reliable system took place when these units were standardized and linked to a numeral system. In Mesopotamia, the system was sexagesimal, based on multiples of six and ten. Therefore, multiples and divisors of a given unit were 60 and 360, 1/60 and 1/360 and so on.

Linking units of measurements to the sexagesimal system made the whole system much more accessible to the administrators of large-scale organisations. For instance, the talent was divided into 60 minas, and each mina was divided into 60 shekels. These changes removed the original concreteness of the system in favour of a more reliable standardisation. This facilitated the calculations necessary for administrative purposes, from additions to multiplications and divisions (by people or units of time). This was especially the case for the distribution of rations, which was a repetitive operation due to its frequency and the large number of people involved. The assets managed by the urban administration (both in terms of income and expenditure) therefore began to be accounted for, both in terms of quantities and time. These aspects could not have been accounted for in individual households, where systems for the record of assets were not needed on such a scale.

Standardised units of measurements required prototypes approved and guarded by the central administration. For instance, the 'palm' had to be equally long for everyone, and always the exact half of a cubit. Therefore, it could not have been measured with one's hand, but with an officially approved palm length. The rise of redistributive organisations of a scale larger than that of family units, then, led to a link between measures and the numeral system. It also led to the development of models, especially smaller stone weights (mostly shekels, rarely minas), which have been recovered *in situ*. On the contrary, measures of lengths were made of more perishable materials. Therefore, they have not survived. Units to measure capacity were at times marked on vases, but are otherwise detectable through the standardised dimensions of containers.

Another step towards this administrative standardisation was the comparison of values. Exchange and redistribution required a system able to measure the value of goods, labour, time and land. Every aspect becoming part of the system had to receive a value in relation to the others. A relation of this kind already existed in a very rudimentary form, namely, through the exchange of a given quantity of a certain commodity for a different quantity of another commodity, according to its accessibility, importance, or the labour needed to produce it. These subjective and variable values allowed the first forms of reciprocal exchanges. However, they could not be transferred onto a larger, long-standing and impersonal redistributive organisation without being simplified and standardised. The central administration therefore established the respective value of the goods and services provided, and based its exchanges and remunerations on this system of equivalences.

Two further operations were essential for the urbanisation process. The first one was the selection of certain commodities as standard units of value, rather than memorising the value of each good in comparison to the others. This standardisation constituted a considerable simplification, and a fundamental one when exchanging on a larger scale. The process led to the memorisation and application of equivalences of all available commodities compared to one unit of value (or two or three). The latter acted as the unit of measure for the other commodities. Therefore, the exchange of any given two commodities had to be calculated against the value of the commodity acting as unit of value, without the latter having to be physically present in the exchange. There were two main units of value in Mesopotamia: barley and silver (and sometimes copper). Barley was readily available, of low value, and thus often present in exchanges. On the contrary, silver was a precious and rare material, but also non-perishable (since it could not be consumed), allowing its accumulation. These were two very different materials, to be used as units on different occasions with different goods, and thus complementing each other.

The second operation was linking this system of values to the numeral system. Equivalences that were too complicated to work out would have made conversions too problematic. The solution was to allocate simple numeral equivalences to the units of value of the local economic system and to calculate them in sexagesimals. Commodities were measured through different systems of measurement (metals and wool in weight, cereals and oil in volume). Therefore, it would have been impossible to calculate correspondences unless the various systems of measurements and the individual values were easy to work out (in terms of being all sexagesimal). The standard Mesopotamian system matched a shekel of silver to a *gur* (300 *sila*, or litres) of barley, or six minas of wool, or twelve litres of oil. Since the multiples and divisors of units of weight and capacity were all roughly linked to the sexagesimal system (6, 10, 12), conversions were relatively easy to work out.

Time was another important factor in this process of quantification. Also in this case, the units of measurement were easily found in nature: the solar year, the lunar month, and the day. This natural way of counting time was then standardised through a sexagesimal system, creating years of 360 days, with 12 months of 30 days each. The same can be said for the subdivision of a day into hours and minutes (on which, however, there is no evidence for the earliest phases). Once it was homogeneous and sexagesimal, time could be easily calculated, especially for the provision of rations. If the daily ration was of two litres of barley, that would become sixty litres a month; similarly, a litre of oil a month corresponded to a shekel of silver a year and so on.

The system of rations gave time a different value according to the work carried out. For basic rations, which repaid the average work in the fields or elsewhere, the main parameters were gender and age. These parameters were used to measure food in terms of the average body weight. The monthly ration of 60 litres for men therefore became 40 for women and 30 for children. The rations also included oil (given on a monthly basis) and wool (provided on a yearly basis), covering the whole range of essentials for survival.

The standardisation and evaluation of labour in relation to the time needed and the payment required led to a standardisation of products. In other words, a potter was paid on a fixed monthly wage, since it was too difficult to check if and how much he actually worked. Consequently, the management established how many pots he had to produce in a given amount of time. The potter knew that by the end of the month he had to deliver a certain number of pots of specified capacity and features. He therefore had to produce them in series (thanks to the existence of the right technology for it), delivering standardised pots. This type of production was able to fulfil a commissioner's wishes in the safest and fastest way possible. Mass production, fixed parameters and fixed wages standardised production on certain types of vases. This process was closely linked to the standardisation of the goods contained in them and their value.

The most studied example of this process is the production of bevelled-rim bowls. The latter were bowls meant for food rations. These bowls were produced through moulds, which gave the external surface of the bowl the rough surface of the mould itself. On the inside of the bowl, fingerprints show how the clay was pressed inside the mould. The border was cut by the potter's thumb (hence the name bevelled-rim bowls). These bowls, made in haste with rough clay and badly fired, have been found in large quantities and concentrations. This proves that they were used for the provision of large numbers of employees in large organisation and therefore not within a family unit. The bowls usually had standardised sizes (large, medium and small), both due to the use of moulds and their intended purpose.

It has been suggested that the capacity of these bowls corresponded exactly to the daily ration, and that the three sizes corresponded to the three categories of people (men, women and children). It has also been suggested that the bowl was thrown away and a new one was provided each time and filled up. However, these suggestions are unacceptable. The bowls were not all the same, not even in terms of size. They were used like normal bowls, thus not filled to the rim and not used to take away a ration (let alone to measure it), but simply to hold the ration to be consumed. They were certainly not thrown away after use, an inconceivable waste for ancient times. They were kept by the palace or temple administration (in fact, the highest concentrations are mainly found around temples) for the meals of their workers, who received their daily ration on location. Therefore, the bowls were for occasional workers (*corvée*), not for regular employees. The latter received a monthly ration. Nonetheless, a high level of standardisation in the production of these bowls remains evident. This derives not only from the production process itself, but also from the purpose (rations) and use of these bowls within a system that was standardised and operated with large quantities.

The administrative needs of the great organisations created a sexagesimal agricultural landscape (made of fields, distances between furrows, simple numeral relations between seeds, harvests, areas, labour units and so on), a sexagesimal division of time and a fixed system of computation and of remuneration. Therefore, they transformed a reality characterised by infinite variables into a computable, impersonal and rational universe, which could be planned and managed successfully.

4 Authentication and record-keeping: the birth of writing

The development of systems of numeration and measurement brought about a concrete need to guarantee and record transactions correctly. The great organisations of the first phase of urbanisation rose to prominence without writing. The latter was developed relatively quickly as a response to these institutions' needs. The creation of a writing system therefore constituted the peak of a long process of labour specialisation and the depersonalisation of work relations and remuneration. Moreover, writing allowed a further move towards new forms of political and economic organisation. These were inaccessible to communities that, despite having experienced processes of labour specialisation, urbanisation and early state-formation, had not yet developed this fundamental instrument.

Initially, seals were the main instruments used to provide a guarantee of authenticity. Already in the Halaf phase (and then in the Ubaid phase) seals were widely used both in Lower Mesopotamia and in the surrounding areas. They were squared or round stamp seals with geometric or animal depictions. The seal impression was the equivalent of a signature, identifying its owner through what it depicted. Subsequently, the Uruk phase brought significant innovations in the shape, decoration and use of seals. First, the cylinder seal substituted the stamp seal. With this new kind of seal, it became possible to obtain long impressions by rolling the seal on wet clay. Consequently, seal impressions became more than mere signatures, guaranteeing the integrity of the product held by the sealed container.

Depictions also changed, representing scenes (real or symbolic) characteristic of early urban communities. These images ranged from scenes depicting agricultural and farming activities, to weaving and pottery making, land and river transport, the arrival of goods in warehouses and temple offerings (Figure 4.5). In addition to that, there were several war scenes (Figure 4.6). This shows the emergence of the image of the heroic king, defender of the temple from enemy attacks, or of the warehouse from wild animals. For instance, the glyptic repertoire found at Uruk usefully summarises the proto-urban society that produced it: from the division of labour to the accumulation of surplus, the development of crafts, the emergence of an elite and a specific leader, with his links to the temple, and the latter's central role in the entire system. These characteristic themes were articulated in such a way that they indicate a clear desire to substitute the former general depictions with a new repertoire. The latter mirrored the ideology of the new society and great organisations to which the owner of the seal belonged.

The most important innovation, however, was in the function of seals. The ability to recognise the owner of a seal impression became an essential aspect in the system of accountability and impersonal guarantees that was fundamental for a large redistributive centre. The sealing of containers (vases and bags) or even rooms (mainly in warehouses), whose locks or bolts were sealed, became a standard practice. The cord closing a container or holding a door was held in place by a 'bulla' (or cretula). The latter was a lump of clay sealed by the appropriate official. Once the bulla dried, it would have been impossible to open the sealed object without breaking the clay seal. Therefore, a bulla made any opening of the object forbidden unless authorised by the owner of the seal, the only one able to replace the bulla. Consequently, sealing and opening became specific administrative acts. The process guaranteed the integrity of the protected content, and required authorisation to use it. This method was practised both on containers destined for trade (vases and bags with goods to be imported or exported) and for the storage of daily commodities (in

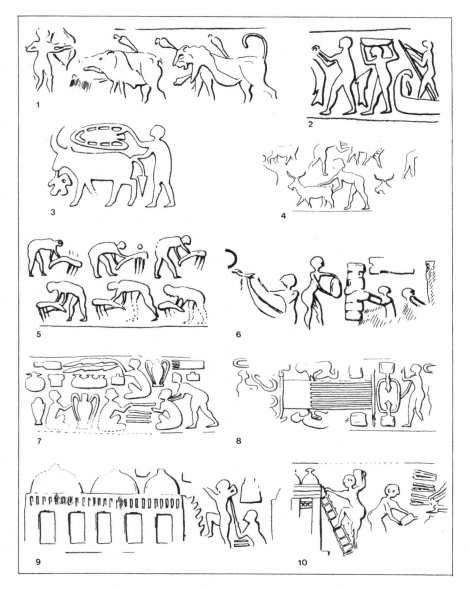

Figure 4.5 Work scenes found on seals from the Uruk phase. 1–2: hunting and fishing scenes; 3–4: farming scenes; 5: agricultural scene; 6: building scene; 7–8: crafting scenes; 9–10: storage scenes.

fact, warehouses could be opened and closed on a daily basis, under the constant supervision of the officer in charge).

As a result of this continuous use, a large number of bullae were used. The broken ones were often kept to calculate and control the frequency of access, and then thrown away in specific areas located near the warehouse. The study of the bullae deposits at Arslantepe is the best example of how a detailed analysis of this kind of evidence can lead to a reconstruction of an entire administrative system, despite the absence of writing. The comparison of the seal (on the outside of a bulla) with the impression of the sealed container

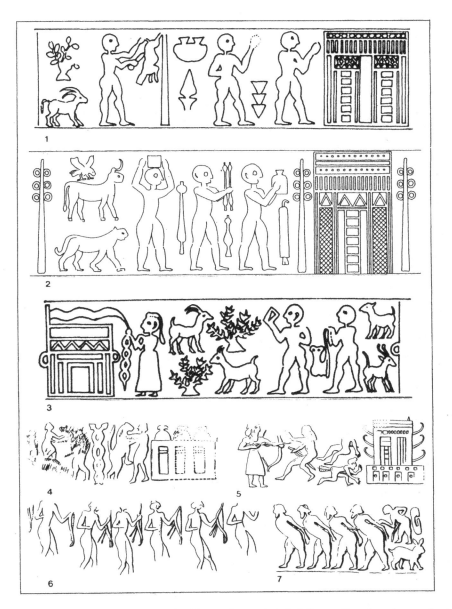

Figure 4.6 Temple and power in seal impressions of the Uruk period. 1–3: delivery of goods to the temple; 4: defence of the warehouses; 5: defence of the temple; 6: row of warriors; 7: row of captives.

or lock (on the inside of a bulla) allows the reconstruction of specific practices. For instance, the constant association of a certain seal to a specific door can provide valuable information about the person and his function in a warehouse.

The bullae placed on containers or doors are mostly concerned with the circulation or storage of goods. However, there were other administrative activities requiring a guarantee of authenticity, despite not being linked to a specific object, such as the giving of orders. These orders mainly came from the central administration and were given to functionaries in the periphery. They could also have provided information and reminders. In these cases, impressions sealed symbolic representations of the commodity and its quantity. Just like seals, these models (tokens) had a long history, pre-dating the Uruk phase. However, these tokens acquired a new role when they entered the redistributive circuit of the great proto-urban organisations. Tokens were made of clay, stone, or bone. Their shape was meant to represent the commodity or quantity involved in the operation. They thus became a sort of writing, though still at a very rudimentary stage. Through the constant interaction of functionaries, a series of small clay tokens held within an unfired clay container and authenticated by a functionary's seal (obviously known to his colleagues) became a perfectly understandable message. If, for instance, a functionary from the periphery had to periodically request cereals for his workmen's rations (say for the construction a canal), he could send a sealed bulla to the central warehouse holding the token for barley in the quantity requested. The functionary at the warehouse, then, could easily decode the request and send the barley, keeping the open bulla for record-keeping.

Clay bulla containing tokens quickly evolved into a more direct and practical system. First of all, in order to know the content without having to break the bulla, the content of the container began to be imprinted on the outside (Figure 4.7). Soon after, people understood that the impressions on the outside of the bulla were authentic enough since they were written while the sealed clay was wet, making the tokens held inside superfluous. Having removed the practice of the tokens, the bulla therefore became a tablet, simply imprinted with the number of goods required and the seal. The tablet was not round anymore, but flatter and with two sides, wide enough to bear the seal and the signs.

A decisive step forward came about with the substitution of a system of tokens with a graphic code, made of the imprint of that same token on clay. This constitutes the origins of writing, a system providing much more flexibility and scope for development. In a short period of time, many signs were created and written with a reed stylus, rather than with the tokens. Apart from numeric signs (divided into units, decimals, sexagesimals and so on), further signs were created to indicate various things (Figure 4.8). Some signs already existed (such as 'sheep', 'fabric' or 'barley'), but as it developed, the process led to the development of pictograms, namely, signs representing in a simplified form of the object meant. Therefore, tablets inscribed with numerals and authenticated with seal impressions were substituted by tablets bearing both numeral signs (imprinted on clay) and pictograms (written with a stylus). Seal impressions soon became superfluous for administrative records, though they remained crucial for important legal tablets, letters and so on. The information provided by the seal could now be expressed through pictograms. Moreover, in order to separate different operations, tablets were divided into boxes, highlighting the total requests and summaries of the amounts requested.

With time, pictograms began to represent not only the object depicted, but also a word that had more or less the same sound. Consequently, an 'arrow' sign could be used to indicate 'life' (since both were *ti* in Sumerian), or a 'reed' sign to indicate 'to give back' (both *gi* in Sumerian) and so on. These peculiarities have allowed us to understand that the language written was Sumerian. These concordances would not have made sense in any other language. At the same time, these associations gave scribes the opportunity to express abstract concepts, actions, personal names and anything else that could not be represented. Therefore, the introduction of morphologic elements (prefixes and infixes) led to the construction of the first written sentences. Writing, then, managed to grow as a response to the administrative needs (commodities, quantities, people, operations successfully accomplished or to accomplish) of the urban societies of the time.

With these new instruments, administration became the most specialised work within the great organisations. The functionary became a 'scribe', who after a highly specialised training was able to write, calculate and perform various administrative tasks. Trainees in workshops learned the secrets of their craft within the first years of apprenticeship. On the contrary, scribes had to train in *bona fide* schools, where teachers taught their students to master a repertoire of hundreds of signs. This training was reserved to the members of the cultural and political elite of the State. This elite was able to control its world through writing and could actively control it on a socio-economic level.

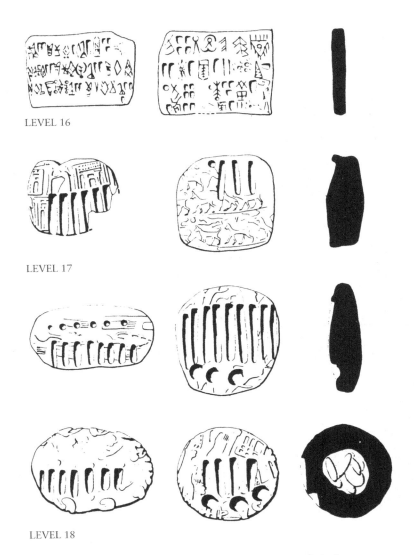

LEVEL 16

LEVEL 17

LEVEL 18

Figure 4.7   The beginnings of writing: administrative records from the acropolis in Susa.
Phase I (level 18): clay bulla with traces of seal impressions and numerals (also enclosed in the bulla in the form of calculi); *Phase II (levels 18 and 17)*: tablets with numerals (not included inside anymore) and seal impressions; *Phase III (level
16)*: tablet with Proto-Elamite writing and numerical signs (without seal impressions or calculi).

Writing did not just provide a way to record information, but also a new way to understand and deal
with the surrounding world. The choice of signs to form a repertoire was a selection process that closely
mirrored the needs of the society developing it. Just like the selection of standard measurements or values,
so the selection of certain realities to be turned into signs transforms an uncontrollable and varied world
into a regulated and simplified set of conventions. There was a selection of 'official models' (objects, plants,
or animals) and a selection of important operations and socio-economic relations. This process transformed
the former chaos of personal relations and individual knowledge into a strictly standardised knowledge,
developed to keep the community together.

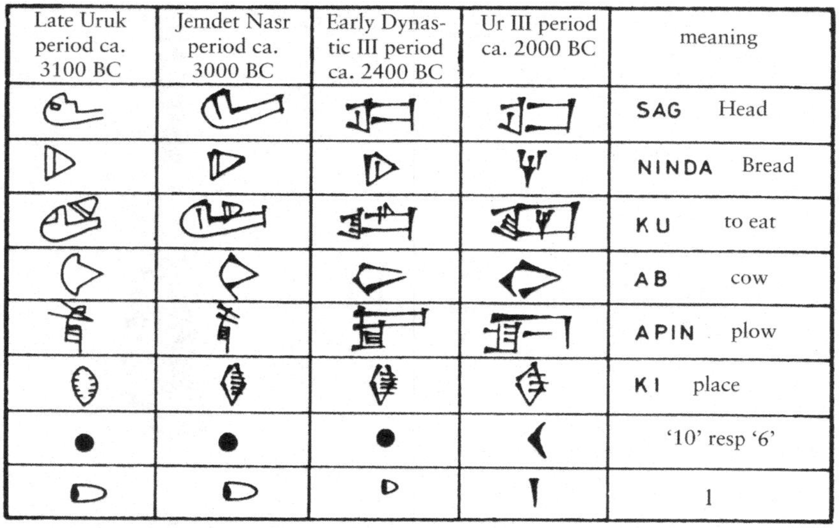

Late Uruk period ca. 3100 BC	Jemdet Nasr period ca. 3000 BC	Early Dynastic III period ca. 2400 BC	Ur III period ca. 2000 BC	meaning	
				SAG	Head
				NINDA	Bread
				K U	to eat
				A B	cow
				APIN	plow
				K I	place
●	●	●		'10' resp '6'	
				1	

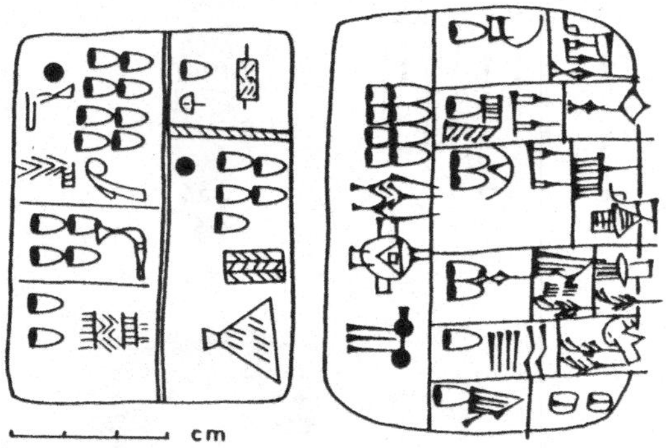

The development of the forms of some selected signs, from the pictograms of Uruk IV to classical Sumerian writing.

Examples of Uruk IV (left) and III (right) tablets.

Figure 4.8   The origins and development of cuneiform writing.

Unsurprisingly, with the development of writing, which was initially meant for administrative texts, a series of scholarly texts began to appear. The latter's aim was that of cataloguing and transmitting writing itself, as well as the knowledge it recorded. These texts were predominantly lists of signs, which were lists of both words and objects. Therefore, even before the appearance of texts that were not administrative records (royal inscriptions, prayers and divinatory texts), there were already lists divided into categories (lists of professions, birds, vases, plants and so on). These were aimed at defining the world these people lived in, making it conventional and functional, and transmitting it in this form to students.

The administrative tablets found in levels IV to III of the Eanna have shown how the main administrative forms that would become well known soon after (especially in the Neo-Sumerian period) were already in existence at this stage (Late Uruk phase), at least in their initial form. Therefore, some tablets regarding land management record the use of fixed estimates of harvests and the payment of two thirds of them to the temple (a third would remain with the manager to cover expenses and keep some seeds for the following year). Other tablets, recording the size of herds, already counted half a lamb per grown sheep, and the alternation of male and female lambs. These approximations would become conventional in the administration, meant to keep track of activities taking place away from the centre. Therefore, what has been so far explained about the economy of this phase derives from administrative sources that would have remained quite difficult to understand without a comparison with later evidence. Just like lists, so administrative conventions developed in the Uruk period then survived in the following periods.

5 Political and ideological aspects of early state formation

The socio-economic stratification of society caused by the rise of labour specialisation was not just a structural change, but also one that affected a society's function. This stratification was 'vertical' (i.e. hierarchical), since the various groups did not have the same degree of access to the city's resources and its decision-making process. However, it was also 'horizontal' (i.e. in terms of space), since privileged groups began to concentrate in cities. Stratification also led to the emergence of a ruling class, in charge of the decision-making process and residing in the city's great organisation. The Urban Revolution therefore led to the formation of the Early State, not just in its decisional function, which already existed in pre-urban communities, but in the fullest sense of the term. The latter is to be understood as an organisation that solidly controls and defends a given territory (and its many communities) and manages the exploitation of resources to ensure and develop the survival of its population. What distinguishes the State is the stratified, yet organically coherent, structure of the human groups constituting it. In other words, the formation of the State placed collective interests above individual ones (or of individual groups such as families, villages and so on), the former being pursued in the various functions and contributions provided by each group.

Early state formation was an organisation centred on a differentiation between groups. In reality, this differentiation was both evident and difficult to accept. Therefore, it became necessary to develop some ideological motivations to convince those carrying out the heavier tasks that social disparity had a key role to play in the overall development of the State. In other words, these explanations tried to portray the exploitation of people as advantageous to those exploited. Early state formation therefore featured both the rise of a ruling class, making decisions and benefiting from a privileged position, and the development of a political and religious ideology. The latter was able to ensure stability and cohesion in this pyramid of inequality.

The ruling class had to work on an operational and ideological front, leading to the formation of a bureaucracy and a priesthood. Bureaucracy, managed by the scribes and hierarchically subdivided, took care of the economic administration of the city-state. It managed and recorded the movement of surplus from the villages to the city. It also determined the redistribution of resources to its workers, and managed the State's land. Finally, the bureaucracy sent orders to specialised workmen, planned and constructed key infrastructures (such as canals, temples, or walls), and engaged in long-distance trade. The priesthood took care of daily and private cultic activities, as well as public festivals. It managed that relation with the divine that provided the ideological justification for the unequal stratification of society. The urban community was already used to justifying events outside human control through its belief in divine entities, and to propitiate them through human acts such as offerings and sacrifices. Consequently, these ideas were applied to the socio-economic organisation of the State and its centralised political structure.

This process led to a sort of parallelism between the accumulation and redistribution of resources and the practice of providing offerings to the gods. The community gave up part of its produce (actually the best part of it, namely the first fruits) to the divine sphere in exchange for the correct and favourable behaviour of natural phenomena. Similarly, it gave up a part of its produce to the ruling class in exchange of a successful organisation of the State. The ruling class therefore managed both the relations with the divine through its priesthood, and the organisation of the State through its bureaucracy, making the two groups overlap. Moreover, just like society was structured into a series of specialised functions, so the divine came to be composed of various characters (polytheism). Each deity had one or more functions and specific responsibilities. Deities therefore formed a pantheon, a structure that organised their various roles into a system of relations (hierarchical and based on kinship). Consequently, relations between gods were expressed through the number and location of temples, indicating different hierarchies in each city.

A third aspect that was fundamental for the functioning of a state was the use and monopoly of defence forces to protect internal cohesion. The wealth and technical knowledge accumulated in cities had to be defended against foreign attacks, both from other city-states and other enemies (for instance, nomadic tribes). This defence system then turned into an offensive tactic. The latter was aimed at getting hold of products, workforce and territories belonging to other city-states or marginal communities. Instrumental for these kinds of activities was the creation of an army, which was divided into two groups. One group was made of full-time workers, specialised in military activities (although this remains purely hypothetical for the Uruk period). In case of war, an army was assembled through military conscription, and was supported by mandatory provisions of military supplies. In this sense, joining an army was not dissimilar to any other kind of work requiring the contribution of the whole population. A certain degree of military intervention was also required to control the community itself. Given the visible inequality of the redistribution of resources, the degree of contribution and the social classes, when ideological beliefs were not enough, the central authorities could establish themselves through coercion. In this way, the State could maintain order in case of rebellion.

The three functions of the State, which were performed by specialised officials (administrators, and priestly and military officials), were united into one figure, namely, the head of the community. The decisions and interdependence of the groups constituting the State had to be represented by a leading figure embodying the power and responsibilities of the State, as well as its ideology. This individual was supported by a communal assembly (*unkin* in Sumerian), which was a legacy of the egalitarian organisation of pre-urban communities. Moreover, he was also supported by specialised advisors and a wide range of functionaries. The latter remained subordinate to his authority.

Therefore, the main role of the king was his administrative function as head of the palace, or 'large house' (*é-gal* in Sumerian). The latter was managed like a large organisation. The king was also responsible for strategic and managerial decisions. However, the king's most visible role was in relation to cults. The king was the high priest (*en* in Sumerian) of the city-god, the human administrator of the city on behalf of the god, the latter being the ideological head of the city. In the Uruk phase, the palace as the exclusive residence of the king did not yet exist. The temple, imagined as the house of the god, was the symbolic and administrative centre of the city. Therefore, as a priest-king, this individual officiated at collective ceremonies, guaranteeing good relations between the human and the divine spheres. In addition to that, the king was in charge of defending his city and his people against foreign attacks. Depictions from the Uruk period show him engaged in more or less symbolic battles against ferocious animals threatening the temple or the city's herds, as well as enemies threatening the warehouses.

The temple was the physical, administrative and symbolic centre of the city. Its sheer size, as well as its façade and furnishings separated it from any other building in the settlement. All these features were meant to highlight the magnificence and richness of the temple. The latter, then, acted as the place in which the community communicated with a deity, as well as the place in which the ruling class presented itself to the rest of the population. Consequently, specific spaces were built around the temple for the performance of processions and festivals. These were the only occasions bringing the population together for ideological purposes. The latter would in turn motivate economic activities. In the case of Uruk, the temple area was particularly developed (see next chapter). The influence of the priesthood on the city's population was closely linked to the strong commitment in the religious justification of socio-economic inequality. This gives us an idea of the actual influence of the central authorities at the expense of the community.

Other forms of political and religious propaganda are not attested for the Uruk period. The temple, as well as the ceremonies dedicated to it and performed around it, seem to have supported the whole ideology of the early State. The image of the king itself, as a priest-king, along with the prestige of his functionaries and priests, is directly linked to the authority of the temple. An enthusiastic religious faith, untarnished by doubts, therefore seems to have been at the core of the formation of the early States' communities in Lower Mesopotamia. Consequently, the king as high priest took advantage of the prestige bestowed upon him through his close connection with the divine sphere.

5

THE RISE AND FALL OF
THE FIRST URBANISATION

1 Long-distance trade

In the Late Uruk phase, the Lower Mesopotamian cities achieved considerable advancements both in terms of social organisation and resources. This allowed them to engage in a type of long-distance trade that was significantly innovative compared to the one attested in the previous Neolithic and Chalcolithic periods. The first factor causing this change was the increased need for raw materials, essential for the new technological and organisational developments taking place at the time: from metals (mainly copper) for tools and weapons, to timber for temples and semiprecious stones. The latter in particular were used for seals and ornaments, which were essential for the specialisation of socio-economic roles, the desire to display wealth ostentatiously and for cultic furnishings.

Another innovative aspect was the structure of long-distance trade, which continued to develop along the same lines throughout the Bronze Age. The great organisations were always the ones initiating trading activities, exchanging their surplus for products that were inaccessible otherwise. However, these organisations did not directly exchange food for raw materials, since the former was difficult to transport and of low value. Therefore, food surplus had to be converted into goods more suitable for trading, such as textiles and other processed products. Moreover, great organisations also began to appoint experts in trading activities: merchants or, better, commercial agents. Each year, the agent left the city with a stock of processed products and travelled to regions rich in raw materials. Once there, he exchanged his products for metals, semiprecious stones, or vegetal products. Subsequently, he returned to his city, where he would work out with his administrators whether the value of the acquired goods was equal to the ones exchanged, following the current charts of correspondences.

Despite being useful to get an idea of the basic dynamics of trade, this brief reconstruction remains heavily biased towards the city acquiring raw materials. One possible correction of this view concerns the existence of privileged trading centres. These acted as intermediaries between Lower Mesopotamia and the regions providing raw materials. Another correction concerns the latter regions, which began to organise their export activities in view of the increasing demand for raw materials from the cities, constituting an unusually large market for the period. Consequently, the export of raw materials increased significantly and was adapted to the demand from the cities. Some materials even began to be sold in semi-processed form (smelted metals or polished stones), or even fully processed. Therefore, trade also had a positive impact on the development of regions located far from the centre.

So far, trade might seem to have been a 'planned' activity, characterised by a direct interaction between the organisation (the palace and the temple) seeking products, and the specialised merchants. However, this view does not cover the whole sequence of operations making trade possible. For instance, distant centres or regions rich in raw materials might have exchanged goods in ways that remain unknown to us, maybe even in a ceremonial form, following the rules of, for instance, gift exchange. Similarly, it remains impossible to evaluate the reasons for exchange in marginal areas. The latter might have had different interests from the ones of the palace or temple administrations, thus providing merchants and other intermediaries with scope for personal earnings.

Whatever the exact practices for exchange and the role of regions rich in resources and intermediary centres were, the administered trade of the cities mostly avoided intermediary steps. It therefore organised commercial expeditions sent directly to the area of origin, concentration, or manufacture of the desired product, thus effectively saving time and cutting down costs. The expeditions mainly took place via navigation (on the Tigris and the Euphrates, as well as the Persian Gulf), and then continued in caravans pulled by donkeys and at times escorted by armed forces.

It has already been mentioned that goods exchanged over long distances had to be valuable enough in relation to their size, and that cereals were not exported. This forced each area to survive on its own food supplies. In this regard, the lack of archaeological data and the existence of attestations from later textual sources documenting trading activities in this period have caused several misunderstandings. In terms of archaeology, imports (metals and semiprecious stones) are far better attested than exports, since the latter were perishable materials (such as textiles) spread across a vast territory.

The problem of the invisibility of exported goods has often been explained through the assumption that these goods were mainly foodstuffs. This conviction is supported by several written sources (especially on the trade between Uruk and Aratta) describing long caravans delivering cereals. In reality, exported goods are invisible to us both because they were perishable and delivered in small quantities and because they were omitted in the texts. Moreover, the small amount of exported goods indicates a typical case of unequal exchange. In other words, the more advanced party (both in terms of technology and organisation) received considerable quantities of raw materials in exchange for small quantities of crafted objects and cheap commodities. This type of trade thus benefited from the different values given to the commodities by the two parties.

It is also possible that written sources did not mention exports because they were ideologically irrelevant. In fact, following the ideology of the early states, raw materials were not seen as obtained through payment. They were seen as acquired through the prestige and power of the city-god and the king, who was the former's human representative and economic administrator. The less inhabited regions in the periphery were therefore seen as the providers of those resources fundamental for the successful functioning of the centre and its symbolic core, namely, the temple of the city-god. Allowing equal exchanges between the centre and the periphery would have meant accepting the existence of other equal political centres. This view would have subverted the idea of the universal centrality of the city and its city-god and the opposition between the civilised and uncivilised world. From this point of view, then, the only acceptable exportable good was food, seen as a product able to 'give life' to those who received it, thus forcing the latter to become part of the redistributive system centred on the urban temple.

Early state formation therefore had a centralising effect on trade, which was only partial in terms of the materials traded and the way trade was pursued, but absolute on an ideological level. It is undeniable that the formation of urban communities in Lower Mesopotamia, characterised by an unprecedented concentration of the population and a marked increase in its needs, caused a significant polarisation in the influx of commodities towards these centres. However, as previously noted, this polarisation does not indicate a total centralisation of resources. It rather indicates the development of a complex system in which the regions rich in resources and the intermediary centres played a prominent role (an aspect which will be better explored later on).

Nonetheless, at least on an ideological level, this composite and polycentric system was seen as univocal, placing the city at the centre of the known world and its resources as distributed around it. The initiatives for the procurement of resources pursued by the centre became the sole motive for exchange. Ideologically, the centre certainly exaggerated this polarity, but at the same time it shows an awareness of the innovative elements of early urban trade: the coordinated exploitation of a series of resources which were underused in their places of origin; the rise of specialised cultivation in response to the demands of the centre; and the unequal aspect of trade, where the imbalance in technical advancement paved the way for a political and cultural inequality.

2 Uruk: the metropolis and its colonies

The impact of the first urbanisation gradually expanded beyond the Lower Mesopotamian centres, roughly creating four concentric zones (Table 5.1). Mesopotamia (constituting the future lands of Sumer and Akkad) was the central nucleus, characterised by a fully developed Uruk culture. Then, there were centres bearing all the traits of Uruk culture, but located, just like 'colonies', in culturally different areas (Khuzistan, Assyria and Upper Mesopotamia and the Middle Euphrates region). In addition to these colonies, there were regions (such as the Upper Euphrates region and certain areas in western Iran) in close contact with Uruk culture, which visibly influenced the local organisation, but not its material culture. Moving further away from the centre, only a limited amount of commercial activities were pursued, with little impact on the local culture.

The most important site in the Lower Mesopotamian nucleus was Uruk. This is not only because it has been better excavated, but also because, judging from its size and the grandeur of its temple area, it must have been the main site of this phase. The temple area (which is the only one that has been extensively excavated at Uruk) was significantly more complex that any other known so far. On the one hand,

Table 5.1 Chronology of the Urban Revolution

	Lower Mesopotamia	Upper Mesopotamia	Western Iran	Syria	Eastern Anatolia
3800					
	Early Uruk Uruk 14–9 Eridu 5–4	Gawra 11–10	Khuzistan: Susa B Zagros: Godin 7 Fars: Early Banesh	Amuq F Hama K	Malatya 7
3400	Late Uruk Uruk 8–4 Eridu 3–2 Nippur 16–15	Gawra 9 Nineveh 4 Tell Brak (Eye-remple)	Khuzistan: Uruk type Zagros: Godin 6–5 Fars: Middle Banesh	Habuba Kebira Jebel Aruda	Malatya 6A Hassek Kurban Hüyük 6 Mersin 14–13
3000	Jemdet Nasr Uruk 3 Nippur 14–12	Gawra 8 Nineveh 5	Khuzistan: Susa C Zagros: Godin 4 Fars: Late Banesh	Amuq G Hama K	Malatya 6B Kurban Hüyük 5 Mersin 12
2800					

the temple of Anu was an example of the individual sanctuary, vertically constructed on top of a terraced mound, whose monumentality expressed a clear mythological and cosmogonic significance.

On the other hand, the large area of the Eanna (dedicated to the goddess Inanna, the most important deity in the city) was more horizontal in its plan. It had numerous sanctuaries, colonnades, courtyards and enclosures, making it the most intricate cultic complex of the period. The sheer size of Uruk, the progressive disappearance of villages in the surrounding countryside, the absence of nearby urban centres and the presence of minor urban settlements scattered from the north to the east of Uruk, are all elements indicating the role of this city as a capital. The city controlled the surrounding countryside and other urban centres depended on it, although not necessarily in a political sense.

As shown by the significant growth of cultic buildings, minor urban centres developed along similar lines, although on a much smaller scale. This is the case for Eridu, where the sequence of temples peaked in a large sanctuary almost as monumental as the one in Uruk. Another example is Tell Uqair and its temple, whose size was comparable to the temples in Uruk. However, its painted decoration was still far from the polychrome mosaics found at Uruk. Excavations in the contemporary layers at Nippur and other Lower Mesopotamian centres should provide evidence for a similar growth and increase in wealth. However, these levels are hard to reach and remain buried under later temple areas.

Fortunately, some 'colonies' of Uruk culture in the Mesopotamian periphery have been successfully excavated. In some cases, Uruk period settlements took over previous local villages. This is the case at Susa, where the Late Uruk levels interrupt the local archaeological sequence, substituting previous cultures (Susiana B and C; Susa A) to then give way to the following Proto-Elamite culture. In other cases, such as in the Middle Euphrates region, new settlements, built in previously uninhabited areas, suddenly became thriving centres, displaying that cultural and organisational complexity elaborated elsewhere and then implanted in the area.

The best examples of these new sites are Habuba Kebira and Jebel Aruda (Figure 5.1). The former was a fortified city located along the Euphrates. Its temple area was built on the south side of the city (Tell Qannas). The rest of the settlement featured a compact and architecturally uniform plan, as well as a type of material and administrative culture of clear Lower Mesopotamian origin (pottery, seals, numeric tablets, inscribed bulla and so on). The construction of an artificial lake has now submerged Habuba Kebira, but not Jebel Aruda, situated on a hill overlooking the same valley. Jebel Aruda was mainly a cultic settlement and its sacred area hosted a variety of temples, whose plans were distinctly Lower Mesopotamian.

While the interpretation of sites like Susa and Habuba Kebira as Uruk colonies is relatively convincing, Uruk's political influence on settlements in Assyria and the Khabur region is less certain. Here, the process of urbanisation, which culminated in the south in the Uruk IV phase, took place earlier, as shown at Tepe Gawra in the Late Ubaid and Early Uruk levels. Therefore, the rise of Late Uruk settlements in the region did not take place on virgin soil (like at Habuba Kebira), or on earlier and culturally different settlements (like at Susa). It rather constituted the culmination of a pre-existent local development.

Unlike Tepe Gawra, which was destined to remain marginalised due to its location on the foothills, Nineveh was another large and developed centre, which would remain the principal city in the area for two and a half millennia. In the Khabur area, the most important sites were Tell Brak, with its Eye Temple (named after the anthropomorphic figurines found there both in the form of offerings and as part of the temple's decoration), Tell Hamukar (recently excavated) and other centres that have not yet been excavated. Nonetheless, their role as 'colonies' is evident through the amount of bevelled-rim bowls found *in situ*. This indicates the presence of organised buildings (temples, storehouses and so on) belonging to the Late Uruk culture.

Considering the distribution of raw materials and the distances covered by the contemporary means of transport, the rise of Late Uruk colonies seems to have had a predominantly commercial aim. It is therefore clear that these settlements, linked to the centre via river, allowed an easier access to areas rich in materials such as timber, metal and semiprecious stones. The region of Susiana was the 'gate' to central and southern

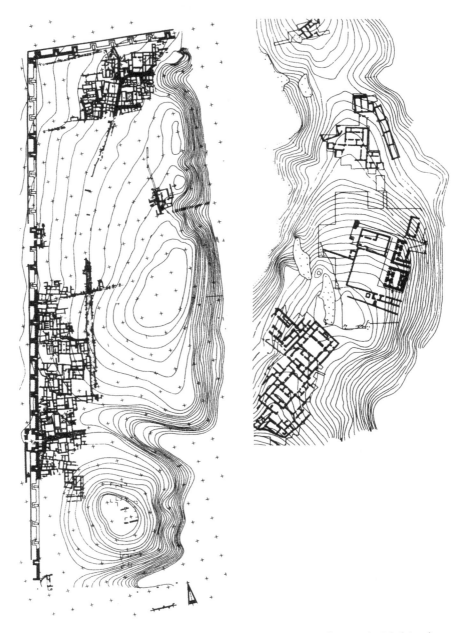

Figure 5.1 'Colonies' of Uruk culture in the Middle Euphrates; *Left*: Habuba Kebira; *Right*: Jebel Aruda.

Iran, Assyria to northern Iran, Upper Mesopotamia to eastern Anatolia and the Middle Euphrates to Syria. Colonies were mainly inhabited by people coming directly from the south, although it is not clear whether this 'south' should always be understood as Uruk. The colonies' political relation with the centre is another difficult matter, since it is not clear whether it was a relation of direct dependence, or of independent integration within a wider inter-regional network. However, the relatively sudden rise and fall of this Late

Uruk colonial system led to the assumption that there must have been a precise political agenda behind this system's organisation and maintenance.

In addition to that, there is a chronological problem, since the elaboration of comparative data from stratigraphic analyses is still in progress. In the past, it was often assumed that the diffusion of Late Uruk culture outside Mesopotamia happened relatively late, during phase III rather than phase IV of the Eanna at Uruk. Today, the widely accepted interpretation sees the diffusion of Late Uruk culture coinciding with the most developed phase of the Eanna (phase IV). Therefore, the later developments of Lower Mesopotamia (Eanna III) are thought to have taken place when the commercial system had already collapsed, thus indicating a tendency towards regression. This chronological reconstruction matches the development of writing in the period: in the colonies, we have the presence of bulla, tokens and the first numeral tablets, but not of more developed written sources, which would be expected with a later dating.

3 The development of the 'periphery'

Outside the areas influenced by Uruk culture, the first urbanisation had a strong impact on the Late Chalcolithic cultures found in Syria, south-eastern Anatolia and south-western Iran. This diffusion developed along two main lines: either through small Uruk commercial junctions located in culturally different territories; or in local centres that began to display a typically urban organisation as a result of their relations with Uruk. Notable examples of the first kind of development are Godin Tepe in the Zagros and Hacinebi and Hassek Hüyük in the Upper Euphrates region. Godin Tepe (level V) was a local settlement hosting a small quarter protected by an enclosure wall. It had few buildings and a large number of bevelled-rim bowls, sealed pots, numeral tablets and seal impressions typical of the period. This material reveals that this quarter was a commercial centre for Uruk. The settlement therefore acted as a crucial junction on the trading route linking Khuzistan and Lower Mesopotamia to the areas providing metals and semiprecious stones. This demonstrates the extent of the commercial influence of the large proto-urban cities on the mountainous peripheries.

A similar development can be found at Hacinebi, which also had an enclosed Uruk quarter and Hassek Hüyük, a small, walled settlement (and therefore more a commercial hub than an actual urban settlement). They both feature strong Uruk influences in their pottery and administration. Evidence from the Upper Euphrates Valley (which has been excavated through salvage operations in areas now submerged by artificial basins) has revealed the progressive nature of the diffusion of Uruk culture and its relations with local cultures. The latter were closely linked to the trade of timber and copper from the Taurus Mountains. Uruk colonies were larger in the valley (like at Habuba Kebira) and then decreased into smaller urban settlements (such as Samsat, which was unfortunately flooded before the Late Uruk layers could be reached) and commercial junctions (such as Kurban Hüyük, Hacinebi and Hassek Hüyük) reaching the Taurus Mountains.

A different situation can be found in the area where the Upper Euphrates Valley opens up in vast basins. Notable is the case of Arslantepe (near Malatya), already an important site in the Late Chalcolithic period (Figure 5.2). In the Late Uruk period, with the rise of inter-regional trade, the settlement became the central commercial junction and political counterpart of Lower Mesopotamian trade, which reached the area following the Euphrates upstream and stopping in the colonies in Syria and around the Taurus region. Although the material culture of Arslantepe remained predominantly local in character, the construction of a Late Uruk temple complex over the previous Late Chalcolithic one marks the impact of the Uruk model on the settlement. Therefore, the temple remained Anatolian in terms of architecture, but its complexity, fortification and structure (with two temples, a fortified gate and storehouses) indicate the implementation of a typically urban model in south-eastern Anatolia.

The same can be said about pottery remains. Certain types of pots (such as spouted bottles) were clearly imported or copied from Uruk. Overall, pottery remained local in character (no bevelled-rim bowls, but wheel-made bowls), but proto-urban in its production, type and quantity. This is particularly true in the

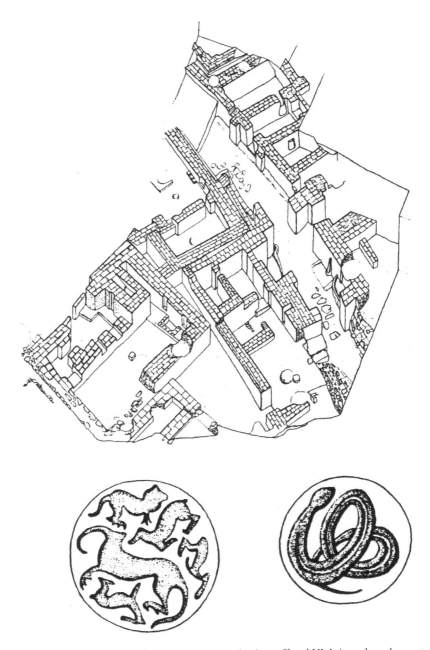

Figure 5.2 Malatya in the Late Uruk period. *Above*: Axonometric view of level VI A (temple, palace entrance, ware-houses); *Below*: Stamp seals.

case of administrative tools, such as bulla bearing seal impressions, which indicate the administrative super-vision of storehouses and individual containers alike. However, the seal impressions continued to feature a strictly local style and design (circular seals with almost exclusively animal depictions), in marked contrast with the few southern examples found there.

As a direct consequence of its proximity to an area rich in copper, metallurgy at Arslantepe was particularly advanced. The area produced copper swords and spearheads of an unparalleled quality in comparison to Mesopotamia. Consequently, Arslantepe was a relatively rich early urban settlement. It featured irrigation agriculture, horticulture, farming (mainly of sheep and goats for wool), the use of timber and metals, an organised administrative body and mass-scale production. In terms of political organisation, the city followed the Lower Mesopotamian model, which was centred on the temple (without a 'non-religious' palace). In terms of size, however, the site remained significantly smaller than the Mesopotamian cities. In the words of Marcella Frangipane, Arslantepe was a 'citadel without a city', namely, an administrative centre supervising a population spread across villages and pasturelands.

A similar development to the one found in the Upper Euphrates had to exist elsewhere, but is unfortunately not as well attested. In certain areas of the Iranian plateau, the spread of Late Uruk material (bevelled-rim bowls, bulla and numeral tablets) allows us to delineate a commercial network. The latter departed from several centres in Khuzistan (Susa, Levels 18–17 of the acropolis; Choga Mish, Tall-i Ghazir) and reached distant centres (Tepe Siyalk, Level IV 1; Godin Tepe, Level V), laying down the foundations for a process of local urbanisation and early state formation which would characterise the following Proto-Elamite phase.

Regarding the Syrian region on the western side of the Euphrates, Late Uruk influences (attested as far as Hama) do not seem to have had an urbanising effect. The Syro-Palestinian area in the south experienced a different phase, influenced by the proximity of semi-arid territories (between the Transjordan plateau and northern Arabia). Consequently, between the fourth and third millennia BC the region experienced the development of pastoral communities. Just like the Ghassulian pastoral culture that had previously risen on the borders of Palestine, so the case of Tell Jawa in this period continued this trend in these semi-arid lands. It was characterised by pastoral activities, political structures and strategies of production that were completely different from the ones found in Lower Mesopotamia. As a result of these differences, when these communities attempted an urban development (such as in the case of Tell Jawa), they rapidly collapsed.

Another important development, despite concerning a region that will not be taken into consideration here, was the appearance of urbanisation and early state formation processes in Egypt. Despite featuring unique characteristics, Egypt displays certain elements of Uruk culture. These can be traced in some iconographic features, pottery types and so on. However, the impact of Mesopotamia on the early state formation of Egypt is currently discredited. This is not only for strictly chronological reasons, which indicate that they were two parallel processes, but also because these similar traits seem to have been purely ornamental, rather than structural. Nonetheless, Egypt experienced a 'primary' urbanisation based on its own resources and not a 'secondary' one based on trade, as was the case in the Mesopotamian periphery.

4 Crisis and regionalisation

The diffusion of the colonial system and of Uruk culture in the Mesopotamian periphery did not last long. Just as quickly as these commercial settlements rose, so they collapsed, bringing about a significant regression of Uruk culture in its later stages (Level III of the Eanna). It is hard to say whether this collapse was due to a crisis of the centre (Uruk), unable to maintain its commercial network the way it was before, or to a rejection of Uruk culture by the local communities, or even rebellions from the periphery. Settlements such as Habuba Kebira quite simply disappeared. At Arslantepe, the large public complex (temples and storehouses) was destroyed by a fire and immediately replaced by a village of simple households. This village shows no sign of a political and administrative organisation and was characterised by Transcaucasian influences. Interestingly enough, on the ruins of the temple complex of Arslantepe, a lavish tomb belonging to a high-ranking individual was constructed, almost symbolising the destruction of this area and its probable cause.

In this way, the wave of 'first urbanisation' collapsed, leaving its technical and administrative legacy only in Mesopotamia. Therefore, the engine stimulating urbanisation, namely, the accumulation of surplus and the strict organisation of labour, seems to have become difficult to sustain in the areas located outside the alluvial plain, which was different both in nature and size. In the mountainous areas, settlements regressed from urban centres to more modest structures, based again on the village model and its strong pastoral component.

In terms of territorial expansion, the diffusion of Uruk culture took place over quite uniform local cultures, namely, the Late Chalcolithic cultures of the northern Ubaid type. Following the decline of Uruk influence, the formerly colonised areas experienced a process of gradual regionalisation. Due to the lack of written evidence, this process can only be traced through pottery and other kinds of material culture. For instance, certain areas on the Armenian plateau were characterised by handmade and polished red-black pottery, as well as roundhouses. In Central Anatolia there was painted pottery, while in some areas of western Upper Mesopotamia, northern Syria and south of the Taurus there was engobed pottery (the so-called Reserved Slip Ware). The latter would eventually be substituted by the so-called 'Metallic Ware'. Finally, Assyria and eastern Upper Mesopotamia (as far as Tell Brak) featured a type of painted and incised pottery called 'Nineveh 5'. The interpretation of these local cultures developing after the collapse of Uruk culture is difficult. There could have been ethnical and political factors at play, as well as re-emerging Late Chalcolithic features and innovative developments. Nonetheless, the degree of cultural diffusion and of inter-regional contacts became significantly more limited than before.

Lower Mesopotamia also experienced some repercussions of this overall process of regionalisation, although it still remained a unique case. In fact, between the end of the fourth and the beginning of the third millennium BC, the Jemdet Nasr phase (named after the site located near Kish, but still linked to Uruk) and the following Early Dynastic I period formed a relatively unitary cycle in Lower Mesopotamia. The Uruk III-Jemdet Nasr phase was still a phase of demographic and economic growth, primarily concentrated in the main centre of Uruk. Moreover, this was a phase of expansion, even in areas that had been previously excluded (the Diyala Valley and the area of Kish). On the contrary, the Early Dynastic I was a period of crisis and regression. This was a delayed consequence of the crisis of the first urbanisation in the Mesopotamian periphery.

Due to their potential in terms of production, the urban settlements of Lower Mesopotamia did not risk extinction. However, between the sudden demographic and organisational growth of the Uruk period and the following growth during the 'second urbanisation' (Early Dynastic II–III), these settlements re-organised their internal structures. Therefore, they virtually interrupted their colonial and commercial networks. Metals and semiprecious stones (such as lapis lazuli) were quite rare in the Early Dynastic I, and Lower Mesopotamia appears as one of the many regional cultures of the area. Nonetheless, it still remained the most conspicuous and advanced culture in terms of demography and organisation.

However, certain aspects of these phases seem to lend themselves to a socio-political interpretation. For instance, while the large temple complexes of the Early Uruk phase peaked in the Eanna III phase (at Uruk, Uqair, Eridu and elsewhere), this period saw the emergence of the 'palace'. The palace was an administrative centre not linked to a cult, an innovation that would lead to significant developments. The institution of the palace first appeared at Jemdet Nasr (after a gap in the evidence in the Early Dynastic I) and would rise to prominence in the Early Dynastic II–III. This innovation caused a certain opposition or complementarity between the 'temple' and the 'palace'. This may indicate the rise of a 'secular' kind of political system in the north (Jemdet Nasr was located by Kish), compared to the temple system of the south.

Therefore, early state organisation continued to operate, with several adjustments and developments, both from the rising palaces and the still prominent temple institutions. Writing remained at the heart of administrative activities, moving on from the pictographic stage of the Uruk IV phase to the logographic and then logo-syllabic ones found on the tablets of the Uruk III and Jemdet Nasr phases. The iconography of seals moved away from working scenes and symbols of power (typical of Uruk IV–III), in favour of geometric depictions in the Jemdet Nasr period (Figure 5.3). These geometric depictions would eventually become more complex in the following period (Early Dynastic I). The information previously provided by depictions on seals, was now delivered entirely in writing. The seal then became just a means for identification, spreading across the population and losing its authority and prestige. Finally, regionalisation became

Figure 5.3 Mesopotamian seal impressions (early third millennium BC). 1–3: Jemdet Nasr style with farming and offer-ing scenes; 4–5: 'brocade' style with ornamental animal motifs; 6–9: Early Dynastic I style from Ur, with farming and offering scenes.

visible in the pottery produced, such as the painted scarlet ware of the Jemdet Nasr and Early Dynastic I phases. This indicates that settlements experienced almost entirely internal developments, both chronologically and regionally.

The other great centre of the first urbanisation, the Susiana region, experienced a similar evolution. After the Late Uruk period, the local sequence reappears with the emergence of Proto-Elamite culture. The latter was characterised by a type of writing that had certainly originated from Uruk IV writing. However, this type of writing experienced considerable changes, in some way contemporary and parallel to those found at Jemdet Nasr. Proto-Elamite writing therefore developed different signs, also due to the need to record the local Elamite language, rather than the Sumerian of Jemdet Nasr. In addition to that, glyptic art and pottery types were considerably different from their Mesopotamian counterparts. This difference marks the development of yet another important regional style, which mirrored the local ethno-linguistic and political features of the area.

Susiana was not the only centre of Proto-Elamite culture, which seems to have had a considerable impact further east. For instance, at Tall-i Malyan (main city of the Anshan region, modern Fars), the settlement extended over 50 hectares, ten times the size of contemporary Susa (Levels 16–13 of the acropolis). The geography of Iran, with its fertile lands surrounded by mountains, or on the margins of the central desert, favoured the rise of local political entities. The latter would eventually unite in a sort of federal system (especially in the following period). Among these various local entities, Susiana remains a unique case, due to its exposure to Mesopotamian influences.

From Tall-i Malyan, Proto-Elamite culture reached a vaster territory than the previous Uruk culture, which had somehow paved the way. Apart from Susa and Tall-i Malyan, Proto-Elamite tablets have been found in the north (Tepe Siyalk IV 2), the east, at Tepe Yahya, and as far as Shahr-i-Sokhta (near the Helmand basin; Figure 5.4). Proto-Elamite trade can be reconstructed studying the distribution of stones and specific types of stone objects (chlorite or steatite vases and so on). Commercial links were distributed across the Iranian plateau, reaching as far as Mesopotamia and the Persian Gulf. Having recently invaded the antiques market, the well-known and lavishly decorated steatite vases have kick-started regular investigations in their area of origin (Jiroft), in the hope of finding the archaeological and socio-political context of the area in this period.

At the beginning of the third millennium BC, pottery of the Jemdet Nasr type began to appear along the Persian Gulf, which was an important area for urban settlements and a source of copper from Oman (the 'Magan' of later Sumerian texts). It is possible that Mesopotamian merchants were in contact with the local communities, stimulating the development of political elite groups. These Oman communities continued to be based in villages. They supported themselves through a combination of fishing, nomadic pastoralism and the earliest cultivation of oases. Typical of the area were the cultivation of date palms and of Sudanese or Yemenite millet, as well as the domestication of dromedaries.

Figure 5.4   Proto-Elamite tablet recording cattle with addends on one side, the totals and a seal impression on the other.

It has to be borne in mind that the innovative use of oases (for the cultivation of date palms) and dromedaries would eventually spread across the Arabian Peninsula and in the Sahara. Among the arid lands extending from Oman to the western coast of northern Africa, Oman rose to prominence for its technological innovations precisely because of its contacts with different and more advanced cultures. Finally, it is important to note how the cultures developing along the Gulf and in Oman, apart from trading maritime materials (mother-of-pearl, shells and turtle shell), enabled an increased interaction between the Sumerian and Elamite coast in the Gulf and the more eastern region of the Indus Valley. In the latter area, the proto-Indian culture of Harappa and Mohenjo Daro (the Meluhha of the Sumerian texts of the third millennium BC) was taking shape.

6

MESOPOTAMIA IN THE EARLY DYNASTIC PERIOD

1 Languages and demography

Following the decline of the Early Dynastic I period (ca. 2900–2750 BC), the Early Dynastic II (2750–2600 BC), IIIa (2600–2450 BC) and IIIb (2450–2350 BC) periods experienced a relatively homogeneous development. This progress can be studied thanks to the increased availability of archaeological evidence and more informative texts, initially only administrative in nature, but then also political and legal. Compared to the previous pre-eminence of Uruk, the Early Dynastic II–III period is characterised by the supremacy of a number of centres, with several city-states of equal size and status competing with each other (Figure 6.1). In the south there were Uruk, Ur (Figure 6.2), and Eridu. In the east, there were Lagash and Umma, and in the centre Adab, Shuruppak, and Nippur. Finally, in the north there were Kish and Eshnunna. Along the Tigris and the Euphrates, Ashur and Mari appeared as new centres of Sumerian expansion. In the Persian Gulf, the Iranian plateau, south-eastern Anatolia and Syria commercial and political links continued to expand.

In this period, the population living in the Mesopotamian alluvial plain was far larger than in any of the earlier periods. The population was more evenly distributed across the territory, despite the survival of ecologic niches (made of arid steppes or marshes), whose economic and political function has already been explained. This integrated territorial system was centred on a network of canals. In the long history of hydraulic interventions in the alluvial plain, which developed alongside local political developments, the Early Dynastic period becomes a phase of friction. This friction caused the difficult integration among neighbouring political entities. Despite their internal unity, there was no overarching unity in the area. Due to the obvious interconnection of water canals and the dependence of settlements in the valleys on those located higher up, the optimisation of water resources for one centre constantly caused significant problems to another. Naturally, such problems caused conflicts between cities over the control of intermediary areas and canals. Over time, this issue caused the shift of privileged areas to the north. This tendency would last until the political unification of the whole area, which perhaps happened too late and did not manage to avoid the eventual crisis of the southernmost centres.

In the irrigated and cultivated areas, a hierarchical division of settlements (capital, intermediary centres and villages) continued to exist. However, it is in this phase that the concept of village changed as a result of its relations with the central administration (a change gathered from the comparative analysis of archaeological data with the textual evidence). Alongside the old kinds of villages, inhabited by 'free' farmers obliged to serve and pay tributes to the central administration, there were now agricultural

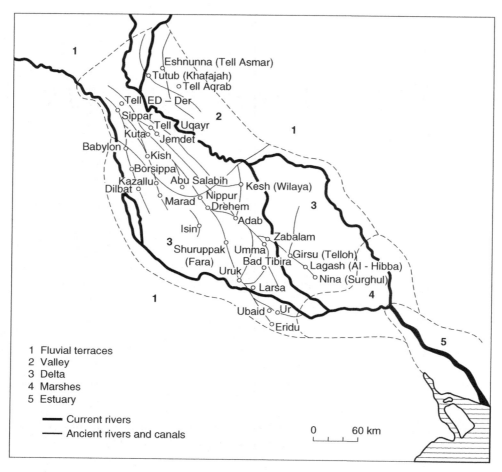

Figure 6.1 Map of Lower Mesopotamia in the Early Dynastic period: cities, canals, and morphological zones.

settlements. These were directly linked to the centre and were designed for the cultivation of the temples' lands through servile labour.

Within this wide range of settlements in the Mesopotamian alluvial plain, pastoral groups continued to provide an important contribution. On a regional level, a marked difference began to appear between north and south, which was both ecologic and socio-political in nature. Ecologically, the north had a distinct advantage in managing and distributing water resources, while the south had the constant problem of marshes. On a socio-political level, the temples in the south continued to acquire lands managed by their administrative centres, while the north left a considerable amount of land at the disposal of the 'free' population.

On top of this variety of settlement types, there was an ethno-linguistic diversity, which is attested in the written sources (and through personal names in particular). However, in view of previous over-simplifications in the study of the relations between languages and cultures, two main points need to be borne in mind. First, the correlations between material culture and ethno-linguistic groups cannot be considered as directly related and univocal. In an area inhabited by a population speaking a wide range of languages such as Mesopotamia, technical progress has to be attributed to the population as a whole. This makes it difficult to attribute certain features to, for instance, the Sumerians and certain others to the Semites. On

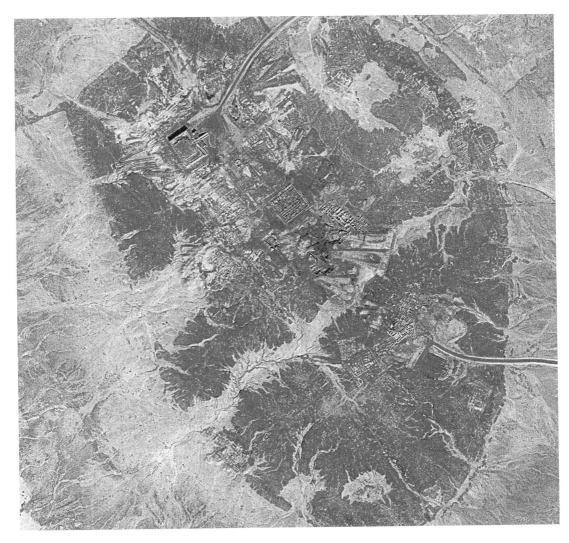

Figure 6.2   Satellite view of the ruins of Ur (Google Earth).

a socio-economic level, differences between the north and the south seem to have arisen from ecologic and historical differences, rather than a different ethnicity. Moreover, on a political level, it has already been demonstrated (by Thorkild Jacobsen) how individual cities were not linguistically exclusive, and their conflicts were not ethnic in nature.

The second point is that the issue of the arrival of ethnic groups in Mesopotamia is a badly formulated problem, if one is looking for a more or less precise 'arrival date'. Lower Mesopotamia has not been inhabited 'all along', but has been the destination of several migration fluxes from its periphery. Therefore, it seems completely arbitrary to wonder whether or not Ubaid culture was Semitic, or whether the Sumerians had 'arrived' at the beginning of the Ubaid or Uruk period. We do not know if their 'arrival' was the consequence of a migration of people that can be precisely dated or, rather, a slow process of infiltration. Most importantly, the Ubaid and Uruk cultures, with their fundamental technological and organisational developments, were closely linked to their territory. They did not 'arrive' from other areas where they had already developed their characteristics traits.

It is necessary to understand that the cultural development of Mesopotamia took place in a mixed ethno-linguistic context as early as the first written evidence appeared (the only type of evidence which can provide a concrete contribution in this matter). This interpretation may, however, seem reductive if compared to the interpretation provided by traditional historiography. The latter prefers to see this development as the result of movements of people, grouped into several 'cultural cycles'. Within this complex mixture of ethnic and linguistic factors, there undoubtedly were significant variations both in time and space. Nonetheless, the correlation of these variations with contemporary technological and organisational developments runs the risk of over-simplifying the actual historical context.

In the Early Dynastic II–III period, texts were normally written in Sumerian, and this aspect alone reveals much about the prevalence of this language over the others. This prevalence leads to the assumption that this culture was 'Sumerian' – a legitimate statement as long as it is clear that this label is in fact a simplification. In reality, the situation must have been much more complex. The distribution of personal names shows that the Semites (Akkadians) were already present in this phase (if not even earlier on). Therefore, the prevalence of Sumerians in the south was counterbalanced by a prevalence of Akkadians in the north, which was a clear consequence of the concentration (formerly defined as the 'primitive seat') of Semitic people in the area.

Similarly, the study of Sumerian vocabularies, especially of more informative terms such as names of services and professions, indicates the presence of at least three different linguistic components (Text 6.1). There were some Sumerian words, in particular those indicating basic functions in terms of production, characteristic of the Chalcolithic stage (thus preceding the process of urbanisation), with a pre-Sumerian origin. These words are attributed to a substrate language with potential links to Iran. Then, there were Sumerian terms, mostly indicating more specialised activities and administrative functions. Last, there were Semitic borrowings, predominantly used for words indicating mobility and control.

Text 6.1 **Population and cultural development in Mesopotamia: the Sumerian lexicon of professions**

1 Substrate terms

engar	'plowman'
nukarib	'gardener'
sipad	'shepherd'
nuḫaldim	'cook'
simug	'smith'
nangar	'carpenter'
tibira	'metal worker'
išbar	'weaver'
ašgab	'leather worker'
ašlag	'launderer'
adgub	'reed weaver'
paḫar	'potter'
šidim	'mason'
kurušda	'fattener of oxen'

2 Sumerian terms

malaḫ	'skipper' (*má* 'ship' + *laḫ* 'to lead')
ár.ár	'mill worker' (*ar* 'to mill')
ka.zida	'miller' (*zid* 'flour')
šim.mú	'perfumer' (*šim* 'perfume' + *mú* 'to produce')
munu₄.mú	'maltster' (*munu₄* 'malt' + *mú* 'to produce')
í.sur	'oil-presser' (*í* 'oil' + *sur* 'to press')
usan.dù	'fowler' (*usan* 'bird' + *dù* 'to make')
zá.dím	'jeweller' (*zá* 'precious stone' + *dím* 'to fashion')
kù.dím	'silver- and goldsmith' (*kù* 'silver' + *dím* 'to fashion')
bur.gul	'stone cutter' (*bur* 'semiprecious stone' + *gul* 'to engrave')
dub.sar	'scribe' (*dub* 'tablet' + *sar* 'to write')
a.zu	'physician' (*a* 'beverage' + *zu* 'to know')
di.kud	'judge' (*di* 'decision' + *kud* 'to cut, decide')
éš.gíd	'surveyor' (*éš* 'rope' + *gíd* 'to stretch')

3 Akkadian terms (linked to Semitic roots)

damgar	'merchant' (Akkadian *tamkārum*, root *mkr* 'to sell')
ragaba	'messenger' (Akkadian *rak(kā)bum*, root *rkb* 'to mount, ride')
ugula	'overseer' (Akkadian *waklum*, root *wkl* 'to entrust')
šabra	'administrator' (Akkadian *šap(i)rum*, root *špr* 'to send')
šagin	'governor' (Akkadian *šaknum*, root *škn* 'to place').

Due to their relations to those diachronic and geographic factors mentioned above, these components have led to the postulation of a division of Sumerian language into a Pre-Sumerian stratum (Proto-Euphratic for Benno Landsberger, and Proto-Iranic for Samuel Noah Kramer), a Sumerian one, and a later Akkadian contribution. Moreover, this division emphasises the north-eastern origin of the first two strata, and the north-western origin of the third one.

It is certain, however, that there was a complex mixture of languages, which was even stronger if one also takes into consideration the surrounding areas. The latter provided an Elamite contribution from the east, a Hurrian one from the north, and a non-Akkadian Semitic one (Eblaite, then Amorite) from the west. The Mesopotamians of the third millennium BC were strongly aware of the variety of languages available to them. This awareness is confirmed by the presence of professional interpreters and scribal tools such as vocabularies in more than one language. In order to explain this multitude of languages, Sumerian culture supported the mythical view of a common original language that existed in a distant past, which was then divided into several languages. In the Akkadian period, another view would be put forward, according to which Akkadian was the central language (since Akkad was at the centre of the known world), Sumerian was the southern one, Elamite the eastern one, Subartean the northern one, and Amorite the western one. In this way, the ethno-linguistic distribution of the Near East was modelled in such a way as to coincide with the Akkadian worldview.

2 The social structure of Mesopotamian temple cities

The evidence from the layout and architecture of the Uruk phase has already demonstrated the centrality of temples in Sumerian cities. The availability of written evidence for the Early Dynastic II–III further clarifies the role of the temple as an ideological, ceremonial and administrative centre. The architecture of

Early Dynastic temples directly reflects their function as a 'total institution' (Figure 6.3). There were spaces dedicated to the gods (such as the cella, only accessible to designated priestly officials), courtyards for communal gatherings, and areas for the accumulation of surplus (storehouses) and economic and administrative activities (archives and workshops).

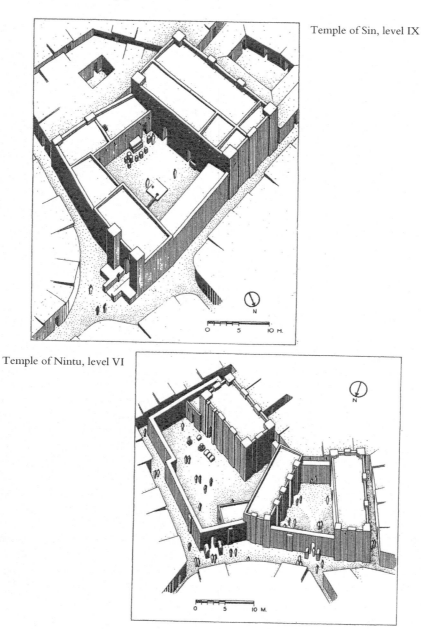

Temple of Sin, level IX

Temple of Nintu, level VI

Figure 6.3 The temple in the Early Dynastic period. The two temples shown were found in Khafaja, Early Dynastic III A.

There is, however, a certain degree of ambiguity between the role of the temple as an administrative centre of the city-state, and an independent nucleus (both in terms of production and organisation) within the city-state. In the Early Dynastic period, the administrative centre moved elsewhere, into the palace. However, temples (each city had more than one) maintained their cultic function as well as their income, although the latter was eventually included within the overarching state administration. In the separation of functions between the temple and the palace, then, the former maintained its ideological supremacy (including the divine legitimation of power), while the latter acquired an executive supremacy.

In terms of internal organisation, it is important to note that Sumerian grouped temples, palaces and households in the unifying category of the 'house' (Sumerian *é*, Akkadian *bītum*). This term clearly indicates that production and administrative unit lying at the core of society. This would remain a fundamental concept throughout Mesopotamian history. On the one hand, a private household ('house of *x*') was owned and inhabited by its owner, who pursued his activities there. On the other hand, a temple ('house of *x* deity') was owned and inhabited by a deity, and was the place where economic activities were pursued on his behalf. By contrast, the palace was simply a 'large house' (Sumerian *é-gal*, Akkadian *ēkallum*), whose plan reproduced a household plan on a larger scale. In this way, this larger household would eventually become the centre of a network of smaller houses (private households or temples), which clearly depended on the palace and had to pay tributes to it.

In the Early Dynastic period, while temples had already existed for a long time, palaces were a relatively recent development. Following the first palace at Jemdet Nasr, other ones were built in the south (Eridu), and especially in the north (Kish, palaces A and P; Mari) during the Early Dynastic IIIa (Figure 6.4). Incidentally, this development took place at the same time as the earliest appearance of royal inscriptions (from king Enmebaragesi to Mesilim and the dynasty of the Royal Cemetery of Ur, which will be considered later on). From the Early Uruk to the Early Dynastic I period, the ruling class (the priesthood) of the temple cities was largely anonymous, due to its role as delegate of the god. Now, however, a new ruling class emerged, which had to assert its legitimacy of rule and to insist on the intelligibility of its abilities (from power to justice).

Even after the rise of palaces, the economic role of temples (alongside their ideological role) continued to be essential, though controlled by the authority of the palace. In fact, a city hosted a number of large and complex cultic buildings (which certainly had an impact on its economy), as well as simpler temples exclusively dedicated to cultic activities. The links between the various temples and between these and the palace was both an ideological and administrative necessity. The gods of these temples (each with a specific personality, gender, competence, mythology and iconography) were initially linked to each other through kinship ties, and then through more 'theological' ties that were different from city to city. At the same time, their property and economic activities were managed through the royal family, whose members acted as human functionaries of the temples, thus imitating the divine family structure.

Having lost its centrality within the new palace state, the temple became a semi-independent unit equal to other similar units. It therefore became a replicable model able to sustain the political expansion of the state itself. Following the structure already laid out in the ancient texts from Uruk (especially the lists of professions from the Uruk III phase), a hierarchy of priestly administrators continued to work within the temple. Below the highest ranks, there were overseers or guards, and then a large number of workers. The temple worked in a variety of sectors: from the transformation of raw materials (around the temple itself), to the storage of goods, the provision of services, and agriculture in the countryside. Therefore, a large number of people working, of lands cultivated, and a large percentage of production were still in the hands of the temples.

Unsurprisingly, the study of the administrative texts of the Early Dynastic period (more precisely the Early Dynastic IIIb at Lagash) led to the interpretation of these systems as 'temple cities'. This is because temples owned all the lands, causing the political and economic dependence of the population on these institutions. However, the lack of private documentation makes this interpretative model untenable, since it is based exclusively on the evidence found in temple archives. For instance, demographic and agricultural

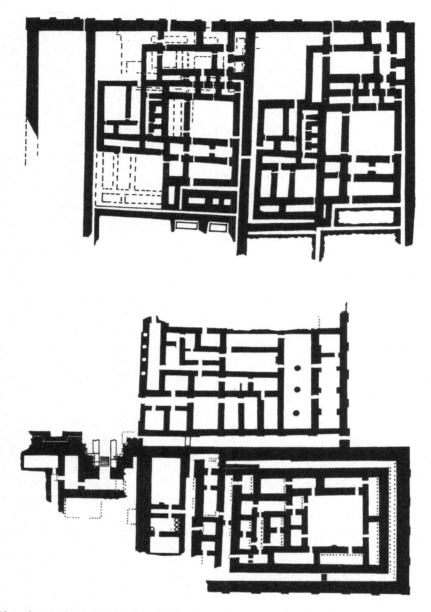

Figure 6.4 The palace in the Early Dynastic period. *Above*: The palace of Eridu; *Below*: Palace A in Kish. Both palaces are from the Early Dynastic III A.

recalculations have proved that temples were not the only institutions governing these cities. Moreover, for the Early Dynastic IIIa period, there are legal documents recording the sale of land not owned by the temple, as well as registrations of seasonal workforce hired by the temple administration. These people must have come from outside the city, and were probably living in the surrounding villages, leading to the hypothesis that the latter owned their own land.

While the idea of the 'temple city' is now considered out-dated, the criticism of the concept has also gone too far. It is clear that the temple was still a fundamental element of the city, one that had a significant socio-economic impact. Therefore, Sumerian cities can be considered temple cities in the same way as Late Medieval Venice can be defined as a commercial city, or nineteenth-century Manchester an industrial city.

The temple or palace administrations had a significant impact not only on the development of cities, but also on village communities. The latter had to contribute to the accumulation of surplus for the centre, either giving up a share of their produce through taxation, or providing additional labour (*corvée*). The central administration had physically changed its countryside through the construction of canals and the creation of new arable land, destined for the temple and its staff. Consequently, this body owned the majority of the land in the surrounding areas. Although the spatial distribution of temple lands compared to village lands is still unknown, it is probable that the temple managed to control new lands located along newly constructed canals, relegating the villages to a more marginal role and lower yields.

The earliest land sales, found in the archives from Fara (ancient Shuruppak, Early Dynastic IIIa), seem to have been an interesting mixture of tradition and innovation (Text 6.2). In terms of tradition, they record the ceremonial rituals making land sales a social act, and the large number of sellers receiving decreasing numbers of 'gifts', according to their kinship ties with the primary sellers. These aspects were residual of a type of ownership that was centred on the family, rather than the individual owner. They therefore required the approval of the extended family before losing a share of the land. The innovative element was the intervention of surveyors and city scribes, paid to provide reliable measures and guarantees during the transaction. Traditionally, this was the responsibility of witnesses. Another innovation was the emergence of buyers able to break down pre-existent family estates, turning them into personal commodities.

Text 6.2   Lower Mesopotamian agriculture in the Early Dynastic period

a) *Contract for the purchase of a field, from Fara (ca. 2550 BC)*

'4 minas of copper: price (*ní-sax*) for the field. This field (measures) 2 *iku*. 4 minas of copper: supplement (*ní-diri*). 52 minas of copper and 2 *ul* of barley: gift (*ní-ba*). 2 minas of wool for cloths, 1 TÚG.ME.GAL garment, 20 loaves of bread, 20 cakes, 4 measures of . . ., 4 measures of . . ., 1 litre of fat (for) Di-Utu and Ur-Elum, those who have 'eaten' the price (*lú-sa_x-kú*, namely, the sellers). 1 *ul* of barley for Nin-Azu. 20 litres of barley, 10 cakes, 1 measure of . . ., 1 measure of . . ., for Ursag-kazida.

Witnesses (*lú-ki-inim*): Ur-abzu the scribe, E-urbidu, Ur-mud the chief fisher and merchant, Lu-kisalsi, Sagantuku, Lugal-nigzu the potter, E-kigala, Ur-mud, . . ., Badada, Ur-Gula the scribe.

1 mina of copper, 10 loaves of bread, 10 cakes, 1 measure of . . ., 1 measure of . . ., for Ige-nugi the surveyor (*dub-sar-gána*).

Ur-Enlil, the *galla* high priest, is the one who bought the field (*lú-gána-sa_x*).

(The year in which) Nammaḫ was *bal*-eponym.

(Name of the field) E-musub.'

b) *Yields (in litres per hectare) of grains in Lagash (Early Dynastic III)*

fields	1	2	3	4	5	6	7	8	9	average
barley	927	1763	2236	2518	2742	2863	3089	3226	3493	2539
emmer	1656	2354	3694	4906	1968	4939	–	–	–	3253
wheat	–	–	–	–	1800	2000	–	–	–	1900

c) Evidence for simple crop rotation (cultivation/fallow land): fields 1–4 are cultivated in one year and fields 5–9 in the next one

Name of the field	Enetarzi		Lugalanda						Urukagina				
	4	5	1	2	3	4	5	6	0	1	2	3	4
Daishgarmud	+		+		+		+		+				
Sagatur	+		+		+		+		+				
Duabuk	+		+		+		+		+		+		+
Daghia	+		+		+		+		+				
Nigin		+		+		+		+		+			
Ugig		+		+		+		+		+			
Sheshdua		+		+		+		+		+			
Kun-Enlilepada		+		+		+		+		+			
Ummezagnusi		+		+		+		+		+			

d) Percentages of grain cultivation (Lagash, Early Dynastic period)

	Early Dynastic period III										Comparisons		
	1	2	3	4	5	6	7	8	9	average	Nuzi 2250	Gudea 2150	Ur III 2050
barley (*še*)	70	75	77	80	83	88	100	100	100	83.7	67	94	98.15
emmer (*zíz*)	30	25	22	20	17	11	–	–	–	15.7	14	5	1.70
wheat (*gig*)	–	–	1	–	–	1	–	–	–	0.6	19	1	0.15

It is clear that large portions of the population remained free in their villages, and only depended on the temple cities as tribute payers, free labourers and worshippers of the city-gods. However, the portion of the population economically and politically dependent on the temple or the palace was rapidly becoming larger and more influential. In fact, a growing class of administrators, merchants, scribes and specialised craftsmen working for the temples was starting to provide a thriving environment for the innovation, organisation and enrichment of Sumerian culture. These people began to leave a significant mark on their cities, archaeologically visible through the increased wealth of tombs, offerings and private households, and the spread of luxury goods (Figures 6.5 and 6.6).

Consequently, the functional division dating back to the Uruk period between temple functionaries (that is, specialised workmen) and free workmen inevitably began to move towards a socio-economic division into classes. The bottom of this pyramid was for now still legally defined. Therefore, there was no confusion between the free members of the village communities and the temple servants forced to cultivate the lands of the specialised workmen and the temples. However, as village communities became increasingly poor, and had to sell their lands, so the two groups began to merge into a large class of farmers without land (whatever their origin and legal status might have been). This new class now depended on the large organisations or its members to survive.

3 Land and labour

The main economic resources of the Early Dynastic period continued to be the cultivation of the alluvial plain and the farming of animals, since both craftsmanship and trade depended on the first two. On their part, the great organisations had a significant impact on both agriculture and farming. This happened

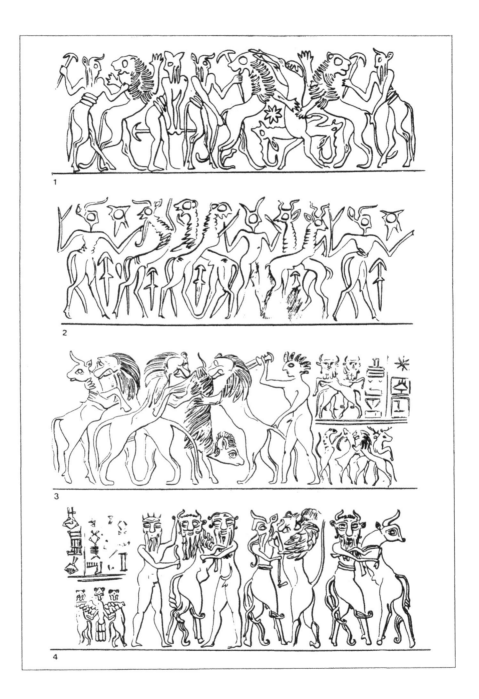

Figure 6.5 Mesopotamian seal impressions of the Early Dynastic II and III. 1–2: Fara style; 3: style of the Royal Cemetery at Ur ('Meskalamdug phase'); 4: style of the First Dynasty of Ur and the Lagash dynasty ('Mesannepadda–Lugalanda phase').

Figure 6.6 Mesopotamian culture of the Early Dynastic period. *Above*: Weapons from the royal tombs of Ur; *Below*: Votive plaque from Khafajah with banquet scene.

through the development of an administration aimed at the optimisation of production. However, this was a long process, which would only reach its zenith towards the end of the third millennium BC, with the Third Dynasty of Ur. The Early Dynastic period provides numerous administrative texts, allowing, together with archaeological and paleo-ecologic evidence, a more detailed reconstruction of agricultural and other activities pursued in Mesopotamia in the second quarter of the third millennium BC.

However, a satisfactory reconstruction of the agricultural landscape of the time remains difficult. Archaeological data have shown that the Mesopotamian landscape was a mixture of lands cultivated through intensive agriculture and irrigation, and marginal territories rich in other resources (steppes and marshes). The layout of individual fields along the irrigation canals can already be seen (through sales texts and land registries) as developing along the same lines as the ones characterising the following periods.

Fields were usually long rectangles of land facing the canal from the shorter side, and were ploughed and irrigated along the longer side. This layout was typical of irrigation agriculture, which aimed at maximising the number of fields along a given canal, creating a row of fields on each side. Fields generally bordered with non-irrigated steppes, un-drained marshes, or even other fields linked to other canals. The areas closest to the canals were generally left for vegetables (garlic, onions and legumes), or trees (such as date-palms), while the largest part of the fields were used for grains, such as barley, wheat and emmer. These three cereals provided different yields, and were different both in terms quality and resistance. In the south, irrigated lands, which were at a high risk of salinisation, were mostly used for barley (in a ratio of 5:1 and above). This grain was used to feed humans and animals alike, as well as for the production of beer. Wheat and emmer were less widespread in the area, thus becoming in a way luxury products. On the contrary, in the north, where rainfall levels were higher, the proportion between the three was more balanced.

Fields were not cultivated all at once. In fact, there is evidence for biennial rotation, a practice requiring a field to be cultivated with grains one year, and then left fallow the following one. Yields remained quite high (with a ratio of 20:1 or 30:1 between seeds and harvest), since many of the degrading factors that would affect Mesopotamian agriculture in the following centuries had not yet arisen. Summer cultivations, such as sesame, were still not widespread. In fact, the agricultural cycle and the system of rotations would be intensified later on, in the second millennium BC, leading to a rapid decline of soil quality. With yields this high, unprecedented not only in the area, but worldwide (for the time), the accumulation of surplus for the maintenance of specialists and the administrative and priestly elite was not difficult. In fact, the largest portion of the harvest (something like two thirds) was sent to the temple or palace storehouses. The rest was put aside to be planted the following year and distributed among the farmers working on the fields.

Just like during the first urbanisation, the availability of surplus kick-started a series of redistributive mechanisms. However, there were marked differences, partly due to the nature of the available evidence (mostly archaeological for Uruk, and textual for the Early Dynastic period). The redistributive system of the Uruk period largely consisted in the direct distribution of food rations. During the Early Dynastic period, food rations were still provided to the seasonal staff (*corvée* farmers), while redistribution for permanent workers took place through other means. These were, among others, the provision of shares of the harvest to the farmers, and plots of land (with farmers) to the specialised workers living in the cities.

Therefore, the system had evolved to become more stable, although this newly acquired stability was to the advantage of the workers. In fact, the temple's lands were divided into lots, which were initially assigned on a temporary basis and in exchange for a service, but eventually began to be inherited. Therefore, the personalised redistributive system of the palace influenced the nature of family properties, while the system of inheritance used by families began to have an impact on the public sector.

Archaeological evidence shows that cities in this period produced artefacts of a very high quality, undoubtedly due to the increased availability of materials through long distance trade. Jewellery, weaponry, refined artefacts to be dedicated as offerings in temples, and musical instruments indicate the increased availability of precious materials and a high level of technical expertise. This expertise clearly reached its peak in Lower Mesopotamia by the Early Dynastic III period. The furniture found in the Royal Cemetery at Ur is the highest example of this development. On the contrary, lower classes produced a much more modest and widespread type of material culture. Administrative texts also provide information on the crafts, their techniques, the terminology of the materials, objects and metal alloys, confirming the supremacy of the palace and the temple in the supervision of these specialised sectors.

Consequently, cities experienced a higher concentration of the workforce, especially in two central sectors of the economy of the time. The first one was the milling of grains. In the absence of a technology able to exploit natural forces, the production of flour was a long and painful process, mostly pursued by women with simple stone grinders – a legacy of the Neolithic period. This kind of work, which was already difficult on a family level, required a large number of women when done within the larger redistributive system of the temple and the palace.

Another sector with a high concentration of workers (mostly women and children) was textile production. Again, the equipment used for spinning and weaving was fundamentally Neolithic, namely, a distaff, a spindle and a horizontal loom. The large quantities of wool arriving in the urban centres were transformed into fabrics, both for internal needs and for trade (textiles were the typical material used for trading), in large workshops. The process required thousands of working days of women reduced to a servile state. These sectors with a high concentration of workers required little skilled knowledge. This was in marked contrast to other sectors, from metalworking to the carving of semiprecious stones, left in the hands of small groups of specialised craftsmen.

4 Between politics and ideology: the administration of cities

Early Dynastic Mesopotamia was divided into a series of relatively small states (with a radius of ca. 30 km), characterised by a virtually equal status and potential for expansion. This regional reorganisation started in the Jemdet Nasr and Early Dynastic I phases in response to the previous pre-eminence of Uruk. Each city had its local ruler, whose title varied from city to city: Uruk was ruled by an *en*, a '(high) priest'; Lagash by an *ensi*, an 'estate manager (for the god)'; while Ur and Kish by a *lugal*, a 'king'. The three terms were not synonymous, each having its own ideological and political implications. The *en* title was clearly meant to underline the continuity and origin of the ruler's authority in the temple, where it found its initial application. The *ensi* title showed the dependence of the ruler to the authority of the god, due to the former's role as delegate of the god. The title of *lugal* (literally, 'great man') emphasised the human qualities of the ruler (both physically and socio-economically), and mirrored the term for 'palace', *é-gal* (meaning 'large house'). While the first two titles are attested in the Uruk and Jemdet Nasr periods, the third one only emerged in the Early Dynastic period. Politically, being an *ensi* also implied relations of dependence on a human level. As a result, more powerful kings, who had a hegemonic and military agenda, would use the title of *lugal*.

With the rise of independent states, problems arose not only on an economic and military level, resulting in conflicts over borders and occasional attempts towards supremacy, but also on a juridical and ideological level. The multitude of deities, which were recognised by the population as a whole, led to the consideration of the presence of a multitude of political centres, roughly one per city (that is, one per god), as legitimate. On an urban level, the local city-god was naturally considered more powerful than those in other cities. This belief led to the rise of local theologies and theogonies (for instance, those at Eridu were different from the ones at Nippur). These ideological differences led to political differences, since states were not strictly seen as equal, but were ranked according to the sets of values of each city.

The multitude of coexisting states was mirrored by the internal developments taking place in each city. Several dynasties followed each other in a sequence of rises and falls that had to be justified theologically. The core unit of power was the *bala*, a 'rotation (of office)' (namely, a 'dynasty'), linked to the respective deity, who would grant or remove his or her support according to the rulers' behaviour. However, just like polytheistic systems featured the supremacy of one god, so kingship developed along a similar line in each city, dynasty after dynasty. Hegemonic strategies therefore originated from, and were legitimised by, the local religious ideology. In this way, the most powerful kings of the period managed to settle controversies in other cities and take over titles, an act that expressed their ability to control cities other than their own.

On a historical level, we know of at least two groups of Sumerian cities, whose function (political or economic) and history remains unclear. The first attempt took place in the Early Dynastic I, and is attested mainly at Ur, through seals called 'City Seals'. These seals depicted the symbols of a variety of cities (Ur, Larsa, Adab, Kesh, the Eanna of Uruk, Lagash and maybe Eridu), some of which have not yet been identified. The cities involved held on to their autonomy and their union could have been for reasons still unknown to us (possibly commercial or even cultic). Far better attested is the second attempt, called the 'Kengir League' (Kengir being the Sumerian term for Sumer) or 'Hexapolis'. It was recorded in a series of texts from Shuruppak (Fara) from the Early Dynastic IIIa period. According to these sources, Shuruppak, Uruk, Adab, Nippur, Lagash, and Umma sent a substantial number of soldiers to Kengir. The most obvious hypothesis is that these cities were allies, possibly against a northern enemy (maybe Kish). The so-called 'Fara Age' (corresponding to the Early Dynastic IIIa) is documented in administrative texts from Fara itself (another name for Shuruppak), located halfway between Uruk and Nippur, and Abu Salabih (north-west of Nippur) in the north.

Nippur held a particularly unique position in the region, due to its mediatory and unifying role. The city never became the seat of a ruling dynasty, but as the main city of the god Enlil, the supreme deity of the Sumerians, it held a central role in the region. Many kings provided votive offerings to the sanctuary of Enlil (the Ekur) and attempted to legitimise their power through the support of Enlil. As Nippur theology spread across Sumer, so Enlil became the ultimate judge of the distribution of power among cities, and began to take on the essential role of mediator among the cities.

Through an internal legitimation of power (public consensus and control of the local priesthood), as well as an external one (through the approval of Nippur, and the establishment of a network of relations with other cities), the rulers of the Sumerian city-states became the administrators of an urban settlement conceived as one large estate. Ideologically, the owner of this 'estate' and its people was the god, while the king was his delegate. However, the king remained the actual leader, as long as he could respect those social and religious conventions necessary to gain the approval of the population. The fundamental duties of the king were the regular management of economic activities, as well as the occasional defence against enemy attacks. His responsibilities were split on two levels, one human and one divine. The king had to implement important decisions and supervise the production and redistribution of commodities. However, successful harvests were attributed to the positive influence of the divine sphere (since harvests depended on natural phenomena). The same can be said about war: the king was responsible for leading military activities, but the conflict's outcome would ultimately be determined by the will of the god (or, better, the conflict of interests between different gods).

However, the god's behaviour was a reflection of human behaviour, since the former's righteousness and justice could not be doubted. If a king, conceptualised as the human representative of the community in front of the divine, committed a violation, the god would have harmed the harvests and would have ceased to protect the city. This link between the king's behaviour and the reaction of the divine led to the third fundamental aspect of kingship, namely, its cultic role. Alongside the management of his land, the king had to ensure positive relations with the divine, thus avoiding the occurrence of natural disasters outside his control. This beneficial relation with the divine only took place when the right individual was heading the community, and through the daily care of this difficult interaction.

The problem of legitimacy was entirely ideological, since one's right to rule was directly linked to one's ability to do so. However, apart from the obvious legitimacy of a ruler inheriting his office from his predecessor, there was a specific need for usurpers or new kings to justify their rule. The solution was to legitimise their rule stating that, if the god had chosen them among all other possible candidates, it was because of their unique qualities, necessary to become good rulers. Even on a daily basis, the king held a central role in cultic activities. Priestly officials managed daily rituals, monthly and yearly festivals (as with most agricultural communities, the new year was a crucial moment) and offerings. However, in this ceremonial repertoire the king held the role of the legitimate intermediary between the community and the city-god.

This inextricable link existing between the administration of cities and its religious justification was a way to overcome visible inequalities. In fact, these would have been impossible to maintain without a strong ideological backing. The Mesopotamian farmer was pressured by uncontrollable natural phenomena harming his fields (from floods to drought, pestilences and locusts) on the one hand, and heavy taxation on the other. He therefore had to be sure that the administration was able to keep the system under control (both efficiently and justly) in view of the common interest, represented by the city-god. While the temple did not require an ideology justifying its existence, the king, whose role could have been performed (or at least coveted) by many other candidates, clearly had to express his qualities, emphasising his strength, justice and ability to rule.

The earliest royal inscriptions were found on temple offerings (stone or metal vases, weapons, statues depicting rulers), or buried under the foundations of buildings founded by kings (temples, canals and so on). They were aimed precisely at advertising the productivity and power of the king, as well as his close dependence on the city-god. These objects, however, due to their small size and their location (buried under a building's foundations), could not have been intended to spread this propagandistic message to the population, but rather for imaginary recipients (the gods and the following rulers). However, the sheer existence and formulation of these inscriptions responded to a concrete royal need, which must have been pursued through other means to reach the population. This period saw the rapid rise of celebrative monuments (victory steles and royal statues). Therefore, their monumentality, location (in the temple), and representations could have been means for propaganda, communicated alongside the implicit message of power delivered by their construction.

Therefore, the performance of rituals and the construction of monuments kick-started the development of the celebratory aspects of kingship. These would further flourish later on, but already had a considerable impact in this period. For instance, the burial of considerable wealth and a large number of individuals in the Royal Cemetery of Ur was the result of the community's acceptance of the role of the king as the legitimate and necessary intermediary between the community itself and that supernatural sphere deciding its fate and survival.

5 The divine foundations of kingship

The Neolithic revolution produced a religiosity centred on fertility issues and animal and vegetal reproduction. The Urban Revolution produced a polytheistic pantheon with deities supervising various aspects of urban life. Therefore, the rise and development of states also necessitated a solid ideological justification of power. In this regard, the earliest religious texts reveal the fundamental characteristics and structure of a fully developed Mesopotamian religion, supported by a complex set of rituals and myths. The texts of the Early Dynastic period already provide a complex picture of Mesopotamian religion. Moreover, many elements found in later texts originated in this period, when Mesopotamian culture acquired those aspects that would characterise it for the following three millennia. Lists of gods, descriptions of temples and hymns reveal the religious heritage of the Sumerian city-states. The historical and religious aspects of Sumerian culture will not be considered here. We will only consider those elements that are important for the understanding of the political and socio-economic phenomena of the time.

It has already been noted how the city-god played a fundamental role in the ideological justification of kingship, ensuring consensus and the collaboration of the population. Moreover, the divine sphere served as a means to explain the world in cultic and mythical terms. This cultic explanation was linked to the system of offerings (food, but also luxury goods). These were provided to the temples on a daily basis, or during festivals and other special occasions. The inequality of the redistributive system was therefore expressed in its fullest form and justified through the system of temple offerings. Redistribution was now too unbalanced to be a mere centralisation of reciprocal relations (such as the exchange of gifts and services). Therefore, it was conceptualised as an investment of present commodities for a future return (which is also the main aim of offerings and sacrifices to the gods). The community, believing that it was supporting the gods to its own advantage, then applied the same ideology to support the ruling elite.

Equally important was the mythical explanation of the world in its current form. The origins of each physical and cultural trait of one's environment were attributed to the intervention of the divine or a hero in a more or less distant past. Similarly, the overall structure of the world was attributed to a creation god acting in a mythical past. Within this view, specific deities created more concrete aspects of daily life, eventually becoming the patrons of that particular sector. Consequently, there were gods protecting animals, cereals, writing and so on. There were also semi-divine characters, mostly idealised as ancient rulers. These figures created the main socio-political aspects of communal life, brought innovative technologies, or simply revolutionised the urban landscape. In this regard, the ruling king was able to provide his own contribution (building a temple or introducing a new festival), thus adding his name to the long and prestigious list of gods or kings who created something important for the community.

The boundary between the contribution of gods and heroes remains an unclear issue. One would expect that, while gods created aspects of life connected with nature, heroes brought more human innovations, mostly related to social institutions. However, it may be worth reconsidering the difference between nature and culture, in order to understand that the separation between gods and heroes was voluntarily blurred. In fact, the mythical foundations of kingship and power inevitably needed the support of the divine sphere. In this regard, certain deities (from Dumuzi to Gilgamesh), who were included in the Sumerian King List, are still considered by some as having a human and historical origin.

Naturally, all foundation myths were subject to a process of reinterpretation and revision for each period, thus reflecting historical and political changes. Therefore, the problems tackled by myths are problems that can be dated, though not with precision. Not all foundation myths were created in the Early Dynastic period, since some of them were developed to provide a background to later situations. Consequently, the issue of the immortality of the king, which is at the heart of the Epic of Gilgamesh, can be contextualised in the deification of the king (whose presumed immortality was disproved by his mortality, and therefore required an explanation), a practice that only appeared in the dynasty of Akkad. On the contrary, a myth such as the one of Adapa, despite having survived only in later texts, could have been a very ancient foundation myth. In fact, it is centred on an ancient problem, namely, that of reassuring the population that priests did not eat the food offered to the god, and were not gods themselves (despite living in the god's house).

The current belief that the heroes of the foundation myths were all created in the Early Dynastic period is therefore inaccurate. Only at the beginning of the second millennium BC, Mesopotamian scholars decided to place these heroes in the dynastic sequences of Uruk and Kish. However, this contextualisation is not historically accurate: it only shows how these mythical kings were placed before kings that were actually attested in the written evidence. The latter is first found (in the form of royal inscriptions and dated archives) at the beginning of the Early Dynastic period IIIa (or at the end of the Early Dynastic II). Consequently, a source such as the Sumerian King List logically placed the mythical kings in the Early Dynastic II period and the flood myth in the Early Dynastic I.

Despite their foundational purpose and their relevance to the problems of their respective contexts, these myths can still inform us on the earliest developments of Mesopotamian society. Since they are attested in later versions, they obviously reveal more (and more reliable details) on these later periods. For instance, the problem of the relations between farmers and shepherds (attested in the myth of Lahar and Ashnan), and of the provision of raw materials from distant lands (attested in the myth of Enmerkar and the lord of Aratta, and of Gilgamesh and Huwawa) were constant issues in Mesopotamian history. However, the presence of certain geographic and technological details indicates that they could have been developed in the Early Dynastic period, and later re-elaborated in their traditional Neo-Sumerian versions.

6 Competition and supremacy

The relative chronology of the Early Dynastic period is based on an analysis of stratigraphic data (the only data available for the Early Dynastic I and II) together with written sources from the Early Dynastic IIIa, and especially IIIb. However, the range of evidence varies greatly from centre to centre. From the settlements in the Diyala (the Oval Temple, and the temples of Anu, Sin, and Nintu at Khafajah; the temple of Abu at

Tell Asmar; the temple of Shara at Tell Agrab) and Nippur (temple of Inanna) we have the longest and more reliable stratigraphic sequences. From Ur we have the monumental complexes (such as the Royal Cemetery), while from Shuruppak and Abu Salabih we have the first administrative archives (Early Dynastic IIIa). Lagash provides a large amount of historical inscriptions and a rich administrative archive (Early Dynastic IIIb), but very little archaeological context, virtually lost during the earliest excavations.

The analysis of this wide range of data coming from a number of centres is not an easy task. Moreover, the chronological reconstruction of this period owes greatly to a later text, namely, the Sumerian King List. This text has provided a rough sequence of rulers. However, it constantly necessitates corrections and integrations. This is due to the unreliability of the dynasties listed before the First Dynasty of Ur, the placement of contemporary dynasties in a chronological sequence, and the lack of dynasties for some important centres (Lagash, Umma and Eshnunna).

Despite the presence of the earliest royal inscriptions (Enmebaragesi of Kish) (Table 6.1), the Early Dynastic II period is mainly attested archaeologically (Table 6.2), with characteristic objects of this period and distinctive styles (such as the Fara-style glyptic; the statues of the temple of Abu at Tell Asmar; the archaic tablets of Ur, and so on). Similarly, the Early Dynastic IIIa period also had distinctive styles and types of objects (the naturalistic sculptures from the temple of Abu, the Imdugud-Sukurru and Meskalamdug glyptic art, inlaid objects linked with the ones from the Royal Cemetery of Ur, votive plaques linked with those from Inanna VII in Nippur, and so on). This phase saw the emergence of the administrative archives at Fara and Abu Salabih, and the dedicatory inscriptions from the Royal Cemetery at Ur (belonging to the '*Kalam*' dynasty, ignored by the Sumerian King List). Only with the IIIb period there is a convergence between the Sumerian King List (which is fairly reliable from this point onwards, but still biased in its selection), and archival evidence (Lagash), royal inscriptions (mainly from Lagash and Ur, and some poorly attested kings of Kish and Uruk), stratigraphic data from temples, and the developments in glyptic art and sculpture.

The Sumerian King List provides a unified, yet selective, sequence of dynasties following and replacing one another. However, the monuments and inscriptions of the time provide a much more complex picture

Table 6.1 Early Dynastic Mesopotamia: chronology of royal inscriptions

	Kish	Adab	Ur	Uruk	Umma	Lagash
2600	Mebaraggesi(+)*					
2500	Uhub Mesilim ab*	Ninkisalsi b				Enhegal Lugalshagengur a
2450	Lugaltarzi*	Merduba Lugaldalu	Meskalamdug° Akalamdug°			Ur–Nanshe
2400	Enbi-Ishtar(+)e*	Eiginimpae	Mesannepadda(+)°·* Aannepadda° Meskiagnunna (+)° Elili (+)°	Enshakushanna (–)e• Lugalkinishedudu (+) f*·° Lugalkisalsi (+)°	Ush Enakale c Urlumma d IIa g Gishakidu	Akurgal Eannarum c Eannatum I d Entemena fg
2350					Wawa	Enannatum II Enetarzi Lugalanda
				Lugalzaggesi (+)h•	Lugalzag- gesi h	Urukagina h

Notes ° "king of Ur"; ★ "king of Kish"; • "king of Sumer"; (+) king attested in the Sumerian King List; a-a= attested contemporaneity.

Table 6.2 Early Dynastic Mesopotamia: archaeological chronology

Period	Khafajah Sin	Khafajah Nintu	Khafajah Oval	Tell Asmar Abu	Nippur Inanna	Architecture	Craftsmanship	Texts	Mari	North Assyria
Jemdet Nasr (3000–2900 BC)	I II III IV	I II		archaic sanctuary I	XIV XIII XII	Uruk Eanna III; Riemchen; Jemdet Nasr "palace"	Seals: Jemdet Nasr style; Pottery: last bevelled rim bowls	Jemdet Nasr tablets		Nineveh 4; Gawra 8
Early Dynastic I (2900–2750 BC)	V VI VII	III		II III IV	XI X IX	first appearance of plano-convex bricks	Seals: "brocade" style; Scarlet Ware		Ishtar E	Nineveh 5; Gawra 7; Ashur: Ishtar H
Early Dynastic II (2750–2600 BC)	VIII	IV V	I	square temple I II III	VIII		Seals: Fara style; "Abstract" sculpture	Archaic texts of Ur; Ennebaragesi	Ishtar D	Nineveh 5; Gawra 7; Ashur: Ishtar H
Early Dynastic IIIa (2600–2450 BC)	IX	VI VII	II	individual sanctuary I	VII VI	Eridu palace; Palace A of Kish; Royal Cemetery of Ur	Seals: Imdugud-Sukurru phase; "Naturalistic" sculpture; Seals: Meskalamdug phase	Mesilim; Texts from Fara and Abu Salabih	Ishtar C; Ishtar B	Nineveh 5; Gawra 7; Ashur: Ishtar G
Early Dynastic IIIb (2450–2350 BC)	X		III	II III	V	End of plano-convex bricks; Temple Oval of Ubaid	Seals: Mesannepadda-Lugalanda phase	Lagash texts (from Ur-Nanshe to Lugalanda)	Ishtar A; Pre-sargonic palace	Nineveh 5; Gawta 7; Ashur: Ishtar G
Proto-Imperial (2350–2300 BC)	IV			IV				Urukagina; Lugalzaggesi		

of co-existing dynasties competing with each other. The latter case is best attested at Lagash, and in particular in its long competition with Umma for control over the Gu-Edinna region, rich in fields and pasturelands. The inscriptions left by the kings of Lagash (mostly celebratory in nature) provide details on the contest between the two from their earliest skirmishes and the intervention of the king of Kish (Mesilim) as mediator between the two, to the later episodes. Naturally, Umma is always described as an aggressive, unjust and dishonest enemy, in stark contrast with Lagash, the just city, which was attacked, but emerged victorious. Unfortunately, nothing has survived of the Umma records on this conflict.

One of the most important moments of this dispute took place under Eannatum. It was recorded in his famous Stele of the Vultures. The inscription is further enriched by the eloquent depiction of the victorious side and the defeated one, as well as the link between human actions and divine intervention. Another important moment took place under Entemena, who left a more complete retrospective account of the conflict. Given the frequency of references to this episode at Lagash, it must have been a dispute with important political and economic implications. It is clear that conflicts such as the one over the Gu-Edinna region were not uncommon in the Early Dynastic period. Therefore, the conflict between Lagash and Umma is only one attested example of the difficulties arising between city-states: disputes over intermediary regions (when these were not mere empty spaces); their ideological interpretation as conflicts between city-gods; and the parallelism between an active military plan and a juridical justification of this plan.

The Lagash material also attests to other kinds of wars, such as incursions, at times without permanent consequences, into distant cities (from Susiana to Central Mesopotamia) in order to gain, or keep, a superior position among the other city-states. The city-state rising above all others would have been the one able to acquire more prestigious titles, such as the one of *lugal*. While support from Nippur was important on an ideological level, the titles *en Uruk* and *lugal Kiš* indicate the supremacy of two main political centres of Lower Mesopotamia: Uruk and Kish. A number of kings, presumably from these two cities, are attested in several inscriptions left in other cities (Nippur in particular). However, these kings could have been local rulers who managed to acquire these prestigious titles after their victories.

The ambition for supremacy soon became an ambition for universal rule. This idea was supported by two concepts. First, there was the idea that the world coincided with Mesopotamia, which was a densely populated, highly productive land surrounded by empty lands. Second, there was the idea of the spread of Sumerian cities, or cities linked to Sumerian culture, in various directions, from Susa, to Mari and Ashur. Through these ramifications, it was deemed possible to reach the edges of the world, identified as the Upper Sea (the Mediterranean) and the Lower Sea (the Persian Gulf). There is a gradual increase in the presence of a universal concept of supremacy. This idea started at the time of Mesilim, king of Kish, who mediated the conflict between Lagash and Umma (Early Dynastic IIIa). The idea survived under the various rulers of the Early Dynastic IIIb (from Eannatum of Lagash, to Lugalkiginnedudu, Lugaltarsi and Lugalkisalsi of Uruk), who combined the titles of king of Kish and of Ur. Finally, the ambition for supremacy peaked at the end of the Early Dynastic IIIb period, which is thus called 'Proto-Imperial'.

There are two significant episodes for this period. First, the king of Adab, Lugalannemundu, appears on the Sumerian King List as the only king of the only dynasty of Adab. An inscription from the Old Babylonian period records the extensive rule of this king, extending across the entire Mesopotamian periphery (Elam, Marhashi, Gutium, Subartu, Martu, Sutium), from Iran to Syria. Obvious anachronisms, however, prove that this is a fake Old Babylonian tablet, but the choice of Lugalannemundu must have been motivated by the supposed greatness of some of his achievements.

The second case, the one of Lugalzaggesi of Uruk, is better attested. We know from his own inscriptions that he defeated and conquered Ur, Larsa, Umma, Nippur and Lagash, thus gaining control over the whole of Lower Mesopotamia. Although his conquests were far from universal, even by Sumerian standards (the Diyala Valley, Central Mesopotamia, Susiana, the Middle Euphrates and Middle Tigris were not under his control), Lugalzaggesi claimed that his rule reached the Lower Sea and the Upper Sea. These statements could have been predictions of future political moves. In fact, they could not have been entirely invented, since that would have caused the king's loss of credibility in front of that part of the audience who knew the truth. It is possible that Lugalzaggesi reached the Mediterranean either in person or through envoys. Alternatively, he could have established military or commercial alliances with other powers (such as Kish, Nagar, Mari and Ebla, which were never conquered by him), although these alternatives were ideologically considered to be secondary. Therefore, the ideology of universal dominion did not need to explain the actual forms of its realisation: imagination not only preceded reality, but was also a powerful stimulus for it.

7 Internal crisis and reform edicts

Before becoming the only king of the Third Dynasty of Uruk, the founder of the first 'empire', Lugalzaggesi, had been king of Umma. Therefore, he inherited the traditional rivalry with Lagash. Unlike his predecessors, Lugalzaggesi managed to solve this rivalry through considerable military contingencies. While there are no records of his achievements from the other conquered cities, Lagash provides its own version of this phase, allowing us to evaluate the real nature of Lugalzaggesi's empire. Even after Uruk's victory, the *ensi* of Lagash, Urukagina, was still able to issue inscriptions, indicating that he must have kept his role in the city. Moreover, in his inscriptions, Urukagina was still able to describe Uruk's victory as a case of abuse of power, pointing out the accountability of the god of Lugalzaggesi against his own god, and hoping in an eventual punishment.

Apart from his clash with Lugalzaggesi, Urukagina is also known for a reform edict informing us of the social problems of the time (Text 6.3). Urukagina was a usurper, and as such he emphasised his difference from his predecessors in two ways. First, these predecessors were portrayed as closely linked to the temple, while Urukagina presents himself as a more 'secular' ruler. Second, Urukagina blamed his predecessors for allowing abuses of power by the priestly elite and administrators at the expense of the population, while the new king was a protector of his people. The legal side of his edict consists in a series of measures aimed at eliminating

---

Text 6.3 The reforms of Urukagina

'Since time immemorial, since life began, in those days, the head boatman appropriated boats, the livestock official appropriated asses, the livestock official appropriated sheep, and the fisheries inspector appropriated . . . and the *guda*-priests paid grain taxes to the town of Ambar. The shepherds of wool sheep paid (a duty) in silver on account of white sheep, and the surveyor, chief lamentation-singer, supervisor, brewer and foreman paid (a duty) in silver on account of young lambs.

The oxen of the gods ploughed the garlic plot of the ruler and the best fields of the gods became the garlic and cucumber plots of the ruler. Teams of asses and spirited oxen were yoked for the temple administrators, but the grain of the temple administrators was distributed by the personnel of the ruler.

When a corpse was brought for burial, the *uḫmuš* took his seven jugs of beer, his 240 loaves of bread, 2 *ul* of *ḫazi*-grain, one woollen garment and one bed; and the *umum* took one *ul* of barley. When a man was brought for the "reed of Enki", then the *uḫmuš* took his seven jugs of beer, his 420 loaves of bread, 2 *ul* of barley, one woollen garment, one bed, and a chair; and the *umum* took one *ul* of barley . . .

The ruler's estate and the ruler's fields, the estate of the "woman's organisation" and fields of the "woman's organisation", and the children's estate and the children's fields all abutted one another. The bureaucracy was operating from the boundary of Ningirsu to the sea.

When the *šublugal* would build a well on the narrow edge of his field, the *iginudu* was appropriated (for the work), and the *iginudu* was also appropriated for (work on) the irrigation channels which were in the field.

These were the conventions of former times!

When Ningirsu, warrior of Enlil, granted the kingship of Lagash to Urukagina, selecting him from among the myriad of people, he replaced the customs of former times, carrying out the commands that Ningirsu, his

---

master, had given him. He removed the head boatman from (control over) the boats, he removed the livestock official from (control over) asses and sheep, he removed the fisheries inspector from (control over) . . ., he removed the silo supervisor from (control over) the grain taxes of the *guda*-priests, he removed the bureaucrat (responsible) for the paying (of duties) in silver on account of white sheep and young lambs, and he removed the bureaucrat (responsible) for the delivery of duties by the temple to the palace.

He installed Ningirsu as proprietor over the ruler's estate and the ruler's fields; he installed Ba'u as proprietor of the estate of the "woman's organisation" and fields of the "woman's organisation"; and he installed Šulšagana as proprietor of the children's estate. From the boundary of Ningirsu to the sea, the bureaucracy ceased operations.'

abuses, bringing back previously lost rights and reinstating the correct relation between the state organisation (and the temple administration) and its subjects. Naturally, this self-legitimating tone was quite evident to the population. Similarly, Urukagina's disassociation from previous governments was equally clear, despite the fact that their dysfunctions and measures were a reaction to the socio–economic crisis of the time.

For now, however, it is inaccurate to speak of reforms, since this would lead to the assumption of an effective change in the juridical or administrative system of the time. The aim of the edict was to re-establish order through a return to the past, idealised (as usual in archaic societies) as a perfect world, characterised by optimal institutions, which were far better at the time of their (divine or kingly) foundation, than later on. In practical terms, the reforms were mainly focused on a reduction of tributes and the abolition of abuses of power. Urukagina was not the first ruler to implement these kinds of measures. At Lagash itself, Entemena proclaimed that 'he caused the son to return to the mother, he caused the mother to return to the son', since he remitted interests on debts, and that he 'established freedom' not just in Lagash, but in Uruk, Larsa, and Bad-tibira (maybe taking advantage of his momentary conquest of these cities).

Apart from the propagandistic aim, these measures reveal the fact that a certain stratum of society was forced to go into debt and sell its property and children to repay interests to a creditor. This downward spiral eventually brought to the disappearance of small family estates and the rise of debt slavery in case of a missing repayment. Debt slavery was considered a serious damage to social order, since it damaged the 'free' portion of the population. Consequently, the solution was to 're-establish freedom'. The ruler issuing a reform edict therefore became a liberator, rejecting the accusation of being accountable for this social deterioration. In the case of Entemena, the causes for slavery are not explained. Urukagina, on the other hand, blamed the crisis (in order to set himself above his predecessors) on the individual abuses of power and the occasional malfunction of the system, rather than the structure of the system. Despite his statement, it is quite clear that this increasing debt of free farmers was a structural problem, linked to the overall tendencies of the period. These led to the disappearance of small family estates and the enrichment of temple and palace estates, as well as their administrators. These problems were actually caused by the rulers' government, forcing rulers to release edicts as a way to keep matters under control and avoid rebellions, without changing too much of the system. The return to the past therefore became a means to mask the profound social changes that were taking place at the time.

These changes led to an unbearable tribute system (in terms of taxes and services) for free inhabitants, and maybe a marginalisation of their lands compared to the areas of development administered by the temple or the palace. It became increasingly difficult for free individuals to maintain this fast pace of contribution and production. A couple of bad years could have destroyed families, irreversibly starting the downward spiral of debt and debt slavery. Members of the highest echelons of society benefited the most from this situation (as lenders), also due to their contacts with the administration, responsible for the accumulation of grains and other products. Blaming priests and administrators for this crisis was aimed at pleasing that part of the population suffering the most from it. The crisis was largely due to the consolidation of large economic organisations, the enrichment of the elite, and the progressive decline of village communities and their farmers. Therefore, aside from individual responsibilities, the crisis remained unstoppable.

7
THE RISE OF EBLA

1 Upper Mesopotamia and the second urbanisation

In the mid-third millennium BC, Upper Mesopotamia, whose urban centres had suffered from the decline of Uruk culture, began to experience a more stable and widespread urbanisation process. This revival took place during the Early Dynastic II and peaked in the Early Dynastic III period. It is worth noting, that the three phases of the Early Dynastic period of Lower Mesopotamia roughly correspond to the three archaeological phases of the Early Bronze Age (whose third phase, however, also includes the Akkadian period). Moreover, a new chronological division has recently come into use, known as Jezira I, II and III.

As previously mentioned, the first urbanisation was characterised by a marked contraposition between settlements closely linked to Uruk culture, from Sumer up along the Tigris and Euphrates, and local settlements influenced by the technical and organisational progress of the south. The latter, however, were still autonomous on a cultural, political and economic level. This distinction disappeared during the second urbanisation. Sumerian influence is only evident in two important centres: Mari, in the Middle Euphrates region, and Ashur, in the Middle Tigris. Their temples and palaces display two types of cultures clearly derived from a Sumerian prototype. However, these two centres were now included in a network of urban settlements extending from Upper Syria and the Balikh and Khabur Valleys to Assyria. This area had higher rainfall levels than the south, leading to more productive rainfed agriculture and farming (mainly goats and sheep).

Excavations and surveys indicate that in the Early Bronze Age II and III both urban settlements and villages grew throughout this area. Moreover, pottery evidence proves that this development was internal. Metallic and Plain Simple Ware substituted the 'Nineveh 5' pottery of eastern Jezira and the Reserved Slip Ware from central and western Jezira. This development led to the formation of a cultural unity embracing a wide area, namely, from the foothills of the eastern Taurus to the northern Zagros. Written evidence would later attest that Hurrian people inhabited these foothills, while Semitic people occupied the rest of the region.

This increase in settlements during the third millennium BC probably benefited from favourable climatic conditions, allowing a better cultivation of the land. However, this area would eventually experience a decline in rainfall. This decline made the local agricultural production levels inadequate for large urban settlements, but more suited to support smaller settlements and less intensive agro-pastoral activities. From a Lower Mesopotamian perspective, this region was defined as the 'high land'. This was due to its location above the Mesopotamian alluvial plain and the plateau, separating irrigated and non-irrigated areas.

Through excavations and surveys, it has been possible to locate areas with high levels of urban concentration. One of these areas was located south of Jebel Sinjar, where rainwater (levels of rainfall being higher in the nearby mountains, which were covered in vegetation) penetrated the foothills, creating aquifers that seasonally brought water to the surface along the Wadi Tharthar. The major centre of the area was Tell Taya (level 9), the largest city of the period (100 hectares). However, there probably were other large centres that still have to be excavated. The second area of high urban concentration was Assyria, not around Ashur, which remains a unique centre in terms of location and culture, but in the agricultural 'triangle' between the Upper Zab and the Tigris. Unfortunately, its centres (from Nineveh to Arbela) have not been excavated for this period.

The Khabur Valley and its tributaries (the so-called 'Khabur triangle') became the main emerging area of Upper Mesopotamia, with several large settlements datable to the Early Bronze Age II and III. The largest one was Tell Brak, ancient Nagar (according to written sources from Ebla), an influential city throughout Upper Mesopotamia (Figure 7.1). Another important centre was Tell Chuera, located along

Figure 7.1. Satellite view of Tell Brak, in the Syrian Jezira (Google Earth).

the western edge of the 'triangle'. There, excavations have uncovered a large city of the Early Dynastic II and III period with obvious Sumerian influences (especially in sculpture) on an equally recognisable local culture, and temples with stone foundations and a non-Sumerian layout. Tell Mozan (ancient Urkish) provides evidence for a Hurrian culture still heavily influenced by the south, but at the same time unique in its characteristics.

One of the main innovations brought from Lower Mesopotamia was writing and everything else that came with it on an administrative level. This is attested in the archives from Tell Beydar, a settlement with an impressive architectural complex. The contemporary texts from Ebla provide a large amount of information on many centres of the Jezira region. For instance, there were Armium (possibly located in the Middle or Upper Euphrates region), Abarsal (around Urfa, possibly identified as Kazane Tepe), and which stipulated a treaty with Ebla to establish commercial boundaries, Urshum, Harran, Irrite, Qattunan and many others.

Of the two most developed centres influenced by Lower Mesopotamian culture, Ashur has not been excavated for the levels dating to the third millennium BC. However, the limited data available leads us to believe that it was a large urban centre. The earliest layers (H and G) of the temple of Ishtar reveal a classic Sumerian-style sanctuary. Its votive statues were similar to the ones found in the Diyala and other centres in the south in the same period.

Much more evidence is available for Mari, where excavations have revealed a large portion of the royal palace (defined by the excavators as 'Pre-Sargonic'). The palace was built in the Early Dynastic IIIa period, and was definitely used throughout the IIIb period (Figure 7.2). Apart from the palace, several temples have been excavated: the temples of Ishtar (with six overlapping layers), Ishtarat, Ninni-Zaza, Shamash and Ninhursag. As in the case of Ashur, the city appears to be just like a Sumerian centre. However, royal votive statues and epigraphic material (further supported by the indirect attestations from Ebla) found at Mari demonstrate that on a linguistic level the city was not a colony of Sumerian immigrants. Mari's personal names were Semitic, as is the language used in its administrative texts. However, it was not Old Akkadian, but the same language found in Ebla, namely, a Western Semitic language used from the Middle Euphrates to the Mediterranean.

Sumerian influences are visible not only on a cultural level (architecture, sculpture and writing), but also through a hoard of precious objects sent from Mesannepadda, king of Ur (known from the Sumerian King List and some attestations from Ur as the first ruler of the First Dynasty of Ur), to king Gansud of Mari. The latter was probably Ansud, founder of the only Mari dynasty attested on the Sumerian King List, and contemporary to the First Dynasty of Ur. This Mari dynasty would then continue with kings attested both in their votive statues (found at Mari) and the Eblaite documentation. However, there are some discrepancies in the titles used by these kings. At Ebla, the king was an *en*, while a *lugal* was a high-ranking royal official, subordinate to the king, or a representative of the Eblaite king outside Ebla. On the contrary, following the Lower Mesopotamian tradition, the king of Mari was a *lugal*.

The Eblaite documentation reveals that Early Dynastic Mari reached its peak of influence on two occasions. The first one was with kings Iblul-Il and Enna-Dagan, who ruled over the whole Middle and Upper Euphrates region. A letter from Enna-Dagan reports a long list of his victories as well as the ones of his predecessors across the entire valley, from Emar to Hashuwa, and with Ebla in a tributary position (Text 7.1). The second moment of Mari supremacy (after a brief period in which Ebla held a hegemonic position in the area) brought to the destruction of Ebla itself. However, Mari would in turn be destroyed under Sargon of Akkad shortly after.

The conflict between Ebla and Mari was rooted in their respective position in the commercial network of the area. Mari was a crucial commercial junction between Lower Mesopotamia and Syria. Ebla controlled those territories that would have allowed the expansion of Mari's commercial network further west. Ebla's position prevented the rise of Mari as a political and economic power in western Syria. Mari was therefore significantly hindered by Ebla, a fact that may be reflected in its alternation of two strategies.

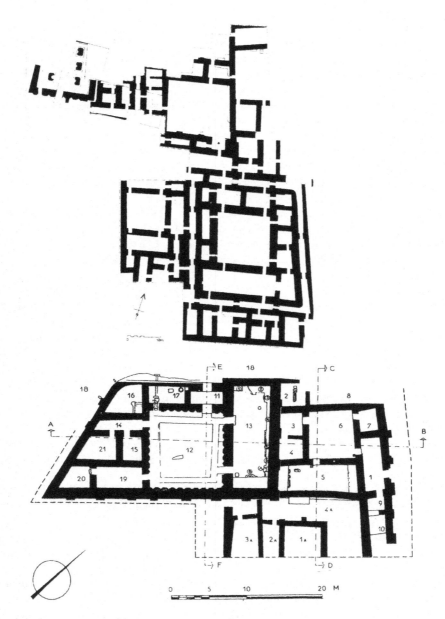

Figure 7.2 Presargonic Mari. *Above*: The palace; *Below*: The temple of Ishtarat and Ninni-Zaza.

The first one was a military strategy against Ebla, aimed at stopping its commercial supremacy in western Syria. The second one was a diplomatic one, aimed at exercising an influential position on the south-eastern trade routes. However, Ebla and Mari were not the only centres in the Upper Mesopotamian regional system: there were also Nagar (Tell Brak), located in the Khabur basin, Armi in the Upper Euphrates, and Kish, a hegemonic power in Middle Mesopotamia at the time. Ebla's alliance with Nagar and Kish against Mari and Armi at the time of the final conflict between the two cities clearly indicates this

---

Text 7.1   A political and military text from Ebla: the letter of Enna-Dagan, king of Mari, to the king of Ebla

'Thus (says) Enna-Dagan, ruler of Mari, to the ruler of Ebla. The cities Aburu and Ilgi, lands of Belan, Sa'umu the ruler of Mari defeated: tells and ruins in the mountains of Labanan he left.

The cities of Tibalat and Ilwani, Sa'umu the ruler of Mari defeated: in the mountain terrain of Angai he left tells and ruins.

The lands of Ra'ak and Nirum, Ashaldu and Badul, Sa'umu the ruler of Mari defeated, in the borders of [. . .], near Nahal, he left tells and ruins.

And the cities of Emar and Lalanium and the *ganum* of Ebla, Ishtup-shar, the king of Mari, defeated: in Emar and Lalanium he left tells and ruins.

And the city of Galalaneni [and the city of . . .] the liberated *ganum* of x (?), Iblul-Il, the ruler of Mari and Abarsal, defeated: in Zahiran he left also seven tells and ruins.

(Regarding) Iblul-Il, the ruler of Mari, Iblul-Il then defeated the city of Shadab, Addalini, and Arisum, in the land of Burman (of the land) of Sugurum and he left tells and ruins.

Then Iblul-il, the king of Mari, defeated the city of Sharan and Dammium: he left two tells and ruins.

Iblul-Il, the king of Mari, came out of the city of Nerat and the fortress (?) of Hazuwan and in the city of Mane received the tribute of Ebla; then he . . . Emar (and) left tells and ruins.

(Regarding) Iblul-Il, the king of Mari, he then defeated the cities of Nahal, Nubat, Shahab, of the land of Gasur (?): in (the land of) Ganane he left also seven tells and ruins.

(Regarding) Iblul-Il, the king of Mari, he defeated the city of Barama – for the second time (?) – Aburu and Tibalat, the lands of Belan: then Enna-Dagan, the king of Mari, left [tells and ruins].

He took (?) . . . the oil of the land. [. . .] Iblul-Il, the king of Mari [. . .].'

---

political and commercial situation (nearby cities being enemies of each other, and forming alliances with cities located around their enemies).

Sargon eventually destroyed 'Pre-Sargonic' Mari around ten years after Ebla's destruction and the end of its archives. With the rise of Naram-Sin, Mari experienced a dynasty of *šakkanakku*. These were rulers who were politically subordinated to the kings of Akkad, and then to the Neo-Sumerian kings of Ur. On an archaeological level, there was a visible decrease in monumental architecture compared to previous periods. Despite being aimed at gaining control on the commercial network of the area, the brutal intervention of Sargon of Akkad actually caused its crisis, allowing the rise of nomadic groups that would eventually bring the whole system to collapse.

2 The kingdom of Ebla: size and structure

Just like in Upper Mesopotamia, the second urbanisation peaked in Syria around the mid-third millennium BC. This period saw the rise of cities and villages across the entire semi-arid plain, as well as in the few irrigated areas and on the coast. This urban growth was already known through some excavations (from Amuq in the north, to Hama in the south, and the coastal centres of Ugarit and Byblos) and the discovery of several necropolises. However, the 'caliciform' ware found there led to the assumption of the existence of standardised palace workshops producing valuable pottery.

In this regard, excavations at Ebla have provided a more detailed picture of the culture and development of the area (Figure 7.3). The archaeological data from third millennium Ebla is quite limited (especially compared to the Middle Bronze Age data), but crucial. This is because the evidence mainly comes from a part of the royal palace (G) that had an Audience Court and administrative quarter (Figure 7.4). Among the many finds, the most important ones are the large archive storing several thousands of tablets, as well as the Rock Temple in the lower city. Despite the lack of private households, the texts and other finds from the palace provide a detailed picture of the cultural, political and economic (in particular, commercial) features of a Syrian state in the Early Dynastic period.

At the peak of its development, Ebla extended over more than 50 hectares (as did Mari and Ashur). The archival material reveals the sheer size and administrative complexity of the city, which must have developed over a relatively long period of time (in fact, under Palace G there are the remains of an earlier palace). Traces of the first urbanisation are not very visible in the area west of the Euphrates. This is because Proto-Syrian culture only took shape later, with a relatively modest Mesopotamian influence (writing aside) and entirely unique features. As shown by the thousands of personal names (not just from Ebla, but from a variety of other localities) found in the administrative texts, the local population was almost entirely Semitic. Both at Ebla and the majority of cities in contact with it, namely, central and western Syria and western Upper Mesopotamia, the population seems to have been relatively homogeneous. In fact, all the names attested are in the same language as the one used in the Eblaite sources.

This homogeneity was not due to Ebla's supremacy, but to the diffusion of this linguistic stratum, namely, 'Eblaite' (whose name is due to its attestation in the Ebla archives). The latter became the main spoken, administrative, and epistolary language of the Syrian and Upper Mesopotamian areas. The Eblaite linguistic stratum was also closely related to Hurrian along the foothills and to Old Akkadian in Central Mesopotamia. Internally, Syria experienced the rise of the Martu, a group bearing strong pastoral connotations, which would have a significant impact in the area in the following period.

Figure 7.3 Aerial view of Tell Mardikh, ancient Ebla (Courtesy: the Italian Archaeological Mission in Syria, Ebla).

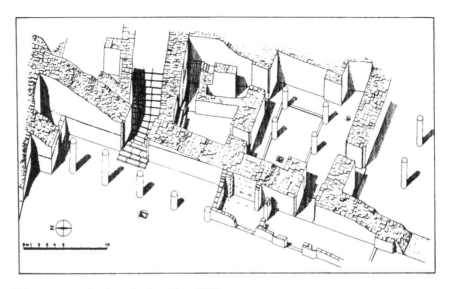

Figure 7.4 Ebla: axonometric view of palace G, ca. 2400 BC.

The kingdom of Ebla extended over a wide area, embracing a large section of northern Syria. The city was able to rely on the fields concentrated in the Matkh Valley and the lands in the surrounding plateau and hills, more suitable for farming, a limited amount of agriculture, and the cultivation of trees. In terms of demography, the data recovered from archival material is incompatible with the archaeological data. Ebla probably had around 15,000 or 20,000 inhabitants at most. The kingdom as a whole (with about a hundred villages with their own administrative functions) probably barely reached 100,000 people. However, the texts attest 11,700 employees working for the central administration, as well as a population of seasonal workers (presumably under *corvée*). The latter were divided into 16 'gates' (that is, districts), with 2,000 'houses' each, amounting to a total of between 130,000 and 150,000 people. Considering the fact that even the number of animals and metals recorded seem extremely high, it may be necessary to examine the way in which the administration determined these numbers.

The kingdom did not reach the Mediterranean coast, ruled by several independent kingdoms such as Byblos, which must have been the most influential one. Similarly, the Eblaite kingdom did not control the Euphrates Valley, where there were several autonomous states, from Carchemish to Emar, Tuttul and Mari. In the south, Ebla did not extend beyond Hama, and bordered with the kingdom of Ibal (near Qatna). Even in the north, the kingdom did not extend beyond Aleppo, where there were other independent states.

Therefore, the kingdom of Ebla was more a large state than a regional one. However, its territory was larger than the one of contemporary Mesopotamian states and with a population of a similar size. However, the lower density of population effectively compensated for the larger size of the Eblaite kingdom. Ebla was a hegemonic centre in the area, and it controlled several of the surrounding states, both politically and economically. Nevertheless, the supremacy of Ebla in the area experienced several fluctuations. At the peak of its expansion, Ebla controlled the Euphrates Valley (from Carchemish to Emar), the Balikh Valley (with the Harran and Irrite kingdoms), and the Taurus foothills (with the Urshum and Hashshum kingdoms, near Gaziantep). The wider commercial network controlled by Ebla will be considered later on, but it reached far beyond the direct political control of the kingdom.

The political structure of the kingdom was also different from the Mesopotamian model, due to the kin-based structure of its society. In fact, since that first urbanisation centred on the rise of temple

121

complexes did not leave a strong mark in Syria, temples did not have the influential political and economic role they had in Mesopotamia (nor would they ever have such a role throughout the Bronze Age or later on). Even the role of cities as promoters of agricultural colonisation, which in Mesopotamia was linked to irrigation and the centralised accumulation of harvests, never appeared in Syria. Consequently, political control seems to have been less centralised, promoting the development of many centres, as well as an agro-pastoral kind of society with a strong kin-based structure (though different from the Mesopotamian one). These aspects would characterise the area for at least two millennia.

Naturally, there was a king, whose title was written with the Sumerogram for 'lord', *en*, read in Eblaite as *malikum* ('king' in Western Semitic), and a queen (*maliktum*). The latter kept her role (as mother of the king) even after her husband's death, and had an important cultic role. After their death, kings were celebrated in funerary cults, and their images and descendancy were preserved. Kings were supported by a group of elders (*abba*), clearly representing the most powerful families in the city. The elders resided in the palace as important guests of the king, and were allotted rations and provisions. Their role was strictly political, but they acted more like an assembly, rather than a set of functionaries supervising certain tasks or administrative sectors.

Alongside the king and the elders, there was another institution, fully administrative in character, headed by a vizier. The latter probably held the title of 'head of the administration' (*lugal sa-za*). The vizier had a very important role, so much so that in the earliest studies on Ebla these men were thought to have been kings (the actual kings rarely appear in the administrative texts). The viziers were in charge of the kingdom's administration, trade, and the army in case of war. The supervisors and governors of smaller cities all held the title of *lugal*, placing them at the same level as the elders and the representatives of the Eblaite kingdom in distant commercial centres or in other kingdoms. These governors were all under the vizier's rule (there were 14 districts, 12 in the kingdom and two at Ebla).

Based on the redistribution of food, the king (as well as the queen), the vizier and the elders seem to have resided in the palace. Therefore, the palace became the home of a series of assembly-type groups. This fact was a reflection of the former decentralisation of power in Syria, as well as its structure as a conglomeration of different settlements. The latter were united under a main city, which was still central, but had to constantly take into account this composite structure. Consequently, the nature of the relation between the elders, the districts and the kin-based structure of the kingdom remains difficult to define. The term 'elders' itself, however, indicates a social structure still centred on the supremacy of powerful families.

3 The kingdom of Ebla: political agenda and war

The archive from Ebla's Palace G covers around 50 years of history and terminates ca. ten years before Sargon's destruction of Mari (ca. 1350 BC). The royal dynasty of Ebla includes the two short reigns of Igrish-Halab and Irkab-Damu, and the long reign (ca. 30 years) of Ishar-Damu. Previous rulers are attested in a list regarding the cult of around ten ancestral rulers, covering a period of roughly a century, thus covering the whole of the Early Dynastic IIIb. Another list mentions further 26 kings, although it is not entirely reliable.

Alongside the last kings of Ebla, the archive records a sequence of viziers. At the time of Igrish-Halab, the office was probably not yet established, but a couple of individuals (Darmiya and Tir) emerged as the most influential in the Eblaite administration. Arrukum was a vizier under Irkab-Damu, while during the reign of Ishar-Damu, Ibrium stayed in office for around 20 years. His son Ibbi-Zikir and grandson Dubbuhu-Adda succeeded him. However, Ibrium remained the most influential figure in this period for his reforms and the establishment of his own dynasty parallel to the royal family of Ebla.

Despite the lack of 'historical' sources (celebratory or narrative), the administrative records provide a considerable amount of information on Ebla's commercial and military activities. The evidence indicates that initially Ebla was under the supremacy of Mari. In fact, following the victorious campaigns of Iblul-Il, the king gained control over the Euphrates Valley and Ebla itself, which had to pay substantial tributes. The situation dramatically changed under Ibrium. He led several campaigns against rebellious vassal-rulers, and more demanding campaigns against Abarsal (at the time of Arrukum), Halsum, Kakmium, and the powerful Armi (on the Upper Euphrates).

Apart from continuing campaigns in the north, Ibrium's son and successor Ibbi-Zikir led some military expeditions to the south (against Ibal). He also fought against Mari through an alliance with Nagar and Kish (which sent their own military contingencies). The war ended with a battle near Terqa, where Mari was defeated and its supremacy removed. Alongside the military and territorial expansion of Ebla, Ibrium and Ibbi-Zikir also increased the kingdom's commercial activities, with a ten-fold increase in investments compared to previous periods. The Eblaite kings expanded their policy of inter-dynastic marriages, first with allies and vassals, and then with the great powers of Nagar and Kish (but never with Mari and Armi).

Having defeated Mari, Ebla never sought to destroy it, and preferred to seal an alliance. This decision was possibly made for commercial reasons, since Ebla was not able to control commercial relations with the east on its own. Moreover, Mari was in a crucial position to control Kish, whose rise under Sargon initiated that expansionistic policy which would characterise the dynasty of Akkad. However, due to a series of events unknown to us, Mari managed to recover from the defeat and to attack Ebla, conquering it and sacking its palace.

This is the most probable hypothesis for the destruction of Ebla. Another suggestion is that Sargon destroyed Ebla, but this seems less plausible. First of all, Sargon himself, celebrating his conquests in the Middle Euphrates, declared that he stopped at Tuttul, while the god Dagan granted him access to the west (Ebla above all). Therefore, Sargon only gained access to the commercial networks of the west. After all, the destruction of a wealthy city such as Ebla would have been celebrated in an entirely different way. Moreover, when, a couple of decades later, Naram-Sin declared his destruction of Ebla (evidently the city that was rebuilt after the time of the Palace G archives), he would state that the achievement was unprecedented, something that he could not have said if Sargon had destroyed the city first. Finally, we know that Sargon conquered and destroyed Mari only a decade after the fall of Ebla, making its destruction militarily impossible with a still powerful Mari in the way.

Be that as it may, after the destruction of the Ebla of Palace G, the city and its entire territory experienced a period of crisis. Therefore, the final phase of the Early Bronze Age (IV, that is, 2300–2000 BC), between the destruction of the palace and the arrival of the Amorites, is relatively unknown. However, following the splendour and power of the Ebla of Palace G and its commercial network, changes in the architecture and organisation of the settlement indicate a visible recession.

4 The economy of Ebla

Unlike other states of the period, at Ebla the redistributive system worked in a slightly different way. It was more ceremonial and personal. The palace provided food rations to a large number (ca. 800 people as well as the king, the royal family and the elders) of *guruš*, 'male attendants', and *dam*, 'female attendants' (responsible for domestic work: cereal grinding, weaving and cooking). Moreover, there were groups of people who received rations without being permanent workers of the palace. For instance, there were the 'villages' (*é-duru* ki), which were teams of workers of 10 to 20 people (supervised by an official) recruited from the villages of the kingdom. The size of this redistributive system based on the direct provision of rations can be estimated through the annual record of cereals reaching the palace. However, sometimes these totals included more than one year. Among the numbers found, the estimate of 90,000 people contributing to this system seems excessive, whereas the 40,000 estimate seems more plausible.

A particular aspect of the Eblaite system is its connection with religious festivals, which became important occasions for the distribution of food to the wider population, and not just the palace attendants and seasonal workers. If in Syria temples were not meant for the accumulation of surplus, they were places for ceremonial redistribution and periodic fairs. Another aspect of the redistributive system was gift-exchange, which further underlines the personal and ceremonial aspects of the transfer of goods in Eblaite economy. However, the system never evolved from the distribution of rations to the allotment of lands (which in Mesopotamia is linked to the development of temple complexes). At Ebla, land allotments were given as a personal gift from the king and remained rather limited, just like the amount of land belonging to the palace. Therefore, lands mainly remained in the hands of villages, which paid a fixed quota to the Eblaite administration.

The base of Eblaite economy was mainly agro-pastoral. Its difference from Mesopotamian economy was largely due to their respective environments. Agriculture in Syria could only rely on rainfall and a few fertile patches available in the area. The yields, which can be deduced comparing the quantity of seeds sown and harvests, were between 1 to 3 and 1 to 5. These are normal rates for this type of agriculture, but still far from the Lower Mesopotamian yields. Due to the fluctuations in rainfall from year to year, the accumulation of surplus to sustain the palace was therefore more difficult and unpredictable. In order to integrate the cultivation of grains and use the lands on the hills, cultivations of typically Mediterranean plants such as vine and olive-trees, as well as several fruit trees, were quite widespread. This separated the Syrian diet from the Mesopotamian one (wine instead of beer, olive oil instead of sesame oil).

The palace managed the large scale farming of sheep and goats. While sheep's wool was used in textile production, stimulating the textile trade, goats were used in agricultural activities (Figure 7.5). Livestock was mainly owned by the *en*, the elders, and other public institutions, as well as the villages. A part of the livestock was directly sent to the central authorities, mainly on the occasion of festivals. The latter required more provisions than the usual distribution of rations (mostly grains). The total number of sheep, goats and cattle farmed is difficult to calculate. Some estimates that have been suggested in the past are physically impossible (400,000 cows and 2,500,000 sheep and goats), since they are similar to the number of livestock of modern Syria. More reasonable estimates still show the presence of a considerable amount of livestock: 9,000 cows and 140,000 sheep and goats.

If agro-pastoral production ensured the survival of the kingdom, the real wealth of Ebla was mainly derived from craftsmanship and trade. The artefacts recovered in Palace G attest to the high quality of craftsmanship in the city: from woodcarvings to inlaid objects, statuettes, ornaments, metal objects and so on. The textual evidence adds detailed information about technical processes (for instant metal alloys), types of products (especially clothes, categorised by shape and quality), and numbers of workers employed. The large number of female servants employed for processing grains and weaving was similar to that of the rest of the Near East. On the contrary, the large number of woodworkers (between 140 and 260) and metalworkers (between 460 and 600) attested is rather extraordinary. Trade remains the best-attested sector of Eblaite economy. This is partially due to the kinds of texts kept in the Palace G archive (other archives might have kept other kinds of sources). The latter was mainly concerned with trade, rather than the management of agro-pastoral activities. Despite this bias in the evidence, trade seems to have held a crucial role at Ebla, as indicated by the particular development of the palace and the spread of Eblaite presence outside its boundaries. Trade had formed a *bona fide* commercial network, with fixed commercial junctions in the cities located along the trade routes. Each of them had a *karum*, a 'port' (namely, a commercial centre), headed by an Eblaite representative (*lugal*) and with a financial and legal organisation meant to support trading activities. Ebla's commercial network was certainly not the only one of the period. There were the ones attested in nearby Abarsal, as well as other similar networks controlled by Ashur in Anatolia, Susa in Iran, and Dilmun around the Persian Gulf.

Relations between commercial networks were difficult to maintain, since each network was striving to grow at the expense of the others, and more than one centre was competing for the control of the same network. The first case is attested in the above-mentioned treaty between Ebla and Abarsal. This treaty lists the *karū* controlled by the Eblaite king, and regulated the way in which merchants from Abarsal were to take advantage of the Eblaite *karū*. There must have been a version of the treaty listing the *karū* belonging

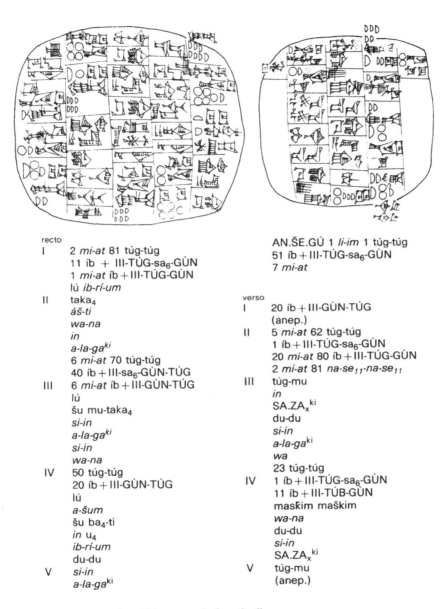

recto

I   2 *mi-at* 81 túg-túg
    11 íb + III-TÚG-sa₆-GÙN
    1 *mi-at* íb+III-TÚG-GÙN
    lú *ib-rí-um*

II   taka₄
    áš-ti
    wa-na
    in
    *a-la-ga*ᵏⁱ
    6 *mi-at* 70 túg-túg
    40 íb+III-sa₆-GÙN-TÚG

III 6 *mi-at* íb+III-GÙN-TÚG
    lú
    šu mu-taka₄
    si-in
    *a-la-ga*ᵏⁱ
    si-in
    wa-na

IV 50 túg-túg
    20 íb+III-GÙN-TÚG
    lú
    a-šum
    šu ba₄-ti
    in u₄
    ib-rí-um
    du-du

V   *si-in*
    *a-la-ga*ᵏⁱ

AN.ŠE.GÚ 1 *li-im* 1 túg-túg
51 íb+III-TÚG-sa₆-GÙN
7 *mi-at*

verso

I   20 íb+III-GÙN-TÚG
    (anep.)

II   5 *mi-at* 62 túg-túg
    1 íb+III-TÚG-sa₆-GÙN
    20 *mi-at* 80 íb+III-TÚG-GÙN
    2 *mi-at* 81 *na-se₁₁-na-se₁₁*

III túg-mu
    in
    SA.ZAₓᵏⁱ
    du-du
    si-in
    *a-la-ga*ᵏⁱ
    wa
    23 túg-túg

IV 1 íb+III-TÚG-sa₆-GÙN
    11 íb+III-TÚB-GÙN
    maškim maškim
    wa-na
    du-du
    si-in
    SA.ZAₓᵏⁱ

V   túg-mu
    (anep.)

Figure 7.5 Administrative texts from Ebla: a record of textile allotments.
Recto '[I] 281 garments, 11 high quality coloured belts, 100 coloured belts: what Ibrium [II] has received from Wana in the locality of Alaga. 670 garments, 40 high quality coloured belts, [III] 600 coloured belts: what has been given in return to the locality of Alaga and to Wana. [IV] 50 garments, 20 coloured belts: what Ashum received when Ibrium went [V] to Alaga. Total: 1001 garments, 51 high quality coloured belts, *Verso* [I] 720 coloured belts. [II] 562 garments, 1 high quality coloured belt, 280 coloured belts for 281 persons: [III] textile allotment (made) in the Treasury (of Ebla) for those who went to Alaga. [IV] Moreover, 23 garments, 1 high quality coloured belt, 11 coloured belts have received as textile allotments the representatives of Wana who went to the Treasury (of Ebla).'

to the king of Abarsal, and the specific clauses for Eblaite merchants using these *karū*. The second case, the one leading to conflicts over the same network, is the one of Ebla and Mari.

Trade was mainly centred on the exchange of textiles and metals. However, the available sources only inform us on the products exported, leaving a substantial gap on the types of products brought to Ebla. Since the area was not rich in minerals, metals must have been both imported and exported. The approach implemented by trade administrators was certainly aimed at making a profit and re-investing it. This approach was therefore very different to the one found in Mesopotamia, aimed at the acquisition of those materials that could not be found in the area. This divergence can be explained. Ebla and other centres located around Mesopotamia monitored the export of processed products and the import of raw materials. They therefore were crucial commercial junctions between Mesopotamia and its periphery. They could count on a wide range of resources and were not cut off from access to raw materials. Consequently, the problem of the acquisition of materials was not as pressing as in Mesopotamia, making the management and control of commercial networks a profitable activity. Certain metals (mainly gold and silver) were used to calculate values and for the accumulation of wealth, while copper and tin were used in the local bronze production.

Even though the palace looked after the commercial network and convoys, and coordinated the commodities brought to Ebla both through official and private agents, trade was not exactly a 'state' activity. In fact, the king, vizier and 'governors' all contributed to the accumulation of commodities alongside private individuals. The commodities (*mu*-DU) given to the convoys departing from Ebla (which were not 'taxes' that the king was, rather absurdly, paying to himself, as previously suggested) were recorded and channelled into the commercial network. They were expected to return with a profit (or a set of goods acquired) to be distributed among its investors.

The texts mainly inform us on the northern (Syrian) and western (Mesopotamian) side of the commercial network (within a radius of 200–250 km), where Eblaite goods (fabrics, clothes and bronze objects) could be sold more profitably, and raw materials (Anatolian metals) were easier to obtain. However, it is clear that the network reached much further than that, as far as Egypt. The latter sent a set of vases with the cartouches of Khefren (ca. 2590–2570 BC), proving that they were kept at Ebla as antique relics) and Pepi I (ca. 2450–2400 BC) as gifts. The network even reached Afghanistan, the main provider of large quantities of lapis lazuli (perhaps after several intermediary commercial exchanges) shaped into small semi-worked blocks.

Eblaite trade with Mesopotamia constituted a considerable problem, due to the presence of two obstacles. The first one was Mari, which controlled the transit over the Middle Euphrates Valley. If we picture the commercial network in the area as shaped like a funnel, Ebla was located at the wider end, while Mari was at the centre of the narrow end. Therefore, Ebla controlled the wider network, but Mari held a key position in allowing the transition of goods to Mesopotamia. This situation naturally caused difficult relations between the two cities, which fluctuated between treaties and conflicts, as mentioned above.

The second obstacle was constituted by Kish throughout the Pre-Sargonic period, and then Akkad from Sargon's reign onwards. Despite the continuity from the supremacy of Kish to the one of Akkad (Sargon continued to call himself 'king of Kish'), considerable changes took place on a political level. The kings of Kish had accepted being one of the many centres contributing to the wider commercial network in the region. On the contrary, the kings of Akkad pursued a far more aggressive strategy. This strategy was first focused on the intermediary areas (Ur on one side and Mari on the other), and then moved on to the main commercial centres located further away (Elam on one side and Ebla on the other).

5 The rise of Proto-Syrian culture

The open character of Eblaite society, less centred on the great organisations (the temple and the palace) than its Mesopotamian contemporaries, and closer to its kin-based structure, is also visible in its architecture, at least judging from its palace. The type of Mesopotamian palace found at Eridu, Kish and Mari was like a fortress. It had narrow entrances and limited access from the outside, and open courtyards inside. On the contrary, the Eblaite palace was designed around its courtyard, the so-called 'Audience Court'. On one side, this courtyard opened up towards the city, and on the other, it provided access to the inside of the palace. This open architecture was both ceremonial, as indicated by the set of stairs reserved for the king's descent towards the external throne, and functional, since the commercial archives were located between the courtyard and the administrative quarter.

Therefore, despite having evolved from an earlier Mesopotamian model in terms of function and architecture, the Eblaite palace was innovative in terms of layout and ideology. This emphasises the more approachable nature of the Eblaite administration. Temple architecture is not well attested for this period, and some information can be gathered from sources describing rituals as well as later architectural developments. It is probable that there were many temples, as many as the deities worshipped in the state cult. However, they were relatively small in size. Therefore, they seem to have been devoid of those economic and administrative structures (storehouses and workshops) that made Mesopotamian temples stand out (also in terms of size and height) as political and economic centres. For instance, the Rock Temple at Ebla was a monumental and visible construction, but lacked those economic buildings characteristic of Mesopotamian temples.

Syrian temples simply were the gods' houses and the focal point of a type of cult that was mainly pursued outdoors. Sacrifices and festivals were not private cults managed by priests, but important redistributive occasions involving the population as a whole. Among the many deities worshipped at Ebla, the most important one for the city and its royal family was the god Kura, a deity exclusively attested in Ebla. He received more offerings than any other deity and his temple was located on the highest point of the city, where royal rituals and important political oaths were performed. Ebla also worshipped popular gods such as Dagan (a typical deity in the Middle Euphrates region), Ishtar/Ishara, Adad (main deity of Aleppo), Shamash, Rashap and Kamish. Other deities were more typical of Eblaite religion, such as the enigmatic Nidabal, who would eventually disappear. Each of these gods had its own temple and cult statue, and regularly received offerings and votive statues. Among the many rituals attested in Ebla, the most important one for the official cult was the enthronement or marriage ritual (attested in many versions, one for each king). This ritual required the king and queen to travel to the shrines of the kingdom.

While Eblaite cults were predominantly local in character, its scribal culture displays a marked Mesopotamian influence. This must have been an obvious consequence of the use of cuneiform writing, with its Sumerian syllabary and logography. Eblaite writing was similar to the cuneiform of the Early Dynastic IIIa period (attested in Fara and Abu Salabih), also found in Pre-Sargonic Mari. This indicates that writing had been in use at Ebla before the construction of Palace G (whose preceding version has only been detected through surveys), possibly in connection with the rise of the Eblaite dynasty (ca. 2500 bc). The Mesopotamian origin of the script was still considered a vital aspect, leading to the training of young scribes at Mari with teachers coming from Kish. Ebla was part of the scribal tradition coming from Central Mesopotamia. This is the tradition defined by Ignace Jay Gelb as the 'Kish tradition', which used the Sumerian system to express the local language.

Scribal training and the need to adapt it to the local languages led to the appearance of lexical texts. These ranged from sign-lists and word-lists (of birds, fish, professions, as well as toponyms), also found in Fara and Abu Salabih, to bilingual lists. The latter were an Eblaite innovation, listing an ideogram with its Sumerian and Eblaite reading (Text 7.2). Due to the standardisation of scribal resources and their transmission through time, the lexical lists of Ebla belong to a tradition dating back to the Late Uruk period. However, these texts had to respond to new needs. Apart from a wider linguistic variety, there was the need to record various systems of numeration and measurement. In fact, Sumerian ideograms could often be used to indicate very different local systems of measurement, making the conversion of an Eblaite measurement into the Mesopotamian system rather inaccurate. Therefore, it was necessary to assign a set of signs to the local systems of measurement, thus separating signifier from signified.

Text 7.2 **Bilingual vocabularies (Sumerian–Eblaite) from Ebla; some exemplary entries, in alphabetical order**

Text		Interpretation	
Sumerian	Eblaite	Reconstruction	Meaning
á-zi	a-me-núm	yaminum	'right'
	a-me-tum	yammittum	»
	ì-me-tum	yimmittum	
baḫar	wa-zi-lu-um	wāṣirum	'potter'
bar-ús	ù-tum	'udum	'stick'
DI	a-a-ga-túm	halāktum	'journey'
	'aₓ-ga-du-um	»	»
	a-la-ag-tum	»	»
eme-bal	a-ba-lu-um	'appālum	'interpreter'
	a-bí-lu-um	'āpilum	»
gaba-ru	ma-ḫa-lu-um	maḫārum	'to receive'
	ma-ḫa-lum	»	
maḫ-muš	ba-ša-mu-um	baṭmum	'snake'
nam-ra-ag	ša-la-tum	ṭallatum	'booty'
ninda-ad₆	'à-mi-zu-um	hamisum	'sour bread'
	'à-mi-zu	»	»
	'à-me-zu	»	»
nin-nì	a-ḫa-tum	'aḫatum	'sister'
nìn-péš	ba-ra-tum	pa'ratum	'mouse'
nì-du₁₀	du-bù-a-tum	ṭūbuwatum	'kindness'
	du-bù-a(?)-túm	»	»
še-àr-àr	da-'à-nu-um	ṭaḫanum	'to grind'
	da-'à-núm	»	»
šeš-mu	a-ḫu-um	'aḫum	'brother'
šu-kus	ba-da-gi i-tim	badāgu yidim	'to cut by hand'
	bí-da-gi i-tim	»	»
tiₘ-mušen	a-bar-tum	'abartum	'eagle'
uru-bar	ì-rí-a-tum	'īriyatum	'outside the city'

Apart from lexical texts, there were divination texts of Mesopotamian origin, and literary texts, also after a Mesopotamian model, but re-elaborated to accommodate local cosmologies and myths. However, writing remained a crucial aspect of the administration, requiring scribes to develop more efficient and clearer ways to record information. In this regard, the Eblaite archive constitutes an important step. It shows a clear desire to store tablets (placed on shelves along the walls, carried in baskets or on trays), to establish clear and consistent types of texts, and to develop a clear way to keep track of accounting records, especially those covering one or more years (Figure 7.6).

However, it has to be said that not everything was yet clear and established. After all, the development of defined and unambiguous types of documents would be the result of later improvements. Nonetheless, Ebla was already on the right path, but its documentation did not manage to reach the exemplary clarity

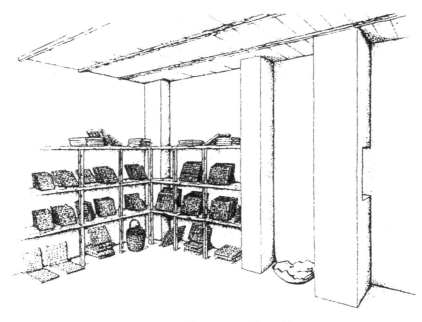

Figure 7.6   Ebla, palace G: reconstruction of one of the rooms of the archive.

that would arise in the Neo-Sumerian period. For instance, in terms of dating systems, the correctness of the calculations, the clarity of the recorded actions, their aim, and the use of a technical terminology only appear through the analysis of several texts. However, these aspects should have been clear after the analysis of only one text, yet they are not.

Even in terms of iconography, Ebla owes greatly to Mesopotamia, and its wealth and refinement was equal to the most important Sumerian centres. Despite having been sacked once it was destroyed, the palace's remains still give us an idea of Ebla's wealth. For instance, there were small sculptures made from a combination of precious materials, from gold to black stone and lapis lazuli. Large sculptures have not been found, probably due to the desire of Eblaite rulers to avoid obvious forms of self-celebration. In terms of material culture, the shell or stone inlays follow Mesopotamian examples, while woodcarvings were typically Syrian and were the forerunners of ivory carvings. Seals were generally similar to the ones of the Early Dynastic II–III, but were filled with local mythological and iconographic motifs (Figure 7.7). Therefore, the city experienced a vivacious intellectual and technical development. This would form the basis for high-quality Syrian craftsmanship, thanks to the use of precious materials from distant lands and earlier Mesopotamian models. Even pottery combined two of the typical features of palace workshops, namely, elegance and standardisation.

6   The second urbanisation in Lebanon and Palestine

As mentioned earlier, the first urbanisation had barely influenced the Palestinian area, but with some iconographic elements even reaching Egypt, although perhaps for other reasons. By the end of the Chalcolithic period, the region only experienced few attempts at urbanisation (such as the one at Jawa). However, these attempts were strategically different from the ones attested in Mesopotamia. Only in the third millennium BC, starting from the Early Bronze Age I and II and peaking in the Early Bronze Age III (thus at the same time as Ebla), had urbanisation begun to have a visible impact on the Syro-Lebanese coast and in Palestine.

Figure 7.7   Ebla: seal impressions from the time of palace G.

This development spread from the north to the south, from the coast and the fertile valleys to the plateaus and hills, from the areas with a more favourable climate to the drier ones (which nonetheless were involved in this process).

For Palestine, the Early Bronze Age III was a phase of growth both in terms of settlements and population. The north–south direction of this process has led us to believe that this growth was due to the immigration of people from the north. However, this idea cannot be substantiated. It is true that there are distinct northern elements in the material culture of the period, such as the Khirbet Kerak pottery, originally from Transcaucasia. However, these northern elements are only one aspect of the gradual development of the area. The demographic, technological and organisational growth of the area was certainly modelled on northern examples, but had to rely on the local availability of people and resources. Just like in Syria, settlements became part of a hierarchic network featuring major centres and villages. From a socio-economic and political perspective, these settlements maintained a tribal structure. Due to the difficult climate, agricultural yields were not high, leading to a diversification of agro-pastoral activities. There were some raw materials available in the region: cedar from Lebanon, copper deposits from Arabah, and semiprecious stones, such as turquoise and carnelian, from Sinai.

The coastal area experienced the rise of important centres (possibly Ugarit), destined to play a major role in the region. One of them was certainly Byblos, whose temples, metal furnishings, votive statues and imported Egyptian artefacts indicate its significant growth and its vast interregional network. Palestine also had important centres, such as Bet Yerah (Khirbet Kerak) near Lake Tiberias, and Megiddo, in the irrigated plains. Other settlements were in fertile oases, such as Jericho, or on the hills, as in the case of Ai and Tell Far'ah. Moreover, the Early Bronze Age III also allowed the development of centres in the far south, such as Tell Areini and Tell Arad in the Negev.

These settlements were fortified, indicating that they were in competition with each other over the control of fertile lands, resources, and trade routes (Figure 7.8). The cities were also smaller than their north Syrian and Upper Mesopotamian counterparts, probably due to the more limited availability of

Figure 7.8 The Early Bronze Age in Palestine: Tell Arad, Area K with its fortification walls.

food. There were public buildings, such as the palace of Megiddo, or the storehouse of Khirbet Kerak. Moreover, these cities had temples, such as the complex Reshef Temple in Byblos. However, temples were generally small, one-roomed structures, with only the essential equipment for cultic activities and no political or economic function.

We do not know which cities held a hegemonic position in the various areas and periods. The Ebla tablets, as well as some Egyptian sources from the Old Kingdom, briefly inform us on the wider contacts of this region. In the north, the area south of the Byblos–Hama axis seems to have been outside the commercial network attested in the Eblaite sources. On the contrary, there seems to have been considerable political and commercial interactions with Egypt, which was beginning to have a significant influence on Palestine.

The Eblaite and Egyptian networks were naturally in contact, as attested by the vases bearing the cartouches of the Egyptian rulers of the fourth and sixth dynasty, generally found at Byblos. As mentioned above, these vases were also found at Ebla, possibly indicating that Byblos must have had an intermediary role between Egypt and Ebla. Since these objects were personalised royal gifts, it cannot be excluded that they were meant for prestigious rulers governing further away. Alternatively, it might have been customary to re-donate these prestigious (and 'named') gifts to third parties living elsewhere. Similarly, the lapis lazuli found in Egypt in the Old Kingdom must have arrived via the Ebla–Byblos–Palestine route, while the gold found at Ebla must have come from Egypt (specifically, Upper Egypt and Nubia). These were all highly prestigious materials, primarily exchanged between rulers.

However, the Egyptian interest in the Levant was chiefly motivated by more practical needs, namely, timber and resins from Lebanon, copper from Arabah, turquoise and carnelian from Sinai, and olive oil and wine. In case of the latter, typically Palestinian wine and oil jars have been found in several Old Kingdom necropolises (Figure 7.9). The Egyptians probably did not necessarily gain access to these resources through trade. First, they could have agreed with the local elite to exchange prestigious objects (both in terms of materials used, and in terms of value, such as magical scarabs), reserved for the local rulers, in exchange for access to Levantine resources. Second, they could have accessed these resources through military interventions, if necessary.

However, Egyptian military interventions in Sinai and Palestine were often aimed at dealing with the incursions of nomadic tribes, defined either with specific names (Shasu or 'Amu) or more general ones (the

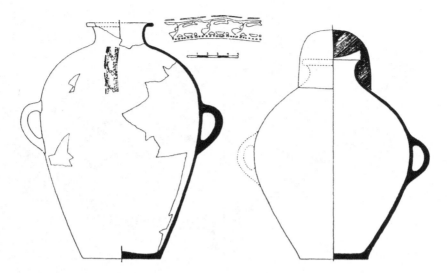

Figure 7.9 The Early Bronze Age in Palestine: Palestinian jars exported to Egypt (Giza necropolis).

'savages' or 'sand-farers'). These people were seen as a cause of turbulence in the activities and interactions of the organised states, due to their mobility, aggressiveness and cultural difference. Nonetheless, Egyptian military campaigns at times targeted urbanised and cultivated areas. For instance, the campaign described in the tomb inscription of Weni took place along the coast, while a relief from Deshasha depicts the siege of a fortified Palestinian city. These were rare cases, since the Egyptian interest in the area was not yet expansionistic, but mainly commercial. Therefore, convoys sent to Palestine, Nubia, or the Wadi Hammamat were meant to access local resources, rather than establishing direct control over these areas. Through the alternation of military interventions with gift-exchange, Egypt established enough control over the area to encourage the local elite to maintain contacts.

Egyptian military interventions in the Levant were much less aggressive than the Akkadian ones from the north, and had no long-term repercussions. The crisis of the Early Bronze Age settlements in Palestine happened more for internal reasons. Their collapse was the result of an excessive exploitation of the natural and technical resources of the period, distributed among too many inhabitants for the available resources. The western corner of the Fertile Crescent was the area most exposed to crisis. Later on, the nomadic people of the area would eventually cause, and take advantage of, the collapse of the Palestinian urban settlements of the intermediate phase between the Early and Middle Bronze Age. Over a couple of centuries urbanisation had caused an unprecedented growth in the area, maybe too much to last. Therefore, this growth drastically diminished for a brief period, only to increase again shortly afterwards.

8

THE AKKADIAN EMPIRE

1 The idea of a 'universal empire'

Sargon, king of Akkad, was a newcomer in the political scene of Mesopotamia. Later accounts would narrate the legends surrounding his obscure and unusual birth, his career as cupbearer of Ur-Zababa, king of Kish, and his rise to power as ruler of the newly founded city of Akkad. Even in his own inscriptions, the complete silence on his predecessors was compensated with statements regarding his personal achievements. The rise of a newcomer from the north facilitated the emergence of a new ideology of kingship, changing the image of the king from that of a cultic and administrative official to that of a war hero. Considerable changes also appeared in the realm of political and military interventions (with an empire that actually managed to reach the Lower and the Upper Sea), and in the rise of Semitic elements alongside Sumerian ones. However, these innovations did not appear all of a sudden. The Akkadian idea of a 'universal empire' included elements that had already appeared in the Proto-Imperial period. Even the commercial networks of the period followed the routes established during the proto-urban and Early Dynastic phases.

Only a few of the royal inscriptions of Sargon and his successors have survived in their original version. More often than not, we possess Old Babylonian copies (from Nippur and Ur) written as a palaeographic and historiographical exercise. These texts reproduced the inscriptions left in the Ekur, the sanctuary of Enlil at Nippur. These were inscribed on votive monuments that still survived half a millennium after the fall of the dynasty of Akkad and were left there for another 500 years. Through these sources, it becomes possible to reconstruct the formation of this empire and to examine the degree of reliability or exaggeration of later legendary accounts of this dynasty.

When Sargon dedicated his first monuments in the Ekur, he did not describe the story of his rise to power. He was already 'king of Kish', a city that he considered his capital, and did not yet use the title of 'king of Akkad'. Sargon's great expedition in the south, reaching as far as the Persian Gulf, constitutes the first phase of the empire's expansion. During that campaign, he defeated Lugalzaggesi, king of Uruk and the other *ensi* ruling the cities of Sumer (Ur, E-ninmar and Umma). In his inscriptions, Sargon claimed that he had won thirty-four battles, subdued fifty *ensi* and washed his bloodied weapons, which now had to be repaired, in the Lower Sea. At the end of this initial phase (Figure 8.1), he already proclaimed that his rule extended from the Lower to the Upper Sea. However, the king admitted that the Akkadians only held control (that is, the *ensi* office) in the area around the Lower Sea, while Elam and Mari remained independent. Kish, which was restored and became the centre of the empire, and Nippur, which received the dedication of celebratory monuments (in exchange for its support of this new dynasty), were the only two cities to receive privileged treatment.

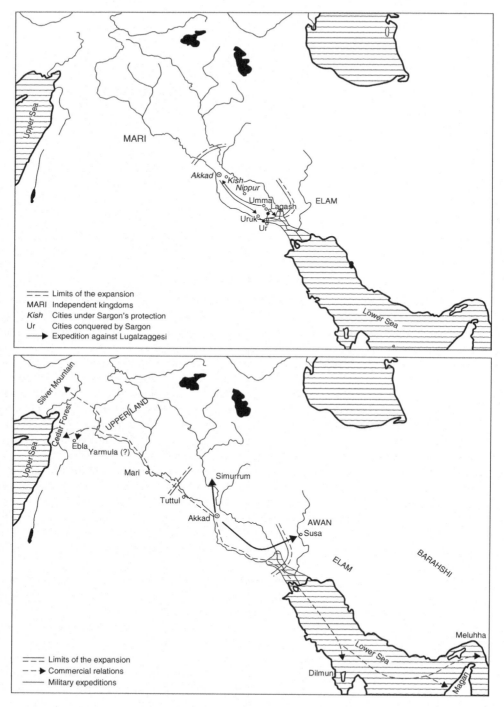

Figure 8.1 The size of the Akkadian empire under Sargon in the first phase (*above*), and the second phase (*below*).

The second phase of the empire's formation was more focused on the re-organisation of commercial routes reaching outside Mesopotamia, rather than on military campaigns. Beyond the Euphrates delta, in the Lower Sea, Dilmun (Bahrain), Magan (Oman) and Meluhha (Indus Valley) were sending their ships and their products to the river port of Akkad. Further north along the Euphrates, Sargon had to stop at Tuttul. Only the god Dagan would grant him access to resources from Mari, Yarmuta, Ebla and the Upper Euphrates region, including the 'cedar wood' and the 'mountains of silver' (the names conveniently given to the Amanus and Taurus regions). Sargon was therefore quite honest, stating that he controlled the area from Tuttul to the Persian Gulf, while his commercial network stretched from the Mediterranean to Magan and Meluhha.

The third phase of the empire's formation laid the groundwork for his successors. Sargon fought Elam and Barahshi, but they still managed to remain independent. The Akkadian expansion inevitably had to collide with Elam and its Awan dynasty. The latter ruled over an aggregation of smaller settlements spread across the Iranian plateau. In terms of size, demography and productivity, Elam was a worthy rival of the Akkadian empire. For now, despite Sargon's victorious expedition against Elam, the two powers continued to confront each other, threatening each other with military interventions in Lower Mesopotamia, as well as commercial ones around the Persian Gulf.

Shortly after, Sargon's son and successor Rimush had to curb the rebellion of several Sumerian cities (Figure 8.2). The first revolts started at Ur, Lagash, Umma and Kazallu (in the north). Rimush also had to deal with a second wave of revolts, possibly initiated and supported by Elam. Once Rimush managed to regain control in Sumer, he directly attacked the alliance Elam-Barahshi-Zahara, winning a battle fought between Susa and Awan. Despite the fact that the Elamites had not been defeated for good, Rimush proclaimed that Enlil had given him 'all the land' (that is, the Mesopotamian alluvial plain) and 'all the mountains' (that is, the periphery), from the Lower Sea to the Upper Sea.

Manishtusu, Sargon's second son, succeeded his brother Rimush and led an expedition beyond the Lower Sea, against Anshan (Fars) and Shirihum. He successfully gained access to the silver mines and the 'mountain of black stone' (diorite). This expedition shows the ability of these rulers to move beyond Susiana and the predominantly commercial interests of Akkad towards the Iranian plateau.

With Manishtusu's successor Naram-Sin, we encounter another influential individual. Like Sargon, Naram-Sin would become a model for later 'historiographical' texts, although with completely different connotations than his grandfather's. Considering the few contemporary sources that have survived, it is possible to see that with Naram-Sin the empire not only did not collapse, but experienced a new surge of expansion. If Sargon had conquered Mesopotamia, if Rimush and Manishtusu had faced Elam, Naram-Sin mainly expanded his territories to the north and north-west. He therefore managed to control an empire that actually stretched from one sea to the other. This was a feat considered to be crucial on an ideological level.

Naram-Sin also managed to consolidate his control to the east. In his inscriptions, he declared his supremacy over Elam 'up to Barahshi'. He therefore controlled the region of Elam, and not its broader confederation. The kings of Awan continued to rule, and relations between Akkad and Awan (described in the inscriptions as subjugated by Akkad) are recorded on an Elamite treaty found at Susa. The agreement was between Naram-Sin and the king of Elam, who is recognised as a political and legal representative of Elam. However, it is true that, after these last attestations, the dynasty of Awan seems to have disappeared. Susa had an Akkadian official in power and Susiana began to be significantly influenced by Akkadian culture. Naram-Sin also guided a military expedition (probably by sea) against the distant Magan. However, he did not conquer the area, but returned with a significant booty and the glory of his victory.

The north experienced two phases under Naram-Sin, documented in various later sources. First, Naram-Sin reached the Upper Mesopotamian city of Talhat and declared that he had conquered Subartu (Upper Mesopotamia), reaching the 'cedar wood' (the Amanus, or at least that whole region surrounding the Mesopotamian plain). Naram-Sin also stated that he subdued the *ensi* of Subartu and the lords

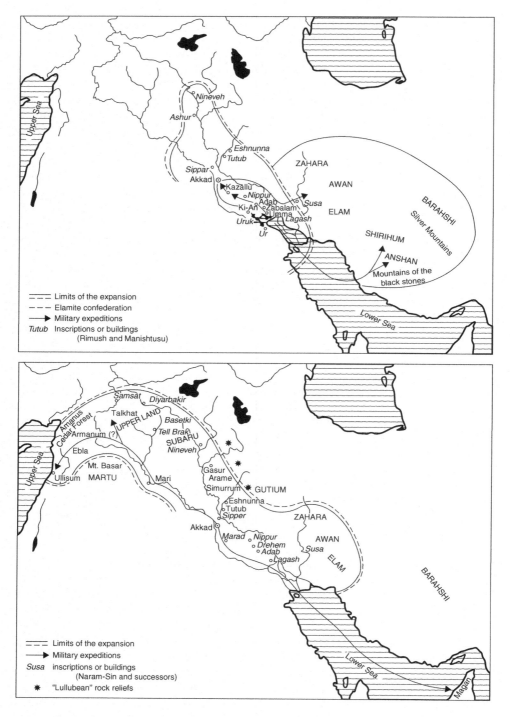

Figure 8.2 The size of the Akkadian empire under Rimush and Manishtusu (*above*), and Naram-Sin (*below*).

of the 'Upper Land'. This division was not really geographic (Subartu being Assyria and 'Upper Land' the Khabur and Middle Euphrates region), but rather socio-political. The *ensi* were local city rulers, while the 'lords' were the tribal chiefs of the steppes beyond the urbanised areas. This control over Upper Mesopotamia is confirmed by the spread of Naram-Sin's inscriptions. Some of them were left in Nineveh, Basetki (north of Assyria) and Diyarbakir. Moreover, one of Naram-Sin's palaces was excavated at Tell Brak, and we know that one of his daughters married the king of Urkish (Tell Mozan).

The second phase of Naram-Sin's expansion was his victorious campaign against Armanum and Ebla. This expedition allowed him to conquer the Amanus (the 'cedar wood') and the Upper Sea. The sources emphatically describe Ebla's destruction as an unprecedented feat. Knowing the wealth of Ebla, this celebratory tone is understandable. However, the Ebla destroyed by Naram-Sin was not the Ebla of Palace G, but the one built immediately after. Summarising Naram-Sin's conquest, he essentially managed to conquer the area from the Euphrates delta to Ullisum (maybe Ullaza, in northern Lebanon) and the Upper Sea.

After Naram-Sin, the empire managed to survive, but began to decrease in size. The date formulas of Shar-kali-sharri attest his wars against Elam, Gutium (Luristan, where one of his inscriptions was found) and the Martu (on the Bishri Mountain). The Sumerian King List places the empire's crisis after Shar-kali-sharri's reign, describing a chaotic phase in terms of rulers and control over the area ('Who was king? Who was not king?'). However, the Akkadian king Shu-Turul is attested shortly after in the Upper Euphrates region, since one of his inscriptions has been found near Samsat. The empire really ended with the arrival of the Gutians. Nonetheless, thanks to its solid structure, largely based on regional control (through strongholds) rather than territorial conquests, the empire managed to maintain a considerable extension up until its final collapse.

2 The structure and administration of the Akkadian empire

The term 'empire' may be misleading when trying to define the territories controlled by the kings of Akkad, especially when comparing it to the territorial empires of the following periods. However, Akkad's imperial ideology was already strong and consistent. The god Enlil and the other gods 'gave' the world's dominion (as far as the seas surrounding it) to the kings of Akkad. However, the actual realisation of this empire was more complicated. The Akkadian empire constituted the first attempt to exercise political control over an extended and diversified territory, with significant linguistic, political, demographic and environmental differences. The composite character of the empire caused more problems than its mere extension. This was a completely different situation than the one of contemporary Egypt. At that time, Egypt was a unified territory with a more homogeneous linguistic, cultural and environmental background.

The most important factor in the formation of the Akkadian empire was military intervention. As a result of that, the king came to be described as a strong and victorious ruler, one that 'has neither equals nor rivals'. Wars were not seen as the result of conflicts between city-gods anymore, but as concrete expressions of the heroism of the king. This aspect of kingship probably finds its roots in the north, in its Semitic background. However, it caused several ideological and religious problems for the Sumerian cities in the south, which saw this self-representation of the Akkadian kings as impious and arrogant.

This change in the ideology of kingship peaked with the deification of Naram-Sin both in his titles and his official iconography. Apart from proclaiming himself a 'strong king' (just like Sargon before him), Naram-Sin also called himself 'god of the land'. He thus became a sort of protective deity that did not replace the traditional gods, but aimed to stand alongside them. This drastic change led to a profound revolution of traditional Sumerian values. This would be attested in later sources, which describe Naram-Sin in a negative light (unlike Sargon), calling him an impious king. He was seen as a ruler who took decisions without consulting the gods, thus causing his own inevitable fall. However, the Sumerian kings would eventually implement (cultically, rather than heroically) Naram-Sin's innovative ideology of kingship for themselves. This proves that it was actually a successful strategy.

137

A different problem from the territorial expansion of the empire was its administration. In this regard, it is necessary to divide the empire into two parts: the centre (from the area slightly north of Akkad to the Persian Gulf) and the periphery. In the centre, Akkadian control was exercised in a compact, yet indirect way. The administration of cities was left in the hands of the local *ensi*. These were under the authority of the king of Akkad, but held a certain degree of autonomy. It is probable that some cities were ruled by an Akkadian *ensi* appointed by the king, while other cities continued to be ruled by a local *ensi*.

In both cases, local dynasties continued to exist. In fact, unlike the following Ur III period, the *ensi* were not yet governors, but were still rulers dependent on Akkadian support and approval. The difficult relations between Akkadian kings and local rulers are visible both on a technical and administrative level and on an ideological and religious one. In terms of administration, there was undoubtedly an Akkadian influence on the economy. The empire's acquisition of new territories and its control of fertile fields in the south, taking these lands away from the temples, initiated a unifying process under the king's authority. This process of unification was further supported by the use of the large number of war prisoners in activities under direct imperial control.

On a religious level, there was a marked contrast between north and south in this period. The new deification of the king and the role of the goddess of Akkad, Ishtar, characterised the north. On the contrary, the south was still centred on the authority of city-gods and of the supreme Sumerian deity, Enlil, god of Nippur. The kings of Akkad paid considerable attention to Enlil and Nippur. The god featured in a prominent position in royal titles. Moreover, the Ekur was restored and enlarged and many monuments celebrating Akkadian victories were left there. These attempts by Sargon and his successors were clearly aimed at inserting their ideology within the political and religious framework of Sumer. This allowed the establishment of a privileged relationship with the head of the Sumerian pantheon, a gesture that automatically placed the Akkadian kings above the other local deities.

The Akkadian kings also took care of their relationships with local city-gods, but in other ways. In this regard, the case of Enheduanna is important as well as symbolic. Enheduanna was Sargon's daughter. She was chosen by her father to become priestess of the city-god of Ur, Nanna-Sin. The presence of an Akkadian priestess from the royal family of Akkad in the prestigious southern city of Ur was probably mirrored by the installation of a Sumerian priestess in the temple of Ishtar in Akkad. These appointments were aimed at uniting the north and the south. However, deities could not be easily identified in other languages (such as the Sumerian Inanna and the Akkadian Ishtar). This problem led to brief periods of rejection in several cities. Nonetheless, in the long run, this strategy would eventually prove to be a winning one (though more for cultural than political reasons). It facilitated the acceptance of a syncretism between the two cultures and the development of a wide network of identifications between them.

The regions outside the centre of the empire, whose collaboration was essential for the celebration of the empire's size, required a different strategy. The periphery was not easy to control either directly or homogeneously. On a political level, it was too vast and varied, with urban centres located in the middle of steppes, mountains and other areas with limited agricultural and demographic concentrations. Therefore, Akkad's interest in the periphery was mainly commercial. This interest was secured through treaties with states too strong to be subdued (such as in the case of Elam), or through the appointment of a local *ensi* (such as the *šakanakku* of Mari). Another possibility was the creation of Akkadian strongholds in foreign territories, such as Naram-Sin's palace at Nagar (Tell Brak). This was probably not the only palace built by Akkadian rulers, and was possibly the most suitable way to keep a vast commercial network under control.

As it can be seen, the Akkadian empire was halfway between the system that supported trade in the Uruk phase, and the more compact and territorial type of organisation that will be encountered with the Third Dynasty of Ur. The Akkadian approach, however, gave the centre of the empire, especially Sumer, too many opportunities to rebel and oppose its religious innovations. Similarly, it gave too much autonomy to the states in the periphery, which should have remained subordinate to the Akkadian strongholds.

3 Demography and administration

Akkad, capital of the Akkadian empire, has never been identified (suggestions on its location vary from the area of Baghdad to the one of Samarra). It therefore remains unexcavated. This fact makes the study of the culture and organisation of the Akkadian empire very difficult. The unavailability of its archives forces us to rely on other archives found elsewhere (Umma, the Diyala region and Gasur in Assyria). Additionally, there are the few buildings attributed with certainty to the kings of Akkad, such as Naram-Sin's palace in Tell Brak. Compared to the Early Dynastic III period, the distribution of Lower Mesopotamian settlements did not undergo significant changes (Figure 8.3). Consequently, the political changes characterising the rise of this new dynasty did not correspond to significant demographic and economic changes in the area. The latter would experience more significant changes with the crisis of the empire.

In the past, Sargon of Akkad's rise was believed to have been the result of the affirmation of Semitic culture over Sumerian culture. Some scholars even suggested an invasion of Semitic people, coming from their 'primitive seat' in the middle of the Syro-Arabian desert, as the reason for Sargon's success. However, these interpretations have now been replaced by our increased knowledge of the period and a more reliable methodology. We know now that Semitic people were already present in Mesopotamia in the Early Dynastic period. Therefore, they did not settle in the region after a mass immigration. Regarding conflicts between cities, it has also been convincingly argued that ethnic differences did not play a significant role. Consequently, there were no ethnic conflicts in Mesopotamia and Sargon was not an advocate of Semitic people fighting against the Sumerians.

It is true, however, that the rise to power of the northern city of Akkad, the centre of a predominantly Semitic population, radically changed the overall situation in the area. Royal inscriptions and administrative texts were now written in Akkadian, rather than (or alongside) Sumerian. The north had its own scribal traditions (the so-called 'Kish tradition'). Therefore, the use of its own language in the imperial administration contributed to the diffusion of its practices, and maybe even its scribes. Moreover, each political change was closely linked to wider trends of the period. The first one was an environmental one. The shift of the political centre to the north was linked to the desire to control water resources. As Upper Mesopotamia became more densely populated and exploited, so the areas further south experienced considerable difficulties. The second tendency was ethno-linguistic. Sumerian, which had been the most influential language for over a millennium, was an isolated linguistic group. On the contrary, Akkadian belonged to the same linguistic group as the languages spoken from Upper Mesopotamia to Syria, not to mention the Arabian Peninsula (for which, however, we do not have any written evidence for this phase). These processes of integration and diffusion, as well as the movement of people, gradually benefited those cultures that could more easily assimilate new immigrating groups. This was the case of the Akkadians, who managed to include those groups coming from the west.

In this regard, then, the rise of Akkad had a cumulative effect. Sargon's conquest of the south was followed by a process of colonisation. This led to the appointment of Akkadian officials to rule several cities and to the movement of farmers and potential tenants to Sumerian territories. The use of another language was only one aspect of the problem. There were also a wide range of customs and legal traditions brought from Akkad, especially regarding property and land management. For this reason, there are more attestations concerning family and royal properties in this period and fewer concerning temple properties (Figure 8.4). As already attested in the Early Dynastic period (also in the south, at Fara), family property was probably more established in the north. In fact, in the north, social structures were more centred on kinship and less subject to the overpowering influence of temples, whose authority was closely linked to the first urbanisation.

Regarding royal land, the Akkadian kings tried to accumulate territories to place them under direct Akkadian control. An important document in this regard is the so-called Obelisk of Manishtusu. The text was written like a typical contract of the period, with a long list of sellers, witnesses and other

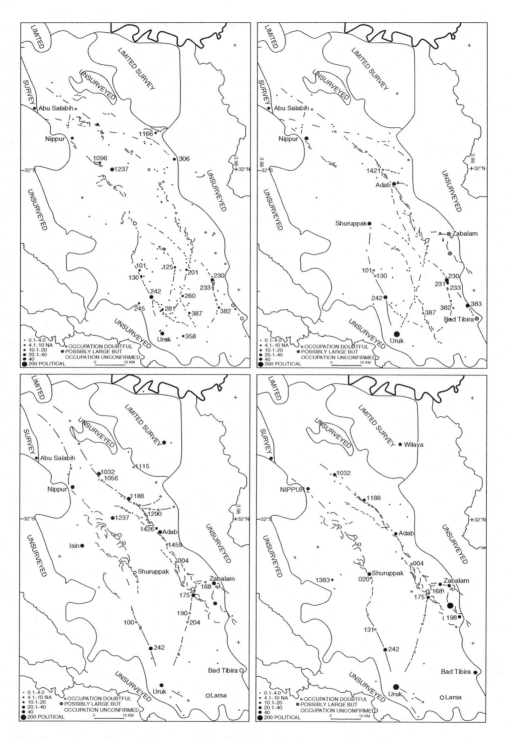

Figure 8.3 Occupation of Lower Mesopotamia in the third millennium BC. *Above, left*: Jemdet Nasr period; *Above, right*: Early Dynastic I; *Below, left*: Early Dynastic II and III; *Below, right*: Akkadian period.

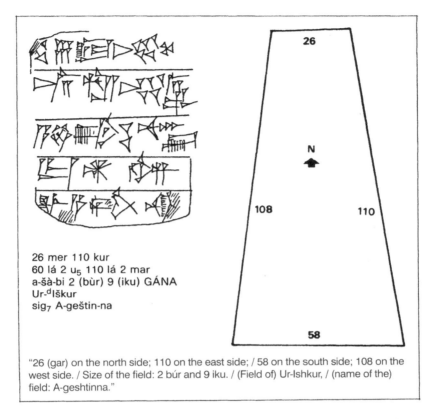

26 mer 110 kur
60 lá 2 u$_5$ 110 lá 2 mar
a-šà-bi 2 (bùr) 9 (iku) GÁNA
Ur-^{d}Iškur
sig$_7$ A-geštin-na

"26 (gar) on the north side; 110 on the east side; / 58 on the south side; 108 on the west side. / Size of the field: 2 búr and 9 iku. / (Field of) Ur-Ishkur, / (name of the) field: A-geshtinna."

Figure 8.4 Agriculture in the Akkadian period: tablet recording the measurements of a field and its reconstruction.

people involved in the transaction. The Obelisk records the king's purchase of a large number of lands. These amounted to more than 2,300 hectares (an incredible amount for that period) in the Mesopotamian region of Marad. On top of these lands bought through private transactions, there were further lands acquired militarily, allowing the royal family to own a large amount of land outside the control of temples. However, despite being politically subordinate to the palace, the latter managed to remain autonomous.

Due to the spread of northern practices, various aspects of the administration – from the various functions within the system to the types of documents and their bureaucratic terminology – underwent considerable changes. Despite the fact that Sumerian and Semitic features coexisted, local varieties in writing and in the shape of the tablets continued to exist. However, an 'imperial' kind of writing gradually became more widespread, due to its homogeneity, elegance and accuracy. This marked the beginning of a Lower Mesopotamian scribal and administrative tradition, which would peak in the Neo-Sumerian period, as a result of another political unification of the area (the Third Dynasty of Ur).

4 Trade and the empire's periphery

In terms of conquests, Sargon personally led his army to Tuttul on one side and the Persian Gulf on the other. Similarly, Naram-Sin reached Ebla (if not even the Mediterranean) and Magan. Comparing the expansion previously achieved through conflicts between neighbouring states with that of the Akkadian empire, it is undeniable that the latter was of a significantly larger scale. Admittedly, early trade and the commercial networks of the Sumerian cities of the Early Dynastic period were already quite far-reaching. These interactions were, however, based more on the presence of intermediary commercial junctions along trade routes. This kind of exchange took longer and was much more expensive. On the other hand, the Akkadian kings attempted to make their political and military plans coincide with their commercial interests. They therefore found a way to directly reach the areas providing raw materials, without relying too much on intermediaries.

In order to achieve this, the Akkadian kings had to take over the main commercial networks of the Near East. Apart from the Lower Mesopotamian one, there were those controlled by Mari and Ebla in the west, by Elam in the Iranian plateau and the ones in the Persian Gulf, centred on the port of Dilmun. The Akkadian military expeditions outside Mesopotamia targeted precisely these three areas. For Sargon, the conquest of Lower Mesopotamia was still mainly a political and military conquest, while commercial activities were pursued either by the Akkadians themselves (in the west), or their partners (in the east).

Manishtusu and Naram-Sin effectively changed this strategy. They managed to take over the commercial networks of Ebla, Elam and, in a less definite way, also Magan (which provided a considerable booty, but the region was left unconquered). To a certain extent, however, the Akkadian takeover of these commercial networks caused their decline. The direct access to resources through plunder and conquest could have drastically damaged commercial networks. The Mesopotamian ideal considered everything outside of it as an uncivilised and deserted source of raw materials at its disposal. This ideal, however, did not take into account the fact that these areas had their own systems to extract materials, process them and exchange them, as well as their own commercial strategies and income.

Consequently, the destruction of Ebla significantly affected the political structure of northern Syria, leading to a higher degree of fragmentation. At the same time, Akkad did not manage to fully control its commercial networks. The conquest of Susiana also altered the confederate structure of the Elamite state. This political change hindered the inflow of commodities from north-eastern Iran, in particular lapis lazuli from Afghanistan and tin from Central Asia. As a result, these materials reached Mesopotamia in smaller quantities and with more difficulties than in the Early Dynastic period.

Unfortunately, the centre of the Elamite confederation, the Awan region, from which the Elamite royal family took its name, has not yet been located. On the upside, other Elamite centres, such as Susa (which was in close contact with Mesopotamia) and Anshan (Tall-i Malyan), have been located. Overall, the Elamite state included a large part of Iran and interacted with other developed centres located further east, such as Tepe Yahya (in the land of Barahshi/Marhashi) and Shar-i Sokhta (possibly the Aratta of Sumerian myths). These were crucial commercial junctions in the network, providing tin, lapis lazuli, diorite and other semiprecious stones to the west.

Within this intricate system, Akkadian action was initially cautious, focused on Susa, and then more ambiguous, alternating military victories with treaties. It is difficult to estimate how damaging Akkadian intervention was in the area. The royal inscriptions of the kings of Akkad attest to the conquest of Elam. However, the Awan dynasty continued to rule and its kings continued to hold important titles. Even the last king of the dynasty, Puzur-Inshushinak, who ruled at the time of Shar-kali-sharri, seems to have held considerable power. During his reign, however, Awan underwent a period of crisis, which spread to the other centres of the Iranian plateau. Shahr-i-Sokhta, for instance, regressed to become a village, effectively blocking the circulation of goods from the east to the west.

The decline of Elam seems to have mirrored the collapse of Akkad. It is difficult to decide whether it was only due to internal factors, or a consequence of continuous Akkadian attacks. The populations living on the Zagros, namely, the Gutians and Lullubeans, played a significant role in this crisis. The Gutians attacked Mesopotamia as well as Elam. Therefore, Elam's decline between the Awan and the following Simash dynasty (originally from Luristan) could have been the equivalent of the Mesopotamian crisis caused by the arrival of the Gutians. However, while Mesopotamia continued to be populated, Elam went through a phase of progressive depopulation.

In the Persian Gulf, prised by the Akkadian kings especially for the tin from Magan, the island of Dilmun seems to have been able to stay safe from violent conquests and destructions. This was precisely because of its role as a commercial junction. Dilmun, however, was a unique case. The area was unable to support itself and had to import the goods needed. The area known as Magan was influenced by the so-called Umm an-Nar culture (in Oman). Magan seems to have had frequent interactions with Mesopotamia, and for this reason Naram-Sin and his army conquered it. Meluhha, influenced by the Harappa and Mohenjo Daro cultures (from the Indus Valley), was a different case. As a source for oils, exotic animals and seashells, all commodities of minor importance, Meluhha's interaction with Mesopotamia was largely indirect. As can be seen, Anatolia, the Syrian coast, Oman, the Indus Valley, Afghanistan and Central Asia constituted a relatively integrated 'world-system'. In this regard, the more-or-less conscious strategy of the Akkadian kings to interfere with the system as a whole did not reach completion. However, considering the territories conquered and the ones that had been destroyed, the Akkadian kings managed to get quite close to their aim.

5 The artistic and literary expressions of kingship

The new image of the king as the heroic ruler naturally left a significant mark in the artistic and literary expressions of the period. The latter indicate a change towards a clearer and more conscious use of iconic and epigraphic monuments as means for propaganda and celebration of a ruler's achievements (Text 8.1). Therefore, elements already developed in the Early Dynastic period, from votive statues to victory steles,

---

Text 8.1   Celebrative inscriptions of the kings of Akkad

1 Inscription of Sargon (Old Babylonian copy from Nippur)

'Sargon, king of Akkad – overseer of Inanna

king of Kish – anointed of Anu

king of the land – governor of Enlil:

he defeated the city of Uruk and tore down its walls, in the battle of Uruk he won, took Lugalzaggesi king of Uruk in the course of the battle, and led him in a collar to the gate of Enlil.

Sargon, king of Akkad:

in the battle of Uruk he won, he defeated the city and destroyed its walls. He defeated E-ninmar and destroyed its walls, conquered its land from Lagash to the sea, he washed his weapons in the sea. He challenged Umma in battle, he defeated the city and destroyed its walls.

Sargon, king of the land:

Enlil gave him no rival; he gave him the Upper Sea and the Lower Sea; from the Lower Sea the sons of Akkad held the position of governors; Mari and Elam stood in front of Sargon king of the land.

Sargon, king of the land:

he restored Kish, and let them (the inhabitants) live in the city.

[Curse:] Whoever will damage this inscription: May Shamash tear out his roots and destroy his seed.

[Caption:] Inscription on the pedestal.

[Caption:] Sargon, king of the land. Lugalzaggesi king of Uruk. Month of the governor of Umma.'

2 Inscription of Rimush (Old Babylonian copy from Nippur)

'Rimush king of Kish:

in the battle against Abalgamash king of Barahshi he won; Zahara and Elam united in battle in Barahshi, but he defeated them. He killed 16,212 men, he captured 4,216 prisoners, he captured Sidgau, governor of Barahshi, he captured Sargapi, governor of Zahara. Between Awan and Susa, in the Upper River, he heaped up a tumulus in their cities, he defeated the cities of Elam, destroyed their walls, and he uprooted the foundation of Barahshi from the people of Elam.

Rimush king of Kish:

Took over Elam according to the will of Enlil, in the third year after Enlil had granted him his kingship. Total: 9,624 men, including the fallen, including the prisoners. By Shamash and Abi I swear: I am not lying, it is true!

[Dedication:] he made this statue at the time of that battle, and dedicated it to his saviour Enlil.

[Curse:] Whoever will damage this inscription: may Enlil and Shamash tear his roots and disperse his seed.

[Caption:] Inscribed on the pedestal, on the left side.

[Curse:] Whoever will damage the name of Rimush king of Kish and will put his name on the statue of Rimush and will say "this is my statue": may Enlil, lord of this statue, and Shamash tear out his roots, destroy his seed, refuse him a male (heir), may he not stand in front of his god.

[Dedication:] 30 minas of gold, 3600 minas of copper, 6 male slaves and (6) female slaves.

[Caption:] Inscription on a silver statue.'

3 Inscription of Naram-Sin (Old Babylonian copy from Nippur)

'From of old, from the creation of men, no one among the kings had destroyed Armanum and Ebla. Nergal opened the way for Naram-Sin, the mighty one: he gave him Armanum and Ebla. He also gave him the Amanus, the Cedar Mountain, and the Upper Sea.

With the weapon of Dagan, the exalter of his royalty, Naram-Sin, the mighty one, defeated Armanum and Ebla, from the bank of the Euphrates to the Ullisum, the men that Dagan gave him from his hand, he smote them: they carried the basket of Abi, his god; Amanus, the Cedar Mountain, he conquered.

When Dagan judged the judgement of Naram-Sin, the mighty one, he delivered Rish-Adad, king of Armanum, into his hand and he bound him to his gate:

(then) he made a statue of diorite, and dedicated it to Enlil, (saying) thus: "Naram-Sin, the mighty one, king of the four quarters of the world, Dagan gave him Armanum and Ebla, and he captured Rish-Adad with his hand. So I dedicated a stone image to Sin."'

4 Inscription of Naram-Sin (original, from Basekti)

'Naram-Sin, the mighty one, king of Akkad:

when the four quarters of the world rebelled together against him, thanks to the love with which Ishtar loved him, he was victorious in nine battles in a single year, and captured the kings that had risen against him.

Since he had strengthened the roots of his city in this difficult (situation), (the inhabitants of) his city, together with Ishtar in the Eanna (Uruk), Enlil in Nippur, Dagan in Tuttul, Ninhursag in Kish, Enki in Eridu, Sin in Ur, Shamash in Sippar, Nergal in Kuta, wished him to become god of Akkad, their city, and in the middle of Akkad they built him a temple.

Whoever will damage this inscription: may Shamash, Ishtar, Nergal overseer of the king, and the totality of those gods tear out his roots, and destroy his seed.'

were remodelled as *bona fide* means of political propaganda. Many votive monuments were built not only in the Ekur of Nippur, but also in the other sanctuaries of the empire, from Sippar to Ur. Statues remained quite simple, with the king in a standing posture on a pedestal often decorated with prisoners of war or defeated enemies. The centrality of the king's image, together with the tone of his inscriptions and dedications, changed the aim of these monuments, which ceased to be the means for a ruler to worship the gods (which had been the aim of votive statues in the Early Dynastic period). Monuments therefore became a way to celebrate the victories of the king.

In victory steles, this change found even more opportunities to express the new role of the king (Figure 8.5). It may be sufficient to compare the stele of Eannatum to that of Naram-Sin to notice the shift from the centrality of the god to that of the king (with the gods only performing a symbolic role, as in Figure 8.6). Even victorious soldiers, who in the Early Dynastic period were depicted as a compact block representing the urban community, were now depicted as individuals with initiative. They were therefore similar to the king, but carved on a much smaller scale. These steles were placed in symbolic locations: either in the centre of the empire or in the main city-temples. Alternatively, they could be left on the edge of the empire, whenever the Akkadian army had reached an insurmountable natural obstacle, beyond which there was nothing left to conquer.

If royal monuments had a clear political function, smaller and more personal objects, such as the seals of Akkadian officials also reflected the new tendencies of the period. Early Dynastic seals with animal patterns (Figure 8.7) were used alongside seals decorated with the new astral deities of the Semitic north (Figure 8.8), such as Shamash and Ishtar. These deities acquired an increasingly influential role, at the expense of the former fertility and chtonic deities. The shift from decorative patterns to narrative depictions also led to the appearance of mythological scenes (which can be sometimes recognised, if they refer to attested myths). This was another innovation compared to the fixed symbolic and cultic iconography of the previous period.

A similar shift can be seen in the inscriptions left on monuments. Very few people could read these texts (namely, scribes and functionaries who were able to read), and the accessibility of the monuments themselves was precluded to the wider public. A strong feature of these texts is their propagandistic tone. However, the latter was not used as a brutal attempt at informing readers or at falsifying information, but as a means for the diffusion of the official ideology. Unfortunately, we only possess the 'tip of the iceberg' of this political propaganda, which reached the wider population in other and simpler ways (orally and ceremonially).

The inscriptions of the Akkadian kings show an increased interest in the narration of events, making the dedication of monuments a pretext for self-celebration. Some Early Dynastic texts were equally rich in narrative details (such as the stele of Eannatum). However, they were so for legal and religious reasons, namely, to explain the rightfulness of the king's actions, justifying them as a defence of the king's rights. These inscriptions were meant to become part of tradition. They portrayed the kings' actions as guaranteed and stimulated through the support of the gods, and therefore made on behalf of the god. On the contrary, Akkadian narrative inscriptions had a completely different tone. They emphasised the central role of the king as the initiator of interventions and as a strong, unrivalled and unprecedented ruler.

The repercussions of this new ideology of kingship are much more difficult to detect in literary texts. Most of these texts were written much later, and the editions that have reached us are the result of changes responding to the tendencies of the following periods. The emergence of a mythical iconography on Akkadian seals has led to the assumption of the central role of this period for the elaboration and narration of myths. This is due to the similarity between the heroic image of the Akkadian king and analogous ideas impersonated by mythical heroes such as Gilgamesh and Enmerkar. The theme of the conflict between north and south can be found in the war between Gilgamesh of Uruk and Agga of Kish. Similarly, military and commercial expeditions in distant lands are attested to in the journey of Enmerkar to Aratta and Gilgamesh to the cedar forest. Even the problem of the partial divinity and problematic mortality of the king are issues attested in these myths.

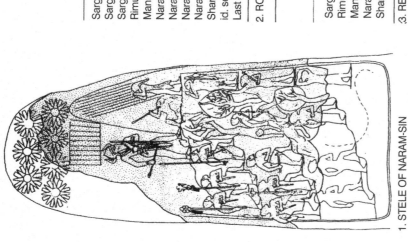

1. STELE OF NARAM-SIN

2. ROYAL TITULATURE OF THE DYNASTY OF AKKAD

	king of Akkad	king of Kish	king of the land	mighty	king of the four quarters	unrivalled	god of Akkad	divine determinative
Sargon, first phase	+	+	+					
Sargon, second phase		+				+		
Sargon, third phase		+				+		
Rimush		+						
Manishtusu						+		
Naram-Sin, first phase	+							
Naram-Sin, second phase				+	+			
Naram-Sin, third phase	(+)			+	+	(+)	+	
Naram-Sin, seals/dedications	+			+	+		+	+
Shar-kali-sharri	+			+				+
id. seals/dedications	+			+				+
Last Kings				+				(+)

3. RELATIONSHIP WITH ENLIL, SUPREME GOD OF SUMER

	Enlil gives the land	dedications to Enlil	subordination to Enlil	interventions in the Ekur	invocation of Enlil in curses
Sargon	+	+	+	-	+
Rimush	+	+	+	-	+
Manishtusu	+	+	-	-	+
Naram-Sin	-	+	-	+	-
Shar-kali-sharri	-	-	-	+	-

Figure 8.5 Akkadian kingship ideology: Naram-Sin's acquisition of a heroic and divine role (1) coincides with a profound revision of royal titulature (2) and of the king's relationship with Enlil (3), head of the traditional pantheon.

Figure 8.6   The victory stele of Naram-Sin, king of Akkad, from Susa, now in the Louvre Museum. © RMN–Grand Palais (Musée du Louvre)/Franck Raux.

Figure 8.7 Farming in the Akkadian period: farming scene carved on a seal.

All these themes seem to belong more to the Akkadian period than the Early Dynastic II period, the time in which these heroes should have lived according to later revisions of these myths. Naturally, on a functional level, these myths were meant to act as models for the kings' behaviour. Nonetheless, the creation of these legends was effectively influenced by the ideology of the Akkadian period. It has to be pointed out, however, that the Sumerian redaction of these poems, with its emphasis on Lower Mesopotamia as the land of the main heroes (Uruk, rather than Kish, for instance), is in marked contrast with the location of the Akkadian dynasty. It is therefore possible that these myths were a result of the influence of Akkadian imperial ideology on Sumerian culture. The latter, then, reformulated its core concepts by applying a Sumero-centric point of view and placing these myths in a distant past. For instance, the tale of Gilgamesh and Agga displays a compromise between the invincibility of the hero from Uruk and the *Realpolitik* attesting the supremacy of the king of Kish. The tale therefore makes more sense if contextualised after the victory of Sargon against Lugalzaggesi. This was the time when the rulers of Uruk tried to reconcile their current subordination to the empire with their former autonomy, rooted in the past splendour of their city.

6 The kings of Akkad in the historical tradition

In the history of the Akkadian dynasty, some elements were bound to stimulate popular culture. Over time, several dynasties were largely forgotten and only remembered by the scholarly works of scribes and priests. On the contrary, the Akkadian dynasty generated a large repertoire of legendary and literary traditions. Sargon and Naram-Sin became model-kings, impersonating, in a positive or negative way, the Mesopotamian ideal of the king. This ideal would become essential for later rulers, who had to compare themselves to these two kings to justify their deeds.

Among the elements aimed at stimulating popular culture, there was the idea of a 'universal empire'. This idea gave a political tone to the Mesopotamian conviction of its centrality in the world. The ideology of the Akkadian triumphal inscriptions therefore became a model for later inscriptions. Even the title of 'king of the four quarters' became a necessary part of the titulature of ambitious kings, while the title 'king of Kish' was reinterpreted to mean 'king of totality'. Then, there was the heroic ideal marshalled by Akkadian inscriptions. This ideal emphasised strength, the ability to subjugate enemies through wars, and culminated with the deification of the king. Heroism, individualism and deification therefore became the main characteristics of these larger-than-life hero-kings. Consequently, everyone wanted to imitate, if not

Figure 8.8   Mythological seal impressions of the Akkadian period.

equal them. Finally, there was the peculiar rise and fall of the power of Akkad. The empire came from nothing, reached unprecedented heights and then collapsed again. This curve inspired considerations on human destiny, the relations of humans and gods and the ability to predict potential crises.

Since the later traditions primarily focused on Sargon and Naram-Sin, these two characters became polar opposites. Sargon represented the positive aspects of the empire's rise to power, while Naram-Sin embodied the negative ones of its decline. Within this oversimplification, Sargon's image was closer to his actual achievements, while Naram-Sin's image was completely distorted. The reasons for this polarisation are understandable. The literary tradition found in Sargon's story the themes of the rise of the 'new man' of non-royal background (aspects that were later enriched with obscure and unusual features), able to build his own fortune and position, which led him to political and military successes.

On the contrary, the negative connotations of Naram-Sin originated from his perceived impiety and arrogance. This behaviour caused the gods to abandon him and bring to an end the empire he inherited. This is, however, a pure deformation of the actual events. The Akkadian empire fell a long time after Naram-Sin's rule. In reality, the king managed to surpass Sargon's conquests. Therefore, the negative portrayal of Naram-Sin must be due to his self-deification. This was an intolerable and shameful behaviour for the temples, since it implied a pretension of being able to achieve greatness by oneself, without the help of the gods. Such behaviour would inevitably cause a punishment from the gods.

The way in which the pseudo-historical tradition of the kings of Akkad was formed can be in part reconstructed. The celebratory monuments, left in the temples and visible to worshippers for over a millennium (until the Elamite attacks in the twelfth century BC), played a central role, since they brought scribes to copy these inscriptions. The creation of *bona fide* studies on these epigraphic texts guaranteed the survival of the heroic and universal phraseology and ideology of the Akkadian empire. In addition to that, Akkadian monuments generated several popular legends and aetiological tales. These are now difficult to reconstruct, but must have played a key role in the survival of these heroes in Mesopotamian tradition.

Alongside the influence of celebratory monuments, there were at least two other sources influencing later accounts on the Akkadian dynasty. First, there were foundation texts buried under temples. These would regularly re-emerge when these buildings had to be restored, becoming the objects of devoted attention. Second, there were omen texts, which recorded particular conformations of the entrails of sacrificial animals. It was widely believed that these phenomena were initially observed in connection to famous political and military events of the Akkadian period. Later specialists would therefore refer to these events to interpret the re-appearance of similar conformations in the entrails. The tendentious nature of these omens can be seen in the fact that the earliest omen texts were quite basic, using phrases such as 'omen of Sargon', inscribed on a liver model (Figure 8.9). Only later on would omen texts become more elaborate and specific (therefore invented or gathered through other means), including historical events linked to particular omens.

The historical tradition on Sargon and Naram-Sin was already fully formed in the Old Babylonian period (ca. nineteenth to seventeenth century BC), when the most famous of these compositions were written. Apart from omen texts, there were false inscriptions, the so-called *narû* (Akkadian for 'stele'). These texts were inspired by the various inscriptions left by the Akkadian kings in temples and their foundations. Moreover, there were epic poems with strong theological features. In virtually all these literary works, there was a strong correlation between historical tradition and omens. This was not just a structural choice, but a thematic one, justifying the existence of this tradition.

In fact, the explanation provided for the rise and fall of the Akkadian empire, and the polarity between Sargon and Naram-Sin, was centred on the latter's different relation to omens, which were considered to be expressions of divine will. Sargon paid attention to omens, an easy task for the ruler, since he kept receiving positive presages. On the contrary, upon receiving negative omens, Naram-Sin, instead of acting upon them, decided not to take them into consideration. He thus deliberately caused his own fall. Omens were therefore considered to be crucial aspects of kingship.

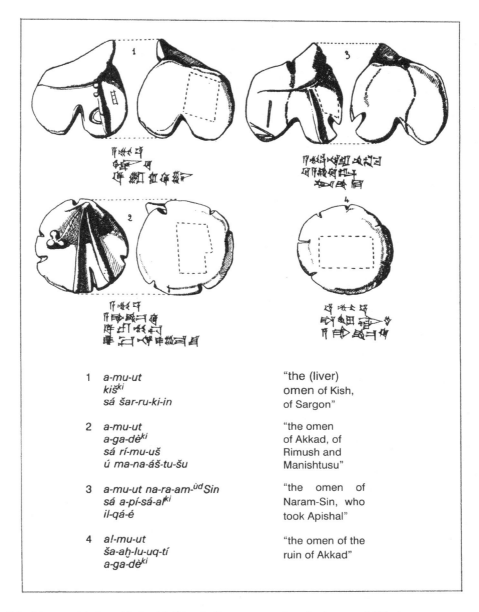

1   *a-mu-ut*
    kiš^{ki}
    sá šar-ru-ki-in

 "the (liver) omen of Kish, of Sargon"

2   *a-mu-ut*
    a-ga-dè^{ki}
    sá rí-mu-uš
    ú ma-na-áš-tu-šu

 "the omen of Akkad, of Rimush and Manishtusu"

3   *a-mu-ut na-ra-am-^{üd}Sin*
    sá a-pí-sá-al^{ki}
    il-qá-é

 "the omen of Naram-Sin, who took Apishal"

4   *a!-mu-ut*
    ša-aḫ-lu-uq-tí
    a-ga-dè^{ki}

 "the omen of the ruin of Akkad"

Figure 8.9 Liver models from Mari, with 'historical' omens regarding the dynasty of Akkad.

Consequently, later kings were required to base their decisions on the paradigmatic example set by the Akkadian kings. In reality, they simply based themselves on the consultation of omens. The link between omens and the examples of previous historical events indicated that favourable omens (such as Sargon's) were positive presages inducing interventions, whilst unfavourable omens (such as Naram-Sin's) signalled caution or the renunciation of the actions that a ruler had in mind. In more practical terms, Sargon was the model to follow for a correct behaviour that respected the will of the gods, while Naram-Sin's behaviour was the one to avoid.

Due to their religious and structural interpretation of the Akkadian empire, these later texts cannot be considered reliable historical sources. Scholars have often attempted to locate the 'historical nucleus' within these texts, using them in relation to the events they recorded. However, in order to understand the reasons why these texts were composed in the first place, it is far more methodologically sound to find the various allusions to the periods in which they were composed, rather than to the time to which they refer.

The most famous tale is probably the 'King of Combat' (*šar tamḫāri*), which recounts Sargon's expedition to the city of Purushhanda, in Central Anatolia. The current interpretation of this story sees some allusions to early Akkadian trade in Cappadocia, several centuries before the Old Assyrian trade in that region. The poem focuses on the problem of omens. Sargon acted correctly because he followed a daring omen (Ishtar's dream), instead of the cautious advice of merchants, acting as his human advisors. He also succeeded because his confidence allowed him to overcome all natural obstacles, reaching this distant land. His feat was so prodigious that the local ruler surrendered without any bloodshed. The reference to Old Assyrian commercial activities is not aimed at attesting an earlier origin of this interaction, but at becoming its exemplary model. Just like Sargon, so the following rulers would have had to follow the advice of the gods and engage in long-distance trade, without fearing human or natural obstacles.

The 'Legend of Naram-Sin' provides a completely different moral. Faced by the invasions of numerous barbaric people from the north (the Umman-Manda), Naram-Sin, before even consulting the omens, sent some of his officials to investigate whether these invaders were human (thus defeatable) or spirits. This first offence was punished through negative omens. At this point, Naram-Sin, instead of following them, decided to follow the advice of his officials and face the enemies. Naturally, he was defeated. The disaster would eventually be fixed thanks to the intervention of the god Ea and Naram-Sin's repentance. However, the invasion was stopped not on the battlefield, but simply through a withdrawal from it. If the 'King of Combat' was a reflection of the various doubts concerning long-distance trade, the 'Legend of Naram-Sin' dealt with the proper way to face an invasion. Therefore, the text advises the reader to hide behind the city wall, rather than confront a strong enemy in battle.

Another famous text, the so-called 'Curse of Akkad', has often been overestimated in its historical significance and underestimated in its implications. The text could have been already composed in the Neo-Sumerian period. It recounts the rise and fall of Akkad, from Sargon's rise to prosperity to Akkad's destruction under Naram-Sin, caused by Enlil's vengeance for the ruler's supposed destruction of the Ekur. In reality, the Akkadian kings restored the Ekur, enriching it with their celebratory monuments and were always respectful of Enlil. Therefore, it is possible to see behind this alleged destruction of the Ekur Naram-Sin's attempt at restoring the sanctuary. However, the decision was considered impious because it was not sanctioned by oracles and was disrespectful of the architectural and cultic tradition of the city. The story reflects a certain degree of criticism on the need of restoration works, possibly from the time of the dynasty of Isin (Ishme-Dagan). The restorations of Ur-Nammu do not, however, contain any criticism on the previous Akkadian interventions. In the 'Curse of Akkad', then, historical facts were drastically modified: the later Gutian invasions were placed at the time of Naram-Sin and the latter's relation with the Ekur was completely misrepresented.

With the emergence of Babylon as a rising power in Mesopotamia, these pseudo-historical texts began to associate Akkad with Babylon. The latter was therefore portrayed as the heir of the former, which largely overshadowed it. Later on, in the Neo-Assyrian period, the destruction of Babylon under Sennacherib would be condemned as a repetition of a supposed destruction of the same city by Sargon to the advantage of the new city of Akkad. In the first millennium BC, while Old Babylonian texts continued to be read and copied by scribes, new compositions were written. They were composed in the form of chronicles delineating the rise and fall of states in relation to their behaviour towards the gods (Marduk in particular). Alternatively, they were written as histories of buildings, whose earliest foundations were made under the Akkadian kings. Each period, then, found ways and reasons to forge links between contemporary events and past models. Unsurprisingly, the kings of Akkad became the ultimate models for later rulers in an area, Mesopotamia, which had been culturally and politically influenced by the dynasty of Akkad more than any other region.

7 The Gutians, Lullubeans and Hurrians

Having kept Mesopotamia united for almost two centuries, the Akkadian dynasty collapsed at the hands of the Gutians, who came from the Zagros Mountains. The Mesopotamian texts describe them as stereotypically barbarian: 'dragons of the mountains', 'enemies of the gods', 'the uncontrolled people', who 'damage land like locusts', 'have no fear of the gods and do not know how to correctly follow the cultic protocol'. The kings of Akkad, from Naram-Sin to Shar-kali-sharri, had conducted various expeditions against Simurrum and Arame (in the Zagros foothills), reaching the land of the Gutians. However, the empire's interest was more focused on the large and wealthy centres in the east (Elam) and west (Mari and Ebla).

Taking advantage of the crisis due to the depletion of resources and the disorganisation of the last Akkadian kings, the Gutians descended the Zagros and ultimately managed to take control over Mesopotamia. The Sumerian King List provides a long list of Gutian rulers. Unfortunately, most of them remain unknown to us, except for one, attested in various inscriptions, but not on the Sumerian King List. This king was Erridu-wizir, 'king of Gutium and of the four quarters'. He dedicated several statues in the Ekur of Nippur and his inscriptions were collected by a scribe of the Old Babylonian period. The scarcity of evidence on the Gutian rule in Mesopotamia probably indicates that their presence did not leave a visible impact on the political and administrative organisation of the region.

It is possible that the Gutians were mainly located in Central Mesopotamia and stayed relatively close to the Zagros Mountains, where they were constantly fighting (Madga, Simurrum, Urbilum). Despite their subordination to the Gutians, however, the Sumerian cities in the south swiftly managed to regain their autonomy. The Gutians actually appointed some local *ensi*, but their control was less political, less oppressive and less efficient than the one of the Akkadian period. Gutian control had less impact on the agricultural activities of the countryside and on the cultic and administrative practices of the cities. Later on, we will see how the southern cities, from Lagash to Uruk, managed to regain their autonomy and initiative, eventually leading to their political rise.

The heartland of the Gutians remained in the mountains. Utu-hegal of Uruk, who would later on defeat them, would accuse them of bringing 'the kingship of Sumer in a foreign land'. We can get an idea of the Gutian ideology of kingship from a relief with a victory scene and inscription of clear Akkadian influence. It was found at Sar-i Pul, on the Zagros Mountains, and belongs to Anu-banini, king of the Lullubeans. Although the Lullubeans and the Gutians were two different populations, they came from the same area. In his inscription, Anu-banini followed the Akkadian model, claiming his control of the territories from the 'Lower Sea to the Upper Sea'. However, his actual dominion was centred on the area around the Zagros Mountains, rather than in the Mesopotamian alluvial plain. Admittedly, empires often influence the regions around them. Consequently, just like the Akkadian empire (and the Ur III dynasty later on) tried to unify Mesopotamia, so the periphery attempted a temporary expansion around Mesopotamia. However, these expansions were structurally fragile and lasted only as long as the military interventions and tribal alliances that created them.

The ethno-linguistic realm of the Hurrians was another example of a political entity with expansionistic ambitions located in the periphery, between the Mesopotamian alluvial plain and the mountains surrounding it. Two late or post-Akkadian inscriptions have been found in this region: the first one belonged to Tish-atal and was found at Tell Mozan (in the Upper Khabur region); the second one belonged to Atal-shenni and was found at Samarra (in the Middle Tigris). Both these kings had Hurrian names, but only the first inscription was written in Hurrian. These kings declared that they controlled the area from Urkish to Nawar. The first city was Tell Mozan itself, while the second one could have been either Nagar (Tell Brak), or a region in the Samarrian hinterland. These early Hurrian states occupied the areas left behind after the fall of the Akkadian empire and not yet occupied by the Third Dynasty of Ur, and therefore surrounded the Gutian territories in the north.

9

THE THIRD DYNASTY OF UR

1 The 'Sumerian renaissance'

Following the decline of Akkadian supremacy after Shar-kali-sharri and throughout the Gutian period, the cities of the Sumerian south, from Ur to Uruk, Umma and Lagash, managed to maintain a considerable degree of independence. The disappearance of a central power must have brought considerable economic advantages. It is true that, due to a general sense of uncertainty, the Gutian period would be remembered as a negative time for trade ('on the highways of the land, the grass grew high'). However, it was also a period of limited tributes levied by kings whose role was more symbolic than anything else, at least in the south. In fact, Gutian rule must have been more solid in the north, where they were a substitute for the Akkadian dynasty, possibly implementing its administrative structure.

Therefore, the south had its own dynasties of *ensi*, who continued the tradition of the Sumerian city-states. The Sumerian King List only attests the 'Fourth Dynasty of Uruk'. The best attested dynasty in the surviving evidence is the one of Lagash, especially for the reigns of Ur-Baba, Gudea and Ur-Ningirsu. We possess a large number of inscriptions and votive statues of Gudea, making him one of the best-attested rulers of this time. Admittedly, if we had a similar amount of evidence from Uruk or Ur, it would have been of a better quality. However, the marginal role of Lagash compared to other more prestigious cities in Sumer makes its documentation more typical of the period, and more useful when trying to reconstruct an overall picture of this period.

Gudea's activities were predominantly local. There is only one conflict attested during his reign, against Anshan and Elam. This was probably due to the proximity of Lagash to Iran, making it an easy target for Elamite incursions. Gudea mainly pursued building and administrative activities, such as the construction of the E-ninnu, the temple of Lagash's city-god Ningirsu. The king described this achievement as a global endeavour. Every land contributed to the temple's construction, and each provided its local materials, from timber to bitumen, metals and semiprecious stones (Text 9.1). Thanks to the prestige of Ningirsu and the ability of Gudea, all these materials managed to travel from the edge of the land to the centre of the world, where the temple was constructed. Naturally, this is a 'world' imagined precisely for the temple's construction, with rivers flowing from north to south to facilitate the arrival of materials at Lagash. This was the point of view of an *ensi* who was neither the most powerful, nor entirely independent in the political situation of the time.

The relative freedom of the city-states explains why the Gutians, considered unbearable by the Sumerians, stayed in power for about a century. Their collapse was caused by a single war and was not particularly difficult. A king of Uruk, Utu-hegal, the only ruler of the 'Fifth Dynasty of Uruk', managed to form an army able to face the one sent by the Gutian king Tirigan, and defeated it. Tirigan fled to the

---

Text 9.1 The *ensi* of Lagash builds the temple of Ningirsu and the entire world participates, donating its materials to the centre of the world (from Gudea, Cylinder A)

'From Elam came the Elamites, from Susa came the Susians; (the peoples of) Magan and Meluhha collected timber from their mountains and – in order to build the temple of Ningirsu – Gudea brought (these materials) together in his town Girsu.

After the god Ninzaga had given him (a pertinent) order: they brought copper for Gudea, the temple-builder, as if he were a transporter of excellent grain; after the god Ninsikil had given him (a pertinent) order: they brought great willow logs, ebony logs together with logs from the sea to the governor, the temple-builder.

In the Cedar Mountain, which nobody had entered before, the lord Ningirsu made a path for Gudea: he cut its cedars with great axes, and he carved the *Shar-ur* (-weapon), the "right arm" of Lagash, his ruler's "storm" weapon, out of it: it is like a giant snake, swimming in water. In the pure quay of Kasurra, he received logs of cedar wood from the Cedar Mountain, logs of cypress wood from the land of cypresses, logs of juniper wood from the land of junipers, tall spruce trees, plane trees, large logs, one larger than the other.

In the land of stones, where no man had ever reached, the lord Ningirsu opened the way for Gudea; (from there) he brought back large stones cut in slabs. From the land of Madga, Gudea gave lord Ningirsu *abal*-bitumen, *igiengur*-bitumen, and gypsum, (and brought them) with *ḫauna*-ships and *nalua*-ships, as if this was what ships (normally) transported, (namely) grain from the fields.

Great things came to support the governor, builder of the E-ninnu: the land of copper, from Kimash, he called, and he mined its copper (and placed it) into large baskets. To the man in charge of building his master's house, the governor, raw gold was brought from its country of origin; for Gudea NE-metal was brought down from its land, light cornelian from Meluhha was laid out before him, and the alabaster arrived from the land of alabaster.

The shepherd builds the temple with precious metals, and the goldsmith participates; he builds the E-ninnu with precious stones, and the jeweller participates; he builds (the temple) with copper and tin: the smith-priest Nintukalamma lays them out in front of him, and the heavy anvil roars for him, like a storm . . .'

---

city of Dubrum, where he was killed. Gutian rule, unable to survive due to its limited presence in the area, inevitably fell. Following this victory, Utu-hegal made Uruk a hegemonic power over the other Mesopotamian cities. However, this supremacy did not last and was soon replaced by the rise of Ur-Nammu, *ensi* of Ur. The latter managed to lay the groundwork for a much more solid and long-lasting rule. This rule combined the independent nature of the Sumerian city-states with an aspiration for universal dominion.

2 The formation and structure of the Ur III empire

Ur-Nammu, who had previously been *ensi* in Ur on behalf of Utu-hegal (and was maybe his brother), supplanted the latter and took on the title of 'strong man, king of Ur, king of Sumer and Akkad'. In the past, supremacy outside the borders of a city-state was seen as an accumulation of different royal titles. Sargon himself had claimed that he managed to unite in his person the role of *en* of Uruk and *lugal* of Kish. Under Naram-Sin, this view was remodelled to become a more universal concept, which is clear in his use of the title 'king of the four quarters'. With Ur-Nammu, supremacy began to be formulated while keeping ethno-linguistic differences in mind. In the south, cities were not considered individually, but as part of the region of Sumer. Akkad represented the north, replacing the role formerly held by Kish. Ur-Nammu therefore tried to emphasise his consolidated kingship over central and southern Mesopotamia. He managed to show that expansionistic and universal ambitions were not particularly significant and that the independent role of city-states was secondary. In other words, the innovation of Ur-Nammu's reign was not in its extension, but in its organisation.

With the rise of Ur, cities lost their traditional autonomy (which is an entirely different concept from their fluctuating state of independence). They were still ruled by an *ensi*. Now, however, the title did not designate a local ruler governing on behalf of the local city-god. The *ensi* became a governor, appointed by Ur and acting on behalf of the king of Ur (Figure 9.1). In this regard, it is rather unsurprising that, among the many Akkadian innovations in kingship ideology, Ur-Nammu and his successors continued the tradition of deifying the ruling king. However, the king was not seen as a hero, like in the Akkadian period, but as a central cultic and administrative figure.

The deified kings of Ur consequently replaced the city-gods as ultimate heads of the land. They therefore controlled the entire production and redistributive system, whose management was inevitably delegated to the local *ensi*. Despite being highly influential on an ideological level, this concentration of resources in the hands of the kings of Ur was difficult to manage on a practical level. The substitution of local rulers with functionaries appointed by Ur could not have been welcomed without opposition and conflict. Nevertheless, apart from the victory of Ur over the *ensi* of Lagash, there are no indications of difficulties in the evidence, which tends to describe the situation *a posteriori*. The kings of Ur actually preferred to avoid mentioning the battles taking place against the Sumerian city-states. They simply celebrated their role as champions of a united and peaceful Mesopotamia.

Ur-Nammu's inscriptions only describe his peaceful endeavours, such as the construction of temples and *ziggurats* (at Ur, Uruk, Nippur and so on), of canals (now connecting cities), the creation of agricultural fields and the revival of trade (Figure 9.2). A commemorative inscription of the king celebrates his popularity following his agricultural interventions: 'The canals you dug, the great fields you sorted, the marshes you drained, the grain you collected, the fortified farms and villages you built, I want the people to look at them in wonder, and that they invoke your name, Ur-Nammu, forever'.

Another fundamental contribution in the organisation of the empire was the creation of the earliest known set of law codes. Even though these laws were inspired by previous reform edicts, their structure was

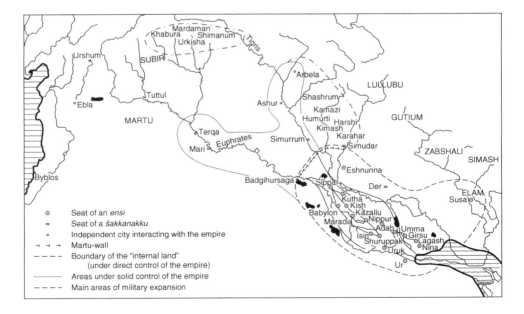

Figure 9.1   The empire of the Third Dynasty of Ur.

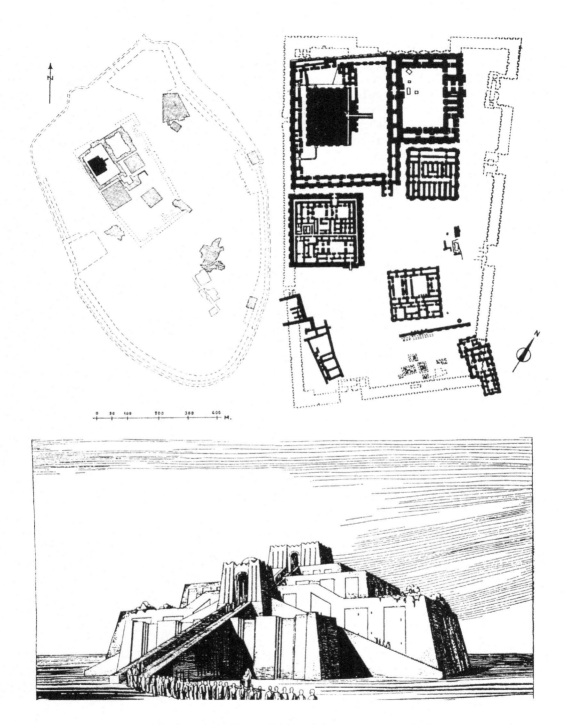

Figure 9.2 Ur in the Neo-Sumerian period. *Above, left*: Plan of the city; *Above, right*: The 'temenos' of the Ur III period; *Below*: The *ziqqurat* of Ur-Nammu.

innovative. In fact, these were not just laws meant to alleviate structural disfunctions in the system. They were an organic and solid re-organisation of the way justice was administered, and it is evident that the intention behind them was to create a uniform system. Ur-Nammu established the standard measure of the sila (a capacity measure), the mina and the shekel (weight measures), and the standard amounts to be paid in case of a homicide, rape, or other crimes. Therefore, instead of occasional reform edicts, Ur-Nammu introduced a unified code, which was also aimed at celebrating the king as the one who established 'justice and fairness' in the land, avoiding abuses and bringing 'freedom'. In other words, the code demonstrated how well organised Ur-Nammu's reign was. Equally important was the land register, a text recording the measures of individual administrative districts, their borders, gods and imperial functionaries.

The size and structure of Ur-Nammu's reign was further consolidated under the rule of his son Shulgi. In the first part of his reign, he continued to present himself as a peaceful builder and administrator both in his votive inscriptions and foundation texts, and in his dating formulas, which always used a religious or civic event as the memorable event of the year. In his self-celebratory hymns, Shulgi emphasises his abilities as a scribe (since he could write in both Sumerian and Akkadian, and knew all five languages of the world), judge, administrator and builder. However, he also stresses his physical strength and military prowess in defending Sumer and Akkad against the attacks of barbarians living in the mountains. In other words, he promoted peace and justice internally ('cities I have not destroyed, walls I have not knocked down' is his emblematic boast), and his victorious might externally.

Following the re-organisation of the army in the twentieth year of his reign, and the creation of a new register in his twenty-first year, the second half of Shulgi's reign focused on a series of campaigns in the north. These expeditions reached several regions located between the Diyala and the Khabur, thus between the alluvial plain and the mountains: Karahar, Simurrum, Harshi, Kimash, Humurti, and Shashrum. Behind this Hurrian-speaking area (which is the reason why these wars are called the 'Hurrian wars'), there were the dangerous mountain people (Lullubeans), against whom the king had to defend his reign. However, within the Hurrian region, there were still fertile lands and important cities (from the Assyrian Urbilum and Nineveh to Urkish) that the empire clearly wanted to conquer.

The number of expeditions sent to the area indicates that the security of the 'Hurrian frontier' and the conquest of Upper Mesopotamia were difficult to achieve. However, in order to justify his title of 'king of the four quarters', Shulgi continued to pursue his expansionist policy outside Sumer and Akkad. On the one hand, this policy ensured more protection to the centre. On the other, it guaranteed the empire's control over the trade routes managed by the three commercial hubs of Susa (for the east), Assyria (for the north and Anatolia) and Mari (for Syria).

In the west, nomadic groups were living among cities similar to the ones of Mesopotamia. In this case, these nomadic groups were not mountain people, but the Martu (Amorites), farmers of the steppes speaking a West Semitic language. Two sons of Shulgi, Amar-Sin and Shu-Sin, who succeeded their father, had to continue the wars on the Hurrian as well as the Amorite front. The Neo-Sumerian mental map of an internal land (Sumer and Akkad) surrounded by a turbulent periphery found its concrete application in the construction of a forti-fication wall crossing the alluvial plain. This wall was located slightly to the north of Akkad, and was meant to protect the empire from the Martu. This small 'Chinese wall' was built roughly at the same time as the Prince's Wall, built by the Egyptian twelfth dynasty to face the same nomadic group. The latter was spreading on both fronts from the Syro-Palestinian region to the areas of greatest urban and agricultural concentration.

Just like the Akkadian kings, the kings of Ur dedicated votive monuments in temples. Their inscriptions were also copied in the Old Babylonian period. A collection of Shu-Sin's inscriptions confirms the impression already described above: the celebratory tone was not directed against Mesopotamian cities or other urban-ised centres (such as the ones in Elam and Syria) anymore. The inscriptions rather focused on those turbulent 'barbarian' groups from the steppes and mountains, considered to be uncivilised and inhuman. Shu-Sin was victorious against Simanum (north of Urbilum), the Lullubeans, the *ensi* of Zabshali (in the Zagros), Shi-mashki (north of Susa, previously read as 'Sua') and other cities and lands within the Elamite confederation.

The empire, which reached its fullest extension during Shulgi's reign, remained the same size until the beginning of the reign of Ibbi-Sin. At that time, the first signs of a crisis began to appear. In these fifty years of consolidated administration and internal peace, Lower Mesopotamia became an ethnically and culturally unified entity, apart from its occasional episodes of political fragmentation. Moreover, the idea of kingship as being only one ruler at any given time began to be increasingly more established (and the Sumerian King List was written in order to support this idea). In this way, there was no political separation among cities, or between Sumerians and Semites, but between this unified system and the surrounding barbarian world.

3 Economy and administration

Despite the difficulties along the borders, the portion of Mesopotamia located between the 'wall of the land' (or the 'wall of the Martu') and the Persian Gulf experienced a phase of great prosperity under the Third Dynasty of Ur. The Akkadian attacks and the more recent incursions of nomadic groups had left a significant mark on Mesopotamia. Consequently, the types of settlements developing in the Ur III period (which would continue throughout the Old Babylonian period) were different from the ones of the Early Dynastic II-III and Akkadian periods. Smaller settlements experienced a period of crisis, mainly due to two main factors. In fact, the foreign incursions of Amorites or Gutians affected more these smaller, unprotected villages, rather than the fortified cities. This caused a mass movement of people towards urban settlements. Moreover, land ownership and management began to be concentrated around temples, which did not hire 'free' workers from villages anymore, but began to employ full-time workers without property who lived in the cities. Overall, the population grew, and it seems that this increase was the highest attested for the entire Pre-Classical period (Figure 9.3).

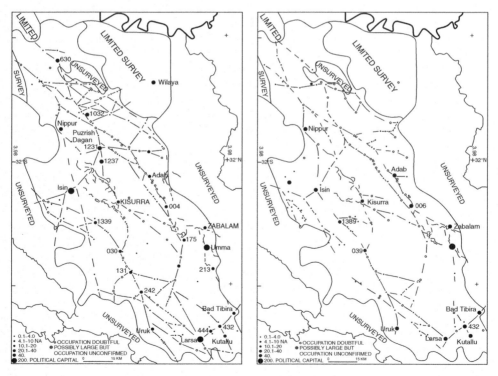

Figure 9.3   The occupation of Lower Mesopotamia from 2100 to 1600 BC. *Left*: Ur III and Isin–Larsa period; *Right*: Old Babylonian period.

Among the cities that had flourished during the Early Dynastic period, many were now in decline, especially in the south (such as Eridu, Uruk and Shuruppak). On the contrary, some cities, such as Umma, Larsa and Isin, experienced a period of significant growth. Moreover, other settlements only now began to rise as influential centres (such as Babylon and other cities in the north). The main axis of Mesopotamia now shifted to the north, balancing the former power struggles between Sumer and Akkad. This fact is clearly shown by the royal titulature of the time. The construction of new canals, favouring certain routes above others, caused considerable migrations to the west, following the slow movement of the Euphrates riverbank in that same direction.

This impressive urban and ideological reorganisation is attested in the texts, which describe several restorations of temples, walls and canals. The building programs of Ur-Nammu and his successors focused on several cities (most importantly in the prestigious Ekur of Nippur), but were predominantly concentrated in Ur. It is there that the main temple complex, which included the most important temples of the city, took its definitive shape. Ur-Nammu built its imposing *ziggurat* (a terraced step pyramid), which was destined to a long history of restorations well into the Neo-Babylonian period (Figure 9.4).

In the Neo-Sumerian period, the population of Ur was ca. 200,000 people. Both this population increase and the urban improvements were largely supported by agricultural activities. This was certainly not new, just like the state's interventions improving hydric infrastructures and the creation of new fields. However, the characteristic feature of all Ur III interventions (and in this regard Shulgi is the ruler deserving most credit) was a clear intention to organise and unify the management of the state. An important indicator of this is the visible increase of Neo-Sumerian administrative texts compared to any other period (unparalleled until the Neo-Babylonian period) and their uniformity (with some local variations) throughout the empire. Therefore, alongside an increase in the quantity of these texts, there was a visible qualitative improvement. This change indicates a desire to keep a thorough account of estimates and results, as well as the workforce employed and their productivity, through the systematic use of fixed parameters. In other words, there was a clear intention to improve economic structures, in order to efficiently and uniformly manage an empire of unprecedented size.

The economy of earlier empires was predominantly based on commercial activities and political relations with states that were controlled by the centre and were dependent on it. However, the empires themselves did not directly control these resources. The direct management of resources was an innovation of the kings of Ur, who applied it throughout the centre of the empire, which was itself no longer divided into several tributary city-states, but into provinces governed by functionaries (the *ensi*) appointed by the kings of Ur. The bureaucratic management of these provinces was uniform and interchangeable, and could be applied throughout the land (although some local variations remained in place).

Figure 9.4 The *ziggurat* of Ur, with modern restorations.

This system was kept in place through an intense exchange of royal messengers. Shulgi's pride in his scribal and administrative abilities therefore acted as a model for his delegates, and clearly expressed the ideology of the empire. The unification and reorganisation of administrative procedures were based both on previous local developments and the Akkadian example. Therefore, they were implemented by combining the previous palace and temple bureaucracies. Regarding land management, the unifying role of the divine king (which was different and innovative compared to the former Akkadian model) led to an ideological inclusion of all 'great organisations' into a single organic system, making them a constitutive part of the empire. Temples in particular continued to be at the centre of Neo-Sumerian economy.

The increased availability of sources allows us to analyse many sectors of the empire's economy. Agricultural activities can be reconstructed thanks to the presence of land registers (from Lagash), which can be analysed in conjunction with other texts (Text 9.2). The resulting social picture is a pyramidal structure starting from individual farmers and moving up to functionaries responsible for the management, taxation and control of the fields. The agricultural landscape was predominantly made of long fields (thin strips of land, whose long side was at least ten times longer than their short side) located along irrigation canals. Their yields were

---

Text 9.2 Neo-Sumerian agriculture: an example of a cadastre, including the measurements of a field (divided into four parts) and an estimate of its yields

'[1.] 660 GAR on the long side, 77 GAR on the short side, 78 *iku* added, 12.75 *iku* detracted: (in total) a field of 573.50 *iku*. (From this:) 91.25 *iku* at 60 (*sila* = litres, of harvest per *iku*), 44.50 *iku* at 180, 38 *iku* at 300; 399.75 *iku* to be left empty. Barley (to be collected) = 2/3 of the harvest) 16,590 litres. Ur-Shulpae is the scribe.

[2.] 670 GAR on the long side, 50 GAR on the short side, 9.50 *iku* added, 58.50 *iku* detracted: (in total) a field of 286 *iku*. (From this:) 30 *iku* at 180 (litres per *iku*), 42 *iku* at 120, 49.50 *iku* at 60; 170.50 *iku* to be left empty. Barley: 8740 litres. Ur-Shaga son of Baada is the scribe.

[3.] 630 GAR on the long side, 36 GAR on the short side, 15.50 *iku* added, 0.75 *iku* detracted: (in total) a field of 241.50 *iku*. (From this:) 37.75 *iku* at 120 (litres per *iku*), 31.75 *iku* at 180, 14 *iku* at 60; 158 *iku* to be left empty. Barley: 7390 litres. Ur-Minmug is the scribe.

[4.] 630 GAR on the long side, 34.50 GAR on the short side, 15.50 *iku* added, 1.25 *iku* detracted: (in total) a field of 234.50 *iku*. (From this:) 25.50 *iku* at 120 (litres per *iku*), 27.25 *iku* at 180, 15.50 *iku* at 60; 166.25 *iku* to be left empty. Barley: 5930 litres. Lu-Suen son of Ur-bagara is the scribe.

Dada will collect (the barley). (Name of) the field: Lugal-namuruna. (Intensity of cultivation) 11 furrows per GAR. Supervisor: the priest of the goddess Nin-MAR.KI. Under the supervision of Baa.

The year following the one in which Kimash was destroyed (= 47th year of Shulgi).'

This table (which does not take into account the additions and detractions of land, since they are difficult to measure and relatively small) displays the agricultural landscape of the time, characterised by long fields. This was the typical layout of planned colonisation, with fields laid out along the irrigation canals. Ca. 2/3 of the land seems to have been left fallow.

300	180	60	empty
180	120	60	empty
180	120	60	empty
180	120	60	empty

carefully calculated following fixed parameters. The administration recorded the size of every field (multiplying the long side by the short side, and taking into account eventual additions or deductions), and was able to estimate yields before harvests by multiplying the area of a field by the established parameters.

In order to maintain an effective control of agricultural production, the administration also established and calculated the quality of the soil, the degree of salinisation, the distance between furrows, the intensity of sowing and the ratio between seeds and harvest. The available evidence only concerns public lands, which were the only ones requiring precise accounting. This is because they were not privately managed and required the involvement of several professionals. Conversely, there is a considerable gap in the evidence on lands owned by individuals or families, including lands given by the state to its workers and the lands owned by 'free' families. Over time, these two categories would eventually converge into one.

The farming of cattle, sheep and goats also underwent careful controls through the re-structuring and standardisation of estimates. This is particularly attested in the specialised administrative centre of Puzrish-Dagan (Drehem) near Nippur. This centre accumulated cattle before sending it to the main temple. The farming of cattle and other animals mainly produced milk and dairy products (butter and cheese). When the administration entrusted a herd to a particular centre, it recorded the composition of the herd, establishing the parameters for the herd's growth each year, as well as the quantity of dairy products to be produced (Text 9.3a). The parameters were purely theoretical. What really happened within the production unit escaped the control of the administration, and was therefore not recorded. The administration's conventions were that a cow never died and gave birth to half a calf a year, alternating between a female and a male calf. The quantity of butter and cheese required from each cow was moderate, but one that had to be provided to the administration, no matter what the actual situation was.

The farming of sheep was mainly focused on the production of wool. When a herd was entrusted to a shepherd, its composition was recorded and the parameters of births and deaths were established. Similarly, the quantity of wool to be produced was calculated, keeping in mind the differences between sheep and rams, as well as their size. Wool was then ranked according to its quality (there were at least six or more categories) and sent to manufacturing centres. Each operation had its own parameters. The administration took into account losses during manufacturing (carding, spinning and washing) and the working days it required. Consequently, a given amount of wool needed a certain number of working days to produce a certain quantity of thread (either warp thread or weaving thread). In order to produce a fabric of given dimensions, then, the administration knew the quantity of working days and warp and weaving thread required. It was then able to calculate the cost and raw materials needed before the whole operation even began.

The monitoring of raw materials, the calculation of the losses and of the working days required were also the core parameters for other sectors in which the workforce was specialised (unlike the textile industry, which employed a large number of female workers, usually slaves, concentrated in hundreds of workshops resembling proper prisons). In pottery production, due to the accessible and inexpensive nature of clay, the administration only established the amount of working days needed to create a vase of a specific type and capacity, leading to a standardisation of pottery types (Text 9.3b). On the contrary, in metallurgy, where working days were not easy to estimate and less important, the administration was mainly concerned with the expensive raw material. Therefore, in order to control the correct and satisfactory use of metal provided to the craftsmen, there were parameters for the ratio between copper and tin, losses during manufacturing and the weight of each piece of equipment.

A different case requiring strict control measures from the administration was the work of merchants. The latter could be defined as commercial agents working for the central administration. Merchants departed with a certain amount of goods to be exported, whose value was known, or just fixed amounts of silver. Upon their return, they had to provide imported goods of an equal value to the ones they exported. The administration therefore had to produce an annual or half-year balance recording the quantity and the single value of the imported and exported goods, their total value and the amount to be credited or deduced from the

Text 9.3 The economic administration of the Third Dynasty of Ur

a) Animal husbandry: expected growth of a herd of cattle in ten years. The uniformity of the sequence (visible from the alternation between births of a male and a female, the fact that no animal dies, and so on), and the modest rates of production and reproduction (1/2 calf a year per cow) show that this was a purely administrative record, rather than an actual reality.

| Year | Cattle | | | | | | | | | | Produce | |
| | Female | | | | | Male | | | | | | |
	Suckling calf	1 year (old)	2 years	3 years	Adults	Suckling calf	1 year (old)	2 years	3 years	Adults	Butter	Cheese
I	1				4	1					20	30
II	1	1			4	1	1				20	30
III	1	1	1		4	1	1	1			20	30
IV	1	1	1	1	4	1	1	1	1		20	30
V	1	1	1	1	5	1	1	1	1	1	20	30
VI	1	1	1	1	6	2	1	1	1	2	25	37.5
VII	2	1	1	1	7	1	2	1	1	3	30	45
VIII	1	2	1	1	8	2	1	2	1	4	35	47.5
IX	2	1	2	1	9	2	2	1	2	5	40	60
X	3	2	1	2	10	2	2	2	1	7	45	67.5

b) Craftsmanship: record of the monthly production of a palace pottery workshop, including times of production for each type of vase.

Total: 3 300 litres kur-GU.DU-jars — work needed: 30 days
Total: 6 300 litres *lahtan*-jars — work needed: 60 days
Total: 9 120 litres pointed vases — work needed: 54 days
Total: 40 110 litres pointed vases — work needed: 220 days
Total: 170 30 litres vases — work needed: 170 days
Total: 320 30 litres wide-rim vases — work needed: 400 days
Total: 54 25 litres wide-rim vases — work needed: 54 days
Total: 62 . . . large — work needed: . . . days
Total: 145 10 litres vases — work needed: 48.3 days
Total: 6 vases with filter — work needed: 6 days
Total: 6 jugs — work needed: 4 days
Total: 12 fixed jars with spout — work needed: 12 days
Total: 12 *lam-ri*$_6$ vases — work needed: 6 days
Total: 85 15 litres vases — work needed: 42.5 days
Total: 3 1 litre vases — work needed: 3 days
Total: 40 5 litres vases — work needed: 13.3 days
Total: 830 1 litre *sa-du*$_{11}$ vases — work needed: . . . days
Total: 12 clay *turuna* objects — work needed: 12 days
Total: 110 large 1 litre vases — work needed: 11 days

In total: 2960.5 working days (needed?)
In total: 3604.3 working days (spent?). Supervisor: . . .
Supplement: X + 25.3 working days
Date (month, year) = fourth year of Amar-Sin

Text 9.4 **Tabular translation of a Neo-Sumerian merchant's balance**

Entries	Quantity	Commodities	Value in silver shekels	grains	Remarks
	12.5 shekels 11 grains	silver	12	101	
	30 gur (= 9000 litres)	barley	30		for the second time from Lu-kalla
Total			42	101	(capital which is on deposit)
Out of which	18.000	feathers	10	–	
	515 litres	sprouted alkali	–	120	
	12.5 litres	*ha-din*-onions	–	75	
	17 litres	'pure' onions	–	60	'intake' of Ur', receipted by Ur-Ninmar via Ur-Shara, son of Lu-igi-shashag
	17 litres	crushed onions	–	60	
	250 mine	gypsum	–	45	
	10 litre	building bitumen	–	20	
	20 litre	cassia	–	10	
	5 shekels	silver	5	–	the price of red silver for eye paint; (which) Ur-Shulpae received
	1 siclo 20 grains	silver	1	20	the price of bronze
	20 shekels 60 grains	silver	20	60	(which) Lu-kalla received
	51 litre	pig's fat	3	174	seal of Ur-Shulpae.
Total			42	104	(was withdrawn)
Credit				3	

(Date:) Year in which the throne of Enlil was fashioned (third year of Amar-Sin).

---

merchant (Text 9.4). The latter amount would be taken into account in the provision for the following year. These records are a fundamental source of information on the types and quantities of goods traded (often within the empire, but sometimes even outside its borders), as well as on the system of equivalences in prices. This information shows how the system previously required a standardisation of weights, measures, quality of goods and their value in silver. Admittedly, the process already had a long history on a local level (as early as the first urbanisation in the Uruk period), but only now was it applied on a wider scale.

Balance records and parameters clearly mirror the type of relation existing between the administration and the merchant, craftsman, or shepherd. However, they are not a faithful representation of the economy of the period. Cows certainly gave birth to more than half a calf a year, but they often died, and the real growth of a herd remains unknown to us. In order to avoid inconveniences, the theoretical values established by the administration therefore had to be lower estimates of the actual values. Consequently, the quantities of wool per sheep, butter per cow, harvest per seed, working days per vase or textile were administrative conventions that left enough margins to the workers. These margins seem to have been quite low for farmers and craftsmen, but much higher for merchants, especially due to the annual pace of returns. Within a single year, a merchant was able to trade goods and silver, investing them in intermediary transactions and interest loans, without having to report back to the central administration.

In the case of trade, then, there was a drastic difference between administrative estimates and reality. Looking at the administrative texts it may appear that the centre supervised trade and that merchants did not have to take risks or decisions and did not earn any profit. In other words, trade may seem to have been intended for the accumulation of raw materials. In reality, what actually happened once the merchant left the centre and before he returned to it, was an entirely different story. In distant lands, there must have been various kinds of exchange, such as barter and gift-exchange. The system of prices established by Sumer had little influence on other values established in areas rich in raw materials. Moreover, the possible intermediary exchanges between merchants, taxes for transit, pre-emption rights of the local elite, and subcontracts are all unknown to us. However, it is clear that the less controlled type of trade pursued by the individual merchant for a profit balanced the type of trade envisioned by the central administration, which was mainly focused on the importation of goods.

4 The scribal tradition

The Third Dynasty of Ur promoted the formation, especially during the reign of Shulgi, of an impressive set of scribal functionaries, responsible for the administration and recording of the empire's economic activities (both in terms of production and redistribution). This process stimulated the creation and development of a scribal culture. Scribal activities were chiefly administrative and for this reason they were mainly employed by the state. However, in the Third Dynasty of Ur, scribes also developed two other areas of expertise, namely, the transmission of scribal knowledge and the writing of literary texts.

The transmission of scribal knowledge took place in the scribal 'school' (the *edubba*, 'house of tablets') under the supervision of expert scribes (the *ummia*, someone similar to a 'professor'). These scribes taught their students to master the difficult scribal repertoire of signs and words (both in terms of writing and memorising), the administrative and legal formulas and various writing styles. The school was an institution linked to the temple. The latter was the unit at the heart of the state administration, and was only accessible to the sons of the ruling class (sons of *ensi* and high officials, as well as scribes).

Therefore, scribal culture was transmitted internally among those people who already belonged to the ruling class. After all, scribal knowledge was an essential prerequisite to access and progress in the administrative profession. Scribal training was tough, and life in the *edubba* inspired the composition of literary texts emphasising the need for full commitment, the relationship between masters and students, and the prospective earnings and social advancements available to the scribe. These aspects turned scribal schools into prestigious intellectual institutions only frequented by a closed caste, who mastered a technical knowledge that was inaccessible to the majority of people. This allowed the scribal elite to control the political and economic activities of the empire.

Scribal culture already existed in the earlier temple-cities in a more or less developed way. Now, however, the pan-Mesopotamian unification of the state made scribal culture more uniform and of a better quality. This was due to the clarity of its conceptualisation and the systematic application of this key structure in any administrative document. The expected outcome of scribal activities was to document the undertakings of the administration. However, by doing that, scribal schools also improved and transmitted those instruments developed from the earliest phases of writing. Sign lists and lexical lists became almost like 'encyclopaedias', organising all the knowledge of the period in a canonical way.

One of the most important collateral productions of scribal schools were texts defined as 'literary', although this 'literary' intent was always a side effect of the original cultic, political, or scholastic purpose of these texts. Collections of literary texts are fundamental for the understanding of Neo-Sumerian culture. In fact, the ambition of scribes to control knowledge and to transmit it to their students resulted in an involuntary transmission of this culture to us. For instance, the Sumerian Georgics (also known as the Farmer's Almanac) was a series of teachings written by a father to his son. It provides information on the Neo-Sumerian agricultural calendar, with a list of operations to be done and the proper way to do them. The educational intent of these texts often provided a platform for the transmission of proverbs and erudite knowledge. These are crucial for the reconstruction of the social context, not of Neo-

Sumerian society as a whole, but at least of its public functionaries. This allows us to catch a glimpse of their attempts to maintain their reputation before their superiors, overcome rivalries, keep their behaviour impeccable, and so on.

Another typical form used for the transmission of knowledge was that of the debate. In these types of compositions, two characters (the shepherd and the farmer) or two personified objects (copper and silver, the date palm and the tamarisk), chosen as opposites or extremes of a certain set of values, debate against each other. They therefore emphasise their own qualities and belittle their opponents'. The general conclusion of the debate is usually that both opponents have useful qualities, and those aspects that at first seemed more prestigious are not necessarily the most desirable ones upon closer examination. The structure of these debates emphasises the competitive nature of Neo-Sumerian society, which was becoming increasingly hierarchical and specialised. It also emphasises the desire to re-examine opposites to develop a more balanced view, able to promote less prestigious functions in the public eye, thus showing a desire for social cohesion.

A large portion of literary texts deal with cults and cannot be treated in detail here. However, these texts contain strong references to the events and ideology of the Third Dynasty of Ur. In this phase, royal hymns began to appear, modelled on earlier hymns of the gods. This was a clear outcome of the deification of the kings of Ur. Royal hymns were usually written in the first person (Text 9.5). Kings spoke in a self-laudatory and self-celebratory tone, indicating that they had not completely taken over the role of the gods. This new form of kingship propaganda complemented royal inscriptions. In the latter, the main focus was on the kings' military victories and building activities. In the hymns, kings emphasised their talents, which were celebrated through anecdotes that had little to do with those accomplishments recorded in the inscriptions. This wider range of celebratory texts perhaps constituted an attempt to appeal to different audiences. In fact, inscriptions visibly displayed and supported by depictions were probably addressed to a wider audience. Royal hymns had a more selected audience, such as functionaries working for the court.

Text 9.5   Royal hymn of Shulgi

'I, the king, from the womb I am a hero, I, Shulgi, from my birth I am a mighty man, I am a fierce-faced lion, begotten by a dragon, I am the king of the four quarters, I am a shepherd, the pastor of the "black-headed people", I am the noble one, the god of all the lands, I am the child born of Ninsun, I am the choice of holy An's heart, I am the man whose fate was decreed by Enlil, I am Shulgi, the beloved of Ninlil, I am he who is cherished by Nintu, I am the one who was endowed with wisdom by Enki, I am the powerful king of Nanna, I am the growling lion of Utu, I am Shulgi, who has been voluptuously chosen by Inanna, I am a mule, most suitable for the road, I am a horse, having its tail on the highway, I am a stallion of Shakan, eager to race, I am a wise scribe of Nisaba.

Like my heroism, like my strength, my wisdom is perfected [as well], its true words I strive to attain.

Righteousness I cherish, falsehood I do not tolerate, words of fraud I hate!

I, Shulgi, the mighty king, superior to all, because I am a powerful man, who rejoices at the strength of his loins, I moved my legs, proceeded along the roads of the land, I determined the *danna*-s, built (lodging-) houses there, planted gardens by their side, established resting places, installed in those places experienced men; he who comes from above, he who comes from below, may refresh themselves in their cool shade; the way-farer who passes the night on the road may seek haven there, like in a well-built city.

That my name be established for distant days, that it never fall into oblivion, that my fame be praised in the land (of Sumer), that my glory be proclaimed in the foreign lands, I, the runner, arose in my strength, (and) in order to test (my speed) in running, from Nippur to the brick-work of Ur, my heart prompted me to traverse, as if it were (the distance) of one mile.

> I, the lion, never failing in his vigour, standing firm in his strength, covered my hips with the *lama ḫussu-*garment, like a dove anxiously fleeing from a *šibbu*-snake, I swung my arms, like the Anzu-bird, when turning its eyes on the mountain, I "opened wide the knees".
>
> The (inhabitants of the) cities, which I had founded in the land, came to (meet) me, the black-headed people, as numerous as ewes, gazed at me with admiration.
>
> Like a kid of the mountain, hurrying to its habitation, while Utu spreads broad daylight over the countryside, I entered the Ekishnugal.
>
> The temple of Suen, the stall which yields plenty of fat, I filled with abundance, oxen I slaughtered there, sheep I lavishly offered there. I caused *sim* and *ala*-drums to resound there, I caused *tigi* drums to play there sweetly, I, Shulgi, the generous provider, presented meal-offerings there; on the "royal stand", clad in terror like a lion, in the lofty-palace of Ninegal, I bowed down and bathed in ever-flowing water, I knelt down and feasted there.
>
> (Then) I arose like a hawk, (like) a falcon (and) returned to Nippur in my vigour.'

Within this closed circle of scribes, functionaries and priests, certain characteristic aspects of Neo-Sumerian kingship left a significant mark. The central issue was the deification of the king and the reality of his human mortality. At the time of Naram-Sin, the problem was dealt with by emphasising the heroic nature of the king. In the Neo-Sumerian period, the answer was more cultic, thus including the divine sphere. Sacred marriages with deities, and burials portrayed as a return to the realm of the gods became focal points of the ideology of kingship. The burial of Ur-Nammu or Shulgi was a moment filled with important implications, as Ur-Nammu's hymns clearly indicate. Gilgamesh was still a model of the mortal divine king, and Shulgi defined him as his own brother, both being sons of the same mother, Ninsun. Instead of mentioning heroic feats, the immortality of the king was portrayed as a descent to the underworld. This descent, then, was clearly visible when the king was ceremoniously buried.

Following the iconographic and literary debut of myths in the Akkadian period, mythological elaborations continued to be developed in response to current events. However, this process began to slow down in the Neo-Sumerian period. After this phase, mythical ancestral kings would cease to be the main models and were replaced by the kings of Akkad. On seals, presentation scenes with a textual description substituted mythological scenes. The standardised, hierarchic position of the characters depicted and the presence of the divine king clearly mirrors the political ideology of the scribal and priestly classes, the main owners of these seals.

Mythological texts also allude to fundamental themes of Neo-Sumerian politics. There were the relations with the people of the west (Martu), the conquest of the north (the Ebih mountain and beyond), the revival of long-distance trade, the re-organisation of agriculture in Mesopotamia and so on. These were not intentional allusions, since they were too indirect to be in any way effective, but were natural influences of that society in the formulation and written transmission of Sumerian mythology.

5 The empire's periphery

The ability of the Third Dynasty of Ur to establish order and unity in its centre was not paralleled by an equal presence in the surrounding regions. The latter were still recovering from the Akkadian interventions and were involved in a series of developments that would eventually spread to Mesopotamia itself. Following the Akkadian expeditions against the Elamite confederation ruled by the dynasty of Awan, a new balance of powers was established in the regions south of the Iranian plateau and in the Persian Gulf (Figure 9.5). Although the role of the kings of Ur there was defined, it was largely marginal. Only during Shulgi's reign, the ruler conquered Susiana, which would remain a province of the empire until the reign of Ibbi-Sin. Under Ur III

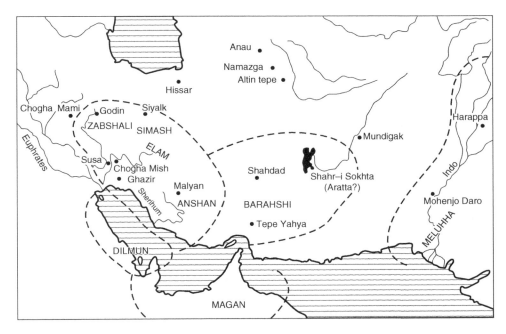

Figure 9.5 Map of the Iranian plateau and the Persian Gulf in the second half of the second millennium BC.

control, Susiana was governed by an *ensi* appointed by the king. The area was therefore included in the Mesopotamian nucleus of the empire and fully integrated both on a political and administrative level.

However, in the surrounding areas, the rest of Elam remained independent. In fact, from an Elamite perspective, Susa was only a marginal city bordering with Sumer. The kings of Ur interacted with the regions of Anshan (Fars), Shimashki and Zabshali (north of Susiana) through a series of peace treaties, containment policies and threats. At times this interaction was expressed through marriages between the daughters of the kings of Ur and the Elamite kings, or military expeditions. However, the kings of Ur never reached a stable control of the area. On the contrary, the necessity to face the Sumerian threat was one of the main catalysts behind the rise of the 'dynasty of Shimashki'. The latter managed to remain independent, and even had a crucial role in the fall of Ur.

Apart from Elam, there were other political and cultural entities with which the Third Dynasty of Ur interacted (though less distant than the ones with which Akkad interacted), although mainly for commercial purposes and not directly. The main state of southern Iran, located east of Anshan, was Barahshi. This area was briefly conquered by the Akkadian kings, but overall remained independent, being far from Lower Mesopotamia. Its centre corresponded to the area of Kerman, and included sites such as Tepe Yahya and Shahdad. Military interventions were then substituted by the frequent exchange of messengers between the area and the kings of Ur. This demonstrates the commercial interaction between the two, at times expressed through some marriages between the two royal families. However, it was Barahshi, rather than Ur, that initiated these interactions. From Ur's perspective, Barahshi was a distant land, only important for semiprecious stones (just like in the Early Dynastic period), animals and exotic plants.

The same can be said about Magan, provider of copper, and the distant Meluhha, provider of exotic and minor products. Also in this case, trade (chiefly by sea) was mainly mediated through other agents, mostly local partners. The main commercial junction was the free port of Dilmun, which in this period was at its peak, at least judging from the archaeological remains. Sumerian merchants did not travel further than Dilmun and mainly acquired raw materials from there. Initiatives were mainly in the hands of Meluhha.

This was the result of the rising influence (which is also visible archaeologically) of Indus culture in the Persian Gulf. Compared to the Akkadian period, there was a concrete change in the degree of commercial activities and political influence, which now moved further east. This allowed Mesopotamia to maintain ties in an indirect and less aggressive way.

A similar situation can be found on the other side of Mesopotamia, with a relatively modest and indirect Neo-Sumerian influence reaching Syria. The crucial centre of interactions with western Syria was the city of Mari. The city had already been conquered by Sargon and was now ruled by a series of 'governors' (Sumerian *šagina*, Akkadian *šakkanakku*), who were more independent than the *ensi*. This line of *šakkanakku* had become completely autonomous after the fall of the Akkadian empire, and continued to remain as such in the Ur III period and after. However, it always maintained its commercial and diplomatic relations with its powerful neighbour.

Apart from Mari, the disappearance of the Eblaite kingdom had left a power vacuum, which allowed the rise of the Martu (Amorites). The latter were a Western Semitic tribal and pastoral group that began to threaten the empire's centre. Within the general influence of the Amorites in Syria, some cities remained autonomous and managed to have a certain degree of commercial interaction with Ur. Some messengers of the *ensi* of Tuttul, Ebla, Urshum and Byblos are in fact mentioned in the administrative texts of Amar-Sin. Despite being defined as such by the Neo-Sumerian scribes, these *ensi* were not dependent on Ur. They were independent rulers, as their limited interaction with the Ur III kings clearly shows.

The Third Dynasty of Ur invested considerably more in its military and political conquest of the north. Despite being far from the territory included by the frontier wall, isolated in a turbulent and hostile territory (as indicated by the many campaigns of Ur in the area), the city of Ashur was fully integrated with the empire. It even had an *ensi* appointed by the king. The strategy of Shulgi and his successors must have been aimed at securing the area around Ashur and other cities further north (Urbilum was also ruled by a *šagina*). In this way, the kings tried to keep the circulation along the Tigris and access to Upper Mesopotamia under control. This strategy was meant to oppose the rise of the Hurrians (Urkish-Nawar) and the incursions of the people inhabiting the Zagros area. At first sight, this effort seems to have been excessive for the results obtained and its apparent aims. It is necessary to note, however, that without these military interventions in the north, the kings of Ur would have become a strictly local power. In their attempt to become an imperial power, they saw Upper Mesopotamia as their main target. Moreover, it is possible that the kings of Ur were trying to reach beyond this difficult area, namely, the mineral deposits of Anatolia.

By the end of the third millennium BC, Anatolia had experienced several movements of people and a dramatic decrease of settlements in a number of areas (mainly in the central plateau, the Konya Basin and Cilicia). However, the area remained an important resource for minerals and metals. Findings such as the royal tombs of Alaca Hüyük indicate the presence of a rich political elite living in areas far from disruptions and migrations (therefore in areas still influenced by Hattic culture). These elite groups, whose main income came from their control of copper ores (Ergani Maden) and silver mines (Bulgar Maden), could have stayed in contact with the Lower Mesopotamian cities throughout the Neo-Sumerian period. This interaction could have rekindled an interest in the area. The latter was already an area of interest for the kings of Akkad, but would be better documented in the Old Assyrian period.

PART III

The Middle Bronze Age

10

THE CRISIS OF THE SECOND URBANISATION

1 The fall of the Third Dynasty of Ur

At the beginning of Ibbi-Sin's reign, the Third Dynasty of Ur was still fully functional. The dating formulas of this period prove this stability, commemorating victories over Simurrum and Huhnur (in the Zagros) and an inter-dynastic marriage with Zabshali. Soon after this, however, the dynasty began to show the first symptoms of a political and economic crisis. First, the tradition, attested in many city-states, of using Ibbi-Sin's dating formulas as a sign of their dependence on Ur began to disappear. The process started in the east of the empire. Eshnunna stopped during Ibbi-Sin's second regnal year, Susa in his third, Lagash in his fifth, Umma in his sixth, and Nippur in his seventh. Around the ruler's seventh year, provincial governors ceased to provide offerings to the gods of Ur. In the previous year, several restoration works are attested on the fortification walls of Ur and Nippur. In other words, by Ibbi-Sin's seventh regnal year, the ruler's kingdom was reduced to his capital and a few other territories. The situation was further worsened by an agricultural crisis which severely damaged the supply systems supporting the Mesopotamian cities. As a result of this scarcity of goods, the prices of basic products increased dramatically.

If the administrative texts carefully recorded these changes, literary texts provided two main explanations for this crisis. First of all, there were natural factors, such as the weak floods of the Tigris and Euphrates. These led to difficulties in irrigation and famine. Second, there were the incursions of barbarian groups. On the one hand, there were the Martu, who had managed to overcome the wall constructed to keep them away. On the other, there were the Gutians and the people of Shimashki. They descended the Zagros and destroyed several Mesopotamian cities (such as Kish and Adab), reaching as far south as Eridu. Moreover, an Elamite incursion caused the fall of Lagash, located in the empire's most vulnerable area.

A collection of royal letters, copied in the Old Babylonian period, informs us of this period of disintegration of central control. Ishbi-Erra, a functionary of Ibbi-Sin originally from Mari, was sent to the north (in the area of Isin and Kazallu) to find grain supplies for Ur. He wrote to his king stating that the operation was impossible because 'all of the Martu have entered the midst of the land, seizing all the great fortresses one after the other.' For this reason, Ishbi-Erra asked the king to be left in charge of the defence of Nippur and Isin. Ibbi-Sin confided to Ishbi-Erra that he was unable to face these dangers, as well as the breakdown of his empire, on his own. Ishbi-Erra, however, took advantage of this situation to become independent.

The Gutian and Amorite incursions only brought temporary destruction and invasions, but the Elamite occupation to the east, and the independence of the north under the newly founded kingdom of Isin, forced the empire to shrink back into a city-state. It is difficult to understand why Ibbi-Sin was unable to fight back, and whether an economic and political crisis preceded or followed the various military attacks on the empire. The literary sources consider the two factors of equal importance. They interpret the various aspects of the crisis as an expression of the gods' decision to abandon their cities and determine the fall of Ur. The city's collapse, however, was not seen as due to a sin committed by its rulers, but simply because: 'Ur was indeed given kingship, but not an eternal reign! From time immemorial, when the land was founded and until the population multiplied, who has ever seen a reign whose kingship was eternal?'

Ibbi-Sin's rule lasted twenty-five years in total, up until Ur's collapse. An Elamite attack against Ur brought Ibbi-Sin to seek refuge within its walls. The city was besieged for a long time, until it collapsed for lack of food supplies. The Elamites broke into the city and plundered it. They profaned its most sacred temples, captured Ibbi-Sin and imprisoned him in Susa. For a while, Ur became an Elamite garrison, until a change in divine support (that is the interpretation given in the sources) brought about its liberation and restoration under Ishbi-Erra. In the later accounts found in collections of omens, Ibbi-Sin's name became synonymous with misfortune and destruction: 'omen of Ibbi-Sin, in whose reign Elam reduced Ur to rubble,' or simply 'destruction omen of Ibbi-Sin.'

The destruction of Ur, which a few years earlier was the empire's capital and the most powerful city in the known world, had an enormous impact. The 'Lamentation over the Destruction of Ur' (Text 10.1) is a long composition written when the reconstruction of the city and its political recovery had already begun (since the text itself ends predicting this recovery). However, the account was close enough to the events surrounding the collapse to provide an organic theological interpretation of it. Despite this theological interpretation, it is still possible to detect some reliable historical information in the text. For instance, there is the division of the crisis into two phases: first, there was a general crisis of the empire (described for each city); and then the destruction of its capital. All aspects of the crisis are described, from the natural phenomena to the agricultural, legal, cultic, political, and military causes of the collapse.

Text 10.1 Lamentation over the destruction of Ur (extract)

'On that day the (good) storm was carried off from the city, that city into ruins;

O father Nanna, that city into ruins was made – the people groan.

In its lofty gates, where they were wont to promenade, dead bodies were lying about;

In its boulevards, where the feasts were celebrated, they were violently attacked.

Who was stationed near the weapons, by the weapons was killed – the people groan.

Who escaped them by the storm was prostrated – the people groan.

Ur – its weak and its strong perished through hunger;

Mothers and fathers who did not leave (their) houses were overcome by fire;

The young lying on their mothers' bosoms like fish were carried off by the waters;

The nursing mothers' bosoms – pried open were their breasts.

The judgement of the land perished – the people groan.

The counsel of the land was dissipated – the people groan.

The mother left her daughter – the people groan.

The father turned away from his son – the people groan.

In the city the wife was abandoned, the child was abandoned, the possessions were scattered about.

Its lady (of Ur) like a flying bird departed from her city;

Ningal, like a flying bird departed from her city.

On all its possessions, which had been accumulated in the land, a defiling hand was placed.

In all its storehouses which abounded in the land fires were kindled.

> At its rivers, the god Gibil, the purified, relentlessly did (his) work.
>
> The lofty, unapproachable mountain, Eresh-shir-gal,
>
> Its righteous house by large axes is devoured.
>
> The Sutians and Elamites, the destroyers,
>
> The righteous house they break up with the pickaxe – the people groan.
>
> Its lady cries: "Alas for my city!", she cries "Alas for my house!
>
> As for me, the lady, my city has been destroyed, my house too has been destroyed!"
>
> – The sixth song –
>
> In her stable, in her sheepfold, the lady utters bitter words:
>
> "The city is being destroyed by the storm"
>
> – Its antiphon –'

This theological interpretation explains the collapse of Ur as a decision taken by the assembly of gods. Despite the reiterative and heartfelt plea of the Moon-god Nanna-Sin for his city, once the decision was taken, it could not be changed until it was carried out in full. Only afterwards was a new propitious phase allowed to begin. Comparing this explanation of Ur's fall with the (almost contemporary) one pertaining to the fall of Akkad ('The Curse of Akkad'), it is possible to see that the latter blamed the catastrophe on the sins of Naram-Sin. Among his many offences, there were his disregard for cultic responsibilities (such as the restoration of the Ekur), behavioural aspects (such as his disregard for omens) and administrative mistakes (such as his abuse of taxation). Both texts share a similar notion of the fluctuation of political entities between a period of growth and a period of collapse. However, the reasons provided to explain the fall are different. One text blamed the Akkadian kings, while the other emphasised the inevitability of Ur's fate. This important difference indicates that, in the eyes of the priestly and scribal classes of Lower Mesopotamia, the dynasty of Ur had managed to achieve a much higher quality of justice and administration in the land than the dynasty of Akkad. In this way, the dynasty of Ur avoided those negative connotations that would have been bestowed upon it otherwise.

2 The nomads and their role: the Martu

The Western Semitic nomads, called Martu in Sumerian and Amurru in Akkadian (from which the name 'Amorites' comes from), played a crucial role in the erosion and definite collapse of the dynasty of Ur. The interaction between cities and nomadic groups was one that had existed for centuries, and this interaction was gradually adapted to the several administrative and economic developments affecting the two. Just like in the Nile Valley, so in the Mesopotamian plain the political and territorial supremacy of the cities and their economy based on agriculture and irrigation had entirely marginalised nomadic groups. They were thus seen as an 'external' presence, especially since farming activities had also become sedentary, or otherwise (whenever transhumance was still necessary) dependent on the economy of the cities.

In comparison, in the Syro-Levantine area, the nature of its environment had allowed the development of a more diverse and complex system, with areas characterised by low levels of urbanisation and intensive agriculture mixed with mountainous areas (with forests and pastures) or semi-arid steppes. Initially, these difficult areas, located between regions cultivated through rainfed agriculture and semi-arid areas, experienced visible growth in the second urbanisation. However, at the end of the third millennium BC, the process came to a sudden halt and a visible decline. It is difficult to understand to what extent this decline was due to the long-term collapse of a kind of urbanisation that was too expensive to maintain compared to its agricultural yields. Moreover, we do not know how much the fluctuations in rainfall actually impacted the overall situation. The latter factor was initially considered an unhistorical supposition. However, thanks to the recovery of more convincing paleo-ecologic evidence, it is gradually becoming more credible.

Following the course of the isohyets, this ecologically and economically 'mixed' Syro-Levantine area extended as far as Upper Mesopotamia. Michael Rowton defined the area as a 'dimorphic zone'. This phrase is now commonly used in this discipline to define an area characterised by a mixed economy based on agriculture and farming. It has to be pointed out, however, that the phrase has been misused. Marcel Mauss first introduced it to define a completely different phenomenon, namely, 'seasonal dimorphism'. The latter is encountered when the same area or population takes on different behavioural patterns at different times of the year. In this sense, our zone was not 'dimorphic' because pastoral groups coexisted with cities and agricultural villages. Rather, it was 'dimorphic' because the agro-pastoral population concentrated in the irrigated lands during the dry summers, and was much more dispersed in the pastures and steppes during the wetter winters and springs. It therefore followed those transhumant patterns that seasonally separated and reunited families and larger kin groups alike.

Consequently, the rise of urban settlements generated a similar rise in the pastoral component of the population. In the first urbanisation, the formation of city-states with an improved political structure had already caused, as a side effect, the formation and political unification of larger tribes. Similarly, the formation of large territorial states was paralleled by the birth of tribal confederations. Nonetheless, city-dwellers continued to see nomadic groups as barbarians devoid of the characteristic aspects of civilisation (such as houses and cities, agriculture and sedentariness, tombs and cults). Despite the ancient ethnographic stereotypes held against them (Text 10.3), however, these pastoral groups had their own culture and political organisation, which gradually become more visible when the sources allow us to catch a glimpse of their real, rather than their stereotypical, image.

Text 10.2 Amorite personal names

1 Phrases with predicate

Verbs in the imperfect tense:

ia-an-ti-in-e-ra-aḫ	yantin-Yaraḫ	'Yarah (= Moon) gives'
ia-ad-kur-AN	yadkur-'El	'El (= god) remembers'
ia-ku-un-su-mu-a-bi-im	yakūn-śumu-'abim	'the name of the father is safe'

Verbs in the perfect tense:

ia-ba-al-ᵈIM	yabal-Haddu	'the god Haddu has brought'

Verbs in the precative mood:

la-aḫ-wi-ba-aḫ-lu	laḫwī-Ba'lu	'may the Lord live!'

2 Noun phrases

In apposition:

i-la-kab-ka-bu-ú	'ila-kabkabuhu	'El is his star'
aś-du-um-la-a-bu-um	'aśdum-la-'abum	'the father really is a lion'

Adjective/stative verb:

a-bi-ṭa-ba	'abī-ṭāba	'my father is good'
ṭà-ab-su-mu-ú	ṭāb-śumuhu	'good is his name'

Participle:

ḫa-am-mu-ra-pi	ammu-rāpi'	'Ammu (=paternal uncle) is a healer'

Preposition:

ba-aḫ-di-li-im	ba-'dī-Līm	'(the god) Lim is behind me'

3 Questions		
a-ia-da-du-ú	*'ayya-dāduhu*	'where is his beloved?'
4 Comparative phrases		
a-bi-mi-ki-AN	*'abī-mi-ki-'El*	'my father is just like El'
la-śi-el-ka-a-bi-im	*lāśū-'el-ka-'abim*	'there is no god like a father'
5 Simple names		
ma-si-ḫa	*maśīḫa*	'anointed'
ia-di-da / ia-di-da-tum	*yadīda/yadīdatum*	'beloved' (both in the masculine and the feminine)
qa-qa-da-an	*qaqqadān*	'stubborn'
6 Genitival phrase		
ab-di-a-mi	*'abd-Ḥami*	'servant of Hami ('father-in-law')'

The pastoral component of the Syro-Levantine and Upper Mesopotamian areas was also recognisable on a linguistic level (known to us from personal names). It was a Western Semitic population (the Amorites) markedly different from the Eastern Semitic one (the Akkadians). Prior to the discovery of the Ebla archives, it was generally believed that in the third millennium BC the Amorites occupied the entire Syro-Levantine area. However, the Ebla archives have shown that the population of northern and Central Syria spoke a language (Eblaite) that was neither Akkadian nor Amorite. It was rather a western language influenced by the Akkadian scribal tradition of Central Mesopotamia (the so-called 'Kish tradition'). The Amorite component therefore remained only secondary up until the fall of the Eblaite kingdom, when it became much more prominent in the area. The influence of the Amorites in Mesopotamia only took place later on, after the fall of the Third Dynasty of Ur.

The secondary role of the Amorite element in Syria requires us to revise once again the old problem of the 'primitive seat' of Semitic people. According to this view, there was an area from which all the populations speaking Semitic languages originally departed, to move to the urbanised and agricultural areas of the Near East. This original region now needs to be searched in the south-western edge of the Near East, following that strip of land between cultivated areas and semi-arid territories extending from Palestine and the Transjordan plateau to western Arabia (from Hejaz to Yemen). This is an area whose Bronze Age settlements have only recently been excavated. The textual and archaeological evidence characterises this territory as an alternation between expansionistic outbursts and recessive phases. This forms a sequence that began with the Ghassulian pastoral groups of the Late Chalcolithic and continued with the Martu and later expansions from the Iron Age onwards.

Apart from the ethnographic stereotypes documented by Sumerian scribes, we know of the Martu from various kinds of evidence. Personal names reveal to us the linguistic aspects of Amorite, such as the conjugation with the prefix *ya-*, rather than the Akkadian *i-* (Text 10.2). Moreover, we are able to understand features strictly pertaining names: the adjectival names ending in − *ānum*; and the bipartite structure of names written as phrases (both with or without a verb), always featuring the name of the god in the second part of the name. The latter aspect is completely different from the tripartite structure of Akkadian names, where the god's name was always at the beginning. To a certain extent, Amorite names also provide us with some information on their tribal structure, especially in terms of kinship and religion. Regarding the former, Amorite names frequently mention the *'ammu*, 'paternal uncle', and *ḫālu*, 'maternal uncle', as well as the phrase *sumu-abim*, the 'father's name'. In terms of religion, Amorite names initially featured the name of a generic 'god', Ila. Only later, they began to assimilate deities such as Adad, Dagan, Ishtar and many others from the Syrian pantheon.

Text 10.3   **Nomads and mountain peoples: the stereotypes of Sumerian literature**

1 The Martu: the nomadic shepherds of the syrian steppes

'Martu of the mountain, that knows not grain'; 'Martu, might of the storm, that never knew a city'; 'tent-dweller'; 'that does not have a city; does not have a house'; 'Martu, that knows not house, knows not city, ghost dwelling in the mountain'; 'Martu: people that dig truffles in the mountain, that never bend their knees, eat raw meat, all their life do not have a house, and when they die they do not have a tomb'; 'Martu, destructive people, whose instincts are like dogs', wolves".

2 Gutians: the nomads of the Zagros mountains

'Unclassifiable as a population, unaccountable as (part of) the (internal) land. Gutians: people that know not relations, whose instincts are human, whose intelligence is canine, and the aspect that of a monkey'; 'mountain dragons'; 'people with the body of a bat, crow-faced men'; 'Gutians (that induce) lamentations, to whom the fear of god has not been shown, who cannot perform rituals and indications properly'; 'who do not ordain priestesses in temples, whose people is as numerous as grass, whose seed is vast, who live in tents, who know not temples, who mate like animals, who know not how to make flour-offerings . . . who desecrate the name of the god and eat what is forbidden'.

3 Unspecified nomads and barbarians

'People that know not metal, people that know not (precious) stones'; 'People that know not oil, people that know not milk'; 'the mountain gods eat people, do not build houses like humans, do not build cities like humans'; 'their hearts know not oven-baked bread, their stomachs know not beer'.

Figure 10.1   A group of Asiatic nomads ('Amu) entering Egypt, ca. 1900 BC.

The second kind of evidence is attested in administrative and historical sources. Administrative texts describe the Martu as working for the cities as shepherds, mercenaries and even sellers of their own products, especially metal objects (such as the typical 'Amorite dagger') and leather. The sources recount the history of the relations between pastoral groups and sedentary communities as a one-sided series of expeditions aimed at pushing these nomadic groups as far away as possible, but in vain. The Martu are already attested in the texts of Ebla, and then in those of the empires of Akkad and Ur. Already at that time their pressure on Mesopotamia was strong, implying their already successful expansion in Syria. From the other side of the Near East, contemporary Egyptian sources of the Middle Kingdom show that the Egyptians had similar worries for these nomadic incursions and took similar measures against them (Figure 10.1). Many military expeditions were sent against them, but these nomadic groups were too mobile and elusive to be completely removed or even conquered. Consequently, several fortifications were built to protect the Nile Delta from incursions coming from the Sinai, clearly mirroring the wall that the kings of Ur had built to protect Mesopotamia.

The sedentary states' attempt at containing these nomadic groups was a recurrent phenomenon in the history of the Near East. On the one hand, in order to reassure the population of their security against incursions, the problem was dealt with by a propagandistic celebration of sedentary states. On the other hand, the administrative texts reveal a completely different picture, whereby nomadic groups contributed to the economy and armies of sedentary states. However, at the end of the third millennium BC the situation became increasingly more dangerous, with nomadic groups placing increasingly more pressure on sedentary states. The situation eventually developed into a series of expansionistic outbursts into urbanised areas, both in Egypt, at the beginning of the Second Intermediate period, and in Mesopotamia, at the time of the fall of Ur.

Traces of this increase in nomadic presence at the end of the third millennium BC have been investigated archaeologically. At this time, Palestine (the region that has been more thoroughly excavated) was experiencing a particular phase, defined as the 'Intermediate Early Bronze–Middle Bronze period'. All of a sudden, the network of cities of the Early Bronze III, which had managed to reach the marginal areas in the south and in the Transjordan Plateau, collapsed. Before the return to urbanisation, through the rise of the Middle Bronze culture coming from the north and the Lebanese coast, the area experienced an intermediate period. The archaeological evidence for this period has been mainly found in necropolises, characterised by grave goods and funerary practices similar to the ones attested for nomadic groups. In particular, Jericho's necropolis features several groups of tombs with different sets of grave goods for different tribal groups. It also shows the practice of secondary inhumations, possibly due to the use of the necropolis by transhumant groups. The

necropolis also features the presence of military elites, equipped with high-quality weapons and types of pottery completely different from the previous or later types known from the area (Figure 10.2).

The consideration of this intermediate period as a phase in which the whole area had recessed from urbanised settlements to pastoral groups has undergone several revisions. First, certain specific points of this analysis have been rectified. Second, it has been discovered that some urban settlements, such as Megiddo, actually managed to survive in this period. Nonetheless, the interpretation of Palestine, located close to the south-western frontier of urbanisation, as a region marked by the strong tribal and pastoral presence in this intermediate period has to be correct, while the application of this interpretation to the whole of Syria and Upper Mesopotamia is far less acceptable.

In Syria, the collapse of the second urbanisation cannot be only due to the fall of Ebla. It was rather the effect of a migration towards more fertile and arable lands. This was generally a long-term phenomenon, but in this case it began abruptly at the end of the Early Bronze Age. In some Syrian areas nomadic pressures managed to spread more easily, causing a strong Amorite influence on Syrian culture. This influence is visible in the personal names attested between the end of the Ebla archives and the Ur III and Isin-Larsa documentation. However, the continuity of the surviving urban centres in Syria is certain and so is the continuity of their pottery types. This continuity remained during that evolution, both in terms of techniques and taste, which marked the beginning of the Middle Bronze Age. A similar situation can be found in Upper Mesopotamia, with the decline and organisational difficulties of its urban centres. Therefore, nomadic incursions took over the territories left vacant by the city-states. There was some sort of cultural continuity, which was however marked by visible changes in production and taste. These changes were not due to external factors, but were the result of an internal development.

The Amorite expansionistic wave developed in successive phases, first invading Palestine, then Syria and Upper Mesopotamia and finally reaching Lower Mesopotamia. The violent nature of the Amorite incursion in Lower Mesopotamia, attested in Neo-Sumerian texts, was a necessity when facing the solid political and military organisation of the Third Dynasty of Ur. Earlier phases of Amorite expansion could

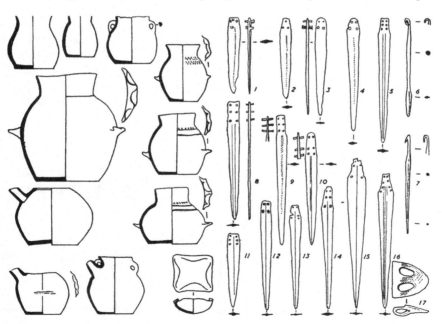

Figure 10.2 Pottery and weapons of the intermediary period between the Early and Middle Bronze Age, from the necropolis of Jericho.

have been different, with situations presenting less resistance and better opportunities to conquer the area. At the beginning of the second millennium BC, however, the Amorite expansion brought a visible predominance of Amorite names in Syria and Upper Mesopotamia and to a lesser degree in Lower Mesopotamia. On a political level, we find Amorite kings ruling over various Syrian and Mesopotamian cities.

Due to the socio-cultural influence of the Amorites taking place in that period, the tribal origins of these kings, however, cannot be assumed *a priori*. This Amorite influence was prevailing in those territories that were formerly part of the kingdom of Ebla and belonged to the 'Kish tradition'. However, in the Sumerian area, Akkadian culture was becoming increasingly influential. The rise of the Amorites in Syria and Upper Mesopotamia was not the reason why the Akkadians moved further south. By then, Akkadian culture was already a strong presence in Lower Mesopotamia. It has to be borne in mind that the scribal and political traditions of the Third Dynasty of Ur over-represented the Sumerian element of the area, which was significantly decreasing. The arrival of the Amorites kick-started a political and cultural fragmentation, which allowed Akkadian culture to rise to prominence. Akkadian culture thus visibly emerged in the scribal tradition, making Sumerian an erudite language only used for religious and literary compositions. Consequently, an Akkadian and Amorite symbiosis substituted the former Sumerian and Akkadian one.

3 Anatolia and Iran: the Indo-European problem

Towards the end of the third millennium BC, the highlands surrounding the Mesopotamian alluvial plain (from Anatolia to Iran), experienced a series of profound transformations. Despite its various micro-regional entities, around 2300 BC (at the beginning of the Early Bronze III) Anatolia experienced a cultural breakdown. Cities were destroyed and subsequently abandoned, leading to a drastic decline of that network of settlements typical of the previous phase. Around 2000 BC, a second breakdown marked the rise of Middle Bronze Age cultures. New pottery types appeared both in the west, in close contact with analogous phenomena taking place in the Aegean, and the east, in the South Caucasus. Tumuli (similar to the *kurgan* typical of the area between the Ukraine and the Caucasus), sometimes equipped with lavish grave goods and high quality metal objects, became increasingly popular.

With the decline of the urban centres of the Early Bronze Age, the area became more open to pastoral groups. These groups influenced several aspects of the material culture of Anatolia. The reappearance of cities and the development of Middle Bronze pottery types would only take place at the beginning of the second millennium BC. This process was the result of the assimilation and integration of new contributions to the ancient cultural heritage of Anatolia. Despite their different location and environment, the processes taking place in the Syro-Arabian steppes and in the Anatolian highlands mirrored each other both in terms of timing and a number of other features. For instance, there were both the crisis of urbanisation, and the assimilation of nomadic elements, which were completely extraneous to the urban and palace organisations of the Early Bronze Age. On the eastern side of the Anatolian plateau, Armenia and the South Caucasus had been completely cut off from the urban cultures of the Early Bronze Age. Now, however, a complementary phenomenon to the one taking place in Anatolia began to appear, bringing about a wider diffusion of cultural elements: from handmade, engobed, polished red-black or black pottery to the above mentioned tumuli with rich metal ware.

Further east, the crisis of urbanisation also affected the Iranian plateau (Figure 10.3). In some regions, especially in Central Iran, which was characterised by more difficult environmental conditions, urbanisation had peaked around 2200 BC and then collapsed. This led to a long period of abandonment, with the reversion of cities to villages and pastoral groups. The more intensely urbanised southern Iran (from Susiana to Fars) managed to survive the crisis. However, Iran still experienced an enormous 'vacuum' in its centre, both on a demographic and political level. This facilitated the infiltration of new groups from the north. Lastly, the Indus Valley civilisation would soon go through migratory movements and reversals to more modest types of settlements and political organisations.

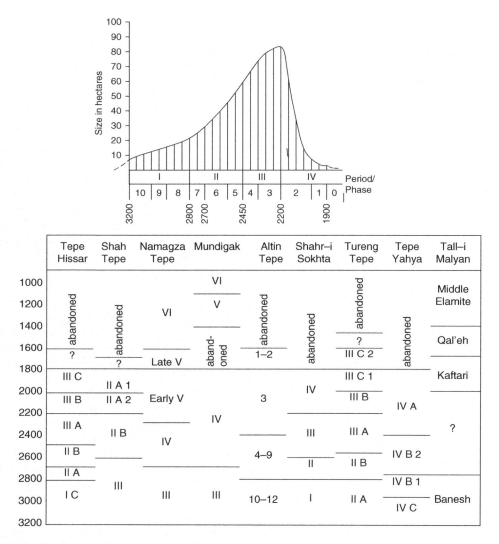

Figure 10.3 The depopulation of the Iranian plateau at the beginning of the second millennium BC. *Above*: Growth and decline of Shahr-i Sokhta; *Below*: Comparative stratigraphy and phases of abandon.

The study of the Syro-Palestinian 'intermediate' period had to take into consideration the diffusion of Semitic people. Similarly, the study of the cultural and demographic changes marking the end of the Early Bronze Age in the highlands has to take into consideration the problem of the Indo-Europeans. The former problem can be analysed more concretely, thanks to the availability of written sources, the contemporary changes in personal names, the circumscribed nature of the area analysed and the similarities in the archaeological evidence. In comparison, the study of the spread of Indo-Europeans and their possible impact on the archaeological evidence is much more difficult to trace. A first difficulty is the spatial (as well as diachronic) diffusion of the problem, which could have extended from Western Europe as far as the Indus Valley, thus affecting different historical and cultural contexts. A second difficulty is the fact that the earliest written evidence available was written at a much later date than the crisis at the end of the third millennium BC. It therefore has to be used retrospectively, with all the difficulties linked to the attempt of gaining a diachronic perspective of a situation presented in a synchronic way (probably due to later changes).

Linguists have often seen a link between the crisis of the Early Bronze Age in Anatolia (and the Aegean) and the spread of the Indo-Europeans. This was a clear attempt to find in the archaeological evidence concrete proof of their theoretical reconstructions. The same can be said of archaeologists, who have tried to find an ethno-migratory explanation for the cultural changes of the period. Moreover, just like in the case of Semitic people, the connection is seen as an 'arrival' of Indo-Europeans in areas previously inhabited by non Indo-European people, who survived as 'substrata'. This view postulates various 'waves' of Indo-Europeans moving from their 'original seat' between south-eastern Europe and Central Asia to the surrounding areas.

This theory is based on the following points, listed in order of decreasing objectivity: 1) personal names found in Old Assyrian tablets from Cappadocia show that Indo-Europeans are attested in Anatolia from 1900 BC, while the Greek dialect of the Linear B tablets and the Indo-Iranian names from Mitanni prove their presence in Greece and Iran from the mid-second millennium BC; 2) in all these areas people of non Indo-European background are attested, such as Pre-Hittites or Hatti in Anatolia and 'Minoani' in the Aegean; 3) the disruptions at the end of the third millennium BC constitute the latest and most visible phase able to provide an archaeological context to the Indo-European migrations in the south; 4) in the study of Indo-European, the group of Anatolian languages (Hittite, Luwian and other similar dialects) is considered part of a more archaic stratum (or at least one that developed before the rise of the larger group of Indo-European languages), compared to Greek and Indo-Iranian groups, which are part of a later stratum.

Within this general overview there are many possible explanations for the presence of Indo-Europeans, although it is not possible to consider them all in detail here. Regarding Anatolia, one of the explanations is that there were several waves, with a Luwian one preceding a Hittite one. Unfortunately, the specific archaeological contextualisation of these waves remains purely speculative. A widely accepted scholarly interpretation was initially suggested by Marija Gimbutas. It links the spread of Indo-Europeans to the diffusion of cultural elements typical of *kurgan* culture from southern Russia. This culture was also characterised by tumulus type graves. In the case of Anatolia, then, the Indo-Europeans were the ones introducing the tumuli, metalwork and black polished pottery typical of the South Caucasus. Both this theory's flexibility and limitations are centred on three main facts: that *kurgan* cultures had a profound diachronic impact; that their grave type was quite widespread both in time and space (being attested in contexts far from the kurganic area); and that the polished black pottery of the South Caucasus survived over a long period of time.

On a methodological level, this type of interpretation invites two fundamental objections. First, even in better-attested historical periods, there is no direct connection between language and material cultures, neither in time nor in space. Chronologically, the linguistic factor is always much more enduring than the cultural factor. Geographically, cultural elements interweave with each other, as well as with other linguistic elements, with a considerable degree of complexity. The second objection is that in better-attested historical periods linguistic changes are not always linked to migratory movements and processes starting from a unified group and leading to its subdivision. In fact, the old model of the linguistic tree itself, which was based on the concept of the development of languages from a single original stock that subsequently spread through migratory movements from a defined original location, has already been abandoned in favour of more complex models. These new models are able to accommodate the various convergences, assimilations, non-migratory diffusions, relations between various languages and so on.

In terms of archaeology, Colin Renfrew's theory deserves to be mentioned, being explicitly against the traditional interpretation. He suggested that Indo-Europeans had 'always' inhabited Anatolia. Therefore, it is worth considering the various fragmentations attested in the material evidence as a result of internal developments. In Renfrew's opinion, the diffusion of Indo-European people should be placed further back in the Neolithic period, when agriculture and village economies spread from Anatolia to south-eastern Europe and beyond. The importance of this theory chiefly lies in its methodological roots. However, the idea of an already Indo-European Anatolia strongly contradicts the linguistic evidence.

It would be much more appropriate to combine the idea of an internal cultural development with the more advanced interpretation of linguistic influences in the Indo-European context. Unfortunately, even when just focusing on Anatolia, the complexity of the problems encountered, the unreliability of the results, and the variety of possible interpretations cannot be considered here. Overall, it cannot be ignored that movements of people took place, especially in the case of Central Asiatic pastoral groups (known for their high degree of mobility). It also cannot be ignored that some fortunate conditions of outstanding insight might one day find reliable evidence for migratory movements in the archaeological evidence. Be that as it may, the highest degree of caution remains necessary. The careless use of ethno-linguistic 'labels' on various aspects of the material culture may lead to the incorrect assumption that there was a direct correspondence between language and culture. For now, there is one acceptable argument in the study of the crisis of the Early Bronze Age in the Aegean, Anatolia and Iran, and its connection with the diffusion of Indo-Europeans. This is the idea that the crisis of Early Bronze urbanised cultures, despite its purely internal nature, could have provided large territories (proper demographic and power 'vacuums') to populations whose lifestyle and economy was suitable for the exploitation of these newly available areas.

4 The diffusion and variety of the crisis

Apart from a number of common elements and implications, which had to be considered as a whole, the crisis of the Early Bronze cultures of the Near East took place over a long period of time and in a variety of different ways. The first clues to the crisis can be seen around 2300 BC, especially in Anatolia, as well as in the increased pressure placed by the periphery on the Akkadian empire. Other regions, such as Iran and Syria, were affected later on. The overall situation regained stability at the beginning of the second millennium BC, with the rise of Middle Bronze cultures. The reciprocal implications between the various phases of the crisis can be cautiously analysed only when the archaeological data (and most importantly comparative chronologies) allow us to understand the relations and directions of the various contributions. Moreover, the reconstruction of an overview of the crisis based on local written and archaeological evidence is not yet reliable enough.

It appears that the causes of the crisis of the second urbanisation were mostly internal processes. For instance, there was the excessive exploitation of the land, the concentration of wealth in the cities and palaces, and the accumulation of this wealth for prestige, which with time led to the ultimate collapse of the system. The crisis mainly affected areas in which urban settlements could not count on a reliable availability of food surplus. On the contrary, Lower Mesopotamia remained virtually untouched by the crisis, and actually attempted to protect itself by getting less involved in external affairs. The abandonment of urbanised areas, whose economy had to revert to a village and pastoral type of economy, was also a long-term phenomenon. Some areas managed to recover from the crisis of the 'intermediate' period, but inevitably collapsed again a few centuries later. It is also possible that the crisis in production had been worsened by climatic factors (higher aridity), which is not mentioned in an attempt to provide a non-human and non-historical explanation to the crisis, but because ecological changes had a long-term impact on the way the land was exploited.

This period of decreasing resources naturally caused the rise of competition and rivalry between groups. This is visibly attested in the belligerent policies of the kings of Akkad. Competition was centred on the control of commercial networks and access to certain raw materials (metals). However, it also had other implications, such as the destruction of agricultural and urban infrastructures. This caused the collapse of several political systems, or at least required expensive works of restoration and readjustment. The forced concentration of resources (both material and human) in the royal palaces made these systems extremely vulnerable to dramatic collapses, especially when their political centres were destroyed. Despite being relatively rare, these episodes had wide-ranging implications extending beyond the boundaries of these cities.

Even during the crisis, some fortunate cases, such as the Third Dynasty of Ur and the Middle Kingdom in Egypt, managed to prosper. However, all the surrounding areas undoubtedly experienced a phase of demographic and urban decline, though at different times and in different ways. The crisis caused a return to simpler and slower strategies for the exploitation of the land. This led to the substitution of cities with villages and pastoral groups. This reversal did not last long in the areas where the recovery had been fast. In other areas, however, this crisis lasted for centuries, and they had to wait for the later regional re-organisations of the Iron Age to become urbanised states once again.

Many groups (pastoral in particular) from linguistically and socially solid areas managed to settle more easily in the open spaces and power vacuums left by the declining cities. On the one hand, there were Semitic groups. On the other, there were the Indo-Europeans. The former managed to enforce and slightly expand the area inhabited by Semitic-speaking peoples in the Syro-Palestinian area and in Mesopotamia. The latter managed to expand their control in Anatolia, Armenia, Transcaucasia and in the Iranian plateau.

As a result, the final crisis of the Early Bronze Age marked the decline of populations that were neither Semitic nor Indo-European. They were therefore living between these two large and expanding groups, and formerly belonged to some of the most important cultures of the period. Some of them, such as the Sumerians in Lower Mesopotamia and the Pre-Hittites in Central Anatolia, went through a visible crisis. Others, such as the Elamites in southern Iran and the Hurrians in Upper Mesopotamia, managed to survive in the course of the second millennium BC. However, their decline was already in sight, due to their position between two groups equipped with virtually endless resources and a strong social and family structure, ensuring their diffusion and supremacy.

11

THE 'INTERMEDIATE PERIOD' OF ISIN AND LARSA

1 The demography and economy of the 'provincial' states

Modern historiography sees the transition from the Third Dynasty of Ur to the Isin–Larsa period as a moment of change in the history of the Near East. However, the people of the time saw it (or tried to see it) as a time of continuity. At first, the elements of a visible 'break' from the past appear prominently: from the break-down of political unity into a fragmentation that has been defined (following the Egyptological terminology) as the 'Second Intermediate period of Babylonia'; to linguistic changes, with Akkadian taking over the role of Sumerian; and changes in the ethnical composition of the population, thanks to the rise of the Amorites.

All these elements, some of which appeared in a very dramatic way (such as the destruction of Ur), had a traumatic effect. In order to overcome the shock, a concrete attempt was made to exorcise it, with a con-scious effort to provide a sense of ideological continuity with the past. This effort was pursued especially by the kings of Isin, who presented themselves as the heirs of the kings of Ur. These kings took over the deification, titulature and ambitions of the kings of Ur and created a king list promoting a direct succession from the dynasty of Ur to that of Isin.

Apart from this sense of continuity, which was promulgated for political reasons, the two periods were actually linked by a profound structural continuity in terms of demography, technology and economy. Due to the radical changes taking place in the surrounding regions in this phase, this continuity was even more significant. Statistical evaluations of the evidence gathered through surveys in the settlements of the time show a marked demographic continuity. However, this continuity might be deceptive. This is due to the technical difficulty in separating the ceramic index fossils of the Neo-Sumerian and early Old Babylonian period.

Changes in each individual sub-system are attested both in the archaeological evidence and in the historical and epigraphic documentation (Figure 11.1). The south experienced the rise of Larsa and the decline of Umma and Lagash. The north experienced the rise of Babylon and the decline of Kish. In the Diyala Valley, Eshnunna became a hegemonic power over the surrounding cities. Despite these changes, the total number of inhabitants and the relations between cities and villages remained roughly the same. A similar continuity can be found in the kings' efforts to build fortification walls, palaces, temples and canals. Unlike the relatively marginal interventions of the Ur kings in provincial centres, there was now an increase in the direct involvement of local kings in these kinds of undertakings. There was also a marked continuity in the architectural styles and plans of cities, visible in the temples and royal palaces of the period, as well as in private households.

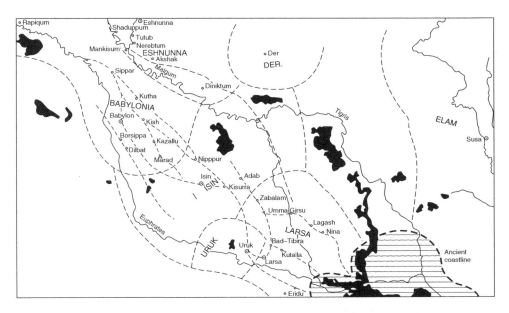

Figure 11.1   Map of Lower Mesopotamia in the Isin–Larsa period (the borders shown are purely indicative).

On a political level, this essentially stable system was structured in a significantly different way. During Ibbi-Sin's reign, imperial control over the surrounding regions broke down. As a result, an increasing number of autonomous centres began to appear. This facilitated the rise of about a dozen of independent States competing with each other. While Isin took over a large portion of the inheritance of the Third Dynasty of Ur, further south Larsa and Uruk remained independent. In the north, Babylon also became an independent centre, eventually conquering other autonomous centres, most importantly Kish. In the Diyala region, Eshnunna was independent, as was Der, located close to the Elam border. Moreover, in this period, the cities that used to be close to the border in the Ur III period became important states gravitating towards Lower Mesopotamia, such as Susa in the east, Ashur in the north and Mari in the north-west.

This was the political framework that developed in the intermediate phase between the Third Dynasty of Ur and the reign of Hammurabi of Babylon. However, the interpretation of this political fragmentation as an intermediate phase between periods of political unification (thus considered to be 'normal') is misleading. In fact, city-states were at the heart of the Mesopotamian political organisation. Consequently, unifications on an imperial level were destined to encounter difficulties within this system, and collapsed after three generations (such as in the case of Akkad and Ur) or fewer (as in the case of Babylonia). In other words, empires could only gradually reach a type of political expansion able to resist even in periods of political fragmentation. By this period, cities were centred on the palace. However, temples continued to maintain their size and role as de-centralised administrative centres. Similarly, kings continued to pride themselves for the restoration and expansion of the most prestigious city-temples. Being by now free from their subordination to the kings of Ur, the temples and sacred areas of the principal Mesopotamian cities began to play an increasingly important role in the formation of a state's identity.

Large sacred areas such as the ones of Ur or Nippur continued to be imposing complexes, despite the fact that the two cities struggled to maintain their pre-eminence. The political role of Ur was by now lost forever. Likewise, the religious role of Nippur lost the support of previous kings (as in the Akkadian period) and also lost its 'amphictyonic' role in relation to the administration of Mesopotamia as a whole (as in the Ur III period). As a result, the temple complexes of other emerging centres began to acquire considerable prestige, from the Ebabbar of Larsa to the 'cloister' of the *nadītu* of Sippar and the Esagila of Babylon. Because of the rivalry among political centres aspiring to supremacy, the former religious and ceremonial role of the centre was taken over by those cities that were temporarily pre-eminent. Ultimately, however, Babylon prevailed.

Less celebrated in propagandistic inscriptions, but far more important and innovative, was the construction and enlargement of the royal palaces (Figure 11.2). In this regard, the Old Babylonian levels of Babylon have not yet been excavated and our knowledge of Isin is still inadequate. Therefore, the best attested palaces of the Isin–Larsa period are the ones of Eshnunna (Tell Asmar), of king Sin-kashid in Uruk and of king Nur-Adad in Larsa. The monumental complex of Eshnunna was made of a southern, a northern and

Figure 11.2 City planning in the Isin–Larsa period. *Above*: The residential district of Ur; *Below*: The administrative district of Eshnunna.

a central palace (Figure 11.3). The latter was probably a continuation of the palace of the *ensi* of the Ur III period, along with the nearby temple of the deified king Shu-Sin. Finally, there was an audience room and other buildings left unfinished or only partially excavated. Even though not all of these constructions were in use at the same time, the dramatic expansion of the palace area in the city compared to the area for temples and private households remains evident.

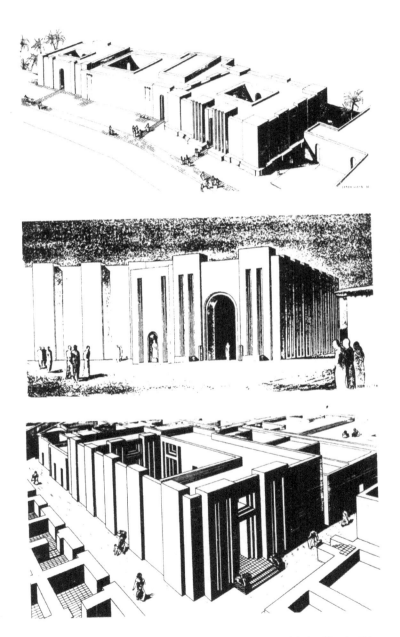

Figure 11.3 Public architecture in the Isin–Larsa period. *Above*: The palace of Ilishu–iliya in Eshnunna; *Centre*: The audience hall of Naram-Sin in Eshnunna; *Below*: Temple of Tell Harmal.

In the countryside, innovations were mainly of a legal nature. On a technological level, there was a marked continuity, with fields, agricultural cycles and equipment staying essentially the same. However, the sources attest to some changes, such as the increasing salinisation of the soil. This seriously affected the southern areas, which were characterised by a longer history of agricultural activities. Similarly, there was a visible decrease in yields. This led to the elaboration of more complex rotations with the introduction of summer cultivations alongside the winter grain cultivations. As a result of the legal changes, the rise of opportunities for private enterprises and the employment of paid workers, this period experienced an increase in the cultivation of plants requiring more care and expertise. For instance, there was the date-palm, which was cultivated alongside vegetables (such as onion, garlic and legumes) in order to make better use the land and water available. This development contributed to the formation of a new agricultural environment along the canals, which was more intensely cultivated throughout the year and therefore more densely inhabited.

The administration of state property developed along the same lines as in the Ur III period. The system still experienced some changes, which were particularly due to the presence of a variety of administrative centres (whose administrative texts differed between the north and the south in terms of writing styles, types and structure), the increasing use of Akkadian (partly disguised under ideographic formulas) and a certain decline compared to the accuracy and consistency of the Ur III scribes. Alongside the administrative documentation of the 'great organisations', there was a consistent rise of texts concerning the private agricultural sector. However, these sources are predominantly legal, rather than administrative. Therefore, due to their inherently different nature, they are difficult to compare with the texts of the state administration.

Trade also experienced a new phase in the private sector. The crucial aim of this new type of trade was to combine aspects of the state administration and its relation with merchants, with a more independent type of trade. In the latter, then, merchants actively oversaw commercial exchanges. This development can be clearly seen in the Isin–Larsa period, which provides important attestations on the maritime trade between Ur and Dilmun. As a southern city easily connected to the Persian Gulf, Ur appears to have been involved in maritime commercial activities organised by its main sanctuary, the temple of Nanna (and his divine consort Ningal). There, dedicatory silver statues in the shape of ships constituted the typical offerings of merchants who had returned alive (and wealthier) from a dangerous journey. Trade between Ur and Dilmun consisted in exporting textiles (as well as silver and other products, like sesame oil or leather) and returning with ingots of copper from Magan. The latter were brought to Dilmun by merchants from the east. Considering the rise of commercial activities in the private sector, the Ur-Dilmun trade indicates a visible development of the roles of the temple and the merchants from the end of the Ur III period (with the texts of Lu-Enlil, a merchant living at the time of Ibbi-Sin), to the time of the dynasty of Larsa (with the letters of Ea-nasir from the reign of Rim-Sin).

Initially, commercial activities were organised just like in the Ur III period, with the temple providing the merchant with a quantity of textiles to be exchanged for copper. By the beginning of the Larsa dynasty, the role of the temple was still visible, but much more marginal. Merchants began to travel to Dilmun independently and to return to Ur to dedicate a tenth of their precious goods (copper, stones, coral and ivory) to the goddess Ningal. Subsequently, trade became an entirely private activity, with contracts and disputes between lenders and travelling merchants, and the temple and palace playing a minimal role.

Therefore, trade evolved from an activity controlled by the state to an independent enterprise that had a purely fiscal relation with the state. Moreover, attestations on the contemporary Old Assyrian commercial activities in Anatolia prove that this evolution was a general trend of the period. With the breakdown of the Neo-Sumerian state, the procurement of raw materials and the income of trade were directly managed by the descendants of those merchants formerly working for the state. The system consequently became decentralised. Due to its strategic location, the old imperial centre of Ur managed to maintain its important role in the trade with Dilmun, Ashur monopolised commercial activities with Anatolia, and Mari remained the central commercial hub for trade with Syria. Finally, Ehnunna and Der, as well as Susa, monopolised the management and control of the exchange of semiprecious stones and tin from Iran.

2 The political pluralism of the Isin–Larsa period

In order to understand the interaction between the many autonomous states of the Isin–Larsa period, ancient scribes and modern scholars alike recognize the passage from the supremacy of Isin (ca. twentieth century BC) to that of Larsa (ca. nineteenth century BC) and then Babylon (from Hammurabi onwards), as the central line of development of the period (Table 11.1). This interpretation implies a transition from city to city of the same ideology of kingship. However, this view, based on the political organisation of Central and Lower Mesopotamia (Sumer and Akkad), does not do justice to those dynasties that rose to prominence in the periphery of Mesopotamia. Moreover, this view does not allow for a broader analysis of the Near East at the time, which should include Elam, Assyria, Mari and other Syrian states beyond Mari. In actual fact, the latter should be the only truly appropriate view of the network of political relations of the period.

Following the Elamite sacking of Ur, the dynasty of Isin, founded by Ishbi-Erra while Ibbi-Sin was still ruling in Ur, rose to power as the heir of the empire of Ur. Ishbi-Erra's titulature was ambitious and clearly inspired by the previous empires ('king of the four quarters of the world', 'god of his land'). He controlled the most prestigious and legitimising locations in the empire: the former capital Ur, which the king soon restored after the considerable damages (especially in its sacred area) caused by the Elamites; and the religious centre of Nippur, with its ideologically unifying function, which continued to be important even in this phase.

This difficult historical moment required considerable effort on two fronts. Outside of Mesopotamia, there were the wars to the east aimed at keeping the Elamites out of Mesopotamia, and the wars to the west against the Martu. Internally, there were restoration works and the administrative and political reorganisation of the state. Despite some good results on both fronts, some of the former influential cities managed to rise to independence as secondary heirs of the empire of Ur. In the south-west, there was Larsa, with a dynasty founded by a certain Naplanum (whose name was Amorite), well before the fall of Ur. In the north-east, there was Eshnunna and maybe Der, acting as a buffer zone between Mesopotamia and Elam. Throughout the twentieth century BC there are few attestations on the area north of Nippur, but it is known that Kish and some other cities were already independent at this stage.

Apart from some marginal and relatively modest exceptions, Isin initially managed to take over a large part of the legacy of Ur. However, this was only within the centre of the former empire. In the periphery, Mari, Ashur and Elam were already completely independent regional powers. Ishme-Dagan, third successor of Ishbi-Erra, tried to expand his rule to the north, but was defeated by Kish. As a result, some cities of his reign were destroyed, Nippur in particular, as attested from a 'lamentation' similar to the 'Lamentation over the Destruction of Ur'. Due to the sacredness of the city and the reconstruction of the Ekur, Ishme-Dagan had exempted Nippur from tributes and military service, claiming that he 'established peace and justice in the land'. This statement alludes to the practice of exemptions, a central feature of the social ideology of the period (many kings of the Old Babylonian period would continue this practice). His self-celebratory hymns therefore show a clear intent in replicating the model established by Shulgi.

Ishme-Dagan was succeeded by Lipit-Ishtar, who managed to keep Nippur and the southern cities of Ur, Uruk and Eridu under his control. He also 'established justice', not only through exemptions and remissions of debts, but also through the creation of a law code (just like Ur-Nammu before him). This law code was aimed at providing a better structure for the implementation of justice, celebrating the exemplary fairness with which justice was administered in his reign (Text 11.1). However, the dynasty founded by Ishbi-Erra disappeared soon after. Lipit-Ishtar was expelled and a new dynasty rose to power in Isin. The city lost a part of its territories in favour of the rising dynasty of Larsa. After just a few generations, the new dynasty in Isin was interrupted. Later accounts would explain that its last king, Erra-imitti, had died sipping hot broth, leaving his reign to a certain Enlil-bani. The latter had been placed on the throne as a substitute king in response to a bad omen (which eventually came true, affecting the real king, rather than his substitute!). With Enlil-bani, Isin also lost control over Uruk, its last city in the south, in favour of a local dynasty.

While Isin moved from being the heir of the Third Dynasty of Ur back to a city-state, Larsa moved in the opposite direction, moving away from its position as city-state clenched between Isin and Elam. Gungunum began his rise to power in Larsa at the end of the twentieth century, taking Ur and Lagash from Isin and Susa from Elam. He took on the title of 'king of Sumer and Akkad', the standard title of the kings of Ur, and led a couple of campaigns against Bashime (located on the Iranian coast facing the Persian Gulf) and Anshan (modern Fars, located in the hinterland of Bashime). Gungunum's successor Abi-sare

Table 11.1 Chronology of the Isin–Larsa period (2000–1750 BC)

	Isin		Larsa		Eshnunna		Babylon		Uruk	
2000	*Ishbi-Erra	2017–1985	Naplanum	2025–2005	Nur-ahum					
			Emisum	2004–1977	Kirikiri					
	*Shu-ilishu	1984–1975			Bilalama	ca. 1980				
			Samium	1976–1942						
	*Iddin-Dagan	1974–1954			Usur-Awassu					
1950										
	*°Ishme-Dagan	1953–1935	Zabaya	1941–1933	°Abi-madar					
	*°Lipit-Ishtar	1934–1924			Azuzum	ca. 1925				
			Gungunum	1932–1906	Ur-Ninkimara					
	*°Ur-Ninurta	1923–1896			Ur-Ningizzida					
1900			Abi-sare	1905–1895	Ipiq-Adad I	ca. 1895	Sumu-abum	1894–1881		
	*Bur-Sin	1895–1874	*Sumu-El	1894–1866	Shiqlanum					
	*Lipit-Enlil	1873–1869			Abdi-Erah					
	*°Erra-imitti	1868–1861			Sharriya					
					Abi-madar		°Sumu-la-El	1880–1845		
					Belakum					
1850			Nur-Adad	1865–1850					Sin-Kashid	1863–1833
	*°Enlil-bani	1860–1837	Sin-iddinam	1849–1843	Warassa				Sin-eribam	1832–1827
	*Zambiya	1836–1834	Sin-eribam	1842–1841	Rubum	ca. 1480	Sabium	1844–1831	Sin-gamil	1826–1824
	*°Iter-pisha	1833–1831	Sin-iqisham	1840–1836	Ibal-pi-El I				Ilum-gamil	1823
	*Ur-dukuga	1830–1828	Silli-Adad	1835			Apil-Sin	1830–1813	Eteya	1822
	*Sin-magir	1827–1817	Warad-Sin	1834–1825	*Ipiq Abad II	1835–1795			Anam	1821–1817
	*Damiq-ilishu	1816–1794			*°Naram-Sin	1794–1785	°Sin-muballit	1812–1793	Irdanene	1816–1810
1800										
	1794: conquered by Larsa		*°Rim-Sin	1822–1763	°Dadusha	1794–1785		1792–1750	Rimanum	1809–1806
					°Ibal-pi-El II	1784–1770			Nabi-ilishu	1806–1802
					Dannum-tahaz		°Ham-murabi		1802: conquered by Larsa	
					Silli-Sin					
			1763: conquered by Babylon		1761: conquered by Larsa					
1750										
					Igish-Tishpak		°Samsu-iluna	1749–1712		
					Iluni					
1700										

* deified king.

° kings that released remission edicts.

managed to oppose the ambitions of the new dynasty of Isin, which was trying to reconquer the cities in the south of Mesopotamia. Abi-sare's successor Sumu-El campaigned in the north, possibly in connection with some hydric projects aimed at channelling the water from the Euphrates to Larsa. Having bypassed Isin, he conquered Nippur (where he was deified) and defeated Kazallu and Kish, thus turning Larsa into a hegemonic power west of the Tigris.

Isin miraculously remained independent, though clenched between Larsa in the south and Kish (and, later on, Babylon) in the north and even tried to reconquer Nippur. At that time, due to the shift of

	Elam		Assyria		Mari		Yamhad		Cappadocia
2000									
	SHIMASHKI DYNASTY		Kikkia		last shakkanakku				
	Kindattu	ca. 2000	Akia		»				
	Idattu I	ca. 2000	Puzur-Ashur I		»				
	Tan-Rukhuratir	ca. 1970	Shalim-akhte		»				
	Ebarti II	ca. 1970	°Ilushuma	ca. 1950	»				
1950									
	Indattu II	ca. 1925			?				
			°Erishum I	ca. 1940–1910					
	SUKKALMAH DYNASTY								
1900									
	Ebarat	ca. 1900	Ikunum						karum II (ca. 1930–1850)
	Shilhaha								(Assyrian trade)
	Addahushu								
			Sargon I						
1850									
			Puzur-Ashur II						karum Ia
			Naram-Sin		Yaggid-Lim				(ca. 1850–1800)
			Erishum II		ca. 1820				(interval)
							Sumu-epuh		
	Shiruktuh	ca. 1800	Shamshi-Adad I	1812–1780	Yahdun-Lim 1815–1799				
1800									
	Shimut-urartash				Yasmah-Addu	1798–1780	Yarim-Lim I	ca. 1790–1770	karum Ib (ca. 1800–1780)
	Siwe-palar-huhpak				Zimri-Lim	1780–1758			(revival of trade)
	Kuduzulush	ca. 1765	Ishme-Dagan	1780–1740			Hammurabi I	ca. 1770–1750	Anum-hirbi
			»		1758: conquered by Babylon				Pithana and Anitta
1750									
			»				»		
			»				»		
			»				»		
			»				»		
			»				»		
1700									

* deified king.

° kings that released remission edicts.

Text 11.1   The 'code' of Lipit-Ishtar, king of Isin

[Prologue]

'On the day when the great Anu, the father of the gods, and Enlil, the king of all the lands, the lord who determines destinies, for Nin-insina, the daughter of Anu, the pious lady, whose kingdom rejoices, whose bright forehead is seen, established the land of Isin, and placed the god Anu, (then) they gave to him a favourable reign and the kingship of Sumer and Akkad.

That day, Lipit-Ishtar, the wise shepherd, was called by Nunamnir in order to establish justice in the land, to banish corruption through "words", to turn back enmity and rebellion by 'force' (of arms), and to (establish) well-being in Sumer and Akkad, (then) Anu and Enlil called Lipit-Ishtar to the princeship of the land.

That day, I, Lipit-Ishtar, the pious shepherd of Nippur, the loyal farmer of Ur, the careful protector of Eridu, the glorious lord of Uruk, the king of Isin, the king of Sumer and Akkad, who am fit for the heart of Inanna, in accordance with the word of Enlil, established justice in Sumer and Akkad.

Verily, in those days, I procured the freedom of the sons and daughters of Nippur, the sons and daughters of Ur, the sons and daughters of Isin, the sons and daughters of Sumer and Akkad, upon whom slaveship had been imposed . . .'

[Laws]

'[§ 6] If a man breaks the door of a house, he who has broken [the door of] the house shall be killed.

[§ 14] If a man went into the garden of another man and was seized for theft, he shall pay 10 shekels of silver.

[§ 15] If a man cut down a tree in another man's garden, he shall pay ½ mina of silver.

[§ 17] If a slave-girl or slave of a man fled into the midst of the city and dwelt in the house of another man for one month and it is proved, slave for slave shall be given.

[§ 18] If he has no slave, he shall pay 25 shekels of silver.

[§ 29] If the second woman that (a man) had married bore him a child, the dowry which she brought from her father's house belongs to her child.

[§ 30] If a man married a wife and she bore him a child, and this child is living, and a slave (also) bore children for her master, the father should grant freedom to the slave and her child; the child of the slave shall not divide the estate with the children of his master.

[Epilogue]

In accordance with the true word of Utu, I have established justice in Sumer and Akkad; in accordance with the pronouncement of Enlil, I, Lipit-Ishtar, son of Enlil, abolished enmity and rebellion through the "word", I eliminated tears, lamentations, corruption, and sin, I have caused righteousness and truth to shine forth, I brought well-being in Sumer and Akkad.

When I had established the wealth of Sumer and Akkad, I erected this stele.' (Several curses against whoever will damage the stele follow).

the Tigris and the Euphrates out of their riverbeds and their later settlement into a new course, the south experienced a violent flood. This must have caused innumerable devastations and reconstructions. There were several conflicts with Babylon, Eshnunna and Elam, while a new independent dynasty was establishing itself in Uruk. Overall, the history of Sumer up until 1830 bc is characterised by states with relatively limited ambitions. These ambitions were in marked contrast to the maintenance of those grand procedures (such as the deification of rulers) and imperial titles used to provide a sense of continuity with the former unity of Mesopotamia.

In the land of Akkad, following the fall of the Ur III dynasty, the ancient and prestigious city of Kish finally regained its independence after a long period of subjugation under both the empires of Akkad and Ur. Alongside Kish, other northern cities became politically autonomous, such as Kazallu, Sippar and Babylon. We know from occasional attestations that these centres were in constant conflict with each other, at least until the rise of Babylon, which was a newcomer in the area. The Babylonian king list begins with Sumu-abum, who controlled Babylon and Dilbat and successfully fought against Kazallu. Sumu-abum's son, Samu-la-El, eventually defeated Kazallu. This king also conquered Kish and managed to unify the whole of Akkad. Consequently, Babylon, Sippar, Dilbat, Marad, Kazallu and Kish all became part of the Babylonian kingdom and were never able to rise as autonomous centres again.

The quick rise of Babylon at the expense of Kish followed the example of the previous and more sudden rise of Akkad at the expense of that same city. The final victory of Babylon, then, led to its identification as a new Akkad, in an attempt to provide an ideological continuation of the latter's political role in Mesopotamia. Sumu-la-El continued the tradition of debt remissions, literally 'breaking the tablets' on which these debts were recorded. In this way, he revived the model established by Sargon and presented himself as a liberator to his subjects in Kish and the other cities under his authority.

The political tensions in the lands of Sumer and Akkad were resolved with a similar outcome. Larsa emerged as the hegemonic state of the south, while in the north Babylon rose to supremacy, ready to tackle southern Mesopotamia. Overall, these tensions were confined to the Mesopotamian alluvial plain, thus mirroring the developments that had taken place in the Early Dynastic period. The imperial phases of Akkad and Ur then became impossible acts to follow. Nonetheless, Akkad and Ur became important ideological models for the north and the south respectively. Outside of Mesopotamia, political developments took a completely different path, characterised by the lesser degree of influence of the city-state structure and the supremacy of the Amorites, who continued to maintain several aspects of their origins as pastoral groups. Consequently, the Mesopotamian foothills experienced a series of sudden expansionistic campaigns (and equally sudden re-adjustments), especially in Assyria, Elam, Eshnunna and Der. These episodes will be taken into detailed consideration later on, but their overall development has to be anticipated here.

After a relatively isolated phase, Assyria suddenly began a campaign, which led king Ilushuma to the far south of Sumer. Then, there was Eshnunna, which had played a relatively small role in the twentieth century bc. In the reign of king Naram-Sin of Eshnunna (an emblematic name emphasizing this king's imperialistic ambitions), the city began its expansionistic conquests in Assyria and Upper Mesopotamia. In the end, the Assyrian king Shamshi-Adad, whose main capital was Shubat-Enlil (in the Khabur region), succeeded in creating a large and complex empire. Even a small centre such as Der, located in a difficult buffer zone between powerful rivals, bravely fought against Eshnunna and Elam.

Despite having been pushed out of Mesopotamia by Ishbi-Erra, Elam, whose political influence reached the east and north of Iran, never gave up on its expansionistic interests in Mesopotamia (especially in the Mari Age). The Shimashki dynasty of Elam was succeeded by a line of *sukkal-mah*. The latter controlled the whole of Elam from Susa to Anshan, including the mountainous regions in the north, shifting the political axis of Elam to the east. The reigns of the Elamite *sukkal-mah* continued to be characterised by a strong political, military and cultural interest in Mesopotamia. Therefore, despite its peripheral location near the border of Elam, Susa became the political centre of this composite kingdom.

Similarly, Akkadian became the main language used in administrative texts. It is clear that the ambition of Elam was to become a constitutive element of an enlarged Mesopotamian territory, extending from the Iranian plateau to northern Syria. However, the original Sumero-Akkadian roots of this area were now combined with a strong Amorite presence. Therefore, the territorial ambitions of the earlier empires now brought a variety of states to interact with each other through ever-changing treaties, rivalries and strategic alliances.

3 The social and legal developments of the Isin–Larsa period

The evolution of family and social relations is generally part of a long-term process, which is difficult to place in a precise historical period. However, certain historical circumstances can provide this evolution with temporary and sudden boosts of development, as well as equally sudden regressions. Regarding the intermediate phase between the Neo-Sumerian and Old Babylonian periods, this boost in the evolution of social relations was provided by the rise of the Amorites. On the one hand, the Amorites had different customs and social structures (closer to a kin-based type of society). On the other, they were less culturally close or even interested in the palace and temple structure, which lay at the heart of Mesopotamian society. These characteristics generated a series of internal phenomena, which can be seen as the result of the mutual influence and close interaction between the social structures of the family and the palace. For instance, there was the inevitable tendency of palace functionaries to leave their posts to their sons. This tendency was clearly aimed at keeping certain professional competencies within one family, as well as benefiting from royal land grants for a longer period of time.

Regarding the first aspect, the transmission of one's professional knowledge from father to son was not a particularly negative tendency for the palace. In the long run, however, it transformed the palace and temple personnel into a series of closed corporations. In other words, members of these elite groups prevented anyone outside this clique from accessing their posts. They also monopolised the technical knowledge needed for the management of these institutions. Consequently, they were able to deal with the central administration with a greater degree of authority, gaining more advantageous positions for themselves and affirming their independence. For example, the fact that scribes were usually sons of scribes created a caste-type of social distinction without harming the state administration *per se*. This is because scribes and administrators were essentially the same people. However, in the case of merchants, the individual management of commercial activities led to the appearance of family-run companies, which were able to continue their business regardless of central control or collective needs. Therefore, these companies could work even when their central administration collapsed (such as at the end of the Ur III period).

The other side of the same phenomenon concerns the private acquisition of lands donated by kings. Initially, palace functionaries were paid through land concessions and these concessions were transmitted together with official posts from father to son. With time, however, concessions became less of a temporary and conditional donation and more of a personal family inheritance. Moreover, the beneficiaries of these lands eventually managed to acquire (through a variety of financial tactics) other lands surrounding their initial concession. This made their estates a combination of palace lands (technically not owned by them) and family property, either inherited or recently acquired. This phenomenon made it difficult to understand the original legal ownership of certain properties and this difficulty was at the heart of several legal disputes. Family legacies (and memories) were therefore contested by records kept in the palace archives and sometimes even by palace functionaries or the king himself.

Family property experienced two parallel developments. First, the increase of privately owned lands (compared to the Neo-Sumerian period) was partly due to non-economic factors, linked to the arrival of the Amorites, the shift of political power in Mesopotamia to the north and the increasing concessions of land to new classes of functionaries, especially those working in the military. This change was an evident result of the frequent conflicts between states and the long-term enrolment of mercenary troops (or even nomadic tribes) that could not be paid through the *corvée* system. Moreover, there was the relentless conquest of cities by hegemonic powers, which took away temple lands to distribute them among the new social classes of soldiers and veterans. The second phenomenon concerns the management and transmission of property within a family. This was the result of an internal socio-economic development. The old system of the enlarged family living in the same property, which was left virtually undivided (in terms of ownership, not management), was by now in crisis. This led to the increasing autonomy of family nuclei. These nuclei had always been a fundamental element in the management of lands. Now, however, they also became crucial players in the issue of land ownership. In other words, brothers began to divide their property among themselves, either at the time of inheriting their share or when they got married.

As a result, while in the third millennium BC inheritances did not require a written text, in the second millennium BC testaments became extremely widespread legal documents for the subdivision of property. There were two types of practices, attested in different areas. In the first tradition, each son received an equal share of the inheritance. In the second tradition, the eldest son received a larger share (usually double) of the inheritance. Inheritance was usually kept within the family, from father to son, unless there were no sons and the inheritance went to other family lines. This phase also saw the increasing 'personalisation' of property, as shown by the concession of temple or palace lands to an individual and not a family. Alongside testaments, real estate transactions became increasingly more widespread. In some areas, more traditional types of transactions remained in place, with the ceremonial and pseudo-legal adoption of the buyer by the seller in order to transfer the land. However, in more legally advanced environments, land sales were agreed on without these ceremonial overtones.

A third type of document (more focused on the establishment of a social relation), typical of the Old Babylonian period, was the land lease contract. In the third millennium BC, temples and palaces already used this form of land management, which required a yearly payment in return. Now, however, these leases were mainly practised by private individuals. This indicates the rise of a class of landowners (mainly upper class functionaries), who owned more land than they could manage on their own, and a class of farmers without land and willing to work on other people's lands. These leases were generally paid either through a fixed percentage of the harvest, or in silver. They also included clauses regarding the duration of the contract, the obligations of both parties and the division of the yields between the owner and the lessee.

However, this practice was only accessible to the wealthier portion of the farming population not owning land, thus still able to pay and work the land independently. Less fortunate families had to find paid work, providing a fundamental service to the large private and public estates. The palace also employed 'hired men' (Sumerian *lú.ḫun.gá*, Akkadian *agrum*) for the construction and maintenance of canals and public infrastructures. The royal administration therefore levied taxes on landowners, kept records of expenditures and incomes, supervised work through contractors, hired large numbers of workmen through intermediaries and paid them with salaries. Consequently, the practice of paying salaries slowly substituted the distribution of rations. Both remunerations were mainly paid in foodstuff (at times converted into silver payments) and only for the periods of actual work, which were usually tasks requiring low levels of technical knowledge, but large numbers of workmen.

In the past, the central administration provided its full-time workmen with rations throughout the year, while its *corvée* workers received temporary rations aimed at compensating for their absence from their own land, which still constituted their core means of sustenance. The situation changed in this period. Salaries were higher than the old rations, since they had to pay for the worker and his family, as well as for those periods in which the worker did not have an income. Despite our lack of information on the exact value of salaries, one still gets the impression that Old Babylonian workers were worse off than the workers paid in rations or providing temporary work through the *corvée* system.

Contemporary texts also attest to the tragic situation of orphans and widows, whose difficult condition became a stereotype throughout the history of the Near East. These were individuals who depended upon the economic role of the father and the husband, but had lost this protection and were now left outside the family system. The crisis of family solidarity also led to the appearance of debt-slavery. Unpaid loans and leases and unfulfilled obligations were covered with the promise of repayment. However, when there was no property to pledge against a loan or lease, the latter could only be paid for through one's own work as a servant. Consequently, the head of the household owing money had to give up his wife, sons and himself as a repayment (Figure 11.4). Since servile work often could only repay the interests and not the initial loan, debt-slavery was virtually irreversible.

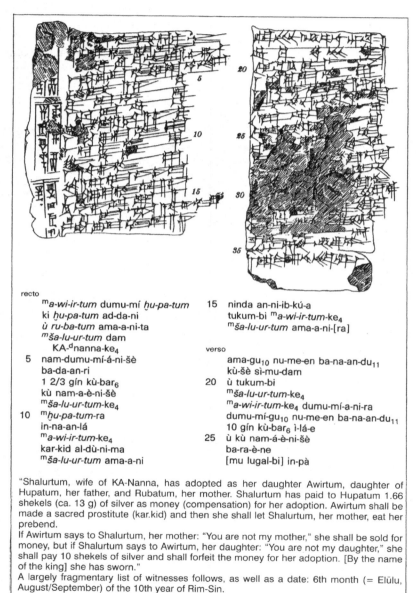

recto

^{m}*a-wi-ir-tum* dumu-mí *ḫu-pa-tum*
ki *ḫu-pa-tum* ad-da-ni
ù *ru-ba-tum* ama-a-ni-ta
^{m}*ša-lu-ur-tum* dam
    KA-^{d}nanna-ke$_4$
5 nam-dumu-mí-á-ni-šè
ba-da-an-ri
1 2/3 gín kù-bar$_6$
kù nam-a-è-ni-šè
^{m}*ša-lu-ur-tum*-ke$_4$
10 ^{m}*ḫu-pa-tum*-ra
in-na-an-lá
^{m}*a-wi-ir-tum*-ke$_4$
kar-kid al-dù-ni-ma
^{m}*ša-lu-ur-tum* ama-a-ni

15 ninda an-ni-ib-kú-a
tukum-bi ^{m}*a-wi-ir-tum*-ke$_4$
^{m}*ša-lu-ur-tum* ama-a-ni-[ra]

verso

    ama-gu$_{10}$ nu-me-en ba-na-an-du$_{11}$
kù-šè sì-mu-dam
20 ù tukum-bi
^{m}*ša-lu-ur-tum*-ke$_4$
^{m}*a-wi-ir-tum*-ke$_4$ dumu-mí-a-ni-ra
dumu-mí-gu$_{10}$ nu-me-en ba-na-an-du$_{11}$
10 gín kù-bar$_6$ ì-lá-e
25 ù kù nam-á-è-ni-šè
ba-ra-è-ne
[mu lugal-bi] in-pà

"Shalurtum, wife of KA-Nanna, has adopted as her daughter Awirtum, daughter of Hupatum, her father, and Rubatum, her mother. Shalurtum has paid to Hupatum 1.66 shekels (ca. 13 g) of silver as money (compensation) for her adoption. Awirtum shall be made a sacred prostitute (kar.kid) and then she shall let Shalurtum, her mother, eat her prebend.
If Awirtum says to Shalurtum, her mother: "You are not my mother," she shall be sold for money, but if Shalurtum says to Awirtum, her daughter: "You are not my daughter," she shall pay 10 shekels of silver and shall forfeit the money for her adoption. [By the name of the king] she has sworn."
A largely fragmentary list of witnesses follows, as well as a date: 6th month (= Elūlu, August/September) of the 10th year of Rim-Sin.

Figure 11.4 Adoption contract from Larsa (Rim–Sin's reign).

The social and legal sensibilities of the time felt the aberration of these situations and recognised the status of the enslaved debtor as a free person. However, only a royal intervention could solve the needs of orphans and widows and free those affected by debt-slavery from this crisis of family solidarity. The latter was significantly under pressure due to the difficult economic situation of the time and the new developments in land concessions.

4 Old Babylonian kingship

In this period of sudden changes, economic growth, political fragmentation, independence, constant exposure to attacks and growing enslavement, kingship became a fundamental point of reference for stability. In this stabilising role, Old Babylonian kingship developed aspects already present in the Neo-Sumerian period, but with new features and nuances. The traditional role of kingship in society was kept, with royal hymns, celebratory inscriptions, codes and amnesties of clear Neo-Sumerian derivation. Even the practice of deifying kings continued to exist, especially in the south. However, it was only limited to a few, more successful kings, or those who felt they were in a solid enough position to acquire a divine role in the eyes of their subjects. In the north, the king continued to be traditionally seen as strong, as a clear expression of his constant military interventions, which were naturally caused by the political fragmentation of the time.

The kings of the Neo-Sumerian period presented themselves as successful administrators. In comparison, Old Babylonian kings preferred the image of the king as 'good shepherd' of his people. This representation not only borrowed the 'pastoral imagery' of the Amorites, but also attempted to present an image of care and consideration for the needs of those less fortunate, who were seen as part of a herd in need of a leader. The central interest of the Neo-Sumerian kings had been the administration of the state and its palace and temple functionaries. Now, however, the central interest of the Old Babylonian kings focused on the population of free people and in particular on those more in need of support.

In a world where solidarity between and within families was slowly breaking down, generating a vast number of people without inheritance, the king presented himself in a 'paternalistic' light. He became a father and mother to orphans and a support for widows. He also became the one who returned the son to his mother, gave freedom to those enslaved, released debts and re-established social order. Edicts celebrating debt remissions and the liberation of debt-slaves thus became the main instruments in the presentation of this new type of kingship ideology. On closer inspection, however, the regular repetition of these measures demonstrates the kings' inability to counter the general economic trends of the period. In fact, these trends were inevitably bringing more and more people into debt-slavery.

The state did not have the right measures to tackle the underlying causes of this socio-economic dysfunction and was only able to work on its effects. Consequently, the causes remained, but at least some of the most unfortunate situations were resolved through royal pardons. Creditors and debtors were aware of the frequency of amnesties, making these royal acts a structural aspect of socio-economic relations. It therefore became a standard royal practice to promulgate a remission edict right at the beginning of a ruler's reign. The phrase 'year in which X established justice in the land' became a common year formula for the second year of a king's reign, the first year being named after his enthronement. In case of long reigns, these types of edicts were repeated on several occasions. The repetition of reforms (though not at fixed intervals) aimed to celebrate the new king and gain the approval of his subjects. They therefore became an integral part of the economic mechanism of the state and were the only way in which the poorer strata of society could avoid life-long slavery.

Just like the amnesties bestowed upon conquered cities, these edicts, with their presentation of the king as 'just', were unapologetically propagandistic. However, the more practical purposes of these measures were always contextualised within a moral and religious 'code'. For instance, it was the god of Sippar Shamash who suggested that Zimri-Lim, king of Mari and conqueror of Kurda, should 'free' the land from debts. Equally propagandistic was the benevolence of the king towards workers involved in construction works, especially of temples. For instance, the king of Larsa, Sin-iddinam claimed that, instead of simple barley, he provided the workers restoring the Ebabbar with a large amount of meat, dates, cheese and oil. The king's involvement in public works therefore became a way to celebrate and advertise the wealth of the state.

In some cases, a king's self-presentation as a 'just' king took on more concrete overtones through the commission of law codes. This was becoming an increasingly popular tradition of the time and was started by Ur-Nammu of Ur. We have the code of Lipit-Ishtar of Isin (Text 11.1), a code belonging to an unknown king of Eshnunna and the famous law code of Hammurabi. The aim of these codes was not strictly legal, since the actual implementation of these laws is dubious and probably did not even take place. At the time, law codes were not the main paradigms for legal verdicts. On the contrary, it was the verdicts that shaped the code. Therefore, these law codes were not aimed at releasing new laws to substitute or unify previous laws. They simply showed how well organised and justly administered the state was under the efficient guide of a certain ruler.

The codes were therefore an analytical demonstration of the fact that justice reigned in the land. In those cases where the prologue of a code has survived, this intention is clearly expressed: 'when the gods entrusted me with the government of the land [. . .] then things happened like this: if a man committed a certain crime, this was the punishment; if a man agreed to this contract, this was the payment' and so on. All these dispositions derived from the current practice of the administration. They also emphasised the model of a good government, where everything was organised according to fair rules, leaving no space for abuses of power. The idea that, in order to achieve a correct development of social relations, it was necessary to reform the state through new reforms was not part of the government's ideology or methodology. The underlying assumption was that the correct implementation of justice, which followed the existing norms, could not fail to create a prosperous reign. Chaos only arose whenever these norms were not applied. The solution, then, was simply to re-establish justice.

Price lists were also an integral part of these codes (from the one of Ur-Nammu to the one of Eshnunna; see Text 11.2). Even in this case, prices were neither new nor more favourable to the current economic climate compared to previous prices. They were not even the highest and lowest prices, but simply fixed and fair prices (fair because stable), organised through basic correspondences (1:1). Therefore, a basic quantity of barley corresponded to one basic quantity of silver. This almost gave the impression that these prices were natural valuations, rather than prices dictated by the economic situation of the time. These 'fair' prices, which to us may seem purely formal and impractical, could have had a significant influence on economic transactions. This is especially due to the presence in the lists of prices for leases, the hiring of workmen and of means of transport. These prices therefore made this type of royal intervention a way to support the weaker party against the abuses of the wealthier stratum of society. Consequently, royal steles were left in market-places as references for the fair prices established by the king. In this way, the economic function of market-places could have increased. This process was further stimulated by the growing number of people who had to depend on exchange in order to survive, and the increasing independence of merchants and craftsmen compared to their former dependence on the palace.

It is true, as Karl Polányi has pointed out, that we have to distinguish between market-place and market: the former is securely attested (Akkadian *maḫīrum*) in Mesopotamia from the Old Babylonian period onwards; the latter can be defined as a self-regulatory mechanism for prices on the basis of the relation between demand and supply. However, it is also true that the market system was known and applied in the market-place. Even before the Old Babylonian period, but especially in this phase of increased freedom from the palace economy and of commoditisation of land and labour, Mesopotamian trade clearly shows the influence of demand and supply in the establishment of prices. This fact led to the development of two stereotypes. On the one hand, phases characterized by political instability, difficult commercial activities

Text 11.2   Old Babylonian price lists

Some Old Babylonian royal inscriptions include 'price lists' for clear propagandistic purposes. For instance, here is what Sin-kashid of Uruk declares:

'During his reign, according to the market rate of the land, one shekel of silver was the price of 3 *gur* (= 900 litres) of barley, 12 minas of wool, 10 minas of copper, 3/30 *gur* (= 30 litres) of sesame oil. His years were years of abundance!'

The propagandistic tone (abundance of goods, thus low prices!) becomes particularly evident when comparing these celebratory statements with more normative, but realistic, price lists (such as the one found in the laws of Eshnunna) and the current prices recorded in the administrative texts of the time. Here are some basic goods one could acquire with one shekel of silver:

	Barley (in litres)	Dates (in litres)	Sesame oil (in litres)	Wool (in minas)	Copper (in minas)
Propagandistic prices					
Sin-kashid	900		30	12	10
Sin-iddinam	1200	3600	30	15	
Shamshi-Adad	600		20	15	
Normative prices					
Eshnunna	300		12	6	3–2
Current prices					
Ur III	300		9–15	10	2–2.5
Hammurabi	150–180	600–120	9–10	5	2–3

and production crises were seen as periods in which prices rose dramatically. For instance, this is the image a literary composition such as the 'Curse of Akkad' used to describe the Akkadian crisis. On the other hand, the typical way to describe a prosperous period, with high levels of productivity and flourishing trade, was to say that with just one unit of silver it was possible to purchase more than one unit of basic products such as barley, wool, oil and copper.

Compared to the prices attested in the contemporary administrative and economic texts, the price lists, such as the one of the Code of Eshnunna, seem quite realistic, while in comparison, the propagandistic price lists included in celebratory royal inscriptions (from the ones of Sin-Kashid of Uruk to Shamshi-Adad of Assyria) provide completely inaccurate prices. The latter were optimistically exaggerated in order to emphasize the prosperity of the king's reign. These stereotypical allusions to extreme situations show that market systems for the determination of prices were in operation. They also show that these mechanisms were somehow considered unfair. This is because they changed prices from the 'right' ones developed by the old system of equivalences established by the palace.

Royal intervention therefore plays a crucial role in re-issuing the 'right' system of prices and in taking care that they were the current prices. The re-issue of the 'right' prices was a purely formal act. However, it was certainly put into practice through the price lists included in the codes and royal inscriptions placed in market-places. Less sure is the idea that the state actually had the necessary means to keep these prices current. There are no traces of concrete interventions (neither preventive nor punitive) to achieve this goal. Therefore, we can only assume that the mere statement of the successful implementation of a state-approved system of equivalences was as far as the royal authorities could go. They therefore relied on the prestige and exemplary role these statements had on inter-personal relations and on the stabilising effect the public sector (where these lists were used) had on the private sector. Equally stabilising was the influence of tradition, namely, the awareness that the prices to apply (apart from extreme cases of shortages or prosperity) were indeed the standard ones. This is shown by the relatively modest fluctuations of prices through time.

5 Old Babylonian culture

In the Old Babylonian period, the school (Sumerian *edubba*) continued to be the heart of Mesopotamian culture. Its highly conservative nature allowed it to pass down those instruments of the scribal profession developed in the third millennium BC. Paradoxically, a large part of Sumerian literature has arrived to us from the *edubba* of Old Babylonian Nippur, when Sumerian was already a dead language. At the same time, however, the school had to take into consideration new problems. These mainly pertained to the definitive transition from Sumerian to Akkadian as the main written language. Syllabaries were adapted to accommodate the characteristics of the Semitic language (the voiced–unvoiced–emphatic triad, the use of long vowels and double consonants and so on). Akkadian morphology therefore began to develop in its classical form.

The problem of bilingualism was not new. However, it had now spread throughout the Mesopotamian scribal tradition, forcing schools to re-formulate bilingual terms and to convert Sumerian conventions into Akkadian. Consequently, we find Sumero-Akkadian bilingual lists arranged in three columns (ideogram, Sumerian reading and Akkadian reading). There even were trilingual lists, such as the ones concerning the *Eme-sal* dialect (of the type *dimmer = dingir = ilu*). The difference between an ideogram and its syllabic writing now made monolingual lists a sort of 'translation', providing an ideogram with its Akkadian reading.

The disappearance of Sumerian as a spoken language forced scribes to develop other forms of recovery and translation of the Sumerian literary tradition. There were interlinear translations, the collection and writing down of the great compositions of Sumerian literature and the teaching of Sumerian. Although it was now a dead language, Sumerian remained a fundamental aspect of scribal training. Apart from its cultural and religious prestige, which made Sumerian a sort of 'Medieval Latin', there was a practical reason for the transmission of Sumerian. In fact, the system used to write Akkadian was originally developed for Sumerian and it kept visible traces of this origin (at least in its ideographic repertoire). In fact, no Akkadian text could have been read or understood without knowing Sumerian.

Alongside the problem of translation, there was the constant need to keep the cultural legacy of the Sumerians updated, expanded and organised. The result of this effort was the development of a large 'encyclopaedia' (which would become a classic), called the *Ḫarra-ḫubullu*. This collection of twenty-two tablets listed all the terms needed by the Mesopotamian scribes: from trees to wooden objects, reeds and objects made of reed, pottery, leather objects, metals and metal objects, wild and domestic animals, body parts, semiprecious stones and stone objects, plants, fish, birds, wool, clothes, places and foodstuffs. In its effort towards classification, this 'encyclopaedia' could be compared to the Chinese one imagined by Jorge Luis Borges (with its incoherent set of categories). However, it should instead be seen as a large 'dictionary', recording the scribal knowledge of the time with all its gaps and overlaps, as well as allowing the constant addition of as many new elements as possible. There were other, more practical, compositions, such as the equally classic, but shorter, *ana ittišu* series. This was a handbook of legal formulas developed for the writing of legal contracts. Then, there were numerical texts (with multiples, multiplications, reciprocals and so on) to facilitate calculations. Another type of text typical of the period was mathematical problems (Text 11.3), such as: 'knowing that a canal is *x* amount long and *x* amount wide, a worker digs *x* amount of land per day and his ration is *x* amount, how many days are needed to dig a canal of *x* length and how much will it cost?'

If the Akkadian and Neo-Sumerian periods were focused on the mythical foundation of the world, the Old Babylonian period developed the concept of a historical foundation. One can assume that

Text 11.3   Administration and scribal education: Old Babylonian mathematical problems concerning the construction of canals

1

'A pit: 5 GAR is the length, 1.5 GAR is the width, 0.5 GAR is the depth; 10 *gín* volume is the assignment, 6 *še* of silver is the monthly wage. What are the area, the volume, the workers (that is, the number of days of work) and the (total expenses in) silver? When you perform (the operations), multiply together the length and the width, and you will get 7.5 SAR (that is, the area); multiply 7.5 by its depth, and you will get 45 SAR (that is, the volume). Take the reciprocal of the assignment, and you will get 6, multiply it by 45, and you will get 4.5 (that is, the working days, to be multiplied by 60). Multiply 4.5 by the wages and you will get 9 *gín* (that is, the total expenses in silver). Such is the procedure.'

2

'A canal: 5 UŠ is its length, 2 *kuš* the width, 1 *kuš* its depth; 1/3 *gín* volume is the assignment, 1 *bán* of barley is the wage of a hired man. What are the area, the volume, the workers (that is, the number of days of work) and the (total expenses in) barley? 1 *ubu* is the area, 1 *ubu* is the volume; 2.5 (to be multiplied by 60) are the workers, the (total of) barley is 5 *gur*.'

3

'The barley for a canal is 5 *gur*, 2 *kuš* the width, 1 *kuš* its depth; 1/3 *gín* volume is the assignment, 1 *bán* of barley is the wage of a hired man. What is the length? 5 UŠ is the length.

4

Chart of the measurements used in the problems

	weight (silver)			
še 'grain'	1			
gín 'shekel'	180	1		
ma-na 'mina'	10800	60	1	
	capacity (cereals)			
sila	1			
bán	10	1		
gur	300	30	1	
	length			
šu-si 'inch'	1			
kùš 'cubit'	30	1		
GAR	360	12	1	
UŠ 'length'	21600	720	60	1
	volume (land)			
gín	1			
SAR (= 1 GAR^3)	60	1		
ubu	3000	50	1	

this development was somehow parallel to the appearance of inherited as well as financially acquired property. These acquisitions required historical proof for the right of ownership. This development was in marked contrast to previous periods, when ownership was either in the hands of the family or the temple. Be that as it may, the Old Babylonian period experienced a surge of the historiographical activities of scribes, normally in connection to current political problems (such as royal legitimacy and royal decisions). This historiographical effort generated at least three types of compositions. First, there were king lists, which developed along two lines: a Sumerian and an Amorite one. The former expressed more traditional southern Mesopotamian ideas, exemplified by the Sumerian King List (as well as the Lagash King List). The aim of this type of list was to provide a single line of kingship and to legitimate the dynasty of Isin. These texts therefore provided the deceptive image of a unified kingship from its mythical foundation ('when kingship descended from the sky') to periods of rivalries and fragmentations. The Amorite line was less traditional, providing the antecedents of the new dynasties through lists of tribal ancestors of a more or less legendary nature (found in the beginning of the Assyrian King List and the one of Hammurabi's ancestors).

The second type of composition consists of the collections of Akkadian and Ur III royal inscriptions (copied from the monuments that still stood in the main Mesopotamian sanctuaries) and from the royal correspondence of the Ur III kings. These texts are fundamental sources for the reconstruction of the history of these periods. They were mainly written down for scholarly purposes, rather than political ones.

The third type of composition, partly derived from the second type, was that of pseudo-historical texts, from 'false inscriptions' (*narû*), imitating authentic inscriptions, to historical poems of the kings of Akkad. As mentioned above, these texts contain more inaccurate than reliable information and provide little evidence on these ancient rulers. However, they contribute to the understanding of the political problems of the periods in which they were composed.

Expressions of increased individualism were also typical of the time. These expressions were linked to that social evolution considered above and can be analysed through two examples. The first one is the iconography of seals. The repetitive Neo-Sumerian scenes depicting the presentation of the seal's owner to the chief deity (or the deified king) by a minor deity continued to be used in the Old Babylonian period. However, since the owner of the seal was identified in writing, the Old Babylonian scenes became even more stereotyped. They therefore depicted the deity introducing the person in question as a generic divine figure (*lamassu*, a sort of personal protective deity or 'guardian angel') and not a recognisable deity. The second example concerns letters written to the gods. These were written by individuals to denounce their state of unjust despair and ask for help. Both mechanisms (presentation and letter to the god) were expressions of an increasing psychological introspection. Through the inclusion of recommendations, official presentations and pleas, these expressions transferred to a religious level what happened in the human sphere. Therefore, there was a clear attempt among common people to develop a personal tie with the divine, effectively avoiding the mediation of the priesthood or the king.

A visible expression of these individual attempts to find explanations through a direct interaction with the divine, unmediated by cults and the state, is the sudden appearance of collections and interpretations of omens (virtually unknown in the third millennium BC). Omens were considered to be visible and perceptible presages of what was happening or was going to happen on an imperceptible level. This connection was possible because these two levels co-existed within the same cosmic order. In the third millennium BC, there were means to communicate with the divine sphere directly, such as premonitory dreams, where a deity appeared to a king in order to tell him what to do. However, these dreams were more than just signs. Dreams were a channel of communication with the divine, using the same language, without the need for interpretation. In the Old Babylonian period this situation changed. Clear dreams continued, but the dreamers were mostly normal individuals, especially women. Therefore, apart from prophetic dreams concerning kings, common dreams also began to be interpreted, in the hope that they contained a cryptic message about the dreamer's future.

The most popular divinatory art of the Old Babylonian period was haruspicy, the inspection of the livers taken from sacrificial animals. This practice would later on develop into extispicy, the examination of all internal organs. The Old Babylonian scribes collected both in writing and through liver models the historical omens of the famous kings of the past. However, despite their conviction, there were few precedents of the practice in the third millennium BC. These artificial historical omens were largely secondary to the large amount of liver omens (Figure 11.5), which came to form a *bona fide* science based on analogies and opposite interpretations, facilitating the discovery of important signs in any liver, object, or ominous situation.

Apart from haruspicy, the Old Babylonian period saw the development of various divinatory sciences. For instance, there was the identification of omens in deformed births (*šumma izbu*), anomalies of the environment or in daily life (*šumma ālu*), incense smoke (libanomancy), physiognomies, astrology, and so on. All these techniques would become part of Near Eastern history and each period would develop its own preferences and differentiations. However, the idea developed at the beginning of the second millennium BC was that anyone, from the king to any of his subjects, could know his fate by interpreting the signs appearing around him.

The study of omens constitutes a fundamental tool for the understanding of the fears and expectations of Old Babylonian society. First, there was a distinction between two spheres, the land (*mātu*) and the house (*bītu*), namely, between the public sphere of the state and the private one of the family. Some divinatory techniques taking place or observed in a cultic context were reserved for the public sphere. Others were accessible to all and were mostly encountered in the private sphere. Sometimes, omens could have a double meaning, being one thing in the *mātu* sphere and another thing in the *bītu* sphere. Apart from this distinction, omens show a high level of conflict between these two spheres, which is unattested in the official documentation. This division is further distorted by the role of omens as outlets for fears and tensions. The public sphere was obviously the place in which usurpations, regicides, revolts and defections took place. The private sphere had the problem of generational conflicts and contests amongst relatives. The main worry was that of cohesion, also in its diachronic aspect, namely, continuity. The values of solidarity and loyalty seem to have been the ones most under threat. This was probably because they were at the heart of society, and were developing in a period when important changes were taking place on an economic and family level.

The structure of the omen (even in its formulation: 'if . . . then . . .') became the typical conceptual structure of Mesopotamian culture. This same structure was applied in collections of laws. The main difference in this case was that the relation between the two hypothetical phrases was not one of sign and interpretation, but of crime and punishment. The structure was also applied to texts of a 'scientific' nature, such as medicine. After all, our modern distinction between science and divination did not exist in Mesopotamia. On the contrary, there were two branches of Mesopotamian medicine, both based on the interpretation of signs. Leo Oppenheim defined the two branches as 'practical' and 'scientific'. The 'practical' branch, typical of the Old Babylonian period, was performed by a physician (*asû*). It consisted in the careful observation of symptoms to develop a diagnosis of the type of illness and the suitable cure (whose efficacy might be dubious, but was based on the use of herbs for healing purposes). The 'scientific' branch was practised by an exorcist (*āšipu*). It consisted in the careful observation of any types of signs, such as signs that the exorcist noticed on his way to the patient's home and an indication of the outcome (survival or death). The latter did not depend on cures, but could be changed through various exorcisms. These magical measures (exorcisms and spells) were for now still relatively marginal, at least compared to the popularity they would experience later on. This indicated a fluctuating preference between an active intervention and a fatalistic acceptance of one's destiny.

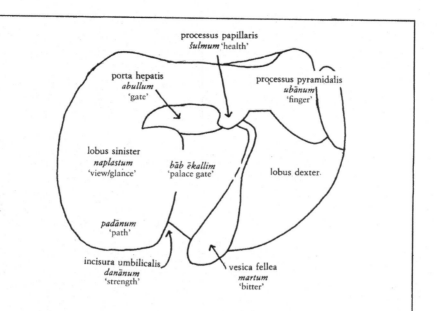

"If the 'path' *(padanūm)* turns around a 'weapon': if you go on a military expedition the enemy...

If the 'path' is present: a famine will come that (will destroy) the enemy ...

If the 'path' is in the middle of another 'path': he who will embark on a journey...

If the 'path' is in a 'sack': end of the reign, last days.

If the 'strength' *(danānum)* is there: the person in question has divine protection.

If the 'strength' is upside-down: the person's house will be ruined.

If the 'strength's' head is detached: betrayal, the palace superintendent will reveal your plans.

If the 'strength's' head is broken: your secret will be revealed.

If the 'strength' is bent but is (still in its place): the army in the foreign land...

If there are two crossed 'strengths': the enemy will be defeated

If there is a blemish on the 'strength': the enemy will take what is in your hunting nets.

If there is a 'foot' on the 'strength': a great house will be torn down.

Figure 11.5 Some examples of Old Babylonian liver omens and picture of a sheep's liver with its Babylonian terms.

12

THE OLD ASSYRIAN PERIOD

1 The origins and structure of the Assyrian state

According to the Neo-Assyrian scribes, who composed a king list covering two millennia, the Assyrian state had tribal and nomadic origins. In this text, the first seventeen kings 'lived in tents' (Text 12.1). A list (in reverse order, that is from son to father) of kings who 'were fathers/ancestors' follows, indicating that this sequence was made in order to link Ila-kabkabi (father of the usurper Shamshi-Adad I) to the last kings 'living in tents', Ushpia and Apiashal. This sequence of kings reflected the cultural and political influence of the Amorites (with its genealogies of tribal chiefs) at the time, and was aimed at legitimising Shamshi-Adad's position. This aspect makes the Assyrian King List a biased and unreliable source for the origins of the Assyrian state. However, it is a much more reliable source for later kings (from Sulili to Erishum II), being based on epigraphic and archival sources. From Sulili to Ilushuma, rulers are said to be 'kings attested in bricks (that is, brick inscriptions), but whose number of eponyms are lost', meaning that the length of their reigns was unknown. For the period from Erishum I to Erishum II, however, the duration of the kings' reigns is also provided, meaning that the eponyms were known.

Text 12.1   The beginning of the Assyrian King List

A: [1] Tudiya; [2] Adamu; [3] Yangi; [4] Kitlamu; [5] Harharu; [6] Mandaru; [7] Imsu; [8] Harsu; [9] Didanu; [10] Hanû; [11] Zuabu; [12] Nuabu; [13] Abazu; [14] Belū; [15] Azarah; [16] Ushpia; [17] Apiashal: Total of 17 kings who dwelled in tents.

B: [26] Aminu son of Ila-kabkabi; [25] Ila-kabkabi son of Yazkur-ilu; [24] Yazkur-ilu son of Yakmeni; [23] Yakmeni son of Yakmesi; [22] Yakmesi son of Ilu-Mer; [21] Ilu-Mer son of Hayanu; [20] Hay-anu son of Samanu; [19] Samanu son of Halê; [18] Halê son of Apiashal; [17] Apiashal son of Ushpia: Total of 10 kings who were their ancestors.

C: [27] Sulili son of Aminu; [28] Kikia; [29] Akia; [30] Puzur-Ashur (I); [31] Shalim-ahhe; [32] Ilushuma: Total of 6 kings attested on bricks, whose eponyms are destroyed.
[33] Erishum (I) son of Ilushuma: ruled for 40 years.
[34] Ikunum son of Erishum: ruled for . . . years.

---

[35] Sargon (I) son of Ikunum: ruled for . . . years.

[36] Puzur-Ashur (II) son of Sargon: ruled for . . . years.

[37] Naram-Sin son of Puzur-Ashur: ruled for . . . years.

[38] Erishum (II) son of Naram-Sin: ruled for . . . years.

D: [39] Shamshi-Adad (I) son of Ila-kabkabi, at the time of Naram-Sin, went to Babylonia. In the eponymy of Ibni-Adad, Shamshi-Adad came back from Babylonia, took Ekallatum, and resided in Ekallatum for 3 years. In the eponymy of Atamar-Ishtar, Shamshi-Adad came from Ekallatum, removed Erishum son of Naram-Sin, seized the throne, and ruled for 33 years.

Analysis

Group A (nomadic rulers): kings 1–12 roughly correspond to the ancestral list of Hammurabi (indicating that it was a general Amorite genealogy), while kings 13–17 were actual kings of Ashur.

Group B: the reverse genealogy aims at linking Aminu and Ila-kabkabi (the brother and father of Shamshi-Adad I respectively) with the old dynasty of Ashur. However, kings 18–26 never ruled in Ashur.

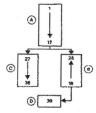

Group C: actual kings of Ashur ruling between the reigns of Apiashal and Shamshi-Adad. However, Sulili (n. 27) could not have been the 'son of Aminu' (who is a much later king) and should rather be 'son of Apiashal'.

Group D: an account of Shamshi-Adad's rise to power (which the addition of group B was meant to anticipate and legitimise), based on a type of text such as the 'Assyrian chronicles' of Mari.

The nomadic origin of the list dates to the time of Shamshi-Adad I and clearly attempts to develop a sort of legitimating 'prehistory'. However, the actual early history of Assyria was that of a region characterised by early urbanisation and intense agricultural activities. Agricultural villages already appeared in Assyria in the Hassuna period, and in the late Ubaid period the first urbanisation prompted the development of the first cities. However, it is necessary to distinguish two centres in Assyria, whose fusion would eventually bring about the rise of the Assyrian state.

The two centres were different both in terms of their environment and their history. On the one hand, there was the fertile 'Assyrian Triangle', located between the Upper Zab and the Tigris, with its main city Nineveh (Figure 12.1). On the other, there was Ashur, the city which gave Assyria its name, located in a more isolated position in the south (Figure 12.2). The Assyrian Triangle was an area of ancient settlements and its levels of urbanisation were high. This was due to the frequency of rainfall in the area and the availability of fertile lands. The region was inhabited by a local population of Hurrian origins. In the late Ubaid and Uruk phases, it received some influences from the south, but managed to assimilate them independently.

On the contrary, Ashur was an isolated city in an arid area, lacking a prosperous agricultural countryside. Its importance lay in its location along the river (Figure 12.3). The southern influences on Ashur were more recent than the ones experienced by Nineveh, and appeared from the Early Dynastic period onwards.

Figure 12.1 Satellite view of modern Mossul, surrounding the ancient city of Nineveh (Google Earth).

However, these were direct influences, turning the city into a *bona fide* centre of Sumerian culture along the Middle Tigris. If Nineveh and the Assyrian triangle were densely inhabited and cultivated, Ashur had to rely on trade. From Ashur it was possible to follow the Tigris towards eastern Anatolia, to cross the Wadi Tharthar to reach Upper Mesopotamia to the west, and to follow the Lower Zab River to reach the Iranian plateau. This strategic position made Ashur the southern commercial junction of Assyria. In a way, then, Ashur acted as an independent entity from the rest of the region. Eventually, the city would manage to rise as the political centre of Assyria, making it one of the most powerful regional powers of the second millennium BC.

The political union of Ashur with the rich Assyrian triangle, and the latter's subordination to the former, was probably caused by the interests displayed by previous empires in this region. Firstly, there was the Akkadian interest in controlling the commercial networks of its periphery. Then, there were the attempts of the Third Dynasty of Ur to turn the *ensi* of Ashur into effective instruments to control the Subartu region, where

Figure 12.2   Satellite view of Qal'at Sherqat, ancient Ashur (Google Earth).

they led numerous campaigns. When the Ur dynasty collapsed, the *ensi* of Ashur became independent. The city became a city-state and an Assyrian dynastic sequence began with Sulili, Kikia and Akia.

The main characteristics of Assyria in Mesopotamian history are therefore already visible in its early phase. Firstly, there was the central inter-dependence between Ashur and the fertile Assyrian Triangle. Then, there was the role of Ashur as southern outpost of the region. This aspect is visible on a political and religious level, as well as in its ethno-linguistic composition. Assyria was a largely Akkadian area in a context dominated by Hurrians along its foothills and Amorites in the steppes. A third aspect was the proximity of Assyria to the Zagros and Taurus Mountains. This profitable position, close to a wide range of raw materials, was not only key to the commercial success of Assyria, but also extremely dangerous. This was due to the threatening pressures (felt by the citizens of Ashur themselves) coming from the people living in these mountains. This aspect would eventually explain the distinct military vocation of the Assyrian state.

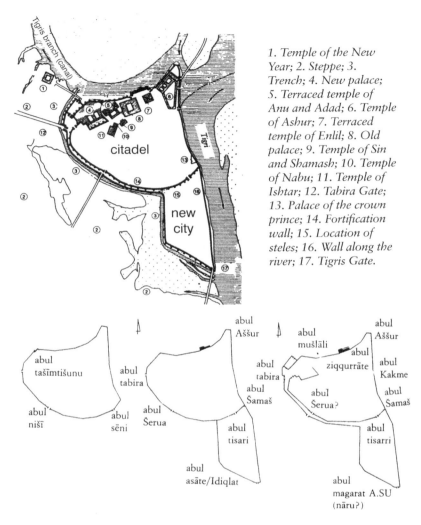

1. Temple of the New Year; 2. Steppe; 3. Trench; 4. New palace; 5. Terraced temple of Anu and Adad; 6. Temple of Ashur; 7. Terraced temple of Enlil; 8. Old palace; 9. Temple of Sin and Shamash; 10. Temple of Nabu; 11. Temple of Ishtar; 12. Tabira Gate; 13. Palace of the crown prince; 14. Fortification wall; 15. Location of steles; 16. Wall along the river; 17. Tigris Gate.

Figure 12.3 Plan of Ashur and development of the city's walls and gates in the Old, Middle, and Neo-Assyrian periods.

To the west, Assyria had easy access to the vast territories of Upper Mesopotamia. The first steps of its rise would therefore be the conquest of the area extending from the Tigris to the Khabur Triangle, the Balikh Valley and the Upper Euphrates region.

Not much is known of the first Assyrian kings (from Sulili to Ilushuma), and the little evidence we have comes from their few surviving building texts. These were found during the excavations in Ashur. We also possess indirect accounts from the so-called 'histories of buildings', written by later kings when, during the restoration of temples, they found previous foundation inscriptions and reported them on their own. Consequently, we know that, from Puzur-Ashur I to Puzur-Ashur II, the Old Assyrian kings worked on the walls of Ashur and the temples of the gods Ashur, Ishtar and Adad. Unfortunately, we do not know the size of the state they governed. However, some information on the period can be found in one inscription of Ilushuma. In this text, the king declared that he 'established freedom (*addurārum*) for the Akkadians and their sons' in cities located east of the Tigris (Der, Awal, Kismar), as well as in Nippur and Ur. A debt release (freeing sons and returning them to their families) that was granted to other cities could only have taken place after a victory. Only then, a king would be able (albeit temporarily) to proclaim an amnesty in order to portray himself as a liberator, rather than a conqueror, to the local population. Ilushuma, then, was the perpetrator of a victorious, yet short-lived, military expedition east of the Tigris and as far as Sumer. This indicates that Assyria was already striving to become a regional power, able to attack far from its heartland.

Immediately after Ilushuma, the city of Ashur was involved in a series of commercial interactions in Upper Mesopotamia and central and eastern Anatolia. This development is attested through documents found in the main commercial junction of the Assyrian merchants, the *kārum* located at Kanesh, in Cappadocia. This commercial network, which could have developed all of a sudden, is well attested during the four reigns of Erishum I, Ikunum, Sargon I and Puzur-Ashur II. Their reigns roughly correspond to the ca. eighty years of the second level of Kanesh (Kültepe). With the reigns of Naram-Sin and Erishum II there is a gap in the evidence, after which a second phase of commercial activities is attested under Shamshi-Adad I (Kültepe, level Ib). The network definitively collapsed under the less powerful successors of Shamshi-Adad. Therefore, this commercial network, which was managed by private merchants, was only able to survive when there was a solid rule in the Assyrian capital, while it collapsed when the Assyrian centre was less powerful.

The commercial nature of the Old Assyrian texts found in Cappadocia runs the risk of obscuring the fact that this was an undoubtedly important, but highly specialised, sector. After all, a more balanced view of the political structure of the early Assyrian state should be based on the documentation found at Ashur. Here, political control was to a certain extent tripartite. At the top of the pyramid, there was the king. His titles were not the ones typical of the period, such as *šarrum* (that is, 'king'), but emphasised his dependence on the city-god. In fact, the Assyrian king was *išši'ak Aššur* (*išši'akku* was the Akkadian version of the Sumerian word *ensi*), 'governor of Ashur (on behalf of the god)'. Considering that the city-god and his city had the same name, this title was particularly significant. It has been noted that under Ilushuma and Erishum I the title gradually changed from 'governor of the city of Ashur' to 'governor of the god Ashur'. The formula that best portrays the close relation between the Assyrian king and this deity is: 'Ashur is king – Silulu/Erishum/etc. is the governor (on behalf) of Ashur'. Similar implications can be found in the title of *waklum*, 'foreman', aimed at presenting the king as the one responsible for the Assyrian community in front of the god. More general titles for the king were *ruba'um*, 'prince' and *bēlum*, 'lord', which were also used to define non-Assyrian rulers.

The second element of Ashur's political structure was the 'city' (*ālum*). The city acted as a single unit represented by an assembly (*puḫrum*), whose members were the heads of free families. The assembly had legal competences and therefore had to deal with disputes or provide legal instructions to its merchants. It was not strictly a political institution, but the voice of the urban community. Like all city assemblies, its importance depended on the importance of activities pursued outside of the palace. In this case, then, the assembly had a considerable role, due to the involvement of the private sector in the Old Assyrian trade.

A third element of the political structure of Ashur was the eponymous official, the *līmum*. His name was used to name years, and his role somehow limited the role of the king. Kingship was hereditary, held by a single family and was legitimated through a privileged relationship with the god Ashur. On the contrary, the eponymous *līmum* was chosen by lot among a limited number of candidates from several families. He was in office for a fixed amount of time and was therefore periodically changed. The duties of the *līmum* are not clear. He could have been a sort of mayor, or the head of the city assembly, or even the receiver of taxes on trade. It is possible, then, that he was more linked to the city than the king.

Overall, the power of the palace was limited. On an ideological level, its role was limited due to the subordination of the king to the city-god. However, this apparent limitation actually consolidated the prestige of kingship in front of its subjects and its priesthood. On a more operational level, kingship was limited by the influence of urban institutions, whose members came from important families involved in the commercial activities that lay at the heart of Ashur's power. Later on, as the role of Ashur deteriorated compared to the agricultural cities of the Triangle, the palace would regain its supremacy at the expense of the assembly. The intensification of military endeavours and the substitution of a military political strategy instead of a commercial one would eventually become significant factors enforcing the authority of the king, at the expense of the other institutions in the city.

2 The Old Assyrian trade

Old Assyrian trade in Anatolia constituted a complex and large-scale process. It is described in detail on thousands of tablets found at Kanesh (Kültepe). It is possible that there were other areas of Assyrian trade, or other contemporary networks belonging to other Mesopotamian or non-Mesopotamian centres, which experienced a similar development. However, these remain unattested. The commercial activities between Ashur and Kanesh therefore constitute our only opportunity to understand the way in which long distance trade was pursued at the time. The intensity and size of this trade allowed it to overcome the initial stage of mere movement of caravans, and led to the stable settlement of Assyrian merchants in Kanesh and in other Anatolian centres. Old Assyrian trade predominantly took place between the Assyrian merchants in Kanesh and their representatives in Ashur (Figure 12.4). Apart from these two main components, there were other important elements: a commercial network extending throughout Anatolia, located between the central *kārum* of Kanesh and other minor commercial junctions; the organisation of production and infrastructure in Ashur; and the presence of intermediaries and agents who moved between the two main centres.

The *kārum* (originally meaning 'harbour', but later applied to any commercial junction) was a structure and, in more concrete terms, a settlement located outside the local city. At Kültepe, where both the city and the *kārum* were excavated, it is clear that there was a local city with a fortification wall and a palace. Outside of it, there was a district of Assyrian merchants. The *kārum* had its own structure and role recognised both by the city of Ashur and the local kingdom. Its role was as guarantor of the operations pursued. It acted as a legal authority in disputes among merchants, or between merchants and locals, and as provider of financial compensations to pay taxes (both to the local city and the *kārum* itself).

The *kārum* had its own structure, general assembly and council. Moreover, a representative from the city of Ashur resided there. This indicates that at the heart of this type of settlement there was an official endorsement from Ashur. It is highly likely that, if we had documents from the palace, we would be able to see the network as a whole as 'administered' by the city, rather than the king. Unfortunately, we only have evidence on the private side of Assyrian trade. Merchants (*tamkārum*) probably had an official role. This was a result of their key role not only as administrators of large assets, but also as individuals originally endorsed by the state. Their main purpose was to manage and make a profit from this trade. In order to achieve this, merchants relied on agents, contractors and individuals in charge of transporting commodities.

This complex organisation is clearly visible from the complexity of the evidence that has been brought down to us. The texts fall into two main categories, namely, contracts and letters. These are two rather predictable categories considering the distance between the people involved and the long-term investment of large amounts of silver and goods. This situation was further complicated by the presence of a variety of individuals with precise functions within a structured system. Moreover, commercial interactions were influenced by minor, yet important, phenomena: from the use of the same caravan by various merchants, to the appearance of credits, contestations on the accuracy of calculations and so on.

Despite these complications, the typical procedure can be seen through three basic types of texts, each with their own sub-categories (Text 12.2). First of all, there is the contract stipulated between the merchant from Kanesh and the caravaneer. This contract states the amount (in weighed silver) that the former entrusts to the latter. Moreover, it records the names of the representatives of the merchant at Ashur to whom the silver had to be delivered, and the caravaneer's promise to return to Kanesh with the goods bought with the silver given to him, at Ashur. When the merchant was a high status individual involved in a large number of deals, the agreement was often pursued by a delegate from Kanesh. Consequently, there are contracts between the merchant and the delegate and between the delegate and the caravaneer. These

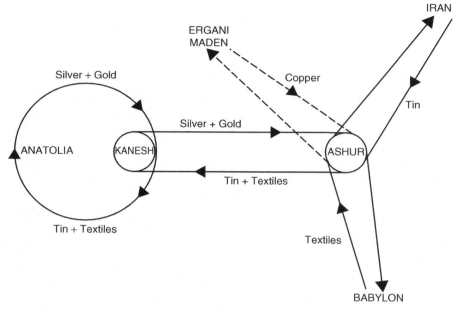

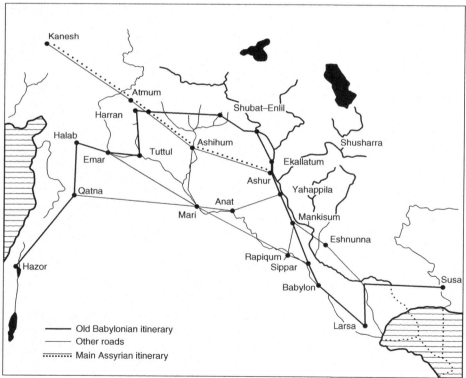

Figure 12.4 Old Assyrian trade. *Above*: A representation of the patterns of exchange; *Below*: Old Assyrian and Old Babylonian road network.

Text 12.2 Old Assyrian caravan procedures: the standard texts

1 The transport contract

'The 30 minas of silver – its *nishatu* tax added, its *šaddu'utu* -tax paid for – which Dadaya entrusted to Kukku-lanum son of Kutaya, and which he carried to the city (Ashur) for buyings – (that) silver belongs to Enlil-bani. Goods will leave the city and cross the country in the name of Enlil-bani again. The goods will arrive at Kanesh and Enlil-bani will receive them. Witness: Baziya son of Ili-kurub; witness: Asutaya, son of Ememe; witness: Ashur-idi, son of Kurub-Ishtar.'

2 The notifying message

'Say to Pilahaya, Irma-Ashur, Mannum-balum-Ashur, Kukkulanum, and Ashur-lamassi (the representatives of Enlil-bani in Ashur); thus (says) Enlil-bani: 30 minas of silver – its *nishatu* tax added, its *šaddu'utu* -tax paid for – with my seal and the seal of Kukkulanum, Kukkulanum is bringing to you. In the silver my hand has been laid. Here in the merchant-office, I have been noted as the warrantor of Kukkulanum and in the 30 minas of silver I have laid my hand. There, place yourselves at the side of Kukkulanum and let him buy textiles for (one) half of the silver, tin for the (other) half of the silver (in) what according to his estimate is a profitable way for him – then have it sealed and with your seals entrust it to Kukkulanum. You are my brothers – as I have laid my hand in the silver here (so) must you there in the towngate, representing me, lay your hands in the goods, and entrust them to Kukkulanum and let Kukkulanum lead the goods to me.'

3 The caravan account

'Thus Pilahaya, Irma-Ashur, and Mannum-balum-Ashur; say to Enlil-bani and Kukkulanum: [a detailed account of the operations follows which will be presented here in the form of a graph for convenience]

silver sent: 30 minas = 1800 shekels	1800–shekels
shortage recorded at arrival: 2/3 minas = 40 shekels	40 = shekels
silver readily available : 1760 shekels	1760 shekels

expenses:

– 114 linen cloths = 7½ minas and 4¼ shekels of silver =	454 1/4 shekels
– 2 talents 15 minas + 40 minas + 8 minas of tin for a total of 13 5/6 minas	
2 5/6 shekels of silver =	832 5/6 shekels
– 6 black donkeys and fodder: 2 minas 8 shekels of silver =	128 shekels
– harness: 16 shekels of silver =	16 shekels
– expenses for the journey: 37 minas of tin = 2 5/6 minas 2 1/16 shekels of silver =	172 1/6 shekels
– working capital of 2 harnessors: 1 mina of silver =	60 shekels
– their garments: 4 shekels of silver	4 shekels
– additions to the capital of PN: 7 shekels of silver	7 shekels
– additions: 12 1/2 shekels of silver	12 1/2 shekels
– payment of the *sa'atu*: 2 1/2 shekels of silver	2 1/2 shekels
– departure toll: 15 shekels of silver	15 shekels
– payment on the account of PN$_2$	6 shekels
– taken by Kukkulanum: 5/6 mina of silver =	50 shekels
Total expenditures:	1760 1/4 shekels

were all composed following the required procedure, specifying the original owner of the silver and were kept by all parties until the end of the operation.

The second type of text is the letter, written by the merchant at Kanesh to his representatives at Ashur. This letter was written for several reasons: to introduce the caravaneer to the representatives, to check that the amount of silver entrusted was correct and to specify how the money was to be invested. In case of the latter, the most popular solution was to invest half of the silver in textiles and half in tin. The goods then had to be entrusted to the same caravaneer.

The third type of text was the letter written by the representatives in Ashur to the merchant in Kanesh, entrusted to the caravaneer on his journey back to Kanesh together with the goods. The letter had the double-aim of reporting how the silver was invested and allowing the merchant to check whether all the goods had been delivered to him. This type of source provides useful evidence on the current prices of goods, delivery costs, the amount of taxes to be paid, the profits gained, and so on. The exchange of orders between merchants often took changes in prices and profit margins into consideration. There are even instructions to pay only in silver or via credit, to buy at any price or only if the price was convenient, to avoid certain types of goods or certain destinations, and so on. Apart from profits derived from trade, there were financial profits from loans and credits, providing monthly interests.

From a commercial point of view, the purpose of the Old Assyrian trade in Anatolia is very simple: the Assyrians brought fabric and tin to Anatolia, and earned silver and gold. The proceeds were normally re-invested in the same goods in order to maintain this commercial cycle. Therefore, this type of trade was not aimed at providing Assyria with goods it did not have, but to export goods for a profit. Silver was used for the accumulation of wealth and as a reference to establish the value of other goods. In other words, silver acted as the pre-monetary equivalent of money, and the Assyrians used it as a means to gain a profit that could be converted into any other good.

From an Anatolian perspective, silver was simply an exportable material. The area was rich in silver mines and therefore acted as the main provider of a metal whose value was quickly increasing in the Near East. In comparison, tin was neither mined nor sold in Assyria, but came from the Iranian plateau, probably the area between northern Afghanistan and Tajikistan. Tin reached Assyria through Shemshara, Eshnunna and Elam with Ashur acting as an intermediary centre. In this regard, it would have been useful to have as detailed evidence on the Iranian commercial network as we possess on the Anatolian one. The other metal needed for the production of bronze, copper, played a marginal role in the Old Assyrian trade. The most probable resources for this metal for Assyria, the mines of Ergani Maden, were closer to Assyria than to Kanesh, cutting out the latter's merchants from this sector of the trade.

Finally, textiles were both produced in Assyria, and imported and re-exported, especially from Babylonia. If Babylonian textiles were often of a higher quality, the majority of textiles exported were from Ashur. They were produced by the same families involved in commercial activities, with the merchants' wives managing the large number of women involved in textile production. According to prosopographic and statistical analyses, a large part of the population of Ashur was directly or indirectly involved in the commerce and production of textiles, which were mainly produced for trade, making Ashur the commercial and 'industrial' city of the period, with little agricultural activity.

Commodities were delivered via donkey-caravans. A caravaneer was generally given a few donkeys, but it is possible that several caravaneers informally joined larger caravans. However, this is not attested in the contracts and the letters. Journeys must have taken place on an annual basis. The inaccessibility of the roads on the Taurus in the winter provided barely enough time to travel from Ashur to Kanesh, to visit other minor cities along the way and return to Ashur. Itineraries had certain fixed crossing points to cross rivers and mountains, but there were alternative routes and deviations to other profitable areas for trade. The route from Ashur to Kanesh was divided into three branches. The first branch was from Ashur to Tell Leilan (Shubat-Enlil), the centre of the kingdom of Apum. This was approximately a 250 kilometre journey up the Tigris and across the Khabur basin. The second branch departed from Apum and reached Abrum, where the Euphrates was crossed. The crossing actually took place at Hahhum (modern Lidar Hüyük, near Samsat). This journey was also 250 km long. The third branch was longer, since Kanesh was located ca. 300 km from the Euphrates, and more difficult, requiring the crossing of several mountains.

Even in the *šar tamḫāri* epic (the King of Battle Epic), merchants warned Sargon on the difficulties of this journey, which required the crossing of 'seven rivers' and 'seven mountains'. The crossing of the Euphrates itself was seen as a heroic endeavour, of which kings should be proud. From Old Babylonian itineraries, datable more or less to the same period as the Old Assyrian trade, we know that on average a caravan could cover 25 km per day, with rest days in certain areas. Therefore, the journey from Ashur to Kanesh must have taken roughly 50 days.

Donkeys carried a large load on each side of the saddle and one on top. Once they reached Anatolia, they were sold for 20 shekels each. On average, a donkey carrying tin had 65 minas of tin on each side and more tin, or four or six pieces of fabric, on the saddle, where some luxury goods were also placed. A donkey carrying fabrics had 12 pieces of fabric on each side, as well as the usual load on the saddle. All textiles were wrapped and sealed according to their owner. The total load was 180 to 190 minas (around 90 kg) per donkey, with bulkier fabric loads being kept lighter and tin loads heavier and more concentrated. The orders to invest half of the silver in tin and half in fabrics indicate that value of textiles and tin roughly followed a 1:1 ratio. However, the bulkiness and lesser value of fabrics required three times the amount of donkeys needed for tin.

Prices in Anatolia were different from the ones in Assyria, a difference that was the entire reason why the trade itself existed. Tin was bought in Assyria at 13 to 16 shekels per shekel of silver and was sold in Anatolia at 6 to 8 shekels per shekel of silver. Fabrics varied in price according to their quality, but normal fabrics cost on average between 3 and 7 shekels of silver each and were re-sold at 10 to 14 shekels. Fabrics of a higher quality cost between 8 and 17 shekels and were sold at 15 to 30 shekels of silver. Even in the case of fabrics, then, merchants tried to get a 100% profit or even more.

Naturally, there were travel expenses, an estimated 10% of the budget, although donkeys and packaging were re-sold. Moreover, there were expenses for food for the caravaneers and the donkeys, requiring 2.5% of the budget, and the many, at times unpredictable, transit taxes. In order to pay them, caravaneers had to carry a certain amount of tin on them. The main taxes were: the *nisḫatum*, which was 5% on fabrics and 3% tin payable at arrival to the king of Kanesh; the *da'tum*, to be paid to the *kārum* and proportional to the journey travelled (10% for the entire journey from Ashur to Kanesh); and the *šaddu'atum*, to be paid at departure to the *kārum*. Overall, however, despite the expenses and taxes, which were at times avoided through smuggling, profits remained quite high.

The wealth of sources on Old Assyrian trade is unparalleled throughout the history of the Near East. However, this network was only one of the many commercial networks in the Near East. A first warning in this regard is that no archaeological reconstruction will ever be able to uncover clues on the credit systems, taxation, organisation and professionals involved in these complex systems. A second warning concerns the specialised nature of the documentation. Despite providing a large amount of information, the archives of the Old Assyrian families involved in trade only concern a small fragment of a larger system. If more evidence were available, the impression of Assyrian trade would be considerably different.

3 The Anatolian states

The Assyrian 'colonial' system in Anatolia involved around ten main *kārum* and ten minor colonies (*wabartum*), all linked to local cities (Figure 12.5). These settlements were mainly distributed in three areas: 1) around the Middle and Upper Euphrates, both on the eastern/ Upper Mesopotamian side (Nihriya, Badua, Zalpah) and the western/Anatolian side (Urshum, Hahhum, Mama); 2) on the Konya plain (Purushhattum, Wahshushana, Wahshaniya, Shalatiwar); 3) along the bend of the river Halys (Hattusa, Karahna, Turhumit), its valley (Samuha) and river mouth (Zalpa). Due to the orographic characteristics of Anatolia, city-states were concentrated in the valleys and plains between mountains and forests, or in the lakes and salt deserts in Central Anatolia. This concentration is confirmed by the archaeological evidence, which attests to a rise of cities at the beginning of the Middle Bronze Age, right after the decline of Early Bronze Age settlements. This was especially the case in Cilicia, in the Konya plain and the Central Anatolian plateau.

There were more local city-states than colonies in Anatolia, with textual evidence attesting to around thirty city-states. While there were probably more, albeit unattested, cities, the number of *kārum* known to us is probably close to their actual number. The local city-states varied in size and power and were independent from one another. However, minor cities gravitated around major centres. Each independent city had its own palace and king. The Assyrian sources call the local political authorities the 'palace' and define the king as a *ruba'um*, the Assyrian term for a ruler, or *šarrum*, a term that implies a higher role.

Figure 12.5 Central and eastern Anatolia in the Old Assyrian period, ca. 1950–1780 BC.

Another title attested only sporadically is *ruba'um rabi'um*, 'great king', implying an extended supremacy over other subordinate cities. In some areas, it is possible to locate some hegemonic cities, such as Kanesh, Wahshushana and Purushhattum. In the period belonging to Level II at Kanesh, the situation seems to have been characterised by a balance of power amongst various independent states. However, in the following phase (Level Ib), expansionistic tendencies began to appear.

Alongside kings, city-states had several important functionaries, the highest ranking one being the 'chief of the citadel' (*rabi simmiltim*), There were other officials linked to those sectors pertaining trade, such as the 'chief of the storehouse', 'chief of the market', 'chief of metals' and so on. These were all Assyrian denominations and all the titles in the local language remain unknown to us. Apart from the few attestations on this administrative organisation, we know of relatively developed palatial states. The latter were able to engage in legal and commercial agreements with the Assyrians (Figure 12.6). These relations were agreed on through treaties sealed by oaths, involving each new local king and the central *kārum* of Kanesh, or the local *kārum*. Treaties certified that the local king allowed the Assyrian colony to stay in his territory and to engage in its commercial activities. The local king also ensured the protection of the colony in his land and along trade routes. Old Assyrian trade was therefore based on a complex set of treaties with all the cities involved in the system. However, the latter was always in danger of breaking down each time there were conflicts between local states, or a new king caused some difficulties.

While a variety of states were involved in these agreements, the other contractual party (the Assyrians) was always the same, represented by the central authority of *kārum* Kanesh and Ashur. The system was relatively stable and homogeneous, with standardised transit taxes and the palace's pre-emption rights on a minor share of the imported stock. There were some disagreements, but they were considerably fewer than the several disputes among the merchants for credit issues. Smuggling itself was meant to avoid the taxes imposed by local rulers, rather than the *kārum*'s ones. However, it was forbidden and punished by the latter, rather than by the local rulers.

If the political status of local rulers was entirely independent from Assyria, it is also clear that Assyrian merchants were not helpless in their relations with the local authorities. Somehow, it is possible to see that these merchants were supported by the Assyrian state. The latter could have even provided a certain amount of military support. This type of Assyrian intervention does not seem to have been required on the other side of the Taurus, although it is well attested in Upper Mesopotamian cities, at least at the time of

Figure 12.6   Anatolian seal impressions on Old Assyrian tablets from Cappadocia.

Shamshi-Adad. Moreover, despite Assyria's potential political and military support, the unity of the colonial system was already strong enough to support its own merchants. Both on a financial and practical level, the system was strong enough to be able to deal with the local states on an equal standing, since the colonies brought tin and textiles to Anatolia. They were also able to exercise a profitable business, which, as far as we can see, was not hindered by obstacles or threats to the caravans travelling across the Near East.

Despite the fact that Assyrians and Anatolians were separate entities, they still remained in close contact. Several mixed marriages are attested and even in terms of material culture, the houses built by the Assyrian merchants were not different from Anatolian houses. Naturally, once merchants had reached a certain age, they usually returned to Assyria, without leaving any ethno-linguistic traces in Anatolia. In this regard, the ethno-linguistic context of Anatolia of the time is only visible to us through the local names attested on the Old Assyrian texts. These personal names partly belonged to dialects somehow related to Hittite, which would begin to be attested shortly after this time. There were also large groups of Luwian names, especially in the south, Hurrian in the south-east and Hittite or pre-Hittite in Central Anatolia. Following the disruptions experienced at the end of the third millennium BC, the Anatolian population thus began to establish itself in a way that will be better attested in the mid-second millennium BC, thanks to the documentation from the Hittite capital at Boghazköi.

In its first eighty years, the Old Assyrian trade enjoyed a period of political stability. The following hiatus of the network was not due to local disruptions, but Assyrian ones, which led to the destruction of the *kārum* of Level II after its sudden abandonment. When the Assyrians returned, possibly supported by a stronger political power in Assyria, they had to deal with a much more complex political situation. This is attested in a letter of the king of Mama, Anum-Hirbi (a king whose name was Hurrian and whose kingdom was located in the south, between the Euphrates and the Taurus) to Warshama, king of nearby Kanesh. The two kings had sealed an alliance through a treaty, but were now accusing each other of plundering each other's kingdoms, either on their own, or through vassals. The latter could have acted independently, but were nonetheless under these kings' jurisdiction. This letter depicts an Anatolia marked by internal conflicts and difficult relations between neighbouring states. Anum-Hirbi must have had territorial ambitions, since he left a stele on Mount Amanus. This stele would eventually be found by Shalmaneser III almost a thousand years later. Having deciphered the name of the unknown ruler, Shalmaneser then left his own stele near Anum-Hirbi's.

If Anum-Hirbi's letter has the advantage of being a direct and authentic piece of evidence, the overall picture of the time can be confirmed considering another source as reliable. Being a later text, this other source has to be used with great caution. Initially, it was believed to be reliable, and later suspicions that it was a fake text, composed by those Hittite rulers who had kept it, now seem excessive. This text was a copy made several centuries after the original inscription of Anitta, king of Kushshara, a king also attested in the Old Assyrian texts from Kanesh (level Ib). On his inscription, Anitta celebrates his victories. He started from his own city, located along the bend of the Halys river and conquered Central and northern Anatolia, reaching Zalpa, near the Halys river mouth and Kanesh (Nesha in Hittite) in the south. The military interventions and destructions of cities were repeated in three campaigns, indicating a situation of local conflicts and the progress of Anitta's expansionistic move.

The succession of local wars similar to the ones attested in Anum-Hirbi's letter or Anitta's inscription explains why the Old Assyrian network collapsed. The network lost the essential prerequisites for this system, namely, political stability and peace, both in Anatolia and in Assyria. This severely hindered the possibility of continuing long-distance trade. However, the significance of Anitta's inscription for Hittite scribes needs to be taken into consideration. Firstly, Kushshara, capital of Anitta's kingdom, was to become the capital of the Old Hittite kingdom. Its kings could have recognised in Anitta's endeavours their own achievements. Secondly, Anitta destroyed Hattusa, the next and most important Hittite capital. He then cursed those who would eventually restore it. Therefore, this text required taking the necessary magic or ritual precautions when the seat of power was moved from a victorious city (Kushshara) to a cursed one.

13

THE MARI AGE

1 Tribes and palaces in the Middle Euphrates

The discovery of the administrative and epistolary archives in the royal palace of Mari has thrown some light on a region and period previously unknown to us. The archives cover a period of three generations in the first half of the eighteenth century BC. Mari's critical position between the Mesopotamian alluvial plain and the west, and its role as an outpost and necessary stop in the journey from Mesopotamia to northern Syria has already been mentioned in the previous chapters (Figure 13.1). In the south, the alluvial plain and its irrigation system enabled the development of an agricultural and densely populated area. In the north, rainfall levels allowed the practice of rainfed agriculture. The Middle Euphrates constituted a sort of corridor linking these two areas, locked between a fertile valley on one side and a semi-arid plateau on the other. This area was characterised by seasonal farming and nomadic settlements in the winter and the spring.

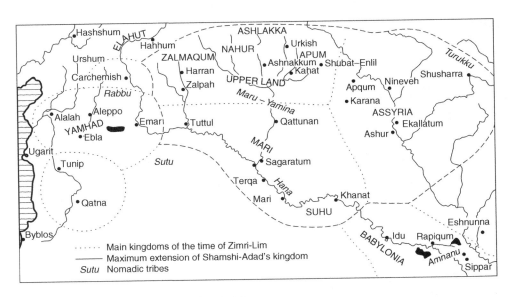

Figure 13.1   Map of Upper Mesopotamia in the Mari Age.

221

The region of Mari was therefore characterised by the close contact and intersection of two contrasting elements, which, for convenience, we will define as nomadic and sedentary. These represent, respectively, the political and organisational structures of the tribe and the palace. In the past, the relation between these two elements has been analysed in terms of their respective anteriority and posteriority, mobility and stability, and aggressive and defensive attitudes. These interpretations were influenced by the partiality of the available documentation, which was written by sedentary scribes, and of the scholars who unintentionally took on this biased point of view. In this way, they consolidated the stereotype of the nomads as uncivilised, aggressive and unstable groups. However, a more anthropological approach has restored the subjective nature of the points of view attested and the diversity and complementarity of these two different lifestyles.

Another misinterpretation was the idea that the presence of pastoral groups in the Middle Euphrates was one of the steps in the wider migration of Semitic people from their 'primitive seat' to their final destination in the Mesopotamian alluvial plain. Consequently, their semi-nomadic lifestyle was interpreted as an intermediary stage in their transition from nomadism to sedentariness. These misinterpretations, which varied between the drastic and naïve to more elaborate and balanced approaches, have survived for a long time. They therefore prevented a full understanding of this semi-nomadic lifestyle, with its transhumant farming and village agriculture, as a characteristic and perfectly suitable lifestyle for the area.

The view that sees mobile groups of nomads as new arrivals in the pre-existent world of the sedentary palaces is also untenable. If there was a secondary and intrusive element in the Middle Euphrates, this was certainly the palace. In reality, both these organisational and economic structures developed alongside each other and influenced one another. Moreover, although the development of palatial states is better documented, tribal groups also experienced an evolution, partly as a response to the evolution of the palaces.

On the issue of aggressiveness, the ancient and modern stereotype of the aggressive nomad has to be reconsidered. In this view, nomads were more dedicated to plundering than to a productive economy and were motivated by the desire to steal the wealth accumulated by the farming communities thus forced to defend themselves. In reality, both economies were focused on production. They both needed the 'other' element and this inevitably led to conflicts over the exploitation of the same territories. There certainly was a degree of nomadic aggression against the palaces. However, the opposite was also present, constituting an attempt to subdue pastoral groups and employ them as an additional workforce or in the military.

In terms of mobility, it is clear that the movements of pastoral groups were not an unplanned wandering in search for food. These movements were the concrete expression in space of their transhumant economy. However, there was also a mobility of the palace. From a structural point of view, palaces depended on various networks that relied on mobility, from communication, to trade and the military. From a diachronic point of view, both the construction of new palaces and political changes required painful modifications of earlier consolidated models for the utilisation of the land.

In the Middle Bronze Age, the pastoral groups of the Middle Euphrates and the Khabur Valley were predominantly Amorite. They were a relatively new presence in the area, substituting previous Eblaite and Akkadian groups. The latter lived in similar conditions and developed a similar economy, based on the farming of sheep and goats, as well as agriculture. Farming included 'horizontal' movements between summer pastures located in the fertile valleys (the *aḫ Purattim*, namely, the 'Euphrates Valley') and winter pastures in the semi-arid plateau (the *mātum elītum*, 'Upper Land'). Only one part of the pastoral group (*nawûm*) moved on a seasonal basis, the rest remained in the villages located in the valley to cultivate the lands. Therefore, there was a typically 'dimorphic' situation, with higher concentrations of people in the summer and lower ones in the winter. The agricultural cycle worked well with the pastoral cycle. The main crops (cereals) were cultivated in winter, allowing fields to be used as pastureland in the summer. Moreover, not all of the land was cultivated, since fields were rotated on a biennial basis. If necessary, groups could move over longer distances, especially towards the north (Upper Khabur), or the west (northern Syria).

The political organisation of these groups was centred on a kin-based structure, with several types of sub-groups, from smaller kin-based groups (the pastoral camp or migratory group) to the tribe and the tribal confederation. Until recently, it was believed that there were three tribal confederations within the kingdom of Mari: the Haneans, who were the ones most integrated with the palace, followed by the Benjaminites and the Sutians. However, Jean-Marie Durand and Dominique Charpin have shown that the term 'Haneans', which gave the name to the homonymous region (Hana), indicated nomads in general. Apart from the more mobile and detached character of the Sutians, who gravitated towards Syria, the two tribal groups of the kingdom of Mari were the Banu-Yamina (Benjaminites), 'sons of the right' (that is, the south) and the Banu-Sim'al, 'sons of the left' (that is, the north). Their names referred to their geographic position in relation to the rising sun. Since the ruling dynasty was of Sim'alite origins, the submission of the Benjaminites seems to have been a difficult task, causing several wars.

Tribes and smaller kin-based groups were normally centred in villages acting as permanent bases. They had their own leaders, whose titles were extraneous to Akkadian and its palatial structure (such as the *sugāgum* and other names). These leaders were military leaders as well as political representatives of the tribes before the palace, which considered these leaders as some sort of local functionaries. The palace provided them with a sort of investiture or formal recognition, requiring the exchange of gifts and payments. Palaces therefore constituted the other side of this complex structure (Figure 13.2). Along the Euphrates

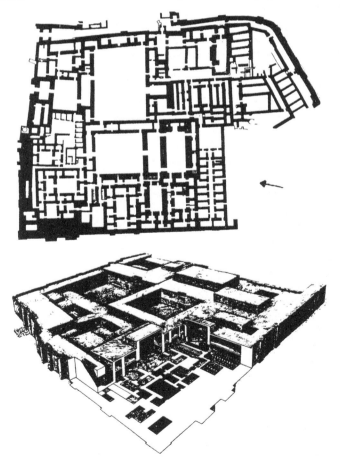

Figure 13.2   Royal palace of Mari: plan and reconstruction.

and the Khabur there was a whole network of walled cities with temples and palaces. These cities were part of a hierarchical system. Some cities had independent rulers, while others were governed by local functionaries. This hierarchy changed over time. The period attested in the Mari archives features the alternating supremacy of Mari and Shubat-Enlil (Tell Leilan). The former controlled the Middle Euphrates and the Lower Khabur region. The latter controlled Assyria and the Upper Khabur region and was chosen by Shamshi-Adad as his own residence.

Following the Mesopotamian model, royal palaces were the seat of the royal administration, with scribes acting as administrators in a variety of sectors. Functionaries appointed by the ruling kings governed the provincial palaces. These provincial palaces had a much more limited bureaucratic structure. Nonetheless, the latter included all functions needed for the correct administration of the city. In the Mari sphere of influence, there were the provincial palaces of Terqa (Tell Ashara), Saggaratum, Qattunan and Tuttul (Tell Bi'a), while in the one of Shubat-Enlil there were Shaghar Bazar and Karana (Tell Rimah). The political structure of all kingdoms belonging to the Amorite cultural sphere, which extended from Syria to Elam, was therefore based on two main components. On the one hand, there was the city with its palace and agricultural fields (*mamlakatum*). On the other, there was the tribal group with its wider presence in the region (*nawûm*). Royal titles such as 'king of Mari and Hana', or 'king of Tuttul and Amnanum' are a clear indication of this double component. The latter is also attested in the Sumerian south in the title of 'king of Uruk and Amnanum'.

The economy of the palaces was partly based on the agricultural activities in the fertile valleys. These were limited, but still able to support the small palaces. Moreover, palaces could rely on taxes on sheep farmed by the tribes and on the north-to-south and east-to-west commercial networks that had to cross this strategic region. The lands directly managed by the palace were not vast compared to their Mesopotamian counterparts. A large share of the surplus was therefore gathered through taxes levied on villages and pastoral groups. Due to its proximity to raw materials, such as wood and metal from Syria and Anatolia, the quality of craftsmanship continued to be as high as the one from Mesopotamia.

Unlike in Mesopotamia, however, life in the palaces of the region seems to have been marked by a scarcity of human, technological and economic resources. This problem is attested in the numerous letters written by royal functionaries and their colleagues in the provincial palaces. In these letters, the functionaries complain about the lack of specialised workforce. They therefore tried to organise the transfer of both specialised and non-specialised workers from one palace to the other and to cope with a wide range of needs (which were difficult to take care of in a stable manner) through the re-organisation of what was available. The situation became significantly worse at the time of Shamshi-Adad. In fact, the construction of his palace at Shubat-Enlil required large amounts of resources. Consequently, the older palaces of Mari and Ashur had to provide parts of their workforce and expertise, worsening a situation that was already unstable.

Another problem was the state of constant conflict caused by the expansionistic ambitions of several kings ruling at the time: from Yahdun-Lim of Mari to Naram-Sin of Eshnunna, Shamshi-Adad of Assyria and Hammurabi of Babylon. In order to pursue these wars, kings relied on copious numbers of tribal troops. Therefore, far from fearing the arrival of nomadic groups, as previously believed, palaces eagerly encouraged their arrival in order to form an army large enough to cope with their various offensive or defensive undertakings. Wars were fought in summer, which was the only season when roads were accessible and food resources were available from the late spring harvests. Just like there was a seasonal complementarity between transhumant farming and agriculture, so there was one between farming and wars. For both agricultural and military needs, the late arrival and reunion of pastoral groups in the valleys caused palaces a great deal of anxiety, often forcing them to resort to several constrictive measures.

The coexistence of two economic and political systems with different characteristics and needs in the same area was based on this territorial and seasonal complementarity. The strategies used by these two systems, however, remained inherently different. The tribe used a more flexible strategy, characterised by a slow pace of development, large territories and a more traditional technical knowledge. Therefore, it produced little surplus in terms of resources, since its main asset was the ownership of herds. However, it still managed to remain safe from sudden crises. On the contrary, the strategy of the palace was much more fast-paced. The palace focused on the effective use of time and space, the over-exploitation of technical and administrative competences and the recruitment (at times even forced) of labour for urban and military endeavours. The palace was also dedicated to the accumulation of surplus to finance the production of luxury products, the maintenance of palatial culture and the exchange of prestigious gifts. In other words, palaces required as much as possible from their territories – a situation that was bearable in favourable times, but that could also cause drastic crises in difficult periods.

It is highly likely that the situation was further worsened by the palaces' introduction of summer cultivations (such as sesame). The latter effectively took away fields formerly used as pastureland. Moreover, the building programs and wars undertaken by the palaces were occasional, yet equally aggravating, initiatives. The economy of the Middle Euphrates could not bear this growing pressure. However, this situation did not affect pastoral groups, which managed to return to their former rhythms. It affected the palaces, which collapsed one after the other, for a variety of reasons. Hammurabi destroyed Mari, while Shubat-Enlil was significantly reduced after Shamshi-Adad's reign. Having kept Mari's legacy alive for a short while, even Terqa suddenly collapsed and so did Tuttul. Around 1800–1750 bc, the Middle Euphrates Valley and the Lower Khabur had been a large network of thriving palaces. However, only a century later, the area became a de-urbanised region. It began to be ruled by pastoral groups that were hindering commercial activities, but could not be conquered by the sedentary states, now located increasingly further away from this region.

2 The reign of Yahdun-Lim

Up until the end of the nineteenth century bc, Upper Mesopotamia had been a politically fragmented region. Following several expansionistic attempts led by a variety of kings, the region found itself unified, though for a short period of time, under the rule of Shamshi-Adad. These expansionistic initiatives were characterised by a certain degree of flexibility and improvisation and were clearly the work of Amorite leaders. These leaders' appreciation for large and unsettled territories was in marked contrast to the aim of Sumero-Akkadian rulers. The latter rather focused on the control of specific agricultural and administrative areas. Although the events took place in the same period, in this section the situation of the western area of the Euphrates Valley will be considered first, to be followed by the one of the eastern area of the Tigris valley.

The creation of the large and powerful kingdom of Mari happened during the reign of Yahdun-Lim, who belonged to the Banu-Sim'al tribe. His father Yaggid-Lim was possibly the king of nearby Suprum. Yaggid-Lim controlled the Middle Euphrates region and had fought for an extended period of time against Shamshi-Adad's father, Ila-kabkabi, who controlled the Middle Tigris. Yahdun-Lim reigned for around fifteen years (ca. 1810–1795 bc) and moved the capital of his reign to Mari. He therefore replaced the dynasty of *šakkanakku* previously governing the city. Yahdun-Lim significantly enlarged his kingdom, becoming 'king of Mari, Tuttul and Hana'. He constructed several canals, in particular the one linking the Khabur to the Euphrates, called Ishim-Yahdun-Lim. He also built several temples and fortification walls, especially in Mari and Terqa, which was the city of the god Dagan and the main religious centre of the region. Finally, he founded a city in the desert, Dur-Yahdun-Lim. A commemorative inscription reports his victory over 'seven kings, fathers of Hana', the leaders of the nomadic tribes located in the region of Mari and Terqa, as the defining moment in the formation of his kingdom. The inscription then continues listing the king's building program.

On a political level, in order to oppose Shamshi-Adad, Yahdun-Lim sealed alliances (through treaties and inter-dynastic marriages) with Yamhad to the west and Eshnunna to the east. Eshnunna controlled

Suhum, a region in the Euphrates Valley south of Mari, where it founded the city of Haradum. At the time, then, the kingdom of Eshnunna bordered with the one of Mari. In the same period, the Mari administration changed its former scribal tradition, inherited from the *šakkanakku*, with a new one, more Babylonian in style and imported from Eshnunna. On a military level, Mari was engaged on two fronts. In the north, the city conquered Tuttul (Tell Bi'a, near modern Raqqa) and Emar (Meskene). This area was formerly ruled by the Banu-Yamina, who rebelled against this expansion.

The foundation texts from the temple of Shamash celebrate this memorable victory against the Benjaminites. The latter are all listed with the name of their city and their tribe: Samanum and the Ubrabum; Tuttul and the Amnanum; Abattum and the Rabbum. These groups were supported by Sumu-epuh, king of Yamhad. The great victory was also celebrated in a year formula, and other formulas commemorated the conquest of the main rebellious centres. The celebratory inscription of Yahdun-Lim even attests his expedition to the Mediterranean. This achievement had both ideological connotations, implying that the king had reached the end of the world, and economic ones, since it allowed him to bring back cedar wood. However, this achievement also implies that Yamhad allowed the expedition to cross its territory.

Much more uncertain was the outcome of Yahdun-Lim's wars against Shamshi-Adad. The king of Mari had a stable control over the Middle Euphrates and Lower Khabur regions. He therefore enlarged his sphere of influence through alliances with Nihriya and Talhayum in the Upper Balikh and with Kurda in the Upper Khabur, reaching as far as the foothills of the Jebel Sinjar. This expansion led to his conflict with Shamshi-Adad. Initially, Yahdun-Lim's army had been quite successful, conquering Nagar (Tell Brak) and reaching Ekallatum, along the Tigris. In the long run, however, it was Shamshi-Adad who eventually succeeded, although the exact circumstances surrounding his victory are unknown to us. As a result of his defeat, Yahdun-Lim's son, Sumu-Yaman, supplanted his father and possibly sought the support of Yamhad. A few years later Sumu-Yaman was also deposed, allowing Shamshi-Adad to conquer Mari.

3 Shamshi-Adad and the 'kingdom of Upper Mesopotamia'

The western side of Upper Mesopotamia was under the supremacy of the king of Mari, the eastern side, from the Tigris Valley to the Upper Khabur, was marked by the several attempts of the kings of Eshnunna to conquer the area. The Eponym Chronicle found at Mari, and the year formulas of Ipiq-Adad of Eshnunna, attest to Ipiq-Adad's fighting in Upper Mesopotamia against the elder brother of Shamshi-Adad, Aminum, and conquering several cities in the Upper Khabur region. Ipiq-Adad's son, Naram-Sin, was previously identified with the homonymous king of the Assyrian King List. However, this hypothesis is now rejected, although the interruption of commercial activities in Cappadocia at the time of Naram-Sin of Assyria could still have been due to the threats posed by Eshnunna. The rise of Eshnunna under Ipiq-Adad and Naram-Sin did not last. The Eponym Chronicle describes the progressive supremacy of Shamshi-Adad, who took over Ekallatum, making it his temporary capital. The king removed Erishum from the throne of Ashur, bestowing upon himself the title of 'king of Assyria' and continued his wars against Eshnunna, now ruled by Dadusha.

The rise of Shamshi-Adad did not take place without opposition, both in terms of the legitimation and the organisation of his reign. On a propagandistic and scholarly level, the rise of Shamshi-Adad was justified both in the Eponym Chronicle and in the Assyrian King List. The former is the story of Shamshi-Adad's family until his definitive rise to power. In its first half, the Assyrian King List constitutes an attempt at placing this usurper and his ancestors within a dynastic sequence that did not originally belong to him.

Shamshi-Adad became king of Assyria only in a second stage. Originally, he belonged to a family of Amorite tribal chiefs. These chiefs had long fought against Yaggid-Lim of Mari and Ipiq-Adad of Eshnunna over the control of the Upper Khabur region. Shamshi-Adad himself had fled to Babylon, seeking political protection against Eshnunna, to then return to power from Ekallatum. At the time, the latter was a historically and geographically marginal centre. Even after his conquest of Assyria, the old religious, political and commercial centre of Ashur had a secondary role in his kingdom.

When Shamshi-Adad managed to expand and consolidate his kingdom, forming what came to be defined as the 'kingdom of Upper Mesopotamia', he entrusted Assyria to his son Ishme-Dagan, who was based in Ekallatum. Shamshi-Adad then moved his residence to Shubat-Enlil (Tell Leilan), to the east of the Khabur Triangle. This was a strategic location to control the routes between Assyria and Upper Mesopotamia. Excavations at Tell Leilan have uncovered a palace and a temple from the reign of Shamshi-Adad, with several cylinder seals belonging to his functionaries. Other administrative centres of his reign that have been excavated are Shaghar Bazar, in the Khabur area, and Tell Rimah, south of the Jebel Sinjar. Alongside administrative texts, numerous buildings and temples have been found there, indicating the remarkable building programs of the Mari Age.

One of the most crucial moments in the rise of Shamshi-Adad was his conquest of Mari. This conquest forced Yahdun-Lim to flee west to Yamhad, which was Mari's enemy, though it was now increasingly concerned about Shamshi-Adad's expansion. After a few years, Shamshi-Adad appointed his own son, Yasmah-Addu, as ruler in Mari. For this reason, the second phase of Shamshi-Adad's reign is best attested in the Mari archives. Mari's administrative structure remained unchanged. However, its subordinate position to a larger kingdom had a strong impact on the city. Parts of the kingdom's resources were moved to support Shamshi-Adad's agenda: from the provision of troops for his military endeavours to the financing and provision of technical and administrative specialists for his building programmes. Relations between Shamshi-Adad and Yasmah-Addu often seem to have been tense. This was due to the Assyrian king's continuous requests, which weighed heavily on Mari's economy. Moreover, there was also Shamshi-Adad's marked intolerance for his son's poor leadership skills. Unlike his more capable elder brother Ishme-Dagan, Yasmah-Addu was considered to be incompetent and immature and in need of constant guidance.

Despite having reached a high point in his political influence, Shamshi-Adad did not want to decrease his political and military engagements, nor was he able to do so. In fact, his expansion could never be fully consolidated. The change between political fragmentation (where power was divided amongst the traditional urban centres) and his 'imperial' unification (based on the mobility and adaptability of the tribal element) had been too abrupt and ambitious to be consolidated successfully.

To the south-east, Shamshi-Adad had to face two powerful states, namely, Eshnunna and Babylon. The latter was still in the process of consolidating itself. Only after the death of Shamshi-Adad did the city became a major political and military player in the Near East under Hammurabi. In comparison, under the leadership of Dadusha, Eshnunna had begun its expansionistic rise in the Khabur and Middle Euphrates regions. At first, Shamshi-Adad managed to keep hold of Me-Turan in the Diyala, and Mankisum in the Middle Tigris. Soon after, however, Dadusha conquered these cities and moved on, conquering Rapiqum and all of the land of Suhum and directly threatening Ekallatum. At this point, Shamshi-Adad decided to sign a treaty and this peace seems to have lasted until his death.

To the north-east, having established control over Assyria with his conquest of Arrapha, Nineveh and Qabra, Shamshi-Adad had to deal with the ever-present problem of this region, which was the pressures from groups living in the Zagros, in particular the Turukku. In this regard, the city of Shusharra (Tell Shemshara) constituted the closest point of economic interaction and military containment of this threatening group. Shamshi-Adad even tried, and for a while succeeded, at restoring commercial activities with Cappadocia, with its high profits. Seals belonging to his functionaries have been found at Acemhöyük (ancient Purushhanda). To the west, having conquered Mari, Shamshi-Adad had to face the powerful kingdom of Yamhad. Its ruler, Sumu-epuh, had already attacked the king on several occasions. As a response, Shamshi-Adad sealed an alliance against Yamhad with Carchemish in the north and Qatna in the south. Yasmah-Addu married a daughter of Ishi-Adad, king of Qatna, from whom Shamshi-Adad sought support on at least two occasions. This was also to boast that he had reached the Upper Sea and the Lebanese forests, just like his son Yasmah-Addu did before him.

On an ideological level, it is clear that Shamshi-Adad followed the example of the Akkadian kings, using the titles of 'strong king' and 'king of Akkad'. Even his military expedition to the Mediterranean followed the same model and so did his aspirations at universal dominion. However, they could not emulate the feat of reaching both the Upper and Lower Sea, since Lower Mesopotamia remained outside the king's reach. It is clear that Shamshi-Adad did not just consider himself king of Assyria. However, in his reign the Assyrian eponym dating system and the Assyrian calendar were implemented in all of his cities, even in those ruled by local dynasts, such as Mari. It is even possible that he substituted the authority of the god Ashur with the one of the god Enlil. His attention to the patron deity of Nippur, who had also been at the heart of Sargon's claim to legitimacy, is evident (like naming his capital after the god).

4 The reign of Zimri-Lim

In his final years, Shamshi-Adad had to face a series of emergencies. These were not particularly relevant on a supra-regional level, but were equally threatening for his state. First, there was the attack of the Turukku, who managed to reach the foothills of the Tur Abdin. Second, there was the revolt of the Zalmaqum region, located in the Upper Balikh. Following the death of Shamshi-Adad's ally Dadusha, a more ambitious ruler, Ibal-pi-El, came to power in Eshnunna. Similarly, in Aleppo the more energetic king Yarim-Lim succeeded king Sumu-epuh. Consequently, the 'kingdom of Upper Mesopotamia' found itself surrounded by threatening neighbours. The now aged Shamshi-Adad delegated more responsibilities to his sons Ishme-Dagan and Yasmah-Addu. He died shortly afterwards, and his death had an immediate impact on the kingdom. Apparently, a tribal chief of the Banu-Sim'al expelled Yasmah-Addu from Mari in favour of the heir of Yahdun-Lim, Zimri-Lim, who also had the support of Yamhad. Shortly after his enthronement, he married Shibtu, daughter of his protector Yarim-Lim.

Of the formerly great kingdom of his father, Ishme-Dagan only managed to keep Assyria, now dramatically reduced to its original size. This was essentially the Tigris Valley, from Ekallatum and Ashur to the area north of the Assyrian Triangle. The territories between Assyria and the Middle Euphrates – the Khabur and Balikh regions, as well as the Jebel Sinjar and Wadi Tharthar – broke down into a network of small independent kingdoms. The strongest contender in the area could then turn these kingdoms into vassal states. The main contest was centred on the rivalry between Zimri-Lim and Ishme-Dagan. From Mari's perspective, this intermediary region was fundamental for its economy. Its water resources, as well as its role as preferred area for seasonal activities, made the Khabur basin a crucial territory for Mari. From an Assyrian perspective, this region was important for strictly commercial reasons, allowing caravans to move from Ashur to Cappadocia.

Zimri-Lim eventually succeeded, conquering the entire Khabur Triangle and the Sinjar's foothills within the first years of his reign. In this way, he cut Ishme-Dagan out of Upper Mesopotamia and its Anatolian trade, which consequently disappeared. The kinglets of Upper Mesopotamia managed to keep the autonomy they enjoyed under Shamshi-Adad. However, the change of overlord brought in many cases a change in the local dynasties. New alliances were enforced by a series of inter-dynastic marriages between several daughters of Zimri-Lim and the kings of Ilansura, Ashlakka, Elahut, Andariq and many more. This was a *bona fide* political strategy, further cemented by the sending of his daughter 'as wife' of Shamash at Sippar, in order to establish friendly ties with Babylonia. There, the princess lived in a cloister of priestesses. The various letters sent by Zimri-Lim's daughters living in Mesopotamia to their father indicate that their situation was not as good as they expected. There were several economic and cultural difficulties, so much so that some marriages had to be annulled.

However, the contest between Mari and Ashur soon became a much wider problem, involving the old state of Eshnunna, Babylon and even Elam. Initially, scholars thought that alliances were roughly separated into two groups: the one of the Euphrates, linking Yamhad, Mari, Babylon and Larsa; and the Tigris one, linking Assyria, Eshnunna and Elam. In reality, it was a much more intricate situation. First, Ibal-pi-El of

Eshnunna attempted to conquer Upper Mesopotamia through a series of expeditions. He followed the Middle Euphrates from Rapiqum to the border of Mari, conquering Suhum. He also fostered a revolt of the Benjaminites against the Sim'Alites of Zimri-Lim. He then followed the Middle Tigris reaching Ekallatum and Ashur, expelling Ishme-Dagan, who fled to Babylon. Ibal-pi-El did not stop there and also reached the Sinjar foothills and the Khabur Triangle.

This expansion, which consisted mainly of sieges rather than conflicts in the battlefield, was energetically opposed by Zimri-Lim. He found the support of Yamhad as well as Babylon, which was alarmed by the threatening rise of Eshnunna. After two or three years, Ibal-pi-El had to retreat, abandoning his conquered cities one after the other and leaving his former allies at the mercy of his enemies. After the peace with Eshnunna and the Benjaminites, Mari went through a relatively stable period for around five years. In this period, Zimri-Lim ordered a 'census' (*tēbibtum*) of the Benjaminites and travelled to Ugarit. This peaceful phase, however, was interrupted by the Elamite *sukkal-maḫ*, who invaded Mesopotamia. At first Mari and Babylon supported Elam in its siege of their old rival Eshnunna. However, the situation completely changed when Elam threatened Babylon and the Sinjar region. This led to the formation of a coalition between Mari and Babylon, along with their allies Larsa, Yamhad, Zalmaqum and all the kings in the Jezira. Within a few years, Elam was forced to retreat, although it still managed to plunder Eshnunna.

A few years later, Hammurabi of Babylon pursued the final expansionistic attempt of this period. Having conquered Larsa, as we will soon see, the king moved against the other surviving states of the time, former allies and enemies alike. He conquered Eshnunna, pushed back Assyria and conquered Mari in his thirty-second regnal year. Two years later, he destroyed it. Despite being a tragic event for the city's inhabitants, the violent destruction of Mari's royal palace managed to preserve an archive with crucial information on the events of the first half of the eighteenth century BC. This has provided us with an unusually detailed account for such a remote historical phase.

5 The Mari Age: wars, alliances and trade

The Mari Age is undoubtedly a period for which it is possible to reconstruct the network of political relations of the 'Amorite' world (Figure 13.3), which can be considered as a cultural and linguistic continuum that spread from Syria to Elam with an unprecedented intensity and breadth of interaction. Akkadian became the preferred language for diplomatic relations and the administration of all the palaces of the area, even where the main spoken language was Hurrian or Amorite. Messengers and ambassadors had to travel extensively to deliver information, requests and gifts, and to prepare the route for merchants or troops. Regarding the letters kings sent to each other, relations between royal houses became formalised through an imaginary sense of 'brotherhood'. This was an intrinsic aspect of the kin-based structure of Amorite society and was further cemented through inter-dynastic marriages. Gift-exchange followed the traditional rules of reciprocity and generosity. Similarly, hospitality was a typical aspect of the way diplomatic relations were established.

The wider political system of the region was divided into two levels, an aspect that will be better documented in the Late Bronze Age. The kings of Yamhad and Qatna in Syria, Mari and Assyria in Upper Mesopotamia, Babylon and Larsa in Lower Mesopotamia and Elam, with its imperial ambitions, had a series of vassal kings depending on them. These states had to swear oaths of loyalty and subordination. Even the ever-changing alliances sealed by rulers were stipulated through oaths and followed the principles of equality. These agreements are attested in their correspondence. We do not possess any of the original texts for this period, with the exception of one treaty from Tell Leilan. After all, many of them must have been formal spoken oaths. We also possess a declaration of war from a letter of Yarim-Lim to Yashub-Yahad of Der. This is a revealing source on a practice that would remain typical of the Middle and Late Bronze Age throughout the Near East.

Figure 13.3 Royal palace of Mari: the fresco defined as the 'investiture of the king' in the throne room.

Upon initiating a war, the king would explain the reason that obliged him to take such a course of action. Normally, this reason was an alleged breach of reciprocal relations, where a friendly and respectful behaviour from one king was returned with hostility and deceitfulness. At the same time, former favours were seen as neither recognised nor returned. At this point, war was viewed as a necessary consequence and the patron deity of the offended party had to act as a judge and participant. This led to the inevitable victory of justice and the punishment of the offender. Apart from this legal and theological justification of war, this phase stands out for the impressive management of military resources. This included a vast mobilisation of troops, enlisted through *corvée* amongst one's own subjects, through semi-nomadic groups, which were encouraged to join in view of rich booties, and through auxiliary troops provided by allies. This exchange of troops between states was a never-ending process, widening the scope of a war to include the entire network of alliances in the Near East.

The deployment of tribal troops was also an opportunity, and an effective way to place nomadic groups within the economic and political system of the kingdoms. Through the so-called 'purification' ritual (*tēbibtum*), the names of individuals were ceremonially inscribed on a tablet, in exchange of land allotments. The census and military deployment of tribal troops constituted a powerful means to break down tribal groups and link each family to specific plots of land. Naturally, while palaces gladly imposed the *tēbibtum* on tribal groups, tribal chiefs disliked the practice, interpreting it as a way to subordinate them to the political and economic authority of the royal palace. These chiefs preferred to keep land undivided, instead of receiving parcels from the nearby kings. In this way, states managed to create large armies of thousands of soldiers, who could travel over long distances, bringing destruction to the places where they needed to find provisions. In this case, village dwellers hid within the large walled cities, which were better prepared to resist the attacks.

The vast majority of wars were pursued through sieges. Battles were relatively rare, despite being much more effective and excellent opportunities for celebratory statements. All the Upper Mesopotamian cities of the period were protected by fortification walls made of high mounds of land on top of which walls were

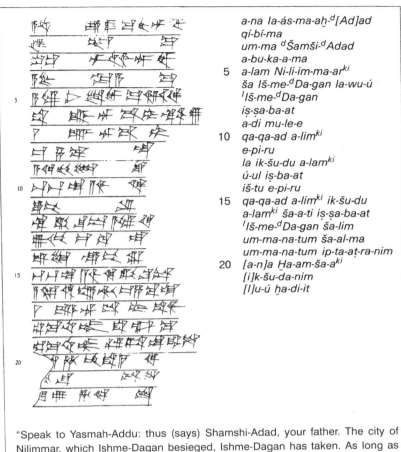

a-na Ia-ás-ma-aḫ-^d[Ad]ad
qí-bí-ma
um-ma ^dŠamši-^dAdad
a-bu-ka-a-ma
5 a-lam Ni-li-im-ma-ar^{ki}
ša Iš-me-^dDa-gan la-wu-ú
^IIš-me-^dDa-gan
iṣ-ṣa-ba-at
a-di mu-le-e
10 qa-qa-ad a-lim^{ki}
e-pi-ru
la ik-šu-du a-lam^{ki}
ú-ul iṣ-ba-at
iš-tu e-pi-ru
15 qa-qa-ad a-lim^{ki} ik-šu-du
a-lam^{ki} ša-a-ti iṣ-ṣa-ba-at
^IIš-me-^dDa-gan ša-lim
um-ma-na-tum ša-al-ma
um-ma-na-tum ip-ta-aṭ-ra-nim
20 [a-n]a Ḫa-am-ša-a^{ki}
[i]k-šu-da-nim
[l]u-ú ḫa-di-it

"Speak to Yasmah-Addu: thus (says) Shamshi-Adad, your father. The city of Nilimmar, which Ishme-Dagan besieged, Ishme-Dagan has taken. As long as the hill did not reach the height of the top of the city, he could not take the city. After the hill had reached the top of the city, he took this city. Ishme-Dagan is well. The troops are well. The troops have been dismissed, and have come to Hamshâ. Rejoice!"

Figure 13.4 Letter from Mari. The siege tactic of the time consisted in the construction of a hill of land against the raised fortification wall, allowing the battering rams and the troops to reach the city.

built. This allowed further protection from siege towers and battering rams. The attacking troops had to use siege ramps long enough to overcome trenches and mounds, which allowed the ramps and towers to move closer to the wall (Figure 13.4). We know of sieges that took only a few days to succeed and others that never reached an outcome.

In times of war, all the information found in the Mari archives seems to be focused on the movements of troops, the outcome of conflicts, logistic problems and changing alliances. In times of peace, messengers and ambassadors travelled back and forth, mainly for commercial reasons. This routine practice, however, has left less visible attestations in the archive. Mari controlled the stretch of land linking Babylonia to Syria. This direct route, however, had a secondary role compared to the main Mesopotamian trade route, which followed the foothills east of the Tigris, to then cross the Khabur Triangle, which was a more densely inhabited area and thus safer, with better provisions and more opportunities for trade. This route is described in the Old Babylonian itineraries, but could have been a much more ancient route. In the Mari Age, however, changes in the levels of security and political unity of Upper Mesopotamia allowed for the deviation of part of the commercial activities to the Middle Euphrates. The route was used by caravans and ships alike, the latter following the river flow to the south. We know that the kings of Mari developed a system to control riverine traffic coming from Syria (Emar and Carchemish). They therefore required payments from ships to cross their territory and to reach Mari or even Sippar and Babylon.

Two routes departed from the Euphrates. One was a land route linking Mari to Qatna. It crossed the Syrian Desert without having to stop at Yamhad first. The other was a system of routes following the Khabur northwards and continuing east towards Assyria and north-west towards Anatolia. There were further ramifications of these routes reaching more distant areas. For instance, we know that ambassadors from far-away Dilmun reached Mari during the rise to power of Zimri-Lim. Surprisingly enough, Egypt was absent in this network and the contacts attested in the Mari archives only reached as far as the Levant. Routes were used to transport agricultural, textile and mineral products. Riverine trade brought products from Upper Syria to Mari, especially highly valued agricultural products such as wine and olive oil, as well as semiprecious stones. There was also an ancient eastern route, which was controlled by Elam and Eshnunna, and reached Syria and Palestine through Mari. This network mainly brought tin, a fundamental metal in the production of bronze.

Trade in copper is far less documented, but it is known that it came from Cyprus and eastern Anatolia. However, since the exportation of bronze artefacts from northern Syria (Yamhad in particular) is well attested, it is possible that bronze production was supported by the delivery of tin to areas close to copper ores. There, the two metals would be combined, manufactured and then delivered elsewhere (thus removing the need for the trading of copper ingots). If this hypothesis is correct, it would explain the importance of northern Syria as the main centre for bronze production in the Near East. In fact, the area received copper from Cyprus and eastern Anatolia and tin from the caravans coming from Ashur and Mari.

6 Yamhad and Middle Bronze Age Syria

Following the demographic and cultural crisis of the 'Intermediate period', Syria experienced a new wave of urbanisation, very similar to the Upper Mesopotamian one. The Proto-Syrian culture of the third millennium BC had certainly been finer and more elaborate. However, the new Old Syrian culture of the Middle Bronze Age was much more stable and established among its population. In this period, numerous walled cities appeared, following the model already developed during the second urbanisation of the Early Bronze Age. The best attested cities of this phase span from Carchemish in the north, whose inner city was built in the Middle Bronze Age, while the outer city was a Neo-Hittite development, to Qatna in the south, with its square ditch and impressive fortification wall. This was a common type of wall, with an earthen rampart. Its construction also provided a ditch surrounding the wall, enforced with stone foundations, and plastered in order to be smooth and solid. On top of this earthen rampart there was the wall, built in stone or bricks. The function of these walls in relation to the introduction of siege machinery has already been mentioned. Naturally, the weakest point of the wall was the gate, which was generally chambered and provided with watchtowers. Amongst the various known examples of this type of fortification, Ebla (Tell Mardikh) is the most complex (Figure 13.5).

Outside the walled cities, villages maintained their communal structure, governed by simple institutions. This was in marked contrast with Mesopotamia, which saw the pre-eminence of the temple and palace economy even in the countryside. States were regional authorities, centred on a fortified capital and its royal palace, which acted as the seat of the king and as a main administrative centre. The Syrian temples of the Middle Bronze Age therefore did not have any function other than the cultic one. They

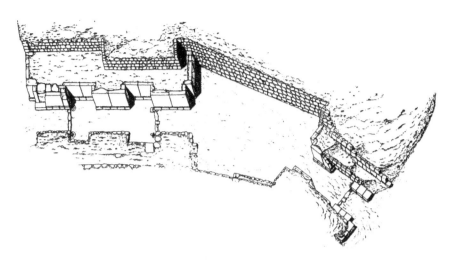

Figure 13.5   Ebla in the Middle Bronze Age: axonometric view of the south-western city gate.

were small, simple structures, with one main room and a portico entrance, or a portico, a main room and a *cella*. On the contrary, palaces were much more complex and considerably larger structures, with storehouses, workshops and administrative buildings. Palaces, then, constituted the nucleus of Old Syrian culture, which expressed itself through a rich and elaborate material culture (from seals to metallurgy, pottery, and so on).

Among the major centres of the region, some remain unexplored for this period (such as Aleppo), or badly excavated (such as Carchemish). Luckily, Qatna (Tell Mishrife), Alalah (Tell Atchana) and Ebla (Tell Mardikh) provide valuable information on this period. Recent excavations in Qatna have only managed to uncover the beginning of the Late Bronze Age (fifteenth century BC). However, it is known that the city was already one of the most important centres in Syria in the eighteenth century, alongside Aleppo, main city of Yamhad. In Level VII of the Alalah excavation, there is the so-called palace of Yarim-Lim, as well as an administrative archive which provides some political information that will be taken into consideration later on. Apart from its impressive fortification wall and gates, Old Syrian Ebla also had three palaces, one on the acropolis and two on the terraces below it. There were also several temples, a fortress, a royal cemetery and a residential quarter with small and standardised houses with simple furniture.

Old Syrian culture had some similarities with Mesopotamian culture, not in terms of a direct influence of the latter, but because of the inclusion of Syria in the political and cultural spheres of the Amorite world, which extended from the Mediterranean to Khuzistan. Despite the fact that Lower Mesopotamia had lost its central role, it still maintained its prestigious status, and Akkadian became the main diplomatic and administrative language of the period. This was mainly because Akkadian had spread in conjunction with cuneiform writing. The diffusion of Akkadian also brought to the diffusion of its administrative procedures. However, they still had to be adapted to different socio-economic needs. Old Syrian culture also had some distinctive features, such as the different role of the temple and the low agricultural yields. The latter limited the amount of available surplus for the palaces and led to the survival of village communities. Moreover, there was the increased role played by commercial and farming activities and the increased instability and exposure to crises of all sorts.

On a political level, following the former supremacy of Ebla and the reconstitution of a system of city-states not far different from the one attested in the Early Bronze Age, Syria experienced a phase of political fragmentation between the twentieth and nineteenth century BC and of increased unity in the eighteenth century BC. At that time, a large part of Syria was under the control of Yamhad and its capital Aleppo. Yamhad was still an emerging state under Sumu-epuh, rival of Yahdun-Lim of Mari and then Shamshi-Adad. However, it was his son Yarim-Lim who became the main leader of a regional political entity, whose power was comparable to the one of Mari, Eshnunna and Babylon. Yamhad was therefore able to become one of the main protagonists in the conflicts and the diplomatic and commercial relations of the period.

Yarim-Lim's army is attested in Mesopotamia during the war that brought an end to Shamshi-Adad's reign. Even at the time of Zimri-Lim, the king of Aleppo declared war to a city as distant as Der, along Elam's border. These distant, yet short-term, conflicts were part of the Amorite tendency to wage war and seal inter-state alliances. It is nonetheless significant that no Mesopotamian state (neither Shamshi-Adad, nor Zimri-Lim), despite being close and involved in the commercial networks of Syria, ever managed to occupy this region militarily. The Euphrates region thus solidly remained under the control of Aleppo, which had Emar as its main harbour and even parts of Mesopotamia as far as the Balikh.

With Zimri-Lim's generation, Mari experienced a more stable period. The matrimonial ties between Zimri-Lim and the royal family of Aleppo, the increased political stability, the succession of the more modest Hammurabi on the throne of the energetic Yarim-Lim, brought a period of increased peace and stable commercial relations. However, the Emar-Balikh line remained the fixed boundary between Yamhad and Mari. When Hammurabi of Babylon ended the royal dynasty of Mari, Yamhad, left untouched by this conquest, would stop its expansionistic ambitions. However, it maintained control of Upper Syria.

The supremacy of Yamhad did not affect the independence of Qatna. Throughout the Mari Age, the latter ruled over a smaller coalition of cities. At the time, relations between Yamhad and Qatna were difficult. This fact led the ruler of Qatna, Ishi-Adad, to seal an alliance with Shamshi-Adad. Yasmah-Addu thus married a princess of Qatna. It is possible that through this alliance Shamshi-Adad was able to claim that he had reached the Mediterranean and Lebanon. The insurmountable presence of Yamhad and Shamshi-Adad's reference to Lebanon (and not to the Amanus, located further north), leads to the assumption that the Assyrian king had reached the Mediterranean by travelling from Mari, through Palmyra, Qatna and Lebanon. Soon after Shamshi-Adad's death, Ishi-Adad also passed away and was succeeded by Amut-pi-El. The latter preferred to seal an alliance with Yamhad, through the mediation of Zimri-Lim.

In the far north of Syria, the kingdom of Carchemish and other centres between the Euphrates and the Taurus (Urshum, Hashshum and Hahhum) were not formally included in the kingdom of Yamhad. These states were important for their commercially strategic position. They seem to have stayed out of the political and military disputes between the larger states, aiming at keeping good commercial relations with whoever was in power in Upper Mesopotamia and Syria. Therefore, just like other northern centres, so Aplahanda, king of Carchemish, maintained good relations with both Shamshi-Adad and Yasmah-Addu, and his son Yatar-Ami did the same with Zimri-Lim.

If the Mari archives provide a picture of the inter-regional relations of the period, the archives from Alalah VII provide information on Syria for the following period. Local Syrian kings are attested recognising the authority of Yamhad. They used the title of *awīlum* ('man') for themselves and of *šarrum* ('king') for the ruler of Aleppo, or, less frequently, the one of 'king' for themselves and that of 'great king' for the king of Aleppo. After all, the first king of the dynastic sequence attested in the Alalah archives was the son of a king of Yamhad. He was placed by the latter on the throne of Alalah following his loss of the city of Irrite (Urfa), due to a revolt.

The archives attest to two generations of kings at Alalah: Yarim-Lim, son of the king of Yamhad Abba-El, and Ammi-taqum. They ruled during the reigns of Aleppo's kings Abba-El (son of the Hammurabi of the time of Zimri-Lim), Yarim-Lim II, Niqmepuh and then Irkabtum, Hammurabi II and Yarim-Lim III. The latter's reigns were shorter and bring us to the first half of the seventeenth century BC, when Alalah VII was destroyed. At the time, the political role of Ebla must have been similar to the one of Alalah, with a relatively wealthy local dynasty (at least judging from the archaeological data), who recognised the supremacy of Yamhad. Just like Alalah, this phase of Ebla abruptly ended in the mid-seventeenth century BC.

More information on the collapse of Yamhad and the destruction of several north Syrian centres comes from Hittite sources, which will be considered later on for the Old Hittite kingdom. At this stage, we can say that by the mid-seventeenth century BC, Hattusili I and Mursili I were in conflict with Yamhad and the other north Syrian states. Initially, Hattusili I attacked the cities in the north, mainly Alalah VII, Hashshum and Hahhum (the burnt level of Lidar Hüyük). The Syrian states tried to join forces against the Hittites, further supported by Carchemish and Yamhad. The Hittite attack was barely held back, but its army had to retreat slightly. In a second phase, Mursili I attacked again, reaching further south, and put to an end the kingdom of Aleppo, destroying several cities, such as Ebla, and taking control over northern Syria.

The conquest of Ebla is attested in the so-called 'Song of Liberation'. This text describes the desire of the conqueror to free and relieve those enslaved, an intention that met the opposition of the main local powers. A few centuries later, the Hittite kings would recall with concern the former power of Aleppo and acted in order to avoid the return of such a great kingdom in northern Syria. This fear, initially acceptable due to the political and military role of Yamhad in the eighteenth and seventeenth centuries BC, became increasingly anachronistic. After its conquest by Mursili I, Aleppo would never regain its former supremacy. Moreover, throughout northern Syria the destructions of the seventeenth century BC accelerated processes of de-population and de-urbanisation in the area.

7 The Hyksos and Middle Bronze Age Levant

In the southernmost part of the Levant, the revival of cities and of state organisation after the Early and Middle Bronze Age took place on a local level, but with a strong Egyptian influence. Having experienced a series of incursions of Semitic nomadic groups from the Sinai and the southern Levant around 2000 BC, Egypt had become a unitary state. It was ruled by the Theban kings of the twelfth dynasty (Middle Kingdom, ca. 1900–1785 BC). These rulers built a fortification wall, the 'Wall of the Prince', to protect the eastern Delta. Moreover, they began to show an interest in Near Eastern resources, such as those used in the Old Kingdom, namely, copper and semiprecious stones from the Sinai and timber from Lebanon (brought to Egypt through Byblos). The kings also displayed a marked interest in products such as wine and oil, and Levantine and Syrian manufactured objects.

The Egyptian presence in southern and coastal Syria and the Levant was relatively strong. This is attested in the recovery of Egyptian scarabs and monuments in a number of cities: Gaza, Gezer, Lachish, Shechem, Megiddo and Beit She'an in the Levant; Byblos, Beirut and Ugarit on the Syrian coast; and Qatna, Ebla and Alalah further inland. At one point, the twelfth dynasty seems to have experienced a phase of decline. While Amenemhat III's monuments are attested in the north in Ugarit and Alalah, the ones of Amenemhat IV have not been found beyond Byblos and Damascus. Moreover, Egypt is not mentioned in the Mari archives (which were contemporaneous with the twelfth dynasty) and the Syro-Mesopotamian commercial networks only reached as far as Hazor, in northern Palestine.

This Egyptian presence in the Near East between the nineteenth and eighteenth century BC used to be interpreted as a form of imperial exploitation. This was allegedly supported by a strong political and military pressure in the area. It is clear now, however, that this presence was purely for commercial reasons, mainly due to the prestige, as well as the economic and military power of Egypt. It did not require military or political interventions. The city that was most influenced by the continuity and intensity of interactions with Egypt was Byblos. Here, a series of local rulers (Abi-sumi, Yapa'-sumu-abi and Yantin) wrote their names in hieroglyphs and used the Egyptian title of ḥ3ty-ꜥ ('governor'). They also received gifts from the Egyptian rulers in exchange for access to the Lebanese forests.

These rulers were independent and an integral part of the commercial network attested in the Mari evidence. In fact, Yantin-'Ammu of Byblos had contacts with Zimri-Lim. A similar influence can be found in Ugarit, where several monuments of Egyptian functionaries have been discovered. These were a clear result of successful commercial relations. Despite being part of the kingdom of Yamhad at the time, in Ebla itself several Egyptian objects with twelfth dynasty cartouches have been discovered. These were undoubtedly prestigious gifts, since they were buried with the local rulers. Even under the thirteenth dynasty, Egyptian commercial relations continued to include Byblos and Ebla. They terminated towards the end of the eighteenth century BC, after which the interaction developed in a completely different way.

Middle Kingdom texts provide some information about the way in which the Egyptians envisioned the political and cultural situation of Syria and the Levant at the time. At the peak of the 12th dynasty, the Near East was still seen as a territory inhabited by nomadic groups and ruled by relatively barbarian tribal chiefs. This is the image portrayed by the famous account of Sinuhe. The latter lived for many years among the Near Eastern 'barbarians', until he returned to Egypt to spend his remaining years and receive an honorable burial. A similar picture of Syria and the Levant comes from the so-called execration texts. These were lists of names of foreign leaders and localities inscribed on figurines. The latter were ritually broken to symbolise the destruction of Egypt's potential enemies.

There are two series of execration texts. The earliest one, belonging to the twelfth dynasty, lists Syrian and Levantine political centers and their tribal groups. This indicates that the area was experiencing a similar situation to the one found in contemporary Upper Mesopotamia, whose states were centered on the interaction of cities with nomadic groups. The later series, belonging to the thirteenth dynasty, only lists city-states. Both lists are important for the Amorite names of the rulers attested and the geographical information provided. These coincide with the areas in which Egyptian scarabs and monuments have been found, namely, the Levant, the Lebanese coast and southern Syria. It is clear that these states were neither subordinate, nor enemies of Egypt, but simply potential enemies. Therefore, despite their contacts with these kingdoms and tribal groups, the Egyptians had learned to fear their unruly and unpredictable reactions.

Throughout the nineteenth century BC, the appearance of the same urban model attested for Syria in the Levant led to a surge of developments in the area. Its political structure must have followed a similar pattern: it started with tribal groups gravitating around urban centers and then concentrated on fortified cities, with their royal palaces and manufacturing and commercial activities. We do not know whether in the south various cities also became unified under the authority of one main city. If that were the case, then the best candidate in northern Palestine would have been Hazor.

By the second half of the eighteenth century BC, relations between Egypt and the Levant changed. In the previous phase (the twelfth dynasty for Egypt and the Middle Bronze IIa for the Levant, ca. 1900–1750 BC), Egypt was a powerful and unified state, while in comparison, the Levant was going through a phase of reorganisation of both its political structure and the relationship between nomadic groups and cities. The following phase (the Second Intermediate period in Egypt and the Middle Bronze Age IIb for the Levant, ca. 1750–1600 BC), however, saw the decline and political fragmentation of Egypt. This was in marked contrast with the Levant, which was now a newly re-organised and prosperous region. From a purely archaeological point of view, this phase seems to have been the peak of ancient Levantine culture. The intensity of commercial activities between Egypt and the Levant remained the same, but underwent several structural changes. This led to a migration of people from the Near East to Egypt, especially in the eastern Delta. This was the area closest to the region used by Levantine shepherds, which was highly desirable for its availability of water and herds even in times of drought and famine.

The fortification wall constructed by the Middle Kingdom rulers had by now lost its efficacy. Therefore, the area between the Delta and the Levant became a sort of cultural continuum where various groups could circulate relatively feely. Consequently, locally-produced Egyptian-style scarabs spread in the Levant, while in Egypt Levantine pottery styles and Near Eastern names began to appear. The

Amorite names of a number of individuals, probably tribal chiefs, are attested in the Delta, bearing the title of *ḥq3-ḫ3swt*, 'rulers of foreign lands', a term that became renowned as Hyksos, its Greek rendering. The Egyptian historiographical tradition, which began in the New Kingdom and culminated in the Hellenistic period with Manetho, saw the Hyksos as Near Eastern leaders, who suddenly attacked Egypt, conquered it and established their foreign rule, which would last until the Theban kings of the seventeenth and eighteenth dynasties managed to drive them out of Egypt. A thorough investigation of the archaeological, onomastic, historical and political evidence, however, shows that the Hyksos' arrival in Egypt, despite not being entirely painless, was neither a mass movement, nor a military conquest.

For a long time, modern historiography has been influenced by the ancient interpretation of the Hyksos. It therefore interpreted their presence in Egypt as one of the steps of a migratory flux moving from the north to the south. It was believed that this was a flux of Hurrian people, bringing to Egypt fundamental technical innovations linked to the use of the horse and the carriage. However, it is clear now that the names of these 'foreign princes' are Semitic (Amorite) and that the infiltration happened well before the arrival of these new techniques. As we will see, these were actually the effect of a cultural diffusion, rather than a mass movement of people.

The 'foreign princes' took advantage of the breakdown of political unity in Egypt after the fall of the thirteenth dynasty and settled in the Delta. For a while (Manetho's fourteenth dynasty), political fragmentation prevailed, with both Egyptian and Near Eastern rulers governing local states. Then, due to a series of internal developments, a dynasty of Near Eastern origins, the 'great Hyksos' kings of the 15th dynasty managed to unify Lower Egypt, although the region continued to be tormented by constant conflicts between rival dynasties. Relations between Egypt and Palestine continued to be complex, though in a completely different way compared to the Middle Kingdom.

The idea of a Hyksos empire that went from Upper Egypt to the Levant and Syria, whose main capital was Avaris (eastern Delta), in between Egyptian and Near Eastern states, is difficult to accept. It is possible, however, that Egypt was partially unified by a dynasty of Near Eastern origins (a fact that is shown by the names of these rulers and the later removal, for religious and nationalistic reasons, of their remains by the following Theban dynasty). This dynasty was clearly deeply Egyptianised, due to its long presence in the area. Meanwhile, it is possible that the Syro-Palestinian area continued to be divided into independent city-states. Therefore, the latter only shared with the Hyksos a type of material culture misleadingly defined as 'Hyksos'. In fact, the latter was simply the material culture of Middle Bronze Age Levant (Figure 13.6). It is true that some Hyksos rulers left their names on objects that reached very distant centres. However, these are just traces of diplomatic or commercial relations and not of actual political control. For instance, the name of the most famous Hyksos king, Hayan, has been found on scarabs scattered from Nubia to the Levant, among fragments of stone vases from Knossos and Hattusa and in an object bought in Baghdad. However, no one could possibly think that his dominion extended from Nubia to Anatolia, Crete and Mesopotamia.

On Hyksos culture, or, better, the infiltration of the Middle Bronze Levantine culture in the Egyptian Delta, the majority of information comes from the excavations at Tell ed-Dab'a, near the Hyksos capital Avaris. The excavations have uncovered not just scarabs and pottery remains, but an entirely unique culture, which combined typically Egyptian elements with typically Levantine ones in the same buildings. Tombs, including burials for horses, and temples in particular were Near Eastern in style (Figure 13.7). In this regard, the stratigraphic evidence shows the progressive appearance of the Levantine style over the prevailing Egyptian one of the earlier phases. Therefore, Tell ed-Daba'a is a clear representation of what the presence of Near Eastern groups, with their own material culture, names and different religion, meant for the Delta. This infiltration, however, would be followed by a sudden reversal of relations. Eventually, at the beginning of the Late Bronze Age, the Near East would become the target of the 'imperial' ambitions of the kings of the Egyptian New Kingdom.

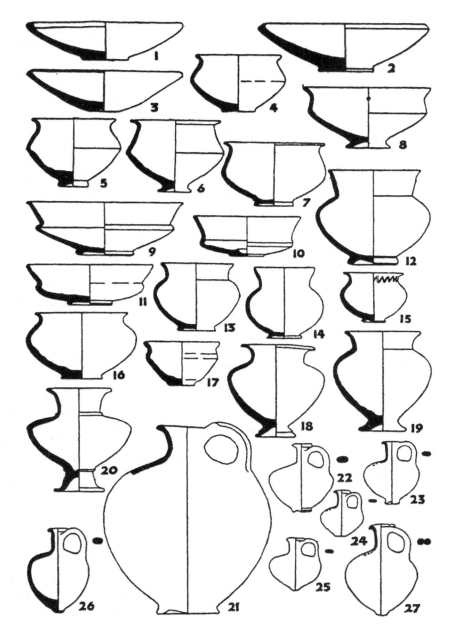

Figure 13.6 Middle Bronze Palestinian pottery from the necropolis of Jericho.

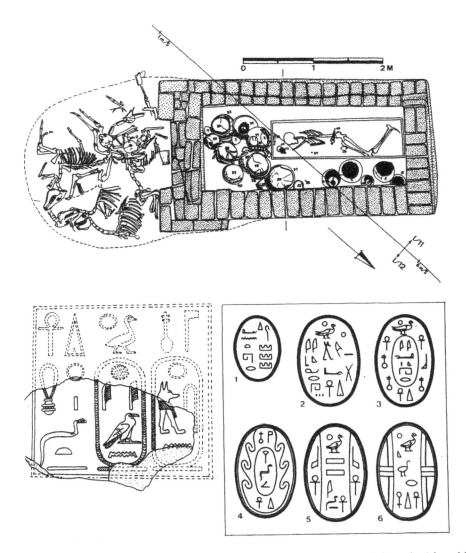

Figure 13.7   The Hyksos. *Above*: Tomb n. 5 at Tell ed-Dab'a, in the eastern Delta, with horse burials and Palestinian-type pottery; *Below, left*: Fragment of an obsidian vase found at Boghazköy, with the cartouche of the Egyptian king Hayan; *Below, right*: 'Hyksos' scarabs, with the signs for ' nt-ḥr' (n.1, followed by the title 'ḥq3 bḫśwt'), 'y qb-ḥr' (n. 2-3); 'w3ḏḏ' (n. 4); 'śšy' (n. 5), 'q3r' (n. 6).

14

HAMMURABI OF BABYLON

1 The unification of Mesopotamia

The regions surrounding Mesopotamia, from Elam to Mari, were often in competition over the conquest of the 'dimorphic' region of Upper Mesopotamia, through constant military expeditions and sudden political changes. Meanwhile, Lower Mesopotamia experienced a different type of political unification, which was marked by a gradual consolidation of power in smaller areas, brought about internally rather than through conquest from outside. Eventually, these areas were united under a single rule. However, at the beginning of the phase considered in this chapter (around 1820 BC), Lower Mesopotamia was still divided into the kingdoms of Babylon, Isin, Larsa and Uruk. There also were some minor centres, such as Der, Kazallu, Malgum, and so on. The two most powerful states were Larsa in the south and Babylon in the north. This situation brought the rulers of Babylon to establish diplomatic ties with Uruk. Despite being a relatively isolated city, Uruk was still an important ally against Larsa. We know of an inter-dynastic marriage between the first king of Uruk, Sin-kashid, with a sister of Sumu-la-El of Babylon. We also know of several military alliances during the reign of Sin-muballit of Babylon and Anam and Irdanene of Uruk.

An initial unification of Lower Mesopotamia came with the reign of Rim-Sin of Larsa, a ruler gifted with exceptional political talent. His father, Kudur-mabuk, was a military and tribal leader who, despite his Elamite name, ruled over an Amorite group. His career, however, remains unknown to us. Kudur-mabuk began his rise controlling the land of the Yamut-bal tribe, until he conquered the throne of Larsa. There, he placed his son Warad-Sin as ruler. The presence of Kudur-mabuk's name alongside his son's in their royal inscriptions indicates, however, that he ruled Larsa with his son. Their military endeavours (including the conquest of Kazallu) and the restoration of the walls and temples of Ur indicate that their reign was largely focused on consolidation. Only with Rim-Sin did Larsa begin its expansion, which we can track down through the many dating formulas of his very long reign. In his fourteenth regnal year, Rim-Sin defeated Uruk and its ally Isin, both supported by Babylon. He also destroyed and conquered Der (in the twentieth year of his reign), Uruk (in the twenty-first year of his reign) and Isin (in his thirtieth regnal year). The conquest of Isin was considered such a prestigious achievement that all the following dating formulas refer to this event.

At this stage, Rim-Sin controlled the whole of Sumer. Despite this, he continued to be surrounded by belligerent neighbours (Elam, Eshnunna and Babylon), which were effectively cutting Larsa out from the diplomatic interactions and manoeuvres of the Mari Age. Just like his father, Rim-Sin also tried to consolidate his kingdom. Following the Sumerian tradition, he ordered the construction and restoration of walls, temples and canals and the dedication of expensive cultic furniture. In terms of political organisation, he introduced something new, ordering tax exemptions, debt releases and the release of debt slavery to 're-establish justice in the land'. These were all common practices in the north (at Isin, Babylon and Eshnunna), but not in the south. Administrative and legal texts from Rim-Sin's reign also attest to the particular care he took to re-organise the management of public land and the revival of trade in the Persian Gulf.

In the year after the conquest of Isin, Hammurabi was enthroned in the city of Babylon. He was to become a much fiercer rival of Rim-Sin than his father Sin-muballit. Rim-Sin, who must have been relatively old at this point, found the second half of his reign marked by the rise of Babylon, although Hammurabi himself was threatened on multiple fronts. This was because Babylon was clenched between the kingdoms of Larsa in the south and Assyria in the north. Both powers, however, were ruled by successful, yet elderly, kings. Eshnunna also constituted a threat to Babylon, especially in the reign of Ibal-pi-El. In the first years of his rule, Hammurabi was particularly engaged in the south. In his seventh regnal year, he took Isin and Uruk away from Rim-Sin, who saw his kingdom being significantly reduced on a territorial level and subordinated to Babylon on a political one. Having secured the south and gained the support of Rim-Sin, now forced to be a subordinate ally, Hammurabi had the opportunity to play an active role in the events of the Mari Age. Consequently, he took advantage of Shamshi-Adad's death to rise as the main player in the entire region.

For around twenty years (1785–1765 BC), the situation remained relatively flexible, though the balance of power always lay between Hammurabi in Babylon and the strong presence of Ibal-pi-El in Eshnunna. In this regard, the Mari archives reveal the string of wars fought along the Euphrates and the Tigris. The tensest front was the border between Babylon and Eshnunna. The two cities were in fact dangerously close to each other. Their respective positions were so consolidated, however, that the majority of conflicts between them took place in Upper Mesopotamia. For the time being, neither contender managed to gather enough force to directly attack the other. In the past decade, the expansionist policy of Eshnunna had commanded a sense of fear throughout Mesopotamia. This fear allowed Hammurabi to gain the support not only of Larsa, but also of Mari and Yamhad, although for a large portion of his reign, Hammurabi was stuck in a political deadlock.

Only towards the end of his reign did Hammurabi see the effects of his gradual rise (Figure 14.1). Within five years, he conquered Larsa (in the thirty-first year of his rule), Eshnunna (in the thirty-second year), and defeated Mari (in his thirty-third year on the throne), which was destroyed after a rebellion in the city (in the thirty-fifth year of Hammurabi's reign). As can be seen, when Hammurabi decided to break out of this deadlock, he did not make a distinction between opponents and former allies: having pitted the one against the other, he condemned them all to the same fate. Towards the end of his reign, he fought wars against Assyria (in the thirty-seventh and thirty-eighth years of his reign), which was now an autonomous yet isolated state. In a way, Assyria was just like Elam. In their former expansionist phases, they had interfered in the Mesopotamian affairs for decades. Now, however, they were in a marginal position.

Hammurabi's unification of Mesopotamia was limited both in terms of time and space. First, the unification was short-lived. Hammurabi's success came towards the end of his reign and his successors did not manage to prevent the breakdown of his kingdom. Moreover, Hammurabi did not hold solid control over all of his conquered territories. A large portion of them had been part of the expansionistic and military tendencies of the Mari Age. For instance, Babylon did not manage to effectively impose its presence in the Middle Euphrates, especially beyond the semi-inhabited territory that separated the northernmost Babylonian centres from the kingdom of Hana, which was heir to the legacy of the kingdom of Mari. The kingdoms of the 'Upper Land' remained even more inaccessible, and would eventually experience the political pre-eminence of the Hurrian element in the area. As mentioned above, Assyria and Elam also remained independent, although considerably reduced in size.

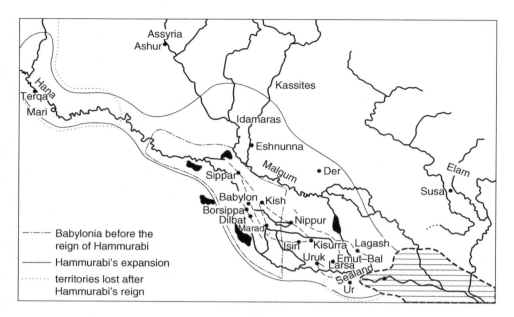

Figure 14.1   Map of the kingdom of Hammurabi of Babylon.

The main Babylonian conquests were therefore centred in the lands of Sumer and Akkad. They coincided in a significant way with the core of the Ur III territory, namely, between the wall built against the Martu and the southern coast of Mesopotamia. Due to this reference to the former Ur III state, the Babylonian unification was effective in eliminating the expansionistic ambitions of individual city-states. Consequently, there were no more expansionistic opportunities for Eshnunna or Uruk, two contemporary and important states of the time, or for smaller independent states, such as Der, Kazallu, or Malgum. Cities now became provincial centres, de-centralised administrative cities of a politically unified land. Therefore, a political fragmentation of the area could not take place on a city-state level anymore, but only through the rise of sizeable territorial states. In other words, with Hammurabi the concept of a land of 'Babylonia', named after its main city, was born. Babylonia thus became the heir of the ancient region of 'Sumer and Akkad'. Eventually, Babylonia would become the southern counterpart of the land of 'Assyria' in the north.

2 The socio-political organisation of the Old Babylonian period

Despite the general rise of the private sector in the economic and socio-political activities of the Old Babylonian period, the kingdoms of Rim-Sin of Larsa and Hammurabi of Babylon led to a visible consolidation of the role of the state. This was a direct consequence of the care these strong rulers took in organising their kingdoms. They both displayed an ability to influence their kingdoms' social structure. This is particularly true when compared to previous phases, marked by instability and political fragmentation.

The central role of the palace developed at the expense of the private sector as well as the temple, which lost a large portion of its privileges. For instance, trade, which the private sector had previously removed from the authority of the temple, was now under royal supervision. Similarly, the administration of justice had formerly been managed by temple judges, in particular those of Shamash, god of justice. However, this task was now practised by royally appointed judges. Even access to temple privileges and income, closely linked to the performance of priestly functions, was often sold or, in a way, 'sub-let'. Because of the gradual disappearance of the ancient redistributive system, this type of access to temple offices gradually became part of a general system in which functions and retributions (which were already part of the redistributive system of the 'great organisations') were converted in economic terms.

The numerous wars and territorial conquests leading to the unification of Mesopotamia led to a significant increase in the allocation of lands to soldiers and veterans in the conquered regions. From the correspondence of Hammurabi with two of his functionaries, Shamash-hasir in Larsa and Sin-iddinam in Sippar, we know of the problems and procedures surrounding the allocation of lands to Babylonian soldiers (Figure 14.2). The king was able to follow individual cases in person, sometimes imposing his own decision over the suggestions of his functionaries. These letters inform us about this process, which was clearly related to the system of personal appeals of subjects to their king, combined with a mixture of abuses and favouritism. The new allocations took place within an ambiguous but highly complex administrative structure, within which there were considerable difficulties in distinguishing between lands personally assigned in exchange for a service to the palace, and those owned by families for generations. It is possible that the numerous allocations of lands to individuals belonging to the poorer strata of society might have

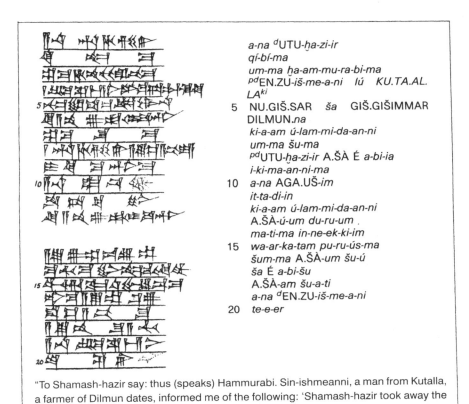

a-na ᵈUTU-ḫa-zi-ir
qí-bí-ma
um-ma ḫa-am-mu-ra-bi-ma
ᵖᵈEN.ZU-iš-me-a-ni lú KU.TA.AL.LAᵏⁱ
5 NU.GIŠ.SAR ša GIŠ.GIŠIMMAR DILMUN.na
ki-a-am ú-lam-mi-da-an-ni
um-ma šu-ma
ᵖᵈUTU-ḫa-zi-ir A.ŠÀ É a-bi-ia
i-ki-ma-an-ni-ma
10 a-na AGA.UŠ-im
it-ta-di-in
ki-a-am ú-lam-mi-da-an-ni
A.ŠÀ-ú-um du-ru-um .
ma-ti-ma in-ne-ek-ki-im
15 wa-ar-ka-tam pu-ru-ús-ma
šum-ma A.ŠÀ-um šu-ú
ša É a-bi-šu
A.ŠÀ-am šu-a-ti
a-na ᵈEN.ZU-iš-me-a-ni
20 te-e-er

"To Shamash-hazir say: thus (speaks) Hammurabi. Sin-ishmeanni, a man from Kutalla, a farmer of Dilmun dates, informed me of the following: 'Shamash-hazir took away the land of my family and gave it to a soldier.' That is what he brought to my attention. When is a land under long-term tenancy ever taken away? Take care of this case, and if this land belongs to his family, give it back to Sin-ishmeanni."

Figure 14.2 Land allocations made by Hammurabi of Babylon in the region of Larsa.

been instrumental in containing the processes of impoverishment and enslavement. In fact, this process created a workforce that was more willing to work in the fields, which were frequently left in a state of abandonment, saturation and decline.

Towards the end of the Old Babylonian period, the area went through an agricultural crisis. This was due to both socio-juridical and physical reasons. Among the latter reasons, there were the long-standing issues of land salinisation, excessive irrigation and cultivation. Moreover, there was the competition over water resources between upstream and downstream regions. Despite the fact that the administrative centre of the region had now moved further north, rulers such as Hammurabi and Samsu-iluna continued to be heavily involved in the restoration of canals throughout their land. Some large-scale programmes, such as the canal named 'Hammurabi-is-the-abundance-of-the-land', were aimed at facilitating the water-flow to the south. However, the majority of interventions seem to have been pursued in the north, in the regions of Akkad and the Diyala. These interventions were more focused on the reinforcement of riverbanks to avoid devastating floods, rather than to promote irrigation. However, these works seem to have been less demanding than the ones celebrated by these kings in their inscriptions or year formulas.

Problems in Babylonia were temporarily held back by the amount of royal interventions in the infra-structure and colonisation of the region. The surrounding regions were in an even worse condition. In the south, where the 'Sealand' was rising as a politically independent power, the processes of de-urbanisation and waterlogging were already at an advanced stage. The Sealand did not have a recognisable urban settlement and was a marginal area, difficult to control and characterised by low population levels. On the other side of Mesopotamia, in the kingdom of Hana, the Middle Euphrates Valley experienced an unstoppable crisis. Again, demographic and urban fluctuations mostly affected marginal areas, while the Lower Mesopotamian centres managed to survive this crisis thanks to their systems of irrigation and production.

Alongside economic difficulties, from the agricultural crisis to the decline of trade, this period saw a reorganisation of social relations along the lines already developed in the Isin–Larsa period. There were two fundamental lines of development: one towards the economic independence of specific privileged groups, originally made of specialised workers, employed by the great organisations; the other towards the enslavement of more vulnerable groups, formerly free families unconnected to the palace. The two processes led to a total overturn of social relations and economic structures. On the one hand, privileged groups, made of scribes, priests, merchants, functionaries and landowners, were attempting to break free from royal control. Consequently, temples and palaces ceased to support themselves through the provision of services performed by their specialised workmen. They therefore developed a complex system of contracts and sub-contracts. This situation led to the centralisation of revenues, rather than of labour.

On the other hand, formerly free men who lost their lands formed a new class of royal functionaries. These individuals worked for the palace in generic roles. They could become soldiers and guardians (*rēdûm*, *bā'erum*), or farmers, fishers and shepherds, in which case they received a 'sustenance field' of the standard size of 1 *bur* (6.5 hectares) (Figure 14.3). In the eyes of these new lower classes of royal workers, the king maintained his image of just ruler, good shepherd and attentive father. A good reflection of the social changes taking place in this period is the change of meaning of the term *muškēnum*, which technically designated a dependant of the palace, but now simply meant 'poor man'.

The famous Code of Hammurabi provides a good picture of Babylonian society under Hammurabi. Apart from the many copies written on tablets, the original Code was written on a diorite stele originally placed in the temple of Shamash at Sippar (Figure 14.4). The stele was recovered in Susa, where it had been brought as booty by the Elamite king Shutruk-Nahhunte around 1200 BC. The Code's structure and length make it the most important source for a reconstruction of Babylonian society. However, this text only provides a glimpse of Hammurabi's period, illustrating a situation that cannot be applied to other places or periods. In particular, the Code describes three different classes, or social conditions: the *awīlum* or '(free) man'; the *muškēnum* or 'dependent of the palace'; and the *wardum* or 'slave'. The latter category

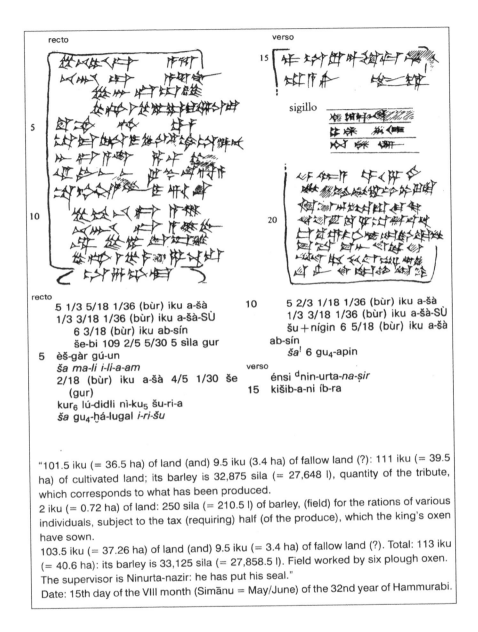

recto

5 1/3 5/18 1/36 (bùr) iku a-šà
1/3 3/18 1/36 (bùr) iku a-šà-SÙ
6 3/18 (bùr) iku ab-sín
še-bi 109 2/5 5/30 5 sìla gur
5 èš-gàr gú-un
ša ma-li i-li-a-am
2/18 (bùr) iku a-šà 4/5 1/30 še
(gur)
kur₆ lú-didli nì-ku₅ šu-ri-a
ša gu₄-ḫá-lugal *i-ri-šu*

10   5 2/3 1/18 1/36 (bùr) iku a-šà
1/3 3/18 1/36 (bùr) iku a-šà-SÙ
šu+nígin 6 5/18 (bùr) iku a-šà
ab-sín
ša¹ 6 gu₄-apin

verso
énsi ᵈnin-urta-*na-ṣir*
15   kišib-a-ni íb-ra

"101.5 iku (= 36.5 ha) of land (and) 9.5 iku (3.4 ha) of fallow land (?): 111 iku (= 39.5 ha) of cultivated land; its barley is 32,875 sila (= 27,648 l), quantity of the tribute, which corresponds to what has been produced.
2 iku (= 0.72 ha) of land: 250 sila (= 210.5 l) of barley, (field) for the rations of various individuals, subject to the tax (requiring) half (of the produce), which the king's oxen have sown.
103.5 iku (= 37.26 ha) of land (and) 9.5 iku (= 3.4 ha) of fallow land (?). Total: 113 iku (= 40.6 ha): its barley is 33,125 sila (= 27,858.5 l). Field worked by six plough oxen. The supervisor is Ninurta-nazir: he has put his seal."
Date: 15th day of the VIII month (Simānu = May/June) of the 32nd year of Hammurabi.

Figure 14.3   Administrative text from Larsa from the time of Hammurabi.

is relatively straightforward, since slaves are attested throughout Mesopotamian history and were the property of other individuals, who had almost absolute power over them. Slaves were originally acquired as war prisoners or bought from foreign lands. Fellow citizens could not become slaves, but only debt servants who worked for a certain amount of time (at times even long periods) without losing their original status.

Figure 14.4. The stele with the laws of Hammurabi, king of Babylon; from Susa, now in the Louvre Museum. ©
RMN-Grand Palais (Musée du Louvre)/Franck Raux.

On the contrary, the difference between the *awīlum* and the *muškēnum* is much more difficult to define, which has led to a variety of scholarly interpretations. This is partly due to the fact that these two classes were composite groups that appeared as a result of the processes mentioned above. 'Free men' were economically independent. They were both free landowners in the traditional sense, or high or middle ranking royal and religious functionaries who managed to own lands and resources formerly only entrusted to them. The *muškēnum* were a different group and depended on the state for support. Economically, then, they were 'semi-free' (though not legally, as often believed), since they did not have the means to support themselves. From the cases listed in the Code and other sources from the period it appears that their status was lower than that of free men and that they were under the protection of the king and subordinate to him.

The Code provides a systematic picture of the current legal disputes of the time (both in terms of criminal and civil law), which in turn allows us to catch a glimpse of Babylonian society. In criminal law, the presence of talion laws has long been emphasised. These laws regulated the types of physical punishments that could be inflicted, quantifying the gravity of the crime committed. This practice has been attributed to the Amorites, since the Sumerian and Akkadian traditions always followed the principle of financial compensation for a crime. Some punishments seem to have been developed more as a speculation than an actual evaluation of the crime. In fact, one gets the impression that they were simply meant to be a deterrent and could not be systematically applied without eliminating the same practices that they were trying to regulate. Regarding civil laws, the Code marks the definite rise of the private sector in land ownership. This aspect had now become a fundamental part of the Babylonian economy. Moreover, the Code emphasises the need to regulate the procedures for leases, salaries, rentals, financial investments and so on. However, the Code does not introduce anything new. It only records the common practices, sealing in the form of rules the practices normally applied, tranforming into norms the prices conventionally used, yet providing them with the royal seal of approval, an aspect that certainly gave them some authority among judges and disputers.

It has been long accepted that Mesopotamian law codes were not intended as prescriptive laws, namely, as a set of rules that had to be applied. Therefore, they do not provide evidence or determine the legal practices they derive from. It is clear from reading the entire Code of Hammurabi, including its prologue and epilogue, that it was a demonstrative celebration of how justly Babylonia was ruled under this king. In other words, the Code was an analytical demonstration, listed case by case, which justified the definition of the king as 'king of justice'. A price list left in a marketplace was not meant to impose official prices, or to simply register the main prices in the market, but to register which prices were 'fair'. Similarly, the Code's stele, left in the temple of Shamash, was a reference for anyone who needed it: 'Let the oppressed, who has a legal dispute, come into the presence of my statue as king of justice and let him read the inscription on my stele and hear my precious words, my stele will make the case clear to him'. It is significant that the stele is dedicated both to the oppressed and to the future king (so that he may not change the clauses on the stele), but not to the judges. It is clear that they would have continued to carry out their verdicts following local practices. These varied from city to city and followed principles that were neither more nor less fair than the ones that were chosen to become part of the depiction of the righteous rule and glory of Hammurabi.

Debt releases and the freeing of debt slaves had a much more direct normative effect. From Rim-Sin's reign to the end of the Babylonian dynasty, the practice, which was now widespread throughout the land, including the south, continued to be implemented. For the first time, we have the text, though incomplete, of one of these edicts, authored by the fourth successor of Hammurabi, Ammi-saduqa (Text 14.1). The edict has a much more technical tone, in marked contrast with the generic propagandistic allusions to similar edicts attested on royal inscriptions and year formulas (i.e. to 're-establish justice', 'break the tablets', 'give freedom', and so on). This technical tone was necessary, since the king wanted to eliminate debts agreed on during difficult times, but did not want to remove loans made for commercial or financial reasons. This technical tone was consequently used in loan contracts. In fact, in a period when it was normal to receive an amnesty at every enthronement (and a long reign would require more than one amnesty), clauses used in contracts were written so as take into account, and eventually avoid, these implications.

Text 14.1   **The Edict of Ammi-saduqa**

A king 'established justice in the land' by abolishing debts on interest loans. However, the edict had to avoid, through specific clauses, the inclusion in the remission of other types of loans, from investments in commercial endeavours to solidarity loans. Here is an abstract from the Edict of Ammi-saduqa:

[§ 2] 'Whoever has given silver or barley to an Akkadian or Amorite as an interest-bearing loan, or to gain a return (*ana melqētim*), and had a written document (lit. a tablet) executed, because the king has established justice in the land (*mīšaram šakānum*), his document is voided (lit. his tablet is broken). He may not collect the barley or silver on the basis of this document.'

[§ 5] 'If anyone had given barley or silver as an interest-bearing loan (*ana ḫubullin*) and had a document executed, but retained the document in his hand and stated: "I have certainly not given it to you as an interest-bearing loan or to gain a return; the barley or silver which I have given you, I have given as an advance on purchases (*ana šīmim*), or without interest (*ana tadmiqtim*), or for some other objective," the person who had received the barley or silver from the creditor shall produce his witnesses to the wording of the document which the lender had denied. They shall speak before the god (that is, under oath). Because he (that is, the creditor) had distorted his document and denied the matter, he must pay six-fold. If he cannot fulfil his duty, he must die.'

[§ 6] 'An Akkadian or an Amorite who has received barley, silver, or (other) goods either as merchandise for a (commercial) journey, or as a joint enterprise for the production of profit (*ana tappûtim*), or without interest, his document is not voided (lit. his tablet is not broken): he must repay (the creditor) in accordance with the stipulations of his agreements.'

[§ 7] 'Whoever has given barley, silver, or (other) goods to an Akkadian or an Amorite either (as an advance) for purchases, for a (commercial) journey, or a joint enterprise for the production of profit, or without interest, and had a document executed, and in the document he had executed he had stated: "At the expiration of the term (of the contract) the money would accrue interest," or if he made any additional stipulations, (the debtor) shall not repay on these terms. He shall repay the barley and silver that he had borrowed, but the (additional) stipulations upon the Akkadian or the Amorite are remitted.'

For now, the king of Babylonia managed to present himself to his subjects and act like a devoted father and a just and fair king (*šar kittim u mēšarim*). However, in this case, justice is not meant as the unchangeable application of the law regardless of whether or not it leads to harmful consequences. Justice meant the care that went into creating a better social balance. In order to maintain it, the king had to pay particular attention to the more vulnerable classes and prevent those developments in the market that would eventually enslave his entire population.

3 Religious reform

The Babylon of the time of Hammurabi and his successors remains buried under the following layers of the city. Due to this severe lack of evidence from the capital, it is difficult to assess the building programme, architecture, monumental art and craftsmanship of the First Dynasty of Babylon. Judging from other centres, it seems that the final phase of the Old Babylonian period was not particularly original. The temple and palace architecture, sculpture and seals of the time continued to follow the schemes developed in the previous periods (Figure 14.5). We know, however, that Hammurabi's reign was a period of significant religious reforms. Firstly, the unification of the region effectively removed the pre-eminence of the local cities' pantheons. In fact, the Amorites preferred different types of deities, in particular those of an astral nature, such as Shamash, Ishtar and Adad. This preference eventually pushed the more chthonic Sumerian

Reign of Ibbi-Sin of Ur.

Reign of Naram-Sin of Eshnunna.

Reign of Shamshi-Adad of Assyria.

Figure 14.5 The 'presentation scene' in Neo-Sumerian and Old Babylonian seals. The personal god or goddess presents the protégé to a major deity. *Above*: From the reign of Ibbi-Sin of Ur; *Middle*: From the reign of Naram-Sin of Eshnunna; *Below*: From the reign of Shamshi-Adad of Assyria.

deities into a secondary role. The cities of the north therefore established their local deities on a regional level: Marduk for Babylon, Nabu for Borsippa, Nergal for Kutha and Shamash for Sippar. In terms of personal religion, the most popular deity seems to have been Shamash, a significant representation of the yearning for justice that characterised Babylonian society at the time.

The pantheon was completely restructured. In the lists and epithets attested in the official inscriptions, many deities were placed on the same level, in an effort to find a connection between each deity and the king. The new structure of the pantheon placed Marduk, god of Babylon, as its head. Since Marduk was a local deity, the operation was not simple to implement, since it was difficult to link him to the previous theologies. The old hierarchy, featuring the supremacy of Enlil and his city Nippur, did not exist anymore. At the same time, the new hierarchy was still under construction. It would only be fully developed during the reign of Nebuchadnezzar I, half a millennium after Hammurabi's reign.

249

Among the many ways of turning Marduk into a national deity, there was an attempt to make Ea, the ancient and prominent god of wisdom, his mythical father. Marduk was then turned into the god of magic, in a somehow complementary position with Shamash, god of justice. The new tendencies in personal religion soon facilitated the development of a direct and heartfelt link between Marduk and his worshippers. This was particularly due to his role as healer and protector. Another innovation was to place Marduk at the centre of the cosmogonical and cosmological worldview of the time. Therefore, Marduk once again substituted Enlil, which eventually led to a syncretism of the two deities. This theological change is attested in the cultic poem *Enūma eliš* (meaning 'when on high', the first words of the text), which was recited during the Babylonian new year festival. As far as we know, however, the change would only be fully implemented under Nebuchadnezzar I.

The third religious reform consisted of the reconsideration of the relationship between theology and politics, and between the human sphere, the king and the divine sphere. Despite replacing the deified Rim-Sin in the south, and in spite of his far more powerful and prestigious role, Hammurabi was not deified. In his inscriptions his name is not preceded by any divine determinatives and some faint traces of his divine status can only be found in some rare epithets. Similarly, Hammurabi's successors would not become deified kings. This led the practice of deifying rulers, which used to be of great religious significance, to disappear. Alongside the decline of the practice, the many manifestations of the kings' deification also disappeared. However, there is still one text, written as a dialogue, which shows Hammurabi involved in practices related to the sacred marriage rite. Similarly, Samsu-iluna had a celebrative hymn written in his honour. These types of texts had been typical expressions of kingship from the Third Dynasty of Ur until the dynasty of Larsa, and therefore belonged to a type of ideology of kingship that was now surpassed.

The king now left the divine sphere to return to the human sphere as a benevolent and just shepherd. If the king did not seek his legitimacy of rule in the divine sphere anymore, he sought it in long genealogies of ancestors. This practice mirrored the kin-based structure of the Amorites. Hammurabi's genealogy partly coincides with the one of Shamshi-Adad. This is not because the two were related, but because, going further back in the genealogical tree, the two had to quote a series of tribal chiefs that were common for all of the Amorites.

The attention to the Amorite component of the kingdom of Hammurabi is very visible. Hammurabi carried the title of 'king of the Martu' alongside the one of 'king of Sumer and Akkad' and used epithets of clear western influence. In his edict, even Ammi-saduqa defined his subjects as 'Akkadians and Amorites' and in this text even some of the provincial cities were given the name of the tribe living there, rather than the actual name of the city (Yamut-bal for Larsa and Idamaras for Eshnunna). All this indicates that the integration of the Amorites was still incomplete and was based on an awareness of their difference. Consequently, the Babylonian kings had a strong interest in paying attention to this western component. These were the last attestations of this kind, however, as by the end of the dynasty, the Amorites were fully integrated into Mesopotamia and Babylonian society had begun to assimilate new incoming groups.

4 The collapse of the empire

Neither Larsa nor Eshnunna ever fully accepted their loss of independence. Consequently, Hammurabi's successor, Samsu-iluna, was heavily engaged in curbing their revolts (Table 14.1). In Larsa, a Rim-Sin II, son of Warad-Sin and nephew of Rim-Sin I, became king. In Eshnunnna, an Iluni, who bore the title of governor and thus was formally dependent on the kings of Babylonia, tried to break free from royal control. Samsu-iluna easily overcame and successfully curbed the first of these rebellions. Meanwhile, the rebellion of the far south led to the unification of the area under Iluma-Ilum, a king defined in the king lists and later accounts as the founder of the dynasty ruling the Sealand (in the far south of Mesopotamia). He therefore prevented Babylonia from having any access to the sea. Even the rebellion of Eshnunna lasted for a long time, until the capture and execution of its leader.

Table 14.1 Chronology of Mesopotamia, ca. 1750–1550 BC

	Sealand	Babylonia		Hana		Hatti	Yamhad
1750	a Rim-Sin II ca. 1735–1720	Samsu-iluna° abc		Isi-sumu-abi	1749–1712 ca. 1750	ca. 1750	d Abba-El ca. 1750–1720
	be Iluma-Ilu ca. 1720–1700			d Yapah-sumu-abi c Yadih-abi	ca. 1720	ca. 1720	Yasin-Lim II ca. 1720–1700
		e Abi-esuh°	1711–1684	Kashtiliash°	ca. 1700	ca. 1700	
1700	Itti-Ili-nibi						Niqmi-epukh
	Damiq-ilishu	Ammi-ditana°	1683–1647	Ammi-rabikh°			
				Shunuhru-Ammu°	ca. 1650		Irkabtum
1650	Ishkibal					Hattusili I ca. 1650–1620	
	Shushi	Ammi-saduqa°	1646–1626	Ammi-Madar	ca. 1625		Yarim-Lim III
		f Samsu-ditana	1625–1595	Abi-Lama	ca. 1610	f Mursili I ca. 1620–1590	
1600	Gulkishar ca. 1600	Kassite dynasty					Hammurabi II
							ca. 1600: Conquered by the Hittites
	Peshgaldaramash				ca. 1550: Conquered by the Kassites	Hantili I ca. 1590–1570	
						Zidanta ca. 1570–1560	
						Ammuna ca. 1560–1550	
1550	ca. 1500: Conquered by the Kassites	Agum II ca. 1550					

° remission edict, a—a = attested contemporaneity

Samsu-iluna boasts of having demolished the walls of Isin (which was therefore also in rebellion) and of all the fortresses in the Diyala Valley. Then, he boasts of having worked on the walls of Uruk, Sippar and Kish. He also claims that he restored the fortresses of Eshnunna and of a new city, Dur-Samsu-iluna (the ancient Tutub, modern Khafajah) after his victories and established a line of fortresses in the south of Babylonia. This frantic involvement in the destruction and restoration of defensive structures, a clear sign of the situation at that time, did not hinder the pursuit of more peaceful endeavours. Samsu-iluna worked on the riverbanks of the Tigris, Euphrates and the Diyala, continuing the large-scale hydric interventions commenced by his father.

However, a new threat was looming from the Zagros. The ninth year of Samsu-iluna's reign is dated after a victory over the Kassites, a mountain community that was beginning to put pressure on the alluvial plain. To the north-west, Samsu-iluna tried to maintain control over the Middle Euphrates and the 'Upper Land', but with limited success. His twenty-third year mentions the destruction of Shehna (the former Shubat-Enlil, capital of Shamshi-Adad's kingdom), where he ended a dynasty that is well attested in the city's archives. His twenty-sixth and thirty-sixth regnal years attest to military activities in Amurru, a term generally indicating the west. The thirty-third year saw Samsu-iluna in Saggaratum, on the Khabur. In the twenty-eighth year of his reign, the king fought a certain Yadih-Abu, a king of the dynasty of Hana. Despite occasional Babylonian expeditions, Yadih-Abu still controlled the Middle Euphrates and Lower Khabur regions from his capital at Terqa.

The long and busy reign of Samsu-iluna was followed by the three reigns of Abi-eshuh, Ammi-ditana and Ammi-saduqa, though information on their military activities are still lacking. We know that Abi-eshuh fought again against the Sealand. Eventually, however, the Babylonian kings did not have the resources to regain control over the whole of their land. Lower Mesopotamia therefore remained divided between the Sealand in the south and the kingdom of Babylonia in the centre and the north. The kings of Hana controlled the Middle Euphrates and the kings of Assyria the Middle Tigris. The famous edict of Ammi-saduqa provides us with information on the administrative structure of the kingdom. It mentions the districts of Numhia, Emut-bal (Larsa), Idamaras (Eshnunna), Isin, Uruk, Kisurra and Malgum. The Sealand must have had its capital at Ur. Despite its presence in the king lists, it is still not well attested in the contemporary sources.

A bit more information is available on the kingdom of Hana, thanks to the contracts from Terqa and the excavations pursued there. Around fifteen kings of Hana ruled the kingdom in the period starting with Hammurabi's destruction of Mari (when Terqa was ruled by a governor appointed by the king of Mari) and ending with the beginning of the Kassite dynasty, around 1600 BC. At that time, Terqa ceased to be a flourishing centre. Only a few of these kings' reigns can be securely dated. Isi-sumu-abum and Yapah-sumu-abum ruled between the end of Hammurabi's reign and the beginning of Samsu-iluna's reign, while Yadih-Abu was a contemporary of Samsu-iluna (twenty-eighth regnal year). A generation later (around 1700 BC) there were Kashtiliash, whose name was Kassite, and then Sunuhru-Ammu and his son Ammi-madar. The remaining kings remain difficult to date, such as Ishar-Lim and Iggid-Lim, whose names seem to be linked to the dynasty of Mari. Despite the restoration of its main temples, the city of Terqa was in visible decline. Nonetheless, it remained an important political and commercial centre, benefiting from its strategic position in the Middle Euphrates.

The archives of Shehna (Tell Leilan) also provide a large amount of information on the period between the destruction of Mari (1961 BC) and of Shehna itself (1728 BC). This evidence informs us of the situation of the Khabur Triangle at that time. The city had been the capital of an independent kingdom, as well as of the state ruled by Shamshi-Adad. After the latter's death, however, Shehna did not fall under Assyrian control, but returned to be the capital of an independent kingdom. The administrative texts and the letters found *in situ* attest to a sequence of three kings: Mutiya, Till-Abnû and Yakun-Ashar. Particularly interesting are some treaties sanctioned with nearby kingdoms: Ashnakkum and Razama, in the Sinjar; Kahat, located south of Shehna; and Ashur. After Samsu-iluna's destruction of the city (1728 BC), however, Shehna fell into a crisis and never recovered.

Towards the end of the century, grave dangers were coming from the north, with the Hittite expeditions against Yamhad. The city was destroyed by the Hittite king Mursili. The kings of Hana probably saw the rise of Hatti positively. Their position in the Middle Euphrates made them obvious rivals and potential victims of both Yamhad and Babylonia. The Hittite conquest of Yamhad made Hatti and Hana neighbouring states. The relations between the two explain the enigmatic expedition of Mursili against Babylonia during the reign of Samsu-ditana, last king of Hammurabi's dynasty. If a Hittite seal found at Terqa is a general indication of the interactions between the two states, the geographical location of Hana made its collaboration essential for the Hittites, allowing the Hittite troops to pass and reach the Babylonian border. A later text on the return of the statue of Marduk to Babylon attests that the Hittites had 'deported' it to Hana, where it remained until a Kassite king of Babylon recovered it. It is therefore possible that the Hittites had waged war against Babylon under Hana's solicitation to resolve the old issues between Hana and Babylonia. Subsequently, the Hittites left the booty, or part of it, at Hana. They then returned to Hatti without taking advantage of the victory, at least politically.

The conquest of Babylon and the sack of Marduk's temple was a deadly blow for the Babylonian dynasty. The Hittites had left, but the reign of Samsu-ditana was now falling apart. The Kassites took immediate advantage of this situation. There is evidence of their presence in Babylonia and Hana both as a group, due to their military pressures, and individually. We do not know how they took control over Babylonia, but it is possible that they did so through a military attack. The king lists developed and recorded a long dynastic sequence beginning with a Gandash and an Agum I, possibly a contemporary of Samsu-iluna (when a Kassite army is first mentioned). The first king who took advantage of the Hittite incursion to take over Babylonia, however, remains unknown to us.

5 The Elamite confederation

The Elamite state, ruled by the so-called *Sukkal-maḫ* Dynasty (the title designating the role of a king), was characterised by a particular administrative structure. Power was distributed among three officials. Firstly, there was the *sukkal-maḫ*, the supreme leader of the confederation, who resided in Susa. Then, there was the *sukkal* of Elam and Shimashki. He usually was the younger brother of the *sukkal-maḫ* and resided in Shimashki. Thirdly, there was the *sukkal* of Susa, normally the *sukkal-maḫ*'s son. The three offices were of decreasing importance. After the death of the *sukkal-maḫ*, his place was taken by the *sukkal* of Elam, his brother, whose place was in turn taken by either a brother or by the son of the deceased *sukkal-maḫ*, namely, the *sukkal* of Susa. In other words, power was transferred from brother to brother. Only after having gone through one generation of brothers it was possible to move on to the son of the first brother, namely, to the next generation.

This strong family solidarity among Elamite brothers is also attested through the practice of levirate marriages, according to which a widow was to be married to the deceased's brother, and of brother-sister marriages. Therefore, under normal conditions, at the death of a *sukkal-maḫ*, the *sukkal* of Elam, his younger brother, inherited his older brother's role and wife, the latter being the sister of both. Naturally, due to the overlap of reigns, the early death of younger siblings and so on, these basic criteria could only rarely be applied in full. This system of distribution and transmission of power was based on the social and legal traditions of the Elamites, which are also attested for the wider Elamite population. Even on a household level, inheritances moved from brother to brother, levirate marriages were practised and the management of family estates remained undivided. However, while in the normal legal practice we see a gradual shift towards subdivisions of inheritances and inheritances from father to son, the royal family stuck to the traditional system for a longer period of time.

Apart from the peculiarity of the family and inheritance system, Elam's political structure was characterised by its confederative nature. This aspect was typical of the region from as early as the Early Dynastic period. Therefore, the role of the *sukkal-maḫ* corresponded to the Elamite confederation and the single *sukkal* corresponded to the individual regional districts. Among these, the role of the *sukkal* of Elam and Shimashki maintained its privilege as a legacy of the former supremacy of the dynasty of Shimashki at the beginning of the second millennium BC. The documentation on Elam predominantly comes from Susa. The city had a central role as the residence of the *sukkal-maḫ*, but also a marginal one from an Elamite perspective, due to its proximity to the Lower Mesopotamian border. Therefore, it is hypothetically possible that other Elamite regions and cities had a similar triad of offices, sharing the same *sukkal-maḫ*, but with different people in the other two roles.

At the beginning of the nineteenth century, the *Sukkal-maḫ* Dynasty replaced the one of Shimashki, perhaps as a repercussion of the incursion of Gungunum of Larsa against Susa. Eparti and Shilhaka, founders of the new dynasty, took on the title of 'king of Anshan and Susa' and made Susa their capital. They also began a phase of intense cultural and political interactions with Babylonia and that vast Amorite 'world' that extended from Elam to Syria and the Levant. They shared the diplomatic practices, commercial activities and military involvements attested in the Mari archives. Susa's scribes used Akkadian not only for their diplomatic correspondence, but also for local legal texts, a large number of which have been found in Susa and some in Malamir (possibly ancient Huhnur), along the route from Susiana to Fars.

On a political level, Gungunum's incursion did not have long-lasting consequences. Elam remained politically independent from the Mesopotamian kingdoms and even relatively superior to them. During the Mari Age, the *sukkal-maḫ* (probably Shirukduh I) was engaged in diplomatic and commercial relations with Mari and the even more distant Qatna. Moreover, in the political and military events of the time, Elam found itself allied to Eshnunna during the siege of Razama, in Upper Mesopotamia, and then leading an invasion of the Jezira. The relationship of Elam with Eshnunna was the most strained one, evidently for disputes over borders.

Elam's influence extended all over the Zagros, reaching Shemshara, which was very close to Assyria. At the death of Shamshi-Adad, when Hammurabi of Babylon began to display his expansionistic ambition, the anti-Babylonian front along the Tigris was under the supremacy of Elam. Hammurabi's victory, however, helped in lowering the expansionistic ambitions and the presence of the *sukkal-maḫ* in the Mesopotamian scene. The Babylonians never conquered Elam and the local dynasty continued to rule, leaving only Susiana vulnerable to the consequences of the military developments taking place in Mesopotamia. Shortly after Hammurabi's reign, the Elamite king Kutir-Nahhunte I successfully led an expedition against the Babylonian cities, showing that the balance of power in the area was still subject to fluctuations. From then on and until the end of the dynasty, which continued after the Babylonian one, there would be no more relevant episodes in the relationship between these two powers. Just like in the rest of the Near East, even in the case of Elam there is a lack of documentation for the sixteenth century BC.

Apart from few royal inscriptions, the evidence on the *Sukkal-maḫ* period is mainly based on legal documents. Apart from the use of the Babylonian language, the Elamite legal system adopted several instruments typical of the Old Babylonian period. At Susa, a fragment of a code has been found, though it is too small for a reconstruction of Elamite society. However, this fragment is clear enough to attest to the royal practice, copied from Eshnunna or Babylon, of producing legal and celebratory texts. For instance, we know that Attahushu (nineteenth century BC), one of the first *sukkal-maḫ*, placed a stele in the market place with a list of fair prices. From the beginning of the sixteenth century BC, we know that some of the last *sukkal-maḫ* 'established justice' in the land, issuing edicts similar to the ones of Ammi-saduqa.

The scribal practices and forms of royal interventions were directly modelled on the Babylonian example. However, the Elamite legal documentation still displays several unique traits and an increased archaism in its style. Firstly, punishments were physical and not financial, cruel and discouraging rather than realistic. Moreover, the evidence used in disputes could be of a magical or religious nature (such as river ordeals). A sworn testimony was more common than the provision of written evidence and nail imprints to sign tablets were used more frequently than seals. The whole conception of justice was based on the religious idea of the *kitin*, or 'divine protection', which could be lost when committing sins and perjuries. Consequently, the divine is strongly present in Elamite legal documentation.

In terms of content, disputes were mainly concerned with the administration and inheritance of family estates. This was an intermediate period between an archaic and a more modern system of Mesopotamian inspiration. This transition brought several difficulties, especially when conciliating the two systems. The archaic system was based on an undivided management of an estate and the transmission of the latter from brother to brother. However, this system was subverted by the appearance of the division of inheritance into shares allocated by lot, the transmission of property from father to son, the sales of real estate outside the family and the use of lands and animals as guarantees against loans. The pledge of someone's life against these loans remains unattested. This is probably because it was the result of a more advanced system of loans anticipating the spread of debt-slavery. As a result of these changes and due to increasing economic pressures, the extended family, united and based on fratriarchy, quickly experienced a crisis. In this regard, we can see the appearance of testamentary clauses assigning inheritances to sons. These clauses also made sure that parents would be taken care of while they were alive, as well as when they passed away. This is the first indication of a non-automatic transmission of inheritance and of the particular attention to respectful behaviour. These two aspects would soon become characteristic throughout the Near East.

15

ANATOLIA IN THE OLD HITTITE PERIOD

1 From political fragmentation to unification

In the history of the Near East, the energetic entrance of the Hittites among the major players in the area happened during the reigns of two kings, Hattusili I and Mursili I. Within fifty years (ca. 1650–1600), these two kings created a strong state, campaigned in the Syro-Mesopotamian lowlands, thus ending two major kingdoms of the time (Yamhad and Babylonia) and began a profound re-organisation of the entire area. Central Anatolia clearly moved from the political fragmentation attested in the Old Assyrian sources (until ca. 1750 BC) to the unified state of Hattusili (around 1650 BC). However, evidence on this political transformation is sparse and varied in terms of types and origins.

Admittedly, Anatolia had been previously unified under Anitta of Kushshara, who led several military expeditions that peaked with the destruction of Hattusa. Anitta made Nesha/Kanesh his capital. His palace in the city is securely documented. Anitta's rise eventually became a model worth remembering and Hittite scribes copied and transmitted his inscription. Barely a century later, another man followed in Anitta's footsteps. It was a 'man of Kushshara', who conquered the Central Anatolian plateau and made one of its cities his capital. However, this man not only made the city that Anitta had destroyed and cursed, Hattusa, his capital, but also took his name from this city (Hattusili). The transfer of the capital of this newly unified kingdom to Hattusa, the construction of a royal palace in the city and the creation of a new administrative system and an archive, are the main reasons why our documentation for this period begins with Hattusili (Figure 15.1). Even Hittite scribes could not access information pre-dating this archive. Therefore, the sequence of Hittite kings and events is only secure from Hattusili onwards. On the contrary, the reconstruction of the formation of the Old Hittite state is based on some obscure, yet reliable, allusions found in Hattusili's texts and on some clear, yet unreliable, attestations from several centuries later.

According to the later Hittite tradition, the Hittite kingdom began with king Labarna and his royal wife Tawananna. Their names, however, were the ancient titles of the Hittite king and queen, also used by other Hittite royal couples. It is etymologically clear that these names were actual titles. Nonetheless, the Hittite tradition explains that Labarna and Tawananna became titles later on. Consequently, they are attested as the first royal couple in the royal lists of ancestors written for cultic purposes many centuries later.

The clearest evidence for this reconstruction of the beginnings of Hittite history can be found on the Edict of Telipinu. This text was written around 1500 BC and recounts past events in connection to current political problems. Telipinu begins his Edict stating: 'Formerly, Labarna was Great King'. In other words,

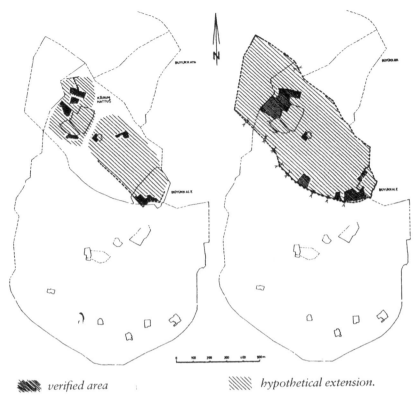

Figure 15.1   Hattusa at the time of the Old Assyrian colonies (nineteenth century BC) and in the Old Hittite period (sixteenth century BC).

it is as if Telipinu had said: 'Once upon a time, there was a king called His Majesty'. The text continues describing Labarna's reign as a model for peace, unity and strength. Immediately afterwards, he describes with almost the same words the reign of Hattusili. However, the latter account is based on evidence from Hattusili's reign (Text 15.1). The unity and peace that Telipinu attributed to Hattusili's reign seems unacceptable considering the evidence from Hattusili's reign. Equally unreliable is the fact that Telipinu copied his idea of Hattusili's reign to create the ancient and archetypal reign of Labarna. The latter never existed as a historical figure, but was a personification of the Hittite ideology of kingship. As we will see later on, this falsification in the Edict of Telipinu can be explained: the king had many problems surrounding his

---

Text 15.1   Historical sources of the Old Hittite kingdom

a) The beginning of the 'Testament' of Hattusili I

'1: The great king, Tabarna, speaks to the troops of the population (of Hatti) and to the dignitaries: I have fallen ill and had proclaimed in front of you the young Labarna: "May he sit upon the throne!"; thus, I, the king, called him "son". I began to instruct him and was fully dedicated to him. But he showed himself as a son without honour: he never shed a tear, he never showed sympathy; he remains cold and ungrateful.

257

2: So I, the king, have summoned him and made him come to my bed: "Well then, what does this mean? No-one will ever try to raise the son of his sister again!" He never gave heed to the word of the king; instead, he always listened to his mother, that snake; his brothers and sisters have never ceased to give him inconsiderate advice, and he has always listened to their words. But, I, the king, have heard them as well. And in front of such hostility I have shown hostility as well.'

b) Extract from the 'Annals' of Hattusili I

'No-one had ever crossed the Purattu river (Euphrates). The great king, Tabarna, crossed it with his feet and his troops crossed it behind him with their own feet. (Only) Sargon (of Akkad) had crossed it before! He had defeated the troops of Hahhum, but he had not damaged the city of Hahhum, had not burnt it down, and he had not shown its smoke to the Storm-god. But the great king, Tabarna, after having destroyed the king of Hashshum and (the king) of Hahhum, burnt (the city) down, showing its smoke to the Sun-god of heaven and the Storm-god, and yoked the king of Hahhum to his chariot!'

---

enthronement. Therefore, in order to present the hostilities within his kingdom as degenerative phenomena that needed to be taken care of, Telipinu had to present a model of a stable and peaceful reign. This model was placed in the ancestral past of the Hittite kingdom.

Both the existence of a mythical Labarna and the idea that the Hittite state was thoroughly united from its beginning are part of an ideal model and an unreliable memory of the origins of the Hittite state. In reality, the situation was completely the opposite. The history of the Old Hittite kingdom is not the history of the breakdown of a formerly united state through rivalries and betrayals. It is the history of a difficult rise towards the unification of Anatolia, which began with local city-states competing with each other (Figure 15.2). The evidence provided by Hattusili's texts regarding the formative process of his kingdom recount the many conflicts fought by him and his predecessors against the Anatolian city-states, and the constant rivalries within the Hittite court. Hattusili, the 'man from Kushshara' who became king of Hattusa, alluded to his predecessors (the kings of Kushshara) being involved in a number of difficult situations. Therefore, the conquest of Anatolia began before his reign. Unfortunately, we do not know how long before then, or whether or not it was a continuation of the hegemonic role that Kushshara had under Anitta a century earlier. Hattusili's reign and the move of the capital to Hattusa marked the realisation of this long process. During his reign, then, the Hittite state was already harbouring expansionistic ambitions. However, this phase still saw numerous conflicts with the cities in Central and northern Anatolia (Shanahuitta and Zalpa).

We do not have enough data to reconstruct the role of each city during the formation of the Hittite state. We can only catch a glimpse of the role of Kushshara, Hattusa and Nesha and the opposing roles of Shanahuitta and Zalpa. The Edict of Telipinu also attests the conquest of Hupishna, Tuwanuwa, Nenasha, Landa, Zallara, Purushhanda and Lushna. Following Hattusili's conquest, the kingdom of Hatti found its centre around the Halys bend. It then reached the coast of the Black Sea (at Zalpa) in the north, the Konya plain in the south-west and the northern side of the Taurus Mountains in the south-east. These territories were part of the regional state known as the 'land of Hatti', while all other territories would continue to be considered conquered territories.

Apart from some historical and political information found in the available evidence, the phase of unification of the Hittite state can also be traced in Hittite myths. A legend recounts the wedding of thirty sons of the Queen of Kanesh, who placed them in a basket and threw them in the Halys until they reached Zalpa. Once these princes unknowingly returned to their homeland, they ended up marrying their thirty

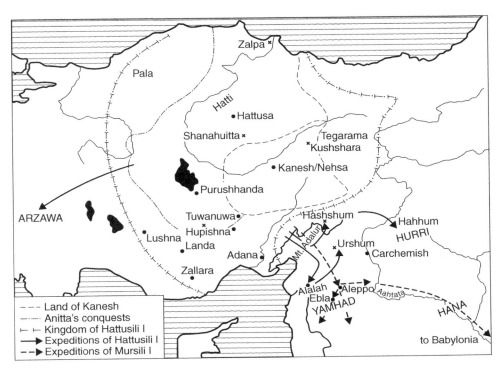

Figure 15.2 The formation of the Old Hittite state.

sisters. The ending of the text has not survived, but it dealt with the problems of kingship and the inheritance system (between the Hittite endogamy and the Indo-European exogamy). It also dealt with the role of Zalpa and Kanesh in the tradition developed by the new dynasty of Hattusa. Even the passage through the Taurus Mountain, which had already inspired several legends in Mesopotamia, became for the Hittites the epitome of a divine deed. Similarly, the crossing of the Euphrates would eventually have the same effect.

The role of some rival cities of Kushshara and Hattusa in the unification of Anatolia also survived in both the mythical tradition and in the ritual texts linked to kingship and enthronement, which indicates that the unification of Anatolia did not just require a sequence of wars and victories, or even destructions. It also had a strong political component, made of kinship ties and a common symbolic and ideological heritage. On a kinship level, two parallel processes were taking place. On the one hand, sons of the Hittite king were sent to the conquered cities as governors. What according to Telipinu took place in a peaceful and idyllic environment, according to the contemporary evidence caused local revolts and tendencies towards independence. On the other hand, the Hittite king married princesses from the cities he conquered and had members of the conquered royal families living in his court. The aim of these measures was clearly to create a more unified environment. However, even in this case serious problems arose, with factions within the Hittite court and its royal family fighting over power and succession. As the political unification of the land was taking place, the Hittite court began to be marked by competition and a multitude of potential candidates to the throne.

This seems to have been the actual way in which the Hittite state was formed both geographically and politically. At the peak of the Old Hittite period, old Hattusili left the throne in favour of young Mursili. In this regard, an important document, the Testament of Hattusili, shows us the dangerous degree of internal conflicts in Hatti. The old king, who unified the land and won over powerful kingdoms in the southeast of Anatolia and in northern Syria, complains that no one, from his wife to the other members of his family, ever listened to his words. Consequently, he had to adopt a stranger, the young Mursili, to cope with the betrayals and assassinations plotted by his relatives. It is a dreadful picture, but the reality could have been even worse. In fact, we have to imagine that the young usurper Mursili was the one directing the words of the old and sickly king lying on his deathbed. This was in order to legitimise his coup, which, unlike the others stated in Hattusili's testament, was actually successful.

2 The expansion of the Old Hittite state

Despite the painful development of the political unification of the Hittite state, at the beginning of his reign Hattusili was also engaged in several military expeditions outside of Hatti. In this regard, valuable information can be found in the bilingual annals of the king. These are written in both Hittite and Akkadian and recount year by year the feats of his first six years of rule (Text 21). The fights with nearby Shanahuitta and the powerful Zalpa took place at the same time as the long-distance expeditions and the disastrous incursions of enemies into the heart of Hatti. At the time, the Hittite state was still poorly unified, but already quite a large state. Consequently, its rise did not take place from a compact centre that was gradually expanding. It happened through ambitious expeditions, followed by the slow consolidation of the centre.

At the beginning of his reign, Hattusili already controlled the central part of Anatolia, possibly from sea to sea. He reached the Black Sea through the conquest of Zalpa, and the Mediterranean through the conquest of Cilicia (Adana, Lawazantiya). To the west, the vast region of Arzawa remained independent. Hattusili led a campaign there in his third regnal year, forcing the region to become part of his kingdom. To the southeast between the Taurus and the Mesopotamian plain, a number of relatively powerful kingdoms remained independent including Hashshum (in the Maraş area), Hahhum (Lidar Hüyük, near Samsat) and Urshum (in the Gaziantep area).

Two major powers were still looming behind these reigns, however. In Syria, there was the Old kingdom of Yamhad. The latter controlled a number of states in south-eastern Anatolia, such as Alalah, Carchemish and maybe Urshum. In Upper Mesopotamia, there was the rising land of Hurri. The latter was defined in the Old Hittite texts more as an ethnical group than a territorial state (i.e. 'the Hurrians', or 'the Hurrian troops'). On the contrary, the Akkadian version of the annals already gives this territory the name of Hanigalbat. The area was divided among small Hurrian states from as early as the Mari Age and even in the Late Akkadian period. The innovation of these Hurrians attested in the Hittite sources was their unification into a state formation destined to play an important part in the history of the Near East.

Hattusili's first expedition south of the Taurus took place in his second year on the throne. Having crossed Mount Adalur (a prosecution of the Amanus), the king marched straight south to Amuq. He destroyed Alalah, an important vassal of Aleppo, leaving no time for the latter to react. Before returning to Hatti, Hattusili moved east to conquer the land of Urshum. The following year, while Hattusili was engaged in conflicts with Arzawa, the Hurrians invaded the land with devastating effect. This action was certainly facilitated by the uncertain loyalty of several cities in the area. In his sixth reigning year, Hattusili again climbed the Adalur, defeated the troops of Hashshum, destroyed Hashshum itself and proceeded to conquer and destroy Hahhum. He then crossed the Euphrates, repeating the famous achievement of the legendary Sargon, though in the opposite direction. The fight against Hahhum had been prepared diplomatically. The Hittite king had the support of Tikunani, a small kingdom in Upper Mesopotamia that was still independent from the Hurrians. The conflicts continued in Syria even after the episodes recounted in the bilingual text. The difficulty of this conquest was mainly due to the active support the city-states between the Taurus and Euphrates received from Yamhad and the Hurrians.

These wars are also attested in some epic and legendary accounts. Some fragments attest to the names of the kings of Aleppo, Yarim-Lim and Hammurabi, as well as a general of Aleppo, Zukrashi, and the troops of the Umman-Manda. The most complete text describes the siege of Urshum. At that time, Hattusili was residing in Cilicia (Lawazantiya), while his generals were trying to conquer the city of Urshum unsuccessfully. This was due to a series of problems and counter-attacks by the besieged and their allies. We do not have the final part of the text, which maybe would have emphasised the decisive intervention of the king to repair for his generals' incompetence. Despite being a literary text, it is based on the events of the time. Whichever way the siege of Urshum ended – the text would logically imply that it was indeed besieged – it is clear that Hattusili found in Syria an arduous opposition, which could not be defeated with the means available to him.

His expansions eventually reached completion under Mursili I, who returned to Syria, apparently to avenge his adoptive father, who was possibly injured in battle, or simply defeated. Mursili successfully managed to defeat the king of Yamhad and his allies. The contemporary sources do not provide as much information as the ones we have for the first wars of Hattusili. Nonetheless, Mursili's success was so resounding that it was remembered in the following centuries. Both Telipinu and a fourteenth century treaty with Aleppo recall Mursili's destruction of the 'great kingdom' of Yamhad as a memorable event. Aleppo itself must have been besieged and destroyed. In that same period, other centres under Aleppo's authority, such as Ebla, were destroyed, probably at the hands of the Hittites themselves, or others linked to those events. This conquest of Ebla has already been mentioned: it is attested in the 'Song of Liberation', a text written in the Hurrian language, but kept in the Hittite archives.

We do not possess the details of the way in which Mursili ruled over his conquered territories. The king probably tried to maintain a Hittite presence there by appointing local dynasts dependent on the Hittite state. Mursili's solid control over Syria is proven by the fact that he moved his troops beyond Syria, reaching Babylonia, which he plundered and then abandoned. After all, it was impossible for Mursili to establish a solid control in Babylonia. Moreover, his ambitions were clearly more modest, namely, to support Hana, maybe in exchange for Hana's support in the Hittite conquest of Yamhad. In the case of Syria, Mursili clearly tried to establish a solid control of the region throughout his reign. Immediately after his reign, we find his successor Hantili engaged in battle with the Hurrians along the Euphrates, in particularly in Carchemish and the land of Ashtata (the valley between Carchemish and Hana). However, Hantili's opposition to the Hurrians failed and northern Syria fell under their control. Therefore, in a way Syria experienced the same fate as Babylonia did with the Kassites: the political gap brought about by the Hittite destruction of Yamhad benefited a third state, a new power destined to last.

The Old Hittite presence in the international scene did not last long, but had important implications. In fact, it confirmed, in a sudden yet influential way, the existence of a new power, able to interact with, or fight against, the major powers in the Near East. This new power had access to resources that had been badly used before. This was largely due to the long political fragmentation of the region, rather than its geographical position. Anatolia certainly had a reputation for its wealth in raw materials and unique local culture. However, in previous phases Anatolia's political fragmentation, which was much more established than in Mesopotamia, made its relations with the latter rather imbalanced. Therefore, once Anatolia was unified, the area inevitably became a major player among the foremost and most ancient powers of the Near East.

3 The social and economic structure of the Old Hittite kingdom

The environment and production processes of the Hittite state were very different from those of Lower Mesopotamia, Syria, or Upper Mesopotamia. Lower Mesopotamia was characterised by fields along canals, intensely cultivated with barley and palm-trees. Syria and Upper Mesopotamia relied on rainfed agriculture and transhumant farming. Anatolia, however, was a mountainous region (the Central Anatolian plateau lies 1000 metres above sea level) with cities and cultivations concentrated in the valleys. The surrounding mountains thus remained forested and largely inaccessible. The presence of forested areas was particularly advantageous. In fact, timber, which other states had to import from elsewhere, was readily available within the Hittite borders. The same can be said for metals, such as copper and silver, as well as stone. Consequently, there was no separation between settled, cultivated areas and areas providing raw materials. Everything was readily accessible within a few kilometres.

Agricultural cultivations in Anatolia were diversified. Grain cultivations developed alongside the cultivation of trees and other plants. Vines, olive-trees, fruits and even bees formed a landscape made of hedged or walled fields. These were completely different from the open fields of the Syro-Mesopotamian lowlands. The farming of goats and sheep was particularly common. However, transhumant farming was different from the one described for the Middle Euphrates. In the latter region, transhumance moved horizontally, with a concentration of people in the summer and dispersion in the winter. In the Anatolian highlands, transhumance moved vertically, with summer pastures on the mountains and winter ones in the valleys. Therefore, dimorphism developed in the opposite direction, with concentrations of people over the winter and dispersions in the summer.

In the forested areas, the farming of pigs was particularly widespread. This animal was not the target of the religious and dietary taboos found in the lowlands. In the valleys, people mainly farmed cattle and, around the mid-second millennium BC, they introduced the farming of horses. With such a variety of natural resources, the main problem was the lack of human labour. Throughout Hittite history, the most recurring problems were the depopulation of the countryside and the pressing need to bring workmen (prisoners and deportees) to Anatolia through military expeditions. This measure was clearly aimed at filling the significant gap formed by the depopulation of the countryside.

Even after the political unification of Anatolia, this agro-pastoral and mining economy remained largely local in character. This was mainly because the area itself was made of several virtually isolated valleys, surrounded by mountains. Cities were not large, but they were well fortified. This was characteristic of the Middle Bronze Age and a clear response to the frequent internal conflicts in the region. The substitution of local political independence with a central authority happened gradually and there was still a certain degree of local autonomy in this phase. Some cities rose as important religious centres, such as Arinna, cult centre of the Sun-goddess, Nerikka and Zippalanda for the Storm-god, then Samuha and many more. Palaces and temples also worked as major economic centres in Anatolia. Many categories of craftsmanship depended on the palaces and trade was probably under royal supervision.

The social stratification attested throughout Ancient Near Eastern society can also be found in Anatolia. On the one hand, there was the 'free' population, which lived in village communities and small urban centres. These settlements had their own political organisation, which was recognised by the king. The 'mayor' and the 'elders' (who had a juridical function) administered the communal and royal lands left momentarily unused and had a tributary relation with the palace. This tributary relation made these communities liable to the *luzzi* service, which was a sort of *corvée* both for normal labour and military purposes. On the other hand, there were artisans, soldiers, administrators and any other category of individuals needed by the palace. These individuals worked full-time for the palace (*šaḫḫan*) in exchange of a plot of land with farmers for their maintenance.

The Hittite Law Code provides the majority of information on this socio-economic system (Figure 15.3). The standard manuscript of the code divided the laws into two series, called 'if a man' and 'if a vine'. These are the initial phrases of the respective sections of the laws. The Code underwent several changes and its formulation often displays considerable innovations of the Hittite legal system. The first version of the Code was written at the time of Hattusili I or Mursili I. This is because some manuscripts were written with the typical writing style of the time. It is clear that the idea to create a code was inspired by previous Mesopotamian examples. However, the political and cultural differences between the two regions made their codes substantially different. First of all, there was no prologue or epilogue. These two aspects essentially made the Mesopotamian codes celebratory inscriptions, though much longer and more specific.

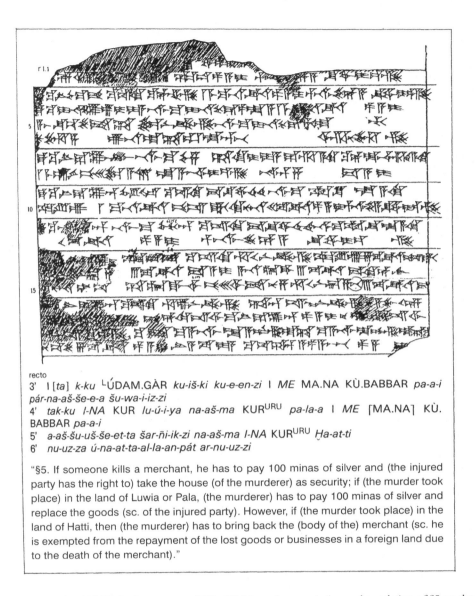

recto

3' I [ta] *k-ku* ᴸÚDAM.GÀR *ku-iš-ki ku-e-en-zi* I ME MA.NA KÙ.BABBAR *pa-a-i*
pár-na-aš-še-e-a šu-wa-i-iz-zi
4' *tak-ku* I-NA KUR *lu-ú-i-ya na-aš-ma* KUR^URU *pa-la-a* I ME [MA.NA] KÙ.
BABBAR *pa-a-i*
5' *a-aš-šu-uš-še-et-ta šar-ñi-ik-zi na-aš-ma* I-NA KUR^URU *Ḫa-at-ti*
6' *nu-uz-za ú-na-at-ta-al-la-an-pát ar-nu-uz-zi*

"§5. If someone kills a merchant, he has to pay 100 minas of silver and (the injured party has the right to) take the house (of the murderer) as security; if (the murder took place) in the land of Luwia or Pala, (the murderer) has to pay 100 minas of silver and replace the goods (sc. of the injured party). However, if (the murder took place) in the land of Hatti, then (the murderer) has to bring back the (body of the) merchant (sc. he is exempted from the repayment of the lost goods or businesses in a foreign land due to the death of the merchant)."

Figure 15.3   From the Old Hittite Laws: copy of KBo VI 2 'recto'; transcription and translation of §5 on the murder of merchants.

The Hittite Code was more of an archival document, whose administrative tone was meant to establish, or change, the norms and prices to be applied.

The casuistic structure ('if . . . then . . .') of the laws remained. This structure, however, was not used to express how well the kingdom was ruled. It was strictly used to specify what constituted a crime and what did not, and, in case it was a crime, what had to be done to repair for it, to compensate the victim and to give back to the culprit his freedom. Moreover, the Code was also meant to change habits and sanc-tions, so that if in the past there was a certain punishment for a certain crime, now it was alleviated. This is in marked contrast with the idea that justice was immutable in its principles and consequences. On the contrary, these laws enabled a development of the system both through time and according to different historical situations.

Almost every entry is linked to price lists. There is no formal distinction between price lists to be used in transactions and rentals and the ones concerned with financial compensations in repair for damages or crimes. These two types of lists form the largest part of the code, while the rest of the Code is concerned with two types of regulations. The first group deals with unlawful sexual relations, either because they were between relatives, or because they were of a beastly nature. The main concern here was to establish a precise distinction between legitimate relations, as in those not liable to sanctions, and illicit ones. Those found guilty of such offences could be condemned to terrible punishments, even death penalties, unless they received a royal pardon.

Then, there was a group of regulations concerned with the management of the land provided by the king, and the types of services to be provided to the Hittite state, such as the *šaḫḫan* and the *luzzi*. This group of laws provides useful information for a socio-economic reconstruction of Hittite society. The system was divided between the *luzzi*, a *corvée* type of service that had to be provided by all subjects, and the *šaḫḫan*, a specialised service repaid through land concessions. The theoretical foundations of this system were constantly hindered and threatened by potentially damaging tendencies and problems. For instance, there was a widespread tendency to sell the lands that had been donated or conceded by the king. In this regard, the main worry of the Hittite kings was to establish who had to continue to provide a certain service, whether that was the person originally appointed, or the new buyer of the land. A mistake here would have cost the palace that particular service.

Another widespread practice was exemption. The priests of Arinna, Nerikka and Zippalanda were exempted from the *luzzi*, but not their employees. Moreover, certain groups of artisans were obliged or not obliged to join the Hittite army and so on. The death or disappearance of either the assignee or the farmer entrusted with a plot of land created several gaps in the royal system of land allotments and the provision of services. There were three possible solutions: 1) either the assignee or the farmer took on the role of the deceased; 2) a prisoner of war was given the land, without having any right to sell the land or avoid the associated service; 3) the land was given to the nearest city, until a more appropriate use of the land was found. The palace was no less powerful than elsewhere, but it seems it was less strongly rooted in the Anatolian economic structure. The complex socio-economic structure of Anatolia, with independent local entities and strong tendencies towards depopulation, made it difficult for the palace to keep its lands and subjects under control.

4 Old Hittite culture

In the Old Hittite period, Anatolian culture was strongly influenced by its prolonged contact with Syrian and Upper Mesopotamian culture and, through them, with the culture of Lower Mesopotamia. Consequently, the Sumero-Akkadian tradition and particularly its scribal culture became an integral part of the culture of the Old Hittite palace, though with considerable Hurrian and Amorite influences. These cultural links underwent several changes and were modified and integrated with considerable originality. A good example of this is writing. At the time of the Assyrian colonies in Anatolia, documents and letters between local kings were written in an Old Assyrian dialect. A century later, in the archives of Hattusa, the texts whose writing style can be dated to the Old Hittite kingdom used a type of writing of clear North Syrian and North Mesopotamian tradition. Moreover, the texts from Hattusa written in Akkadian were not written in the Assyrian dialect, but in the Babylonian one. Hattusa was thus the most distant ramification of the Syro-Mesopotamian culture of the Amorite period.

However, the Old Hittite civilisation's greatest innovation, which was not achieved by the Amorite and Hurrian centres, was the use of the Babylonian syllabary to write the local Hittite language. This was a clear indication of the active reception of the Mesopotamian writing system in Anatolia and of the ability to distinguish writing and language, utilising an already existing system to deal with new requirements. This development may seem banal, but it was an innovation that did not appear elsewhere. Old Hittite formulas and prologues and the structure of Hittite documents were equally original. The scribal tradition of sign lists, word lists and literary texts, was reformulated in response to local needs. Therefore, word lists were bilingual, providing a translation of each word in Hittite, and literary texts were translated.

Among the Mesopotamian literary texts, the most popular ones in the Old Hittite period were the ones linked to Anatolia or, more generally, with the lands west of Mesopotamia. This seemingly Hittite preference could, alternatively, have been pre-filtered by north Syrian scribes. Consequently, the Epic of Gilgamesh was copied and translated, especially the episode concerned with the expedition to the cedar forest and the battle against Humbaba. Also the pseudo-historical tales concerning Sargon and Naram-Sin were copied, in particular Sargon's expedition in Anatolia (the *šar tamḫāri*), or the battles of Naram-Sin against Syro-Anatolian coalitions. However, there is no identification of the Hittites with the Anatolian enemies of the kings of Akkad. On the contrary, the Hittites identified with the latter, at least to compete with the kings of Akkad, using them as a model worth imitating and surpassing.

In terms of city plans, architecture and craftsmanship (metallurgy, pottery and so on) it is clear that Old Hittite culture was connected to the contemporary cultures of the Syrian and Upper Mesopotamian Middle Bronze Age. However, many elements of local continuity from the Anatolian Early Bronze Age are even more visible, possibly due to the geographical position of Anatolia, close to rich natural resources (timber, stone, metals and so on). Consequently, the walled cities of the Anatolian Middle Bronze Age were different from their contemporary counterparts in Syria and Upper Mesopotamia. In particular, the structure of the Old Hittite acropolis (Büyükkale) in Hattusa was very different from the ones in other important centres, such as Mari and Alalah. The entire acropolis of Hattusa was used as the administrative centre of the Old Hittite state. The many functions of the palace as royal residence, and cultic and administrative centre were not included into one large building. Its archives, storehouses and open spaces for audiences were here subdivided into many free-standing buildings.

Old Hittite architecture mainly used timber and stone, not only for foundations, but also for the walls themselves. The local pottery (first Cappadocian and then properly 'Hittite') and seals show the originality of Anatolian culture, especially if compared to the contemporary developments in the Syro-Anatolian area (such as the Khabur pottery and the Old Syrian seals). The originality of Old Hittite culture was the consequence of the survival of the local tradition. However, Hittite literature emphasises the ethno-linguistic distinction between the Hattic element (that is, the pre-Hittite Anatolian element) and the Indo-European one.

In the realms of religion, mythology, literature, society, kingship, the military and historiography, great emphasis is placed on the Hattic tradition, characterised by strong feminine elements (such as the chthonic nature of Hattic religion, centred on the worship of the Great Mother) and Indo-European patriarchal and military contributions. In other words, the Hattic tradition was considered to be matriarchal (a legitimate heir is the son of one's sister), while the Indo-European one was patriarchal (one's son is his legitimate heir). This Hittite worldview desperately tried to find a compromise between the two traditions. Therefore, it is possible that the vast majority of litigations and disputes over the rightful heir to the throne derived from these two very distinct traditions. This theory has some important implications for the study of Hittite history, but it cannot be the only explanation for the troubles surrounding the Hittite throne.

In the formation phase of the Old Hittite state, the symbiosis of Hattic and Indo-European elements in the local culture had already existed for centuries, perhaps even longer than is generally believed. The two elements were never explicitly placed in opposition to each other, neither in conflicts between cities, nor as opposing traditions or customs. For instance, the interpretation of Nesha's conflicts against Zalpa or Hattusa as essentially conflicts between Indo-Europeans and Pre-Hittites constitutes an arbitrary and erroneous interpretation of the historical context of the time. Similarly, seeing the competition between a son and a son-in-law over the Hittite throne as an ethnic conflict between a Hattic and Indo-European tradition is an interpretation that is not supported by the available evidence.

An even worse misinterpretation of Hittite culture is the understanding of some of its characteristic traits as more or less linked to an Indo-European tradition. If we accept that the Indo-European linguistic groups derived from the third millennium 'Kurgan IV' culture from southern Russia (thus preferring a 'lower' interpretation, implying a better survival of this cultural heritage), this culture was nonetheless made of Chalcolithic shepherds and warriors. The latter did not live in cities, were not organised into states and had far less complex modes of production and inheritance systems than the ones that developed in Anatolia over the millennia. For instance, how is it possible to attribute to the Indo-Europeans a specific historical value for the Old Hittite period? This historical value is already closely linked to the legal and political system of Middle Bronze Age Anatolia, in which it had a specific purpose. Similarly, if the Hittites were indeed more belligerent than their neighbours, how is it possible to attribute the seemingly belligerent nature of the Hittites to an Indo-European heritage? The wars of the Syro-Anatolian Middle Bronze Age were fought in political and technological contexts that could not have existed in the 'primitive seat' of the Indo-Europeans. This strongly 'ethnical' view of the cultural development of the Hittites is therefore outdated. It is the result of a historiography that produced and emphasised the myth of the Indo-Europeans, influencing the reconstruction of the history of the Hittites.

Unlike the Mesopotamian and Syrian contexts, which have been considered in the previous chapters, Old Hittite kingship and power were characterised by three main aspects: the instability and contentiousness surrounding the transmission of power; the role of institutional bodies; and the pre-eminent role of the female element. The rivalries surrounding the palace over the succession to the Hittite throne are clear not only from the retrospective descriptions provided by Telipinu. They can already be detected in Hattusili's and Mursili's texts, in particular the testament of the former in favour of the latter. It is clear that the murderous plots described in the sources, which paradoxically saw the succession system as one requiring the son-in-law to kill the son of the previous king, were not the norm. They were violations that were severely punished.

The constant reappearance of these murder plots and violations began to form a system *de facto* and Hittite kingship continued to be exposed to the ambitions of others. These issues, however, did not appear simply because the system of succession was not strong enough or exclusive enough. It was also because of the survival within the Hittite court of that fragmentation and competition typical of Anatolian culture. The political unification may have begun to eliminate this fragmentation in the rest of Anatolia, but it continued to exist in the capital. The political use of marriages by the Hittite royal family, then, made this a constant problem throughout Hittite history.

The role of institutional bodies should not be overemphasised, but it does remain an important aspect of the Hittite state. The testament of Hattusili and other texts from the period mention a general assembly (*pankuš*) that acted as a kind of guarantor of the king's decisions and a court (*tuliyaš*) acting as a juridical assembly. However, it is not clear whether the latter's decisions were applicable to the royal family. The *pankuš* had nothing to do with the problem of the Indo-European aristocracy (military in particular). On the contrary, it was the opposite of those functionaries working for the state's administration on its highest levels, who were mainly related with the royal family. The *pankuš* was an assembly embracing more than just the aristocracy, and, together with the king, was able to stop the ambitions and abuses of the most powerful Hittite families.

The king was not 'first among equals' and his alleged 'equals' were certainly not part of the *pankuš*. The king was one and held absolute power. However, access to kingship remained highly desirable for a large portion of the royal family. Consequently, the 'assembly' and the 'tribunal', the former influencing the public opinion and the latter having a more juridical role, could limit abuses of power and potential damages to the unity of the Hittite state. However, the *pankuš* would eventually disappear. This was not because the alleged Indo-European heritage was dying out, but because the aristocracy, which was both military and administrative, and largely coincided with the many relatives of the king, managed to rise above it.

Finally, the importance of the feminine element was expressed through the role of the *tawananna*, which was the counterpart of the *tabarna*. The *tawananna* was not just the king's wife, since she held the title until her death. Therefore, there was normally a *tawananna* older than the queen, namely, the mother of the king, and the two were in competition with each other. The *tabarna/tawananna* couple mainly had a cultic role, probably as a human representation of a divine couple, envisioned as the Storm-god (male) and the Sun-goddess (female). The king, just like the queen or queen mother, was neither deified nor identified with a deity, and it was only after his death that it was said that he had 'become a god'. In this regard, the Hittites dedicated an entire cult to their royal ancestors, who were paired into couples of *tabarna* and *tawananna*. These cults are attested in later inventories and ritual texts, which provide diachronic sequences of these pairs, updated after each generation. Therefore, the royal couple was frequently involved in cultic ceremonies, and descriptions of rituals are some of the most widespread types of texts in the archives from Hattusa. These rituals mainly took place in the capital, where many temples and various cults could be found. However, there were also many ceremonial peregrinations to the sanctuaries of the land of Hatti.

The persistence of local cults was deeply rooted in Hittite culture, and the royal family took charge of them. In this way, the royal family was able to present itself to its subjects as the heir of the previous local monarchies and as an intermediary between the human and the divine spheres. The 'thousand gods of the land of Hatti' were extremely similar in type. Each city had a storm-god, always called with the same name or, better, with the same writing, but specified for each city. In terms of function and types of gods, then, there were many similarities among the many gods of Hatti. However, the maintenance of their local identity and temple organisation was equally strong. The divine couple that took on the official role of state couple was made of the solar goddess of Arinna, a city near Hattusa and the Storm-god of Hatti. Oddly enough, this choice does not provide a privileged position to the capital of the Hittite state. It was rather based on the selection of the most common types of deities, rather than the pre-eminence of a specific couple over the others. Therefore, the main problem of the Old Hittite monarchy was to keep united a region that in its historical and cultural tradition, as well as geographically and ethnically, was prone to disintegrate into smaller autonomous states and communities.

PART IV

The Late Bronze Age

16

THE LATE BRONZE AGE
Technologies and ideologies

1 The 'mountain people' and the 'dark age'

In the study of the history of the Ancient Near East, it is common to define the period roughly comprising the sixteenth century BC as a 'dark age'. This phase separates the First Dynasty of Babylon from the beginning of the Late Bronze Age, which is far better attested. The length of this 'dark age' depends on whether one chooses a short or a long chronology. This preference also becomes a way to evaluate this 'dark age'. The supporters of a long chronology emphasise the drastic cultural changes taking place between the Old Babylonian period and the Late Bronze Age. These changes would explain the long interval between the two phases. On the other hand, the supporters of a short chronology emphasise the elements of cultural continuity and the scarcity of documentation for this phase. Thankfully, now that the study of the Old and Middle Hittite evidence has drastically improved, the obscure character of the sixteenth century BC has been partly reduced.

The Mitannian kingdom (a.k.a. Hurri or Hanigalbat) already existed at the time of Hattusili I. Therefore, Upper Mesopotamia, which experienced the majority of changes in this phase, does not constitute a total gap in our knowledge anymore. Nonetheless, this phase shows a visible decrease of textual evidence. Broadly speaking, for Babylonia there is a gap between the Old Babylonian and the Kassite documentation. The latter only provides evidence from the Amarna Age onwards. Equally vast is the gap between the Assyrian kings Ishme-Dagan and Ashur-uballit, while the Hittite gap between Mursili and Telipinu is far shorter. On a local level, there is the gap between the texts of Alalah VII (ca. 1700–1650 BC) and Alalah IV (ca. 1550–1450 BC), since levels VI to V have not yielded any texts. This drastic reduction in the available sources cannot be entirely due to chance in the excavations. The sixteenth century BC must have been a consolidating period for new state administrations, such as the ones of the Hurrian kingdom of Mitanni and of the Kassite kingdom of Babylonia. These new state formations must have needed some time to implement an effective system to control their territories and manage their economy.

While the character of the sixteenth century BC is to a certain extent destined to remain obscure, several formerly accredited interpretations regarding this phase are now largely discredited. The old interpretation saw the appearance of this sort of 'middle age' of the second millennium BC as the result of the irruption of new populations in the Near East, mainly coming from the Anatolian and Iranian highlands. For this reason, these populations were conventionally called the 'mountain people' and were considered of Indo-European origins. The rise of the Hittites, Hurrians and Kassites in the political scene of the Near East was therefore arbitrarily considered as a single phenomenon, and thus placed in the same period and within the same ethno-linguistic group. However, there were considerable differences between the Indo-European groups of Anatolia and the Indo-Iranian ones of the Hurrians and the Kassites. Moreover, these groups had several non-Indo-European features.

The Hittites and the other Indo-European groups from the Anatolian plateau were part of an archaic branch of the Indo-European language. They were already settled in that region by the end of the third millennium BC (perhaps even earlier). Consequently, their migration to Anatolia already took place at least half a millennium before the sixteenth century BC. Moreover, the Hittite state was already under development towards the end of the Old Babylonian period. It already had the opportunity to express its political and military influence in the Near East through its conquests of Yamhad and Babylon.

Similarly, in the mid-second millennium BC, the Hurrians were not a new population. They are attested in Upper Mesopotamia in the earliest evidence concerning the area, namely, from the mid-third millennium BC. Finally, the Kassites were one of the many populations inhabiting the Zagros (like the Gutians and Lullubeans), constantly pressing on the Mesopotamian alluvial plain. Consequently, their rise in Babylonia was not the result of a consistent migratory movement. It was a political and military intervention of a small group of Kassites, who were thus unable to completely alter the ethnic composition of Babylonia.

The ethno-linguistic innovation of the sixteenth century BC was rather brought about by the appearance of Indo-Iranian terms in the personal names from Mitanni and other states connected to it. Alongside these personal names, there was the appearance of a specific terminology linked to the breeding and training of horses for the two-wheeled horse-drawn chariot (Text 16.1). These names had a clear Indo-Iranian etymology, very similar to Ancient Persian and Sanskrit, such as Shuwardata ('given by the sky'), Biryashshura ('valiant hero') and Indaruta ('supported by Indra'). Moreover, new names of gods appeared, such as Indra, Mitra, Varuna, Nashatya (invoked in a treaty between Hatti and Hurri) and Shurya, the Sun-god of the Kassites. Similarly, Indo-Iranian terms and phrases regarding the training of horses began to appear in treaties, such as *aika-wartanna* ('one turn'), *tēra-wartanna* ('three turns'), *panza-wartanna* ('five turns'), and so on. Even the etymology of the word used to indicate chariot warriors, *maryannu*, was of Indo-Iranian origins (from the Sanskrit *marya*, 'young warrior'). This Indo-Iranian element was therefore very different from the Indo-European linguistic group found in Anatolia, since it was more recent and of eastern origins.

Text 16.1 Indo-Iranian words and personal names linked with the training of war-horses and light chariots

1 Indo-Iranian words linked to chariots and horses from the treaty of Kikkuli and the Nuzi texts

aššuššanni	'horse trainer' (Sanskrit *aśvas* 'horse')
ašuwaninni	'charioteer (?)' (same as above?)
maryannu	'chariot warrior' (Sanskrit *marya* 'youth')
babrunnu	'brownish-red' (the colour of a horse) (Sanskrit *babhru* 'reddish-brown')
barittannu	'grey' (Sanskrit *palitá* < * *paritá* 'grey')
pinkarannu	'tawny' (Sanskrit *pingalá* < * *pingará* 'reddish')
aika-wartanna	'one turn' (Sanskrit *éka* < * *aika* 'one' + Old Iranian *vartaní* 'turn, track')
tēra-wartanna	'three turns' (*trí* + *vartaní*)
panza-wartanna	'five turns' (*pánca* + *vartaní*)
šatta-wartanna	'seven turns' (*saptá* + *vartaní*)
nā-wartanna	'nine turns' (*náva* + *vartaní*)

---

2 Potential Indo-Iranian etymologies of the personal names of the royal family of Mitanni

Tushratta = Sanskrit *tveṣá-ratha* 'whose war-chariot advances impetuously'

Shattiwaza = Sanskrit * *sāti-vāja* 'he who acquires war booties'

Artatama = Sanskrit * *R̥ta-dhāmam* 'whose residence is R̥ta (truth, justice)'

Artashumara = Sanskrit * *R̥ta-smara* 'he who remembers R̥ta'

These innovations, however, were not part of those types of invasions once envisioned by historians, who pictured a wave of Indo-Iranian warriors who, equipped with chariots and horses, spread in the Near East, reached Egypt (as the Hyksos) and conquered the Hurrian and Semitic populations. Their success, then, was attributed to their superior armament and increased mobility. In reality, there are no traces of such an invasion. The invasion of the Hyksos in Egypt not only took place well before the sixteenth century BC, but also took place in a completely different fashion. Similarly, the formation of the Mitannian kingdom, which would have been the centre of the Indo-Iranian people, was the result of the unification of a variety of Hurrian groups that had lived in the area for centuries.

The real innovation of the sixteenth century BC, then, is the diffusion of a new trend in terms of personal names and technical terminology linked to the introduction of the chariot and horses. These were indeed innovations of the seventeenth century BC, probably from the vast territories of the Iranian plateau and Central Asia. At the beginning of the second millennium BC, the urban settlements in these regions had experienced a crisis that caused a demographic and power vacuum, which in turn facilitated the settlement of groups of shepherds and warriors from the area of the *kurgan*. From there, military innovations spread to the Near East. Then, the Upper Mesopotamian and north Syrian states adapted these innovations to fit the technical standards and socio-economic needs of more complex types of urban settlements.

The real gap in our knowledge appears at the end of the third millennium BC, with a marked discontinuity in the archaeological evidence between the Early and Middle Bronze Age. In comparison, the transition between Middle and Late Bronze Age in the sixteenth century BC was an entirely internal process, which did not experience any discontinuity. The urbanisation process, its rise and decline, was a unitary process and even the material culture from the time developed coherently and without interruptions. The distinction between a Middle and a Late Bronze Age is in fact a mere convention, while the cultural developments of the time constituted a unitary process. An interruption of this process only took place in the twelfth century BC, with the transition from Late Bronze to Iron Age. Therefore, this seemingly 'dark age', placed in the middle of this cultural development, was not interrupted by strong migratory movements. It was simply the result of political consolidations and socio-economic changes, changes which were partly brought about by the new military innovations from the east and partly by specific historical events.

2 Technological innovations and their implications

Some *equidae* had been used in the Near East from as early as the Neolithic Revolution, or, better, Andrew Sherrat's 'secondary revolution'. In fact, the donkey was the most widespread draught animal, while the far stronger onager was used for four-wheeled carts. Horses remained undomesticated until the end of the seventeenth century BC. This was mainly due to the areas in which wild horses could be found and the difficulties encountered in their domestication. Naturally, there were some isolated cases in which horses were used. Overall, up until the seventeenth century BC the horse did not have any reason to be historically attested. Its Sumerian designation as 'mountain donkey' (anše kur.ra) proves that back then the horse was seen as a wild and exotic variation of the more common and docile donkey.

Around 1600 BC, the horse finally appeared in the Near East, quickly spreading as far as Egypt. The horse was used to pull light chariots with two spoked wheels. This type of chariot was made of a selection of hard woods. The lightness of this vehicle allowed two horses, connected to the chariot via a yoke, to carry two people (a charioteer and an archer) and to move at a considerable speed. The chariot has a long and well-attested history in the Near East. The earliest models were mainly four-wheeled carts with disk wheels, used to transport goods. Two-wheeled carts were relatively rare, usually drawn by onagers and driven by a warrior. The latter was too focused on driving the chariot and staying on it to be able to simultaneously use a bow or other weapons effectively.

The origins of the two-wheeled horse-drawn chariot are mainly attributed to the Iranian plateau. This is because the technical terminology used in Hittite or Akkadian sources to describe this particular and difficult training borrowed Indo-Iranian terms and phrases. This technique was therefore developed by the Indo-Iranians living in the Iranian plateau or even in Central Asia. However, the spread of the practice to Mesopotamia, Anatolia and Syria brought about several technical and socio-political adjustments and improvements. Horses and light chariots could be used for hunting activities, which could have had a symbolic meaning (especially when the king was involved), but not a political one. However, the chariot and the horse found their main application in the military, where they completely revolutionised the fighting techniques of the time.

The wars fought in the third millennium BC and in the first half of the second millennium BC were mainly fought on the battlefield. Armies of soldiers fought with short weapons and were at times supported by the throwing of arrows and javelins. More often than not, these types of conflicts ended with the siege of walled cities through increasingly effective siege engines. These machines were designed to destroy the ever-improving fortifications of the cities. From the mid-second millennium BC to the end of the Bronze Age (the Iron Age would experience further improvements), however, the typical battle was centred on the charge of an army of chariots against other chariots or troops of soldiers. The army, then, began to be divided into two groups, characterised by a different social and military prestige: the infantry and the chariotry. The former always had more soldiers, but the latter was far more mobile and effective.

The chariot had a variety of functions. It acted both as a mobile platform for archers and as an effective tool to break infantry lines and to follow fleeing enemies. While its use as a mobile platform has been widely accepted by scholars, the idea that it was used to break down troops has been considered impracticable. Logistically, the horses would have refused to charge a stationary obstacle. However, the iconographic and written evidence from the Late Bronze Age consistently indicates that this was a common practice and even the most effective and bravest one. The formation of foot soldiers was not compact enough to constitute a single stationary obstacle. Moreover, the horses' fear must have been preceded by the soldiers' terror of being charged by an entire troop of chariots. In other words, the flight and subsequent havoc created by fleeing foot soldiers must have overridden the horses' refusal to move forward.

Therefore, Late Bronze Age battles began with the initial charge of the chariots of the attacking army on the opposing troops of foot soldiers. They then continued with the attacking army's infantry moving forwards in the gaps created by the chariots. Meanwhile, the other army's chariots would have proceeded along the flanks, in order to surround the enemy. Naturally, it is always the winning side that narrates battles, giving us the impression that this assaulting, frontal tactic was successful. However, it is not necessarily true that defensive tactics, supported by strategically located mountains or rivers, were any the less effective.

The beginning of the Late Bronze Age brought other innovations. For instance, there was scale armour, used on both men and horses. This type of armour has been found in excavations, on representations, and is also mentioned in administrative texts. This innovation was the result of the spread of the composite bow, made of two horns linked at the base. The composite bow was able to throw arrows at a greater distance and with much more power than the simple bow. Frontal combat between foot soldiers armed with short weapons thus became less essential. On the contrary, siege engines and techniques continued to be central and of the same type as the ones developed in the Mari Age.

These innovations had a considerable impact on the social structure of Late Bronze Age communities due to the combination of ideological implications with economic ones. On an ideological level, the creation of an army of charioteers playing a significant role in battles made them a heroic ideal and thus part of a specific social class. In the ideological conception of the time, battles were not won by the king anymore, nor by the patron deity of a city, with soldiers merely acting as an anonymous mass following the orders of their leaders. On the contrary, battles were won by troops of charioteers with specific instruments and training, whose essential talent was their bravery. The king shared with the *maryannu* these essential and elitist ideals of bravery and valiantness, clearly expressed in the literature and iconography of the Near East, from Egypt to Babylonia (Figure 16.1).

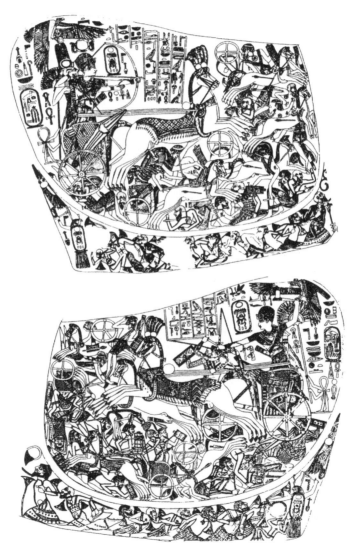

Figure 16.1 The king as a hero, fighting alone on his chariot and defeating a multitude of enemies (panels from Tuthmosis IV's chariot).

275

The costliness of the equipment (chariots, horses, metal armours for men and horses, weapons and so on) and the complexity of the training process required palaces to employ full-time charioteers with considerable economic means. Thus, palaces resorted to the old system of assigning plots of land with farmers in exchange for the charioteers' service. This also allowed the training of horses together with the charioteers. The amount of land given, the nature of this service and the solidarity (either through friendship or kinship) between the king and the *maryannu*, made the old system of royal land grants more 'feudal' in nature. This definition is certainly anachronistic, but it is nonetheless useful to approximately summarise the system's development. For the first time in the history of the Near East the ruling elite included a military class holding a privileged socio-economic position among the classes of functionaries, scribes, priests and merchants.

The birth of this military aristocracy of landowners embodying a heroic ideal coincided with another radical change in the socio-political systems of the Syro-Mesopotamian region. From as early as the Mari Age, but especially in the texts from Hana and Alalah VII, documents providing personal guarantees for debt repayments began to include new types of clauses. These ensured that 'even in case of a liberation (that is, an edict of liberation), he (the debt slave) will not be freed'. The spread of these clauses caused the disappearance of the royal edicts after the end of the seventeenth century BC. By then, edicts had become completely ineffective. If kings were still interested in the emanation of edicts, they could have banned these clauses, or found ways to make them ineffective. However, they were not interested in maintaining social order through measures considered to be 'just' in the Old Babylonian period anymore.

Therefore, the key elements in the formation of common interests between the king and the elite at the expense of the farming population were: the new solidarity between the palace and the military aristocracy; the shift of the military class from groups of farmers providing a *corvée* type of service to military specialists; and the role of the palace and the military as main money lenders and acquirers of debt servants. Consequently, the farming population was obliged to incur substantial debts and become debt slaves, without any support from the palace. The ideal of the 'just and fair king' thus left the Late Bronze Age kingship ideology and its propaganda in favour of the ideal of a strong and brave king, who alone on his chariot terrorises the enemy's infantry. Even on a practical socio-economic level, the Late Bronze Age was a much more difficult period than the previous one. Debt slavery visibly increased, causing an equal increase in the amount of slaves trying to escape. A counter-reaction to these flights was the development of a process of capture and return of the escaped slaves. This procedure, however, would eventually bring the Near Eastern communities of the Bronze Age to an end.

Other technological innovations of the period had less of an impact on the political and socio-economic organisation of Late Bronze Age communities, although they are still useful for the understanding of Late Bronze Age culture. Basic architectural and production techniques, from metallurgy to pottery, developed internally without outstanding innovations. New advances were achieved in a sector that could be defined as 'applied chemistry'. In this regard, an interesting case is the development of the production of coloured glass. In the Early Bronze Age, a coloured glaze was used to cover the surface of terracotta objects. Now, however, objects (initially small in size, such as small vases and jewellery) entirely made of glass began to be produced, with sand, natural ashes and mineral dyes fused through various firing stages in the kiln (Text 16.2).

Text 16.2   The first attempts at glassmaking

An instruction text describing how to make glass (Middle Babylonian period, ca. 1600 BC)

'If you want to produce *zagindurû* -coloured (green lapislazuli) glass, you grind finely, separately, ten minas of *immanakku* -stone and 12 minas of *ahussu* -plant (ashes). You mix (these) together, you put (the mixture) into

---

a cold kiln which has four fire openings and arrange (the mixture) in between the four openings. You keep a good and smokeless fire burning. As soon as your mixture glows red, you take it out into the open air and allow it to cool off. You grind it finely again. You collect (the powder) in a clean *dabtu* -pan. You put (it) into a cold chamber kiln. You keep a good and smokeless fire burning. As soon as it glows golden-yellow, you pour it on a kiln-fired brick. (This first stage) is called the *zukû* ("pure" vitreous paste).

Collect ten minas of "slow" copper compound in a clean *dabtu*-pan. You put (it) into a hot chamber kiln. You close the door of the kiln and keep a good and smokeless fire burning until the compound glows red. (Meanwhile) you crush and grind finely ten minas of *zukû* -glass. You open the door of the kiln and throw (the ground glass) upon the copper compound and close the door of the kiln again. As soon as the glass and the copper compound become mixed, and the copper compound settles underneath the glass, you stir it a couple of times with the rake. You pour it inside the fire in a new *ḫaragu* -pan. On the tip of the rake you will see some drops (form). When the glass assumes the colour of ripe (red) grapes, you keep the glass boiling with the copper compound (for a time). You pour it on a kiln-fired brick. (This second stage) is called the *tersītu* ("preparation").

You grind finely, separately, ten minas of *tersītu* -preparation, ten minas of *būṣu* -glass, and sifted *aḫussu* -plant ashes, 2/3 minas of mother-of-pearl (? "sea-white"), and coral. You mix (them) together. You collect (the mixture) in a clean *dabtu* -pan. You put it in a cold kiln which has four fire openings and place it on a stand between the openings. The base of the *dabtu* -pan must not touch the (bottom of the) kiln. You keep a good and smokeless fire burning. The fire should come out of the openings like [. . .]. As soon as your mixture is melted you pull the (burning logs of the) fire apart. You take (the mixture) out of the cold kiln and grind it finely. You collect (the powder) in a clean *dabtu* -pan and put it into a cold chamber kiln. You keep a good and smokeless fire burning. Not until the glass has become red you close the door of the kiln and while it glows yellow you stir it once "towards you". After it has become yellow, and you see some drops (form) and when the glass is homogeneous, pour it in a new *dabtu* -pan and out of the cooled-off kiln emerges *zagindurû* -coloured glass.'

Glass production began as an artificial substitute to semi-precious stones (mainly lapis lazuli), which were difficult to get in this period, due to the crisis of the settlements and commercial networks of the Iranian plateau. This decrease in the availability of semi-precious stones throughout the Near East is attested archaeologically, especially when compared to their spread in the mid-third millennium BC. Texts consequently began to distinguish between the genuine 'mountain lapis lazuli', from the artificial ones, called the 'lapis lazuli of the kiln', or 'boiled lapis lazuli'. The same distinction can be found for a variety of semi-precious stones, all with different colours or a mixture of colours that the various glass pastes tried to imitate. If the genuine stones continued to be of a higher value, the artificial ones became much more widespread in the production of jewellery, seals and small vases, becoming more affordable alternatives.

Coloured dyes were also used on textiles. Apart from mineral and vegetable dyes, there were animal dyes. The most expensive one was purple dye, extracted from shellfish. This type of dye was also linked to the Akkadian term for lapis lazuli (*uqnû*), whose colour could at times be close to purple and at times to a deep red. Another development during this phase was in the production of perfumes and spices, which were at this time used more for healing than for cooking. Perfumes and spices were produced from plants that were sometimes imported from distant lands, providing a new impulse for the commercial networks of the time.

The fact that these innovations were not developed in Lower Mesopotamia, which had been the epicentre of technical advances until then, but in Upper Mesopotamia and Syria, is particularly striking. Horse training was centred in Mitanni, glass working in the area extending from Upper Mesopotamia to the Levant and purple dye in the Lebanese coast. From these original centres, these techniques quickly spread throughout the Near East. Since these were all high quality, refined and expensive techniques, they appealed to the palaces and their elite. This aspect explains the extraordinary pace of their diffusion, which developed through the contacts and exchanges between specialised artisans and royal palaces that would characterise the Late Bronze Age.

However, there was another fundamental way in which innovations began to spread. These were recorded on texts that can be considered *bona fide* treatises. The most ancient and basic techniques were developed well before the invention of writing and were by this point already established and well-known practices. In comparison, new techniques had to be written down, probably as a result of the interaction between specialists and scribes, who had previously only produced 'scientific' texts regarding mathematics or medicine, two important sectors for administrators, or for learned groups of medical practitioners and exorcists.

Now, however, there were treatises on horses, the most famous one being the Hittite text found in Hattusa. This treatise is attributed to a certain Kikkuli from Mitanni, who used the above-mentioned Indo-Iranian terms and phrases. Other treaties on horses have been found in the Middle Assyrian archives from Ashur, while Ugarit provides a number of hippiatric texts. Regarding the production of glass, there are some texts from the Middle Babylonian period, written during the reign of Gulkishar, king of the Sealand (Text 16.2). These texts contained indications of a magical nature, but also retained some concrete, technical information. Following their instructions, it has been possible to produce a glass paste. Finally, the Middle Assyrian archives yielded texts on the production of perfumes and spices. This development was a response to the new needs of the royal courts (or new solutions to old problems), located in the new epicentres of technical advances and commercial interactions, such as Syria, Anatolia and the Jezira. As such, these new types of texts constitute a clear expression of a cultural environment that was increasingly technical and practical, rather than scientific and scholarly.

3 The regional system

The transition from the Middle to the Late Bronze Age was affected by the gradual reduction of the urbanised and settled areas of the Middle Euphrates, Upper Mesopotamia and the Syrian and Transjordan plateaus. This had been a long-term phenomenon following the one already described for the beginning of the second millennium BC. Semi-arid areas, where the great cities of the Early and Middle Bronze Age had flourished, were now abandoned. Their cities were reduced to settlements mainly based on semi-nomadic farming. In the Middle Euphrates, Mari, Tuttul and Terqa experienced a similar decline, alongside Shubat-Enlil and other centres of the Khabur, as well as Ebla and Qatna in Central Syria. In comparison, this decline was not experienced by cities located in areas characterised by high rainfall levels, near rivers, or the sea.

Overall, this phenomenon led to a depopulation of the Near East, though the extent of this differed from area to area. Central and Lower Mesopotamia also experienced a demographic concentration. This was due to the decline of the urban settlements in the Middle Euphrates and the crisis of the area around the Persian Gulf. Consequently, the total amount of inhabitants significantly decreased from the Old Babylonian period to the Kassite period. In the irrigated and urbanised areas, however, agriculture seems to have survived the overall decline. The same can be said regarding Middle Elamite Susiana and maybe even for some of the regions of southern Iran, although these areas must still have suffered from the demographic and power vacuum in the Iranian plateau. In Upper Mesopotamia, depopulation did not affect some areas, in particular the Assyrian Triangle, where the majority of the population was concentrated and managed to grow even further. Also in the Levant, the depopulation of the semi-arid plateaus was opposed by an increased concentration of people in the cities of the valleys and the coast. Consequently, the development of these settlements reached the highest peak of their history.

In Anatolia, only a few cities in the valleys managed to grow significantly, while the remaining mountainous territories remained largely depopulated. Some of these valley settlements, however, experienced a period of crisis compared to the early second millennium BC. The regions surrounding the Near East also experienced considerable changes. Both the Aegean and Egypt saw a demographic and urban growth, while Central Asia and the Indus Valley declined, due to the implications of those movements of people that had begun further west a couple of centuries earlier. Overall, the situation led sedentary states and pastoral groups alike to reinforce their respective political structures. This was a process of differentiation and contraposition that was lacking those former interactions characteristic of the Middle Bronze Age. The reciprocal hostilities between palaces and tribes, then, peaked in the Late Bronze Age.

Another local, yet significant, change was the isolation of Babylonia from long-distance contacts with Syria and Anatolia, as well as Iran and the Persian Gulf. Babylonia thus experienced a significant demographic, economic and military decline, as well as in terms of production, compared to other developing areas. The former central position of Babylonia, which had been a constant from the first urbanisation of the Uruk phase to the reign of Hammurabi, had by now disappeared. The centre of political and commercial activities shifted to the west, along an axis extending from Upper Mesopotamia to the Levant. This area was the focus of the expansionistic interests of the Hittites in the north and the Egyptians of the New Kingdom in the south. Commercial networks with the Mycenaean and Cypriot cultures also began to appear at the expense of interactions with Assyria, Babylonia and Elam.

The former central role of Mesopotamia, then, was substituted by a more balanced distribution of power in the Near East (Figure 16.2), a move that was characteristic of the Late Bronze Age as a whole. This new balance was made of a mosaic of medium-sized states, which held a hegemonic role over the smaller states in their sphere of influence. This process formed a two-level structure. Regional powers remained relatively stable in time (from 1600 to 1200 BC). Starting east, there was Elam, which controlled a large part of the Iranian plateau. Beyond the plateau, the regions located alongside the Gulf and the Indus Valley ceased to be

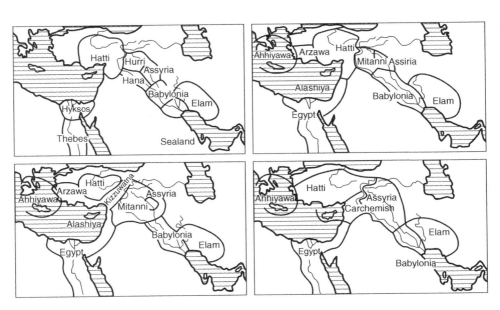

Figure 16.2   Fluctuations in the Near Eastern 'regional system' of the Late Bronze Age. *Above, left*: The formation period, c. 1600 BC; *Below, left*: The hegemony of Egypt and Mitanni, ca. 1450 BC; *Above, right*: The hegemony of Egypt and Hatti, ca. 1350 BC; *Below, right*: The final stage, ca. 1220 BC.

279

involved with the Near East, whose interaction with the area had been fundamental up until the first quarter of the second millennium BC. Then, there was Kassite Babylonia and its unstable control of the Sealand. In Upper Mesopotamia, the supremacy of the Mitannian kingdom was taken over by the Middle-Assyrian kingdom around 1350 BC. The Hittites continued to rule in Anatolia and still held control of the regions in western Anatolia and northern Syria. Finally, in this phase we catch a first glimpse of the regional power of the Mycenaeans, though mainly for commercial purposes; of the island of Cyprus, an important source for copper; and of New Kingdom Egypt, which held control of several Syro-Palestinian states.

This regional system had its original roots in the Amorite Age, when there already were regional states controlling minor states. However, there were two fundamental differences. First, the Late Bronze Age system was more specific in the formalisation of its political interactions and more stable compared to the fleeting hegemonies of the Middle Bronze Age. Second, the system was now enlarged to include formerly marginal regions, such as western Anatolia, Egypt and the Aegean. There were two types of formalisation of political relations: 'horizontal' ones established between powers of equal status; and 'vertical' ones, namely, relations of subordination. Kings of regional states held the title of 'great king' (*šarru rabû*), which technically designated independent rulers who controlled other rulers. The latter held the title of 'small king' (*šarru ṣiḫru*), which defined autonomous but not independent rulers, 'servants' of their 'masters', the great kings. The role of small kings is better understood in the Levant, Upper Mesopotamia and Anatolia. In areas where there had been an established centralisation for centuries these local states were more like administrative units without political autonomy.

Among kings of equal status, especially the great kings, political relations were centred on equality. Despite their demographic, political, military and economic status, which varied in time and space, great kings saw themselves as equals. They defined this equality using a language of 'brotherhood' (*aḫḫūtu*), 'friendship' (*ra'amūtu*) and 'goodness' (*ṭābūtu*). These characteristics responded to an ideology of kinship that owed a great deal to the practice of establishing family relations through a complex network of inter-dynastic marriages. Reciprocity and equality were particularly important features of commercial and diplomatic relations (Text 16.3). Late Bronze Age palaces expressed this sense of reciprocity through gift-exchange and hospitality. Therefore, what had to be done by one party, also had to be done by the other party, just like 'brothers' had to provide for one another, rather than acting selfishly.

Text 16.3   The treaty between Idrimi of Alalah and Pilliya of Kizzuwatna (ca. 1500 BC)

This is a typical example of a treaty of the period, both in terms of its structure (reciprocity expressed through repetitions) and its subject matter (the capture and return of fugitives).

'Tablet of the treaty, when Pilliya and Idrimi swore divine oaths and sealed this treaty. They will return fugitives to each other: Idrimi will seize the fugitives of Pilliya and will return them to Pilliya; Pilliya will seize the fugitives of Idrimi and will return them to Idrimi. Whoever will capture a fugitive, he will return him to his master: if it is a man, (the master) will pay 500 shekels of copper as a ransom, if it is a woman, he will pay 1000 shekels of copper as a ransom. If a fugitive of Pilliya enters the land of Idrimi, and nobody seizes him, but his master seizes him, he shall not pay a ransom to anyone. And if a fugitive of Idrimi enters the land of Pilliya, and nobody seizes him, but his master seizes him, he shall not pay a ransom to anyone. In whichever town they are hiding a fugitive, the town leader and 5 notables will swear divine oaths. The day in which Barattarna will have sworn divine oaths with Idrimi, from that day on the extradition of fugitives will begin. He who will violate the instructions of this tablet, may Teshub, Shumegi, Ishhara (and) all the gods destroy him!'

Statements expressing reciprocity and equality clearly represent the nature of political relations of the time. These can be found in letters with greeting formulas written following the diplomatic etiquette of the time, in formal treaties, featuring a meticulous attention to reciprocity, and in calculations of the value of gifts given and received. In the case of the latter, ideals of generosity, expressed through counter-gifts of higher value, were in marked contrast with the attention great kings paid to maintaining the economic stability of their kingdoms. This issue might have been indelicate to express, but it was nonetheless important.

Even 'vertical' relations were based on specific shared ideas. They followed a precise protocol based on inequality, rather than reciprocity, as was more fitting in the case of relations between a 'servant' and his 'master', rather than between 'brothers'. The dependence of the small king on his master was based on 'loyalty' (*kittu*, a term that in the Old Babylonian period was used to indicate 'justice'). The small king was completely devoted to the great king and tried to serve him in every possible way, with all his heart and without reservations or ambiguities. Everything, from his own person to his wealth and any information at his disposal, had to be offered to his great king. A small king had no way of being released from his obligations, since he could not leave his rank among the other kings and regain his freedom of action. Therefore, his secondary role was based on a forceful play of powers. His only alternative was to betray his master to join another neighbouring master. Similarly, paying tributes to a great king did not constitute an inconvenience, but a necessary choice.

In order to consolidate the fundamental nature of Late Bronze Age political relations as based on exchange, the loyalty and tributes provided by the small kings had to be returned in some way by the great kings. Therefore, great kings guaranteed 'protection' (the verb *naṣāru*), namely, the preservation of the small kings' kingdoms against internal or external attacks. As long they remained loyal, small kings could demand to be allowed to continue their rule and to choose their successors. Another term dramatically used to express this 'vertical' interaction was 'life' (*balāṭu*), since the great king made his loyal small king 'live'. Politically, the great king made him live because he allowed him to rule over his kingdom. Physically, the great king protected him. A rebellion or a betrayal, such as an attempt to change master, was punished with the small king's removal from his throne or even his death.

The network of relations based on loyalty and protection ensured a considerable local stability for the great powers of the Near East, while the network of 'brothers' provided stability for the system as a whole. This stability was also the result of a vast number of breaches of this system of interactions, from internal betrayals and removals of kings from their seat, to the many inter-regional wars. However, these glitches never managed to damage the basic structure of the system. This period therefore becomes a concrete expression of the remarkable proximity between brotherhood and hostility.

Peaceful and normal diplomatic and commercial relations were characterised by a high degree of conflict. Marriage negotiations and commercial calculations seem to have constantly brought relations to the brink of breakdown, although this was often more due to the kings' behaviour than to specific issues. None of the kings wanted to appear too complacent or too submissive. After all, these were not the characteristics of a great ruler. Consequently, negotiations were deliberately protracted in time. This came at the expense of messengers and ambassadors, due to the established practice of keeping them in one's court as a sign of dissatisfaction. The exchange of letters, gifts and women kept political relations alive, especially when they were in process, rather than when they terminated. For this reason, negotiations took a long time and, as soon as they were completed, new ones followed.

Even wars did not require the basic rules of interaction to be removed, but simply new ones to be implemented. Wars were heroic acts, but also ordeals to ascertain who was right. They therefore required a continuation of diplomatic relations (though with a different meaning than the one envisioned by Carl von Clausewitz) through other means. Heroism and ordeals both required kings to follow the rules of equality, without those deceits and ambushes employed by barbarians. Only mountain or desert nomads attacked unannounced, suddenly and at night, or behind someone's back, when an enemy was not ready. Among civilised kings, wars were declared, explaining the ethical and legal causes emphasising that the challenger was right and the enemy a traitor.

Wars were waged through the deployment of armed forces at the time and place agreed upon, with a precise division between who had to attack and who had to defend himself. If the outcome of the battle showed who was right, the defeated enemies, at least the ones belonging to the military aristocracy, could be freed after paying a ransom. The enemies were respected if they had fought correctly and bravely, or despised if they acted in cowardly manner, without following the established rules. Everyone was seen as belonging to the same civilisation and to the same social stratum. Enemies were not barbarians or invaders, but warriors able to win a war through the support of their respective gods. Contempt for inferior peoples was directed towards nomads and mountain people, the latter of whom were considered outside of this civilisation due to their refusal to accept the political hierarchy and rules governing the Near East, and their compensation for their inferiority through deceit.

4 The age of international relations: trade and culture

The increasing separation between palaces and the wider population in the kingdoms of the Late Bronze Age was in contrast to the increasing interaction between royal palaces, which were linked to each other in a series of personal, commercial and cultural relations, creating a stronger international environment than in previous periods. This general tendency led to the development of a concept of social 'caste', indicating that certain individuals were aware of the fact that they belonged to a superior social stratum. This development was shared by different cultural traditions and nationalistic and ethno-centric behaviours. It was expressed through a widespread tendency towards the accumulation of the best products made for the palaces.

The appreciation for beautiful horses, chariots, weapons, clothing, jewellery and perfumes led to the spread of locally produced goods and of a concrete effort to gain the best products directly from the place where they were produced (Figure 16.3). Regarding high-end craftsmanship, it therefore becomes difficult

Figure 16.3   Maritime trade in the Late Bronze Age: Syrian merchant ships unload their goods in an Egyptian harbour (Thebes, tomb n. 162).

to establish the origins of the objects discovered in Late Bronze Age palaces. For instance, chariots found in Egyptian tombs can be attributed to Mitanni or northern Syria thanks to the identification of the types of woods used, rather than the objects' features and style. On the contrary, jewellery and glass are so homogeneous in style throughout the area that establishing their origins remains an extremely difficult task.

This network of communication and exchanges extended as far as Egypt and the Mycenaean world. The far east remained largely marginal in this period. The elitist nature of these interactions made them completely different from the ones attested in the Early and Middle Bronze Age. The system was more centred on royal courts and less on organised groups of merchants, while the former competition between different commercial networks was replaced by a single overarching network. This network was not aimed at undermining rivals from their privileged positions, but at providing a type of exchange designed to increase the prestige of the main political players (that is, the royal courts) in the eyes of the population. Consequently, commercial and diplomatic networks began to overlap. In particular, diplomatic networks took over the high-end and more prestigious side of trade. Naturally, utilitarian exchanges continued to exist and prevailed on a quantitative level, but they were almost entirely concealed on a propagandistic level. Overall, the network was articulated into three sub-systems, namely, the exchange of messages, people and commodities.

The exchange of messages was developed to support the other two sub-systems. In fact, the vast majority of royal correspondence was centred on marriage negotiations, requests of specialists and gift-exchange. However, messages still had an intrinsic value, as demonstrated by letters simply containing greetings and by the importance of formalities in these letters. Despite the cultural differences existing between Babylonia, Egypt, Hatti and Syria, the formulation of an address to a king still had to follow certain international formulas considered to be the correct ones. The Egyptian principle was to address the king simply mentioning the name of the sender and of the receiver. The Near Eastern one focused on rank, so that the name of the more important person had to come before the less important one, or on courtesy, where the name of the receiver preceded the one of the sender. The different combinations of these three principles were highly dependent on etiquette otherwise there would have been serious political consequences.

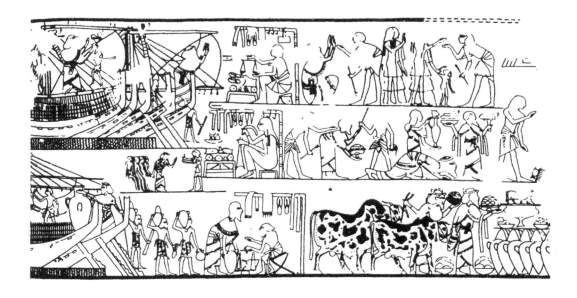

The same can be said about greetings. Among great kings, letters begin with an exchange of wishes and information on the sender's health, from the king himself to his family, the most important officials in his court and even chariots, horses and the entire kingdom. Small kings greeted Egyptian kings with a self-deprecating statement. This was not part of the Egyptian custom and the Egyptians themselves saw it as a typically Near Eastern practice. However, in the Near East, small kings did not greet Hittite or Mitannian kings in this same way, indicating that this type of greeting was developed to address the semi-divine Egyptian king.

Just like in the Mari Age, the *lingua franca* was Akkadian, written in cuneiform. The practice of communicating in Akkadian even reached Cyprus and Egypt and was used as a 'third' language among non-Babylonians. For instance, the small kings of Canaan wrote to the king of Egypt in Akkadian and vice versa and the same happened in their correspondence with the Hittite king. Consequently, bilingual and multilingual lists reappeared. The only difference was that previous examples of these types of texts were developed in already bilingual areas (Sumerian and Akkadian in the third millennium BC; Hurrian and Hittite in Anatolia). Now, however, these texts were used in areas speaking one language, in order to be able to understand the diplomatic language of the time (such as the Egyptian-Akkadian texts from El-Amarna). Alongside these texts, used in scribal schools, there were interpreters used for direct communication. This category of specialist has been attested from as early as the third millennium BC, but by this phase it became much more frequently attested and needed.

This 'international' Akkadian was not particularly consistent. In the better equipped courts, which had probably used Akkadian for a longer period of time, the Akkadian used is generally correct. However, it is still filled with local variations, expressing the Hurrian, Hittite, or Western Semitic origins of the scribes writing the texts. In more marginal areas, which had become part of the system more recently, such as the Levant and Egypt, the influence of the local language had a much stronger influence. This led to the development of several glosses, the incorrect use of verbs, of literary references that made little sense in Akkadian and so on. Finally, as frequently happens in cases such as these, the 'third' language used by people speaking different languages generated serious misunderstandings on the connotations and denotations of words and phrases. This is especially the case with more technical terms, fundamental in any political discourse.

Letters were delivered by messengers, who were more akin to emissaries and ambassadors than simple message-bearers. Their role was not just limited to the physical delivery of the tablet. It required them to be tactful enough when adding the necessary explanations to the negotiation, understanding and responding to the reactions of the receiver. They therefore acted as mediators of an often complex long-distance interaction, constantly kept on the brink of fracture. Emissaries were protected in their journeys through letters of safe-conduct and by the norms of hospitality in foreign courts, where they dined at the king's table and were treated with high regard. However, as soon as a problem arose, emissaries were the first to suffer the consequences. It was common practice for kings to keep them at their court, sometimes for years, in order to put pressure on the other king. Being an emissary was therefore both a prestigious and dangerous role. This difficulty often led these men to request exemptions through documents signed by the king.

The role of messengers and their frequent detention in foreign royal courts is closely connected to the practice of exchanging people in the political relations of the Late Bronze Age. The most important and concrete expression of this practice can be found in the frequent inter-dynastic marriages (Text 16.4). Normally, the practice had to be reciprocal and this is the way it is described in the sources, although the complex network of inter-dynastic marriage was often far from being reciprocal in actuality. For instance, an Egyptian king explicitly proclaimed that he was glad to marry a Near Eastern princess, but that no foreign king could marry Egyptian princesses. In this way, Egyptian kings placed themselves on a superior level compared to the rest of the Near Eastern kings. Even among the latter, however, at least as far as the sources reveal, reciprocity was not practiced. In fact, it seems that princesses only moved in one direction, so that a king who gave a princess in marriage to another king, would in turn receive one from a third king. Consequently, mutual kinship ties between two courts were an exception, rather than a rule.

Text 16.4   Late Bronze Age marriage agreements: a letter of Kadashman-Enlil, king of Babylon, to the Egyptian king Amenhotep III

'Behold, since you, my brother, did not allow your daughter to marry and wrote to me saying: "From of old, a daughter of the king of Egypt has not been given to anyone", (I say): "Why do you speak like this? You are a king; you can do according to your heart's desire. If you give, who shall say anything?" When they had told me this, I wrote to my brother as follows: "(In your land) there are grown up daughters and beautiful women. Send me any beautiful woman, as if she were your daughter. Who shall say: She is not a king's daughter?! But you have not sent anyone at all. Did you not seek brotherhood and friendship? Just like you wrote to me to (arrange) a marriage, so that we be nearer related to one another, so I wrote to you for this same reason, for brotherhood and friendship, so that we be nearer to one another through marriage. My brother, why did you not send me a woman? Perhaps, since you have not sent me a woman, should I deny you a woman, thus behaving like you? No! There are daughters of mine, and I shall not deny them to you. [. . .] Regarding the gold for which I have written to you, send me gold, as much as there is, in large quantities, before your envoy comes to me, now, immediately, this summer, in the month of Tammuz or the month of Ab, so that I may finish the work I have begun. If you, during this summer, in the month of Tammuz or the month of Ab, will send me the gold for which I have written to you, I shall give you my daughter: but you, please, send me the gold accordingly. If, however, you will not send the gold in the month of Tammuz or the month of Ab, I will not be able to finish the work I have begun. I beg of you: why should you send me (the gold) once I have completed the work I have begun? Why would I want gold? Even if you sent me 3000 talents (= 90 tons!) of gold, I would not accept it, I would send them back and I would not give you my daughter in marriage.'

Initial negotiations were filled with enthusiasm and willingness in engaging into an inter-dynastic marriage, only to be followed by complaints about problems and delays in the process. Admittedly, a certain degree of quarrel was fundamental to the maintenance of diplomatic relations, but inter-dynastic marriages presented three specific difficulties. First, there was the issue of the value of the dowry, marriage gifts and counter-gifts, which made marriage negotiations very similar to economic transactions. The second issue concerned rank: there was a fundamental difference between providing a princess who would eventually become queen and one who would become just another woman in a large royal harem. The third issue was the fate of the princesses that had already been given in marriage to foreign courts, who tended to be lost without a trace. Moreover, there was a concrete realisation that the prestige and political interest expected from the marriage never appeared afterwards.

All these negotiations shared several common features, such as the role of the protagonists of the negotiations. The king requiring a bride was generally insistent and aggressive, while the father of the bride was complacent but meticulous. The bride became a passive participant, almost like a beautiful object. Each court had its own matrimonial strategy. The Egyptian one was to acquire Near Eastern princesses, to express the centrality and superiority of Egypt. The Babylonian strategy was to give princesses to the Egyptian kings in exchange for gold. The Hittite strategy was to seal a network of kinship ties for strictly political reasons, in order to mark a preliminary intervention, a guarantee of loyalty, or at the beginning of an alliance.

Inter-dynastic marriages were an influential channel for acculturation, maybe even more influential than their participants imagined. The impact of a second-ranking wife, who lived in a harem as living proof of the power of her new husband, was completely different from that of a queen who would mother the king's successor. Therefore, the link between the queen and the successor to the throne was a very delicate issue, due to its potential political implications. From a more general perspective, foreign wives had a strong influence on the education of their sons, the cultural climate of the court, the introduction of new deities and the kings' decisions.

Apart from princesses and emissaries, specialists were often requested by foreign kings and they were sent to foreign courts with a combination of pride and worry. This is because they promoted the spread of specialised knowledge from court to court. Specialists were required from regions known for a specific expertise. Naturally, this gave an enormous sense of pride to the kings providing these individuals. However, foreign kings could keep the specialists for an extended period of time, at times without ever letting them return home. This could be a cause for concern for the kings who sent the specialists. Physicians and exorcists were requested from Egypt, while musicians, sculptors and specialised craftsmen circulated throughout the Near East. The formerly redistributive system attested in the Mari archives originated from the local shortage and frequent movement of specialists within the same kingdom. In the Late Bronze Age, it was replaced by a reciprocal system, which responded to the kings' interest in acquiring foreign specialists. These could be experts in new and prestigious techniques, often inaccessible otherwise.

An extreme example of a request for a specialist was the request for a healing deity. The latter was delivered in the form of a cultic statue, which had to be returned. Even Egypt, which sent human physicians, requested the statue of Ishtar of Nineveh. Another indication of this practice is the case of the statue of Marduk, which had been 'deported' by the Hittites, Assyrians and Elamites. To justify this, the sources would say (as a result of a pious pretence of his priesthood) that the god wanted to travel to those foreign lands and extend the radius of his beneficial influence, following the example of other healing deities.

Finally, there was the third sub-system, gift-exchange, one of the paramount types of commercial exchange of the Late Bronze Age. The exchange of gifts between kings opened the way for new commercial networks and in a way the gifts themselves were effectively commercial in nature. The commercial networks available at the time are relatively obvious (Figure 16.4). Egypt mainly provided gold, as well as ebony, carved ivory and other typically African goods. Babylonia (or rather, through the mediation of Babylonia) provided lapis lazuli, while Hatti had silver. Mitanni and Syria provided chariots, horses, weaponry and glass. Finally, the Syrian coast had wool and purple dye.

This 'code' of behaviour had its intrinsic value. The careful calculation of the value of gifts and counter-gifts were hidden behind declarations of selflessness, generosity and joy in giving rather than receiving, and of a desire to please one another. Gifts had to be personal, made on special occasions and could only be requested to face particular needs. Naturally, these were all just pretexts, repeated over the years and inherited by the kings' successors in case of prolonged negotiations. The formality of the interaction therefore had to be maintained at all costs and it was unacceptable to greedily request gifts without a concrete reason or, rather, a pretext. If, in the case of equal exchanges, gifts concealed (or emphasised) trade, in the case of unequal exchanges gifts concealed (or emphasised) tributes. The terminology and nature of the sources clearly show an attempt to conceal tributes in the form of gifts. The only difference was that these so-called gifts were established beforehand and that the counter-gift was not material. The latter fell into that category of life and protection provided by the great king to his subjects.

The distinction, however, between equal and unequal relations and thus between tributes and trade, could have been quite ambiguous and one-sided. For instance, Egypt and its Near Eastern contacts maintained an ambiguous type of relation with one another. In the realm of international relations, the Egyptian king accepted not only the formalities surrounding gifts, but also the implications of reciprocity and of the need for the counter-gifts to be of equal value. Nonetheless, when addressing his own subjects about the arrival of exotic goods from foreign lands, the Egyptian king openly described them as tributes, concealing the fact that he had to provide counter-gifts and act in a reciprocal manner. The king therefore advertised these gifts as a result and proof of the superiority of Egypt on an international level. There was a radical difference between the way in which political relations were pursued and the way in which they were presented to the population. When comparing a letter or a treaty with a celebratory inscription, it is

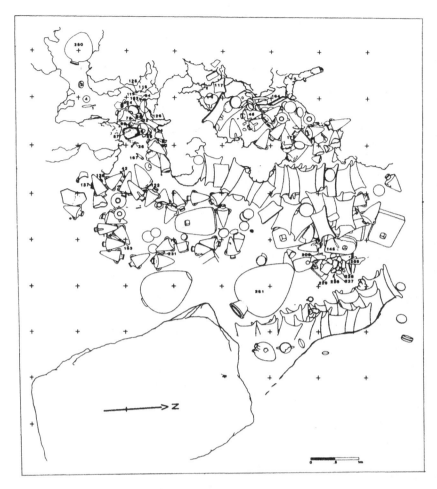

Figure 16.4   Metal trade in the Late Bronze Age: copper and tin ingots, amphorae, and other materials found in the shipwreck of Ulu Burun (fourteenth century BC), near Kaş (Turkey).

almost impossible to believe that they are presenting the same episodes. This is because their presentation and interpretation of the events and the relations between the two parties appear to have been completely different.

However, not all interactions took place between royal courts or were presented in contrasting ways. Trade between merchants was stipulated through contracts completely lacking ceremonial formalities. In this case, there was a pressing need to establish equivalences between various systems of weight and value. This allowed merchants to trade in regions that counted the same goods in different ways or simply used a different measuring system. The presence of foreign merchants was at times relatively conspicuous and permanent, giving the impression that these individuals lived in proper colonies. For instance, the concentration of Cypriot and Mycenaean pottery in the harbour of Ugarit has led to the belief that there was a nucleus of Aegean merchants in the city (Figure 16.5). Similarly, sources attest to the conspicuous presence of merchants from Ugarit in Cyprus. Political developments had a strong impact on these types of concentrations. Consequently, the Mycenaean merchants in Ugarit came from an elusive and distant political

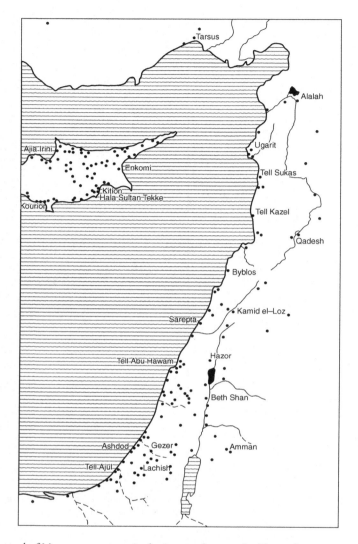

Figure 16.5 The spread of Mycenaean pottery in the Levant, fourteenth–thirteenth century BC.

power and could only count on their abilities and goods. On the contrary, Hittite merchants, sometimes emissaries of great kings to whom the small king had to swear allegiance and obedience, could trade in a much stronger position. They could thus establish a financial influence that could have jeopardised the interests of the king of Ugarit.

Politics and trade were therefore closely connected, both in ceremonial and official contexts and in trade itself. The possibility for merchants to travel along a certain commercial route was hindered by the presence of political borders, since no one could cross them without the consent of the local ruler. Therefore, despite the great kings' interest in expanding their network of contacts at the expense of other kings, interactions were effectively blocked or at least mediated by neighbouring states. The system of regional jurisdiction thus led to intense commercial interactions. However, it extended over relatively short distances, due to the difficulties encountered in crossing neighbouring states.

The strict regional jurisdiction also had some positive effects. The great king was responsible for the safety of merchants and messengers crossing his territories on behalf of his colleague. Specifically, each small king was accountable to his great king for everything that happened in his kingdom. In turn, each village was accountable for whatever happened in its surroundings to its king. Killings of merchants or robberies of caravans were very frequent. The palace supervision over settled areas still left caravans crossing large portions of land (especially semi-arid and mountainous areas) at the mercy of nomadic attacks. Even the crossing of cultivated areas was not without considerable risks, due to the considerable distance between palaces and villages.

The wealth of goods carried by mercantile caravans was such as to encourage assaults, especially by the poorer farmers and shepherds, but the palace was unable to prevent or solve the problem. The only way to keep commercial networks up and running was to take on the responsibility to take care of the problem, each ruler acting in his local sphere of influence. This procedure followed the horizontal and vertical ranks that characterised the period and through it victims were compensated for their misadventures and their losses by the palaces, which would punish the village where the accident took place, without ever trying to find the culprits. Therefore, compared to the Old Assyrian trade, Late Bronze Age trade not only had a different socio-political value, but was also far more dangerous. The subconscious decision of palaces to separate themselves from the population thus led to several problems. In fact, the palaces' exploitation of villages was compensated by the 'taxation' imposed by farmers and shepherds on caravans.

17

THE RISE OF MITANNI

1 The Mitannian kingdom: structure and history

From as early as the mid-third millennium BC, Upper Mesopotamia had experienced the development of a series of Hurrian city-states and several attempts at political unification, from the kings of Urkish and Nawar to the empire of Shamshi-Adad. However, by the end of the seventeenth century BC, the region was finally unified under a single kingdom. The latter was defined in the sources as Mitanni (or Mittani/Maitani), its political name, as Hurri, which refers to the name of its people, or as Hanigalbat, the name of the region (Figure 17.1). Even before 1600 BC, in Hattusili I's annals, the Hurrians who invaded Anatolia appear as a politically unified group (the Akkadian version uses Hanigalbat, the geographic term). Similarly, the Hurrians fighting the Hittites in northern Syria were considered a distinct political entity.

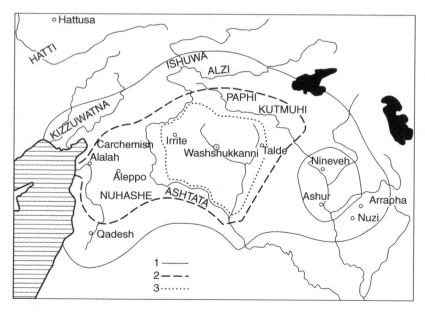

Figure 17.1   Map of the kingdom of Mitanni (1: maximum expansion of Barattarna; 2: territories held by Tushratta; 3: territories held by Shattiwaza).

At the heart of the unification of the Hurrians to form the kingdom of Mitanni there was the Indo-Iranian wave linked to the introduction of the horse-drawn chariot. Even the personal names used by the royal family of Mitanni are consistently Indo-Iranian, as if these rulers were consciously associating their names with the greatest military innovation of the time. Prior to the rise of Mitanni, no Indo-Iranian names are attested in the Near East and this trend would eventually fade with the decline of this kingdom. In this phase, then, the chariot spread quickly in the Near East, and was already used by both sides in the Syro-Hittite wars of Hattusili I. The military victories of the Old Hittite kings in Syria, which effectively ended the supremacy of Yamhad, constituted another fundamental factor in the rise of the Mitannian kingdom. The Hittites had been unable to fill the power vacuum created by the fall of Yamhad. Consequently, they quickly lost control over the area south of the Taurus. In this way, Mitanni, which had previously opposed the Hittites and supported the north Syrian states, took advantage of the fall of Yamhad. The rising kingdom invaded the whole region and reached the Mediterranean coast. To the east, the profound crisis of Assyria that followed Ishme-Dagan's reign allowed Mitanni to establish its control over the area, reaching as far as the eastern side of the Tigris.

At the centre of this vast kingdom there was the capital of Mitanni, Washshukkanni, located in modern Tell Fekheriye, near Ras el- 'Ain, at the source of the Khabur River. This *tell* has a vast rectangular city, with a wall that could have been built at the end of the Middle Bronze Age. Previous levels have not survived, indicating that the city was built in this phase as the capital of the new Mitannian kingdom. Unfortunately, the Mitannian levels are submerged in the groundwater beneath the *tell* and are therefore difficult to excavate. The Mitannian kings ruling in the fifteenth century BC continued to use the seal of a king Shuttarna, son of Kirta. It is therefore possible to identify this ruler as the founder of the dynasty and its capital, and as the one who first unified the region. However, we do not possess any more information on the formation of the Mitannian kingdom prior to the mid-sixteenth century BC.

From the sixteenth century BC onwards, we possess a certain amount of information. The latter mainly comes from kingdoms dependent on the Mitannians, such as Alalah in the far west, Nuzi in the far east, or even from other kingdoms, such as Hatti, Egypt and, later on, Assyria (Table 17.1). The Nuzi evidence provides information on Hurrian society and its economy in the Mitannian phase. The texts from Alalah (Level IV) provide important information on the political structure of Mitanni and its relations with its vassals. The inscription of Idrimi, king of Alalah, was written on a statue found under the floor of a temple. It narrates how Idrimi, a son of a king of Aleppo who had lost his throne after an internal revolt, became king of Alalah. Prior to the rebellion against Idrimi's father, Aleppo controlled a vast territory. However, after Idrimi's adventure, an unknown usurper ruled the city. Consequently, Idrimi took over the throne of the kingdom of Mukish, whose capital was Alalah. In order to consolidate his position, Idrimi had to gain the support of Barattarna, king of Mitanni, who controlled the entire area. The great king of Mitanni and the small king of Alalah therefore sealed a treaty.

Under Barattarna, Mitannian control had successfully reached the south. When the Egyptian kings of the eighteenth dynasty expanded in the Levant, the most important kingdoms of Central Syria, Qadesh and Tunip, sought the support of the Mitannian king against the Egyptians. Barattarna is also attested in Nuzi, indicating that during his reign Mitanni had already reached its maximum extension. Barrattarna was probably a contemporary of Tuthmosis I, the Egyptian king who reached the Euphrates, trespassing into Mitannian territories. However, the Egyptian incursions were short-lived and each time they retreated Mitanni promptly regained control over the area.

Two generations later, the situation was still the same, with Niqmepa, king of Alalah, ruling as a vassal of the Mitannian king Shaushtatar. The latter was a contemporary of Tuthmosis III and therefore had to face the Egyptian military expansion at its height. The constant and successful campaigns of this Egyptian king reached Ugarit, along the coast, and Qadesh, in the Orontes Valley. However, Mitanni still held control over Central and northern Syria. Niqmepa sealed several treaties with other powerful states within the Mitannian sphere of influence, such as Tunip in the south and Kizzuwatna in the north.

Table 17.1 Anatolia, Syria, Upper Mesopotamia, ca. 1600–1350 BC

	Hatti	Kizzuwatna	Alalah	Mitanni
1600	Mursili I a ca. 1620–1590		ca.1600: destruction of level VII a	ca.1620: beginning of the kingdom of Mitanni
	Hantili I			Kirta (?)
	Zidanta I		level VI ca. 1600–1540	Shuttarna I (?)
	Ammuna	ca.1550: beginning of the kingdom of Kizzuwatna		»
	Huzziya I		level V	»
	Telipinu b	Ishputahshu b	ca. 1540–1480	
1500	Tahurwaili c	Eheya c		»
	Alluwanna		ca. 1480: beginning of	»
	Hantili II	Paddatishshu	level IV	»
	Zidanta II d	Pilhiya de	Idrimi ef	Barattarna
	Huzziya II			Parshatatar
	Tudhaliya I	Shunashshura g	Niqmepa gh	
	Hattusili II	ca. 1400: end of the kingdom of Kizzuwatna	Ilim-ilimma II	Shaushtatar h
1400				Artatama I
	Tudhaliya II		»	Shuttarna II
	Arnuwanda I		»	(Artashumara)
	Tudhaliya III		»	
	Suppiluliuma I il ca. 1370–1342		Itur-Addu i	Tushratta I ca.1375–1350
1350				

a—a= attested contemporaneity.

Shaushtatar was also involved in several successful conflicts against Assyria and managed to establish some sort of control over the area. We know that the Mitannian king took away some precious gold and silver doors from Ashur as booty for his own city. Having established Mitanni's frontier with Egypt, Shaushtatar's reign marks the peak of Mitannian supremacy. Assyria and Kizzuwatna, formerly great powers, were reduced to mere vassals, equal to the smaller Syrian states. Considering the contemporary Hittite and Kassite crisis, Mitanni became one of the most powerful states in the Near East. Moreover, it became the only power able to face the ever-increasing Egyptian military expansion in the Levant.

Relations between Egypt and Mitanni, which had been hostile for over a century (from the mid-sixteenth to the mid-fifteenth century BC), suddenly changed. The frontier established in Syria satisfied both parties. This was partly because it was becoming increasingly difficult for both to move beyond this point. Moreover, both parties were probably content with the tributes they received from the states within their respective territories. The Mitannian dynasty and the Egyptian dynasty (which by now had become less interested in a military expansion) began to arrange inter-dynastic marriages and began to regularly exchange gifts, envoys and letters. Marriages, however, were only arranged in one direction. A daughter of Artatama I married Tuthmosis IV, a daughter of Shuttarna II married Amenhotep III, and Tushratta's daughter married Amenhotep IV.

This situation was highly advantageous for Egypt. Its bridgehead in Syria and the Levant guaranteed the protection of the Egyptian border, and brought Near Eastern goods as tributes to Egypt. It also allowed matrimonial, commercial and political interactions between Egyptian rulers and the great kings of the Near East. These measures confirmed the centrality and superiority of Egypt in the political milieu of the time. Egypt's alliance with Mitanni, and the support of its army, ensured that the northern border of Egypt was safe.

Even for Mitanni the security of its southern frontier and its alliance with Egypt constituted an advantage, allowing the kingdom to concentrate on the turbulent Anatolian front. There, Kizzuwatna acted as a buffer zone between Mitanni and Hatti. The Hittites were therefore blocked beyond the natural barrier of the Taurus, but were always ready to promptly regain control over the former territories of the Old Hittite kingdom. There were considerable fluctuations in the relations between Mitanni and Hatti. Kizzuwatna itself was eventually lost to the Hittites, but overall Mitanni kept a solid, and often hegemonic, position, at least up until the accession of Suppiluliuma to the Hittite throne.

At this point, from a Mitannian point of view the situation was still under control. Tushratta managed to successfully defeat one of the first Hittite incursions and even sent part of his booty to Egypt. In fact, the Amarna archive indicates that Tushratta was heavily involved in marriage negotiations and the exchange of gifts and letters with the Egyptian king. The second Hittite attack was sudden and arrived on an unexpected front. Instead of crossing Kizzuwatna, the Hittite king crossed the Euphrates further north, in the kingdom of Ishuwa, and descended straight to Washshukkanni. Tushratta refused to face the Hittites in the battlefield and instead stayed inside the capital.

From then on, Tushratta lost control over the following moves of the Hittite army. The latter marched on to Syria, conquering all the Mitannian vassal states, and stopped on the Upper Orontes, at the Egyptian frontier. Ugarit and Amurru, formerly under Egyptian control, 'spontaneously' submitted to the rising Hittites. Meanwhile, Tushratta was killed, and replaced by Artatama II, who was supported by the Hittites. However, this king immediately submitted to the Assyrians, who had taken advantage of the Mitannian crisis to regain power. Consequently, the Hittites began to support the Mitannian Shattiwaza, who had sought refuge in the Hittite court and was now the son-in-law of the Hittite king. As a pawn in the wider Hittite scheme, Shattiwaza attempted to regain control over Mitanni. An expedition led by Shattiwaza and Suppiluliuma's son Piyashshili, king of Carchemish, removed Artatama from the Mitannian throne and the Assyrian control of the region.

In this way, the penultimate phase of Mitannian history began. Shattiwaza's subordination to Hatti forced him to give up the territories on the western side of the Euphrates to Carchemish. This was mainly as a sign of gratitude towards Piyashshili for his role in Shattiwaza's rise on the Mitannian throne. The Mitannian king also had to give up the aspirations and attributes of a great king. However, Hatti still respected the former prestige of Mitanni. This phase of Hittite dependence did not last long. The Assyrian kings (as we will see more in detail later on) began repeatedly to attack Mitanni. The Hittites were unable to hold their position effectively. This is because the Assyrians were better placed for sending troops into Upper Mesopotamia than were the Hittites. The Assyrian army was in fact able to use those roads formerly employed for military and commercial interactions with that region. Consequently, the Hittite presence in the area was forced to gradually step down and retreat to the other side of the Euphrates. The last chapter of Mitannian history therefore began with its conquest by the Assyrians, who would eventually annex the area in the thirteenth century BC.

In its three centuries of supremacy in the Near East, apart from successfully unifying the marginalised Hurrian groups settled in Upper Mesopotamia, Mitanni provided an important contribution to the structure of the region. However, due to the lack of direct evidence from the area, it is still difficult to establish with precision the degree of this contribution. It appears that Mitanni was responsible for the introduction of chariots and horses, which eventually became a fundamental part of Near Eastern societies. Moreover, Mitanni seems to have played a crucial role in the creation of the military aristocracy of the *maryannu*, whose diffusion roughly coincided with the Mitannian sphere of influence. However, without the archives from Washshukkanni we are unable to establish and fully appreciate the Mitannian contribution to the cultural and political structure of the time. Nonetheless, the spread of Hurrian elements in Syria and Anatolia, where they would survive even after the fall of the independent kingdom of Mitanni, was a direct consequence of Mitannian supremacy and socio-political influence.

2 Nuzi and Mitannian society

Due to the lack of evidence from the centre of the Mitannian kingdom, we have to reconstruct Hurrian society and economy in the fifteenth century BC from the texts found in the Syrian city of Alalah (level IV), and in Nuzi (Yorghan Tepe), east of the Euphrates (Figure 17.2). In both cities, society was structured in relation to its proximity to the palace. The administrative structure of Alalah is fairly clear. The population

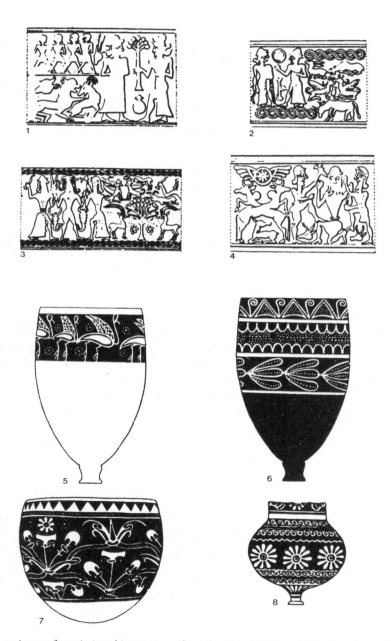

Figure 17.2   Mitannian artefacts: 1–4: seal impressions (from the Kirkuk tablets); 5–8: palace pottery from Alalah.

was divided into four categories: the *maryannu*, the military elite of charioteers; the *eḥele*, lower ranking palace functionaries; the *ḥupšu*, free farmers; the *haniaḥḥu*, poorer farmers. For each village, the state administration knew the number of members belonging to each class and the names of the heads of households who had to provide certain services and tributes.

Nuzi society had a similar structure, although its legal documentation is more focused on specific issues and problems. The city of Nuzi was not large. A palace and some private households occupied a large portion of the city. Nuzi was a rural administrative centre. Therefore, in the hierarchic structure of the time, it was a third-class settlement. The city was part of the kingdom of Arrapha (modern Kirkuk), which had a king and a royal palace. In turn, Arrapha depended on the great king of Mitanni. Mitanni/Hanigalbat is mentioned in the Nuzi texts as a distant entity from which messengers and other palace guests arrived, as well as horses, armour and specific types of clothes. However, Nuzi functionaries were rarely required to travel to Mitanni. Similarly, the king of Arrapha is rarely mentioned in the texts. This indicates that the Nuzi archives are fairly local in nature.

The tablets from the palace and the temple area are mainly concerned with the economic issues of the central administration. These were, for instance, the storage and distribution of military equipment (weapons, armour and horses), textile production, and the management of the palace's lands. Alongside lands belonging to the palace, there were lands allotted to palace functionaries in exchange for their services. However, the majority of lands were generally privately owned by families. Similarly, the majority of sources from Nuzi do not come from the palace archives, but from private archives. These belonged to wealthier citizens, actively involved in the acquisition and management of properties.

The archives concern the whole territory of Nuzi, made of villages grouped into districts (*dimtu*) and separated by pasturelands and uncultivated areas. Agriculture partly relied on irrigation, but was predominantly rainfed. The Nuzi texts provide considerable information on cultivation, from yields (generally on a ratio of 1:5 to 1:8, with a theoretical 1:10 ratio used in legal clauses) to the shape and dimension of fields (similar to the ones found in Lower Mesopotamia), the various crops cultivated, transhumance and so on. The vast majority of texts, however, are mainly concerned with the legal and economic relations of Nuzi society. The latter had reached a state of advanced disintegration, with an increasing separation of families and lands, labour and ownership. The class of small owners of family lands, generally living in village communities, formed the main part of Nuzi society. This class was experiencing a profound debt crisis. One measure implemented to cope with this debt crisis was interest loans (50 per cent). These were usually stipulated on an annual basis and repaid from the harvests. Another measure was the personal loan (*tidennūtu*), repaid through one's service (in the form of prolonged slavery, although not for life) or pledging one's land (Text 17.1a). Failed repayments must have been frequent, since interest loans were already difficult to repay. The third measure was the selling of one's land. However, the former owners, now disowned, generally tended to stay on their lands as farmers working for the new owners.

Text 17.1 Three legal contracts from Nuzi

a) Loan contract with personal antichretic guarantee (tidennūtu)

'*Tidennūtu* tablet of Tehip-tilla, son of Puhi-shenni. Halu-shenni, son of Shattu-kewe, has taken 8 *imērū* of barley and in return of the barley his son Ar-tidi will reside for 8 years in the house of Tehip-tilla. When the 8 years are over, Halu-shenni will return the 8 *imērū* of barley and will take his son. If he (Ar-tidi) will leave the work of Tehip-tilla for a single day, he will pay a mina of copper per day. If Ar-tidi dies, (Tehip-tilla) will take another son of Halu-shenni. If Halu-shenni will not respect the agreements, he shall pay 1 mina of silver. (10 witnesses). These are the men who gave the barley. (4 seals).'

b) *Real estate adoption* (tuppi mārūti)

'The adoption tablet with which Wur-Teshub, son of Akip-tashenni, has adopted Tarmi-tilla, son of Shukri-tilla. As his share of the inheritance, he has given Tarmi-tilla 9 *aweḫari* (ca. 1 hectare) of land in the rural district of Birishanni of PN, to the east of the field of Tiesh-urhe, to the north of the field of the same Tiesh-urhe, to the south of the field of Zike, to the west of the road leading to the rural district of Nawiya. On his behalf, Tarmi-tilla, has given Wur-Teshub 4 *imērū* (= 270 litres) of barley as gift. Wur-Teshub will take over the *corvée* for the field. If the field will become the object of a dispute, Wur-Teshub will release it and hand it over to Tarmi-tilla. Whoever will not fulfil the agreement, he will have to pay 1 mina of silver and 1 mina of gold. This tablet was written after the agreement, in Nuzi, at the entrance gate. (7 witnesses, 7 seals).'

c) *Lawsuit for defamation*

'Akawatil, son of Wullu, appeared in a lawsuit before the judges against Akkul-enni, son of Mush-teya. Thus (spoke) Akawatil: "Akkul-enni said to me: You are full of leprosy!" The judges questioned Akkul-enni and he (declared): "I did not say that". So the judges said to Akawatil: "Bring your witnesses (who saw) that Akkul-enni said to you that you are full of leprosy!" Akawatil brought PN_1, PN_2, PN_3: the three witnesses of Akawatil presented before the judges. This is their declaration: "Akkul-enni said the following to Akawatil: You are full of leprosy! Do not come close to me!" So the judges sent these three men, PN_4, PN_5, PN_6 – three legal officials – together with Akkul-enni so that he may "lift up the gods" (that is, performed an oath ritual to free himself from the accusation); but Akkul-enni turned away from the gods. Akawatil won the case, and the judges condemned Akkul-enni to pay 1 ox to Akawatil. (3 seals, name of the scribe).'

Regarding this third stage, the standard practice in Nuzi was to disguise this transaction as an adoption: either as a transfer from father to son (*marūtu*; Text 17.1b), or, less frequently, between brothers (*aḫḫūtu*). The adopted gave the adopter a 'gift', namely, the price of the land. In turn, the adopter ensured the adopted a share of the inheritance. The latter could have been partial if there were other sons (the new brothers of the adopted person), or even total. Apart from this sort of legal fiction, there was a concrete loan provided by the adopted to the adopter. This was returned later on, after the death of the adopter, when the inheritance was divided. The fictitious character of these adoptions is not only visible from the payment of the gift (or, rather, the price), but also from the fact that there were many adopters, usually small landowners, and few adopted individuals, generally wealthy landowners. The most famous of these, a certain Tehip-tilla, was adopted by his debtors around a hundred times. He therefore acquired thousands of hectares of land. The reason for the creation of this fiction is clear. These lands formerly belonged to private families that could not dispose of these lands freely, since they were obliged to keep them within the family. However, the gradual breakdown of economic and family relations led to the creation of these fictitious adoptions. In this way, it became possible to bypass those scruples opposing the spread of land sales. The practice, also attested elsewhere, became so widespread in Nuzi that it had a devastating impact on the entire system.

Nuzi also provides evidence for actual adoptions, which can be recognised from the inclusion of a number of specific clauses. Just like elsewhere in the Near East, real adoptions were not meant to find a family for an orphan child unable to survive on his own. On the contrary, the adopted was usually a self-sufficient adult, while the adopters were generally old and without descendants. The adopters were therefore forced to adopt someone that could take care of them for the remaining part of their lives. Real adoptions clearly paved the way for the fictitious ones. In both cases, the adopters received a support, be it a 'gift' (in the fictitious adoptions) or food and clothes until their death (in the case of real adoptions), which could only be repaid by pledging their inheritance.

However, despite the similarities, the two types of adoptions had completely different implications on a personal level. This is particularly noticeable in a number of clauses attested in the sources. In case of real adoptions, the adopted took over the duties of a biological son. Therefore, he had to take care of his new parents, respect them while they were alive, mourn them after their death, look for them if they disappeared, and so on. The 'fake' adopted was not responsible for any of these duties, since the latter had been paid for through his 'gift' or loan. Therefore, he just had to wait until he could receive his adopters' inheritance.

The same can be said about public duties. Private landowners had to provide a *corvée* (*ilku*) type of service to the palace. This service could vary from occasional military service to agricultural duties on the palace lands, and other types of work which the palace might have needed. In the adoption contracts it is often specified that the *ilku* had to be provided by the adopter and not the adopted. In fact, Tehip-tilla could not have provided a *corvée* service on behalf of hundreds of adopters. Moreover, unless otherwise specified, the adopters normally continued to work on their lands. The change of ownership, then, would only have taken place after they had died.

An external observer analysing the management of land in Nuzi might get the impression that these adoptions had little impact on the system. After all, the same people cultivated fields and property continued to be parcelled out for heirs, while the palace continued to receive tributes and services. The real change actually took place on an ownership level, since land began to be owned by a small portion of society. The palace had long ceased to emanate edicts aimed at solving the problem of debt slavery, which meant that the incidence of such labour was now growing without any means to control it. The fact that Tehip-tilla, a landowner and adoptive son by profession, and the 'king's son' Shilwa-Teshub, living in the palace, belonged to the same class meant that they shared the same economic interests. These interests were also shared by all the *maryannu* and the other members of the aristocracy. In this way, an aristocracy that was ideologically 'military', actually became a landowning class.

The situation was no worse in Nuzi than in other kingdoms. Many fugitives from Akkad (that is, from the Babylonian kingdom) and elsewhere even sought refuge in Nuzi. These people had lost everything in their native countries, becoming servants without lands, and had preferred to escape. However, they did not find a better situation in Nuzi and were forced to sign contracts of self-enslavement, promising to work for a landowner in exchange of a life annuity. Personal relations were therefore economically regulated. Those coping mechanisms formerly implemented by families and village communities had by now become impracticable. Kings, for their part, had ceased to play the fatherly role of the 'good shepherd'. They became an integral part of that elite group taking advantage of the difficulties encountered by farmers, thus significantly increasing their wealth and power.

Even among the judiciary corruption was spreading (Text 17.1c). An entertaining legal text records how a mayor of Nuzi had taken advantage of his role by accepting bribes. Reading the text it becomes evident that the practice of bribing officials to take care of a matter was not just common, but even considered legitimate. The illegitimacy of the case was not that the mayor had received a bribe, but that he had not done what he was paid to do. It is therefore clear that there was a parallelism between a 'gift' given in order to be adopted or looked after, and a 'bribe' paid to obtain a favour from the authorities. Likewise, there are considerable similarities between the documents specifying that Tehip-tilla did not have to mourn his deceased adoptive parents, and those accusing the mayor of not having done the favours in exchange of which he accepted bribes.

3 Kizzuwatna and the Hittite Middle Kingdom

In the two centuries of Mitannian supremacy in Upper Mesopotamia, Anatolia remained politically divided and went through several complex political developments. Unfortunately, the available documentation only allows a partial reconstruction of these complex events. Therefore, there are still several problems in the reconstruction of the chronology and dynastic sequences of the time. We know that, between the unification of Anatolia under Mursili I and Suppiluliuma, the Hittite kingdom constituted only one of the many states of Anatolia. The latter were constantly competing and sealing alliances with each other. The Edict of Telipinu explains that the crisis following the death of Mursili I was the reason for the development of internal problems, and that the intervention of the king resolved them. However, these rivalries, which already existed at the time of Hattusili I and Mursili I, were not terminated by the reforms of Telipinu. The competition within the Hittite court was an endemic phenomenon, characterised by regicides and usurpations. Apart from this internal instability, the success of the Hittite state depended on its relations with other states, which also experienced a series of crises and recoveries.

Mursili's usurper and successor, Hantili, had a long and active reign, albeit one with considerable difficulties. He fought Mitanni along the Euphrates (from Tegarama, west of Malatya, to Carchemish), fortified several cities and the Hittite capital itself. To the north-east, Hantili had to face for the first time a turbulent mountain population, the Kaska. They destroyed cities and sanctuaries from Nerikka to Tiliura, making Hittite control difficult across the Pontus and threatening Hatti itself. However, the crisis peaked under Ammuna. According to Telipinu, this king murdered his father to seize the Hittite throne and was therefore punished by the gods. During his reign, Hatti faced several internal problems, such as poor harvests and attacks from the Kaska. Because Ammuna's army was unable to oppose the attacks, the Hittites lost control over many territories.

In south-western Anatolia, Arzawa, a kingdom that had already been difficult to control in the Old Hittite kingdom, finally became independent. Similarly, Cilicia, in south-eastern Anatolia, was unified as the independent kingdom of Kizzuwatna. This predominantly Luwian kingdom, with clear Hurrian and Indo-Iranian influences, became a buffer state between Hatti and Mitanni. Consequently, Kizzuwatna's size and authority made this state a power equal to both Hatti and Mitanni. Even for Telipinu, relations with Kizzuwatna constituted one of the main problems of his reign. The reason for this was that the Hittites were refusing to give up on their expansionistic ambitions in the south-east. Initially, Telipinu led several campaigns to Hashshum and Lawazantiya, interfering with the sphere of influence of Kizzuwatna. However, he eventually sealed an alliance with Ishputahshu, king of Kizzuwatna. This king clearly considered himself equal to the kings of Hatti and Mitanni. On a seal found in the city of Tarsus the latter held the title of great king, implying a total independence from both Hatti and Mitanni.

Telipinu is best known for his Edict, which reformed the rules for succession to the Hittite throne (Text 17.2). According to Telipinu, the internal problems of the Hittite state were caused by the lawlessness of the royal succession. The king therefore decided to put an end to the recent problems, to return to the unity and solidarity characterising the early history of Hatti, and to regulate the rules of succession. In reality, Telipinu himself was a usurper, involved in the murder of the previous king. Therefore, his proposal to set new rules for succession was aimed at defending his unstable position and avoiding conspiracies, which had threatened every king before him. In order to be accepted as rightful ruler, Telipinu reminded his court that: regicides had been common in the Hittite court; that the entire elite had been involved; and that it was time to put an end to all the revenges and conspiracies. Therefore, the 'reform' of Hittite royal succession was simply a formalisation of what was already done in practice: the first candidate to the throne was a first ranking prince, then there were the second ranking sons, and then the sons-in-law. It was the same system that had previously encouraged sons-in-law to kill the kings' sons in order to seize the throne. After Telipinu's reign, these dynastic conspiracies not only continued, but became even worse.

Text 17.2   From the Edict of Telipinu: the model and anti-model of kingship

'Thus Tabarna Telipinu, Great King. Once Labarna was Great King, and his sons, his brothers, his in-laws, and the men of his clan and his soldiers were united. The land was small, but wherever he went to wage war he held with (his) arm the lands of the conquered enemies. He destroyed region after region, gained control over lands, and conquered lands as far as the frontier of the sea. Whenever he returned from his campaigns, each of his sons was sent to each of the (conquered) lands: Hupishna, Tuwanuwa, Nenasha, Landa, Zallara, Parshuhanda, Lushna – they governed the various regions and the great cities were nourished with maternal milk.

Then, Hattusili reigned: also his sons, his brothers, his in-laws, and the men of his clan and his soldiers were united. Wherever he went to wage war, he also held with (his) arm the lands of the conquered enemies. He destroyed region after region, gained control over lands, and conquered lands as far as the frontier of the sea. Whenever he returned from his campaigns, each of his sons was sent to each of the (conquered) lands, and also in his hand the great cities were nourished with maternal milk. However, when the servants of the princes became rotten, they began to devour their houses, began to constantly plot against their overlords, and began to shed an increasing amount of blood.

When Mursili reigned in Hattusa, also his sons, his brothers, his in-laws, and the men of his clan and his soldiers were united: he held with (his) arm the lands of the conquered enemies, gained control over lands, and conquered lands as far as the frontier of the sea. He fought against Aleppo, destroyed Aleppo, and brought the population of Aleppo and their possessions back to Hattusa. Then he fought against Babylon, destroyed Babylon, defeated the Hurrians, and he brought back to Hattusa the population of Babylon and its possessions.

Hantili was a cup-bearer, he had the sister of Mursili as his wife. Zidanta rose up with Hantili and they pursued an evil action: they killed Mursili and shed blood . . . When Hantili was old and was about to become a god, Zidanta killed Piseni, the son of Hantili, together with his sons, and he also killed his most important servants. Zidanta became king, but the gods sought revenge for the blood of Piseni: the gods made his son Ammuna his enemy, and he killed his father Zidanta . . . The blood of the Great Clan expanded, queen Istapariya died, and then also the crown-prince Ammuna died. The men of the gods were saying: "Behold, in Hattusa blood has spread!"

Then, I, Telipinu, called the assembly in Hattusa: "In the future, may there be no one harming the son of the (royal) clan. May there be no one drawing a knife on him! May only a prince of the first rank become king. If there is no son of the first rank, may a second rank son become king. If there is no male heir, may the husband of a first rank daughter become king. In the future, to whoever will become king after me, may his brothers, his sons, his in-laws, and the men of his clan and his soldiers be united, and so he will be able to hold with (his) arm the lands of the (conquered) enemies!"'

The most effective and credible part of the Edict of Telipinu can be found at the end of the text. This part is concerned with the reform of lands owned by the elite in exchange for their service to the palace. According to Telipinu, in a land partly destroyed by invasions (from the Kaska to other enemies) and inadequate defences, and partly afflicted by internal conspiracies, many estates had fallen into the hands of 'servants'. The latter took advantage of the murderers owning the estates and their subsequent convictions. During Telipinu's reign, land grants for palace functionaries, already common in the Middle Hittite kingdom, significantly increased. These were allotments guaranteed by the royal seal and by the solemn statement of the inalterability of royal decisions (Figure 17.3). Moreover, these land grants were in fact definitive and based on loyalty, rather than on the actual performance of the service. In this way, the king effectively placed the entire elite under his authority, bringing forward the overall process of unification

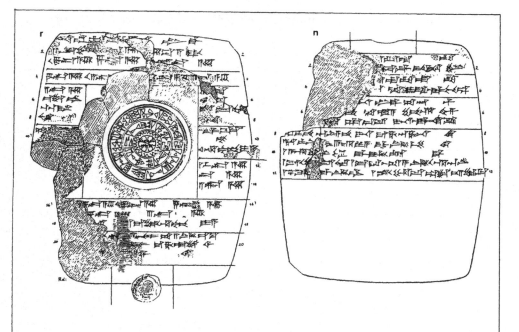

recto
List of the allotted lands, with their size and characteristics.

verso
Gift formula:
1 [LUGAL.GAL *IŠ-ŠI-MA A-NA* ᵐ*a*] *t-ta-at-ta*
2 [...................*A-na* N] *Ì.BA-ŠU ID-DI-IN*
3 [*UR-RA-AM ŠE-E-RA-AM A-N*]*A* ᵐ*at-ta-at-ta*
4 [*A-NA* DUMUᴹᴱˢ-*ŠU MA-AM-MA-*] *A-AN LA I-RA-AG-GU-UM*
5 [*A-WA-AT ta-ba-ar-*]*na* LUGAL.GAL *ŠA* AN.BAR
6 [*ŠA LA-A NA-A-DI-A-*]*AM ŠA ŠE-BI-RI-IM*
7 [*ŠA UŠ-PA-A*] *Ḫ-ḪU* SAG.DU-*SÚ I-NA-AK-KI-SÚ*

"[(all of this) the great king has taken and given to A]ttata [...a]s a gift.
[In the future no]one [will be able to] contend this against Attata [and his sons].
[The words of Tabar]na, great king, [are] iron;
[they cannot be cast] off and cannot be broken.
He who alters [them] will have his head cut off."

Cuneiform label of the seal (in the middle of the recto):

Outer circle   ᴺᴬ4KIŠIB *ta-ba-ar-na* LUGAL GAL *ḫu-uz-zi-ya*
Inner circle   *ŠA A-WA-TE*⁽ʔ⁾ *UŠ-PA-AḪ-ḪU* BA.ÚŠ

Figure 17.3 Land grant of the Hittite king Huzziya II, fifteenth century BC.

and consolidation that begun under Hattusili I. However, it is important to bear in mind that Telipinu's contribution to this process is more significant as a source than as an exceptional (and actual) contribution to the development of the Hittite state.

After Telipinu, and throughout the first half of the fifteenth century BC, the Hittite crisis continued unchanged. The kingdom remained weak, and suffered from the pressure of the Kaska in the north. Moreover, Hatti was surrounded by a network of independent states of equal power and size, from Arzawa to Kizzuwatna and Mitanni. Within Hatti itself, the dynastic sequence for this period is uncertain. The only available source, the royal lists of ancestors found in the cultic texts of the imperial period, contains several gaps and even inversions. For instance, king Tahurwaili, attested in an important treaty, does not appear in these lists. This indicates that the latter were edited following later ideals of legitimacy or for other reasons.

Similarly, we have some evidence on the dynastic sequence of the kingdom of Kizzuwatna. A Shunashshura was a contemporary of Niqmepa, king of Alalah, and both were subjects of king Shaushtatar of Mitanni. Then, there is an entire sequence of treaties between Hatti and Kizzuwatna, whose chronological order relies heavily on the Hittite dynastic sequence. However, it is sure that Pilliya was a contemporary of the Hittite king, Zidanta II. Eheya was a contemporary of Tahurwaili, and Paddatishshu was a contemporary of an unknown Hittite king. These treaties regulated borders and the extradition of refugees, which was a central issue in the political relations of the period. Just like the treaty between Pilliya and Idrimi, the agreements between Hatti and Kizzuwatna were reciprocal, with clauses repeated for both parties and a particular emphasis on the equal status of the two rulers.

Around 1450 BC, Hatti revived its military and political ambitions. This altered the balance of power between the various independent states of Anatolia that had characterised the first half of the century. The main protagonist of this revival was Tudhaliya, conventionally considered to be Tudhaliya II, but probably the first ruler with this name. In the dynastic lists, this ruler was married to queen Nikkal-mati. She is attested in a number of fragments of annals, which provide important information on this phase. Tudhaliya led a successful campaign in Arzawa in his first regnal year, in Ashshuwa (in western Anatolia) in his second year, against the Kaska in his third year, and in Ishuwa in his fourth year.

During his reign, Hatti became a power superior to both Kizzuwatna and Aleppo. While Kizzuwatna was submitted via treaties, Aleppo was successfully conquered. These feats had strong implications on Hatti's relations with Mitanni. The conquest of Kizzuwatna is well attested in the treaty between Tudhaliya and Shunashshura. This agreement continued the long tradition of sealing treaties among equals to express a new type of relation, namely, that of submission of one party to the other. This submission was presented diplomatically, without a request for tributes and with an emphasis on the prestige and authority of a kingdom (Kizzuwatna) that had a glorious and independent past as a major power in the area. However, this apparent respect does not conceal the actual submission of Kizzuwatna to Hatti. This was a mere prelude to the eventual annexation of the kingdom to the Hittite state shortly after. Even the historical introduction of the treaty was extremely tactful in presenting the events preceding the treaty in a way that appeared as a 'liberation' for Shunashshura. Nonetheless, the treaty clearly stated that the former equal status of Kizzuwatna was now ended and that its role was now that of a mere pawn between Hittite and Hurrian relations.

Regarding the conquest of northern Syria, already attested in a later treaty, the discovery of the texts from Tell Munbaqa (Ekalte), on the Middle Euphrates, can be now dated to the reign of Tudhaliya. Alongside these important successes, the reigns of Tudhaliya and his successor Arnuwanda I (whose queen was, according to the lists, Ashmu-Nikkal) encountered serious difficulties in controlling the far east (such as in the case of the Hittite vassal Mita in Pahhuwa) and especially the south-west (with king Madduwatta of Arzawa). The west, from Arzawa to Alashiya/Cyprus, experienced several revolts supported by the kings or leaders of Ahhiyawa, namely, the Mycenaeans. In its sudden expansion, the Hittite Middle Kingdom did not manage to consolidate control in its periphery. In the latter, there still were strong independent tendencies, different strategies, and hostile coalitions against the Hittites. This phase was therefore characterised by intense military endeavours, unstable alliances and sudden changes in political and diplomatic relations.

The reigns of Tudhaliya and Arnuwanda were fundamental for the consolidation of the Hittite state. They therefore constituted the culmination of a long path towards the political and administrative unification of the Hittite state, formerly rooted on the political fragmentation of Anatolia. In particular, during Arnuwanda's reign, many texts providing 'instructions' to royal functionaries, oaths for the troops, and treaties establishing subordinate relations within the Hittite state were composed. The entire system was in fact based on oaths of loyalty, and on loyalty as a fundamental aspect of behaviour. This ideal formed a system that could only be kept under control through a complex network of personal relations. It is almost as if the entire state were a large family, kept together through kinship ties, but constantly threatened by ambitions, betrayals and plots. Instructions and oaths would become a fundamental part of the relations between the Hittite ruler and his subjects even later on. However, it is important to understand that Tudhaliya and Arnuwanda were the rulers who successfully managed to shape and consolidate this system.

Not long after the reigns of Tudhaliya and Arnuwanda, Aleppo and Kizzuwatna were lost to the Mitannians during the reign of Hattusili II. Similarly, the western Anatolian states reclaimed their independence, which meant that the heart of Hatti was under threat from every direction. A later text recounting this phase of Hittite history attests that Arzawa conquered the Konya plain, while further enemies from the south-east conquered Kizzuwatna. Moreover, Ishuwa invaded Malatya, Hayasha invaded the Upper Lands and the religious centre of Samuha. Finally, the Kaska attacked and burned Hattusa.

The entire period remains difficult to reconstruct. Later sources often listed as contemporaneous events that actually happened at different moments in time, with various implications and duration. At the same time, sources emphasising the effectiveness of the Hittite intervention do not contribute to a more accurate reconstruction of this phase. The 'Deeds of Suppiluliuma', written in the reign of Mursili II, begins with the wars that the young soon-to-be king had fought during his father's reign (Tudhaliya III). The Hittite troops seem to have been engaged in difficult campaigns without definite outcomes. They fought the Kaska in the north and the treacherous and 'barbarian' people of Hayasha in the north-east. The latter lived in a mountainous land that was difficult to cross. This was the situation around 1400 BC, with the Hittites being threatened in the heart of their state and fighting the mountain populations in the north. Kizzuwatna was under Mitannian control, while Arzawa controlled western Anatolia and became part of the wider network of international relations through its correspondence with the Egyptian king Amenhotep III.

18
THE HITTITE EMPIRE

1 Suppiluliuma and the empire's formation

When Suppiluliuma became king of Hatti, taking advantage of the death of the chosen heir to the throne (his brother, Tudhaliya), the kingdom's situation was precarious. During his father's reign, Suppiluliuma had led several campaigns in the north against Hayasha and the Kaska. The young king incessantly continued his military campaigns for about twenty years, at least according to later sources. This relatively obscure phase of Hittite history played a fundamental role in the development of the Hittite state (Figure 18.1). Before venturing into more ambitious endeavours, it was necessary to face the Kaska, who were too close a threat for the Hittite capital, and to deal with the tribes living in the Anatolian highlands.

While they dealt with the Kaska militarily, the Hittites managed to come to an agreement with Hayasha. This agreement was sealed through the marriage of Suppiluliuma's daughter with the king of Hayasha. The

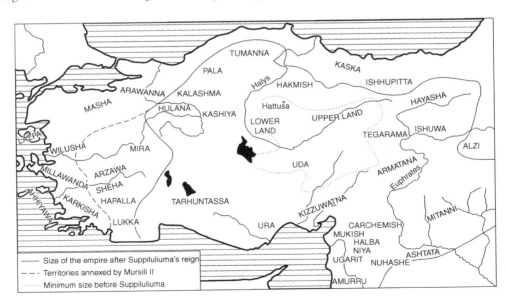

Figure 18.1   Map of the Hittite empire, fourteenth–thirteenth century BC.

303

treaty was, however, atypical and marked by the constant worry about the 'barbarian' customs of Hayasha. These concerns not only could have tainted the reputation of the Hittite princess, but also her political role, making the agreement rather pointless. Hayasha was a kingdom in Anatolia of marginal importance. However, it had a crucial strategic position, able to prevent the campaigns against the Kaska. Hayasha also provided access to Ishuwa (on the Upper Euphrates), a region through which the Hittite kingdom could reach Mitanni. Ishuwa, located in the Keban and now submerged by a dam, was partly subject to Hatti's authority. Nonetheless, the usual problems of expatriation, trespassing and raids made relations between the two very difficult. Further south, Kizzuwatna, a 'protectorate' during the reign of Tudhaliya II, was now fully annexed to the Hittite state. The role played by Suppiluliuma in this regard remains unattested, but we know the outcome: the Hittite state fully controlled the area extending from the Euphrates to the Amanus and the Mediterranean.

By establishing his position in the Pontus regions, the Hittite king had managed to consolidate his kingdom enough to get involved in more expansionistic ventures. Consequently, once interests in western Anatolia (Arzawa) were cast aside, this talented and ambitious Hittite ruler was able to focus on Mitanni and Syria. This interest could have been motivated by the remote (under Mursili I) and more recent (Tudhaliya II) history of Hittite control over the area, and by the crucial role of this territory in the international relations of the period. Therefore, the only way for Hatti to become a great power in the Near East and overcome its marginal position was to participate in the Syro-Mesopotamian interactions, forging relations with Egypt and Babylonia.

In this regard, scholars have often overestimated the significance of a victory against the Hittites boasted by the Mitannian king Tushratta in a letter to the king of Egypt. It is possible that both sides trespassed and raided each other's territories without the direct involvement of their rulers. One gets the impression that during the twenty years spent fighting in Anatolia, Suppiluliuma had already developed an interest in Syrian affairs, though more diplomatically than militarily. Due to the loyalty of Mitanni's Syrian vassals (Carchemish, Aleppo, Mukish, Nuhashe and Qatna) to their lord Tushratta, Suppiluliuma forged relations with two vassal kings under Egyptian control. These two vassals were interested in breaking free from their ties with Egypt and in gaining independence. As a result, the neighbouring states denounced the betrayal of Aziru, king of Amurru, and Aitakama, king of Qadesh, to the Egyptian king.

Suppiluliuma's ambitious military campaign led him from the Euphrates to Lebanon 'in one year'. It was undoubtedly a sudden military intervention, but by no means improvised. The Hittite king had already managed to seal alliances to support other candidates to the throne within the royal families of both Mitanni and at least one Syrian kingdom, Nuhashe. These agreements thus acted as pretexts for military interventions. The Hittite army began in the north and crossed the Euphrates at Ishuwa. From there, they descended towards the enemy's capital, Washshukkanni. Tushratta refused to face the Hittite army and remained within his capital's walls. Through the support of Suppiluliuma, the Mitannian, Artatama II, soon replaced Tushratta. However, the new king subsequently became involved in the grander scheme of the emerging Assyrian king, Ashur-uballit. At this point, Suppiluliuma left Mitanni and focused on Syria. The vassals still loyal to Mitanni fiercely opposed the king's expansion, but the latter could rely on the support of Amurru and Ugarit. The Hittite army defeated all his enemies, crossed the Orontes Valley, reached Qatna and Qadesh, and stopped there in order not to interfere too much with the Egyptian sphere of influence. After all, the campaign had been already too long and the Hittite military bases were too far.

For six years, Suppiluliuma remained in Syria to consolidate his conquests. In this regard, there were three main problems. The first was to make sure that the former Egyptian vassals, who had not been conquered militarily, understood that there was no space for independence. Consequently, Amurru, Ugarit and Qadesh became Hittite vassals, equal to the former Mitannian vassal states. To force them to submit, however, Suppiluliuma had to resort to his army, replacing the dynasties ruling these vassal states. The second problem was purely military: Hatti had to conquer the last cities standing in its way while defending itself from Mitannian attacks. Military control was consolidated through the siege and conquest of Carchemish, the last city able to resist thanks to its strategic position along the Euphrates. The third problem was to keep

Egypt at bay. In fact, Egypt was increasingly worried by the loss of its vassals in the north, and of the arrival of the ambitious Suppiluliuma in place of Tushratta, who had been an ally of the Egyptian king.

Some battles between Hatti and Egypt took place, but Suppiluliuma's expansion was facilitated by Egypt's internal crisis. The latter was linked to the end of the 'heretic' cult of the Aten, the return of the court to Thebes, and the revival of the cult of Amun. At the peak of Suppiluliuma's interventions in Syria (that is, the siege of Carchemish), the widow of Amenhotep IV (Tutankhamun, for some scholars, despite the chronological problems) wrote to the Hittite king to marry one of his sons. This request was clearly against the interests of the Egyptian court at Thebes, which was trying to regain control in Egypt. Despite the initial hesitation, Suppiluliuma agreed to send a son, who was killed en route. The Hittite reaction was violent and resulted in a couple of fights at Beqa, near Damascus. This episode benefited the consolidation of the Hittite position in Syria, effectively justifying the Hittite conquest of Egyptian territories and the establishment of a Hittite border extending from the source of the Orontes to Lebanon.

The conquered states received different treatments. Suppiluliuma appointed two of his sons as kings in two important cities: Aleppo, for its prestige; and Carchemish, for its strategic position. The two kings settled in these cities with a large retinue of Hittite functionaries. The enthronement of Telipinu in Aleppo was aimed at containing the ambitions of a city that had previously held a hegemonic position in Syria and that was still respected by the Hittites. This contrasted with the appointment of Piyashshili in Carchemish which was predominantly aimed at creating a Hittite base in northern Syria. This position would allow an area to be kept under control, which was otherwise too distant from Hattusa (in case of sudden attacks from that front). The first and most important occasion in which Piyashshili had to prove his role as Hittite viceroy in Syria was the expedition that defeated the Mitannian king, Artatama II in favour of Shattiwaza. Carchemish's location in the Middle Euphrates therefore made it the centre of the newly conquered territories which extended from Mitanni to Syria.

In the other cities conquered by Hatti, local kings were kept in place. The rulers of states that deliberately surrendered to the Hittites and contributed to their success (such as Amurru and Ugarit), had to pledge their loyalty to Suppiluliuma and pay tributes in order to keep their thrones. The states that opposed the Hittites, however, saw the appointment of new pro-Hittite rulers, who were chosen from among the members of the local royal families. This different treatment of states did not affect inter-state relations. In both cases, states had to become Hittite vassals and pay tributes. Personal enmities and loyalties were punished or rewarded through the removal of, or the permission to keep, one's throne. Overall, however, the submission of a 'small kingdom' always followed the same pattern. In this way, the Hittite king took over the legacy of the Mitannian king he had defeated and part of the Egyptian legacy, without any dramatic changes for the smaller states of the area.

Soon after these conquests and the political and legal consolidation of power (that is, the selection of rulers and the stipulation of treaties), Suppiluliuma died. After thirty years of constant campaigns, he left a remarkably larger kingdom than the one he had inherited. This kingdom, however, was also extremely exhausted, both in terms of energy and resources. In this regard, the pestilence that spread throughout Anatolia, brought by soldiers and war prisoners from Syria, is only one representative symptom of an exhausted state. The maintenance and consolidation of Suppiluliuma's conquests (or their loss and the subsequent reduction of the kingdom) was hanging by a thread and constituted a great responsibility for Suppiluliuma's successors.

2 The Hittite empire

Shortly after the death of Suppiluliuma, his successor, Arnuwanda II, also died. The young Mursili II ascended the throne, but found himself in a difficult situation. The king reports upheavals in all the lands conquered by his father. In fact, these states clearly doubted Mursili's ability to subdue them once again. Within Hatti, the pestilence had not just physically hindered the land, but had also harmed its overall morale. It was believed that such a divine punishment must have had an original cause, to be found in the reign of Suppiluliuma. Even on a personal level, it is possible that such a strong, yet largely absent, father figure must have had an impact on his young successor.

Therefore, on the one hand, Mursili began an intense military campaign, almost to prove to his subjects that he was no less than his father. On the other hand, Mursili questioned himself and the gods on the cause of the pestilence, and on the sins supposedly committed by his father. Perhaps, the latter had failed to perform some of his cultic duties due to his campaigns, or just broke an oath for political reasons. Be that as it may, Suppiluliuma had left an empire that was as vast as it was infested with pestilence. Mursili wanted to be both heroic and pious, and attributed all his successes to Ishtar, his protector. We also owe to Mursili the redaction of his annals in two versions, the Ten Year Annals (Text 18.1) and the Detailed Annals, as well as the account of the deeds of his father Suppiluliuma.

Text 18.1 Hittite historiography: from the Ten Year Annals of Mursili II (years 6 and 7)

'The following year I went into the land of Zihariya. The Kaska, who had occupied Mount Tarikarimu by force during the reign of my father, had become a threat to Hattusa: they came and attacked Hattusa, and caused severe damage. I, His Majesty, went and attacked the Kaska that had conquered Mount Tarikarimu; the Sun-goddess of Arinna, my lady, the mighty Tarhunta, my lord, Mezzulla and all the gods marched before me: I defeated the Kaska of Mount Tarikarimu, I destroyed them, I laid waste to Mount Tarikarimu, and devastated with fire the entire region of Zihariya; then, I returned to Hattusa. I did this in one year.

The following year I went to the land of Tipiya. While my father was in the land of Mitanni, Pihuniya, a man of Tipiya, began to march and pursued several incursions in the Upper Land, he reached Zazisha, took up the Upper Land, and deported it to the land of Kaska; he conquered the entire land of Ishtitina and turned it into land for his pastures. Moreover, Pihuniya did not rule in the Kaskean manner: among the Kaska one man did not hold power alone, but all of a sudden that Pihuniya began to rule like a king. I, His Majesty, went to him, I sent him a messenger and wrote to him: "Send me my subjects that you took and deported among the Kaska!" But Pihuniya answered thusly: "I will not give anything back to you! And if you will wage war against me, I will not prepare for battle in my land: I will march against you in your territory and will prepare for battle against you in your territory!" When Pihuniya answered me in this way and did not return my subjects, I marched against him and attacked his territory; the Sun-goddess Arinna, my lady, the mighty Tarhunta, Mezzulla and all the gods marched before me: I conquered the entire land of Tipiya and destroyed it with fire, I captured Pihuniya and deported him to Hattusa. Then, I returned to the land of Tipiya and restored the region of Ishtitina that Pihuniya had taken, and turned it once again into the land of Hattusa.'

Apart from the endemic turbulence of the Kaska, Mursili had to engage on two fronts, namely, Syria and Arzawa. Thankfully, not all recently conquered Syrian states were rebelling. After all, Hittite control was left in the hands of Mursili's brothers, Telipinu, king of Aleppo, and Piyashshili, king of Carchemish. While the former brother died prematurely, the latter, who had already proved his abilities in his conquest of Mitanni, acted as the real leader of the Hittite resistance. The Syrian rebellion began in Nuhashe and Qadesh, reaching Ugarit, but not Amurru. The king of Amurru, Aziru, actually remained loyal to the Hittites, and so did his son.

On their part, the Egyptians tried to take advantage of the upheavals in Syria. The new Egyptian king Horemheb campaigned in the north, fought against the Hittites, but had to retreat. Despite the death of some of the most important players in Syria, from Aziru to Piyashshili, Mursili managed to consolidate Hittite control once again. He appointed new functionaries in Syria and signed a series of treaties. We possess the treaties signed with Talmi-Sharruma of Aleppo, Niqmepa of Ugarit and Duppi-Teshub of Amurru.

Carchemish, the main stronghold of Hittite control in Syria, received a considerable amount of territories, from the ancient kingdom of Mukish to Siyannu, south of Ugarit.

In Arzawa the situation was different. Suppiluliuma had never managed to establish solid control in the area, even though Hatti's supremacy was effectively recognised throughout Anatolia. Mursili therefore had to face a composite state. Arzawa, ruled by Uhha-ziti, held a hegemonic position over the other kingdoms of south-eastern Anatolia: Mira, Kuwaliya, Hapalla and the Land of the Sheha River. Mursili thus moved his troops towards the Aegean Sea, forced Uhha-ziti to flee, accepted the surrender of some states, and conquered the others. In the end, Mursili was able to consolidate control over the area through a series of treaties (similar to the ones stipulated in Syria) with Manapa-Tarhunta of Sheha, Mashhuiluwa of Mira-Kuwaliya, and Targashnalli of Hapalla. In the second half of Mursili's reign, however, Mashhuiluwa betrayed him. This forced Mursili to lead new campaigns and sign treaties with new vassals. However, Hittite control over Arzawa remained solid.

At the end of Mursili's reign, Central and southern Anatolia, from the Aegean to the Euphrates, was under Hittite control, either directly or through its vassals, linked to the empire through treaties. However, the Pontus and the Black Sea coast remained unconquered and a constant worry for the Hittites. Admittedly, it was a predominantly mountainous area, largely uninhabited and not technologically advanced. Nonetheless, the proximity of this turbulent area to the Hittite capital Hattusa was still threatening. The loss of control over prestigious sanctuaries in the north, Nerikka in particular, was also a problem for the empire. Moreover, the constant intrusions of the Kaska and the shift of the main political interests of the Hittites to the south had made the capital relatively marginal and thus exposed to attacks.

Mursili's son and successor, Muwatalli, tried to formalise the complex management of the empire. Control over the northern territories and the border with the Kaska was delegated to his brother, Hattusili. He held the title of king of Hakpish and ruled over Pala (in north-western Anatolia), Kaska, and the 'Upper Lands' (in the Upper Halys area). Hattusili led a war against the Kaska until the liberation of Nerikka and other sanctuaries, and the removal of potential threats to Hattusa. At the peak of the war, Muwatalli abandoned the capital. He moved his court to Tarhuntassa, further south, and got involved in the events taking place beyond the Taurus Mountains.

In fact, the beginning of the thirteenth century BC saw the revival of Assyria's and Egypt's expansionistic campaigns. Under Adad-nirari I and Shalmaneser I, Assyria immediately conquered Mitanni/Hanigalbat and, despite Hittite intervention, managed to consolidate its control over the region. As a result, the Euphrates became the frontier between Hatti and Assyria, and Carchemish, formerly chosen to be at the centre of the Hittite territories south of the Taurus, now became the stronghold of the Hittite border with Assyria, a position that the city would keep for a long time. Even Egypt revived its campaigns in the Near East under the kings of the nineteenth dynasty. Seti I and Ramses II both tried to move north to remove Qadesh and the Upper Orontes Valley from Hittite control. Despite its celebration in his inscriptions, Seti's attempt did not have a concrete outcome. On the contrary, Ramses II's campaign had been more solid, relying on the betrayal of the king of Amurru, Benteshina, in favour of Egypt. Muwatalli fiercely reacted to this betrayal and faced Egypt in battle. Ramses II arrived north with a large army, clashed with the Hittite army at Qadesh, and had to retreat, leaving Amurru to the Hittites. The border was kept south of Qadesh, despite the fact that the Hittite counter-attack moved as far as Damascus.

When Muwatalli died, the bipartition of the Hittite state caused several dynastic problems. Hattusili wanted at least to keep control over the northern territories, and perhaps hoped to be able to influence his young nephew, Urhi-Teshub, son and successor of Muwatalli. However, Urhi-Teshub could not accept the supremacy of his uncle and tried to keep him under control, even moving the Hittite capital back to Hattusa. Hattusili rebelled and, with the support of many members of the elite and several vassals, faced his nephew in war, seizing the throne and exiling Urhi-Teshub to Syria and then Egypt. This move truly was a *coup d'état*, which the usurper (yet another one in the history of Hatti) justified through his Apology. This text pointed out Urhi-Teshub's illegitimate claim to the throne, since he was a 'bastard son', and his arrogance. However, these were more Hattusili's 'sins', rather than his nephew's. Moreover, the text describes the divine support and omens used to justify Hattusili's claim to the throne. The latter was described as legitimate simply because it succeeded not just on a political level, through the support of the elite and Hattusili's military victories, but even on a theological level. Considering the fact that the gods had allowed a 'small king' to succeed a 'great king', how could Hattusili's claim not have been legitimate?

Having seized the throne, Hattusili tried to defend himself from the branch of the royal family that had been damaged by his usurpation. He gave the kingdom of Tarhuntassa to one of Urhi-Teshub's brothers, Ulmi-Teshub (whose throne name was Kurunta), who had supported his uncle during the civil war. Tarhuntassa was a vast kingdom, extending from the salt lakes' area to the Mediterranean coast. It received a privileged status, comparable to the one of Carchemish. Hattusili's rise to power also drastically changed the kingdom's foreign affairs. Hattusili reinstated Benteshina, who meanwhile had become his son-in-law, on Amurru's throne. Moreover, the Hittite king took advantage of Egypt's reduced involvement in the Near East. In fact, after the outcome of the battle of Qadesh, Ramses II seems to have been more interested in celebrating his achievements within Egypt (Figure 18.2), than in pushing his border in Syria a couple of kilometres to the north.

Hattusili and Ramses therefore sealed a friendly alliance, which envisioned the two empires as equal, and used Hittite diplomatic formulas (completely unknown to the Egyptians). This peaceful treaty constitutes a real success for Hattusili. He achieved that formal equality considered unacceptable for the eighteenth dynasty kings during Suppiluliuma's reign, barely a century earlier. The alliance was further strengthened by the marriage of Ramses II with a daughter (or maybe two) of Hattusili. This gesture gave the Egyptian king the opportunity to celebrate within Egypt his apparent supremacy in the Near East. At the same time, it assured the Hittites that the border in Syria was now established, and that normal commercial and diplomatic interactions were to substitute former expansionistic attempts. With regards to relations between Hatti and Babylonia, a letter of Hattusili to the young Kassite king, Kadashman-Enlil, begins with a paternalistic and protective attitude towards the Babylonian king. The letter then moves on to examine a series of commercial and political controversies.

Problems with Assyria mainly arose with the reign of Hattusili's son and successor, Tudhaliya IV. The situation had become increasingly tense after the Assyrian conquest of Hanigalbat and the consolidation of the frontier between Hatti and Assyria along the Euphrates in the reign of Tukulti-Ninurta I. The two empires were therefore at war. Amurru was forbidden to allow merchants (both local and foreign, especially Mycenaean merchants from Ahhiyawa) to reach Assyria. Ugarit was exempted from sending troops in aid of the war against Assyria in exchange for a large tribute. Hatti mobilised large military contingents and economic contributions to face the Assyrians in war. However, both armies were too strong to move beyond the Euphrates frontier. Contentious letters were exchanged, and important battles were fought. Especially in Assyria, there was a concrete attempt at celebrating their military achievements, in order to compensate for the lack of definitive outcomes. Unlike the fictitious propaganda attested in Egypt and Assyria, Hatti did not need to take such measures. After all, preventing the expansionistic attempts of its two powerful neighbours constituted an achievement in itself. Further wars were fought by Tudhaliya in the Mediterranean. He first led an expedition to Cyprus, recounted by his son when he returned to the island. He then sealed diplomatic alliances in order to cease the revolts (supported by the Mycenaeans) taking place on the Aegean coast of Anatolia. These revolts are attested in the so-called 'Letter of Milawata'. The Hittites were therefore facing threats on several fronts, but for the time being managed to resist.

Internally, Tudhaliya was suffering the consequences of his father's usurpation, and tried to protect himself from his subjects' betrayals, He thus pointed out the negative example set by those who supported his father. In reality, the usurpation actually granted the throne to Tudhaliya himself. Above all, Tudhaliya confirmed the privileged status of Kurunta, king of Tarhuntassa, who began to use the title of 'great king'. We exceptionally possess the original copy, written on a bronze tablet, of a treaty between Hatti and Tarhuntassa defining the borders of this kingdom. Among the greatest achievements of Tudhaliya's reign,

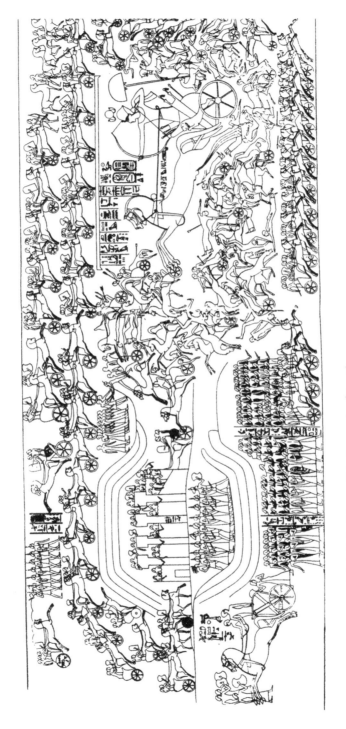

Figure 18.2   The battle of Qadesh (reliefs of Ramses II in the temple of Luxor).

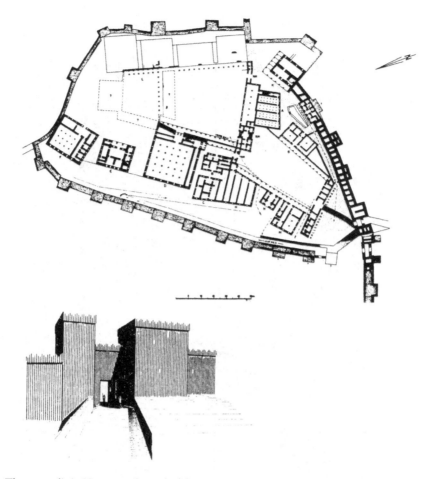

Figure 18.3   The acropolis in Hattusa at the end of the Hittite empire, ca. 1200 BC. Plan (*above*) and reconstruction
of the south-western gate (*below*).

however, there was the enlargement (almost to double its original size) of the Hittite capital. The king
commissioned the addition of a wall that included the sacred upper city (Figure 18.3), and the construction
of the sanctuary of Yazilikaya, near Hattusa.

Despite some successes, the situation worsened in the reigns of the last two Hittite kings, Arnuwanda
III and Suppiluliuma II. Suppiluliuma managed to conquer Alashiya (Cyprus) through a naval battle and
disembarked troops on the island. It was such a sensational achievement that it was recorded both in a
written treaty and an inscription (written in Luwian hieroglyphs) left in the upper city of the Hittite capital.
However, on a political level the conquest probably did not last long. By now, Syria was no longer under
direct Hittite control. This was partly due to the delegation of control to Carchemish and the consolidation of exemptions and disengagements, which had been granted or at least tolerated, when the political
situation was still relatively solid.

Even in Anatolia control seems to have slipped from the hands of the last Hittite kings, who were constantly engaged in ensuring a loyalty that was becoming increasingly difficult to achieve. There were too
many claimants, too many bad examples and too many dangers to effectively establish a system of loyalties
in the Hittite state. 'Loyalty' could only be an effective means to establish political control when it was

balanced in a complex network of reciprocal support. It was in the interest of everyone involved to keep this balance alive. Therefore, the great king ruled through the support of his subjects and vassals, and the latter survived thanks to the great king's support. Reading the sources from the last phase of the empire, the loyalty expected by the king from his subjects seems not to have been reciprocated anymore. It therefore became a simple moral and legal obligation, and not the result of a reciprocal interaction. The tone of these texts thus seems increasingly concerned, almost panicked, by the fear of being abandoned.

It is not easy to understand how this deterioration could have taken place in such a short period of time. The political decline of the Hittite state certainly developed in parallel with the depopulation of Hatti. The land was exhausted by the constant effort of maintaining solid control over the conquered territories from a relatively unpopulated centre. Moreover, this deterioration was also contemporaneous to the overall decline of the powers ruling in the Near East. As we will see, this sudden decline will involve Hatti, its subjects, and even its enemies, in a general process of reorganisation of the entire area.

3 Political control in the Hittite empire

At its peak, the Hittite empire extended from the Aegean to the Upper Tigris, and from the Black Sea to Lebanon. It therefore constituted one of vastest empires that had ruled in the Near East until then, only to be overcome later on by the Egyptian empire. The nature and systems of cohesion used by the Hittite empire require some consideration. The Hittite empire did not belong to the old type of commercial empire, typical of the third and second millennium BC (such as in the case of the Old Assyrian commercial network, or even some aspects of Egyptian presence in the Syro-Levantine area). In fact, despite considering the commercial aspect important, Hatti never placed it at the heart of its hegemonic system. Moreover, the solid system of control over conquered territories used by later empires (the Neo-Assyrian one in particular) was not yet developed in the Late Bronze Age. Therefore, while the centre was a politically unified area, the conquered territories, whose subjugation and dependence was fundamental for the empire's survival, continued in their efforts towards independence. Nonetheless, the administrative and political organisation of Anatolia greatly improved during the Hittite empire (from Suppiluliuma I onwards). By now, then, the empire ruled over a large portion of Central and eastern Anatolia and was as large as Kassite Babylonia or Assyria.

The key element holding the empire together was of a legal and personal nature. It was centred on a series of subordinate personal relations expressed following a specific legal protocol. It is likely that the kingdoms of Mitanni, Kizzuwatna and Arzawa used a similar system. However, Hatti provides us with the largest amount of evidence for this system and the justified impression that it was more broadly and systematically applied there. These personal ties were formalised through an 'oath' (*lingai*). The latter included a series of detailed clauses, developed in order to leave nothing to chance, and to leave out those who did not swear the oath or the events not included in the oath. This was in marked contrast with the Egyptian system, where oaths of dependence were kept deliberately vague, allowing the Egyptian king to interpret it whichever way he wanted. Moreover, Egyptian treaties were verbal agreements, and less related to the person swearing the oath, and more to his function in connection to the Egyptian king.

Hittite oaths are attested in a series of documents that scholars tend to divide according to type. However, the Hittites probably conceived these texts as part of a unitary system. The 'instructions' regulated the system of dependencies within the Hittite state, while the 'treaties' regulated external relations. Instruction texts, which were mainly developed before Suppiluliuma's reign, were in use throughout the empire. They were mainly concerned with important aspects of the state and military administration. They focus in particular on the upper strata of Hittite society. This elite is divided between the 'great ones', the sons of the most influential families in the Hittite elite, and the 'king's sons', the relatives (biological or not) of the king. The latter mainly held offices within the Hittite court, in the administration of the empire's periphery, and in the army.

Each member of this elite group had to swear a loyalty oath to the king. These oaths included general principles, such as the loyalty to the king and his chosen heir, and more detailed principles on the correct fulfilment of their office (Text 18.2). This wide network of oaths developed an equally wide system of reciprocal ties. After all, the king could only rule through the support and loyalty of his functionaries, and the latter were kept in their places through the support and loyalty of the king towards them. This network of loyalties was closely linked to the network of kinship relations of the Hittite court. The latter network is clearly expressed by the group called the 'king's sons'. The Hittite royal family always had a strong interest in inter-dynastic marriages, giving and taking wives from the Anatolian elite. This process eventually made kinship ties extremely ideological. However, despite being useful in forging a strong political cohesion internally, these kinship ties also promoted competition. This was due to the large number of individuals who could theoretically claim the throne, or at least other important positions within the Hittite court.

Text 18.2   From the loyalty oath sworn by Tudhaliya IV's eunuchs

'Thus Tudhaliya, Great King: I have become king, and you, eunuchs, have to swear on the person of His Majesty: "We will protect His Majesty for kingship, and then we will protect the sons of His Majesty and (his) royal line!" To you, who are eunuchs, and the men equal to you: His Majesty is in your hands; protect His Majesty and then protect the royal line of His Majesty! His Majesty has many brothers, the sons of his ancestors are numerous, and Hattusa is full of the royal line: within Hattusa there are many descendants of Suppululiuma, descendants of Mursili, descendants of Muwatalli, descendants of Hattusili. Do not look for another man for kingship! For the future kingship protect only the royal line of Tudhaliya! If something evil ever happened to His Majesty – and His Majesty has many brothers – and you are more or less responsible for this, and you approach someone else saying: "Is he whom we select ourselves not the son of our lord as well?", that is unacceptable! With respect to future kingship, you must only protect the royal line of His Majesty! Do not approach anyone else, protect the kingship of His Majesty and the descendants of His Majesty! . . . Or, if a disgrace (were to threaten) the life of His Majesty, you find out about it and throw him a bridge, saying: "On this day, I have not been assigned to any service, thus it is not my sin": may this be sworn through a divine oath! Or, since I will often send you, eunuchs, as envoys together with princes and lords in the lands of a neighbouring (king), do not change the words of His Majesty: may this be sworn through a divine oath! Or, if someone is favourable towards His Majesty, but an enemy of His Majesty takes you aside (saying): "Make that man fall into disgrace in front of His Majesty!" and you make him fall into disgrace; or, someone is your enemy, but he has His Majesty's favour, and you deliberately make him fall into disgrace and harm him in some way: may these gods destroy you! To you, eunuchs, who have immediately come here, I, His Majesty, have made you swear: "If you hear from someone something evil or suspicious regarding His Majesty, inform His Majesty!", but if you do not inform His Majesty as soon as you hear it: may this be sworn through a divine oath! Now, to you who have not been here and have sworn individually; if you hear from someone something evil regarding His Majesty, do not hide it: may this be sworn through a divine oath! His Majesty has many brothers (that is, the kings of equal status): my brothers are many and there are many neighbouring kings. If I send one of you, eunuchs, to someone, and the latter gains his favour and he opens his mouth and reveals the things of the king: may this be sworn through a divine oath! Or if he sees something suspicious from him and hides it: may this be sworn through a divine oath! Or, as it is customary among the Hittites, instead of the kingship of His Majesty, they secretly prefer the kingship of another man: may this be sworn through a divine oath! Or, if a friend hears from a friend something evil about His Majesty, and does not disagree: may this be sworn through a divine oath! . . .'

The king's activities and movements throughout the empire were another important element for internal cohesion. One gets the impression that in some periods of Hittite history the king was often far from the Hittite capital. First, this was because of the typical practice of celebrating religious festivals in all sanctuaries of Hatti. Many of these were important and prestigious cultic centres on a regional level, and therefore required the presence of the king. Second, there were the king's military duties. The king was not only involved in the most important campaigns, able to provide him with international fame and opportunities to celebrate his feats, but also in more modest expeditions against the elusive mountain tribes.

The king's cultic responsibilities throughout Hatti derive from an ancient tradition. They were also closely linked to the early unification of the land. The king's itinerant cultic responsibility was partly solved through the concentration of a variety of temples and cults in Hattusa. However, it still required the constant peregrination of the king and queen (who also held a crucial role in Hittite cults) to the sanctuaries of the land. On the other hand, military responsibilities were closely linked to the heroic image of kingship in the mid-second millennium BC. In this period, the king effectively belonged to the military aristocracy and had to prove his extraordinary prowess and valiance to both his people and rivals. This military and cultic movement of the king was a clear reflection of the fragmented nature of Anatolia and the decentralised position of the Hittite capital. In more practical terms, had the king remained permanently in the capital it would have isolated him from the rest of the land.

If kingship in the Hittite empire had lost its original features and was partly influenced by other kingship ideologies of the time, it still continued to be more personal compared to the Egyptian and Mesopotamian traditions. The 'great ones' and the 'king's sons' constituted a key resource used by the king to choose his administrative, cultic and military collaborators. These did not need to have a particular expertise. As a result, some titles that clearly originated in the Hittite court, such as 'cupbearer' or 'steward', did not correspond to their initial functions anymore, but became purely formal titles. Therefore, specific duties were bestowed on individuals specifically chosen by the king, without the need of bureaucratic protocol or a political career.

The periphery still maintained a residual system inherited from its former independence, with palaces, storehouses (the so-called 'houses of the seal'), local cultic centres and local legal and administrative practices. The management of centres located in the periphery was left in the hands of a 'mayor' (*ḫazānu*), a 'provincial governor' (*bēl madgalti*), and the 'elders'. The mayor was responsible for civic duties, while the governor focused on military concerns. The elders dealt with legal issues and represented the local community. The instruction texts sent by the king to mayors and provincial governors were typically strict on their guidance over the management of the area and the issue of security from external threats. However, they were quite flexible on legal measures to be taken, allowing their delegates to follow local practices.

The Hittite state applied the same principles and means at the heart of its internal organisation to foreign relations. Personal oaths linking the 'small king' to the 'great king', and vice versa, were expressed through written oaths of loyalty with specific clauses (Text 18.3). The Hittite king thus promised to protect the throne of the small king and to transmit it to the latter's designated heir. In turn, the small king agreed to pay a tribute, provide military contingents and return fugitives (usually a one-sided aspect of the agreement). Moreover, the vassal had to provide key information, support in case of internal revolts, and so on.

Text 18.3 Treaty between Mursili II and Niqmepa of Ugarit

Example of a treaty between a Hittite 'great king' and a Syrian 'small king' (extract)

'You shall be a friend to my friend, and an enemy to my enemy! If the king of Hattusa goes against the land of Hanigalbat, or Egypt, or Babylonia, or the land of Alshi, whatever enemy land located near the borders of your land that is hostile to the king of Hattusa; and whatever land located near the borders of your land that is friendly to the king of Hattusa: Mukish, Aleppo, Nuhashe, turn and become hostile to the king of Hattusa, when the king of Hatti goes out to attack them, if you, Niqmepa, do not intervene wholeheartedly with your troops, your chariots, and if you do not fight with all your heart (you will transgress the oath)! And if I send to your aid, Niqmepa, a prince or a high-ranking nobleman with his troops and his chariots, or if I send him to attack another land: if you, Niqmepa, do not intervene wholeheartedly with your troops and your chariots, and do not fight the enemy; and if you commit something evil and say this: "I belong to the oath and am subject to the treaty: let the enemy defeat them, or let them defeat the enemy, I do not know anything about it," and if you send a message to that enemy, saying: "Behold, the Hittite troops are coming to attack: be on guard!" you will transgress the oath! And if some other enemy rises against the king of Hattusa, and attacks Hittite territories, or if he carries out a personal attack against the king of Hattusa and you, Niqmepa, hear of it, then you must immediately come to the aid of the Great King with your troops and your chariots. If it is not possible for Niqmepa himself to come, his son or his brother shall immediately come to the aid of the king of Hattusa with troops and chariots! . . . If some tribe (?) sets out and comes to your land, and you, Niqmepa, speak unfavourable words before them and turn their faces to the mountains or to another land – speak favourable words before them! Show them the road with benevolence! Give them beer and provisions! If the king of Hattusa oppresses in battle some enemy land, and the latter sets out and enters the land of Ugarit, Niqmepa shall seize them and give them to the king of Hattusa! If he does not seize them and give them to the king of Hattusa, he will transgress the oath. If a fugitive flees from the land of Hatti and comes to the land of Ugarit, Niqmepa shall seize him and return him to the king of Hattusa. If he does not return him, he will transgress the oath. If a fugitive flees from the land of Ugarit and comes to the land of Hatti, the king of Hatti will not seize him and return him: it is not permitted for the king of Hattusa to return a fugitive. If a fugitive comes to the land of Ugarit from the land of Hanigalbat or from another land, you, Niqmepa, will not detain him, but will allow him to go to the land of Hatti. If you detain him, you will transgress the oath. Everything Niqmepa wants, he shall request from the king of Hattusa: he shall take whatever the king of Hattusa will give to him, he shall not take whatever the king of Hattusa will not give him! . . .'

In its conventional form, this type of treaty was developed by Suppiluliuma's court, and was consolidated by Mursili. It would be in use until the end of the empire. This type of treaty derived from the treaties of equality in use in the fifteenth century BC, with several substantial adaptations and changes. In this regard, the treaty of Shunashshura marked the passage from equal treaty to a treaty of subordination. Having become inherently unequal, a treaty still had two parties tied by an oath, but was only commissioned by the Hittite king. Therefore, it became a sort of one-directional edict, similar to those internal instruction texts, which were also a form of royal edict. The 'classic' Hittite treaty was a suitable form of agreement to define the relations of the Hittite king with his Syrian and Anatolian small kings. However, there still were special treaties, which had to take into account particular political situations. For instance, there were treaties stipulated with formerly powerful states. The latter would have resented the classic form of Hittite treaty. Therefore, treaties stipulated with Kizzuwatna and Mitanni allowed exemptions, and emphasised their prestigious and long tradition. However, these were not equal treaties. The only truly equal treaty was stipulated with Egypt, another empire belonging to the great powers of the time. Only in the case of Egypt did the Hittite king find a ruler of equal stature.

Another special type of treaty was the one agreed with non-monarchic states. These lacked a single figure of authority to act as the community's representative. Nonetheless, their personal relation with the Hittite king had a political value. Consequently, when the Hittites stipulated treaties with the city of

Ishmerikka or the Kaska tribes, they had to sign them with a wide range of elders and tribe leaders. This was an attempt to link via oath all the people they represented. Therefore, these oaths were meant to diplomatically subjugate all these composite political entities.

Alongside formal treaties, the Hittites sealed their foreign relations even further through a complex network of inter-dynastic marriages. These were aimed at linking the various small kings under their control on a personal level. Moreover, they established favourable successions to local thrones through the queens of Hittite descent (destined to be the successors' mothers). Finally, inter-dynastic marriages introduced Hittite culture and religion in their vassals' courts. The examples of Shattiwaza of Mitanni, who married a daughter of Suppiluliuma, or Benteshina of Amurru, married to a daughter of Hattusili III, are clear indicators of this matrimonial strategy. Therefore, the latter was carefully applied on political fugitives in view of their future enthronement. Consequently, these individuals would be considered reliable enough to participate in the resolution of local issues in favour of the Hittites.

The same means (treaties and marriages) to seal relations were also employed to seal relations between great kings. However, these were exceptional cases. The treaty between Hatti and Egypt is in itself unparalleled. It was a later re-use of a fifteenth-century practice to regulate border issues (such as the return of fugitives and so on) among equals, but that was by now used to establish unequal relations between states. Despite being an anomaly for the period, it was gladly accepted by Ramses in order to celebrate his achievements to his people. Similarly, through this treaty, Hattusili was able to ensure the new southern border of the Hittite empire. This constituted a major success compared to his predecessor's achievements. With regards to inter-dynastic marriages, the provision of Hittite princesses to the Egyptian king, or the arrival of Babylonian princesses in Hattusa, could not have been more than a mere celebration of already friendly relations between these states.

4 The economy of the Hittite empire

The agricultural and demographic levels of growth in the Hittite empire were similar to the ones attested for the Old Hittite kingdom, but encountered more difficulties. In this phase, there was a marked tendency towards the concentration of settlements in more favourable areas and their considerable reduction in size. Apart from the more general causes for these changes, some areas also had specific reasons, such as the constant conflicts in the northern territories. These issues were damaging the economy and the population alike. This was true both from the Hittites' perspective, which saw in the turbulence, mobility and aggression of the Kaska the motive for the war, and the Kaska's perspective, which did not accept the imperialistic ambitions of the Hittites, determined to control and include the mountain tribes within their political sphere of influence.

The growing ambitions of the Hittites worsened the increasing difficulties of the time. The empire's expansionistic efforts brought about the enlargement of the capital. This generated a centripetal movement of labour and resources, both in terms of food and other materials. In the Old Assyrian period, Hattusa barely extended over a dozen of hectares (plus five hectares of its *kārum*). By the Old Hittite period, the city had grown, reaching around forty hectares. However, in the Imperial period (thirteenth century BC), a further extension of the capital added around a hundred hectares, making Hattusa not just the largest city in Anatolia, but one of the largest in the Near East. Temples, fortifications, storehouses and other non-residential buildings took up a considerable amount of land (Figure 18.4). Therefore, the capital's population must have reached around 20,000 people. This demographic concentration was nothing compared to the concentration of resources and labour needed for the construction of public buildings and the defensive system. Moreover, there was the maintenance of the royal palace and the entire state and cult administration. To make matters worse, Hattusa was located in a mountainous area. The city was therefore difficult to access and had few agricultural fields in its surroundings.

The empire's efforts in the centre were paralleled by an effort alongside the Hittite borders. The Hittite kings' annals recount a long sequence of wars. These wars were mainly defensive in the sixteenth and fifteenth centuries BC, but more expansionistic in the fourteenth and thirteenth centuries BC. The expansionistic campaigns required larger armies and greater movements, and brought logistics problems, as well as considerable losses. This military effort, of which the king and the elite were proud, had a negative impact on the Hittite economy and its population. The internal wars of Anatolia were also meant to deport the Anatolian population, in an attempt to make up for previous losses. Rather than describing the conquests and booties gathered, the sources always emphasise the number of war prisoners (NAM.RA) taken by the king. They stereotypically add that the ones taken by the soldiers were innumerable (namely, uncounted by the administration and numerous in appearance). Tens of thousands of prisoners were taken from the conquered lands to Hatti. This was mainly to fill the ever-growing depopulation of the Hittite countryside (Text 18.4). However, overall, these deportations were moving around an insufficient number of people, a number that was further reduced through the constant wars, deportations and re-settlements of people in new territories.

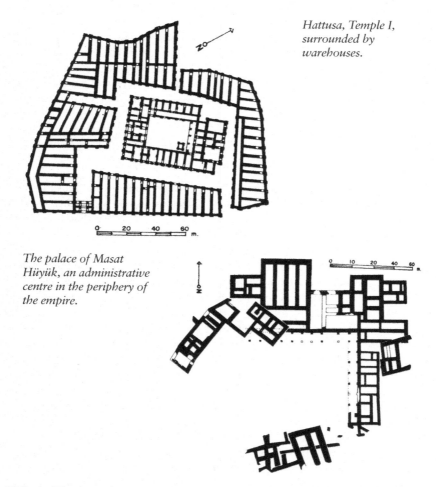

Hattusa, Temple I, surrounded by warehouses.

The palace of Masat Hüyük, an administrative centre in the periphery of the empire.

Figure 18.4 Hittite architecture. *Above*: Hattusa, Temple I, surrounded by warehouses; *Below*: The palace of Maşat Hüyük, an administrative centre in the periphery of the empire.

Text 18.4 The internal colonisation of the land of Hatti: Deportees fill the gaps in the countryside caused by the constant military campaigns

a) *The reorganisation of the northern districts*

'In the district of Turmitta. In the town of Lihshina, His Majesty has instituted the following things: 50 houses for a total of 500 deportees, 1 town, 3 tell, previously owned by the priests, 3 houses of deportees from Hatuhina, men of Azzi; 1 house of 10 deportees from the palace of Hariyasha.

In the town of . . .: 3 houses of 30 deportees of Zipishhuna, 3 houses of 30 deportees from Tazipa, men of the *upati* (land); . . .; 3 houses of 30 deportees, herdsmen (they look after Takashipa); 2 houses of 20 deportees, men of Kazaha, servants of Daduili, men of the *upati* (land). Total: 16 houses of 160 deportees (that) His Majesty has added. 50 cows, 400 animals of which 120 goats. They will perform the service. The main storehouse will provide 150 *parisu* of seeds.

In the town of Nenasha, His Majesty has instituted the following things: 140 deportees that already belonged to the god. The king of Tumana will provide 24 oxen and 200 sheep.

To the gods of the town of Walma, His Majesty has instituted the following: 1 house of 10 deportees; . . .; 1 house of 16 deportees, mountain people; 1 house of 10 deportees, servants of Inara; 1 house of 4 deportees, of the priest; 1 house of 10 deportees, the king's weavers. Total: 5 houses of 50 deportees, 50 heads of sheep, previously. The king of Tumana will provide 14 oxen of which 4 plough oxen.

In Tenizadasha, to the god Pirwa, His Majesty has instituted the following: 4 houses of 40 deportees, farmers of horses. The king of Tumana will provide 4 oxen and 30 sheep. The main storehouse will provide 30 *parisu* of seed . . .'

b) *From the donation of Queen Puduhepa to the Goddess Lelwani*

'The woman (called) Abbâ; 1 of her daughters called Niwa; 1 (other) daughter is dead; 1 son called Dudu. Total: 4 people. The woman receives a prisoner of war. (This family) was already assigned to the service of the temple (of Lelwani).

The woman (called) Mamma; 1 of her daughters called Shaushkatti; 2 of her sons called Teshmara and Yarraziti. Total: 4 people. Mamma receives a prisoner of war. She was already assigned to the service of the temple.

. . .

1 young girl named Titai I have given as fiancé to Apallu; I have given to Apallu a young boy to raise, Tatili brother of Titai, but I have not released him yet.

1 newborn baby called Pitati; 1 boy called Temetti: given to Piya, son of Pitawiya, to raise them.

1 young boy named Tuttu: given to . . .; he has not been given yet.

1 woman called Utati (daughter) of Pitagatti; 1 young boy called Nuhati; 1 woman called Kattittahi (daughter) of Tatili; 1 daughter of her brother, also called Kattittahi; 1 woman called Utati (daughter) of Temetti; 1 young girl called Udati, daughter of the brother of her husband; 1 woman called Udati (daughter) of Zakappauti; 2 of her sons called Happanu and Sharaduwa; 1 woman called Utati (daughter) of Zaga . . .; 1 of her daughters called Mamma; 1 woman called Udati (daughter) of Piptarawashi; 1 of her sons called Pittatta; 1 young girl called Kumiya I have given to Mulla to raise. In total: 23 people (that) Haranaziti has brought from the expedition against the town of Zikeshara.'

Another type of movement of people pervading the Hittite evidence is the problem of fugitives. The latter were slaves, debtors, people who committed a crime, political opponents, and many other individuals from all strata of Hittite society. Naturally, the state receiving these fugitives had strong interests in keeping them. If they were from a lower social background, they could have been labourers. If they came from the elite, they could become useful political pawns for manoeuvres over neighbouring states. The reciprocal need for stability had led the Syro-Anatolian states of the sixteenth and fifteenth centuries BC towards a reciprocal practice of extradition. However, once the Hittites managed to rise above all other states in the area, and the population decreased even more, the practice became more one-sided. Therefore, Hittite fugitives had to be returned, while the Hittites kept foreign fugitives in their land.

Some temple inventories from the time of Hattusili III are a clear example of the demographic problem of the time. The problem had become particularly serious. Since women were often left alone, perhaps having been widowed by war, they were given a war prisoner as a replacement for their husband. Families were destroyed, and the numbers of children was not high enough to ensure an adequate generational cycle. If the assumption that this problem afflicted Anatolia as a whole is correct, then the crisis was particularly worrying.

Admittedly, Hittite history had been marked by a demographic and production problem from the start. A depopulated countryside necessarily brought difficulties in providing the most basic resources to larger urban centres. When demographic levels were the highest, we see Telipinu making sure that the agricultural centres owned by the elite were productive. However, at the lowest demographic levels, we see the great famine towards the end of the empire. Anatolia did not produce grain, which had to be imported from Syria (Mukish) and even Egypt. Ships from Ugarit were even sent to bring grain to the Cilician port of Ura. 'It is a matter of life or death,' said the Hittites to their vassals, while the Egyptian propaganda boasted of having 'kept the miserable land of Hatti alive'

It is probable that the crisis did not affect all of Anatolia in the same way. The south-western regions (Arzawa), the Konya plain, the Cilician plain and the areas along the Euphrates seem to have been better off. However, Central Anatolia (Phrygia and Cappadocia) and northern Anatolia experienced a growing crisis. This internal crisis was closely linked to the fall of the empire. The sources (which will be considered later on) record the arrival of enemies, forcing the Hittites and their remaining vassals to engage in military campaigns, both on land and sea, in south-western Anatolia. Be that as it may, not long after this Hattusa was destroyed (or even abandoned) and the archives cease to provide any information. The fall of the capital caused the breakdown of the entire state, which was dependent on this centre and was already fragile and depopulated.

It is not sure whether the fall of Hattusa was caused by the Sea People. However, their presence so far north would seem a deviation from their attested route. Alternatively, it could have been the Kaska, who could have taken advantage of the concentration of Hittite troops in the south-west. Otherwise, it could have been the people arriving from the west, such as the Phrygians. Once written sources from the area reappear, the Phrygians would appear to be already settled in the area. Be that as it may, by the end of the thirteenth century BC the land was worryingly depopulated. It was only able to survive thanks to its great capital and its redistributive system. Once the Hittite state collapsed, new people from the west settled in Central Anatolia. The Luwians and Hittites moved to the south-east, the only area that had managed to survive the crisis and to be less affected by the arrival of new populations.

5 Magic and politics, law and historiography

Even in the Imperial period, propagandistic expressions of kingship (that is, through celebratory monuments and inscriptions), typical of the Mesopotamian and Egyptian ideology of kingship, were far more modest. This avoidance of excessive propaganda was due to the Hittite kings' lack of interest in addressing their people, and the inability of the latter in having any impact on the former. Propaganda was exclusively addressed to the court, the royal family and the state administrators. Therefore, the Hittite ruling class saw the king as a hero, who respected the core values of the legal and personal network of relations constituting the Hittite state. These values could all be synthesised into one simple idea, namely, 'justice' (*parā ḫandandātar*), which required the respect of ethical, religious and legal principles.

Compared to their vassals and enemies, the Hittite kings display a *bona fide* obsession in trying to demonstrate that their decisions were right. Since there would always have been disagreements on who was right in any given situation, the kings tried to regulate each social or political interaction through a sworn agreement. Therefore, he who followed the oath by the letter would have been right, while the one who breached it would have been wrong. If everyone respected the oath, there would have been no social, political or military dispute. Since these treaties were all in favour of the Hittite ruler, it is clear that the observance of the treaties would have implied a passive acceptance of the superior role of the Hittite ruler and of Hatti as a whole.

When agreements were stipulated without writing them down, the criteria used were the most common ones. These were centred on the idea of analogy (in the sense of proportionality). On the one hand, there was a 'horizontal' analogy, namely, the idea of reciprocity, according to which something was right in one direction, if it was right in the opposite direction. Therefore, if one sacked the other's land, he could not complain about the latter sacking his land in return. Similarly, if one state held the other's fugitives, it was fair that the other state did the same. However, there was also a 'vertical' analogy, which was more diachronic. According to this concept, something was right if it had been done in the past, especially in a distant and mythical past, which acted as a model for current behaviour. Therefore, despite the lack of treaties, reciprocity and tradition should have been enough to provide the right criteria to solve controversies.

If controversies were too difficult to solve, there was always war. War was seen as a conflict by ordeal (a common idea in the Late Bronze Age), namely, as a way to see who was ultimately right. In our view, the winner is right in the sense that he imposes his reasons, forcing them on the potential reasons provided by the losing side. The Hittite idea, however, was completely different: he who was right would have won because he was supported by the gods, and would have demonstrated that his argument was right through his victory. This vision of military victories as some sort of ordeal made war extremely ritual in nature. There was a ritual to declare war, which had both operational and religious consequences. War officially began with a notification sent to the enemy recounting the offences suffered, the goodwill of the sender bestowed in vain, and the inevitability of war. Similarly, a notification of war was also sent to the enemy's gods, in the form of legal texts. In these notifications, the sender explained the enemy's offences and invited the gods to abandon the land, to side with the fair king, facilitating the victory of the Hittite king and his gods.

Battles were also conceived as ordeals, since they were fought over long periods of time and in well-known areas, with the two armies facing each other, without betrayals or deceptions. This was, at least, the ideal battle. However, it did not come as a surprise if the 'unfair' enemy was equally unfair on the battlefield. Therefore, by continuing to behave incorrectly even when justice was being ascertained, the enemy confirmed his lack of moral values and made the outcome of the battle even more evident. The battle was therefore resolved quickly, since divine support made it a pure formality, forcing the unfair and godless enemy to die or flee.

Although the outcome of a battle was taken for granted and seen as relatively easy *a posteriori*, it required extreme caution beforehand (Text 18.5). This caution was propitiatory and reinforced by specific rituals. These were developed to prefigure the future victory by making the Hittite warriors, clad in bronze, symbolically fight the enemy, armed with reeds. Alternatively, there were magic rituals, meant to transform the enemy's soldiers into harmless women. Above all, there was an ascertaining caution, made of mantic rituals, which were of Mesopotamian (mainly hepatoscopy) and Anatolian origins (ornithomancy and the so-called KIN-oracle, where lots were placed on a diagram covered with symbols). Long texts predicted entire military campaigns on the basis of oracular verifications before the wars were even begun. Each movement, attack and strategy was tested through oracles and, if the outcome was negative, an alternative was tested, until the right prediction was in place.

Text 18.5   Hittite magic rituals in preparation for war

a) *Ritual for the evocation of enemy gods*

'When they want to perform, a magical ritual at the enemy border, they offer one sheep to the Sun-goddess of Arinna, to the Storm-god, to Inar, to all the gods, to Telipinu of Turmitta, to the male gods and the goddesses, to the gods of the assembly, to all the gods, to all the mountains and rivers, and they offer a sheep to Zithariya, saying: "Behold, the god Zithariya keeps prostrating himself to the gods: the lands that were legitimate and eternal possession of Zithariya, the lands in which he wandered, where great festivities were celebrated, now have been taken by the Kaska. The Kaska have started the war: they boast of their might and of their bones, and they have humiliated you, o gods . . . Here, Zithariya keeps bringing his case to you, to all the gods: welcome in your heart your case, judge your case, judge the cause of Zithariya! O gods, destroy the land of the Kaska!" . . . Then, they recite this: "O gods of the land of the Kaska, behold! We have called you to assembly, come, eat, drink; and here listen why we have brought a case against you. The gods of the land of Hatti have not taken anything away from you, o gods of the land of the Kaska, nor have they done anything wrong against you. You, gods of the land of the Kaska, have started the war, you have sent away the gods from the land of Hatti and you have taken their territories. The Kaska have started the war: you have taken away from the Hittites their cities and you have driven them away from their fields and vineyards. The gods and the men of the land of Hatti demand that blood may be shed" . . .'

b) *Planning a military expedition through oracles*

'(3) From Hanhana to Hatina; he spends the night in the ruins of Katruma. In Pitakalasha, but may it remain out of the investigation whether he should attack Pitakalasha or whether he will conquer it peacefully. The next day, he destroys Shunapashi and Pitalahshi, then he sleeps in the fortified camp of His Majesty's father. The following day he attacks Tashinata. In Hatinzuwa, in Tapilusha; he attacks Kashkama; in Nerik, I rebuild Nerik. From Nerik, I will ask the oracle on whether to attack the enemies immediately, or celebrate the *wurulli* -festival first. If, o god – like above, the investigation is favourable . . . Result: Unfavourable. (4) From Hanhana he spends the night in the ruins of Katruma. The following day the troops of chariots attack Pikauza and the troops of the tribes advance before him. His Majesty sleeps in the fortified camp of His Majesty's father and the troops of chariots and the troops of the tribes return to His Majesty in the fortified camp of His Majesty's father. The following day he sets Shunapashi and Pitalahshi on fire and he sleeps in the fortified camp of His Majesty's father. The following day, in Pikauza; he changes direction, in Ishtahara, he does not go to Kashkama anymore. In Nerik, he rebuilds the city. From Nerik I will again ask the oracle on whether to attack the enemies immediately, or celebrate the *wurulli* -festival first . . . (unfavourable answer). (5) From Hanhana to . . . he spends the night in Pikanunusha. In . . ., further away from Pitakalasha, but may it remain out of the investigation whether he should attack Pitakalasha or whether he will conquer it peacefully. He sleeps in the fortified camp of His Majesty's father. The following day he attacks Shunapashi and Pitalahshi, then he sleeps in the fortified camp of His Majesty's father. In Pikauza, he changes direction, in Ishtahara, in Nerik he rebuilds the city. From Nerik I will again ask the oracle on whether to attack the enemies immediately, or celebrate the *wurulli* -festival first . . . (unfavourable answer). Etc.'

Oracles and magic rituals were not limited to military endeavours, but also pervaded and influenced Hittite politics. We have already mentioned how the pestilence led Mursili II to embark on a series of oracular and mantic investigations to discover the reason for the plight. Even political struggles within the Hittite court and the capital were largely dealt with through magic. Moreover, it was even possible to eliminate one's political rival by accusing him of using 'black' magic to destroy his opponents. These allegations naturally led to the development of 'white' magic counter-measures (otherwise the accusations would not have been credible). Therefore, political competition, just like battles, developed along two lines, first on a ritual level, then in reality. Consequently, the outcome of the symbolic confrontation would have set the mood of the participants involved in the real confrontation.

The Hittite idea of battle as a verification of justice by ordeal can also be found in its historiography. First, there were 'premonitory anecdotes', recounting more or less famous characters (or even unknown or fictitious) that acted in a certain way, committed a certain sin, and had to suffer a specific consequence. These anecdotes were mentioned to whomever found himself in a similar situation and could learn to behave correctly, avoiding those mistakes that ruined others before him. In a way, these anecdotes were a 'secular' version of the Mesopotamian historical omens. In fact, it was not the appearance of an ancient omen at the time of a certain outcome that taught an individual what to do anymore, but the human and rational connection between behaviour and result, cause and effect.

However, the exceptional development of Hittite 'historical' literature was not aimed at establishing models of behaviour for the future, but at justifying present actions. In this sense, the Hittite attitude towards history was a consequence of their attitude towards justice and their obsession in being right. The historiography of the Middle Hittite kingdom and the Hittite empire were a clear reflection of their respective periods. The complaints against the enemy and proclamations of innocence were at the centre of war declarations and invocations of the enemy's gods. They therefore became 'historical preambles' of those means used to seal new relations, namely, treaties of subordination. Having been defeated or, alternatively, having surrendered, Hittite vassals also had to endure the idea that their subordination was the rightful consequence of their previous behaviour or noncompliance to the treaty. Naturally, these reconstructions were highly tendentious, since they selected and twisted facts in order to support a point of view aimed at justifying what the Hittites did.

Another application of Hittite historiography can be found in the internal documents of the state administration, such as royal edicts and apologies. The tradition seems to have begun at the time of the founder of the Hittite state, namely, Hattusili I, who justified the selection of his adoptive son, Mursili, as heir on his deathbed. Then, there was the Edict of Telipinu. In order to justify his usurpation and avoid future usurpations, Telipinu rewrote the entire history of the Hittite state and its alliances or betrayals, and invented the model-king, Labarna. He also dealt with the issue of usurpation through imaginary future reforms. Finally, there was the Apology of Hattusili III, a clear usurper in the eyes of everyone, from Urhi-Teshub's supporters to his own supporters and even his son. The king therefore tried to demonstrate that his illegitimacy was nothing compared to that of his nephew. Moreover, his armed revolt is described as an act of defence. Finally, Hattusili points out that divine support had ultimately proved his righteousness and fairness.

Deeds and annals are the last type of historical texts. They are already attested in the reign of Hattusili I and in the Middle Hittite kingdom. These types of texts peaked in the reign of Mursili II, with the Deeds of his father, Suppiluliuma, and his own Ten Year Annals and Detailed Annals. In these sources, the king's self-justification is clearer in the inscription's context (whenever it survived). Thus, Mursili's Ten Year Annals were aimed at demonstrating that the king, despite being a 'small king', could rely on Ishtar's support to solve a very difficult situation. When this overall framework is missing (the other texts are rather fragmentary), single episodes demonstrate the wider celebratory and justificatory intentions of the king. They strongly emphasise Hittite righteousness, the enemy's immorality, and the centrality of divine intervention for Hatti's success. However, annals were not simply apologetic texts, but an advanced stage in the development of continuous historical accounts. Therefore, they were written down to commemorate remarkable, heroic moments, filled with lessons for the future.

There are very few Hittite celebratory or monumental inscriptions. However, towards the end of the empire, Luwian hieroglyphs, which had been in use from as early as the Middle Hittite kingdom on seals, began to be used on monuments. In this regard, towards the end of the thirteenth century BC, there is a text of king Suppiluliuma II on his conquest of Cyprus and linked to the construction of a funerary monument for his father. The tone of this text was somehow similar to the monumental inscriptions found in Mesopotamia. Overall, Hittite historical or, better, political literature was more aimed at justifying the kings' deeds rather than celebrating them, and was written for the court, rather than the wider population. However, there was still a propagandistic intent, although it was aimed at a much smaller circle of people. This was a reflection of the times, but was also a typically Hittite characteristic. For instance, contemporary Assyria translated its heroic and religious deeds into a much more celebratory literature. Therefore, in the case of the Hittites, the contrast between the external version of a particular course of events used in international relations, and the shamelessly celebratory internal version directed towards a state's population, was not as strong. Having removed the broader population as a relevant audience, the Hittite or foreign (and internal or external) members of the international aristocracy received the same message from the Hittite ruler, namely, the self-justification of a king who sensed problems in his palace, his family and on an international level.

6 Cultural and religious syncretism

Ever since the diachronic study of Hittite writing has allowed us to establish the chronology of Hittite sources with more precision, it has become possible to distinguish the linguistic and writing characteristics of each phase of Hittite history. In turn, this has allowed us to reconstruct the evolution of Hittite culture from its earliest developments to the innovations linked to the administration of this vast empire. However, the dating of a number of sources to the Old Hittite kingdom has revealed the aspects of Hittite culture that developed in its earliest phases. In this way, it has become possible to see a considerable degree of cultural continuity until the fall of the empire. Even Hittite involvement outside Anatolia is already attested in the reign of Hattusili I and Mursili I, especially in terms of their interest in Mesopotamian heroes (from Gilgamesh to Sargon), law codes and so on.

The intensification of contacts outside Anatolia therefore led to an increase in foreign influences on Hittite culture. Contacts with prestigious, yet distant, lands, such as Egypt, Babylonia and Assyria, remained relatively modest. They mainly affected scribal culture, which saw in the Babylonian centres the origins of cuneiform culture. Alongside the diffusion of Babylonian scribal texts (such as bilingual word lists and so on) and literary texts, Hatti experienced the spread of deities such as Marduk of Babylon, Shamash of Sippar, or even the healing powers of Ishtar of Nineveh. Moreover, foreign mantic techniques and practices began to be implemented and some specialists even came to Hatti, from sculptors, physicians, exorcists and so on.

In case of areas directly under Hittite control, such as the Syrian vassal states (speaking Hurrian or Canaanite) and Kizzuwatna, the situation was different. The thirteenth century BC was marked by a strong Hurrian influence departing from Kizzuwatna, Mitanni and the north Syrian states and reaching the Hittite capital, well beyond its original region. One of the main reasons for this diffusion was the prestige of some sanctuaries, myths and rituals in the region. In more practical terms, however, the influence of certain functionaries and priests of Hurrian origins must have facilitated the spread of this phenomenon. The most famous example of this is Puduhepa, wife of Hattusili III and priestess of the goddess Hebat at Kummani (in Kizzuwatna). She greatly influenced her husband in the inclusion of Hurrian cults. The traditional divine triad in the Hittite state cult was made of the solar goddess, Arinna, her husband, the Storm-god of Hatti, and their son, the Storm-god of Nerikka and Zippalanda. The Hurrian counterpart of this triad thus became Hebat, Teshub and Sharruma.

This interest in incorporating Hurrian religion within Hittite state religion was a consequence of the century-long effort in making Anatolian culture (Hittite and Pre-Hittite) a sort of official syncretism of different local cults and traditions. A monumental expression of this desire to assimilate Hurrian religion within the official Hittite pantheon is the sanctuary of Yazilikaya (Figure 18.5). The latter was located

Figure 18.5 The sanctuary of Yazilikaya, near Hattusa. *Above*: Reconstruction of the exterior from the south; *Centre*: The main room; *Below*: A procession of deities.

right outside Hattusa and linked to it through a processional way. The sanctuary had a set of gateways and stairs leading to the main entrance, and a complex of sculpted stone gorges. On the latter, there are several depictions of the processional meeting between female and male deities. This was a typically Hurrian interpretation of the pantheon, as indicated by the names given to the figures, each represented through his or her main characteristics (from attributes, to clothes and symbolic animals). The sanctuary was built during the reign of Tudhaliya IV, son of Puduhepa and Hattusili.

The Hittite archival tradition reveals a similar attempt to assimilate the composite tradition of Anatolia. Hittite cult inventories are already an interesting example in this regard. These inventories of cultic objects provided a description of cultic statues (of either local or foreign origins). They therefore were a bureaucratic manifestation of that iconographic knowledge at the heart of sanctuaries such as Yazilikaya. This knowledge was normally obvious within one's own culture, but was far more complicated in the case of Hatti and its constant foreign influences. Even more typical is the category of texts describing cultic festivals. These were long, detailed day-to-day descriptions of the actions to be performed by each participant, the offerings to provide, and the words to be said during religious festivals. The latter were part of the cultic calendar of a series of localities. Some of these rituals became part of the capital's cultic calendar. However, even if they were not included, they were still important, since the king had to personally travel and officiate at the ceremonies.

Rituals were not only written in Hittite, but also in Hattic (either in part or through the use of some Hattic words), Luwian and Hurrian. This aspect shows how the presence of a variety of local cults was made even more difficult by the variety of languages in use (partly spoken and partly present in the form of cultic residues). The same can be said concerning mythology. Having absorbed some Mesopotamian elements during the Old and Middle Hittite kingdom, the fourteenth and thirteenth centuries BC saw the assimilation of Hurrian myths (from the Song of Ullikummi to the Myth of Kumarbi). These myths were normally set in Upper Mesopotamia and northern Syria. There was even a myth of West Semitic origins (El-kunirsha), a clear assimilation from the more distant Syrian vassals.

Considering the aggravating depopulation of the centre of the empire, the persistence of local cultures, the extraordinary extension of the empire, and the growth of its capital, the syncretism of cults and foreign cultures also had a political value. The wider population spoke Hittite and mainly lived in the capital and its surroundings, but was constantly reduced in number by the Kaska incursions and the continuous wars. Consequently, the empire's population saw the increasing influence of Luwian people, especially from Arzawa to Kizzuwatna, and of Hurrians, from Kizzuwatna to Hanigalbat. Hittite culture did not manage to prevail over these other cultural waves and was forced to accept their influence by making them 'official'. After all, within Hatti itself, Hattusa, despite its size and power, never managed to complete the process of unification and centralisation. Local cults therefore survived, local functionaries continued to stay in power, and temples kept their lands. This forced the Hittite kings to forge a purely formal cultural unification, concentrating several local cults in the capital, and travelling throughout the land to confirm their priestly role in all of the kingdom's cults.

19

SYRIA AND THE LEVANT IN THE LATE BRONZE AGE

1 Demography and settlements

In the Middle and Late Bronze Age, settlements in Syria and the Levant maintained a certain degree of continuity. Virtually no major new settlement was built in this period and city plans practically remained the same, surrounded by the same fortification walls. In other words, cities did not grow enough to require the construction of new walls, so that the strong walls built at the beginning of the second millennium BC only required a few improvements and some restoration works on the gates. Within these walls, public buildings, and palaces in particular, became larger and richer at the expense of residential areas (Figures 19.1 and 19.2). Temples, both of the tripartite rectangular type and the 'temple-tower' type, remained relatively small.

Within this overall continuity, however, there was a general tendency leaning towards settlements located in more fertile and favourable areas, either along the coast or in river valleys. This led to the partial abandonment of settlements located further inland. Therefore, Syrian settlements east of the Orontes and Levantine settlements east of the Jordan River declined, with few exceptions in areas with higher rainfall levels. While in the Early Bronze Age III Syro-Levantine settlements experienced their period of maximum expansion, in the Late Bronze Age these same settlements reached their lowest levels of growth. Areas that had been inhabited for centuries were now abandoned, and only in the Iron Age would people begin to settle in the surrounding hills and mountains. The formerly prestigious Syro-Levantine cities, such as Ebla and Qatna, also visibly declined, and large fields used for intensive agriculture had now become pastureland.

This decline led to a visible increase in animal farming, but a considerable decrease in the number of inhabitants. Animal farming itself was an activity characteristic of smaller communities that did not need to exploit their resources to the full. Combining the available textual and archaeological evidence, it is possible to estimate the number of people living in the area at the time. For some cities we know their perimeters and the size of their residential quarters. Other areas have been surveyed, confirming the overall tendency towards the concentration of people in cities, and providing information for minor settlements existing alongside the larger cities of the region. In this regard, sources from Alalah IV and Ugarit provide reliable information, which can be integrated with further estimates found in the Egyptian evidence.

For instance, the kingdom of Mukish, located in the Amuq Plain, had around 200 villages. These are attested in a number of detailed lists, which provide the number of houses or adult males living there, subdivided into categories. Villages were small and had between three and 80 houses, and between six and 100

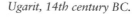

Ugarit, 14th century BC.

Alalah, 15th century BC.

Figure 19.1 Syrian palaces of the Late Bronze Age. *Above*: Ugarit, fourteenth century BC; *Below*: Alalah, fifteenth century BC.

adult males, averaging at around 30 houses and 190 inhabitants per village. Overall, the population living in the countryside included ca. 30,000 people, while the capital Alalah probably added a further 5000 inhabitants. The same can be said for Ugarit, located on the coastal plain near Latakia. In this case, we do not possess many detailed sources. However, it is safe to assume that it had around 200 villages as well, varying in size, but reaching up to a few hundred inhabitants. It has been estimated that the population living in Ugarit's countryside was around 25,000 people and that the capital had a maximum 10,000 inhabitants.

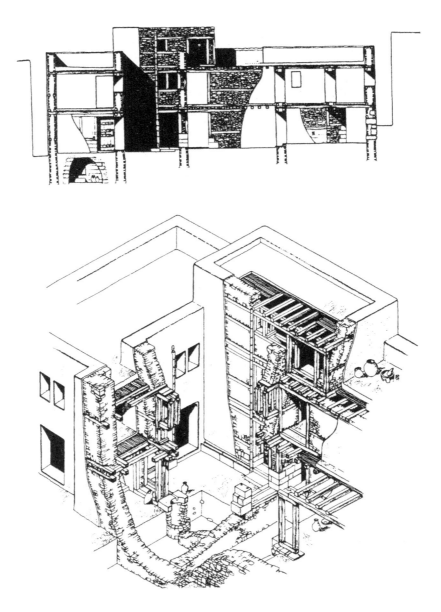

Figure 19.2   A private household in Ugarit, thirteenth century BC. *Above*: Reconstruction; *Below*: Axonometric view
with details of the building techniques used.

A stele of Amenhotep II, recording the dozens of people captured or killed, provides a summary in
which his 'prisoners' amount to around 90,000. This number could not have just included actual prisoners,
but the entire population conquered and left in their land as Egyptian subjects. In particular, the stele mentions 15,000 inhabitants in Nuhashe (the area east of the Orontes). This is a reasonable estimate compared
to the ones calculated for the more densely populated regions of Mukish and Ugarit. Overall, by comparing the archaeological and textual evidence, it has been suggested that there were around 200,000 people
in the Late Bronze Age Levant, and therefore around 750,000 people in the entire Syro-Levantine area.

Apart from this estimate of the total population in the area, there were important local differences. Some city-states were completely imbalanced in their population's distribution. The city of Tyre, located on an island, was an extreme example of a small city with limited control over its hinterland. However, most coastal states had a large number of inhabitants concentrated in cities, and the rest of the population living in the farming villages, while there were virtually no semi-nomadic groups. The Syrian states located in semi-arid areas (such as Nuhashe) or more mountainous ones (such as Amurru) constituted completely different cases, with fewer inhabitants in the cities and a stronger pastoral, rather than agricultural, component.

Overall, the marked preference for settlements in fertile areas provided more land to pastoral activities. This type of occupation was much more difficult to control for the palace administrations. Moreover, the territories separating cities and agricultural fields, made of forests, hills or steppes, were politically 'outside' the control of the state. Consequently, they became increasingly dangerous to cross, especially for merchants and royal messengers, and impossible to control, becoming the preferred refuge for bandits and fugitives.

The lists of villages from Alalah IV provide (as already mentioned in the case of Mitanni) a useful overview on the social structure of the area. The administration divided the population into four categories, which have to be divided into two groups. The first group mainly included the population living outside the palace, divided between the *ḫupšu*, farmers and landowners, and the *ḫaniaḫḫu*, 'shepherds' (the term derives from the name of the Haneans) or even poor individuals without lands. The second group was that of palace functionaries, either charioteers (*maryannu*) or other specialists (*eḫele*). Comparing the various lists available, it can be inferred that the free population amounted to 80 or 90 per cent, of which ca. 85 per cent were farmers and 15 per cent shepherds and poor individuals. Of that 10 or 20 per cent who were palace functionaries, these were mainly *eḫele*, while the *maryannu* were concentrated in the major cities. In the capital the percentages would have been different, with a prevalence of *eḫele* and *maryannu*.

Demographic levels must have been low, especially considering the fact that from the Middle to the Late Bronze Age the total population number declined, and dropped even further from the fifteenth and fourteenth centuries to the thirteenth century BC. It is often believed that the reasons for this decline were wars, in particular the wars of the Egyptian kings, and internal struggles. However, there were also socio-economic factors, such as the overwhelming labour and tribute system, debt slavery, the rising number of fugitives, and the increasing abandonment of entire villages. These were all factors that contributed to these low demographic levels.

In a few cases, one senses a marked difference between families belonging to the palaces, characterised by polygamy and a multitude of children, and farming families, usually monogamous and with few children. Moreover, the gradual deterioration of relations between manufacturers and non-manufacturers would explain the rise in taxes and the resulting breakdown of entire families, from slaves without families to groups of deported people and individual fugitives. Having established the main internal reasons for this decline, it becomes clear that the crisis of the Syro-Levantine area constituted a more passive reaction to the process that had already caused the depopulation of Anatolia, namely, the imperialistic activities of the Hittite state.

2 Socio-economic organisations: the palace and the countryside

Differences in landscape and demography had a strong influence on the local economic tendencies of the Late Bronze Age Syrian and Levantine states. The increasing lack of agricultural workforce and the rise of palace administrations to increasingly high standards caused a marked social, economic and political separation between palaces and villages. This division had never been as obvious in the previous, or even the following, periods. Nonetheless, palace economies ultimately relied on the productivity of the primary sector, which in turn provided for the palaces through their tributes.

Unfortunately, Syro-Levantine agricultural yields in this period were very low. For the Late Bronze Age, we have yields on a ratio of 3:1 or 5:1 between planted seeds and harvests. These low yields, together with a lack of agricultural workforce, led to the abandonment of fields located in semi-arid areas, whose harvests were far too unpredictable. Therefore, this period saw the rise of more specialised cultivations, requiring even more labour and irrigated fields. The texts from Ugarit and Alalah, close to the Mediterranean coast, and from Emar and Ekalte, in the Euphrates Valley, portray a landscape made of square or rectangular fields (not as elongated as the ones found in Mesopotamia) for the rainfed cultivation of cereals, of small irrigated gardens surrounded by an enclosure wall (especially in Emar, on the Euphrates, and in Ugarit, in a coastal area with water springs), and of vineyards (especially in Alalah and Ugarit) and olive-groves in hillier areas.

However, the characteristics of the region's agricultural landscape were not as influential as the legal administration of these lands. The basic separation between lands belonging to the palace and lands owned by private families continued to exist. The former lands were partly used by the palace, through the employment of servants without families (and thus without offspring). These farmers had to give up 50 per cent of their harvests to the palace, while the remaining half was used to cultivate the lands the following year, as well as to provide food to people and animals. Alternatively, the palace allotted its lands to palace functionaries on a temporary basis. Eventually, these lands remained within the same families, forming a class of absent landowners working for the palace.

Regarding lands belonging to villages, the palace required them to pay a tithe, thus far less than what the palace required from its own employees. In fact, the palace could not extend its control over the villages' lands. Villages were a crucial source of labour, needed to work on palace lands full-time whenever necessary, or for seasonal and intensive work (as it would have been inconvenient for the palace to maintain permanent servants for this purpose). Therefore, palace lands were productive because they used part of the economic and social resources of the villages. Other palace activities, such as the farming of sheep for the production of wool or various types of workshops, were not producing food surplus, but simply transforming raw materials. Consequently, the value of payments in food rations, fundamental for workshops that did not produce food, could have been equal to the value of the goods produced. However, the overall advantage of this system was the production and availability of a wider range of products.

With an agro-pastoral productivity that did not provide wide margins for surplus, the palace economies, especially in coastal areas such as Ugarit, Byblos and Tyre, and more northern ones, such as Carchemish and Aleppo, largely relied on craftsmanship and trade. Just like in the Eblaite period, the main sectors were two, namely, textiles and bronze. The textile sector was centred on transhumant wool production, which gained significant value and prestige through specific techniques, such as dying fabrics in various shades of purple (produced from Mediterranean molluscs). Bronze production was also highly developed, thanks to the availability of copper from nearby Cyprus. Moreover, bronze was continuously exported to Mesopotamia, Egypt and even Anatolia. The tributes Syrian states had to pay to the Hittites, and Levantine states to the Egyptians, show that the main products required were purple dyed woollen fabrics and bronze objects and weapons. In the case of gift-exchanges between royal courts, there were also high-quality luxury products, such as glass, jewellery, gold and silver cups, specific items of clothing, or chariots.

In the Late Bronze Age, the palace and family sectors experienced significant social changes. These were mainly due to the above-mentioned economic and political problems of the period, which affected the Near East as a whole, but had a particular impact on Syria and the Levant. From as early as the sixteenth century BC, the palace was characterised by the solidarity existing between the king and his elite. This resulted in the marginalisation and exploitation of the rest of the population. This solidarity was further strengthened by those processes of accumulation of lands in the hands of few wealthy individuals and debt slavery. The king had in fact ceased to take care of these processes. The solidarity of the elite also did not manage to preserve the ancient system according to which specialised labourers guaranteed their services to the palace in exchange for their maintenance. Between the fourteenth and thirteenth centuries BC, then, three phenomena developed alongside each other, whose combination eventually threatened the entire system.

The first phenomenon, the most ancient and obvious one, was the transmission from father to son of the service to the palace and the land allotted with it. In the long run, those who were born in lands belonging to their families for generations naturally believed that it was a particular type of family property requiring royal approval, such as a document signed by the king. Consequently, the former service to the palace was simply turned into a heavy tribute, which completely upset the relation between service and retribution.

The second phenomenon, which was more recent and problematic, was the spread of exemptions from service. These were originally granted as a repayment for special services to the king. However, with time the exemptions began to be inherited as well, becoming closely linked to a particular land, rather than a specific beneficiary. The third phenomenon was typical of cities like Ugarit, where economic and commercial activities were more important than military campaigns. It was the practice of paying the palace instead of providing a service, especially when the latter was military (such as being a *maryannu*, or other), and therefore too dangerous.

The accumulation of unlawful inheritances, exemptions and payments for services, at first every year, then only once, brought the palace to lose its specialised labourers. The phenomenon mainly involved the upper classes, while craftsmen seem to have been less involved in this particular development. Different exemption strategies began to appear, clearly exemplified by the two opposite groups of the merchants and the *maryannu*. As commercial agents working for the palace, merchants would have generally departed with a grant from the palace to bring back goods from abroad. However, they started to combine this institutional activity, which provided them with considerable wealth, with more commercial and financial activities, such as interest loans and counter-guarantees. The aim of these merchants was to increase their personal wealth at the expense of the palace. They thus obtained service and tax exemptions, which made them more like independent dealers than palace functionaries. When palace administrations collapsed at the beginning of the twelfth century BC, merchants were therefore able to continue their activities, restructuring the system formerly centred on the palace. The strategy used by the *maryannu* was simply based on a combination of exemptions and inheritances. They 'paid' for their freedom and generated an income from their lands, through a system that by now did not require them to work. By the time palaces collapsed, partly because of these military exemptions, the class of the *maryannu* was completely swept away, disappearing from the sources.

While the inheritance of lands and services had moved from the family sector to the palace, the latter's attention for personal merits rather than family history began to spread among its free citizens. The head of the household therefore became an independent landowner, rather than the owner of a land that belonged to his entire family. This is due to the spread of land sales, which were by now free of all those obsolete symbolic and ceremonial practices in use in the past. As we have already seen for Nuzi, but without all the juridical fiction, in many cases these alienations happened out of necessity, greatly benefiting those who could lend money (either merchants or other members of the palace). Even in case of inheritances within a family, the old criteria of transferring one's estate to one's sons (and a privileged share to one's eldest son) were gradually substituted by choices based on merit and personal preferences. The first idea was that there was no elder or younger son, and the eldest son could not rely on his innate privilege anymore. The second criteria was that, in order to inherit, it was necessary to 'honour' (*kabādu*, as one would say in Ugarit) or 'fear' (*palāḫu*, as one would say in Emar) one's parents, namely, take care of them and obey them, acting respectfully towards them.

Being one's son, thus one's biological heir, was therefore not enough anymore, since procedures of disinheritance and alienation were now relatively common and easy to implement. Especially in case of the death of a father, the respectful behaviour of sons towards their widowed mother, who in Emar became 'both mother and father', was crucial to ensure them their inheritance. No one could rely on a right by birth on his inheritance anymore, but had to earn this right through work and obedience to one's parents.

Moreover, when birth rates were low and families were extremely small, adoptions and emancipations of female slaves became increasingly common. This practice contributed to the transformation of the old family solidarity, based on a network of mutual support allowing families to overcome financial or demographic difficulties within a wider community, into a mere issue of financial management. This forced the former system of communal solidarity to slowly disappear. Therefore, this social solidarity was substituted by personal achievements and the commodification of land and labour. The process thus allowed the strongest to survive and left the weakest to perish.

Debtors unable to repay their loans and forced to become slaves for life thus became incredibly numerous. In this regard, the political authorities did not develop any measures to protect them or free them. Instead of commissioning remission edicts, palaces were too busy promulgating agreements for the search, capture and return of fugitives to their owners. Unable to flee from one state to the other, fugitives tried their luck in areas outside palace control. In the steppes, mountain and forest fugitives, called the *ḫabiru*, found refuge in tribal groups involved in transhumant farming and banditry at the expense of palace caravans. The consequences of this process were serious. Villages, which the majority of fugitives came from, found an alternative to the authority of the palace. At the same time, shepherds began to play a less marginal and more conflictual role towards the palace. The merciless exploitation of rural classes by the palace and the increasingly low demographic levels, together with the increasing exemptions of palace functionaries and the changes in family relations, laid the groundwork for significant social changes. The latter, however, were waiting for the definite collapse of the palaces' authority to become fully effective.

3 The structure and political dependences of the Syro-Levantine states

Within the typically two-level political system of the Late Bronze Age, the entire Syro-Levantine region appeared as a land of small kings and the only region not to be politically unified under one great king (Table 19.1). After the collapse of the kingdom of Yamhad at the hands of Mursili I, the area became a highly desirable target for all the surrounding great powers. The latter were clearly trying to take advantage of the political fragmentation of the area. After the short-lived control of the area by the kings of the Old Hittite kingdom, from 1600 to 1200 BC the region was split between the Mitannians, the Egyptians and the Hittites, three completely different political entities.

The Mitannian presence in the area is not well attested. We know that Mitanni established its control in northern Syria when the Old Hittite kingdom collapsed. From there, Mitanni expanded further, conquering southern Syria. There, Tunip and Qadesh took advantage of Mitannian support to oppose the Egyptian campaigns in Syria. However, the Mitannian influence in the region was put to an end by the memorable expedition of Suppiluliuma against Tushratta. Mitannian control was based on the prestige of its charioteers (the *maryannu*), who spread from Mitanni to Syria. The military interventions of the Mitannians in Syria, however, are not documented. We can only catch a glimpse of them once they had already established their control over the area.

At that time, small Syrian kings like Idrimi (Text 19.1) could only rule if they were recognised by the Mitannian king. They therefore had to seal some sort of agreement with him, although the details of these treaties remain unknown to us. We know that it was a personal type of agreement of reciprocal loyalty between lord and vassal, forging a relation loose enough to allow small kings to seal treaties among themselves. This indicates that the Syrian states had a certain degree of freedom in their foreign relations. Nonetheless, the vassals also benefited from Mitannian support in case of external attacks, such as the Egyptian expeditions against Qadesh, and internal ones, such as in the case of Idrimi, a usurper who had to wait for 'seven years' to be accepted as legitimate ruler.

Shortly after, the Egyptians established their control through the expeditions of the first kings of the eighteenth dynasty, who had just defeated the last Hyksos rulers. The first military campaigns in Syria were demanding, since they reached almost the heart of the Near East. Tuthmosis I even left a stele along the

Table 19.1 The chronology of Syria and Anatolia, ca. 1350–1200 BC

	Hatti	Carchemish	Aleppo	Ugarit	Amurru	Egypt
1400						
	Suppiluliuma ca.1370–1342	Piyashshili (Sharri-Kushuh) ca.1345–1335	Telipinu ca. 1345–1330	Ammistamru I ?–1370 Niqmadu II ca.1370–1335	Abdi-Ashitta ca.1400–1370 Aziru ca.1370–1335	Amenhotep III 1402–1364 Amenhotep IV 1364–1347
1350						
	Arnuwanda II ca.1342–1340 Mursili II ca. 1340–1310	Shahurunuwa (and/or XX-Sharruma) ca. 1335–1270	Talmi-Sharruma ca. 1330–?	Ar-Halba ca. 1335–1332	Ari-Teshub ca. 1335–1332 Duppi-Teshub ca. 1332–1300	Tutankhamun 1347–1338 Ay 1338–1334 Horemheb 1334–1306
1300						
	Muwatalli ca. 1310–1280 Urhi-Teshub ca. 1280–1275 Hattusili III ca. 1275–1260	Ini-Teshub ca.1270–1220	Halpaziti ca. 1250	Niqmepa ca. 1332–1270 Ammistamru II ca. 1270–1230	Benteshina ca. 1300–1285 Shapili ca.1285–1276 Benteshina ca. 1275–1250	Ramses I ca. 1306–1304 Seti I ca. 1304–1290 Rameses II ca. 1290–1224
1250						
	Tudhaliya IV ca. 1260–1220 Arnuwanda III ca. 1220–1200	Talmi-Teshub ca. 1220–1190		Ibiranu ca. 1230–1210 Niqmadu III ca.1210–1200	Shaushgamuwa ca. 1250–1220 »	Merneptah ca. 1224–1210
1200						
	Suppiluliuma II ca. 1200–1182	Kuzi-Teshub ca. 1190–?		Ammurapi ca. 1200–1182	» »	Seti II and others 1210–1190 Ramses III 1190–1159
1150						

Text 19.1   The autobiography of Idrimi, king of Alalah

'I am Idrimi, the son of Ilim-ilimma, servant of Adad, Hebat and Ishtar, the lady of Alalah, my ladies. In Aleppo, my paternal home, a hostile incident occurred, and we had to flee to the people of Emar, my mother's relatives, and we stayed in Emar. My brothers, who were older than me, stayed with me, but none of them thought the things I thought. I thought this: whoever will gain control over the paternal home will be the true first-born son, and whoever will not, will remain the servant of the people of Emar. I took my horses, my chariot, my groom, and rode in the desert, entering the land of the (nomadic) Sutians. There, I spent the night in my covered chariot. The next day I departed and arrived in the land of Canaan, where there is the town of Ammiya. In Ammiya, there were people from Aleppo, Mukish, Ni' and Ama'u: as soon as they realised that I was the son of their lord, they joined me, and thus I increased the total number of my companions. For seven years, I lived among the Habiru (fugitives), releasing birds (for omens) and examining (sacrificial) entrails, until in the seventh year Adad turned towards me. So I made ships, filled them with my soldiers, and proceeded via sea towards the land of Mukish and reached land at Mount Casius. I marched inland, and my land found out, and they brought me oxen and sheep. In a single day, in unison, Ni', Ama'u, Mukish, and Alalah, my city, came to me. My brothers found out and they came to me: since they concluded a treaty with me, I confirmed them as my brothers.

For seven years, Barattarna, the mighty king, king of the Hurrians, was hostile to me; but in the seventh year I wrote to King Barattarna, king of the Umman-Manda, reminding him of the services of my ancestors, when they were at their service and our actions were pleasing to the kings of the Hurrians, and they had made a binding agreement between them. The mighty king paid heed to the previous services and the oath between them, respected the (previous) agreement – both in terms of the structure of the oath, and in terms of our services – and accepted my regards. I increased my loyalty even further, which was already considerable, and through my valiantness and my loyalty I returned to him a (otherwise) lost dynasty. I swore the binding agreement and (so) became king in Alalah.

The kings of the south and the north came to me: since they had heaped on the ground the . . . (?) of my fathers in their lands, I picked it up from the ground and raised it even more. I took my soldiers and marched against the land of Hatti. Seven of their fortified cities: Pashahu, Damarut-re'i, Haluhhan, Zisal, Ie, Uluzina, and Zaruna, these were their cities and these I destroyed. The land of Hatti did not assemble against me, so I did what I wanted. I captured their prisoners, I took their valuables, their possessions, their things, and I divided them among my auxiliaries, my brothers, and my friends: their parts I provided. I returned in the land of Mukish and entered my city Alalah.

With the prisoners and the valuables, possessions, and things that I brought from the land of Hatti, I built a palace. I made my throne like the throne of (other) kings, I made my brothers like the brothers of the king, my sons like their sons, I made my companions their companions. The inhabitants of my land I made to live in favourable places; those who did not have a dwelling, I made them dwell, thus consolidating my reign. I made my cities like they were before, at the time of the ancestors. The signs that the gods of Alalah had established, and the sacrifices that our ancestors used to perform, I performed them regularly: these things I did, and I entrusted them to my son Adad-nirari.

I ruled for twenty years. I wrote my deeds on my statue, (so that everyone) may see them and bless me.'

Euphrates to mark the fact that he had reached the edge of the world. However, these incursions did not last long. Only with Tuthmosis III would the Egyptians eventually implement a more methodical and progressive strategy to subdue the Levant and southern Syria, achieving several military successes. Having consolidated their control as far as Ugarit and Qadesh (Figure 19.3), the Egyptians developed a conflictual relation with Mitanni. However, the situation was soon turned into a peaceful agreement between the two powers.

Egyptian control in the Near East was divided into three levels. There were a few areas under direct Egyptian control, such as some ports, the fertile area of Yarimuta (on the plain between Acre and Megiddo), used to provide for the troops, and some cities in strategic locations, such as Beit She'an (the best attested city archaeologically). The entire region was divided into three provinces, whose main centres were: Gaza, in the province of Canaan; Sumura, in the province of Amurru, on the Lebanese coast; and Kumidi, in the province of Ube, Beqa and Damascus. These three cities hosted Egyptian governors, their storehouses and garrisons. They were the main centres of Egyptian control, especially for the secondary and more widespread type of dependence on the Egyptians.

This system allowed local small kings to continue to rule in their states by sealing a treaty of dependence to the Egyptian king. This treaty forced the vassal to obey the great king. The agreement was entirely one-sided. In fact, the Egyptian king was not interested in local conflicts in the area, as long as the winners remained loyal to him. In other words, Egypt did not provide support to his vassals. In terms of tributes, the amounts required were sent in letters and then collected each year, or on other occasions in case of further requests (Figure 19.4). If the local king was able to control the city entrusted to him, pay the tributes and ensure military support to the Egyptian troops in the area, the Egyptian king was satisfied and did not require more.

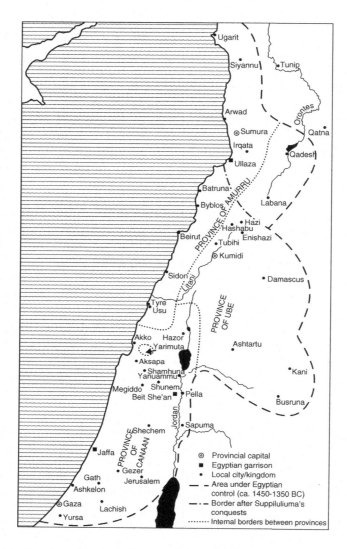

Figure 19.3 Map of the Egyptian territories in Syria and Palestine between the fifteenth and thirteenth centuries BC.

However, the Egyptian indifference to the frequent conflicts among vassals caused a progressive deterioration of the political organisation of the Syro-Levantine states, with several usurpations, conquests and plunders.

The third level of political control was applied on some marginal states, located along the borders of the Egyptian territories, such as the Sinai (on the other side of the line of coastal fortresses protecting the passage between the western Delta and the southernmost Levantine cities), the Transjordan plateau, the hills in the West Bank, and the forests of northern Beqa and the Upper Orontes. In these areas, the Egyptian ruler could not exact a fixed tribute, due to the lack of palaces and recognisable political leaders. Moreover, the groups living in these areas frequently hindered the network of communications that had to pass through their territories. This problem led to several Egyptian expeditions in these areas, as a response to the continuous raids at the hands of these 'bandits'.

Figure 19.4   Syrians presenting their tribute to the Egyptian king (tomb of Menkheperresoneb, from the reign of Tuthmosis III).

Hittite control developed along different lines. The system was established during the reign of Suppiluliuma. The latter partly took control over the Syrian states formerly under Mitannian control, and partly gained the support of states formerly under Egyptian control, such as Ugarit, Amurru and Qadesh (Figure 19.5). The Hittite system was very similar to the Mitannian one. It was based on mutual loyalty established through written treaties. The Hittite king ensured protection to his loyal vassals and contributed to the consolidation of political relations among the north Syrian states. Hittite presence, however, was more invasive than Mitannian presence in the area. It did not allow alliances between small kings, and every problem had to be dealt with directly by the king. Therefore, any controversy inevitably required the intervention of the Hittite ruler. This allowed him to modify the local political structure of the Syrian states, from the borders between states to the relations of dependence between small kings and their own vassals. Just like the Egyptians, the Hittites also required the yearly payment of a tribute, which was not collected, but personally delivered to the Hittite court. Apart from these standard practices, there were specific agreements developed to deal with particular or exceptional cases.

In many cases, on top of this system of dependences, another type of control was implemented. This was a characteristic aspect of Hittite policy, namely, the appointment of members of the royal family of Hattusa in the conquered states. In the two key cities of the region, Aleppo and Carchemish, Suppiluliuma appointed two of his sons as kings. Moreover, he gave a pivotal role to the king of Carchemish. Eventually, the latter became so powerful as to become almost a Hittite viceroy in Syria. When Aleppo's power declined, Carchemish managed to acquire even more territories, from Aleppo itself to the former kingdom of Mukish (where a son of the previous king was appointed), the region of Ashtata and Emar (in the Euphrates Valley, south of Carchemish) and Siyannu (on the Mediterranean coast). Another type of political control was implemented through the establishment of actual kinship relations, such as the marriage that linked Hattusili III to the royal house of Amurru. The name and personal seal of Shaushgamuwa, king of Amurru, shows that he was of Hittite descent on his mother's side.

Regarding the small kingdoms, rivalries continued in the Mitannian area (as in the case of Idrimi), and significantly increased in the Egyptian area. There were conflicts between Amurru and Ugarit, Amurru and Byblos, Tyre and Sidon, and the expansionistic campaigns of Qadesh, Shechem and Jerusalem. Only the Hittites managed to keep these rivalries under control, although mainly in the north. In

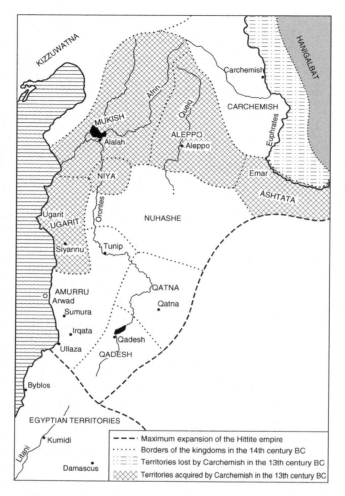

Figure 19.5 Hittite territories in Syria, ca. 1350–1190 BC.

these conditions, the attempts of the Syro-Levantine kingdoms to rise to power only took place before the consolidation of the great powers' control (for instance in the case of Aleppo and Qadesh at the beginning of the Mitannian control in the region), or in marginal areas (such as the attempt of Amurru to rise to independence from both the Egyptians and the Hittites). The only attempt that managed to last was the one of Carchemish. However, this was simply because it did not rise against the system, but as an integral part of it. In fact, the 'viceroyalty' of Carchemish in the thirteenth century BC laid the foundations for the Neo-Hittite state, a power that would last even after the fall of the empire.

Each kingdom followed the dynastic rule according to which no one could seize the throne (not even a usurper), if he did not belong to the royal family. This principle, however, still allowed a wide range of individuals to rise to power. A throne undoubtedly constituted an indissoluble inheritance. The two principles by now widespread on a family level, namely, personal merit and the non-biological theory about inheritances, caused bitter fights among brothers. These fights were worsened by the kings' polygamy and the influence of mothers in the selection of the heir to the throne.

Once on the throne, the king was still conditioned by a series of factors. The first factor came from his superiors, since a lesser king was always a vassal to a great king. Second, the king was influenced by his subjects, since the 'city', with its high concentration of elite groups (from the *maryannu* to merchants, scribes and priests), was powerful enough to express its opinions and disapproval. Finally, there was the king's own family and social class, made of the 'great ones' and the 'sons of the king', potential rivals and leaders of internal revolts. The situation was therefore quite unstable. On an ideological level, the situation emphasised those ideals of valour and initiative. However, from a practical point of view, it entailed several internal conflicts. Together with the political dependence to a great king, these conflicts worsened an already difficult economic and demographic situation.

The palace administration was based on a highly bureaucratic and hierarchic structure, led by a governor (*šakin māti*), a series of functionaries responsible for specific sectors (such as the harbour, chariots, fields and so on), and several professional groups (which should not be considered proper 'corporations'). Outside the palace, villages and cities had their own political microstructure, led by a delegated official appointed by the king (*ḫazānu*), the institution of the 'elders', which was a legacy of the ancient pluralistic and kin-based political organisation of the area and an assembly. The elders, usually five, represented the village when dealing with requests from the palace, such as searches for fugitives or when merchants were killed. In these cases, the village rested on its communal solidarity and remained silent in front of the royal judges. The elders would state that they knew nothing about the events, and the village paid the compensations required, to then deal with the problem internally. Therefore, below the great and small kings, there was a third level of political organisation. This was constituted by local communities, with their collective structure made of communal fields, wells, and pastures, their contributions to the palace (the payment of tithes and the dispatch of men for *corvée* work), their collective responsibilities, and their kin-based structure. More than anywhere else, in Syria and the Levant village communities still held a role in the Late Bronze Age that had long disappeared elsewhere, suppressed by the intrusive nature of the great urban organisations, namely, the temple and the palace.

4 Political developments and the local states

The politically fragmented and dependent states of Syria and the Levant experienced modest local developments, but monumental conflicts between the great powers of the time. In this regard, the sixteenth century BC remains poorly documented. In the north, the Mitannians established their control at the expense of the Hatti of Hantili and Ammuna, and developed a network of relations with the states of the area. Some of these were involved in coalitions. This was the case of Aleppo, which at the time of the plot against Idrimi's father controlled a large portion of northern Syria (from Aleppo to Mukish, Niya, and Ama'u). Qadesh was in a similar situation. Egyptian sources describe its hegemonic position over other important kingdoms in the area, such as Megiddo and Tunip.

This was a transitional phase from a system of medium-sized coalitions led by local kingdoms (Yamhad, Qatna, and Hazor in the Mari Age), to a system of dependency on a single foreign great king. The majority of evidence for this phase comes from the texts found in Level IV at Alalah. Its kings (Idrimi and Niqmepa) sealed alliances with Kizzuwatna and Tunip in order to recover and return some fugitives. Other sources come from Qatna. Apart from the well-known temple inventories from the fifteenth century BC, other texts have been recently discovered, such as the so-called Idanda archive (alongside its rich royal underground cellars and palace). These texts fill the gap in the documentation between the temple inventories and the Amarna period, when Akizzi was king of Qatna. After the destruction of the city by Suppiluliuma, Qatna's role, which had been important in the Middle Bronze Age, gradually declined. Just like Ebla, the city became a field of ruins in a semi-arid steppe, and its monumental walls ceased to enclose anything anymore.

Around the same time, the first Egyptian kings of the eighteenth dynasty began their first expeditions. These campaigns covered a considerable distance, but failed to establish a solid Egyptian presence in the Near East. These first attempts would turn out to be in vain, due to the lack of foreign expeditions during the reign of Hatshepsut. It is pointless to try to date the expeditions of Tuthmosis I and III so that they do not overlap with the sources from Alalah IV. In actual fact, they can very well overlap, since these expeditions were occasional and did not threaten the Mitannian supremacy in the area. The southern Levant was a different case, since the area was already under Egyptian control from the sixteenth century BC.

In the first half of the fifteenth century BC, the expeditions of Tuthmosis III brought to the consolidation of Egyptian control throughout the Levant and over a large portion of Syria. These systematic and continuous campaigns can be divided into three phases. In the first phase, there was the great campaign of Tuthmosis III's first regnal year. It culminated in the battle of Megiddo, which ensured Egyptian control in the Levant. In the second phase, there were the campaigns of the fifth to seventh years. These led to the conquest of Qadesh and southern Syria. The remaining campaigns constitute the third phase (eighth year onwards), leading Tuthmosis to the Euphrates, well within Mitannian territories, from which the Egyptian ruler took the entire coast up to Ugarit, and the Orontes Valley (with Tunip and Nuhashe). The following campaigns of Amenhotep II simply consolidated control over these areas, perhaps with some losses. When the border between Egypt and Mitanni was established and the two powers came to an agreement, possibly as a reaction to the Hittite expansion of Tudhaliya II, Mitanni kept Aleppo, Mukish, and Nuhashe, while Egypt kept Ugarit, Tunip, Qadesh and the southernmost states.

The Amarna Age has often been depicted as a period in which Egypt had lost some of its control in the Near East. However, a closer look at the sources, especially the letters from the Amarna archive, shows that Egyptian control in the Near East continued to exist in its usual form (Text 19.2). The latter was considerably frustrating for the small Syro-Levantine kings, who did not receive any support in return for their loyalty to the Egyptian king. They denounced the Egyptian king's indifference, in the hope of receiving some sort of support. However, these denunciations were more the result of a constant misunderstanding of the nature of Egyptian presence in the Near East. They do not indicate that the Amarna Age was a phase of particular Egyptian indifference for Near Eastern affairs.

Text 19.2 The epistolary protocol of the archive of el-Amarna

Themes: a) protection; b) listening; c) preparation (military).

Egyptian request

'Say to Indaruta, man of Achshaph: thus (speaks) the king. I made this tablet reach you to tell you:

a   Make sure to protect the place of the king where you are.
b   Behold, the king has sent you to Hanni, son of Mayriya, head-groom of the king of Canaan. Listen carefully to the things he will tell you: may the king not catch you doing something wrong! Listen carefully to everything he says and do it accurately!
c   Beware not to be negligent: may you be prepared in anticipation (of the arrival) of the troops, food being plentiful, wine, and everything else being plentiful.

He will arrive very soon and will behead the enemies of the king. Be aware that the king is well, like the Sun in the sky, and his troops and chariots are very well.'

Positive answer

'To the king, my lord, my god, my Sun, the Sun in the sky, thus speaks Yidya, man of Ashkelon, your servant, the dirt under your feet, the groom of your horses. I prostrate myself at the feet of the king, my lord, the Sun in the sky, seven and seven times I prostrate myself on the back and on the stomach.

a   I am indeed guarding the place of the king and the city of the king, my lord, where I am.

b   Who is the dog that would not obey the orders of the king, the Sun in the sky?!

c   I am indeed preparing absolutely everything: food, drinks, oxen, grain, straw, everything that the king, my lord, commanded, I am indeed preparing it. And I am indeed preparing the tribute of the Sun, in accordance with the command of the king, my lord, the Sun in the sky.'

Negative Answer

'Rib-Adda says to the king, my lord: I prostrate myself at the feet of my lord, seven and seven times I prostrate myself.

c   Since my lord has written to me asking me for *taskarinnu* -wood, this can be found in Zalhi and Ugarit, but I cannot send ships over there because Aziru is hostile to me and the rulers of all the cities are allied to him: their ships move as they wish and take whatever they want.

. . .

a   Since the king, my lord, says: "Protect them, and protect the city of the king who is with you," how can I protect it? I have written to the king, my lord: "All the cities are taken, only Byblos and another one are left." I have sent a messenger to the king, my lord, but troops have not been sent to me and the messenger has not been released either . . .'

It is probably true that more than a decade of control in the area would have lowered Egyptian military presence in the Near East, turning the rounds to collect tributes into a mere routine. It is also true that the rumblings of Suppiluliuma's interventions in Syria sparked several reactions in the small kingdoms along the border. Consequently, Aitakama of Qadesh and Aziru of Amurru chose an aggressive strategy. This led to the protests of their neighbours and a certain degree of concern in the Egyptian court. Their activities were not much different from those of other kings, such as Lab'aya of Shechem or Zimrida of Sidon, but while the latter acted within the Egyptian territories without threatening Egyptian supremacy, Aitakama and Aziru acted on the border, a fact that could have led to their separation from the Egyptian sphere of control.

When Suppiluliuma's presence was consolidated and Mitannian supremacy suddenly collapsed, the states began to ask for support from each other. The former Mitannian vassals (Qatna and Nuhashe) close to the Egyptian border asked for help from the Egyptian king, recalling their ancient dependence to the dynasty. On the contrary, the Egyptian vassals located along the border (Qadesh, Amurru, and Ugarit) abandoned the Egyptian king and swore their loyalty to the Hittite king. Eventually, Suppiluliuma's success led to the inclusion of both groups under Hittite control. The Egyptian border, then, moved from Ugarit to Byblos, and from Qadesh to Beqa.

From the second half of the fourteenth century to the thirteenth century BC, Hittite and Egyptian control remained stable. This stability was initially the result of a hostile balance of power, with continuous attempts by the Egyptian kings (from Seti I to Ramses II) to regain control over Qadesh and Amurru. The most famous episode in this regard is the battle of Qadesh, where Ramses II's attempt to move north was put to a halt. The king had to give up on Qadesh and Amurru, and suffered some incursions reaching as far as Damascus. Despite these setbacks, the Egyptian kings, such as Ramses II in the case of Qadesh, still celebrated their feats or their easy victories over the rebellious cities and tribes on a monumental scale. They did not give up this internal propagandistic agenda even when the border of their territory was established through a treaty between Hattusili III and Ramses II, sealed through an inter-dynastic marriage, rather than military combat.

In the north, it is important to follow the history of Carchemish, Amurru and Ugarit, each significant for different reasons. Carchemish is a unique case. The city had always been important for its strategic location. Suppiluliuma chose it as a privileged seat of power and entrusted it to his son Piyashshili. The latter showed great military talent in placing Shattiwaza on Hanigalbat's throne, and in dealing with the revolts in Nuhashe and Qadesh. Under his and his successor's rule, Carchemish became a delegate of Hatti for the control of Syrian affairs. The process culminated in the second half of the thirteenth century BC, with the reigns of Ini-Teshub and Talmi-Teshub.

At that time, the kingdom of Carchemish extended from Emar (whose texts clearly show the dependence of its kings to the kings of Carchemish) to Mukish and Aleppo, and supervised all Syrian affairs. From Tudhaliya IV's reign onwards, then, Carchemish effectively cut off the Hittite kings' power over the area. The inter-dynastic legal texts found at Ugarit show that Carchemish's political and commercial presence in northern Syria became hegemonic. Its kings were therefore able to take full advantage of the delegation of power received from their cousins, the Hittite kings. In the final phase of the empire, and within the overall tendency towards political fragmentation, the kings of Carchemish were able to act independently and to take over the role, as well as the title, of great king.

On the contrary, Amurru was a new kingdom, created in the Amarna period by a talented tribal and military leader, Abdi-Ashirta. The centre of this new state was located in the Lebanese mountains, which acted as the military base for fugitives (ḫabiru) and shepherds. There were no cities and Abdi-Ashirta never held the title of king. Through an intense propaganda addressing fugitives and village farmers, Abdi-Ashirta managed to rise to power, threatening the coastal cities, especially Byblos (whose king Rib-Adda recorded Amurru's rise in his heartfelt and in vain appeals to the Egyptian king), and the cities in the Orontes Valley. Taking advantage of an attack to the city of Sumura, Abdi-Ashirta volunteered to reconstruct the city and to take on the role of Egyptian delegate over the whole of Amurru, which was the name of the Egyptian province headed by Sumura.

After the death of Abdi-Ashirta, the situation successfully evolved under the leadership of his son Aziru. He consolidated control over Tunip and Sumura, conquered Ugarit and Byblos, and played on the Egyptian fear of his potential alliance to the Hittites. Aziru therefore made Amurru a hegemonic power along the Egyptian border. Suppiluliuma's victory brought Amurru to leave the Egyptian sphere of control to join the Hittites. However, this new ally turned out to be much more actively involved and demanding in terms of loyalty. Therefore, through his alliance with Hatti, Amurru's hegemonic role was drastically reduced. Nonetheless, at the beginning of the thirteenth century BC, Amurru's position alongside the border inspired Benteshina to follow the example of his predecessor Aziru. Benteshina's alliance with Egypt was the main cause of the war between Ramses and Muwatalli and the battle of Qadesh. Benteshina lost his kingdom, but he regained control over it after cleverly siding with the winner in the conflict between Hattusili and Urhi-Teshub. Having established kinship ties with the Hittite royal family, the last kings of Amurru would maintain the peace until the end of the empire.

Ugarit was a smaller kingdom compared to Amurru, and less powerful than Carchemish. However, it remains particularly important for us ever since excavations uncovered its royal palace, complete with its diplomatic, epistolary, legal and administrative archives. These constitute the main source for the reconstruction of the historical and social developments of Late Bronze Age Syria. As an Egyptian vassal until the Amarna period, Ugarit endured the military pressures of its southern neighbour, Amurru. Not long after this, Ugarit pledged its loyalty to the Hittites. This took place during the reign of king Niqmadu. He restored the city's royal palace, re-organised its archives, and copied many literary texts. After Niqmadu's death, Ugarit was involved in the revolts of Mursili II's early years, thus losing the territories it had previously obtained. During Niqmepa's and Ammistamru's reigns, Ugarit's dependence to Hatti, and more specifically Carchemish, became even more explicit. On top of the standard treaty sealed between Mursili and Niqmepa, further agreements were signed to guarantee the permanence of Hittite merchants in the city, the return of fugitives to Ugarit, and the sanctions to apply in case merchants got killed.

Ugarit's primary role was commercial. It was the most important Syrian port within the Hittite realm, with privileged relations with Cyprus, the entire Syro-Levantine coast, and Cilicia, reaching the Egyptian Delta on the one side and Crete on the other. Hittite interest in the commercial activities and wealth of Ugarit was in marked contrast with Ugarit's military involvement. The city often preferred to pay large tributes instead of sending troops to war against the Assyrians. Therefore, Ugarit showed an increasing military and political indifference, which by the last decades of the thirteenth century BC became so evident that it caused several complaints. However, in the final crisis, Ugarit was still able to deploy its fleet and troops to defend the Hittite ruler.

5 Art and scribal culture

The marked political and socio-economic separation between ruling and rural classes is also attested in Syrian and Levantine culture. The material culture of Late Bronze Age Syria and the Levant, visible in the most popular products of the time, shows a marked decline in quality in comparison to the Middle Bronze Age. It is probable that rural settlements and modest residences experienced an overall process of impoverishment. On the contrary, royal palaces and elite residences show the highest concentration of wealth ever attested in the Near East. If the Levantine palaces were not comparable to the abodes of the other Near Eastern great kings in terms of size, wealth and grandeur, they could be compared to the latter in terms of quality. Local palace craftsmanship was highly desirable and appreciated by foreign great kings, who tried to acquire it in the form of tributes or gifts.

The cultural heart of the palaces was the scribal school, which was responsible for the administration and organisation of archives. Syllabic cuneiform continued to be the most popular type of writing not only for diplomatic correspondence, but also for internal administrative and legal texts. Knowledge of Akkadian was not well developed and locally adapted in smaller marginal centres. However, it was of a very high standard in the great centres in the north, which could count on a long tradition and a rich and established scribal style. In the royal palace of Ugarit, as well as the private archives belonging to important members of the scribal and priestly elite, a good apparatus of scholastic instruments and literary texts has been found.

Babylonian epic and mythological texts became part of the local culture, especially when they were relevant to Syria, such as in the case of the deeds of Gilgamesh or Sargon (which even managed to reach Amarna). Local scribal circles also took on the values and texts of the scribal culture of Kassite Babylonia. Texts like the 'Poem of the Righteous Sufferer' and other texts concerned with human nature and social relations not only appeared in Syria and the Levant in their original versions, but also had a significant influence on the local writing style, especially in letters (such as the ones of Rib-Adda).

From a technical point of view, the usual diffusion of bilingual and multilingual word lists significantly increased. These texts combined the knowledge of learned languages (that is, Akkadian and Sumerian) belonging to the scribal circles with local languages (Hurrian and Canaanite). This increase was due to the intense inter-state relations of the time and the influence of foreign rule over these states. For instance, the Ugarit archives have provided texts written in a large variety of scripts and languages, giving us an idea of all the languages and scripts existing at the time. There were texts written in Akkadian and Sumerian, in Hurrian and Ugaritic (the local language), texts written in Luwian hieroglyphs, Hittite cuneiform, Egyptian hieroglyphs and the Cypro-Minoan script.

The coexistence of so many languages and scripts could have promoted the development of new scripts. Some of them, like the Middle Bronze Age hieroglyphics from Byblos, developed along traditional lines. However, Late Bronze Age Syria and the Levant also constitute the first areas where something far more innovative appeared, namely, alphabetic scripts. All previous writing systems had been a mixture of syllabic and logographic signs (such as cuneiform) or hieroglyphic signs (such as Egyptian or similar writing systems). The Egyptian system already had some monoconsonantal signs, which could have formed the basis for a writing system that was purely consonantal, and thus alphabetic. Alphabetic writing was what scripts such as the Proto-Sinaitic and Proto-Canaanite were trying to achieve, and what Ugaritic eventually achieved.

The Ugaritic script was the only example of the official use of an alphabetic writing system. In fact, it was employed in administrative and literary texts, as well as for the description of local rituals. Since Ugarit was not used to separate language from script these rituals could not be written in Sumerian and Akkadian. In all other cases, the Babylonian scribal tradition relegated alphabetic scripts to marginal areas, allowing their use only outside the palace administration. Only after the decline of the palaces' scribal schools, alphabetic writing would eventually spread and become more popular.

The decision of Ugarit's scribes to use an alphabetic script to record the local literary tradition has allowed the survival of rare and interesting sources. These texts were copied in the mid-fourteenth century BC. They could have been written earlier, as usual in the case of mythical and religious texts whose authority was centred on their long-standing tradition. However, some elements found in these literary texts clearly belong to the Late Bronze Age. For instance, the poem of Keret is the story of a legendary king of Ugarit who obeyed the orders the gods gave him in a dream and set out on a journey to find and marry a princess. Keret would eventually succeed in his quest, but only after overcoming several obstacles, even his own son's attempt to remove him from the throne. The happy ending of the story is typical of a fairy-tale. However, its underlying ideology of kingship is typical of the Late Bronze Age, with its religious connotations closely linked to the heroic and adventurous ideals of the time.

The legendary adventure of Keret is remarkably similar to the real story of Idrimi. The narration of the latter's adventure also follows the structure of a tale, being the young prince who had to endure an injustice, but had the ambition and talent to regain his throne. In this way, he not only proved his valour and overcame all adversities until his authority was recognised by the great king, but also defeated his enemies, reconstructed his palace, and reinforced his kingdom. However, while Keret's epic constituted a foundation myth for Ugaritic kingship ideology, Idrimi's tale is a usurper's apology, aimed at presenting the latter in a better light in the eyes of the population.

In another text written shortly afterwards in Egypt, a similar story became an opportunity to describe the exotic world of Syria and Mitanni. The story tells of an Egyptian prince who sets out with his chariot and horses (the fundamental equipment for any princely adventure) to find a princess living far away. The prince naturally had to overcome all sorts of difficulties and to face a prophecy regarding his death. These heroic stories, closely linked to the ideology of kingship of the time, clearly travelled from court to court. Their influence can be traced not only in Syrian inscriptions, but also in Hittite historical texts and Egyptian royal inscriptions.

Another Ugaritic poem, the Aqhat Epic, was also centred on characters from the royal family and issues of descendancy. Despite being more difficult to place in a specific historical context or to compare to other similar 'true' stories (such as Idrimi's story), the Aqhat Epic shares the adventurous and fairy-tale tone of Keret's story. They almost seem like stories written and narrated to entertain the court, where hunting, wars, bows and chariots, as well as faraway princesses, were real topics. By now, these stories lacked any religious connotations.

However, clear religious connotations can be found in other Ugaritic poems, centred on the god Baal. There was his battle against Mot, namely, Death, which alludes to the alternation between a season of death and a season of life. This was a crucial aspect in the agro-pastoral religion of the time. Then, there was

Baal's battle against Yam, the Sea, which alludes to the cosmologic idea of the chaotic sea surrounding the world. Finally, there were the story of the reconstruction of Baal's temple and other religious stories, some of which were also used during religious festivals (one of these stories even dedicates some sections on this aspect). A similar picture is attested in the iconography of the time, which was largely religious, but also related to hunting and wars. This type of iconography was centred on the figure of the king on his chariot, throwing arrows against enemies or wild animals, while his horses galloped in a quite idealised way. This

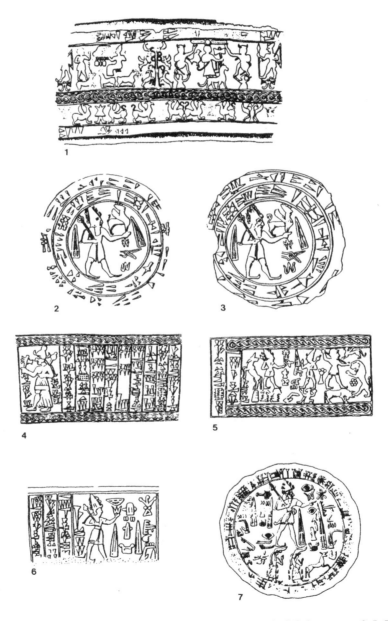

Figure 19.6   Royal seals of Carchemish in the thirteenth century BC. 1: Seal of Shahurunuwa; 2–5: Four seals of Ini-Teshub; 6: Seal of Talmi-Teshub; 7: Seal of Kuzi-Teshub.

iconography would eventually be copied from the Aegean to Egypt. However, it was originally developed in Syria, at the time when the use of chariots and horses became an essential requirement of kingship.

Apart from its iconography, Levantine craftsmanship of the Late Bronze Age was also renowned for its refinement. Some of it is lost forever, such as the multi-coloured fabrics, woven or embroidered with typical iconographic motifs, which we can make out from some Egyptian depictions. Other objects have survived and are well known, such as carved ivories. These developed in the Early Bronze Age (the Eblaite carved wood figurines), but were now revived thanks to the Egyptian influence in the area. Then, there were metal cups decorated with hunting and war scenes. Fabrics, worked metals, coloured glass, jewellery and carved wooden and ivory figurines were typical products of the high-end craftsmanship of the Syrian courts. They appear in the inventories of gifts, dowries, tributes and booties, as products that the intense exchange of goods made internationally renowned, but were originally from the Levant.

Alongside the circulation of goods, there was also a circulation of craftsmen, which led to the diffusion of several iconographic motifs, styles, techniques and prized raw materials. This makes a reconstruction of the exact origins of certain objects difficult. Despite some superficial assessments of Syrian art as lacking originality, one has to concede that this prestigious type of craftsmanship combined a wide range of influences. The latter were greatly facilitated by the commercial and political scene of the period. For instance, carved ivory was an Egyptian influence, especially since ivory came from Egypt (Figure 19.6).

In terms of Syro-Hittite seals, the kings and functionaries of Carchemish began to use stamp seals, originally from Anatolia, as well as cylinder seals, typical of northern Syria (Figure 19.7), and Luwian hieroglyphs as well as cuneiform in their inscriptions. Moreover, the local iconography started to include both Syrian and Anatolian elements. However, influences roughly stayed within their political borders: the south and the Mediterranean coast had strong Egyptian influences; northern and Central Syria was much more influenced by Hittite culture. This division would survive even after the fall of the great powers that created it.

Apart from external influences on local art, Syria and the Levant also influenced neighbouring kingdoms. The most obvious example of this is the art of New Kingdom Egypt, which had a strong Syro-Levantine influence in its iconography, the structure of the scenes, and the choice of backgrounds, landscapes and settings. This taste for the exotic, along with the appreciation of non-Egyptian styles and products, became an integral part of the decorative arts of the time, of official celebratory reliefs and even temple architecture. Similarly, Egyptian literature and language were heavily influenced by Syria. This aspect is also visible in the spread of Near Eastern cults, especially in the Delta.

Figure 19.7   Syrian kingship iconography: ivory panel of the king of Ugarit, ca. 1360 BC.

6 Urban, rural, and nomadic religion

Despite being far away from his population on a cultural and socio-economic level, the king regained his central role and connection to his subjects in his religious role and his participation in cults and rituals. The latter was aimed at obtaining a favourable response from the gods, the ultimate guarantors of the kingdom's well being. Alongside sources from Ugarit, we also have texts from Emar, which include long and detailed descriptions of rituals. These reveal strong Hittite and Mesopotamian influences, since the city was located on the eastern Syrian border.

The king's religious role was twofold: to defend the kingdom from external dangers, and to promote the fertility and reproductive cycle of the land. In order to face the first aspect, the king was involved in rituals against enemies, or to defend the city walls. He thus ideologically embodied his practical role in leading the army and in the defence of his kingdom. In order to deal with the second aspect, the king was the main actor in a series of festivals (such as the *hieros gamos*) aimed at stimulating and enforcing natural forces. This was again a conceptualisation of his economic role in the land, even though the latter was quite neglected at the time.

The kings of Syria and the Levant were not deified while alive, and actually seem to have preferred a more secular and practical ideology of kingship. However, they were deified to some extent after their death. They became part of a category of beings (the *refa'im*) that were part of a dynastic cult and were believed to be contributors to the well-being and security of the land they once ruled. The practice of burying the dead under the living's homes led to the development of a series of funerary rituals (such as funerary offerings), which were also applied in the palace and royal tombs. The dynastic lists written for ritual purposes are the only record of this continuity with the past, which cannot be attested in the legal and administrative sources. This is due to the absence of dates (texts used the phrase 'from today and forever') and the use of dynastic seals inherited from father to son, marking one's legitimacy of rule and the eternal nature of royal decisions.

The king could count on a sort of identification with the principal deity of his pantheon, normally called Baal, namely, 'lord'. In some cities, this god was equalled to Hadad, Dagan, or other deities. The identification was twofold, since the king ritually embodied the god, but the god in turn acquired a kingly role in myths. In other words, the god was king in front of the other gods, acted like a king, and held royal epithets, weapons and attributes. Just like the human king, Baal was fundamental for two reasons. First, he had to keep external dangers at bay, such as malefic and chaotic forces. Second, he had to ensure the fertility of plants and animals by becoming a god of rain, the core element stimulating agriculture in the region, and a dying and resurging god, imitating the seasons. The god's female counterpart was the 'lady', Baalat, often identified with Astarte or Anat. If official religion emphasised the male deity, popular religion focused on his female counterpart, a typical preference in cults linked to agriculture. Figurines of this goddess are common in Syria, and were frequently reproduced in smaller sizes. This indicates their importance in popular religion. On the contrary, the official religion preferred to represent the god in bronze or stone depictions placed in palaces and temples.

Alongside the 'lord' and the 'lady', there was a third deity completing this divine triad, usually an old and relatively absent deity simply called the 'god' (El). He was the creator of the world, who fathered gods and humans. This third deity was as central in the theology of the time, as absent in iconographic and mythological attestations. However, he was the clearest expression of the religious beliefs of pastoral and nomadic groups. Regarding the religious beliefs of these groups, there is little evidence. Moreover, it is often difficult to interpret, due to the obvious lack of direct attestations. Nonetheless, it is clear that pastoral religion was different from agrarian religion. Despite being both concerned with fertility, farmers focused more on the dualistic unity of land and water, symbolised by the reproduction of humans and animals. On the contrary, shepherds focused on the reproductive cycles of herds and the ideology of kinship, a core concept in their social organisation.

Alongside the father god El, there were probably other father gods of Amorite origins and centred on kinship. These deities embodied a legacy of those divine and kinship elements (the 'father', 'brother', 'paternal uncle', 'maternal uncle', and so on) typical of Middle Bronze Age names attested in pastoral communities. This type of religion was much more abstract, less concerned with rituals, myths and depictions, but far more interested in sacred locations, such as tombs of ancestors, sacred areas for seasonal meetings, temples located outside cities. This preference was a clear consequence of the transhumant nature of these communities, providing sacred meetings points for the various tribal groups living in the area.

20

THE MIDDLE ASSYRIAN
KINGDOM

1 The Assyrian revival in the Amarna Age

The four centuries separating Ashur-uballit from Ishme-Dagan constitute a badly attested phase of Assyrian history, both in terms of local inscriptions and external evidence. The kingdom was reduced to its core, with few opportunities for expansion. The rising kingdom of Mitanni reached Ashur and compromised the latter's full independence. A certain degree of political continuity in the area is attested in the Assyrian King List. The latter continued to be updated for legitimacy purposes throughout this phase of usurpations and internal revolts. This political continuity is also attested in the sequence of eponyms, and in texts mentioning the kings' restorations of Ashur's temples. Alongside building programmes, there was considerable commercial activity, such as the relations between king Ashur-nadin-ahhe and Egypt. There were also military interventions, such as the establishment of the border with Kassite Babylonia under Puzur-Ashur and Ashur-bel-nisheshu. However, military endeavours initially ended up in Mitanni's favour, which resulted in winning Washshukkanni the gold and silver gates of Ashur as booty.

During the reign of Ashur-uballit, Assyria suddenly rose out of this subordinate position, in a prodigious revival that could only be explained if we had more information on the events immediately preceding it (Figure 20.1). Suppiluliuma's expedition had unwillingly subverted the already difficult relations between Assyria and Mitanni. This led to the latter's collapse and the death of its king, Tushratta. Having seized the Mitannian throne through Hittite support, Artatama II eventually had to submit to the Assyrian king, Ashur-uballit, who was already powerful enough to pursue expansionistic campaigns in Upper Mesopotamia. Within a few years, Hanigalbat became the centre of a heated dispute over which power had to take over the gap left by Mitanni. Ashur-uballit's plan to keep the area under control through Artatama was ruined by the campaign of Piyashshili and Shattiwaza against Artatama's son. For now, this move benefited the branch of the Mitannian royal family supported by Hatti. Ashur-uballit still held control over the eastern side of Hanigalbat, closer to Assyria. However, for the time being, the Assyrian king did not try to do anything else.

Despite this setback, the energy with which Ashur-uballit and his ruling elite entered the international scene remains extraordinary. Before then, the Assyrian monarchy had experienced a long depression. Moreover, it was originally conceived as a form of subordination to its main city-god, with the king acting as a mere administrator and custodian on behalf of the god Ashur. All of a sudden, Ashur-uballit took on the title of 'great king', thus clearly stating his intention to enter the international scene as a major player. However, neither the other great kings nor their immediate successors recognised his title. This reaction

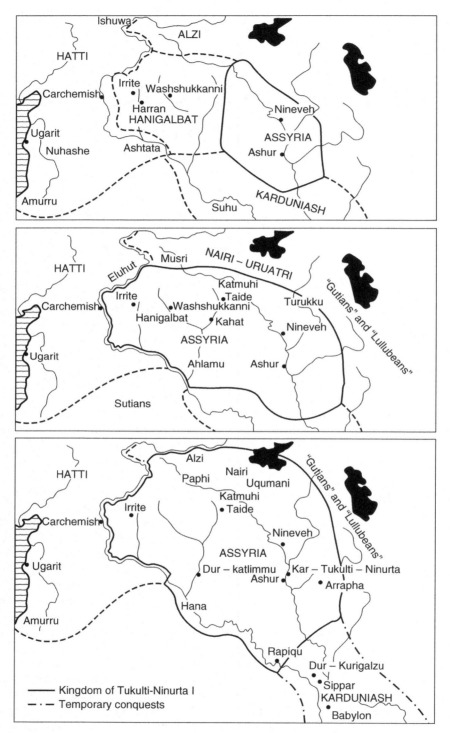

Figure 20.1 The Middle Assyrian kingdom. *Above*: Reign of Ashur-uballit I; *Centre*: Reigns of Adad-nirari I and Shalmaneser I. *Below*: Reign of Tukulti-Ninurta I.

instigated a long controversy that only the military superiority of Assyria would eventually bring to an end.

Apart from this new titulature, Assyria's entrance in the network of international relations of the time is attested in two letters found in Amarna. The letters were written by the Assyrian king to Amenhotep IV in order to establish diplomatic and commercial relations with Egypt. In the first letter, the Assyrian king used a cautious and humble tone, as was appropriate for whoever wrote to someone one did not know, unaware of his customs and possible reactions. However, in the second letter, which followed the positive outcome of the first, Ashur-uballit already defined himself as great king. He also called the Egyptian king by name, and defined him a 'brother', the standard practice among kings of equal rank. The Assyrian king also began to make demands about the amount of gold he expected to receive, the timing of emissaries, and the efficiency of the system, which in his opinion was not enough even to repay the emissaries' journeys.

Ashur-uballit had therefore managed to establish relations with Egypt. However, he had also shown a certain degree of tactlessness in his dealings, since he explicitly expressed his economic interests in this interaction. This aspect was in marked contrast with the diplomatic tone and customs of the great kings of the time. As soon as the Kassite king, Burna-Buriash, found out that the Egyptian king had established diplomatic relations with Ashur-uballit, Burna-Buriash wrote to the Egyptian king. In the letter, he claimed that the Assyrians were his subjects and that the Egyptian king could not bypass him in this way. Although this request was unrealistic, Burna-Buriash rightly stated that the Assyrians were simply after economic gains, and were inadequate for those ceremonial and diplomatic relations established among great kings. Therefore, the tactlessness of the Assyrians and their intrinsic interest in business affairs must have been an internationally renowned stereotype.

Egypt was a distant land and not particularly interested in the issues of status among Near Eastern kings, which were anyway considered inferior to the Egyptian kings. The real rivals of Ashur-uballit were the Hittites and the Kassites. As mentioned above, the Assyrians were openly at war with the Hittites, fighting for control over Hanigalbat. This contrasts with the fact that, despite the indignant reaction of Burna-Buriash over the rise of the Assyrian king as great king, the Assyrians and the Kassites managed to come to an agreement. Burna-Buriash's son, Kara-hardash, married Ashur-uballit's daughter, Muballitat-Sherua. Her son, Kadashman-Harbe, was destined to succeed his father on the Babylonian throne. Even in this case, the ambition and effectiveness of Ashur-uballit's strategy comes to the fore, showing how he used an established means to seal relations among kings, such as inter-dynastic marriages, to obtain concrete and immediate advantages.

However, this strategy caused a severe Kassite reaction, leading to the death of Kadashman-Harbe. It is not certain whether or not his Assyrian lineage was the reason for the revolt, but we can be sure that Ashur-uballit interpreted the reaction in this way. The Assyrian king marched to Babylonia, placing king Kurigalzu, the 'little one' and infant son of Kadashman-Harbe, on the throne. The now old Assyrian king and his daughter, a truly Assyrian *éminence grise* in the Kassite court, were counting on influencing the infant king, seeing in him a malleable, if not subdued, neighbour. This was indeed the situation during Ashur-uballit's reign and throughout Kurigalzu's childhood. However, once the young king grew up, he would eventually cause some problems to the Assyrian side of his family.

By the time Ashur-uballit died, Assyria had become a high-ranking power in the Near East in practice, but was not yet recognised by its neighbours. However, the more this recognition was delayed, the more evident and threatening the Assyrian aggressiveness and ambition became. Nonetheless, the equal status of Assyria with Babylonia, Hatti, and Egypt had by now become a reality. It was also expressed in a variety of ways, from marriages to war and trade. Ashur ceased to be a Mesopotamian outpost on the way towards a fragmented Anatolia, which was a source for raw materials and a profitable market for Assyrian and Babylonian textiles. Assyria became a regional power in a complex network of regional powers. This network offered two alternatives. One option was to integrate in the network of relations among great powers, made of contacts between palaces, and exchanges of messages and gifts, paving the way for commercial relations. The second option was the expansion in that power 'vacuum' in Upper Mesopotamia, which lent itself to the establishment of an exclusively Assyrian network. At the moment, however, this area was contended by the Hittites in the north and the Kassites in the Middle Euphrates. Moreover, east of Assyria there still were those tumultuous mountain populations, preventing contacts with Iran, which had been so fundamental a millennium earlier.

2 The Upper Mesopotamian empire

In the second half of the fourteenth century BC, Assyria, blocked by Hanigalbat to the west, had to deal with two main issues: keeping the mountain tribes at bay (Gutians, Lullubeans, Turukku); and fighting against the Kassites, in order to move the border further south and away from Ashur. The uncertain outcome of the battle of Sugagu, fought by Enlil-nirari against Kurigalzu, was followed by the battle between Arik-den-ili and Nazi-Marutash. However, only with the battle at Kar-Ishtar in Ugarsallu, fought between Adad-nirari I and Nazi-Marutash, would Assyria succeed in pushing the frontier from the Lower Zab Valley to the Diyala Valley.

With Adad-nirari I, Assyria also revived its expansion in Upper Mesopotamia. An initial campaign brought defeat to king Shattuara I, who became an Assyrian vassal. A second intervention defeated Wasashatta, Shattuara's son, who rebelled against the Assyrians as soon as he came to the throne. The Assyrians conquered the entire territory 'from Taite to Irrite', namely, from the Khabur and Balikh basins to the border of Carchemish. Adad-nirari took on the title of 'king of totality', indicating his control over Upper Mesopotamia as a whole. He proclaimed that his conquests extended from Rapiqum in the south to Elahut, the Euphrates Valley north of Carchemish.

The Hittites were unable to provide military support to their vassal and an adequate opposition to the Assyrian army. Adad-nirari mockingly stated that Wasashatta had asked Hittite support by paying a 'tip', and that the Hittites had accepted the payment, but did not help him. Wasashatta had clearly ceased to pay tributes to the Assyrians in order to pay the Hittites instead. From an Assyrian, and highly idealised, perspective, payments that in the right direction were 'gifts' ensuring good political relations became humiliating and useless 'tips' when paid to the enemy. This was seen as particularly true if in times of necessity the patron proved to be powerless. It is probable that this episode happened during the reign of Urhi-Teshub, whose problems were preventing him from dealing with these troubles in Upper Mesopotamia. Be that as it may, for the first time the Assyrians managed to face the Hittites along the Euphrates.

Once Hattusili III seized the Hittite throne, he received a proposal from Adad-nirari I to establish friendly relations and even a request for permission to visit the Amanus Mountain. This request was either aimed at gaining access to its timber, or at leaving a stele on this mountain located on the edge of the known world. The Hittite king replied that the Assyrian king was by all means a great king after his conquest of Hanigalbat. However, the 'brotherhood' was out of the question ('Were you and I born from one father or mother?' asked the king sarcastically, deliberately ignoring the conventional meaning of this kinship tie), as well as the expedition to the Amanus. The latter was in fact a threatening request despite its commercial and ideological justifications.

Towards the end of Adad-nirari's reign, it is possible that Hanigalbat momentarily slipped out of Assyrian control. This forced Adad-nirari's son, Shalmaneser I, to conquer it again, defeating Shattuara II, who was supported (this time actively, but still in vain) by the Hittites. This time, Shalmaneser changed tactic. Instead of establishing a vassal state in Hanigalbat, the king preferred to establish direct control, putting a definite end to Hanigalbat's independence. Initially, the local dynasty was substituted by an Assyrian functionary (the *sukkallu rabû*, whose title was 'king of Hanigalbat'). Later on, the region was divided into districts ruled by Assyrians governors (*šaknu*), who resided in newly built palaces.

The Assyrians also deported the defeated populations and attempted to place them in new agricultural territories. Having relegated the local population to the countryside, the Assyrians settled in the cities, taking over the region's economy. The Middle Assyrian archives from the area were found at Sikannu (Tell Fekheriye), Amuda, Harbe (Tell Chuera), Giricano, and especially Dur-Katlimmu (Tell Sheikh Hamad). Their archives show that these cities were inhabited by Assyrians and run with an Assyrian administrative system. This system was implemented in the course of a few years. Perhaps, this prompt 'Assyrianisation' was meant to imitate the ancient commercial activities in the area. In fact, it partly maintained its role as a sort of 'network' of palaces linked by specific itineraries in the middle of an ethnically composite country-side. Be that as it may, the colonisation and administrative unification of the area allowed for the prompt assimilation of Upper Mesopotamia in the Assyrian kingdom.

The new westernmost border of Assyria along the Euphrates was now close to the Hittite empire. Relations between the two powers continued to be difficult, however. First, this difficulty was due to the expansionistic ambitions of the Assyrians, and the Hittite desire to reconquer Hanigalbat. Both goals were completely unrealistic at that time. Second, there were the turbulences of the smaller states located on the border between Assyria and Hatti. These states were taking advantage of their position along the border, with its usual problems with fugitives and raids from the other side of the border.

This was the case of Turira, which caused the Hittite king to complain to the Assyrian king following the practice established among great kings: either the Assyrian king intervened to keep his vassal at bay, or the Hittite king would have intervened himself, trespassing across the border as a just defence and reaction to the constant provocations. A far more serious issue was the case of Nihriya, an important centre on the Upper Euphrates. In order to gain control over it, the Assyrians and the Hittites eventually had to face each other in the battlefield. Attempts to avoid the clash had already failed, and the classic formula of being 'friend of friends and enemy of enemies' now showed its true artificiality. Since Nihriya is my enemy – said the Assyrian king – you cannot help it, thus leave and let me conquer it. Since Nihriya is my friend – replied the Hittite king – you cannot attack it, thus go away. However, Shalmaneser did not leave, and attacked Nihriya, defeated the Hittites, and had the opportunity to triumphantly notify the outcome of the war to the Hittite vassals.

3 Political consolidation and the Babylonian problem

The Middle Assyrian empire, which reached its maximum extension under Tukulti-Ninurta I (1243–1207 BC), bordered with three different types of frontiers. To the north-east, in the northern Zagros and the Upper Tigris Valley, there were a series of mountain populations, organised into small states. On the one hand, these states could not oppose the mighty Assyrians and tended to gravitate around them. On the other hand, the nature of this territory was inaccessible for an army and full of hiding places. Therefore, it prevented a definite conquest and re-organisation of the area in the same fashion as Upper Mesopotamia.

To the west, the border was defined by the Euphrates, with the Assyrian settlements of the eastern riverbank facing the Hittite vassals of the western riverbank. This border was difficult to overcome, and gave a certain degree of security against the Assyrian expansion in that direction. Finally, there was the southern border with Babylonia, a kingdom with a similar political structure and equal military strength (Table 20.1). This border was not fixed, and constantly moved further north or further south, according to whoever was more powerful at the time.

Tukulti-Ninurta was active on all three fronts, though in different ways. The north-eastern border was the most crucial for the survival of Assyria, despite being the one whose conquest brought the least glory. The tribes and chiefdoms of the Zagros and Upper Tigris were dangerously close to the Assyrian country-side. They constantly harassed it with incursions and raids, the latter being the ultimate reason used by the Assyrian propaganda to justify its military interventions. However, Assyrian interventions in the mountains were far more damaging than the incursions of these mountain people in Assyria. Moreover, the Assyrians had further reasons to attack other than to simply defend themselves. The area was rich in timber, especially on the Mehru Mountain. Tukulti-Ninurta needed timber to support his intensive building programme,

Table 20.1 Mesopotamian chronology, ca. 1550–1200 BC

	Sealand	Babylonia		Assyria		Mitanni/ Hanigalbat
1550						
1500	Adara-kalamma Ekurduanna Melamkurkurra	Agum II a Burna-Buriash I Kashtiliash III	ca. 1550	Ashur-nirari I a Puzur-Ashur III Enlil-nasir I		
1450	b Ea-gamil	b Ulam-Buriash Agum III		Nur-lli Ashur-shaduni Ashur-rabi I		Barattarna Parshatatar
		c Karaindash		Ashur-nadin-ahhe I Enlil-nasir II Ashur-nirari II c Ashur-bel-nisheshu Ashur-rim-nisheshu	1430–1425 1424–1418 1417–1409 1408–1401	Shaushtatar Artatama I
1400		Kadashman-Harbe				
		Kurigalzu I		Ashur-nadin-ahhe II Eriba-Adad	1400–1391 1390–1364	Shuttarna II (Artashumara)
1350	ELAM	Kadashman-Enlil I	1374–1360	def Ashur-uballit I	1363–1328	Tushratta Artatama II
	g Hurbatilla Pahir-ishshan Attar-Kittah	Burna-Buriash II d Kara-Hardash c Nazi-Bugash gf Kurigalzu II	1359–1333 1333 1333 1332–1308	f Enlil-nirari Arik-den-ili	1327–1316 1317–1306	Shuttarna III Shattiwaza
1300	ca. 1330 ca. 1300					l Shattuara I
	Humban- numena Untash-GAL	h Nazi-Marutash i Kadashman –Turgu Kadashman-Enlil II Kudur-Enlil	1307–1282 1281–1264 1263–1255 1254–1233	Adad-nirari I hilm n Shalmaneser I	1305–1274 1273–1244	m Wasashatta n Shattuara II
1250	Umpatar-GAL	ca. 1250				
	p Kidin-hutran ca. 1230	Shagarakti- Shuriash o Kashtiliash IV op Enlil-nadin- shumi op Kadashman- Harbe II op Adad-shum- iddina	1245–1233 1232–1225 1224 1223 1222–1217	oTukulti-Ninurta I Ashur-nadin-apli	1243–1207 1206–1203	
1200		oq Adad-shum- usur	1216–1187	q Ashur-nirari III q Enlil-kudur-usur q Ninurta-apil-Ekur	1202–1197 1196–1193 1192–1180	

a–a = attested contemporaneity

which included temples as well as palaces and fortifications. The region was also rich in copper in the Diyarbakir area, and in horses around lake Urmia, both fundamental resources for the Assyrian army.

Through this pretext of defending the Assyrian countryside, Tukulti-Ninurta's army reached deep into the region. This was in order to ensure, through effective deterring interventions, free access to these strategic resources. The lands first affected by the Assyrian attacks (Alshe/Alzi, Paphi, Amadani and so on) became tributary states. Beyond the Upper Tigris, the land became almost inaccessible and military expeditions became less frequent. In this area, there were a variety of small states (the 'forty kings') belonging to the land defined by Shalmaneser as Uruatri, and by Tukulti-Ninurta as Nairi (Text 20.1). In order to face the Assyrian threat, these states began to establish some form of organisation, which was not yet politically unified, but far more coordinated than before.

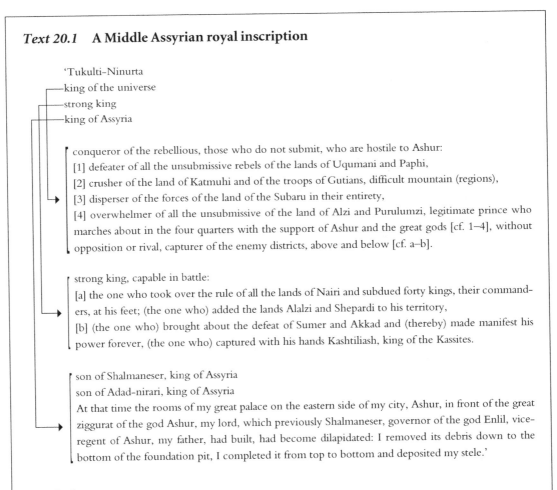

Text 20.1   A Middle Assyrian royal inscription

'Tukulti-Ninurta
king of the universe
strong king
king of Assyria

conqueror of the rebellious, those who do not submit, who are hostile to Ashur:
[1] defeater of all the unsubmissive rebels of the lands of Uqumani and Paphi,
[2] crusher of the land of Katmuhi and of the troops of Gutians, difficult mountain (regions),
[3] disperser of the forces of the land of the Subaru in their entirety,
[4] overwhelmer of all the unsubmissive of the land of Alzi and Purulumzi, legitimate prince who marches about in the four quarters with the support of Ashur and the great gods [cf. 1–4], without opposition or rival, capturer of the enemy districts, above and below [cf. a–b].

strong king, capable in battle:
[a] the one who took over the rule of all the lands of Nairi and subdued forty kings, their commanders, at his feet; (the one who) added the lands Alalzi and Shepardi to his territory,
[b] (the one who) brought about the defeat of Sumer and Akkad and (thereby) made manifest his power forever, (the one who) captured with his hands Kashtiliash, king of the Kassites.

son of Shalmaneser, king of Assyria
son of Adad-nirari, king of Assyria
At that time the rooms of my great palace on the eastern side of my city, Ashur, in front of the great ziggurat of the god Ashur, my lord, which previously Shalmaneser, governor of the god Enlil, vice-regent of Ashur, my father, had built, had become dilapidated: I removed its debris down to the bottom of the foundation pit, I completed it from top to bottom and deposited my stele.'

Analysis

Note that the three basic titles are repeated and further elaborated in the three sections of the text: (1) 'king of the universe' through an account of the vast expeditions of the king (with a strong emphasis on rebels, totality, borders, conquest, lack of rivals); (2) 'strong king' through an account of the personal valiantness of the king ('at his feet' – 'with his hands'); (3) 'king of Assyria' through an emphasis on dynastic continuity and the restoration of the capital's building. Among other aspects: the 'four quarters' re-iterate a quadripartite structure; 'above and below', the phrase concluding the first section, is specified in the second section (Nairi is in the north and Babylonia is in the south with respects to Assyria, following the course of the Tigris). Regarding the relationship with the god Ashur: the relationship is passive in the first section (the king wins through divine support), absent in the second section ('strong' is a secular and autonomous title), active in the third section (the king takes care of the buildings in the god's city).

The Euphrates front was by nature quite fixed. Once problems along the border were solved (such as in the cases of Nurira and Nihriya), the great river continued to remain difficult to cross for both empires' armies. The latter could have tried to cross further north, but the area was as difficult to access as it was politically problematic. When Tukulti-Ninurta came to the throne, he received a letter from Tudhaliya IV. In an attempt to provide sound advice to the young king, the Hittite king wrote to discourage him from sending a military expedition against Paphi, a piece of advice that the Assyrian king promptly dismissed. This was a rather small episode, yet very significant. Both kings were unable to fully control the area between the Upper Euphrates and Upper Tigris, but both feared that the opponent would eventually succeed, or become too influential in the area.

Later on, Tukulti-Ninurta and Tudhaliya would become fully-fledged enemies. This forced the Hittite king to mobilise his Syrian vassals economically (through the military exemption of Ugarit in exchange of an expensive payment), commercially (through the treaty with Shaushgamuwa, which prevented him from sending and allowing merchants to and from Assyria), and militarily. Despite the tension, there were no direct wars between the two powers. Therefore, Tukulti-Ninurta could not do anything else other than resuming his first year expedition against Paphi for purely propagandistic purposes. He described the expedition with an anti-Hittite tone and stated that on the other side of the Euphrates he had captured 28,800 'Hittite' prisoners. In fact, from an Assyrian perspective, everything on the other side of the Euphrates was automatically considered Hittite.

In the second half of his reign, Tukulti-Ninurta was engaged in the fight against Babylonia. While the Assyrian king was dealing with the north-eastern border, the Kassite king, Kashtiliash IV, conquered some territories along the Assyro-Babylonian border. He therefore broke the solemn oath sealed between the two states after Adad-nirari I's victory at Kar-Ishtar, which established the frontier in favour of the Assyrians. As soon as the Assyrian king was able to intervene in the south, he waged war against Kashtiliash to punish his betrayal. He therefore promptly regained control over the territories lost to the Kassites. The clash on the battlefield ended with an Assyrian victory, and Kashtiliash was captured and brought as prisoner to Ashur.

Tukulti-Ninurta continued his intervention and conquered Babylon. He destroyed its walls and temples, and deported the cultic statue of the god Marduk and a part of the city's population. Then, the king tried to conquer the entire land of Akkad as far as the Persian Gulf. Tukulti-Ninurta proclaimed himself king of Babylon, of Sumer and Akkad, and even of the distant Dilmun and Meluhha. He thus claimed that his dominion extended from the 'Lower Sea (that is, the Persian Gulf) to the Upper Sea' (that is, the lake Van, or even the Mediterranean itself, which was symbolically reached thanks to his 'victory' over the Hittites).

While Tukulti-Ninurta was officially king of Babylon (for seven years), he had some time to dedicate to his ambitious building programme in Assyria. After several temple restorations in the old city of Ashur, he built a new city, Kar-Tukulti-Ninurta. This was the first new capital of Assyrian history, and was located close to Ashur, on the other side of the Tigris. In this way, the king marked his desire to separate himself from the traditional balance between the various components of Assyrian power: from Ashur's temple and its priesthood, to eponyms, powerful families, and the rising bureaucracy, who had long been part of the Assyrian political system.

This was an authoritative change, especially due to the considerable effort put into the new capital, both in terms of economic investment and labour. Consequently, a rebellion broke out, further provoked by the reaction to Tukulti-Ninurta's achievements in Babylonia, which for some reason were not seen in a good light. The old king was killed in his new capital by a group of conspirators. In turn, the latter enthroned one of their sons. Babylon, which had effectively already regained its independence, was abandoned. The rest of the empire stayed united, but under the obscure successors of Tukulti-Ninurta, the great political, military, building and administrative interventions of the great kings of the thirteenth century BC faded away. These later kings probably had little power. However, it has to be borne in mind that at that time the Near East suffered an unprecedented crisis. During this crisis, Assyria managed to remain relatively stable, and was still able to intervene in Upper Mesopotamia, while the Hittites disappeared for good.

4 Palace culture and political propaganda

The Middle Assyrian state was different from the Early Dynastic temple cities, the commercial colonies of the Old Assyrian period, or even the fleeting empire of Shamshi-Adad I. Nonetheless, the structure of the Assyrian state owed a great deal to all these previous experiences. Having ceased to be a strategic commercial link between southern Mesopotamia and the mountainous periphery, the Middle Assyrian state became the centre of its own world and its own imperialistic ambitions. Ashur had the opportunity to increase its wealth through its commercial network and the agricultural and demographic wealth of the Assyrian Triangle and its main city, Nineveh.

Subsequently, Assyria managed to expand in Upper Mesopotamia and to revitalise the region by colonising it. Finally, the Akkadian language and culture, a legacy of the former status of Ashur as northern outpost of Lower Mesopotamia, had placed the Assyrians in marked contrast to their neighbours, namely, the mountain tribes of the Zagros and the Hurrian groups of the Upper Tigris and the Khabur. This inevitable position of Assyria, surrounded by threatening powers, was actually a crucial economic and human resource. It therefore allowed the Assyrians to turn this situation around, gaining a hegemonic role.

Due to the variety of cultural influences affecting Assyria, Middle Assyrian culture developed some unique characteristics. The first was a certain stratification of cultural influences and contributions. These can be detected, but were nonetheless well integrated within a culture characterised by a strong individuality. In terms of influences, there were ancient elements deriving from local traditions, which dated back to the Early Dynastic city-state structure. Then, there were Mitannian influences, which dated back to the formation of the Assyrian kingdom, when it was surrounded by the Mitannians, and then to the Assyrian conquest of Hanigalbat. Finally, there was a Babylonian influence, a recurring phenomenon that intensified in periods in which the two powers were fighting against one another, such as during the reign of Shamshi-Adad I, and now with Tukulti-Ninurta I.

The local cultural legacy of Assyria was mostly concerned with the main economic and political structure of the land. Mitannian contributions were mainly technological and social. Finally, Babylonian influences belonged to the learned realm of the scribal school, literature and religion. In terms of literature, Tukulti-Ninurta brought several important texts from Babylon and commissioned his celebratory poem describing his victory to be written in the Babylonian dialect. However, Assyrian scribes continued to use their writing style and language, as well as their eponymous dating system and local calendar.

The second characteristic of Middle Assyrian culture was that it was well aware of the tendencies of the time. Middle Assyrian culture therefore absorbed some features of Late Bronze international relations. At the same time, it established the basis of what would become the culture of the Assyrian empire in the first millennium BC. For instance, the use of chariots was a clear tendency of the time. In Assyria, chariotry became the core of its army, preventing improvisations and heroic virtuosities. This change laid the foundations of that lethally efficient army able to support the Assyrian imperial expansion. The palace glassware and pottery, the elegant and unequivocally Assyrian seals (Figure 20.2), the ceremonial weapons and the jewellery made the Middle Assyrian court one of the greatest of its time. Moreover, its choices would remain more stable compared to elsewhere, thanks to the survival of Assyria after the fall, or complete change, of all other Late Bronze Age kingdoms.

Figure 20.2   Middle Assyrian seal impressions of the fourteenth (1–2) and thirteenth (3–8) centuries BC.

The third characteristic of Middle Assyrian culture was the fact that it developed as a mouthpiece of Assyrian political control and its ideological justifications. The latter were crucial to force the Assyrian population through an endless string of wars without losing its dynamism and national appeal. In this regard, two of the most characteristic aspects of Middle Assyrian culture were its monumental architecture and political literature. Except for Egypt, Middle Assyrian monumental architecture was unparalleled at the time, both in terms of scale and quantity.

Fortunately, the available archaeological and epigraphic evidence has provided considerable information on Ashur. Being the capital, the city must have been the most striking example of Middle Assyrian monumental architecture. Functional constructions such as city walls or embankments along the Tigris developed alongside equally impressive restorations, or foundations *ex novo*, of palaces and temples dedicated to Ashur, Ishtar and many other deities (Figure 20.3). These buildings were clearly designed and built to be imposing and to impress the population. However, they required an astounding amount of material. This scenographic effect was further emphasised by the explicitly ideological purpose of naming the city gates, providing epithets to temples, and celebrating festivals in various sanctuaries, strengthening the political and religious symbolism of this growing empire.

Unfortunately, we do not have enough evidence on the other Assyrian cities. However, it is impossible to believe that key cities like Nineveh or Arbela were not the object of similar monumental building

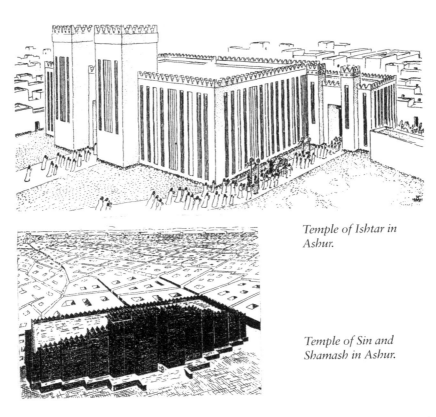

Temple of Ishtar in Ashur.

Temple of Sin and Shamash in Ashur.

Figure 20.3 Middle Assyrian temple architecture. *Above*: Temple of Ishtar in Ashur; *Below*: Temple of Sin and Shamash in Ashur.

programmes, and there are some clues confirming this assumption. Far better documented is the interest of Shalmaneser and Tukulti-Ninurta in providing an Assyrian organisation to the new provinces. The textual evidence attesting the construction of a network of palaces is also confirmed by the archaeological evidence. For instance, the excavation of the Middle Assyrian levels at Dur-Katlimmu, Sabi Abyad, Harbe, Tille and elsewhere have revealed several palaces and administrative archives. These discoveries concretely show what the Assyrian kings were celebrating in their inscriptions.

However, the greatest achievement of this architectural political strategy was the construction of new cities. We are well informed on the foundation of Kar-Tukulti-Ninurta from its eponymous king and we hear that the foundation of Kalhu took place during the reign of Shalmaneser I. This leads us to ask the question of whether or not the latter king wanted to found a new city like his son. If this were the case, the attempt would have been twice as revolutionary, requiring the movement of the court from Ashur to the triangle of land formed by the Tigris and the Upper Zab. By returning to Ashur and founding his new residence in front of the old southern centre, then, Tukulti-Ninurta would have expressed his desire to go in the opposite direction from his father's decision. This decision would have showed that the core of the Assyrian state had to stay closer to Babylonia, rather than to the mountain tribes in the north.

Middle Assyrian building programmes were all directed to the Assyrians (as well as the conquered populations and potential enemies) and were simply celebrating their strong presence. On the contrary, functionaries, scribes and courtiers had to go through a much more comprehensive process of acculturation. In terms of political literature, the Middle Assyrian kings were influenced by the general tendencies of the period (for instance, the effort put by contemporary Hittite and Egyptian rulers into their political propaganda), but expressed themselves in their own unique way, destined to survive even after this phase. Foundation texts became a clear means of celebrating the kings' political and military achievements. Moreover, the first chronicles began to appear. These texts were more or less written with the same tone of foundation inscriptions, but with the king acting and speaking in the third person instead of the first person.

Different, but equally clear, is the political function of the Middle Assyrian coronation ritual. On the one hand, the ritual reiterated the archaic subordination of the king to the god, considered to be the true king of the city that delegated power to the king as mere administrator (and in fact at the peak of the ritual the participants would shout 'Ashur is king! Ashur is king!'). On the other hand, the ritual placed the king in a network of personal relations with the city's major institutions and its population. This network was symbolised by a ritual gift exchange, during which the king's subjects offered their gifts to their new ruler. The latter returned the gesture, probably more generously. These allusions to the balance of power that developed around the function of the king were expressed in the ritual through a complex system of religious symbolic gestures. However, in reality, this balance of power was purely fictional, due to the increasingly central role of the king.

The Assyrian reaction to external dangers is well represented in a prayer of Tukulti-Ninurta, which is an exemplary expression of that 'obsidional complex' mentioned above (Text 20.2a). The situation described in the text is that of a set of enemy lands avidly interested in plundering the riches of Assyria, accumulated thanks to the efficient work of an organised society. These enemy lands are seen as inhabited by evil and destructive enemies, barbarians and parasites. In other words, these enemies were the complete opposite of the Assyrians, who respected the gods, were just, civilised, productive and organised. The siege seems lethal, but the prayer was aimed at seeking divine support so that Assyria could succeed, expanding cosmic order over chaos. The ideological tone of the prayer, a true manifestation of Assyrian expansionism, is evident. The Assyrian success over the surrounding enemies, which the Middle Assyrian kings achieved with systematic efficiency, is therefore justified as an act of defence, civilisation and justice.

However, the masterpiece of Middle Assyrian political literature was the poem of Tukulti-Ninurta, celebrating his victory over Kashtiliash. The poem is a true manual on the sacred nature of the Assyrian wars, a repertoire of commonplaces on the correct or incorrect way of waging war and on maintaining peace. From an Assyrian perspective, Kashtiliash was responsible for the war, since he broke his solemn oath. He was an impious king, abandoned by his own gods, who left him to face his own mistakes. He was also a coward, who did not want to face the Assyrian king in the battlefield, having attacked the Assyrians when they were not ready to defend themselves. On the contrary, Tukulti-Ninurta respected his oaths and was forced to wage war to establish justice and order. He is therefore portrayed as the valiant and brave king, supported by the gods, who recognised him as a champion of piety and justice.

The accusation of the defeated enemy was a widespread practice, since the winner felt the need to demonstrate the fact that, despite being innocent, he was forced to overthrow the enemy to defend the ideals of peace, justice and freedom. In this sense, Tukulti-Ninurta's poem was a post-victory version of Hittite rituals aimed at preventively accusing the enemy for the war. However, in Tukulti-Ninurta's case there must have been some specific reasons leading to the composition and diffusion of the poem. Some reasons can be found in the Babylonian realm, since the poem was written in Babylonian and not Middle Assyrian. For instance, the poem could have acted as a justification of the deportation of the cultic statues as an expression of the gods' abandonment of Kashtiliash. Other reasons can be found in Assyria, or at least in its elite, which possibly disapproved of the intervention for religious or other reasons, and did not accept the breach of the peace treaty with Babylonia.

On the contrary, the motives behind the letter written by Shalmaneser to the king of Ugarit after the battle of Nihriya are obvious, and it is possible that the king wrote similar letters to all of Hatti's vassals (Text 20.2b). In this case, the opposition between the just and valiant Assyrian king and his disloyal and cowardly enemy is much more stereotypical. The use of letters for a celebratory and apologetic message is worth noting, since letters were commonly used for diplomatic communications. Shalmaneser's letter was not written using the terminology and style of the royal correspondence of the time, but using the typical tone of royal poems and inscriptions. After all, in terms of its purpose and genre, this letter is more similar to the latter types of texts. The only difference was that the recipient of this particular text was a vassal king and not the king's subjects.

Text 20.2   Middle Assyrian ideology and political propaganda

(a) *A prayer of Tukulti-Ninurta I to the god Ashur*

'You have taught your land not to transgress the oath, to observe norms. They (the Assyrians) do not cross the lines you have traced, and conform to your judgement. They are respectful and careful towards the firm decision of your supreme power. They trust your benevolent judgement, they seek your divinity. You are their great and good support, their vast protection. Trusting in your lordship, they consult in the middle of the sky your solution (to their problems).

(On the contrary) the other lands in unison surround your city, Ashur, with a circle of evil, and together they hate the shepherd you have chosen to keep the people in order. All the lands to which you have provided a benevolent support, despise you; while you have extended your protection over them, they reject your land. The kings you have filled with good things continue to disobey you; those to whom you have allowed your favour, prepare to do battle against you.

For your city, Ashur, battle is continuously ready, a mass of attacks is moving against it. Enemies and rivals do not cease to look at your residence with evil intentions, and they make arrangements to sack your land, Assyria. Day and night, all the (foreign) lands desire the destruction of your wonders, they pester everywhere to destroy your cities, they plot to defeat you. All the wicked ones gather in a dark day, without sun; hostile hands are stretched to break the Assyrian armies. As wicked people, they plot against their benefactor; they transgress the norms of the lord of all the lands; forcefully, they gather princes (allies) and auxiliary troops.

Of your land, of Assyria, you are the lord: be a mighty lord, a vindictive prince! May your supreme power always be its protection, and may it support its fight! O lord, for your land Assyria, do not leave your beneficial arm inactive! O Ashur, great lord, king of the gods, Assyria is yours! O Assyrian Enlil, lord of all the lands, Assyria is yours!'

(b) Letter of Shalmaneser I to the king of Ugarit

'Thus, Tudhaliya, king of Hatti, wrote to me: 'Why are you hostile towards me? Why do you approach one of my allies to conquer it? Come then, let us fight! Otherwise I will be the one to come and bring you battle.' I answered thusly: 'Why would you have to come? I will be the one to come.' So, that same day I gathered the troops and chariots (and went) towards Taide, but did not reach it. Tudhaliya, king of the Hittites, sent me a second envoy, bearer of two threatening and one peaceful letter. He showed me the two threatening letters. As soon as my soldiers heard the hostile words, they began to prepare to march; and the envoy of the king of Hatti saw that too. After three days, the envoy of the king of Hatti brought me the peaceful letter, in which it was written: 'Adad and Shamash know this: I am not at war with my brother the king of Assyria, I am at peace. I will return his fugitives, and those who have fled in front of the king of Assyria and have sought refuge in the land of Hatti, I will make them return to the king of Assyria. Why would we, brothers, be hostile to one another?' [. . .] Since the king of Hatti had written me this, and the city of Nihriya was my enemy, I led my troops to lay siege on Nihriya. But an official (?) of the king of Hatti was inside Nihriya with Hittite troops. So, I wrote to the king of Hatti: 'Nihriya is my enemy. Why are your troops inside Nihriya? If you really are my friend, not my enemy, why are your troops supporting Nihriya? I will lay siege on Nihriya, order your troops to exit the city.' But he did not agree and did not even reply to me, but in the presence of my envoy raised his hand to the god Shamash saying: 'Shamash, you already know: I cannot do this, because the king of Assyria is (already) lined up for battle.' When I heard about these words, I wrote a tablet with an oath and sent it to him (saying): 'To (demonstrate) your good faith, touch this tablet in front of Shamash.' But he did not want to touch the tablet in front of Shamash. (Anyway) I made my troops retreat on that same day, and placed the camp (?) of my troops at Shura, and there were 120 leagues until the camp (?) of the troops of the king of Hatti. But a fugitive of the Hittite soldiers came to me and said: 'The king of Hatti is ready to attack, (even though) he never stops sending you swift messages to let you know you should have trust.' As soon as I heard these words of the fugitive, I said to the herald of my camp: 'Put on your armour, climb on your chariots! The king of Hatti is ready to attack!' I yoked the horses to my chariot myself and left saying: 'The king of Hatti is ready to attack! My soldiers and my chariots should not leave the camp if not after me!' I entered the [fight] and inflicted a painful defeat [to the king of Hatti], and his troops [escaped] in my presence [. . .]'

5 Middle Assyrian society

The shift from commercial to agricultural activities, alongside the conquests and the expansion of the Middle Assyrian state, led to the formation of a class of wealthy landowners. These individuals received lands through royal grants, and belonged to the military and administrative aristocracy. Fortunately, we possess some of these royal land grants, which were very similar to those described for the Hittite kingdom and Syria, and those attested in Kassite Babylonia. Royal grants were part of a mechanism typical of the Late Bronze Age. Apart from these grants, lands were freely sold, without any royal intervention to reduce the debts incurred by farmers. Consequently, we still encounter in the evidence debt slaves or farmers who gave up wives and daughters as slaves.

The population was divided into three categories: palace functionaries, 'free' (*ḫupšu*) village farmers, and owners of lands allocated by the king. Even the Assyrian army had members from all three categories, who held various titles relating to their ownership of land, or other means of sustenance. The class of free farmers, however, was in the process of becoming a secondary class. This class was afflicted by economic difficulties and debt slavery. The latter was progressively becoming a type of slavery connected to a specific land. Individuals receiving royal land grants belonged to the elite, a class closely linked to the palace, but able to personally manage royal lands. This was unlike lower ranking palace officials, who were not as privileged. Consequently, the elite was able to access those military and administrative roles in the provinces offered by the rising empire.

The palace was the heart of Middle Assyrian society. It was a large building with an equally large staff, but had a more restricted role compared to elsewhere in the Near East. The palace was simply a royal residence that had eventually expanded. From the instruction texts written to provide guidance on the internal management of the palace, and in particular of its harem, we gather a relatively unpleasant picture of life in the palace (Text 20.3a). The latter appears as a sort of prison, in which its residents, such as women and servants, were kept under constant control by a network of guards and informers. However, the accusation of individuals constituted an equally serious offence as the one perpetrated by the offenders. Eunuchs became typical functionaries of the Assyrian palace, both for their efficiency in managing the harem, and their close dependence and loyalty to the king.

Comparing Middle Assyrian instruction texts, which are attested from the reigns of Ashur-uballit to Tiglath-pileser I (who collected them), to the earlier Hittite ones, we note two completely different situations. Middle Assyrian society was extremely close, while Hittite society was much more open. However, they both emphasised personal relations of loyalty, which held the entire political system together. The instructions were called *riksu* ('bond'), a term that was also used in the establishment of a state as one's vassal, and both situations were sealed through an oath (*mamītu*).

A broader, yet incomplete, picture of Middle Assyrian society can be found in a collection of laws whose final edition was probably written in the reign of Tiglath-pileser I (just like the collection of edicts), although it was originally from the fourteenth to the thirteenth centuries BC. This collection is quite different from the Old Babylonian ones. Despite the fact that it was also written, copied and stored in the palace, the collection was not part of a royal edict. It lacked the standard prologue and epilogue, and the propagandistic or celebratory tone. Moreover, each law lacked that desire to regulate socio-economic relations, which was typical of the Old Babylonian period, but was now completely unsuitable for the conceptualisation and administration of power.

The Middle Assyrian Laws did not have price lists or measures to alleviate economic difficulties or liberate debt slaves. Therefore, the overall aim of these laws remains unclear. Since they were not celebratory in an obvious way, they could have been more normative, yet not necessary innovative, measures. It is possible that, having seen the Old Babylonian codes, Middle Assyrian scribes decided to develop an Assyrian code. However, they clearly misunderstood the implications of the Old Babylonian codes, which were rooted in a completely different ideology of kingship.

The Middle Assyrian Laws are mainly concerned with civil penal law, with a particular attention to the behaviour of women (Text 20.3b). The resulting picture is quite crude. The patriarchal structure of Middle Assyrian society was very imposing and centred on the absolute subordination of women to men (first the father and then the husband). Punishments were cruel, ranging from the frequent executions to the widespread practice of mutilations, beatings and forced labour, while payments were rarely required. Equally crude was the list of possible crimes (especially sexual abuse) and the frequent violence. It has been often believed that this picture is a good reflection of the aggressive and military nature of Middle Assyrian society. In this regard, it has to be pointed out that this same insistence on physical and humiliating punishments is also attested in the way the Assyrians treated the enemies they defeated in battle.

Text 20.3   Middle Assyrian legal texts

a) An example of a palace decree

'Tukulti-Ninurta, overseer (*aklum*), son of Shalmaneser, overseer, has issued the (following) decree for the palace personnel (lit. those who stand in front of him): the day in which the god goes into procession, when he enters the Palace, the Palace Supervisor, the Palace Herald, the Chief of the *zarīqu* -functionaries, and the Physician of the Inner Quarters should inspect the (new) court attendants, and report which ones are the king's eunuchs or the palace functionaries that are not yet ready (lit. acute). (In this case) they will be entrusted to court attendants for a second time. If these officials should not make a report (as they should), they are held responsible for a punishable offence.'

b) Extracts from the Middle Assyrian laws

Tablet A, §12 (carnal violence): 'if a married woman has passed along the streets, and a man has seized her (and) said to her, 'Let me lie with you,' if she is not willing (and) strenuously defends herself, but by force he takes her and lies with her, whether he has been found upon the married woman, or witnesses have brought charge against him of having lain with the woman, the man shall be put to death, (while) for the woman there is no punishment.'

§13–14 (adultery): 'if a married woman has come out of her house and gone to a man, where he is dwelling, (if the man) has lain with her (and) knew that she was a married woman, both the man and the woman shall be put to death.

If a man has lain with a married woman, either in a tavern or in the street, and knew that she was a married woman, the man who lay with her shall be treated as the (married) man declares that his wife shall be treated. If the man who lay with her did not know that she was a married woman (and) has lain with her, he is quit, (while) the (married) man shall charge his wife and shall treat her as he will.'

Tablet B, §12–13 (cultivation on another man's property): 'If a man has laid out an orchard (or) [dug] a well (or) grown trees in [. . .] field, (and) the owner of the field looks on (and) does not [come forward], the orchard is free to (be taken by) him who laid it out; (but) he shall give field for field to the owner of (the field which is now) the orchard.

If a man has either laid out an orchard or dug a well or grown vegetables or trees on waste land which is not his (and) charge (and) proof have been brought against him, when the owner of the field comes forward, he shall take the orchard together with the (produce of) his labours.'

Other laws of the code depict a socio-economic environment made of farming villages, which had their own organisation (each had a mayor and group of elders), their disputes and frequent breaches of borders between fields, as well as irrigation problems between neighbouring fields and temporary serfdom. The Middle Assyrian family was still based on a unity of brothers, who, if divided, still gave double the inheritance to the eldest son. Moreover, there was the practice of levirate marriage, which was clearly aimed at maintaining women and estates within one's own family.

These laws also emphasise the influence of military activities, with soldiers who never returned from war, or were lost. Consequently, widows had to wait five years before they could re-marry, but meanwhile had serious difficulties in supporting themselves and their children. Assyria was therefore still at the initial stage of that breakdown of family unity attested in this phase. In this sense, it was more traditional than Syria. However, the relentless imperial expansion began to create serious gaps in the Assyrian population (which the deportation of people was meant to compensate). The expansion, then, kick-started those processes which were eventually to lead to the accumulation of lands in the hands of the highest ranking officials. The latter was another serious issue, though more on a social rather than a demographic level.

21

KASSITE BABYLONIA

1 The political developments

Following Mursili I's expedition in Babylonia, Samsu-ditana continued to rule for a few years over a reduced and devastated kingdom. This situation paved the way for the rise of the Kassites, who had already attempted some military expeditions in Babylonia during the reign of Samsu-iluna. Unfortunately, we do not possess any information about the way in which a Kassite dynasty managed to establish itself on the Babylonian throne. Later chronicles would report that the dynastic sequence of Kassite kings had begun with some individuals (Gandash, Agum I and Kashtiliash I) that remain unattested in Babylonia. Hypothetically, they could have been contemporaries of the last kings of the First Babylonian Dynasty. These kings must have belonged to a Kassite dynasty that was already established, but was based in the original land of the Kassites, namely, the Zagros Mountains, and not in Babylonia. Be that as it may, the name of the Kassite conqueror of Babylon remains unknown to us.

However, a later source attests that 24 years after Marduk's statue was 'exiled' to Hana at the hands of the Hittites, the Kassite king, Agum II, successfully brought it back to Babylon. Both the dynastic sequence of the kings of Hana and the epigraphic and archaeological evidence from Terqa suddenly stop at the beginning of the sixteenth century BC. Therefore, it is possible to deduce that Agum II, one of the first Kassite kings of Babylon, had destroyed Terqa. In this way, the king put an end to the kingdom of Hana, and brought back to Babylon the booty and the statue of Marduk. The Babylonian kings would continue to hold an theoretical supremacy over the Middle Euphrates, especially in the Suhu area (immediately south of Hana), despite the subsequent Assyrian interest in the area.

Similarly, the Kassites managed to keep a hold of the Sealand, thus unifying Lower Mesopotamia under their authority. Ulam-Buriash and Agum III (whose distinction from Agum II is still under debate) defeated the last kings of the Sealand and proclaimed themselves kings of that region. The royal titles of the Kassite kings still attest their control over their original land and the foothills between the Zagros and the Tigris (Padan and Arman). The Babylonian kingdom, which was called Karduniash in Kassite, was now a relatively vast territory, worthy of being considered a 'great kingdom' in the Late Bronze Age international system. To the north, we have some attestations on a number of conflicts with Assyria. As a result of these clashes, several treaties were signed between Burna-Buriash I and Puzur-Ashur III, and between Kara-indash and Ashur-bel-nisheshu.

The official entrance of the Kassites in the long-distance diplomatic network of the time took place during the reign of Kara-indash. According to some retrospective mentions found in the Amarna correspondence, Kara-indash was the first Babylonian ruler to establish relations with Egypt. Amenhotep II (a contemporary of Kara-indash) states that after his conquests in Syria, even the king of Shanhara (the Egyptian name for Babylon) sent him gifts. Later on, Amenhotep III married a daughter of Kurigalzu I. This king began an ambitious building programme in Babylonia. He founded the city of Dur-Kurigalzu, and built and restored temples in many cities, even in the far south. However, these achievements might not have been all his, since it is not always easy to distinguish his inscriptions from the ones of Kurigalzu II.

The Amarna letters also attest negotiations for another inter-dynastic marriage. They began with Kadashman-Enlil and Amenhotep III, but were only agreed on at the time of Burna-Buriash and Amenhotep IV. This is mainly due to the Babylonian insistence on receiving an adequate payment in gold, since the Egyptians were refusing to send one of their princesses in marriage. The attitude of the Babylonians seems ambiguous, since the great care in the formal issues of rank, reciprocity and tradition was combined with an equally great, almost uncouth, avidity to receive Egyptian gold. As a result of that, in the other important courts of the time it was commonly believed that the Kassite kings deliberately sold their daughters for gold.

At the time, Babylonia suffered greatly from the divide existing between its long-standing tradition and its limited opportunities for expansion. This was due both to its distance from the heart of inter-dynastic relations, now located further west, and its reduced power. Having lost its former central role, Babylonia was now a marginal and almost secondary state compared to the other great powers of the time. For instance, when the Babylonian king complained that the Egyptian king had not sent him gifts when he was ill, he was clearly unaware of how far Egypt was from Babylonia. He therefore had to ask messengers and merchants if it was possible that the Egyptian king was oblivious to his situation.

The revival of Ashur-uballit's Assyria marked the beginning of a difficult phase for the Kassite kings. Burna-buriash, unable to obtain an Egyptian princess, gladly accepted the Assyrian king's daughter, Muballitat-Sherua, as daughter-in-law. However, when a palace revolt eliminated her son once he had become king, the Assyrian ruler attacked Babylon. He then placed the infant Kurigalzu II ('the little one'), another son or nephew of Muballitat-Sherua, on the throne. However, once of age, Kurigalzu felt closer to his Kassite lineage, being the son of Kara-hardash, than his Assyrian one on his mother's side. Therefore, he fought against the Assyrians in the battle of Sugagu (whose outcome remains uncertain), just as he had fought against the Elamites, successfully reaching Susa.

From the mid-fourteenth to the mid-thirteenth century BC, the Kassite rule in Babylonia remained relatively stable. The kingdom had to contain the expansionistic ambitions of the Assyrians and the Elamites, and kept good relations with the Hittites. Commercial relations with the latter are attested in the long letter of Hattusili III to Kadashman-Enlil II. The route passed through the Euphrates Valley (to avoid crossing Assyrian territories), where it encountered problems with local nomadic groups, and reached northern Syria. Once there, however, Babylonian merchants could access the western resources in precarious conditions, given the great distance of Babylonia and the little influence the latter had outside of Mesopotamia.

Assyria remained the biggest problem for the Kassites, especially in the area east of the Tigris. The Assyrians managed to defeat the Kassite Nazi-Marutash under the leadership of Adad-nirari I. This victory only allowed a minimal shift of the border between the two kingdoms, which still maintained control over their own territories. Following the conventions of the time, the alternating victories of one kingdom or the other led to the establishment of several treaties defining the border, and the composition of heroic poems. The latter were aimed at celebrating within one's own kingdom the king's successes. When Kashtiliash IV took advantage of Tukulti-Ninurta I's coronation to move the border further north, he clearly outraged the wrong enemy. The reaction of the young Assyrian king was incredibly determined and aggressive: he not only defeated Kashtiliash in the battlefield, captured him and brought him back to Ashur, but also reached Babylon and conquered it.

The Assyrian rule in Babylon lasted for seven years. Tukulti-Ninurta held the nominal title of king, while he delegated control of the area to his trustees. Tukulti-Ninurta's intervention was similar to Ashur-uballit's attempt to control Babylonia through a puppet king. At the same time, however, it was far more drastic and hostile, causing great damage to Babylon and the deportation of Marduk's statue. Even Tukulti-Ninurta's poem, with its polemic and apologetic tone, was probably a response to the Babylonian reaction against this harsh Assyrian intervention.

While an Assyrian revolt eliminated Tukulti-Ninurta, a Babylonian revolt eliminated his representative in Babylon. The latter was replaced by Kashtiliash's son, Adad-shum-usur. However, the Assyrian rule in Babylonia, emphasising its internal instability, encouraged a third international power to intervene, namely, Elam. The coronation of Adad-shum-usur seems to have been a reaction of the Kassite aristocracy against the Assyrian as well as the Elamite invasions. Adad-shum-usur fought the Assyrians with moderate success and managed to consolidate his position. However, the stability of his long reign, just like the one of his successors Meli-shipak and Marduk-apla-iddina, was due to the momentary weakness of both Assyria, ruled by the weaker successors of Tukulti-Ninurta, and Elam.

After this phase, the Kassite dynasty quickly began to collapse. First, the Assyrian king Ashur-dan successfully attacked Babylonia. Then, the Elamite Shutruk-Nahhunte conquered and plundered the eastern and northern Babylonian cities (Eshnunna, Sippar, Akkad and Dur-Kurigalzu). He brought a large booty back to Susa, including some ancient monuments kept in the Babylonian temples. The Elamite king then left his son, Kutir-Nahhunte, to rule northern Babylonia alongside the residual Kassite power that was still surviving in the south. A few years later, Kutir-Nahhunte delivered the final blow to the Kassite dynasty, conquering Babylon and deporting the prestigious statue of Marduk to Susa, together with the statue of Nanaya from the sanctuary of Uruk.

In this way, the Kassite dynasty ended. Despite being originally foreign to Babylonia, this dynasty had been able to rule there for half a millennium, thus much longer than any of the local Babylonian dynasties. The fall of the Kassite dynasty happened around a decade after the fall of the other major players of the Late Bronze Age, but for other reasons. The upheavals marking Syria and Anatolia in the thirteenth century BC did not reach Mesopotamia. There, the difficult political triangle established in the thirteenth century BC between Assyria, Babylonia and Elam continued in the following centuries, though with new dynasties.

2 The socio-demographic crisis

The mid-second millennium BC marked a severe crisis of Lower Mesopotamian demography, economy and production. After the demographic peak reached in the Ur III and Isin–Larsa periods, the First Babylonian Dynasty had experienced serious difficulties in maintaining this growth. The Kassite period, then, saw a visible decline. Despite its unique characteristics, this decline was an integral part of the overall crisis marking the Late Bronze Age throughout the Near East.

A number of marginal areas, especially the Middle Euphrates Valley, were largely abandoned. This aggravated the isolated position of Babylonia. Other areas, especially in the south, experienced the decline of their irrigation systems and soil fertility, and the transformation of vast areas into pasturelands or marshes. The Diyala Valley, despite being located outside this scenario, experienced around a 50 per cent decline in its population. This decline was worse in cities than in villages. In Central Mesopotamia, which managed to resist this decline better, settlements diminished by 75 per cent in the Old Babylonian levels, with cities more than halved. The centre of power was now in the north, extending from Babylonia to Dur-Kurigalzu, Borsippa and Nippur.

The unification of Babylonia had drastically reduced the power of individual cities. Babylon was the only city hosting the royal court and accommodating the flux of goods and activities linked to the palace. Unfortunately, Kassite Babylon (just like the Babylon of the time of Hammurabi) is not well attested archaeologically, and its evidence could have provided a more positive picture of this period. The other cities were turned into provincial capitals, but were first and foremost cultic centres. The division of the region into 20 provinces took place in the Kassite period. Each province had a governor (*šaknu*), who supervised a hierarchy of functionaries with titles that were different from the ancient ones (*kartappu*, *šakrumaš* and so on). Only some of these provinces, mainly in the centre of the kingdom, had a Babylonian city as their capital (from Dur-Kurigalzu to Isin and Nippur). Other provinces were centred on tribal or family groups, defined as the 'House of' a certain ancestor or founder. They thus reproduced a social structure of clear Kassite origins. Finally, some provinces were more marginal entities, especially in the area between the Tigris and the Zagros.

Overall, the Kassite kingdom was largely de-urbanised, and maybe even fragmented, due to the impact of the arrival of foreign and mountain people within a society already in a critical situation. Kassite infiltration was not particularly significant in terms of number. However, it found its strength in the socially compact nature of its groups (divided into 'houses'), and their politically influential role, represented by their military aristocracy. These groups partly imposed their habits and their concept of state on Babylonia. Even in terms of production, the area experienced the rise of 'corporations' modelled around the family structure and named after eponymous ancestors. Both these aspects were extraneous to Sumerian and Akkadian culture. When the Kassites lost political control over the Zagros area, due to the marked economic and administrative differences between the alluvial plain and the mountains, the Kassite groups already settled in Babylonia were soon integrated into the local community.

As mentioned above, Babylonian cities became increasingly important as cultic centres. Therefore, they somehow lost the role they once had in the Neo-Sumerian period, with temples acting as production and redistributive centres of a vast state, whose economy could not have been managed by one single centre. The Kassite kings went through considerable efforts to restore Babylonian sanctuaries in the north as well as in the south. In fact, temples soon took on the role of functional administrative centres. The temple archives from Nippur provide us with this picture, attesting the introduction of more complex and sensible accounting methods (Figure 21.1). It is highly likely that other cities, even in the far south (Ur, Uruk), experienced a similar development. Despite this role, Kassite economy was highly diversified, adaptable and personal, following the typical tendencies of the Late Bronze Age.

In the Kassite period, Babylonia also experienced the influence of new military techniques (chariots and horses). The latter benefited a small group of military professionals, who received generous land grants from the king. Apart from the large plots of land administered by the temples and located around the old Babylonian cities, another type of land ownership developed. The latter was made of royal land grants given to the members of the military, administrative and religious elites. This type of grant was much more personal. It featured the usual characteristics of hereditary transmission and the transformation of the temporary land allocations into fully-fledged ownership guaranteed by the king.

These allocations are particularly well attested in a type of monument typical of the Kassite period (and afterwards), namely, the *kudurru*. It is probable that these stone steles were originally boundary stones, used to define the borders of lands. However, Kassite *kudurrus* were left in temples, displaying in an influential and sacred location whatever was written on them. These *kudurrus* were royal land grants, briefly describing the land provided and eventual tax exemptions, but only rarely reporting the reason for this allocation (Text 21.1). The text was accompanied by symbols of those gods called upon to seal the validity of the agreement, and by curses against whomever moved, usurped or abolished this decree. It is likely that these texts also had an archival copy, sealed by the king and not much different from those sources we have encountered throughout this period, especially in Syria, Anatolia and Assyria.

Unlike this class of privileged dignitaries, the farming population experienced a drastic impoverishment, losing that political role characterising the Old Babylonian sector outside the palace. Just as in the other Near Eastern regions, in Kassite Babylonia titles and royal epithets, as well as royal inscriptions, show the kings' lack of interest in the wider population. Therefore, kings emphasised their privileged connection with the (predominantly Kassite) military and administrative aristocracy. Similarly, legal texts show

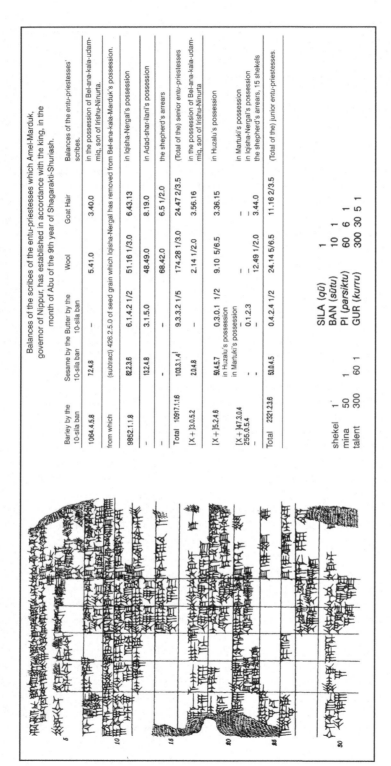

Balances of the scribes of the *entu*-priestesses which Amel-Marduk, governor of Nippur, has established in accordance with the king, in the month of Abu of the 9th year of Shagarakti-Shuriash.

Barley by the 10-sila ban	Sesame by the 10-sila ban	Butter by the 10-sila ban	Wool	Goat Hair	Balances of the *entu*-priestesses' scribes.
1064.4.5.8	7.2.4.8		5.41.0	3.40.0	in the possession of Bel-ana-kala-udam-miq, son of Irishu-Ninurta.
from which	(subtract) 426.2.5.0 of seed grain which Iqisha-Nergal has removed from Bel-ana-kala-Marduk's possession.				
9852.1.1.8	82.2.3.6	6.1.4.2 1/2	51.16 1/3.0	6.43.13	in Iqisha-Nergal's possession
–	13.2.4.8	3.1.5.0	48.49.0	8.19.0	in Adad-shar-ilani's possession
–	–	–	68.42.0	6.5 1/2.0	the shepherd's arrears
Total 10917.1.1.6	103.3.1.4¹	9.3.3.2 1/5	174.28 1/3.0	24.47 2/3.5	(Total of the) senior *entu*-priestesses
[X +]3.0.5.2	2.0.4.8	–	2.14 1/2.0	3.56.16	in the possession of Bel-ana-kala-udam-miq, son of Irishu-Ninurta
[X +]5.2.4.6	50.4.5.7 in Huzalu's possession in Martuki's possession	0.3.0.1 1/2	9.10 5/6.5	3.36.15	in Huzalu's possession
[X +]47.3.0.4 255.0.5.4 –	0.1.2.3	–	12.49 1/2.0	3.44.0	in Martuki's possession in Iqisha-Nergal's possession the shepherd's arrears, 15 shekels
Total 2321.2.3.6	53.0.4.5	0.4.2.4 1/2	24.14 5/6.5	11.16 2/3.5	(Total of the) junior *entu*-priestesses.

	SILA (*qû*)	1		
	BAN (*sūtu*)	10	1	
	PI (*parsiktu*)	60	6	1
	GUR (*kurru*)	300	30	5	1

shekel	1	
mina	50	1
talent	300	60	1

Figure 21.1 Administrative text from Nippur, Kassite period. The accounting records of the time stand out for their exemplary clarity and their tabular structure, an innovation compared to the traditional arrangement of accounts in columns (in the translation: in columns 1–3 the numbers represent, in order, GUR, PI, BAN, SILA; in columns 4–5, the numbers represent talents, minas, shekels).

Text 21.1 A limestone kudurru from Susa recording the land grants of the Kassite king Nazi-Marutash

r. 1 1) *na-zi-múru-taš* 2) *šar kiššati* 3) *mār ku-ri-gal-zu* 4) *liplippi* 5) *bur-na-bu-ri-aš* 6) *šar la ma-ḫar* 7) *eqlēti^{mes} ša mehret^{mes}* 8) *^{uru}bābili* 9) *a-na ^dmarduk be-li-šu* 10) *id-id-in-ma* 11) *^{uru}TUR.ZA.GIN* 12) *ša bīt-muq-tar-is-saē* 13) *a-di 4 alān^{mes}Š* 14) *ù 7 me zēri-šu* 15) *a-na ^dmarduk iddin-ma* 16) *i-na lib-bi* 17) *^ughga-za-an-na-ti* 18) *qa-ti bīt-muq-tar-is-saḫ* 19) *ú-ter-ru* 20) *70 zēru* 21) *ugār ^{uru}ri-is-ni* 22) *kišād ^{i7}su-ri rabî* 23) *30 zēru* 24) *ugār ^{uru}ti-ri-qa-an* 25) *kišād ^{i7}da-ba-an* 26) *napḫâtu 1 me zēru 1 iku ṣimid* 27) *1 ammatu rabītu^{u4}* 28) *piḫât bīt-^dsîn-ma-gir* 29) *70 zēru* 30) *ugār ^{uru}dūr-šarri* 34) *kišād ^{i7}da-ba-an* 35) *napḫāru 1 me zēru 1 iku ṣimid* 36) *1 ammatu rabītu^{u4}* 37) *piḫat ^{uru}dūr-^dpap-sukkal*

II 1) *1 ŠU zēru* 2) *ugār ^{uru}pi-la-ri-i* 3) *kišād nār-šarri* 4) *piḫât ^{kur uru}ḫu-da-di* 5) *1 me zēru 1 iku ṣimid* 6) *1 ammatu rabītutu4* 7) *ugār ^{uru}dūr-^dnergal* 8) *kišād ^{i7}mi-ga-ti* 9) *piḫât dup-li-ia-aš* 10) *50 zēru 1 iku ṣimid* 11) *1 ammatu rabītu^{tu4}* 12) *ugār ^{uru}dūr-^dšamaš-ilu-ban ǔ* 13) *kišād ^{i7}su-mu-un-der* 14) *piḫât bit-^dsîn-ašared* 15) *84 zēru 1 iku ṣimid* 16) *1 ammatu rabītu^{tu4}* 17) *ugār ^{uru}ka-re-e* 18) *kišād nār-šarri* 19) *piḫât ^{uru}u-pi-l* 20) *i-na lib-bi* 21) *7 me zēru* 22) *ša ^{uru}TUR.ZA.GIN* 23) *4 me 94 zēru* 24) *i-ru-um* 25) *me 6 zēru re-ḫu* 26) *na-zi-mú-ru-taš* 27) *šar kiššati* 28) *mār ku-ri-gal-zu* 29) *šar bābili* 30) *^mka-sag-ti-šu-gab* 31) *mār aḫu-bāni?* 32) *arad-su* 33) *i-ri-mu.*

'Nazi-Marutash, king of totality, son of Kurigalzu, descendant of Burna-Buriash, king without rivals, has donated the fields in front of Babylon to Marduk, his lord, and he has donated the city of T. (of the district) of Bit-muqtarissah with 4 towns and land (arable) with 700 *gur* of seeds (that is, 7000 *iku*, 2520 hectares) to Marduk. This the mayors responsible of Bit-muqtarissah have given up (?).

Land (arable) with 70 *gur* of seeds, irrigation district of Risni on the banks of the 'Great ditch' (and) land (arable) with 30 *gur* of seeds, irrigation district of Tiriqan, on the banks of the Daban. Total: land (arable) with 100 *gur* of seeds, at 30 *sila* for 1 *iku*, (measured) according to the 'large cubit' (that is, ca. 76 cm), in the administrative district of Bīt-Sîn-magir.

Land (arable) with 70 *gur* of seeds, irrigation district of Shasai on the banks of the Daban (and) land (arable) with 30 *gur* of seeds, irrigation district of the 'Fortress of the king', on the banks of the Daban. Total: land (arable) with 100 *gur* of seeds, at 30 *sila* for 1 *iku*, (measured) according to the 'large cubit', in the administrative district of the 'Fortress of Papsukkal'.

Land (arable) with 60 *gur* of barley, irrigation district of Pilari, on the banks of the 'King's canal', administrative district of Hudadi.

Land (arable) with 100 *gur* of seeds, at 30 *sila* for 1 *iku*, (measured) according to the 'large cubit', irrigation district of the 'Fortress of Nergal', on the banks of the Migati, administrative district of Dupliash.

Land (arable) with 50 *gur* of seeds, at 30 *sila* for 1 *iku*, (measured) according to the 'large cubit', irrigation district of the 'Fortress of Shamash-ilu-banu', on the banks of the Sumundar, administrative district of Bīt-Sîn-ashared.

Land (arable) with 84 *gur* of seeds, at 30 *sila* for 1 *iku*, (measured) according to the 'large cubit', irrigation district of Karê, on the banks of the 'King's canal', administrative district of Upī.

Of the land (arable) with 700 *gur* of seed of the city of T., (the king) has donated the (above mentioned) lands (arable, in total) with 494 *gur* of seeds. The remaining lands (arable) with 206 *gur* of seeds, Nazi-Marutash, king of totality, son of Kurigalzu, king of Babylon, has donated to Kasagti-Shugab, his servant.'

Several curses against the potential violator of these instructions follow.

the re-organisation of private land management, land sales, paid labour, land leases and of all the practices common in the Old Babylonian period. Having already lost their lands, the farming population, now transformed into simple paid labourers, was relegated to rural serfdom, working both in temple lands and lands belonging to royal functionaries (Figure 21.2). Servile labour soon substituted paid labour, permanent dependence substituted temporary (seasonal and daily) contracts, and rations substituted salaries.

Overall, this process appears like a return to a distant past, but the phenomenon affected different parts of the population. Rations were not provided to 'free' labourers obliged to provide *corvée* service anymore, but to permanent servants. Dependence on the temples did not affect specialised workers, but did affect farmers, who had fewer opportunities to be heard on economic and political issues. Due to the spread of exemptions, along with the hereditary transmission of royal land grants, the ancient class of palace and temple attendants began to neglect the situation in which the farmers now found themselves. These factors brought about the formation of conspicuous and well protected family estates. The latter were outside the control of the official administration. It was an almost entire overturn of the former situation in Babylonia: once, palace functionaries inhabited the cities, and a community of free private landowners inhabited the countryside; now, relatively free functionaries resided in the cities, and the countryside only had a population of servants dependent on cities and temples.

There was also a third issue affecting the socio-economic environment of Mesopotamia, which was not as united as it once was. From the mountains to the steppes, foreign groups, Kassites on the one hand, Sutians on the other, began to settle in marginal areas and marshes. These groups brought different social structures, which were new to the temple cities and their organisation. The latter were not used to the kin-based structure and the mobility of pastoral groups. The decline of the agricultural landscape therefore brought about the collapse of the ancient social organisation. At the moment, however, it did not seem possible to envision the rise of a new social organisation able to replace it.

3 Standardisation and wisdom literature

The Kassites had little influence on the literary culture of the Middle Babylonian period. They were completely extraneous to this Mesopotamian tradition. In the eyes of the Sumero-Akkadian scribes, the Kassites were representatives of those mountain people who did not know Mesopotamian culture and how to perform important rituals. Within the scribal sector of the period, Kassite influence can only be found in

Figure 21.2 Farming scene with seed-plough, found on a seal from the Kassite period.

some names for the various coat colours of horses, whose training constituted the main innovation of the period. There was, however, a problem in translating the names of Kassite deities into their corresponding Babylonian counterparts. This practice was linked to the assumption that other cultures' deities were none other than one's own, but with different names. Even in the case of the names of Kassite kings, Babylonian scribes supplied a translation in Akkadian, in order to display their linguistic knowledge.

Babylonian language had meanwhile evolved along internal lines, developing from Old Babylonian to Middle Babylonian. However, this language was used in more practical documents (letters and legal and administrative texts). For literary texts, the Middle Babylonian scribes developed Standard Babylonian, an artificial compromise between Old and Middle Babylonian. Standard Babylonian was therefore characterised by several archaisms. This was a scholarly attempt to keep Old Babylonian alive as a literary language, since many of the literary compositions written in this language had by now become classics worth imitating.

Alongside Standard Babylonian, during the Kassite period scribes also began the standardisation of literary compositions. Both literary texts and more practical treaties (such as omen and medical series, lexical lists, collections of phrases and so on) had been written in the Old Babylonian period. However, over time they experienced several modifications and adaptations, at times with important additions and omissions. With the Kassite period, scribes began to believe that the formation phase of Babylonian literature had ended. It was therefore time to preserve and pass on the work of the great masters of the past. This required scribes to correctly copy, without variations, an entire corpus. In this way, the Middle Babylonian scribes developed a series of standard editions.

Many centuries later, in the library of Ashurbanipal, some editions would be referred to with the names of the scribe and his school ('after *X*, from *X* city'). These were renowned master scribes from the Kassite period, and many later scribes considered themselves their descendants. It is not a coincidence, therefore, that the few names of 'authors' of literary compositions that have survived to us come from the Kassite period. These individuals could also have been responsible for the standardisation of previous works and series.

From a Neo-Assyrian and Neo-Babylonian point of view, the Kassite period was the time in which the great master writers and curators (known by name and by personality traits) of Mesopotamian literature lived, while the previous anonymous literature remained unclassifiable. However, it is worth noting that Old Babylonian literature remained anonymous because it was centred on the *edubba*, namely, the scribal school. The latter was therefore seen as the central institution responsible for the compositions of the time. Through the individualist spirit of the Kassite period, the desire to pass one's name to posterity developed alongside a certain degree of pedantic overload in terms of contents. This further proves that the main scribal activity of the time was the standardisation of knowledge, rather than its composition.

However, the limited creativity of Kassite scribes should not be measured against their close connection to classic compositions. In the reconstruction of the chronology of Mesopotamian literature, the large majority of works are concentrated in the libraries of Nippur (Old Babylonian texts) and Nineveh (Neo-Assyrian texts). This fact initially brought scholars to simplistically separate texts between 'old' and 'late' works. Only subsequently, was it clarified that the Kassite period was not only responsible for the standardisation of Babylonian knowledge. It was also responsible for the composition of new and original works, as well as entirely new re-interpretations of earlier works.

The characteristic features of this period were pessimism and individualism. The crisis of social values and the attempt to resort to personal values were the result of this period of crisis (which affected the area in terms of demography, productivity and family values), and of the decline of the centrality of the Babylonian state. This brought about the beginnings of more individualistic interests. In emergent states, these interests were usually heroic in nature. However, in a state in crisis, they became more anti-heroic, even intimate, being concerned with the differences between merit and success, and between achievement and recognition. The answers provided were either an intellectual meditation on the validity of social norms, or the simplistic provision of magical or fideistic explanations and remedies. However, these two extremes often met, forming a sort of 'double truth'. The latter provided a constructive solution through magical remedies or theological explanations. However, overall, it left an unresolved situation on the personal level.

It is known that the Epic of Gilgamesh was turned into an organic cycle in the Old Babylonian period. Among the many re-editions, it seems that it was re-written in the Kassite period with several scholarly and anti-heroic nuances, right before it was turned into its standardised edition. The poem's series of failures (which would have been considered as such from a heroic view of life, aimed at reaching immortality) became a way to reach a deeper awareness of one's limits and to search for more realistic models. Similarly, the Legend of Naram-Sin was originally centred on the relation between the compliance of omens and success. It therefore provided a negative depiction of the king, who sinned because of his arrogance and was punished through his failure. However, in the standard edition, the Legend's conclusion emphasises the anti-heroic ideal of passive resistance, namely, the typical behaviour of whoever tries to do some damage control. This conclusion, which had little relevance in the Legend and was different from the Old Babylonian one, was clearly a Kassite addition. This attitude is also attested in a letter from Ugarit, in which the same ideals of passive resistance were passed on as practical advice.

Regarding omens, the large corpus of Old Babylonian omens was collected and arranged into standardised series. Some creative additions, however, can be found in physiognomic omens, as well as those concerned with behavioural characteristics. In terms of physiognomic omens, the previous period had emphasised the most visible ones, such as moles, which were considered obvious 'signs'. The Kassite period was probably the time in which the attention turned towards physiognomic features such as the face, hair, hands and feet. This was an attempt to read an individual's fate from these revealing clues on his personality and character. This principle is even more evident in omens gathered from an individual's behaviour and opinion of himself. A typical expression of the Kassite scholarly environment was the fact that the omen always went against one's opinion of oneself. In other words, whoever thought of himself as a great man would have suffered a decline, whoever was shy would have been successful, and so on.

The difficulties and existential doubts of the period led to the development of the idea that a man, together with his own talents, was the maker of his own destiny. Alternatively, he had his destiny written on him or inside him, rather than in the entrails of sacrificial victims. However, this attitude, which clearly belonged to the more learned portion of society, was not as popular as the spread of formalism and magic typical of the Kassite period. All these traits would become an integral part of Babylonian culture in the first millennium BC. As mentioned above, in terms of medical advice, the focus on therapies attested in the Sumerian and Old Babylonian periods was now substituted by the Kassite attention for diagnoses. The latter were based on often irrelevant 'signs' and cured through magic and faith in the gods.

In the scribal milieu, the combination of individualistic tendencies (which were common in the period) with the crisis of the Kassite state (which was particularly worrying for the Babylonians) led to a growing tendency towards a consideration of greater themes, such as the nature of divine justice and of human destiny. These themes essentially formed what has been defined as 'wisdom literature'. This type of literature was expressed in various ways, from dialogues to collections of proverbs, but was marked by an overall sense of pessimism and indifference. The resignation and passive resistance attested in the Legend of Naram-Sin can also be found in one text that was part of this wisdom literature, namely, the Counsels of Wisdom. This text reformulated the issues of resignation and passive resistance to suit a more personal and court environment, rather than a military one. It provided advice such as not to oppose enemies, to be accommodating, and to always appear polite, while honouring the gods through prayers and sacrifices. Therefore, the former ideals of affirming one's valour and fairness through active interventions were substituted by a disenchanted realisation that true merits all too often remain unrecognised, thus making any exposure to dangers pointless.

The main composition of Babylonian wisdom literature is the so-called Babylonian Theodicy. It was based on this relinquishment of responsibilities in order to realise that success did not depend on merit, but on wealth. In the Theodicy, the Sumerian structure of the debate between two speakers championing opposite values was reformulated into a dialogue between the sufferer and his wise friend. Each speaker champions different points of view. Therefore, the debate was not a contraposition of two realities (such as, copper and silver, shepherd and farmer), but of two ways of seeing the same reality, following the psychological views of the time.

Of the two points of views, that of the sufferer is emotional and pessimistic, but adheres to the reality of social relations of the time. It emphasises the uselessness of active involvement in view of the poor results gained. In contrast, his wise friend shows a more optimistic and rational attitude, often accusing the sufferer of madness and lack of understanding. However, the wise friend debates on a level completely detached from the social situation of the time. This was the divine sphere, a realm that cannot be fully understood, forcing human beings to completely trust the gods in hope of a better future. The text also emphasises the idea that some sort of relation between behaviour and success still exists, hidden behind an unknown sin. The latter, then, was the cause for all the unjustifiable problems. This attitude was necessary because otherwise one would have to doubt divine justice, thus making life unbearable.

The other great composition of Babylonian wisdom literature, the *Ludlul bēl nēmeqi* (Text 21.2), follows the same structure: the protagonist, a high court functionary vilified by his envious rivals, removed from his post, enslaved as a result of the subsequent economic difficulties, ill and depressed, was evidently punished for a sin committed against the god Marduk. Only through several dreams and exorcisms he managed to regain, through Marduk's intervention, his health, status, power and wealth. As in the Theodicy, so the *Ludlul* emphasises the imperfect relation between social life and theological remedies. On the one hand, there was the realistic court environment, with its fierce competition among functionaries, the defamations, the career jumps, the rise or fall in royal favour. This was a typical representation of Near Eastern courts, but a particularly aggravated one in this competitive and more individualistic phase. In this view, the court was a meritocratic environment, yet at the same time deprived of that protection once guaranteed by tradition and kinship relations. On the other hand, there was the re-interpretation of this situation through the ideas of sins, exorcisms and divine interventions.

Text 21.2   The wisdom literature of the Kassite period: extracts from the Poem of the 'Rightful Sufferer' (*Ludlul bēl nēmeqi*)

Tablet I, 1–12: Hymn to Marduk

'I will praise the lord of wisdom, the deliberative god (?)
Who lays hold of the night, but frees the day,
Marduk, the lord of wisdom, the deliberative god (?),
Who lays hold of the night, but frees the day,
Whose fury surrounds him like the blast of a tornado,
Yet whose breeze is as a morning zephyr,
His anger is irresistible, his fury is a hurricane,
But his heart is merciful, his mind forgiving,
The (beneficial) source whose hands the heavens cannot hold back, but whose gentle hands sustain the moribund.'

Tablet I, 43–58: The Case of the Rightful Sufferer

'My god has forsaken me and disappeared,
My goddess has failed me and keeps at a distance.

The benevolent angel who (walked) beside [me] has departed,

My protecting spirit has taken to flight, and is seeking someone else.

My strength is gone; my appearance has become gloomy;

My dignity has flown away, my protection made off.

Fearful omens beset me.

I am got out of my house and wander outside.

The omen organs are confused and inflamed for me every day.

The omen of the diviner and dream priest does not explain my condition.

What is said in the street portends ill for me.

When I lie down at night, my dream is terrifying.

The king, the flesh of the gods, the sun of his peoples,

His heart is enraged (with me), and cannot be appeased.

The courtiers plot hostile action against me,

They assemble themselves and give utterance to impious words.'

Tablet I, 78–89: Forsaking Friends and Relatives

'Though a dignitary, I have become a slave.

To my many relations I am like a recluse.

If I walk the street, ears are pricked;

If I enter the palace, eyes blink.

My city frowns on me as an enemy;

Indeed my land is savage and hostile.

My friend has become foe,

My companion has become a wretch and a devil.

In his savagery my comrade denounces me,

Constantly my associates furbish their weapons.

My intimate friend has brought my life into danger;

My slave has publicly cursed me in the assembly.'

Tablet IV, 9–30: The Healing Process

'He who smote me

Marduk, he restored me.

He smote the hand of my smiter,

It was Marduk who made his weapon fall.

. . . (13–28)

The Babylonians saw how Marduk restores to life,

And all quarters extolled his greatness.'

An extreme example of these learned interpretations is the Dialogue of Pessimism, where the usual scheme of contraposition was reinvented to contrast the various pros and cons of any human activity. The dialogue takes place between a master and his servant. The former invited the latter to agree with his every statement, and suggests to him a series of pairs of opposite objectives. However, the servant is always able to provide pros, making good use of the large collection of Babylonian proverbs and commonplaces. The contrast does not really take place between master and servant, and there is no theological interpretation counterbalancing realistic statements. The Dialogue simply demonstrates that everything is true and fair, and so is the opposite of everything. Only suicide, then, is the answer to a useless life. Therefore, in a text lacking the formal use of divine justice, the crisis of the Kassite state appears to us in its most extreme expression.

4 Magic and religion

The lack of specifically Kassite elements in Babylonia is also attested in Babylonian religion. The only frequently cited Kassite deities, who would survive within the Babylonian pantheon, were Shuqamuna and Shumaliya. These were the guardian deities of the ruling dynasty. Other deities, such as Harbe, Marutash and Buriash are attested in the names of Kassite kings, and in lists providing their Babylonian equivalents. It is highly significant that these names frequently changed and were still uncertain. This is because the Kassite deities were difficult to identify with Mesopotamian deities.

In the pantheon of Nippur, the city from which the vast majority of Kassite texts come from, Enlil remained the main deity. However, the now consolidated role of Babylon as political capital allowed the rise in popularity of its patron deity, Marduk. This tendency had already begun under Hammurabi, and would acquire a more systematic coherence under Nebuchadnezzar I. The important role of Babylon as a political centre was therefore mirrored by its equally important role as a cultic centre, with the gods of the other cities gravitating around it. Alongside the prestigious gods of the previous period, such as the moon-god, Sin of Ur, or the solar god, Shamash of Larsa and Sippar, new gods entered the pantheon, most notably Nabu of Borsippa and Nergal of Kutha.

Apart from geo-political factors, this evolution was a consequence of the general tendencies of the time. The cult of Shamash, god of justice, and Adad, the heroic and belligerent god, had been widespread in the previous period, due to their largely social and positive qualities. Within the characteristic mentality of the Kassite period, Marduk, the exorcising god, Nabu, the god of wisdom, and Gula, goddess of medicine, became the most popular deities of Babylonia. This is because they took care of an individual's moral and physical evils. In other words, justice and heroism ceased to be the prevailing models, and each person began to have faith in exorcisms or learned considerations about life.

In the Old Babylonian period, gods had already visibly evolved from mere expressions of natural forces to expressions of moral values. This evolution became even more prominent in the Kassite period. This period shows a marked preference for a more personal type of deity. The latter could have had the name and personality of one of the great deities of the official pantheon. However, this type of deity was willing to establish a personal tie with an individual, becoming his confidant, the receiver of his prayers and sacrifices, his advisor on the correct remedies to implement, and his saviour. Consequently, personal prayers became a common way to express this personal relation between man and god. While scribes standardised the 'classical' list of the Babylonian pantheon, listing thousands of gods, each individual worshipper began to prefer a single deity, able to embody the divine sphere as a whole, so as to successfully interact with people's lives.

Man became the object of a fight between the negative forces (from illness to failure, defamation, poverty and impotence) afflicting him, and the positive forces meant to remove evils through exorcisms. Diagnostic interventions (such as omens) and remedies (such as exorcisms) could not entirely solve the problem, since the ultimate cause of the difficulties or successes was the person's sin or faith in the gods. In theory, this moral and theological aspect was essential. However, the practical aspect of diagnostic and curative measures had a far more crucial role in daily life and popular opinion.

Evil forces were provided with their own personality. Some gods, at times even major ones, belonged to negative realms, such as Nergal, god of pestilence, while illnesses and accidents became minor demons. Similarly, divine positive forces aimed to support humankind became some sort of personal 'guardian angels', divided into four figures: *ilu*, a protective god; *ištaru*, some sort of goddess of fortune; *lamassu*, the protective genie; and *šēdu*, a sort of personification of the *élan vital*. Therefore, alongside the strong tendencies towards formalism and exorcism, the Kassite period also shows a considerable degree of introspection, placing those divine forces formerly external to people on an internal and personal level.

Formalism and standardisation were also the cause for the increased importance of the symbolic representations of gods and their diffusion in the private sphere, mainly in the form of seals and *kudurrus*. The *kudurrus*, the boundary stones mentioned above, left considerable space to curses. In the depicted section, the *kudurrus* also left space to divine symbols, as if the measures established by the king would not have been followed without mentioning divine punishments. The repetitiveness and lack of space on these *kudurru* led to the transformation of symbols and curses into specific stereotyped formulas for each deity. In some cases, the symbols represented animals, such as Adad's bull or Gula's dog. In other cases, there were astral symbols (mainly for Sin, Shamash and Ishtar), a clear mark of a tendency towards that astral interpretation of the divine sphere that would peak in the first millennium BC. Finally, there were symbols depicting typical divine weapons or tools, such as Marduk's spade and Nabu's stylus, at times chosen as a result of peculiar word games. All these exorcisms, amulets, symbols and formulas indicate how Babylonian religion moved its attention from political relations to interpersonal relations, and, finally, intrapersonal ones.

5 The rise of the Middle Elamite kingdom

Between 1550 (the end of the sequence of *sukkal-maḫ* and of legal texts from Susa) and 1350 BC, Elam experienced its own dark age. However, this phase was different from the one attested in the rest of the Near East. In reality, this presumed 'dark age' appears to be so more in terms of textual evidence, rather than historical developments. The end of the previous period had already shown the presence of Hurrian personal names, which now appeared alongside Kassite names. Considering the proximity of Elam to the Zagros (home of the Kassites) and the area east of the Tigris (where the Hurrian elements originally came from), these influences are not surprising.

The linguistic relations between Elamite, Hurrian and other languages spoken in the Zagros are not clear enough to prove a Mesopotamian origin of these personal names. After all, they could have reached Elam directly from the mountains. Similarly, we do not know for sure the reach of Elamite influence to the north-west and the political status of the mountain tribes in relation to Elam. It is possible that the constant conflicts between Elam, Assyria and Babylonia were fought to gain control over the commercial routes crossing Iran, as well as the foothills between the Tigris and the Zagros.

In the mid-fourteenth century BC, Kurigalzu II defeated the Elamite king Hurba-tilla. However, the latter does not appear in the Elamite dynastic sequences. Therefore, it is possible to assume that he was a king of Susiana with a Hurrian name, and that his defeat and Kurigalzu's expedition to Susa did not threaten the stability of the Elamite confederation. Shortly after, when Middle Elamite sources reappear, we find a completely different situation from the period of the *sukkal-maḫ*. Susa ceased to be the political centre of Elam. The seat of power moved further inland, beyond the mountains, in Anshan (modern Fars). Consequently, Middle Elamite kings began to use the title of 'king of Anshan and Susa'.

The official language (also for royal inscriptions) was once again Elamite, and not Babylonian, as it had been before the dark age. Finally, the succession was by now patrilineal, a predictable result of that evolution of Elamite society that began in the seventeenth and sixteenth centuries BC. Another particular aspect of the Middle Elamite kingdom was its local character compared to the time of the *sukkal-maḫ*. At the time of the *sukkal-maḫ*, the choice of Susa as capital showed a clear intention of becoming a constitutive part of the Mesopotamian political system and of Babylonian culture. Now, however, following a tendency that has been attested in Hatti and Mitanni, Elam strived to maintain its uniqueness, while presenting itself as one of the protagonists in this decidedly polycentric Late Bronze Age Near East.

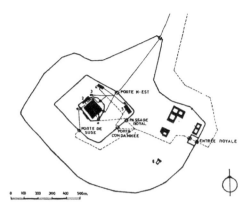

Figure 21.3 Dur-Untash (Choga Zanbil): plan of the city with the processional roads, the royal palace (east), and the sacred complex (within the walls) featuring a ziqqurat in the middle.

The founder of the new Elamite dynasty was Ike-Halki. He was succeeded by Pahir-ishshan and Attar-kittah, possibly two contemporaries of Nazi-Marutash and Kadashman-Turgu. Elam was therefore part of that coexistence of different powers characteristic of the second half of the fourteenth century BC. At the same time as the rise of the Middle Assyrian state, the Middle Elamite state grew under Humban–nimena, Untash-Humban, Unpatar-Humban and Kidin-Hutran. Internally, the most influential Elamite king was Untash-Humban, who founded the city of Dur-Untash (Choga Zanbil, south-east of Susa). Dur-Untash was a small city, but certainly an important religious centre, with a *ziqqurat* that could have competed with the Babylonian ones and a rich set of temples and public buildings (Figure 21.3). Therefore, Elam was clearly influenced by the tendencies of the time (such as the foundation of Dur-Kurigalzu in Babylonia and Kar-Tukulti-Ninurta in Assyria), founding royal residences and artificial capitals *ex novo*. The buildings of Dur-Untash constitute the most imposing and significant remains of Middle Elamite culture (also due to their state of conservation). Even a single monument, such as the bronze statue of queen Napirasu, confirms that the reign of Untash-Humban constituted the apogee of the Middle Elamite period.

Meanwhile, the conflict between Assyria and Babylonia, and the subsequent decline of the Kassite dynasty, provided Elam with the perfect opportunity to embark on several military expeditions in Babylonia. Untash-Humban himself led an incursion against several Babylonian cities, taking away a considerable booty. The expedition of Tukulti-Ninurta against the Kassite king, Kashtiliash, constituted the crucial moment opening up an array of opportunities for the Elamites. Kidin-Hutran thus led two important expeditions, destroying the area east of the Tigris (Der and the Diyala Valley). He subsequently reached Nippur and other cities in the heart of Babylonia. The incursions did not provide long-lasting results, but allowed the Elamites to control certain areas in the Zagros foothills, especially the lands of Padan and Yalman (Arman). The latter had been the main regions of the earliest Kassite kings and a crucial link between their native land and Babylonia. Not even Tukulti-Ninurta's reaction and attack, reaching as far as the Persian Gulf, succeeded in removing these newly conquered lands from Elamite control.

We have already mentioned that the final fall of the Kassite dynasty, which took place in the twelfth century BC, was the result of further Elamite incursions led by Shutruk-Nahhunte and Kutir-Nahhunte. However, these expeditions, marking the highpoint of the Middle Elamite kingdom, took place after the Late Bronze Age. They therefore took place in a different political scenario, which has to be taken into consideration later on.

PART V

The Early Iron Age

22
CRISIS AND REORGANISATION

1 The internal factors of the crisis

Shortly after 1200 BC, the entire political system of the Near East, which had been relatively stable for centuries, collapsed rather abruptly. This collapse was due to the arrival of foreign invaders from the west. Modern historiography has been initially satisfied with the external and migratory explanation of the crisis. However, it then started to question the extent to which the explanation was sufficient to justify such a large-scale decline and subsequent reorganisation. The crisis of the twelfth century BC completely re-shaped the political organisation, the distribution of settlements, the material culture, the social relations and the ideologies of the Near East.

The change was so drastic that in the nineteenth century (AD) the division of the early history of human-kind into technological epochs considered the crisis of the twelfth century BC as the watershed moment between the Bronze and Iron Age. It is now a well-accepted fact that the clash of invaders against the powerful states of the time had devastating effects and drastic consequences precisely because these states were to a certain degree already weakened. External factors (migratory in particular) certainly played an important role. However, they are now either reformulated in their scale (such as the number of Sea Peoples), or reinterpreted as internal factors (nomads), which are considered to be effects rather than causes, or even constitutive aspects rather than ultimate reasons for this collapse.

With regards to each individual region, the demographic crisis that affected Late Bronze Age communities has already been mentioned. The semi-arid Transjordan and Upper Mesopotamian plateaus reverted to a predominantly nomadic lifestyle. Anatolia and Syria experienced the abandonment of large cities, and settlements began to be concentrated in the fertile valleys. Finally, in Central and southern Mesopotamia the population was virtually halved. Therefore, the fundamental basis of this crisis must have been due to internal factors (such as low birth rates, since other demographic factors were already low), and closely linked to low production levels and several social problems.

These internal demographic issues must have been worsened by certain political developments. Although human and material resources were decreasing, palaces refused to lower their expectations and their needs, which actually increased. On the contrary, palaces began to weigh even more on the population, leading to the ultimate decline of an entire class of people that was already experiencing severe economic difficulties. The conquest of entire regions forced to pay tributes, the widespread deportations and increasing international competition (which was also military) were all means through which the strongest states attempted to compensate for their own crisis. However, they inevitably transferred these problems to the weakest regions.

Wars, deportations, depopulations and production crises led to famines and pestilences, which became an endemic problem in the Late Bronze Age. The available documentation reports that these issues were particularly prominent in the mid-fourteenth century BC and the end of the thirteenth century BC. The desperate cries for grain of the last Hittite rulers to their remaining vassals, or the Egyptian intervention 'to maintain the miserable land of Hatti alive', both describe an exceptionally severe crisis. Moreover, the dendrochronologic sequence from Gordion records a sequence of particularly dry years around 1200 BC. This would explain the severe famine affecting an already weakened Anatolia. In Lower Mesopotamia, the progressive collapse of the network of canals led to an agricultural crisis. The latter left the marshes and semi-arid areas to semi-nomadic pastoral activities. Alongside the agricultural decline and the spectacle of formerly great cities reduced to empty walls in the steppes, was a crisis of commercial caravans. These caravans met increasing difficulties in crossing ever-expanding areas outside palace control (the latter being unable to deter or punish robbers).

Demographic and production difficulties grew at the same pace as the overall social crisis of the time. From a logical and chronological point of view, this social crisis can be considered the fundamental reason for the entire collapse. For instance, there was the above-mentioned increase of private individuals losing their lands and the subsequent intensification of debt slavery. The decline of family and village solidarity led to the enrichment of the palace elite and the subsequent ruin of the rest of the community. This led to the separation of members of the same family (especially wives and sons given away as debt slaves), forcing people coerced into debt slavery (or just about to be) to flee. The decline of the village population into a class of slaves therefore greatly contributed to the demographic decline, the lack of motivation in production and the decreased acceptance of royal authority.

It has already been noted how Late Bronze Age kings were rather indifferent to the economic difficulties of the farming population. They therefore ceased to commission remission edicts and even took advantage of the situation by acquiring more wealth, in a blind strategy aimed at achieving results quickly. In this task, kings were also supported by an equally blind elite solidarity. Even within the family, the end of the traditional sense of communal solidarity was expressed by the addition of clauses obliging sons to assist and obey their parents in order to gain a share of the inheritance. In all fairness, this overall situation was to a certain extent coherent. At least from an individual perspective it demonstrates a clear attempt to gain a larger percentage of a set of resources that were decreasing in number. However, from a wider perspective, this same situation emphasises the negative effects of an attitude that, despite being aware of the obvious need to maintain the minimum levels of survival and political freedom, still ignored these concerns. This deliberate negligence was meant to maintain a mechanism centred on the concentration of surplus in the hands of the elite.

The enormous gap existing between the ruling elite and the rest of the population also had an impact on an ideological level. The king ceased to portray himself as a good father of his people, in favour of a more heroic depiction of himself. The latter emphasised his strength and military prowess, as well as his refined and international taste. As a result of this change, the population ceased to recognise the king as the protector of those in need, ensuring justice and fairness to his people. The population could neither rebel nor forge an alternative social organisation, due to the lack of the necessary prerequisites, means and ideology. The only reaction available was therefore to flee, leaving behind all those intolerable difficulties in search of a new life elsewhere. The rise in the number of fugitives was so dramatic that it forced states to seal a network of inter-state agreements aimed at searching, capturing and returning those who escaped. Consequently, people ceased to escape to other states, and preferred to hide in areas outside palace control, making the steppes and mountains their ideal refuge.

These areas were mainly used by transhumant pastoral groups, who were seen by those in palaces as robbers, simply because they were able to live outside palace control, assaulting caravans and protecting fugitives. Consequently, tribal groups became an alternative to the unjust state administrations, a model of non-palatial social organisation impossible to find in the now declining villages. The compromised communal solidarity supporting the palace was in some cases even substituted by a solidarity against the palace. For individual fugitives, or small groups of them, this new communal life required constant movement and a life in hiding. When entire villages moved from palace dependence to tribal solidarity, however, then entire communities virtually 'became *ḫabiru*' without having to leave their lands. They therefore avoided the excessive political and economic impositions simply by shifting their allegiance, changing their solidarity and obedience, and depriving their former states of material as well as human resources.

2 The migration of peoples

By the time the internal processes of socio-economic and political decline had reached worrying levels, the Near East was afflicted by an external wave of migrations. In order to evaluate the impact of this factor, it may be sufficient to compare the outcome of the crisis in the west and in Mesopotamia. The west was affected by these migrations, while Mesopotamia remained relatively untouched by these invaders. However, in Mesopotamia the demographic and economic crisis would last for centuries, and its political and cultural traits would continue to survive. Meanwhile, the west (from Anatolia to Cyprus, Syria and the Levant) experienced a radical change through several technological, ideological and social innovations, opening up to new ethnical, political and linguistic influences.

The ultimate place of origin of these migratory movements affecting the Near East in the twelfth century BC was probably the Balkan Peninsula. This area never had any contact with the Near East. These movements of people had to cross the eastern Mediterranean, an aspect that gave them their characteristic maritime connotation. The eastern Mediterranean had long been an integral part of a political and commercial network that included the Near Eastern and Egyptian coasts. One of the most important participants in this network was the Mycenaean state. The latter was divided into a series of autonomous city-states, possibly linked to each other in some form of hegemony. In fact, the Hittites knew of a kingdom of Ahhiyawa (namely, Achaia), located on the other side of the sea (Greece/Peloponnese). Ahhiyawa was the centre from which Mycenaean elements reached the coast of Asia Minor. This kingdom was considered powerful enough by the Hittites to make them wonder if it should be considered a great kingdom within the Near Eastern network of great powers. Ahhiyawa had certain distinctive characteristics (such as its archives written in Linear B, a reflection of the Near Eastern administrative system) and acted as a bridge between the non-urbanised areas of Europe and the Central Mediterranean.

Mycenaean relations with Egypt and the Levant were predominantly commercial and followed different practices from those characterising the rest of the Near East in the Late Bronze Age. In this case, the diplomatic, political and 'administrative' aspects of trade were downplayed in favour of actual trade. The latter pursued by private merchants, some of which privately acted for the palaces. This type of trade led to a visible increase in the exportation of Mycenaean pottery to the Anatolian and Syro-Levantine coasts, reaching as far as Egypt. These exchanges were normally peaceful and were delivered by a variety of commercial fleets (Mycenaean, Syro-Levantine, Cypriot, or Egyptian ones). However, there still were groups of robbers attacking fleets and coastal cities in a similar fashion to the nomads assaulting caravans. The boundary between piracy and organised military endeavours, and between the indifference of the palaces and their participation in these activities, was not always clear. Even in the fifteenth century BC (Madduwatta) and the fourteenth century BC (Amarna), we know of this involvement of palaces, especially in the southern coast of Anatolia (from Lydia to Cilicia). For the Hittites, this area was difficult to control (due to the proximity of the Taurus Mountains to the coast) and would continue to be a land of pirates in the following centuries.

More serious symptoms of increasing turbulence from the eastern Mediterranean marked the second half of the thirteenth century BC. The most important one was the support provided by populations from the Mediterranean to the Libyans. The latter tried to invade Egypt, but were defeated by the Egyptian king, Merneptah, around 1230 BC. This 'coalition' included the Eqwesh (Achaeans), the Lukka (Lycians), and three groups typically associated with the Sea Peoples, namely, the Teresh, the Shekelesh and the Sherdana. Of the latter three groups, only the last one was already known in the Amarna Age. Back then, the Sherdana constituted a group of mercenaries working in the Egyptian and Syro-Levantine area. The Merneptah episode bears several similarities with the following invasion of the Sea Peoples. However, this particular invasion can be contextualised in the Mycenaean expansion of the Eqwesh and the commercial activities of specialised groups (Sherdana) or bandits (Lukka) roaming in the eastern Mediterranean.

Another interesting episode was the Hittite conquest, celebrated by Suppiluliuma II, of Alashiya (Cyprus) around 1200 BC. Alashiya had a particular status and role in the regional system of the Late Bronze Age. It was the main provider of copper for the entire region and was considered an important commercial partner. Its king was powerful enough to be able to address the Egyptian king as his 'brother'. Alashiya was therefore a kingdom that had been able to remain relatively independent, despite being 'used' by Hatti or Ugarit as the preferred destination for exiled political figures. Suppiluliuma II's decision to conquer the island must have been a reaction to a change in the latter's political situation. This could have been due to the waves of Mycenaean immigrants reaching the island, which made Alashiya a troublesome power for the Hittite empire, especially in terms of its maritime connections between Cilicia and Syria.

The third symptom has been attested archaeologically. In fact, it has been noted that typical elements of 'Philistine' culture in the Levant (such as anthropoid terracotta sarcophagi) (Figure 22.1) appeared before the invasion (whose date is securely attested). It therefore seems that groups of Philistines or other groups closely related to them, such as the Sherdana from the previous century, were mercenaries at the service of Ramesside Egypt. These mercenaries were mainly deployed in Syria and the Levant. These groups were so large in number that they left an archaeological trace of their presence.

These symptoms show that, at the beginning of the twelfth century BC, the invasion was not entirely unexpected. However, it was sudden enough to bring panic to the Near Eastern courts, which were frantically trying to find the adequate measures to defend themselves. On the invasion, we possess two types of documents. First, there are the inscriptions and reliefs left by Ramses III to celebrate his victory on the invaders in the eighth year of his reign (1190 BC). These sources provide some information on these invaders' composition and on the succession of events. Second, there are a group of letters from Ugarit, which attest the frantic preparations to resist the attack. On the one hand, Ramses III's inscriptions have been known for longer and are more explicit in their narration of the invasion and have therefore always been the main source for the historical reconstruction of this event. On the other hand, the letters from Ugarit provide a more realistic picture of the situation, untarnished by the celebratory aims of the Egyptian reliefs, which consequently appear less credible.

The letters from Ugarit inform us that the small groups of ships raiding the Syrian coast constituted the first symptom of the imminent invasion. Ugarit and Alashiya, both dependent on the Hittites and main providers of the empire's ships, exchanged information and gave each other advice. The appeals of the Hittite king to unite forces against the common enemy were welcomed by Ugarit, which sent ships and troops in aid of the great king. The Hittite intervention against the invaders took place in the westernmost Anatolian region, namely, the land of Lukka, clearly in order to protect the Hittite territories. However, this attempt did not succeed. This was either because the conflicts ended badly for the imperial army, or because the invaders managed to infiltrate or bypass the enemy lines. The invaders managed to spread in the Near East, overcoming the coastal regions of Cilicia, Cyprus, Ugarit and Amurru. The latter were all unable to face the enemies, due to their lack of warships and troops. The only option left was to hide inside the walled cities, in the hope that the invaders would march on. However, in the case of Ugarit and several other cities, the invaders managed to overcome these fortifications and destroy the cities.

The information from the Ugarit letters, written in a way 'the day before' the invasion, partly differ from the ones provided by Ramses III, which left his inscriptions after the invasion. According to the Egyptian king, a 'confederation' of Mediterranean peoples (Philistines, Zeker, Shekelesh, Danuna and Weshesh) had invaded and destroyed one after the other the states of the Hittite empire, from Hatti to

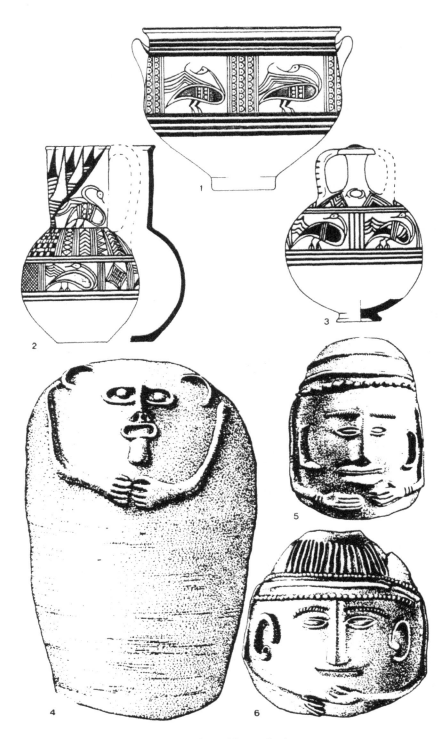

Figure 22.1   Philistine culture. 1–3: Pottery; 4–6: Anthropoid sarcophagi.

Qode (namely, Cilicia), Arzawa (south-western Anatolia), Alashiya (Cyprus), and Carchemish (namely, northern Syria). The invaders had stopped along the coast of Amurru and were threatening to invade Egypt. These individuals are carefully depicted on their ships or their ox-drawn carts carrying their belongings and their families. They are shown with their traditional headgear, which was plumed for the Philistines or horned for the Sherdana, and their typical weapons, such as long swords and small round shields. The reliefs therefore depict a large invasion led by both sea and land. Apparently, the Egyptians faced the enemies in a naval battle, preventing them from disembarking, and successfully defeated them (Figure 22.2).

However, several features of this Egyptian celebratory account are more traditional than accurate. Concepts such as 'coalition' and 'plot' are an integral part of the Egyptian narrative and the description of the battle as the key moment in the fight against the enemy is in this case entirely fictitious. This is also indicated by the lack of any specific location for this battle or a thorough description of the events. It is possible that Ramses III wanted to synthesise into a single and sensational event a series of far less heroic clashes (both on land and sea) between smaller groups of invaders and the Egyptian troops in Syria, the Levant and the Delta (Figure 22.3).

This picture would not be very different from what is attested in the letters from Ugarit, because the invasion must have lost a large part of its élan and resources once it reached the Levant and the Delta. Be that as it may, the invasion certainly took place and was relatively compact and sudden, enough to explain the panic of the letters from Ugarit and the sense of relief attested in Ramses III's celebratory inscriptions. However, the invasion was far more diversified than it was described by the Egyptian king in his attempt at emphasising his heroic and reassuring role as the only bulwark able to defeat the invaders.

The obvious opposition presented by Ramses III between the Hittite empire, which succumbed to the invasion, and the Egyptian empire, which successfully managed to defeat the invaders, is only partly true. Egypt itself remained unharmed, but all its Syro-Levantine territories were lost. The largest group of invaders, the Philistines, successfully settled in the Levant. Later on, we will see that the Philistines ruled

Figure 22.2 The naval battle between Ramses III and the Sea Peoples (relief from the temple of Medinet Habu).

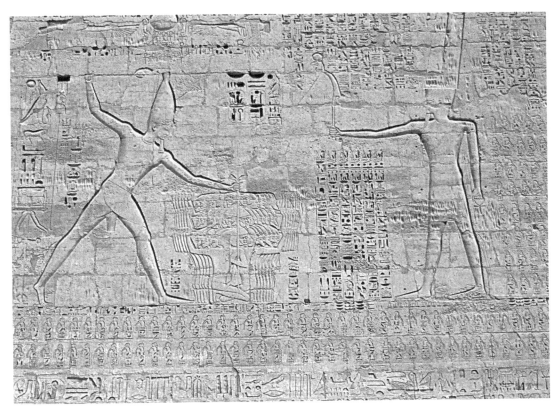

Figure 22.3 Relief of Ramses III in the temple of Medinet Habu (Thebes West): the victorious king smashing the enemies, in front of the god Amun.

from the five cities of Gaza, Ashdod, Ashkelon, Gath and Akkaron. These cities constitute the so-called Philistine Pentapolis. These key cities covered the Mediterranean coast from the Egyptian border to the area of Jerusalem. The Zeker settled further north, towards the Carmel. Alongside the textual evidence, we also possess some archaeological data concerning the destruction of coastal cities and the appearance of sub-Mycenaean pottery similar to Philistine pottery. Some areas experienced more violent destructions. Ugarit and Alalah, for instance, disappeared forever. Other areas, such as Cyprus, Cilicia and Amuq saw the settlement of groups of immigrants. Finally, areas such as the Lebanese coast from Byblos to the Carmel remained less affected by the invasion.

The number of invaders could not have been too large, especially of those who arrived by sea. Moreover, with time all the immigrants would become part of the local population, at least from an ethno-linguistic point of view. However, at this point in time, their military strength, social cohesion and their determination were enough to make them prevail over the fortified cities. These aspects placed them in a stronger position and even influenced the material culture of the invaded areas. In this context, Egypt's role seems ambiguous. The employment of Sea Peoples as mercenaries took place both before and after the invasion. It is possible that the Egyptian kings allowed the Philistines to settle in the Levant to substitute the Egyptian legions based there, thus granting them the management of those territories that Egypt was unable to keep on its own. However, the Philistines quickly turned the situation to their advantage.

Following the invaders' journey backwards, the cause of their irruption in the eastern Mediterranean should be searched in some development or gap in the Balkans, or even Europe in general. Their place of origin remains difficult to establish and is anyway outside the geographic scope of this book. The infiltration of Philistines and other groups as far as the Levant and the Delta was neither the only one, nor the most important one. In terms of migrations and ethnical changes, it has to be borne in mind that the fall of the Mycenaean world is closely linked to the arrival of new peoples in Greece. In fact, the 'Doric migration', with all the new information provided by modern historiography, certainly remains a very important event, parallel both in terms of time and features to the migrations taking place in the Near East.

In Anatolia, the proximity of the fall of the Hittite empire to the fall of Ugarit indicates that the two powers collapsed for the same reasons and in the same (or similar) way. The military events mentioned above, namely, the establishment of a military front in western Anatolia against the invaders, probably resulted in a defeat for Hatti. This defeat was enough to kick-start the disintegration of the empire as a whole. The Sea Peoples alone, however, are not enough to explain the fall of the empire and the destruction (or sudden abandonment) of Hattusa, the latter being the decisive moment of the decline from a strictly political point of view.

There are two possible scenarios able to explain this collapse. They both take into account the ethno-linguistic features of Anatolia in the following centuries, with Neo-Hittite centres located in the southeast and the Phrygians settled in the central plateau. The first scenario takes into account the fact that, alongside invaders from the Mediterranean, there were other groups, namely, the Phrygians. The latter, then, attacked the empire by land, infiltrating in Anatolia from Troas and spreading in the north and centre of the Anatolian Peninsula. In this scenario, the Phrygians would have been the ones who destroyed Hattusa, taking advantage of the military expedition keeping the Hittite army along the coast.

The second scenario takes into account the fact that the effort of the Hittite army against the invaders had removed those defences meant to protect Hattusa against its ancient enemy, the Kaska. The latter indeed dwelled extremely close to the capital. The Phrygians, then, would have settled in Anatolia, only at a later stage, taking advantage of the power vacuum caused by the invasion and the ever-increasing demographic problems of the area. Admittedly, the two scenarios are not very different. They constitute different assessments of the impact of internal factors, such as the demographic and production crisis, and the significant setback caused by the arrival of the Sea Peoples in the southern provinces of the empire. Be that as it may, the Phrygians would eventually be the ones to ultimately take advantage of the power vacuum created by the fall of Hatti. They would provide a more complex ethno-linguistic composition to Anatolia, with some elements of continuity as well as more recent innovations.

3 The collapse of the regional system

Up until the invasion, the regional system of the Late Bronze Age, with its two levels of kings (small and great kings) and its complex network of equal and unequal relations, had managed to survive well despite its difficulties and adaptations. However, the arrival of the Sea Peoples and other internal migratory movements led to the destruction of many palaces, the essential centres of this system. In many cases, these destructions were not followed by reconstructions, but created even more gaps in the territory. Consequently, the entire system of inter-regional relations collapsed without being reconstituted. It would take a long time for a different system to be implemented.

The simultaneous destruction of several palaces in the Near East marked the end of diplomatic relations, its correspondence and formal political relations. Therefore, it removed both the protagonists of these interactions (namely, the kings residing in these palaces) and their instruments (scribes, messengers and administrative centres). Tributary relations linking small kings to great kings ceased to exist, since they either collapsed or were anyway unable to provide or expect tributes. The commercial activities of the palaces also ceased to exist. These activities required the physical presence of a palace and its administration, responsible for the provision of grants, warranties, protection and presentations. The destruction of palaces, then, which had an impact on a system inextricably linked to the palaces, also meant the destruction of the political system of inter-regional relations.

Among the great kingdoms, the most significant collapse was the fall of the Hittite empire. The destruction of its capital (no matter who was responsible for it) was much more effective than the arrival of the Sea Peoples, who only devastated the southern Hittite territories on the Mediterranean coast. Following the collapse, the entire region was forced to return to far simpler forms of political organisation and relatively elementary administrative systems. This decline was also due to the momentary disappearance of writing.

It is, however, necessary to make a distinction between two different situations attested within Anatolia. In the southeast, in the territories dependent on Tarhuntassa and Carchemish, a certain continuity of the imperial legacy was maintained. The area from the Konya plain to the Euphrates also experienced a division of the land into local kingdoms, roughly mirroring the Hittite 'provinces' or vassal states. The rest of the peninsula was far more sparsely inhabited and more directly affected by the arrival of groups from the Balkans. It therefore began to develop political formations more influenced by ethnic factors. A visible effect of the collapse of the Hittite empire was the reversal to pre-urban settlements, both in terms of structure and organisation. Only later on, would new urban centres, belonging to the new type of cities characteristic of the Iron Age, begin to spread in Anatolia.

A similar picture could be reconstructed for the Aegean, which is relevant here only in comparison to the situation in the Near East. This area also experienced the fall of palaces and their administrative structure. This led to the temporary reversal to smaller settlements. The arrival of new groups from the north also led to the slow formation of political organisations based on new concepts. Cyprus itself, which in the Late Bronze Age had experienced political unity and a strong participation in the network of commercial and diplomatic relations of the time, was now broken down into small city-states. Moreover, the island experienced the arrival of new groups from the west and the first conflicts between different ethnic groups.

As far as Egypt was concerned, despite being internally unharmed by the invasion, it still had to give up its territories in the Near East and reduce its inter-regional relations. The Philistines established themselves in the Levant. The entire Syro-Levantine region experienced a period of political autonomy, without great kings requiring tributes and threatening the local population with their armies. Assyria survived unharmed on the other side of the Euphrates. However, it did not have the strength to take advantage of the power vacuum created by the invasion to fulfil the dream of reaching the Mediterranean. This distant ambition belonged to the Middle Assyrian kings of the thirteenth century BC, in a time when this dream was impossible to achieve. The problem was that even areas located more inland, which therefore were left unaffected by the invasion of the Sea Peoples, were affected by other phenomena. Before resuming their inter-regional contacts, they also experienced a critical adjustment period.

On a political level, the crisis of the twelfth century BC led to a marked bipartition of the Near East. East of the Euphrates, despite the constant raids of nomadic groups, the three regional powers of Assyria, Babylonia and Elam continued to rule. These three powers also maintained their tri-polar relations. The latter were characterised by an alternation of phases of peace with phases of war and equally interchanging alliances, such as the one of Babylonia and Elam against Assyria, or the one of Babylonia and Assyria against Elam. All these elements determined these powers' long-term stability. West of the Euphrates, the marked fragmentation, without hierarchies or agreements between states, replaced the old regional system with a new one. The latter was partly based on previous political divisions. In this regard, it may be worth remembering that in the Late Bronze Age the Syro-Levantine area was a region of small kings, while Anatolia had been ruled by local kinglets even at the time of the Hittite empire. However, this new system also acquired new connotations, due to the impact of new ethnical groups and tribes settling in the area.

4 Technological innovations and territorial interventions

The transition from the Bronze Age to the Iron Age was marked by some technological innovations. These innovations had strong implications on the territorial, socio-economic and political structure of the Near East. They were not brought from the outside or linked to the migratory waves from the Balkans, but internal innovations, whose earliest stages are attested in the Near East. The twelfth century BC breakdown gave leeway to the spread of innovations formerly hindered by the rigidity of the Late Bronze Age system. Therefore, the destruction of many urban centres, along with their palaces, workshops, scribal schools and commercial centres, brought the development of alternative cultural and operational elements to the ones affected by the crisis. As a result, Iron Age culture was less centred on the palace than Bronze Age culture. It was much more widespread both socially and geographically, and thus more accessible and less exclusive. Moreover, the different ways in which areas located east or west of the Euphrates were affected by the crisis and participated in the various technological innovations of the period led to the division of the Near East into a more conservative east and a more innovative west.

The main innovation traditionally associated with the transition from the Bronze to the Iron Age is the introduction of iron metallurgy. Some scholars still support the hypothesis of the spread of iron metallurgy from the west and the assumption that it was brought by the Sea Peoples. In this view, the latter would have succeeded over the powers of the Near East precisely because of their use of iron weapons against their enemies' bronze weaponry. However, the slow and progressive spread of iron objects seems to have moved from the Near East to Europe, thus in the opposite direction to the that of the Sea Peoples. The first experimentations in iron metallurgy took place in the Near East, mainly in Mitanni, Kizzuwatna and Syria. The metal used was not only meteoric iron, but also smelted iron. The former was pure, easy to work with, and used to produce small items of jewellery from much earlier periods. The latter was extracted from iron ores and thus required a technical knowledge of the processes and equipment needed. As long as the bronze workshops of the palaces and the inter-regional trade for copper and tin continued to exist, bronze metallurgy remained prominent, while iron weapons were rare luxury objects.

The crisis of trade and palace workshops allowed the spread of iron metallurgy. The latter was meant to compensate for the resulting gap in the production of metal objects. Iron was much more suitable to this new historical context for several reasons. With the exception of the Mesopotamian alluvial plain, iron ores were widespread in the Near East, though concentrated in smaller quantities. These natural resources could provide iron to many small production centres, while bronze metallurgy necessarily required an efficient commercial network able to link the few regions rich in copper and tin with the production centres. The transition from Bronze to Iron Age was therefore marked by a renewed interest in mineral prospecting, not only for iron, but also for copper and tin. Copper and tin began to be found in formerly neglected areas (such as the Sinai and Arabah), or in distant regions (such as the western Mediterranean, as we will see later on).

This intensification in mineral prospecting must have contributed to the discovery of iron ores, which were much more modest and widespread, but perfectly adequate to provide for the needs of the time. Once the processes for the refining, carburisation and quenching of iron had been discovered, the necessary equipment for the casting and manufacture of iron was far simpler and more accessible than the equipment required for bronze metallurgy. Consequently, iron could be worked in small village (or temporary) workshops, while bronze was exclusively worked in palace workshops. Overall, then, apart from providing far harder weapons than bronze, iron metallurgy became much more widespread and accessible. The regional monopolies linked to the efficient commercial networks of the palaces were therefore substituted by the diffusion of the extraction and manufacture of iron, a more 'autarchic' and readily accessible type of metallurgy.

A similar situation appeared in a completely different sector with the diffusion of the alphabet. Even in this case, both in its theoretical foundations and in its initial applications, the alphabet had already been in use in the Syro-Levantine area during the Late Bronze Age. However, the survival of scribal schools and palace administrations, closely linked to the transmission of syllabic cuneiform, had delayed the diffusion of the alphabet. In its simplicity, the alphabet had a far broader social appeal than the complex ideographic–syllabic system, whose study took many years and was very expensive. This difficulty in learning, linked to the limited access to this type of training, had made the scribal class a closed elite group, jealously guarding the privilege of writing as well as its economic and prestigious benefits. The diffusion of the alphabet, then, could only take place at a time when the collapse of palaces caused the destruction of their archives and libraries, the dispersion of the scribal elite, and the disappearance of the main commissioner of administrative texts, namely, the palace.

The diffusion of writing in the Late Bronze Age palaces was therefore contrasted by the sporadic attestations of written texts in the Early Iron Age. The few alphabetic texts do not belong to the realm of the administration. This aspect indicates a continuity in the marginal use of alphabetic writing, which was already attested prior to the crisis. Some of these written attestations record the ownership of arrowheads and spearheads, while others are just small graffiti on pottery. There were also funerary and votive inscriptions, which display no significant differences between royal inscriptions and the ones left by lower-ranking individuals. Only later on, the administrative use of alphabetic writing would begin to appear, with alphabetic inscriptions on *ostraka*.

Despite these difficulties, the most significant innovation brought about by alphabetic writing was its accessibility to non-professional scribes. In this regard, graffiti (either signatures or short inscriptions) are a typical expression of the accessibility of alphabetic writing. Graffiti were left by visitors in cultic places, on monuments, or elsewhere. This was an unthinkable practice in the cuneiform scribal realm of the Late Bronze Age. Also in the case of writing, then, the Near East appeared split into two groups. Mesopotamia and Egypt continued with their complex writing tradition, while alphabetic writing began to be used in Syria, the Levant, Anatolia and the Aegean, that is, the more innovative areas (Figures 22.4 and 22.5). The only exceptions were the inscriptions in Luwian hieroglyphs, a clear legacy from the past and an obvious attempt at reviving it.

Other technological innovations had a considerable impact on the distribution of settlements and the agro-pastoral activities of the region. Also in this case, these changes developed internally and over a long period of time, but were dramatically accelerated and re-evaluated after the crisis of the twelfth century BC. A wide range of technical interventions on the Near Eastern landscape suddenly became extremely important at the beginning of the Iron Age. First, there was the construction of terraces on hilly and mountainous lands. These terraces paved the way to the cultivation (mainly arboriculture, especially of olive-trees, in connection with the cultivation of cereals) of areas covered by forests or formerly used as summer pasturelands in the Late Bronze Age. The construction of terraces was closely linked to the intensification of deforestations, which created mountain clearings and transformed seasonal lands into permanent fields.

Equally important was the revival and improvement of irrigation techniques in dry lands (*wadis* in particular), with the construction of transversal dams and a system of canals to distribute water. This intervention was characteristic of the south-western 'border' zone (northern Arabia, the Transjordan plateau, Negev and Sinai) (Figure 22.6). In the north, especially between Iran and Armenia, a new method of irrigation began to be implemented, namely, the underground *qanat*. The latter brought water across long distances with less evaporation. These hydraulic techniques in semi-arid and mountainous areas followed the first hydraulic innovations developed several millennia earlier in the alluvial plains, bringing about a considerable increase in the number of fertile lands available.

Thanks to the appearance of iron tools, the excavation of deeper wells, possibly caused by short-term climatic difficulties, became less arduous, and led to the increased spread of pastures in semi-arid areas. Rather than the anonymous excavation of wells by tribes of shepherds, the epigraphic evidence clearly attests wells excavated by kings. It is highly significant that the transition between the Bronze and the

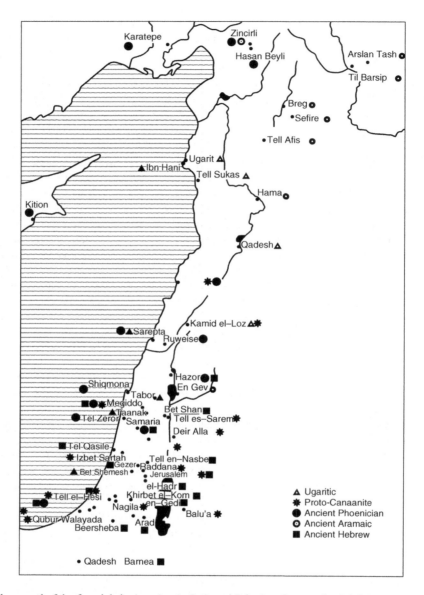

Figure 22.4 The spread of the first alphabetic scripts in Syria and Palestine, fourteenth–eighth century BC.

Iron Age saw a significant increase in the excavation of wells both in Egypt and Assyria. A problem linked to this development was the plastering of wells in order to make them waterproof, and thus more efficient than Bronze Age wells. This ensured that cities and fortresses had a reserve of winter rainwater that could last an entire year. Admittedly, the excavation of wells, the use of waterproof plasters, and the development of hydraulic systems for the provision of water to cities are all phenomena that still have to be better clarified through archaeological investigations. However, it can already be said that the end of the second millennium BC marked a pivotal moment in the development of these types of interventions in the land.

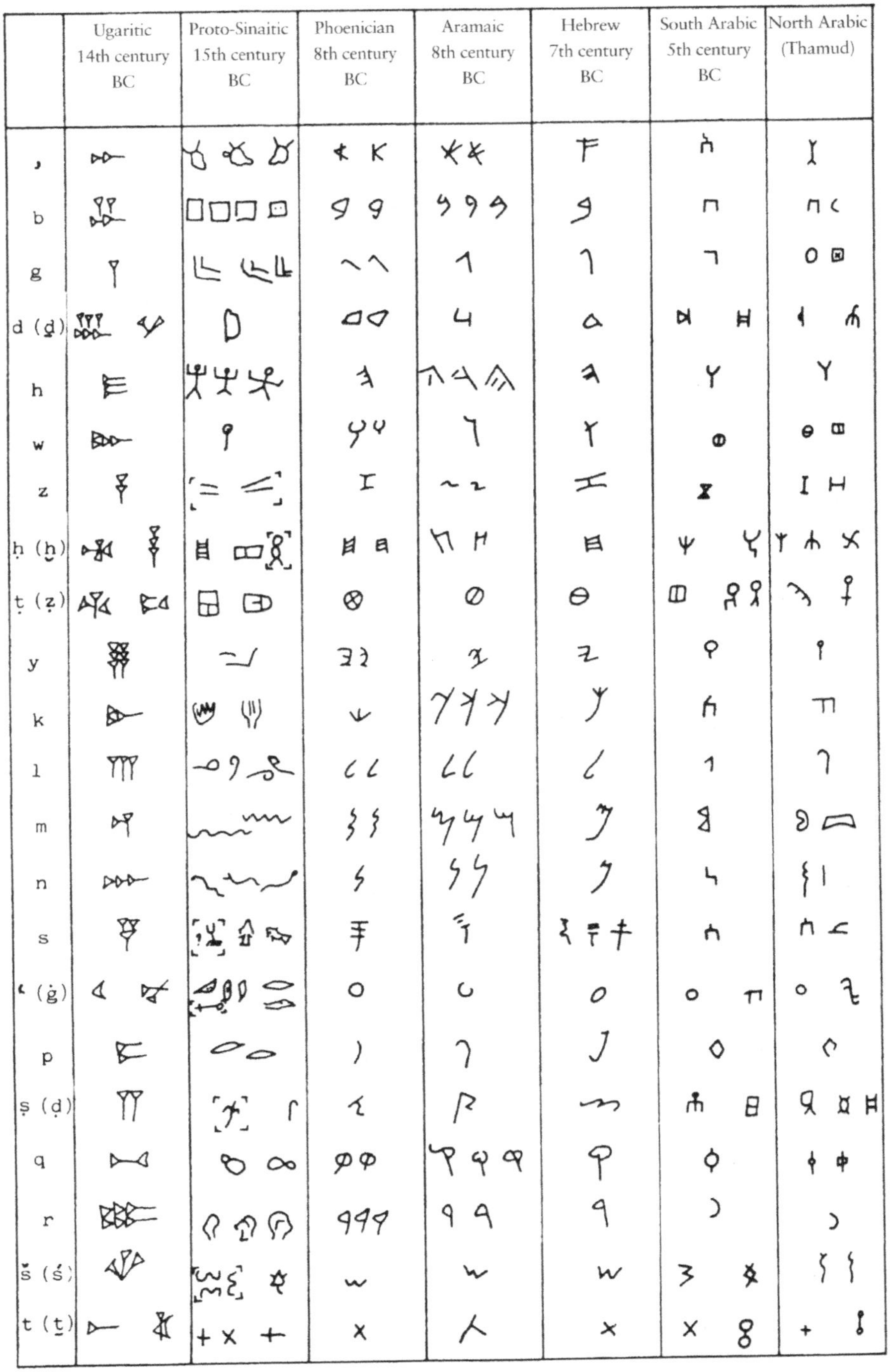

	Ugaritic 14th century BC	Proto-Sinaitic 15th century BC	Phoenician 8th century BC	Aramaic 8th century BC	Hebrew 7th century BC	South Arabic 5th century BC	North Arabic (Thamud)
ʾ							
b							
g							
d (ḏ)							
h							
w							
z							
ḥ (ḫ)							
ṭ (ẓ)							
y							
k							
l							
m							
n							
s							
ʿ (ġ)							
p							
ṣ (ḍ)							
q							
r							
š (ś)							
t (ṯ)							

Figure 22.5   Diffusion and evolution of the alphabet in the Semitic world.

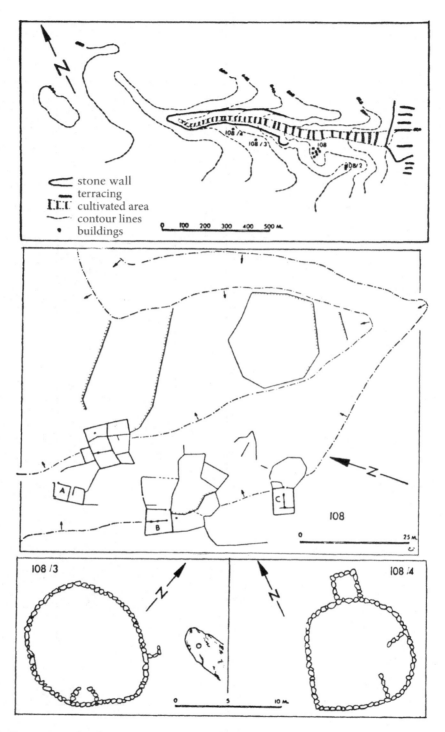

Legend within figure:

- ⊏⊐ stone wall
- —— terracing
- ⊏⊏⊏ cultivated area
- - - - contour lines
- • buildings

0 100 200 300 400 500 M.

108/4
108/3
108
108/2

A

B

C

108

0   25 M.

108/3

108/4

0   5   10 M.

Figure 22.6 Ramat Matred in the Negev: an Iron Age agricultural farm in an arid environment. *Above*: Plan; Centre: Plan of the settlement; *Below*: Sheepfolds.

Finally, the Iron Age saw the large-scale domestication of the camel and the dromedary. Both animals had been known for a long time and were occasionally used in the Bronze Age. The initial spread of the camel began in the highlands of Iran and Central Asia, while the dromedary spread from the Syro-Arabian desert. Both areas were directly linked to the Fertile Crescent, but located outside this urbanised region. The domestication of the camel and the dromedary opened up new modalities of transport for men and goods in the desert. It was well known that these animals could resist for several days without water, while donkeys, sheep and goats had to drink water at least every other day. In this way, it became possible to create a network of caravans reaching distant oases, previously cut off from commercial interactions because the caravans had to cross fertile areas.

These oases now became important stops for travellers, providing them with water. Oases also became important centres for the intensive cultivation of various plants, especially the date palm. Moreover, a camel was able to carry a far heavier load than a donkey (which had been the only means of transport in the Bronze Age). Apart from the Arabian caravans, which travelled along the main route linking Central Syria to the Hejaz and Yemen, there were the caravans crossing the Iranian desert, thus reviving commercial activities in the area. It has to be borne in mind that the end of the Bronze Age marked the introduction of riding horses (instead of draught horses), a significant innovation in the fast transport of messengers. This development became increasingly widespread in the Iron Age, generating a new specialty and military technique, and bringing to an end the use of war chariots. In addition to that, the camel also became an important animal for fighters, not to break down infantry enemy lines, but as an effective means for the fast incursions (and equally fast escapes) of raiders.

The effects of these innovations on the Near Eastern landscape were dramatic. On the one hand, hilly and mountainous areas that had previously been cut off from important historical events were now converted into stable settlements. On the other hand, those abandoned Early Bronze Age settlements in the internal plateaus were now reoccupied and hosted several stable agricultural centres. Finally, this enlarged territory and these new stable settlements developed alongside the rise of an important peripheral area crossed by caravans. Overall, the Late Bronze Age pattern of settlements, characterised by concentrated settlements surrounded by wide uninhabited spaces, was completely turned upside-down. Occupation became much more widespread across the entire region, though with varying degrees of intensity according to each individual case.

However, within this extensive occupation of the Near Eastern territory, settlements became smaller. At least in the western regions, where the new model rose to prominence, the large cities of ten thousands of inhabitants, which had been at the heart of the political systems of the Bronze Age, were not as popular anymore. The cities of the Early Iron Age were rather well fortified citadels, with fewer inhabitants and small public buildings. The percentage of the 'urban' population dramatically dropped, while villages acquired a new role, strengthening their defences and structures. Therefore, the marked difference between cities and villages characterising the Bronze Age was now visibly reduced.

As far as the exploitation of the land is concerned, the main innovation of the time was the appearance of the 'fully' nomadic lifestyle of camel farmers. The latter developed alongside the 'closed' nomadic lifestyle (semi-nomadic) of the transhumant farmers of sheep and goats. The two lifestyles were drastically different in terms of economy, geography and their relations with cities. We are already familiar with the economic structure of semi-nomadic groups: transhumant farming of sheep and goats was alternated in time and space with agriculture, originating that 'double morphology' characteristic of these social groups. Semi-nomadic groups, however, were not major players in commercial activities, which they rather hindered through raids. They were more involved in military expeditions, for which they were recruited by city-states as auxiliaries. As a result they continued to have a largely conflictual relation with the cities, while at the same time depending on them.

'Fully' nomadic groups were mainly specialised in the farming of camels and dromedaries, the intensive agriculture of oases, and independent commercial and military activities. The use of camels and the control of caravans allowed these nomadic tribes to become the preferred mediators for inter-regional trade, which they facilitated rather than opposed. The availability of fast animals with long autonomy also facilitated the pursuit of successful military expeditions and of fast raids of sedentary settlements which thus provided a more balanced opposition to powerful city-states. These two types of nomadic lifestyle developed in different areas. Transhumant groups lived in close contact with agricultural settlements, developing strong linguistic, ethnic and political similarities between shepherds and farmers. On the contrary, the 'fully' nomadic lifestyle developed outside the Near East, in areas that constituted an Iron Age addition to the areas interacting with the Near East. Moreover, these nomadic groups constituted the agents linking areas that had been previously cut off from the Near East.

In this regard, Yemen is a case in point. Its climate significantly facilitated its agricultural and urban development, but its location had initially left it outside the great network of contacts of the Near East. These interactions were only possible through complex and secondary sets of interactions. Yemen's products, such as gold, incense and myrrh, could only reach the Near East through Egypt, and it was only in the Iron Age, that Yemen managed to actively participate in the great commercial networks and political relations of the time. The same can be said of the intermediary area of the Hejaz. Similarly, the lands located on the other side of the Iranian deserts, either in the north (Turkmenistan) or the east (Indus Valley), had experienced a long period of isolation after the interruption of their commercial relations in the third millennium BC. This was due to the movement of entire populations and the decline of their powerful local cities. The Iron Age therefore revived this situation allowing a better commercial, and then political, integration of the various cultures and centres of south-western Asia.

A similar situation should be envisioned in terms of maritime relations, although the specific documentation on this aspect remains inadequate. It seems that in the Mediterranean the introduction of more advanced navigation techniques (namely, the connection between sail, keel and rudder) had opened up new sailing opportunities. These were far more audacious than the Bronze Age type of navigation along the coasts. The end of regional interferences and the search for metals contributed to the rise of Greek and Phoenician navigation in the western Mediterranean from as early as the first millennium BC. Something similar must have taken place in the Indian Ocean, although with completely different winds (monsoons). Even in this case, it may be worth wondering whether the coastal navigation that had kept Dilmun, Magan and Meluhha in contact with the land of Sumer was not substituted in the Early Iron Age by a more complex and wider system. The latter could have linked the Persian Gulf and the Iranian and Indian coasts with Yemen and eastern Africa, thus closing that circle of commercial activities moving around the Arabian Peninsula. In turn, the latter could be linked to the networks of land routes connecting Egypt, the Transjordan plateau and Yemen. Therefore, it seems that the beginning of the Iron Age brought about the unprecedented expansion of commercial activities in virtually every direction.

5 Kinship and 'nation' states

The crisis of cities and palaces, and the availability of innovative technologies in semi-arid regions significantly increased the political influence of nomadic groups. This was the case both for the 'new' nomads (camel farmers) and for the old transhumant groups: the former settled in previously uninhabited areas and were thus an entirely new entity; the latter managed to gain a more central role compared to their marginal role in the Late Bronze Age. Pastoral groups had now become an attractive alternative political organisation compared to the palaces, which had become too demanding and in many cases disappeared.

The movement of villages towards pastoral groups instead of the cities was a process whose effects are almost invisible in terms of settlements. Pastoral groups had always settled in fertile fields on a seasonal basis, thus developing a strong interaction with the local farming communities. However, once the villages' subordination to the palaces, which had been purely tributary, had fallen apart, pastoral groups suddenly became a desirable alternative for villages. Therefore, the villages, which had initially experienced a phase of relative autonomy, then of subordination to the palaces and of administrative unity, were now transformed into clans or sub-groups of these pastoral tribes. They therefore entered the tribal system as a kin-based unit.

This process did not lead to a 'sedentarisation' of nomadic groups or a 'rise to power' of these tribes, but rather to a re-elaboration of socio-political relations according to new parameters. The Early Iron Age therefore saw a shift from the administrative system, at the heart of the Bronze Age palace states, to the kinship system. The latter was at the heart of a new type of state formation developing in this period, eventually leading to the birth of the 'nation' state. Admittedly, this reconstruction is largely based on Biblical evidence, which was compiled much later. However, the little evidence there is from this period seems to broadly confirm these developments. Members of a state identified themselves as such because they believed that they descended from one eponymous ancestor. Therefore, the 'charter' of this kinship state was genealogy. The latter was able to link the mythical patriarch to the current members of the tribe, following kinship and marital ties that had a precise meaning in this genealogical code. Primogeniture, adoptions, marriages and every other form of kinship then indicated various types and degrees of socio-political integration.

Consequently, in order to integrate individual villages as clans of a tribe, the villages' names were linked to an intermediate eponym (often the son of the tribal eponym, or a descendant of the confederal eponym, or an ancestor of the family eponyms). This process led to the establishment of a network of descendancy and brotherhood with other groups. However, the remaining cities were normally too large and important to be integrated in this way. Their position was therefore established through stories that made the tribal eponyms and these cities come to an agreement or to conflictual relations, thus explaining the current situation. Overall, this phase saw the increased implementation of aetiologies. These were used as charters of all those elements constituting this type of political formation: from borders between neighbouring communities to alliances, rivalries, the privileged status of certain groups or places, the acknowledgement of the communal nature of certain cults, prohibitions, norms and the importance of some specific localities. All these aspects were rooted in stories explaining the origins of these practices and the topographic features of the places representing, or simply using, these practices.

This kin-based reorganisation of the political system ruling in sedentary settlements developed alongside the occupation (or re-occupation) of new territories, where these new political structures were founded *ex novo*. This process had already begun in the thirteenth century BC and was further developed in the following centuries. In Palestine, the main protagonists of this expansion and territorial re-organisation were a series of populations linguistically related and linked to the previous groups living in the area in the Late Bronze Age (the 'Canaanites'). Each one of these populations now began to develop an individual 'nationality' of their own. Further north, similar processes led to the formation of Aramean states. The latter expanded to the east and revived the old agricultural landscape, significantly improved by the construction of terraces.

The new 'nation' states of the Canaanites (to the south) and Arameans (to the north) already expressed their kin-based structure in their names, which were usually 'House of' followed by the name of the eponymous ancestor. Similarly, the names of these states' members were the 'sons of' the same eponymous ancestor. Otherwise, the state formation was named after the name of a mountain or a region. Be that as it may, these names were completely different from the ones of Late Bronze Age states. The latter were usually taken from the names of their capitals, a practice that now became secondary, since the seat of power was not located in a specific palace, but was held by a specific group or lineage.

This transition from city-state to kin-based state was characteristic of the Syro-Levantine area (Figure 22.7). Elsewhere, the two processes existed alongside each other, and were different in their origins and nature. This aspect requires a closer examination. A first difference concerns the area east of the Euphrates, home of the great regional states of Assyria and Babylonia. In this area, tribal groups of Aramean origins began to infiltrate. These groups had to a certain extent been in these areas before (especially in the Middle

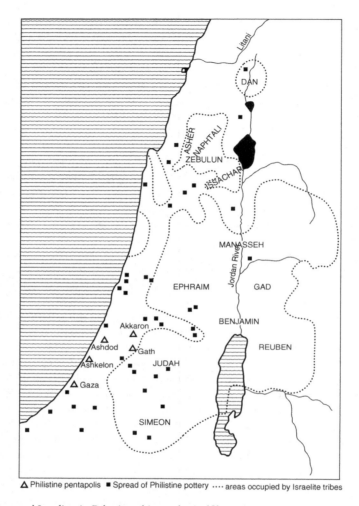

Figure 22.7   Philistines and Israelites in Palestine, thirteenth–twelfth century BC.

Euphrates and the Khabur Valley) as the Sutians and Ahlamu. However, now they moved further south, occupying vast territories in Lower Mesopotamia.

The relationship between these emerging tribal groups and the powerful states of Assyria and Babylonia could not have followed the same practices developed in the west by the small Syro-Levantine states. In the east, the tribes remained relatively extraneous to the great state formations of the area. The sedentary states, unable to assimilate them within their own administrative structure, tried to push them outside their borders and continued to consider them a hostile and foreign presence. The 'sedentarisation' of the eastern Arameans was therefore a much more arduous and partial process compared to its western counterpart, preventing their transition from tribe to state.

A second difference concerns the area outside the Fertile Crescent, alongside the Zagros and the Armenian plateau. At the end of the second millennium BC, this area was not yet densely populated. However, its people began to organise themselves into more stable state formations. This development was in part a reaction to the imperial attacks of the Assyrians, Elamites and Babylonians. It was mainly a response to the overall tendencies of the time, with the development of 'national' entities centred on kinship, and named after a population or a region. These entities were able to establish internal cohesion through a combination of kinship, linguistic and religious ties. Despite the fact that the evidence for these mountainous regions is far less than that for the semi-arid plateaus, it appears that the two processes developed at the same time. In both cases, they resulted in the formation of tribal states, finally getting rid of the marginal role they had in the Bronze Age.

A third difference concerns the political organisation of populations who recently established themselves in the Near East. Their foreign nature compared to the local population made 'national' features, such as language, religion and common origin, determining factors in the establishment of their socio-political identity. A case in point is that of the Philistines. Despite having followed a Canaanite model settling into a network of city-states, they continued to be seen as a population that had recently settled in the area and spoke a foreign language. Something similar could have taken place in Anatolia with the arrival of the Phrygians. However, two points have to be borne in mind: the first one, is that the evidence on the political structure of the Phrygians does not immediately appear in the twelfth century BC, but emerged only later on; the second one, is that the area occupied by the Phrygians was vast (roughly central and north-western Anatolia), so that their relations with the surviving local population could not have been easy, thus developing varying degrees of assimilation.

Be that as it may, after the Bronze Age crisis, also in Anatolia we do not encounter city-states anymore, but 'national' political entities, defined by the names of their populations: Phrygians, Lydians, Carians, Lycians and many more. When attempting to distinguish old features from new ones, at least from an ethno-linguistic point of view, one normally resorts to an analysis of the linguistic evidence of the first millennium BC. The Phrygians, then, constituted a new linguistic stratum, while the Lydians, Lycians and Carians were more or less linked to the Luwian populations of the second millennium BC. However, old communities and new groups experienced a complex series of contacts and assimilations, now impossible to reconstruct for each case.

This tribal kind of kinship therefore changed the nature of states in the Early Iron Age compared to the ones attested in the Bronze Age. The latter had been territorial states in which every individual who lived within a specific territory controlled by a certain palace was automatically its subject. Within the territorial state, there were two main criteria for differentiation. First, there was a division between cities and the surrounding farming villages, and possibly some marginal pastoral groups. Second, there was the division between members of the palace and 'free' individuals. An individual therefore belonged to a state regardless of the language he spoke, the religion he believed in or his origins. Moreover, the border between two states was defined through military interventions and tributes, and not through the identity of the communities living on either side of it. A sense of 'national' identity was only attested in case of major state formations (such as 'the Egyptians' and 'the Assyrians'), but this self-identification was not placed in opposition to other populations, considered to be equal. This identification was rather placed in opposition to the world outside of this system, creating a contraposition between a central population of 'humans' and a periphery of sub-humans.

On the contrary, the 'nation' State of the Iron Age adopted the descendancy from a common ancestor, namely, the kinship ties existing between its current members, as a parameter of appurtenance. It is obvious that descendancy and kinship could be artificially established. However, this aspect further supported the idea that kinship expressed political relations. This national identity therefore led to an emphasis not on the control of a certain territory (the population could have migrated), but on the shared language, religious beliefs (a tribal god who would become a national god), customs, dress codes, taboos and so on. Within the 'nation' state, distinctions in terms of settlements and lifestyle among citizens, farmers, shepherds, or between palace functionaries and free citizens, ceased to be important. This was also because administrative and tributary dependencies were temporarily reduced. The state centred on the palace and its tributary and administrative system, typical of the first and second urbanisation, was therefore substituted by a kin-based state. The latter clearly revived pre-urban (or, better, 'peri-urban') values. A typical example of this can be found in the army. The Bronze Age army was an army of specialists and *corvée* soldiers. The army of the Early Iron Age was a 'military population' charged with enthusiasm, guided by the decisions of kin-based groups united in council and not by impositions from the state administration. Moreover, this army chose its charismatic leaders, who would return to their previous occupation once the danger was overcome.

23

ISRAEL

1 The problem of the origins of Israel

Among the populations of the Ancient Near East, the case of Israel is peculiar. Its historiographical evidence has been preserved in both the Christian and Jewish traditions. Therefore, archaeological and epigraphic discoveries pertaining to Israel have not uncovered some forgotten historical data *ex novo*. They have only provided further clarifications to be individually compared with the attestations found in the Old Testament. Moreover, archaeological and epigraphic contributions to the reconstruction of the history of Israel have been relatively modest so far. This is especially the case when compared to the history of the Assyrians, the Hittites, the Egyptians or the Sumerians. Without the Old Testament, then, it would be incredibly difficult to provide a historical reconstruction of ancient Palestine, whose history would otherwise be rather vague and uncertain for us.

The fortunate survival through time of a certain historical memory of Israel is clearly due to its importance in a book that is holy for both Judaism and Christianity. However, this aspect has caused several problems in the critical use of this crucial source. These problems have constantly affected the reconstruction of the history of Israel and continue to prevent the use of an unbiased and critical approach today. The main problem is the fact that, for the believers of these religions, this corpus of sources records a 'truth', revealed by God through a number of human agents. This view makes it impossible for these believers to question the historical value of holy books such as the Old Testament. For centuries, historiography could not overcome the nature of 'revealed truth' attributed to the historical memories of Israel. This interpretation continues to exist in more traditional Judaic circles, or among Catholic and Protestant fundamentalists, thus indirectly affecting even the most secular of scholars.

In particular, the analysis of the archaeological and non-biblical evidence in conjunction with the accounts attested in the Bible has frequently been pursued as a search for rather arbitrary 'confirmations' or, vice versa, 'contradictions'. The contradiction between a 'true' account and 'real' archaeological evidence can often lead to a historical deadlock. In reality, biblical accounts are later (often considerably later) historical elaborations of the events described. Moreover, they are not only based on indirect and uncertain evidence, but also motivated by a specific purpose, which was often an expression of its own time.

Therefore, it is necessary to contextualise biblical sources in their period of composition, uncovering their political and cultural setting, as well as the problems, that led to their creation. It is indeed possible that these later historiographical reconstructions preserve some traces of documentary evidence or reliable memories. However, this is difficult to ascertain even after removing all the later political and religious

401

interpretations from the original facts. On the contrary, non-biblical material is far more immediate in its use, since it was contemporary to its events and was normally guided by simpler and more obvious motives.

These difficulties become even more problematic when addressing the issue of the origins of Israel. On the one hand, biblical accounts on this issue were written much later than the period which they were trying to reconstruct. On the other hand, non-biblical sources are not very informative and quite rare. Moreover, as far as biblical accounts are concerned, the issue of the origins of Israel is a topic that has attracted the greatest number of biased interests (from national identity to political propaganda and religious explanations), thus further concealing those few traces of historical evidence.

Broadly speaking, the historical and archaeological context of Palestine at the beginning of the history of Israel can be summarised in the following way. The Egyptian empire had ruled over the Levant from the mid-sixteenth century to the beginning of the twelfth century BC. After the empire's collapse, the local populations experienced a phase free of foreign rule and the intense exportation of resources. The Philistines settled in one portion of the territory left by the Egyptians, and tried to establish their supremacy over the remaining Canaanite cities, succeeding along the coast and in the valleys (Jezreel and the Middle Jordan). However, the hills remained outside their control. In the hilly and mountainous areas of the West Bank and the semi-arid Transjordan plateau, a typical Iron Age process began to be implemented. The latter involved considerable deforestations, the construction of terraces, canals in the *wadis*, wells and cisterns, and the spread of fortified cities and villages. This 'new' human element appearing in the Levant has been defined as the 'Proto-Israelites'. These were tribal and pastoral groups who were not yet defined as Israelites. As mentioned above, the crisis of royal palaces led to a mass movement towards tribal groups of refugees. In this regard, it is possible to deduce an etymological connection between the name given to these refugees (ḫabiru, or 'br/ 'pr) and the name for the Hebrews ('br). The latter were probably seen by the Canaanite citizens as refugees without any specific geo-political position.

On a regional scale, it is difficult to match the micro-systems of settlements, which are archaeologically attested, with the tribal and political entities attested in the Bible. As a legacy of the Late Bronze Age, we have the surviving 'Canaanite' cities. At the end of the Late Bronze Age, not all palaces were destroyed, or, at least, not all at the same time. Nonetheless, the progressive impoverishment of these administrative structures is evident. As a new element, we have newly colonised areas, new villages and mountain citadels. These were all the result of the sedentarisation of pastoral groups. With the marked exception of the Philistine Pentapolis, the system was based on a composite balance, without a single seat of hegemonic power. If one accepts later biblical attestations, it is possible that there were several associations between tribes in the same fashion as the ones attested in the Middle Bronze Age. Moreover, it is equally probable that several tribes and cities signed some agreements to establish terms for farming, marriage and trade. Finally, it is possible that the tribes living in the central highlands developed a precocious sense of national identity to oppose other powers, particularly to the west (Philistines) and east (Ammonites).

This formative (pre-monarchic) phase of the ethno-political entity constituting 'Israel' became in its own historical tradition the phase in which all the foundation stories justifying later events and problems took place. With time, then, a genealogical structure was developed to act as a 'charter' of inter-tribal relations. In its final formulation, a single genealogical tree united the eponymous patriarchs of Israelite national identity (Abraham, Isaac and Jacob) with the eponyms of each individual tribe (a dozen of sons of Jacob), all the eponyms of clans and villages, and the ones of individual heads of households. At this point, each individual family tree would take over. These genealogies were embedded in aetiological stories, meant to explain the reasons for the existence of certain rituals, borders and institutions. These stories, however, need to be repositioned in the period in which they were formulated (which varies for each individual case), rather than the period to which they refer.

Regarding the period of composition of these texts, some specific events further contributed to the deformation of the actual origins of Israel. First, there was the later Babylonian exile and return to Israel.

In order to justify their return to their homeland, and to support territorial claims over groups who stayed in the Levant, the foundational story of the initial immigration of Israelite groups from the outside became far more accredited. In this story, the ancient patriarchs, who were wandering in lands that did not belong to them, received the divine promise of becoming an immense population settling throughout the land. Then, there was the first exile in Egypt, and the exodus (or return) to the Levant (ca. thirteenth century BC), which mirrored the historical exile and return of the seventh century BC.

Joshua's conquest, supported by aetiological stories such as the conquest of Jericho (which at that time had already been abandoned for centuries), was therefore used to justify the actions of the survivors of the Babylonian exile. The latter took possession of the land upon their return. By then, the Canaanites had long settled in this land, but were considered unrightful dwellers, since the divine promise condemned them to be exterminated. They were therefore considered to be the precursors of the 'Samaritans' and other groups. The survivors of the Babylonian exile saw both groups as foreigners who unrightfully settled in the land. The story of the exodus and the conquest of Israel, including the issue of the foreign origins of the people of Israel and their relations with the local populations, is therefore a composition created in response to the problems of the seventh century BC. Consequently, it has nothing to do with the issues surrounding the events of the twelfth century BC.

Another clearly datable element, thanks to the pro- and anti-monarchic controversies surrounding it, is the creation of a time of the Judges. This was a time when 'there was no king in Israel, and everyone did what he saw fit.' The Judges were non-hereditary tribal leaders. Their rule should have taken place between the time of the Canaanite monarchies, destroyed by Joshua, and the formation of the Israelite monarchy of Saul and David. The time of the Judges became the object of several debates between those who considered the lack of a king as a period of weakness and political chaos, and those who saw this period as the epitome of the ideals of freedom, equality and lower fiscal and administrative pressures.

This group of biblical sources also suffered from the problems of the post-exilic phase. At that time, there were no monarchies, and it was only possible to either hope for their return to re-establish the nation, or to hope for the consolidation of new types of government. In the twelfth and the eleventh centuries BC, however, a real 'time of the Judges', as described in the homonymous book, did not exist. In the Levant, kings continued to rule in the surviving ancient Canaanite city-states. These cities were seen as enemies by the tribal groups. However, the latter were not able to replace them. Certain accounts of the Book of Judges are purely mythical, and are meant to transmit ethical and religious values, rather than historical facts. Naturally, some authentic memories of that time, and even some lines from ancient poems, could have survived in these sources.

A third group of anachronisms concerns the projection back to the origins of Israel of the religion characteristic of later phases, first of the pre-exilic and then the post-exilic phase. Moses was seen as the founder of Yahwism as a revealed religion, thus already perfect in its final form, well before the return of the Israelites in the Levant. Not only would the people of Israel have entered the Promised Land already perfectly structured into a socio-political association of tribes ruled by common leaders. They would have done so perfectly formed into a monotheistic religious community of devotees of Yahweh, the national and exclusive deity of the Israelites. In reality, it had been a gradual process, which experienced fundamental developments in the religious reforms of Hezekiah and Josiah (seventh century BC), and especially within the exilic and post-exilic community. For the latter, religious faith constituted the main element of national cohesion after the disappearance of a solid political organisation.

Regarding the 'pact' (*běrīt*) agreed between Yahweh and his people and the foundation of a nationalistic religious community, its placement at the time of Moses and Joshua is completely artificial and anachronistic. Later legal texts could have preserved some ancient traditions, such as the reference to the social debate surrounding debt slavery. However, the 'pact' between Yahweh and his people resembles more the 'pacts' sealed between the Assyrian king and his subjects, rather than the Late Bronze Age agreements between great and small kings. Be that as it may, the identification of those elements that can be securely attributed to the twelfth century BC continues to be arduous. This is due to the nature of our main source, which experienced a long history of modifications and adaptations, mostly datable from the seventh century BC onwards.

2 A unitary state

Israelite historiography saw the time of the Judges as the initial phase of the consolidation of a new ethnical and political entity (the tribal league). The latter developed in the highlands of the West Bank and partly in the Transjordan plateau. The conflicts of this new entity with the surviving Canaanite and other emerging city-states were re-interpreted as phases of 'oppression', meant to punish the sins of its people, or phases of 'liberation', which were the result of divine forgiveness. Similarly, this consolidation process saw the rise of temporary individual or group governments, the experimentation of non-bureaucratic decisional procedures (oracles and selections by lot), and finally the progressive formation of a new type of monarchic state. The latter was characterised by the earliest attempts (by Jephthah, Gideon and Abimelech) to adapt the tribal element of this new entity into a centralised type of government. Meanwhile, as a result of similar processes, the Transjordan plateau saw the rise of other 'national' entities: the Ammonites to the east of the Middle Jordan; the Moabites to the east of the Dead Sea; and the Edomites further south. Apart from these groups, there were the tribes dealing with camels (Midianites, Amalekites), which practised the new type of 'full' nomadism typical of the Iron Age, and were able to move deep into the West Bank through ruthless incursions.

The transition from the relatively flexible time of the Judges, characterised by its strong tribal legacy, to a unitary monarchy, in which some aspects of the previous palace systems reappeared, was embodied by the figures of Samuel and Saul (ca. 1000 BC). The coronation of Saul mirrors in its timing (i.e. war) and its forms (i.e. divine appointment by a 'prophet' and the subsequent acclamation of his people) the appointment of the Judges. However, his authority was far more influential and led to very different implications. The tribal league was held together by kinship and religious ties as well as its enmity for the surviving city-states. When it began to merge the institutions of the tribe with those of the city, it essentially lost its *raison d'être* as an opponent of a sedentary type of order and became a representative of this same order. Consequently, authority had to become more consistent and complex. Post-exilic historiography would idealise this problem in the dialogue between the prophet/judge Samuel and the people on the advantages and disadvantages of the establishment of kingship. Samuel recalls the oppression and abuses of the Canaanite kings against whom the league rose. However, the people suggest a new type of kingship, which envisions the king as a judge of his people, leader in his people's wars, and an expression of their political independence.

According to the Bible, Saul ruled over the small court of Gibeah (a mountain city). He was supported by a circle of military leaders (his son Jonathan, his cousin Abner and David, his armour-bearer). Saul managed to succeed against the Amalekites and Ammonites to the east and the Philistines to the west, and integrated the tribes into a unitary system. The Philistines, more worried by this unification than Saul's military successes, organised a counter-attack that peaked with the battle of Gilboa. The defeated Saul killed himself, and the Philistines established their authority in his kingdom.

However, this conquest did not cause a reversal to the previous political organisation of the area. The northern tribes (Israel) recognised Saul's son, Ish-Baal, as king, while the south (Judah) became the centre of David's kingdom under concession of the Philistines, who found the division advantageous. However, when Ish-Baal died, the tribes' elders encouraged David to become king over the whole of Israel and crowned him at Hebron. The response of the Philistines, however, arrived too late and was ineffective. David managed to relegate the Philistines to the coast, establishing his control over the mountains, where the majority of Israelites lived. This is the Biblical version of the facts. In reality, the kingdom of Saul, even if it actually existed, was limited to the small territories of the tribes of Ephraim and Benjamin.

The Bible also attests that, on an institutional level, Israel began its first definitive steps during the reign of David (1000–960 BC). The heart of the kingdom was not the tribal league alone anymore, and other elements became part of a system held together by proximity and obedience to a single ruler. Overall, this move indicates a return to a more territorial type of state, but with two main differences. First, in terms of dimension, the Davidic state included that part of Palestine previously broken down into city-states. Second, the survival of the tribes' national identity allowed the prevailing element (Israel) to gather within its tribal structure other formerly extraneous elements, such as cities and minor tribal groups.

This overcoming of the tribal state could only have taken place through a thorough process of consolidation and military expansion. Apart from Judah and Israel, then, David conquered the city-state of Jerusalem. The latter became his capital, since it was a city extraneous to the tribal system and thus 'neutral'. David conquered even more territories, which were all tied in some way to the king: Edom was annexed, Ammon was subdued, and Moab became a vassal state. The Arameans in the north-east and the Philistines in the south-west were kept under control. The Biblical tradition, overestimating the size of the Davidic kingdom in order to make it the ultimate example of national pride, recounts a garrison in Damascus and a tribute sent by the king of Hama.

The military and political successes of David led to an idealisation of Israel as a land extending from the Egyptian border to the Euphrates, well beyond the border of the Promised Land and the actual location of the Israelite tribes. Internally, the kingdom would have experienced the establishment of a group of mercenaries independent from the tribes' army, as well as of a class of administrators. Similarly, the palace and its functionaries would have regained their role at the heart of the state, leaving the rest of the population outside the political milieu and merely acting as a resource for taxation and labour. However, this scenario continues to remain utopic. The local archaeological data and the evidence from outside the Levant show that it is impossible that such a large kingdom with such a structure existed between the eleventh and tenth centuries BC. The only supporting evidence for this phase comes from a later Aramaic inscription found at Tel Dan. This inscription mentions a 'House of David' only to indicate the kingdom of Judah alone.

The Bible provides an even more utopic and anachronistic portrayal of the reign of Solomon (ca. 960–920 BC), David's son and successor. Once the war ended, political relations became more diplomatic. In this regard, the marriage of Solomon with the daughter of the king of Egypt was a particular mark of prestige. Thanks to the commercial ties with the Phoenicians of Tyre, trade was thriving and displayed a particular interest in southern Arabia, chief provider of gold and incense. Initially, merchants followed the old sea routes under Egyptian control. Expeditions departed from the seaport of Ezion-geber and descended the Red Sea to Ophir. From there, the expeditions would continue via land along routes linking Yemen to the Transjordan plateau, which had now become viable thanks to the domestication of the camel. Consequently, the biblical account of the visit of the queen of Sheba to Jerusalem, despite its fairy-tale connotations, has a plausible commercial background.

The public buildings begun by David were greatly improved by Solomon. This is one of the aspects in which the archaeological evidence could confirm the Bible's account, but fails to do so. The description of 'Solomon's temple' appears to have been, in actual fact, a plan for the construction of a 'second' temple in the Achaemenid period. This temple followed the model of the great Babylonian temple complexes with storehouses and workshops. Even the plan of the palace imitates a Persian *apadana* (a large hypostyle hall). Moreover, the dimensions of these complexes as a whole were out of proportion for Palestine in the tenth century BC. Actually, they would have taken up the entire area occupied by the city of Jerusalem at the time. It has to be borne in mind that the Levantine temple was relatively modest in size and linked to the royal palace. Therefore, it is clear that the idea of the absolute centrality of Solomon's temple and its independence from the palace were inspired by later events, making this view largely anachronistic for this phase.

In order to face the new financial situation of the palace and the state, the entire kingdom was allegedly divided into twelve districts, which united cities and tribes, namely, Canaanites and Israelites. Both were equally obliged to contribute through payments and labour, practices already common for the farming and urban communities of the area, but difficult to accept for the tribal groups. The situation led to an overall dissatisfaction with the 'House of David', which was accused of having abandoned the ancestral traditions not only for economic purposes, but also in terms of religion, worshipping foreign deities alongside Yahweh. After the death of Solomon, then, this sense of unrest led to the breakdown of the kingdom. This fall is, however, simply a fictional construction meant to explain the end of a unitary state that had never existed, and the subsequent division between a kingdom in the north (Israel) and in the south (Judah). This political division is the only fact attested in the Bible that is confirmed by the evidence.

3 The political context

The existence of a kingdom that united Palestine as a whole (or even the entire Levant) is anachronistic and justified by post-exilic nationalistic interests (as well as other interests linked to them). On the contrary, the presence of two kingdoms, Judah in the south with its capital, Jerusalem, and Israel in the north with its capital, Samaria, is confirmed by other contemporary sources. Moreover, it follows the overall development of the Levant in the Iron Age until the Assyrian conquest (that is, from the tenth to the mid-eighth centuries BC) (Table 23.1). The complex network of powers in Palestine, then, found consolidation through six important elements: the Philistine Pentapolis, the kingdom of Judah, the kingdom of Israel, Ammon, Moab and Edom (Figure 23.1).

Despite the failure of its hegemonic ambitions in Palestine, the Philistine Pentapolis was strong enough to remain independent from the larger kingdom of Israel and the neighbouring one of Judah. The former differences between the Philistines and the prevailing local Semitic population had gradually diminished through a process of linguistic assimilation and acculturation. After the disappearance of Aegean (found on Philistine pottery) or Egyptian (anthropoid sarcophagi) elements, characterising the first phase of Philistine presence in the Levant, Philistine material culture became similar to the one found in the Levantine cities located further inland. Similarly, personal names became Semitic and deities took on local names (such as Dagon at Gaza and Ashdod, and Astarte at Ashkelon).

Political leaders held a Philistine title, namely, *seranīm*, which has been compared to the Greek *tyrannos*. We do not, however, know if and to what extent this Philistine leadership was different from Canaanite kingship. Other elements of the Philistine socio-political system (such as armies of mercenaries, land allotments to vassals and so on) were originally Canaanite. Despite having an elite of foreign descent, the Philistine city-states ended up becoming an element of continuity with the Late Bronze Age. This is especially the case when they are compared to the more innovative 'nation' kingdoms developing further inland.

Among the latter, the kingdom of Judah (from the ninth to the eighth centuries BC) was initially a small and marginal kingdom. It was dependent on either Israel, or Damascus in an anti-Israel position, or Assyria in an anti-Israel and anti-Damascus position. From an economic point of view, the kingdom was cut off from the Mediterranean by the Philistine cities and from the Transjordan caravan routes by Edom and Moab. Therefore, the kingdom of Judah could only count on the few agro-pastoral resources available in its hilly (mountain of Judah) and semi-arid (Negev) territory (Figures 23.2 and 23.3). The alleged dynastic continuity of the 'House of David' and the prestige of the temple of Yahweh are all later fictionalisations. The latter were probably developed at the time of Josiah and then further expanded by exilic and post-exilic ideologies.

On the contrary, the kingdom of Israel ruled over a far larger and varied territory, which included plains (Jezreel and the Middle Jordan), mountains and access to the Mediterranean (south of the Carmel) and to the Transjordan caravans (Gilead). Consequently, up until the Assyrian conquest of the area, the kingdom of Israel held a hegemonic position in Palestine. The historical and institutional development of the kingdom went through various stages. First, the kingdom was a tribal state, run by a group of elders. The

Table 23.1 Palestine and southern Syria, ca. 1000–700 BC

	Judah	Israel	Tyre	Byblos	Damascus	Bama
1000	David ca.1000–900			Ahiram ca. 1000 Itto-Baal ca. 979 Yehi-Milk ca. 950	Hadad-ezer of ca. 970 Zobah Rezon ca. 950	Toi ca. 970
950	Solomon ca. 960–920 Rehoboam 922–915 Abiya 915–913 Asa 913–873	Jeroboam 922–901	Hiram I 976–930 » » » »	Abi-Baal ca. 925 Eli-Baal ca. 915 Shipit-Baal ca. 900	Hezyon Tab-Rimmon	
900	Jehoshaphat 873–849	Nadab 901–900 Basha 900–877 Zimri 876 Tibni 876–873 Omri 876–869	Itto-Baal 891–859 »		Bar-Hadad I ca. 900–873 Adad-idri Bar-Hadad II ca. 855–845	Urhilina ca. 850
850	Joram 849–842 Ahaziah 842 Atalia 842–857 Jehoash 837–800	Ahab 869–850 Ahaziah 850–849 Joram 848–842 Jehu 842–815 Jehoahaz 815–801	Baal-manzer ca.840			Uratamis
800	Amaziah 800–783 Uzziah 783–742	Jehoash 801–786 Jeroboam II 786–746			Haza-El ca. 845–800 Mari (Bar-Hadad III) ca. 800–780 Hadyanu ca. 780–750	Zakir ca. 800
750	Ahaz 735–715 Hezekiah 715–686	734 Dor, Megiddo, Gilead Assyrian provinces 722 Samaria Assyrian province	Hiram II ca. 740 Mitinnu ca. 730	Shipit.Baal ca. 740	Rahyanu ca. 750–730 732 Damascus Assyrian province	Eni-Ilu ca. 740–730 732 Hata- rikka Assyrian province Yaubi'di ca. 720 720 Hama Assyrian province
700			Luli ca. 700	Uri-Milk ca. 700		
650	Manasseh 686–642		Baal ca. 675–600	Milk-ashap ca. 670		
600	Amon 642–640 Josiah 640–609 Jehoakaz 609 Jehoiakim 609–598 Jehoiachin 597 Zedekiah 597–586		Itto-Baal ?–574 Baal 574–564			

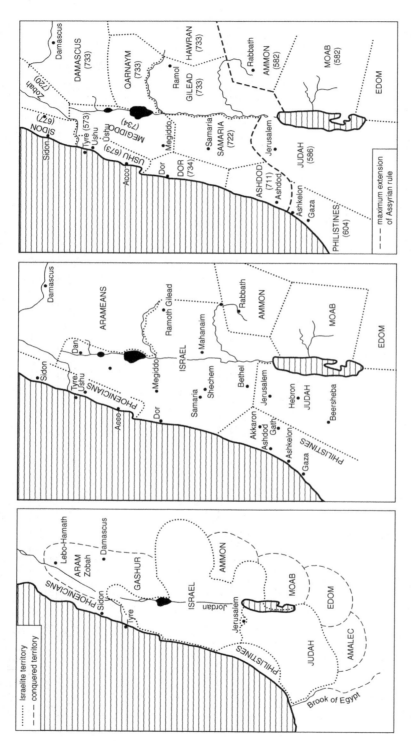

Figure 23.1 Iron Age Palestine. *Left:* The kingdom of David, tenth century; *Centre:* Map of Palestine between the ninth and eighth centuries BC; *Right:* The Assyrian and Babylonian provinces.

Figure 23.2 Beersheba, a typical example of Iron Age urban settlement in Palestine. 1: Water system; 2: Circular street; 3: Storehouses; 4: Gate; 5: Well.

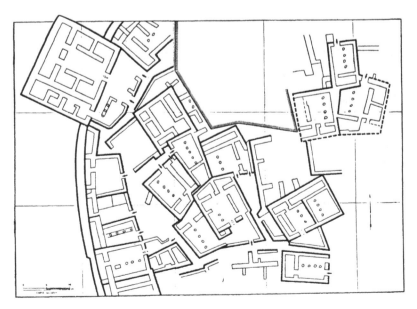

Figure 23.3 The standardised household plan of Israelite cities. Tell Beit Mirsim, stratum A, north–western quarter.

kingdom was at war with Judah over the border between the two (land of Benjamin), and was without a capital, a dynasty and a stable structure. The situation degenerated into a series of usurpations, short-lived reigns and internal conflicts. However, by the mid-ninth century BC Israel was a stable kingdom, ruled by the dynasty of the 'House of Omri'. This dynasty made Samaria its capital and built a palace with a royal court, a bureaucracy and a state administration.

The reigns of Omri and Ahab were characterised by considerable building programmes and saw establishment of kinship ties with the royal family of Tyre. Israel got involved in commercial activities and turned the kingdom of Judah into a protectorate. Moreover, Israel was involved in military conflicts with Damascus over the strategic region of Gilead and had to suffer the initial stages of the Assyrian expansion. This swift transformation of the kingdom of Israel triggered several internal problems. These problems were caused by the division between a 'modernising' effort championed by the court at Samaria and a more conservative attitude. The latter's religious, ethical and social arguments were championed by prophets accusing rulers of idolatry and corruption. The Yahwistic revolt led by the general Jehu caused a change in the ruling dynasty, but failed to alter the political organisation of Israel, which continued along the same lines. However, the Assyrian conquest of Syria soon put Israel in a difficult position, being forced to choose between submitting to or opposing the Assyrians.

The other kingdoms along the Transjordan plateau (Ammon, Moad and Edom) had less of an impact on the political developments of the area. Their main problem was maintaining their independence. In the case of Ammon, the threat came from Israel and Damascus. This forced the Ammonites to get involved in the Syro-Ephraimite wars for the control of Gilead and the 'King's Highway'. In the case of Moab, this kingdom initially almost fell under the control of Israel. The stele of the Moabite king, Mesha, provides a rare opportunity to compare the Israelite version of the events, which has survived in the Bible, with the Moabite one. The two appear to be opposite versions of the facts, but share a similar theological view. Edom experienced several phases of submission to the kingdom of Judah. Moreover, its proximity to Egypt provided it with some scope for political manoeuvre. Among the three Transjordan kingdoms, Edom was the most marginal, weakest and least organised one. However, it had a key position, linking Judah to the Red Sea, and controlled areas rich in minerals, especially copper and iron. The economy of all three Transjordan kingdoms was centred on animal farming and the passage of caravans travelling from Yemen to Syria, and vice versa. These kingdoms were therefore far wealthier than they would have been had they relied solely on what their local resources could provide, an aspect that explains the precocious Assyrian interest in the area (Figure 23.4).

Throughout this phase of independence and political pluralism, Palestine became an integral part of a network of Aramean, Phoenician and Neo-Hittite states further north, which are here separated according to their location and ethno-linguistic features for convenience. In terms of political relations and material culture, very few elements distinguished the courts of Jerusalem, Samaria or Rabbath Ammon from the courts of Tyre, Damascus or Hama. The rise of 'national' traits, however, became a much more influential factor in this period. These national traits were centred on the choice of language used and the dynastic or national deity worshipped, namely, Yahweh for Jerusalem, Milkom for the Ammonites, Chemosh for the Moabites, Baal for Tyre, and Hadad for Damascus. These political and national entities had interacted with each other for centuries, taking advantage of their relative distance from the surrounding empires. The Egyptians led their last military expedition in the area under Sheshonq, and the Assyrians would lead their first incursions with Shalmaneser III. Therefore, between 1200 and 750 BC the provision of Levantine resources as a tribute to the surrounding empires or the occasional booties were modest in scale and in their impact on the local economy. This was in marked contrast with the situation of the area after the Middle Bronze Age.

Relations among the kingdoms and ruling houses of the Levant naturally fluctuated between alliances and wars. External alliances often met with violent reaction from the local population, mainly for religious and nationalistic reasons. The latter acted as the main motives for wars. The issue was that alliances between

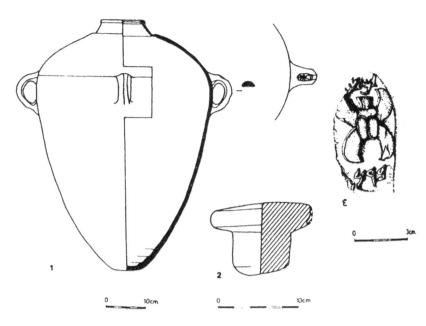

Figure 23.4   Storage jar with its stopper and a royal stamp on the handle, kingdom of Judah (Lachish, seventh century BC).

ruling houses from different national backgrounds (in terms of language, religion or culture) tended to link courts, thus bypassing the rest of the population. In fact, these alliances were sealed through inter-dynastic marriages, gift exchanges, dispatches of specialists and commercial activities.

All these interactions brought a large number of foreign products and trends to the royal courts, as well as people speaking foreign languages and with different cultural backgrounds (such as the kings' wives and their retinues). These influences ultimately led to the introduction of foreign cults. The population was far more committed to national and religious values than the appreciation of exotic products. Therefore, it condemned its rulers. The main advocates of these criticisms were the prophets loitering in the courts, who became the spokespersons of anti-royal opinions. Even in case of serious problems in regional wars, such as the measures to be taken in the face of the Assyrian threat, we encounter constant clashes of opinion. These disagreements not only took place within the court, but also outside of it, and adopted the typical 'code' of the prophetic message

The outcome of wars (from victory to defeat, one's own destruction or the opponent's, foreign interventions and so on) was always explained theologically, more as a result of ethical and religious factors, rather than military prowess. Just as in the Bronze Age, war was always a 'sacred war', apparently fought by soldiers, but ultimately fought by the gods of each party. Bronze Age wars were also sacred in the sense that they were an ordeal meant to show who was right and who was wrong in the political and diplomatic disputes preceding the conflict. In the Iron Age, however, wars were sacred because they were essentially a clash between national deities (personified by their respective armies) who prevailed depending on their strength. The enemy would therefore be beaten not because he was wrong, but because he had sinned by worshipping the wrong deity and not being part of the 'chosen' people. Consequently, in the Iron Age, national identity was cemented more through wars than through peace. In this sense, it was easier to mobilise the population through the words of prophets championing a fight until death, than through the courts implementing more realistic and opportunistic measures.

4 The empires' impact

The Assyrian intervention in the Levant initially contributed to the internal conflicts among the Palestinian kingdoms, but then became increasingly more forceful, moving from the north to the south. Already in 853 BC, Ahab of Israel participated in the alliance of Syrian states that successfully defeated Shalmaneser III's army. This reaction may have been a sporadic event, a simple pause from internal conflicts in order to unite old rivals against a common danger. In reality, it was a symptomatic reaction to a threat whose impact would have soon deeply affected the northernmost states. For Palestine, the Assyrian danger only became a real issue around the eighth century BC, when the choice between paying tributes and seeing one's territory devastated became a recurrent issue.

Overall, the Assyrian conquest developed in three stages. First, a local kingdom was forced to provide an annual tribute. Then, taking advantage of supposed rebellions, the Assyrians would impose a king chosen by them in place of the rebels. Finally, still after more rebellions or oppositions, the Assyrians would destroy the kingdom, turning it into a mere province. Within 25 years, from Tiglath-pileser III to Sargon II, all the areas surrounding the kingdom of Israel, namely, Megiddo, Dor and Gilead (734 BC), and Qarnaym and Hauran (733 BC) became Assyrian provinces. Then, it was the turn of the heart of Israel, namely, Samaria (722 BC), and Ashdod (711 BC).

Instead of coalescing against the invaders, the Palestinian states went for different political strategies. Some submitted to the Assyrians, while some others opposed them. The Palestinian states therefore tried to take advantage of the invaders in order to solve old disputes. In turn, they were used by the invaders as auxiliaries and fifth columns, possibly in the hope of participating in the division of the booty. In this phase (as well as during the Babylonian intervention), relations among local states and groups worsened. This is attested in numerous prophecies against foreign peoples, in which the destruction of the enemy was seen as a demonstration of their sins, while the enemy's profit of one's own ruin was lamented. These prophecies also saw the arrival of imperial invaders as a divine intervention to destroy and punish the Israelite people.

Even within each individual kingdom, there were considerable debates on the best strategy to implement. Some people wanted to resist the invaders, while others, at the risk of being considered pro-Assyrian or, later on, pro-Babylonian, suggested submitting to these powers. Considering the superiority of the Assyrian army over the Levantine fortifications, it has to be said, alas *a posteriori*, that submission (as in the case of Judah) at least allowed the maintenance of a certain degree of autonomy. Armed resistance (as in the case of Samaria) only led to a quicker defeat. Moreover, it was far easier to resist for the southernmost states (Judah, Edom and Gaza), which were further away from the Assyrian threat and supported by Egypt. Jerusalem, for instance, managed to overcome a difficult siege (701 BC), despite losing a portion of its territories.

The Assyrian conquest of the Southern Levant had a significant impact on the economy and demography of the area. Palestine had already experienced long periods of submission to foreign empires, Egypt in particular (throughout the Late Bronze Age), without dramatic consequences. This was due to the modest levels of damage and exploitation, and the maintenance of political independence on a local level. Now, however, the regular payments of large tributes significantly impoverished states that could count on very limited local resources. Nonetheless, the greatest damage to the economy of the area came from the destruction of fields, cultivations, agricultural villages, irrigation systems and terraces. Moreover, devastations and deportations caused a serious impoverishment of the local demography, its culture and knowledge.

The Assyrians mainly deported citizens, while farmers remained in their devastated lands. Alongside the depopulation of the Levant, the people in the Levant experienced a sense of overall discouragement and a phase of de-culturation. Cities were not dynastic seats of power anymore, with their ostentation and accumulation of wealth that stimulated local craftsmanship as well as trade. This caused a decline in the overall sense of cohesion and nationalism of the people. Now, cities hosted Assyrian governors, administrators, garrisons and cults. They thus became mere 'terminals' of a complex mechanism of centralisation of resources in aid of the development of the imperial capitals and the re-population of the Assyrian countryside.

The whole of Palestine therefore experienced the same process, although the transformation of Judah (as well as Gaza, Moab and Edom) into an Assyrian province happened much later, due to its position and the support of the Egyptians. Its temporary submission to the Assyrians was at times substituted by a braver reaction. The latter was inspired by the international scene (that is, Egyptian support and the Assyrian difficulties in Babylonia) and was aimed at reacquiring an independence that began to be seen in religious terms (as cultic reforms). In other words, the Jewish people and their political representatives began to believe that a more rigorous faith in Yahweh would have led to a better political situation. Therefore, dangers began to be seen by some as a consequence of religious mishaps.

A case in point is the reign of Hezekiah (715–687 BC), who re-organised the state and its cults, and fortified and enlarged Jerusalem. He resisted the siege of Sennacherib (701 BC), avoiding the total destruction of the city, but lost a large portion of his kingdom. Another significant episode took place during the reign of Josiah (640–609 BC), who took advantage of the fall of the Assyrian empire to restore his state. This was just a short-lived phase in which the Syro-Levantine territories were relatively free, right before the Babylonians (coming from the north) and the Egyptians (from the south) would contend control over the Levant. Josiah tried to re-conquer the Israelite territories and dreamed of restoring the Davidic kingdom. Through him, the identification of the state with the national god reached its highest levels, with a single god (Yahweh) dwelling in a single temple (that of Jerusalem), and with a drastic elimination of different or foreign cults. However, this political autonomy did not last long, and Josiah died in a battle against the Egyptians. Nonetheless, the religious reforms, which Josiah wanted to support following the discovery in the temple of the ancient divine laws, laid the groundwork for the developments that would take place in the exilic age.

A few years later, the Babylonians achieved what the Assyrians had failed to achieve. Nebuchadnezzar conquered Jerusalem, making it one of his vassals (597 BC), and then re-conquered it, putting a definite end to its independence (586 BC). Solomon's temple was destroyed, the city walls dismantled, and the local elite was deported to Babylonia. Gaza, Ammon and Moab had a similar fate. The Babylonian deportations were of a smaller scale compared to the Assyrian ones. In 701 BC, the latter seem to have moved ca. 27,290 people from Samaria and 200,150 from Judaea. On the contrary, the Babylonians deported from Jerusalem 3000 people in 597 BC, and 1500 in 586 BC. However, unlike the Assyrians, the Babylonians did not repopulate the devastated countryside with people deported to the Levant from elsewhere, but brought all the deportees to Babylonia. Therefore, while the northern countryside (Israel and the Aramean states) was re-colonised by a mixture of surviving farmers and new immigrants, the south (Judah) remained empty, but more ethnically compact.

Moreover, while the deportees in Assyria eventually integrated with the local population, the exiles in Babylonia kept their cohesion and individuality. Despite being exiled as well, their king was still considered their ruler. Apart from the different durations of the exiles, differences in the ways the deportees were employed and in the process of de-culturation also had a considerable impact. The Assyrian system was tremendously effective in matching various ethnical groups and cultures, but was also able to colonise new areas and re-organise entire systems of production. The Babylonian system was more moderate and permissive, but also less interested in the conditions of the conquered areas. From the Assyrian conquest in the second half of the eighth century BC to the Babylonian one in the mid-sixth century BC, the Palestinian settlements and their population abruptly declined, reaching the lowest levels in the history of the Ancient Near East.

This demographic and power vacuum led to the movement of peoples. The Edomites moved from their ancient seat, east of Arabah, to the southern part of the former kingdom of Judah (in the Hebron and Beersheba). The latter would become the Idumaea of the classical period. The entire area east of the Jordan became increasingly affected by the arrival of Arab-speaking populations, former tribes involved in the farming of camels. These groups were now on their way to sedentarisation and occupied those urban and commercial centres abandoned by previous inhabitants. Especially in the north, the Assyrian deportations allowed the penetration of Aramaic-speaking groups from Central and northern Syria, as well as Upper Mesopotamia and Chaldea.

The deportees who came to the Levant also imported their deities and customs. These were initially extraneous, but eventually managed to integrate within the local culture. Therefore, the northern Levant was characterised by a culturally mixed population of local farmers and foreign deportees, but without a ruling elite (with the exception of the Assyrians governing the provinces). This population spoke Aramaic and their religion was a syncretism of a variety of cults that converged in the area. On the contrary, the nucleuses of learned Jewish deportees, former members of the Levantine palace or temple elite, tried to maintain the purity of their language, customs and religion throughout their Babylonian exile. In this way, the Jewish exiles were trying to avoid any assimilation with the surrounding and prevailing population, without realising to what extent this rigour and cultural isolation were in fact innovative.

These nuclei of exiles considered themselves, and not the farmers who stayed in the Levant, to be the authentic survivors of this national disaster. They continued to see Palestine, and in particular Jerusalem, as their homeland, imbuing it with at times quite unrealistic symbolic values. Once these deportees returned from their exile at the beginning of the Persian period, they would try to regain their land, without realising that they had created something entirely new and innovative. Just as the empires were reducing Palestine into a culturally uniform territory, depriving it of its former cultural centres of national identity, the initial conditions for the rise of invisible (but not less drastic) frontiers were starting to appear on a social and ethnical level. These invisible frontiers were centred on theological formulations, convictions and personal behaviour.

5 The uniqueness of Israelite religion

The greatest legacy of ancient Israel is its monotheistic religion, which has survived to this day both in its direct branch, namely, Judaism, and its collateral one, namely, Christianity. Our culture has long been (and is still) afflicted by the problem of the 'uniqueness' of the religious developments of Israel. The descendants of Israel's people express this idea through their conviction of its originality and a resistance to any form of assimilation. However, from a secular point of view, once the theological explanation has been discarded (namely that of the Chosen People), it becomes necessary to find a historical explanation.

A historical explanation of this uniqueness (and its subsequent 'normalisation') has to avoid any anachronistic data, which would make unique in a specific historical context something that actually developed later on. This danger is not at all abstract, but a consequence of what has been already explained above. The religious innovators lurking behind the practice of providing authority to an account by dating it back in time, simply turned the evolution of an entire population into a fixed state. The latter seemingly appeared fully developed from its beginnings. In addition to that, we run the risk, after millennia, of flattening the picture even further if we compare the final result of this religious development, which peaked with the rise of Judaism, with the development of a generic 'Near Eastern world'. However, the Near East also had its diachronic depth spanning across at least three millennia, and a vast variety of local experiences and evolutions.

The religious reformers of the sixth to the fourth centuries BC therefore projected the origins of their theological and cultic re-organisations in the formative phase of the ethnic and political community of Israel. They condensed all these factors into the figure of Moses, who would have allegedly received the 'Tablets of Law' directly from Yahweh. From this point of view, then, Yahwism did not experience any evolution from Moses to Judaism, namely, from the thirteenth to the fourth centuries BC. Naturally, this is a purely artificial invention. From the little contemporary data available, it appears that Palestinian religion in the thirteenth to the tenth centuries BC was highly complex. Each city hosted a variety of deities and their cults. They were all structured into similar pantheons (but different in their specific details), and had a common iconographic and mythological repertoire, at least in their general features. Therefore, the agrarian and urban religion of the Canaanites existed alongside the religion of pastoral groups. The latter was a different kind of religion, based on different premises.

The foundation of the temple of Jerusalem as a building annexed to the royal palace led to the selection of one deity as the head of the official pantheon of the kingdom of Judah. This deity thus became the chief deity of Judah's dynasty. The chosen deity, Yahweh, was possibly not new in the area. He was, however, certainly not among the major deities linked to the established mythological and cultic tradition of the area. In this regard, it appears that Yahweh was not the pre-existing patron deity of Jerusalem. Some of the main features of this god, such as his aniconism, demythicisation and a clear connection with genealogical ancestors, seem to belong to a nomadic and pastoral type of religion, rather than an agrarian religion. Naturally, the presence of a dynastic deity did not preclude the presence of other deities' cults. The latter continued to be maintained, especially in the other cities and regions more closely connected to their local traditions, but also in the capital itself, due to its central role in the kingdom.

There were other temples of Yahweh outside of Jerusalem, which were mainly ancient sanctuaries of other deities whose characteristics began to be associated with Yahweh. These cultic buildings, however, continued to maintain their cultic, mythological and priestly traditions. What was most important was that Yahweh was not yet a monotheistic deity. In fact, a female deity associated with him has been epigraphically attested. This indicates that Yahweh was originally part of a polytheistic pantheon. Therefore, in the course of the monarchic phase of Israel, Yahweh's prestige rose at the expense of other deities. This sometimes happened through assimilations, such as in the case of El, Elyon and other pastoral deities. Alternatively, it happened through a subordination and demonisation of other deities, such as in the case of Reshef and other healing deities. On the contrary, in the case of the divine pair Baal-Astarte, who were at the centre of the local agrarian religion, the rise of Yahweh caused a significant degree of conflict and opposition.

Clashes with the neighbouring states had theological implications. These religious consequences became increasingly evident once the Assyrians began to threaten the area. It has already been noted how war was envisioned as a conflict between national deities, leading to a theological interpretation of both victories and defeats. It is understandable that a victory would increase a national deity's prestige, and a conquest would lead to the spread of the cult of the winner's god. Nonetheless, it is peculiar how in this case defeat brought about the most important theological development. Surprisingly enough, a sporadic defeat was not interpreted as another deity's prevalence over one's own, but as the latter's decision to punish his people for some sin committed against him. Therefore, after a complete national disaster at the hand of the rising empires of the Near East, the most accredited theological justification was that the national deity was so powerful as to be able to 'use' the enemies' armies and their powerful rulers to punish his people. This is a significant ideological change. In a normal polytheistic environment, the outcome of a war was the result of the opposition of two rival deities. However, this theological utilisation of the victors' foreign deities and the preference for an explanation focused on the relationship between a national deity and his people indicate an essential lack of interest for any deities other than one's own.

It is possible that all the populations conquered by the Assyrians experienced this theological development (including northern Israel). As these populations became part of the Assyrian imperial system, however, their cultic and cultural individuality, as well as their ability to recover from the attacks, diminished. In this regard, the case of Judah was significantly different. At the peak of this theological process, the kingdom resisted the Assyrians. It also experienced the reforms of the kings Hezekiah and Josiah, who tried to respond to this negative turn of events through religious measures.

These measures can be synthesised into two main reforms: the idea of the uniqueness of the kingdom's cult, and the definition of the 'law'. The faith in a single national god therefore became the only path to salvation. Any compromise or preference for other deities became a sin provoking a divine punishment. In other words, the more negative a situation was turning out to be, the more it became necessary to implement an exclusive type of religiousness. The cult began to be concentrated in the temple of Jerusalem, thus emphasising its national implications. Other cultic centres were eliminated, and priesthoods other than the one dedicated to Yahweh were persecuted and disbanded. For the first time, then, the concept of a kingdom worshipping a single god in a single place was developed.

An ancient manuscript containing the 'divine law' was 'accidentally' found in the temple. If the cause of a success or a defeat depended on the community's behaviour, it became necessary to unambiguously know in detail what had to be done, what had to be avoided, and what were the possible 'sins' and objections of the god. Therefore, the king's legitimacy of rule and his efficiency ceased to be the defining factors in a community's relations with the divine. This indicates that the prestige of kingship, formerly the exclusive mediator between the human and the divine sphere, had greatly diminished. Now, the potential cause for a national crisis was the behaviour of the population as a whole. Therefore, at the eve of the final collapse of the kingdom, monolatrism, a central temple, a codified set of laws and a sense of collective responsibility emerged.

Shortly after Josiah's reforms, the Babylonian army destroyed Jerusalem and Solomon's temple. This brought to an end the Davidic monarchy, which in its final phase had become a central presence also for the former Israelite subjects in the north. The temple's destruction, the end of national independence, and the deportation of the elite largely eliminated those aspects at the heart of this national identity. After all, these imperial measures were aimed precisely at destroying different national identities. If there were no land, state, king and temple anymore, the only point of reference was the law. Therefore, religion became a practice requiring an organised cult, requiring an increased internalisation of its principles and a certain degree of individual formalities (taboos, circumcision, Sabbath and so on). A member of the Israelite community, which had by now become a religious community, therefore had to distinguish himself within a heterogeneous world. Whoever loyally observed the law (and was therefore worshipping the only true god, Yahweh) considered himself a member of a group that survived a national disaster and lived in a world of 'pagans' (namely, worshippers of false gods). This group was only apparently defeated and marginalised, while in reality it continued to be aware of its profound prestige in being a nucleus of individuals loyal to Yahweh.

However, this conceptualisation only made sense if there was a chance to overturn the current situation. This was a hope to once again make the faith in one god and his laws coincide with an economic and political prosperity that at the moment was benefiting the 'pagans'. This point of view could be seen in two ways. On the one hand, there was the political view of restoring national unity, regaining control of one's former territory, reconstructing the temple, and restoring the monarchy. On the other hand, the overturn of the situation could be seen in a more personal, eschatological sense, rather than a political one. In this view, one would hope that in the end the divine judge would finally and rightly bestow prizes and punishments by taking into account merits and sins, without meddling with historical events.

When the Persian empire allowed the return of the exiles to Judaea, the prospects of a political renaissance seemed to be close to fulfilment. This renaissance would have featured the re-foundation of the temple of Jerusalem (the 'second' temple), the adoption of the divine laws in the land, and the development of an autonomous national entity. However, the nucleus of Judaean exiles who managed to return to the land of their fathers found a mixed population composed of previous inhabitants and new immigrants. This mixed population was worshipping syncretistic cults, intermarried and was relatively demotivated. The survivors, who were fervent Yahwists, tried to tackle this situation by restoring the temple and the law, forbidding mixed marriages and religious syncretisms, and by considering illegitimate the presence of those who did not belong to the Yahwist community. They therefore dreamed of a political restoration, which was hindered by the current situation.

With the decline of the monarchic ideal, the priesthood became the figurehead of national identity. The priesthood therefore took on the task of providing the authentic interpretation of the law, and dismissing all the cults that did not take place in the temple of Jerusalem. The second temple was very different from the first one. The latter had been an important cultic place in connection to the palace. The second temple followed the Babylonian example, exacting the tithe, owning land and administering justice. It therefore became the only focal point of its national community. Discriminations, religious conflicts, dismissals and persecutions of anything different were the consequences of the historical context of the 'second' temple (up until its destruction under Titus and the Roman diaspora). On the contrary, eschatological solutions of the contradiction between ethical values and reality, and the emergence of an individual sphere first within a strong sense of nationalism, and then outside of it, only emerged as long-term developments.

The issue of the 'uniqueness' of Israelite religion can then be reformulated and restructured: why did other nations and other religions that experienced the same treatment of deportation and de-culturation not react in the same way? Why was there no 'Bible' of Tyre or Damascus? In this regard, it may be worth bearing in mind the differences between Assyrian and Babylonian imperialism both in terms of duration and methods applied. The Assyrian deportees were many more, were distributed in various provinces, and were substituted in their homeland by other deportees from other provinces. This situation brought to a (at times forced) symbiosis on both a social and family level, eventually leading to a religious syncretism. The Judaean deportees in Babylonia were fewer and all members of the elite. They remained united in their exile and they returned after a few decennia to a Judaea emptied of its population. Having survived the fiercely de-culturative treatment of the Assyrians, Jerusalem managed to transform the Babylonian exile and the loss of its political identity as an opportunity to strengthen its religious national identity, leaving us a corpus of generic religious texts. This was a clear effort to rewrite its history as a response to its difficult situation.

6 The historiographical re-elaboration of Israelite history

Compared to the rest of the Near East, pre-exilic Israelite culture is poorly attested. Archaeological investigations have provided far clearer and more monumental remains for the cultures of Egypt and Mesopotamia and for the rest of the Levant than for Israel. However, Palestine has been the target of much more thorough archaeological investigations than any other region of the Near East, and maybe even of the world. If one had to reconstruct the history of Israel on the basis of these findings, the resulting picture would be relatively brief and poor. The reason for this is the nature of the area. The latter was in a marginal position both in terms of natural resources and of political developments, with small-scale settlements and political and cultural developments, especially in comparison with the surrounding areas in the Iron Age.

Then, there were more specific reasons. First, despite having been repeatedly excavated, the capital Jerusalem has provided (and will always provide) very little evidence for the monarchic phase. This is due to the presence of later buildings over the layers of the temple, the palace and the Davidic city. Moreover, the lack of figurative monuments partly derives from the presence of religious movements that were against iconographic representations. Despite the fact that these movements were not so absolute and widespread as the Old Testament would make us believe, they still had a considerable impact. Vaguely similar is the peculiar lack of royal inscriptions, which have been found in many contemporary sites further north. This absence must be due to the cultural choices made with regards to the type of kingship and the relationship existing between the king and his subjects in Israel.

Finally, there was the strong cultural influence of flourishing centres, in particular that of Tyre, and Phoenicia in general. At least this is what can be understood from the Biblical account of the construction of the temple of Solomon, which was supposedly built by workers from Tyre, and the discovery of Phoenician ivories in Samaria. In contrast, the basic material culture of the area is far better attested than in other areas. This is mainly due to the intense excavations in Palestine. In this regard, we possess a detailed and diachronic development of pottery types, houses and building techniques, fortresses and city fortifications, and the overall layout of the cities in the area during the Iron Age.

It is undeniable that the written sources and official monuments found in Palestine may be rather limited. However, the Bible continues to play a crucial role in the reconstruction of the religious, political, literary and institutional history of Israel. Therefore, the importance of the transmitted literary corpus known as the Old Testament could not be more evident. There are two strategies that can be implemented to analyse this complex collection of texts, which is characterised by numerous adaptations and a noticeable distance between the time of the episodes narrated and of the narrator. The first one is to give in to the temptation of using the historical data provided by the Old Testament to reconstruct the periods to which they refer. In other words, one could use the Book of Genesis to reconstruct the 'Patriarchal' age, the Book of Joshua to reconstruct the conquest of Israel, the Book of the Judges to reconstruct the homonymous phase, and so on. The second strategy consists in using these various texts to reconstruct the time in which they were written and the problems that led to their composition. This strategy is far more difficult to implement. It requires the rearrangement of the individual texts, and even the individual textual additions, to precise phases and precise problems, following their internal developments. Despite these issues, this procedure is the only correct one. The first strategy, which has been frequently applied, implies a degree of reliability of the sources that still needs to be demonstrated and is so far not plausible.

Rearranging individual texts, which together form the Old Testament, according to the time they were composed, one notices that the majority of them were written considerably after the time period considered in this book, namely, in the post-exilic phase (that is, the Achaemenid and Hellenistic period). Only a few of them were composed in the exilic phase. Without a doubt, the Old Testament can be better evaluated and appreciated in the context of the second temple rather than the first. It constitutes a monumental example of a re-formulation of the past, and its rewriting as a response to the present, the latter being a much later phase compared to the time narrated.

However, the consideration of the Old Testament here is justified for various reasons. In the critical and textual analysis of the Bible, the (mainly prophetic and historiographical) texts of the exilic and pre-exilic phase, namely, the time of the reformers, correspond to the Deuteronomy. They constitute a precious set of evidence on the final phases of the history of Israel within the historical reconstruction embarked on in this book. Moreover, the entire Old Testament reused and re-organised ancient material, which can be reconstructed and to a certain extent 'dated', contextualising it in earlier phases. Moreover, the historiographical re-organisation of the history of Israel in the post-exilic phase was the result of the political and cultural developments of the previous phases, and constitutes a significant aid for the comprehension of its most important aspects. However, it remains crucial to avoid the influence of the pre-dating of developments for theological reasons and the simplifications of a complex history in its final reconstruction.

For the phase of the 'origins' of Israel, its actual historical development and its Biblical account are completely different. This is due to the lack of reliable sources for this period, the considerable amount of time that passed when the account was written, and the strong influence of 'foundational' motives. For this period, then, our own archaeological and contextual evidence is far more reliable than that which the authors of the sixth to the fourth centuries BC had at their disposal, such as ancient legends, memorised genealogies and aetiologies.

For the monarchic phase it is necessary to make a distinction. The account of the reigns of David and Solomon is largely idealised and overestimated. It was originally developed as an archetypal and optimal model of rule, and is therefore not more reliable than the account on the origins of Israel. The divided monarchy is a different case. Naturally, ideological modifications are also attested for this phase. For instance, the sequence of kings is entirely modelled on their perceived qualities. Therefore, there is a distinction between 'good' and 'bad' kings, according to the extent to which they worshipped Yahweh. However, regarding the factual information recorded in the Bible, whenever external contemporary evidence has been discovered, this seems to largely confirm the Biblical account of the facts. The stele of Mesha or the Assyrian annals naturally provide a different point of view on the historical developments of the time. Moreover, these interpretations often differ from those provided by the Bible. Nonetheless, the main events recorded largely correspond to the ones attested in the Bible.

Consequently, the biblical authors must have had access to some of the written evidence of the time, possibly some palace 'chronicles' or 'annals'. Perhaps they even accessed some royal inscriptions, the ultimate expressions of an official historiography from the monarchic age. The formal tone and the historiographical maturity of the Bible, however, can only be part of a later development. This makes it impossible to accept the widespread assumption that Israelite historiography had prodigiously anticipated Greek historiography, and had abandoned Near Eastern historiography. Following the current interpretations on the matter, the main historiographical arrangements are the so-called 'deuteronomistic' ones of the pre-exilic and exilic phase (sixth to fifth centuries BC), and the 'sacerdotal' ones of the post-exilic phase (fourth century BC). Therefore, older material should be understood as part of an ancient tradition, rather than reliable written sources.

The prophetic texts constitute a second set of valuable documents (having removed any later additions or adaptations), due to their proximity to the events narrated. The literary genre of the 'prophecy' is simply a strongly theologised 'code' of political, rather than ethical or religious, messages. They therefore provide information on both the internal political developments of the kingdoms of Judah and Israel, and their involvement in the events affecting the Near East as a whole, from their relations with neighbouring kingdoms and populations to the imperial attacks.

The emerging picture is one that could not be attested in official accounts of these events, recording contrasting opinions, alternative strategies, and internal conflicts. Moreover, this picture also emphasises the presence of that theological history mentioned above, and through it the presence of contrasts among the Syro-Levantine nations. The opportunity to catch a glimpse of (for instance) the arguments of the 'pro-Egyptian' and 'pro-Babylonian' side, or the impact the Assyrian destruction of a kingdom had on the surrounding kingdoms, are extremely rare. This is not because similar situations or debates did not occur elsewhere, but because the Israelite ones are the only ones that have survived to us. They therefore give us an idea of the political climate of the Near East in the Iron Age.

The imperial attacks, the deportations and the exiles, and then the return and the national renaissance of Israel, acted as a stimulus for a large portion of ancient Jewish literature. The three main stages were: 1) the debate over the political strategies to be implemented on a local level, the destiny of the neighbouring states and the function of empires; 2) then, during the exile, the influence of Babylonian (and maybe even Iranian) culture in the realms of historiography, wisdom, narrative and cultic literature; 3) and finally, the great re-writing of the past as part of the political masterplan centred on the second temple. Before these important, yet short, phases, what has survived of ancient Jewish literature is not very different from the rest of Near Eastern literature of the time. The literary, as well as religious, originality of Israel was after all the result of its final phase. The latter led to the political breakdown of the kingdom and the birth of Judaism. Therefore, the idea that the Bible safeguarded a legacy of ancient knowledge is a phenomenon that needs to be considered, at least in part, as an illusion.

24

THE PHOENICIANS

1 The independent cities

The term 'Phoenicians' indicates those peoples who spoke a north-western Semitic language, lived on the Syro-Lebanese coast from 1200 BC, and later on spread throughout the Mediterranean. This was their Greek designation (*Phoinikes*). Locally, they were either defined as Canaanites, without any distinction from the people living in the hinterland, or even Sidonians, after the name of one of their main cities. This multiplicity of designations already indicates that the Phoenicians did not have a specific or official name for themselves. This is hardly surprising, considering the fact that the Phoenicians were never politically unified and constituted a network of cities acting as independent kingdoms.

Phoenicia was a long strip of land located between the mountains and the Mediterranean Sea. In some points, the land features some coastal plains, while in others the mountains reach the sea, or slowly turn into hills along the coast. In the Iron Age, these mountains were mainly forested areas, especially in Lebanon, which was renowned for its cedar, an excellent wood for construction works used from as early as the third millennium BC. Alternatively, the area was covered by maquis shrubland. The plains and hills were intensely cultivated with olive trees, vines, fruits and vegetables, integrating the main cultivation of cereals. The area was densely populated and divided into villages. These villages were politically and economically dependent on the main cities of the local dynasties. The main cities of Phoenicia were Arwad, Byblos, Sidon and Tyre. Among the minor cities, there were Siyannu and Usnu in the north, Sumura and Arqa between Arwad and Byblos, Beirut between Byblos and Sidon, Sarepta between Sid and Tyre, and Ushu and Acre to the south of Tyre.

The beginning of the history of the Phoenicians and their own ethnical and cultural identity is conventionally dated around 1200 BC. However, this does not indicate that they arrived in the region around then, as the Classical tradition often stated, or that they organised themselves in new ways around that time. On the contrary, the Phoenicians of the Iron Age were direct descendants of those people inhabiting the area in the Bronze Age. This aspect is particularly visible on a cultural level. In the Bronze Age, the coastal cities were part of kingdoms that included the cities in the hinterland. Around 1200 BC a process of division between the cities along the coast and the ones in the hinterland began to occur. This process was mainly caused by other populations, such as the Neo-Hittites and the Philistines, and the pastoral groups of the Aramean, Israelite and Transjordan hinterland. The change provided a new cultural climate and new forms of political organisation. Meanwhile, the Phoenicians stood as the direct descendants of the 'Canaanite' culture of the Late Bronze Age.

This turning point was further emphasised by the invasion of the Sea Peoples, who broke down the consolidated system promoted by the regional empires of the time. In this way, the Phoenician cities managed to regain their long lost independence. The main city in the north, Ugarit, was destroyed by the Sea Peoples. Therefore, it never became a 'Phoenician' city. On the contrary, the other cities in the area between Arwad and the Carmel apparently managed to survive the invasion. They separated themselves from the Southern Levant, now occupied by new populations. Moreover, by then the nomadic element had affected the hinterland, leading to substantial changes in the way in which states were organised. Meanwhile, the coastal cities, which were protected from these tribes by the Lebanese mountains, continued to maintain their division in city-states centred on royal palaces. The survival of this ancient type of organisation is also visible from the presence of an assembly alongside the king, and the return of an ideology of kingship centred on the ideals of 'justice and fairness'.

We have various attestations on the first phase of Phoenician history (twelfth to tenth centuries BC). The Egyptian tale of Wenamun, who went to the king of Byblos Zakar-Baal to ask for cedar wood, provides the most elaborate picture of the time. While Egypt proclaims the (theological rather than political) dependence of Lebanon to the cult of Amun, Byblos shows a preference for a more pragmatic and purely commercial approach. Despite the fact that Byblos' dependence on Egypt had now ceased to exist, the city remained a privileged commercial centre for Egyptian trade, just like it had been from its earliest phases. A series of royal inscriptions left by local kings (Ahi-ram, Abi-Baal, Eli-Baal, Shipit-Baal and Yehi-Milk) show the development of a new type of kingship. Some of them were inscribed on monuments left by Egyptian kings, confirming this interaction with Egypt (Figure 24.1).

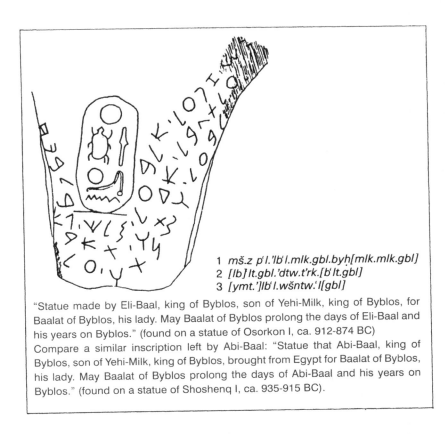

1 *mš.z p'l.'lb'l.mlk.gbl.byḥ[mlk.mlk.gbl]*
2 *[lb]lt.gbl.'dtw.t'rk.[b'lt.gbl]*
3 *[ymt.']lb'l.wšntw.'l[gbl]*

"Statue made by Eli-Baal, king of Byblos, son of Yehi-Milk, king of Byblos, for Baalat of Byblos, his lady. May Baalat of Byblos prolong the days of Eli-Baal and his years on Byblos." (found on a statue of Osorkon I, ca. 912-874 BC)
Compare a similar inscription left by Abi-Baal: "Statue that Abi-Baal, king of Byblos, son of Yehi-Milk, king of Byblos, brought from Egypt for Baalat of Byblos, his lady. May Baalat of Byblos prolong the days of Abi-Baal and his years on Byblos." (found on a statue of Shoshenq I, ca. 935-915 BC)

Figure 24.1 Inscription of Eli-Baal, king of Byblos, ca. 900 BC.

Regarding the northernmost cities of Phoenicia, king Tiglath-pileser I (ca. 1100 BC) informs us that he had travelled to Arwad for wood. Moreover, some sources attest that an ancient supremacy of Sidon ceased around 1000 BC in favour of Tyre. The Old Testament provides some information on Tyre. The king of Tyre, Hiram, provided wood and specialised workers for the construction of the temple of Jerusalem during the reigns of David and Solomon. He also participated in some commercial endeavours in the Red Sea. The overall picture is fragmentary, but still fairly coherent. A series of independent cities in the Levant were active in terms of trade and production. They were also involved in reciprocal relations with the states in the hinterland, as well as the more distant and powerful kingdoms of Assyria and Egypt.

Even at the beginning of the first millennium BC, there is little historical evidence about the Phoenician cities, due to an almost total lack of local attestations. In the case of Tyre, the abstracts of the city's 'Annals' recorded by Josephus Flavius, who claimed that they derived from Menander of Ephesus, only provide the name of its kings. However, these attestations are unreliable. This is partly because they coincide with those of the Old Testament (which were known to Josephus), but not with the information provided by the Assyrian annals, which were unknown to him. The Bible also attests the inter-dynastic marriage arranged between the royal family of Tyre at the time of king Itto-Baal with the royal family of Samaria. It also attests the commercial, cultural and religious influence of Tyre on the kingdom of Israel.

For the other Phoenician cities, the available evidence is mainly Assyrian, and is more concerned with their relations with Assyria, rather than their history. Admittedly, the continuation of the Assyrian expansion from the ninth to the seventh centuries BC became the central issue of the history of the region. If the isolated expeditions of Tiglath-pileser I and Ashurnasirpal II were mainly commercial and peaceful, this Assyrian attitude completely changed with Shalmaneser III (mid-ninth century BC). The new expansionistic ambitions of the Assyrians meant that the Phoenician cities were forced to pay heavy tributes, in order to avoid any Assyrian attack. There were cases in which the Phoenician cities resisted the invasion. This is the case of the battle of Qarqar (852 BC), fought by the northern Phoenician cities (Siyannu, Usnu, Sumura and Arqa), which were more directly affected by the invasion. In general, however, the Phoenician cities preferred to pay the tributes to keep away the Assyrians and any threat of war.

Almost a century later, in the mid-eighth century BC, the Assyrian threat returned in a more concrete form with Tiglath-pileser III. The Assyrian king directly annexed the area to his empire. In 743 BC, the entire northern coast, reaching as far as Byblos, was turned into an Assyrian province, whose capital was Sumura. Being an island, Arwad managed to remain independent, while Byblos and the southernmost cities continued to pay tributes. However, the rivalry among the Phoenician cities, especially between Sidon and Tyre, facilitated Assyrian expansion. In 700 BC, Sennacherib managed to expel from Sidon Luli, king of Tyre, who at the time also ruled over Sidon. The Assyrian king then appointed a new king chosen by him. In 677 BC, Esarhaddon conquered Sidon with the support of Tyre, captured its last king, Abdi-Milkutti, and turned it into a province. He also made Tyre and its king Baal his vassal. A few years later (671 BC), however, Tyre, supported by the Egyptians, managed to rebel. The reaction of the Assyrian was ruthless, and Tyre lost a portion of its territories. The mainland was turned into an Assyrian province whose capital was Ushu, while Tyre remained independent on its own little island.

At the time of Ashurbanipal, further conflicts with Tyre and Arwad took place, the former being continuously supported by the Egyptians. On several occasions, the kings of Tyre and Arwad had to formally submit to the Assyrians, although they still managed to keep their independence. By the end of the Assyrian empire (612 BC), Phoenicia was divided into the three provinces of Sumura in the north, Sidon in the centre and Ushu in the south. Meanwhile, Arwad, Byblos and Tyre continued to be autonomous states forced to pay tributes to the Assyrians.

During the final collapse of the Assyrian empire, Tyre tried to regain its commercial and political position, taking advantage of the power vacuum existing between the Babylonians and the Egyptians. However, soon enough, the expansion of Babylonia over the entire Levantine coast also affected the Phoenician coast. Tyre was besieged for a long time and eventually collapsed in 573 BC, although the city continued to have its local dynasty. The latter ruled alongside a Babylonian governor, except for a period in which the king of Tyre was exiled to Babylonia, and several 'judges' ruled the city.

It is probable that the Babylonian empire also conquered Arwad and Byblos. Eventually, the whole area would become part of the Persian empire, but even then it would maintain (as in the case of Tyre) or re-establish (as in the case of Sidon) its local dynasties. However, they remained strongly dependent on the Achaemenid ruler. The inscriptions of these later rulers clearly imitated some of the motifs of the former political independence of Phoenicia, though re-adapted in the context of their political dependence within a new imperial system.

2 Trade and manufacture

More than in any other region of the Near East, in Phoenicia cities were significantly more important than the countryside, as was the manufacture of products compared to agricultural production. Phoenician economy was based more on the manufacture and selling of products originally from other areas, than the resources from its own land. This activity was further aided by the favourable position of Phoenicia, located between the Near Eastern hinterland, with its ancient cultural and commercial centres (Mesopotamia, Egypt, Anatolia and Syria), and the western Mediterranean, with its mineral and agricultural resources ready to be explored and exploited.

Even before 1200 BC, the Syro-Levantine coastal cities, in particular Ugarit, were already involved in maritime trade. The latter developed alongside land trade. Some products such as purple-dyed fabrics, bronze objects and carved ivory had already become typical of the area and were exported as luxury products. Although Phoenician trade was based on previous traditions, the Iron Age brought about a series of innovations. The crisis of royal palaces caused a reorganisation of commercial activities. This reorganisation forced merchants to continue their trade without the administrative and financial support of the palace. Moreover, the overall decline of the palaces, which had constituted the main centres of commercial activity in the past, brought merchants to build their own, less official and more fragmented, 'markets'.

The breakdown of the regional system of accountability and protection certainly made trade far more dangerous and banditry far more widespread. Nonetheless, it still constituted an important opportunity for Phoenician trade. In the Late Bronze Age, both the Egyptian and Mycenaean fleets hindered Syrian navigation to the south, around the Egyptian Delta, and to the west, around Cyprus, Cilicia, or at least at the access point to the Aegean. Following the crisis of the twelfth century BC, while Egypt was in difficulty and the Mycenaeans completely disappeared from the international political scene, the Phoenician ships were finally able to sail far into the Mediterranean (Figure 24.2). They thus could take advantage of the experience accumulated and developed in the previous centuries by the Egyptians in the Red Sea, and the Mycenaeans in the Mediterranean.

The tale of Wenamun provides a good picture of the commercial activities in the eastern Mediterranean in the mid-eleventh century BC. Egypt remained loyal to the 'bureaucratic' style of trade, with a palace functionary setting off with a 'donation' to gather materials that could not be found in the region. On the contrary, the Levant had several active fleets owned by private 'firms'. These were more or less linked to, or protected by, the local authorities. Moreover, the area experienced a considerable amount of retaliations, rivalries and piracy (Phoenician pirates are well known, for instance, from the Homeric poems). The king of Byblos acted as the political authority in the city, and the Lebanese forests continued to be under his supervision. The agreement the king stipulated with the Egyptian envoy shows his preference for commercial interests. This was, however, in marked contrast with the political and theological arguments presented by Wenamun.

The picture depicted by this tale is interesting. It not only shows the presence of new elements typical of the political and commercial scene of the Iron Age, such as the city 'assembly' and the commercial 'firm', but also a certain degree of continuity with the Late Bronze Age procedures. The latter, however,

Figure 24.2   A Phoenician fleet in a relief of Sennacherib in Nineveh.

were adapted to the new developments of the time. The main issue was the ambiguous role of the king of Byblos (as the commercial partner of Wenamun, but judge in his controversy with the Zeker). Similarly, there was the problem of the ambiguous legal position of the port and the ship in terms of their place in the local jurisdiction. Moreover, this phase saw the deterioration of negotiations compared to the old gift-exchange system, now tainted by strictly financial calculations. Overall, then, the tale of Wenamun provides a relatively realistic picture, showing the rise of Phoenician trade away from the old palace trade of the Late Bronze Age.

The geographic information provided by the tale of Wenamun is limited to the Egyptian Delta, the Phoenician coast and Cyprus. However, it is probable that in its first phase (eleventh to ninth centuries BC) Phoenician trade had sailed far, taking over the old Egyptian and Mycenaean routes. Regarding southern routes, which were already Egyptian, we only possess attestations from the Bible. This is due to the fact that the Phoenician cities did not have direct access to the Red Sea. In the joint ventures of Hiram and Solomon to reach the distant Ophir region (Yemen and/or the Somalian coast), rich in gold and incense, Jerusalem contributed by allowing the crossing of its territories and the use of its port, Ezion-geber, in the Gulf of Aqaba. In turn, Tyre provided ships and its maritime and commercial expertise. This type of trade took place every three years. It required one summer to get to Ophir, and another summer to return from it. This trade was also heavily supervised by the state, and did not need intermediary ports. It therefore reached Ophir directly. The city was rich in precious materials, which were managed by a political power that was still in its earliest stages.

The timing and organisation of these expeditions to the distant region of Ophir provides us with some information on similar expeditions to the equally distant land of Tarshish. This was the name given to the western Mediterranean, namely, southern Spain (the Greek Tartessos), which was rich in metals (mainly silver and tin). The Greek tradition dates the foundation of the most ancient Phoenician colonies in the west (such as Cadiz and Utica) to slightly after the Trojan War (eleventh century BC). This dating, however, is too early for *bona fide* colonies, an institution that at that time did not even exist. However, it is plausible that the Phoenicians began their commercial contacts with the west around this time, and were probably similar to those with Ophir. Every three years and without intermediary stops, then, the Phoenicians could directly reach regions rich in minerals (such as Sardinia and southern Spain). There, they encountered states that were still in their formation stages. The Phoenicians could then seal agreements with these states to access metals in exchange for precious objects (weapons and jewellery) for the local leaders.

In the following centuries, from the ninth to the seventh centuries BC, Phoenician presence in the Mediterranean increased so much that it can be confirmed archaeologically. The main regions of interest for the Phoenicians were those rich in mineral resources, such as Sardinia, southern Spain, and, obviously, Cyprus. Cyprus remained the main provider of copper, and was located immediately to the west of Phoenicia. There were also some intermediary regions not rich in metals, such as Tunisia and Sicily, which would become the main centres of colonisation. Already in this phase, it is possible to note a certain degree of commercial rivalry between Phoenicians and Greeks. This rivalry would eventually become visible in terms of colonisation. The Greeks had a similar technical knowledge and similar interests, which resulted in a division of routes and centres. This phase also saw the emergence of increasingly more developed local states. Therefore, Phoenician trade acted as a stimulus for the rise of more complex states, which developed through several advances both in terms of settlements and technology. Consequently, some areas, and Etruria in particular, became fierce competitors for both the Greeks and the Phoenicians in terms of trade, piracy and craftsmanship (especially of metals).

Phoenician presence in the Mediterranean is particularly marked by the export of particular types of objects (Figures 24.3). Among the most valuable were bronze objects (plates, decorated paterae, tripods, cauldrons and weapons), carved ivories (combs, handles, small containers and furniture parts), embroidered or dyed fabrics (obviously lost to us), and glassware (small phials, but especially a large amount of coloured glass beads, small jewellery, Egyptianising scarabs and so on). The spread of these Phoenician products started the whole 'orientalising' fashion attested throughout the Mediterranean, and adopted by the Greeks. Decorated metal paterae, carved ivories and embroidered fabrics became important means for the diffusion of an entire iconographic repertoire. In this iconography, heroes, mythical creatures, landscapes and various filling elements formed scenes that initially had clear mythological references, but now became purely decorative and only secondarily symbolic (Figure 24.4).

In the Phoenician workshops, this iconographic repertoire had been the result of the inclusion of a vast number of Egyptian motifs alongside Syro-Levantine ones. Later on, the repertoire would also include Assyrian and Urartian motifs. Since Cypriot, western Anatolian and Aegean workshops borrowed these motifs, it has become increasingly difficult to distinguish direct or indirect contributions and influences. Consequently, it is virtually impossible to detect the place of origin of simpler objects, such as Egyptianising scarabs, and jewellery in general. In this 'orientalising' world, the Phoenicians acted as the main, but not only, protagonists in a complex network of relations and rivalries both with the Greeks and the local populations.

While 'orientalising' products spread in the Mediterranean through trade, similar products spread to the east, especially in Assyria. Between the eighth to seventh centuries BC, Assyria had decorated paterae similar to the ones found in Cyprus, Greece and Italy, and carved ivories. The latter constitutes the most conspicuous documentation of this Phoenician product. Moreover, written evidence attests the presence of embroidered or dyed fabrics, bronze cauldrons and tripods, weapons and jewellery. However, these products did not spread in the same way as in the Mediterranean. The contexts of these findings (that is, in palaces) and the written evidence recording tribute payments show that the spread of these Phoenician products to the east took place in the context of the Assyrian imperial rule, and its subsequent economic

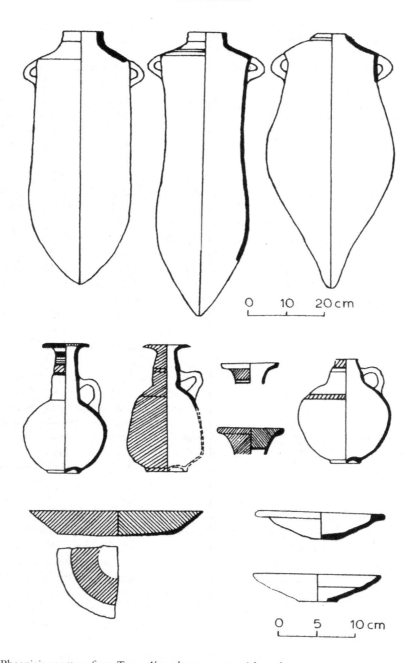

Figure 24.3   Phoenician pottery from Tyre. *Above*: large commercial amphorae.

pressure on the Phoenician states. Moreover, many craftsmen from Tyre and Sidon worked in Nimrud to build or decorate Ashurnasirpal II's new capital.

It has to be pointed out, however, that since there are still very few attestations of private activities, the sources may have overrepresented the tributary aspect of this influence. The 'imperial' interest in Phoenician goods alone implies their spread and appreciation in Assyria. Therefore, it is likely that

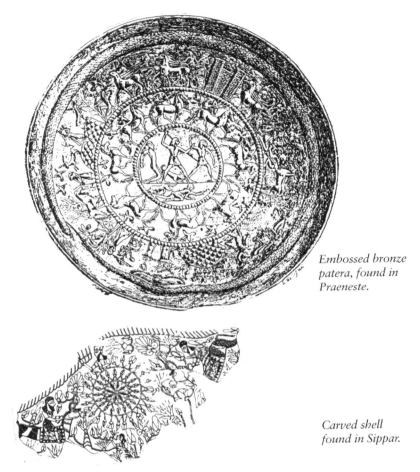

*Embossed bronze
patera, found in
Praeneste.*

*Carved shell
found in Sippar.*

Figure 24.4   Phoenician craftsmanship. *Above*: Embossed bronze patera, found in Praeneste; *Below*. Carved shell found
in Sippar.

these tributary attestations are the only surviving records of a commercial network whose unattested
side was pursued by private individuals. Nonetheless, it is also worth considering that trade tends to
adapt to the specific requirements of its recipients. In other words, it is possible that the freer type of
trade attested in the Mediterranean was counterbalanced by a more 'bureaucratic' type of trade. This
is because in the latter case the recipient was an eastern kingdom governed by an established palace
administration.

Another clue of the prestige of Phoenician craftsmanship and culture was the spread of inscriptions written in the Phoenician language in areas speaking other languages. These are the well-known inscriptions of
Kilamuwa (king of Sam'al, ninth century BC) and Azitiwadda (Karatepe, eighth century BC), and the more
recently discovered ones in Cilicia (Çineköy, near Adana, and Incirli, near Maraş, eighth century BC). The
introduction of the alphabet in Phrygia and Greece is clearly due to the prestige of the Phoenician model.
In this regard, the Greek tradition speaks of 'Cadmean letters', where Cadmos was the Semitic Qedem,
namely, the 'East'.

The prophet Ezekiel provides a picture of Tyre's commercial activities at the end of the seventh century
BC (Figure 24.5). The passage informs us on both the horizons and procedures of Phoenician trade at that

time. Regarding the former, it is possible to see four concentric zones: a more internal zone (Judah, Israel and Damascus) provided agricultural products (cereals, wine, olive oil and honey); the intermediary zone (Upper Euphrates and northern Arabia) provided animals (horses, sheep, goats, mules and wool); a third zone (Greece, Anatolia, Upper Mesopotamia, Assyria, Edom and Arabia) provided crafted objects (bronze

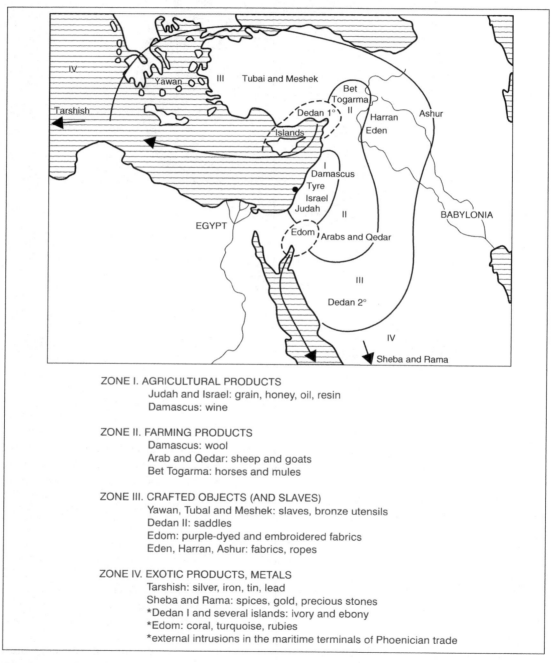

ZONE I. AGRICULTURAL PRODUCTS
Judah and Israel: grain, honey, oil, resin
Damascus: wine

ZONE II. FARMING PRODUCTS
Damascus: wool
Arab and Qedar: sheep and goats
Bet Togarma: horses and mules

ZONE III. CRAFTED OBJECTS (AND SLAVES)
Yawan, Tubal and Meshek: slaves, bronze utensils
Dedan II: saddles
Edom: purple-dyed and embroidered fabrics
Eden, Harran, Ashur: fabrics, ropes

ZONE IV. EXOTIC PRODUCTS, METALS
Tarshish: silver, iron, tin, lead
Sheba and Rama: spices, gold, precious stones
*Dedan I and several islands: ivory and ebony
*Edom: coral, turquoise, rubies
*external intrusions in the maritime terminals of Phoenician trade

Figure 24.5 The commercial network of Tyre according to Ezekiel 27, 12–24.

utensils, textiles, harnesses and iron objects) and slaves; finally, the last zone (Tarshish in the west and southern Arabia in the south) provided metals (silver, tin and gold) and exotic products (spices, precious stones, ebony and ivory).

The point of view is genuinely that of Tyre (which is placed at the centre of this world), though perhaps a bit biased by the Israelite nature of the text that has survived to us. Nonetheless, the passage balances our partial view, attested in the Classical sources, of the prevalence of maritime trade for the Phoenicians. This attestation therefore proves that the majority of their commercial activities were in fact pursued on land. Phoenician presence in the Mediterranean, then, appears to have been relatively marginal compared to the commercial network extending from Anatolia to Arabia.

An important absence is that of the Mesopotamian empires and Egypt. This perceived absence is partly due to the probable historical context of the passage, namely, the renaissance of Tyre between the collapse of the Assyrian empire and the rise of the Babylonian empire. It was also partly due to the fact that the passage emphasises the importation of materials (following the ideal of a central land acquiring products from all over the known world), rather than the markets outside of it. Apart from its ideological bias, the technical terminology used in the passage introduces the importance of a financial base and of the manufactured objects exported by Tyre. Moreover, the passage seems to allude to that 'silent trade' also described by Herodotus regarding Phoenician merchants. The manufacture of high-end products and the spread of exotic products and raw materials by the Phoenician cities peaked amid the pressures of the powerful empires in the hinterland. A large part of Phoenician commercial activities was clearly directed towards the eastern markets. However the maritime trade for which the Phoenicians are renowned undoubtedly opened up the entire Mediterranean coast to more complex interactions. In this way, the Phoenician cities became the ultimate representation of Near Eastern culture in the west.

3 The colonial expansion

When in 700 BC Sennacherib removed king Luli of Tyre from Sidon, the latter fled to Cyprus. Through an inscription of the time, we know that the city of Kition was a Phoenician colony with a governor (*skn*) under the authority of Tyre. The case of Cyprus is unique. Its proximity to the Phoenician coast (so much so as to be visible from the Lebanese mountains) meant that the island had been in close contact with the Near East from the Late Bronze Age, especially with Ugarit. Ugarit kept a group of its representatives in Cyprus, and had in its own port a group of Cypriot and Mycenaean merchants. In the Early Iron Age, Phoenician presence in Cyprus, attested through pottery remains and inscriptions, significantly increased. This increase first happened around the coast, but then mainly in the south-east, around Kition. The rest of the island saw the settlement of the Greeks, while the hinterland saw the rise of local independent states. The former unity of this island (namely, Late Bronze Age Alashiya), then, began to be broken down into a network of city-states of different origins and speaking different languages. Among these city-states, the Phoenician element became one of the prevailing ones.

In the tenth and ninth centuries BC, Cyprus was the only place in which the Phoenicians had already established some settlements. In the rest of the Mediterranean, they did not yet have fixed colonies. This indicates that there were no waves of migrations in this phase. However, the situation changed in the eighth century BC, with the appearance of Phoenician 'colonies' in several areas of the Mediterranean. These colonies are partly attested in Greek sources, which sometimes provide us with a foundation date, and partly attested archaeologically. The quantity and typology of the archaeological remains indicate a fixed presence of Phoenician groups. Phoenician colonisation is a phenomenon that developed, both chronologically and in terms of procedures, alongside Greek colonisation. The latter also took place after a previous pre-colonial phase of trade and navigation to specific areas of the Mediterranean. Moreover, in some areas, the Phoenicians had preceded the Greeks, and vice versa. Be that as it may, the two developed around the same time, leading to a *bona fide* division of the coasts and other influential areas throughout the Central and western Mediterranean.

It is clear that this phenomenon was an innovation in the way trade was pursued in the Mediterranean. It would be anachronistic to date colonisation to an earlier phase in which trade was more flexible. Similarly, it is equally clear that at a certain point it became impossible to maintain the old system without adapting it to the developments of the time. Generally speaking, the causes for these changes were probably linked to the context of the colonisers' homeland, that of the lands colonised, and the types of resources sought after. In the early first millennium BC, the political organisation of the local populations living in the western Mediterranean significantly improved. This development led to their increasingly important role in both production and trade. Between the eleventh and ninth centuries BC, Phoenician merchants monopolised the means required for commercial activities (from ships to commercial expertise) and benefited from a marked divide in the value of goods. In the eighth century BC, however, the rising local kingdoms became far more active participants, making a seasonal trade of few ships insufficient. From a purely economic, political and military perspective, these changes also led to the necessity of a far stronger presence in the area. Regarding the materials required by the merchants from the east, the rise of colonies marked the shift from a phase mainly concerned with the acquisition of metals, to one that appreciated agro-pastoral products as well as the availability of abundant land and workforce. The latter were still underused compared to the Phoenician coasts.

Admittedly, colonisation could have been a phenomenon promoted by the colonisers' homeland. This initiative, then, could have been aimed at convincing the latter to leave their lands and venture in riskier, but more promising, endeavours. Unlike Phoenicia, we possess better attestations on the potential internal causes of colonisation from Greece. In this case, colonisation was linked to internal political conflicts and the emergence of new social classes unable to find an adequate place in their homeland. The legend of the foundation of Carthage (Tunisia), according to which the city was founded by a number of political figures who had escaped some internal conflicts in Tyre, is attested in the Greek (and then Roman) tradition. It is probable, however, that it mixed up the causes for Phoenician colonisation with those of Greece.

The little evidence we have on relations between Tyre and Carthage (*qrt-ḥdšt*, literally, 'new city') indicates that, just like for the Greeks, a colony was not an autonomous political entity. It was dependent on its homeland. We know that Carthage continued to send a yearly tribute to Tyre centuries later. This indicates that the city was taxed just like the other cities of the kingdom of Tyre. Moreover, Carthage did not have a 'king' like the Phoenician cities, but was ruled by 'judges' (*šptm*, or *sufetes* in Latin). Its government was therefore similar to the other subordinate centres and Tyre itself in those few years in which its legitimate king was captive in Babylonia. The distance from the homeland undoubtedly made colonies virtually autonomous. However, this political dependence implies an official foundation of these colonies, rather than one pursued by rebellious groups seeking freedom and independence from Phoenicia.

Some scholars have suggested that the establishment of colonies could have been due to the increasing Assyrian pressure on the Phoenician cities, although this is a rather late explanation of the beginnings of Phoenician colonisation. After all, up until the time of Esarhaddon, Tyre (the main protagonist of this colonising process) does not seem to have suffered excessive pressures from the Assyrians. Moreover, later on, relations between the Phoenician cities and the Mesopotamian empires allowed the maintenance of a certain degree of political and economic autonomy. The latter allowed the maintenance of those processes that benefited the empires themselves, but that could not take place through direct imperial control. Just as in the case of the Greeks in Asia Minor escaping the Persians, the few groups of refugees escaping imperial pressure could only have moved to already colonised areas. Overall, then, internal socio-economic problems and external imperial pressures do not seem enough to justify Phoenician colonisation. It is most likely, then, that the latter developed in order to adapt to the developments taking place in the Mediterranean.

Colonisation led to a clear division of the Mediterranean between the Greeks and the Phoenicians. The Phoenician colonies 'skipped' the Central Mediterranean, both in the north (in the Aegean and Ionian Sea) and in the south (Cyrenaica). As modern scholars have pointed out, this distribution of colonies indicates that there was no technical need for colonies to be so close to each other as to require just one day to reach them by sea. Therefore, Phoenician colonies were mainly concentrated in western Sicily (Motya, Panormos, Soluntus), Malta, Pantelleria, Tunisia (Carthage and Utica), Sardinia (Nora and Tharros among others), the Balearic Islands, and southern Spain (Cadiz and others). It was a compact network, concentrated on the central archipelagos and on peninsulas (without moving further inland). It also combined areas rich in minerals (Sardinia and Spain) with densely populated areas and strategic points for the control of maritime routes.

The prompt separation of the colonies from Phoenicia led one of them, Carthage, to take on a hegemonic role. In turn, Carthage became the starting point of another wave of colonisation focused on the African coast (Tripolitania, Algeria and Morocco) and on already Phoenician areas, such as Spain and Sardinia. The history of the Phoenician colonies and of Carthage is outside the scope of the present volume both in terms of its geographic and chronological delimitations. The rise of the Carthaginian empire and its clash with the Romans is well known. For now, it is only important to note that through these colonial outposts the Phoenicians managed to continue their exploration of distant lands in a constant search for new routes and materials. Around 600 BC, the Near Eastern Phoenicians even prolonged the Red Sea route by circumnavigating Africa on behalf of the Egyptian king, Necho. In turn, the Carthaginians passed the Pillars of Hercules, reaching England in the north (Himilco, ca. 450 BC) and the Gulf of Guinea in the south (Hanno, ca. 425 BC).

4 The ports and the empires

Looking at a map of the Assyrian empire at the peak of its expansion, it is surprising how the minuscule territories of Arwad (a small island), Byblos (with its small territory in the hinterland) and Tyre (again an island) managed to remain autonomous. It is clear that a mainland empire struggled in sieging coastal cities and conquering maritime states. This difficulty would also be encountered by the Persian empire with the Greek cities. It is likely that the Assyrian empire deliberately desisted from subduing the few surviving Phoenician cities. After all, if the Assyrians had been willing to conquer them, they would have succeeded. The type of dependence deemed sufficient for the Assyrians is attested in the treaty between Esarhaddon and Baal, king of Tyre (Text 24.1).

Text 24.1   A treaty between Esarhaddon, king of Assyria, and Baal, king of Tyre (between 675 and 671 BC)

Column I: only the beginning has partially survived:

'Treaty of Esarhaddon, king of Assyria, eldest son of Sennacherib, king of Assyria, with Baal, king of Tyre . . . eldest son of . . .'

Column II: unreadable.

Column III: § 1 unreadable.

§ 2 '. . . The royal deputy whom I have appointed over you . . ., the elders of your country, . . . the royal deputy with them . . . do not listen to the words of his mouth without the royal deputy; nor must you open a letter which I send you without (the presence of) the royal deputy; if the royal deputy is absent, wait for him and then open it, but do not . . .'

---

§ 3 'If a ship of Baal or of the people of Tyre is shipwrecked off (the coast of) the land of the Philistines or anywhere on the borders of the Assyrian territory: everything that is on the ship belongs to Esarhaddon, king of Assyria, but one must not do any harm to any person on board of the ship, and their names . . .'

§ 4 'These are the ports of trade and the trade roads which Esarhaddon, king of Assyria, granted to his servant Baal: toward Akko, Dor, in the district of the Philistines, anywhere; in all the cities within the Assyrian territory, on the seacoast; in Byblos of Lebanon, all the cities in the mountains, anywhere. All the cities of Esarhaddon, king of Assyria, Baal and the people of Tyre, the people of Esarhaddon, king of Assyria, can go to (?). In their ships or in any city of Esarhaddon they go to, his cities, his towns, his wharves, which to the land [. . .], in any of the outlying regions, as in the past [. . .] they should be received peacefully. Any working group . . . nobody should harm their ships. Inland, in his district, in his manors . . . just like in the past in the land of Sidon . . .'

Column IV: invocations to the gods, both Assyrian and Phoenician (Baal Shamim, Baal Malagē, and Baal Saphon).

According to this treaty, Tyre was recognised as autonomous, and both Phoenician and Assyrian deities were called upon to guarantee the validity of the oath. The treaty deals with the regulation of Tyre's commercial activities, such as the Assyrian ports the city was allowed to use, the foreign states it could visit, and the procedures allowed by the treaty between Assyria and Tyre. The Assyrian interest in controlling the political scene of Tyre is clear, since the local king had to rule alongside an Assyrian functionary. Moreover, Assyria clearly wanted to minimise Phoenician trade with the Egyptians and the Philistines. This was a clear attempt to concentrate the majority of goods in Assyria. Control over the income of Phoenician trade was therefore more important than control over the small Phoenician territory. An annexation, with all the destruction that came with it, ran the risk of ruining a mechanism that had to be maintained and exploited. Therefore, Assyria followed the standard policy implemented by an empire towards commercial ports. It consequently left them with enough autonomy to allow the continuation of commercial activities. This decision ultimately benefited the empire itself, guaranteeing provisions and products that were otherwise inaccessible.

A couple of Neo-Assyrian letters show how these measures were applied in practice and how they could cause problems. In the Phoenician cities, Assyria could access valuable craftsmen for the decoration of its new capital, and capable seamen for the navigation of the Persian Gulf (against Elam). Moreover, the Assyrians could benefit from merchants able to bring western products, and financial entrepreneurs able to provide food supplies to Assyria. Overall, then, the empire tolerated the autonomy of the Phoenician cities, and saw the arrival of Phoenician financial and commercial activities in the heart of its own territory positively. The Babylonian empire followed the same policy. Despite having conquered Tyre, Nebuchadnezzar left its local dynasty in place. The importance of Phoenician trade for the Babylonian empire is attested in some sources on the importation of metals from the west. It is also symbolised by the presence of a certain Hanunu, whose name was Phoenician, as head of merchants.

When the Babylonian empire was replaced by the Persian empire, this attitude towards the Phoenicians was maintained and even improved. Therefore, the Achaemenid rulers allowed the Phoenician cities to have a certain degree of local autonomy. Sidon had once again a dynasty of its own, alongside those of Tyre, Byblos and Arwad. Having been part of the imperial system for a long time, Sidon even became the capital of Phoenicia, namely, a privileged seat of imperial presence in the land. The Achaemenid improvements in the Phoenician cities were focused on a couple of them, chosen as main centres of development. In Cyprus, the kings of Kition received new cities and managed to gain control over the entire Phoenician side of the island. In the mainland, Tyre and Sidon received various localities in the Syrian and southern Levantine coast, and the same happened to Arwad and Byblos.

The buildings excavated for the Achaemenid phase at Sidon, Byblos and Arwad reveal a significant rise in building activities. These activities were partly in response to commercial developments (fortifications and ports), and partly ceremonial (the sanctuaries of 'Amrit at Arwad, and Bustan esh-Sheih at Sidon). Judging from these monumental and public remains, while the rest of the region struggled to recover from the crisis of the eighth and seventh centuries BC, the coastal cities experienced a period of considerable flowering. The Achaemenid empire also counted on the Phoenician fleet in both its military endeavours, such as the wars against the Greek cities and the difficult control over Cyprus and Egypt, as well as its commercial enterprises.

We have crossed the chronological boundaries of this book in order to show how the policies applied by the Assyrians continued to be implemented in the Achaemenid period. Although forms and procedures changed over time, the Phoenician cities continued to maintain their intermediary role between the Near Eastern empires and the Mediterranean world. This role naturally developed and took on different forms according to the needs of the time: from the navigation of individual ships to the foundation of colonies; from the importation of metals to financial intermediation and so on. In order to better fulfil this role, the Phoenicians developed or adopted new instruments (such as coinage), which led to their fame and characterisation as merchants (or, at times, pirates) in the Mediterranean, a stereotype that constantly vacillated between admiration and denigration.

25

THE ARAMEANS IN SYRIA AND MESOPOTAMIA

1 From tribe to state

In the past, the relatively sudden appearance of the Arameans after the crisis of the twelfth century BC led scholars to look for their beginnings in the second or even the third millennium BC. These allegedly early beginnings, however, were later on discredited and the Arameans are now believed to have been a new presence in the Near Eastern scene of the Iron Age. Admittedly, there have been several misconceptions even regarding their sudden appearance. These misconceptions led to the assumption that the Arameans were part of the migrations of Semitic populations taking place at the end of the Late Bronze Age. Moreover, the Arameans have often been compared to the Amorites, who appeared a millennium earlier, and the Arabs, who would appear a millennium later. From this point of view, these three populations were envisioned in opposition to the sedentary Canaanites and connected to each other in a typological and linguistic continuity within a large-scale pattern of migrations from deserts to fertile areas.

As has already been seen for Palestine, in reality the contraposition between new populations and the Canaanites is more social than based on their 'arrival date'. The Arameans were the offspring of those pastoral groups already inhabiting the region and interacting with the sedentary groups living there. During their expansion following the crisis of the twelfth century BC, they began to integrate with the people already living in the region. This process led to a certain degree of assimilation, although this assimilation happened more with the Canaanites, who spoke a similar language, rather than the Neo-Hittites, Hurrians, Assyrians and Babylonians, who had very different cultures and languages.

From a linguistic point of view, there was a continuity of personal names between Canaanites and Arameans, a continuity that had nothing to do with the significant influence on personal names brought by the Amorites a millennium earlier. Moreover, the linguistic differences existing between Aramaic and Canaanite do not indicate the arrival of new groups, but rather a process of progressive differentiation between the two. These differences were either conservative traits typical of a pastoral environment (which was more conservative than the urban one), such as the retaining of interdentals and the long *a* (rather than changing it into an *o* like in Phoenician and Hebrew); or the result of different developments from the same linguistic family, such as in the case of the use of a postpositive rather than the Phoenician and Hebrew prepositive article.

Therefore, the Arameans were the descendants of those tribes known as the Sutians in Syria and the Ahlamu in Upper Mesopotamia, which pursued semi-nomadic pastoral activities (alongside occasional raids) in the Late Bronze Age. The earliest Assyrian sources (eleventh century BC) mentioning the 'Ahlamu of the land of Armaya' clearly show the transition from the old to the new reality. Moreover, there are Assyrian sources (Tiglath-Pileser I) claiming that the Assyrians sent the Arameans away to the other side of the Euphrates for 28 times in 14 years. This clearly shows the unstoppable movement of the Arameans against which the imperial armies were ultimately powerless. In fact, they could defeat them in battle, but could not stop this pervasive wave of infiltration.

Due to the impact of the crisis and reformation at the end of the twelfth century BC, there were profound differences between the Sutians and Ahlamu of the fourteenth and thirteenth centuries BC and the Arameans of the eleventh and tenth centuries BC. In terms of demography and settlements, the areas that were not particularly suitable for irrigation (such as semi-arid plateaus, hills and mountains) that declined in the Late Bronze Age suddenly became the preferred areas for Iron Age settlements. Sedentarisation, then, led to a significant change in the areas formerly used as pastureland in the Late Bronze Age and to an increase of settlements in the highlands and the hinterland. On a political level, the local power vacuum created by the crisis of the palaces, and the wider vacuum brought about by the fall of regional powers provided the Arameans with unprecedented opportunities and freedom of action. The changes in agricultural settlements and the new interest of nomadic groups in commercial activities allowed tribes to develop and gain an unprecedented importance. Therefore, having ceased to be marginal groups acting against the economic system of the Bronze Age, in the Iron Age tribes (not just pastoral groups) acquired a new role and considerable wealth. Moreover, the new commercial routes placed the Aramean city-states in Syria at the heart of the Near Eastern commercial network.

Among the Aramean city-states there were: Bet Rehob, Ma'akah and Geshur in the Upper Jordan; Damascus; Zobah in the Beqa Valley; Hama in the Orontes Valley; Bit Agushi and its capital Arpad in the Aleppo area; Bit Adini and its capital Til Barsip (Tell Ahmar) on the Euphrates; and Ya'udi and its capital Sam'al (Zincirli) in the Taurus foothills. In Upper Mesopotamia the situation was similar, with Bit Bahyani and its capital Guzana (Tell Halaf), Nasibina and other states in the Khabur Triangle and Bit Zamani in the Upper Tigris (Figure 25.1).

Meanwhile, the situation in Lower Mesopotamia was very different. This was due to the marked contrast between the desert and the alluvial plain, and the strong political unity and level of urbanisation of the area. The Aramean tribes thus remained marginalised and had minimal access to cultivated areas, leading to a slow and partial sedentarisation. Instead of becoming states centred on cities, the tribes continued to exist. There were: Laqe in the Middle Euphrates, Hatallu in the Wadi Tharthar, Utuate in the Middle Tigris, Puqudu, Gambulu and other groups to the east of the Lower Tigris. As we will see, the rise of the Chaldeans in Lower Mesopotamia was different in terms of their origins (in that they came from the south), their later arrival in Mesopotamia, their more flourishing economy with several commercial traits and their gravitation towards the old Babylonian cities.

In the Canaanite areas, the Aramean element constituted a local development, characterised by continuity in terms of language and personal names. This continuity facilitated the assimilation of the old nomadic groups and the old agricultural communities into homogeneous national entities. The situation was very different in areas where the Aramean element had to assimilate with completely different cultures. This was the case of the Neo-Hittites of northern Syria, the Hurrians in the Khabur and Upper Tigris, the Assyrians in the Middle Euphrates and Middle Tigris and the Babylonians in Lower Mesopotamia. In these cases, we see a juxtaposition of Aramean and local elements. For instance, Syrian states such as Hama or Sam'al used Aramaic and Neo-Hittite in their texts and personal names, whilst in Lower Mesopotamia, there is a visible distinction between Chaldeans and Babylonians. This distinction, however, does not mean that the urban population marginalised these nomadic groups, but that the new tribal element constituted a political and military elite supported by an unchanged local economy.

On an ideological and institutional level, the kinship model became the core aspect of the territorial state, making blood relations and descendancy (expressed through linguistic and religious affinities) important criteria for social identity. In this regard, the formulas 'house (*bīt/bēt*) of *X*' and 'sons of *X*', used to

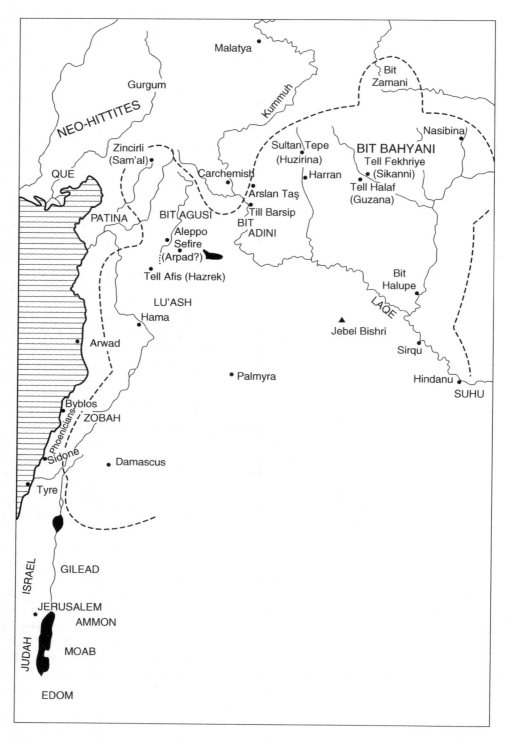

Figure 25.1   The Arameans in Syria and Upper Mesopotamia, ca. 900–700 BC.

designate a state and its members, are a clear expression of this phenomenon. The division between a tribal elite and the groups responsible for production is also expressed in the inscriptions from Sam'al. The latter make a clear distinction between the 'fierce/wild' (*b'rrm*), namely, the nobility of nomadic origins and the farmers (*mškbm*). Similarly, the inscriptions from Sefire distinguish in more general terms the 'population' ('*m*) from the 'lords' (*b'lm*). Therefore, the members of the leading family in the city, made of former tribal leaders, ruled this composite entity. The king thus ruled alongside the leaders of the tribal clans he came from. These leaders maintained a certain degree of (mainly kin-based) authority. For this reason, we find the king of Arpad, Matti-El, ruling alongside the 'kings of Arpad' and the king of Zobah, Hadad-ezer, with his servants, the 'kings of Zobah'.

This new type of government followed the procedures characteristic of city-states. On an ideological level, however, it still maintained its kin-based tribal aspects, which had been characteristic of the Amorite phase and were later abandoned in the Late Bronze Age. The king was seen as both mother and father of his people and his main requirements were a sense of justice, wisdom and kindness. Moreover, the king became the proclaimer of utopic social changes, such as 'whoever never saw the face of a sheep, I made him owner of a flock'. The Late Bronze Age gap between rulers and subjects was now in part solved. After all, the reaction to this issue constituted one of the main factors allowing the rise of this new social and political order. Propagandistic expressions therefore marked the renewed attention of the king towards the interests of his subjects. The role of the king was, however, balanced by the role of his subjects, who, through their kin-based hierarchy, were responsible for the selection of the king and the administration of power.

2 The history and culture of the western Aramean states

Our knowledge of the historical developments of the Aramean states is not homogeneous. It is partly based on inscriptions left by the local kings and partly on external sources, such as the Old Testament for the southernmost states, and Assyrian inscriptions for the northern ones. For the earliest phases of their history (eleventh–tenth century BC), however, we do not possess local inscriptions. This is because, at that time, these states were still in their formative phase and had not yet developed those administrative and celebrative forms necessary to leave monumental marks. Similarly, we lack attestations in the Assyrian sources, due to the fact that Assyria had to keep a hold of its territories against the spread of Aramean groups.

We possess more evidence on the southern Aramean states, mainly regarding their conflicts against Israel. The important role of Zobah (in the Beqa Valley) at the time of Saul and David seems a reliable memory, also because it had no other purpose for the later editors of the Bible. Zobah lacked urban settlements and was articulated into a network of 'kings', who recognised the authority of Hadad-ezer. Following David's victory, Zobah was broken down, allowing the rise of Damascus, a far more solid state. The city rose in the middle of a vast oasis watered by the rivers flowing down from the Anti-Lebanon Mountains. It was more productive in terms of agriculture and more compact in terms of settlements than the other Aramean centres. Moreover, from a commercial point of view, Damascus' location to the east made it a privileged commercial junction in the caravan route departing from southern Arabia. This route passed through the states in the Transjordan plateau and, once in Damascus, was divided into various routes moving to the west, towards the Mediterranean Sea, or the north, towards the Orontes Valley and northern Syria, or the north-east, crossing Palmyra to reach the Middle Euphrates and then Babylonia.

The commercial importance of Damascus is evident in the Bible, according to which David tried to take advantage of his victories by establishing a garrison and a commercial centre in Damascus. However, Rezon, a general of Hadad-ezer, managed to establish his authority in the area and began a dynasty that held control over the whole of northern Syria. In the Bible, the rulers of Damascus are all called Ben-Hadad (Hadad was the chief deity of Damascus), making it extremely difficult to distinguish between them. One Bar-Hadad I (which is the Aramaic form of Ben-Hadad, the Jewish version attested in the Bible) is attested on a stele found near Aleppo and dedicated to the god Melqart (surprisingly, a deity of Tyre).

He must have been the same individual who sealed an alliance with Asa of Judah and devastated Israel. A Bar-Hadad II established a sort of supremacy in Israel at the time of Omri, but was defeated by Ahab, who managed to turn the situation around. The aim of these so-called 'Syro-Ephraimite' wars was to gain control over the area of Gilead. The latter was the only Israelite point along the caravan route crossing the Transjordan plateau. Therefore, Israel was trying to become one of the states benefiting from this trade. At the same time, Damascus was trying to expand its commercial presence in the south, removing all rivals. It is highly significant that the kingdom able to momentarily succeed always established commercial junctions in the defeated states. Therefore, Damascus established commercial bases in Samaria, while Israel established commercial bases in Damascus.

These local conflicts did not change the overall organisation of the area. Meanwhile, Assyria was still unable to intervene. Assyrian intervention only took place after the mid-ninth century BC with Shalmaneser III, who forced local disputes to a temporary halt. Consequently, old enemies such as Damascus and Samaria suddenly found themselves allied against a common enemy. Before Shalmaneser, northern Syria must have experienced a similar situation. Shalmaneser's predecessor, Ashurnasirpal II, only reached the Mediterranean in one campaign. It was a relatively peaceful incursion, aimed at the establishment of a commercial colony in the Middle Orontes and of establishing relations with the cities along the coast.

On the contrary, the situation of the Aramean states east of the Euphrates was very different. These states had suffered from the pressure of the Assyrian expansion, aimed at controlling the entire Mesopotamian territory, well before the mid-ninth century BC. Therefore, the former alternation between Assyrian and Aramean settlements was gradually transformed into a more homogeneous territory forced to pay tributes to the Assyrians. The expeditions of Tukulti-Ninurta II, Adad-nirari II and Ashurnasirpal II in the Khabur Valley, the Middle Euphrates and the foothills of the Tur Abdin, led to the conquest of all the small Aramean states which had developed in those areas in the previous two centuries.

The Assyrian conquest lasted for a long time and the results were relatively ambiguous. A clear example of this situation is the bilingual inscription in Aramaic and Assyrian found at Tell Fekheriye. The author of the inscription, who defines himself as 'king' (*mlk*) of Sikannu and Guzana (Tell Fekheriye and Tell Halaf respectively) in the Aramaic version, defines himself as 'governor' (*šaknu*) in the Assyrian version. There are several aspects worth noting: the bilingualism of the inscription; the Aramaic name of the king (Hadad-yis'i) in contrast with the Assyrian one of his father (Shamash-nuri); the Assyrianising nature of the statue in contrast with its local style; and the Assyrian style of the first part of the inscription compared to the Aramaic one of the second part. All these aspects show the politically and culturally ambiguous position of the Aramean states, stuck between being Aramean states conquered by the Assyrian expansion and Assyrian provincial states of intrinsic Aramean tradition.

The inscription from Tell Fekheriye can be dated to the mid-ninth century BC, shortly before the military endeavours of Shalmaneser III west of the Euphrates. This expedition was an attempt to extend to Syria those tributary relations established in Upper Mesopotamia. The state most affected by this expansion was Bit Adini. Its strategic location allowed the crossing of the Euphrates, making Bit Adini one of the main targets of Shalmaneser's expeditions. Having gained free access to the Euphrates crossing, Shalmaneser made his way to the Aramean states in the centre and the south of Syria. All these states tried to oppose him. The most famous conflict of this phase is the battle of Qarqar, which took place near the colony founded by Ashurnasirpal a few years earlier. The following years saw an increasing sequence of battles, which are described as victorious by the Assyrian ruler. Judging, however, from the sheer fact that there was a sequence of conflicts, it is clear that the battles were not enough to establish absolute Assyrian control in the area. The anti-Assyrian coalition, which included Israel and the Phoenician cities, was centred on the two main Aramean states in Syria, namely, Damascus, ruled by Hadad-ezer, and Hama, ruled by Irhuleni (also attested in some inscriptions in Luwian hieroglyphs). They were, respectively, the hegemonic centres of southern and central Syria.

After the death of Shalmaneser, the Assyrians retreated, the local states resumed their local conflicts and the major centres attempted once again to gain a hegemonic position in the area. In the south, under the leadership of Hadad-ezer and especially Haza-El, Damascus reached a visible supremacy, with Israel, Judah and even the Philistine states recognising its authority, while northern Jordan was directly annexed. In central Syria, Hama was aspiring to a similar role and gained control over the entire region of Lu'ash (the Nuhashe of the second millennium BC) and the city of Hazrek (Tell Afis). A stele of Zakir, king of Hama, celebrates his successful survival after the siege of Hazrek by a coalition between the king of Damascus, Bar-Hadad III, and all the Syro-Anatolian rulers (Bit Agushi, Que, Amuq, Gurgum, Sam'al and Malatya) who united to put an end to the rise of a new power in the area, or maybe to punish the pro-Assyrian policy of Hama at the time of Shalmaneser III.

In northern Syria, the main centre was Bit Agushi (Aleppo). We are, however, much more informed about a small marginal state, located in the valley linking the Amuq with eastern Anatolia. This was the kingdom of Sam'al (Zincirli). The inscription of king Kilamuwa indicates that the situation was unstable both internally, with social conflicts and economic instability and externally, with the request of Assyrian intervention against the neighbouring Danunim. The names of the kings of Sam'al are partly Anatolian (such as Kilamuwa) and partly Semitic (Kilamuwa's father Haya' or the founder of the dynasty Gabbar). Moreover, the inscription was written in Phoenician, another indication of how in this marginal corner of its diffusion the Aramean element was struggling to find a cultural and political identity.

With the beginning of the eighth century BC, the local conflicts had to decrease due to the impact of more dangerous struggles. Syria found itself at the centre of the aggressive ambitions of Urartu, with its south-western expansion, and Assyria, which was going through a period of reorganisation. The way in which these new hegemonic relations were organised has partly survived. In fact, we have two treaties. The first one, written in Assyrian, was sealed between Ashur-nirari V and the king of Arpad (Bit Agushi) Matti-El. The second one is in Aramaic and was sealed between the same Matti-El and a certain Bar-Ga'yah, king of Katka. The Assyrian treaty is a straightforward expression of the situation at the time: the constant Assyrian incursions in Syria forced Bit Agushi to become a tributary state, although the growing concern surrounding the rise of Urartu led Assyria to turn a verbal agreement into a written treaty, aimed at guaranteeing the loyalty of the key-state of Aleppo.

There are several interpretations of the Aramaic treaty. This is due to the intrinsic problems surrounding the identity of Bar-Ga'yah (which means literally, 'son of majesty', and is a title rather than a personal name) and in identifying the unknown state of Katka with an important state of the time. It is clear that in this treaty Bar-Ga'yah was in a dominant position. The most likely hypothesis is that it was Assyria, represented by the powerful *turtanu* Shamshi-Ilu, who ruled the western provinces of the empire and was facing the Urartian expansion between 805 and 750 BC. Another Aramaic inscription, similar to the one of Sefire, has been found in Bukan (Mannea) and is probably another piece of evidence attesting to Shamshi-Ilu's interventions against Urartu.

At the time of Tiglath-pileser III's enthronement, the system of alliances was in favour of Urartu. Its king, Sarduri, was in an alliance with Matti-El of Arpad and all the Neo-Hittite states of eastern Anatolia and Syria. The decisive victory of Tiglath-pileser in 743 BC, however, completely turned the situation around, cutting Urartu off the west. In this way, the Assyrians established their control in Syria and put an end to its independence. Aleppo was besieged, conquered and turned into an Assyrian province. The states still able to remain independent, including Damascus, were forced to pay tributes.

The condition of those states that were still autonomous is exemplified by the case of Sam'al. Its last local kings, Panamuwa and Bar-Rakib, managed to keep the royal title, but were in fact completely overshadowed by the authority of the Assyrian king (Figure 25.2). They owed him the 'independence' of their kingdom. They were therefore linked to the Assyrian ruler through ties of loyalty and gratitude, and provided him with military support and tributes. These were destined to be the last autonomous endeavours of the western Aramean states The Assyrians continued to relentlessly annex these states to

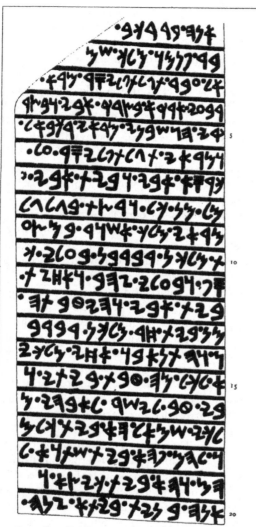

1 'nh.brrkb.
2 br.pnmw.mlk.šm
3 'l.'bd.tgltplysr.mr'.
4 rb'y.'rq'.bṣdq.'by.wbṣd
5 qy.hwšbny.mr'y.rkb'l.
6 wmr'y.tgltplysr.'l.
7 krs'.'by.wbyt.'by.'
8 ml.mn.kl.wrṣt.bglgl.
9 mr'y.mlk.'šwr.bmṣ
10 t.mlkn.rbrbn.b'ly.k
11 sp.wb'ly.zhb.w'hzt.
12 byt.'by.whyṭbth.
13 mn.byt.hd.mlkn.rbrb
14 n.whtn'bw.'hy.mlky
15 '.lkl.mh.tbt.byty.w
16 by.tb.lyšh.l'bhy.m
17 lky.šm'l.h'.byt.klm
18 w.lhm.ph'.byt.štw'.l
19 hm.wh'.byt.kyṣ'.w
20 'nh.bnyt.byt'.znh.

"I am Bar-Rakib, son of Panamuwa, king of Sam'al, servant of Tiglath-pileser, king of the four quarters of the world. Through the loyalty of my father and my own loyalty, my (divine) lord Rabik-El and my (earthly) lord Tiglath-pileser caused me to reign on the throne of my father. The house of my father profited more than any other, and I ran at the wheel of my lord, the king of Assyria, in the midst of mighty kings, possessors of silver and possessors of gold. I took over the house of my father and I made it better than the house of any other mighty king, and my brothers, the kings, were desirous of all that is the beauty of my house. My fathers, the kings of Sam'al, did not have a beautiful house: they had the house of Kilamuwa, which was their winter house and their summer house. Instead, I have built this house."

Figure 25.2 Aramaic royal inscription: the inscription of Bar-Rakib, king of Sam'al, vassal of Tiglath-pileser III of Assyria.

their territories, taking advantage of any vacillation from their vassals. Tiglath-pileser III thus annexed Arpad in 740 BC, Hazrek (the northern region of the kingdom of Hama) in 738 BC and Damascus in 732 BC. Sargon II completed the process with the annexation of Hama and possibly Zobah in 720 BC. Consequently, in about twenty years, all the Aramean states were conquered and turned into Assyrian provinces.

The culture of the Aramean states is not well attested. The main Aramean centre, Damascus, has not been excavated for this period. In the case of Aleppo, the discovery of a temple in its citadel shows more of the Hittite legacy of this city than the Aramean contributions. A better idea of the Aramean cities in the region can be gained from relatively important centres, such as Hama and Sam'al. The acropolis of Hama had a monumental complex constructed shortly before the Assyrian conquest of the city. It was built over a settlement that had existed for around a millennium, thus maintaining its basic plan. In comparison, the citadel of Sam'al was planned and built *ex novo*. The external city walls formed a circle at the centre of which was the citadel, protected by a defensive wall, with more walls protecting each part of the citadel. Moreover, the citadel had the porticoed palaces (*bīt hilāni*) considered by the Assyrians to be a typical north Syrian type of building. Both Zincirli and Tell Halaf (Guzana) had a regular city plan, a similar division between outer and inner city (i.e. the citadel) and the same style of palace architecture (Figures 25.3 and 25.4). While the western city of Zincirli preferred a circular plan, however, the more eastern Tell Halaf preferred a square plan. This was a clear mark of Assyrian influence, which had a long history and a strong influence on the settlement east of the Euphrates.

At its height, Aramean culture in Syria developed as a response to the Assyrian empire, against which it was politically opposed, even though it was still heavily influenced by the Assyrian presence. Nonetheless, local features prevail and can be found throughout Aramean culture: from architecture to urban planning; ivory production; and even in terms of the characteristics and language used in royal inscriptions. There were, however, two trends closely linked to the hegemonic role of Assyria in the area. On the one hand, Assyria had a fascination for western culture and made sure to take advantage of it. Initially, Assyria expressed this fascination in a non-destructive way: from the imitation of the *bīt hilāni* to the acquisition of techniques and luxury goods such as ivories, bronze ware and embroidered fabrics. However, the Assyrians soon began to directly interfere with the Aramean states, which led to the depletion of local resources and an overall cultural decline in the area. On the other hand, there is also a strong 'Assyrianising' tendency attested amongst the last Aramean states. These acted as imperial outposts and partly tried to tailor the production of luxury goods to the needs of the prevailing Assyrian market. It is therefore highly significant that the peak of Aramean culture in Syria can be dated to the eve of its destruction at the hands of the Assyrians, as if the empire had initially stimulated, then abused and destroyed, its western territories.

3 The eastern tribes

East of the Euphrates, in the Assyrian territories and Lower Mesopotamia, the Arameans found a different situation both in terms of resources and culture. This situation led to a much more marked separation from the Akkadian-speaking population. Therefore, the Arameans managed to maintain their tribal structure and to remain separate from the powerful centres of the area for a longer period of time. As an extraneous presence in Mesopotamia, the Arameans spread from the north-west to the south-east. They thus followed a path similar to that of the Amorites a millennium earlier. This similarity was due to the location of pasturelands and transhumant areas along the so-called 'dimorphic zone', a low rainfall area which was relatively large in Syria, and was located between deserts and cultivated areas. In Mesopotamia, however, this area was reduced to a sort of corridor between the Tigris and the Zagros.

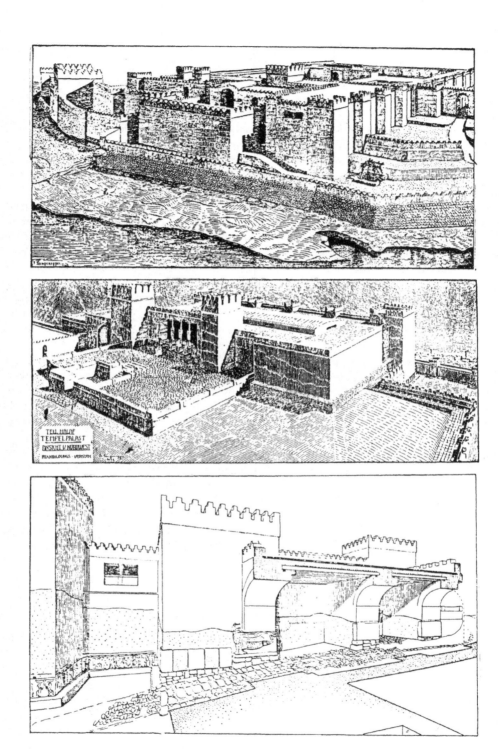

Figure 25.3 The Aramean centre of Guzana (Tell Halaf). *Above*: Reconstruction of its fortification walls; *Centre*: Reconstruction of the temple-palace; *Below*: Cross-section of the citadel gate.

Figure 25.4   The citadel of Zincirli (Sam'al) in the eighth century BC, and the entrance gate with sculpted orthostats.

Around 1100 BC, the inscriptions of Tiglath-pileser I record the presence of Arameans throughout the Middle Euphrates, from Bit Adini, Laqe and Suhu to Rapiqum, near the northern border of Babylonia. These attestations mainly mark the Aramean presence close to Assyria. The heart of the Aramean presence was still located further west, in the Syrian desert (Palmyra and Jebel Bishri). From there, the Aramean tribes frequently led dangerous incursions (especially during famines) into cultivated lands and even close to larger cities. A clear picture of this, precisely because of the critical timing of this violent incursion, is provided by the so-called 'Broken Obelisk' (Ashur-bel-kala, ca. 1060 BC), and by a Babylonian chronicle (referring to Tiglath-pileser I, ca. 1080 BC). These sources record the clashes between Assyrians and Arameans from the Euphrates to well beyond the Tigris.

443

A similar situation should be envisioned for Babylonia. The decline of the irrigation system and the weakness of the central government gave enough space, both politically and in terms of settlements, to the Arameans. When this process ended, between the ninth and eighth centuries BC, a series of Aramean tribes were settled in Babylonia. These tribes settled especially in the above-mentioned 'dimorphic corridor', extending from the eastern side of the Tigris to Elam and the Persian Gulf. The inscriptions of Tiglath-pileser III and Sennacherib provide the names of around forty Aramean tribes and some personal names, thus confirming their western origins (with *ya-* prefixes; *-ān* and *-a'* suffixes). These were all small tribes, which were unable to form a large and stable entity, but kept their tribal leaders. The latter were defined in the Assyrian sources as *nasīku*.

Judging from the tribute paid to the Assyrians by these tribes, their economy was mainly based on agriculture and farming, especially transhumant farming. Some tribes (especially the Utu') even specialised to become mercenary troops. The linguistic and socio-economic assimilation with the Babylonian population, however, remained relatively modest. This assimilation was further worsened by the raids of nomadic groups, who were seen by the Babylonians as bloodthirsty and dangerous bandits. Even the attempts of the Aramean tribes to become more sedentary were seen as an illegitimate appropriation of arable lands at the expense of the Babylonians. At least, this was the propagandistic representation provided by the Assyrian kings, who wanted to depict themselves as liberators and restorers of justice in the land. At times, the sources define the Arameans as Sutians, an archaic term that by then simply meant 'nomads'. For instance, the Aramean invaders were presented as Sutians in the Poem of Erra, which we will analyse later on in relation to Babylonia.

The Chaldeans of Lower Mesopotamia were closely linked to the Aramean tribes. The Arameans and Chaldeans were two distinct ethnic groups and the Assyro-Babylonian sources never confused them with each other, or considered them to be the same. They settled in different areas, with the Chaldeans concentrated around the lower end of the Euphrates (from Nippur to Ur and Uruk) and the Arameans concentrated in the north. Moreover, they settled in Mesopotamia at different times. There is no mention of the Chaldeans before the first half of the ninth century BC. Their political structure was mainly tribal, but larger than the one seen for the Aramean tribes. We only know of five Chaldean tribes: Bit Yakini, Bit Dakkuri, Bit Ammukani, Bit Sha'alli and Bit Shilani. They were all very powerful groups and imposed themselves in a dominant role in Babylonia. This aspect caused many problems for the Assyrians.

Chaldean leaders were defined as 'kings' (in the plural *šarrāni*) or 'chiefs' (*ra'sāni*) – a clear allusion to a structure similar to that of the Arameans, although some of their most powerful chiefs managed (as we will see later on) to gain control over the area, including its cities. They therefore bestowed upon themselves grander titles such as 'king of Chaldea' or 'king of the Sealand' and even ones related to Babylonian kingship, becoming the leaders of Babylonia against the Assyrian invaders. Unlike the Arameans, the Chaldeans quickly managed to assimilate with Babylonian culture. They thus took on Babylonian names and do not seem particularly involved in farming activities. Judging from the tributes paid to the Assyrians, one of the main aspects of their economy was a considerable availability of exotic products from India or southern Arabia, such as gold, incense, ivory, ebony and rosewood. Consequently, the Chaldean tribes must have been involved in commercial activities linked to the caravans reaching Arabia, Yemen and the ports overlooking the Indian Ocean. This involvement must have been partly a legacy of the networks reaching Ur and the Sumerian south and partly the result of new Iron Age developments (especially in Arabia), such as the domestication of camels and the appearance of oases and wells.

The hypothesis according to which the origins of the Chaldeans should be placed more in the far south of the Arabian Peninsula, rather than among the Aramean tribes of Syria, is therefore highly plausible. A migration to Mesopotamia from the south rather than the west would explain their settlement in different areas compared to the Arameans. Similarly, a different origin would explain the clear distinction made by the Assyrians between the two groups. Having said that, however, the few surviving Chaldean personal names show some similarity to Aramaic names. Nonetheless, it is also true that the ethnic and linguistic identity of the whole of eastern Arabia in this period remains largely unknown to us.

4 The spread of the Aramaic language

The progressive diffusion of the Aramaic language is such an important phenomenon, that it has to be mentioned in passing, even if it affects a period of time outside the one considered in this chapter. At the beginning of the first millennium BC, the Aramaic dialects were only one of the many linguistic groups in the Near East. Moreover, the Arameans were in contact with areas speaking a variety of languages, from Phoenician to Hebrew, Neo-Hittite and Assyrian. At the time, the characteristic features of Aramaic were not yet fully developed within the group of Western Semitic languages. In the course of half a millennium, through a slow yet unstoppable process, the entire Syro-Levantine and Mesopotamian region became Aramaic, making this language one of the official ones of the empire. Aramaic texts would spread even outside this region, reaching Anatolia, Egypt, Arabia, Iran and even the borders of India. At the same time, other languages, from Canaanite dialects to Assyrian and Babylonian, were experiencing the opposite phenomenon and began to disappear. This process was long and complex and went through several stages.

The first phase took place between the second and first millennium BC, coinciding with the infiltration and sedentarisation of Aramean groups mentioned above. As a result, an Aramaic-speaking zone appeared in Syria and the northern Levant, including the desert hinterland, which remains sparsely documented. In this phase, Aramaic only stood out from the other north-western Semitic languages of the area through a few emerging traits. It was subdivided into a variety of local dialects, which the inscriptions from various sites occasionally display in writing.

The second phase took place in the following centuries, through the progressive movement of the Aramean groups. In Upper Syria, Aramaic rose at the expense of the Neo-Hittite language (which was already precarious on a demographic level). In Upper Mesopotamia, it rose at the expense of the last remainders of Hurrian languages and in clear competition with the Assyrian expansion. Finally, in Lower Mesopotamia, Aramaic appeared alongside or instead of Babylonian. The degree of infiltration in this phase is difficult to quantify, since the previous dominating languages and cultures had a considerable staying power in the documentation. One of the clues of this Aramean infiltration, however, is the growing presence of Aramaic personal names and glosses in the Akkadian texts. The survival of the official written languages therefore only partly obscures this changing situation, which was primarily affecting the spoken language.

The third phase is linked to the imperial deportations of the Assyrians and the Babylonians and the later returns granted by the Achaemenids. These deportations led to a gradual integration of the local population with the newcomers. In the long run, this process benefited the Aramaic language, which was the most widespread element among those deported. Also in the heart of the empires, deportations, which were aimed at repopulating areas experiencing a demographic crisis, caused linguistic changes in favour of the prevailing language. Moreover, when some groups of deportees managed to return from Babylonia to their original lands, they brought back a new Aramaic language, which had become theirs during the exile. This is true for the well-known case of Judaea, but it was certainly not the only one.

Naturally, each region gradually accumulated the impact of the various factors and the various stages of infiltration. For instance, Babylonia first experienced the arrival of entire nomadic tribes that settled in marginal areas. Then, there was the progressive infiltration of Aramean groups in the countryside and in the Akkadian-speaking Babylonian cities in search of work and land. Finally, there was the arrival of deportees from western Aramaic lands, who were superimposed on a population that had already begun to integrate and was already used to the Akkadian/Aramaic bilingualism. By the end of the process, the weakest and smallest groups were assimilated within the predominant Aramaic groups, leading to the emergence of a unified Aramaic dialect (the so-called Imperial Aramaic). Imperial Aramaic first appeared in Assyria and then spread throughout the empire, substituting and changing pre-existing local dialects. All the following Aramaic dialects, from the Biblical to the Egyptian variety (which were in reality more written variations than actual dialects) of the Achaemenid period were derived from Imperial Aramaic.

Aramaic therefore became the language spoken by the majority of people in Syria, the Levant and Mesopotamia. Consequently, the empires (the Babylonian and especially the Persian empires) began to use it as their official language alongside the persistent use of Akkadian. This linguistic problem naturally led to the (different yet closely linked) issue of the writing system used by Aramaic. While Akkadian remained closely connected to the complex cuneiform system and its enormous list of signs, Aramaic used an alphabetic writing, far easier to learn and use (Figure 25.5). Already in the Assyrian period, cuneiform tablets began to provide notes in the Aramaic alphabet, providing an easier identification of the text. By the Neo-Babylonian period, Aramaic was fully used alongside Akkadian in administrative texts (Figure 25.6).

It is worth bearing in mind, however, that the different materials used to write each language has led to an imbalance in the surviving documentation. While clay tablets normally survive virtually intact, of the papyri used for Aramaic usually only the clay 'bulla' survives. The latter preserve the seal impression of the functionary, placed on the knot holding the now decayed papyrus. If we did not have these issues in the survival of the evidence, we would be in a far better position to assess the growing role of Aramaic in the imperial administrations of the time. On a spoken level, the unification and de-culturation of the provinces, brought about by the imperial conquests, facilitated the rise of Aramaic in every area inhabited by a Semitic-speaking population. Aramaic thus developed alongside Persian, which had by then prevailed in the Iranian plateau and the last surviving Anatolian languages, destined to be supplanted by Greek later on. Apart from Aramaic, the often elusive reservoir constituted by the Arabian Peninsula was experiencing the rise of Arabian-speaking peoples. The latter would eventually impose on Aramaic the same processes of superimposition and assimilation that the latter had imposed on Canaanite and Akkadian.

Figure 25.5 Assyrian/Aramaic bilingualism: a 'cuneiform' scribe writes (in Assyrian) with a stylus on a clay tablet, while an 'alphabetic' scribe writes (in Aramaic) with a brush on a papyrus or parchment.

ASSYRIAN (Side A)

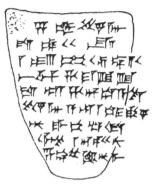

5 ANŠE ŠE.PAD.MEŠ
ša DUMU.MAN ŠU²
ᵀTa-qu-u-ni ˡᵘ2-u
ina IGI ᵀḪa-ma-tu-ṭu
Ša ᵘʳᵘ Ḫa-an-du-a-te
ŠE.PAD.MEŠ a-na 1 ANŠE 5-BÁN-šá
tar-GAL-bi ⁱᵗⁱDU₆
lim-mu ʳᵈPA.MAN.PAP
5 ˡᵘŠE.KIN.KUD.MEŠ

"5 *emāru* of barley belonging to the crown prince, managed by Taquni, the "deputy", (are given) to Hamatutu of Handuate. The (interest of the) barley increases by 1.5 *emāru*. Month VII; eponym Nabu-shar-usur. 5 harvesters (also owed)."

ASSYRIAN (Side B)

š rn snh zy
br mlk'ʾl
ḥmṭṭ mn ḥdwh
5 b 6.5
ḥsdn 5
l'm rbsrs
nbsrṣr

"Barley. The 'deputy' of the crown prince (has given) to Hamatutu of Hadduwah 5 (*emāru*) a(t the rate of) 6.5, and 5 harvesters. Eponym the chief eunuch Nabu-sar-usur."

Figure 25.6   Bilingual tablet (Assyrian and Aramaic), with a record of a loan in barley.

26

THE NEO-HITTITE STATES

1 The origins of the Neo-Hittite states

Following the collapse of the Hittite empire, the Central Anatolian plateau saw the arrival of new peoples (the Phrygians), which settled alongside the local population. Meanwhile, the political organisation and culture of the area was reduced to the village level. However, the area was beginning to acquire the innovative forms of social organisation and ethnic and national identity characteristic of the Iron Age. On the contrary, in south-eastern Anatolia, particularly in the regions under the control of Carchemish and Tarhuntassa, the population speaking Hittite (and especially Luwian) managed to resist these changes. It developed into a series of local states centred on a city, but including a large territory in the foothills (Figure 26.1).

The most visible sign of continuity with the imperial Hittite phase is the survival of the so-called 'Luwian hieroglyphs', which the new states inherited from the Hittite empire. This writing system was already in use in the fifteenth century BC (in the Hittite Middle Kingdom and in Kizzuwatna), and then between the fourteenth and thirteenth centuries BC, particularly on inscriptions left on the seals of kings and functionaries (thus relatively small in size). Towards the end of the empire, Luwian hieroglyphs began to be used on rock monumental inscriptions, such as the 'historical' inscription of Suppiluliuma II, found in Hattusa (*Südburg*), and other inscriptions left in several locations, including Aleppo. With the rise of the Neo-Hittite kingdoms, the monumental use of Luwian hieroglyphs increased, sometimes even in relatively long texts. These were left both inside cities (on the gates of palaces and citadels) and outside of them (on rock monuments, near wells, sanctuaries, and other important locations). The visibility of these extra-urban inscriptions made Luwian hieroglyphs known to us (yet still undeciphered) well before cuneiform. They therefore made Neo-Hittite monuments famous before the archaeological rediscovery of the Hittite empire. This led to the development of more or less interesting interpretations, such as the one identifying the authors of these inscriptions as the Amazons. The travellers of the eighteenth and nineteenth centuries (AD) clearly borrowed this idea from Greek mythology.

As an ideographic system, hieroglyphic writing can be easily adapted to write a variety of languages, for instance Hurrian, used in some personal names of the imperial age. Therefore, while the monuments of the Hittite empire were presumably written in Hittite, the Neo-Hittite inscriptions used a language closely related to Luwian. Even personal names seem more Luwian than Hittite, with the exception of those royal names that were clearly imitating the names of Hittite rulers. This phenomenon can be easily explained. The location of the Neo-Hittite states corresponds to the south-eastern portion of the Hittite empire, where the Luwian element was already prevailing in the second millennium BC. After all, Hittite was only

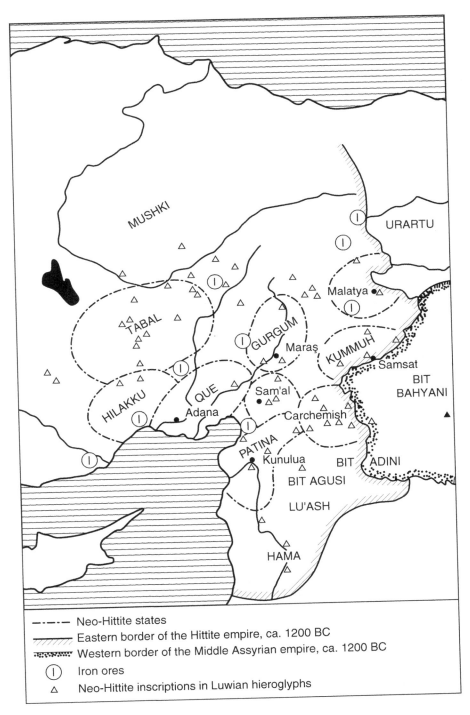

Figure 26.1 Map of the Neo-Hittite states, ca. 1000–700 BC.

important because it was the language of the Hittite capital. In reality, even before the destruction of the empire, Hittite language had little impact on the local population.

The general movement to the south-east becomes visible through a comparison between the area occupied by the Hittite empire and the one occupied by the Neo-Hittite states. This shift has led to the assumption that the origins of the Neo-Hittite states was linked to a migration from Anatolia to northern Syria. This movement should have taken place when the empire collapsed, as a reaction to the migration of Phrygians in the central plateau. However, this assumption is not only unfounded, but also unnecessary. The area in which the Neo-Hittite states developed was well within the ancient borders of the Hittite empire. Therefore, the impression of migrations is largely due to the loss of the western and northern territories, and not to a migration of people to the south-east. The Neo-Hittite states bordered to the east with the Euphrates, on the other side of which were the Assyrians. Therefore, the capitals of the Neo-Hittite states overlooking the Euphrates (Carchemish, Kummuh, Melid) were all located along the 'Hittite' (that is, western) side of the Euphrates. To the south, the states were barred by the old border between Egypt and Hatti (the southernmost inscriptions are the ones from Hama), and had to move further north due to the movement of Aramean groups.

It is important to make a distinction between the states located to the north or the south of the line formed by the Amanus and the Anti-Taurus. North of this line (Hittite Tarhuntassa) and up to the Halys and salt lakes (beyond which there were the Phrygian territories), a Luwian population had inhabited the region well before the fall of the empire, at a time when the area was part of the Hittite state. South of the Amanus/Anti-Taurus line (Hittite Carchemish), the majority of the population was Semitic with a Hurrian component. The area used to be divided into autonomous kingdoms dependent on the great king of Hatti. In the course of the fourteenth and thirteenth centuries BC, these kingdoms experienced a certain degree of infiltration of Hittite and Luwian elements. The Hittite dynasties ruling over Aleppo and Carchemish had brought a retinue of functionaries, scribes, soldiers, and merchants. This left a marked Hittite imprint on the palace culture of these two cities. In some areas, from the former kingdom of Mukish (Alalah III) to Emar, their direct dependence on the Hittite viceroys in Carchemish led to a considerable degree of acculturation, attested in the surviving texts and monuments. In the thirteenth century BC, Hittite influence also affected centres such as Ugarit and Amurru, the former through merchants, and the latter through the royal family.

This 'Hittitisation' was in a way relatively superficial or, better, only affected the elite. This is because it mainly influenced the palace courts and their administrative and celebrative expressions. The rest of the population remained largely unaffected. Nonetheless, this process was enough to provide the necessary premises for the development of Neo-Hittite culture in centres such as Carchemish and Patina, where it even affected their official expressions. Moreover, the process had a secondary and less obvious impact on centres such as Hama or Bit Adini. In Carchemish, where the cultural and political continuity from the thirteenth century BC to the Neo-Hittite period is evident, the Hittite element pervades its remains. On the contrary, in newer centres, such as Sam'al, the Hittite element was complementary to the predominant Aramean element. This caused a difficult coexistence between official Hittite manifestations and the more widespread Aramean culture.

Despite individual differences, in northern Syria, the Neo-Hittite element mainly affected those areas that had been under direct control of Carchemish in the thirteenth century BC: Carchemish itself, the area of Mukish (which had now become Patina), and partly that of Aleppo. Further south, in the ex-kingdoms of Ugarit, Amurru, Nuhashe, and Qadesh, the rise of the Arameans was facilitated by the common Semitic background they shared with the local population. On the contrary, in the Upper Euphrates, the Taurus, Cilicia, and Cappadocia, the fall of the unifying authority of the Hittite empire had provided autonomy to areas formerly lacking independence. Overall, the collapse of the Hittite empire strengthened both old (Carchemish) and new autonomous states. It is interesting to note that from the collapse to the conquest of the Neo-Hittite states, the Assyrians continued to define the territory west of the Euphrates as Hatti. Carchemish in particular was defined as the 'great Hatti'. Therefore, despite the fact that each Hittite kingdom was autonomous, the prominence of Carchemish remained, being rooted in the important role the city had in the Hittite empire.

2 The history of the Neo-Hittite states

The Neo-Hittite territory bordered with the Arameans to the south, the Phrygians to the north-west, and the Euphrates to the east. On the other side of the Euphrates, there were the Assyrian and Urartian territories. The region was subdivided into around ten states. In northern Syria, Carchemish was the most obvious heir of the Hittite empire. The kingdom of Patina, which the Assyrians called Unqi (modern Amuq), was the heir of the kingdom of Mukish. Between these two Hittite strongholds, the Aramean presence was seeping through from Arpad/Aleppo to Sam'al. Further north, still west of the Euphrates, there were Kummuh (whose capital was in modern Samsat) and Melid. West of these two kingdoms there was Gurgum and its capital Marqasi (modern Maraş), while Cilicia was subdivided into two kingdoms. To the east, in the plains, there was Que, while to the more mountainous west there was Hilakku. Beyond the Taurus there was Tabal, a confederation of minor kingdoms, which at times managed to gain independence. All these states were concentrated in the valleys and the plains between mountains, and were separated from each other by the Taurus Mountains. Therefore, the states were located in key positions, allowing control over cultivated areas, the necessary routes for communication, and access to those natural resources necessary for the manufacture of iron.

The period between 1200 and 1000 BC remains relatively obscure. This is mainly because the Neo-Hittite states were still under formation and in the process of overcoming the effects of the collapse of the empire. The collapse had indeed provided new opportunities for independence and growth, but at the same time brought those negative effects caused by the fall of a consolidated government. For instance, it is possible to see the difficult relationship between change and continuity in the older centres. In Melid (Arslantepe), the sequence of city gates from the Hittite empire to the Assyrian conquest is markedly discontinuous. In Carchemish continuity prevails, and the names of the local rulers continued with the personal names of the royal family of Suppiluliuma, with an Ini-Teshub II (attested in the texts of Tiglath-pileser I) and a Talmi-Teshub II (attested in a local inscription). Moreover, one of the first dynasties of Melid was related to the one of Carchemish. However, the majority of the kingdoms and their capitals were new, and thus unable to leave a significant mark in their earliest stages.

Between 1000 and 850 BC, some local royal monuments began to appear. Their style and typology partly mirror the imperial style of the Hittites, but at the same time seem innovative in their characteristically Neo-Hittite style, not yet influenced by the Assyrians. This style even managed to influence both the Aramean centres in Syria and the Assyrians themselves, once they came into contact with the Neo-Hittite states. Thanks to these local monuments, it is partly possible to reconstruct some dynastic sequences (Table 26.1). The sequence of rulers in Carchemish was: Suhi I, Astuwatananza, Suhi II, then Katuwa. These kings commissioned important inscriptions, monuments, and building interventions. Gurgum was ruled by a dynasty whose sequence can be found in the genealogy of its last king, Halparuntiya III. For Melid, one ruler worth mentioning is Sulumeli, who built the so-called 'Lion Gate' monumental complex. The overall impression is that of a progressive development, which was still protected from the devastating Assyrian incursions. This development can only be traced in the architecture and improvements attested in the cities. Nonetheless, it certainly affected the political and economic sectors as well.

The first Assyrian crossing west of the Euphrates, led by Ashurnasirpal II at the end of his kingdom, did not affect the Neo-Hittite territories. It just crossed the kingdoms of Carchemish and Patina as far as the Orontes Valley. Patina's capital, Kunulua, should in all probability be identified with Tell Taynat, in the Amuq. There, important public buildings dating to this period have been found, though without any inscriptions providing the names of the rulers who commissioned these works. A particularly important religious centre belonging to this pre-Assyrian phase was that of 'Ain Dara (whose ancient name remains unknown), where a temple and an impressive series of reliefs have been found.

Just like the Aramean states, in the Neo-Hittite states the situation dramatically changed with the reign of Shalmaneser III. Having ensured the crossing of the Euphrates at Bit Adini, the Assyrian king conquered

Table 26.1 Chronology of the Neo-Hittite kingdoms, ca. 1100–700 BC

	Arpad	Patina	Carchemish	Sam'al	Gurgum	Que	Kummuh	Malatya	Tabal
1100			Ini-Teshub II ca. 1100; Talmi-Teshub II ca. 1000					Allumari ca. 1100	
1000			Suhi I						
950			Astawatananza; Suhi II; Katuwa	Gabbar ca. 920	Palalam ca. 950; Muwanza; Halparuntiya I				
900	Gusi ca. 870	Lubarna I ca. 870; Sapalulme ?–858	Sangara 870–848	Bamah ca. 890; Hayanu ca. 860–850	ca. 900 Muwatalli II ca. 860–850; Muwatalli 858; Halparuntiya II 853		Qatazilu 860–857	Lalli 853–836	
850	Arame 858–834	Qalparunda 858–?; Lubarna II ?–831; Surri 831; Sasi 831–?	Astiruwa	Kilamuwa ca. 840–830	Palalam II 805; Halparuntiya III	858–833 Kate 805 Kirri 833	Kumzshpi 853; Ushipil-ulme 805–773		Tuwati I 832; Kikki
800	Atar-shumki 805–796		Yariri; Kamani	Panamuwa I ca. 780; Bar-Sur				Shahu Hilaru-atta ca. 780–750	Tuwati II ca. 800
750	Matti-El 754–740; 740: Arpad Assyrian province	Tutammu 738; 738: Patina Assyrian province	Pisiri 738–717; 717: Carchemish Assyrian province	Panamuwa II ca. 750–730; Bar-Rakib ca. 730–710; ca. 710: Sam'al Assyrian province	Tarhulara 743–711; Mutallu 711; 711: Gurgum Assyrian province	Urikki 738–710; ca. 710: Que Assyrian province	Kushtashpi 755–732; Mutallu 712–708; 708: Assyrian province	Sulumeli 743–732; Gunzinanu 730–720; Tarhunazi 720–712; 712: Malatya Assyrian province	Wassurme 739–730; Hulli 730–?; Kummuh/Ambaris ?–713; Ishkallu
700						696: revolt of Kirua; 689: revolt of Sanduarri		675: revolt of Mugallu	675: Mugallu of Malatya

Syria through a series of annual campaigns. The first ones were mainly focused on Central and southern Syria, leaving the Neo-Hittite states unaffected by the incursions. However, all states in the region felt this rising threat, an issue that made the Neo-Hittite states send contingents to the battle of Qarqar. In the final ten years of his reign (around 840–830 BC), Shalmaneser focused his attentions on the northern states (Unqi/Patina, Melid, Que, Tabal), directing the Assyrian incursions towards Anatolia. For the first time, the Assyrian army overcame the Taurus and followed the routes used by the Old Assyrian merchants a millennium earlier. In this regard, the stele Shalmaneser III left on the Amanus was placed right next to the one of king Anum-Hirbi, who ruled at the time of the Old Assyrian colonies. The continuous incursions of Shalmaneser were enough to turn the Neo-Hittite states into tributary states without affecting their autonomy. The reaction of each individual kingdom was different. The two kingdoms more directly in danger, Carchemish and Kummuh, seem to have preferred a policy of submission. They therefore paid the tributes without having to be forced by the Assyrians militarily. On the contrary, the fiercest fights were put up by more marginal states, which thought to be able to avoid the tributes.

After the death of Shalmaneser, the Assyrian presence west of the Euphrates decreased. By the end of the ninth century BC, Adad-Nirari III faced a coalition of Aramean states, led by Arpad, and Neo-Hittitte states. Following his victory, the Assyrian king managed to establish the border between the vassal state of Kummuh and the rebellious state of Gurgum. The entire first half of the eighth century BC is dominated by the figure of Shamshi-Ilu. He was the Assyrian *turtānu* who resided in Til Barsip (the former capital of Bit Adini) and held the north-western territories under control through military expeditions or diplomatic interventions. The political orientation of the local kingdoms continued along the same lines as in previous phases. Carchemish (where the monuments of king Yariri and king Kamani, unattested in the Assyrian sources, were built in this phase) and Kummuh (where a Suppiluliuma was king, though we do not know to what extent he was aware of his illustrious name) remained prone to submission to the Assyrians. Other kingdoms, such as Gurgum, ruled by that Halparuntiya III, whose inscription has allowed the reconstruction of the kingdom's dynastic sequence, remained determined to resist the Assyrians.

Admittedly, the Assyrians were not yet able to march beyond Gurgum, and by the mid-eighth century BC the power threatening the Neo-Hittite states was rather Urartu. For the latter, Melid constituted a key crossing point. Therefore, Argishti I and Sarduri II conquered it. Sarduri placed an inscription on a cliff overlooking the Euphrates not only to mark the border of the Urartian territory, but also to indicate his ambitions in that direction. From Melid, Urartian influence moved in two directions. To the west, beyond the Taurus, there was the confederation of Tabal, where Tuwati held the title of 'great king'. He therefore controlled the small local kings. Tabal constituted for Urartu a relatively strong opponent (enough to discourage any military intervention) interested in an anti-Assyrian coalition. However, the additional involvement of Kummuh in this large anti-Assyrian coalition centred on Urartu led to an Assyrian intervention. Tiglath-pileser III had barely been crowned when he decided to confront the coalition in the kingdom of Kummuh. The Assyrian king defeated the coalition in a battle (Kishtan, 743 BC). This victory had a double effect: it cut out Urartu from the territories west of the Euphrates, and placed the Neo-Hittites states at the mercy of the Assyrians.

It took the Assyrians thirty years to consolidate the outcomes provided by the victory in Kishtan in full. Tiglath-pileser preferred to secure his direct control over Central and southern Syria, while the Neo-Hittite states were under a less restrictive type of control. We have already seen the case of Sam'al, whose kings Panamuwa II and Bar-Rakib were loyal vassals of Assyria. It is likely that Kummuh, Gurgum, Melid, and even the more distant Tabal, Tuwana, Atuna, Ishtunda, and Hubishna were in a similar situation. The only Neo-Hittite kingdom that was turned into a province already at the time of Tiglath-pileser is Unqi/Patina, which was directly involved in the fight against Arpad and other Aramean kingdoms.

A unique document marking this final phase of independence is the bilingual inscription (in Phoenician and Luwian hieroglyphs) from Karatepe. It was written in the second half of the eighth century BC.

The inscription belongs to a certain Asatiwata, who celebrated the construction of his fortress, Asatiwatiya (Karatepe), located along the border with Sam'al. Asatiwata was not an independent ruler, but a vassal of Urikki of the 'House of Mopsos', a king of Que (known as Adana in Hittite and Danunim in Phoenician) also attested in the Assyrian annals. The problems Asatiwata had to face in his reign were mainly internal or predominantly local. In his inscription, there is no trace of the imminent Assyrian threat that would soon affect both Que and Sam'al. We know that in Sargon II's reign they both became Assyrian provinces, although the copious quantity of historical accounts about this king does not explicitly record their annexation.

With the reign of Sargon II, the Assyrians finally managed to put a definite end to the independence of the Neo-Hittite states. Sargon's decisive intervention was a reaction to the rebellions in the area, which were backed up by the Phrygians. Consequently, the king annexed one after the other, first Carchemish (717 BC), then Tabal and Hilakku (713 BC), Que (if he did not submit it beforehand), Melid (712 BC), Gurgum (711 BC), and Kummuh (708 BC). Some centres were turned into capitals of the Assyrian provinces, but even these cities suffered the consequences of this drastic political change. They quickly began to decline, giving up their role as active centres of political, commercial, and building initiatives. Therefore, these cities lost their former role of stimulators of local culture, and became mere terminals of the imperial administration. As a result, the construction of royal monuments and buildings ceased, and Luwian hieroglyphs, designed for monumental inscriptions, slowly began to disappear.

Assyrian control over the new provinces was not easy to implement. The alliance between Assyria and Phrygia left the areas between the two states without any external support. Nonetheless, Assyria found itself unable to establish a solid presence beyond the Taurus. While the Syrian territories along the Euphrates and in the Cilician plain continued to be Assyrian provinces, the kingdoms of Tabal and Hilakku regained to a certain extent their autonomy. Sargon's successors repeatedly tried to re-establish Assyrian control in these distant lands, but with little success. In the reign of Ashurbanipal, at the eve of the final collapse of the Assyrian empire, Tabal and Hilakku were fully independent nucleuses of what would become the kingdoms of Cappadocia and Cilicia in the Neo-Babylonian and Median periods. Cappadocia eventually became part of the Median empire, while Cilicia remained independent until it became part of the Achaemenid empire (whose kings respected its unique status).

These forward glances into the fate of these states show how, even when annexed, these distant lands were relatively protected from the impact of imperial administrations. The latter often crushed and combined populations through deportations and the imposition of their own administrative systems. The survival of Luwian personal names (and probably of the language itself) in southern Anatolia up until the Hellenistic period is a significant clue of the vitality of Anatolian culture. The latter benefited from its marginal position and the difficult access to its territories. Anatolia therefore managed to avoid those processes of annexation and de-culturation far better than the more vulnerable Syrian territories.

3 The culture of Neo-Hittite centres

The rise of Neo-Hittite centres between 1000 and 700 BC clearly shows the unusual growth of a region that in the previous and following phases remained largely marginal. This is due to the obvious limitations imposed by a mountainous territory upon political and demographic developments. The rate of demographic growth is not quantifiable, but there are indications of a distinct growth, possibly due to the autonomy of the region and the availability of important natural resources for Iron Age technology. The valleys surrounding the Taurus provided minerals and timber, which now became crucial and strategic resources. Similarly, in Cilicia and Cappadocia horse breeding developed in parallel with the more eastern centres of Armenia (Urartians) and the Zagros (Mannaeans).

The new technologies and military equipment of the Iron Age are closely linked to the most characteristic materials of the Early Iron Age in Anatolia. The bronze industry began to specialise in the production

The Neo-Hittite States

of large and medium-sized ware, especially cauldrons and tripods, for which the Neo-Hittite centres were as renowned as the Phrygian and Urartian ones. The Neo-Hittite states also produced shields and belts of the same quality and in the same quantities as the ones commonly associated with Urartian culture. Less prestigious, but equally important from a technological point of view, were iron objects and weapons. The latter are largely underrepresented in the archaeological evidence, just like 'invisible' remains such as textiles and horses.

Following the general trends of the Iron Age, the typical Neo-Hittite settlement was a well-protected, but small, citadel. The only exception is Carchemish, which more than doubled in size compared to the already large Middle and Late Bronze Age settlement (Figure 26.2). Therefore, the area within the new fortification wall surrounding the 'lower city' now reached around a hundred hectares. All the other capitals were far smaller in size. However, they were well protected with fortification walls and pincer gates, often angled to the left in order to force the attacking armies to expose their flanks. Even minor centres were fortified, thus reducing the typical Late Bronze Age contraposition between fortified capitals and

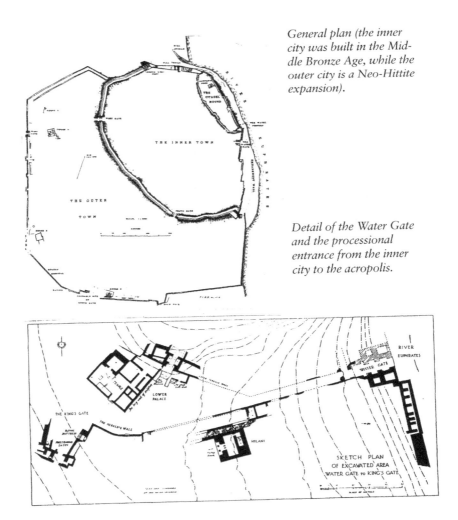

General plan (the inner city was built in the Middle Bronze Age, while the outer city is a Neo-Hittite expansion).

Detail of the Water Gate and the processional entrance from the inner city to the acropolis.

Figure 26.2 Carchemish.

455

unprotected villages. These minor centres often became fortresses protecting valleys and strategic access points between mountains.

The reduced size and defensive systems implemented made the citadels a sort of crossing between a city and a castle. City gates were decorated with carved reliefs, kick-starting a large-scale artistic trend, which would eventually be imitated and improved by the Assyrian empire. The reliefs decorating the entrances of large sites (Carchemish) and medium-sized ones (Melid), as well as simple fortresses (Karatepe), are one of the most iconic aspects of Neo-Hittite culture (Figure 26.3). These reliefs recorded several aspects of the local culture, from mythological to celebratory scenes (with soldiers, dignitaries, and kings), and simple animals, depicted in an apotropaic function. The same can be said about monumental inscriptions. They were not placed inside palace and temples or on statues and steles like in the Bronze Age, but on

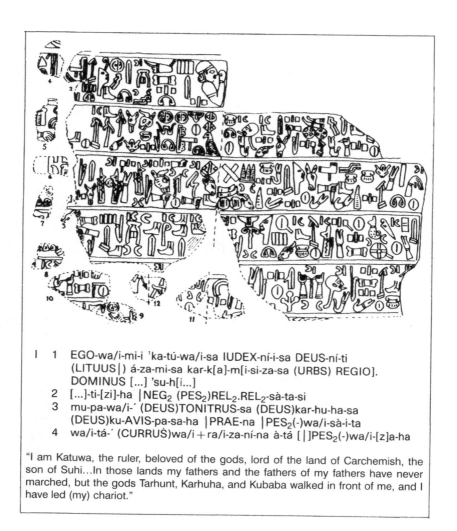

> I 1 EGO-wa/i-mi-i 'ka-tú-wa/i-sa IUDEX-ní-i-sa DEUS-ní-ti (LITUUS|) á-za-mi-sa kar-k[a]-m[i-si-za-sa (URBS) REGIO]. DOMINUS [...] 'su-h[i...]
> 2 [...]-ti-[zi]-ha |NEG₂ (PES₂)REL₂.REL₂-sà-ta-si
> 3 mu-pa-wa/i-' (DEUS)TONITRUS-sa (DEUS)kar-hu-ha-sa (DEUS)ku-AVIS-pa-sa-ha |PRAE-na |PES₂(-)wa/i-sà-i-ta
> 4 wa/i-tá-' (CURRUŚ)wa/i+ra/i-za-ní-na à-tá [|]PES₂(-)wa/i-[z]a-ha

> "I am Katuwa, the ruler, beloved of the gods, lord of the land of Carchemish, the son of Suhi...In those lands my fathers and the fathers of my fathers have never marched, but the gods Tarhunt, Karhuha, and Kubaba walked in front of me, and I have led (my) chariot."

Figure 26.3 Inscription in Luwian hieroglyphs of Katuwa, king of Carchemish (early ninth century BC), originally left on the Herald's Wall of the Royal Gate (cf. Figure 26.2).

large outdoor surfaces. This change was possibly in response to the long tradition of rock monuments and inscriptions in Anatolia, but it was now improved even further.

Neo-Hittite culture seems to express the political ideology of closed centres, committed to defend a considerable wealth and prised technologies. At the same time, these cities addressed a population that was relatively small, but highly responsive and influential regarding the decisions of the state. The overall picture is, however, influenced by the fact that the majority of the evidence comes from the royal citadels. Therefore, the role of temples and rock sanctuaries remains largely unknown. Nonetheless, it may be worth assuming that the latter's role was quite important. After all, they constituted the link between the religious institutions of the Hittite empire in Anatolia and those that would characterise the same area in the following periods (especially the Hellenistic period). It is also relatively easy to suppose that palaces managed craftsmanship and trade, the exploitation of forests and mines, and military endeavours. Meanwhile, temples managed agricultural and farming activities, the latter being less visible even in the Assyrian records, but nonetheless essential for the local population.

Neo-Hittite kingship must have been relatively complex, but this complexity is not fully expressed in celebratory inscriptions. Rulers defined as 'kings' controlled the area alongside other rulers defined as 'judges' (*tarwani*). The latter were at times in a subordinate position, and might not have belonged to the royal family. The king of Carchemish held the title of 'governor of the land'. We also know that the title 'great king' was revived both in Carchemish and Tabal. These titles seem to combine ancient traditions with innovative elements. Indeed, the Neo-Hittite states had to create an ideology of kingship that was partly inspired by the Hittite imperial tradition, and partly a response to the local administration in which they developed.

The celebration of justice and well-being was typical of the Iron Age as a whole. However, alongside the Aramean expressions of this ideology, which have been studied for longer, it has become necessary to add the Neo-Hittite expressions, which are equally significant and direct. Unlike Syria, however, which remained relatively 'secular', Anatolia combined socio-political issues with a particular interest in the cultic aspects of kingship. This is particularly visible in the rock inscriptions left outside the city and linked to the many cultic locations in the area.

27

ASSYRIA, BABYLONIA AND ELAM IN THE TWELFTH TO NINTH CENTURIES BC

1 The Middle Elamite apogee

Following the crisis of the twelfth century BC, the lands west of the Euphrates experienced a phase of reformation. Throughout this period, Mesopotamia continued to endure its slow decline and its traditional conflicts. From as early as the fourteenth century BC, the Kassite, Middle Assyrian, and Middle Elamite kingdoms were competing in a sort of 'power triangle' (Table 27.1). This complex interaction was marked by sudden changes within a generally stable balance of power, and by the difficult position of Babylonia, caught between its two fierce rivals. Since these powers remained unaffected by what was going on in the west, this 'triangle' continued to exist well after the twelfth century BC. Moreover, the end of the Kassite dynasty and the rise of the Second Dynasty of Isin were more a consequence of this 'power triangle', than a mark of new turmoils. Similarly, although the Aramean infiltrations in Upper Mesopotamia and Babylonia brought new internal disorders, they did not bring about the rise of new political powers.

Among the three kingdoms, Elam was the power least (or even not at all) interested in the western turmoils. Elam reached the peak of its power in the twelfth century BC, taking advantage of the damage Assyria and Babylonia inflicted upon each other during the fierce conflicts between the successors of Tukulti-Ninurta and the last Kassite kings. In Elam, a new dynasty made Susa the centre of its kingdom, and chose the god of Susa, Inshushinak, as its main deity. Shutruk-Nahhunte managed to considerably strengthen his entire kingdom, which now extended from the coast of the Persian Gulf (Liyan) and Anshan to the Mesopotamian border. Shutruk-Nahhunte brought to Susa the monuments of the previous Elamite kings, and constantly emphasised the dynastic (and inter-dynastic) continuity and unity of Elam.

The victorious expedition of the Assyrian king Ashur-dan against Babylonia and the subsequent collapse of the Kassite dynasty provided Shutruk-Nahhunte with the perfect opportunity to campaign in Mesopotamia. The extent of his incursion can be reconstructed from his celebratory inscription. The latter also recorded the origins of the monuments that were brought back to Susa as booty. The Elamite king first crossed the areas east of the Tigris, in particular the Diyala Valley (Eshnunna). He then moved west, beyond the Tigris reaching northern Babylonia (Opis, Dur-Kurigalzu, Sippar). Finally, he descended south through Akkad and Kish, and reached Babylon. Shutruk-Nahhunte left his son Kutir-Nahhunte as governor of Babylonia, and returned to Susa with a large booty. This booty included several 'historical' monuments taken from the Babylonian temples, the most renowned ones being the stele of Naram-Sin, the Code of Hammurabi, and the Obelisk of Manishtusu.

Table 27.1 Chronology of Mesopotamia, ca. 1200–900 BC

	Assyria		Dynasty	Babylonia		Elam	
1200			last Kassite kings	Adad-shum-usur	1216–1187		
				Meli-shipak	1186–1172	Hallutush-Inshushinak	
				Marduk-apla-iddina I	1171–1159		
	ab Ashur-dan I	1178–1133		bc Zababa-shum-iddina	1158	acd Shutruk-Nahhunte	ca. 1170–1155
				d Enlil-nadin-ahi	1157–1155		
1150				Marduk-kabit-ahheshu	1154–1140	Kutir-Nahhunte	ca. 1155–1140
	Ninurta-tukulti-Ashur		Second Dynasty of Isin	Itti-Marduk-balatu	1139–1132	Shilhak-Inshushinak	ca. 1140–1120
	Mutakkil-Nusku			c Ninurta-nadin-shumi	1131–1126		
	ef Ashur-resh-ishi	1132–1115		fg Nebuchadnezzar I	1125–1104	g Hutelutush-Inshushinak	ca. 1120–1100
				Enlil-nadin-apli	1103–1100		
1100	h Tiglath-pileser I	1114–1076		h Marduk-nadin-ahhe I	1099–1082	Shilhina-Hamru-Lagamar	
	il Asharid-apil-Ekur	1075–1074					
	Ashur-bel-kala	1073–1056		i Marduk-shapik-zeri	1081–1069		
	Eriba-Adad II	1055–1054					
	Shamshi-Adad IV	1053–1050		l Adad-apla-iddina	1068–1047		
1050	Ashurnasirpal I	1049–1031	Second Sealand Dynasty	Marduk-ahhe-erriba	1046		
	Shalmaneser II	1030–1019		Marduk-zer-X	1045–1034		
	Ashur-nirari IV	1018–1013		Nabu-shumlibur	1033–1026		
				Simbar-shipak	1025–1008		
				Ea-mukin-zeri	1008		
				Kashu-nadin-ahhe	1007–1005		
1000	Ashur-rabi III	1012–972	Bazi Dynasty	Eulmash-shakin-shumi	1004–988		
				Ninurta-kudur-usur I	987–985		
				Shirikti-Shuqamuna	984		
	Ashur-resh-ishi II	971–967		Mar-biti-apla-usur	984–979		
				Marduk-mukin-apli	978–943		
950	Tiglath-pileser II	966–935	various dynasties	Ninurta-kudur-usur II	943		
	Ashur-dan II	934–912		Mar-biti-ahhe-iddina	942 ?		
900	Adad-nitari II	911–891					

a – a = attested contemporaneity.

Kutir-Nahhunte's stay in Babylonia proved to be difficult. In the south, a new dynasty rose to power in Isin. For three years the Elamites were forced to fight, bringing destructions that would be long remembered for its ruthless ferocity. They 'deported' cultic statues to Susa, in particular the one of Marduk from Babylon and of Nanâ (Inanna) from Uruk. When his father died, Kutir-Nahhunte returned to Susa to replace him and left a governor in Babylonia. The region was now reduced into an Elamite vassal, but continued to be rebellious. In Susa, the new king mainly focused his attention on his building programme, with construction and restoration projects in the capital and other important centres.

Kutir-Nahhunte was succeeded by his brother Shilhak-Inshushinak. In his reign, the Middle Elamite kingdom reached its peak both in terms of extension and monumental splendour. Following a series of campaigns attested in one of his celebratory inscriptions, the king took on, deservedly, the title of 'expander of the empire'. Although many of the places mentioned by him remain unknown, it is clear that he expanded to the west. He conquered the entire region between the Zagros and the Tigris, reaching the Lower Zab and the Assyrian border. He annexed the regions of the Diyala, mount Ebih (Jebel Hamrin), Yalman, and Kirkuk. These areas were inhabited by Akkadian, Kassite, and Hurrian populations. This was the maximum extension ever reached by the Elamite kingdom, which also controlled the eastern territories from the Persian Gulf to the deserts in central Iran. The only areas unconquered by the Elamites were Assyria (which was considerably reduced in size) and the Mesopotamian south, ruled by the Second Dynasty of Isin. Babylonia itself suffered incursions, but its occupation was not consolidated. Therefore, the Tigris and Lower Zab became the westernmost borders of the empire at its peak.

The Middle Elamite apogee is marked by the intense building activities of Shilhak-Inshushinak, especially in Susa. The two temples of Ninhursag and Inshushinak on the acropolis of Susa were rebuilt and expanded. The same happened to other temples in Susa and other centres. An important example is the Middle Elamite public building of Tall-i Malyan (Anshan) (Figure 27.1). Anshan was the capital of the eastern part of the state. Several administrative texts and palace workshops, with remains of flint and semi-precious stones, have been found there. The building activities on the acropolis of Susa were further enriched with furniture, mainly in bronze, and the concentration of war trophies, celebratory steles, and votive foundation texts.

From a technical point of view, it is interesting to see how Shilhak-Inshushinak proudly proclaimed that he turned old buildings made of unbaked bricks into buildings made of baked bricks. The latter were indeed far more resistant, but much more expensive. In terms of wall decorations, this phase saw the spread of coloured reliefs on glazed tiles (already a Kassite innovation) and of embossed bronze panels. Therefore, the Elamite kingdom managed to reach a level of power comparable to the one of the great Mesopotamian powers. Moreover, it employed similar celebratory and monumental expressions. However, Elam also had access to resources that remained too distant and scarce for Mesopotamia, from bronze (which was even used for building decorations) to fuel (to bake the thousands of bricks used) and semi-precious stones. All these materials were accessible thanks to the mountains covering a large portion of the Elamite territory.

This apogee, however, did not last long. Despite taking on the title of 'expander of the empire', the successor of the great Shilhak-Inshushinak, namely, Kutelutush-Inshushinak, had to endure a marked reduction of his territories. This is at least what we gather from a Mesopotamian perspective. It is therefore possible that the situation was different in the east. In Tall-i Malyan, this king is well documented, and it is possible that he focused most of his efforts on the east of Elam. Meanwhile, in Mesopotamia the situation had drastically changed. Ashur-resh-ishi's Assyria and the Second Dynasty of Isin of Nebuchadnezzar I had enough initiative to regain their lost territories.

The Assyrian intervention at the expense of Elam, which lost its westernmost territories (in the Kirkuk area and in the region between the Zab and the Diyala), is not well documented. It probably took place without important conflicts and affected only the more marginal Elamite territories. On the contrary, Nebuchadnezzar I's first attack caused an effective reaction. Nonetheless, this episode showed

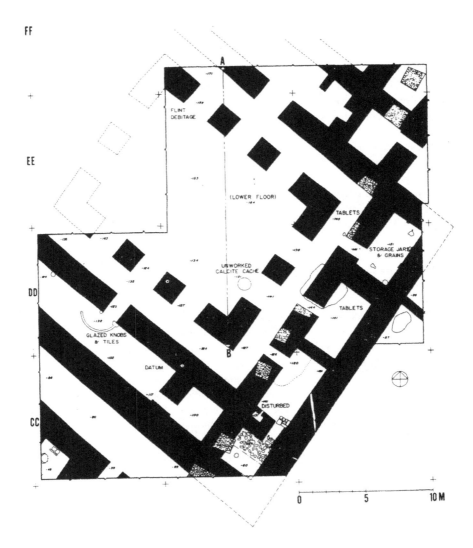

Figure 27.1 Middle Elamite building from Anshan (Tall-i Malyan).

how the expansionistic initiative had now switched sides. A second attack brought the Babylonian king to the Elamite capital of Susa. A symbolic mark of this victory was Nebuchadnezzar's retrieval of Marduk from his Elamite 'exile'. A more concrete mark of this conquest was the confirmation of the power of Isin in the heart of Elam. Consequently, Elam ceased to be a power capable of interfering with Mesopotamian affairs.

A gap of three centuries (1100–700 BC) marks the transition from the Middle Elamite to the Neo-Elamite kingdom. This lack of evidence is far more drastic than the one affecting Babylonia, but it is not entirely dissimilar. The gap is a concrete consequence of a crisis (in terms of demography, production, and political control) that particularly affected Susiana. It is likely that Anshan was less affected by the crisis. Overall, in this phase the entire area experienced a movement of populations, which left a mark on the local political structures and settlements of Elam.

2 Nebuchadnezzar and the Second Dynasty of Isin

The first kings of the new dynasty of Isin had to face the Elamite pressures of Kutir-Nahhunte and Shilhak-Inshushinak. They were also affected by some incursion west of the Tigris. However, they managed to establish their authority, moving the capital to Babylon and acquiring control over the entire area west of the Tigris. The definitive removal of the Elamite threat from the Mesopotamian territories happened during the reign of the most important king of the dynasty, Nebuchadnezzar I. The account of the final battle has survived on a *kudurru*. On this kudurru, the victorious king allotted lands and important political roles to one of his 'vassals', Lakti-Shihu (or Lakti-Shipak; in the old reading: Ritti-Marduk), head of the house of Bit-Karziabku. This vassal played a crucial role in leading the chariots in the right wing of the Babylonian army. In the text, it appears that Nabuchadnezzar had prepared for the conflict through a political and diplomatic move. He therefore sealed alliances with the local leaders of the area between the Tigris and the Elamite border. This was a composite area both from a political and ethno-linguistic point of view, with Kassites (like Lakti-Shihu), Elamites, Arameans, and Babylonians living alongside each other. Nebuchadnezzar's victory led him to Susa, where he achieved a brief victory and managed to return the statue of Marduk to Babylon. Nonetheless, all his military victories and political moves also led to the Babylonian conquest of the region between the Tigris and the Zagros.

Having removed the Elamites, the area between the Diyala and the Lower Zab saw the convergence of the ambitions of both Assyria and Babylonia. In this case, however, Nebuchadnezzar was less fortunate. The Assyrian sources record his defeats near the Tigris, at Zanqu and Idu, where the border was established. Meanwhile, the Middle Euphrates region saw the rise of a series of Aramean states (the main one being Suhu). Theoretically, these states were dependent on Babylonia, but in actual fact they were independent. Even in the west, then, Nebuchadnezzar re-established the old Babylonian border. Further wars are implied from his epithets, such as 'conqueror of Amurru' and 'plunderer of the Kassites'. These epithets allude to his victories on the Aramean invaders and the people from the Zagros.

The grand titles held by Nebuchadnezzar and the other (far less successful) kings of the dynasty of Isin are in marked contrast with the reduced involvement of Babylonia in international affairs in comparison to the Kassite period. These titles varied from the obvious 'king of Babylon', 'king of Karduniash', or 'king of Sumer and Akkad' to 'king of kings', 'king of totality', 'king of the four quarters'. The political situation of the time had drastically changed, since some powers had disappeared (Hatti) or were now inaccessible (Egypt). In addition to that, the Babylonian kingdom itself had changed, and internal difficulties precluded an involvement in foreign affairs. With the disappearance of Elam from the international scene, Babylonia's foreign relations were focused on the consuming fight with Assyria between the Adhaim and the Zab. Moreover, the movement of nomadic groups precluded access to the network of interregional commercial routes. In particular, the two traditional commercial routes of Babylonia, that of the Middle Euphrates leading to Syria, and that of the Persian Gulf towards Dilmun, were difficult to access. It therefore appears that for many centuries there were no consistent commercial activities with these regions.

The only commercial activity for Babylonia in this period had to cross the Zagros. In Luristan, apart from the traditional local 'bronze' objects (which have a substantial diachronic history), several swords, arrowheads, and spears bearing inscriptions of Babylonian kings have been found. These objects began to appear around the late Kassite period, peaked during the dynasty of Isin, and continued in the following dynasties. A century after Nebuchadnezzar I's reign, the Babylonian king Simba-Shihu was able to intervene in the valley of Zamua, close to Assyria. The reasons for the fierce conflicts between Assyrians and Babylonians in the Zagros foothills are understandable. The issue at stake was not just the control of these territories, but also the control of the Iranian commercial routes, their outlets in the alluvial plain, and the relations with the mountain tribes.

Within the land of Sumer and Akkad, the administration of the dynasty of Isin continued along the same lines as in the Kassite period. We know of around twenty provinces ruled by a governor (*šakin māti*, then *šakin tēmi*). Some of these provinces were named after their main city (Nippur, Isin, Dur-Kurigalzu, and so on). There were also other territorial entities and tribal 'houses' (defined with the term *Bīt* plus the name of the ancestor). The 'urban' provinces were mainly in the north (in the former land of Akkad), and less in the south, where Ur seems to have been the most vital city. 'Tribal' provinces were mainly located in the area east of the Tigris. It is possible that, within the land, the traditional duties of the 'governors' were taking care of irrigation systems and temple architecture. In the provinces along the borders, these tasks were more military and governors had a more personal, rather than administrative, relationship with the king.

After Nebuchadnezzar I, the dynasty of Isin continued to survive for a couple of decennia. A series of kings managed its legacy and continued the fight with Assyria in the Zagros foothills though an alternation of wars and truces, and the capture and release of several cultic statues. At the same time, however, the progressive and unstoppable Aramean infiltrations were eroding part of the countryside away from Babylonian control.

The reign of Nebuchadnezzar I is particularly important for its theological aspects. These are closely linked to the return of the cultic statue of Marduk from its Elamite 'exile'. The Babylonian interpretation of this deportation of the god was seen in a positive light, namely, as a voluntary peregrination of the statue. The latter had been taken by the Hittite king Mursili I, then by the Assyrian king Tukulti-Ninurta I, and then by the Elamites. The purpose of this alleged 'peregrination' was the spread of the god's prestige and his power throughout the world. The full affirmation of Marduk as chief deity of Babylonia, a process that had begun with Hammurabi, was consecrated in the final edition of the 'Epic of Creation' (*Enūma eliš*, a title taken from the first line of the text). In the poem, Marduk defeated the primordial chaos, embodied by Tiamat, thus becoming the god responsible for the order of the universe. After his victory, he gained the respect of the other gods, who were forced to bow in front of Marduk's superiority, proven in the battlefield.

Taking over the place of Enlil on a cosmological level, Marduk became the most important deity on a ceremonial level. The poem had a fundamental role in the grand festival of the 'New Year' (*Akītu*). During this festivity, the statue of Marduk was moved in procession from the Esagila to the Bit Akiti, located outside the city (where Marduk would meet his son Nabu from Borsippa). The *Akītu* festival would remain the most important festivity in Babylonian history, constituting a moment bringing crowds of worshippers together, and exorcising the concern for the correct progress of the seasons, of harvests, and of the survival of order over chaos.

3 Tiglath-pileser I and the end of the Middle Assyrian period

In the mid-twelfth century BC, Assyria was clearly experiencing difficulties. The infiltrations of the Ahlamu/Arameans across the Euphrates were threatening Assyrian control in Upper Mesopotamia. Meanwhile, the last repercussions of the Phrygian invasions in Anatolia had come close to the Upper Tigris, taking some territories (Alzi and Purulumzi) from the Assyrians. At the same time, the expansion of Elam in the Zagros foothills had reached the Lower Zab. Assyria therefore found itself significantly reduced in size, roughly extending from Arbela to Nasibina. However, Assyrian kings continued to claim their supremacy over the area extending from Upper Mesopotamia to the Euphrates.

A certain degree of stability was reached under Ashur-resh-ishi. The king managed to strengthen Nineveh and other key cities, such as Arbela, along the Zagros border, and Apqu, in Upper Mesopotamia. In terms of expeditions, Ashur-resh-ishi tried to push away the Aramean infiltrations along the Euphrates, from Carchemish to Suhu. He also fought against the Babylonians over certain territories along the Euphrates and the Tigris. In the battles at Zanqu and Idu, the Babylonians had to retreat, severely hindering the ambitious plans of Nebuchadnezzar I. The military endeavours of the king of Isin and his removal of the Elamites from foreign affairs had actually benefitted Assyria. This situation allowed the Assyrians to take over the areas left vacant by Elam.

The long reign (almost forty years) of Tiglath-pileser I continued and expanded the ambitions of the Assyrians with a much higher drive and rate of success (Figure 27.2). The king led Assyria through one of its most successful phases, similar to the one under Tukulti-Ninurta I (one and a half centuries earlier) or Ashurnasirpal II (two and a half centuries later). Unfortunately, being between two phases of crisis, the

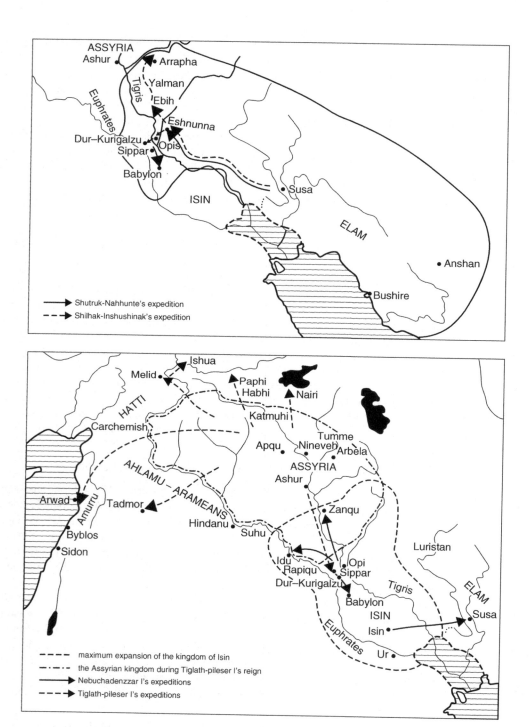

Figure 27.2 *Above*: The apogee of the Middle Elamite period, ca. 1150–1120 BC; *Below*: The apogee of the Second Dynasty of Isin, ca. 1120–1105 BC, and Assyria during the reign of Tiglath-pileser I, ca. 1115–1075 BC.

reign of Tiglath-pileser I appears as a brief success. Nonetheless, his reign is a good indication of the ease through which an energetic political leadership could guide a still intact state (such as Assyria) to great success, even in a phase of international instability. Five years of Tiglath-pileser's military expeditions are documented in his annals. In the thirteenth century BC, Assyrian royal inscriptions had already begun to be much more narrative. From Tiglath-pileser's annals, however, these texts began to be organised by year, becoming much more articulated and detailed historical sources.

There were two trends in the military efforts of Tiglath-pileser I. Firstly, there was an obscure and continuous military effort in the mountains. The latter stood dangerously close to the Assyrian countryside. This effort was essential for the survival of the state and the Assyrian access to raw materials, but brought little glory and many difficulties. Secondly, there were far more visible and rewarding efforts on an ideological level, but also less crucial. These efforts were mainly aimed at two coveted and distant destinations, namely, Babylonia in the south, and the Mediterranean in the west. Both destinations were 'liminal', the first one being a more political conquest, and the other a cosmic one.

The mountains extending from the Upper Tigris to the Upper Zab presented the same problems as the ones attested for the reigns of Shalmaneser I and Tukulti-Ninurta I. However, these problems were now further complicated by the military pressures of the Phrygians (the 'Mushki' in Assyrian) in the area and the rise of confederations of mountain tribes. Tiglath-pileser defeated the Mushki and re-conquered Alzi and Purulumzi. This victory constituted a crucial moment in the Assyrian expansion, so much so that the annals provide a topographic description of it. The first campaign was fought against Katmuhi (a state located on the Tigris close to the Assyrian border). This choice indicates the precarious state of Assyrian control at that time, even in the areas surrounding its heartland. The second campaign was fought against the land of Paphi, north of the Upper Tigris. The third campaign affected the Nairi lands, in the Armenian plateau, near Lake Van. The Assyrian king only imposed an annual tribute there, including bronze cauldrons and horses. The local political organisation remained intact, with a network of small local kings (whose names are mainly Hurrian, such as Kili-Teshub and Shadi-Teshub), who were part of larger political entities (the largest one being Nairi). The latter probably developed as a response to an emerging sense of tribal and linguistic 'nationalism'.

In the fourth year, the king began to focus his attention to the west and as far as the Mediterranean. However, the Aramean tribes constituted the first obstacle in this direction. These tribes now ruled in the Middle Euphrates, the Khabur Valley, and throughout Upper Mesopotamia. The (largely ideological) ambition of the Assyrian king was to push them back to the west of the Euphrates, the ideological boundary of the empire, towards Palmyra and Jebel Bishri, where they came from. The policy implemented, and maybe the only one possible, was that of ensuring communication among the Assyrian administrative centres. This allowed the interception and identification of tribal groups whenever possible, although their mobility made their subjugation or definitive destruction difficult to achieve.

Having somehow overcome the issue of the safety of the routes allowing communication between Assyria and the Euphrates, the remaining issue was the crossing of the river. This problem was not only technical, but also political. It marked the exit of the Assyrian army from the empire's territories and the entrance into someone else's territory, such as the one still defined as 'Hatti', even though the rival empire had long ceased to exist. The Assyrian king claims that he had imposed an annual 'tax' (paid in timber) on the king of Carchemish Ini-Teshub (II). It is clear, however, that it was a peaceful commercial agreement, even though the presence of the Assyrian army constituted an element of constant pressure. The third step was reaching the Mediterranean, which happened in Arwad. There, the Assyrian king received the 'tributes' of the other Phoenician cities, and ventured into an exciting trip by sea, reaching Sumura.

The Babylonian campaign took place in the final phase of his reign and was preceded by the usual fights east of the Tigris, in the area between the Lower Zab and the Diyala. The balance of power had visibly changed from the time of Nebuchadnezzar. The Assyrians were now able to reach the Diyala and then cross the Tigris, moving towards Babylonia itself. The northern Babylonian cities (Dur-Kurigalzu, Opis, Sippar) were conquered. The same fate befell the capital, but the episode did not have any important political consequences. The Assyrian king retreated, being content with his increased prestige and fully aware of his inability to consolidate control in Babylonia both militarily and politically.

The ideology lurking behind the military endeavours of Tiglath-pileser I was emphasised in his own inscriptions and expressed in several ways (Text 27.1). Firstly, there were the steles left (or carved on rocks) at the edge of the world, for instance, at the source of the Tigris. Then, there was the hunting of wild animals (lions, elephants, and buffalos) in the marshes of the Euphrates, or the capture of dolphins and narwhals in the Mediterranean. Symbolically, a hunt was meant to express the king's ability to dominate the wild forces of nature. However, another significant aspect was the king's ability to capture these animals and bring them to the heart of Assyria. The animals would then be left in 'parks' full of vegetation and with

---

Text 27.1   The campaigns of Tiglath-pileser I in a summarising inscription

'Tiglath-pileser, strong king, king of the universe, king of Assyria, king of the four quarters of the world . . . (further epithets and the king's genealogy follow):

Thrice I marched to the lands of Nairi and conquered extensive lands of Nairi from Tumme to the lands of Dayenu, Himua, Paiteru, and Habhu. I received their tribute of horses in harness.

I conquered 12,000 of the troops of the land of the extensive Mushki (that is, Phrygia) in battle. I laid out by means of the bow the corpses of their fighting men right through the plain.

I took and uprooted 4,000 Urumu and Apishlu, insubmissive Hittite troops, and regarded them as people of my land.

I completely conquered the entire land of the Lullumu, the lands Salua, Qummenu, Katmuhu, and Alzi.

By the command of the gods Ashur, Anu and Adad, the great gods my lords, I marched to Mount Lebanon. I cut down and carried off cedar beams for the temple of the gods Anu and Adad, the great gods my lords. I continued to the land of Amurru, and conquered the entire land of Amurru. I received tribute from the lands of Byblos, Sidon, and Arwad; I (also) received a crocodile and a large female ape of the sea coast. Finally, upon my return I became lord of the entire land Hatti and imposed upon Ini-Teshub, king of Hatti (that is, king of Carchemish), a tax, a tribute, and cedar beams.

I marched to the city Milidia (Malatya) of the great land of Hatti. I received the tribute of Allumaru. I conquered the city Enzatu of the land of Ishuwa and the land of Suhmu. I uprooted prisoners from their midst and brought them to my land.

I have crossed the Euphrates 28 times – twice in one year –in pursuit of the Ahlamu Arameans. I brought about their defeat from the city Tadmor (Palmyra) of the land Amurru, Anat and the land of Suhu, as far as Rapiqu of Karduniash. I brought their booty and possessions to my city Ashur.

I marched against Karduniash (Babylonia): I conquered from the other side of the Lower Zab, the city Arman of Ugar-Sallu, as far as the city of Lubdu. I crossed over the River Radanu. I conquered the cities at the foot of Mounts Kamulla and Kashtilla. I took out their booty and possessions and brought them to my city Ashur.

On this campaign of mine I marched to the land of Suhu: I conquered (from) the city Sapiratu, an island in the Euphrates, as far as the city of Hindanu. I took prisoners from them, and brought them to my city Ashur.

By the command of the god Ninurta who loves me I marched to Karduniash. I conquered the cities Dur-Kurigalzu, Sippar of Shamash, Sippar of Annunitu, Babylon, Opis, which is on the far side of the Tigris, the great cult centres of Karduniash together with their fortresses. I brought about the defeat of their multitudes and took prisoners without number from them. I captured the palaces of Babylon which belonged to Marduk-nadin-ahhe, king of Karduniash, and burnt them. In the eponym of Ashur-shumu-eresh and in the eponym of Ninuaya, twice, I drew up a battle line of chariots against Marduk-nadin-ahhe, king of Karduniash, and defeated him.'

[A description of the buildings (temples and a royal palace) constructed thanks to the booty brought back from the campaigns follows.]

artificial irrigation. In these parks, animals and plants from the conquered lands were brought as a representation of the diverse world conquered by the king. Stone representations of the hunted and killed animals (bulls and lions) were even left at the entrance of temples and palaces. These animals acted as protective (and deterrent) figures at the service of the king, who proved that he was able to control them.

One of the main purposes of the Assyrian expeditions in the mountains was the crucial access to the raw materials (especially timber) necessary for the king's building programme. The latter included the restoration and expansion of Assyrian temples. In this regard, the 'Annals' were meant to be the foundation text left in the temple of Anu and Adad. In terms of architecture, Tiglath-pileser I's reign constitutes the peak of the Middle Assyrian period, and was in marked continuity with the reign of Tukulti-Ninurta. This is the case not only for architecture, but also for seals and the other artistic expressions. After all, the reign of Tiglath-pileser I belonged to the Middle Assyrian period and it ended it with pride.

The same can be said for literary and administrative texts. It is probable that the Middle Assyrian Laws were written during the reign of Tiglath-pileser I. It is sure, however, that the collection of palace edicts belongs to his reign. This collection clearly displays the marked continuity between Ashur-uballit's and Tiglath-pileser's edicts. Alongside the collection and organisation of legal texts, the king also took care of literary texts, with the establishment of the first 'library'. This library contained several Babylonian works brought back as booty by Tukulti-Ninurta and Tiglath-pileser himself. It has already been mentioned that Middle Assyrian 'political' literature, which peaked with the Tukulti-Ninurta Epic, provided now, in its final phases, the basis for further developments. Despite fitting perfectly in the constant development, both in terms of its elaboration and complexity, of Middle Assyrian royal inscriptions, annalistic literature constituted an innovation of this phase.

After Tiglath-pileser I, Assyria went through another obscure phase. It is possible that no sensational endeavour, like the one in Babylonia or the Mediterranean, took place. However, it is equally probable that Assyria continued to maintain its presence in the northern highlands and to establish relations in Upper Mesopotamia against the Aramean infiltrations. In this regard, the so-called Broken Obelisk clearly shows the Assyrian difficulty in keeping areas such as the Khabur Valley and the foothills of Tur Abdin under control. The Broken Obelisk is a monument that presents clear similarities with the texts of Tiglath-pileser I, but was probably written later, perhaps in the reign of Ashur-bel-kala. It attests to the constant effort and the relative success of the Assyrians in trying to turn into a reality the ideal of controlling Upper Mesopotamia, a dream that Assyria did not give up even in times of crisis. Even the archive of Giricano, from the reign of Ashur-bel-kala, clearly portrays how an Assyrian centre in the Upper Tigris functioned normally in this phase, at the eve of a major crisis.

4 The demographic and political crisis

The three great figures of Tiglath-pileser I for Assyria, Nebuchadnezzar I for Babylonia, and Shilhak-Inshushinak for Elam, give the illusion that the great crisis, which affected the western regions of Near East at the beginning of the twelfth century BC, had not affected the powers east of the Euphrates. In reality, the crisis was only postponed by a couple of centuries, and definitely affected all three states at the beginning of the tenth century BC. As mentioned above, Elam entered a completely obscure phase, while Babylonia and Assyria both experienced the worst phase of their history. The delay of the crisis of the three powers was partly due to its general movement from west to east. It was also partly due to the ability of these three great powers to react to a degree that may appear useless and unrealistic from a long-term perspective. However, at that moment, this reaction was the result of the intervention of talented leaders, extensive mobilisations, and high levels of cultural originality.

The great crisis that followed had demographic, political, and cultural consequences. In terms of demography and production, the crisis is particularly visible in Babylonia (Figure 27.3). Archaeological evidence (in terms of surveys of settlements) reveals a further decline from the Kassite period. The latter phase had

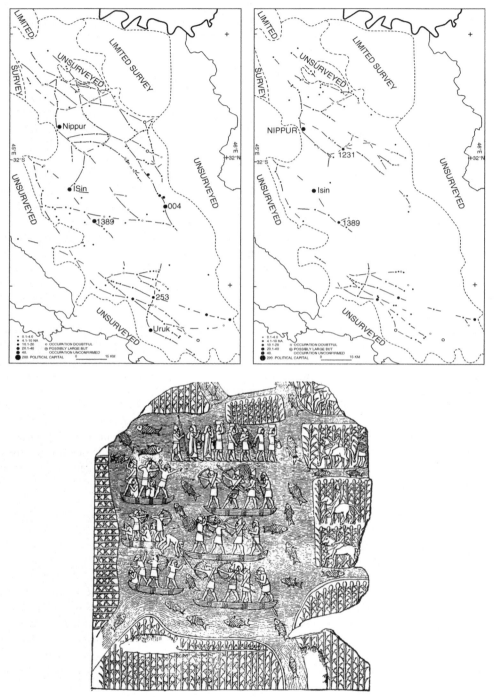

Figure 27.3 The crisis of Lower Mesopotamia. *Above, right*: De-population in the Kassite period (1200–700 BC); *Below*: The marshes of Lower Mesopotamia in a relief from Nineveh.

been already in decline in comparison to the Old Babylonian period. The decline from the Kassite to the 'Middle Babylonian' period has been quantified on the basis of the reduction to a half of its production levels for the Nippur area (which was relatively protected from wars and invasions and quite productive), and to less than a quarter for the Diyala region (more exposed to Assyrian and Elamite destructions). In both cases, the crisis affected more the cities than the villages. It is conceivable that, in proportion, areas more exposed to nomadic infiltrations or devastations from the Elamite wars, namely, the south and east, experienced a more visible decline. Overall, there was a truly sudden decline, and the total population regressed to the levels of the Early or Proto-urban phase (ca. 2500 years earlier).

The causes and characteristics of the crisis were both old and new. The long-term causes (the salinisation of agricultural fields, the collapse of the network of irrigation canals, and the decline of the local administrative systems) were combined with the effects of the more recent wars, the political instability, and the invasions. The latter eventually led to famines and epidemics, a drastic reduction of the population, and low birth rates. A symbolic example of this decline is the appearance of cannibalism as a literary *topos*. This *topos* was clearly developed to show the extent of the crisis among the population, whose undernourishment almost led them to the tragic decision of 'eating their own children'.

The issue of political instability did not affect Assyria (which was rather afflicted by dynastic rivalries), but brought to the collapse of Elam to the point of making any evidence for this phase inaccessible. However, it predominantly affected Babylonia. After the end of the dynasty of Isin, a sequence of short-lived dynasties of different and often foreign origins came to power, but their authority was not well established in the land. Firstly, three kings of the 'Second Dynasty of the Sealand' re-emerged from the far south to control Babylonia. They ruled for around twenty years (ca. 1025–1005 BC). Then there were three kings of the dynasty of Bazi, originally from somewhere along the Tigris. This dynasty ruled for another twenty years (ca. 1005–985 BC). It was followed by only one king of an 'Elamite' dynasty, who ruled for only six years. Finally, there was the 'dynasty of E', whose enigmatic name is documented in the Babylonian King List. The exact duration of this dynasty is uncertain, due to a break in the King List.

The already scanty evidence for this phase progressively leads us into a completely obscure phase. This gap in the evidence lasts until some Assyrian attestations from the end of the ninth and the beginning of the eighth centuries BC provide further evidence to date a number of Babylonian kings: Shamash-mudammiq (contemporary to Adad-nirari II), Nabu-shum-ukin (contemporary of Adad-nirari II and Tukulti-Ninurta II), and Nabu-apla-iddina (contemporary of Ashurnasirpal II and a relatively important ruler). The lack of evidence is not due to the archaeological excavations. The lack of archival and administrative texts, which were already decreasing during the Second Dynasty of Isin, is a clear reflection of the administrative chaos of the time. Unsurprisingly, the only royal inscriptions from this phase have been found on *kudurrus* (Figure 27.4), weapons from Luristan, bricks, and rare votive inscriptions. This was also due to the very few military expeditions and building programmes pursued.

Considering this severe lack of detailed evidence, a 'sense' of this phase can be partly gathered from pseudo-historical and religious/literary texts. These texts not only refer to, but also partly originated in this period. Chronicles reflect the political uncertainty and poverty of the time. They provide the characteristic 'indicators' of the crisis, such as prices or the celebration of the New Year festival. At times, the festival could not be celebrated, indicating that the inhabitants could not leave the city and travel between Borsippa and Babylon. Chronicles and omens brought to the development of the so-called 'prophecies'. These prophecies narrated the history of past kingdoms as if they still had to develop in the future, mainly in order to predict their uncertain outcome. The kingdoms are anonymous and often difficult for us to identify due to our lack of information for this phase (which would have been known to the audience of the time). However, they are often characterised by a sequence of misfortunes (from famines to invasions, wars, and usurpations), recoveries, and fleeting successes.

It therefore appears that the society of the time had lost its former confidence in the centrality and continuity of kingship. The latter used to be the guiding force and the ultimate authority in the land, due

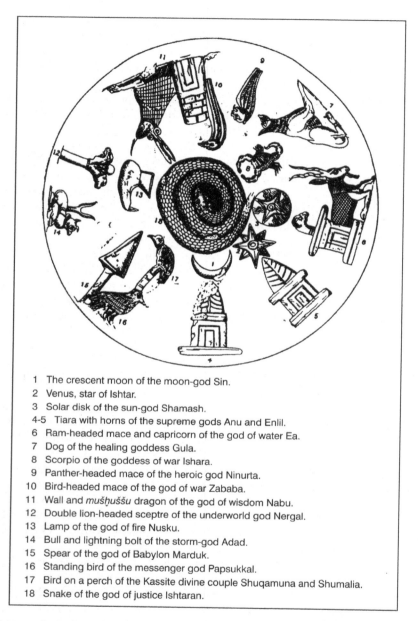

1 The crescent moon of the moon-god Sin.
2 Venus, star of Ishtar.
3 Solar disk of the sun-god Shamash.
4-5 Tiara with horns of the supreme gods Anu and Enlil.
6 Ram-headed mace and capricorn of the god of water Ea.
7 Dog of the healing goddess Gula.
8 Scorpio of the goddess of war Ishara.
9 Panther-headed mace of the heroic god Ninurta.
10 Bird-headed mace of the god of war Zababa.
11 Wall and *mušḫuššu* dragon of the god of wisdom Nabu.
12 Double lion-headed sceptre of the underworld god Nergal.
13 Lamp of the god of fire Nusku.
14 Bull and lightning bolt of the storm-god Adad.
15 Spear of the god of Babylon Marduk.
16 Standing bird of the messenger god Papsukkal.
17 Bird on a perch of the Kassite divine couple Shuqamuna and Shumalia.
18 Snake of the god of justice Ishtaran.

Figure 27.4 The top of a kudurru from the reign of Marduk–apla–iddina found in Susa, showing eighteen divine emblems.

to its exclusive connection with the divine. Kingship now became an ambiguous institution, combining positive and negative aspects, in a fluctuation that was difficult to understand. The only possible solution was to hope in a better future, which could arrive all of a sudden and without any particular reason, just like the misfortunes afflicting the land. This genre of texts mainly seems to belong to the Neo-Babylonian period, but it is likely that its roots originated in this critical phase of Babylonian history.

Finally, there are two literary texts that best represent the main characteristics of this phase. Regarding the Poem of Erra, it is difficult to establish whether it refers to a particular episode or it is more concerned with a general account of the devastations and destructions caused by nomadic incursions in the Babylonian cities. The poem's tone is theological. It explains an episode of destruction and revival that afflicted Nippur, Babylon, Uruk, Sippar, Dur-Kurigalzu, and Der (namely, the entire Babylonian kingdom). These cities were at the centre of the destructive attack of the god Erra and his subsequent withdrawal. The agents of these destructions are the nomads (Sutians), famines, and plagues. Erra was the god of plagues and many passages from this poem were later inscribed on amulets to protect from diseases, further increasing this deity's popularity. Therefore, apart from a potential connection with the destruction brought by the Arameans, the poem provides a useful representation of the overall sense of insecurity in Babylonia. This insecurity was caused by the nomadic incursions in Babylonia, and the overall decline in terms production and demography resulting from this situation. The poem's theological interpretation of the crisis (namely, divine anger) recommends fideistic and magical remedies. Political and military solutions are seen as even more unrealistic and pointless. Admittedly, this was a common problem in Babylonian history. However, the centuries of Aramean infiltration (tenth to eighth century BC) made the situation far more unstable and worrying.

The other important literary text is the so-called 'Advice to a Prince' (Text 27.2). It deals with the topic of good government, and provides an interesting point of view on Babylonian internal political affairs. The Poem of Erra has been tentatively dated between the reigns of Adad-apla-iddina (eleventh century BC) to Nabu-apla-iddina (ninth century BC) on very little evidence, but still represents the condition of the Mesopotamian world during the Aramean invasions. Similarly, there have been some attempts at dating the Advice to a Prince with precision (even as late as the reign of Sennacherib). Despite the fact that this text cannot be dated with any precision, it is still a useful text for a general reconstruction of the first millennium BC.

The text is interesting both in terms of structure and content. In terms of the former, the text re-uses the genre of omens applied to a series of relatively homogeneous causes and effects. These are mostly socio-political, thus easy to connect to each other: if a king behaves in a certain way in the administration of justice, or of exemptions, and so on, he will succeed; if, however, a king is too strict and arrogant, he will fail. The text therefore shows an implicitly polemic attitude towards the tradition of predicting the future from external phenomena (such as the position of stars or the characteristics of livers). On the contrary, it displays a distinct desire to provide a political reason to political developments. This is the pinnacle of a tendency that had brought personal omens to become more physiognomic and behavioural in the Kassite period. In other words, it was a long process that slowly shifted from more artificial and magical omens to more human and social ones. The process therefore moved from an idea of the existence of a connection between every aspect of nature, to the careful analysis of only the pertinent aspects.

In terms of content, the Advice to a Prince provides a window into the relationship between royal control and the autonomy of the cities. The political and administrative crisis had forced each city to look after itself. Rather than governors appointed by the kingdom, temples acted as the real centres of local resources and activities. Indeed, temples could rely on their millenary tradition, administrative structure, prestige, and ability to motivate the population. They therefore required and obtained from the kings (probably the weakest ones) a certain degree of autonomy and various exemptions from tributes and obligations (defined with the terms *kidinnu* in Kassite and *zakûtu* in Akkadian). They also had a certain degree of self-government for the administration of justice and of the cities' internal affairs.

When a 'strong' (an adjective that had a negative connotation in the omen tradition from as early as the Old Babylonian period) king attempted to abolish exemptions, and regain control over the situation and over the cities' resources, the cities would react accusing the king of bad government, arrogance, disregard of the ancient traditions, and arbitrariness in the abolition of exemptions solemnly promised by his predecessors. The image of the unfair and arrogant king depicted in the Advice to a Prince is so negative, that it has been suggested that it represents a foreign king (maybe Assyrian) provoking a reaction on a national scale. However, it is possible that this image referred to any Babylonian king who was trying to enforce the central structure of the kingdom, but whose interests were by now too far from the ones of the land's temples and cities.

Text 27.2   The Advice to a Prince

In the form of omens, the urban and temple authorities react to royal attempts at establishing the central structures of the state.

'If a king does not heed justice, his people will be thrown into chaos, and his land will be devastated. If he does not heed the justice of his land, Ea, king of destinies, will alter his destiny and will not cease from hostilely pursuing him. If he does not heed his nobles, his life will be cut short. If he does not heed his adviser, his land will rebel against him. If he heeds a rogue, the *status quo* in his land will change. If he heeds a trick of Ea, the great gods in unison and in their just ways will not cease from prosecuting him.

If he improperly convicts a citizen of Sippar, but acquits a foreigner, Shamash (god of Sippar), judge of heaven and earth, will set up a foreign justice in his land, where the princes and judges will not heed justice.

If citizens of Nippur are brought to him for judgement, but he accepts a present and improperly convicts them, Enlil (god of Nippur), lord of the lands, will bring a foreign army against him to slaughter his army, and the prince and chief officers will roam his streets like vagabonds.

If he takes the silver of the citizens of Babylon and adds it to his own coffers, or if he hears a lawsuit involving men of Babylon but treats it frivolously, Marduk (god of Babylon), lord of heaven and earth, will set foes upon him, and will give his property and wealth to his enemy.

If he imposes a fine on the citizens of Nippur, Sippar, or Babylon, or if he puts them in prison, the city where the fine was imposed will be completely overturned, and a foreign enemy will make his way into the prison in which they were put (to free them).

If he mobilises the whole of Sippar, Nippur, and Babylon, and imposes forced labour on the people, exacting from the *corvée* at the herald's proclamation, Marduk, the sage of the gods, the prince, the counsellor, will turn his land over to his enemy, so that the troops of his land will do forced labour for his enemy, for Anu, Enlil, and Ea, the great gods, who dwell in heaven and earth, in their assembly affirmed the freedom of those people (of Sippar, Nippur, and Babylon) from such obligations.

If he gives the fodder to the citizens of Sippar, Nippur, and Babylon to (his own) steeds, the steeds who eat the fodder will be led away to the enemy's yoke. If those men will be mobilised with the king's men when the national army is conscripted, mighty Ea, who goes before his army, will shatter his front line and go at this enemy's side.

If he loosens the yokes of their oxen, and puts them into other fields, or gives them to a foreigner, . . . will be devastated. If he seizes their . . . stock of sheep, Adad, canal supervisor of heaven and earth, will extirpate his pasturing animals by hunger and will amass offerings for Shamash.

If the adviser or chief officer (the eunuchs) in the king's presence denounces them and obtains bribes from them, at the command of Ea, king of the abyss, the adviser or chief officer will die by the sword, their place will be covered over as a ruin, the wind will carry away their remains, their achievements will be given over to the storm wind.

If he declares their treaties void, or alters their inscribed treaty stele, sends them on a campaign or . . . to the oaths, Nabu, scribe of Esagila, who organizes the whole of heaven and earth, who directs everything, who ordains kingship, will declare the treaties of his land void, and will decree hostility.

If either a shepherd or a temple overseer, or a chief officer of the king, who serves as a temple overseer of Sippar, Nippur or Babylon, imposes *corvée* labour on them in connection with the temples of the great gods, the great gods will quit their dwelling in their fury and will not enter their shrines.'

PART VI

Empires and Unification

28

THE RISE OF THE NEO-ASSYRIAN EMPIRE

1 Revival and consolidation (934–859 BC)

In the two and a half centuries (ca. 1200–950 BC) of slow disintegration of the Middle Assyrian kingdom, Assyria experienced a sort of division between the traditions and ambitions of the Assyrian kings and reality. These kings continued to consider themselves rulers over the entire territory conquered by Tukulti-Ninurta I. In reality, they only controlled the heart of Assyria and some isolated strongholds within the wave of Aramean infiltrations and the independent local centres. As a result, the first phase of the Assyrian revival, which lasted a century (from the mid-tenth to mid-ninth century BC), focused on the progressive consolidation of this gap. This led to the effective control of the areas believed to be under Assyrian control, regaining the positions previously lost, and consolidating the structure of the Assyrian state. These results were achieved through an uninterrupted series of campaigns. These took place *within* the territories conceived to be part of the empire. These campaigns were not expansionistic per se, but rather a reclaim of Assyrian authority. The Assyrians therefore felt that their authority had been put into question by the 'rebellions' of cities and peoples that should have recognised their authority instead.

The initial steps of this process were taken in the reign of Ashur-dan II (934–912 BC), even though evidence on his endeavours is discontinuous and uncertain. Ashur-dan's inscriptions show that his aim was the recovery of lands lost to the Aramean invaders. In more than one instance, we are clearly informed of when control over a certain area was lost. The inscriptions also attest that a large portion of the Assyrian population had escaped due to the instability of the situation and famine. However, the Assyrian population was now reinstated, protected, and reassured. One gets the impression that in Upper Mesopotamia the remainders of the Assyrian colonisation, established between the reigns of Shalmaneser I and Tukulti-Ninurta I, were surrounded by the new invaders. The Assyrian colonies were therefore in need of support and reinforcements. The main conflicts took place in Katmuhi and Habruri, which were immediately adjacent to the Assyrian cities and countryside, between the Upper Tigris and Upper Zab.

A similar situation is attested for the reign of Adad-nirari II (911–891 BC), although by then the Aramean siege had already been pushed further away. Adad-nirari intervened on the three traditional fronts: the northern highlands, the Babylonian border, and Upper Mesopotamia. Having already gained control over Katmuhi in the north, the Assyrian army moved into the lands of Habhu and Nairi (thus emulating the expansion achieved under the reign of Tiglath-pileser I). This was the Hurrian mountainous area that Assyria had considered under its control from the Middle Assyrian period. However, the area was now becoming better structured and organised. Due to the nature of the area, the maximum achievement conceivable was limited to the acquisition of horses and timber for the army and various Assyrian building programs. The situation in the Babylonian border was very different. The border divided two solid territorial states and had been moving forwards and backwards for centuries, in an alternation of wars and treaties whose sequence is attested in the 'Synchronous History'. In this regard, then, the treaty between Adad-nirari and the Babylonian Nabu-shum-ukin is yet another proof of the inability of either party to prevail.

On the Aramean front, Adad-nirari's intervention followed two trajectories. The first one moved from the west to the east along the foothills of Mount Kashyari (Tur Abdin). The king began several building activities in the key city of Apqu (Tell Abu Mariya). He also obtained a victory over a certain Nur-Adad, the most dangerous 'rebel' in the area. This victory led to the Assyrian control of Nasibina, Guzana, and Huzirina, through which the great commercial route crossed the Khabur and Balikh. Then, there was the north–south trajectory. This trajectory descended the Khabur from Nasibina, crossing a series of Assyrian centres and Aramean tributary centres, and reaching the Middle Euphrates (Hindanu). Although the problems encountered and measures taken were the same as the ones of Ashur-dan, their application was much broader. Assyrian control reached the farthest borders of the idealised empire, namely, from the Babylonian border to the Euphrates and the mountains of Nairi.

Tukulti-Ninurta II (890–884 BC) continued to rule along the same lines (Figure 28.1). In the north, following the Upper Zab, the Assyrian ruler re-established his control over Habruri, and following the Tigris, he conquered Bit Zamani (near modern Diyarbakir). The king also reached the source of the Tigris (an achievement of great ideological importance). Considering the fact that the territories both to the left (Habhu) and the right (Kashyari) of the river remained outside Assyrian control, this was a relatively brave infiltration. In one of Tukulti-Ninurta II's boldest campaigns, he descended the Wadi Tharthar and crossed the Babylonian territory as far as Dur Kurigalzu and Sippar without meeting any opposition. He then followed the Middle Euphrates (via Anat and Hindanu) and arrived in the Khabur, as far as Nasibina. The king's inscriptions at Terqa (Tell Ashara) and Kahat (Tell Barri) confirm his presence and building activities in Upper Mesopotamia. Just like in the case of Adad-nirari II, detailed annalistic accounts allow a precise reconstruction of Tukulti-Ninurta II's itinerary and the type of political relations established between the centres involved and Assyria.

The reign of Ashurnasirpal II (Ashur-nasir-apli; 883–859 BC) is much more well documented. His annals constitute the longest, most detailed and accurate Assyrian historical account (Text 28.1). However, its style is rather simple and repetitive when compared to more elaborate texts from the eighth and seventh centuries BC. With Ashurnasirpal, the operation of recovery of lost territories and consolidation of the empire reached its peak and can be considered completed. This led to a couple of campaigns outside the Middle Assyrian borders. Mapping the itineraries of his campaigns, it is possible to note how they were perfectly connected to each other, covering the entire circumference of the empire, as if they were the result of a specific project. However, it is more convenient to examine them by geographic sector, rather than in chronological order.

The first area experiencing a significant intervention is Zamua, an intermountain basin in the valley of the Lower Zab that joins the Diyala River. It was a key area both strategically and commercially. It appears that Assyria had never managed to access this area, while there are traces of Babylonian influence. A mountain pass (the pass of Babite) separated Zamua from Assyria, and it was a fortified pass, almost like a 'gate' difficult to cross. Ashurnasirpal forced his way through, defeated and conquered the local leaders in a couple of campaigns, and founded some Assyrian centres (Dur-Ashur and Tukulti-Ashur-asbat). These cities were collection points for tributes and goods, as well as administrative and military centres. Control over Zamua allowed to cut off Babylonia from its communications with Lake Urmia (and generally with the lands of Nairi-Urartu), and from the great route crossing the Zagros from the Diyala to the Iranian plateau.

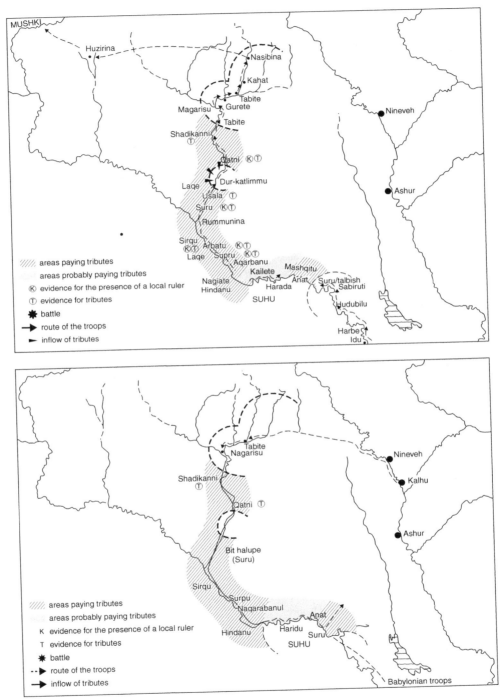

Figure 28.1 The military campaigns of Tukulti–Ninurta II (885 BC) and Ashurnasirpal II (878 BC) in the Khabur and Middle Euphrates region. The territories solidly under Assyrian control (Dur-Katlimmu; Nasibina – Tabite – Magarisu) did not have to pay tributes; Suhu relied on the support of Babylonia (whose frontier was between Anat and Suru).

Text 28.1 The seventh campaign of Ashurnasirpal II: an example of an Assyrian annalistic account of the ninth century BC

'While I was in Kalhu, this report was brought back to me: 'All of the men of the land of Laqe, Hindanu, Suhu, have rebelled and crossed the Euphrates.' On the eighteenth day of the month Sivan, I moved from Kalhu. After crossing the Tigris, I took to the desert and approached the city of Suru which belongs to Bit-Halupe. I built my own boats in the city of Suru and made my way towards the Euphrates. I went down as far as the narrows of the Euphrates. I conquered the cities of Henti-Ilu and Azi-Ilu, (leaders) of the Laqeans. I massacred them, carried off captives from them, razed, destroyed, and burnt (their) cities.

In the course of my campaign I turned aside and razed, destroyed, and burnt the cities which are on this bank of the Euphrates and which belong to the land of Laqe and the land of Suhu, from the mouth of the river Khabur as far as the city Sibatu of the land of Suhu. I reaped their harvests. I felled with the sword 470 of their fighting men. I captured 20 alive and erected them on stakes. I crossed the Euphrates at the city Haridu by means of the boats which I had made, rafts made of inflated goatskins which had moved along the road simultaneously with the army. Suhu, Laqe, and Hindanu, trusting in the massiveness of their chariotry, troops, and might, mustered 6,000 of their troops and attacked me to wage war and battle. I fought with them and inflicted upon them a defeat. I destroyed their chariotry, I felled 6,500 of their men-at-arms with the sword, and the rest of them the Euphrates consumed because of the thirst they suffered in the desert. I conquered from the city of Haridu in the land of Suhu as far as the city of Kipinu, the cities of Hindanu and Laqe which were on the other bank. I massacred them, carried off captives from them, razed, destroyed, and burnt their cities.

Azi-Ilu of Laqe, trusting in his own might, seized the crossing at the city Kipinu. I fought with them and away from Kipinu I brought about his defeat. I massacred 1,000 of his fighting men, destroyed his chariotry, carried off many captives from him, and brought away his gods. To save his life he took a rugged mountain, Mount Bisuru (Jebel Bishri), in the direction of the Euphrates. For two days I went after him. I felled with the sword the rest of his soldiers and their remains the mountain of the Euphrates consumed. I went after him as far as the cities Dummetu and Azmu, cities of Bit Adini. I felled with the sword the rest of his troops and carried off him valuable booty, oxen, and sheep which, like the stars of heaven, had no number. At that time I uprooted Ila of Laqe, his harnessed chariots and 500 of his troops. I brought them to my land Ashur. I conquered, razed, destroyed, and burnt the cities Dummetu and Azmu. I emerged from the narrows of the Euphrates.

In the course of my campaign, I turned aside. Azi-Ilu vanished in the face of my mighty weapons in order to save his life. I uprooted Ila, leader of Laqe, his troops and his chariots with teams. I brought them to my city Ashur. I confined Hemti-Ilu of Laqe in his city. With the support of Ashur my lord he took fright in face of my mighty weapons, my fierce battle, and my perfect power, and I received the property of his palace – silver, gold, tin, bronze, bronze casseroles, garments with multi-coloured trim – his valuable booty. In addition, I imposed upon them more tribute and tax than ever before.

At that time, I killed 50 strong wild bulls on the other bank of the Euphrates. I captured eight wild bulls alive. I killed 20 ostriches. I captured 20 ostriches alive. I founded two cities in the Euphrates, one on this bank of the Euphrates, which I called Kar-Ashurnasirpal and one on the other bank of the Euphrates, which I called Nibarti-Ashur.'

The second area of intervention was the one of Habhu and Nairi, and along the entire mountain range. This intervention took advantage of the previously conquered, yet still unstable, strongholds of Habruri (Upper Zab) and Bit Zamani (Upper Tigris). Ashurnasirpal enforced the Assyrian centres in the Upper Tigris Valley (Tushhan) and led a series of military expeditions in the mountains. There, the kingdoms were able to resist the Assyrian conquest. They were also on the verge of shifting from being an anti-Assyrian confederacy, similar to the one of Nairi, to a compact state like the one of Urartu. From an Assyrian point of view, in order to ensure the safety of the Assyrian centres at the bottom of the valley, it was important to consolidate control of the Upper Tigris. On the left side of the valley, Habhu and Nairi could not be overcome, and were anyway not part of the territories traditionally reclaimed by the empire.

The Kashyari Mountains, located between the valleys of the Tigris and Euphrates and the Upper Mesopotamian plateau, constituted a different case. They were cutting off communications between Tushhan and Nasibina. This area therefore had to be under Assyrian control at any cost. Ashurnasirpal led several violent campaigns there. The outcome of these campaigns initially seemed uncertain. However, judging from the progress of the Assyrian expansion, the king probably considered the area securely under his control. Naturally, the most inaccessible mountain areas would remain unreachable for the Assyrian functionaries and administrators. Nonetheless, the fortified cities and routes were securely under Assyrian control.

The centres in the southern foothills of the Kashyari (from Nasibina and Kahat to Guzana and Huzirina) were already under Assyrian control. Therefore, Ashurnasirpal was able to retrace the routes followed by his predecessors, and repeat the expeditions on the Khabur and Middle Euphrates (Figure 28.1). These expeditions were essentially a mixture of tribute collection, display of military power, and actual conquest. Apart from specific cases, such as local successions used as an excuse for Assyrian intervention, the situation was clear: all Aramean centres of the Khabur, as well as the ones along the Euphrates, on the 'Assyrian' left bank, could not escape Ashurnasirpal's army. They were forced to submit to the Assyrians, accepting to pay the tribute. They therefore became part of the empire, in the same way as the other Assyrian centres amongst which they were located. The centres on the 'Aramean' right bank felt protected by the river and the support from Babylonia (for the southernmost cities) and Bit Adini (for the ones further north), and refused to pay the tribute. Ashurnasirpal promptly intervened on the other side of the Euphrates, against Hindanu and Suhu (Figure 28.2), and fought both the Babylonian army and the one of Bit Adini. He thus gained control over the entire Euphrates Valley from Jebel Bishri to Anat and the Babylonian border.

Ashurnasirpal spared Babylonia, but decided to march against Bit Adini, which was by now an anomalous state, with territories on both side of the Euphrates (its capital, Til Barsip was on the 'Assyrian' bank). It therefore prevented the crossing of the river, and occupied a portion of the land within the theoretical borders of the empire. In order to complete the re-conquest of the empire, then, Bit Adini had to be pushed back to the other side of the river. Ashurnasirpal led two campaigns against Bit Adini. The first, relatively small, one was aimed at regaining the territories on the left bank, although Til Barsip remained untouched. The second one brought Ashurnasirpal to cross the Euphrates and achieve the dream of gaining access to the Mediterranean.

The crossing of the river led to several clashes with Bit Adini. On the contrary, Carchemish (the other key state for the crossing of the river) did not oppose the Assyrian ruler. This was also because the latter did not wish to claim Carchemish's territory, being located on the right bank, in the 'land of Hatti'. The Assyrian army proceeded through the land of Patina, in a journey that was largely peaceful. The army also received tributes, although we do not know to what extent they were imposed or traded. Along the southern border of Patina, the Orontes could be crossed, allowing access to the Mediterranean. The Assyrian king founded an Assyrian colony there (repeating an operation already implemented in Zamua and Bit Zamani). He then reached the Mediterranean, where he received 'tributes' from the Phoenician cities. Finally, he returned, crossing the Amanus and collecting precious timber. Despite its mainly commercial purpose, this expedition outside the Assyrian borders is important. It marked a desire for stable control that had never before gone so far, and paved the way for the far stronger interventions of Shalmaneser III.

Figure 28.2 Relief of Ashurnasirpal II, with Assyrian soldiers crossing a river towards a city under siege. From Nimrud, now in the British Museum, Reg. No. 1849,1222.10. © The Trustees of the British Museum.

In Assyria, the greatest achievement of Ashurnasirpal II was the construction of a new capital in the site of Kalhu (modern Nimrud). The site already had some buildings from the time of Shalmaneser I. His predecessors had resided either in the ancient religious and political centre of Ashur or in Nineveh. The latter was more centrally located within the agricultural 'triangle' and now safe after the conquest of Katmuhi. Ashurnasirpal initially resided in Nineveh, but soon after began working on the new capital. The latter was inaugurated with a grand banquet, attended by guests from all over the known world, as well as new colons, artisans, and constructors. The royal palace was lavishly decorated with sculpted orthostats inscribed with the king's deeds. Despite having suffered considerable modifications and damages, it still stands as a testimony of the pinnacle of Assyrian political and military power, of its economic and labour mobilisation, and of its celebratory and propagandist expression. This expression was often meant to be a deterrent. In fact, the Assyrian kings even prided themselves on the ruthless punishments they inflicted over the populations they defeated. Overall, the precariousness afflicting Assyria a couple of decennia earlier now seems overcome. The centre of the world was now solid, with materials, workforce and the most talented artists travelling from the margins of the empire to contribute to the construction of Assyrian monuments.

If the excavations at Nimrud provide good evidence on the centre of the empire, the margins of the empire can be better understood through the comparison of contemporary accounts with the archaeological remains. In particular, the site of Dur-Katlimmu (Tell Sheikh Hamad, on the Khabur) is an excellent example of a site that remained 'Assyrian' from the Middle Assyrian period to the reign of Ashurnasirpal, while nearby centres were increasingly influenced by the Aramean infiltrations. Further south, in the Suhu area, the Assyrian 'twin' sites Sur Jur'a and Glaya, located opposite each other along the banks of the Euphrates, clearly show the problem of the crossing of this river, which constituted a serious barrier.

Both archaeologically and textually, it is possible to catch a glimpse of the progressive consolidation of the network of communication and administrative centres that constituted the empire. Therefore, the former mosaic now became more homogeneous, though still ambiguous. The 'governors' (*šaknu*) ruling over individual cities were sometimes of Assyrian, and sometimes of local origin. Their loyalty was constantly ambiguous and their desire for autonomy can be clearly seen in the case of Tell Fekheriye. The empire did not yet have an established division into provinces like in the following periods. It continued to survive through a combination of tributes from the periphery and military expeditions. The latter were so expensive (in terms of people and means) as to become unsustainable in the long run. Having regained the 'traditional' empire, Assyria now faced two problems: the first one was its internal structure; the second one was in terms of growth. The first issue seems to have been the most urgent one. However, the successors of Ashurnasirpal II did not know how or did not want to deal with the problem, preferring to expand a not yet consolidated empire.

2 The first expansion and its crisis (858–745 BC)

In his annals, Shalmaneser III (Shulmanu-asharedu; 858–824 BC) records an endless list of yearly campaigns. Initially, he led them in person, but then he partly delegated them to his generals, especially in the great expeditions to the north and the west. The frequency and effort put into these campaigns brought debatable results. It seems as if Assyria, having suddenly 'discovered' the existence of other lands and riches beyond its traditional borders, and its marked military superiority over its neighbours, had not been able to resist the temptation of expanding further. The accounts of Shalmaneser's campaigns lack those details that make Ashurnasirpal's annals so unique, but several later versions of them have survived. The latest ones cover the entire sequence of thirty-two campaigns (from his accession to 828 BC). We also possess valuable depictions of them (with a certain degree of parallelism in the written sources), in the so-called Black Obelisk, the Balawat Gates, and the reliefs in the residence of Fort Shalmaneser at Nimrud. The development of narrative forms for the celebration of the king's deeds therefore appeared alongside the development of more iconic expressions. After their privileged placement in the orthostats decorating gates and palaces in the reign of Ashurnasirpal II, these expressions found other suitable locations.

The first area of interest for Shalmaneser's campaigns was that of the mountains in the north. The now consolidated positions acquired in the northern valleys of the Upper Zab (Habruri) and the Tigris (Bit Zamani) were used as bases to turn the surrounding areas into 'vassals'. The latter thus became systematic and resigned payers of tributes, which included horses and bronze cauldrons. The regions most directly affected in the Zab area were Gilzanu and Hubushkia, in the Lake Urmia basin. In the Upper Tigris area, beyond the river source, one could reach the Upper Euphrates Valley, in the area of Melid, Alzi, and Dayaeni. The Lake Van area, the political centre of the people of Nairi, which by now had a 'king' (a certain Arame) and a name (Urartu), was more difficult to access. Shalmaneser's incursions in the heart of Urartu, the battles won, and the cities conquered not only show the extent of the Assyrian effort in the area, but also Urartu's strength and ability to resist.

Although in a relatively different way, Shalmaneser III put a similar effort west of the Euphrates. While Ashurnasirpal II had paved the way in this direction, Shalmaneser fiercely revived the westward expansion. Commercial presence was substituted by a strong military presence, which led to destructions and heavy tributes. In this expansion, it is possible to detect three phases. The first one was mainly aimed at weakening the opposition of Bit Adini and ensuring the Assyrians a crossing point on the Euphrates. The second phase focused on the south, against the coalition headed by Damascus. The third one focused on the northwest, in the area of the Neo-Hittite kingdoms. There were several battles with uncertain outcomes (such as the one of Qarqar), and several different reactions to the Assyrians: from the pro-Assyrian Kummuh, Carchemish, and Hama, to the violent opposition of the other local states. Moreover, Assyria continuously brought local resources to its heartland, although the costs of these endeavours must have been extremely high even for Assyria.

Looking at both the northern and western front, it can be said that Shalmaneser III's policy was one of intense expansion of the area paying tributes outside the traditional borders. Those 'tribute collection rounds' made within the empire's territory during the reign of Ashurnasirpal II, were now made outside of it. However, the overall reactions and oppositions to these tributes were now very different. The states outside the empire also had their traditions, resources, and strategies to protect. Some of them, like Urartu and Damascus, were powerful states. Benefiting from the fact that they acted within their own territory, they became the centres of a resistance able to stand up to the Assyrian army as an equal rival. Consequently, 'tribute collection rounds' became far more demanding, expensive, and even unpredictable than the traditional rounds. Once Assyria began to expand outside its boundaries and request tributes from other states, the political position of Upper Mesopotamia also changed. It therefore became an integral part of Assyria itself. This fact led to the development of the practice according to which internal territories were governed by Assyrian functionaries loyal to the king. Their careers and roles could not be inherited. However, the lands and responsibilities granted to these provincial 'governors' remained relatively fluid, eventually leading to the overall crisis of this structure.

Finally, there was the Babylonian problem. Shalmaneser's immediate predecessors had opted for a cautious policy mainly aimed at consolidating the border. This strategy was characterised by little provocations from both parties, and a marked preference for written treaties rather than wars. Precisely because of the treaty with the Babylonian king Marduk-zakir-shumi, Shalmaneser intervened in Babylonia upon request of its king. The state was threatened by a revolt led by Marduk-bel-usate, brother of Marduk-zakir-shumi. The military intervention of the Assyrians (851–850 BC) followed the previous policy. However, it still managed to establish a kind of presence and intrusion in Babylonia that would eventually become rather intense. For now, the visit paid to the prestigious Babylonian deities and the 'police-style' intervention against the turbulent Chaldeans show that the Assyrian king wanted to appear kind and supportive towards the Babylonians.

The reign of Shalmaneser III, now fairly old, ended in chaos. The war of succession that saw the chosen heir Shamshi-Adad fight his brother Ashur-da'in-apli lasted six years, from the last three years of the old king and the first three of his successor. The revolt affected numerous important cities both in Assyria and its provinces. Shamshi-Adad eventually managed to prevail and rule as fifth ruler with this name (823–811 BC). The king's rule in Assyria, however, was still rather unstable. To make matters worse, he was forced to be in Babylonia, due to the usual series of treaties (a fragment of his treaty with the Babylonian king Marduk-zakir-shumi has survived) and Assyrian interventions in Babylonia.

Interventions in Babylonia, the pious worship of Babylonian deities, and the campaigns against the Chaldean tribes continued under Adad-nirari III (810–783 BC). The sheer continuity of the Assyrian presence in Babylonia throughout the ninth century BC brought to an increasing influence of Babylonian religion in Assyria. The god Nabu, who was the most 'popular' deity in Babylonia, even more than Marduk, also became popular in Assyria. Consequently, Adad-nirari built him a temple in Ashur. It is also possible to date the composition of the 'Synchronous History' to his reign, since the text ends recounting episodes from this phase. This fact is emblematic. With the beginning of the eighth century BC, the phase of equal relations between Assyria and Babylonia effectively ended. Former interactions had allowed each state to prevail over the other, forming a rivalry between essentially equal powers. In the following period, however, a 'Synchronous History' could not have been written. This is because Assyria eventually managed to gain a hegemonic role, displaying a more or less open intention to annex Babylonia to its territories.

Adad-nirari III's reign also saw the continuation of the policy of expansion to the north and west initiated under Shalmaneser III. We lack the annalistic evidence, but the Assyrian Eponym Canon continues to attest a relatively continuous sequence of expeditions well within Syria and as far as the Mediterranean. The Assyrian king was also able to act as a judge in disputes among local states, establishing the borders between Arpad and Hama, and Gurgum and Kummuh.

Shalmaneser III had therefore left an ambiguous legacy. On an international level, Assyria certainly held a strong, hegemonic position outside its borders, especially in Babylonia, Syria, and Urartu. Internally, however, the wars of succession at the end of the king's reign kick-started a marked process of disaggregation. Adad-nirari III still managed to control it. However, the process spread in the following three reigns (Shalmaneser IV, 782–773 BC; Ashur-dan III, 772–755 BC; Ashur-nirari V, 754–745 BC). This problem would only be solved through the drastic innovations brought by Tiglath-pileser III.

The 'strongest' figure of the first half of the eighth century BC was the *turtānu* (the commander-in-chief of the Assyrian army) Shamshi-Ilu. He developed a trend that had already begun with the *turtānu* Dayyan-Ashur. The latter had led the expeditions and managed the policies of the old Shalmaneser. Shamshi-Ilu settled in Kar-Shalmaneser (Til Barsip, the old capital of Bit Adini that allowed control over the Euphrates crossing) and acted as a sort of 'viceroy' for western affairs. He also led campaigns in several regions (from Syria to Urartu), and kept the prestige of Assyria alive in the lands of the foreign tribute-payers. However, he certainly took over a large portion of the power belonging to the legitimate Assyrian kings, whom he continued to formally respect. The campaigns that the Eponym Canon continued to record therefore have to be attributed to him. The absence of a celebratory literature from the reigns of Adad-nirari III to Tiglath-pileser III further proves the passive position of the Assyrian kings in this phase.

It is possible to attribute to Shamshi-Ilu the treaty, written in Aramaic on a stele found at Sefire, that he imposed on Matti-El of Arpad under the mysterious name of Bar-Ga'yah, king of Katka, and the fragment from a similar Aramaic stele from Bukan (in the region of Lake Urmia). Both attestations are a clear reflection of his interventions in Syria and against Urartu. The other treaty of Matti-El, this time written in Akkadian, was sealed with Ashur-nirari V, namely, the official king, regardless of the *de facto* powerful position of Shamshi-Ilu.

Other influential individuals are attested on their own commemorative steles. These sources clearly indicate the difficult and ambiguous balance between royal approval and the emphasis on individual power, and the actual usurpation of those iconographic and celebratory expressions traditionally reserved for the king. The ambiguous position of certain local leaders of the ninth century BC is exemplified by the figure of Hadad-yi'si. He is attested on the bilingual inscription found on a statue from Tell Fekheriye. In this inscription, Hadad-yi'si declared himself 'king' in the Aramaic version and 'governor' in the Assyrian one. He also used the iconography of the king, thus becoming a model for those governors of Assyrian origins, who did not feel inferior. An emblematic example of this is the case of Nergal-eresh, whose stele has been found at Tell Rimah (Figure 28.3). As governor of Rasappa and Hindanu, he controlled the area between the Wadi Tharthar, the Khabur Valley, and the Middle Euphrates, namely, the entire southern half of the empire. A part of this territory would later be in the hands of another great 'liege', Bel-harran-beli-usur, who left his stele at Tell Abta, in the Wadi Tharthar.

These cases are somehow anomalous, since they consisted in the accumulation of several territories under a single 'governor'. However, despite remaining within the limits allowed, other functionaries still managed to accumulate a large amount of property for themselves. This is the case of the governor of Guzana Mannu-ki-Ashur, of the *abarakku* Shamash-nasir, or the governor of Kalhu Bel-tarsi-iluma. Even the figure of queen Shammuramat (the legendary Semiramis) can be understood as part of an overall tendency that led to the increase of the number of politically influential people. These individuals effectively took power away from a type of kingship that had previously monopolised control over the state administration.

An exception to this tendency is Suhu, where a local dynasty of 'governors' who pretended to descend from Hammurabi ruled between 830 and 745 BC. Their political status, however, was rather ambiguous. On the one hand, they were formally dependent on Babylonia, although the latter did not have any influence on the region anymore. On the other hand, they were in close contact with the Assyrian governors in the Middle Euphrates. In essence, they were autonomous rulers, governing over a strategic location and leaving interesting celebratory inscriptions. These inscriptions document the arrival of caravans from southern Arabia, conflicts with the Aramean tribes, and the foundation of citadels.

Overall, the Assyrian 'feudalisation' between the mid-ninth century BC and the mid-eighth century BC was the result of a somehow 'savage' exploitation of the economic and political opportunities that the administration of the empire provided to its ruling class. These opportunities were neither regularised into an organic structure at this stage, nor kept under control by strong kings. This allowed the development of abnormal forms of political control. Therefore, in its first phase of expansion outside the old borders,

"To Adad, great lord, hero of the gods, first-born son of Ashur, who alone is fiery, lofty irrigator of heaven and earth, who provides fertility, who dwells in Zamahi, the great lord, his lord:
(3-12) I, Adad-nirari, the mighty king, king of the world, king of Assyria, heir of Shamshi-Adad, the king of the world, king of Assyria, son of Shalmaneser the king of the four quarters, mobilised chariots, troops, and camps, and ordered a campaign against Syria (Hatti). In (my) first year I made the lands of Amurru and Hatti in its entirety kneel at my feet; I imposed tribute and regular tax for future days upon them. He (sic) received 2000 talents of silver, 1000 of copper, 2000 talents of iron, 3000 multi-coloured garments and (white) linen garments as tribute from Mari' of the land of Damascus. He (sic) received the tribute of Ia'asu of Samaria, and of the (rulers) of Tyre and Sidon. I marched to the great sea where the sun sets, and erected an image of my royal self

in the city of Arwad, which is in the middle of the sea. I went up the Lebanon Mountains and cut down timbers: 100 mature cedars, material needed for my palace and temples. He (sic) received tributes from all the kings of the Nairi land.
(13-21) At that time I ordered Nergal-eresh, the governor of Rasapa, Laqe, Sirqu, Anat, Suhi and ... of ... (build?) Dur-Ishtar with its 12 villages, Kar-Sin with its 10 villages, Dur-bel-X with its 33 villages, Dur-Ashur with its 20 villages, Dur-Nergal-eresh with its 33 villages, Dur-Marduk with its 40 villages, Tell-Adad-nirari with its 126 villages, Dur-bel-Sangari with its 28 villages (all) in the district of Azalla, Dur-Adad-nirari with its 15 villages in the district of Laqe, the city of Adad with its 14 villages in the district of Qatni, a total of 331 towns which Nergal-eresh founded and built in the name of his lord. Whoever shall blot out a single name from among these names, may the great gods fiercely destroy him."

Figure 28.3 The stele of Nergal-eresh from Tell Rimah. Despite the final curses, lines 13 to 21 were defaced when Nergal-eresh lost power.

the Assyrian empire ran the risk of breaking down into a confederation of influential governors each attempting to gain power for themselves. They were only kept together by their formal recognition of the authority of the Assyrian monarchy and the convenience of intervening as a unity in foreign territories. Assyrian control west of the Euphrates remained relatively solid, and continued to exploit local resources and regulate relations with and among local states. However, the loss of initiative left considerable space for the interventions of other powers.

3 The second expansion and the provincial system (744–705 BC)

Towards the mid-eighth century BC, at the peak of the Assyrian crisis, Sarduri I, king of Urartu, crossed the Urartian border and intervened in the network of Neo-Hittite states, forming a vast anti-Assyrian coalition. In terms of potential of intervention and deterrence, a strong and active Urartu could have opposed a now divided and paralysed Assyria. In fact, even Matti-El, who was already tied to Ashur-nirari through a formal treaty, switched sides and sealed an alliance with Sarduri.

In this difficult situation, the Assyrian throne was seized by Tiglath-pileser III (Tukulti-apil-Esharra; 744–727 BC). He may have been a usurper, but was certainly a talented and energetic individual. The king had to face a double challenge: first, he had to provide the empire with a solid structure and internal unity; second, he had to face the enemies outside Assyria, in Babylonia and Urartu in particular (Table 28.1). Even before consolidating his internal position, Tiglath-pileser managed to deploy an effective army, indicating that Assyria was internally solid and was only lacking a powerful leader (Figure 28.4). A few months after his enthronement, Tiglath-pileser was already fighting in Babylonia. Barely two years later, he faced and defeated Sarduri, Matti-El, and the other members of the coalition in one of those decisive battles that mark the course of history for several decennia (Kishtan, 743 BC). Sarduri remained cut off from the political developments west of the Euphrates. This provided Assyria with the opportunity to take advantage of the situation throughout the second half of the eighth century BC. Just like Shalmaneser III a century earlier, Tiglath-pileser first focused on the Aramean states in the centre and the south, rather than the Neo-Hittite states in the north. Arpad was immediately sieged and its punishment was exemplary. In the following years, the king conquered Unqi/Patina, then Hatarikka (the northern half of the kingdom of Hama), Damascus, and the external provinces of Israel, just to mention his main conquests.

From an Assyrian point of view, the conquered states were all 'traitors', since they were previously tied to Assyria through relatively recent and more or less formal agreements. In these agreements, they had sworn their loyalty and their payment of tributes to the Assyrians. Their 'rebellion' and subsequent punishment paved the way for the development of a new system, namely, their transformation into Assyrian provinces. Local dynasts were systematically replaced with Assyrian governors, and local palaces were reconstructed as Assyrian provincial palaces. The latter had an Assyrian administrative system, Assyrian

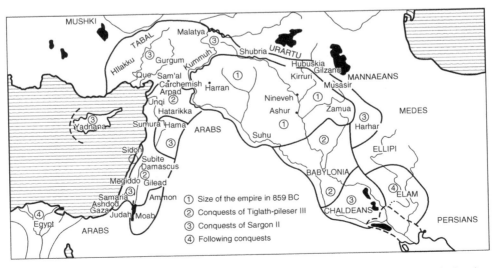

Figure 28.4 Map of the Assyrian empire, ninth to seventh century BC. The borders are conjectural, also due to the short-term duration of some conquests (Egypt, Yadnana, Hilakku and Tabal, Babylonia and Chaldea before Sennacherib).

Table 28.1 Chronology of Mesopotamia, ca. 900–600 BC

ca. BC	Assyria	Babylonia	Elam	Urartu
900	Adad-nirari II 911–891; Tukulti-Ninurta II 890–884	Shamash-mudammiq ca.905; Nabu-shum-ukin I ca.895		
	Ashurnasirpal II 883–859	Nabu-apla-iddina ca.870		
850	Shalmaneser III 858–824	Marduk-zakir-shumi I 854–819		Arame 858–844
				Sarduri I 844–832; Ishpuini 832–816; Ishpuini-Menua 816–810
	Shamshi-Adad V 823–811	Marduk-balatsu-iqbi 818–813; Baba-akh-iddina 812–?		
800	Adad-nirari III 810–783; Shalmaneser IV 782–773	Ninurta-apla-X; Marduk-bel-zeri; Marduk-apla-usur		Menua 810–786
	Ashur-dan III 772–755	Eriba-Marduk ?–760; Nabu-shum-ishkun 760–748	Humban-nimena II ca.770	Argishti I 786–764
750	Ashur-nirari V 754–745	Nabu-nasir 747–734	Humban-tahra ca.750	Sarduri II 764–734
	Tiglath-pileser III 744–727	Nabu-nadin-zeri 733–732; Nabu-shum-ukin II 732; Nabu-mukin-zeri 731–729; Pulu (Tiglath-pileser III) 728–727	Humbanigash ca.742–717	
725	Shalmaneser V 726–722	Ululayu (Shalmaneser V) 726–722; Marduk-apla-iddina II 721–710		Rusa I 734–714
	Sargon II 721–705	Sargon II 709–705; Sennacherib 704–703; Marduk-zakir-shumi II 703; Marduk-apla-iddina II 703	Shutruk-Nahhunte II 717–699	
700	Sennacherib 704–681	Bel-ibni 702–700; Ashur-nadin-shumi 699–694; Nergal-ushezib 693; Mushezib-Marduk 692–689; Sennacherib 688–681; Esarhaddon 680–669	Hallutash-Inshushinak 698–693; Kudur-Nahhunte 693–692; Humban-nimena III 692–689; Humban-Haltash I 688–681; Humban-Haltash II 680–675	Argishti II 714–680
675	Esarhaddon 680–669			
	Ashurbanipal 668–631	Ashurbanipal 668; Shamash-shum-ukin 667–648	Urtaki 674–664; Tepti-Humban-Inshushinak 664–653; Tammaritu 652–650	Rusa II ca.680–640
650			Atta-Hamiti-Inshushinak 650; Indabibi 649–648; Humban-Haltash III 648–642	
	Ashur-etil-ilani 630–627	Kandalanu 647–627; "no king" 626; Nabopolassar 625–605		Sarduri III ca.640–610
600	Sin-shar-ishkun 627–612; Ashur-uballit II 611–609			Rusa III ca.610–590; Rusa IV(?) ca.590–585

garrisons, and Assyrian cults. Regarding the population, the old system of deportations was revived, applied on a larger scale, and over long distances. These deportations had the double intent of breaking down the political and cultural role of the local elite, and of repopulating and keeping up the production standards of the conquered territories.

The new provinces continued to be located among local kingdoms (such as Sam'al, Carchemish, and Kummuh in the north, or Judah in the far south). The latter either survived thanks to their submissive attitude towards the Assyrians, or were reduced but not yet entirely eliminated (such as Hama and Samaria). The process was long and experienced several difficulties. However, it allowed Tiglath-pileser to reach southern Palestine (Judah and Gaza), in a progression that turned into a reality a project that initially seemed rather utopic. Beyond the Palestinian states, new powerful entities were on the rise: the Egyptians, who instigated and supported the southernmost and coastal Levantine states; and the Arabs, who supported their partners along the commercial route connecting Yemen with the Transjordan plateau and Central Syria.

The Neo-Hittite states in the north remained partly autonomous. However, they were still forced to submit and pay tributes to the Assyrians due to their defeat in the battle of Kishtan. Further east, Urartu had lost many of its territories, but for Tiglath-pileser III was not yet adequately deterred. The Assyrian army therefore entered the Armenian plateau and sieged Tushpa (Van), the Urartian capital. The ferocity of the destruction of Urartu, however, did not lead to concrete results, except for the separation of Urartu from the buffer zone extending from Musasir to Gilzanu. To the south-east of Lake Urmia, Tiglath-pileser faced the new Iranian populations that were substituting the pre-Indo-European ones. The Mannaeans and the Medes had now reached the Zagros foothills. The Assyrians did not realise the extent of the territory these populations controlled. Crossing the land of the 'distant Medes' from tribe to tribe, Tiglath-pileser reached Mount Bikni, the 'mountain of lapis lazuli', probably Mount Demavend. Just like the Arabs in the south, so the Medes in the north opened (or re-opened) immense opportunities, moving the border of the world even further.

Despite the positive results of the first campaign, Babylonia continued to be a problem and required more decisive interventions. It is clear that a Babylonian monarchy, exponent of the Akkadian and urban element of Babylonia, did not exist anymore, since it had died out through dynastic wars. Nonetheless, Babylonia experienced the rise of the Chaldeans. Various tribal leaders began to emerge one after the other as opponents of the Assyrians. These leaders had far less powerful armies, but were still rather elusive in their marshy southern lands, making them difficult to defeat once and for all.

Tiglath-pileser managed to defeat the first and strongest of his opponents, Ukin-zer of Bit Ammukani. Then, he defeated Bit Sha'alli and Bit Shilani, and obtained the surrender of Bit Dakkuri and of the new emerging leader of Bit Yakini, Marduk-apla-iddina (the Merodach-baladan of the Bible), who remained independent *de facto*. Having temporarily cast aside the Chaldean problem, Tiglath-pileser took on the title of king of Babylon, with the name of Pulu. This was little more than a formality that emphasised the disappearance of a Babylonian kingship. However, it was not enough to consolidate the Assyrian presence in Babylonia. Tiglath-pileser naturally had to return to Assyria. The gap he left behind was filled by Marduk-apla-iddina. Consequently, at the moment in which the traditional elements of Babylonia were dissolved, the Babylonian problem became even more difficult to solve.

The internal reorganisation of the Assyrian state developed alongside the creation of a new set of external provinces. In the first phase of his reign, Tiglath-pileser began a drastic reorganisation of those governors who had been able to gain a dangerous degree of independence. The new king personally led his army and managed to re-conquer control over his empire. The old Upper Mesopotamian provinces were redefined following a similar model to the one implemented in the new provinces. The latter were entrusted to the main functionaries of the centre, in an automatic system that did not allow abuses of power at the expense of the central authority. Finally, in Kalhu, the capital, Tiglath-pileser revived the celebrative repertoire of inscriptions and wall reliefs placed on official buildings. These interventions clearly conveyed a message of strength and wealth as an expression of his imperial ideology. This apparatus had not been in use in a monumental way ever since the death of Shalmaneser III, a century earlier.

Tiglath-pileser's successor, Shalmaneser V, had a short reign (726–722 BC). He dedicated part of his efforts to Babylonia, where he was king Ululaya of Babylon. He also completed the submission of the Palestinian states (Israel). According to Sargon II's account, it is probable that Shalmaneser's consolidating efforts went too far: he removed the traditional privileges and exemptions of the 'sacred cities' of Ashur and Harran. This move caused a series of reactions that the king was unable to control, leading to his death and the rise of the usurper Sargon II (Shurru-kîn; 721–705 BC).

Being a usurper, Sargon had to repay the forces that supported his rise to power. A good indication of this duty was the re-establishment of the exemptions for Ashur and Harran. The latter was an ancient cultic centre of the god Sin that was now becoming the main Assyrian stronghold in the west. Overall, Sargon's reign continued the process of centralisation and reorganisation initiated by Tiglath-pileser III. This process also saw the foundation of a new 'artificial' capital, Dur-Sharrukin (Khorsabad) (Figure 28.5). This city was

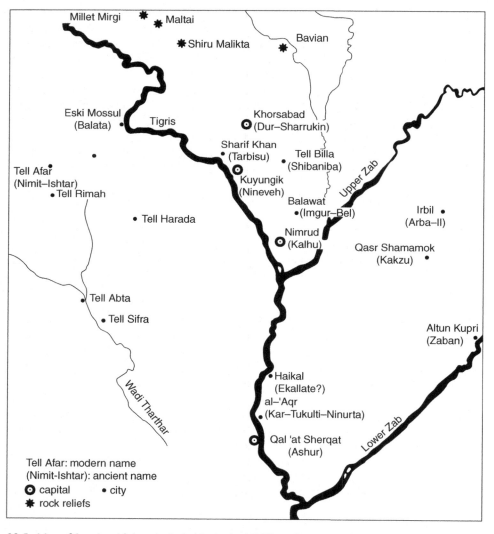

Figure 28.5 Map of Assyria with its principal cities in the Middle and Neo-Assyrian period.

built *ex novo* in a site without any previous settlement history (Text 28.2). The city's plan had a rectangular layout, an orthogonal structure, and featured a clear isolation of the city centre in a decentred citadel. The plan was clearly designed to be a new model, in marked opposition with the chaotic plans of older cities such as Ashur and Nineveh. The new capital also constituted an opportunity to develop a new celebrative repertoire made of annals and carved orthostats. These two standard genres of Assyrian iconography of kingship found under Sargon a 'classical' style. This style fully exploited the results of a long maturation process already begun in the ninth century BC, and then revived under Tiglath-pileser.

Text 28.2 Neo-Assyrian letters of the reign of Sargon II (from Nineveh and Dur-Sharrukin)

1 *Urzana of Musasir, a buffer state between Assyria and Urartu*

'Tablet of Urzana to the palace overseer. May it be well with you. (Regarding that) which you have written: 'Is the king of Urartu with his mass of troops coming? Where does he tarry?' – the governor of the city of Uasi and the governor of the district of the land of Ukka have come; they performed the ritual in the temple. They say: 'The king (of Urartu) is coming; (now) he is staying in the city of Uasi. The (other) governors will come later; they will offer sacrifices in Musasir.' (Regarding that) which you have written: 'Without the favourable opinion of the king let no one put his hand to the rite,' when the king of Assyria came, did I oppose him? What he wanted to do, he did. (Then) how would I be able to hold this (other) one back?

2 *The wood of Lebanon*

'To the king, my lord, (from) your servant Qurdi-Ashur-lamur. Regarding (the king of) Tyre, about whom the king said: "Speak (to him), (but) be kind with him" – Well, then, all the wharves are at his disposal, his subjects come and go in the wharves as they please; they sell and buy. Mount Lebanon is at his disposal, and they climb up and down as they please, and bring down wood. To whoever brings down wood, I impose a tax. I have put some tax collectors in charge of all the wharves of Lebanon (and) they supervise the mountain. I have (also) put a tax collector in charge for those who descend to the wharves that are in the city of Sidon, but the Sidonians sent him away. Afterwards, I sent the (corps of the) Ituayu on Mount Lebanon, and they have made people crawl on the ground for fear. In the end they wrote to me, (saying that) the tax collector, who had left, they had brought back into Sidon. Thus I said to them: "Have the wood brought down here, do your work with it, but do not sell it to the Egyptians or the Philistines, otherwise I will not allow you to go up into the mountain" . . .'

3 *Lack of workforce*

'To the king my lord, (from) your servant Ashur-dur-paniya. May it be well with the king my lord. Concerning the workers the king my lord wrote to me about (saying) "Give them to the chief of the servants, so that they will do their work": my workers are sixteen. Three are with the palace herald, three are working in the citadel, ten are working by the city wall: a total of sixteen workers that are all engaged. And their sons are helpers and trainees: not one of them knows how to work, (but) they bring baskets (of bricks) to the wall. (Thus) I say: for (these) workers there is enough work; I cannot give them away. I have (already) given up some of my workers for the construction of the citadel, and for the palace herald. But my own work, that under my supervision, is already too much. These ten workers that have (stayed) with me, are not moving: they have to break bricks here.'

Even in terms of military activities, Sargon continued with the same level of personal involvement and continuity as Tiglath-pileser. In Syria and the Levant there was now very little to complete, since the siege of Samaria, begun under Shalmaneser V, had ended the same year as Sargon's enthronement. Hama became an Assyrian province, moving the Assyrian border as far as Judah. However, the main Phoenician and Philistine cities remained autonomous. The revolts in the area were still supported by Egypt, which was soon defeated (Raphia). Sargon also ventured into the Mediterranean, understanding that the coast of the 'Upper Sea' was not the end of the world, but the beginning of another one equally rich in people, commercial networks, techniques, and interesting materials.

The king managed to conquer Cyprus, but control over the island remained difficult to consolidate for a continental power such as Assyria. Nonetheless, this conquest allowed the expansion of the Assyrian sphere of tributary states and the increase of the propagandistic celebration of the king's achievement. The distance of the destinations reached and those glimpsed naturally led to the reminiscence of an almost mythical past. In this regard, Egypt and Nubia, which were now ruled by an 'Ethiopian' dynasty (the Kushite dynasty), were called Magan and Meluhha, reviving an ancient terminology whose original meaning was now lost. By sailing in the Mediterranean, the expedition in Cyprus allowed the king to surpass the traditional Assyrian pride of just reaching the sea.

The conquest of Cyprus (Yadnana) in the middle of the Upper Sea was mirrored by the tribute from the king of Dilmun, in the middle of the Lower Sea. The homage of Dilmun was a consequence of the position achieved by Sargon II in Babylonia. There, a new triangle of power appeared between Assyria (whose king formally claimed to be king of Babylonia), the Chaldeans, the only local (intrusive, but by now established and integrated) power able to oppose the Assyrians, and Elam. The latter reappeared in Mesopotamia as a military support for the Chaldeans against the Assyrians. In particular, Sargon had to face Marduk-apla-iddina. The latter was now the hegemonic leader of the Chaldean tribes, and had the support of the Elamite kings Humbanigash and Shutruk-Nahhunte. The Assyrian military interventions in 720 and 710 BC managed to provide Sargon with a temporary supremacy. However, they failed to solve the problem once and for all. This was due to the elusiveness of the Chaldeans and the inaccessibility of Elam. Consequently, the Assyrian presence in Babylonia continued to be difficult and unstable.

Sargon's main efforts, then, were focused on the northern front, from the Neo-Hittite states in the north-west to Urartu, the Zagros, and the Iranian plateau. Under Tiglath-pileser III, the Neo-Hittite states had managed to remain autonomous (although they still had to pay a tribute). With Sargon, they became Assyrian provinces. Carchemish, Gurgum, and Kummuh, and perhaps even Sam'al and Que (although we lack the evidence on the decisive moment of their annexation), became relatively stable provinces. Hilakku and Tabal, located in the Taurus and thus less easily accessible for the Assyrian army, were less solid provinces. Indeed, behind the resistance of Tabal, Sargon could sense a Phrygian support. Mita, king of Mushki (the Phrygian king Midas attested in Greek mythology) now bordered with the Assyrian territories in Cappadocia, supported Tabal, but remained far enough to avoid a direct Assyrian intervention. This led to a diplomatic agreement between Mita and Sargon. In this way, the Assyrian king managed to deal with the last oppositions of the westernmost Neo-Hittite states under his control.

The support provided by Urartu to the Neo-Hittite states and its influence over the states bordering with Assyria, such as Musasir or Gilzanu, was a far more serious problem. The victory of Kishtan may have removed the Urartian presence west of the Euphrates, but did not compromise the kingdom's stability and its ability to intervene outside its borders. King Rusa controlled Musasir, an Urartian cultic centre and a strategic city posing a serious threat to Assyria. He also extended his influence on the Mannaeans (southeast of Lake Urmia), taking away an important provider of horses from Assyria. Sargon thus decided to intervene in the heart of the Urartian state. His 'eighth campaign' (714 BC) is well known for its political and military achievements. However, it is also remarkable for the detailed, first-hand account about the campaign in a letter that the victorious king wrote to the god Ashur. There, the king provided an account of the war commissioned by the deity. In a long and victorious expedition, Sargon regained control over the Mannaeans, and punished Rusa and his allies (Zikirtu in particular). Then, he sacked Musasir, bringing a rich booty back to Assyria. This was a severe blow for Urartu and in particular for Rusa, who, according to Sargon, killed himself out of despair.

Just like Tiglath-pileser, Sargon came into contact with the Indo-Iranian groups and the tribes of the 'distant Medes'. He also reached Mount Bikni and described new and wonderful places. However, a new population appeared north of the lands of the Urartians and Mannaeans, namely, the Cimmerians (Gimir-raya). Their rise was worrying the Assyrians (their concern is attested in their oracular consultations). For a while, the Cimmerian expansion was partly contained by the Urartians, whose presence protected the Assyrian empire from the waves of infiltrations from the north. However, a clamorous victory of the Cimmerians over the Urartians threw Assyria into panic.

Sargon died in battle in the land of Tabal in a minor conflict, and his body was left unburied. This was an extraordinary situation that required an explanation. Sargon therefore must have committed a 'sin' (perhaps his usurpation of the throne, or maybe something else?) to arise such a drastic divine punishment. Sargon's successor, his son Sennacherib, was chosen by his father and was already involved in the government of the state. The new king took care not to mention his father in his inscriptions, and launched an inquiry on his father's 'sin'. Moreover, Sennacherib immediately abandoned the new capital Dur-Sharrukin, in order to show his detachment from his cursed father.

4 The seventh century BC: the peak of the empire

For three quarters of a century (ca. 705–630 BC), during the reigns of only three kings and with the capital firmly established in Nineveh, Assyria ruled an empire that, after Sargon's annexations, could not expand further (Figure 28.4). The number of states that could be conquered and turned into provinces was by then fairly limited. Therefore, the seventh century BC only saw few additions to the empire. In other words, the system had reached a saturation point. There still were three great kingdoms (Egypt, Urartu, Elam) outside the empire's borders. However, they were too difficult to conquer. There also were several new and unruly populations, such as the Arabs in the south and the Medes in the north. However, they eluded the standard forms of control and exploitation. Within the empire itself, the Babylonian problem continued to be unresolved. The issue at stake was not the conquest of the old southern capital, but rather the submission of the elusive Chaldean tribes, hiding in their refuges in the marshes and steppes.

The reign of Sennacherib (Sin-ahe-eriba; 704–681 BC) is well attested in his annals and other inscriptions, as well as on his palace reliefs, characterised by their distinctive landscapes. The king's military expeditions in the north and the west were few. This, however, was because of the political situation at the time, and not because of a lack of evidence on our part. Despite reaffirming the tributary agreements with the small independent kingdoms of the coast (the Phoenician cities) and the south (Judah and the Philistine cities), the only great expedition in Syria and the Levant did not achieve its main objective. Of the two most important enemies, the king of Sidon escaped his capture by fleeing to Cyprus, and Hezekiah of Judah survived the siege of Jerusalem. However, he lost part of his territories to the neighbouring pro-Assyrian states. The campaign was emphatically celebrated on the enormous depiction of the siege of Lachish, which was placed in a highly visible position. Nonetheless, the actual results of the campaign were relatively modest.

Sennacherib never went to Anatolia in person, possibly because of the curse surrounding his father Sargon's death there. His generals led a few campaigns in Cilicia and Cappadocia, while Urartu remained untouched. Assyrian control was lost in several areas: Tabal became independent, Musasir returned to Urartu, and Ellipi and other areas of the Zagros fell under Elamite control. Sennacherib probably thought that these were natural adjustments, and that the recovery of certain borders would have been more costly than convenient.

The only significant and continuous military involvement of the Assyrians was focused on Babylonia, with several, not always successful, expeditions. The first phase still saw Marduk-apla-iddina as 'king of Babylon' and supported by Elam. Sennacherib would polemically remark that Marduk-apla-iddina had impiously 'bought' Elam with the treasury from the Esagila. An Assyrian victory at Kish and the first escape of the Chaldean king allowed the enthronement in Babylon of a certain Bel-ibni, an Assyrian trustee. Marduk-apla-iddina swiftly eroded Bel-ibni's power, provoking yet another Assyrian intervention. The latter resulted in the appointment of Ashur-nadin-shumi, son of the Assyrian king, in Babylonia, and the flight of the Chaldean king to Elam. A third intervention led to an Elamite counterattack and the capture of Sennacherib's son.

After the disappearance of Marduk-apla-iddina, a new Chaldean leader, Nergal-ushezib rose to power in Babylonia with the support of the Elamites. Sennacherib defeated both the Chaldeans and the Elamites at Nippur. He was about to continue towards Elam to avenge his son, but he was stopped by the oncoming winter. The subsequent death of the Elamite king proved to be enough for Sennacherib, who simply declared that the gods had completed his punishment. The third Chaldean enemy was Mushezib-Marduk, who managed to form a coalition able to threaten Sennacherib (again 'buying' allies with Marduk's treasures). The battle of Halule (691 BC), which was described by the Assyrian king as a great victory, in fact led to a stalemate. Nonetheless, two years later Sennacherib returned and reached a 'final solution', relieving his resentments accumulated through the many military failures and the death of his son. Babylon was destroyed, its remains flooded, and the most glorious city of the time was condemned to be eternally forgotten.

The destruction of Babylon was contrasted by the king's building program in Nineveh. The latter had long been the largest city in Assyria, but was now further enlarged and embellished as the true capital of the empire. Nineveh was therefore seen as the centre of the world, accumulating tributes from the empire's periphery. In his celebratory expressions, Sennacherib insists on his enlargement and improvement of the city. The city was inhabited by around 100,000 inhabitants, and had serious problems of supply. The king tried to increase the productivity of the surrounding countryside by transforming the already extensive grain production into an even more intensive cultivation. Consequently, he commissioned several hydraulic interventions, channelling additional canals (gathered through various tunnels and a *bona fide* aqueduct) in the Khosr River, which passed through Nineveh. Within the capital, Sennacherib's activities also included a new enlarged city wall, a royal palace (found during the old nineteenth century excavations), and restorations and enlargements of various city temples.

The succession to the throne had long become enough of a problem to involve a large part of the kingdoms and the entire ruling class, both in the centre and the provinces. Sennacherib designated his youngest son Esarhaddon (Ashur-ah-iddina) as successor. This selection was certainly influenced by the latter's mother, the Aramean Naqi'a (Zakutu in Babylonian). In fact, Sennacherib clearly preferred him to his other children, sons of previous wives. This decision, inscribed in the stars and accompanied by every sort of favourable omen, was put into action through the participation of everyone involved (from the members of the royal family to court functionaries) in an oath of loyalty to the king and his designated successor. This colossal formality, however, did not appease the ambitions of the other brothers of Esarhaddon. One of them even killed the old Sennacherib to seize the throne. This led to a civil war between the chosen heir and the alleged parricide, which resulted in the victory of Esarhaddon (680–669 BC).

The issues of succession, however, became intertwined with the problems in Babylonia. The destruction of Babylon had serious consequences, even religious ones. This was due to the prestige of Babylon's temples and deities in Assyria itself. Esarhaddon was particularly influenced by religious and magical considerations (and had a growing obsession for every sort of verification through omens). Consequently, he was extremely worried by his father's 'impious' behaviour. Compared to his father's interventions, Esarhaddon completely changed his policies. He generously allowed exemptions to Ashur, thus reviving Sargon's policy (which Sennacherib had seemingly interrupted). He also began the restoration of Babylon, returning to the Babylonians their property, and to the Babylonian temples their cultic statues, previously deported by Sennacherib to Assyria.

Other Babylonian centres were also restored and granted exemptions and privileges. More repressive interventions were led against the Aramean and Chaldean tribes. In particular, the king focused on Bit

Dakkuri and Gambulu, which had threatening leaders in power. Elam was relatively under control and had to reduce its pressures in the west compared to the previous period. Esarhaddon remained king of Babylonia throughout his reign, and managed to keep the situation under control better than his predecessor. However, it is difficult to understand whether this was an effect of Esarhaddon's benevolent behaviour towards Babylonia, or a consequence of the harsh final intervention of his father.

Having established control over Babylonia, Esarhaddon led an expedition in eastern Arabia (Bazu). This area was described as an impenetrable desert, a kingdom of death, and the true edge of the world. The Assyrian expedition in Arabia is a significant mark of the time. It implies that, alongside the more well-known commercial route along the west of the Arabian Peninsula (Yemen-Hejaz), there was a route along the Persian Gulf, in an area that had been barely visited for centuries.

There are no annalistic accounts for Esarhaddon, but his military activity was much more substantial than his father's. In the north, Assyrian interventions were provoked by several difficult and not always solvable situations. In Anatolia, Mugallu, king of Melid and Tabal, had become independent. Assyrian control in the area was further threatened by the rebellions of the populations in the Taurus and the incursions of Cimmerians and Scythians. Having reached Urartu, the latter spread in the Anatolian Central plateau and moved against the kingdom of Phrygia. In Urartu, Esarhaddon had issues with the kingdom of Shubria, a buffer state between Urartu and Assyria. This episode is attested in a 'letter to the God', written by Esarhaddon to inform the god of the just punishment inflicted on the treacherous vassal. The letter shows the theological interpretation of facts in terms of a violation of a sacred oath and the subsequent divine punishment. This interpretation is also attested in an episode recounting the welcoming, rather than the extradition of refugees. This story would seem relatively banal, but it is probable that the refugees were the king's brothers (or their supporters) defeated in the war of succession.

Further east, the Mannaeans continued to worry Esarhaddon. They had significantly evolved from the time of Sargon. The Mannaeans thus ceased to be a buffer state between Assyria and Urartu, subject to the harassment and tributes of both, and punished by one state when the other was approaching. They now became an important political presence, fully aware of its own resources. They expanded at the expense of Assyria (Zamua), and were now able to control the commercial networks coming from Iran. The Medes experienced a similar development. While in the reign of Sargon they were considered as a generic group, now they were known tribe by tribe, together with the name of their leaders and the region they controlled. The power of the Medes was both economic (horses, metals, and other products from Iran) and military. Relations between Assyrians and Medes were sealed through sworn treaties, and required the latter's service to guard the Assyrian palaces. Contrary to prior belief, it is certain that the Median territories were not annexed to the empire.

Finally, in the Syro-Levantine front, Esarhaddon added a further state to his provinces through the annexation of Sidon. He also regained some sort of control over Cyprus, although this control was as temporary as the one in the reign of Sargon. The king continued to fight the independent Palestinian states in the south, and then decided to intervene in Egypt. At the time, the latter was supporting (if not instigating) all the Levantine rebellions, and welcoming the defeated refugees. However, Egypt was relatively vulnerable and reduced to a 'broken reed' (as they used to say in the Levant at the time). It thus was better in promising support to the Phoenician and Levantine kingdoms rather than providing it. Egypt was ruled by a Nubian dynasty (headed by king Taharqa). However, the Egyptian and Libyan princes of the Delta were eager to break free from Nubian control. Esarhaddon's expedition was therefore an easy success. He marched as far as Memphis, while Taharqa retreated in Thebes (Upper Egypt). Following the campaign, the princes of the Delta became Assyrian vassals and Esarhaddon returned to Assyria. If the conquest had been relatively easy, control over Egypt proved to be difficult to maintain. As soon as the Assyrians left Egypt, Taharqa swiftly re-conquered Lower Egypt, regaining his previous position. A few years later, Esarhaddon organised a new expedition to Egypt, but died on the way, leaving the Egyptian problems in the hands of his successor.

Esarhaddon's succession had been prepared following a similar procedure as the one implemented by Sennacherib. The decision was still influenced by the queen mother Naqi'a/Zakutu. Esarhaddon had chosen Ashurbanipal (Ashur-ban-apli), leaving his eldest son Shamash-shum-ukin as king in Babylonia. This was an equally prestigious role from a religious and cultural point of view, but definitely secondary on a political level. All members of the royal family and the court, as well as all the Assyrians, had to swear an oath (*adê*) of loyalty to the king's decision. Apart from Ashurbanipal's account, this oath is attested in a number of letters from his functionaries, and has fully survived (in a long and articulated text) in the oath taken by the leaders of the Medes. This oath, commonly misunderstood as a vassal treaty, was instead an oath of loyalty that the Medes swore as the crown prince's bodyguards, thus ensuring the loyal execution of royal orders. After a reign spent worrying for any 'sign' on his fate and that of his empire, and appointing 'substitute kings' to divert negative omens, Esarhaddon, probably already ill, died on his way to Egypt. Ashurbanipal therefore became king while still young, ruling for forty years (668–629 BC).

Unlike his predecessors, Ashurbanipal did not lead his military expeditions in person, but simply devised the necessary orders from his palace. However, he prided himself on other personal achievements, namely, on being an expert scribe, able to understand even ancient and difficult Sumerian and Akkadian texts. He also proclaimed his ability to work with multiplications and divisions, and to quote and interpret the canonical series of liver and astronomical omens. His palace in Nineveh was the last building of this kind in Assyria to reach high levels of complexity and quality. There, the king ordered the collection of all renowned literary and religious texts, especially from Babylonia, in order to build a 'library'. Despite the fact that this initiative had some modest antecedents (Tiglath-pileser I), Ashurbanipal's collection exceeded them for the systematic conception, the quantity of texts accumulated, and the amount and quality of the philological work needed. Moreover, we owe Ashurbanipal's library, found during the nineteenth century excavations at Nineveh, a large part of our knowledge of Babylonian literature.

Despite not being led by the king in person, Ashurbanipal's military campaigns were numerous. They were depicted and narrated on inscriptions and reliefs, as if they were led by the king himself. These celebratory expressions were highly innovative, breaking from the traditional schemes through wider landscapes and detailed depictions, and ceasing the traditional year-by-year accounts or scene-by-scene depictions. Ashurbanipal's most urgent problem, however, left unresolved at the time of his father's death, was Egypt. The expedition begun by Esarhaddon was resumed and led to completion by Ashurbanipal's generals. Taharqa was pushed out of Egypt. The Delta princes that had supported Taharqa were removed with the exception of Necho, who was left as ruler in Sais (almost as an Assyrian viceroy in the Delta), and his son Psamtik, ruler of Athribis. As usual, the Assyrian retreat from Egypt allowed the intervention of the Kushite king Tantamani, successor of Taharqa. This time, however, the Assyrians reacted immediately and marched into Upper Egypt. Having regained control over Memphis, the Assyrian army reached and conquered Thebes.

Despite having effectively ended the Kushite rule in Egypt, Assyrian control could not be consolidated. The Assyrian sources skip the following developments: Psamtik gained control over Egypt, expelling the Assyrians, and establishing a new dynasty that controlled the entire Nile Valley from the Delta to Thebes (663 BC). This time, Ashurbanipal did not intervene. This indicates that the Assyrians were unable to lead systematic interventions this far. After all, the Phoenician and Levantine states, which had initially sparked the conflict between the Assyrians and the Egyptians, continued to remain independent even when they were sieged, such as in the case of Tyre or Arwad.

If Egypt was a distant problem and overall a superfluous conquest, Babylonian control and the rise of Elam in Lower Mesopotamia continued to be a main reason for concern. The rise to power of Shamash-shum-ukin in Babylon did not solve the problem, but made it worse. The 'unfaithful brother', as Ashurbanipal describes him in his inscriptions, acted independently and attempted to free himself and his land from Assyrian control. He formed a coalition against Ashurbanipal with all the other powers outside the empire, from Elam to Egypt, the Arabs, and the Iranian tribes. Apart from the propagandistic exaggeration, the main support of Shamash-shum-ukin undoubtedly came from Elam. The latter was in the middle of internal power and succession wars. The former pro-Assyrian policy established under Esarhaddon was therefore abandoned, in the hope of isolating Assyria and drastically reducing its hegemonic role.

The sequence of events is complex. At the beginning, Shamash-shum-ukin was still peaceful, while Elam was supporting various 'rebels' in southern Mesopotamia. Ashurbanipal's generals defeated a coalition between the Elamite Urtaku, Nippur, and Gambulu (665–663 BC). Ten years later, the most threatening Elamite attempt (under Teumman) was countered by a more serious Assyrian intervention that led the Assyrian army to Elam. As a result, Ashurbanipal forced the traditionally composite political structure of Elam to accept Assyrian control. This caused difficult relations among the internal factions. The 'mosaic' of factions extended as far as Lower Mesopotamia, where Shamash-shum-ukin ruled in the north (in the area around Babylon), while the Chaldean Nabu-bel-shumate ruled in the Sealand. At this point, the king of Babylon put the above-mentioned anti-Assyrian coalition together. The coalition was impressive, but inconsistent, due to the conflicting ambitions of the kings of Babylon and Elam. Therefore, the intervention of the Assyrian general Bel-ibni was decisive. Babylon was conquered, Shamash-shum-ukin died in his burning palace, and a certain Kandalanu was enthroned as an Assyrian governor in his place. Soon after, at the peak of a long campaign in which the Assyrian army devastated Elam (Figure 28.6), Susa was conquered and ruthlessly destroyed.

The destruction of Elam constituted a crucial moment in Mesopotamian history. The Chaldeans now lacked an external support. Consequently, for the remaining fifteen years of Ashurbanipal's reign, they were unable to intervene. The repercussions of Elam's disappearance, however, went far beyond the Lower Mesopotamian scene and the Assyrian presence in Elam. The fall of Elam created a power vacuum that not even Assyria was able to fill. Emblematically, soon after the sack of Susa, Ashurbanipal received a tribute from a king Cyrus of Parsumash (namely, Persis or modern Fars), an ancestor of the great Cyrus II. Already at this stage, the Persian nation occupied the land of Anshan, the ancient eastern centre of Elam.

The sack of Susa could have marked the peak of the Assyrian empire, but at the same time it signalled the beginning of the empire's decline. Of the three other powers of the time, one, Egypt, was increasingly unable to intervene in Syria and the Levant, but was also too distant for another Assyrian intervention. The second power, Elam, had fallen, facilitating the rise of even more dangerous enemies. The third power, Urartu, was going through considerable difficulties. The latter, however, were more due to the pressures from the north than the Assyrians. Having defeated his rivals, now turned into 'regular' (non-expansionistic) powers, Assyria was more than ever exposed to the pressures from the new populations of the south and the north. Indeed, the latter were now free from the opposition of the former rivals of Assyria. The people of the south, namely, the Arabs, could not threaten Assyria. The Assyrian army easily overcame the Arabic troops on camels, which were inferior both in terms of weaponry and military tactics. The large booty brought back to Assyria led to the fall of prices in slaves and camels (following the typical celebrative *topos*). However, the centres, wealth, and human resources of the Arabs were still too far from Assyria. Therefore, their crucial commercial role in the Arabian Peninsula remained unshakeable.

The Iranian tribes in the north were a far more dangerous threat for Assyria, while Anatolia was still under the influence of the Cimmerians. After the fall of the kingdom of Phrygia, the new kingdom of Lydia contacted Assyria to seal an alliance against the common enemy. Gyges sent an embassy to Ashurbanipal. Allegedly, this move was inspired by a dream. However, the embassy's messengers spoke an unknown language and came from too far to be included in the 'mental map' of the Assyrians. The embassy was therefore ignored. Soon after, the Assyrians faced the Lydian and Ionian mercenaries of Psamtik's army, which made them retreat from Egypt.

Urartu was still standing, but was forced to ask for help to the Assyrians in order to face the Scythians and Cimmerians. Assyrian support, however, never materialised. This was not because Urartu was distant, but because it was considered a traditional enemy of Assyria. This reaction indicates that the Assyrians were clearly unable to cast their sense of rivalry aside – a decision that would soon prove to be a mistake. Further east, the Mannaeans and the Medes were also on the rise. Ashurbanipal sent his generals and achieved some

Figure 28.6 Relief of Ashurbanipal, with the siege of an Elamite city. From Kouyunjik, now in the British Museum, Reg. No. 1856,0909.17–18. © The Trustees of the British Museum.

successes. However, these campaigns only managed to contain their expansion. They did not avert the transformation of the Mannaeans and Medes into organised states with considerable military and economic power.

At the eve of Ashurbanipal's death, the empire seemed larger and stronger than ever before. Everything seemed under control or, at least, almost everything. Who could have predicted, then, that new problems on the rise, combined with old unresolved issues, would have brought the empire to a sudden and definitive collapse?

29

THE STRUCTURE OF
THE NEO-ASSYRIAN EMPIRE

1 City and countryside

Despite being a wealthy and populated land, the territory of Assyria was fairly limited in size. It therefore encountered some organisational and demographic problems when ruling over a large portion of the Near East. In this phase, the heart of Assyria reached the peak of its expansion. This development was not entirely due to a demographic growth in the countryside, but rather to the presence of a network of considerably large cities located a few kilometres away from one another. Despite the construction of its 'new city' and a marked increase in sacred buildings, Ashur did not reach the fifty hectares mark, thus remaining in the class of Bronze Age cities. The city was located in a relatively isolated area and was not a privileged commercial junction anymore. Therefore, it now became a prestigious sacred city in constant need of special treatments and exemptions.

The real development took place in the triangle of land between the Tigris and the Upper Zab. This area became the preferred location for the three Neo-Assyrian capitals of Kalhu (for Ashurnasirpal II and his successors), Dur-Sharrukin (Sargon II), and Nineveh (especially for the final phase, from Sennacherib onwards). Kalhu was a city of 360 hectares, 20 of which were occupied by the citadel, with its royal palaces and main temples (Figure 29.1). Following the standard evaluation of a hundred inhabitants per hectare, Kalhu must have had around 35,000 inhabitants. Ashurnasirpal's text celebrating the city's foundation attests that the monumental opening banquet had 16,000 citizens, 47,000 builders, 5,000 foreign guests, and 1,500 officials. However, the first number is far too low and has to be added to the last number, since the court and administration were moved to the new capital. It is also possible that a number of builders working on the city eventually settled there.

Dur Sharrukin was of a similar size, reaching 320 hectares, 20 of which belonged to the citadel (Figure 29.2). However, the sporadic occupation of this artificial capital meant that its number of inhabitants constantly changed. Nineveh, an already important and ancient city, was far larger and was further enlarged in the Neo-Assyrian period, reaching 750 hectares (20 hectares for its citadel) under the last Sargonids (Figure 29.3). The round and exaggerated number of inhabitants attested in the Book of Jonah (120,000) seems excessive, but it is possible that this large metropolis reached 70,000 inhabitants, becoming an unusually large settlement for its time.

These great capitals were not the only Assyrian urban phenomenon of the time. A series of minor centres appeared in a sort of circle surrounding the main cities. These minor centres were still relatively large and equipped with the administrative and cultic apparatus characterising a city. Some centres emerged

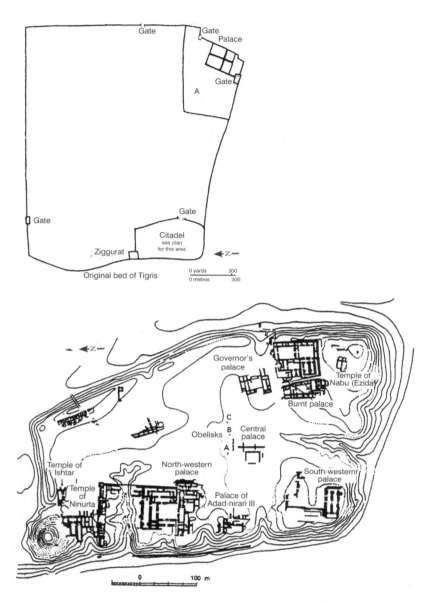

Figure 29.1 Kalhu (Nimrud). *Above*: Plan of the city; *Below*: The citadel.

west of the Tigris, where Balatu (Eski Mossul), Apqu (Tell Abu Mariya), and Nimitti-Ishtar (Tell Afar) controlled the routes towards Upper Mesopotamia and the populated production district at the foothills of the Jebel Sinjar. Other centres emerged to the south-east, beyond the Zab, where Kilizi (Qasr Shamamok) and especially Arbela (buried under the homonymous modern city) were already frontier cities and main junctions for communications with Iran and the area between the Tigris and the Zagros. All these cities, and the capitals in particular, caused serious supply issues. Consequently, relations between the cities and the Assyrian countryside drastically changed, with cities in constant growth and villages in decline, further

Schematic plan of the city

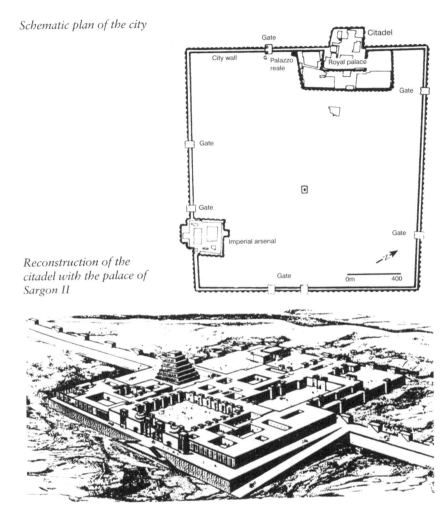

Reconstruction of the citadel with the palace of Sargon II

Figure 29.2 Khorsabad (Dur-Sharrukin). *Above*: Schematic plan of the city; *Below*: Reconstruction of the citadel with the palace of Sargon II

worsening the latter's situation. In terms of supplies, the cities also saw a marked increase of the 'parasitic' component of the population, namely, state and religious functionaries, craftsmen and soldiers.

Through the foundations and enlargements of cities, the Assyrian kings denounced the problem of supplies, boasting of having increased the productivity of the countryside through the colossal construction of canals (from the Zab and its minor western tributaries) (Figure 29.4). These interventions were meant to irrigate the Assyrian countryside, allowing a wider range of cultivations alongside the already intensive cereal farming. Food had to be produced within a few kilometres from the cities. This aspect is confirmed by the monumental efforts of the Assyrian kings in this regard. However, it is possible that kings, or individual functionaries owning land in the provinces, imported part of the supplies from further away, especially via river. It is clear that the role of the Assyrian metropolises as the heart of the empire facilitated more an accumulation of workforce and raw materials, rather than food supplies, but it could have contributed to the latter as well.

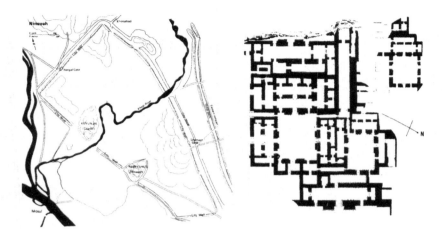

Figure 29.3   Nineveh. *Left*: Plan of the city, with its fortification wall and the two citadels of Kouyunjik (royal palaces) and Nabi Yunus (arsenal); *Right*: The palace of Sennacherib.

In terms of technology, the great hydric interventions were certainly innovative, with rock-cut canals and tunnels built with the new type of technical knowledge developed in the Early Iron Age in the mountainous areas. However, it appears that there were no other significant innovations in this phase, apart from possibly some developments in irrigation and the introduction of a few new plants (such as cotton). On the contrary, Assyria experienced profound socio-economic changes. The impact of this internal evolution and the empire's efforts seriously affected the Assyrian countryside. The expropriation of the local village communities at the advantage of public and private creditors, and the mixture of enslaved farmers with actual slaves, led to the formation of one general class of slaves. The latter were linked to their owners and the land they worked on (Figure 29.5). Great landowners were mainly high functionaries of the court or state administration. They received lands from the king and at times even received exemptions. These individuals managed to increase their estates and clientele through interest loans. The military and imperial efforts of Assyria affected all these processes, thus increasing their impact. Moreover, the population in the countryside was significantly decreasing due to the Assyrian military service. The latter was a continuous and dangerous duty, costing many people their lives. Their absence from the countryside was filled through the deportations of people from conquered territories. These deportees immediately became slaves to the palace or the great landowners receiving these individuals from the palace.

Landowners lived in the city, held various types of offices as 'servants of the king', had considerable wealth, and were involved in the empire's military and administrative activities. Consequently, an enormous gap was formed between the landowners and the servile class of farmers. Villages underwent significant changes, with the assimilation of private lands into larger landed estates owned by wealthy landowners. Farmers became mere workers, whose number was recorded in the registries of the time according to gender and age. Children were measured in spans, in order to predict the time needed until they became an additional workforce in the fields. The marked growth of cities in contrast with the countryside thus corresponded to the contrast between the ruling elite living in the cities and the enslaved mass of farmers living in the countryside. This growth of the elite found new opportunities in each newly conquered land, quickly expanding the process of enslavement to the countryside outside the Assyrian borders.

This production system (which did not work as well in the reproduction cycle for the workforce and the military) underwent a relatively reasonable taxation (apart from exempted areas), at least compared to the normal Near Eastern standards. This system of taxation was able to maintain the king and his court on

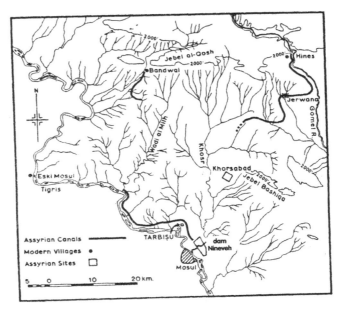

Figure 29.4 The irrigation system of the Assyrian countryside. *Above*: The Jerwan aqueduct, built by Sennacherib (plan); *Below*: Reconstruction of the site of Hines (Bawian), where the canal began.

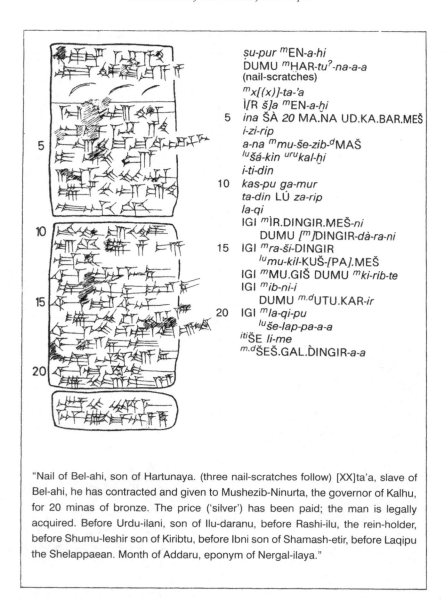

```
              ṣu-pur ᵐEN-a-ḫi
              DUMU ᵐHAR-tu?-na-a-a
              (nail-scratches)
              ᵐx[(x)]-ta-'a
              ÌR š]a ᵐEN-a-ḫi
        5     ina ŠÀ 20 MA.NA UD.KA.BAR.MEŠ
              i-zi-rip
              a-na ᵐmu-še-zib-ᵈMAŠ
              ˡᵘšá-kin ᵘʳᵘkal-ḫi
              i-ti-din
        10    kas-pu ga-mur
              ta-din LÚ za-rip
              la-qi
              IGI ᵐÌR.DINGIR.MEŠ-ni
                 DUMU [ᵐ]DINGIR-dà-ra-ni
        15    IGI ᵐra-ši-DINGIR
                 ˡᵘmu-kil-KUŠ-[PA].MEŠ
              IGI ᵐMU.GIŠ DUMU ᵐki-rib-te
              IGI ᵐib-ni-i
                 DUMU ᵐ·ᵈUTU.KAR-ir
        20    IGI ᵐla-qi-pu
                 ˡᵘše-lap-pa-a-a
              ⁱᵗⁱŠE li-me
              ᵐ·ᵈŠEŠ.GAL.DINGIR-a-a
```

"Nail of Bel-ahi, son of Hartunaya. (three nail-scratches follow) [XX]ta'a, slave of Bel-ahi, he has contracted and given to Mushezib-Ninurta, the governor of Kalhu, for 20 minas of bronze. The price ('silver') has been paid; the man is legally acquired. Before Urdu-ilani, son of Ilu-daranu, before Rashi-ilu, the rein-holder, before Shumu-leshir son of Kiribtu, before Ibni son of Shamash-etir, before Laqipu the Shelappaean. Month of Addaru, eponym of Nergal-ilaya."

Figure 29.5   Neo–Assyrian contract for the purchase of a slave (end of the ninth century BC).

unprecedented levels of luxury. Contributions varied in kind depending on the status of the lands, which were subdivided into three types: there were lands directly managed by the centre or the provinces; royal lands assigned to court administrators; and private lands that had entered the real estate sector, which could be bought and taken away from village communities. Lands belonging to the state probably had to provide a 'quota' (*iškaru*), a mechanism that was particularly suitable for animal farming and workshops. In other words, having determined the means of production (lands, livestock, materials) and the parameters of productivity, the state administration required an established amount of the finished product, regardless of profits or losses.

Lands managed by private individuals or assigned to functionaries had to provide a certain percentage of their estimated produce. This quota used different terms when it referred to livestock (*ṣibtu*) or corn and straw (*nusaḫē* and *šibšu*), which were the main produce requested by the state. Labour services were as important as contributions in kind. They followed the general concept of the *ilku*, both in the case of agricultural, construction, or other works (*tupšikku*), and military service (*ṣab šarri*). A system of royal exemptions benefited privileged individuals. This fact clearly affected the farming population, already without lands and enslaved.

The farming population would have been close to extinction, but the process was slowed down by the frequent deportations. These deportations, however, could not solve this structural problem. Deportations simply displaced the crisis elsewhere, from the centre of Assyria to its periphery (which in fact experienced drastic declines), slowing down the crisis but not eliminating its effects in Assyria. Moreover, these constant deportations ultimately changed the internal social structure and the ethno-linguistic background of the Assyrian population. The latter had to endure a *bona fide* genetic mutation, an aspect that explains its sudden and complete disappearance after the empire's collapse.

2 The army and the administration

The importance of military interventions is not only attested in the empire's celebratory texts, but also in its administrative texts. The current image of the Assyrian empire, then, is that of a military machine bringing terror and destruction throughout the Near East. Admittedly, the continuity and number of Assyrian campaigns led by the king or his generals are impressive. On top of that, there was the less celebrated, but equally demanding, series of minor conflicts, patrols, garrisons, and so on. In the critical formative phase of the empire (under Shalmaneser III, Tiglath-pileser III, and Sargon II), the practice of leading one campaign per year seems to have been followed. Campaigns were only pursued in the summer, when it was easier for the army to cross mountains and rivers, and to gather supplies. This effort naturally weighed on the Assyrian population, since the Assyrian army was essentially a *corvée* army, with very few auxiliary troops sent from the allies in the areas attacked. There were few professional soldiers, which were enlisted in small specialist corps. The Assyrian army was led by court functionaries. Just like the king himself, the latter normally combined political and military activities and expertise.

Despite their obvious approximations and exaggerations, celebratory inscriptions provide more information regarding the size of the Assyrian troops than administrative texts. It appears that in the ninth century BC the majority of conflicts were fought with an army of 10,000/20,000 men per side. These numbers give us an idea of the size of Assyrian expeditions in the more demanding campaigns. An extreme case was that of the battle of Qarqar, where the Syrian confederation put together an army of 4,000 chariots, 2,000 cavalrymen, 1,000 camels, and 55,000 infantrymen. In this case, the Assyrian army was definitely smaller, but not by much.

Sources from the eighth to the seventh century BC lack precision and reliability on this issue. For instance, Sennacherib was clearly exaggerating when he claimed that his army killed 150,000 men in the Babylonian and Elamite armies during the battle of Halule. However, it is true that the armies of the seventh century BC were far larger (at least five times more) than the ones of the ninth century BC. Consequently, the number of casualties increased. Moreover, the number of deaths by natural causes, which were an equally severe problem at the time, needs to be added to the number of people killed in battle. The build-up of losses, which amounted to a few thousands per year, was enormous, especially when compared to the number of inhabitants considered above. The final passage of the letters to Ashur of Sargon and Esarhaddon declare that '1 charioteer, 2 cavalrymen, 3 infantrymen' were killed, a statement indicating that the kings were trying to exorcise in a ceremonial way a very serious problem.

The army was subdivided into various specialist troops. Especially in the eighth century BC, the mass of infantrymen was generally divided into archers and soldiers with spear and shield. Chariot troops continued play an important role, but it was not as decisive as in the Late Bronze Age. The cavalry thus became the main mobile element of the Assyrian army. The latter also had to adapt to the type of enemy encountered. In fact, there were substantial differences between armies with chariots and heavy infantry (Babylonia, Elam, and the Syro-Levantine states), and armies mainly composed of archers and cavalrymen (such as the Iranian tribes), or troops with camels (such as the Arabs). Pitched battles remained relatively rare, and expeditions generally peaked in the siege of enemy citadels. Consequently, sappers, who also had to clear mountain routes and organise the crossing of rivers, played an important role in the Assyrian army. They operated siege engines (such as battering rams and siege towers), which were placed in front of city walls through ramps or dikes.

Weapons are documented in celebratory reliefs and through actual archaeological finds. The Assyrian cities stored large amounts of weapons and chariots in their armouries. The Assyrian army predominantly needed horses and bronze, a fact that explains the frequent expeditions in the north. These expeditions were meant to ensure these important resources, following a circular process. Other information on the Assyrian army, such as its exact organisation, its hierarchy, its subdivisions into fixed modules, and their displacement on the battlefield remain badly attested. It has been suggested, for instance, that chariots were divided into squadrons of 53 chariots (106 men), but this reconstruction is based on a single source. However, the latter was not necessarily recording the standard practice.

In keeping with the ideology of kingship of the Middle Assyrian period, the leadership of the army was a responsibility of the king (or a general acting on his behalf). Alongside the king, there were court dignitaries and state administrators, allowing us to catch a glimpse of their hierarchy. Of the five highest-ranking dignitaries, the first one was the *turtānu*. This term is commonly translated as 'general' or 'generalissimo', due to his visibly important role, but it actually meant 'second (in command)' or 'deputy', indicating the most important assistant of the king. Then, there was the *nāgir ēkalli* ('palace herald'), the *rab šaqē* ('chief cupbearer'), the *rab ša rēši* ('chief eunuch'), the *masennu* (*abarakku* in the old reading, a 'supervisor'), and the *sukkallu* ('steward'). All these titles show that their origin was in the palace environment, but their functions now covered the entire state and military administration of Assyria.

These high-ranking functionaries ruled over the most ancient and prestigious provinces in Upper Mesopotamia, such as the one of Harran/Til Barsip. The latter was the most important one and was in the hands of the *turtānu*. All other provinces were also given to state functionaries, as we will see later on. The people holding these high-ranking offices managed to get a hold of them after a long activity (or, better, a career) at the service of the king, mainly in two categories: as *šūt ziqni*, literally, the 'bearded ones'; and as *šūt rēši*, 'eunuchs'. The latter were appreciated both for their loyalty and their inability to produce any heirs who could take over their wealth and positions. It seems that there were no fixed sectors in the administration of the state (at least in terms of management). This aspect allowed the king to personally keep the entire system under his control. The relationship between the king and his functionaries was direct and personal. It was centred on loyalty and sealed through an oath, placing each functionary at the mercy of the king's personal opinion on his work. This situation encouraged a sense of envy and rivalry among functionaries, resulting in constant defamations and accusations. Through the latter, personal fortunes were built and destroyed in a matter of seconds. Consequently, those who felt suspected, unfairly accused, or fell in disgrace, developed a syndrome of the 'rightful sufferer'. Generally, this led to a marked preference for a more cautious and conformist behaviour, strictly following the king's will.

The local administrations had a completely different structure. Minor centres maintained their old structure, with a 'mayor' (*ḫazānu*) and a group of 'elders' (*šībūti*), responsible for the administration of justice and economic issues (namely, the relations with the central administration). The practice of using judges in disputes, favouritisms, and various kinds of oppressions spread in both sectors. In these instances, an appeal to the king was allowed. However, in practice, this opportunity to appeal to the highest power in the kingdom, justice personified from the point of view of the population, must have been relatively unrealistic. This appeal to the king is attested in a story, 'The Poor Man of Nippur'. The latter managed to beat the local authorities by appealing to the king. To a certain extent, this fictional picture and reality could have coincided. This could have been true especially since the king was seen as a fair judge not because of his particular love for justice, but rather because he generally had to solve far more intricate disputes. Therefore, the king's occasional intervention against the moderate power games of his low-ranking functionaries could have been beneficial for his popular image.

3 Forms of dependence

A diachronic consideration of Assyria has already shown how the organisation of conquered territories can be divided into two major phases, separated by the passage into the mid-eighth century BC. Before then, the empire was clearly separated into two distinct areas. The first area (defined as *māt Aššur*, 'the land of Ashur') was the territory conquered in the Middle Assyrian period, located between the Euphrates to the west and the Zagros foothills to the east. In this territory, the Assyrian presence was consolidated into a network of Assyrian centres (with an Assyrian population) mixed among centres inhabited by the local population (which in the case of the Arameans constituted a later infiltration). The control and economic exploitation of this area was entrusted to functionaries (the *šaknu*) ruling over individual centres or small areas. These functionaries remained integrated with the local leaders recognised by the Assyrian authorities. Then, there was a second area outside the traditional borders (metaphorically called *nīr Aššur*, 'the yoke of Assyria'), made of neighbouring kingdoms forced to pay tributes, which constantly became more expensive due to the frequent rebellions. In this second area, Assyrian presence was limited, with representatives of the Assyrian ruler (*qēpu*) stationed in the courts of the local rulers. Therefore, the latter were allowed to maintain a certain degree of autonomy. The formal means to acquire a tributary state was the oath sworn by the local kings to their Assyrian overlord, promising the payment of yearly tributes.

The reforms of Tiglath-pileser III provided the empire with a more uniform organisation. The provincial system was expanded outside the traditional borders of Assyria, where formerly independent kingdoms were turned into provinces. The size of these new provinces roughly corresponded to the one of the kingdoms they took over. With larger kingdoms, more provinces were created. Each province had a capital with a palace for the Assyrian governor (still defined as *šaknu*, or *bēl pīḫāti*, a term that was at times synonymous, although it also indicated a lower ranking provincial governor), an Assyrian garrison, and a series of administrative offices. Provincial capitals also acted as centres for the collection and distribution of tributes, and for the performance of Assyrian cults. The provinces were entrusted to governors appointed by the king, in a concrete attempt to avoid the formation of dynasties in the Assyrian provinces.

There was a marked difference between the provinces located within the 'land of Ashur' and the ones outside of it. The ancient provinces located east of the Euphrates, which had been long influenced by Assyrian culture, began to take on several cultural and structural features, whose style can be defined as 'provincial Assyrian'. These traits can be found in the provincial palaces of the ninth to seventh century BC from this area. A clear example of this is Harran, which almost became the western capital of the empire. It was ruled by the *turtānu*, was home of the prestigious temple of Sin, and was thus granted several exemptions. Moreover, several administrative texts from Harran (found in Nineveh) record its lands and agricultural personnel. Not far from Harran, there was Huzirina (Sultantepe), where another Assyrian provincial palace, with its administrative archives and a library of literary texts, has been found. Close to the Euphrates, the excavations at Til Barsip (Tell Ahmar) and Hadattu (Arslan Tash) have also uncovered Assyrian palaces with paintings and sculptures. In the Khabur Triangle, we know of Guzana (Tell Halaf), where an Assyrian provincial centre replaced an earlier palace belonging to a local dynasty. Further south, Dur-Katlimmu (Tell Sheikh Hamad), Shadikanni (Tell Ajaja), and other centres around the Haditha Dam are also well known. This complex of palaces, fortified cities, archives, and celebrative inscriptions shows the spread of Assyrian culture throughout Upper Mesopotamia. It also shows the advanced stage of assimilation and colonisation that brought to the formation of a 'Great Assyria', extending from the Euphrates to the Zagros.

The 'yoke of Assyria' was in a different position. There, the Assyrian provincial system survived for around a century (from the end of the eighth to the end of the seventh century BC) and was never fully consolidated, since Assyrian influence was more limited and almost irrelevant. Throughout the external provinces, Assyrian presence is archaeologically attested more in its negative connotations, rather than its building interventions. For instance, there were the considerable destructions in the ninth century BC, marking the military presence of the Assyrians in the area. These destructions became even worse in the eighth century BC. The Assyrians destroyed city walls and palaces, devastated the countryside, and dispersed the local elite and its craftsmen. They also deported the local population, and abolished every aspect of local activities (celebrative or other). All these interventions led to the sudden collapse of the local population and its economy, the disappearance of all local religious and artistic expressions, and the spread of an overall sense of demotivation and discouragement. In other words, the area experienced a fast and drastic process of de-culturation. The area was once a rich and culturally varied land, with a variety of different ethnical groups and artistic expressions, with local traditions and structures. However, all of a sudden, this territory was impoverished and turned into a homogenous entity by the Assyrian army and administration. The characteristic features of the Assyrian re-organisation did not have enough time or means to establish themselves in these new provinces. The latter, then, continued to be plagued by processes of depopulation and de-culturation even after the empire collapsed.

The Assyrian deportations are an important and renowned aspect of the process of de-culturation. Their double aim has been already pointed out. The solution to the depopulation of the Assyrian cities and the countryside, currently in crisis due to the constant wars, was to rehome farmers in the countryside. Similarly, the Assyrians acquired individuals with technical competences for the court administration and the construction of buildings. Moreover, in an attempt to suppress the national and cultural identities of the conquered populations, crossover deportations were often implemented, moving people from one province to the other. This practice combined the discomfort of the survivors, who saw their land being occupied by new people (seen as an instrument of imperial oppression), with the usual difficulty of the deportees, who were left in a new land among unknown people. The size of these deportations was often considerable. The numbers attested on celebrative inscriptions appear unreliable in some cases, but relatively reliable in others (Figure 29.6). Nonetheless, these were generally high figures (around tens of thousands of people) especially for cities or regions whose total population was not particularly high. Deaths during deportations must have been extremely common, and the birth and production rates of the deportees remained rather low. Therefore, it is clear that deportations had more negative than positive consequences.

The Assyrian administration was essentially a system for the collection of tributes. It was also one of the causes for the imperial transformation of the conquered territories into a homogeneous entity. The tribute system evolved alongside administrative developments, which in turn were largely stimulated by the former. Following a loyalty oath, the tributary relations required were very specific. Tributes had to be provided each year, and had to be paid in specific amounts and types of goods, depending on the local resources. Goods were generally easy to transport, either because of their nature (such as in the case of horses), or because they were valuable even in small quantities (such as metals, either in ingots or in the form of objects). Some goods were necessary and not available in Assyria (such as timber, delivered as much as possible via river). The delivery of horses and metals (for military purposes), and timber and stones (for building purposes) from the periphery to Assyria caused several technical issues. These are attested in administrative, epistolary, and celebrative texts, each reporting the problem from a different point of view.

In the Neo-Assyrian period, the types of tributes provided, as well as the terminology used, were still influenced by the origins of tributes as voluntary contributions (that is, 'gifts') or commercial ones. Tributes thus maintained a distinction between a '(main) contribution' and an '(additional) gift' (*biltu/maddattu* and *nāmurtu* respectively), even though both were now compulsory, pre-established, and one-directional

Relief from Nineveh depicting a siege and deportation.

Table of the numerical data provided by the Assyrian inscriptions.

King	number of deportations	number of deportees		number of unquantified deportations.
		totals reported in the sources	incomplete totals reported in the sources	
Ashur-dan II	2			2
Adad-nirari II	1			1
Tukulti-Ninurta II	2			2
Ashurnasirpal II	13	12,900		5
Shalmaneser III	8	167,500		3
Shamshi-Adad V	6	36,200		2
Adad-nirari III	1			1
Tiglath-pileser III	37	368,543	x + 25,055	19
Shalmaneser V	1			1
Sargon II	38	217,635	x + 21,650	24
Sennacherib	20	408,150	x + 61,000	17
Esarhaddon	12			12
Ashurbanipal	16			16
Total	157	1,210,928	x + 107,705	105

Figure 29.6 Assyrian deportations of conquered peoples.

(namely, they were not reciprocal, other than ensuring the avoidance of an Assyrian military intervention). Those who refused to submit were plundered. The subsequent booty roughly corresponded to the same type of resources the Assyrians would have required in the form of tributes. Moreover, these interventions showed how the Assyrian 'machine' was able to get what it wanted one way or another. When the provincial system was installed, a land was mainly required to provide 'corn and straw'. This is also because the destruction of the local palace workshops brought to a decline of local craftsmanship. Horses and timber were mainly collected from regions that remained difficult to control, or were still outside Assyrian control.

Even at the peak of its expansion, the empire recognised subordinate, yet autonomous, powers, with which spoken oaths were recorded in detailed written treaties. The first example, from the pre-provincial phase, comes from the treaty between Ashur-nirari and Matti-El of Arpad. This treaty can be considered a paradigmatic example of these types of formalisations. It is even possible that these treaties originated in northern Syria. In the Sargonid phase, then, it is not surprising that the surviving treaties only concern states outside the Assyrian borders, such as the Phoenician city of Tyre, which was never sieged and was still thriving through its maritime trade. The city sealed a treaty with Esarhaddon that certainly placed it in a subordinate position, but still recognised its autonomy. The Medes agreed to seal a series of 'loyalty oaths' with Esarhaddon, mainly in connection with the problem of succession (Text 29.1). Another fragmentary treaty was sealed between Ashurbanipal and the North Arabian tribe of Qedar. Therefore, it is clear that subordination treaties remained a fundamental

---

Text 29.1   The loyalty oath required by Esarhaddon from the Median leaders in occasion of the selection of Ashurbanipal as heir to the throne (extract, I 41–II 91)

'The treaty (*adê*) which Esarhaddon, king of Assyria, has made with you in the presence of the great gods of heaven and earth, concerning Ashurbanipal, the crown prince, son of Esarhaddon, king of Assyria, your lord, whom he named and appointed to the crown-princeship. When Esarhaddon, king of Assyria, dies, you will seat Ashurbanipal, the crown prince, upon the royal throne, he will exercise the kingship and lordship over you. You will protect him in country and in town. You will fight and will die for him. You will speak with him in the truth of your heart, you will give him sound advice loyally. You will set fair path at his feet. (You swear) that you will not be hostile to him nor will you seat one of his brothers, older or younger, on the throne of Assyria instead of him. That the word of Esarhaddon, king of Assyria, you will neither change nor alter. That you will serve only Ashurbanipal, the crown prince, whom Esarhaddon, king of Assyria, your lord (hereby commends), that he will exercise the kingship and dominion over you.

(You swear) that you will protect Ashurbanipal, the crown prince, whom Esarhaddon, king of Assyria, has designated to you (and of whom) he has spoken to you, and concerning whom he has firmly imposed the treaty upon you. That you will not sin against him; that you will not bring your hand against him with evil intent. That you will not revolt (or) do anything to him which is not good, and not proper. You will not oust him from the kingship of Assyria by helping one of his brothers, older or younger, to seize the throne of Assyria in his stead. You will not set over you any (other) king or any (other) lord, nor will you swear an oath to any (other) king or any (other) lord.

(You swear) that you will neither listen nor conceal any improper, unsuitable or unseemly word concerning the exercise of kingship, which are unseemly and evil against Ashurbanipal, the crown prince, either from the mouth of his brothers, his uncles, his cousins, his family, members of his father's line; or from the mouth of officials or governors, or from the mouth of an officer or courtiers, or from the mouth of any skilled person or from the mouth of any of the masses, as many as there are, but you will come (and) report (these things) to Ashurbanipal, the crown prince.

(You swear) that, should Esarhaddon, king of Assyria, die while his sons are minors, you will help Ashurbanipal, the crown prince, to take the throne of Assyria, (and) will help to seat Shamash-shum-ukin, his "twin"-brother, the crown prince of Babylon, on the throne of Babylon. The kingship over the whole of Sumer, Akkad (and) Karduniash (Babylonia) you will hand over to him. Whatever gift Esarhaddon, king of Assyria, his father, gave him he will take with him. Do not hold back even one.'

means for the formalisation of relations with political entities that were not easy or convenient to include in the Assyrian provincial network. This was either because these entities were elusive (such as the nomadic groups of the Arabian desert or the Iranian plateau), or because it was more convenient to keep them in a subordinate, yet autonomous, state (such as in the case of Tyre) than to conquer and destroy them.

Then, there were some anomalous cases. The first one was Babylonia, where the personal rule of the Assyrian king, or the appointment of local rulers loyal to the Assyrians, show that it was deemed impossible to turn Babylonia into an Assyrian province. Some marginal portions of the Babylonian kingdom were at times turned into provinces. Overall, the kingdom continued to be seen as a single entity that could not be broken down, no matter how ardently the Assyrian kings wanted to secure control over the area. The failed annexation of Babylonia was mainly due to its influential political and cultural (i.e. religious) traditions. It therefore left the problem unresolved, a fact that would eventually lead to the collapse of the empire. Other issues left unresolved were Egypt and Elam. In both cases, Assyrian control did not last. It appears that the Assyrians preferred to encourage the fragmentation of these powers into a series of local statelets, thus weakening these powers without having to conquer them. In Egypt, the Delta fiefdoms provided the basic framework for a political fragmentation under Assyrian control. However, the attempt eventually failed due to the rise of one of them. In Elam, political fragmentation was also based on the traditional divisions of the land into individual political entities. However, the Assyrian strategy of encouraging local autonomies at the expense of a unified organisation made Elam an easy target of new emerging forces in the Iranian plateau.

4 The Assyrian imperial ideology

Just like every empire, the Assyrian state was based on the exploitation of local differences. A small elite managed to subdue larger groups, first internally, and then outside Assyria, in a process based on an increase of needs and expectations. The centre monopolised decisions, imposing them on groups that did not contribute to their formulation and were actually placed in a worse position because of these decisions. The centre also acquired wealth, taking it away from those who produced it. This system based on inequality was possible thanks to both physical and technical aspects: Assyria had a superior organisation, a better army, and a range of human and economic resources that was larger and more compact than those of the conquered groups.

However, an aspect that cannot be ignored in the maintenance of the empire was its ideological interpretation of reality. This view provided its centre with further reasons for its actions other than sheer convenience, and the exploited groups (who re-employed these ideas for the exploitation of other groups) with reasons to accept this unequal system, convincing them that it was also at their advantage. This process of Assyrian self-motivation seems to have worked. However, its effects on conquered groups remain debatable. It is certain that they kept their own ideologies, which justified their defeat in different terms than the ones used by the Assyrians. Apart from its success, the Assyrian elite developed an organic worldview, within which conquests became coherent and acceptable. The analysis of Assyrian ideology, then, can be broken down into a series of dualisms in terms of space, time, men, and resources.

This geographic duality saw a contraposition between an 'internal' world, which was ordered and civilised, and a chaotic, culturally backward periphery. The latter – be it the Iranian or Anatolian mountains, the Syro-Arabian desert, or the Lower Mesopotamian marshes – seems impracticable, unsuitable for living, sterile, and unproductive. The interaction between centre and periphery took place in two ways. The polarisation of centre and periphery (and its resources) already gave the latter a certain degree of functionality and a purpose. However, when the interventions of the Assyrian kings led to the expansion of the centre, they gradually reduced the chaotic periphery to the point of making it disappear completely. The king organised expeditions through the difficult routes leading to the far end of the world, where he left a boundary stele to demonstrate his right to universal control. In this way, an unknown world became known, an unproductive world became productive, an uninhabited world was colonised, and a hostile world had to submit to the might of the Assyrian king. Assyrian conquests were therefore seen as a way to bridge the gap between the centre and the periphery. This process made the latter more similar to Assyria, giving it the same functionaries, tributes and royal orders.

Apart from being limited in terms of space, the world's correct functioning was limited in terms of time. In fact, the rise of the Assyrian empire brought about a phase of cosmic order, after which, if one was not careful enough, chaos could return. The current world was ordered because the gods (for the basic natural elements) and the ancestral heroes (for a variety of institutions) established the constitutive foundations of the empire. The role of the king was therefore twofold: to maintain in functioning order what already existed (restoring crumbling temples, ensuring the performance of festivals, and so on); and to introduce further innovative (or 'creative') elements. The latter role explains the kings' common assertion of having been the first to introduce a certain institution, or the first to walk a certain route, or the first to introduce a certain type of workmanship or constructing a certain temple, and so on. The peak of the creative/foundational role of the king was the construction of a new capital in the centre of the world. The capital was to become the point around which the rest of the universe revolved, and whose construction required the contribution of men and materials from all over the world.

The third element of the Assyrian imperial ideology was centred on the diverse range of people conquered by the empire. Naturally, the Assyrians kept a clear distinction between them and the barbarians. Just like its internal world, so its people were the epitome of every positive quality, while all negative qualities typically characterised foreigners. The latter, then, had weird customs, spoke incomprehensible languages, and were seen as barely human. The typical moment of confrontation between these two worlds was war. On the one hand, the Assyrians were alone, certain of their technical and moral superiority, and their divine support. On the other hand, the enemies were always in large number, composite, and united into coalitions, in an effort to overcome in quantity their qualitative inferiority. However, once on the battlefield, they were irremediably overcome, so that it could not be said that a battle even took place, but only a devastating attack and the enemies' flight.

The reason for this idea was that the Assyrian king had a direct and legitimate link with the gods, and with Ashur in particular. On the contrary, the enemies were 'godless' or were abandoned by their gods, or were supported by inferior deities. The Assyrians simply had to rely on their king, and in turn the Assyrian king simply had to rely on the god (who in fact claims: 'Go, do not fear, I shall stand by your side'). The enemies, however, had to absurdly rely on the help of others, or on the inaccessibility of their lands or the number of their troops. The comparison between these two 'faiths', one being the correct one and the other simply delusional, brought an obvious outcome. However, through conquest and submission, even foreigners were believed to acquire more positive characteristics, as long as they remained loyal to the Assyrian king and submitted to becoming part of the empire. Therefore, foreigners were placed in new cities and houses, became part of the Assyrian administration, and were even integrated both in terms of language and aims, slowly becoming more 'human' and less barbarian.

Finally, as an obvious consequence of the spatial and human differences between the Assyrians and the rest of the world, there was the distinction between centre and periphery in terms of resources. The centre was an urbanised and agricultural region, where life was thriving and food was produced. The periphery was subdivided into several 'monocultures' (there were areas devoted to growing cedars, or cypresses, or to mining lapis lazuli or copper), and was thus an unsuitable living environment. In fact, who could live off cedar or lapis lazuli alone? Naturally, all these resources were seen as distributed throughout the periphery, so that they would eventually find their way to the centre.

This influx of raw materials from the periphery to the centre therefore gave the former some sort of dignity and purpose. Prior to the Assyrian 'discovery' of these resources, then, they were treated as if they had never existed. In return of this influx, the centre provided cultural and ideological contributions, such as protection, justice, and order. This interaction between material resources and ideological contributions could not have taken place anywhere else but in the centre and through the intervention of the central administration. Therefore, the latter stood as yet another proof (as if there was any need for it) of the central role of Assyrian kingship and its political power, and the inevitability of the empire's expansion.

Whenever the Assyrians conquered a new territory, submitted new populations to their power, or forced a centralisation of new human and economic resources, they envisioned it as a necessary and benevolent act of civilisation and world colonisation. This process led to the unification of the entire territory under the only legitimate power in the name of the Assyrian gods. Therefore, these interventions were seen as instrumental for the completion of the gods' creation and organisation of the world. Once the empire's borders coincided with the far ends of the world, all the resources were gathered in the centre and every population was ruled by the only legitimate power, then this divine process of creation would have been deemed complete. Consequently, the world would have become perfect.

5 The Assyrian celebrative system

The concrete expression of the Assyrian imperial ideology can be found in its celebrative system. The latter was directed to both an internal and external audience, while we stand as its anomalous and accidental audience. Scholars have often wondered about the actual accessibility of these celebrative expressions to their intended audience. In particular, scholars have wondered about the problem of the accessibility of royal inscription to a largely illiterate public (since cuneiform remained a knowledge reserved for the scribal class). Those who could access these texts and understand them in full were mainly those who wrote them. From a more practical point of view, the placement of many inscriptions prevented public access (especially foundation texts, buried under the corners of buildings). The texts themselves are addressed to a surreal or as yet inaccessible audience, such as the gods or future kings. These observations are indeed correct, but it still remains impossible to separate the overall aim of the Assyrian celebrative system, namely, to justify the king's actions (which is evident to anyone looking at any Assyrian celebrative inscription), from its ability to reach its target audience. Moreover, the channels and expressions through which this system is known to us are inaccurate (and biased) and do not cover the entire spectrum.

It is necessary, then, to establish the various circles of potential audiences and the corresponding forms of communication. The most internal circle was that of the scribes and palace functionaries. The latter were the administrators and managers of the Assyrian state, and the authors and audience of these texts, in a process of self-education, fundamental for the stability of the empire's elite. This internal circle was not only the only one able to read these texts, but also the only one able to understand the ideological subtleties written in them. Then, there was a larger circle of residents of the Assyrian cities. Despite their illiteracy, the latter were affected by the content of these celebrative expressions and the reasons provided for the king's interventions in two ways. Firstly, these messages were orally transmitted. Secondly, they were expressed during celebrations (such as after expeditions or during regular festivals) with parades of prisoners and exotic products. For instance, the 'letters to Ashur' could have been written for a public celebration in which the king read his report to the god out loud in the presence of the priesthood and several representatives of the population. This second circle of Assyrian citizens and foreign visitors (envoys, merchants, and messengers) was also affected by an effective visual channel. The latter was made of the monumental temples and palaces, as well as their decorative scheme, which emphasised Assyrian opulence, power, and might, and the miserable fate (and the ferocious treatment) of rebels.

Finally, there was a third circle, made of farmers living in the countryside. The latter constituted the majority of the population. This circle was not only illiterate, but also lacked the means to participate in festivals in the cities. Therefore, farmers only felt the repercussions of these events and their motivations. They only knew that in the distant capital, which they had heard of, but never seen, the king ensured his good relations with the gods, that dangerous enemies had been removed from the borders, and so on. These mere simplifications of the celebrative apparatus were enough for the position of this circle in the

Assyrian political hierarchy. Therefore, each member of the system received the type of message that he was able to gather, thus receiving a level of understanding of the system that was appropriate to his position. As a secondary and intrusive audience of these messages, we are forced to base our understanding of the Assyrian celebrative apparatus from the expressions reserved for the 'first' circle. Therefore, we tend to underestimate the simpler and more effective means implemented to spread the message to the rest of the population.

It has already been mentioned that celebrative texts (such as royal inscriptions, both annals and summaries, which usually were votive inscriptions for new buildings) are quite sophisticated and contain subtle political messages. Admittedly, this is not immediately evident. The texts have a simple narrative structure (which would only become more stylistically complex under Ashurbanipal), based on the obvious cycle starting with an initial offence (a rebellion or other), followed by the decision to intervene and the acquisition of the necessary materials and divine support. The cycle peaked with the victory and the reinstatement of the correct order, which resulted in a triumph and celebration. Each individual episode is repetitive and outcomes are predictable. It seems that the choice of words and phrases used was so rooted in the ancient scribal conventions to leave little space to the narrator's creativity or the details of the episode. Only when we have various versions of the same episode, we are able to see how the process of rewriting responded to some subtle changes that took place over time, and how the omission or addition of some details did not take place by chance. These changes led to a complete reformulation (or even omission) of episodes that could not be presented the way they were in the past. In other words, the past was constantly rewritten in response to present events. This is the typical way for totalitarian regimes to manipulate the past.

In this regard, titulature was an area displaying visible changes. At first, one gets the impression that titles were chosen at random and taken from a long legacy of ancient titles. Therefore, they were added one on top of the other to emphasise the quantity, rather than the meaning, of titles. On the contrary, the choice of titles was the result of a conscious and ideologically aware selection. Apart from the basic, relatively fixed, titles (such as 'great king, mighty king, king of the universe, king of Assyria, king of the four quarters'), each king chose the titles characterising his policies at the beginning of his reign. These titles were meant either to differentiate a king from his predecessor, or to deliberately imitate the latter. Moreover, specific titles were only acquired after a particular achievement. For instance, an allusion to Assyrian control 'from the Lower Sea to the Upper Sea', as stereotypical as it may seem, had to be justified through campaigns in the Persian Gulf and the Mediterranean. This leads to a two-way interaction: titles mirrored a king's intentions and actual achievements, and the latter were planned and executed in order to be able to use a title. An equally careful selection concerns gods, chosen according to the location in which the inscription was placed, the type of achievement celebrated, the relations with the city of a certain deity, and so on.

If inscriptions allowed control over the terminology used and precise connotative effects, the other category of celebrative works, the sculpted reliefs, also display several conventions and expressions. Despite belonging to a different technical sphere, they insisted on the same themes and the same results. It has often been noted how texts and reliefs to a certain extent overlap, especially in terms of themes and connotations. This overlap of themes mainly concerns the recurrence of standard themes (such as the overcoming of a difficult route, the reaching of the edge of the world, the reception of tributes, the account of killed enemies, and many others). However, it also concerns the representation of single episodes, with their unique and recognisable features, often described in captions. An actual overlap rarely took place (mainly under Ashurnasirpal II, while it was avoided later on), with the texts carved over the reliefs, but without a precise reference to the episodes accounted.

Just like texts, reliefs were the expression of a coherent celebrative program. However, the latter remains less evident for us due to the state in which the reliefs have survived after a long series of ancient destructions and more modern dispersions. The reconstruction of each relief in the right iconographic cycle clarifies the main principles of Assyrian celebrative programs. It has to be pointed out, however, that the placement of these reliefs inside palaces (at least in the case of more complex cycles) excludes their role as a 'poor man's Bible' (like in the case of depictions in medieval cathedrals). Only those who had access to the palace could see these reliefs. It has been posited that, in terms of foreign audience, the reliefs must have been seen by foreign envoys, who had the opportunity to meditate over the ferocious scenes depicted in the corridor and antechamber of the throne room in the palace of Kalhu (Figure 29.7).

Having lost the oral accounts and ceremonial aspects of this celebrative apparatus, the last clues survive in the palaces and temples, as well as the urban plans themselves, especially in the case of new and 'artificial' capitals. The ideological message concealed behind the architecture and plans of buildings and cities is emphasised by the names given to the buildings and their parts. These names normally contained celebrative indications. For instance, there are the names of the gates of Nineveh or Dur-Sharrukin, which emphasise Assyrian opulence and a sense of security and defence. These are pertinent

Figure 29.7   Assyrian 'terror' propaganda. *Above and Centre*: Atrocities inflicted by the Assyrians on their prisoners; *Below*: Counting chopped heads.

topics for gates and city walls. Texts also help us to define the positive aspects of the kings' building programs. They insist on the substitution of something small with something larger, of something bent with something straight, of something precarious with something solid, of something superficial with something profound, of something unadorned with something decorated (Figure 29.8). Therefore, texts emphasise order and perfection. Comparing city districts that developed spontaneously (such as in the case of Ashur) with the regular plan of the newly founded citadels, it becomes possible to see how urban planning was meant to convey a message of cosmic perfection. This was in marked contrast with the chaos of what existed beforehand.

Architectural and urban interventions were concentrated in the centre of the Assyrian world, mainly its capital and, to a lesser extent, the other Assyrian cities. However, there are some examples from the periphery, mainly those provincial palaces mentioned earlier. In these cases, the contrast of the Assyrian palaces with the overall decay of the surrounding world (a decay which the Assyrians contributed to with destructions and plunders) is even more evident, almost reaching the effect of a 'cathedral in the desert'. This was an exemplary statement of that order the Assyrians wanted to spread throughout the world. The realisation of this order, however, was hindered by the rebellions in the chaotic periphery, which only true champions could overcome. When the Assyrian king reached the far end of the world, at the source of the Tigris, or a mountain close to the sea, or another typically 'liminal' location, it was not necessary to build a palace. It was enough to leave a stele commemorating the achievement and marking the new border. This border marked the frontier of the cosmos over chaos. Since this border coincided with the far end of the world, it ensured the fact that the expansion was complete, and that no further lands had to be reached or ordered. In terms of propaganda, the rock steles left at the edge of the world were not useful and were seen by few people. However, they would be mentioned by future kings who would reach the same location and leave their own stele.

In contrast with the spread of the central presence of the Assyrian king in the periphery, there was the celebrative concentration of elements of the periphery in the centre. This aspect had an important and visible economic significance, marking the influx of resources (raw materials, labour, and so on) from the periphery to the centre of the empire. However, it was also expressed in ceremonial and symbolic terms. Firstly, there was the emphasis of the universal provenance of the carpenters building Assyrian palaces, and

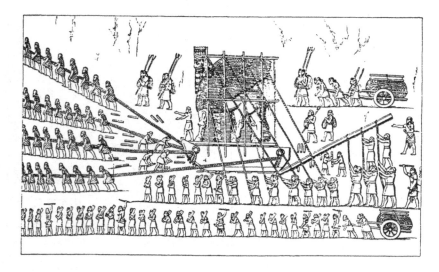

Figure 29.8 The transportation of a colossal bull, from a relief of Sennacherib in Nineveh.

of the valuable and exotic raw material with which they were built. Then, there was the concentration of exotic plants and animals in actual parks, the predecessors of the 'paradises' of the Achaemenid kings. In these parks, the Assyrian kings tried to recreate exotic landscapes (through irrigation) with animals from all over the world. These animals were used both for the royal hunt (which was also a symbolic event) and to affirm universal control, achieved through an exemplary sample collected and imprisoned in the centre of the empire.

6 Magic and politics

For the planning and execution of political and military interventions, the Assyrian king largely relied on human information and instruments. He possessed a large amount of information from the remotest parts of the empire, as well as the closest palace rooms (equally unreliable). Letters and 'voices' were constantly circulating and constituted the base of his decision-making process, from the destitution of a functionary to the start of a military campaign. However, the ideology of the time was convinced that human information was neither reliable nor sufficient, unless it was supported by further information from the divine sphere. The latter was gathered through thousands of possible channels, due to the interconnection of every constitutive part of reality. It was therefore impossible to intervene without a positive omen. However, when there was a contradiction between the human and divine channels, the king had to follow the latter. In their celebrative inscriptions, the Assyrian kings constantly emphasise that they faithfully followed the indications provided by the god Ashur and other important deities. They therefore allude to the standard practice of consulting omens before any intervention.

There was a wide range of techniques and 'sectors' through which omens were taken. The examination of the entrails (mainly the liver) of sacrificial animals continued to be highly prestigious. However, in the first millennium BC, astrology acquired absolute pre-eminence. The careful observation of the positions of planets, as well as more meaningful phenomena such as eclipses, became a constant means to predict the future and a useful guidance on the decisions to be taken. All the observations taken in the past centuries, with their respective previsions, were collected in enormous canonical treaties, copied from scribe to scribe. Indeed, there were specialised scribes who only focused on this essential and enormous area of late Mesopotamian knowledge, namely, the astrological series *Enūma Anu Enlil*. If other techniques were available to private individuals (from dreams to the observation of daily life), astrology, which was based on observations requiring a specific type of equipment and knowledge, was typically a temple/priestly technique. Therefore, it was predominantly used to serve the king and the Assyrian state. Only secondarily, astrology found a way to spread among private individuals, leading to the creation of horoscopes based on dates of birth.

Regarding the popular use of divination, the consultation of omen lists, written in an archaising language and largely concerning a remote past, was problematic. This was due to the necessity of adapting its geographic terminology to the current age. For instance, if a certain omen was negative for the king of Amurru, there was a need to understand the current significance of this omen. In fact, who was this 'king of Amurru' (a geo-political entity that had long disappeared) in the Neo-Assyrian period? Therefore, specialists had to interpret omens in light of the current events of the time, and supposed that the king of Amurru (the West) could have been Tyre, Tabal, or Egypt. A relatively large number of texts from the reigns of Esarhaddon and Ashurbanipal attest the great care (almost obsessive in the case of Esarhaddon) in searching any possible information, decoding it, and translating it into practical answers (Text 29.2). These were letters written by specialised astrologists to the king, requests from kings to specialists, or prayers to the gods asking for support. There were even oracular responses (which culminated in the exhortation 'Go, do not fear, I shall stand by your side') delivered from the gods to the king through the mediation of priests or prophets. Only through this support was the king able to engage in any intervention and be sure of its success.

Text 29.2   Politics and divination in the reign of Esarhaddon

1 The political interpretation of the stars

'The lunar eclipse which occurred in the month of Tebet, afflicted Amurru. The king of Amurru will die, and his land will decrease, or will be destroyed. Perhaps the masters can tell the king my lord something about (what should be understood as) "Amurru". Amurru means Hatti (that is, Syria), or the Sutians, or Chaldea. Someone among the kings of Hatti, Chaldea, or Arabia, will bear the evil of this sign. For the king, my lord, all is well: the king my lord will attain his desires, the rites and prayers of the king my lord are well accepted by the gods. (In practical terms:) Either the king of Kush (that is, Ethiopia), or the king of Tyre, or Mugallu will die, or the king my lord will capture him, or the king my lord will reduce his country, and the women of his harem will enter the service of the king my lord. The king my lord can be happy.'

2 Consultation of the god Shamash for political issues

'Shamash, great lord, that I am invoking, give me a truthful answer: regarding Kashtaritu, the city ruler of Kar-kashshi, who sent to Marmiti-arshu, the city ruler of the Medes, the following message: "Let us seal an alliance with one another against Assyria!" (Now,) will Marmiti-arshu listen to him? Will he agree with him? Will he pay attention (to the plan) of hostilely marching against Esarhaddon, king of Assyria, this year? (Only) your great divinity knows it.'

3 Oracle of the goddess Ishtar of Arbela, spoken by a priestess

'O Esarhaddon, king of all the lands, do not fear! Which wind has ever blown against you, whose wings I have not broken? Your enemies fall like ripe apples at your feet. I am the Great Lady, I am Ishtar of Arbela, who throws your enemies at your feet! Which of my words, that I ever said to you, you could not rely on? I am Ishtar of Arbela, I will set up an ambush for your enemies, I will give them to you. I am Ishar of Arbela, I walk before you and behind you: do not fear! (Spoken by Ishtar-la-tashiat, (woman) of the city of Arbela.)'

Apart from positive responses, there were negative omens. If they were discovered as a response to a request on whether or not to engage in an action, they naturally discouraged it, with limitative and negative consequences. Moreover, there were negative omens containing worrying predictions of misfortunes. In these cases, it was necessary to implement magical counter-interventions, meant to remove the effects of the omen, or at least divert them. When negative omens affected the king himself, the practice of substituting the king was resumed. Therefore, an individual formally took over the role of the king for the period predicted by the omen, while the king stayed in a safe place. At the peak of the dangerous phase, the substitute king was killed, in order to remove the predicted misfortune once and for all.

This procedure, as rare and extreme as it was, clearly shows the marked formal and ritualistic tendencies of the Assyrians. These tendencies were typical of this period, and developed alongside a variety of magical measures. On a private level, there were the apotropaic *namburbû* rituals, which provided individuals with the means (namely, incantations to be recited and actions to be executed) to face any kind of risk. The 'classical' magical rituals, such as the *Šurpu* and *Maqlû* series, were widespread in this period. These series standardised the incantations to be pronounced while burning the 'magical material', which symbolised the evil or the enemy. This formality peaked with the endless lists of possible enemies, made in order to include all possibilities, ensuring that the protective barrier meant to guard the person had no defects. Spells and exorcisms were made on the enemy's tracks, his clothes, hair, nails, and so on. In order to prevent the dangerous use of this magic, the nails of the Assyrian king were cut, placed in a small bottle, and thrown away at the far end of the world, where nobody could find them or use them.

On a more historical and political level, apart from these common practices, which provide a good representation of the time, the tendency towards magical formalities gradually acquired more importance. Sources from the ninth century BC still present political and military relations between the Assyrians and their neighbouring populations in a realistic way. Thus, we have sequences of rebellions and punitive expeditions, of missed tributes and destroyed cities, of atrocities and triumphs. All of this was certainly achieved through the superior support of the gods, but was led with a human point of view. With the eighth and seventh century BC, the presentation of events changed. The enemy did not rebel against the Assyrians, but violated the oath sworn in the name of the gods. Therefore, the enemy was not punished by the Assyrian king *per se*, but by the intrinsic effectiveness of the oath. This was because divine punishment was able to reach beyond human intervention. The oath (*adê*) became the heart of all political relations, both within the state and outside of it. The fundamental importance of the oath intrinsically justified any reaction. This means that the enemy was to blame not for disrespecting the Assyrian king, but the gods. Therefore, an enemy, traitor, or rebel, was not defined from a subjective and interpersonal point of view anymore, but from a more objective and cosmic one.

The Assyrian king maintained his central role in the religious system of his land. This centrality was ancient, and was based on the figure of the king as 'delegate' of the god Ashur. The king was the protagonist of the rituals of the Assyrian cultic calendar. With the eighth century BC, he was at the centre both of the system of sworn loyalty oaths, and of the network of information (omens) and magical solutions. In this system, the role of the priesthood from the numerous Assyrian temples seems rather marginal. Naturally, the number of temples increased. Alongside the traditional Assyrian ones, several temples of Babylonian origins were added. The Assyrian kings continued to restore, decorate, and enlarge them, and boast about these changes. However, the influence of the priesthood of the individual temples on the political management of the empire seems to have become rather limited. A centre such as Ashur (or even Harran, about which we know far less) was predominantly seen as a temple-city, and for this reason was granted exemptions. Meanwhile, the political centre of the empire was moved to 'virgin' sites, in which the surface occupied by the palace, deposits, storehouses, and fortifications was far superior than the area occupied by temples. The expressive code of the Assyrian political ideology remained predominantly religious, but the divine sphere was purely a hypostasis of Assyrian kingship and its political power. After all, it is sufficient to move our attention from the celebrative inscriptions to other administrative texts and letters to note the secular nature of the Assyrian state. The latter indeed featured the absence of priests in the imperial elite, the purely figurative formality of invocations to the gods, and the absolute centrality of the king.

30

THE PERIPHERY OF
THE NEO-ASSYRIAN EMPIRE

1 The southern border: the first Arabs

We have already considered the history and characteristics of the populations that were living at the time of the Neo-Assyrian empire, and were then conquered and destroyed by the latter (the Arameans, Neo-Hittites, Phoenicians, Israelites, Babylonians and Chaldeans). However, since every empire generates a periphery, the end of the Neo-Assyrian empire saw the survival of several ethnic groups and political formations. Some of them were old neighbours of Assyria that had managed to resist annexation by the empire. Others were new entities emerging with unique characteristics or, better, whose 'civilised' centre was becoming more consolidated in this phase.

This is what we see in the case of the Arabs, who came into contact with the Assyrian empire along its southern border. The latter extended from the Euphrates river mouth to Palestine, separating the 'Fertile Crescent' from the Arabian Peninsula. The central section of this border, located to the south-west of the Euphrates, was the least accessible, due to the presence of the desert. For this reason, this area was largely barren and rarely crossed throughout the Bronze Age. However, thanks to the new technological developments of the Iron Age (from the dromedary to wells in oases), this inaccessibility was partly overcome, especially for nomadic groups. Nonetheless, commercial routes and settlements remained rooted elsewhere. Therefore, the edges of this southern border remained the easiest to cross in both directions. The eastern side was relatively narrow and less important. There, the Arabian Desert ended on the coast of the Persian Gulf. Consequently, Lower Mesopotamian centres reached Dilmun (Bahrain) and Oman following the coast or by sea, and from there reached the Indian Ocean. However, during the Iron Age, both the Lower Mesopotamian cities and the populations settled in Oman (and in the Gulf in general) were in crisis.

The wealth of contacts characterising this network in the third millennium BC was now completely lost and forgotten, so much so that the names of Magan and Meluhha were re-used in Neo-Assyrian texts to designate Egypt and Nubia. Only with the Achaemenid empire (fifth century BC) would commercial interactions (especially maritime ones) in the Gulf be revived. In the Neo-Assyrian period, the most resounding attempt in this area was Esarhaddon's expedition. After a long journey through the desert, his troops reached the land of Bazu, where they defeated some local kings (and queens), destroyed settlements, and brought back booty and prisoners. Bazu was located on the coast opposite Dilmun and extended as far as Qatar. Therefore, the Assyrian expedition managed to campaign far into the peninsula. This indicates that the Assyrian interest in the area and its local political formations were far more important than what the lack of evidence on the matter would lead us to believe.

Be that as it may, the most consistent interaction between Arabs and Assyrians was without a doubt the one frequently mentioned earlier. The caravans (or series of caravans) travelled from Yemen to the north along the western border (Hejaz) of the Arabian Peninsula, and reached the Transjordan plateau and mainland Syria. From an Assyrian perspective, the Arabs were associated with the mainland Syro-Palestinian states, with which they engaged in commercial interactions. In the battle of Qarqar, Shalmaneser III already had to face a thousand camel riders belonging to the Arab Gindibu. From Tiglath-pileser III to Sargon II and Sennacherib, the military and commercial presence of the Arabs in the west is repeatedly documented. Their clashes with the Assyrians thus became frequent. With Ashurbanipal, the entire southern border, from Chaldea to Palestine, seems in movement, with the western side of the border remaining the main point of contacts and clashes. The great Assyrian attack and raid east of Damascus severely damaged the Arabic tribes, leading to a fall of the price of camels and slaves in the Assyrian markets.

For a long time, the Assyrian written evidence on the Arabian tribes and political formations of the eighth and seventh centuries BC lacked any supporting archaeological evidence. Until recently, archaeological excavations in the Arabian Peninsula mainly focused on the search of South Arabian inscriptions, neglecting the rest or being limited by the political restrictions imposed by Saudi Arabia. Hopefully, current excavations (especially the one of Tayma) will soon uncover some useful evidence. It is clear that the Proto-Arabian world of the first half of the first millennium BC had its own prehistory, whose traces are coming back to light in several sites, from Yemen to the Hejaz and Oman. We know that the Neolithic cultures documented in particular near the Persian Gulf were succeeded by a sequence of Bronze Age cultures (covering the second millennium BC). These Bronze Age cultures established relations with Mesopotamia in the east, and Syria and the Levant along the Hejaz-Yemen axis. However, they were relatively poor in terms of settlements and technological developments, which remained those typical of transhumant farmers. Historically, this Bronze Age 'Proto-Arabian' context remained relatively marginal, becoming more the object rather than the protagonist of commercial interactions.

The technological developments of the Iron Age paved the way to a new phase in the Arabian Peninsula. This provided its populations with commercial and military opportunities that the states of the Fertile Crescent were forced to take into account. The presence of a Yemenite 'centre' can be seen from the beginning of the first millennium BC (and the legend of Salomon and the queen of Sheba are a clear proof of this). In the ninth and eighth centuries BC, a South Arabian civilisation was gradually developing, with its own writing, walled cities, monumental temples and irrigation canals. This culture reached its classical style in the seventh century BC. On the one hand, the entire system was based on intensive agriculture. The latter was facilitated by the climate on the Yemenite highlands and the great dams between the mountain *wadis* and the desert. On the other hand, the system benefited from the trade of gold and spices.

Towards the end of the seventh century BC, Assyrian sources mention Ita'amar and Karibilu, kings of Sheba. Thanks to the available archaeological evidence, which have invalidated the previous short chronology based on the epigraphic sources, it is now certain that these kings should be identified with the *mukkaribs* of Sheba Yatha'-amar Bayyin and Karib'il Watar. The latter are well attested in monumental inscriptions and belong to a relatively long genealogy. Between 775 and 400 BC (the period belonging to the timeframe of this book), Yemen was ruled by the so-called *mukkaribs* (a royal and religious title). They resided in the region's capital, Sheba. These rulers commissioned several urban and architectural interventions, as well as the construction of imposing dams (such as the first construction of the famous Marib Dam). Following a series of victories, they held a hegemonic position in Yemen and were involved in caravan trade. Later on, in the Achaemenid and Hellenistic period, the kings (not *mukkaribs* anymore) of Sheba, as well as other reigns and dynasties of Ma'in (the Minaeans), Qataban, Hadramawt, and Himyar would take over.

Overall, it is possible to provide some indications on the characteristics of those Arabs that were in contact with the Assyrians. Firstly, names of individuals and locations are entirely Arabic (both South and North Arabic). The Arabian population was Semitic and there are no indications of other linguistic substrates. Secondly, the image of these Arabs was very distinctive. For instance, several 'queens' are attested guiding (even in war) the north Arabian tribes. This aspect is so anomalous that is has to reflect some sort of historical reality, possibly misunderstood by the Assyrians. Overall, the technical repertoire (such as the use of dromedaries), the clothing and weaponry of the Arabs, as well as their combat style and their economic resources, were presented in marked contrast with the 'normal' Mesopotamian standards (Figure 30.1). The Arabs implemented particular strategies for political unification and organisation. The latter were based more on the 'tribe' and its mobility, rather than a precise geographic location. Naturally, there were some 'cities' in the Bazu area, in the Hejaz (with important centres, from Tayma to Dedan, and Yathrib), and in southern Arabia. These were all political and cultic centres dedicated to the management of caravan trade, either as terminals or as strategic points providing supplies along the commercial routes. Moreover, the sheer size of the site of Tayma indicates a considerable concentration of inhabitants, while the irrigated agriculture of the south Arabian cities indicates substantial levels of agricultural production.

Assyrian and Syro-Levantine interests in the Arabs were predominantly commercial. Trade was very specific both in terms of its products (gold, incense, spices and precious stones) and means of transport (caravans). The resources partly came from Yemen and partly from elsewhere, providing the Near Eastern 'market' with products from India and Africa. This allows us to catch a glimpse of a network of land and maritime commercial networks that went well beyond the Yemen-Hejaz-Transjordan-Syria route. It also included other lands around the Indian Ocean. This vast network, however, would only begin to be fully recorded in the sources in the Achaemenid and Hellenistic period.

Finally, there is another, far from secondary, aspect, namely the demographic pressure of the Arabian Peninsula over the Fertile Crescent. Despite the rejection of the anachronistic and simplistic belief that the Arabs 'emigrated' to the north, it has to be conceded that certain phases experienced 'waves' of movement. The latter led the areas along the border of the Fertile Crescent to be directly involved with the border of the Arabian Peninsula. The latter was a largely semi-arid and nomadic area. Waves such as the one of the Ghassulians or the Martu have already been considered. Now, a similar long-term wave appeared, which led the Arabian people closer to the north-western Semitic populations, namely, the Chadeans in Lower Mesopotamia and the groups living in the Transjordan plateau. The Nabayate that the Assyrian sources mentioned as living in the Transjordan plateau have a name that is vaguely similar to the one of the later Nabateans. Structurally speaking, they were both part of a similar development: North-Arabic speaking

Figure 30.1   An Assyrian depiction of the Arabs when they were defeated by Ashurbanipal's troops (relief from Nineveh).

people, following the commercial caravans and the routes of transhumant farmers, began to concentrate close to the fertile lands of Syria and the Levant, gradually taking them over. The Nabayate and Qedarites (in the Wadi Sirhan) mentioned in the Assyrian texts or the Midianites of the Old Testament were therefore at the forefront of a pressure that would significantly increase in the following centuries.

2 The political history of Urartu

Throughout the Bronze Age, the Armenian highlands east of the Upper Euphrates and north of the Upper Tigris played a relatively marginal role in the history of the great kingdoms (from Hatti to Mitanni and Assyria) surrounding them. For the Hittites, the lands east of Melid and Ishuwa were rather primitive in terms of customs and political organisation. From their point of view, the Kaska on the Pontic Mountains and the peoples of Hayasha (near Erzincan) were 'barbarians' that could not be included in their hegemonic political system. They had to be kept at bay either militarily or through treaties. The Mitannian kingdom possibly had more contacts with its northern neighbours, at least because of their similar ethno-linguistic background. This assumption has led to the belief that the Hurrians had originally descended in Upper Mesopotamia from the mountains of the lowlands, and had kept in contact with the populations in the north. The Middle Assyrian kingdom mainly waged wars in the area and benefited from its economic resources, but concealed these intentions behind a defensive policy against the threat of incursions from the north.

Already in the Middle Assyrian period (Shalmaneser I), the term Uruatri (the archaic form of Urartu), and more frequently the term Nairi, were used to designate a whole series of political entities located in the mountains north of Assyria. The majority of clashes were fought in areas located between the Assyrian and the northern populations: from Shubria and Habhu (north of the Upper Tigris) to Habruri (the northern valley of the Upper Zab). Tiglath-pileser I moved well into these territories, marking his presence with the steles left at the Tigris source and near Malazgirt (to the north-west of lake Van). Dayaenu (Upper Euphrates) and Tumme (south-east of Urmia) constituted the two extreme borders (to the west and the east respectively) of the lands of Nairi and of Assyrian interventions.

From the early first millennium BC to the reign of Ashurnasirpal II, the Assyrian policy continued along the same lines implemented in the thirteenth century BC. Meanwhile, the area was developing those innovative characteristics of the Iron Age. In terms of settlements, there was a significant increase of fortified cities guarding intermontane regions. The latter underwent an agricultural development through improvements in irrigation and cultivations. In the individual valleys and lakes (Lake Van, Lake Urmia and Lake Sevan), a series of political and 'national' entities (tribal seems a reductive term at this point) were beginning to take shape, with a sequence of ruling kings. From an Assyrian perspective, the unity of these states was nothing more than a way to face their powerful common enemy. Therefore, apart from the times in which Nairi had to face Assyria, its nature as a permanent confederal entity remains dubious.

In the mid-ninth century BC, the area visibly experienced a political unification. Shalmaneser III had to face first a certain Arame of Urartu (858–844 BC) and then Sarduri I (Sheduri in Assyrian), king of Urartu. Therefore, Urartu, formerly a part of the Nairi 'mosaic' of powers, eventually gained a hegemonic position over the surrounding states. This power established a well-protected political centre at Tushpa, in the Lake Van, and was able to coordinate an anti-Assyrian resistance. Apart from Tushpa, Arame had other 'royal cities' at the centre of each neighbouring state. Shalmaneser claims his destruction of Arzashkun, capital in the Malazgirt area, and Sagunia, capital in the Musharea. This indicates that the Urartian unification had removed the local kinglets close to the Van Basin. The supremacy of Urartu eventually spread to the west, reaching Enzite and Ishuwa in the Upper Euphrates, and to the south-east, reaching Lake Urmia and the northern valley of the Upper Zab (Habruri and Musasir, an ancient cultic centre). If at the time of Arame Shalmaneser was able to reach the heart of Urartu, at the time of Sarduri, the Assyrian king only managed to touch the southern states (Hubushkia and Musasir). The Assyrian influence over the rising Urartian kingdom is evident in its architecture, royal titles, the practice of writing its earliest inscriptions in Assyrian (a practice started by Sarduri I), and presumably in the structure of the state itself (the administration and the army).

In the following 90 years (ca. 830–740 BC), the kingdom of Urartu managed to consolidate its position and extend its hegemony over the Armenian highlands, thus taking advantage of the relative weakness of Assyria (Figure 30.2). With Ishpuini (832–810 BC; the Ushpini of Shamshi-Adad V) and Menua (810–786 BC), royal inscriptions were written in Urartian (or in two languages, Urartian and Assyrian, like the Kelishin Stele), although their structure still shows a certain degree of Assyrian influence. During the reign of Melua in particular, Urartu went through a monumental building programme, focused on three characteristic interventions: royal cities protected by walls, fortresses to defend mountain passes and valleys, and canals. Urartian expansion focused on a west-east axis, following the mountains in the north. To the west, Urartu established its control over Alzi and Melid, which was the 'gate' to the land of Hatti (Neo-Hittite states). To the east, the kingdom established control over Lake Urmia and the Upper Zab (the Kelishin Stele was placed in the passageway between these two basins), and reached the land of the Mannaeans, south-east of Lake Urmia (archaeologically attested in the site of Hasanlu). Urartu's expansion to the north was equally important, leading to a substantial increase of the Urartian sphere of control. The latter included Transcaucasian areas that until then had been outside the control of any state known to us. To the north of Mount Ararat (whose Biblical name reproduces the name of Urartu itself), the Urartians began their systematic 'colonisation' of the Araxes Valley and Lake Sevan.

In the reign of Argishti I (786–764 BC), Urartian expansion reached its peak. The king's annals record his military campaigns in detail. Having firmly established Urartian control in Lake Urmia and Melid (where Argishti came into contact with another great political entity in the Anatolian plateau: the Phrygians), the king focused his efforts on the north. The Urartian kingdom established its control and provided the necessary urban and defensive improvements to the lands of Diauehi (in the area of Erzurum), Eriahi (Arpa Çay Basin), Etiuni (in the Erivan/Yerevan area, whose name cane from the Urartian Erebuni),

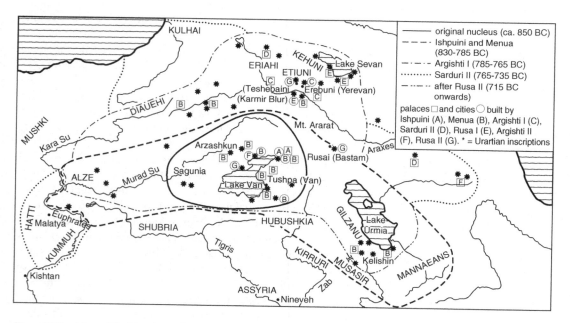

Figure 30.2 Map of the kingdom of Urartu and its expansion, ca. 850–650 BC.

and Kihuni (Lake Sevan). The original centre of the kingdom, Van, was now decentred to the south, a direction in which any form of expansion was impossible due to the presence of Assyria. With the latter, Argishti tried to limit the inevitable rivalry and occasional clashes. It was the time when the *turtānu* Shamshi-ilu was trying to deal with the northern and western borders of Assyria to compensate for the negligence of the Assyrian rulers.

Argishti's policy was continued by Sarduri II (764–734 BC; whose annals have also survived), who reached and conquered the northern region of Kulhai (the Colchis of the Greeks), on the coast of the Black Sea. However, unlike Menua and Argishti, Sarduri II did not fear to interfere with the Assyrian interests. Consequently, the kingdoms of Melid and Kummuh were conquered, and an anti-Assyrian alliance was established with Arpad and Gurgum, as well as Melid and Kummuh. The reign of Tiglath-pileser III, however, changed the situation. The Assyrians defeated Sarduri in a memorable battle (Kishtan, 743 BC), forcing the Urartian king out of the Euphrates Valley. A few years later, the Assyrian army reached Tushpa, sieging (albeit without a clear outcome) the Urartian king, and showing that the situation was now overturned. Despite this retreat in the western front, the size of the Urartian kingdom remained largely unchanged. However, from now on, Urartu had to take into account an aggressive Assyria, which had far superior economic and human resources at its disposition.

We do not know if these military defeats led to the fall of Sarduri II. His successor, Rusa I (734–714 BC, Ursa in the Assyrian sources), was a usurper, who claimed that he had conquered the kingdom only with his own horses and his charioteer. He was also a religious reformer, substituting the official god Tesheba of Van with the god Haldi of Musasir as head of the Urartian pantheon. Rusa was undoubtedly a talented politician, who tried to re-conquer territories from Assyria by establishing new alliances. The king regained control over Musasir, close to the Assyrian border, and removed the Mannaeans from Assyrian control (meaning that the rich tribute paid in horses was now sent to Urartu). Finally, he established diplomatic relations with Mita of Mushki and Ambari of Tabal, in order to take away from Assyria control over Central and eastern Anatolia.

This Urartian revival was roughly contemporary to the efforts of Tiglath-pileser III and Shalmaneser V in Syria and the Levant. However, when Sargon II focused his attention to the north, Rusa's policy proved to have been quite impracticable. Consequently, the Assyrian annexation of the Neo-Hittite states once and for all cut Urartu off from any control in the Euphrates Valley (from Melid to Carchemish). Moreover, a memorable expedition of the Assyrian king (namely, his 'eighth campaign') brought destruction in the eastern territories of the Urartian kingdom, and regained control over the Mannaeans. This expedition peaked in the sack of Musasir and the temple of Haldi, after which a rich booty was brought back to Assyria.

However, the Assyrian expansion and the transformation of the Neo-Hittite states into Assyrian provinces were not the only reason for the change of the position of Urartu in the west. Urartu also suffered from the impact of the invasion of the Cimmerians. It is possible that Rusa died while fighting them, and it is peculiar that both Sargon of Assyria and Mita of Mushki/Phrygia met a similar fate. Therefore, the three great kings competing over control in eastern Anatolia were caught off guard by the incursion of the Cimmerians and the subsequent turbulence in the area. Assyria sealed alliances with both Phrygia and Urartu. This was possible mainly because the boundaries delimiting these powers were now consolidated. In fact, now these borders did not separate ever-changing spheres of influence anymore, but consolidated territorial empires.

Due to the lack of Urartian annals or detailed Assyrian sources on Urartu, the phase between the death of Rusa I and the end of the Urartian kingdom is often considered a period of decline and crisis. It is undeniable that there was a marked decline in the tensions along its southern and western borders. For example, when the buffer state of Shubria refused to return some fugitives to Assyria, Esarhaddon ferociously punished it, but he still showed his respect for Urartu and did not expand further. Even under Ashurbanipal, at the peak of Assyrian power, Urartu was recognised as an equal power. At the same time, the Urartian kings Argishti II and Rusa II (ca. 714–680 BC and 680–640 BC) were actively engaged along their northern and eastern borders. In particular, Rusa II commissioned several fortifications in Urartu, strengthening the kingdom's position in its three most important fronts: Lake Urmia (with the construction of the royal fortress of Bastam), the Araxes Valley, and Lake Sevan (with the construction of the royal city of Teshebaini/Karmir Blur).

This increase in building and military interventions in the north-east was a direct consequence of the new developments taking place in the Iranian plateau. These developments were threatening Urartu's position. In reality, the first incursions of the Cimmerians had simply been a prelude to the invasions of the Cimmerians and Scythians in the mid-seventh century BC, the formation and expansion of an autonomous Mannaean state threatening Urartu's position in Lake Urmia, and finally the rise of the Medes. Urartu and Assyria may have intervened together, or at least did not hinder each other in their interventions. When Ashurbanipal defeated Elam, the king of Urartu, Sarduri III (ca. 640–610 BC) congratulated him, an act that was presented by the Assyrians as a sign of submission.

However, Assyria, the vaster and stronger power of the two, would be the first to collapse under the joint attack of the Chaldeans and the Medes. Having already destroyed Assyria, in 608 BC Nabopolassar led an incursion in Urartu simply to protect the northern flank of his advance towards Syria. Despite this, between the end of the seventh and the beginning of the sixth centuries BC, Urartu still managed to resist under the leadership of a series of Sarduri III's successors. We do not have any textual evidence on the fall of Urartu. The latter took place around 590 BC, at the hand of several Iranian tribes that managed to break through the line of fortresses and citadels protecting Lake Urmia and the Araxes Valley. It has been suggested that the Scythians were the ones who destroyed the Urartian cities, involuntarily leaving as their mark a typically Scythian kind of arrowhead. This hypothesis is plausible, but it seems that the elimination of Urartu was rather finalised by the Medes. The latter already controlled Upper Mesopotamia and the northern Zagros (Zamua and the Mannaeans) after the fall of Assyria (610 BC), and in 585 BC faced the Lydians in Cappadocia.

Having become part of the Median kingdom, Urartu eventually became a satrapy of the Achaemenid empire under the name of Armenia. This onomastic change was neither secondary nor a mere formality. It was a direct consequence of a change in the ethnic composition of the area. In other words, the Armenians (whose language was Indo-European) substituted the Hurrian-speaking Urartians. However, it would be far too simplistic to blame this change on the destroyers of the Urartian cities, or to see it as a change that took place in a couple of years. On the contrary, this shift constituted a long-term phenomenon, which developed alongside the infiltration of the Phrygians in Anatolia and the Indo-Iranians in Iran. There-fore, the political supremacy of Urartu and the traditional tone of its official inscriptions have managed to conceal what was actually happening to its population. Once the Urartian state was destroyed, however, the new Armenian people, supported by the Medes and Persians, eventually gained the upper hand in the area.

3 The economy and culture of Urartu

Urartu was a network of regions separated by mountains. This aspect has led to its designation as a 'conti-nental archipelago'. Its mountains were covered by forests (far more than today, after millennia of defor-estation) and largely uninhabited. The majority of the population was therefore concentrated in the valleys and lakes, at an altitude of 1000/1500 metres. Communications between basins were difficult and had to be interrupted during the winter. In the Pre-Urartian period, the area had low population levels, which significantly rose and peaked in the eighth and seventh centuries BC. However, on an archaeological level, this development is only partially 'invisible', since a large portion of the population was made of transhu-mant farmers and farmers living in small villages. The Assyrian sources distinguished three types of Urartian settlements: 'fortified cities', 'fortresses' and the 'neighbouring villages'. The first group was made of cities that in the Iron Age, and especially in Urartu, were particularly small. In fact, the 20 hectares of Bastam constituted the maximum size for an Urartian city, which could only be surpassed by the capital (Tushpa). Archaeological surveys have located several Urartian fortresses, providing their plans and sizes. These were imposing fortresses and effective strongholds, but mainly hosted garrisons. Therefore, the majority of the population lived in unfortified villages and seasonal camps.

It appears that the Urartian state made a great effort to provide its territory with fortified strongholds, meant to defend strategic access points, control agro-pastoral lands, and protect the accumulated resources. This effort is a representation of the building aspect of the Urartian state from its formative process to its hegemony, and its defence from Assyrian and then Scythian attacks. The 'royal cities', capitals of the Urartian cantons, had 'palaces', where the products accumulated through internal taxation and war booties were stored. There were warehouses for foodstuffs, such as the imposing ones found intact at Karmir Blur, which have allowed an estimation of the amount of food stored. In addition to that, there were armouries for chariots and weapons, and treasuries, mainly located in temples. In this regard, Sargon's description of his sack of the temple of Haldi at Musasir provides the most informative and impressive indications of the wealth stored in Urartian temples.

At the centre of the Urartian state there was the king, whose titles were of Assyrian inspiration ('mighty king'; 'great king'; 'king of Nairi' in Assyrian and 'of Biaini' in Urartian; 'king of kings'; 'king of the lands'; and so on). He was supported by a series of functionaries both in the centre and the periphery of the kingdom. The king's celebrative repertoire (also Assyrian-inspired) was made of votive and annalistic inscriptions placed in emblematic locations. At times, these inscriptions were even left outside palaces or cities, as steles left in mountain passes, rock reliefs near river crossings and so on. Nonetheless, the means and stages that led to this centralisation of power, which started from a number of small 'nations' forming the constitutive elements of the Urartian state, remain largely unknown.

The centralisation of power in Urartu must have been due to two essential elements: the army and the exploitation of 'strategic' resources. Urartu must have required a larger standing army to guard the numerous fortresses and fortified cities, and to ensure a continuous defence against foreign invaders and local raiders. Due to the nature of Urartu's territory, invaders and raiders were a constant threat. Judging from the Urartian annals, during campaigns the Urartian army followed the common division into chariotry, cavalry and infantry. Despite being an integral part of Urartian iconography, chariots were few in number and difficult to use in a largely mountainous territory. It appears that the Urartian army normally relied on around a hundred chariots, a few thousands horsemen and around 20,000 soldiers. The Urartian army, then, was certainly adequate for the local demographic resources, but far from the size of the Assyrian army. Therefore, the latter could only be stopped through the inaccessibility of the Urartian territory and fortresses.

An influx of deportees and animals, taken during the Urartian campaigns against the small neighbouring states, refilled the local supplies through planned redistributions and allocations. The availability of 'strategic' resources explains the wealth of Iron Age Urartu. These resources were mainly metals and horses, as well as timber for buildings. The latter was less desired by foreign states, due to the lack of rivers able to carry timber to the south. Copper and iron, the two main metals of the time, were available in a number of areas controlled by Urartu, from eastern Anatolia to the south Caucasus. Afghan tin reached the Near East through Iran, and control over it was one of the reasons for the rivalry between Urartu and Assyria.

It is possible that metals were a royal monopoly, while horses were a different case. The latter were bred near the river basins of the Armenian highlands, and especially near Lake Urmia and east of it (Mannaeans). Horse breeding was largely left in the hands of pastoral groups, but the king had a right to request them. This royal right was another reason for disputes between Urartians and Assyrians. It would be inherited by the Median kings, Achaemenid emperors and Hellenistic rulers. Therefore, Urartu had an advantage over Assyria, namely, of having in its own land the necessary resources for its military and building interventions. The Assyrian empire gathered these resources with great difficulty. From a long-term perspective, however, the formation of the Urartian state was stimulated by this Assyrian interest in Armenian resources. Therefore, Urartu partly developed imitating Assyria, and partly relied on a different balance of resources (that is, less workforce and more raw materials).

The demographic growth of Urartu was partly due to animal farming, which provided sheep, goats, and cattle alongside the 'strategic' breeding of horses. It was also partly due to agricultural developments. The latter mainly involved the construction of irrigation systems, which were different (yet not less important) to the ones developed in the Mesopotamia Alluvial Plain from as early as the proto-historic age. Irrigation in the highlands is a development typical of the Iron Age, and consists of the deviation and artificial channelling of rivers, directed towards wider stretches of arable land. These were hydraulic interventions adapted to the Urartian mountainous territory. Certain Neo-Assyrian building interventions were partly the result of these same experiences.

A particular system, which would eventually spread in Iran but is first attested in Urartu, is that of the *qanat*. The latter was a subterranean tunnel connected to the surface through vertical wells (built for the construction of the tunnel itself and for aeration). This system allowed the delivery of water over long distances, avoiding evaporation, regardless of the varying inclination of the surface. Springs, *qanat*, surface canals and aqueducts formed a remarkably efficient landscape, but still relatively vulnerable. Thanks to these infrastructures, the area experienced significant agricultural development. The latter was characterised by the intensive cultivation of crops and trees (especially vines), with a particular attention for royal or even temple supplies (Figure 30.3). Sargon's account of his eighth campaign shows the king's admiration for Urartian agriculture, as well as its fortresses and the wealth of its treasuries.

Urartian metalwork is well documented in the archaeological evidence, not so much in terms of iron, which was a more practical and constantly reused metal, but in terms of bronze, which presents several characteristic features of Urartian craftsmanship (Figure 30.4). Large cauldrons (with handles in the form of 'sirens') and tripods were valuable objects, often used as assets to facilitate the circulation of wealth. Some of them 'emigrated' to Assyria, in the form of tributes, or to Greek sanctuaries as votive offerings. Bronze was also used in the decoration of valuable furniture, such as in the case of the renowned throne of Toprakkale. Moreover, a large portion of Urartian weaponry was still made out of bronze, such as shields, helmets, belts and harnesses decorated with war and hunting scenes, rows of soldiers and chariots, fortresses, mythical animals, or divine symbols. These valuable items also spread alongside similar Neo-Hittite and Phrygian objects through trade, gift exchange, tributes and plunders.

Architecture is another sector showing Urartu's great originality, despite its reuse of Mitannian, Middle Assyrian and Neo-Assyrian elements. Fortresses display the clever exploitation of their difficult location, establishing a sort of continuity between rocks and artificial constructions. This aspect is particularly visible in the fortress of Van. Even individual buildings display unique characteristics, such as the great columned halls in palaces, or the Urartian tower-temples, two elements that would be borrowed in Median and Persian architecture. Therefore, despite owing much to Assyria and Syria, Urartian art still managed to develop its own individual traits, rooted in the cultural and geographic features of the area. Moreover, Urartu became in turn a centre for the diffusion of iconographies and styles towards Iran and Greece.

4 The Neo-Elamite kingdom: history and culture

In the mid-eighth century BC, after almost four centuries of silence, Elam reappeared in the Near Eastern scene. It took on an important role up until the final destruction of Susa by Ashurbanipal shortly after the mid-seventh century BC. Despite the obvious continuity between the two phases, this last century of Elamite history is defined as the Neo-Elamite kingdom to separate it from the Middle Elamite kingdom of the thirteenth and twelfth century BC. The gap in the evidence between the Middle and Neo-Elamite kingdoms, then, remains an unresolved issue. On the one hand, the lack of Mesopotamian attestations corresponds to the decline of Elam into a local power. However, this does not imply a complete separa-

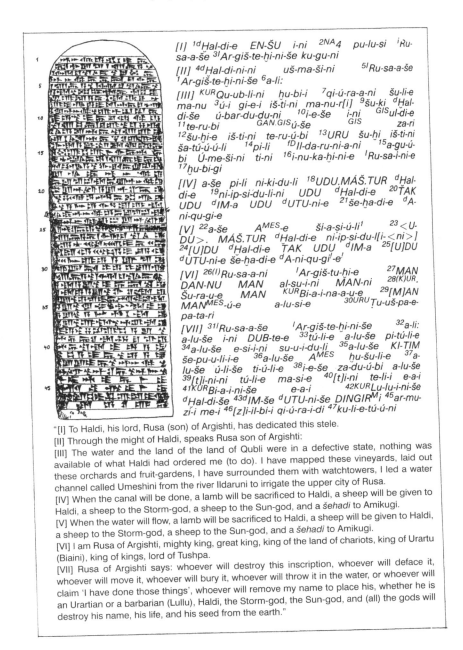

[I] ¹ᵈHal-di-e EN-ŠU i-ni ²NA₄ pu-lu-si ⁱRu-sa-a-še ³ⁱAr-giš-te-ḫi-ni-še ku-gu-ni

[II] ⁴ᵈHal-di-ni-ni uš-ma-ši-ni ⁵ⁱRu-sa-a-še ⁱAr-giš-te-ḫi-ni-še ⁶a-li:

[III] ᴷᵁᴿQu-ub-li-ni ḫu-bi-i ⁷qi-ú-ra-a-ni šu-li-e ma-nu ³ú-i gi-e-i iš-ti-ni ma-nu-r[i] ⁹šu-ki ᵈHal-di-še ú-bar-du-du-ni ¹⁰i-e-še i-ni ᴳᴵˢul-di-e ¹¹te-ru-bi ᴳᴬᴺ.ᴳᴵˢú-še ᴳᴵˢ za-ri ¹²šu-ḫi-e iš-ti-ni te-ru-ú-bi ¹³URU šu-ḫi iš-ti-ni ša-tú-ú-ú-li ¹⁴pi-li ᶠᴰIl-da-ru-ni-a-ni ¹⁵a-gu-ú-bi Ú-me-ši-ni ti-ni ¹⁶i-nu-ka-ḫi-ni-e ⁱRu-sa-i-ni-e ¹⁷ḫu-bi-gi

[IV] a-še pi-li ni-ki-du-li ¹⁸UDU.MÁŠ.TUR ᵈHal-di-e ¹⁹ni-ip-si-du-li-ni UDU ᵈHal-di-e ²⁰ŤAK UDU ᵈIM-a UDU ᵈUTU-ni-e ²¹še-ḫa-di-e ᵈA-ni-qu-gi-e

[V] ²²a-še ᴬᴹᴱˢ-e ši-a-ṣi-ú-li¹ ²³<U-DU>. MÁŠ.TUR ᵈHal-di-e ni-ip-si-du-l[i-<ni>] ²⁴[U]DU ᵈHal-di-e ŤAK UDU ᵈIM-a ²⁵[U]DU ᵈUTU-ni-e še-ḫa-di-e ᵈA-ni-qu-giⁱ-e

[VI] ²⁶⁽ⁱ⁾Ru-sa-a-ni ⁱAr-giš-tu-ḫi-e ²⁷MAN DAN-NU MAN al-su-i-ni MAN-ni ²⁸⁽ᴷ⁾ᵁᴿ Šu-ra-u-e MAN ᴷᵁᴿBi-a-i-na-a-u-e ²⁹[M]AN MANᴹᴱˢ-ú-e a-lu-si-e ³⁰ᵁᴿᵁTu-uš-pa-e-pa-ta-ri

[VII] ³¹ⁱRu-sa-a-še ⁱAr-giš-te-ḫi-ni-še ³²a-li: a-lu-še i-ni DUB-te-e ³³tú-li-e a-lu-še pi-tú-li-e ³⁴a-lu-še e-si-i-ni su-u-i-du-li ³⁵a-lu-še KI-TIM še-pu-u-li-e ³⁶a-lu-še ᴬᴹᴱˢ ḫu-šu-li-e ³⁷a-lu-še ú-li-še ti-ú-li-e ³⁸a-lu-še za-du-ú-bi a-lu-še ³⁹[t]li-ni-ni tú-li-e ma-si-e ⁴⁰[t]li-ni te-li-i e-a-i ⁴¹ᴷᵁᴿBi-a-i-ni-še e-a-i ⁴²ᴷᵁᴿLu-lu-i-ni-še ᵈHal-di-še ⁴³ᵈIM-še ᵈUTU-ni-še DINGIRᴹⁱ ⁴⁵ar-mu-zi-i me-i ⁴⁶[z]i-il-bi-i qi-ú-ra-di ⁴⁷ku-li-e-tú-ú-ni

"[I] To Haldi, his lord, Rusa (son) of Argishti, has dedicated this stele.
[II] Through the might of Haldi, speaks Rusa son of Argishti:
[III] The water and the land of the land of Qubli were in a defective state, nothing was available of what Haldi had ordered me (to do). I have mapped these vineyards, laid out these orchards and fruit-gardens, I have surrounded them with watchtowers, I led a water channel called Umeshini from the river Ildaruni to irrigate the upper city of Rusa.
[IV] When the canal will be done, a lamb will be sacrificed to Haldi, a sheep will be given to Haldi, a sheep to the Storm-god, a sheep to the Sun-god, and a *šehadi* to Amikugi.
[V] When the water will flow, a lamb will be sacrificed to Haldi, a sheep will be given to Haldi, a sheep to the Storm-god, a sheep to the Sun-god, and a *šehadi* to Amikugi.
[VI] I am Rusa of Argishti, mighty king, great king, king of the land of chariots, king of Urartu (Biaini), king of kings, lord of Tushpa.
[VII] Rusa of Argishti says: whoever will destroy this inscription, whoever will deface it, whoever will move it, whoever will bury it, whoever will throw it in the water, or whoever will claim 'I have done those things', whoever will remove my name to place his, whether he is an Urartian or a barbarian (Lullu), Haldi, the Storm-god, the Sun-god, and (all) the gods will destroy his name, his life, and his seed from the earth."

Figure 30.3　Urartian royal inscription: the stele of Rusa II.

tion of the latter from the Mesopotamian scene. On the other hand, the lack of local attestations implies an interval in building and celebrative interventions, at least in Susa, which remains our main source of information. Even in the case of Tall-i Malyan, the main centre of eastern Elam (Anshan), we know that the city collapsed after the Middle Elamite period. This proves that this gap in the evidence affected both major political centres of the Elamite confederation. Therefore, it remains unclear where and for how long

Figure 30.4   Urartian bronze disk with war scenes.

Elam survived as a political entity in its 'obscure' phase (ca. 1100–800 BC). Elam experienced profound ethno-linguistic changes in this period, with Indo-European groups rising in the Iranian plateau (inhabited by Elamites, Lullubeans and Gutians) and extending as far as the Zagros Mountains.

The reappearance of Mesopotamian information took place during the reign of Sargon II, a contemporary of the Elamite kings Humbanigash I (742–717 BC) and Shutruk-Nahhunte II (717–699 BC), who was succeeded by Hallutash-Inshushinak (699–693 BC). During the reign of Shutruk-Nahhunte, Elamite royal inscriptions reappeared in Susa and in the monumental complex of Malamir, a mountain pass midway between Susa and Esfahan. The three Elamite kings were brothers on their mother's side and cousins on their father's side, and we only have the names of their fathers (who were brothers as well), Humban-nimena II (ca. 770 BC) and Humban-tahra (ca. 750 BC). This indicates that the new dynasty must have begun in the eighth century BC. There are many elements showing the Neo-Elamite desire to evoke the glory of the Middle Elamite phase. Firstly, there is a revival of ancient royal names and of the Middle Elamite royal titulature. Moreover, when describing the sack of Susa, Ashurbanipal mentions the presence of Elamite monuments alongside those monuments brought back after the ancient Elamite incursions in Babylonia, including a statue of Nanâ (Inanna), probably taken from Uruk 1635 years earlier.

In other words, one gets the impression that there was a dynastic and architectural continuity between the Neo-Elamite period and its earlier phases. The royal titulature included the ancient titles of 'king (*sunkik*) of Anshan and Susa', 'master (*katri*) of Elam', 'governor (*hal-menik*, translated as *šakkanakku* in Akkadian) of Elam', and the title of 'magnifier of the realm'. The latter emphasises the revival of Elamite expansion. The centre of the kingdom was clearly moved to Khuzistan, with Susa as its capital, centre of the kings' building programmes, treasures and monuments. Further east and further north, however, it remains unclear to what extent the Neo-Elamite kings controlled Fars (Anshan), which was included in their titles, and Esfahan. On the contrary, Neo-Elamite expansion to the south-west is well attested, and brought Elam to participate once again in the dispute over Babylonia, leading to its clash with Assyria and its final collapse.

The structure of the Neo-Elamite kingdom was still suffering from the fragmentation and complexity of its landscape, and the 'fratriarchal' nature of the Elamite family and royal succession. The old characteristic triad of the *sukkal-maḥ* is not attested anymore, or at least is not as visible. However, it is still possible to see a system in which the ruling king (residing in Susa) was surrounded by a series of high functionaries. These were all more or less his relatives, ruled over regions and cities, and were involved in the succession to the throne. Consequently, in this century of Neo-Elamite history (ca. 740–640 BC), Elam had twelve kings, while Assyria had only four. This visible political instability and the fragmentation of the Elamite state clearly contributed to Elam's weakness. Another potential weakness was in the kind of values supported by the Elamite elite, which accumulated and flaunted wealth, and created 'paradises' (parks pre-dating the Persian ones) where one could practise hunting.

Even in war, the elite saw an opportunity to parade an armament that was more opulent than practical. This, at least, was the opinion of the Assyrians, who derided the Elamite soldiers for being so lavishly attired as to be unable to fight. This characteristic eventually formed a *topos* that would be bestowed on the Persians, who were described in this way by the Greeks at the time of Alexander's campaigns, and the Sassanians, described in this way by the Arabs. Apart from personal ostentation, Ashurbanipal's description of Susa, its temples, treasures and royal necropolis, clearly shows that the Assyrians considered these levels of Elamite wealth and ostentation excessive. The final century of the Elamite kingdom was marked by a revival of building activities, both in Susa and elsewhere, with buildings decorated with glazed bricks, which rivalled Assyrian palaces more in refinement than size. However, these interventions were suppressed and almost erased by the radical intervention of Ashurbanipal, so that there are very few remains of the Neo-Elamite level in Susa (a site that has been extensively, yet badly, excavated).

The Neo-Elamite policy in Mesopotamia can be reconstructed from the Assyrian sources, although only partially and with obvious exaggerations in certain crucial episodes. Overall, it is possible to detect a territorial strategy centred on the conquest of border territories between Susiana and Lower Mesopotamia, and a strategy of consolidation of communication and commercial routes. The latter developed along the Zagros, competing with Assyria for the key-areas of Ellipi and Zamua, and descended to the mouth of the Tigris and Euphrates (the Sealand, ruled by the Chaldean tribe of Bit Yakini), in order to cut Assyria off maritime trade. The aim of the entire strategy was to control (even indirect control) Babylonia, in order to prevent Assyria to establish a stable control over the region. This explains the constant Elamite interventions supporting any anti-Assyrian 'rebel' claiming his rule over Babylonia in place of the puppet monarchs appointed by the Assyrians.

The Neo-Elamite phase began in the second half of the eighth century BC. The texts of Tiglath-pileser III, who was involved in the issues surrounding Babylonia, do not mention Elam. However, all of a sudden, during the reign of Sargon II, the Elamite king Humbanigash I is attested sealing an alliance with Marduk-apla-iddina, and fighting the Assyrians at Der (720 BC). Ten years later, Sargon defeated the Chaldean-Elamite alliance and the Elamite king Shutruk-Nahhunte II. Consequently, Assyria was able to resume relations with Dilmun in the Persian Gulf, and to regain control over Ellipi in the Zagros, thus hindering Elamite commercial relations in the south and the north. When Sennacherib succeeded his father on the Assyrian throne, Shutruk-Nahhunte tried to regain his previous position, supporting once again the anti-Assyrian forces in Babylonia. However, he was defeated in Kish and had to retreat. The following year, the Assyrians returned in Ellipi to enforce their control in the area. Alongside the pre-existing fortress of Harhar (Kar-Sharrukin), the Assyrians founded the city of Kar-Sennacherib, acting as another political and commercial centre.

Meanwhile, Hallutash-Inshushinak became king in Elam, but supremacy continued to fluctuate between the two powers. An expedition of Sennacherib reaching the Elamite coast on the Gulf was countered by an Elamite incursion in northern Babylonia and the siege of Sippar. Then, there was an Assyrian victory in Nippur and an expedition up to the border of Elam. This intense Assyrian military pressure brought to the fall of Hallutash-Inshushinak and Kudur-Nahhunte III. The following king, Humban-nimena III (Menanu in the Assyrian sources), revived the coalition and faced Sennacherib in the battle of Halule (near Samarra, in the north). Sennacherib celebrated this battle as an Assyrian victory. In reality, the battle constituted a real setback for the Assyrian king, which would only be overcome two years later with the destruction of Babylon.

The stalemate resulting from these constant conflicts was followed by around twenty-five years of relatively peaceful relations (689–664 BC) under the rule of Humban-Haltash I, Humban-Haltash II and Urtaku. This situation was mirrored by the rule of Esarhaddon, whose policy in Babylonia also proved to be less aggressive. Regarding the periphery, the land expedition to Bazu indicates that Esarhaddon could probably not cross the Gulf by sea. Meanwhile, in the Central Zagros, the local populations (the Medes in particular) began to take control over commercial relations, removing Elamite and Assyrian control in the area.

Urtaku was persuaded to break the long truce by supporting a Lower Mesopotamia coalition against Ashurbanipal, but failed. He was substituted on the Elamite throne by his nephew Tepti-Humban-Inshushinak (Teumman in the Assyrian sources). This sudden death and political change was naturally seen by the Assyrians as a divine punishment of their treacherous rivals. This interpretation was not very far from the truth, considering the typically Neo-Elamite link between military defeats and loss of the Elamite throne. Teumman, who would be described by the Assyrians as the worst Neo-Elamite king, was probably not a legitimate heir to the throne, since Urtaku's sons escaped to Assyria. Teumman ruled in Elam for around ten years and managed to move his army into Lower Mesopotamia. Ashurbanipal led a violent attack against the ruler and reached Elam, defeated Teumman at the Ulai River (the modern Karkheh River) and took over control of the region. Teumman died in battle, and Ashurbanipal placed Urtaku's sons as rulers in Susa, Madaktu and Hidalu, in the hope that this political fragmentation and the dependence of each ruler on the Assyrians would be enough to keep Elam under control.

However, Elam was not yet tamed. The kinglets somehow managed to deal with internal struggles and support the Babylonians, making Ashurbanipal's solution ineffective. Humban-Haltash III finally managed to gain control over Susa and Madaktu in 648 BC, re-unifying Elam. Unfortunately, the unification happened at the most inconvenient time. Ashurbanipal had just managed to solve the Babylonian problem with the death of Shamash-shum-ukin and the appointment of Kandalanu, and could not allow the situation to be overturned once again through an Elamite intervention. The king therefore sent a double Assyrian expedition. In 647 BC, Humban-Haltash fled, the Assyrians invaded the area, and when they retreated, the Elamite king returned. The second Assyrian intervention in 646 BC was ruthless: the Assyrian army entered Elam, destroyed the land and its cities, and then focused all its efforts on Susa, which was sacked and burnt to the ground. In this case, alongside the celebration of the value and size of the booty brought back, the Assyrians curiously emphasised their desire to desecrate Elamite cultic centres and the royal necropolis. This behaviour indicates their will to once and for all end this long-standing rival and its unusual culture.

The devastation brought by Ashurbanipal's army had the desired outcome. For a couple of years, Humban-Haltash continued to rule from Madaktu over a destroyed Elam. After all, even from an Assyrian perspective, Elam could not be turned into a new province. The Persians were already established in

Anshan. Their king Kurash (Cyrus, the homonymous ancestor of the founder of the empire) sent gifts to the Assyrian king, benefiting from the substitution of the neighbouring Elamite ruler with a more distant overlord. The fall of Elam, then, created a political vacuum that could not be filled by the Assyrians, a situation that was very advantageous for the new Iranian populations. If the Medes had long managed to claim their space between the spheres of control of Urartu, Assyria and Elam, the Persians had to wait for the fall of Elam to be able to intervene. In a few years, the political strategy of Ashurbanipal proved to be particularly short-sighted, ultimately damaging Assyria's position. Assyria thus ceased to be protected by Elam, the land that had long kept away part of the populations coming from the north.

5 Phrygia and Lydia

In the twelfth century BC, the first expansion of the Phrygians (Mushki) reached the Upper Tigris, but was pushed back by Tiglath-pileser I. From then until the beginning of the eighth century BC, the silence of the written evidence corresponds to the slow development of the material culture and socio-political organisation of Central Anatolia, which is archaeologically attested. The peak of this process was the formation of the Phrygian kingdom. The latter became a hegemonic power in Central and western Anatolia, and to some extent the heir of the Hittite kingdom, which collapsed half a millennium earlier. Around the mid-eighth century BC, evidence on the Phrygian kingdom becomes more consistent. We possess Assyrian sources from the reigns of Tiglath-pileser III and Sargon II, local inscriptions, and important archaeological remains, such as the royal tumuli of Gordion (Figure 30.5). However, considering the fact that the Phrygian kingdom collapsed at the beginning of the seventh century BC at the hand of the Cimmerians, its documented history only covers the span of around fifty years.

The eastern border of the kingdom was well defined. The Upper Halys and the salt lakes separated the Phrygian kingdom from the Neo-Hittite states (and later on from the Assyrian provinces established there). The northern border reached the Pontic Mountains or even the Black Sea. Only the western border, however, cannot be defined with certainty. It appears that Lydia and the Greek cities on the Aegean coast were never conquered by the Phrygians, but remained autonomous. Similarly, it is possible that the Phrygians never controlled the populations in the south, from the Carians to the Lycians and other populations living in the Taurus area.

The kingdom's capital was Gordion (on the Sakarya River). Further Phrygians centres extended from 'Midas City' (Yazilikaya, between Afyon and Eskisehir) in the west to post-Hittite Boghazköi and Pazarli to the east (Figure 30.6). In terms of archaeology, Phrygian remains are attested over a far longer period of time than the fifty years attested in the written sources. This indicates that Phrygian culture had a formation phase and a phase following the collapse of the kingdom. In terms of diffusion, it is difficult to establish the spread of Phrygian culture. The most distinctive aspects of Phrygian culture – from its painted pottery (thus the name 'Phrygian pottery') to bronze objects – are attested well beyond the Phrygian borders. Therefore, local variations in style did not necessarily correspond to ethno-linguistic or political differences.

According to Greek sources, the names of the kings of Phrygia alternated between Midas and Gordion. However, the Assyrians only attest one 'Mita of Mushki', but it is not excluded that this 'Mita' combined a number of individuals. Unlike Greek sources, which were far later and more anecdotal, the Assyrian sources are contemporary to the Phrygians. They therefore provide more reliable historical and political information on the kingdom. The latter appears to have been involved in a clash of powers (the other two being Assyria and Urartu) over the control of the Neo-Hittite states, especially Tabal and Hilakku, which were the nearest of these states to Phrygia.

While the situation was unstable and an expansion was still possible, Mita tried to get involved in the affairs of the Neo-Hittite states. However, once the Assyrian provincial system was implemented in the entire area south-east of the Taurus, the Phrygian policy had to change. The kingdom tried to seal diplomatic relations with the Assyrians, and tacitly recognised Assyrian supremacy in Cilicia and the Euphrates.

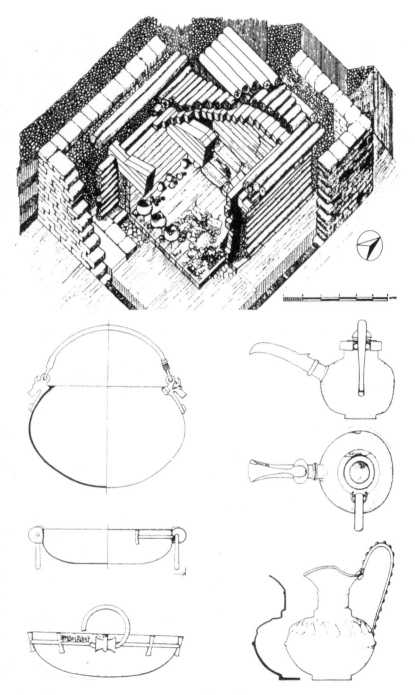

Figure 30.5 The royal tumulus (attributed to Midas) in Gordion. *Above*: Plan of the burial chamber; *Below*: A selection of the metal ware found in the tumulus.

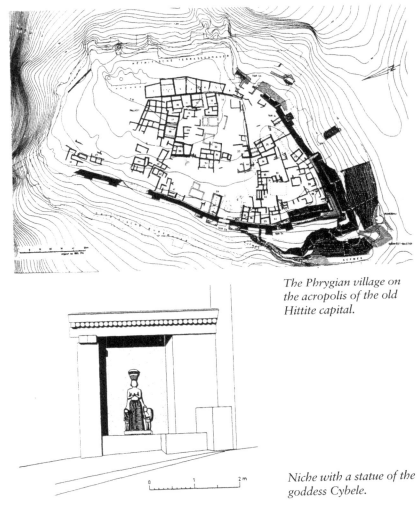

The Phrygian village on
the acropolis of the old
Hittite capital.

Niche with a statue of the
goddess Cybele.

Figure 30.6 Büyükkale in the Phrygian period. *Above*: The Phrygian village on the acropolis of the old Hittite capital; *Below*: Niche with a statue of the goddess Cybele.

This strategy was possibly implemented in exchange of a certain degree of influence over Tabal, which remained (or returned) autonomous. Eventually, the incursions of the Cimmerians destabilised the entire political asset of the area. Having pushed back the Urartians and the Assyrians, the Cimmerians moved to the west at the beginning of the seventh century BC. Gordion fell and was destroyed, and a horde of Cimmerians farmers and soldiers reached the coast of the Aegean.

The collapse of the Phrygian kingdom did not mark the end of Phrygian culture, just like the Cimmerian invasion did not cause a significant change in the ethnic composition of Anatolia. Shortly after, around 670 BC, a new power rose to prominence. The latter was partly an heir of the legacy left by the kingdom of Phrygia, but was located further west. It was the kingdom of Lydia, whose capital was the city of Sardis. The founder of its ruling dynasty was Gyges. The latter gained control over Central and western Anatolia. Greek sources attest the existence of an earlier 'Heraclid' dynasty. This dynasty supposedly ruled in the phase between the 'heroic' age after the Trojan War and the reign of Gyges, and thus was contemporary to the Phrygian kingdom. However, this dynasty remains unattested elsewhere. Only with Gyges, both the Assyrian and Greek sources begin to be more reliable, except maybe for Herodotus' account of Gyges' rise to power. It appears that, following a premonitory dream, Gyges wrote to Ashurbanipal asking for support against the Cimmerians, but then sealed an alliance and supported Egypt in their fight against the Assyrians. Soon after, the Lydian king had to face another incursion of Cimmerians and Scythians, and died in 652 BC during the siege of Sardis.

According to Herodotus, his successors were Ardys, Sadyattes and Alyattes. These kings managed to consolidate the kingdom of Lydia, expel the last Cimmerians, and conquer the Greek cities in Asia Minor and other Anatolian states south and east of Lydia, reaching the borders of Tabal and Hilakku. The long reign of Alyattes probably constituted the peak of development and stability of the Lydian kingdom. Following the collapse of Assyria and Urartu, the rising Median kingdom and its expansion to the west clashed with the Lydians of Alyattes. The outcome of the war was uncertain, but the mediation of Cilicia and Babylonia eventually led to a peace between the two powers, sealed through inter-dynastic marriages. The final battle preceding this truce has been dated with precision, thanks to the solar eclipse of 585 BC, which happened on the day of the battle.

Croesus was the last king of Lydia and a legendary symbol of wealth and misfortune. Under the leadership of Cyrus, the Persians defeated the Medes and resumed expansion to the west, this time with remarkable determination. Croesus tried to form an anti-Persian coalition with all the powers threatened by the Persian expansion, from Egypt to the Greeks, Cilicia and Babylonia. However, Cyrus' swift intervention precluded any coordination. Sardis was sieged and the Lydian kingdom was annexed to the empire.

The main Phrygian and Lydian political developments known to us concern their relations with their Near Eastern neighbours (Assyrians, Medes and Persians). However, it seems that on a cultural and commercial level interactions with the west were equally, if not more, intense. Around the eighth century BC, the Phrygians adopted an alphabet substantially similar to the one developed by the Greeks slightly earlier. Although some Phoenician inscriptions are attested in Cilicia and even close to the Phrygian border, it remains likely that the Phrygians developed their alphabet through their contacts with the Greek World. The same phenomenon would again appear with the Lydians, who would also adopt an alphabetic writing of Greek origins. Due to Lydia's position, relations with the Greek cities of Asia Minor were even more intense. We know that Phrygian and Lydian kings left several valuable dedications in Greek sanctuaries, especially at Delphi. Moreover, it is highly significant that the kingdoms of Lydia and Phrygia were contemporary to the phase of increased oriental contacts and influences in the Greek World. Bronze cauldrons, tripods, washbowls, cups and weapons were imported to Greece for their material and symbolic value (as prizes or votive offerings) as well as their quality. They therefore acted as crucial means for the spread of Near Eastern figurative, mythical and technological elements. Naturally, other means (such as textiles and carved wooden objects) also contributed to this diffusion, but have not survived in the archaeological evidence.

At this point, it has become necessary to at least mention the presence of Greek colonies on the Anatolian coast. Mycenaean presence in the fourteenth and thirteenth centuries BC, the Ahhiyawa of Hittite texts, was re-instated through the so-called 'Ionian migration' around 1000 BC. This migration led to the formation of the 'twelve' cities of Ionia (from Miletus to Ephesus and others mainland cities, and the nearby islands of Chios and Samos). Further minor centres were the Eolic ones in the north (Lesbos and the nearby coast) and the Doric ones in the south (Rhodes and its nearby coast). These centres developed alongside the mainland kingdoms, though with variations according to their size and origins.

The beginning of the eighth century BC constituted an important change also for the Greek cities in Asia, with the introduction of the alphabet and the development of their political organisation, trade, and 'orientalising' craftsmanship. While Phrygia (and then Lydia) was strongly affected by the political and commercial development of these Greek cities, the more distant Assyrian empire barely took notice.

Sargon, Sennacherib and Esarhaddon mention the Ionians in passing (Yaman/Yawan), after having come across them in Cyprus and occasionally in Cilicia. Greek merchants tried to found some trading colonies on the coast of Syria, such as the one of Al-Mina. These colonies were meant to avoid the Anatolian middlemen and establish direct contacts with the Neo-Hittite, Aramean and Phoenician states (which in the mid-eighth century BC were still independent), and then with the Assyrians. As we have seen, the latter eventually conquered the entire area, but to a certain extent impoverished it.

Throughout the eighth century BC, while Greek colonisation in the west was in full swing, a real colonising movement to the east was lacking. This lack was due to the different political structures of the Mediterranean and Near Eastern world. In the Mediterranean, the Greeks, just like the Phoenicians, were dealing with populations whose organisation and technology were not yet fully consolidated. Moreover, they still had virtually 'untouched' natural resources. The Greeks and Phoenicians therefore needed to found colonies able to manage the exploitation of the local resources and interact with the local rulers. On the contrary, in the Near East, the Greeks had to deal with kingdoms with sophisticated administrations. The latter were governed by a trained elite that did not welcome the formation of foreign colonies. These elites preferred that trade passed through the traditional intermediaries of the local 'palace' or the 'port'. Therefore, Near Eastern kingdoms prevented any form of consolidation of Greek commercial presence, and examples such as the one of Al-Mina were rare and relatively modest.

Up until the seventh century BC, the Greeks only managed to settle in Ionia and Cyprus. However, towards the end of the seventh century, the Anatolian coast experienced a wave of colonisation (mainly from Miletus). The latter was relatively modest in the southern coast (Cilicia), but far more intense in the north (Sinop, Trabzun and others), in areas far from the control of the great kingdoms and empires. This wave of colonisation had two main characteristics, namely, that it was late and marginal. The lateness may indicate that this colonisation was impracticable (or unnecessary) before the collapse of the three great kingdoms of Phrygia, Urartu and Assyria, which monopolised the Near Eastern resources and markets. The marginality of the colonisation also shows that these colonies had no intention to interact with the Babylonians and the Medes. They preferred to avoid them, focusing on the areas between the mountains (Taurus and Pontus) and the sea. These areas were inhabited by mountain people that not even the Medes or the Persians could control. In these marginal areas, the Greeks sought direct access to natural resources (such as metals), avoiding imperial supervision. In this regard, the story of the Argonauts seeking the 'Golden Fleece' of the mythical Colchians (along the former north-western border of Urartu) constitutes the 'foundation myth' of these commercial networks and settlements near metal ores.

As much as the commercial and cultural interactions between the Greeks and the Anatolian kingdoms were intense and effective in influencing each other, there were still considerable differences. The latter led to the interpretation of the Phrygians and the Lydians as carriers of different economic and value systems. Some legendary motifs, based on archaic traditions (the tripod of the Seven Sages, the ring of Polycrates), formed some sort of 'economic anthropology' of the Greeks. Similarly, other stories, based on customs seen as 'different' by the Greeks, formed an 'economic anthropology' of the Anatolian kingdoms.

For instance, there is the renowned legend of Midas, who received from the gods the gift of turning anything he touched into gold, thus running the risk of dying of hunger. This was the sentence of what anthropologists would call the 'upward conversion', namely, the exchange of low value, but essential, products for high value, but unnecessary, products. The latter were destined for storage in treasuries or for opulent display. Indeed, this was the economic strategy of the Phrygian elite, at least judging from the wealth left in the funerary tumuli of Gordion, or in the Phrygian palaces, or the votive objects and gifts provided to seal diplomatic relations. This strategy was implemented at the expense of the needs of the wider population. It was therefore despised by those who did not belong to the social circle benefiting from this ideology and economic and political strategy.

The same can be said regarding the legend of Croesus, the wealthiest man in the world, destined to be punished (in a sort of compensating nemesis) by being burned alive. The story of Croesus shows many orientalising elements (according to the Babylonian Theodicy, the rich who accumulated excessive wealth would be burned alive) and intellectual complications. However, the criticism of the excessive accumulation of wealth and power, which placed someone at the top of a pyramid far too steep to last, remains. Therefore, in the eyes of the Greeks, the kingdoms of Phrygia and Lydia inspired the image of an excessive accumulation of wealth. Since they both disappeared in a couple of centuries (750–550 BC), they became an example of a strategy not worth following.

31

THE FALL OF THE EMPIRE AND THE RISE OF THE CHALDEANS

1 The fall of the Neo-Assyrian empire

Ashurbanipal's celebrative inscriptions may have ended around 635 BC, but the king had already achieved his greatest accomplishments by 646 BC, with his victory over Elam and the Arabs (ca. 645 BC?). The following years of his reign were spent gaining ceremonial recognition of his authority from the surviving kingdoms in the empire's periphery: from the Persians in Anshan to the Urartians and the Lydians. In the final years of Ashurbanipal's reign, however, the first signs of the empire's crisis began to appear, at least in the western regions, which were devastated by the Scythians, who descended in the Levant. Moreover, the crisis spread throughout the mountains north of Assyria, now controlled by the local populations (especially the Medes).

Unfortunately, we do not know with precision when Ashurbanipal's reign ended. It is likely that the old king retired in 631 BC, leaving the Assyrian throne to his son Ashur-etil-ilani and then died in 627 BC, the same year as the Babylonian king Kandalanu. The phase between 635 and 626 BC remains relatively obscure due to the lack of evidence, but was probably marked by a civil war in Assyria and the loss of Assyrian control in Babylonia. In the year defined by the Babylonian Chronicle as 'without a king' (626 BC), the civil war ended with the rise as king of Assyria of another son of Ashurbanipal, Sin-shar-ishkun. From 626 BC, the lack of evidence is resolved by a series of tablets providing an annalistic account of Babylonian events. These tablets must have formed a continuous sequence, although the ones that have survived to us present several gaps. Between 626 and 623 BC, the constant Assyrian incursions in the south only managed to strengthen the anti-Assyrian rebellions in the Babylonian cities (from Uruk to Nippur, Babylon and Der). This situation greatly benefited the leader of the Chaldeans, Nabopolassar of Bit Yakini, who would eventually be recognised as king of the Babylonians (625–605 BC).

Following a gap in the chronicles, the series continues with the year 616 BC (and ends in 594 BC), describing an entirely new situation (Text 31.1). Nabopolassar gained full control of the south, defeating the last Assyrian garrisons in Babylonia, and marched north in the Assyrian territory. The Babylonian king's expansion mainly moved in two directions. Along the Euphrates, the king conquered Suhu and Hindanu, and reached the Balikh River without encountering any opposition. By then, Assyria had lost control of Syria and the Levant to Egypt, but had gained its military support. The Egyptian army is already attested as fighting in Mesopotamia alongside the Assyrians around 616 BC. Assyria had also lost control of the Middle Euphrates, which Nabopolassar promptly crossed to surround his rival and separate him from Egypt. The other and more decisive direction of Babylonian expansion was along the Tigris. This move first forced the

Assyrians to retreat near the Zab. Then, Nabopolassar attacked the southernmost Assyrian cities, namely, Arrapha and Ashur. In this direction, however, the Babylonian king had to face the interference of the local mountain populations. At the time, the Mannaeans were supporting the Assyrians, while the Medes were fighting against them. The Mannaeans and the Medes were clearly fighting (or at least competing) over control of the Iranian plateau. Consequently, their choice of allies was to become a defining factor in the events to come. In the end, the collapse of the Neo-Assyrian empire led to the fall of the Mannaeans and the subsequent victory of the Medes.

Text 31.1   The collapse of the Assyrian empire as described in the *Babylonian Chronicles*

In years 12 to 16 of the reign of Nabopolassar, Ashur, Nineveh, and Harran were destroyed, and the coalition between the Medes and the Babylonians replaced the great empire.

'The twelfth year: In the month of Ab the Medes, after they had marched against Nineveh . . . hastened and they captured Tarbisu, a city in the district of Nineveh. They went along the Tigris and encamped against Ashur. They did battle against the city and . . . destroyed it. They inflicted a terrible defeat upon a great people, plundered and sacked them. The king of Akkad (Babylonia) and his army, who had gone to help the Medes, did not reach the battle (in time). The city . . . The king of Akkad and Umakishtar (Cyaxares, king of the Medes) met one another by the city and together they made an entente cordiale. Cyaxares and his army went home. The king of Akkad and his army went home.

The thirteenth year: In the month of Iyyar, the Suheans rebelled against the king of Akkad and became belligerent. The king of Akkad mustered his army and marched to Suhu. On the fourth day of the month of Sivan he did battle against Rahilu, a city which is on an island in the middle of the Euphrates, and at that time he captured the city. He built his . . . The men who live on the bank of the Euphrates came down to him . . . he encamped against Anat and the siege engines he brought over from the western side . . . he brought the siege engines up to the wall. He did battle against the city and captured it . . . the king of Assyria and his army came down and . . . The king of Akkad [went home] with his army.

The fourteenth year: The king of Akkad mustered his army and marched to . . . The king of the Umman-Manda (that is, the Medes) marched towards the king of Akkad . . . they met one another. The king of Akkad brought across [the army] of Cyaxares and they marched along the bank of the Tigris. They encamped against Nineveh. From the month of Sivan until the month of Ab – for three months – they subjected the city to a heavy siege. On the xth day of the month of Ab, they inflicted a major defeat upon a great people. At that time, Sin-shar-ishkun, king of Assyria, [died (?)] . . . They carried off the vast booty of the city and the temple, and they turned the city into a ruin heap. The . . . of Assyria escaped from the enemy and embraced the feet of the king of Akkad to save his own life. On the twentieth day of the month of Elul, Cyaxares and his army went home. After he had gone, the king of Akkad [despatched his army] and they marched to Nasibina. Plunder and exiles of . . . and they brought the people of Rusapa to the king of Akkad at Nineveh. On the xth day of the month of . . . [Ashur-uballit (II)] ascended the throne in Harran to rule Assyria. Up until the xth day of the month of . . . in Nineveh . . . from the twentieth day of the month of . . . the king of . . .

The fifteenth year: In the month of Tammuz, the king of Akkad mustered his army and marched to Assyria . . . victoriously . . . of the land of . . . and of the land of Shu- . . . he plundered it and carried off its vast booty. In the month of Marchesvan the king of Akkad took the lead of his army and marched against Ruggulitu. He did battle against the city and on the 28th day of the month of Marchesvan captured it. He did not leave a single man alive . . . he went home.

> The sixteenth year: In the month of Iyyar the king of Akkad mustered his army and marched to Assyria. From the month of . . . until the month of Marchesvan he marched about victoriously in Assyria. In the month of Marchesvan the Umman-Manda, who had come to help the king of Akkad, put their armies together and marched to Harran against Ashur-uballit (II) who had ascended the throne of Assyria. Fear of the enemy overcame Ashur-uballit (II) and the army of Egypt which had come to help him and they abandoned the city and crossed [the Euphrates]. The king of Akkad reached Harran and . . . captured the city. He carried off the vast booty of the city and the temple. In the month of Adar the king of Akkad left their . . . he went home. The Umman-Manda who had come to help the king of Akkad, withdrew.'

Already by 614 BC, the Medes of Cyaxares (Umakishtar in the Babylonian Chronicle) had invaded the Assyrian cities, conquering Tarbisu and then Ashur, which was brutally sacked. Nabopolassar moved north to help Cyaxares, but reached Ashur after the siege. Nonetheless, the Babylonian king sealed an alliance with the Median king and returned to Babylonia. Two years later (612 BC), the two armies attacked Nineveh for the final blow on the Assyrians. After three months of siege, the Assyrian capital was taken, sacked and destroyed. Sin-shar-ishkun died during the siege. The Medes returned to their land, but Nabopolassar still had the strength to march to Nasibina and conquer it. The Assyrian court sought refuge in Harran. There, an Ashur-uballit II, whose name recalled the founder of the Middle Assyrian kingdom, was made king of the deteriorating empire. In 610 BC, the Medes and Babylonians reached Harran and conquered it. Ashur-uballit and his Egyptian allies retreated west of the Euphrates.

This was effectively the end of the Neo-Assyrian empire. Despite the fact that the remaining Assyrian troops continued to fight alongside the Egyptians for a couple of years, Ashur-uballit was effectively removed from power, disappearing from the sources. At this stage, the real confrontation was among the surviving states in the empire, which were fighting over its remains. The alliance between Cyaxares and Nabopolassar was still in place, but was becoming increasingly less functional on a military level, although the alliance clearly implied a division of the respective areas of influence. The Babylonians gained control over the Mesopotamian plain, while the Medes gained control over the Iranian and Anatolian highlands. The third power was Egypt, which had controlled the Syro-Levantine area from 616 BC and was competing with the Babylonians along the Euphrates, in an attempt to regain control over Harran. Before dealing with the Egyptians in the west, Nabopolassar, supported by his son and designated heir Nebuchadnezzar II, decided to consolidate his presence to the north of his empire with a series of expeditions into Kummuh, reaching the borders of Urartu. This kingdom would survive another couple of years. To a certain extent, Urartu was trying to take part in the division of the former Assyrian territories, especially in the area between the Upper Euphrates and the Upper Tigris.

The last year of Nabopolassar's reign (605 BC) marked the decisive victory of the Chaldeans. Nebuchadnezzar crossed the Euphrates at Carchemish, the operative centre of the Egyptians. The city was sieged, the Egyptians retreated and Nebuchadnezzar followed them to Hama, where he defeated them again. At this point, the prince found out that his father had died. He thus returned to Babylon to take the throne, having already conquered Syria as far as Hama and placed the Egyptians in a difficult position.

2 The Chaldean dynasty

Following his father's death, Nebuchadnezzar continued to be engaged in Syria and the Levant (the 'land of Hatti' in the Babylonian Chronicle). It took around ten campaigns to conquer the small local kingdoms. Some of them had managed to remain independent and had even taken advantage of the collapse of the Neo-Assyrian empire to regain control over their territories and acquire even more autonomy. This was the case of Tyre and especially the kingdom of Judah with its ruler Josiah. The latter's ambitions, however, were crushed by the Egyptians, while the Babylonians besieged Jerusalem (586 BC). Apart from the conquest of the former Assyrian territories and the ones the Assyrians had left autonomous, Nebuchadnezzar also had to push back the expansion of Egypt, which was clearly taking advantage of its proximity to the Levant. This was in marked contrast with the Babylonians, who each year had to endure a long journey to reach the same area. Despite this logistical difficulty, the two armies were not equal and Nebuchadnezzar managed to gain control over the Levant as far as the Egyptian border.

Following this victory, the borders were consolidated: the Babylonians controlled Mesopotamia, Syria and the Levant; Egypt had to retreat back in its land; and the Medes ruled in the highlands, conquering the Urartian territories and bordering with Lydia on the Halys (Table 31.1). However, there is an anomalous and significant piece of information: in year 9 of Nebuchadnezzar's reign, a 'king of Elam' marched against the Babylonians and the two armies almost fought on the Tigris. The precise account in the chronicle attests that the two armies were just a day's march from each other, but the 'king of Elam' panicked and retreated. This 'king of Elam', then, must have been a Persian king, unhappy with the division of the former Assyrian territories between Medes and Chaldeans.

Even after 594 BC, when the Babylonian Chronicle ends, Nebuchadnezzar had to continue his campaigns in Syria and the Levant. We know of his conflicts with Egypt (588 and 568 BC), his final siege and the destruction of Jerusalem (586 BC) and his long siege of Tyre (585–572 BC). The latter city was not conquered, but had to come to an agreement with the Babylonians by accepting the presence of a Babylonian governor alongside the local ruler. Moreover, the Cilician plain (Hume, or Que for the Assyrians) was annexed to the Chaldean kingdom. We also have some information on Lebanon and its cedar forests, which, despite being impoverished, were still a valuable asset. Nebuchadnezzar, emphasising his beneficent impact on the inhabitants of Lebanon, stated that he turned the forests into royal property and reserved the right to use its timber for himself. Moreover, he declared that he improved the route from Lebanon to the Euphrates, through which cedar wood flowed to the Arahtu canal, thus reaching Babylon. All the western provinces, already drained by the Assyrian conquest and provincial system, had to suffer new destructions, deportations and increasingly severe exploitation. The Babylonians reduced the Syro-Levantine population to its lowest attested levels. They also failed to intervene in the repopulation of the countryside or the reconstruction of cities. They only brought back to Babylonia the remaining resources. This would soon prove to be a remarkably short-sighted policy.

Table 31.1 Chronology of the Ancient Near East, ca. 650–500 BC

	Babylonia		Media		Persia		Lydia	
650			Kashtaritu /Phraortes	ca. 670–625	Kurash/Cyrus Teispes	ca. 645 ca. 635–620	Gyges Ardys Sadyattes	682–644 644–630 629–618
	Nabopolassar	625–605						
600			Cyaxares	ca. 625–585				
	Nebuchadnezzar II	604–562			Cyrus I	ca. 620–600		
	Amil-Marduk	561–560	Astyages	585–550			Alyattes	617–561
	Neriglissar	559–556			Cambyses I	ca. 600–559	Croesus	560–546
	Labashi-Marduk	556						
550								
	Nabonidus	555–539			Cyrus II	559–530		
					Cambyses II	529–522		
500					Darius I	521–486		

Unlike Assyrian royal inscriptions, Neo-Babylonian royal inscriptions do not focus on military achievements, but on building activities. Even its royal titulature moved from the emphasis on world conquest to the management of temples. However, this does not indicate that the Chaldean kings were peaceful, not even in their ideology. The chronicles attest to the military campaigns of Nebuchadnezzar, and the Old Testament shows that their ideology and propaganda was not far from the ferociousness of their Assyrian predecessors. The main difference was that Babylonia had a different local political tradition, which was largely non-imperialistic. Moreover, the intended 'audience' (real or not) of these inscriptions, and the wider audience receiving the broader message were different. The Assyrian kings addressed an 'external' audience that had to be persuaded or intimidated, from neighbouring kings to disloyal vassals, and new and still unstable provinces. At the same time, the Assyrian empire did not have fixed borders and its ideology was focused on constant expansion, even though its centre was never fully consolidated. Therefore, the Assyrian kings were forced to emphasise their military achievements, the relentlessness of their interventions and the proven uselessness of any opposition against their might.

In comparison, the Chaldeans had reached the maximum expansion possible by the tenth year of Nebuchadnezzar's reign. This was due to the maintenance of the alliance, and the division of the territories with the Medes, and the untouchable position of Egypt. Provinces were depopulated and exhausted, and there were no more powers to persuade or intimidate. Therefore, the audience of Babylonian royal inscriptions was almost exclusively the priestly circles of the Babylonian cities. The credibility of the king was (almost paradoxically) based on the execution of the *akītu* festival, or on the adequacy of a certain divine statue according to traditional parameters. After centuries in which Babylonia was merely the object of competition between Assyrians, Elamites and Chaldeans, it suddenly found itself ruling an empire without adequate means. Even the destruction of Assyria was largely due to the intervention of the Medes. Similarly, the conquest of the Syro-Levantine states virtually happened without strong enough opposition. Babylonian control, then, lasted for 60 years, largely thanks to the energetic leadership of Nebuchadnezzar. After his reign, the empire began to encounter increasing difficulties and collapsed without any opposition. In these 60 years, the empire's policy was centred on cultic issues: from the restoration of buildings to the execution of festivals, the return of statues to their original location and the interpretation of 'signs'.

One of Nebuchadnezzar's inscriptions provides some information on the empire's structure. This included court functionaries, followed by provincial governors and then the vassal kings of the coastal cities – mainly the Phoenician cities of Tyre, Sidon, Arwad and the Philistine cities of Gaza and Ashdod. The Babylonian provinces were mainly located in Lower Mesopotamia and corresponded with the main Chaldean tribes: the Sealand (Bit Yakini), Puqudu, Bit Dakkuri, Gambulu, Bit Ammukani and a few cities east of the Tigris (Der, Dupliash and a couple of unknown ones). A list of officials placed in minor centres, still within the land of Akkad, follows, alongside a list of *qēpu*, who were governors placed in marginal cities or alongside local rulers. The overall impression is that between the 'land of Akkad', namely Babylonia, and the independent coastal cities, there was little more than the desert, or at least nothing remotely comparable to the Assyrian provincial structure.

From the sack of the Assyrian cities, which turned Assyria into a virtually abandoned territory between the Babylonians and the Medes, and the income from the western territories, Nebuchadnezzar managed to pursue an intense building programme. This programme was mainly focused on Babylon itself. The king built a large royal palace and restored and strengthened the city's fortifications (in particular, a fortification wall with a large fortress in the north and the fortification wall in the south). Moreover, the main religious centres of the city, the *ziqqurat* (the biblical 'Tower of Babel') Etemenanki and the Esagila (the temple of Marduk), were enlarged and placed in a large *temenos* in the centre of the city. In comparison with previous interventions, this was an unparalleled building programme both in terms of scale and prestige, requiring an enormous amount of workers and supplies. Equally demanding were the smaller interventions made in the other cities, from Sippar to Ur, with particular attention to the cultic city of the god Nabu, Borsippa.

The route between the Ezida (the temple of Nabu in Borsippa) and the Esagila (the temple of Marduk in Babylon) and the processional way connecting the Esagila through the gate of Ishtar to the *bīt akīti*, a temple located outside the city, were the backbone of Babylonian official religion on its most important occasion, which was the New Year festival.

After 43 years of rule, Nebuchadnezzar's death heralded a period of instability in Babylonia. His son Awil-Marduk only ruled for a couple of years. He celebrated his enthronement releasing Jehoiachin of Judah and other three prisoners captured by his father during his campaigns 30 years earlier. Then, the king is suspected to have been killed, and was in any case succeeded by a usurper, the general Nergal-shar-usur (Neriglissar in Greek), who managed to rule for four years, celebrating the construction of some buildings and leading some expeditions to the kingdom of Pirindu. This expedition is attested in the only surviving chronicle about him. The kingdom of Pirindu was located in Cilicia Aspera and had taken over the old kingdom of Hilakku (which had never been conquered by either the Assyrians or the Phrygians). Cilicia Aspera bordered with Cilicia Campestris (Hume), which was under Babylonian control. An incursion of Pirindu in Hume and Syria led to the intervention of Neriglissar, who destroyed the Cilician cities and reached the Lydian border. Neriglissar was succeeded by his son Labashi-Marduk, but he was murdered in a conspiracy a few months later.

The plot brought another usurper to power, Nabonidus (Nabu-na'id), who was not related to the royal family and was from the old Assyrian centre of Harran. In Harran, his mother Adad-guppi was priestess of the moon god Sin in the sanctuary of Ehulhul, destroyed by the Medes in 610 BC. Having come to power through a *coup d'état*, Nabodinus had to justify his enthronement despite being a usurper as well as a foreigner, and lacking the support of the priesthood of Marduk. One of his inscriptions summarises his ideological strategy to overcome these problems, a strategy that was in part defensive and in part critical towards Marduk. According to him, the violent destruction of Babylon 130 years earlier remained an unforgiveable Assyrian offence; Sennacherib had followed the will of Marduk and was then punished by the deity. In Nabonidus' view, then, the Assyrians were not at fault. Moreover, when the Medes destroyed Assyria, they also destroyed the Babylonian cities that were not supporting Nabopolassar. Therefore, Marduk attacked other Babylonian cities, so much so that the Babylonian king had to go into mourning.

Then, Nebuchadnezzar and Neriglissar began to restore temples and re-instate the ancient cults, but much of these interventions remained provisional and questionable. Despite being heir of these benefactors, both Awil-Marduk and Labashi-Marduk were impious, since their rule was not allowed to last long. Nabonidus therefore concludes by stating: 'I am the true legitimate heir and the continuator of Nebuchadnezzar and Neriglissar (an aspect proved by signs written in the stars and dreams), I have continued and finished the restoration of temples, the sacred furniture and the cults'. At this point, Nabonidus goes into details. Having recalled what has been done for the triad Marduk-Nabu-Nergal, the triad at the heart of the Babylonian state (Babylon, Borsippa, Kutha), he provides a new astral triad: Shamash-Sin-Ishtar. These gods ruled more marginal cities, namely, Larsa and Sippar for the sun god Shamash, Ur and Harran for the moon god Sin, and Uruk and the mythical Akkad for Ishtar (Venus). This broader contextualisation of religion allowed the king to justify his reconstruction of the temple of Sin at Harran, which had remained in ruins for 54 years. Marduk himself allegedly commissioned its restoration.

This complex cultic explanation recognises the central role of Marduk as the god bestowing Babylonian kingship to the king and deciding one's future. However, it clearly enlarges the spectrum by including other marginal gods, thus pleasing more cities and priesthoods and criticising the role of Marduk. If this compromising decision certainly displeased the priesthood of Marduk, Nabonidus' position is even more marked in his Harran inscriptions, which commemorate his mother and place Sin in a central role, attributing to him a connection to kingship that in Babylon would have been unacceptable, or even 'heretic' (Text 31.2).

Text 31.2   The Harran Inscription of Nabonidus

The celebration of Sin, the move to Arabia, the emphasis on the relationship between Syria and Babylonia, are all elements aimed at pleasing the 'audience' in Harran, but difficult to accept in Babylonia.

'The operation of Sin, greatest of the gods and goddesses, nobody knows it, since from distant days it came not down to the land, wherefore the people of the land saw it indeed, but wrote it not on a tablet and set it not down for days to come: that you, Sin, lord of the gods and goddesses, dwellers of the heavens, came from the heavens in front of me, Nabonidus king of Babylon. I, Nabonidus, the lonely one, who have not the honour of being a somebody, and kingship is not within me, but the gods and goddesses prayed for me, and Sin called me to the kingship. In the ninth season he caused me to behold a dream saying this: "Quickly restore the E-hul-hul, the temple of Sin in Harran, and I shall give you all the lands."

But the sons of Babylon, Borsippa, Nippur, Ur, Uruk, Larsa, the administrators and inhabitants of the Babylonian cities, acted wickedly and offended his divinity, they knew not the terrible wrath of the Moon-god, king of the gods. They disregarded his rituals and dedicated themselves to impious and disloyal discourses. Like dogs, they devoured one another, they brought fever and famine in the midst of them. He (Sin) decimated the people in the land, he made me leave my city of Babylon, and led me to Tayma, Dadanu, Padakku, Hibra, Yadihu, as far as Yatribu. Ten years I went about amongst them, and did not enter my city Babylon.

At the word of Sin, king of the gods, lord of the lords of the gods and goddesses, dwellers of the heavens, they accomplished the word of the Moon-god, Sin, and made Shamash, Ishtar, Adad, and Nergal guard my safety and life. In a single year, in the month of Nisan and the month of Teshrit, the people of Babylonia and of Syria the produce of the plains and of the sea received. In all those years without ceasing, Adad, lockkeeper of heavens and the netherworld, at the command of Sin waters of rain gave them to drink, even in the rigour of summer, in the months of Sivan, Tammuz, Ab, Elul, and Teshrit, so that they brought their property and possessions in peace before me.

At the word of Sin, Ishtar, lady of battle, without whom hostility and peace exist not in the land, and a weapon is not forged, placed her hand over them (the Babylonians); the king of Egypt, the Medes, the lands of the Arabs, and all hostile kings, for peace and good relations sent messengers before me. Regarding the Arabs [eternal enemies] (?) of Babylonia, ever ready to plunder and capture its wealth, at the word of Sin, Nergal shattered their weapons and all of them he bowed down at my feet. Shamash, lord of the oracle, without whom a mouth is not opened and a mouth is not shut, accomplishing the command of the Moon-god, the father who created him, made the people of Babylonia and Syria, whom he had committed to my hands, (to be) of true mouth and heart with me, so that they kept guard for me, they accomplished my command in the seclusion of tracts far distant and roads secluded which I travelled.

After ten years the appointed time arrived on the day in which the king of the gods, the Moon-god, had predicted, namely, the seventeenth day of the month of Teshrit, (the day) which is called the 'day in which Sin is favourable'. (A hymn to Sin follows.)

Before that day, my consultations with the diviner and dream interpreter never ceased, but wherever I slept, my dreams were confusing; until the word became true, the time arrived, the right moment predicted by Sin arrived. Then, I sent a messenger from Tayma to Babylon, my seat of lordship. When they saw him, the Babylonians brought gifts and offerings before him; the kings of the neighbouring lands came up and kissed my feet, and those far away heard it, and feared his great godhead. The gods and goddesses who had escaped (from Babylon) returned back and brought their blessings. In the oracle of the diviner the organs were disposed favourably for me.

I made my subjects as far as the most distant lands live in wealth and abundance, and I took the road to my own land. The word of his great godhead I observed, without being negligent: I let summon the peoples of

Babylonia and Syria, from the border of Egypt on the Upper Sea as far as the Lower Sea, whom Sin, king of the gods, had committed to my hands. The E-hul-hul temple of Sin anew I built, I finished its work. I led in procession Sin, Ningal, Nusku, and Sadarnunna from Shuanna (Babylon), my royal city, and with joy and gladness I made them enter (the E-hul-hul) and dwell in their lasting sanctuary. Generous libations before them I poured out and I multiplied gifts. Thus, I filled the E-hul-hul with joy and brought pleasure to the heart of its (priestly) personnel. I accomplished the command of Sin, king of the gods, lord of lords, dwelling in the heavens, whose name surpasses that of the other gods in heaven: of Shamash, who is his brightest (peer), of Nusku, Ishtar, Adad, and Nergal, who accomplished the command of the Moon-god, their surpasser.'

The Babylonian priesthood presents a different point of view in a text written at the time of Cyrus, when Nabonidus was already defeated. This text summarises all the complaints against the Babylonian king. In essence, the text was an apologetic statement of the conqueror of Babylon, Cyrus, and an accusation against the overthrown king Nabonidus. The accusations are mainly religious and cultic, focusing on the introduction of Sin's cult and divine image, which were not part of the Babylonian tradition and were described as grotesque. Nabonidus was accused of having failed to celebrate the New Year festival in Babylon because he was too busy restoring the E-hul-hul. He was also accused of being an ignorant king unable to read, write, or understand rituals, and of interpreting omens the way he wanted. Moreover, the text provides a political accusation, namely, that he had abandoned Babylon to rule from Tayma, in Arabia. In Tayma, Nabonidus allegedly killed its king and citizens and rebuilt the city almost as a rival Babylon.

If the first years of Nabonidus' reign were spent consolidating his power in the centre and restoring temples, in the following ten years the king indeed moved to Arabia (551–541 BC). He left his son Belshar-usur (the biblical Belshazzar) to rule in Babylon. The move to Arabia coincides with Cyrus' victory over Astyages, marking the transition from Median to Persian rule. It is therefore possible that Nabonidus' move was a reasonable reaction to this political change. It has been suggested that this move to Arabia was meant to mobilise the western half of the empire (Aramean and Assyrian) with the addition of an Arabian component. This was necessary because the eastern half of the empire (the Babylonian and Chaldean half) was unreliable due to the above-mentioned religious problems. It has also been suggested that the transfer of the court to Tayma constituted a more secure position than Babylon. However, if these were Nabonidus' intentions, they completely failed. On the eve of Cyrus' attack, Nabonidus had to return to Babylonia. He was forced to (rather ineffectively) resist the attack with Babylonian troops and not with the (rather utopic) Aramean and Arabian forces of the west.

It is clear that Nabonidus' transfer to Tayma marked a separation of the king from Babylon and Marduk's cult, and it was seen as such by the Babylonians themselves. The king may have followed a religious path that remains unknown to us, but he clearly showed an attention towards the political and economic rise of Arabia. The latter had previously played a marginal role in the Near East and was considered a land of elusive nomads. Nabonidus found several thriving cities in the Hejaz, from Tayma itself (where current excavations have shown its remarkable size) to Dedan, Khaybar and Yathrib (Muhammad's Medina). All these centres were ruled by local kings and had a stable population. These cities were important for the control of caravans travelling from Yemen to Syria. Nabonidus therefore made sure to control a substantial section of this journey, expanding close to the Yemenite centres and eliminating intermediaries. In this sense, Nabonidus' move, far from being an anti-Persian defensive strategy, appears as an active strategy in the opposite direction. In other words, it appears that Nabonidus underestimated the gravity of the developments taking place in the north, focusing instead on expanding towards the south.

When indicating the many years that the king stayed in Tayma, the Babylonian Chronicle implicitly emphasised the fact that the New Year festival was not celebrated. Unsurprisingly, then, as soon as the king returned to Babylon (in his seventeenth regnal year), his first concern was to celebrate the festival. However, the situation quickly deteriorated: the Persians, who in the previous years made several efforts towards expansion, intervened once again. Ugbaru (Gobryas in Greek), governor of Gutium (the chronicle here uses an archaic term), led the Persian troops and won a battle in Opis, at the Tigris crossing. Without encountering any opposition, he then conquered Sippar and Babylon. Soon after the conquest, Cyrus arrived and was welcomed as a liberator, while Nabonidus was captured. The king's most visible intervention in Babylon was predominantly cultic. It is attested both in the chronicle and the Cyrus Cylinder (mentioned above). Despite the fact that the invading 'Gutians' (namely, the Persians) entered the Esagila, they did so unarmed and did not interrupt the ritual calendar of the city. Cyrus proclaimed that he followed Marduk's will, acting as the restorer of those traditional cults that Nabonidus had subverted. Babylon was neither destroyed nor sacked, but was only annexed to the rising Persian empire, becoming one of its main centres. The end of an entire world thus happened with a sense of continuity and great care in concealing the progressive loss of status of the city whose decline in power would only become evident later on.

3 Economic growth

The 60 years between the fall of the Assyrian cities and the arrival of Cyrus in Babylon constituted a period of economic growth. This growth did not affect the empire as a whole, but was limited to two areas. The main area was naturally Lower Mesopotamia. The end of the wars and destructions, which over the centuries had become a sort of routine, led to a growth in production and population. The latter was naturally modest in the short Neo-Babylonian phase, but would continue under the Achaemenids. Since Babylonia was the centre of the empire, resources gathered from tributes and war booties flowed from the periphery to Lower Mesopotamia. As mentioned above, these resources, combined with the increased availability of labour, were destined for the construction of the kings' cultic and defensive building programmes. Commercial activities were also concentrated in the political capital of the empire, Babylon.

Another area of development was that of the autonomous Phoenician and Philistine cities on the Mediterranean coast. These centres took advantage of their intermediary role between the empire and the rising Mediterranean world, their contacts with Egypt and their role as major access points to the sea for the caravans coming from Arabia. If Babylonia was mainly an agricultural, political and redistributive centre, the west of the empire was predominantly a commercial one. With the Persians, the west would experience an urban development in terms of fortifications, administration and religion. The areas located between these two centres (Central Syria and the Levant, Upper Mesopotamia and Assyria) became virtually deserted. This is due to the fact that both the surviving local population and the deportees struggled to develop economically and culturally.

Babylonia experienced a visible growth (Figure 31.1). The land was overcoming a long phase of decline and de-population. This decline had reached its lowest levels between the tenth and seventh century BC. With the end of the seventh century BC and the beginning of the sixth century BC, Babylonia was on the path of recovery. Population levels grew, but did not reach the density of the time of Hammurabi, or the levels of the Ur III and Isin-Larsa periods. Admittedly, it is difficult to separate (through archaeological surveys) the growth that took place in the 60 years of the Chaldean dynasty from the following growth under the Achaemenids. This is due to the fact that their ceramic index fossils are difficult to distinguish. In terms of settlements, the growth mainly affected the cities, which were the main focus of the kings' building programmes. The farming population remained modest in size (thus its percentage declined). After all, some aspects of decline were irreversible at this stage. The increasing waterlogging of Lower Mesopotamia, which was a result of the collapse of the network of irrigation canals, the silting of the Gulf's coast and the advance of the desert in the west towards the Euphrates, were all factors weighing on the Babylonian cities and cultivations, which therefore became a sort of 'island' of agricultural productivity surrounded by

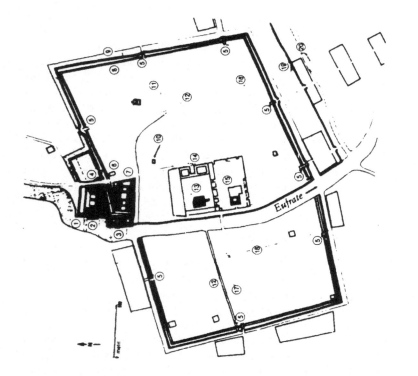

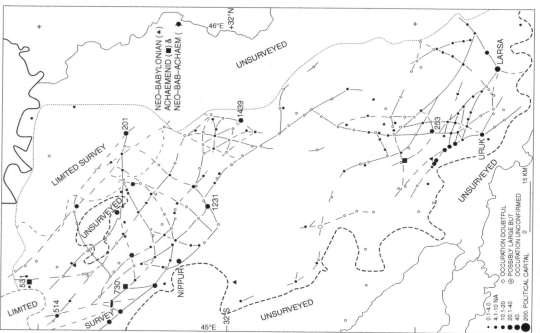

Figure 31.1 The revival of agriculture and construction. *Left:* Lower Mesopotamian settlements in the Neo–Babylonian and Achaemenid period; *Right:* Plan of Babylon.

desolated areas, from sandy dunes in the west, to the marshes in the south, the political border in the east and the war-related de-population in the north.

In these conditions, apart from the thriving building activity, agriculture experienced a decent growth. However, the Babylonian landscape was far from the one attested in its golden age. Small private properties had virtually disappeared and even the large properties belonging to royal functionaries ceased to be an important element of the agricultural landscape of Babylonia. Instead, the large temple and palace estates dominated the area and were the main employers of the farming population. Alongside slaves and paid farmers, there were deportees (from the ones brought by the Assyrians to more recent ones), debt slaves and the new class of unfree serfs bound to the temple (*širku*). All these people worked on lands that they did not own and were ruled by a class of temple and palace 'administrators' (*šatammu* and other lower categories), who did not own the land either, but managed it on behalf of the temple and the palace.

In this network of large public farming estates, administrators constantly tried to gather some income for themselves. Overall, land management was based on pre-fixed parameters, such as the productivity of the land, fixed rates of taxation and fixed percentages for the administrators and farmers (Figure 31.2). Therefore, agriculture became an essentially financial endeavour. There were calculations of profits over several years and the evaluation of the benefits of drainage interventions, of introducing a new cultivation and so on. However, this calculation of the division of shares between workers and public institutions led to a visible clash between the temple and the palace over each other's percentages. It is possible that many disagreements in the cities, including the clash between Nabonidus and Marduk's priesthood, derived from issues of this kind.

Nabonidus and his son Bel-shar-usur issued an edict meant to define the shares due to each individual and the palace. This edict must have caused disdain in the temple administration. It was followed by local rebellions and the departure of the king to Tayma. However, we know, at least for the area of Uruk, that the public farming estates entrusted by the king to functionaries/entrepreneurs were moderately successful, cultivating fields that had been long abandoned, and managing agricultural productivity. This structure, based on large farming estates managed by a single administrator, did not have too much of an impact on a practical level. Of the two main crops cultivated at the time, grain and palm-trees, the latter required the division of the land into smaller plots. The unification of land management, then, was mainly a financial matter. Land management was placed in the hands of fewer individuals, in an attempt to deal with the serious problem of supplying the Babylonian cities. This situation was characterised by a marked difference between the amount of food produced in the countryside and the food consumed by the citizens, who were able to access supplies in the markets or through participation in public activities, but not as a direct retribution for their specialised labour.

Craftsmanship and production also experienced considerable socio-economic changes in this period. The groups of specialist workers divided by specialisation, organised into a hierarchical order and working for the palace, were now structured into a kind of free 'corporations', which united specialists of the same area, possibly following an internal hierarchical order. However, these 'corporations' were not part of the palace administration anymore and thus needed commissioners. Naturally, the palace and the temple remained the main commissioners, but now there were also private individuals. Nonetheless, even in the case of public commissions, they were established via some sort of contract defining the economic remuneration of the service. The palace and temple administrations, the former being a larger unity and the latter being smaller and divided among all the Babylonian cities, continued to employ only three types of professionals: scribes, administrators and priests.

In the commercial sector, the importance of financial issues over purely commercial ones, far from being a deformation of the documentation, seems to be a reflection of the time. The great commercial networks of the time did not pass through Babylonia. The route moving from the south to the north departed from Yemen, crossed the Hejaz and reached the Syro-Levantine coast or the Nile Delta. Similarly, the route moving from the east to the west crossed the highlands in the north, gathering the flux of resources from

A contract recording the king's provision of fields to private individuals in return for a regular payment to the Eanna of Uruk

"Shum-ukin, son of Bēl-zeri, a descendant of Basiya, and Kalbâ, son of Iqishâ, have prayed Nabonidus, king of Babylon, the king their lord, with these words: 'May the king our lord give us 6,000 kur of seed field, and land for date-farming, 400 workmen, 400 oxen, 100 adult cows for ... of the 400 oxen. We will give back on a yearly basis, in the season of the high waters, to the Divine Lady of Uruk, the sum of 25,000 kur of barley and the 10,000 kur of dates.'
Nabonidus, the king their lord, favourably accepted their request and gave Shum-ukin, son of Bēl-zeri, a descendant of Basiya, and Kalbâ, son of Iqishâ, 6,000 kur of seed field, including fallow land – of which half needs to be left each year -, 400 workmen, 400 oxen, 100 adult cows for ... of the 400 oxen. The oxen and adult cows should not perish. They (i.e. Shum-ukin and Kalbâ) will show the king's representative the increase, what will be born, of the adult cows; and he will mark them with the iron star of the Divine Lady of Uruk and will return them to Shum-ukin and Kalbâ. They will take on (the responsibility o)f fixing the deteriorating ploughs. Each year, during the season of high waters, Shum-ukin and Kalbâ will give the Divine Lady of Uruk the sum of 25,000 kur of barley and the sum of 10,000 kur of dates, in total 35,000 kur of barley and dates according to the unit of the Divine Lady of Uruk. Only once, in the first year, will be given to them from the Eanna temple 3,000 kur of barley to be sown and 10 talents of iron (for the ploughs). ... Shum-ukin and Kalbâ are responsible for each other in everything they will do. (Witnesses...). (Agreed in Larsa), month of Nisan, 28th day, first year of Nabonidus, king of Babylon (= 555 BC)."

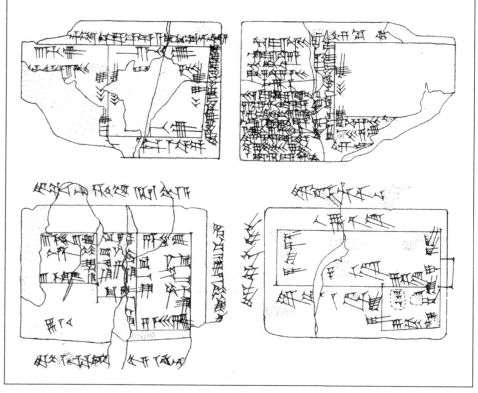

Figure 31.2 Neo–Babylonian agriculture. *Above*: The 'general farms' of the Eanna of Uruk; *Below*: Field plans of the Neo–Babylonian and Persian periods.

India and Central Asia in Persis and Susiana. These goods were then brought to Lydia and the Aegean. Babylonia therefore ran the risk of being cut off, staying in a rich and important niche of land, but isolated by the marshes separating it from the Gulf (which was mainly accessed through Susiana, rather than the Sealand) and by the post-war desolation of the Middle Euphrates and Middle Tigris regions.

If Babylonia managed to avoid being entirely cut off, it was mainly because it was the final destination of the resources gathered through trade. It therefore acted as a first-class 'market' (one of the main ones of the time) and political centre. Commercial activities were mainly in the hands of the Phoenicians (one of them, a certain Hanunu, was the chief of the royal merchants under Nebuchadnezzar), the Arabs and the Iranian populations. Even in terms of financial activities, Babylon delegated them to foreigners and ex-deportees (Jewish groups in particular), such as in the case of the famous 'houses' of the Egibi and then the Murashu in the Achaemenid period. These were more financial, rather than purely commercial, institutions, which gathered a large share of their profits through moneylending and the management of agricultural production.

Neo-Babylonian cities had therefore become complex socio-economic realities. They were ruled by the temple, or the palace in the case of Babylon, namely, by a public institution. The latter's praxis, strategies and interests, were however private. Alongside these institutions there were corporations of specialist workers, commercial and financial 'houses' and public administrators. These were all professions formerly belonging to the category of the 'servants of the king', who once formed the public sector, but now worked as 'private' individuals (*mar-banūti*). Therefore, the cities' economic and legal administration was entrusted to the temple and the city council, which represented the 'corporations' and the 'houses'. The former category of 'free' private landowners had long become a class of employed workmen, insolvent debtors, unfree serfs (or oblates), deportees and slaves. The progressive enslavement of the farming population, combined with the formal status of specialists and administrators, mirrors that 'mass slavery' described by the Greeks about the Persian empire. This impression is only partly acceptable. It has to be pointed out that the development of a private economic sector outside the palace and the temple was an innovation of this phase both in terms of organisation and structure.

4 Neo-Babylonian culture

In a letter from the Neo-Assyrian period, Babylon proudly proclaimed its long history of 'freedom' and cosmopolitanism: regardless of one's privileges, whoever entered the city, Babylonian or not, sedentary or nomadic, man or woman, human or animal, would be protected. Far from the kings' abuse of power, and thanks to its privileged religious and cultural status, Babylon became the meeting point of different populations, traditions and experiences. In this regard, Babylon was visibly different from the Assyrian capitals, especially the newly founded cities. The latter were predominantly inhabited by Assyrians, who were too involved in the management and unification of the empire. The centre of the Assyrian empire also experienced the influx of people and goods from all over the world. However, this influx was paraded for propagandistic purposes, used for various purposes, or at least placed in zoological and botanic parks. Therefore, Assyrian society did not consider these foreign people and elements as equal. On the contrary, Babylon can be considered a sort of 'park', but a lively and non-artificial one, gathering elements from all over the world. Therefore, Babylon juxtaposed its own ideology of unification that welcomed the 'other', against the Assyrian imperial ideology of unification. The latter was more focused on the elimination of the 'other'.

Neo-Babylonian culture and society were largely the result of an international ethno-linguistic, social and cultural syncretism. The composite nature of the population derived from the survival of the ancient Akkadian nucleus and the addition of new populations through migrations (such as in the case of the Aramean and Chaldean tribes) and deportations. Over time, the Akkadian nucleus had decreased in size due to the post-Kassite demographic crisis. Apart from the settlement of new ethnic groups, which led to the rise of Aramaic as the main spoken language (to a lesser degree in writing), there were further move-ments of people. These were smaller in size, but nonetheless significant for the cities. These people were mainly political refugees, merchants, artists, specialists of all sorts and messengers from all over the known world (Egypt, the Phoenician cities, Arabia, or Iran). Some sectors, such as trade, were fully in the hands of foreign communities. The ancient communities of deportees, who had few chances to integrate and develop in Assyria, therefore managed to settle well in Babylonia, where they acquired important social and economic positions.

The ethnical composition of Babylonia and the merging of different traditions did not, however, man-age to form a coherent cultural model. Consequently, it was largely obliterated, at least officially, by a more archaising and nationalistic model. This official archaism and the revival of ancient traditions appeared precisely when the vitality of the local Babylonian culture declined. Apart from Sumerian, which had been a dead language for over a millennium and a half, now Akkadian also became a dead language. Aramaic thus became the main spoken language. Nonetheless, Akkadian continued to be used in all sorts of texts, in an attempt to revive the classical language of Hammurabi's age. Sumerian also continued to be studied, though with increasing difficulty. Therefore, in a world that knew and used an alphabetic writing, Baby-lonia continued to write in cuneiform, a script inextricably linked to Akkadian. The scribal class was even proud of this choice. They emphasised the prestige of the meaning of the cuneiform signs, the abundance of logograms and their use for cryptographic purposes, especially in certain types of texts (such as astro-nomical, hepatoscopical and medical texts), knowledge of which was an exclusive privilege of scribes and priests.

Until the Neo-Babylonian period, Babylon had long ceased to provide any kind of contribution in the fields of architecture, sculpture and seals. Therefore, the city's rise as imperial capital led to the revival of building and decorative activities (Figures 31.3 and 31.4). These interventions focused on three main aspects: size and number, the imitation of ancient models and the use of post-classical decorative tech-niques, such as glazed brick reliefs and decorations. The latter were unknown in the Old Babylonian period, mainly because they developed in the Kassite period, and in Elam. The iconographic repertoire visible here, especially on seals, was made up of revived (and largely imitated) ancient motifs, with a par-ticular attention to prestigious phases such as those of Akkad and of the First Dynasty of Babylon. This same tendency is visible in royal inscriptions, royal titulature and other expressions of Babylonian kingship ideol-ogy. Ancient works of art and royal monuments were recovered and restored, or even gathered in collec-tions (such as the 'museum' in Babylon's new palace). The latter stood alongside libraries (such as the one of Sippar in the Achaemenid period), which were filled with the literary and religious masterpieces of the past. This obsession with ancient models led to the production of fake ancient relics (such as the 'Cruciform Monument' of Manishtusu), aimed at providing a foundation to current privileges and exemptions.

Mesopotamian kings had always made an effort towards the recovery of previous foundation inscrip-tions buried under the buildings they restored. They even mentioned them in *bona fide* 'histories' of build-ings. However, the Chaldean kings turned this effort into a relentless and voluntary quest for ancient foun-dation texts, especially the ones dating to the Akkadian period, which was considered the first and most prestigious phase of Babylonian history. This view led to the identification of Akkad with Babylon, which also had a long history that was now largely taken for granted. This historical and antiquarian interest rose at the expense of a more historical and celebrative narration of facts, a tendency that had peaked during the Neo-Assyrian period. Not only do Neo-Babylonian royal inscriptions lack annalistic accounts describing military expeditions, but they also lack 'historical' depictions in the fashion of the Assyrian palace reliefs.

Apart from its archaism, another characteristic of Neo-Babylonian culture was its symbolism in depic-tions and ritualistic behaviour. Precisely because this culture was unable to develop new elements, Neo-Babylonian culture focused on issues of formality. This formality is visible in its religion, with its obsessive attention to the execution of rituals, the way gods, their statues and symbols were represented and the pronunciation of their epithets and appropriate formulas. All these aspects became an intrinsic part of

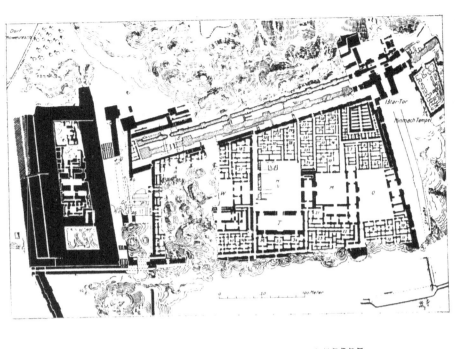

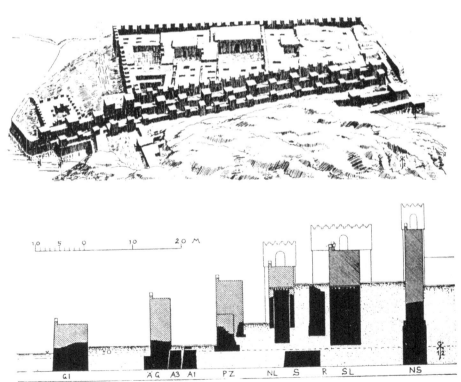

Figure 31.3 Babylon, southern fortress. *Above*: Plan; *Centre*: Reconstruction; *Below*: Cross-section of the northern walls.

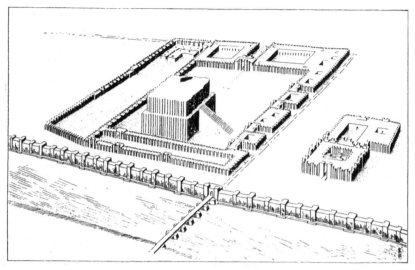

Reconstruction.

*Depiction on a relief
of Ashurbanipal from
Nineveh.*

Figure 31.4   The 'Tower of Babel'. *Above*: Reconstruction; *Below*: Depiction on a relief of Ashurbanipal from Nineveh.

public and private religion and a testing ground for the king. Therefore, the use of symbols was increased at the expense of anthropomorphic representations of gods, while the repetition of ancient formulas was increased at the expense of the development of new mythical or ceremonial aspects. This marked formality of official representations corresponds to the shift of personal religion away from official religion. Popular religion had long moved towards more magical beliefs and practices, developing effective actions (first to find out and then to correct or avoid a certain issue) to manipulate reality through the interpretation of parallel phenomena. Moreover, Mesopotamian religion had long been attracted by omens and exorcisms. This tendency, then, peaked in the Neo-Babylonian period.

Among the various divinatory techniques, astrology became the most popular, being the most rational and stable one. Every event was linked to a specific movement of the stars, whose regularity and repetitiveness was soon discovered. Other techniques, such as hepatoscopy, were based on exceptional signs and their unique and unpredictable conformations. However, the latter were always different, leaving more space for personal interpretation. In a more rigid system, such as astrology, the future became predictable and the past retrievable. Unsurprisingly, in the first phase of the Neo-Babylonian period (in the mid-eighth century BC), the king Nabu-nasir commissioned the daily recording of the position of the stars and the corresponding events taking place. These events were both 'historical' and daily life episodes and even included price fluctuations. The composition of these 'Astronomical Diaries', parts of which have survived to us, continued for many centuries, well into the Hellenistic period. It therefore constitutes one of the most ambitious research projects conceived in antiquity.

In the Neo-Babylonian period, this astronomical interest led to the formulation of horoscopes, according to which the position of the stars at the moment of one's birth determined an individual's personality and fate. According to the Greeks, who only encountered the remains of this long Mesopotamian cultural tradition, the typical sciences of the 'Chaldeans' were astrology and magic. The first was conceived as a science for the study of the future, providing it with a rigid, unquestionable, structure. The second provided practical remedies, imposing on something already happening an even stronger influence, from a paralysing effect to a forced liberation. In other words, magic altered the prefixed course of events through an anomalous intervention. While in a world of flexible presages magical measures were compatible and useful, in a world determined through astronomical observations magic must have become less influential. Magic therefore became not just an anomalous intervention, but a maleficent and subversive one.

32

THE MEDES AND THE RISE
OF THE PERSIANS

1 The Iranian tribes from the migrations to the Assyrian period

As mentioned above, the prosperous urban cultures of the Early Bronze Age in Iran experienced a crisis around the eighteenth century BC, with the abandonment of cities and a return to village communities. These villages were characterised by an agro-pastoral economy and a local socio-political organisation. This process of decline did not just affect Iran, but also Central Asia and the Indus Valley. This fact indicates that the decline was probably not just the result of strictly local phenomena, but of far more complex factors. Therefore, the internal crisis, which eventually led to the development of new ways to exploit resources, could have been the context, rather than the outcome, of the change in the people inhabiting the area, featuring the spread of Indo-Iranian peoples in the south.

It is believed that a first 'wave' of Proto-Indo-Iranians had already reached south-western Iran a little after the beginning of the crisis and revival of the area. This first wave led to the spread of 'Indo-Iranian' names among the *maryannu* and in Mitanni, and of the light war chariot and horse as far as the Fertile Crescent. If Syria and Mesopotamia only saw the spread of new types of personal names and techniques, it is possible that Iran also experienced the diffusion of the 'carriers' of these innovations. This initial and influential wave (due to its military and technical contributions) was followed by other waves, in a process spread through time. However, the subsequent impact of these later waves on the archaeological cultures of the Middle/Late Bronze Age and Early Iron Age remains difficult to establish and quite problematic to postulate with any certainty. According to the texts of Shalmaneser III, in the mid-ninth century BC, the Assyrians were in contact with the populations of the Iranian 'second wave' (now separated from the Indian element, which moved in other directions) living in the Zagros, most importantly the Medes. It is therefore likely that the linguistic 'Iranisation' of the Iranian plateau took place between 1300 and 900 BC. This led to the progressive disappearance of the Pre-Indo-European stratum. The latter was particularly strong in the Zagros area, from Urartu to Elam.

Thanks to the growing availability of written sources identifying peoples and states, the distribution of the Iranian populations becomes increasingly clear. Therefore, it becomes possible to identify a series of ethno-linguistic entities. We can define them as 'nations' in the Iron Age sense, namely, as entities that considered themselves united through kinship as well as linguistic and religious aspects. Each 'nation' was subdivided into tribes and minor entities. This structure varied according to the types of production and settlements, and implied various levels of political organisation. The principal 'nations' were: the Medes in the northern Zagros; the Persians in the ancient region of Anshan; the Hyrcanians and Parthians east of the Caspian Sea; the Bactrians and Sogdians north of the Hindu Kush; and the Aryans, Drangianians and Arachosians in Central Iran. A complete picture of the Iranian tribes would only emerge in the Achaemenid period, with the division of the empire into satrapies under Darius I. Nonetheless, almost all the names of these Iranian 'nations' already appear in previous sources (especially Assyrian ones) or in tales (especially Greek ones) set before the rise of the Achaemenids. However, the final collocation of these groups does not always match the original one. It is therefore possible that in the Assyrian period (from the ninth to the seventh centuries BC) these groups were still relatively mobile, and it was only later that these groups gradually converted to more sedentary forms of settlement and production. This led to the formation of a political system in which each 'nation' occupied a specific territory.

According to archaeological and textual evidence, the economy of the Iranian peoples of the period from 1300 to 600 BC was predominantly agro-pastoral. Farming played an important role. The farming of cattle (in the fertile valleys), sheep and goats (in more mountainous and semi-arid areas) continued alongside new forms of farming: the farming of horses, especially in the northern Zagros (Mannaeans, Medes), and the farming of 'Bactrian' camels (with two humps). The Bactrian camel spread from Central Asia to the Iranian plateau, reaching the area of diffusion of the Arabian dromedary. Horses and camels may have significantly increased the military and commercial potential of Iranian groups, but they also increased the interest of the Mesopotamian empires in the area (Text 32.1). The latter were not only interested in gaining control over these precious resources, but also over the new commercial routes created by the Iranian groups. These routes linked the Fertile Crescent to Central Asia, from which a large quantity of Afghan lapis lazuli and tin once again reached the Near East (after a an intermission of around a millennium).

Text 32.1   The royal monopoly of war horses in Armenia and Media: Sargon (late eighth century BC), Xenophon (early fourth century BC), Strabo (late first century BC)

Sargon II, eighth campaign, 170–173

'The people who dwell in this district (Zaranda) have no equal in the whole land of Urartu in terms of their ability in riding horses. Each year they take the foals, born in this vast land, which they train for the royal army. Until (the foals) are brought to the district of Subi – which the Urartians call the land of the Manneans – and their performance is not observed, they do not ride them: they do not teach them the "exit", "turn", and "return" (namely, the riding movements) necessary for battle, and the yoke remains loose.'

Xenophon, Anabasis, IV 5.34

'When Cheirisophus and Xenophon asked the village chief, through their Persian-speaking interpreter, in which land they were, he replied: "In Armenia". They also asked him for whom the horses were being reared. He answered that they were the tribute for the king (of Persia) . . . The horses of this region were smaller than the Persian horses, but much more spirited. It was here that the Greeks learned from the village chief about wrapping small bags around the feet of their horses and beasts of burden when they were going through the snow: otherwise, they would sink in up to their bellies.'

Strabo, XI, 13.7

[On Media] 'Just like in Armenia, the land provides exceptionally good pastures for the rearing of horses. In particular, a certain meadow there is called "Horse-pasturing," and those who travel from Persia or Babylon to the Caspian Gates pass through it. At the time of the Persians, it is said that this meadow hosted fifty thousand mares, which constituted the royal herd. As for the Nesaean horses, reserved for the king because they were the best and the largest, some say that the breed came from here, while others say from Armenia. Just like the horses now called Parthian horses, their particular appearance distinguishes them from the Helladic horses and the other horses in our country. Further, we call the grass that makes the best food for horses by the special name "Medic", from the fact that it abounds there.'

Strabo, IX, 14.9

[On Armenia] 'The country is so very good for pasturing horses – for which it is not inferior to Media – that the Nesaean horses, which were used by the Persian kings, are also bred there. Every year, at the time of the festivals for Mithra, the satrap of Armenia used to send twenty thousand foals from these herds to the Persian king.'

In terms of agriculture, the formation of these Iranian 'nations' in the Iron Age facilitated the spread of new irrigation systems. The latter were different from the ones implemented by the urban cultures of the Early Bronze Age. This change was clearly a response to a different eco-system. Surface irrigation, typical of the alluvial areas or around the delta, was further supported by the construction of subterranean canals (*qanat*). These were much more suitable to hilly and mountainous areas. Moreover, the area experienced the development of a network of oases in semi-arid areas. Despite the inherent difficulty in dating *qanat* and oases, it seems certain that they first appeared in the Iron Age.

Through these agro-pastoral foundations and their socio-political unity and efficiency, the Iranian peoples managed to grow at the expense of Pre-Indo-European groups. However, Western 'Eurocentric' historiography has often overestimated the impact of the socio-political aspect of the Iranian groups. These 'successful' social aspects are partly linked to the above-mentioned economic and technological developments. Innovations in irrigation ensured the cultivation of new territories. Similarly, the training of horses, which were not attached to chariots anymore, but ridden, ensured their military superiority in terms of mobility, disengagement and success. Apart from these technical points, the influence of a particularly strong kinship and social unity based on the division of the community into inheritable 'functions' (that led to the development of *bona fide* 'castes') is a modern interpretation of the facts. For instance, the theory of a 'tripartite ideology' and the subsequent division of Iranian society into three groups, namely, a class of warriors, priests and farmers (G. Dumézil), is largely debatable and based on later evidence. On the one hand, this tripartite social structure would be completely different from the one attested in other urbanised cultures characterised by labour specialisation. The social structure of these other urbanised cultures was far more sophisticated (apart from the basic division between producers and specialists), but not inheritable or linked to any form of kinship ideology. On the other hand, this reconstruction would also be different from the less structured organisation of those non-urbanised and 'marginal' populations, which would have been replaced by this tripartite division of Iranian society.

A more simplistic application of this theory would imply that, first, the class of warriors was linked to war, horses and the management of the various embryonic nationalistic structures. Second, the class of farmers was linked to irrigation and the increase of agro-pastoral productivity. Finally, the class of priests, represented by the magi, was exclusively responsible for cultic activities (sacrifices, exorcisms and so on) and the interpretation of signs from the gods. This priestly function, and its marked separation from other traditional religions, led to the development (possibly already in the seventh century BC) of a new religious ideology. This ideology was based on strong moral values and a dualistic view of the world. The latter was separated into the principle of good (and truth), embodied by Ahura Mazda, and the principle of evil (and lies), embodied by Ahriman. This new religion replaced previous cults and was aimed at fighting evil through the mobilisation of Ahura Mazda's followers. Traditionally, this new religious ideology is attributed to the works of Zoroaster. His life and the first manifestations of Mazdaism are difficult to date. They therefore remain the object of several hypotheses, based on the analysis of the most ancient texts from the Avesta, the holy book of this new religion. The type of society and political organisation characterising the original context of Mazdaism is relatively simple, and does not involve a unitary state and large cities. Several linguistic aspects indicate that Mazdaism originated in north-eastern Iran (Bactria), but the tradition points to Media.

The traditional dating, which places Zoroaster in the seventh century BC, seems appropriate. Mazdaism appeared in the sources with the first Achaemenid rulers (mid-sixth century BC), when it became the official religion of the empire. Suggestions for a far earlier dating seem anachronistic even in terms of the type of religion, since dualism is a form of monotheism. It is possible to detect an early political manifestation of Mazdaism close to the time of Zoroaster in the Median intervention against the 'evil' Assyrian empire. This interpretation has been put forward on the basis of rather ancient Iranian traditions and legends regarding the origins of the Kurds as descendants of the Medes.

2 The kingdom of Media: formation and expansion

Between the ninth and seventh centuries BC, the historical and political developments taking place in the Iranian plateau are mainly attested in the Assyrian sources. The latter only inform us on the western side of the plateau, close to the Zagros. Even the archaeological evidence seems to be conspicuous and accurate more for the western, rather than the northern and eastern side of the Iranian plateau. The best attested states are: the kingdom of the Mannaeans, located to the south-east of Lake Urmia and tucked in-between Urartu, Assyria and the Medes; the kingdom of Ellipi in Luristan; and the Median tribes, settled in a large area between the Zagros, the central deserts and the Demavend (the Bikni mountain attested in the Assyrian sources). The rise of these western Iranian kingdoms, however, is not simply an impression given by the amount of evidence available. Being so close to the Assyrian empire, these states were constantly under pressure and strongly influenced by Assyrian culture. This situation, then, forced their transformation from tribal groups to more solid and defined political entities.

The Assyrian pressure led to several military expeditions, which peaked in the reigns of Sargon II and Esarhaddon, although it should be pointed out that these interventions were only the most extreme expressions of a vast series of commercial and political interactions. These interactions demonstrate the Assyrian interest in the strategic resources of the area and in transforming the aggressive nature of these peoples into a manageable and instrumental force for the empire. Direct Assyrian control did not manage to move far beyond the Zagros. The majority of attempts continued to be concentrated on the route (the Khorasan Highway) that from Babylon followed the Diyala River, passed through Kermanshah, crossed the watershed at Behistun, touched Ecbatana/Hamadan and continued to the north-east, reaching Central Asia. The initial plan, which proved to be short-lived, was to install a series of Assyrian provinces and centres along this route, transforming local Harhar into Kar-Sharrukin, and Elanzash into Kar-Sennacherib. The Assyrian attempt did not last, and led to a regression that affected even Zamua (which was part of the empire from the time of Ashurnasirpal II). However, it still brought several administrative, tributary and political improvements into the heart of Ellipi and Media.

Excavations have uncovered the monumental complexes of Hasanlu for the Mannaean kingdom, and of Godin Tepe, Nush-i Jan and Baba Jan for Media (where the capital Ecbatana has not yet yielded any remains for this phase) (Figure 32.1). These settlements feature tower temples, hypostyle halls, warehouses and fortifications suitable for local centres whose population was spread out throughout the territory. The nature of these cities recalls the Assyrian title of *bēl āli* ('lord of cities'), used to designate the leaders of the Median tribes. In terms of settlements, the presence of villages and seasonal camps corresponds to an agro-pastoral economy, while these fortified cities filled with storage spaces indicate a more commercial

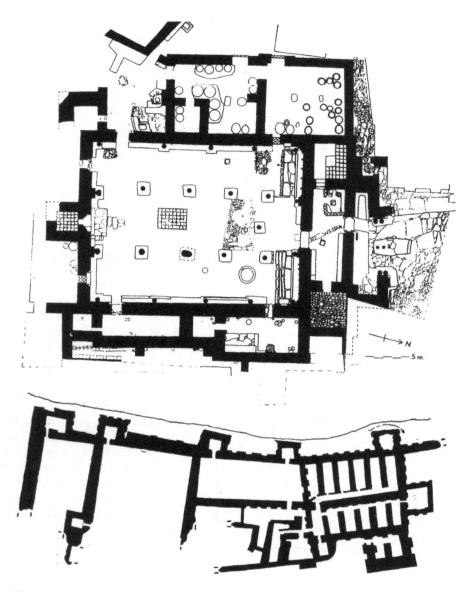

Figure 32.1 The architecture of the Mannaeans and the Medes. *Above*: The palace of Hasanlu (level IV); *Below*: For-tifications and storehouses of Godin Tepe (period IV, phase 4).

and military economy. For instance, the renowned Ziwiye hoard (a collection of ivories and metal ware originally placed in a tomb and then sold in the illegal market) should be attributed to the Mannaeans. This treasure is a clear mark of the tendency towards the ostentation and accumulation of luxury goods existing among the tribal leaders of those mountains (Figure 32.2). This tendency was largely due to their control of the commercial activities existing between the Assyrian empire and the Iranian plateau. It also gives us an idea of the progressive, but fast formation of a local culture. The latter was marked by the prevailing Assyrian and Urartian influences alongside contributions from Central Asia.

Figure 32.2   Decorated bronze quiver from Luristan, eighth–seventh century BC.

Unfortunately, the other two important centres of development of Iranian 'nations' remain less well attested for the Assyrian period. The one in Persis (Anshan/Anzan) remained a part of the Elamite political system, but its population gradually declined (at least according to the archaeological evidence). This situation led to the almost sudden appearance of a Persian population and royal dynasty. The latter came into direct contact with Assyria once Elam collapsed. In the other centre of Iran, Bactria, some sort of unification of the eastern Iranian 'nations' is attested. For the time being, however, it seems precocious to define this unification as a 'kingdom of Bactria' or even a 'Greater Bactria', ruling over other 'nations'. Due to its distance from the Mesopotamian empires, the political unification of north-eastern Iran would happen later on. On the other hand, influential examples from Central Asia could have inspired the hydraulic and urban interventions of the time.

Until the reign of Esarhaddon, the Medes remained a 'distant' (that is how they were stereotyped) and divided population for the Assyrians. In the historical sources, Esarhaddon lists three Median leaders: Uppis of Partakka (in the Esfahan area), Zanasana of Partukka (possibly Parthia), and Ramataya of Urukazabarna (possibly in the Hamadan area). In the loyalty oaths sealed in view of the succession to the Assyrian throne, the Median leaders, who provided bodyguards for the Assyrian crown prince, were far more numerous. In fact, having eliminated Partakka and Partukka (probably because these regions were too far away), Ramataya is attested alongside the leaders of Elpa (Ellipi), Karzitali, Nahshimarta, Zikrisi, Zamua and Izaya. This list, featuring a mixture of Iranian and Elamite personal names, covered the entire Zagros area. This confirms the political fragmentation of the area and its recognition of Assyrian hegemony around 670 BC.

This situation is in marked contrast with the account provided by Herodotus, who speaks of a single dynastic sequence for the Medes. The latter was allegedly established by Deioces (who united the Medes and built Ecbatana), and continued with Phraortes (who annexed Persia and died in a battle against the Assyrians) and Cyaxares. Considering the fact that Cyaxares is well attested between 625 and 585 BC, Herodotus' chronology would place Deioces (who ruled for 53 years) and Phraortes (who ruled for 22 years) between 705 and 625 BC. This reconstruction would partly overlap with the Median phase described by the Assyrians as marked by fragmentation. In order to confirm Herodotus' account, it has been suggested that Deioces should be identified with Daiukku (who, however, was a governor of Mannaea). In turn, Phraortes should be identified with Kashtaritu, attested in Assyrian oracles as a threat to Assyria. However, this Kashtaritu was not a king of the Medes, but a ruler of the city of Kar-Kashi. Moreover, the threats attested in the oracles mention several populations, from the Medes to the Mannaeans, Cimmerians and so on. Overall, it has to be pointed out that Herodotus' account cannot be matched to the attestations in the Assyrian sources. Therefore, the latter, being contemporary to the events, should be considered the most reliable.

Only with Cyaxares, the Medes finally had a single ruler. According to Herodotus, Cyaxares initially had to face an invasion of the Scythians, but managed to defeat them, marking the end of their dominion. Moreover, he possibly managed to gain control over Bactria and other north-eastern 'nations' through diplomatic marriages. Be that as it may, it is certain that in 614 BC, beneath the walls of a destroyed Ashur, he sealed an alliance with the king of Babylon, Nabopolassar. Two years later, the allies destroyed Nineveh and effectively ended the supremacy of the Assyrian empire. Following this memorable achievement, Cyaxares enlarged his network of coalitions and his sphere of expansion. He then clashed with the kingdom of Lydia in a battle marked by an eclipse (thus allowing its precise dating) in 585 BC.

Greek historiography modelled its image of the state ruled by Cyaxares on the Achaemenid empire, and conceived it as part of a sequence of empires (from Assyria to Media, Persia, Alexander and then Rome). In other words, the image of Media was one of a large territorial empire extending from Bactria to Central Anatolia. Once again, it is far more sensible to use the evidence provided by the Assyrian sources and the archaeological excavations. Cyaxares appears to have been a charismatic leader, who managed to gain a prestigious position among an unstable coalition of peoples thanks to his anti-Assyrian interventions. Herodotus himself describes the kingdom of Media as characterised by banquets, hunts, hospitality, gift-exchange, betrayal and revenge, rather than a formal and organised administration (possibly due to the absence of writing). In this regard, even the archaeological evidence debunks the myth of a Median 'empire'. The cities in the Central Zagros, which had been prosperous political and economic centres in the Assyrian period, seem to have experienced a crisis towards the end of the seventh century BC. Due to the collapse of military and commercial relations with their powerful neighbour

(Assyria), these cities began to be occupied by 'squatters'. Therefore, it seems that the Assyrian empire's collapse also affected its periphery (which, ironically, inflicted the final blow on the empire), forcing it to return to a tribal state.

Cyaxares' son and successor, Astyages, found himself at the centre of a network of matrimonial, military and commercial alliances tying Media with Babylonia, Lydia, Cilicia and Egypt (Figure 32.3). This situation led to around 30 years of peace in the Near East. Just as during the reign of his father, Astyages ruled over a state formation that is difficult to define as an 'empire'. This was mainly for two reasons. First, the territories controlled by Media did not include the areas with the highest rates of concentration in terms of population and cities, namely, Mesopotamia, Egypt and the Indus Valley. On the contrary, from a demographic point of view, the Median kingdom ruled over relatively 'empty' areas (or only inhabited in the many oases scattered throughout the kingdom), that were rich in resources. All these territories had always been part of the periphery of previous empires, rather than empires themselves. Second, the internal cohesion of the kingdom remained difficult throughout its history. Median hegemony was centred on a network of relations with the leaders of the various Iranian 'nations', thus preventing the creation of a tribute or provincial system. Therefore, the political traditions of the Medes could not support an imperial system. Despite being militarily superior (and equipped with specific traditions in this regard), the Medes do not seem to have been interested in pursuing an imperial strategy.

The few decades marking the hegemony of the Medes in the Near East, however, do show a considerable degree of political stability. This situation would change with the intervention of Cyrus II the Great, king of Persia. In a few years (between 553 and 550 BC), the king rebelled against Median control, ultimately achieving hegemony. Unlike the Medes, the Persians were supported by a far stronger tradition, namely, that of Elam (Susa and Anshan). Elam's history was marked by military and political interventions in the heart of the Mesopotamian alluvial plain, and its control over the nearby mountain regions. Therefore, taking advantage of these Elamite political and organisational experiences, and combining them with the new military and ideological impetus of the Iranian 'nations', Cyrus paved the way for a new phase of the history of the Ancient Near East.

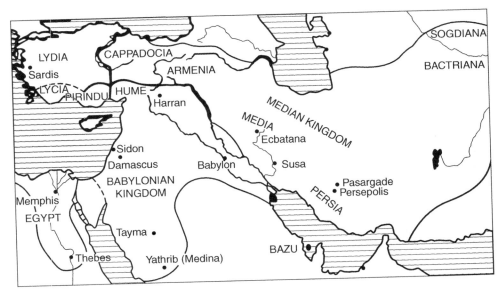

Figure 32.3 The Near East under the Medes and the Chaldeans, ca. 600–550 BC.

3 The Persians and the conquest of the Near East

The peaceful coexistence between Medes and Babylonians, Lydians and Egyptians, was brutally interrupted by the initiative of an Iranian 'nation' that was dissatisfied with its secondary role as a subordinate of the Medes. At the time of the collapse of the Assyrian empire, the Persians had already attempted some interventions. They replaced the Elamites in the region of Anshan (the Classical Persis, modern Fars) with a dynasty belonging to the clan of the Achaemenids and related to the Median royal family. This dynasty was already ruling with the title of king of Anshan (an archaic title now referring to the kingdom of Persia) for a few generations.

Suddenly, at least as far as we can tell, soon after the rise of Nabonidus in Babylonia, the king of Persia, Cyrus II (nephew of Cyrus I, a contemporary of Nabopolassar), rebelled against Astyages and faced him in battle. Due to the collapse of the network of loyalties and supporters of the Median king, Cyrus obtained an easy victory. The Nabonidus Chronicle reports that this decisive moment happened in 550 BC. The capture of Astyages (whose life was spared) and the conquest of Ecbatana were followed by a swift substitution of Median supremacy with a Persian one. Consequently, kings and nations that had formerly recognised the supremacy of Astyages, now accepted the supremacy of Cyrus. Initially, the latter's victory only brought an internal change of power within a large political formation marked by fragmentation. For the time being, then, the Persians seemed willing to recognise the independence of each local 'nation' and their dynasties.

The situation then rapidly changed. Internally, while Media's historical background was centred on a network of tribes, Persia benefited from the experience and political structure of Elam. Externally, while inheriting the alliances of Astyages within the Iranian confederation, Cyrus rejected the previous foreign alliances. He thus brought the 30 years of peace in the Near East to an end. In 547 BC, Cyrus attacked Lydia. He therefore crossed the Halys River and faced Croesus in a battle. The outcome was uncertain, and Croesus, being used to other rules of war, returned to Sardis and dismissed his troops. However, Cyrus followed him, besieged Sardis, captured (but spared) the king, and annexed Lydia. The king then left one of his governors to complete the annexation. Cilicia, now surrounded by Cyrus' territories, was also annexed, although it appears that it was never defeated and enjoyed a privileged status.

In the following years (545–539 BC), Cyrus focused on the margins of the empire. Some 'nations' were automatically annexed through the king's victory over Astyages, although the political role of the Persians in north-eastern Iran remained uncertain enough to require a decisive intervention. This intervention not only clarified that the 'king of kings' was now Persian and not Median, but also that the situation had changed, and was now far more demanding. The submission of Bactria (the main 'nation' in the north-east) was probably followed by the conquest of new territories (compared to the boundaries of the Median kingdom), namely, Gandhara and Arachosia. In this way, Cyrus' dominion reached the borders of the Indus Valley.

As we have already seen in the previous chapter, the third step of Cyrus' expansion was the conquest of Babylon (539 BC). This conquest allowed Cyrus to control the Mesopotamian and Syro-Levantine territories, while northern Arabia remained autonomous. For various reasons, then, Cyrus' conquests, as extraordinary in terms of time and extension as they may have been, required relatively modest military intervention. In the Greek tradition, his fame as conqueror was presented alongside his magnanimous and moderate nature: defeated kings were spared, conquered cities were not destroyed, local deities and cults were maintained and even taken on by Cyrus himself. This was a clear attempt to take full advantage of that peaceful coexistence already established through the alliance between the Medes and the Babylonians. However, the Persian strategy was clearly imperialistic, expansionistic and focused on unification.

Cyrus' expansionistic ambitions were continued under his successors. His son Cambyses conquered Egypt (525 BC) and Cyprus. After Cambyses' death, a *coup d'état* led to the rise of the usurper Darius (who belonged to another branch of the Achaemenid clan). Despite his focus on the empire's internal consolidation, Darius also continued and completed the Persian expansion. In the last 20 years of the seventh century BC, the Persian empire conquered Thracia (Skudra) and the Aegean islands (Yauna), but failed to conquer

Greece. Libya (Put) and Nubia (Kush) soon followed as an extension of Persian control in Egypt. The empire also conquered parts of the Indus Valley (Hindush). The Persians also defeated the Scythians (Saka) in northern Iran, probably reaching as far as the Jaxartes River and Lake Aral. The empire experienced several internal revolts, first in its heartland (Elam, Babylonia and Media), and then in more distant lands (Egypt, Cyprus and Ionia). Moreover, the Persians suffered some setbacks. Certain marginal populations continued to be difficult to control (especially nomadic groups), from the Arabs to the Scythians and the populations in the Caucasus Mountains. However, overall, the 50 years of conquests from Cyrus to Darius marked a radical expansion of the Near Eastern political scene.

The Persian empire included regions that in the previous centuries (or even millennia) had developed different socio-economic and political structures, and were linked to each other through commercial, diplomatic and military ties. For a long time, all these regions managed to remain distinct, allowing us to follow their individual history. However, from the second half of the seventh century BC, this becomes impossible. The important centre of Mesopotamia (which is the main focal point of this book) was sided by the centres of the Nile Valley, the Aegean, the Indus Valley and Central Asia. Moreover, other centres began to emerge, from southern Arabia, Ethiopia and the Central Mediterranean.

Within this polycentric 'universal empire', several ancient contrapositions continued to exist. The contraposition between lowlands (Syria and Mesopotamia) and highlands (Iran and Anatolia) was partly overcome, since these two groups were now part of the same political entity. The Zagros foothills ceased to be a political, as well as ethno-linguistic, boundary between states. The states in the highlands (and not the ones in the lowlands) were therefore responsible for the removal of this frontier. Consequently, the contraposition between centre and periphery was reformulated. The political centre of the world (or the empire) used to be part of this periphery, but now acquired its central role due to the inclusion of several other ancient 'centres of the world' placed in a single, enlarged world. The barycentre of this world, then, was not one specific area, but the cumulative intersection of several important centres.

Finally, the old contraposition between 'palaces' and 'tribes', namely, between areas with high demographic concentration and areas for the exploitation of resources, was reshaped. Having ceased to be a consistent ethnic and regional contraposition, the empire became a mixture of urban and mountain components within the same nation and the same economic system. However, in the central area of the empire, the Persians failed to conquer the several tribes of 'bandits' living in the mountains. This fact clearly indicates how these concepts of 'centre' and 'periphery' responded to different political structures and the flux of goods. Therefore, they were not objective geographic locations.

Of the old imperial ideologies, the Persian empire maintained the concept of the centripetal movement of resources and the centrifugal movement of ethical and political contributions. Achaemenid palaces (in Pasargadae and then Persepolis) were built with materials and craftsmen from all over the world. Each population contributed with their best and most characteristic products. However, these resources only found their optimal application when, through the coordination of others, they contributed to the construction of the central nucleus of the world. In return, the latter provided the world with security, laws, divine approval and civilisations.

Compared to previous empires, the Persian empire reached an unparalleled expansion (five or ten times larger than the previous empires). It may suffice to note that the former territories of the Chaldean empire eventually became two satrapies out of 20 Persian satrapies, while the ones of the Neo-Assyrian empire became four. This unparalleled size naturally required a new balance between unification and division into provinces. While Cyrus, building on the structure of the Median kingdom, allowed a considerable degree of local autonomy, Darius's strategy was far more centralising, systematic and focused on unification. Even the capitals remained more than one. The Persian court therefore constantly travelled between Susa, Babylon, Ecbatana, Pasargadae and Persepolis. Formally, as well as in terms of the monumentality of their celebrative and building programmes, the Persian cities (Pasargadae with Cyrus and Persepolis with Darius) continued to hold a privileged position, although it is likely that the king (and his harem) passed the majority of his time in Susa. Susa was not only equipped with better administrative structures, but also located at the crossing between the highlands and the lowlands, the boundary between the Iranian and Semitic world.

The use of summer and winter residences (Ecbatana and Persepolis, and Susa and Babylon respectively) was a direct consequence of the pastoral customs and transhumance between highlands and lowlands typical of the Iranian tribes. Pasargadae and especially Persepolis were constructed as large ceremonial complexes (Figure 32.4). Their architecture borrowed Urartian and Median features, but enlarged them. This was the case of the tower temples and the hypostyle halls surrounded by hypostyle porticoes, which generated the *apadana* type of architecture (Figure 32.5). Masters and expertise from Mesopotamia, Egypt and even Lydia and Ionia, contributed to the creation of palace complexes that fully displayed the universal nature of the empire and its various components.

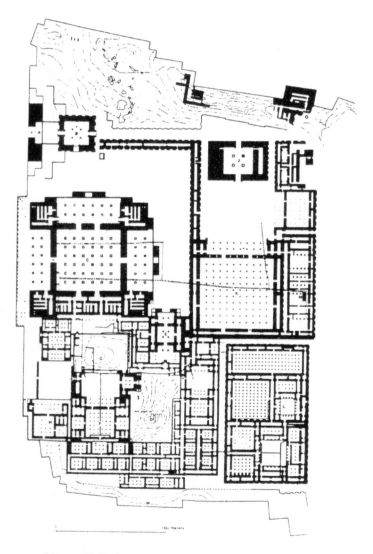

Figure 32.4 The terrace of Persepolis (A: Stairway access; B: Gate of Xerxes; C: Apadana; D: Palace D; E: Tripylon; F: Palace of Xerxes; G: Palace G; H: Palace H; I: Palace of Darius; J: Gate (incomplete); K: Throne room; L: Treasury; M: Storehouses; N: Royal stables; O: Fortress).

Figure 32.5   Persepolis, the Apadana, general view.

Apart from the urban and administrative tradition, the Persian empire was also marked by its nomadic and military origins, which survived in its kingship ideology. The centre of the empire was wherever the king resided. However, the king was constantly on the move, both in military and peaceful expeditions, improving cities as well as other locations. The construction of palaces was commissioned alongside the creation of parks (the 'paradises') for hunting and in order to display, almost in an exemplary way, the luxuriance of its vegetation. Similarly, the typical examples of royal propaganda were rock inscriptions (an ancient tradition in the Zagros from the time of Anu-banini and the Akkadian kings) placed in mountain passes, such as the renowned rock reliefs at Behistun (Bisutun).

The extension and polycentric nature of the empire soon led to a linguistic problem. This was not solved through the selection of one *lingua franca*, but through the inclusion of a selection of languages in inscriptions. Persian celebrative inscriptions are usually trilingual. Elamite, Babylonian and Old Persian were considered equal in status, while some inscriptions also feature Aramaic and Egyptian. It is worth noting that Darius was the first king to introduce Old Persian (Cyrus did not use it in official inscriptions). This decision required the adaptation and simplification of cuneiform to suit this new language. Nonetheless, the language of administrative texts remained Akkadian in Babylonia, Egyptian in Egypt, Aramaic in Syria, while Old Persian slowly substituted Elamite in Persepolis and then Susa.

Aramaic gradually became the *lingua franca* of the empire, able to fulfil local needs in a vast portion of the empire and to act as an intermediary among neighbouring regions, from Egypt to Anatolia and Iran itself. Old Persian spread especially in the Armenian and Anatolian highlands (less in the Babylonian and Aramean lowlands) as a consequence of the allocation of a number of Persian (and Median) governors in these areas, from administrators to military officials. These were all members of the Persian aristocracy who received lands and official roles in the most challenging areas of the empire. Iranian names, cults and languages thus reached the most distant provinces of the empire, far beyond the original spread of the Iranian 'nations'.

From an administrative point of view, Darius was responsible for the definitive structure of the empire, which was subdivided into 20 'satrapies'. The list provided by Darius in the Behistun Inscription does not fully coincide with the one provided by Herodotus (Figure 32.6). However, the latter's account seems to

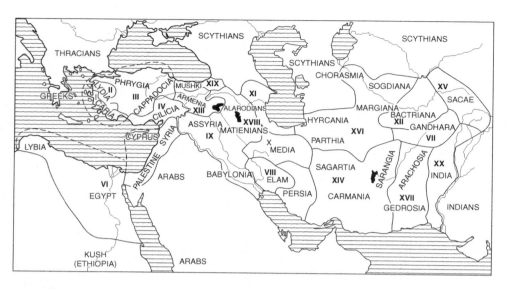

Figure 32.6 Map of the Persian empire under Darius I (I–XX: sequence of satrapies according to Herodotus; cf. the 'source' to Text 32.2).

be based on reliable sources as well. It is likely that the definitive organisation of the empire experienced a number of modifications and additions through further conquests. The size, population and potential contribution of satrapies varied and were affected by the empire's historical developments. Egypt and Babylonia, with their high concentration of people and resources, were each a satrapy. The same can be said about more modest mountain areas, where the Persian kings were eager to maintain and recognise local ethnic and 'national' identities.

The list of tributes attested in Herodotus, but reliable, is a clear reflection of this situation (Text 32.2). They probably represent the most concrete contribution from Darius' reign in terms of the empire's organisation. Previous empires had a different practice, which varied from region to region. Moreover, they required the imposition of fixed tributes in some cases, and the provision of more or less ceremonial 'gifts' or reserves of key resources (forests and horses) in others. On the contrary, with Darius the system became more homogeneous and balanced in terms of impositions. Persia was the only region exempted from tributes and extraneous to the division into satrapies. The system of gift-exchange continued for some marginal populations (Arabs, Colchians and Scythians) that were not yet subjected to a more demanding political and fiscal relation with the empire, nor were they likely to be any time soon.

Text 32.2   The annual tributes of the satrapies of the Persian empire, calculated in silver talents (according to Herodotus, III, 89–94)

I.	Caria, Lycia, Pamphylia	400
II.	Mysia, Lydia	500
III.	Phrygia, Cappadocia	360
IV.	Cilicia	500 + 360 white horses
V.	Syria, Palestine, Cyprus	350
VI.	Egypt, Libya	700 + income in silver from fishing in lake Moeris +120,000 measures of grain

VII. Sattagydians, Gandhara, etc.	170	
VIII. Susiana	300	
IX. Assyria and Babylonia	1000 + 500 youths, future eunuchs	
X. Central Media	450	
XI. Northern Media	200	
XII. Bactriana	360	
XIII. Armenia	400	
XIV. Sagartians, Sarangians, etc.	600	
XV. Sacae	250	
XVI. Parthia, Chorasmia, Sogdiana	300	
XVII. Gedrosia, Arachosia	400	
XVIII. Matienians, Saspires, Alarodians	200	
XIX. Mushki, Tibareni, etc.	300	
XX. India	–	360 talents of gold dust

Cf. Figure 32.6.

Apart from a couple of exceptions, tributes were estimated in weighed silver, which was already the main currency of exchange. The fiscal unification of the empire brought to the unification of measure and value systems (or at least the imposition of one fiscal system over local systems). The peak of this unification was the spread of coinage, which made its first appearance in Lydia and Ionia. The gold and silver 'daric' soon became the official currency of the empire, being weighed metal whose weight and purity was guaranteed by the royal stamp. Coinage developed more as a response to administrative rather than commercial needs, such as the payment of taxes and tributes and the payment of mercenaries. Alongside imperial coins, other forms of payment and accounting continued to exist on a local level. However, with time, the issue of imperial coins brought to the issue of coins from other governors and cities. This development led to the commercial as well as the administrative and tributary use of coins.

The administrative, tributary, linguistic and monetary unification of the empire led to a material unification in terms of buildings and transports. Palaces and paradises were built throughout the empire. After all, satrapies had to be modelled upon the example of the empire's original centre. In the areas characterised by a long history of urbanisation, building activities were conspicuous, but simply restored what was already there. In the Achaemenid period, then, both Sidon and Sardis received their unmistakable Persian traits, but simply replaced the previous (local or provincial) constructions. In contrast, throughout Iran and Central Asia, the consolidation of imperial control required the formation of new urban and palace centres, as well as agricultural infrastructures. This marked a definitive step towards the unification of the entire area to standards previously reserved for distinct areas.

Prior to Darius' reign, a road network already existed to cater for the growing commercial interactions between regions. Moreover, in the previous empires (the Assyrian one in particular), this network was improved for military and administrative purposes. With Darius, however, this road network became increasingly more organic, with the designation of 'royal roads' (originally an Assyrian designation) to the main routes. These routes had resting stations equipped with fresh horses and fortresses protecting river crossings or mountain passes. A renowned contribution of Darius is his postal system, described with admiration by Herodotus for its efficiency and rapidity. Equally renowned are the interventions in road engineering, which expanded what was begun under the Assyrians and the Babylonians.

The Persians restored mountain roads and built fixed or pontoon bridges to cross rivers or even the sea (the Hellespont under Xerxes). From a Greek point of view, the main section of the Royal Road was the one linking Sardis to Susa. It crossed Anatolia, Armenia and Media. However, other sections must have been equally essential. For instance, an important road was the one going from Susa to Persepolis. Similarly, the Khorasan Highway from Babylon to Ecbatana and the Caspian Gates was the main route going north. The King's Highway in Syria and the Transjordan plateau was the main route going south, meeting the South Arabian caravan routes. Finally, from a strictly Persian perspective, the routes linking Ecbatana with Bactria, or Persepolis with Drangiana and Arachosia must have been equally important to reach the far-eastern borders of the empire.

The consolidation of the empire's road network developed alongside the consolidation of maritime routes. The previous mainland empires had long considered the Persian Gulf, the Red Sea and the Mediterranean Sea as branches of a circular Ocean encompassing and delimitating the known world. These branches penetrated towards the centre of the world, but remained separate from one another. The Achaemenid period constitutes the peak of a process of exploration. This process was begun by the Phoenicians (in the Mediterranean) and the Egyptians (in the Red Sea), who managed to link to each other the various internal branches of this Ocean. The circumnavigation of Africa and the excavation of a channel linking the eastern Nile to the Red Sea in Darius' reign managed to improve the navigation of the Mediterranean and the Red Sea. Finally, the expedition of Scylax of Caryanda, who followed the course of the Indus River, reaching the Arabian Peninsula and the Isthmus of Suez, completed the circle.

The awareness of the connection between the Indus Valley and the river mouth of the Tigris and Euphrates certainly brought back an ancient route that had been vital at the time of Akkad and Meluhha. However, the discovery of the connection between Mesopotamia and Egypt through the circumnavigation of the Arabian Peninsula was even more important. Therefore, alongside the mainland caravan routes, south Arabia introduced maritime routes reaching Ethiopia on the one hand, and the Persian Gulf and India on the other. Classical sources tend to focus on the exploration of the Mediterranean. However, it is probable that the exploration of the Indian Ocean happened at the same time and with a similar intensity, though with completely different technical problems (such as monsoons and the ocean itself).

4 The reformulation of imperial ideology

The evidence on Median kingship and its possible Zoroastrian links are uncertain. In fact, the evidence partly comes from elements attested in the Persian empire that were seen as originally Median, largely from linguistic similarities. A certain degree of similarity and continuity between the structure of the Median kingdom and the one of Cyrus (thus prior to the substantial innovations under Darius) can be surmised. The latter could have exploited these Median features to ensure the automatic acceptance of Persian hegemony by the other Iranian 'nations'. Moreover, it is worth bearing in mind that the Greeks continued to call the Persians 'Medes' and their Greek supporters 'medising'.

As mentioned above, the Classical (and in part the modern) tradition tends to conceive the state ruled by Cyaxares and Astyages along the same lines as the one ruled by Cyrus. This led to the definition of the Median kingdom as a *bona fide* empire. Nonetheless, the short span of Median supremacy, its decline, and the gap in the documentation seem to support a more reductive interpretation of the Median kingdom. The Median kingdom, then, must have been more similar to previous examples, than to the following ones. Therefore, the Median kingdom should be seen as a political entity similar to the Mannaeans or Ellipi. The only difference was that the Medes extended their control much further, thanks to the military expeditions of Cyaxares and the resulting network of inter-dynastic relations. As a result, Median kingship ideology could not have been far from the kinship and military ideals characterising its Iranian hinterland. After all, Near Eastern models must have been too foreign for the Medes.

On the contrary, Achaemenid kingship was far more complex and can be distinguished into two types: one for Cyrus and one for Darius. Naturally, certain Iranian elements continued to survive. First, there was the military role of the king, which led to the emphasis on his physical, heroic and military prowess. Then, there was the emphasis on kinship and the fact that the king belonged to a privileged and distinguished Iranian clan. Finally, there was the ethical aspect of kingship, which led to the interpretation of clashes with enemies as a clash between good and evil. This resulted in the inevitable victory of justice and truth over falsehood (a typical aspect of Zoroastrian religion).

Elements derived from Assyrian and Babylonian kingship ideologies are equally evident. These provided the Persian kings with the most visible administrative and celebrative means to express their kingship: from royal titulature (Cyrus was 'king of totality', 'great king', 'mighty king', 'king of Babylon', 'king of Sumer and Akkad', 'king of the four quarters of the world') to the structure of the court, the central and provincial government, the system of tributes and the military. Even the idea of a universal empire and the expectation (or dream) to make it match with the size of the entire known world, was of clear Mesopotamian derivation.

Other relevant contributions, yet more difficult to detect, are the ones of those states that had already begun a cultural syncretism between Iranian and Mesopotamian traditions, namely, Elam, Urartu and even Media itself. These cultures combined the tradition of the Mannaeans with the one of the Assyrians. In this case, it may be worth mentioning two cases in point. The first is an anecdote reported by Herodotus on the way in which Darius (thanks to a trick of his charioteer) managed to win a 'horse race' for kingship. This account derives from an inscription left on one of his monuments stating how, 'with the aid of his horses and his charioteer, his hands conquered the kingdom of Persia'. This inscription was clearly modelled upon the one by Rusa of Urartu, inscribed on one of his statues in the temple of Musasir and which Sargon found and copied. In turn, this inscription imitated far more ancient examples (as early as the second millennium BC) from Mitanni and north Syria (Idrimi). Therefore, Herodotus' anecdote is not a reflection of Iranian ideology, but a Greek misunderstanding of a century-old Hurrian and Urartian motif attested in the Near East.

Another example is the *topos* reported by the historians of Alexander the Great, according to which the Persians went to war lavishly dressed. For this reason, then, they were considered unable to face their enemies (in this case, the Greeks), who were less opulent and elegant in their attire, but more practical and effective. This same *topos* is attested in Assyrian sources (such as Sennacherib regarding the battle of Halule) describing Elamite soldiers. The latter, then, were seen as the predecessors of the Persians not only geographically, but also in their tendency of going to war as if they were attending a sumptuous parade.

Therefore, as the Persians were gaining control over the other Near Eastern kingdoms, they also acquired their political and ideological models. This fact led Cyrus and his successors to present themselves as legitimate heirs to the local dynasties. They even promoted themselves as the restorers of these states at the expense of corrupt rulers, who were rightly removed from their thrones. This strategy led to the formation of the idea of a universal empire through acquisition rather than through the elimination of other centres of power. This was in marked contrast with the approach used by the Assyrian empire: it was a direct consequence of the considerably larger size of the Persian empire.

The Assyrians could still conceive a universal dominion built on the destruction of previous kingdoms and their capitals, the deportations of their ruling classes, the destruction of their culture and the elimination of their deities. In this regard, Esarhaddon emblematically stated: 'Before me cities, behind me heaps of ruins.' However, even the Assyrians had to revise their strategy in one particular centre (Babylon), whose cultural and religious importance prevented its destruction. The Persians, however, had to face the same problem on a far larger scale. Moreover, they had to deal with their cultural inferiority compared to kingdoms with more ancient traditions, more complex economic and social structures, and more sophisticated ideologies and cultures. Therefore, they preferred not to destroy, but rather to assimilate, implement and reformulate.

This Persian attitude is particularly significant with regards to local cults. It is certain that Darius, and possibly even Cyrus, were Zoroastrians. Therefore, their one and only god was Ahura Mazda. All other gods (turned into demons) were only his counterpart, representing the sphere of evil and falsehood. Despite this religious ideology, the Persians tolerated the cults and deities of the people they defeated. Cyrus tried to gain the approval of those he defeated by proclaiming himself a worshipper of Marduk when he conquered Babylon, and emanating an edict allowing the return to Jerusalem of Yahweh's population (at least according to the Bible). Therefore, the Persians subscribed to the ideals of plurality and tolerance in their empire: each region and population had its own gods, and had the right to worship them; cult statues were returned to their original temples; religious festivals were celebrated; and temples were restored. In this view, then, the emperor of this universe acted as a benevolent patron of the various religions of his empire, although one is left to wonder whether the Mazdaist beliefs of the Persian kings clashed with this policy. In fact, what may appear to us as a just and fair policy, from a strictly Mazdaist perspective was essentially a surrender to falsehood.

Naturally, it is necessary to distinguish Cyrus from Darius. The former was more prone to syncretisms and more enthusiastic about adapting to each local tradition he encountered. Even his personal belief in Mazdaism is more of an *argumentum e silentio*. On the contrary, Darius visibly placed Ahura Mazda in a prominent position, without rejecting Cyrus' strategy and concessions. Nonetheless, Darius acted with all that intolerance and ruthlessness typical of a dualistic ideology aimed at the repression of the 'evil' and 'false' ones, especially when they were threatening his position. The political and religious ideologies of the Persians formed the core of the Achaemenid imperial ideology. The tolerance displayed towards other cults was simply a reflection of an imperial ideology that envisioned dominion through accumulation rather than elimination. The official cult of Ahura Mazda, with its abstract features and dynastic exclusivity, was a reflection of the superior and unifying role of the 'great king' and his central administration. Finally, the Mazdaist dualism between Good and Evil, Truth and Lie, Order and Chaos, was a reflection of the dynamic and punitive aspects of the empire, its ambition towards further conquests and its repression of revolts and oppositions. The latter in particular were seen as attacks of evil peoples against the difficult and deserving success of the supporters of Good in their rule of the world.

33

CONCLUSION

1 A new geopolitical reality

We have now seen the progressive growth of Near Eastern states and their history in the course of three millennia (3500–500 BC), from the Urban Revolution to the Achaemenid empire. In this long process, individual villages and transhumant groups gradually became part of larger local systems (or city-states) featuring one city as the main centre of a mainly agro-pastoral hinterland. With time, states turned into regional entities, ruling over several areas and cities. Sometimes, they even became 'nation' states, namely, states where political and ethnical identities coincided. Finally, towards the end of this long process, some states grew even larger, becoming the centres of 'universal' empires.

This political growth was not part of a single and homogeneous transition. Some areas clearly experienced a process of unification early on, while others kept their internal political divisions for a longer period of time. Similarly, some phases saw the early formation of pseudo-imperialistic entities, while others experienced a marked tendency towards fragmentation. Broadly speaking, the average size of political formations undoubtedly experienced a progressive growth. Conversely, the number of independent states within the Near East gradually decreased. However, the moment in which a single political entity managed to control the Near East as a whole, and even crossed its boundaries, evidently marks the end of this book. This is mainly due to the fact that this book's perspective is far too narrow to deal with the development of larger territorial states. If the development of the Persian empire and the Hellenistic period had been included in this volume, it would have been necessary to not only consider their Near Eastern premises, but also their Aegean, Mediterranean, Egyptian, Iranian, Central Asian and Indian ones. In other words, with these phases, the point of view becomes so broad as to require an entirely different approach and methodology.

There are several reasons why this progressive geopolitical growth took place. The first factor, linked to technological developments, was the marked increase of opportunities across a variety of sectors in terms of knowledge, communication and transport (of people and goods). Moreover, there was the increased mobility of caravans and troops. A state was essentially based on the management of a series of movements (of men, messages and goods). Therefore, technological developments allowed the establishment of the optimal dimension of these interactions for each state. This factor, however, was relatively modest in size. After all, between the Akkadian and Neo-Assyrian period, geographic knowledge, techniques for communication and means of transport did not change very much. Only the beginning (in the Urban Revolution) and the end (in the Persian empire) of this period really show the remarkable developmental 'jump' accomplished in the span of three millennia. These two moments therefore mark the beginning and end of a moderate, yet consistent, growth.

A far more influential factor was state administration, a sector that is closely linked to the degree of socio-economic complexity of a state. Initially, the administration was focused on the simple partition of food produced or harvested by an enlarged family, and the responsibilities of each individual member in case of external dangers. Therefore, villages and transhumant groups were still able to cope on their own. However, at one point it became necessary to establish and regulate quotas to be given to each individual, developing a system based on a social and spatial division of labour. Consequently, the 'county' or 'region' became the smallest unit of a state, characterised by a city acting as the centre of specialist labour and leadership, and a network of villages acting as agricultural centres. Later on, when a state's identity gradually began to include linguistic and religious elements, these entities became 'nation' states. Therefore, it can be said that each political development in a state's ideology and administration brought, or could have brought, territorial expansion.

In this expansion, conceived as a progressive acquisition by social units of increasingly more complex functions, the most basic units continued to maintain their original size. On the one hand, this led to the progressive movement of formerly important roles outside a state's sphere of direct control, which were left in the hands of smaller, relatively apolitical, groups (social classes, specialised groups, or families). On the other hand, this situation led to a type of structure similar to the one of 'Chinese boxes', where the larger and politically unifying 'box' contains a series of smaller 'boxes'. From a structural point of view, this series of 'boxes' mirrors the varying influence of these functions. From a historical point of view, these 'boxes' mark the stages that led to the formation of the largest political entities in the Near East. Therefore, the main political formation of the Neolithic period, namely, the village, survived as part of larger local, regional and imperial states. However, the village essentially maintained the same responsibilities. At the beginning, the functions performed by the village seemed the only and most fundamental ones. Later on, these same responsibilities became largely secondary, strictly local and politically irrelevant. The same can be said for the city. Following a period in which the city acted as the ultimate centre of political power, it subsequently became a local branch of a larger state. At the same time, the city maintained its characteristic decisional and administrative competences. Finally, the same process affected regions, defined through geographic boundaries or common ethno-linguistic or cultural features. These regions, then, became provinces or satrapies of larger empires, without losing their size or competences.

The increased complexity of these historical and political developments led to the growth of their population and production base. The two main indicators of this phenomenon are the size of the population and the overall production levels. Unfortunately, we lack a systematic and extensive collection of data on this matter (both in terms of time and space). However, one still gets the impression that long-term growth of population and production levels in the Near East appeared alongside several fluctuations. These fluctuations were characterised by sudden rises and declines, whose scale significantly affected the overall process of growth. Naturally, short-term fluctuations were linked to occasional factors, while long-term growth was centred on fundamental changes in modes of production. These changes ensured a drastic surge in production and survival rates. The marked demographic and production growth of the Urban Revolution led to the almost tenfold growth of the levels attested for the Neolithic period. However, the phase covered in this book substantially constitutes a period of stasis or, more accurately, an alternation between evolution and crisis, which did not bring about sudden or drastic changes in production levels. This fact shows that the period between 3500 and 500 BC constitutes a phase marked by a single fundamental mode of production. In this regard, intermediate fluctuations cannot be ignored and are particularly visible in major centres. This indicates that they were the result of waves of 'urbanisation' (first in the Uruk period, then the Early Bronze Age, the Middle and Late Bronze Age, and, lastly, in the Iron II period), separated by phases of demographic and documentary decline (the so-called 'dark ages').

The end of this long journey (roughly covering the third quarter of the first millennium BC) shows again a remarkable development, not just within the Near East, but also outside of it. Once again, this sudden change remains difficult to quantify, but one can assume that its population and production levels tripled. Unlike previous, largely local, and temporary developments, this surge led to the establishment of new production and demographic levels. The latter would remain the same throughout the Classical period, Late Antiquity and the Medieval period, until the appearance of new developments. Therefore, the choice of 500 BC as the moment to end this volume can also be justified from this point of view, being a visible mark of a historical and structural change that was not momentary, but would last for the following centuries.

The geopolitical growth of states also led to the expansion of the Near Eastern borders. For three millennia, the Near East remained a sort of urbanised island. It was characterised by a concentration of people and production processes in their centres, and surrounded by a more primitive and less inhabited periphery. When the above-mentioned processes began to affect the periphery as well, the nature of borders in the Near East began to change. In other words, the edge of the Near East ceased to separate inhabited areas from deserted ones, or an organised world from a chaotic one, or settled areas from regions simply rich in natural resources. Borders began to separate different inhabited areas structured in a variety of ways.

From a Western (largely Eurocentric) perspective, one of the most powerful images of the Near East in the Pre-Classical period is that of a centre of technological and administrative innovation, which eventually spread to the west, stimulating the growth of the European periphery. After 500 BC, however, this image is replaced by the contraposition between East and West. In fact, in the meantime, the West reached a position able to oppose the former centrality and privileged stance of the Near East. Naturally, apart from this opposition between Europe and the Near East, there were new frontiers that developed around the same time: the frontier between the Iranian and Chinese world, which affected Central Asia; the frontier between the Near East and India; and the southern border of the Classical World, Christianity, and then Islam, in Africa. However, these other areas did not affect the Western world as much. On the contrary, the opposition between East and West would continue to hold a discriminative value and a place of absolute importance in the European tradition.

It is certain that the ideas of 'ex Oriente lux' (literally, 'light from the East') and of the cultural rivalry between the East and the West are based on Eurocentric and misleading simplifications, or even *bona fide* falsifications of the evidence. The same can be said of the so-called *leitmotif* of world history, which sees the progressive movement from the east to the west of the centre of civilisation (from the Near East to Greece, then Rome, then Western Europe). All these stereotypes do not fit within a balanced and exhaustive evaluation of the evidence. The concept of 'border' itself is largely subjective, since it is based on the establishment of an 'inside' and 'outside', of an 'us' and 'them'. Consequently, the resulting historical images based on these oppositions are inevitably biased. However, an awareness of the subjective bias of these images allows these Eurocentric simplifications to provide a certain degree of insightful self-analysis. From an objective and simplified point of view, then, the direct heir of the civilisations of the Ancient Near East is the Hellenistic world, then the Christian East, the Iranian empires, and Islam. From a purely Eurocentric perspective, it is highly significant that this book ends when the Near East 'passed the baton' over to Greece and the Mediterranean world.

2 The new cultural developments

The end of our journey is not just marked by the expansion of historical developments outside the Near East. It is also marked by the sudden appearance of significant intellectual and religious innovations. The sixth century BC (or, better, the two centuries between 650 and 450 BC) is the heart of what has been defined as the Axial Age of world history. In this phase, a series of reformers and innovators rose to prominence, from Confucius in China (550–480 BC) to Buddha in India (560–480 BC), Zoroaster in Iran (seventh century BC), and the Ionian philosophers and scientists in Greece (sixth century BC). The latter laid the foundations of the Classical philosophy, tragedy and historiography of the fifth century BC. Then, there were the great prophets of Israel (Deutero-Isaiah, Jeremiah and Ezekiel) linked to the Babylonian exile (587–539 BC), and preceded by the first formulation of Yahwism by the Deuteronomist (in Josiah's reign, 640–609 BC). The protagonists and trends of the Axial Age are as different from each other as their respective cultural backgrounds and traditions. Even their innovations varied from rationalism to ethics. This concentration of cultural changes in the Axial Age is more than just a mere coincidence: it developed out of common situations and a common need to define the role of human beings in the world. In other words, this phase constitutes a significant separation from previous traditions and lifestyles.

The Axial Age developed alongside the formation of 'universal' empires, from the Assyrian to the Persian empires in the Near East, and similar states in India and China. All these territorial states were the result of similar processes developing over millennia, and were based on premises that had by now lost their potential. Therefore, it is no coincidence that the Axial Age tried to overcome the founding principles of empires, and developed on the margins or even against the empires themselves. Consequently, the great traditional cultures and their privileged centres were cut off from this process, and even antagonised it. For instance, Babylonia or Egypt did not have 'Axial' innovators. They were fully dedicated to the standardisation and archaising revival of their cultural legacy, from the esoteric expressions of Chaldean astrology to Egyptian Hermeticism. In contrast, the main centres of innovative cultural developments were located in new or marginal areas: from the Greek poleis on the edge of the Persian empire to the deportees within the Mesopotamian empires, the new communities in the Iranian mountains, and the new political and religious environments outside the traditional seats of power in India and China.

In terms of religion, the innovations of the Axial Age produced new ideologies. These ideologies eventually substituted polytheism, the latter being an important outcome of the Urban Revolution. However, Judaic monotheism (then Christian and Islamic monotheism, which derived from it) or Iranian dualism (Mazdaism and then Manichaeism) did not mark a 'reduction' of the divine sphere, but the birth of a different divine model. The increased influence and size of empires had not reduced the number of deities at the expense of the conquered cultures. On the contrary, empires had increased the number of deities through accumulations and syncretisms. Monotheism and dualism (the latter being a particular form of monotheism) do not unify a wide range of divine figures, but remove this variety. They therefore reject all the distinctive features of deities in favour of a more general and ethical characterisation of the divine. Up until the Axial Age, religion had been firmly in the hands of those in power. These individuals acted as the only legitimate mediators in the relations between the human and the divine sphere. The rise of universal empires, however, gradually increased the gap existing between the ruling elite and the rest of the population. Consequently, the former mediatory role of rulers was (or had to be) removed in favour of a direct connection between the individual and the divine. For this reason, the new religions developed in the Axial Age were 'ethical' and closely linked to the individual. They therefore were in marked contrast with previous religions, which were far more 'ceremonial' and concerned with the maintenance of the official socio-political structure of a state.

The other great legacy of the Axial Age is the rationalisation and secularisation of knowledge. Science and philosophy developed along internal lines, through their own methods and without those practical or cosmological connections that had previously hindered intellectual research. In other words, 'mythical thought', or at least the tendency to explain or envision reality in mythical terms, was replaced by 'rational thought'. A cumulative type of knowledge was replaced by a structural interest in the understanding of the world, both in its physical and conceptual aspects. Consequently, historiography, ethnography and political theory developed alongside science and philosophy. All these new disciplines had pre-Axial precedents in the Near East, but lacked more comprehensive and conscious formulations.

The emergence of moral concerns in religion and the rational aspects of knowledge can be linked to the emergence of the individual. This phase saw the development of the individual personality, and of a direct link between the individual and his own issues, outside family, social, communal and political structures. This development can be seen in high status expressions as well as in the wider population, in the tip of the iceberg as well as in the mass below the surface of the water. Stylistically, there is a marked tendency towards originality and creativity (for instance, in sculpture). Moreover, an attention for unique physical traits substituted stereotyped and standardised depictions. Now, then, the ultimate goal of a narrator or a poet was originality. This was in marked contrast with the earlier obsession for the reproduction of ancient traditional models. The content of literary works itself tends to be more specific, rather than based on previous models.

Prior to the Axial Age, the only renowned figures were rulers. This was due to their constant efforts in placing themselves in a super-human category alongside gods and founding heroes. Kings therefore always emphasised their contribution to the order of the world, its correct management and their fight against the forces of chaos. The few other personalities or the few authors we know of are simply early efforts at anticipating the eventual changes that would take place in the Axial Age. However, these painful efforts could only have succeeded by becoming models and founding prototypes of later literature. Pre-Axial literature therefore developed together with political power, and was actually funded by the palace. On the contrary, post-Axial literature would (or could) become not only autonomous, but even in opposition to the palace administration.

In terms of *longue durée* (if one can accept the application of Braudel's approach here), the Axial Age constitutes a suitable development to mark the end of the phase treated in this book (3500–500 BC) and to open a new one (ca. 500 BC–1500 AD). It is, however, necessary to understand in what way this marked change relates to the previous phase. The Axial Age displays elements of both continuity and change. The 'revolutions' of the Axial Age, then, may have developed against the traditional cultures and empires (although they would become an integral part of the following empires), but they were also the final outcomes of tendencies that existed throughout the previous three millennia.

In this book, we have tried to follow a coherent line of development and its repercussions on a material (namely, the ownership and management of means of production), social and ethical level. Consequently, it has been possible to follow the gradual rise of the role of the individual from its anonymous presence within kinship and family groups. The latter controlled means of productions, managed them according to strictly traditional practices, and only categorised its members according to gender or age groups. The process continued throughout the Urban Revolution and its subsequent developments. This rise was initially (and, to a certain extent, always) limited to adult males, and mainly within specialist classes. In this process, the idea that a man's destiny was written in his family and in his social position was slowly replaced with the conviction that a man's destiny depended on his behaviour and abilities. In this regard, the evolution of inheritance systems is a significant indication of the evolution of legal responsibility (from collective to family and personal responsibility) and socio-economic mobility (both vertical and horizontal). This evolution also contributed to the appearance of other criteria, such as the importance of originality in literary works, and the marked transition from state religion to a more intimate and personal type of religion.

Thanks to the gradual accumulation of functional, socio-economic, ethnic, cultural and religious differentiations, the emergence of the individual from the group continued throughout the Bronze Age. This gives us the impression that a non-traumatic turn of events was still possible, at least in terms of the development of the individual's rationality, moral values and introspection. On the contrary, the process came to an abrupt standstill in the Early Iron Age, when the rise of nomadic and pastoral groups marked the return to tribal structures and kinship values. This situation led to a different regression in the Late Iron Age at the hand of the rising empires. The latter conquered and essentially suppressed thriving cultural and political centres, imposed a sort of 'mass slavery', and revived archaisms. Moreover, they only allowed the practice of magical (for example, prophecy and exorcisms), cumulative and theosophical (astrological or not) wisdom.

This regression, which was controlled by the empires' centres, brought about the 'revolutionary' reaction of the great prophets, religious reformists, scientists and philosophers of the Axial Age. Despite their opposition to the great cultural centres of a tradition in decline, however, these innovators did not fail to draw from previous experiences (after all, they could not have done otherwise). The latter allowed them to bring change, further emphasised by the overall cultural regression of the time. Therefore, the search in the previous millennia of Ancient Near Eastern history for the religious, scientific and philosophical precedents and premises of the Axial Age cannot be considered a merely arbitrary or useless thought experiment.

3 A static legacy: the 'elementary forms'

With these ethical, intellectual and religious innovations (which, from our point of view, seem the normal legacy of individuals and societies), the history of Ancient Near Eastern cultures drastically changed. However, one may wonder if these innovations have preserved anything that can enlighten us on the ideas and values of the previous phases. It may be sufficient to think of the way (and the amount of time) in which the Western World rediscovered and reconstructed the history of the Ancient Near East to realise an essential fact: the history of the Greek and Roman World always remained an intrinsic part of the cultural legacy of the Western World, even in the various forms in which it had been revisited. On the contrary, Pre-Classical history originally emerged out of an anthropological investigation of the 'primitive' cultures that still survived at the time. On a side note, it is striking how this revival took place in the last phase in which it was physically possible to do so. Soon after the discovery and study of 'other' world cultures, the impact of colonialism, and the Industrial Revolution (and, then, world economy) led to the irreversible mutation or elimination of these cultures. The same can be said for the recovery of ancient archaeological and historical remains, which slightly anticipated the savage destruction of their original environment in favour of new forms of exploitation and settlement. These interventions fatally compromised earlier forms of human settlement. In other words, the study of these cultures foreshadowed and preceded their imminent destruction. This pattern is attested both for ancient and modern imperialism in its military, economic or intellectual connotations alike.

During this phase of global unification and intense interaction with 'other' cultures, Western culture established a comparative relationship with ancient cultures. Consequently, through the identification of similarities and differences, Western culture either tried to demonstrate how things have never changed or, alternatively, how things have changed, thus proving the uniqueness of the Western World. These extreme interpretations may appear naïve and unacceptable, but their more detailed and thorough elaborations constitute the core of structuralism and historicism. These two approaches cannot be ignored, regardless of one's preference for one or the other. As much as one tries to unify historical developments, one inevitably encounters exceptions. Similarly, as much one tries to establish universal 'laws', one has to realise that in history these rules are more often broken than followed. Yet despite one's effort to focus on the historical context of specific customs, events, centuries and regions, one notices the existence of common institutional, phenomenological and fundamental categories. After all, if that were not the case, it would be impossible to discuss them in our own language and with our own approach.

In order to identify these 'elementary forms' constituting a sort of basic grammar of history, one has to admit that the Near East provides us with a relatively complex and complete sample of evidence. This has the added advantage of showing us elementary forms in their early formation and their later developments, relatively free of further complications. As already pointed out earlier, the Near East has become a sort of privileged historical 'workshop'. This allows (to a certain extent) the study of certain phenomena in their purest state possible, avoiding those interferences that make these same phenomena difficult to identify or analyse in later phases. Elementary forms can therefore be easily identified in their earliest stages and simplest forms. Moreover, once identified, they can be easily recognised as elementary forms within more sophisticated phenomena.

In this volume, we have encountered various forms of human aggregation, first in their formative and then in their later stages. Thus we have moved from villages and transhumant groups to cities, tribes, ethnic groups, nations, confederations and empires. Within them, we have identified and explored the formation of centres of power: from the temple to the palace, the warehouse, the scribal school, the fortress and the armoury. We have also seen the establishment of a wide range of ways to establish control and subordination: from social stratification within a single community to foreign conquest, at times in its more drastic forms of annexation or destruction. We have discovered the way labour was subdivided and rewarded (from rations to salaries), and surplus was accumulated (from tributes to taxes). We have seen the way (or the 'rules') in which war was waged and peace was established. We have followed the development of the means for the justification of power and inequality: from legal reforms to usurpers' apologies; from the celebrations of victories to the descriptions from the point of view of the defeated; and from punitive interventions to alluring alliances.

In terms of communication, we have seen the development of the 'elementary forms' of the message, both in its transmission and recording. We have therefore explored the development of messages from letters to administrative reports, from receipts to payment orders, from lists to summaries, from archives to libraries. In more general terms, we have seen the transition from a visual or monumental language to a written (and then alphabetic) one, from interlineal translations to the rise of a *lingua franca*, and from diplomatic agreements to commercial barter.

In terms of socio-political organisation, we have explored the development of codes and edicts, assemblies and courts, councillors and delegates, inheritances and testaments, adoptions and donations, and confiscations and exemptions. All these 'elementary forms' did not exist before. The necessary conditions for the development and implementation of these practices first appeared in the portion of history considered in this book. Despite their natural evolution in response to changing socio-economic, political and cultural developments, all these innovations remained relatively stable. Therefore, they can be recognised today as more elementary forms of our own, alas more structurally and historically complex, achievements.

Today, it would be impossible to conceive a study, be it a comparative or a phenomenological one, on the great themes of the city, the state, imperialism, communication, writing, social stratification, production economy or trade in which the Near East does not hold a privileged position. Apart from providing a set of documentation equal to any other (later) historical context, the Near East also provides the *origins* of the city, the state, imperialism, writing, administration and so on. If the term 'origin' is inevitably shrouded in myth, we can at least state that with the Near East we can experience for the first time (similar developments would appear later on elsewhere) the progressive development of the elementary forms of the organisation and interaction of communities.

4 A dynamic legacy: progress and crisis

Alongside the static and structural acquisition of elementary forms, the history of the Ancient Near East also presents the problem of the general interpretation of historical developments, namely, the impact of dynamic and evolutionary factors. In this regard, it is possible to identify two models of development. The first one is that of exponential growth through gradual accumulation at an increasingly fast pace. This model is the result of the historiographical approach of the late nineteenth and early twentieth centuries (AD). These were the earliest phases of the systematic reconstruction of the history of the Ancient Near East, and were dominated by the concept of 'progress'.

This idea came out of the development of European culture after the Industrial Revolution and modern colonialism. The latter brought a significant economic and political growth (though limited to the Western World) through the exploitation of the non-Western world. For decades, this seemingly unstoppable growth led to the illusion that this progress was never-ending, almost like a steep curve in a graph. This optimistic view, centred on the idea of progress, naturally led to the appreciation of the technical and cultural developments of the Ancient Near East. The latter, then, became the distant originator of this progress. From this perspective, the Near East was seen as a sequence of cultural and technological inventions and innovations, of increasingly efficient modes of production, of increasingly complex political formations, and of freer and higher forms of human expression.

Then, the concepts of crisis and catastrophe, and of the 'limits of progress' were introduced (or re-introduced) in the study of Ancient History. This was due to the global crises following the First World War, the economic depression and the political recessions. Moreover, the spread of these issues to the rest of the world, and the more recent demographic, productive and energy crises continue to enforce this view. In other words, these historical developments led to the idea of an upward and downward development determined by the difficult interaction between various factors, eventually causing regressions. The negative elements of crisis, then, are not seen as accidents within a largely exponential growth, but structural traits (equal to elements of growth) of the overall system. Today, this growth can be simulated through information technologies and systems theory.

The over-exploitation of the land, the depletion of resources, the economic cycles, the difficult relations between centre and periphery within an integrated global economy, all contributed to a radical change of our worldview. Therefore, the simple (and more optimistic) historical interest in the cultural achievements of the elite, the urbanised and imperial centres, technological innovations and the developments of ever-profitable systems expanded to include less sophisticated areas, phases of stalemate and recession, and the so-called 'dark ages' and 'intermediate periods'. In other words, historical interest began to consider all those submerged areas (especially in terms of evidence) of that 'iceberg' of ancient cultures.

However, it would be far better to suggest a composite model. The latter would still focus on progress in terms of long-term effects, but would be more cyclical in the short-term. The history of the Ancient Near East covers some of these cycles, roughly one for each part of this volume. Our interest in this phase should not be limited to positive accomplishments. It should not consider growth as the only factor providing us with information, or as a premise of our own progress. We should focus on the variety of development strategies (which depend on different ecologic and historical contexts) and especially on the different outcomes, some 'winning' and others more 'regressive', leading to the marginalisation and disappearance of entire communities.

This enlarged model also shows how the real legacy of the Ancient Near East is not the progressive type of sequence starting from Greece to Rome, the Christian Medieval Age and Modern Western Europe, but the following phases of the Near East itself. These later phases also had their sequence of growth and were affected by socio-political, technological and economic decline. Moreover, there were issues such as the de-population, desertification and destruction of the landscape, cultural dogmatism, political dependence and subsistence economies in critical zones. All these factors are not secondary in an overall evaluation of the history of the areas under analysis.

This new historiographical model allows a better understanding and a more reliable interpretation of the past. Unsurprisingly, the old Eurocentric point of view was based on the tripartite division of history into Ancient, Medieval and Modern history. All three phases were seen as developing along the same lines. Now, however, history has overcome the issue through the historical evaluation of prehistoric phases. In addition to that, there is the introduction (once impossible to apply) of the concept and study of contemporary history, as well as the historical understanding of future developments. Another addition is the renewed interest in other cultures, whose history is relevant, but often neglected. Finally, there is also the sociological development of the history of marginal social classes, of women, of all sectors that remain unattested in the evidence, and of daily life.

In order to make this enlarged and empowered model effective, it is necessary to understand the dynamics of progress and recession, and of cultural evolution in its broadest connotations. Unfortunately, this is only possible with a balanced and sufficient set of evidence. This is not the case for the Near East, and it is likely that the problem will never be fully fixed. Therefore, it may seem that the positive consideration of the Near East as a useful source of 'elementary forms' does not apply for an interpretation of its dynamic legacy. However, our historical investigation appeared well equipped for the study of these elementary forms. This was due to their intrinsic simplicity and proximity to the phase in which these various phenomena were introduced, and to the fact that they are extraneous (which allows us to not get too involved in the interpretation), yet similar to 'our' own forms. In this regard, then, the study of the dynamic legacy of the Near East, far from being able to provide anything transferable elsewhere, has to depend on models developed elsewhere. These other models can rely on more statistical documentation, and support the study of the Near East by interpolation, allowing us to make sense of the surviving evidence.

What remains is the great contribution that the Ancient Near East can give to history in general. It expands our perspective in terms of time and space, and of types of phenomena. This new perspective is now part of 'our own' culture, which remains the first one to be able to provide interpretations that are not excessively self-centred. This prevents the presentation of other cultures as mirrors of our own culture. These cultures, then, are presented as autonomous entities. Much has been done towards a 'normalisation' and 'simplification' of the earliest Eurocentric and finalistic histories of the Ancient Near East (whose approach now survive in high school textbooks). However, there is still much to be done.

ANNOTATED BIBLIOGRAPHY

Abbreviations

AfO	*Archiv für Orientforschung* (Graz)
AnSt	*Anatolian Studies* (London)
AoF	*Altorientalische Forschungen* (Berlin)
BASOR	*Bulletin of the American Schools of Oriental Research* (New Haven)
BO	*Bibliotheca Orientalis* (Leiden)
JA	*Journal Asiatique* (Paris)
JAOS	*Journal of the American Oriental Society* (Boston)
JCS	*Journal of Cuneiform Studies* (New Haven)
JESHO	*Journal of the Economic and Social History of the Orient* (Leiden)
JNES	*Journal of Near Eastern Studies* (Chicago)
MARI	*Mari: Annales de recherches interdisciplinaires* (Paris)
MDOG	*Mitteilungen der Deutschen Orient-Gesellschaft* (Berlin)
MIOF	*Mitteilungen des Instituts für Orientforschung* (Berlin)
OA	*Oriens Antiquus* (Rome)
OBO	*Orbis Biblicus et Orientalis* (Freiburg–Göttingen)
Or	*Orientalia* (Rome)
RA	*Revue d'Assyriologie* (Paris)
RAI	*Rencontre Assyriologique Internationale. Comptes-rendus.*
RHA	*Revue Hittite et Asiatique* (Paris)
SMEA	*Studi Micenei ed Egeo-Analotici* (Rome)
SS	*Studi Storici* (Rome)
UF	*Ugarit-Forschungen* (Neukirchen)
WO	*Welt des Orients* (Göttingen)

1 The Ancient Near East as a historical problem

For a long time, the main publication on the history of the Ancient Near East has been the *Cambridge Ancient History*, vol. I (1970–71); vol. II (1973–75); and vol. III (1982). However, this publication is now quite out of date. In contrast to this, P. Attinger and M. Wäfler are working on a far more philological publication, entitled *Annäherungen* (OBO 160), Freiburg–Göttingen 1999, and so far have

580

published volumes 1 to 5 (referenced in the relevant chapters). A recent Italian publication worth mentioning is *Storia d'Europa e del Mediterraneo*, I–II, Rome 2006, edited by S. De Martino. Among the publications by individual authors on the topic I would like to mention P. Garelli, *Le Proche-Orient Asiatique*, I–II, Paris 1969–74; A. Kuhrt, *The Ancient Near East c. 3000–330 BC*, I–II, London–New York 1995; M. van de Mieroop, *A History of the Ancient Near East*, Oxford 2007. A. L. Oppenheim's *Ancient Mesopotamia*, Chicago 1977, is atypical, but remains a core reading. Another excellent publication is J. N. Postgate's *Early Mesopotamia*, London–New York 1992, but unfortunately it only focuses on the phase between 3000 and 1500 BC.

Among more archaeological introductions, I would like to mention A. Invernizzi's *Dal Tigri all'Eufrate*, I–II, Florence 1992; P. Matthiae, *La storia dell'arte dell'Oriente Antico*, I–III, Milan 1996–2002; L. Huot, *Une archéologie des peuples du Proche-Orient*, I–II, Paris 2004. On archaeological issues see R. Matthews, *The Archaeology of Mesopotamia: Theories and Approaches*, London–New York 2003; and S. Pollock and R. Bernbeck (eds), *Archaeologies of the Middle East*, Oxford 2005. On specific regions, see J.-C. Margueron, *Les Mesopotamiens*, I–II, Paris 1991; S. Pollock, *Ancient Mesopotamia*, Cambridge 1999; P. Akkermans and G. Schwartz, *The Archaeology of Syria*, Cambridge 2001. A useful encyclopaedia is E. M. Meyers (ed.), *The Oxford Encyclopaedia of Archaeology in the Near East*, I–V, Oxford 1997.

Chronology, textual evidence: W. Eder and J. Renger (eds), *Chronologies of the Ancient World* (Brill's New Pauly, Supplements), Leiden–Boston 2007. **Archaeological evidence:** R. W. Ehrich, *Chronologies in Old World Archaeology*, I–II, Chicago 1992; M. Bietak (ed.), *The Synchronization of Civilizations in the Eastern Mediterranean in the Second Millennium BC*, I–II, Wien 2000–2003. **On chronological debates:** P. Aström (ed.), *High, Middle or Low?*, Gothenburg 1987; H. Gasche, J. A. Armstrong and S. W. Cole, *Dating the Fall of Babylon*, Ghent 1998; H. Hunger and R. Pruzsinszky (eds), *Mesopotamian Dark Age Revisited*, Wien 2004.

Bibliographies: *Orientalia* (Rome) has been publishing a *Keilschriftbibliographie* each year since 1941, while the one published in *AfO* includes archaeology, but is published less regularly. **Encyclopaedia:** the *Reallexikon der Assyriologie*, I–XI, Leipzig–Berlin 1928–2008, is still a work in progress and has reached entries beginning with *Sam-*. **Guide to publications of cuneiform literature:** R. Borger, *Handbuch der Keilschriftliteratur*, I–III, Berlin 1967–75 (now rather out of date). **Archives:** O. Pedersen, *Archives and Libraries in the Ancient Near East, 1500–300 BC*, Bethesda 1998.

Anthologies (from various periods): J. B. Pritchard, *Ancient Near Eastern Texts*, Princeton 1955 (and its *Supplement*, 1968); O. Kaiser (ed.), *Texte aus der Umwelt des Alten Testament*, I–III, Gütersloh 1982–97; the series *Littératures anciennes du Proche Orient*, Paris 1968 onwards, and *Testi del Vicino Oriente Antico*, Brescia 1990 onwards; B. Foster, *Before the Muses*, I–II, Bethesda 1993; J. Black et al., *The Literature of Ancient Sumer*, Oxford 2004.

2 The geography of the Ancient Near East

A structural approach to the civilizations of the Ancient Near East can be found in *L'alba della civiltà*, I–III, Turin 1976. A more recent and broader publication is J. M. Sasson's (ed.) *Civilizations of the Ancient Near East*, I–IV, New York 1995. See also H. Klengel (ed.), *Kulturgeschichte des alten Vorderasien*, Berlin 1989; G. Leick (ed.), *The Babylonian World*, London–New York 2007.

Law and society: see R. Westbrook (ed.), *A History of Ancient Near Eastern Law*, I–II, Leiden 1999; M. Liverani and C. Mora (eds), *I diritti del mondo cuneiforme*, Pavia 2008. On earlier phases see C. Wilcke, *Early Ancient Near Eastern Law*, München 2003. **Law codes:** M. T. Roth, *Law Collections from Mesopotamia and Asia Minor*, Atlanta 1995.

Geography: on the Ancient Near East in general see X. de Planhol, *Les fondements géographiques de l'histoire de l'Islam*, Paris 1968; P. Sanlaville, *Le Moyen-Orient arabe*, Paris 2000. **Paleoecology:** see W. C. Brice (ed.), *The Environmental History of the Near and Middle East*, New York–London 1978; W. Frey and H. P.

Uerpmann (eds), *Beiträge zur Umweltsgeschichte des vorderen Orients*, Wiesbaden 1981; K. Verhoeven in H. Gasche and M. Tanret (eds), *Changing Watercourses in Babylonia*, Ghent 1998, pp. 159–245. **Cartography:** Tübinger Atlas des vorderen Orients, Wiesbaden 1990 onwards; *Atlante storico del Vicino Oriente antico*, Rome 1982 onwards. **Cultural atlas:** M. Roaf, *Cultural Atlas of Mesopotamia and the Ancient Near East*, New York 1990. Toponyms are subdivided by periods and published in the series *Répertoire Géographique des Textes Cunéiformes* (*Tübinger Atlas des vorderen Orients*, Reihe B7), I–XII, Wiesbaden 1974–2001.

Settlement history: R. McCormick Adams, *Land Behind Baghdad*, Chicago 1965; *The Uruk Countryside*, Chicago 1972; *Heartland of Cities*, Chicago 1981; also the *Northern Akkad Project Reports* 1–10, Ghent 1987–1996; P. J. Ucko, R. Tringham and G. W. Dimbleby (eds), *Man, Settlement and Urbanism*, London 1972; G. M. Schwartz and S. E. Falconer (eds), *Archaeological Views from the Countryside*, Washington 1994. On archaeological surveys cf. I. Hodder and C. Orton, *Spatial Analysis in Archaeology*, Cambridge 1976; F. Hole in *Paléorient* 6 (1980), pp. 21–44; C. L. Redman in *Journal of Field Archaeology* 9 (1982), pp. 375–382. **Ethnography:** C. Kramer (ed.), *Ethnoarchaeology*, New York 1979, and *Village Ethnoarchaeology*, New York 1982; J. N. Postgate in *Cambridge Archaeological Journal* 4 (1994), pp. 47–65.

On the city: C. H. Kraeling and R. McCormick Adams (eds), *City Invincible*, Chicago 1960; G. Wilhelm (ed.), *Die Orientalische Stadt*, Saarbrücken 1997; M. Novak, *Herrschaftsform und Stadtbaukunst*, Saarbrücken 1999; M. van de Mieroop, *The Ancient Mesopotamian City*, Oxford 1997.

On the palace: E. Heinrich, *Die Paläste im alten Mesopotamien*, Berlin 1984; J.-C. Margueron, *Les palais de l'âge du bronze en Mésopotamie*, I–II, Paris 1971; P. Garelli (ed.), *Le palais et la royauté*, RAI 19, Paris 1974; E. Lévy (ed.), *Le système palatial en Orient, en Grèce et à Rome*, Strasbourg 1987; I. Nielsen (ed.), *The Royal Palace Institution in the First Millennium BC*, Athens 2001; J. N. Postgate et al., *Palast*, in *Reallexikon der Assyriologie* X (2003–05), pp. 195–276.

On the temple: E. Heinrich, *Die Tempel und Heiligtümer im alten Mesopotamien*, Berlin 1982; E. Lipinski (ed.), *State and Temple Economy in the Ancient Near East*, I–II, Louvain 1979; V. A. Hurowitz, *I Have Built You an Exalted House*, Sheffield 1992; A. R. George, *House Most High*, Winona Lake 1993; C. McCormick, *Palace and Temple*, Berlin 2002. **On divine kingship:** N. Brisch (ed.), *Religion and Power*, Chicago 2008.

Villages: I. M. Diakonoff in *JESHO* 18 (1975), pp. 121–133; M. Liverani in RAI 44, Venezia 1999, I, pp. 37–47; otherwise W. F. Leemans in *Recueils de la Société Jean Bodin*, 41, Paris 1983, pp. 43–106; G. van Driel, in *Festschrift Veenhof*, Leiden 2001, pp. 103–118.

Households: K. R. Veenhof (ed.), *Houses and Households in Ancient Mesopotamia*, RAI 40, Leiden 1996; P. Brusasco, *Mesopotamian Domestic Architecture and Its Textual Dimension*, Oxford 2007. **On house plans:** E. Heinrich and U. Seidl, *MDOG* 98 (1967), pp. 24–45. **Models:** J. Bretschneider, *Architekturmodelle in Vorderasien*, Kevelaer 1991; B. Muller, *Les maquettes architecturales du Proche-Orient Ancien*, I–II, Beyrouth 2002. **On foundation rituals:** C. Ambos, *Mesopotamische Baurituale*, Dresden 2004.

On food: D. Brothwell and P. Brothwell, *Food in Antiquity*, London 1979; for a more detailed treatment of the topic, see H. Hoffner, *Alimenta Hethaeorum*, New Haven 1974; L. Milano in *Dialoghi di Archeologia* 3 (1981), pp. 85–121; L. Milano (ed.), *Drinking in Ancient Societies*, Padova 1994; L. Milano and C. Grottanelli (eds), *Food and Identity in the Ancient World*, Padova 2004; J. Bottéro, *The Oldest Cuisine in the World*, Chicago 2004.

Technology: R. J. Forbes, *Studies in Ancient Technology*, I–IX, Leiden 1955–64 and Ch. Singer, E. J. Holmyard and A. R. Hall (eds), *History of Technology*, Oxford 1955 are now out of date; for more recent studies see P. R. S. Moorey, *Ancient Mesopotamian Materials and Industries*, Oxford 1994; D. T. Potts, *Mesopotamian Civilization: The Material Foundations*, London 1997; and *Storia della Scienza*, I/3, Rome 2001 (on the Ancient Near East see pp. 193–535).

On the structural problems of ancient economy: A. Bongenaar (ed.), *Interdependency of Institutions and Private Entrepreneurs*, Leiden 2000; J. G. Manning and I. Morris (eds), *The Ancient Economy*, Stanford 2005; and the proceedings edited by M. Hudson et al., *Privatization in the Ancient Near East*; *Urbanization* *and Land Ownership in the Ancient Near East; Debt and Economic Renewal in the Ancient Near East; Creating Economic Order in the Ancient Near East*, Cambridge (MA) 1996–2004.

On 'modes of production' in the Ancient Near East: M. Liverani in *L'alba della civiltà*, II, pp. 1–126; C. Zaccagnini in *Dialoghi di Archeologia* 3 (1981), pp. 3–65; P. Briant, *Rois, tributs et paysans*, Paris 1982. **Independent Marxist approaches:** A. L. Oppenheim in *JESHO* 10 (1967), pp. 1–16; I. J. Gelb in *JAOS* 87 (1967), pp. 1–8. **Influential studies on economic anthropology:** K. Polanyi, *Trade and Market in the Early Empires*, New York 1957; K. Polanyi, *The Livelihood of Man*, New York 1977; M. Sahlins, *Stone Age Economics*, London 1972.

Trade and finance: J. G. Dercksen (ed.), *Trade and Finance in Ancient Mesopotamia*, Leiden 1999; C. Zaccagnini (ed.), *Mercanti e politica nel mondo antico*, Rome 2003; H. D. Baker and M. Jursa (eds), *Approaching the Babylonian Economy*, Münster 2005. **Agriculture:** K. Butz and P. Schröder in *Baghdader Mitteilungen* 16 (1985), pp. 165–209; M. A. Powell in *ZA* 75 (1985), pp. 7–38; R. M. Jas, *Rainfall and Agriculture in Ancient Mesopotamia*, Leiden 2000; and especially the *Bulletin on Sumerian Agriculture*, I–VIII, Cambridge 1984–1995. **Landscape:** M. Liverani in *JESHO* 39 (1996), pp. 1–41.

Unity and variety: L. Levine and T. C. Young (eds), *Mountains and Lowlands*, Malibu 1977; H. Nissen and J. Renger (eds), *Mesopotamien und seine Nachbarn*, RAI 25, I–II, Berlin 1982; M. Rowlands, M. T. Larsen and K. Kristiansen (eds), *Centre and Periphery in the Ancient World*, Cambridge 1987; B. Geyer, *Conquête de la steppe*, Lyon 2001. **Collapse:** N. Yoffee and G. L. Cowgill (eds), *The Collapse of Ancient States and Civilizations*, Tucson 1988; J. Tainter, *The Collapse of Complex Societies*, Cambridge 1988.

Nomadic and sedentary societies: H. Klengel, *Zwischen Zelt und Palast*, Leipzig 1972; P. Briant, *Ètat et pasteurs au Moyen Orient ancien*, Paris–Cambridge 1982; O. Aurenche (eds), *Nomades et sédentaires: perspectives ethnoarchéologiques*, Paris 1984; R. Cribb, *Nomads in Archaeology*, Cambridge 1991; O. Bar-Yosef and A. Khazanov (eds), *Pastoralism in the Levant*, Madison 1992; R. Bernbeck, *Steppe als Kulturlandschaft*, Berlin 1993; and the studies of M. B. Rowton in *Or* 42 (1973), pp. 247–258; *JNES* 32 (1973), pp. 201–215; *JESHO* 17 (1974), pp. 1–30; *OA* 15 (1976), pp. 17–31; *JNES* 35 (1976), pp. 13–20. See also Ch. Nicolle, *Nomades et sédentaires dans le Proche-Orient ancien*, RAI 46, Paris 2004; W. H. van Soldt (ed.), *Ethnicity in Ancient Mesopotamia*, RAI 48, Leiden 2005; J. R. Robertson in *Studies in Honor of E. Leichty*, Leiden 2006, pp. 325–336.

Ideologies and historiography: M. Liverani in *L'alba della civiltà*, I, pp. 275–414; III, pp. 437–521; *Or* 42 (1973), pp. 178–194; J. J. Finkelstein and A. L. Oppenheim in *Propaganda and Communication in World History*, I, Honolulu 1979, pp. 50–144; H. Tadmor and M. Weinfeld (eds), *History, Historiography and Interpretation*, Jerusalem 1983; A. R. Millard, J. K. Hoffmeier and D. W. Baker (eds), *Faith, Tradition and History*, Winona Lake 1994; M. van de Mieroop, *Cuneiform Texts and the Writing of History*, London 1999. **Studies based on archaeological evidence:** P. Matthiae, *Il sovrano e l'opera*, Rome–Bari 1994; M. Novák, *Herrschaftsform und Stadtbaukunst*, Saarbrücken 1999.

3 The Neolithic and Chalcolithic periods

On the origins of agriculture: D. R. Harris and G. C. Hillman (eds), *Foraging and Farming*, London 1989; D. O. Henry, *From Foraging to Agriculture*, Philadelphia 1989; A. B. Gebauer and T. D. Price (eds), *Transitions to Agriculture in Prehistory*, Madison 1992; C. Wesley Cowan and P. J. Watson (eds), *The Origins of Agriculture*, Washington 1992; D. Zohary and M. Hopf, *Domestication of Plants in the Old World*, Oxford 1994. On domestication, after the introductions by F. E. Zeuner, *A History of Domesticated Animals*, London 1963 and B. Brentjes, *Wildtier und Haustier im Alten Orient*, Berlin 1962, cf. P. Ducos, *L'origine des animaux domestiques en Palestine*, Bordeaux 1968; P. J. Ucko and G. W. Dimbleby, *The Domestication and Exploitation of Plants and Animals*, London 1969; D. R. Harris (ed.), *The Origins and Spread of Agriculture and Pastoralism in Eurasia*, Washington 1996. For an ideological approach see J. Cauvin, *Naissance des divinités, naissance de l'agriculture*, Paris 1997.

583

On the Neolithic, see the introduction by J. Mellaart, *The Neolithic of the Near East*, London 1975 now needs revisions. For a bibliography on individual phases and regions (too long to reference here) see M. Frangipane, 'Il neolitico e la protostoria nel Vicino Oriente antico' in De Martino (ed.) *Storia d'Europa e del Mediterraneo*, I, pp. 258–265. **Households:** O. Aurenche, *La maison orientale: L'architecture du Proche Orient ancien dès origines au milieu du quatrième millénaire*, I–III, Paris 1981; O. Aurenche in *Paléorient* 7/2 (1981), pp. 43–55.

Early urbanisation: Ch. L. Redman, *The Rise of Civilization: From Early Farmers to Urban Society in the Ancient Near East*, San Francisco 1978; G. Stein and M. S. Rothman (eds), *Chiefdoms and Early States in the Near East*, Madison 1994.

4 The Urban Revolution

Two fundamental readings are V. G. Childe in *Town Planning Review* 21 (1950), pp. 3–17 and R. McCormick Adams, *The Evolution of Urban Society*, Chicago 1966. For more recent publications see H. Nissen, *The Early History of the Ancient Near East, 9000–2000 BC*, Chicago 1988; M. Liverani, *L'origine delle città*, Rome 1986; J. L. Huot, *Les premiers villageois de Mésopotamie: du village à la ville*, Paris 1994; M. Frangipane, *La nascita dello Stato nel Vicino Oriente*, Rome–Bari 1996; J.-D. Forest, *Mésopotamie. L'apparition de l'état VIIᵉ–IIIᵉ millénaires*, Paris 1996; M. Liverani, *Uruk: The First City*, London 2006.

Some influential models on the origins of the state: E. Service, *Origins of the State and Civilization*, New York 1975; R. Cohen and E. Service (eds), *Origins of the State: The Anthropology of Political Evolution*, Philadelphia 1978; H. Claessen and P. Skalnik (eds), *The Early State*, Paris 1978; N. Yoffee, *Myths of the Archaic State*, Cambridge 2005.

Uruk culture: see Chapter 5. **On the system of rations (even for later periods):** see I. J. Gelb, *JNES* 24 (1965), pp. 230–243; L. Milano in R. Dolce and C. Zaccagnini (eds), *Il pane del re*, Bologna 1989, pp. 65–100.

Seals: P. Ferioli and E. Fiandra (eds), *Archives before Writing*, Rome 1994; in particular M. Frangipane, *Arslantepe: Cretulae*, Rome 2007. **On the origins of writing:** A. Le Brun and F. Vallat in *Cahiers de la Délégation archéologique française en Iran* 8 (1978), pp. 11–59; D. Schmandt Besserat, *Before Writing*, I–II, Austin 1992; a different approach is presented by J. J. Glassner, *Écrire à Sumer: L'invention du cunéiforme*, Paris 2000.

Uruk texts: M. W. Green and H. J. Nissen, *Zeichenliste der archaischen Texten aus Uruk*, Berlin 1987; H. J. Nissen, P. Damerov and R. K. Englund, *Frühe Schrift und Techniken der Wirtschaftsverwaltung im alten Vorderen Orient*, Berlin 1990 [English translation: *Archaic Bookkeeping*, Chicago 1993]. An excellent treatment of the topic is R. K. Englund, *Texts from the Late Uruk Period*, OBO 160/1 (1998), pp. 13–233.

5 The rise and fall of the first urbanisation

On Uruk culture and its expansion: G. Algaze, *The Uruk World System*, Chicago 1993; G. J. Stein, *Rethinking World-Systems: Diasporas, Colonies, and Interaction in Uruk Mesopotamia*, Tucson 1999; M. S. Rothman (ed.), *Uruk Mesopotamia and Its Neighbors*, Santa Fe–Oxford 2001; J. N. Postgate (ed.), *Artefacts of Complexity: Tracking the Uruk in the Near East*, Warminster 2002; G. Algaze, *Ancient Mesopotamia at the Dawn of Civilization*, Chicago 2008; M. Frangipane, *Economic Centralization in Formative States*, Rome 2011.

On the process of regionalisation: A. Palmieri in *Studi S. Puglisi*, Rome 1985, pp. 191–214. Jemdet Nasr: U. Finkbeiner and W. Röllig (eds), *Ǧamdat Naṣr: Period or Regional Style?*, Wiesbaden 1986; K. R. Englund and J. P. Grégoire, *The Proto-Cuneiform Texts from Jemdet Nasr*, Berlin 1991. Nineveh 5: E. Rova and H. Weiss (eds), *The Origins of North Mesopotamian Civilization: Ninevite 5 Chronology, Economy, Society (Subartu 9)*, Turnhout 2003. **On Elam (also for the following phases):** F. Vallat,

Suse et l'Elam, Paris 1980; E. Carter and M. Stolper, *Elam: Surveys of Political History and Archaeology*, Berkeley–Los Angeles 1984; P. Amiet, *L'âge des échanges inter-iraniens*, Paris 1986; D. Potts, *The Archaeology of Elam*, Cambridge 1999.

6 Mesopotamia in the Early Dynastic period

Sumerians and Semites: F. R. Kraus, *Sumerer und Akkader*, Amsterdam 1970; B. Landsberger, *The Conceptual Autonomy of the Babylonian World*, Malibu 1976. **On the Semitic origins of Mesopotamian culture:** P. Fronzaroli in *Rendiconti dell'Accademia Nazionale dei Lincei* 19, 20, 23, 24, 26 (1964–71), *passim*. **Sumerians:** H. Crawford, *Sumer and the Sumerians*, Cambridge 1991; G. Pettinato, *I Sumeri*, Milano 1992.

Temple cities: A. Falkenstein in *Cahiers d'Histoire Mondiale* 1 (1954), pp. 784–814; I. J. Gelb in *Studi E. Volterra*, VI, Milano 1969, pp. 137–154. **On their political structure:** T. Jacobsen in *ZA* 52 (1957), pp. 91–140. **Society:** I. M. Diakonoff, *Ancient Mesopotamia*, Moscow 1969. **Settlement models:** M. Ramazzotti in *CMAO* 9 (2003), pp. 15–72.

Land sales: D. O. Edzard, *Rechtsurkunden des III Jahrtausend*, München 1968; I. J. Gelb, P. Steinkeller and R. M. Whiting, *Earliest Land Tenure Systems in the Near East*, I–II, Chicago 1991; cf. J. Glassner in *JA* 273 (1985), pp. 11–59; E. Cripp, *Land Tenure and Social Stratification in Ancient Mesopotamia*, Oxford 2007.

Architecture: H. Crawford, *The Architecture of Iraq in the Third Millennium BC*, Copenhagen 1977; Ö. Tunca, *L'architecture religieuse protodynastique en Mésopotamie*, I–II, Leuven 1984; E. F. Henrickson in *Mesopotamia* 16 (1981), pp. 43–140; 17 (1982), pp. 5–33. **On the Royal Cemetery of Ur:** H. Nissen, *Zur Datierung des Königsfriedhofs von Ur*, Berlin 1966; S. Pollock in *Iraq* 47 (1985), pp. 129–158.

Royal inscriptions: H. Steible, *Die altsumerischen Bau- und Weihinschriften*, I–III, Wiesbaden 1982–83; J. Cooper, *Presargonic Inscriptions*, New Haven 1986; D. Frayne, *Pre-Sargonic Period (2700–2350 BC)*, Toronto 2008. **Royal titulature:** W. Hallo, *Early Mesopotamian Royal Titles*, New Haven 1957. **On the mythical foundation of the state:** T. Jacobsen, *The Treasure of Darkness*, New York–London 1976. **On the Sumerian King List:** T. Jacobsen, *The Sumerian King List*, Chicago 1939; P. Michalowski in *JAOS* 103 (1983), pp. 237–248; P. Steinkeller in *Festschrift C. Wilcke*, Wiesbaden 2003, pp. 267–292.

On the history of the Early Dynastic II period: H. P. Martin, *Fara*, Birmingham 1988; R. J. Matthews, *Cities, Seals and Writing*, Berlin 1993; G. Visicato, *The Bureaucracy of Shuruppak*, Münster 1995; M. Krebernik, *Die Texte aus Fara und Tell Abu Salabih*, OBO 160/1 (1998), pp. 235–427. **On the Early Dynastic III:** J. Bauer, *Der vorsargonische Abschnitt der mesopotamischen Geschichte*, OBO 160/1 (1998), pp. 429–585. **On the Lagash–Umma conflict:** J. Cooper, *The Lagash–Umma Border Conflict*, Malibu 1983.

7 The rise of Ebla

On Upper Mesopotamia: H. Weiss (ed.), *The Origins of Cities in Dry-Farming Syria and Mesopotamia in the Third Millennium BC*, Guilford Conn. 1986. **Pre-Sargonic Mari:** A. Parrot and G. Dossin, *Les temples d'Ishtarat et de Ninni-Zaza*, Paris 1967, and *Le trésor d'Ur*, Paris 1968; and various articles in the *MARI* and *Amurru* series. **Tell Chuera:** A. Moortgat and U. Moortgat Correns, *Tell Chuera in Nord-Ost Syrien*, I–III, Berlin 1967–1988. **Tell Beydar:** the texts were published by W. Sallaberger et al., in *Subartu* 2 (1996) and 12 (2004), and the excavation by M. Lebeau et al. in *Subartu* 10 (2003) and 15 (2007). **Tell Brak/Nagar:** D. Oates, J. Oates and H. McDonald, *Excavations at Tell Brak*, II, London 2001 (texts by J. Eidem, pp. 99–120).

Ebla: P. Matthiae, *Ebla, un impero ritrovato*, Torino 1995, and *Gli Archivi Reali di Ebla*, Milano 2008; P. Matthiae, F. Pinnock and G. Matthiae Scandone, *Ebla: Alle origini della civiltà urbana*, Milano 1995; G. Pettinato, *Ebla: Nuovi orizzonti della storia*, Milano 1986. Fundamental readings on the reconstruction of the history of Ebla are A. Archi and M. G. Biga in *JCS* 55 (2003), pp. 1–44; M. G. Biga in *Or* 72 (2003), pp. 345–366 and 77 (2008), pp. 289–334. See also the numerous articles on *Studi Eblaiti* I–IV (1979–81); L. Cagni (ed.), *La lingua di Ebla*, Naples 1981; L. Cagni (ed.), *Il bilinguismo a Ebla*, Naples 1984; L. Cagni (ed.), *Ebla 1975–1985*, Naples 1987; P. Fronzaroli (ed.), *Studies on the Language of Ebla*, Florence 1984, and *Literature and Literary Language at Ebla*, Florence 1992; *Miscellanea Eblaitica*, 1–4, Florence 1988–1997; C. H. Gordon (ed.), *Eblaitica*, I–IV, Winona Lake 1987–2002. **Eblaite texts:** A. Archi et al., *Archivi reali di Ebla, Testi*, I–XVI, Rome 1985–2008; *Archivi Reali di Ebla, Studi*, I–IV, Rome 1988–2008. **Archaeological remains:** P. Matthiae (ed.), *Materiali e Studi Archeologici di Ebla*, I–VI, Rome 1992–2005.

On the second urbanisation in Lebanon: M. Saghieh, *Byblos in the Third Millennium* BC, Warminster 1983. **In Palestine:** P. de Miroschedji, *L'époque pré-urbaine en Palestine*, Paris 1971; A. Kempinski, *The Rise of an Urban Culture: The Urbanization of Palestine in the Early Bronze Age*, Jerusalem 1978. **On foreign relations:** J. B. Hennessy, *The Foreign Relations of Palestine during the Early Bronze Age*, London 1967; A. Ben-Tor in *Essays Y. Yadin*, Toronto 1983, pp. 3–18.

8 The Akkadian empire

On settlements, apart from the above-mentioned works by R. McCormick Adams, see also Mc G. Gibson, *The City and Area of Kish*, Miami 1972; H. Weiss in *JAOS* 95 (1975), pp. 434–453. **History:** A. Westenholz, *The Old Akkadian Period*, OBO 160/3, pp. 15–117.

Royal inscriptions: I. J. Gelb and B. Kienast, *Die altakkadischen Königsinschriften*, Stuttgart 1990; D. Frayne, *Sargonic and Gutian Periods*, Toronto 1993. **Royal titulature:** M. J. Seux in *RA* 59 (1965), pp. 1–18; T. Maeda in *Orient* 20 (1984), pp. 67–82. **On the legacy of the Old Akkadian period:** J. S. Cooper, *The Curse of Agade*, Baltimore 1983; M. Liverani (ed.), *Akkad: The First World Empire*, Padova 1993; J. Goodnick Westenholz, *Legends of the Kings of Akkade*, Winona Lake 1997.

Economy and administration: B. Foster, *Umma in the Sargonic Period*, Hamden 1982 and *Administration and Use of Institutional Land in Sargonic Sumer*, Copenhagen 1982. **On the Obelisk of Manishtusu:** I. J. Gelb, P. Steinkeller and R. M. Whiting, *Earliest Land Tenure Systems*, cit. I, pp. 116–140.

On Mesopotamian and Iranian trade in the third millennium BC: M. Tosi in *Studi G. Tucci*, Napoli 1974, pp. 1–20; G. Pettinato in *Mesopotamia* 7 (1972), pp. 43–166; C. Lamberg-Karlowsky in *Ancient Civilization and Trade*, Albuquerque 1975, pp. 341–368; Ph. Kohl in *Current Anthropology* 19 (1979), pp. 463–475; Sh. Ratnagar, *Trading Encounters*, Oxford 2004.

On the periphery of the empire, the Lullubeans: H. Klengel in *MIOF* 11 (1966), pp. 349–371. **The Hurrians:** see Chapter 17; for Tell Mozan see the excavation reports by G. Buccellati and M. Kelly Buccellati, and those by H. Dohmann and P. Pfälzner in *MDOG* 132 (2000)–137 (2005). **Elam:** T. Potts, *Mesopotamia and the East*, Oxford 1994; K. de Graef, *De la dynastie de Simaški au Sukkalmaḫat*, Ghent 2006. **Dilmun:** D. Potts (ed.), *Dilmun*, Berlin 1983. **Magan and Meluhha:** D. Potts, *The Arabian Gulf in Antiquity*, I–II, Oxford 1990. **Marhashi:** P. Steinkeller in *ZA* 72 (1982), pp. 237–265. **Tepe Yahya:** C. Lamberg-Karlowsky and D. Potts, *Excavations at Tepe Yahya: The Third Millennium*, Cambridge (MA) 2001. **The Iranian periphery:** M. Tosi and R. Biscione, *Protostoria degli Stati turanici*, Napoli 1979; Ph. Kohl, *L'Asie centrale dès origines à l'âge du fer*, Paris 1984.

9 The Third Dynasty of Ur

Gudea: C. Suter, *Gudea's Temple Building*, Groningen 2000; B. Pongratz-Leisten, in *Baghdader Mitteilungen* 37 (2006), pp. 45–59. **Inscriptions:** H. Steible, *Die neusumerischen Bau- und Weihinschriften*, I, Stuttgart 1991; D. O. Edzard, *Gudea and His Dynasty*, Toronto 1997. **On Utu-hegal:** H. Sauren in *RA* 61 (1967), pp. 75–79; W. Römer in *Or* 54 (1985), pp. 274–288.

Ur III history: W. Sallaberger, *Ur III-Zeit*, OBO 160/3 (1999), pp. 121–390 (including a detailed presentation of the sources). **Geography:** F. R. Kraus in *ZA* 51 (1955), pp. 45–75; J. P. Grégoire, *La province méridionale de l'état de Lagash*, Luxembourg 1962; H. Sauren, *Topographie der Provinz Umma*, Heidelberg 1966; F. Carroué in *Acta Sumerologica* 15 (1993), pp. 11–69; J. Dahl, *The Ruling Family of Ur III Umma*, Leiden 2007.

Royal inscriptions: H. Steible, *Die neusumerischen Bau- und Weihinschriften*, II, Stuttgart 1991; D. Frayne, *Ur III Period*, Toronto 1997. **Hymns:** G. R. Castellino, *Two Shulgi Hymns*, Rome 1972; J. Klein, *Three Shulgi Hymns*, Ramat Gan 1981; E. Flückiger-Hawker, *Urnamma of Ur in Sumerian Literary Tradition*, Freiburg–Göttingen 1999. **Royal correspondence:** P. Michalowski, *The Correspondence of the Kings of Ur*, Winona Lake 2011.

Legal texts: A. Falkenstein, *Die neusumerische Gerichtsurkunden*, I–III, München 1956–57; J. Krecher in *ZA* 63 (1974), pp. 145–271; F.R. Kraus in *WO* 8 (1976), pp. 185–205. **On Ur administration:** J. P. Grégoire, *Archives administratives sumériennes*, Paris 1970; T. Sharlach, *Provincial Taxation and the Ur III State*, Leiden–Boston 2004. **Correspondence:** E. Sollberger, *The Business and Administrative Correspondence under the Kings of Ur*, Locust Valley 1966; P. Michalowski, *Letters from Early Mesopotamia*, Atlanta 1993.

Agriculture: M. Civil, *The Farmer's Instructions*, Barcelona 1994; G. Pettinato, *Texte zur Verwaltung der Landwirtschaft in der Ur-III-Zeit*, Rome 1969, *Untersuchungen zur neusumerischen Landwirtschaft*, Napoli 1967, and in *Studia Orientalia* 46 (1975), pp. 259–290; K. Maekawa in *Zinbun* 13 (1974), pp. 1–60, and in *RA* 70 (1976), pp. 9–44; M. Powell in *ZA* 75 (1985), pp. 7–38; see also the *Bulletin on Sumerian Agriculture* vols 1–3 (1984–1987). **Labour:** see P. Steinkeller and H. Waetzold in M. A. Powell (ed.), *Labor in the Ancient Near East*, New Haven 1987, pp. 73–115 and 117–141.

Production: H. Neumann, *Handwerk in Mesopotamien*, Berlin 1987. **Textile production:** H. Waetzoldt, *Untersuchungen zur neusumerischen Textilindustrie*, Rome 1972; K. Maekawa in *Acta Sumerologica* 2 (1980), pp. 81–125. **Pottery:** H. Waetzoldt, in *WO* 6 (1971), pp. 7–41; P. Steinkeller in *AoF* 23 (1996), pp. 232–253. **Metalworking:** H. Limet, *Le travail du métal au pays de Sumer au temps de la III dynastie d'Ur*, Paris 1960. **Farming:** I. J. Gelb in *JCS* 21 (1967), pp. 64–69; M. Sigrist, *Drehem*, Bethesda 1992; R. K. Englund in *Or* 64 (1995), pp. 377–429. **Fishing:** R. K. Englund, *Organisation und Verwaltung der Ur III-Fischerei*, Berlin 1990. **Trade**: D. Snell, *Ledgers and Prices*, New Haven 1982; M. van de Mieroop in *JCS* 38 (1986), pp. 1–80.

10 The crisis of the second urbanisation

The crisis of 2000 BC: cf. J. W. Meyer and W. Sommerfeld (eds), *2000 v. Chr.: Politiche, wirtschaftlkiche und kulturelle Entwicklung im Zeichen einer Jahrtausendwende*, Saarbrucken 2004. **On the Ur III collapse:** T. Jacobsen in *JCS* 7 (1953), pp. 36–47; T. Gomi in *JCS* 36 (1984), pp. 211–242; C. Wilcke in *WO* 5 (1969–70), pp. 1–31, and in *ZA* 60 (1970), pp. 54–69; J. van Dijk in *JCS* 30 (1978), pp. 189–208. **Lamentations**: P. Michalowski, *The Lamentation over the Destruction of Sumer and Ur*, Winona Lake 1989; W. Römer, *Die Klage über die Zerstörung von Ur*, Münster 2004; M. Green in *JCS* 30 (1978), pp. 127–167, and in *JAOS* 104 (1984), pp. 253–279.

The Amorites: G. Buccellati, *The Amorites of the Ur-III Period*, Napoli 1966. **Archaeological evidence:** K. Kenyon, *Amorites and Canaanites*, London 1966; W. G. Dever in *BASOR* 237 (1980), pp. 35–64. **Personal names:** H. Huffmon, *Amorite Personal Names in the Mari Texts*, Baltimore 1965; I. J. Gelb, *Computer-Aided Analysis of Amorite*, Chicago 1980; M. P. Streck, *Das amurritische Onomastikon der altbabylonischen Zeit*, Münster 2000.

The Indo-European problem: see J. P. Mallory, *In Search of the Indo-Europeans*, London 1989; F. Villar, *Gli Indoeuropei e le origini dell'Europa*, Bologna 1997. **Amorite words:** E. Benveniste, *Le vocabulaire des institutions indo-européennes*, I–II, Paris 1969. **The spread of the Amorites:** M. Gimbutas in *Journal of*

Indo-European Studies 1 (1973), pp. 163–214, 5 (1977), pp. 277–338, 18 (1990), pp. 197–214; A. Martinet, *Des steppes aux oceans: L'indo-européen et les 'Indo-européens'*, Paris 1986. On C. Renfrew's theory see *Archaeology and Language*, London 1987, based on the model of A. J. Ammermann and L. Cavalli Sforza, *La transizione neolitica e la genetica delle popolazioni in Europa*, Torino 1986. **Tripartite ideology:** G. Dumézil, *L'idéologie tripartite des Indo-européens*, Bruxelles 1958, and *Mythe et épopée*, Paris 1968. **Indus civilisation:** B. Allchin and R. Allchin, *The Rise of Civilization in India and Pakistan*, Cambridge 1982. **On its crisis:** Sh. Ratnagar, *The End of the Great Harappan Tradition*, Manohar 2000.

11 The 'Intermediate period' of Isin and Larsa

See D. O. Edzard, *Die 'zweite Zwischenzeit' Babyloniens*, Wiesbaden 1957; M. Stol, *Studies in Old Babylonian History*, Leiden 1976; and especially D. Charpin, *Histoire politique du Proche-Orient amorrite*, OBO 160/4 (2004), pp. 23–480. **Royal inscriptions:** D. Frayne, *Old Babylonian Period 2003–1595 BC*, Toronto 1990.

Social and legal developments: H. Klengel in *Acta Antiqua* 22 (1974), pp. 249–257, and, pp. 39–52; D. O. Edzard in *ZA* 60 (1970), pp. 8–53; J. Klima in *ArOr* 46 (1978), pp. 23–35; I. M. Diakonoff in *ZA* 75 (1985), pp. 47–65, and in H. Klengel (ed.), *Beiträge zur sozialen Struktur des alten Vorderasien*, Berlin 1971, pp. 15–31; A. Seri, *Local Power in Old Babylonian Mesopotamia*, London 2005. **Edicts:** F. R. Kraus, *Königliche Verfügungen in altbabylonischer Zeit*, Leiden 1984.

Economy: M. van de Mieroop, *Society and Enterprise in Old Babylonian Ur*, Berlin 1992; A. Goddeeris, *Economy and Society in Northern Babylonia in the Early Old Babylonian Period*, Leuven 2002; M. Stol, *Wirtschaft und Gesellschaft in altbabylonischer Zeit*, OBO 160/4 (2004), pp. 641–678.

Real estate: Das Grundeigentum in Mesopotamien, Berlin 1987. **Irrigation:** S. Walters, *Water for Larsa*, New Haven 1970. **On the role of the state:** N. Yoffee, *The Economic Role of the Crown in the Old Babylonian Period*, Malibu 1977; M. de Jong Ellis, *Agriculture and the State in Ancient Mesopotamia*, Philadelphia 1976. **Farming:** F. R. Kraus, *Staatliche Viehhaltung im altbabylonischen Lande Larsa*, Amsterdam 1966; J. Postgate in *Journal of Semitic Studies* 21 (1975), pp. 1–21. **Craftsmanship:** M. van de Mieroop, *Crafts in the Early Isin Period*, Leuven 1987. **Trade:** W. F. Leemans, *The Old Babylonian Merchant*, Leiden 1950, and *Foreign Trade in the Old Babylonian Period*, Leiden 1960; M. San Nicolò, *Die Schlussklauseln der altbabylonischen Kauf- und Tauschverträge*, München 1974; J. Renger in A. Archi (ed.), *Circulation of Goods in Non-Palatial Context*, Rome 1984, pp. 31–124.

Scribal culture: A. Sjöberg in *JCS* 24 (1972), pp. 126–131, and *Studies T. Jacobsen*, Chicago 1975, pp. 159–179; H. Vanstiphout in *JCS* 31 (1979), pp. 118–126; F. R. Kraus, *Vom mesopotamischen Menschen der altbabylonischen Zeit und seiner Welt*, Amsterdam 1973; D. O. Edzard, *Altbabylonische Literatur und Religion*, OBO 160/4 (2004), pp. 481–640. **Priesthood:** J. Renger in *ZA* 58 (1967), pp. 110–188, and 59 (1969), pp. 104–203; D. Charpin, *Le clergé d'Ur au siècle d'Hammurabi*, Geneva 1986.

Divination (including the following periods): J. Bottéro in J. P. Vernant (ed.), *Divination et rationalité*, Paris 1974, pp. 70–197; J. Bottéro in A. Finet (ed.), *La voix de l'opposition en Mésopotamie*, Bruxelles 1973, pp. 117–162 and *Les pouvoirs locaux en Mésopotamie*, Bruxelles 1982, pp. 6–28. **Extispicy:** U. Jeyes, *Old Babylonian Extispicy*, Leiden 1989.

12 The Old Assyrian period

The Assyrian King List: F.R. Kraus, *Könige die in Zelten wohnten*, Amsterdam 1965. **Eponyms list:** K. R. Veenhof, *The Old Assyrian List of Eponyms*, Ankara 2003.

General overviews: K. R. Veenhof, *The Old Assyrian Period*, OBO 160/5 (2008), pp. 13–264. **The Old Assyrian state:** M. T. Larsen, *The Old Assyrian City State and Its Colonies*, Copenhagen 1976; J. G. Dercksen, *Old Assyrian Institutions*, Leiden 2004. **Trade:** M. T. Larsen, *Old Assyrian Caravan*

Procedures, Istanbul 1967; K. Veenhof, *Aspects of Old Assyrian Trade and Its Terminology*, Leiden 1972; J. G. Dercksen, *The Old Assyrian Copper Trade in Anatolia*, Leiden 1996. **Texts:** C. Michel, *Correspondance des marchands de Kaniš au début du IIe millénaire*, Paris 2001.

The Anatolian states: K. Balkan, *Letter of King Anum-Hirbi of Mama to King Warshama of Kanish*, Ankara 1957; E. Neu, *Der Anitta-Text*, Wiesbaden 1974.

13 The Mari Age

Sources on Mari: Archives royales de Mari, I–XXVI, Paris 1950–1988; J.-M. Durand, *Documents épistolaires du palais de Mari*, I–III, Paris 1997–2000; numerous texts and studies are published in the journal *MARI*, vols 1 (1982) and following, and in the series *Florilegium Marianum*, I–VIII, Paris 1992–2005; see also *Amurru*, I–III, Paris 1996–2004, and W. Heimpel, *Letters to the Kings of Mari*, Winona Lake 2003.

Other archives: J. Eidem, *The Shemshara Archives*, I–II, Copenhagen 1992–2001; O. Loretz, *Texte aus Chagar Bazar und Tell Brak*, Neukirchen 1969; S. Dalley, C. Walker and J. Hawkins, *The Old Babylonian Tablets from Tell al Rimah*, London 1976; M. Krebernick, *Ausgrabungen in Tall Bi'a-Tuttul, II: Die altorientalischen Schrifturkunde*, Saarbrücken 2001.

Nomadic groups: J. R. Kupper, *Les nomades en Mésopotamie au temps des rois de Mari*, Paris 1957; J. T. Luke, *Pastoralism and Politics in the Mari Period*, Ann Arbor 1965; V. H. Matthews, *Pastoral Nomadism in the Mari Kingdom*, Cambridge (MA) 1978; M. Heltzer, *The Suteans*, Napoli 1981.

History: D. Charpin and N. Ziegler, *Mari et le Proche-Orient à l'époque amorrite*, Paris 2003; also M. Anbar, *Les tribus amurrites de Mari*, Fribourg–Göttingen 1991; Wu Yuhong, *A Political History of Eshnunna, Mari and Assyria during the Early Old Babylonian Period*, Changchun 1994. **Diplomatic relations:** C. Zaccagnini in *Studi F. Pintore*, Pavia 1983, pp. 189–253. **War:** J. Sasson, in *Mélanges Birot*, Paris 1985, pp. 237–256. **Assemblies:** D. E. Fleming, *Democracy's Ancient Ancestors: Mari and Early Collective Governance*, Cambridge (MA) 2004.

Provincial centres, Tell Shemshara: J. Laessoe, *Peoples of Ancient Assyria*, London 1963. **Tell Rimah:** S. Dalley, *Mari and Karana: Two Old Babylonian Cities*, London 1984.

Alalah VII: F. Zeeb, *Die Palastwirtschaft in Altsyrien nach den spataltbabylonischen Getreidelieferlisten aus Alalah (Schicht VII)*, Münster 2001, and in *UF* 23 (1991), pp. 405–438, 24 (1992), pp. 445–480, 25 (1993), pp. 461–472. **Hittite intervention:** A. Kempinski, *Syrien und Palästina in der letzten Phase der Mittelbronze II-B Zeit*, Wiesbaden 1983; E. Neu, *Das hurritische Epos der Freilassung*, Wiesbaden 1996.

The Hyksos and the Middle Bronze Age in the Levant: J. van Seters, *The Hyksos: A New Investigation*, New Haven 1966; E. Oren (ed.), *The Hyksos: New Historical and Archaeological Perspectives*, Philadelphia 1997. **Tell ed-Dab'a:** M. Bietak, *Avaris, The Capital of the Hyksos*, London 1996; id., *Tell ed-Dab'a*, II, Wien 1975; E. van den Brink, *Tombs and Burial Customs in Tell ed-Dab'a*, Wien 1982.

14 Hammurabi of Babylon

Babylonia: H. Gasche, *La Babylonie au 17. siècle avant notre ère*, Ghent 1989; R. Pientka, *Die spätaltbabylonische Zeit*, Münster 1988; for more concise publications (including the following periods) see M. G. Biga, *I Babilonesi*, Rome 2004, and M. Jursa, *Die Babylonier*, München 2004. **Hammurabi**: H. Klengel, *Hammurabi von Babylon und seine Zeit*, Berlin 1976; D. Charpin, *Hammu-rabi de Babylone*, Paris 2003; M. van de Mieroop, *King Hammurabi of Babylon: A Biography*, Oxford 2005.

Genealogy: J. Finkelstein in *JCS* 20 (1966), pp. 95–118. **Code:** J. Bottéro in *Annali della Scuola Normale Superiore di Pisa* 13 (1982), pp. 409–444. **Royal inscriptions:** D. R. Frayne, *Old Babylonian Period*, Toronto 1990. **Correspondence:** F. R. Kraus (ed.), *Altbabylonische Briefe*, I–XI, Leiden 1964–86.

State and economy: apart from the references mentioned for Ch. 11, see M. Stol in *JCS* 34 (1982), pp. 127–230; D. Charpin in *BO* 38 (1981), pp. 517–547, and in *JA* 270 (1982), pp. 25–65. **Sippar:**

R. Harris, *Ancient Sippar*, Istanbul 1975, and in *JESHO* 6 (1963), pp. 121–157; E. Stone in *JESHO* 25 (1982), pp. 50–70. **Dilbat:** H. Klengel in *AoF* 4 (1976), pp. 63–110. **Kutalla:** D. Charpin, *Archives familiales et propriété privée en Babylonie ancienne*, Genève 1980.

Edicts: F. R. Kraus, *Ein Edikt des Königs Ammisaduqa von Babylon*, Leiden 1958, and in *Studies B. Landsberger*, Chicago 1965, pp. 225–231; J. Bottéro in *JESHO* 4 (1961), pp. 113–164; J. Finkelstein in *Studies B. Landsberger*, Chicago 1965, pp. 233–246.

Kingdom of Hana: G. Buccellati and O. Rouault, *L'archive de Puzurum*, Malibu 1984; A. Podany, *The Land of Hana*, Bethesda 2002. **Kingdom of Shehna:** J. Eidem, *Apum: A Kingdom on the Old Assyrian Route*, in OBO 160/5 (2008), pp. 265–352. **The Sealand:** S. Dalley, *Babylonian Tablets from the First Sealand Dynasty*, Bethesda MD 2009.

15 Anatolia in the Old Hittite period

For the Hittites see Ch. 18. **On the formation of the Hittite state:** H. Otten, *Eine althethitische Erzahlung um die Stadt Zalpa*, Wiesbaden 1972; F. Starke in *ZA* 69 (1979), pp. 47–120; M. Liverani in *OA* 16 (1977), pp. 105–131.

The Annals of Hattusili: A. Kempinski and S. Košak in *Tel Aviv* 9 (1982), pp. 87–116; Ph. Houwink ten Cate in *Anatolica* 10 (1983), pp. 91–109, 11 (1984), pp. 47–83; S. de Martino, *Annali e Res Gestae antico ittiti*, Pavia 2003. See also E. Neu, *Das hurritische Epos der Freilassung*, Wiesbaden 1996; M. Salvini, *The Habiru Prism of King Tunip-Teššup of Tikunani*, Rome 1996.

Kingship: S. Bin-Nun, *The Tawananna in the Hittite Kingdom*, Heidelberg 1975; I. Kloch-Fontanille, *Les premiers rois hittites et la représentation de la royauté dans les textes de l'ancien royaume*, Paris 2001.

Hittite law code: H. A. Hoffner, *The Laws of the Hittites*, Leiden 1997. On problems with the Hittite writing style, see S. Heinhold Krahmer et al., *Probleme der Textdatierung in der Hethitologie*, Heidenberg 1979; S. de Martino in *La Parola del Passato* 47 (1992), pp. 81–98.

16 The Late Bronze Age: technologies and ideologies

On Indo-Iranian elements: M. Mayrhofer, *Die Indo-Arier im alten Vorderasien*, Wiesbaden 1966; A. Kammenhuber, *Die Arier im vorderen Orient*, Heidelberg 1968; I. M. Diakonoff in *Or* 41 (1972), pp. 91–120; M. Mayrhofer, *Die Arier im vorderen Orient: Ein Mythos?*, Wien 1974.

Chariots and horses: W. Nagel, *Der altmesopotamische Streitwagen und seine Entwicklung*, Berlin 1966; J. Zarins in *JCS* 20 (1978), pp. 3–17; M. Littauer and J.H. Crowel, *Wheeled Vehicles and Ridden Animals in the Ancient Near East*, Leiden–Köln 1979; H. P. Uerpmann and R. H. Meadow (eds), *Equids in the Ancient World*, Wiesbaden 1986; R. Drews, *Early Riders*, New York–London 2004. **Treatises on horses:** A. Kammenhuber, *Hippologia hethitica*, Wiesbaden 1961.

The Hittite regional system: M. Liverani, *Prestige and Interest*, Padova 1990; *International Relations in the Ancient Near East, 1600–1100 BC*, New York 2001; R. Cohen and R. Westbrook (eds), *Amarna Diplomacy*, Baltimore 2000; S. Roth in D. Prechel (ed.), *Motivation und Mechanismen des Kulturkontaktes in der späten Bronzezeit*, Florence 2005, pp. 179–226; M. van de Mieroop, *The Eastern Mediterranean in the Age of Ramesses II*, Oxford 2007.

Trade: C. Zaccagnini, *Lo scambio dei doni nel Vicino Oriente durante i secoli XV–XIII*, Rome 1973; M. Liverani in *OA* 11 (1972), pp. 297–317; J.D. Muhly, *Copper and Tin*, New Haven 1973. **Glass:** A. L. Openheim in *Glass and Glassmaking in Ancient Mesopotamia*, Corning 1970. **Marriages:** F. Pintore, *Il matrimonio interdinastico nel Vicino Oriente durante i secoli XV–XIII*, Rome 1978; J. van Dijk in *Or* 55 (1986) pp. 159–170; Ph. J. Houwink ten Cate in *AoF* 23 (1996), pp. 40–75. **Exchange of specialists:** E. Edel, *Ägyptische Ärtze und ägyptische Medizin am hethitischen Königshof*, Opladen 1976; C. Zaccagnini in *JNES* 42 (1983), pp. 245–264.

Navigation and shipwrecks: G. Bass, *Cape Gelidonya: A Bronze Age Shipwreck*, Philadelphia 1967; in *American Journal of* Archaeology 90 (1986), pp. 269–296. **Mycenaean and Cypriot pottery:** The Mycenaeans in the Eastern Mediterranean, Nicosia 1973; A. Leonard in *BASOR* 241 (1981), pp. 87–101; A. B. Knapp and T. Stech (eds), *Prehistoric Production and Exchange*, Los Angeles 1985; M. Marazzi, *La società micenea*, Rome 1994. **Maritime trade:** N. H. Gale (ed.), *Bronze Age Trade in the Mediterranean*, Jansered 1991; E. H. Cline, *Sailing the Wine-Dark Sea*, Oxford 1994; C. M. Monroe, *Scales of Fate*, Oxford 2009.

17 The rise of Mitanni

The Hurrians: G. Wilhelm, *Grundzüge der Geschichte und Kultur der Hurriter*, Darmstadt 1982; RAI 24 = RHA 36 (1978); *La civiltà dei Hurriti* (= *La Parola del Passato* 55) (2000). **Origins:** T. Richter in J. W. Meyer and W. Sommerfeld (eds), *2000 v. Chr.: Politiche, wirtschaftlkiche und kulturelle Entwicklung im Zeichen einer Jahrtausendwende*, Saarbrucken 2004, pp. 263–312. **Mitanni:** J. Freu, *Histoire du Mitanni*, Paris 2003.

Nuzi: M. Morrison and D. Owen (eds), *Studies on the Civilization and Culture of Nuzi and Hurrians*, I–XVII, Winona Lake 1981–2008. **Landscape:** C. Zaccagnini, *The Rural Landscape of the Land of Arraphe*, Rome 1979; A. Fadhil, *Studien zur Topographie und Prosopographie der Provinzstädte des Königsreichs Arraphe*, Mainz 1983; R. Kolinski, *Mesopotamian dimātu of the Second Millennium BC*, Oxford 2001.

Socio-economic relations: N. Yankowska in *JESHO* 12 (1969), pp. 233–282; B. L. Eichler, *Indenture at Nuzi*, New Haven 1973; M. P. Maidman, *A Socio-Economic Analysis of a Nuzi Family Archive*, Philadelphia 1976; C. Zaccagnini in *SS* 25 (1984), pp. 697–723. **Agriculture:** C. Zaccagnini in *OA* 14 (1975), pp. 181–225, and in *JESHO* 22 (1979), pp. 1–31. **Farming:** M. Morrison in *Studies Lacheman*, Winona Lake 1981, pp. 257–296.

Kizzuwatna: after A. Goetze, *Kizzuwatna and the Problem of Hittite Geography*, New Haven 1940, cf. M. Liverani in *OA* 12 (1973), pp. 267–297; G. Del Monte in *OA* 20 (1981), pp. 203–221; R. Beal in *Or* 55 (1986), pp. 424–445; P. Desideri and A. M. Jasink, *Cilicia*, Torino 1990.

Middle Hittite kingdom: Ph. Houwink ten Cate, *The Records of the Early Hittite Empire*, Istanbul 1970; O. Carruba in *SMEA* 18 (1977), pp. 137–185, and *Studies H. G. Güterbock*, Istanbul 1974, pp. 73–93; I. Hoffmann in *Or* 53 (1984), pp. 34–51; J. Freu, in *Hethitica* 8 (1987), pp. 123–175; S. de Martino, *L'Anatolia occidentale nel medio regno ittita*, Florence 1996. **The Edict of Telipinu:** I. Hoffmann, *Das Erlass Telipinus*, Heidelberg 1984; K. Riemschneider in H. Klengel (ed.), *Beiträge zur sozialen Struktur des alten Vorderasien*, Berlin 1971, pp. 79–102; M. Liverani in *OA* 16 (1977), pp. 105–131; R. Beal in *JCS* 35 (1983), pp. 115–126; G. Beckman, in *Tribute to H. G. Güterbock*, Chicago 1986, pp. 13–31. **Land allotments:** K. Riemschneider in *MIOF* 6 (1958), pp. 321–381; D. Easton in *JCS* 33 (1981), pp. 3–43.

18 The Hittite empire

General overview: O. R. Gurney, *The Hittites*, Harmondsworth 1980; H. Klengel, *Geschichte des hethitischen Reiches*, Leiden 1999; S. de Martino, *Gli Ittiti*, Rome 2003; T. Bryce, *Life and Society in the Hittite World*, Oxford 2004, and *The Kingdom of the Hittites*, Oxford 2005; B. J. Collins, *The Hittites and their World*, Atlanta 2007. **Sources:** E. Laroche, *Catalogue des textes hittites*, Paris 1971, in *RHA* 30 (1972), pp. 94–133, and 33 (1975), pp. 63–71. **On Hattusa:** P. Neve, *Hattuša: Stadt der Gotter und Tempel*, Mainz 1993.

Kingship: H. G. Güterbock in RAI 19, Paris 1974, pp. 305–314; A. Archi in *SMEA* 1 (1966), pp. 76–120; M. Giorgieri and C. Mora, *Aspetti della regalità ittita nel XIII secolo a.C.*, Como 1996. **Royal titles:** H. Gonnet in *Hethitica* 3 (1979), pp. 3–108.

Hittite history: K. Kitchen, *Suppiluliuma and the Amarna Pharaohs*, Liverpool 1962; H. Klengel in *Or* 32 (1963), pp. 32–55; A. Ünal, *Hattušili III*, Heidelberg 1974; H. Otten, *Die Apologie Hattušilis III*, Wiesbaden 1981; A. Archi in *SMEA* 14 (1971), pp. 185–215; Ph. Houwink ten Cate in *Studies H. G. Güterbock*, Istanbul 1974, pp. 123–150; I. Singer in *ZA* 75 (1985), pp. 100–123; H. Otten in *MDOG* 94 (1963), pp. 1–23.

Political structure, edicts: E. von Schuler, in *Festschrift J. Friedrich*, Heidelberg 1959, pp. 435–472. **Treaties:** G. Kestemont, *Diplomatique et droit international en Asie occidentale (1600–1200 av. J.-C.)*, Louvain 1974; H. Otten, *Die Bronzetafel aus Boğazköy*, Wiesbaden 1988; G. Beckman, *Hittite Diplomatic Texts*, Atlanta 1996. **Instructions and oaths:** E. von Schuler, *Hethitische Dienstanweisungen*, Graz 1957; F. Imparati in *RHA* 32 (1974), pp. 1–210; N. Oettinger, *Die militärische Eide der Hethiter*, Wiesbaden 1976.

Diplomatic correspondence: A. Hagenbuchner, *Die Korrespondenz der Hethiter*, I–II, Heidelberg 1989; E. Edel, *Die ägyptisch-hethitische Korrespondenz*, Opladen 1994; C. Mora and M. Giorgieri, *Le lettere tra i re ittiti e i re assiri*, Padova 2004; H. Hoffner, *Letters from the Hittite Kingdom*, Atlanta 2009.

Economy: H. Hoffner, *Alimenta Hethaeorum*, New Haven 1974; H. Klengel in *SMEA* 16 (1975), pp. 181–200 (temple), in *AoF* 6 (1979), pp. 69–80 (trade). **Society:** I. M. Diakonoff in *MIOF* 13 (1967), pp. 313–366.

Sites and archives in the periphery, Maşat: T. Özgüç, *Maşat Höyük*, I–II, Ankara 1978–1982; S. Alp, *Hethitische Briefe aus Maşat Höyük*, Ankara 1991; J. Klinger in *ZA* 85 (1995), pp. 74–108. **Ortaköy:** A. Ünal, *Hittite and Hurrian Tablets from Ortaköy*, Istanbul 1998. **Kuşakli:** A. Müller-Karpe in *MDOG* 132–138 (2000–06), passim.

On the surrounding lands, the Kashka: E. von Schuler, *Die Kaškäer*, Berlin 1965. **Ishuwa:** H. Klengel in *OA* 7 (1968), pp. 63–76. **Arzawa:** S. Heinhold-Krahmer, *Arzawa*, Heidelberg 1977, in *Or* 55 (1986), pp. 47–62, and 52 (1983), pp. 81–97. **Alashiya:** I. Vincentelli in *Bibliotheca Cipriota* 3 (1976), pp. 9–49; L. Helbing, *Alasia Problems*, Göteborg 1979; A. B. Knapp, *Copper Production and Divine Protection*, Göteborg 1986. **Ahhiyawa:** H. G. Güterbock in *Proceedings of the American Philosophical Society* 128/2 (1984), pp. 114–122; W. Helck, *Die Beziehungen Aegyptens und Vorderasiens zur Aegäis*, Darmstadt 1979.

Historiography: H. Cancik, *Grundzüge der hethitischen und alttestamentlichen Geschichtsschreibung*, Wiesbaden 1976; G. Del Monte, *L'annalistica ittita*, Brescia 1993, and *Le gesta di Suppiluliuma*, Pisa 2008. **Magic and politics:** A. Kammenhuber, *Orakelpraxis, Träume und Vorzeichen bei den Hethitern*, Heidelberg 1976; A. Archi, in *OA* 13 (1974), pp. 113–144; A. Ünal, *Ein Orakeltext über die Intrigen am hethitischen Hof*, Heidelberg 1978. **Cult and politics:** O. R. Gurney, *Some Aspects of Hittite Religion*, Oxford 1977; V. Haas, *Der Kult von Nerik*, Rome 1970; R. Lebrun, *Samuha*, Louvain 1976; V. Haas, *Geschichte der hethitischen Religion*, Leiden 1994.

19 Syria and the Levant in the Late Bronze Age

History: H. Klengel, *Geschichte Syriens im 2. Jahrtausend v.u.Z.*, I–III, Berlin 1965–70, and *Syria 3000 to 300 BC*, Berlin 1992. **Geography:** J. Sapin in *JESHO* 24 (1981), pp. 1–62, and 25 (1982), pp. 1–49, 114–186; W. H. van Soldt, *The Topography of the City-State of Ugarit*, Münster 2005.

Socio-political organisation: G. Buccellati, *Cities and Nations of Ancient Syria*, Rome 1967; M. Heltzer, *The Internal Organization of the Kingdom of Ugarit*, Wiesbaden 1982, and *The Rural Community in Ancient Ugarit*, Wiesbaden 1976; M. Liverani, in *JESHO* 18 (1975), pp. 146–164. **Modes of production:** J.-A. Zamora, *Sobre el modo de producción asiático en Ugarit*, Madrid 1997; J. D. Schloen, *The House of the Father*, Winona Lake 2001.

Kingship: M. Liverani in RAI 19, Paris 1974, pp. 329–356 (Ugarit) e H. Klengel, *ibid.*, pp. 273–282 (Alalah); J. C. de Moor in *Zeitschrift für die alttestamentliche Wissenschaft* 88 (1976), pp. 323–345; K. Kitchen in *UF* 9 (1977), pp. 131–142; J. Sapin in *UF* 15 (1983), pp. 157–190.

Habiru: O. Loretz, *Habiru-Hebräer*, Berlin 1984. **Nomads:** R. Giveon, *Les Bedouins Shosou des documents égyptiens*, Leiden 1971.

Emar: M. Chavalas (ed.), *Emar*, Bethesda 1995; M. Adamthwaite, *Late Hittite Emar*, Louvain 2001; L. Mori, *Reconstructing the Emar Landcape*, Rome 2003. **Ekalte:** W. Mayer, *Tall Munbaqa-Ekalte, II. Die Texte*, Saarbrücken 2001.

Ugarit: various authors in *Supplément au Dictionnaire de la Bible*, IX, Paris 1979, pp. 1124–1466; M. Yon and M. Sznycer and P. Bordreuil, *Le pays d'Ougarit autour de 1200 av. J.-C.*, Paris 1995; M. Yon, *La cité d'Ougarit*, Paris 1997; W. Watson and N. Wyatt (eds), *Handbook of Ugaritic Studies*, Leiden 1999 (history: I. Singer, pp. 603–731). **Texts:** P. Bordreuil and D. Pardee, *La trouvaille épigraphique de l'Ougarit*, Paris 1989; S. Lackenbacher, *Textes akkadiens d'Ugarit*, Paris 2002; W. H. van Soldt, *Studies in the Akkadian of Ugarit*, Kevelaer 1991; I. Márquez Rowe, *The Royal Deeds of Ugarit*, Münster 2006; S. Parker, *Ugaritic Narrative Poetry*, Atlanta 1997.

Alalah IV: E. von Dassow, *State and Society in the Late Bronze Age at Alalaḫ*, Bethesda 2008; Ch. Niedorf, *Die mittelbabylonischen Rechtsurkunden aus Alalaḫ*, Münster 2008. **Idrimi:** M. Dietrich et al. in *UF* 13 (1981), pp. 201–290; M. Liverani, *Myth and Politics in Ancient Near Eastern Historiography*, London 2004, pp. 85–96, 147–159.

Qatna, history: H. Klengel in *MDOG* 132 (2000), pp. 239–252. **Excavations:** M. Novak and P. Pfälzner in *MDOG* 132–139 (2000–2007), *passim*; D. Morandi and M. Luciani in *Akkadica* 124 (2003), pp. 65–120, 143–204. **Texts:** Th. Richter, *MDOG* 135 (2003), pp. 167–188.

Amurru: I. Singer in Sh. Izre'el, *Amurru Akkadian*, II, Atlanta 1991, pp. 135–195.

On the Egyptian presence in Syria: W. Helck, *Die Beziehungen Aegyptens zu Vorderasien*, Wiesbaden 1962; D. B. Redford, *Egypt, Canaan and Israel in Ancient Times*, Princeton 1992. **The Amarna correspondence:** W. L. Moran, *The Amarna Letters*, Baltimore 1992; M. Liverani, *Le lettere di el-Amarna*, I–II, Brescia 1998–99. **The battle of Qadesh:** W. Mayer and R. Mayer-Opificius in *UF* 26 (1994), pp. 321–368; M. C. Guidotti and F. Pecchioli (eds), *La battaglia di Qadesh*, Livorno 2002. **On the treaty between Egypt and Hatti:** E. Edel, *Der Vertrag zwischen Ramses II. und Hattusili III.*, Berlin 1997.

20 The Middle Assyrian kingdom

Royal inscriptions: K. A. Grayson, *Assyrian Rulers of the Third and Second Millennia BC*, Toronto 1987; R. Borger, *Einleitung in die assyrischen Königsinschriften*, I, Leiden 1961. S. Maul, *Die Inschriften von Tall Taban*, Tokyo 2005. **Chronology:** C. Saporetti, *Gli eponimi medio-assiri*, Malibu 1979; J. Boese and G. Wilhelm in *Wiener Zeitschrift für die Kunde des Morgenlandes* 1 (1979), pp. 19–38. **History:** A. Harrak, *Assyria and Hanigalbat*, Hildesheim 1987; H. Freydank, *Beiträge zur mittelassyrischen Chronologie und Geschichte*, Berlin 1991.

Archives: O. Pedersen, *Archives and Libraries in the City of Assur*, I, Uppsala 1985; J. N. Postgate in RAI 30, Leiden 1986, pp. 168–183. **Provincial centres:** E. Cancik-Kirschbaum, *Die mittelassyrischen Briefe aus Tall Šeh-Hamad*, Berlin 1996; W. Röllig, *Land- und Viehwirtschaft am Unteren Habur in mittelassyrischer Zeit*, Berlin 2008; K. Radner, *Das mittelassyrische Tontafelarchiv von Giricano* (Subartu 14) 2004; P. Akkermans in *Akkadica* 66 (1990), pp. 13–66, and 84–85 (1993), pp. 1–52 (Sabi Abyad); S. Jacob, *Die mittelassyrische Texte aus Tell Chuera*, Wiesbaden 2009.

Trade: B. Faist, *Der Fernhandel des assyrischen Reiches zwischen dem 14. und 11. Jh. v.Chr.*, Münster 2001. **Administration:** H. Freydank in *AoF* 1 (1974), pp. 55–89, and 4 (1976), pp. 111–130; J. N. Postgate in *AoF* 13 (1986), pp. 10–39; J. Klein, *Mittelassyrische Verwaltung und Sozialstruktur*, Leiden–Boston 2003.

Political propaganda: P. Machinist, *The Epic of Tukulti-Ninurta I*, PhD. Yale University 1978; S. Lackenbacher in *RA* 76 (1982), pp. 141–156. **Urban planning:** T. Eickhoff, *Kar Tukulti-Ninurta*, Berlin 1985.

Code: C. Saporetti, *Le leggi medioassire*, Malibu 1979. **Edicts:** E. Weidner in *AfO* 17 (1954–56), pp. 257–293. **Land allotments:** P. Garelli in *Semitica* 17 (1967), pp. 5–21; J. N. Postgate in *Bulletin of the School of Oriental and African Studies* 34 (1971), pp. 496–520, and in *Studies I.M. Diakonoff*, Warminster 1982, pp. 304–313.

21 Kassite Babylonia

Sources, chronology, history: J. A. Brinkman, *Materials and Studies for Kassite History*, I, Chicago 1976; K. Balkan, *Studies in Babylonian Feudalism of the Kassite Period*, Malibu 1986. **Kudurru:** K. E. Slanski, *The Babylonian Entitlement Narûs (Kudurrus)*, Boston 2003.

Agricultural crisis: Mc G. Gibson in *Irrigation's Impact on Society*, Tucson 1974, pp. 7–19. **Labour:** J. A. Brinkman in *Studies F.R. Kraus*, Leiden 1982, pp. 1–8. L. Sassmannshausen, *Beiträge zur Verwaltung und Gesellschaft Babyloniens in der Kassitenzeit*, Mainz 2001.

Standardisation: W. G. Lambert, in *JCS* 11 (1957), pp. 1–14, 16 (1962), pp. 59–77; E. Reiner in *Or* 30 (1961), pp. 1–11; F. Rochberg-Halton, in *JCS* 36 (1984), pp. 127–144. **Wisdom literature:** W. G. Lambert, *Babylonian Wisdom Literature*, Oxford 1960; G. Buccellati, in *OA* 11 (1972), pp. 1–36, 81–100, 161–178; J. Sasson (ed.), *JAOS* 101/1 (1981).

22 Crisis and reorganisation

Sea Peoples: W. W. Ward and M. S. Joukowsky (eds), *The Crisis Years: The 12th Century*, Dubuque 1992; R. Drews, *The End of the Bronze Age*, Princeton 1993; E. Oren (ed.), *The Sea Peoples and Their World*, Philadelphia 2000; B. U. Schipper, *Die Erzählung des Wenamun*, Freiburg–Göttingen 2005. **Philistines:** T. Dotan, *The Philistines and Their Material Culture*, New Haven 1982; J. Brug, *A Literary and Archaeological Study of the Philistines*, Oxford 1985, G. Garbini, *I Filistei*, Milano 1997.

Internal factors: M. Liverani in M. Rowlands, M. T. Larsen and K. Kristiansen (eds), *Centre and Periphery in the Ancient World*, Cambridge 1987, pp. 66–73, and in M. Molinos and A. Zifferero (eds), *Primi popoli d'Europa*, Firenze 2002, pp. 33–48. **Technological innovations, iron:** J. Waldbaum, *From Bronze to Iron*, Göteborg 1978; T. A. Wertime and J. Muhly, *The Coming of the Age of Iron*, New Haven 1980. **Agriculture:** L. Stager in *BASOR* 221 (1976), pp. 145–158; D. C. Hopkins, *The Highlands of Canaan*, Winona Lake 1983. **Camels:** R. Bullit, *The Camel and the Wheel*, Cambridge (MA) 1975; D. T. Potts in *JESHO* 47 (2004) 144–145. **Alphabet:** J. Naveh, *Early History of the Alphabet*, Leiden 1982; M. G. Amadasi Guzzo, *Scritture alfabetiche*, Rome 1987; B. Sass, *The Genesis of the Alphabet*, Wiesbaden 1988, and *The Alphabet at the Turn of the Millennium*, Tel Aviv 2005. **Re-urbanisation:** S. Mazzoni (ed.), *Nuove fondazioni nel Vicino Oriente antico*, Pisa 1994.

23 Israel

Among the many histories of Israel, see G. W. Ahlström, *The History of Ancient Palestine*, Minneapolis 1993; M. Liverani, *Israel's History and the History of Israel*, London 2005. **Based on archaeological evidence:** I. Finkelstein and N. A. Silberman, *The Bible Unearthed*, New York 2002.

Patriarchal traditions: D. B. Redford, *A Study of the Biblical Story of Joseph*, Leiden 1970; T. L. Thompson, *The Historicity of the Patriarchal Narratives*, Berlin 1974; J. van Seters, *Abraham in History and Tradition*, New Haven 1975; T. Römer, *Israels Väter*, Göttingen 1990.

Tribes of Israel: C. de Geus, *The Tribes of Israel*, Amsterdam 1976; N. K. Gottwald, *The Tribes of Yahweh*, New York 1979; B. Halpern, *The Emergence of Israel in Canaan*, Chico CA 1983; N. P. Lemche, *Early Israel*, Leiden 1985. M. Rowlands, M. T. Larsen and K. Kristiansen (eds), *Centre and Periphery in the Ancient World*, Cambridge 1987. **Archaeological evidence:** I. Finkelstein, *The Archaeology of the*

Israelite Settlement, Jerusalem 1988, and *Living on the Fringe*, Sheffield 1995; I. Finkelstein and N. Na'aman, *From Nomadism to Monarchy*, Jerusalem 1994.

On the formation of Israel's monarchy: F. S. Frick, *The Formation of the State in Ancient Israel*, Winona Lake 1985; B. Halpern, *The Constitution of the Monarchy*, Chico CA 1981; V. Fritz and Ph. Davies (eds), *The Origins of the Ancient Israelite States*, Sheffield 1996. **United monarchy:** T. Ishida (ed.), *Studies in the Period of David and Solomon*, Tokyo 1982; J. K. Handy (ed.), *The Age of Solomon*, Leiden 1997. **Divided monarchy:** J. Hayes and J. Miller (eds), *Israelite and Judaean History*, Leiden 1977. **Neighbouring groups:** A. van Zyl, *The Moabites*, Leiden 1960; B. Routledge, *Moab in the Iron Age*, Philadelphia 2004; E. A. Knauf, *Ismael*, Wiesbaden 1985, and *Midian*, Wiesbaden 1988; J. R. Bartlett, *Edom and the Edomites*, Sheffield 1989; D. Edelman (ed.), *Edom and Seir in History and Tradition*, Atlanta 1995; B. McDonald and R. Younker (eds), *Ancient Ammon*, Leiden 1999.

Archaeological evidence: Y. Aharoni, *The Archaeology of the Land of Israel*, Philadelphia–London 1982; H. Weippert, *Palästina in vorhellenistischer Zeit*, München 1988; A. Mazar and E. Stern, *Archaeology of the Land of the Bible*, I–II, New York, 1990–2001; E. Stern (ed.), *The New Encyclopaedia of Archaeological Excavations in the Holy Land*, I–IV, Jerusalem 1993. **Biblical geography:** Y. Aharoni, *The Land of the Bible*, London 1967; S. Mittmann and G. Schmitt (eds), *Tübinger Bibelatlas*, Stuttgart 2001.

Imperial conquest: M. Cogan, *Imperialism and Religion*, Pittsburg 1971; H. Spieckermann, *Judah unter Assur in der Sargonidenzeit*, Göttingen 1982; E. Stern, *Material Culture of the Land of the Bible in the Persian Period*, Warminster 1982; L. Grabbe (ed.), *Leading Captivity Captive*, Sheffield 1998; H. M. Barstad, *The Myth of the Empty Land*, Oslo 1996.

Society: R. de Vaux, *Les institutions de l'Ancien Testament*, I–II, Paris 1960–61; P. M. McNutt, *Reconstructing the Society of Ancient Israel*, Louisville–London 1999; Ph. J. King and L. Stager, *Life in Biblical Israel*, Louisville–London 2001. **Kingship:** J. Soggin, *Das Königtum in Israel*, Berlin 1967; T. Ishida, *The Royal Dynasties in Ancient Israel*, Berlin 1977; T. N. Mettinger, *King and Messiah*, Lund 1976.

Historiographical re-elaborations: M. Smith, *Palestinian Parties and Politics That Shaped the Old Testament*, New York 1971; P. Sacchi, *Storia del mondo giudaico*, Torino 1976; G. Garbini, *History and Ideology in Ancient Israel*, London 1988; N. P. Lemche, *The Israelites in History and Tradition*, London 1998; Th. L. Thompson, *The Bible in History*, London 1999.

24 The Phoenicians

G. Garbini, *I Fenici: Storia e religione*, Napoli 1980; M. Gras, P. Rouillard and J. Teixidor, *L'universo fenicio*, Torino 2000; G. Markoe, *Phoenicians*, London 2000; M. E. Aubet, *The Phoenicians in the West*, Cambridge 2001; cf. *Studia Phoenicia*, I–III, Leuven 1983–85. **Overviews:** *Dictionnaire de la civilisation phénicienne et punique*, Turnhout 1992; V. Krings (ed.), *La civilisation phénicienne et punique*, Leiden 1995; **Trade and colonisation:** G. Bunnens in *JESHO* 19 (1976), pp. 1–31; *L'expansion phénicienne en Méditerranée*, Bruxelles 1979; W. Röllig (ed.), *Phönizier im Westen*, Mainz 1982; various authors in *Aula Orientalis* 3 (1985), 4 (1986); M. Liverani in *Studies H. Tadmor*, Jerusalem 1991, pp. 65–79.

Inscriptions: H. Donner and W. Röllig, *Kanaanäische und aramäische Inschriften*, I–III, Wiesbaden 1964–68; J. Gibson, *Phoenician Inscriptions*, Oxford 1982; M. G. Amadasi Guzzo, *Le iscrizioni fenicie e puniche delle colonie in Occidente*, Rome 1967. **Wenamun:** H. Goedicke, *The Report of Wenamun*, Baltimore 1976.

25 The Arameans in Syria and Mesopotamia

H. Sader, *Les états araméens de Syrie*, Beirut 1987; P. E. Dion, *Les Araméens à l'âge du fer*, Paris 1997; E. Lipinski, *The Aramaeans*, Leuven 2000; W. Pitard, *Ancient Damascus*, Winona Lake 1987. **Origins:** K. Lawson-Younger in W. Pitard (ed.), *Ugarit at Seventy-Five*, Winona Lake 2007, pp. 131–174. **On the Arameans in Babylonia:** M. Dietrich, *Die Aramäer Südbabyloniens in der Sargonidenzeit*, Neukirchen

1970; J. A. Brinkman, *A Political History of Post-Kassite Babylonia*, Rome 1968, pp. 260–288, and *Or* 46 (1977), pp. 304–325; F. Malbran-Labat in *JA* 267 (1980), pp. 11–23.

Ancient Aramaic inscriptions: H. Donner-W. Röllig, *Kanaanäische und aramäische Inschriften*, I–III, Wiesbaden 1964–68; J. Gibson, *Aramaic Inscriptions*, Oxford 1975; A. Lemaire and J. M. Durand, *Les inscriptions araméennes de Sfiré*, Genève 1984; A. Abu Assaf, P. Bordreuil and A. Millard, *La statue de Tell Fekheryé*, Paris 1982. **On the spread of Aramaic:** E. Lipinski, *Studies in Aramaic Inscriptions and Onomastics*, Louvain 1975; F. M. Fales, *Aramaic Epigraphs on Clay Tablets of the Neo-Assyrian Period*, Rome 1986; F. Altheim and R. Stiel, *Die aramäische Sprache unter den Achaimeniden*, Frankfurt 1964.

26 The Neo-Hittite states

A. M. Jasink, *Gli stati neo-ittiti*, Pavia 1995; H. Craig Melchert, *The Luwians*, Leiden 2003. **Inscriptions:** D. Hawkins, *Corpus of Hieroglyphic Luwian Inscriptions*, Berlin–New York 2000. **Reliefs:** W. Orthmann, *Untersuchungen zur späthethitischen Kunst*, Bonn 1971; H. Genge, *Nordsyrisch-südanatolische Reliefs*, Copenhagen 1979.

Karatepe: F. Bron, *Recherches sur les inscriptions phéniciennes de Karatepe*, Genève 1979; J. D. Hawkins and A. Morpurgo Davies in *AnSt* 28 (1978), pp. 103–119; I. Winter in *AnSt* 29 (1979), pp. 115–151; J. Deshayes and M. Sznycer and P. Garelli in *RA* 75 (1981), pp. 31–60. **Tabal:** S. Aro, *Tabal*, Helsinki 1998.

27 Assyria, Babylonia and Elam in the twelfth to ninth centuries BC

On the Middle Elamite apogee see Chapter 5; on Tiglatpileser I (codes and edicts) see Chapter 20. **Post-Kassite Babylonia:** J. A. Brinkman, *A Political History of Post-Kassite Babylonia 1158–722 BC*, Rome 1968. **Royal inscriptions:** G. Frame, *Rulers of Babylonia 1157–612 BC*, Toronto 1995. **Litearature:** L. Cagni, *L'epopea di Erra*, Rome 1969.

Nebuchadnezzar I: W. G. Lambert, *Essays T. Meek*, Toronto 1964, pp. 3–13, and in *Iraq* 27 (1965), pp. 1–11; J. Roberts in *Essays J. Finkelstein*, Hamden 1976, pp. 183–187. On the prophecies of Marduk cf. also R. Borger in *BO* 28 (1971), pp. 3–24. **New Year festival:** B. Pongratz-Leisetn, *Ina šulmi īrub: Die kulttopographische und ideologische Programmatik der akītu-Prozession*, Mainz 1994; J. Bidmead, *The Akitu Festival*, Piscataway 2002.

28 The rise of the Neo-Assyrian empire

Royal inscriptions: W. Schramm, *Einleitung in die assyrischen Königsinschriften*, II, Leiden 1972; A. K. Grayson, *Assyrian Rulers of the Early First Millennium BC*, I–II, Toronto 1991–1996; H. Tadmor, *The Inscriptions of Tiglath-pileser III*, Jerusalem 1994; A. Fuchs, *Die Inschriften Sargons II. aus Khorsabad*, Göttingen 1993, and *Die Annalen des Jahres 711 v.Chr.*, Helsinki 1998; W. Mayer in *MDOG* 115 (1983), pp. 65–132; D. D. Luckenbill, *The Annals of Sennacherib*, Chicago 1924; E. Frahm, *Einleitung in die Sanherib-Inschriften*, Wien 1997; E. Leichty, *The Royal Inscriptions of Esarhaddon, King of Assyra*, Winona Lake 2011; R. Borger, *Beiträge zum Inschriftenwerk Assurbanipals*, Wiesbaden 1996.

Letters and other archival sources are published in the series *State Archives of Assyria*, I–XVIII, Helsinki 1987–2003; cf. also S. Parpola, *Letters from Assyrian Scholars to the Kings Esarhaddon and Assurbanipal*, I–II, Neukirchen 1970–83. **Legal and administrative texts (other than the SAA):** J. Postgate, *Fifty Neo-Assyrian Legal Documents*, Warminster 1976; *Cuneiform Texts from Nimrud*, I–III, London 1972–1984; K. Radner, *Die neuassyrischen Privatrechtsurkunden*, Helsinki 1997. **Provincial archives:** S. Dalley in *Abr Nahrain* 34 (1996–97), pp. 66–96 (Tell Ahmar); F. M. Fales et al., *The Assyrian and Aramaean Texts from Tell Shiukh Fawqani*, Padova 2005; K. Radner, *Die neuassyrischen Texte aus Tall Šēḫ Ḥamad*, Berlin 2002.

Royal grants: J. Postgate, *Neo-Assyrian Royal Grants and Decrees*, Rome 1969.

History: for a general overview see F. M. Fales, *L'impero assiro*, Rome–Bari 2001; for a concise introduction see E. Cancik-Kirschbaum, *Die Assyrer: Geschichte, Gesellschaft, Kultur*, München 2003; R. M. Fales and G. B. Lanfranchi, 'L'impero neoassiro' in S. de Martino (ed.), *Il mondo antico, I. La preistoria dell'uomo. L'Oriente mediterraneo, Vol. II. Le civiltà dell'Oriente mediterraneo (Storia d'Europa e del Mediterraneo)*, Rome 2006, pp. 505–575. **On individual phases:** S. Ponchia, *L'Assiria e gli stati transeufratici*, Padova 1991; B. J. Parker, *The Mechanics of Empire*, Helsinki 2001; Sh. Yamada, *The Construction of the Assyrian Empire*, Leiden 2000; R. Lamprichs, *Die Westexpansion des neuassyrischen Reiches*, Neukirchen–Vluyn 1995; H.-U. Onasch, *Die assyrische Eroberungen Ägyptens*, I–II. Wiesbaden 1994. Many studies are collected in S. Parpola and R. M. Whiting (eds), *Assyria 1995*, Helsinki 1997, and in H. Waetzoldt and H. Hauptmann (eds), *Assyrien im Wandel der Zeiten*, Heidelberg 1997.

Historical topography: K. Kessler, *Untersuchungen zur historischen Topographie Nordmesopotamiens*, Wiesbaden 1980; M. Liverani, *Studies on the Annals of Ashurnasirpal II*, Rome 1992; M. Liverani (ed.), *Neo-Assyrian Geography*, Rome 1995; D. Morandi Bonacossi, *Tra il fiume e la steppa*, I–II, Padova 1996. **Atlas:** S. Parpola and M. Porter, *The Helsinki Atlas of the Near East in the Neo-Assyrian Period*, Helsinki 2001.

29 The structure of the Neo-Assyrian empire

City and countryside: D. Oates, *Studies in the Ancient History of Northern Iraq*, London 1968; J. Reade in *RA* 72 (1978), pp. 47–72, 157–180; A. Bagg, *Assyrische Wasserbauten*, Mainz 2000. **Land and labour:** F. M. Fales, *Censimenti e catasti di epoca neo-assira*, Rome 1973, and in *OA* 14 (1975), pp. 325–360, *SAAB* 4 (1990), pp. 81–142; N. Postgate in *JESHO* 17 (1974), pp. 225–243; J. Zablocka in *AoF* 1 (1974), pp. 91–113; S. Parpola in *ZA* 64 (1975), pp. 96–115.

Kingship and imperial ideology: M. Liverani in M. T. Larsen (ed.), *Power and Propaganda*, Copenhagen 1979, pp. 297–317; M. F. Fales (ed.), *Assyrian Royal Inscriptions*, Rome 1981; B. Oded, *War, Peace and Empire*, Wiesbaden 1992; B. Pongratz-Leisten, *Herrschaftswissen in Mesopotamien*, Helsinki 1999; W. Holloway, *Assur is King!*, Leiden 2002; G. W. Vera Chamaza, *Die Omnipotenz Aššurs*, Münster 2002. **Royal titulature:** M. J. Seux, *Epithètes royales akkadiennes et sumériennes*, Paris 1967. **The empire's structure:** M. Liverani in *SAAB* 12 (1999–2001), pp. 57–85; J. N. Postgate in *World Archaeology* 23 (1992), pp. 247–263.

War: F. Malbran-Labat, *L'armée et l'organisation militaire de l'Assyrie*, Genève 1982; M. Weippert in *Zeitschrift für die alttestamentliche Wissenschaft* 84 (1972), pp. 460–493. **Deportations:** B. Oded, *Mass Deportations and Deportees in the Neo-Assyrian Empire*, Wiesbaden 1979.

Ruling class: A. Millard, *The Eponyms of the Assyrian Empire*, 1994; R. Mattila, *The King's Magnates*, Helsinki 2000; K. Radner and H. D. Baker, *The Prosopography of the Neo-Assyrian Empire*, I–III, Helsinki 1998–2002.

Architecture: B. Menzel, *Assyrische Tempel*, I–II, Rome 1981; S. Lackenbacher, *Le roi bâtisseur*, Paris 1982, and *Le palais sans rival*, Paris 1990; J. M. Russell, *Sennacherib's Palace without Rivals at Nineveh*, Chicago 1991; P. Matthiae, *Ninive*, Milano 1998. **History of the earliest excavations:** M. T. Larsen, *The Conquest of Assyria*, London 1994.

Taxation: J. N. Postgate, *Taxation and Conscription in the Assyrian Empire*, Rome 1970; F. M. Fales in *Studi F. Pintore*, Pavia 1983, pp. 49–92 (timber), in *Assur* 1/3 (1974), pp. 5–24 (horses). **Tributes:** M. Elat in *AfO Beiheft* 19 (1982), pp. 244–251; J. Bär, *Der assyrische Tribut und seine Darstellung*, Neukirchen 1996. **Foreigners:** M. Wäfler, *Nicht-Assyrer neuassyrischer Darstellungen*, Neukirchen 1975.

Archives, Ashurbanipal's library: O. Pedersen, *Archives and Libraries in the City of Assur*, Uppsala 1986; S. Parpola in *JNES* 42 (1983), pp. 1–29; J. Reade and S. Parpola and T. Kwasman in *RAI* 30, Leiden 1986, pp. 213–222, 223–236, 237–240.

30 The periphery of the Neo-Assyrian empire

The Arabs: I. Eph'al, *The Ancient Arabs*, Leiden 1982; E.A. Knauf, *Ismael*, Wiesbaden 1985; Ch. Robin, *L'Arabie antique*, Aix-en-Provence 1991; M. Elat in *Festschrift für R. Borger*, Groningen 1998, pp. 39–57; J. Retsö, *The Arabs in Antiquity*, London–New York 2003; S. Cleziou, M. Tosi and J. Zarins, *Essays on the Late Prehistory of the Arabian Peninsula*, Rome 2002. **South Arabian civilisation:** A. de Maigret, *Arabia Felix*, Milano 1996; Ch. Robin and I. Gajda (eds), *Arabia Antiqua*, Rome 1996; A. Avanzini, 'I regni sudarabici' in S. de Martino (ed.), *Il mondo antico, I. La preistoria dell'uomo. L'Oriente mediterraneo, Vol. II. Le civiltà dell'Oriente mediterraneo (Storia d'Europa e del Mediterraneo)*, Rome 2006, pp. 691–728.

Urartu: P. Zimanski, *Ecology and Empire: The Structure of the Urartian State*, Chicago 1985; V. Haas (ed.), *Das Reich Urartu*, Konstanz 1986; M. Salvini, *Geschichte und Kultur der Urartäer*, Darmstadt 1995, and 'Il regno di Urartu', in S. de Martino (ed.), *Il mondo antico, I. La preistoria dell'uomo. L'Oriente mediterraneo, Vol. II. Le civiltà dell'Oriente mediterraneo (Storia d'Europa e del Mediterraneo)*, Rome 2006, pp. 459–503. **Historical geography:** P. Pecorella and M. Salvini, *Tra lo Zagros e l'Urmia*, Rome 1984; H. F. Russell in *AnSt* 34 (1984), pp. 171–201. **Inscriptions:** M. Salvini, *Corpus dei testi urartei*, I–III, Rome 2008.

The Mannaeans: R. Böhmer in *BaM* 3 (1964), pp. 11–24. **The Medes:** M. Liverani, in *JCS* 47 (1995), pp. 57–62. **The Cimmerians:** G. B. Lanfranchi, *I Cimmeri*, Padova 1990; A. Ivantchik, *Kimmerier und Skythen*, Moscau 2001

The Neo-Elamite kingdom: M. W. Waters, *A Survey of Neo-Elamite History*, Helsinki 2000; also P. de Miroschedji and W. Hinz in *Mélanges P. Steve*, Paris 1986, pp. 209–225 and 227–234. **The collapse of Elam:** P. de Miroschedji in *ZA* 75 (1985), pp. 265–306, and in *Iranica Antiqua* 25 (1990), pp. 47–95.

Phrygia, inscriptions: C. Brixhe and M. Lejeune, *Corpus des inscriptions paléo-phrygiennes*, I–II, Paris 1984. On Gordion see R. S. Young, *Three Great Early Tumuli*, Philadelphia 1981. **Lydia:** C. Talamo, *La Lidia arcaica*, Bologna 1979. **On languages and texts from Asia Minor:** R. Gusmani, O. Carruba and G. Neumann in *Annali della Scuola Normale Superiore di Pisa* 8 (1978), pp. 833–886. **On Late Luwian culture:** cf. Ph. Houwink ten Cate, *The Luwian Population Groups of Lycia and Cilicia Aspera*, Leiden 1961.

31 The fall of the empire and the rise of the Chaldeans

F. Joannès, *La Mésopotamie au 1er millénaire avant J.-C.*, Paris 2000; S. Graziani, *L'età neobabilonese*, in S. de Martino (ed.), *Il mondo antico, I. La preistoria dell'uomo. L'Oriente mediterraneo, Vol. II. Le civiltà dell'Oriente mediterraneo (Storia d'Europa e del Mediterraneo)*, Rome 2006, pp. 621–661. **On Babylonia before the Neo-Babylonian dynasty:** J. A. Brinkman, *Prelude to Empire. Babylonian Society and Politics, 747–626 BC*, Philadelphia 1984; G. Frame, *Babylonia 689–627 BC: A Political History*, Istanbul 1992; S. Cole, *Nippur in Late Assyrian Times*, Helsinki 1996. **On the collapse of the Neo-Assyrian empire:** S. Zawadzki, *The Fall of Assyria*, Delft 1988; M. Liverani in S. Alcock (ed.), *Empires*, Cambridge 2001, pp. 374–391, and in *SS* 49 (2008), pp. 277–292.

The Neo-Babylonian dynasty: D. J. Wiseman, *Nebuchadrezzar and Babylon*, Oxford 1985; P.-A. Beaulieu, *The Reign of Nabonidus*, New Haven 1989; F. D'Agostino, *Nabonedo, Adda-guppi, il deserto e il dio Luna*, Pisa 1994; D. Arnaud, *Nabuchodonosor II, roi de Babylone*, Paris 2004. **Babylonian topography:** A. R. George, *Babylonian Topographical Texts*, Leuven 1992.

Babylonian institutions: G. Barjamovic, in *Studies Larsen*, Leiden 2004, pp. 47–98. **Royal inscriptions:** P. Berger, *Die neubabylonische Königsinschriften*, Neukirchen 1973; H. Schaudig, *Die Inschriften Nabonids von Babylon und Kyros' des Grossen*, Münster 2001. **Archives:** O. Pedersen, *Archive und Bibliotheken in Babylon*, Saarbrücken 2005.

Economy, agriculture: D. Cocquerillat, *Palmeraies et cultures de l'Eanna d'Uruk (559–520)*, Berlin 1968; K. Nemet-Nejat, *Late Babylonian Field Plans*, Rome 1982; M. Powell in *AfO* 31 (1984), pp. 32–66;

G. Ries, *Die neubabylonischen Bodenpachtformulare*, Berlin 1976; M. Jursa, *Die Landwirtschaft in Sippar in neubabylonischer Zeit*, Wien 1995; C. Wunsch, *Das Egibi-Archiv, I: Die Felder und Gärten*, Groningen 2000; K. Kleber, *Tempel und Palast. Die Beziehungen zwischen dem König und dem Eanna-Tempel im spät-babylonischen Uruk*, Münster 2008.

Craftsmanship: D. Weisberg, *Guild Structure and Political Allegiance in Early Achaemenid Mesopotamia*, New Haven 1967. **Slavery:** M. Dandamaev, *Slavery in Babylonia from Nabopolassar to Alexander the Great*, De Kalb Illinois 1984. **Trade:** A. L. Oppenheim in *JCS* 21 (1967), pp. 236–254; H. Lanz, *Die neubabylonischen harranu-Geschäftsunternehmen*, Berlin 1976; C. Wunsch, *Die Urkunden des babylonischen Geschäftsmannes Iddin-Marduk*, I–II, Groningen 1993. **Temple:** A. Bongenaar, *The Neo-Babylonian Ebabbar Temple at Sippar*, Leiden 1997; M. Jursa, *Der Tempelzehnt in Babylonien*, Münster 1998. R. da Riva, *Der Ebabbar-Tempel von Sippar*, Münster 2002.

Foreign minorities: R. Zadok, *On West Semites in Babylonia during the Chaldaean and Achaemenian Periods*, Jerusalem 1977; I. Eph'al in *Or* 47 (1978), pp. 74–90; S. Kaufman, *The Akkadian Influences in Aramaic*, Chicago 1974.

Historiography, chronicles: K. Grayson, *Assyrian and Babylonian Chronicles*, Locust Valley N.Y. 1975; J. J. Glassner, *Mesopotamian Chronicles*, Atlanta 2004. **Diaries:** H. Hunger and A. Sachs, *Astronomical Diaries and Related Texts from Babylonia*, I–V, Wien 1988–2001. **Prophecies:** A. K. Grayson and W. G. Lambert in *JCS* 18 (1964), pp. 7–23; R. Biggs in *Iraq* 29 (1967), pp. 119–132. **Astronomy and astrology:** E. Reiner and D. Pingree, *Babylonian Planetary Omens*, I–III, Malibu–Groningen 1956–1981–1998; H. D. Galter, *Die Rolle der Astronomie in den Kulturen Mesopotamiens*, Graz 1993; U. Koch-Westenholz, *Mesopotamian Astrology*, Copenhagen 1995; H. Hunger and D. Pingree, *Astral Sciences in Mesopotamia*, Leiden 1999; D. Brown, *Mesopotamian Planetary Astronomy-Astrology*, Groningen 2000.

32 The Medes and the rise of the Persians

Migrations: R. Girshman, *L'Iran et la migration des Indo-Aryens et des Iraniens*, Leiden 1977; I. Medveskaya, *Iran: Iron Age I*, Oxford 1982. **On the pre-imperial phase:** P. Briant, *L'Asie centrale et les royaumes proche-orientaux du premier millénaire*, Paris 1984. And in *Iranica Antiqua* 19 (1984), pp. 71–118; S. C. Brown in *JCS* 38 (1986), pp. 107–119. **On the supposed Median empire:** H. Sancisi-Veerdengurg in *Achaemenid History*, III, Leiden 1988, pp. 197–212; B. Lanfranchi (ed.), *Continuity of Empire: Assyria, Media, Persia*, Padova 2003. **On Zoroaster:** M. Boyce, *A History of Zoroastrianism*, I–II, Leiden–Köln 1982; G. Gnoli, *Zoroaster in History*, New York 2000.

The Persian empire: J. Wiesehöfer, *Ancient Persia*, London 1996, and the more concise *Das frühe Persien*, München 1999. A broader treatment of the subject can be found in I. Gershevitch (ed.), *The History of Iran*, II, Cambridge 1985; P. Briant, *Histoire de l'empire perse*, Paris 1996. Several studies are collected in A. Kuhrt and H. Sancisi Weerdenburg (eds), *Achaemenid History*, I–VIII, Leiden 1987–1994.

Imperial ideology: P. Frei and K. Koch, *Reichsidee und Reichsorganisation im Perserreich*, Freiburg–Göttingen 1984; P. Briant in *Dialogues d'Histoire Ancienne* 2 (1976), pp. 163–239; G. Gnoli in *Acta Iranica* 1 (1974), pp. 117–190, in *Studi G. Tucci*, Napoli 1974, pp. 23–88. **Tributes and satrapies:** P. Briant and C. Herrenschmidt (eds), *Le tribut dans l'empire perse*, Paris 1989; P. Högemann, *Das alte Vorderasien und die Achämeniden*, Wiesbaden 1992; B. Jacobs, *Die Satrapienverwaltung im Perserreich*, Wiesbaden 1994.

On the 'Axial Age' cf. S. N. Eisenstadt (ed.), *The Origins and Diversity of Axial Age Civilizations*, Albany N.Y. 1986; J. P. Arnason, S. N. Eisenstadt and B. Wittrock (eds), *Axial Civilizations and World History*, Leiden 2005.

INDEX

The names in italic are names of deities

Index

Arinna (Anatolian city) 262, 264, 267
Arman (a region in the Zagros, *see also* Yalman) 364, 377,
Armanum (a city associated to Ebla, *see also* Armi) 137
Armaya (*see also* Arameans) 435
Armenia 17, 38, 45, 89, 181, 185, 391, 454, 465, 487, 521–2, 524–5, 565, 568
Armenians (Indo-European population) 524
Armi (Upper Mesopotamian kingdom) 118, 123
Arnuwanda I (Hittite king) 301–2
Arnuwanda II (Hittite king) 305
Arnuwanda III (Hittite king) 310
Arpa Çay (a river in eastern Turkey) 522
Arpachiya (prehistoric site in Assyria) 48, 54
Arpad (North Syrian city and kingdom, *see also* Bit Agushi) 435, 437, 439, 441, 451, 453, 482–3, 485, 508, 523
Arqa (city in Lebanon) 420, 422
Arrapha (Assyrian city, modern Kirkuk) 227, 295, 538
Arslan Tash (archaeological site on the Middle Euphrates, ancient Hadattu) 505
Arslantepe (archaeological site on the Upper Euphrates, *see also* Malatya) 56, 58, 74, 86, 88, 451
Artatama I (Mitannian king) 292
Artatama II (Mitannian king) 293, 304–5, 347
Arwad (Phoenician city) 420–3, 431–433, 465, 494, 541
Aryans (Iranian population) 555
Arzashkun (Urartian city) 521
Arzawa (a region in south-western Anatolia) 260, 298, 301–2, 304, 306–7, 311, 318, 324, 386
Asa (king of Israel) 438
Asatiwata (local king of Karatepe) 454
Asatiwatiya (ancient name of Karatepe) 454
Ashdod (Philistine city) 387, 406, 412, 541
Ashkelon (Philistine city) 387, 406
Ashlakka (city and kingdom in Upper Mesopotamia) 228
Ashmu-Nikkal (Hittite queen, wife of Arnuwanda I) 301
Ashnakkum (Upper Mesopotamian region) 252
Ashnan (Sumerian goddess) 109
Ashshuwa (ancient region in north-western Anatolia) 301
Ashtata (region on the Middle Euphrates, *see also* Emar and Meskene) 261, 335
Ashur-ah-iddina, *see* Esarhaddon
Ashur-ban-apli, *see* Ashurbanipal
Ashur-bel-kala (Assyrian king) 443, 467
Ashur-bel-nisheshu (Assyrian king) 347, 364
Ashur-da'in-apli (brother of Shamshi-Adad V) 482
Ashur-dan II (Assyrian king) 366, 458, 475–6
Ashur-dan III (Assyrian king) 482
Ashur-etil-ilani (Assyrian king) 537
Ashur-nadin-ahhe (Assyrian king) 347
Ashur-nadin-shumi (Assyrian king) 492
Ashur-nasir-apli, *see* Ashurnasirpal

Ashur-nirari V (Assyrian king) 439, 482–3, 485, 508
Ashur-resh-ishi I (Assyrian king) 460, 463
Ashur-uballit I (Assyrian king) 271, 304, 347, 349, 361, 365, 467
Ashur-uballit II (Assyrian king) 539
Ashur (chief god of Assyria) 211–2, 228, 347, 355, 357–8, 490, 503, 505, 510–11, 515, 517
Ashur (city located on the Middle Tigris, modern Qal'at Sherqat) 93, 112, 115–17, 120, 124, 170, 187, 190–1, 208–13, 216–17, 219, 224, 226–9, 232, 252, 278, 292, 347, 349–50, 354–5, 357–8, 365, 480, 482, 488–9, 492, 497, 514, 517, 538–9, 560
Ashurbanipal (Assyrian king) 371, 422, 454, 494–6, 508, 512, 515, 519–20, 523–4, 526, 528–31, 534, 537
Ashurnasirpal II (Assyrian king) 422, 426, 438, 452, 463, 469, 476–7, 479–81, 497, 512, 521, 557
Asiab (prehistoric site in Luristan) 36
Assyria (region and kingdom) 12, 19, 48, 54, 83–4, 89, 115–6, 137, 139, 159, 191, 195, 201, 207–12, 216–7, 219–20, 224, 226–9, 232, 241–2, 252, 254, 279, 291–3, 307–8, 311, 322, 347, 349–51, 354–6, 358–9, 362, 364–7, 376, 389, 392, 397–8, 406, 413, 422, 425, 428, 432, 437–9, 441, 443, 446, 453–4, 458, 460, 462–3, 465–7, 469, 475–6, 480–3, 485, 487, 490–3, 495, 497, 503–5, 506, 509–10, 512, 521–6, 529–31, 534–5, 537, 541–2, 545, 550, 557, 559–61
Assyrians 3, 219–20, 286, 293, 308, 341, 349–51, 355, 357–9, 361, 363, 365–6, 398–9, 401, 410, 412–5, 417, 422, 426, 430–3, 434–5, 438–9, 441, 443–5, 450–1, 453–4, 462–3, 465, 467, 475, 479, 481–2, 487, 490–1, 493–5, 506–7, 509–11, 514, 516–7, 519–20, 523–5, 529–31, 533–5, 537–42, 547, 549, 554, 560, 567, 569
Astarte (Canaanite and Phoenician goddess) 345, 406, 415
Astyages (Median king) 544, 561–2, 568
Astuwatananza (king of Carchemish) 451
Atal-shenni (king of Urkish and Nawar) 153
Athribis (Egyptian city) 494
Attahushu (king of Susa) 254
Attar-kittah (Elamite king) 377
Atuna (small kingdom in the Tabal region) 453
Avaris (capital of the Hyksos) 237
Awal (ancient city east of the Lower Tigris) 212
Awan (Elamite region and dynasty) 135, 142, 168
Awil-Marduk (Babylonian king) 542
Aziru (king of Amurru) 304, 306, 339–40
Azitiwadda (Phoenician king) 427

Baal (Canaanite and Phoenician god) 342–3, 345, 415
Baal (king of Tyre) 422, 431
Baalat (Canaanite and Phoenician goddess) 345
Baba Jan (archaeological site in Luristan) 557
Babel (Biblical name of Babylon) 4, 541
Babylon 152, 161, 186–8, 191, 193, 195, 224, 226–9, 232, 234, 240–2, 248–9, 253–4, 271–2, 322, 354–5, 364–6, 375, 458, 460, 462, 469, 471, 487–8, 491–2,

602

Made in the USA
Columbia, SC
19 February 2019